Fodor's 2003

Caribbean

The Guide
for All Budgets

Completely
Updated

Where to Stay, Eat,
and Explore

On and Off
the Beaten Path

When to Go,
What to Pack

Maps, Travel Tips,
and Web Sites

Fodor's Travel Publications • New York, Toronto, London, Sydney, Auckland
www.fodors.com

Fodor's Caribbean 2003

EDITORS: Douglas Stallings, Jane Driesen, Laura M. Kidder, Mark Sullivan

Editorial Contributors: Isabel Abisláiman, Pamela Acheson, Carla Armour, Carol Bareuther, John Bigley, Kathy Borsuk, Karen W. Bressler, Mary Dempsey, Michael de Zayas, Suzanne Gordon, Delinda Karle, Lynda Lohr, John Marino, Elise Meyer, Richard B. Meyers, JoAnn Milivojevic, Caryn Nesmith, Paris Permenter, Vernon Ramesar, Eileen Robinson Smith, Jordan Simon, Cristina Cordova Suarez, Jane E. Zarem

Editorial Production: Taryn Luciani

Maps: David Lindroth, *cartographer;* Rebecca Baer and Robert Blake, *map editors*

Design: Fabrizio La Rocca, *creative director;* Guido Caroti, *art director;* Melanie Marin, *photo editor;* Jolie Novak, *senior picture editor*

Cover Design: Pentagram

Cover Photograph: Stephen Frink/Corbis, *cover (Virgin Gorda, British Virgin Islands).*

Production/Manufacturing: Robert B. Shields

Copyright

Special Sales

Important Tip

Although all prices, opening times, and other details in this book are based on information supplied to us at press time, changes occur all the time in the travel world, and Fodor's cannot accept responsibility for facts that become outdated or for inadvertent errors or omissions. So **always confirm information when it matters,** especially if you're making a detour to visit a specific place.

CONTENTS

Maps and Charts

ON THE ROAD WITH FODOR'S

THE MORE YOU KNOW before you go, the better your trip will be. The island's most fascinating small museum (or its best duty-free shop or most authentic creole restaurant) could be just around the corner from your hotel, but if you don't know it's there, it might as well be on the other side of the globe. That's where this book comes in. It's a great step toward making sure your next trip lives up to your expectations. As you plan, check out the Web as well. Guidebooks have been helping smart travelers find the special places for years; the Web is one more tool. Whatever reference you consult, be savvy about what you read, and always consider the source. Images and language can be massaged to make places appear better than they are. And one traveler's quaint is another's grimy. Here at Fodor's, and at our on-line arm, Fodors.com, our focus is on providing you with information that's not only useful but accurate and on target. Every day Fodor's editors put enormous effort into getting things right, beginning with the search for the right contributors—people who have objective judgment, broad travel experience, and the writing ability to put their insights into words. There's no substitute for advice from a like-minded friend who has just come back from where you're going, but our writers, having seen all corners of the Caribbean, are the next best thing. They're the kind of people you'd poll for tips yourself if you knew them.

After almost two decades in New York, husband and wife team **Pamela Acheson** and **Richard B. Myers** now divide their time between Florida and the Caribbean. They write extensively about both areas and are regular contributors to Fodor's guides. They are co-authors of *The Best Romantic Escapes in Florida* volumes 1 and 2.

Carla Armour, a native Dominican, has worked in the island's tourism industry for more than 25 years. She has been president of the Dominica Hotel & Tourism Association and vice president of the Dominica Writer's Guild.

St. Thomas–based writer and dietitian **Carol M. Bareuther** publishes two weekly columns on food, cooking, and nutrition in the *Virgin Islands Daily News* and serves as the USVI stringer for Reuters. She also writes about sports and travel for several publications. She's the author of two books, *Sports Fishing in the Virgin Islands* and *Virgin Islands Cooking.*

Although a native of the Windy City, **Kathy Borsuk** now enjoys the much-warmer trade winds of the Turks and Caicos Islands. She is managing editor of *Times of the Islands* magazine, a quarterly publication covering the stunning natural resources, fascinating history, interesting personalities, and varied hotel and restaurant choices in the Turks and Caicos.

New York–based **Karen W. Bressler** enjoys escaping the northeastern winters to write about Aruba. Karen has written for many magazines. She is the author of *Fodor's Pocket Aruba* and has contributed to *Fodor's Brazil* and *Fodor's Israel,* and has published several books of her own.

Suzanne Gordon followed her bliss and moved to Nevis, leaving behind a career with the *Philadelphia Inquirer,* to travel and write about the islands. She contributes to several publications. She's also completing a guide to architecture in the Caribbean and is involved in historic preservation projects throughout the islands.

Long time St. John resident **Lynda Lohr** lives above Coral Bay in a hurricane-resistant house she and her significant other are building themselves. A reporter by trade, her work has appeared in numerous publications as well as travel Web sites. On her rare days off, she swims at Great Maho Bay and hikes the island's numerous trails.

Friends of **Elise Meyer,** who updated the St. Barths chapter, often joke that her middle name is "Let's Go." In addition to being an enthusiastic traveler, art historian, independent curator, Internet enterpreneur, event planner, architectural consultant, and cookbook writer, Elise has contributed articles to myriad newspapers, magazines, and Web sites. She lives in Connecticut with her husband and children.

JoAnn Milivojevic is a writer and photographer living in Chicago. She's produced videos in the Cayman Islands and on St. Kitts & Nevis. Her travel articles have appeared in publications nationwide. She recently released a CD of her travel experiences, "Confessions of a Caribbean Addict: A Woman's Sexy and Sensual Tales of the Tropics."

After honeymooning in Jamaica, **Paris Permenter** and **John Bigley** decided to specialize in writing about and photographing the Caribbean. They've authored numerous Caribbean guidebooks, the latest of which is *Lovetripper.com's Guide to Caribbean Destination Weddings*. Their work has appeared in publications nationwide. From their home base in Texas, they edit Lovetripper.com Romantic Travel Magazine.

Vernon O'Reilly-Ramesar is a broadcaster and writer who divides his time between Trinidad and Canada. He has come to love the natural treasures of Trinidad and Tobago, spending much of his time exploring the miracles of the rain forest. Vernon updated the Trinidad and Tobago, Bonaire, and Curacao chapters for this edition.

Jordan Simon began his West Indies love affair as a child when his artist mother took him to Haiti. He has since visited and written about nearly every Caribbean island. He writes regularly for national magazines and newspapers. He has authored several books, including *Fodor's Colorado, The Gousha/USA Today Ski Atlas,* and (with Pam Bell) *Astronumerology: Your Key to Empowerment Using Stars and Numbers*.

In 1995, Hurricane Marilyn blew **Eileen Robinson Smith** out of the Caribbean and back to her lakeside home in Charleston, South Carolina. For two years she lived in St. John and wrote for *The Virgin Island Journal*. Before that she lived in St. Thomas, St. Croix, and Tortola. Her articles on food and travel have appeared in local, regional, and national publications.

Jane E. Zarem travels frequently to the Caribbean from her Connecticut home. Among the score of islands she has explored, she finds it difficult to pick a favorite— she loves them all. She has contributed to numerous Fodor's guides, among them *New England, USA, Cape Cod, Bahamas, Healthy Escapes* and *Great American Sports and Adventure Vacations*.

Michael de Zayas, who hails form Miami, spent his childhood vacations exploring the beaches of the Caribbean. He updated St. Martin/Sint Maarten and Anguilla for this guide and also contributes to *Fodor's Bahamas*.

Several writers contributed to the Puerto Rico chapter. **Isabel Abisláiman,** a San Juan–based freelance writer, investigated her city's sights, hotels, and shops. **Mary Dempsey,** who has written about Latin America for such publications as *Condé Nast Traveler,* covered the island's eastern reaches. **Delinda Karle,** a former features editor at the *San Juan Star,* visited the territory south of the mountains. **John Marino,** the city editor at the *San Juan Star,* covered his town's dining and nightlife/arts scenes. His colleagues, writer **Caryn Nesmith** and researcher/copy editor **Cristina Cordova Suarez,** put their talents to work on the northwestern and A to Z sections, respectively.

Don't Forget to Write

Your experiences—positive and negative— matter to us. If we have missed or misstated something, we want to hear about it. We follow up on all suggestions. Contact the Caribbean editor at editors@fodors.com or c/o Fodor's, 280 Park Ave., New York, New York 10017. And have a fabulous trip!

Karen Cure
Editorial Director

x

Island Finder

	Cost of Island	Number of rooms*	Nonstop flights	Cruise ship port	U.S. dollars accepted	Historic sites	Natural beauty	Lush	Arid	Mountainous	Rain forest	Beautiful beaches	Good roads
Anguilla	$$$	1,046			•				•			•	
Antigua & Barbuda	$$$$	3,500	•	•	•	•			•			•	
Aruba	$$	7,500	•	•	•		•		•			•	•
Barbados	$$$	6,000	•	•	•	•	•					•	•
Bonaire	$$	800	•	•	•		•		•				•
British Virgin Islands	$$$	1,302	•	•	•	•	•	•	•	•	•	•	
Cayman Islands	$$$$	3,453	•	•	•				•			•	•
Curaçao	$$	2,000	•	•	•	•			•			•	•
Dominica	$	800		•			•	•	•	•	•		
Dominican Republic	$	49,000	•	•	•	•	•	•		•	•	•	•
The Grenadines	$$$	500			•		•			•		•	
Grenada	$$$	2,300	•	•	•	•	•	•		•	•	•	
Guadeloupe	$$	5,800		•			•	•	•	•	•	•	•
Jamaica	$$$	16,103	•	•	•		•	•		•	•	•	•
Martinique	$$$	4,800	•	•			•	•		•	•	•	•
Nevis	$$$	400			•	•	•	•		•		•	
Puerto Rico	$$	11,909	•		•	•	•	•		•	•	•	•
Saba	$	96					•	•		•	•		•
St. Barthélemy	$$$$	715		•	•		•			•		•	
St. Eustatius	$	95			•	•				•			•
St. Kitts	$$	1,400		•	•	•	•	•		•		•	•
St. Lucia	$$$	3,300	•	•	•	•	•	•		•	•	•	
St. Maarten/St. Martin	$$$	6,146	•	•	•					•		•	•
St. Vincent	$$	730		•	•	•	•	•		•	•		
Trinidad	$	1,462	•	•	•			•		•	•	•	
Tobago	$$	1,500	•			•	•	•			•	•	
Turks and Caicos	$$$	1,300	•		•	•	•			•		•	
U.S. Virgin Islands:													
St. Croix	$$	1,495		•	•	•	•	•		•	•		•
St. John	$$	1,003		•	•	•	•	•		•		•	•
St. Thomas	$$	3,038	•	•	•	•				•		•	•

Figures based on 2000 estimates

Public transportation	Fine dining	Local cuisine	Shopping	Music	Casinos	Nightlife	Diving and Snorkeling	Sailing	Golf	Hiking	Ecotourism	Villa rentals	All-inclusives	Campgrounds	Luxury resorts	Secluded getaway	Good for families	Romantic hideaway
	●	●	●	●			●	●				●	●		●	●		●
●	●		●			●	●	●		●			●		●	●	●	
●	●	●	●	●	●	●	●	●	●	●	●	●	●		●	●		●
●	●	●	●			●	●	●		●	●	●	●		●	●		●
					●		●	●		●	●	●	●					●
●	●	●	●	●		●	●	●	●	●	●	●	●		●	●		●
	●		●				●		●		●	●	●	●	●			
●	●	●	●		●	●	●	●	●	●	●	●	●		●		●	●
●		●		●			●			●	●	●	●				●	●
●	●	●	●			●	●	●		●	●	●	●		●		●	●
	●	●					●			●		●			●			
●	●	●	●			●	●	●	●	●	●	●	●		●	●	●	
●	●	●	●	●		●	●	●	●	●	●	●	●	●		●	●	
●	●	●	●	●	●	●	●	●	●	●	●	●	●	●			●	●
●	●	●	●	●	●	●	●	●	●		●	●					●	
●	●						●	●	●	●		●			●	●		
	●						●			●	●	●			●	●		●
		●	●	●			●	●				●			●	●		●
		●					●			●	●					●		
	●	●	●			●	●	●	●	●		●		●				●
●	●	●	●	●		●	●	●	●	●	●	●	●	●	●	●	●	●
●	●	●	●			●	●	●	●	●	●	●	●		●	●		●
●	●				●	●	●	●			●	●			●	●		
●		●			●		●	●		●		●					●	
	●	●	●		●		●	●		●	●	●	●	●		●		●
		●				●		●	●	●	●	●			●		●	●
●	●	●	●	●		●	●	●	●	●	●				●		●	
●	●	●	●			●	●	●	●	●	●			●	●	●	●	●
●	●	●	●				●	●	●	●		●	●		●		●	

ESSENTIAL INFORMATION

ADDRESSES

"Whimsical" might best describe Caribbean addresses. Street names can change for no apparent reason, and most buildings have no numbers. Addresses throughout this guide may include cross streets, landmarks, and other directionals. But to find your destination, you might have to ask a local—and be prepared for directions such as, "Go down so, turn at the next gap (road), keep goin' past the church, and you'll see it right down the hill."

AIR TRAVEL

BOOKING

When you book, **look for nonstop flights** and **remember that "direct" flights stop at least once.** Try to avoid connecting flights, which require a change of plane, or connections to other airlines. The more connections you make, the more likely your luggage won't keep up with you. For more booking tips and to check prices and make on-line flight reservations, log on to www.fodors.com.

CARRIERS

➤ FROM THE U.S. AND CANADA: **Air Canada** (☎ 800/776–3000 in the U.S.; 888/247–2262 in Canada, WEB www.aircanada.ca). **Air Jamaica** (☎ 800/523–5585, WEB www. airjamaica.com). **Air ALM** (☎ 800/ 327–7230, WEB www.airalm.com). **American Airlines** (☎ 800/433–7300, WEB www.aa.com). **BWIA** (☎ 800/ 538–2942, WEB www.bwee.com). **Continental** (☎ 800/231–0856, WEB www.continental.com). **Delta** (☎ 800/241–4141, WEB www. delta-airlines.com). **Northwest Airlines** (☎ 800/447–4747, WEB www. nwa.com). **United Airlines** (☎ 800/ 538–2929, WEB www.united.com). **US Airways** (☎ 800/428–4322, WEB www.usairways.com).

➤ FROM THE U.K.: **Air Jamaica** (☎ 0208/570–7999, WEB www. airjamaica.com). **British Airways** (☎ 0845/77–333–77, WEB www. britishairways.com). **BWIA** (☎ 0171/ 745–1100, WEB www.bwee.com). **Virgin Atlantic** (☎ 0129/374–7747, WEB www.virginatlantic.com).

➤ FROM ELSEWHERE IN THE WORLD: **Air France** (☎ 0/802/802–802 in Paris, WEB www.airfrance.com). **British Airways** (☎ 02/8904–8800 in Sydney; 03/9565–8133 in Melbourne; 07/3223–3123 in Brisbane, WEB www.britishairways.com). **KLM** (☎ 31/20–4–747–747 in Amsterdam, WEB www.klm.com). **Qantas** (☎ 13–13–13 in Australia; 0800/808–767 in New Zealand, WEB www.qantas.com).

➤ CARIBBEAN INTERISLAND CARRIERS: **Air Caraïbes** (☎ 0590/824–700, WEB www.aircaraibes.com). **American Eagle** (☎ 800/433–7300, WEB www. aa.com). **Air Jamaica Express** (☎ 800/523–5585, WEB www. airjamaica.com). **BWIA Express** (☎ 800/538–2942, WEB www.bwee.com). **Caribbean Star** (☎ 268/461–7827; 800/744–7827 within the Caribbean, WEB www.flycaribbeanstar.com). **LIAT** (☎ 800/468–0482, WEB www. liatairline.com). **SVG Air** (☎ 784/ 457–5124, WEB www.svgair.com). **Winair** (☎ 800/634–4907, WEB www. windwardislandsairways.com).

CHECK-IN AND BOARDING

Always **ask your carrier about its check-in policy.** Plan to arrive at the airport about two hours before your scheduled departure time for domestic flights and 2½ to 3 hours before international flights. Checking in, paying departure taxes (which are usually *not* included in your airfare in the Caribbean), clearing security, and boarding can take longer than you expect at some island airports. **Expect security personnel to hand-search all your carry-on items**—sometimes a second time at the gate. When heading home, **get to the airport at least 1½ hours ahead of time** (2 hours if you plan to squeeze in some duty-free shopping). From most islands, there's often only one flight per day going in the direction you're headed.

Assuming that not everyone with a ticket will show up, airlines routinely overbook planes. When everyone does, airlines ask for volunteers to give up their seats. In return, these volunteers usually get a certificate for a free flight and are rebooked on the next flight out. If there are not enough volunteers, the airline must choose who will be denied boarding. The first to get bumped are passengers who checked in late and those flying on discounted tickets, so **get to the gate and check in as early as possible,** especially during peak periods.

Always **bring a government-issued photo I.D. to the airport;** even when it's not required, a passport is best.

CUTTING COSTS

The least expensive airfares to the Caribbean must usually be purchased in advance and are nonrefundable. It's smart to **call a number of airlines,** and when you are quoted a good price, **book it on the spot**—the same fare may not be available the next day. Always **check different routings** and look into using alternate airports. Also, price off-peak flights, which may be significantly less expensive than others. Travel agents, especially low-fare specialists (☞ Discounts and Deals), are helpful.

Use the Internet to compare fares and schedules and buy tickets. Most airlines offer discounted prices or bonus frequent flyer miles if you purchase tickets on-line. General travel sites, such as www.expedia.com, www.orbitz.com, or www.travelocity.com, let you compare current fares for all airlines serving a particular destination and will also book your flights. In fact, many airline sites now show you competitive routings and fares. You can also **bid for cheaper fares over the Internet** through companies such as www.priceline.com, which are legitimate sources for seats on major airlines. The more flexible you are with

your timing and destination, the better the deal you can make.

Ask about island-hopping passes. Air ALM's 30-day "Visit Caribbean Airpass," for example, may be used for five destinations, including Miami. Air Jamaica's "Stop Over Free" program allows you to stop over in Jamaica for part of your vacation when you fly round-trip to any of the airline's other Caribbean destinations. American Airlines and American Eagle offer a "Caribbean Explorer" fare to 23 Caribbean destinations out of San Juan. BWIA offers a 30-day "Caribbean Traveller" air pass for travel to its 12 Caribbean and South American destinations. LIAT has three categories of interisland "Explorer" passes for different durations.

Consolidators are another good source. They buy tickets for scheduled international flights at reduced rates from the airlines, then sell them at prices that beat the best fare available directly from the airlines, usually without restrictions. Sometimes you can even get your money back if you need to return the ticket. Carefully read the fine print detailing penalties for changes and cancellations, and **confirm your consolidator reservation with the airline.**

➤ CONSOLIDATORS: Airline Consolidator (☎ 425/485–1355 or 888/468–5385, WEB www.airlineconsolidator.com). Cheap Tickets (☎ 800/922–8849, WEB www.cheaptickets.com). Discount Airline Ticket Service (☎ 800/576–1600). Economy Travel (☎ 888/222–2110, WEB www.economytravel.com). In the U.K.: Flights 4 Less (☎ 020/7400–7097, WEB www.flights4less.co.uk). Unitravel (☎ 800/325–2222, WEB www.unitravel.com). Up & Away Travel (☎ 212/889–2345, WEB www.upandaway.com).

ENJOYING THE FLIGHT

State your seat preference when purchasing your ticket, and then repeat it when you confirm and when you check in. For more legroom, you can request one of the few emergency-aisle seats at check-in, if you are capable of lifting at least 50 pounds—a Federal Aviation Administration requirement of passengers in these seats. Seats behind a bulkhead also offer more legroom, but they don't have under-seat storage. Don't sit in the row in front of the emergency aisle or in front of a bulkhead, where seats may not recline.

If you have dietary concerns, **ask for special meals when booking.** These can be vegetarian, low-cholesterol, or kosher, for example. It's a good idea to pack some healthy snacks and a small (plastic) bottle of water in your carry-on bag. On long flights, try to maintain a normal routine, to help fight jet lag. At night, **get some sleep.** By day, **eat light meals, drink water** (not alcohol), and **move around the cabin** to stretch your legs. For additional jet-lag tips consult *Fodor's FYI: Travel Fit & Healthy* (available at bookstores everywhere).

Smoking policies vary from carrier to carrier. Many airlines prohibit smoking on all of their international flights; others allow smoking only on certain routes or certain departures. Ask your carrier about its policy.

FLYING TIMES

The flight from New York to San Juan, Puerto Rico, takes 3½ hours; from Miami to San Juan it's 1½ hours. Flights from New York to Kingston or Montego Bay, Jamaica, take about 4 hours; those from Miami, about an hour. Nonstop flights from London to Antigua and Barbados and from Paris to Guadeloupe, Martinique, and St. Martin are about 7 hours. Once you've arrived in the Caribbean, hops between islands range from 20 minutes to 2 hours.

HOW TO COMPLAIN

If your baggage goes astray or your flight goes awry, complain right away. Most carriers require that you **file a claim immediately** before leaving the baggage claim area. Be sure to get a receipt for your baggage check, which the airline may retain, and a phone number (not reservations) where you may inquire about the status of your bag. Although it's a special nuisance when you're en route to your vacation destination, it's good to know that lost bags are merely delayed and rarely lost forever.

➤ AIRLINE COMPLAINTS: U.S. Department of Transportation **Aviation Consumer Protection Division** (✉ C-75, Room 4107, Washington, DC 20590, ☎ 202/366–2220, WEB www.dot.gov/airconsumer). **Federal Aviation Administration Consumer Hotline** (☎ 800/322–7873).

RECONFIRMING

Check the status of your flight before you leave for the airport. You can do this on your carrier's Web site, by linking to a flight-status checker (many Web booking services offer these), or by calling your carrier or travel agent. Always confirm international flights at least 72 hours ahead of the scheduled departure time. Be sure to **reconfirm your flights on interisland carriers.** You may be subject to a small carrier's whims: if no other passengers are booked on your flight, you may be requested (actually, told) to take another flight or departure time that's more convenient for the airline, or your plane may make unscheduled stops to pick up more clients or cargo. It's all part of the excitement—and unpredictability—of Caribbean travel. In addition, regional carriers use small aircraft with limited baggage space, and they often impose weight restrictions; **travel light,** or you could be subject to outrageous surcharges or delays in getting very large or heavy luggage, which may have to follow on another flight.

AIRPORTS

Airports on most of the islands are modern facilities, with comfortable waiting areas, restaurants, duty-free shops, and other services. The smaller, more remote island destinations, of course, have tiny airfields and few services.

BIKE TRAVEL

Many Caribbean islands are mountainous, and their narrow, steep, winding roads already have difficulty accommodating cars, pedestrians, and occasional livestock. Serious bikers, of course, will take all this in stride. If you're a more laid-back biker, however, good bets include: Antigua, Aruba, Bonaire, Puerto Rico, Grand Turk and Providenciales (Turks and Caicos Islands), St. Croix (USVI), and

St. Martin. Most islands have at least one bike-rental company (rates are usually reasonable), and some resorts offer guests the use of bikes at no additional charge.

BIKES IN FLIGHT

Most airlines accommodate bikes as luggage, provided they are dismantled and boxed. Airlines sell bike boxes, which are often free at bike shops, for about $5 (it's at least $100 for bike bags). International travelers can sometimes substitute a bike for a piece of checked luggage at no charge; otherwise, the cost is about $100. Domestic and Canadian airlines charge $25–$50.

BOAT AND FERRY TRAVEL

Ferry travel is an inexpensive way to island-hop. Ferries ply the waters of the Grenadines, for example, and you can take a day-trip or spend a week or more cruising from one lovely island to another. Cargo schooners and mail boats are even less expensive and more adventuresome modes of interisland travel, but you can't be in a hurry. High-speed ferries or catamarans link neighboring islands, such as Grenada with Carriacou; Martinique with Dominica, Guadeloupe, and St. Lucia; St. John with St. Thomas; and St. Maarten/St. Martin with Anguilla, St. Barths, and Saba. Reservations aren't usually necessary.

BUS TRAVEL

Some islands, such as Puerto Rico, St. Thomas, the Dominican Republic, Aruba, and Barbados have convenient, inexpensive bus service along regular routes—and with regular schedules. On smaller islands, "bus" service may be provided by privately owned vans that follow regular routes but not necessarily regular schedules—they just keep coming, one after another, all day long. Fares are inexpensive (some buses require exact change in local currency), and this mode of transport is a good way to absorb the local culture.

BUSINESS HOURS

Though business hours vary from island to island, shops are generally closed Saturday afternoon and all day Sunday. Some shops close for an hour at lunchtime during the week, as well, although this practice is becoming increasingly rare. Farmers markets are often open daily (except Sunday), but Saturday morning is always the most colorful and exciting time to go.

CAMERAS AND PHOTOGRAPHY

Frothy waves in a turquoise sea and palm-lined crescents of beach are relatively easy to capture on film if you **don't let the brightness of the sun on sand and water fool your light meter.** You must compensate or else work early or late in the day when the light isn't as brilliant and contrast isn't such a problem. Try to **capture expansive views** of waterfront, beach, or village scenes; consider shooting down onto the shore from a clearing on a hillside or from a rock on the beach. Or **zoom in on something colorful,** such as a delicate tropical flower or a craftsman at work—but always **ask permission to take pictures of locals or their property.** **Use a disposable underwater camera** to make your snorkeling and diving adventures more memorable. The *Kodak Guide to Shooting Great Travel Pictures* (available in bookstores or from Fodor's Travel Publications) is loaded with tips.

➤ PHOTO HELP: Kodak Information Center (☎ 800/242–2424).

EQUIPMENT PRECAUTIONS

Keep your film and videotape out of the sun, and be advised that sand and sea water are no friends to most camera workings. Carry an extra supply of batteries, and **be prepared to turn on your camera or camcorder** to prove to airport security personnel that the device is real. **Keep all film, exposed or unexposed, in your hand luggage.** High-tech security scanners used on checked luggage can adversely affect film. Always **ask for hand inspection of film,** which becomes clouded after successive exposures to airport X-ray machines, and **keep videotapes away from metal detectors.** Although thievery isn't a major concern in the Caribbean, don't invite problems: **never leave your gear unattended on the beach or in a rental car,** and **lock up your**

camera or video equipment when you leave your hotel room.

FILM AND DEVELOPING

Film, batteries, and one-time-use cameras are available in camera stores, souvenir shops, hotel boutiques, and pharmacies—although such items can cost twice as much as at home. In all but the most remote areas, you can find 24-hour film-developing services, as well.

CAR RENTAL

Major firms, such as Avis, Hertz, and Budget, have agencies in many islands of the Caribbean. But **don't overlook local firms**; their cars are mechanically sound, and prices are competitive. Cars often have standard transmission, although automatic is usually an option. It's not crucial to reserve a rental car prior to your arrival. Many hotels, especially those far from the airport, include airport transfers, and taxis are always an option. Besides, you may only want a rental car for a day or two of on-your-own sightseeing. For exciting treks into remote areas where roads are hilly or unpaved, **rent a four-wheel-drive vehicle.**

➤ MAJOR AGENCIES: **Alamo** (☎ 800/522–9696; WEB www.alamo.com). **Avis** (☎ 800/331–1084; 800/879–2847 in Canada; 02/9353–9000 in Australia; 09/526–2847 in New Zealand; 0870/606–0100 in the U.K.; WEB www.avis.com). **Budget** (☎ 800/527–0700; 0870/156–5656 in the U.K.; WEB www.budget.com). **Dollar** (☎ 800/800–6000; 0124/622–0111 in the U.K., where it's affiliated with Sixt; 02/9223–1444 in Australia; WEB www.dollar.com). **Hertz** (☎ 800/654–3001; 800/263–0600 in Canada; 020/8897–2072 in the U.K.; 02/9669–2444 in Australia; 09/256–8690 in New Zealand; WEB www.hertz.com). **National Car Rental** (☎ 800/227–7368; 020/8680–4800 in the U.K.; WEB www.nationalcar.com).

CUTTING COSTS

Ask about required deposits and cancellation penalties. Plan to **pay by credit card to avoid a hefty cash deposit.** If you're traveling during a holiday period, **make sure that a confirmed reservation guarantees you a car.** To get the best deal, **book** through a travel agent who will shop around.

INSURANCE

When driving a rented car you are generally responsible for any damage to or loss of the vehicle. You may also be liable for any property damage or personal injury that you may cause while driving. Before you rent, see what coverage you already have under the terms of your personal auto-insurance policy and credit cards.

REQUIREMENTS AND RESTRICTIONS

An international driver's license or a temporary permit, which you can get at rental agencies or local police offices upon presentation of a valid license and a small fee, is often required.

SURCHARGES

Before you pick up a car in one city and leave it in another, **ask about drop-off charges or one-way service fees,** which can be substantial. Note, too, that some rental agencies charge extra if you return the car before the time specified in your contract. To avoid a hefty refueling fee, **fill the tank just before you turn in the car,** but be aware that gas stations near the rental outlet may overcharge. It's almost never a deal to buy the tank of gas in the car when you rent it; the understanding is that you'll return it empty, but some fuel usually remains.

CAR TRAVEL

Although exploring on your own can give your sightseeing excursions a sense of adventure, tentative drivers should instead consider hiring a taxi for the day. Locals, who are familiar with the roads, often drive fast and take chances. You don't want to get in their way.

EMERGENCY SERVICES

Major-brand gas and service stations, where you can use your credit card, are found throughout the Caribbean but mainly in the larger towns. Before driving off into the countryside, **check your rental car for tire-changing equipment,** including an inflated spare. Roadside assistance may be unavailable.

ROAD CONDITIONS

Island roads, particularly in mountainous regions that experience heavy tropical rains, are often potholed and bumpy—as well as narrow, winding, and hilly. **Drive with extreme caution,** especially if you venture out at night. You won't see guardrails on every hill and curve, although the drops can be frighteningly steep. And pedestrians (including children and the elderly) and livestock often share the roadway with vehicles.

ROAD MAPS

Road maps are available from car-rental agencies and often at your hotel. Small islands have few roads—often one main road around the perimeter and a couple that cross the island. It's hard to get lost.

RULES OF THE ROAD

On islands with a British heritage, **be prepared to drive on the left.** Speed limits are low, because it's often hard to find a road long and straight enough to *safely* get up much speed. And always **wear your seatbelts,** which are required by law. Drivers are generally courteous; for example, if someone flashes car headlights at you at an intersection, it means "after you."

CHILDREN IN THE CARIBBEAN

Kids of all ages love the beach and, therefore, love the Caribbean. Resorts are increasingly sensitive to families' needs, and many now have extensive children's programs and can arrange for a baby-sitter when parents need some time alone. On sightseeing days, try to include some activities that will also interest children. Sights and attractions that children will particularly enjoy are indicated in the Exploring section of each island chapter by a rubber-duckie icon (🐤) in the margin. For general advice about traveling with children, check out the family travel tips in the Family Travel section of www.fodors.com and consult *Fodor's FYI: Travel with Your Baby* (available in bookstores everywhere).

If you are renting a car, don't forget to **arrange for a car seat** when you reserve. For general advice about traveling with children, consult *Fodor's FYI: Travel with Your Baby* (available in bookstores everywhere).

FLYING

If your children are two or older, **ask about children's airfares.** As a general rule, infants under two not occupying a seat fly at greatly reduced fares or even for free. When booking, **confirm carry-on allowances** if you're traveling with infants. In general, for babies charged 10% of the adult fare you are allowed one carry-on bag and a collapsible stroller; if the flight is full, the stroller may have to be checked or you may be limited to less.

Experts agree that it's a good idea to use safety seats aloft for children weighing less than 40 pounds. Airlines set their own policies: U.S. carriers usually require that the child be ticketed, even if he or she is young enough to ride free, since the seats must be strapped into regular seats. Do **check your airline's policy about using safety seats during takeoff and landing.** Safety seats are not allowed everywhere in the plane, so get your seat assignments as early as possible.

When reserving, **request children's meals or a freestanding bassinet** (not available at all airlines) if you need them. But note that bulkhead seats, where you must sit to use the bassinet, may lack an overhead bin or storage space on the floor.

FOOD

Even if your youngsters are picky eaters, meals in the Caribbean shouldn't be a problem. Baby food is easy to find (although often pricier than you might find at home, and brands may be limited). Hamburgers and hot dogs are available at many resorts. Chicken legs, fried or baked, are ubiquitous throughout the Caribbean; restaurants offer pasta and vegetarian dishes, pizza, sandwiches, and ice cream—all of which appeal to kids. Supermarkets have cereal, snacks, and other packaged goods that you'll recognize from home. At outdoor markets, a few dollars will buy you enough bananas, oranges, and other tropical fruit to last your entire vacation. Just watch out for overly spicy food that may be upset children's sensitive stomachs.

LODGING

Children are welcome in most Caribbean resorts; exceptions are couples-only and adults-only establishments and the ultra-exclusive properties. Some places have only limited children's activities and may not welcome kids during peak season. Other properties offer fully supervised kids' programs, in-room baby-sitting, kids' menus and other family-friendly features. Children under 12 or 16 can often stay free in their parents' room (be sure to **find out the cutoff age for children's discounts** when booking).

Families should also **consider booking a condo or a villa**; a two-bedroom condo (and sometimes even a one-bedroom condo, with a sleeper sofa in the sitting room) is often suitable for two parents and two children traveling together and may also be cheaper than a larger room or suite in a hotel or resort for a similar time period. Meal preparation in the condo's kitchen can save substantially on the cost of meals. Some condo resorts even have children's programs. In some islands, such as Grand Cayman, condos and villas actually outnumber hotel rooms.

PRECAUTIONS

Don't underestimate the tropical sun. Throughout the day, even away from the beach, lather plenty of sunscreen—with a sun protection factor (SPF) of 15 or higher—on all exposed areas. Small children should also wear a hat. Mosquito bites can become infected when scratched, so **use bug spray** and avoid the problem. To prevent dehydration, **carry plenty of bottled water** at the beach and on sightseeing excursions.

To avoid immigration problems when a child carries a last name that's different from that of an accompanying parent, **bring identification that clarifies the family relationship** (e.g., a birth certificate identifying the parent or a joint passport). If a child is traveling without both birth parents, a notarized letter should accompany the child from the nonpresent parent(s) authorizing permission for the child to travel.

SIGHTS AND ATTRACTIONS

Places that are especially appealing to children are indicated in the Exploring section of each island chapter by a rubber-duckie icon (🦆) in the margin.

SUPPLIES AND EQUIPMENT

Suites at many resorts and even small hotels have sofas suitable for children sharing a parent's room. High chairs and cribs are also generally available. Supermarkets sell common brands of disposable diapers, baby food, and other necessities. Bookstores and souvenir shops have activity books and toys that kids will enjoy on vacation and back at home.

COMPUTERS ON THE ROAD

Bring an adapter for your laptop plug. Even if your computer can be used on either a 100v or 220v system, the prongs on your U.S. standard plug won't fit into Caribbean 220v wall outlets. Adapters are inexpensive and generally available in hardware stores at home and in the Caribbean. Some hotels will lend adapters to guests for use during their stay.

At the airport, **be prepared to turn on your laptop** to prove to security personnel that the device is not a security risk. The security X-ray machines aren't damaging to a laptop, but **keep computer disks away from metal detectors.** In your hotel, **stow away and lock up your laptop when you're out of the room.** Although thievery isn't a major concern in the Caribbean, don't invite a problem.

CONSUMER PROTECTION

Whether you're shopping for gifts or purchasing travel services, **pay with a major credit card** whenever possible, so you can cancel payment or get reimbursed if there's a problem (and you can provide documentation). If you're doing business with a particular company for the first time, **contact your local Better Business Bureau and the attorney general's offices** in your state and (for U.S. businesses) the company's home state as well. Have any complaints been filed? Finally, if you're buying a package or tour, always **consider travel insurance** that includes default coverage (☞ Insurance).

➤ BBBs: **Council of Better Business Bureaus** (✉ 4200 Wilson Blvd., Suite 800, Arlington, VA 22203, ☎ 703/276–0100, FAX 703/525–8277, WEB www.bbb.org).

CRUISE TRAVEL

Cruising is a relaxing and convenient way to tour this beautiful part of the world. You get all of the amenities of a luxury hotel and enough activities to guarantee fun, even on the occasional rainy day. All your important decisions are made long before you board. Your itinerary is set, and you know the total cost of your vacation beforehand.

Ships usually call at several ports on a single voyage but are at each port for only one day. Thus, although you may be exposed to several islands, you don't get much of a feel for any one of them.

To learn how to plan, choose, and book a cruise-ship voyage, consult *Fodor's FYI: Plan & Enjoy Your Cruise* (available in bookstores everywhere).

➤ CRUISE LINES: **American Canadian Caribbean Line** (✉ Box 368, Warren, RI 02885, ☎ 401/247–0955 or 800/556–7450, WEB www.accl-smallships.com). **Carnival Cruise Lines** (✉ 3655 N.W. 87th Ave., Miami, FL 33178, ☎ 305/599–2600 or 888/227–6482, WEB www.carnival.com). **Celebrity Cruises** (✉ 1050 Caribbean Way, Miami, FL 33122, ☎ 305/539–6000 or 800/722–5941, WEB www.celebrity-cruises.com). **Clipper Cruise Line** (✉ 7711 Bonhomme Ave., St. Louis, MO 63105, ☎ 314/727–2929 or 800/325–0010, WEB www.clippercruise.com). **Costa Cruise Lines** (✉ World Trade Center Bldg., 80 S.W. 8th St., Miami, FL 33130, ☎ 305/358–7325 or 800/462–6782, WEB www.costacruises.com). **Crystal Cruises** (✉ 2049 Century Park E, Suite 1400, Los Angeles, CA 90067, ☎ 310/785–9300 or 800/446–6620, WEB www.crystalcruises.com). **Cunard Line** (✉ 6100 Blue Lagoon Dr., Suite 400, Miami, FL 33126, ☎ 305/463–3000 or 800/7–CUNARD, WEB www.cunardline.com). **Disney Cruise Line** (✉ 210 Celebration Pl., Suite 400, Celebration, FL 34747, ☎ 407/566–3500, WEB www.disneycruise.com).

Holland America Line (✉ 300 Elliott Ave. W, Seattle, WA 98119, ☎ 206/281–3535 or 800/426–6593, WEB www.hollandamerica.com). **Norwegian Cruise Line** (✉ 7665 Corporate Center Dr., Miami, FL 33126, ☎ 305/436–4000 or 800/327–7030, WEB www.ncl.com). **Princess Cruises** (✉ 10100 Santa Monica Blvd., Suite 1800, Los Angeles, CA 90067, ☎ 310/553–1770 or 800/421–0522, WEB www.princesscruises.com). **Radisson Seven Seas Cruises** (✉ 600 Corporate Dr., Suite 410, Fort Lauderdale, FL 33334, ☎ 954/776–6123, 800/285–1835, or 800/477–7500, WEB www.rssc.com). **Regal Cruises** (✉ 300 Regal Cruises Way, Palmetto, FL 34221, ☎ 941/721–7300 or 800/270–7245, WEB www.regalcruises.com). **Royal Caribbean International** (✉ 1050 Caribbean Way, Miami, FL 33132, ☎ 305/539–6000 or 800/327–6700, WEB www.royalcaribbean.com). **Seabourn Cruise Line** (✉ 6100 Blue Lagoon Dr., Suite 400, Miami, FL 33126, ☎ 305/463–3000 or 800/929–9391, WEB www.seabourn.com). **Silversea Cruises** (✉ 110 E. Broward Blvd., Fort Lauderdale, FL 33301, ☎ 954/522–4477 or 800/722–9055, WEB www.silversea.com). **Star Clippers** (✉ 4101 Salzedo St., Coral Gables, FL 33146, ☎ 305/442–0550 or 800/442–0551, WEB www.star-clippers.com). **Windjammer Barefoot Cruises** (✉ 1759 Bay Rd., Miami Beach, FL 33139, ☎ 305/672–6453 or 800/327–2601, WEB www.windjammer.com). **Windstar Cruises** (✉ 300 Elliott Ave. W, Seattle, WA 98119, ☎ 206/281–3535 or 800/626–9900, WEB www.windstarcruises.com).

➤ ORGANIZATIONS: **Cruise Lines International Association** (CLIA; ✉ 500 5th Ave., Suite 1407, New York, NY 10110, ☎ 212/921–0066, WEB www.cruising.org).

CUSTOMS AND DUTIES

When shopping abroad, **keep receipts** for all purchases. Upon reentering the country, **be ready to show customs officials what you've bought.** If you feel a duty is incorrect, appeal the assessment. If you object to the way your clearance was handled, note the inspector's badge number. In either case, first ask to see a supervisor. If the problem isn't resolved, write to the appropriate authorities, beginning with the port director at your point of entry.

IN AUSTRALIA

Australian residents who are 18 or older may bring home A$400 worth of souvenirs and gifts (including jewelry), 250 cigarettes or 250 grams of tobacco, and 1,125 ml of alcohol (including wine, beer, and spirits). Residents under 18 may bring back A$200 worth of goods. Prohibited items include meat products. Seeds, plants, and fruits need to be declared upon arrival.

➤ INFORMATION: **Australian Customs Service** (Regional Director, ✉ Box 8, Sydney, NSW 2001, ☎ 02/9213–2000 or 1300/363263; 1800/020504 quarantine-inquiry line, FAX 02/9213–4000, WEB www.customs.gov.au).

IN CANADA

Canadian residents who have been out of Canada for at least seven days may bring in C$750 worth of goods duty-free. If you've been away fewer than seven days but more than 48 hours, the duty-free allowance drops to C$200; if your trip lasts 24 to 48 hours, the allowance is C$50. You may not pool allowances with family members. Goods claimed under the C$750 exemption may follow you by mail; those claimed under the lesser exemptions must accompany you. Alcohol and tobacco products may be included in the seven-day and 48-hour exemptions but not in the 24-hour exemption. If you meet the age requirements of the province or territory through which you reenter Canada, you may bring in, duty-free, 1.5 liters of wine *or* 1.14 liters (40 imperial ounces) of liquor *or* 24 12-ounce cans or bottles of beer or ale. If you are 19 or older you may bring in, duty-free, 200 cigarettes and 50 cigars. Check ahead of time with the Canada Customs and Revenue Agency or the Department of Agriculture for policies regarding meat products, seeds, plants, and fruits.

You may send an unlimited number of gifts (only one gift per recipient, however) worth up to C$60 each duty-free to Canada. Label the package UNSO- LICITED GIFT—VALUE UNDER $60. Alcohol and tobacco are excluded.

➤ INFORMATION: **Canada Customs and Revenue Agency** (✉ 2265 St. Laurent Blvd. S, Ottawa, Ontario K1G 4K3, ☎ 204/983–3500; 506/636–5064; 800/461–9999, WEB www. ccra-adrc.gc.ca/).

IN THE CARIBBEAN

Although customs inspectors in some countries inspect all baggage to allay their concerns about smuggling or drug running, many islands wave those tourists who have no goods to declare through customs inspections with only a cursory question or two. Exceptions include major hubs within the Caribbean, such as Jamaica, Puerto Rico, and Antigua. If you're yachting through the islands, note that harbor customs are often thorough, as well.

These rules generally apply throughout the Caribbean: Individuals are limited to bringing *in* 2 liters of alcohol, two cartons of cigarettes, and a reasonable amount of duty-free goods for your personal use. More than that, and you'll be asked to pay a hefty import tax.

IN NEW ZEALAND

All homeward-bound residents may bring back NZ$700 worth of souvenirs and gifts; passengers may not pool their allowances, and children can claim only the concession on goods intended for their own use. For those 17 or older, the duty-free allowance also includes 4.5 liters of wine or beer; one 1,125-ml bottle of spirits; and either 200 cigarettes, 250 grams of tobacco, 50 cigars, *or* a combination of the three up to 250 grams. Meat products, seeds, plants, and fruits must be declared upon arrival to the Agricultural Services Department.

➤ INFORMATION: **New Zealand Customs** (Head Office, ✉ The Customhouse, 17–21 Whitmore St., Box 2218, Wellington, ☎ 09/300–5399 or 0800/428–786, WEB www.customs.govt.nz).

IN THE U.K.

Although some Caribbean nations are part of the British Commonwealth, they are not part of the

European Union (EU) with regard to customs. From countries outside the European Union, including those in the Caribbean, you may bring home, duty-free, 200 cigarettes or 50 cigars; 1 liter of spirits or 2 liters of fortified or sparkling wine or liqueurs; 2 liters of still table wine; 60 ml of perfume; 250 ml of toilet water; plus £145 worth of other goods, including gifts and souvenirs. Prohibited items include meat products, seeds, plants, and fruits.

➤ INFORMATION: **HM Customs and Excise** (✉ Portcullis House, 21 Cowbridge Rd. E, Cardiff CF11 9SS, ☎ 029/2038–6423 or 0845/010–9000, WEB www.hmce.gov.uk).

IN THE U.S.

U.S. residents who have been out of the country for at least 48 hours may bring home, for personal use, $400 worth of foreign goods duty-free, as long as they haven't used the $400 allowance or any part of it in the past 30 days. This exemption may include 1 liter of alcohol (for travelers 21 and older), 200 cigarettes, and 100 non-Cuban cigars. Family members from the same household who are traveling together may pool their $400 personal exemptions. For fewer than 48 hours, the duty-free allowance drops to $200, which may include 50 cigarettes, 10 non-Cuban cigars, and 150 milliliters of alcohol (or perfume containing alcohol). The $200 allowance cannot be combined with other individuals' exemptions, and if you exceed it, the full value of all the goods will be taxed. Antiques, which the U.S. Customs Service defines as objects more than 100 years old, enter duty-free, as do original works of art done entirely by hand, including paintings, drawings, and sculptures. If you're returning from the U.S. Virgin Islands (USVI), the duty-free allowance is $1,200. If your travel included the USVI and another country—say, the Dominican Republic—the $1,200 allowance still applies, but at least $600 worth of goods must be from the USVI.

U.S. residents 21 and older may bring back 2 liters of alcohol duty-free as long as one of the liters was produced in a CBI country. In addition, regard-

less of your age, you are allowed 200 cigarettes and 100 non-Cuban cigars. Antiques, which the U.S. Customs Service defines as objects more than 100 years old, enter duty-free, as do original works of art done entirely by hand, including paintings, drawings, and sculptures. You may also send packages home duty-free, with a limit of one parcel per addressee per day (except alcohol or tobacco products or perfume worth more than $5). You can mail up to $200 worth of goods for personal use; label the package PERSONAL USE and attach a list of its contents and their retail value. If the package contains your used personal belongings, mark it PERSONAL GOODS RETURNED to avoid paying duties. You may send up to $100 worth of goods ($200 from the U.S. Virgin Islands) as a gift; mark the package UNSOLICITED GIFT. Mailed items do not affect your duty-free allowance on your return.

➤ INFORMATION: **U.S. Customs Service** (for inquiries, ✉ 1300 Pennsylvania Ave. NW, Washington, DC 20229, WEB www.customs.gov, ☎ 202/354–1000; for complaints, ✉ Customer Satisfaction Unit, 1300 Pennsylvania Ave. NW, Room 5.5A, Washington, DC 20229; for registration of equipment, ✉ Office of Passenger Programs, 1300 Pennsylvania Ave. NW, Room 5.4D, Washington, DC 20229, ☎ 202/927–0530).

DINING

The Caribbean islands offer dining experiences that will delight any palate. You'll find French cuisine with exquisite service, lavish buffets featuring local dishes, fresh seafood served by the waterfront, Italian pasta with a modern twist, Chinese cuisine to eat in or take out, vegetarian dishes of just-picked produce, and more. Fast-food restaurants usually feature fried chicken, not burgers, but pizza is everywhere. The restaurants we list in the island chapters are the cream of the crop in each price category.

MEALS AND SPECIALTIES

Give your taste buds a vacation and try local cuisine, which could be Spanish-style in Puerto Rico and the Dominican Republic, French creole in St. Lucia, Martinique, and Dominica, Indian in Trinidad, Indonesian in

Aruba, spicy barbecue in Jamaica, and fresh seafood everywhere. Vegetarians can expect a treat, as the fresh fruit and vegetables, both usual and unusual, are plentiful.

Resort breakfasts are frequently lavish buffets that offer tropical fruits and fruit juices, cereal, fresh rolls and pastries, hot dishes, such as codfish, corned beef hash, and potatoes, and prepared-to-order eggs, pancakes, and French toast. Lunch could be at a beachfront café or a picnic at a secluded cove. But dinner is the highlight, often combining the expertise of internationally trained chefs with local know-how and ingredients.

MEALTIMES

Expect breakfast to be served from 7:30 AM to 10 AM; lunch from noon to 2 PM or so; and dinner from 7 PM to about 10 PM—perhaps later on Spanish-heritage islands. Some restaurants have specific mealtimes; others serve continuously all day long. Unless otherwise noted, the restaurants listed in this guide are open daily for lunch and dinner.

PAYING

Major credit cards (Access, American Express, Barclaycard, Carte Blanche, Diners Club, Discover, EnRoute, Eurocard, MasterCard, and/or Visa) are accepted in most restaurants. Exceptions are noted in the reviews.

RESERVATIONS AND DRESS

Reservations are always a good idea; we mention them only when they're essential or not accepted. Book as far ahead as you can, and reconfirm as soon as you arrive. (Large parties should always call ahead to check the reservations policy.) We mention dress only when men are required to wear a jacket or a jacket and tie. Beach attire is universally frowned upon in restaurants throughout the Caribbean.

WINE, BEER AND SPIRITS

The Caribbean is where "de rum come from," so rum is the base of most cocktails—often fruity, festive ones that really pack a punch. Many islands also have their own breweries, and the local beers are light and refreshing—perfect for hot summer afternoons at the beach.

DISABILITIES AND ACCESSIBILITY

Very few attractions and sights in the Caribbean are equipped with ramps, elevators, or wheelchair-accessible toilets. Exceptions include places on Puerto Rico and the USVI, which must abide by the Americans with Disabilities Act—although not all facilities are well-equipped.

LODGING

Resorts in hilly or mountainous regions are particularly difficult for travelers with disabilities. Many hotels and resorts have accessible ground-floor guest rooms; others, particularly newer ones, offer some guest rooms with extra-wide doors and bathrooms with grab bars and easily accessible shower stalls. Some hotels may also help arrange rentals of special equipment. Be sure to **make your special needs known when reserving your room.**

RESERVATIONS

When discussing accessibility with an operator or reservations agent, **ask hard questions.** Are there any stairs, inside *or* out? Are there grab bars next to the toilet *and* in the shower/tub? How wide is the doorway to the room? To the bathroom? For the most extensive facilities meeting the latest legal specifications, **opt for newer accommodations.** If you reserve through a toll-free number, consider also calling the hotel's local number to confirm the information from the central reservations office. Get confirmation in writing when you can.

TRANSPORTATION

At most Caribbean airports, passengers board and disembark aircraft directly from and onto the tarmac, which requires negotiating a steep staircase. Puerto Rico is one exception, although even there some small planes can't use the connected jetways. It can be a rather long walk to immigration, customs, and the airport exit. Aircraft operated by U.S. carriers must provide accessible lavatories, movable aisle armrests (on planes with 30 or more seats), an on-board wheelchair (on planes with 60 or more seats), and space to store a passenger's own folding wheelchair in the cabin (on planes with 100 or more seats). If you require a special in-flight accommodation (e.g., respirator hook-up), the airline may require up to 48 hours' advance notice. Be sure to **request wheelchairs or escort assistance when booking your flight.**

➤ COMPLAINTS: **Aviation Consumer Protection Division** (☞ Air Travel) for airline-related problems. **Departmental Office of Civil Rights** (for general inquiries, ✉ U.S. Department of Transportation, S-30, 400 7th St. SW, Room 10215, Washington, DC 20590, ☎ 202/366–4648, FAX 202/366–3571, WEB www.dot.gov/ost/docr/index.htm). **Disability Rights Section** (✉ U.S. Department of Justice, Civil Rights Division, 950 Pennsylvania Ave. NW, Washington, DC 20530, ☎ ADA information line 202/514–0301 or 800/514–0301; 202/514–0383 TTY or 800/514–0383 TTY, WEB www.usdoj. gov/crt/ada/adahom1.htm).

TRAVEL AGENCIES

In the United States, the Americans with Disabilities Act requires that travel firms serve the needs of all travelers. Some agencies specialize in working with people with disabilities.

➤ TRAVELERS WITH MOBILITY PROBLEMS: **Access Adventures** (✉ 206 Chestnut Ridge Rd., Scottsville, NY 14624, ☎ 716/889–9096, dltravel@ prodigy.net), run by a former physical-rehabilitation counselor. **CareVacations** (✉ No. 5, 5110–50 Ave., Leduc, Alberta T9E 6V4, Canada, ☎ 780/ 986–6404 or 877/478–7827, FAX 780/ 986–8332, WEB www.carevacations. com), for group tours and cruise vacations. **Flying Wheels Travel** (✉ 143 W. Bridge St., Box 382, Owatonna, MN 55060, ☎ 507/451– 5005, FAX 507/451–1685, WEB www. flyingwheelstravel.com). **Tomorrow's Level of Care** (✉ Box 470299, Brooklyn, NY 11247, ☎ 718/756–0794 or 800/932–2012), for nursing services and medical equipment.

➤ TRAVELERS WITH DEVELOPMENTAL DISABILITIES: **New Directions** (✉ 5276 Hollister Ave., Suite 207, Santa Barbara, CA 93111, ☎ 805/967–2841 or 888/967–2841, FAX 805/964–7344, WEB www.newdirectionstravel.com). **Sprout** (✉ 893 Amsterdam Ave., New York, NY 10025, ☎ 212/222–9575 or 888/222–9575, FAX 212/222–9768, WEB www.gosprout.org).

DISCOUNTS AND DEALS

Visit during the off-season, when prices usually plummet at even the glitziest resorts; you'll realize savings of up to 50% between April 15 and December 15. Moreover, you'll usually find fewer tourists, it's easier to rent a car, the sea tends to be calmer and clearer, and you might stumble onto local festivals.

Remember that your budget will go further on some islands (Dominica or Saba, for example) than on others (St. Barths or Anguilla). And more developed islands (St. Thomas, St. Maarten/St. Martin, Aruba, Puerto Rico, Jamaica, Grand Cayman) tend to be more competitive and creative in their package pricing. You'll also find that smaller hotels and guest houses or those that are a short walk from the beach offer very pleasant accommodations that are priced considerably lower than their larger, beachfront neighbors.

Be a smart shopper and **compare all your options** before making decisions. A plane ticket bought with a promotional coupon from travel clubs, coupon books, and direct-mail offers or purchased on the Internet may not be cheaper than the least expensive fare from a discount ticket agency. And always keep in mind that what you get is just as important as what you save.

DISCOUNT RESERVATIONS

To save money, **look into discount reservations services** with Web sites and toll-free numbers, which use their buying power to get a better price on hotels, airline tickets, even car rentals. When booking a room, always **call the hotel's local toll-free number** (if one is available) rather than the central reservations number—you'll often get a better price. Always ask about special packages or corporate rates.

When shopping for the best deal on hotels and car rentals, **look for guaranteed exchange rates,** which protect you against a falling dollar. With your rate locked in, you won't pay more, even if the price goes up in the local currency.

➤ AIRLINE TICKETS: ☎ 800/AIR–4LESS.

➤ HOTEL ROOMS: **Hotel Reservations Network** (☎ 800/964–6835, WEB www.hoteldiscount.com). **Turbotrip. com** (☎ 800/473–7829, WEB www. turbotrip.com).

PACKAGE DEALS

Don't confuse packages and guided tours. When you buy a package, you travel on your own, just as though you had planned the trip yourself. Fly/drive packages, which combine airfare and car rental, are often a good deal.

DIVING

The Caribbean offers some of the best scuba diving in the world. The waters around Bonaire's entire coast, for instance, are a protected marine park, with scores of dive sites accessible from the beach. The Cayman Islands, Turks and Caicos, the British Virgin Islands, St. Lucia, Dominica, and St. Vincent and the Grenadines also offer world-class diving experiences. The water throughout the Caribbean is crystal clear, often to 200 ft (61 m), and the quantity and variety of marine life is astounding.

Resorts often offer guests introductory scuba instruction in a pool, followed by a shallow dive; some hotels have on-site dive shops. All shops offer instruction and certification according to the standards set by either the National Association of Underwater Instructors (NAUI) or the Professional Association of Diving Instructors (PADI). Dive operators offer day and night dives to wrecks, reefs, and underwater walls.

DIVERS ALERT

Don't fly within 24 hours after scuba diving.

➤ ORGANIZATIONS: **NAUI Worldwide** (✉ Box 89789, 1232 Tech Blvd., Tampa, FL 33689, ☎ 813/628–6284 or 800/553–6284, WEB www.naui.org). **PADI** (✉ 30151 Tomas St., Rancho Santa Margarita, CA 92688, ☎ 800/729–7234 or 949/858–7234, WEB www.padi.com; ✉ 3771 Jacombs Rd., Bldg. C, #535, Richmond, British Columbia, Canada, V6V 2L9, ☎ 604/273–0277 or 800/565–8130; ✉ Unit 7, St. Philip's Central, Albert Rd., St. Philip's, Bristol, United Kingdom BS2 0PD, ☎ 0117/300–7234; ✉ Unit 3, Skyline Pl., French's Forest, Sydney, NSW, Australia 2086, ☎ 2/9451–2300).

ECOTOURISM

Travelers are being lured to the Caribbean as much by the natural beauty of beaches, rain forests, and even desertscapes (on Aruba or Bonaire) as by the fancy resort life. Island governments are becoming increasingly aware of the value of their unique natural resources and are continuing to create national parks, bird sanctuaries, and marine preserves. For example, Bonaire's entire coast is a national marine park, its northern third is a nature preserve, and its southern third a protected salt flat. Two-thirds of St. John, USVI, is national parkland.

Dominica, the Dominican Republic, Grenada, Guadeloupe, Puerto Rico, Saba, St. Vincent, and St. Lucia are other Caribbean leaders in environmental awareness, each with vast forest preserves and hiking trails. Botanical gardens welcome visitors on St. Lucia, St. Vincent, Barbados, and many other islands. Nearly all islands have special programs, hikes, and tours that promote a better understanding of and a deeper appreciation for nature.

ELECTRICITY

On many islands, the electric current is 110–120 volts alternating current (AC), and wall outlets take the same two-prong plugs found in the United States. Exceptions include the French islands and those with a British heritage. **Check with your hotel about current** when making reservations. If the current isn't compatible with your appliances, **bring a converter and an adapter.** With dual-voltage items (such as many laptop computers), you'll need only an adapter. Some hotels will lend adapter plugs to guests for the duration of their stay. Many establishments also have hair dryers and irons either in their rooms or available for borrowing, so you can leave yours at home. Don't use the 110-volt outlets marked FOR SHAVERS ONLY for high-wattage appliances such as blow-dryers.

FURTHER READING

Caribbean Style (Crown Publishers) is a coffee-table book with magnificent photographs of the interiors and exteriors of homes and buildings in the Caribbean. Short stories—some dark, some full of laughs—about life in the southern Caribbean made *Easy in the Islands*, by Bob Schacochis, a National Book Award winner. Schacochis has an ear for local patois and an eye for the absurd. In *Coming About: A Family Passage at Sea*, author Susan Tyler Hitchcock details her family's adventures sailing for nine months in the Bahamas and the Caribbean; it's an intimate look at the islands and a wonderful meditation on marriage and family. Thinking of running away and starting a business on a sun-drenched island? *A Trip to the Beach* by Robert and Melinda Blanchard is the ultimate inspiration. This funny, adventurous tale of how the Blanchards moved to Anguilla, started a restaurant, and learned innumerable lessons (including how to liberate fresh ingredients from the customs warehouse) will have you fantasizing about your own escape. To familiarize yourself with the sights, smells, and sounds of the West Indies, pick up Jamaica Kincaid's *Annie John*, a richly textured coming-of-age novel about a girl growing up on Antigua. The short stories in *At the Bottom of the River*, also by Kincaid, depict island mysteries and manners.

Omeros is Nobel Prize–winning St. Lucian poet Derek Walcott's imaginative Caribbean retelling of the *Odyssey*. Anthony C. Winkler's novels, *The Great Yacht Race*, *The Lunatic*, and *The Painted Canoe*, provide scathingly witty glimpses into Jamaica's class structure. *Wide Sargasso Sea*, by Dominica's Jean Rhys, is a provocative novel set in Jamaica and Dominica that recounts the early life of the first wife of Edward Rochester (pre–Jane Eyre). James Michener depicted the islands' diversity in his novel *Caribbean*. To probe island cultures more deeply, read Trinidad's V. S. Naipaul, particularly his *Guerrillas*, *The Loss of El Dorado*, and *The Enigma of Arrival*; Eric Williams's *From Columbus to Castro*; and Michael Paiewonsky's *Conquest of Eden*.

Though it was written decades ago, Herman Wouk's hilarious *Don't Stop the Carnival* remains as fresh as ever in its depiction of the trials and tribulations of running a small Caribbean hotel. Mystery lovers should pick up a copy of Agatha Christie's *A Caribbean Mystery*. And kids might enjoy reading the Hardy Boys mystery *The Caribbean Cruise Caper*. If you're keen on specific subjects, such as history, cuisine, folklore, bird-watching, or diving, you'll find wonderful books by local authors on each island.

GAY AND LESBIAN TRAVEL

Some Caribbean islands are more welcoming than others as travel destinations for gays and lesbians. Puerto Rico is the most gay-friendly island in the Caribbean—and the only one with extensive gay-oriented nightlife. San Juan has gay and lesbian guest houses, bars, clubs, and two gay-popular beaches. The USVI are also a good choice. St. Thomas has a few gay bars and discos, and the West End of St. Croix has quietly become gay- and lesbian-friendly. Otherwise, the French and Dutch islands are the most tolerant of gay and lesbian travelers. Attitudes are changing, albeit incrementally. The Cayman Islands, which once banned a gay-chartered cruise ship, now makes it a point to emphasize that all visitors are welcome if they respect the islands' conservative sensibilities. This is good advice to follow throughout the Caribbean, where nearly every island frowns upon same-sex couples strolling hand in hand down a beach or street, beach attire is welcome only at the beach, and most public displays of affection (either straight or gay) are frowned upon. Upscale resorts for adults, where privacy and discretion are the norm, are often the most welcoming to gay and lesbian travelers, but individually rented villas, many of which have private pools, are another good option. Couples-only resorts throughout the Caribbean, such as the all-inclusive Sandals and Couples resorts, do not, as a rule, welcome same-sex couples.

➤ GAY- AND LESBIAN-FRIENDLY TRAVEL AGENCIES: **Different Roads Travel** (✉ 8383 Wilshire Blvd., Suite 902, Beverly Hills, CA 90211, ☎ 323/651–5557 or 800/429–8747, FAX 323/651–3678, lgernert@tzell.com). **Kennedy Travel** (✉ 314 Jericho Turnpike, Floral Park, NY 11001, ☎ 516/352–4888 or 800/237–7433, FAX 516/354–8849, WEB www.kennedytravel.com). **Now, Voyager** (✉ 4406 18th St., San Francisco, CA 94114, ☎ 415/626–1169 or 800/255–6951, FAX 415/626–8626, WEB www.nowvoyager.com). **Skylink Travel and Tour** (✉ 1006 Mendocino Ave., Santa Rosa, CA 95401, ☎ 707/546–9888 or 800/225–5759, FAX 707/546–9891, WEB www.skylinktravel.com), serving lesbian travelers.

GUIDEBOOKS

Plan well and you won't be sorry. Guidebooks are excellent tools—and you can take them with you. You may want to check out the color photo–illustrated *Fodor's Exploring Caribbean*, thorough on culture and history, and *Fodor's Caribbean Ports of Call*, a pocket primer for cruisers—both available at on-line retailers and bookstores everywhere.

HEALTH

Health-care standards vary from island to island. The staff at your hotel can recommend a doctor, dentist, clinic, or hospital should a need arise. Sometimes, particularly at family resorts, a nurse is on-site during the day and a doctor is on-call. Doctor visits, incidentally, can be costly—even on islands where the general cost-of-living would make you think otherwise. Doctors and hospitals may require cash payment or take a major credit card; Medicare, Medicaid, and many U.S. medical insurance policies are not valid outside the U.S.

FOOD AND DRINK

Traveler's diarrhea, caused by consuming contaminated water, unpasteurized milk and milk products, and unrefrigerated food isn't a big problem in the Caribbean—unless it happens to you. So **watch what you eat,** especially at outdoor buffets in the hot sun. Make sure cooked food is hot and cold food has been properly refrigerated. As a rule, tap water is pure and food is wholesome in hotels and local restaurants throughout the Caribbean—except in the Dominican Republic—but **be cautious when buying food from street or beach vendors.** And just as you would at home, **wash or peel all fruits and vegetables** before eating them.

Mild cases of diarrhea may respond to Imodium (known generically as loperamide) or Pepto-Bismol (not as strong), both of which can be purchased in local pharmacies. Drink plenty of bottled water, which is readily available, to keep from becoming dehydrated. A salt-sugar solution (½ teaspoon salt and 4 tablespoons sugar) per quart of water is a good remedy for rehydrating yourself.

MEDICAL PLANS

No one plans to get sick while traveling, but it happens, so **consider signing up with a medical-assistance company.** Members get doctor referrals, emergency evacuation or repatriation, hot lines for medical consultation, cash for emergencies, and other assistance.

➤ MEDICAL-ASSISTANCE COMPANIES: **International SOS Assistance** (WEB www.internationalsos.com; ✉ 8 Neshaminy Interplex, Suite 207, Trevose, PA 19053, ☎ 215/245–4707 or 800/523–6586, FAX 215/244–9617; ✉ 12 Chemin Riantbosson, 1217 Meyrin 1, Geneva, Switzerland, ☎ 22/785–6464, FAX 22/785–6424; ✉ 331 N. Bridge Rd., 17-00, Odeon Towers, Singapore 188720, ☎ 338–7800, FAX 338–7611).

OVER-THE-COUNTER REMEDIES

Island drug stores and supermarkets are well-stocked with familiar over-the-counter medicines and other health products that you might need. If you don't see precisely what you want, **ask the pharmacist** to recommend an appropriate substitute. If you can only use a specific or an uncommon medicine, be sure to bring a sufficient supply with you.

Smart Travel Tips A to Z

PESTS AND OTHER HAZARDS

The major health risk in the Caribbean is sunburn or sunstroke. Having a long-sleeve shirt, a hat, and long pants or a beach wrap available is essential on a boat, for midday at the beach, and whenever you go out sightseeing. **Use sunscreen** with an SPF of at least 15—especially if your complexion is fair—and apply it liberally on your nose, ears, and other sensitive and exposed areas. **Make sure the sunscreen is waterproof** if you're engaging in water sports, **limit your sun time** for the first few days, and **drink plenty of liquids,** monitoring intake of caffeine and alcohol, which hasten the dehydration process.

Even experienced swimmers should **exercise caution in waters on the windward (Atlantic Ocean) side of the islands.** The unseen currents, powerful waves, strong undertows, and rocky bottoms can be extremely dangerous—and lifeguards are rare. Even in the calmest water, **watch out for black, spiny sea urchins**; stepping on one is guaranteed to be painful for quite some time.

The small lizards native to the islands are harmless (and actually keep down the bug population), and poisonous snakes are hard to find, although you should exercise caution while bird-watching in Trinidad. **Beware of the manchineel tree,** which grows near the beach and has green applelike fruit that is poisonous and bark and leaves that can burn the skin. The worst insect problem may well be the tiny no-see-ums (sand flies) that appear after a rain, near swampy ground, and around sunset; mosquitoes can also be annoying. **Bring along a good repellent.**

SHOTS AND MEDICATIONS

No special shots or vaccinations are required for Caribbean destinations.

➤ HEALTH WARNINGS: **National Centers for Disease Control and Prevention** (CDC; National Center for Infectious Diseases, Division of Quarantine, Traveler's Health Section, ✉ 1600 Clifton Rd. NE, M/S E-03, Atlanta, GA 30333, ☎ 888/232-3228 general information, 877/394-8747 travelers' health line, 800/311-3435

public inquiries, FAX 888/232-3299, WEB www.cdc.gov).

HOLIDAYS

Most islands observe an annual independence or other national day, certain Christian holidays (Easter weekend, various feast days, and Christmas), and New Year's Day. On many islands the biggest holiday of the year is the last day of Carnival (traditionally the Tuesday before Ash Wednesday), a festival that's no longer limited to mid-February. Banks, shops, and offices are closed on holidays.

INSURANCE

The most useful travel-insurance plan is a comprehensive policy that includes coverage for trip cancellation and interruption, default, trip delay, and medical expenses (with a waiver for pre-existing conditions).

Without insurance you will lose all or most of your money if you cancel your trip, regardless of the reason. Default insurance covers you if your tour operator, airline, or cruise line goes out of business. Trip-delay covers expenses that arise because of bad weather or mechanical delays. Study the fine print when comparing policies.

If you're traveling internationally, a key component of travel insurance is coverage for medical bills incurred if you get sick on the road. Such expenses are not generally covered by Medicare or private policies. U.K. residents can buy a travel-insurance policy valid for most vacations taken during the year in which it's purchased (but check pre-existing-condition coverage). British and Australian citizens need extra medical coverage when traveling overseas.

Always **buy travel policies directly from the insurance company**; if you buy them from a cruise line, airline, or tour operator that goes out of business, you probably will not be covered for the agency or operator's default, a major risk. Before making any purchase, **review your existing health and home-owner's policies** to find what they cover away from home.

➤ TRAVEL INSURERS: In the U.S.: **Access America** (⊠ 6600 W. Broad St., Richmond, VA 23230, ☎ 800/284–8300, FAX 804/673–1491 or 800/346–9265, WEB www.accessamerica.com). **Travel Guard International** (⊠ 1145 Clark St., Stevens Point, WI 54481, ☎ 800/826–1300; 715/345–0505, FAX 800/955–8785, WEB www.travelguard.com).

➤ INSURANCE INFORMATION: In the U.K.: **Association of British Insurers** (⊠ 51 Gresham St., London EC2V 7HQ, ☎ 020/7600–3333, FAX 020/7696–8999, WEB www.abi.org.uk). In Canada: **RBC Travel Insurance** (⊠ 6880 Financial Dr., Mississauga, Ontario L5N 7Y5, ☎ 905/791–8700 or 800/668–4342, FAX 905/813–4704, WEB www.rbcinsurance.com). In Australia: **Insurance Council of Australia** (⊠ Level 3, 56 Pitt St., Sydney, NSW 2000, ☎ 02/9253–5100, FAX 02/9253–5111, WEB www.ica.com.au). In New Zealand: **Insurance Council of New Zealand** (⊠ Level 7, 111–115 Customhouse Quay, Box 474, Wellington, ☎ 04/472–5230, FAX 04/473–3011, WEB www.icnz.org.nz).

LANGUAGE

It becomes obvious that the Caribbean's history is linked with that of European and African countries when you consider all the languages that are spoken on the islands. As for "official" languages, English is well-represented (14 island nations), followed by Dutch (6 islands, though English is widely spoken), French (3 islands), and Spanish (3 islands). St. Maarten/St. Martin is split geographically, culturally, and linguistically—Dutch (as well as English) is spoken on one side, and French on the other.

You'll also find a variety of idiomatic expressions, West Indian lilts and patois, and French Creole dialects that transform the official languages. On both St. Lucia and Dominica, for example, English is the official language, but most locals also speak a patois that's a mix of English, French, and African words; on French-speaking St. Barths, some people use the Norman dialect of their ancestors; and on the Dutch islands, you'll encounter perhaps the most worldly tongue of all, Papiamento—a mixture of African languages, as well as Dutch, English, French, Portuguese, *and* Spanish. There are also places, such as Barbados, where early Irish and Scottish settlers affected the island accent; and in Trinidad, East Indian and Chinese arrivals have contributed to culture, food, and terminology.

LANGUAGES FOR TRAVELERS

A phrase book and language-tape set can help get you started. *Fodor's French for Travelers* and *Fodor's Spanish for Travelers* (available at bookstores everywhere) are excellent.

LODGING

Decide whether you want a hotel on the leeward side of an island (with calm water, good for snorkeling and swimming) or the windward (with waves, good for surfing, not good for swimming). Decide, too, whether you want to pay the extra price for a room overlooking the ocean. At less expensive properties, location may mean a difference in price of only $10–$20 per room; at luxury resorts on pricey islands, however, it could amount to as much as $100 per room. Also **find out how close the property is to a beach.** At some hotels you can walk barefoot from your room onto the sand; others are across a road or a 10-minute drive away.

If you go to sleep early or are a light sleeper, **ask for a room away from the entertainment area.** Air-conditioning isn't a necessity on all islands, many of which are cooled by trade winds, but it can be a plus if you enjoy an afternoon snooze or are bothered by humidity. Breezes are best in second-floor rooms, particularly corner rooms. If you like to sleep without air-conditioning, make sure that windows can be opened and have screens. If you're staying away from the water, you'll want a ceiling fan. You'll likely notice a candle and box of matches in your room. In even the most luxurious resorts, there are times when things simply *don't* work; it's a fact of Caribbean life. And no matter how diligent the upkeep, humidity and salt air take their toll.

The lodgings we list are the top of the line in each price category. We always list the available facilities—but we don't specify whether they're all included in the rates. When pricing accommodations, always ask what's included and what costs extra.

Assume that hotels operate on the **European Plan** (EP, with no meals), unless we specify that they use either the **Continental Plan** (CP, with a Continental breakfast), **Breakfast Plan** (BP, with a full breakfast), or the **Modified American Plan** (MAP, with breakfast and dinner) or are **all-inclusive** (including all meals and most activities).

APARTMENT AND VILLA RENTALS

If you want a home base that's roomy enough for a family and comes with cooking facilities, **consider a furnished rental.** These can save you money, especially if you're traveling with a group. Home-exchange directories sometimes list rentals as well as exchanges.

➤ INTERNATIONAL AGENTS: **At Home Abroad** (✉ 405 E. 56th St., Suite 6H, New York, NY 10022, ☎ 212/421–9165, FAX 212/752–1591, WEB www.athomeabroadinc.com). **Hideaways International** (✉ 767 Islington St., Portsmouth, NH 03801, ☎ 603/430–4433 or 800/843–4433, FAX 603/430–4444, WEB www.hideaways.com; membership $129). **Vacation Home Rentals Worldwide** (✉ 235 Kensington Ave., Norwood, NJ 07648, ☎ 201/767–9393 or 800/633–3284, FAX 201/767–5510, WEB www.vhrww.com). **Villanet** (✉ 1251 N.W. 116th St., Seattle, WA 98177, ☎ 206/417–3444 or 800/964–1891, FAX 206/417–1832, WEB www.rentavilla.com).**Villas and Apartments Abroad** (✉ 1270 Ave. of the Americas, 15th floor, New York, NY 10020, ☎ 212/897–5045 or 800/433–3020, FAX 212/897–5039, WEB www.ideal-villas.com). **Villas International** (✉ 4340 Redwood Hwy., Suite D309, San Rafael, CA 94903, ☎ 415/499–9490 or 800/221–2260, FAX 415/499–9491, WEB www.villasintl.com).

CAMPING

Camping is a big draw on St. John, USVI, and many other islands have facilities if you want to fend for yourself and sleep under the stars. Some islands have no camping facilities at all and, in fact, discourage campers.

HOME EXCHANGES

If you would like to exchange your home for someone else's, **join a home-exchange organization,** which will send you its updated listings of available exchanges for a year and will include your own listing in at least one of them. It's up to you to make specific arrangements.

➤ EXCHANGE CLUBS: **HomeLink International** (✉ Box 47747, Tampa, FL 33647, ☎ 813/975–9825 or 800/638–3841, FAX 813/910–8144, WEB www.homelink.org; $106 per year). **Intervac U.S.** (✉ 30 Corte San Fernando, Tiburon, CA 94920, ☎ 800/756–4663, FAX 415/435–7440, WEB www.intervacus.com; $90 yearly fee for a listing, on-line access, and a catalog; $50 without catalog).

HOTELS

All hotels included in this guide have guest rooms with private baths, unless otherwise noted. Major hotel chains listed below have properties on one or more of the islands.

➤ TOLL-FREE NUMBERS: **Best Western** (☎ 800/528–1234, WEB www.bestwestern.com). **Choice** (☎ 800/424–6423, WEB www.choicehotels.com). **Club Med** (☎ 888/932–2582, WEB www.clubmed.com).**Comfort Inn** (☎ 800/424–6423, WEB www.comfortinn.com). **Days Inn** (☎ 800/325–2525, WEB www.daysinn.com). **Divi Resorts** (☎ 888/367–3484, WEB www.diviresorts.com). **Four Seasons** (☎ 800/332–3442, WEB www.fourseasons.com). **Hilton** (☎ 800/445–8667, WEB www.hilton.com). **Holiday Inn** (☎ 800/465–4329, WEB www.sixcontinenthotels.com). **Hyatt Hotels & Resorts** (☎ 800/233–1234, WEB www.hyatt.com). **Inter-Continental** (☎ 800/327–0200, WEB www.intercontinental.com). **Marriott** (☎ 800/228–9290, WEB www.marriott.com). **Le Meridien** (☎ 800/543–4300, WEB www.lemeridien-hotels.com). **Radisson** (☎ 800/333–3333, WEB www.radisson.com). **Renaissance Hotels & Resorts** (☎ 800/468–3571, WEB www.renaissancehotels.com/). **Ritz-Carlton** (☎ 800/241–3333,

WEB www.ritzcarlton.com). **Rosewood** (☎ 888/767–3966, WEB www.rosewoodhotels.com). **Sandals** (☎ 800/726–3257, WEB www.sandals.com). **Sheraton** (☎ 800/325–3535, WEB www.starwood.com/sheraton). **Sol Meliá** (☎ 800/336–3542, WEB www.solmelia.com). **Sonesta** (☎ 800/766–3782 in the U.S. and Canada; 00800/4000–1000 in the U.K.; 1300/727–220 in Australia, WEB www.sonesta.com). **Westin Hotels & Resorts** (☎ 800/228–3000, WEB www.starwood.com/westin). **Wyndham Hotels & Resorts** (☎ 800/822–4200, WEB www.wyndham.com).

MAIL AND SHIPPING

Airmail between Caribbean islands and cities in the United States or Canada takes 7–14 days; surface mail can take 4–6 weeks. Airmail to the United Kingdom takes 2–3 weeks; to Australia and New Zealand, 3–4 weeks.

OVERNIGHT SERVICES

Courier services (such as Airborne, FedEx, UPS, and others) operate throughout the Caribbean, although not every company serves each island. "Overnight" service is more likely to take two or more days, because of the limited number of flights on which packages can be shipped.

MONEY MATTERS

Prices throughout this guide are given for adults. Substantially reduced room rates, meal charges, and admission fees are almost always available for children; students and senior citizens often receive reduced admission fees. For island-specific information on banks, currency, service charges, taxes, and tipping in the Caribbean, *see* the A to Z sections *in* individual island chapters.

ATMS

Debit cards aren't widely used in the islands, although you can use bank cards and major credit card to withdraw cash (in local currency) at automatic teller machines (ATMs). ATMs can be found on most islands at airports, cruise ship terminals, bank branches, shopping centers, gas stations, and other convenient locations. Although ATM transaction fees may be higher abroad, the rates are excellent because they're based on wholesale rates offered only by major banks.

CREDIT CARDS

Major credit cards are widely accepted at hotels, restaurants, shops, car-rental agencies, other service providers, and ATM machines throughout the Caribbean. The only places that might not accept them are open-air markets or tiny shops in out-of-the-way villages.

It's smart to **write down (and keep separate) the number(s) of the credit card(s) you're carrying** and the toll-free number to call in case the card is lost or stolen.

Throughout this guide, the following abbreviations are used: **AE,** American Express; **D,** Discover; **DC,** Diners Club; **MC,** MasterCard; and **V,** Visa.

CURRENCY EXCHANGE

The U.S. dollar is the official currency on Puerto Rico and the USVI, as well as the British Virgin Islands. On Grand Cayman, you will usually have a choice of Cayman or U.S. dollars when you take money out of an ATM and may even be able to get change in U.S. dollars. On most other islands, U.S. paper currency (not coins) is usually accepted. When you pay in dollars, however, you'll almost always get change in local currency; so it's best to carry bills in small denominations. Canadian dollars and British pounds are occasionally accepted, but don't count on this as the norm. If you do need local currency (say, for a trip to one of the French islands), **change money at a local bank** for the best rate.

Travelers to the Caribbean from countries other than the United States might want to purchase a small amount of local currency (or U.S. dollars) before leaving home to pay for incidentals until you can get to a local bank.

➤ EXCHANGE SERVICES: **International Currency Express** (☎ 888/278–6628 orders). **Thomas Cook Currency Services** (☎ 800/287–7362 orders and retail locations, WEB www.us.thomascook.com).

TRAVELER'S CHECKS

Do you need traveler's checks? It depends on where you're headed. If you're going to rural areas and small towns, go with cash; traveler's checks are best used in cities. Lost or stolen checks can usually be replaced within 24 hours. To ensure a speedy refund, buy your own traveler's checks—don't let someone else pay for them: irregularities like this can cause delays. The person who bought the checks should make the call to request a refund.

PACKING

Travel light. Dress on the islands is generally casual. Bring loose-fitting clothing made of natural fabrics to see you through days of heat and humidity. Pack a beach cover-up, both to protect yourself from the sun and as something to wear to and from your hotel room. On all islands, bathing suits and immodest attire off the beach are frowned upon. A sun hat is advisable, but you don't have to pack one—inexpensive straw hats are available everywhere. For shopping and sightseeing, bring walking shorts, jeans, T-shirts, long-sleeve cotton shirts, slacks, and sundresses. Night-time dress can range from really informal to casually elegant, depending on the establishment. A tie is practically never required, but a jacket may be appropriate in the fanciest restaurants and casinos. You may need a light sweater or jacket for evenings and at higher altitudes.

Leave camouflage-pattern clothing at home. It's not permitted for civilians, even children, in some Caribbean countries and may be confiscated if worn.

If you're making one or more airline connections, it's smart to pack some toiletries, a change of clothes, and perhaps a bathing suit in your carry-on bag—just in case your checked luggage doesn't make the connection until a later flight (which may be the next day).

In your carry-on luggage, **pack an extra pair of eyeglasses or contact lenses and enough of any medication** you take to last the entire trip. You may also ask your doctor to write a spare prescription using the drug's generic name, since brand names may vary from country to country. In luggage to be checked, **never pack prescription drugs or valuables.** And don't forget to carry with you the addresses of offices that handle refunds of lost traveler's checks. Check *Fodor's How to Pack* (available in bookstores everywhere) for more tips.

To avoid customs and security delays, carry medications in their original packaging. Don't pack any sharp objects in your carry-on luggage, including knives of any size or material, scissors, manicure tools, and corkscrews, or anything else that might arouse suspicion.

CHECKING LUGGAGE

You are allowed one carry-on bag and one personal article, such as a purse or a laptop computer. Make sure that everything you carry aboard will fit under your seat or in the overhead bin. Get to the gate early, so you can board as soon as possible, before the overhead bins fill up.

If you are flying internationally, note that baggage allowances may be determined not by piece but by weight—generally 88 pounds (40 kilograms) in first class, 66 pounds (30 kilograms) in business class, and 44 pounds (20 kilograms) in economy.

Airline liability for baggage is limited to $2,500 per person on flights within the United States. On international flights it amounts to $9.07 per pound or $20 per kilogram for checked baggage (roughly $640 per 70-pound bag) and $400 per passenger for unchecked baggage. You can buy additional coverage at check-in for about $10 per $1,000 of coverage, but it excludes a rather extensive list of items, shown on your airline ticket.

Before departure, **itemize your bags' contents** and their worth, and label the bags with your name, address, and phone number. (If you use your home address, cover it so potential thieves can't see it readily.) Inside each bag, **pack a copy of your itinerary.** At check-in, **make sure that each bag is correctly tagged** with the destination airport's three-letter code. If your bags arrive damaged or fail to arrive at all, file a written report with the airline before leaving the airport.

PASSPORTS AND VISAS

When traveling internationally, **carry your passport** even if you don't need one (it's always the best form of I.D.) and **make two photocopies of the data page** (one for someone at home and another for you, carried separately from your passport). If you lose your passport, promptly call the nearest embassy or consulate and the local police.

U.S. passport applications for children under age 14 require consent from both parents or legal guardians; both parents must appear together to sign the application. If only one parent appears, he or she must submit a written statement from the other parent authorizing passport issuance for the child. A parent with sole authority must present evidence of it when applying; acceptable documentation includes the child's certified birth certificate listing only the applying parent, a court order specifically permitting this parent's travel with the child, or a death certificate for the non-applying parent. Application forms and instructions are available on the Web site of the U.S. State Department's Bureau of Consular Affairs (www.travel.state.gov).

ENTERING THE CARIBBEAN

On most Caribbean islands, vacationers who are U.S., Canadian, or British citizens must have either a valid passport or prove citizenship with a birth certificate (with a raised seal) as well as a government-issued photo I.D. Visitors from other countries must present a valid passport. All visitors must have a return or ongoing ticket.

PASSPORT OFFICES

The best time to apply for a passport or to renew is in fall and winter. Before any trip, check your passport's expiration date, and, if necessary, renew it as soon as possible. Current U.S. passport holders may renew by mail; forms are available at local post offices or can be downloaded and printed from the Internet.

➤ AUSTRALIAN CITIZENS: **Australian State Passport Office** (☎ 131–232, WEB www.passports.gov.au).

➤ CANADIAN CITIZENS: **Passport Office** (to mail in applications: ✉ Department of Foreign Affairs and International Trade, Ottawa, Ontario K1A 0G3; ☎ 800/567–6868 toll-free in Canada or 819/994–3500, WEB www.dfait-maeci.gc.ca/passport).

➤ NEW ZEALAND CITIZENS: **New Zealand Passport Office** (☎ 0800/22–5050 or 04/474–8100, WEB www.passports.govt.nz).

➤ U.K. CITIZENS: **London Passport Office** (☎ 0870/521–0410, WEB www.passport.gov.uk).

➤ U.S. CITIZENS: **National Passport Information Center** (☎ 900/225–5674; calls are 35¢ per minute for automated service, $1.05 per minute for operator service; WEB www.travel.state.gov).

REST ROOMS

Rest rooms in hotels, restaurants, and public buildings are, as a rule, clean and well-equipped. Pay toilets aren't customary nor are staffed rest rooms.

SAFETY

Be as cautious as you would at home in terms of not walking alone in unfamiliar places, locking away valuables, and not flaunting expensive jewelry in public places. **Don't swim alone in unfamiliar waters,** and don't swim too far offshore; most beaches have no lifeguards.

SENIOR-CITIZEN TRAVEL

To qualify for age-related discounts, **mention your senior-citizen status up front** when booking hotel reservations (not when checking out) and before you're seated in restaurants (not when paying the bill). Be sure to have identification on hand. When renting a car, ask about promotional car-rental discounts, which can be cheaper than senior-citizen rates.

➤ EDUCATIONAL PROGRAMS: **Elderhostel** (✉ 11 Ave. de Lafayette, Boston, MA 02111-1746, ☎ 877/426–8056, FAX 877/426–2166, WEB www.elderhostel.org). **Interhostel** (✉ University of New Hampshire, 6 Garrison Ave., Durham, NH 03824, ☎ 603/862–1147 or 800/733–9753, FAX 603/862–1113, WEB www.learn.unh.edu).

SHOPPING

Shopping in the Caribbean can mean duty-free bargains on watches and jewelry, perfume, designer clothing, china and crystal, and other luxury goods from around the world. It can also mean buying locally produced straw items, wood carvings, original art, batik beachwear, clay pottery, spices, coffee, cigars, and rum.

Bargaining isn't expected (and is considered insulting) in shops, but at open-air markets and with street vendors it may be acceptable. Keep in mind, however, that selling handicrafts or home-grown produce may be a local person's only livelihood. When bargaining, consider the amount of work or effort involved and the item's value to you. Vendors don't set artificially high prices and then expect to bargain; they bargain so you'll buy from them instead of their neighbor.

KEY DESTINATIONS

On some islands, such as St. Maarten, St. Barths, St. Thomas, and Aruba, all shopping is duty-free. Other islands, like Barbados and St. Lucia, have certain shops or specific areas where you can purchase duty-free items upon presentation of your passport and/or ongoing ticket; still others, such as Puerto Rico, St. Vincent, and Grenada, have very limited duty-free opportunities—one or two stores or just shops in the airport departure area.

SMART SOUVENIRS

Bring home a pantry full of spices from Grenada, pottery from Barbados, lace from Saba, woven-grass mats from St. Vincent, cigars from the Dominican Republic and Puerto Rico, fashions made of hand-printed fabric from St. Lucia, Blue Mountain coffee from Jamaica, Carib straw baskets from Dominica, aloe from Aruba, Angostura bitters from Trinidad—and rum from just about everywhere. St. Maarten and St. Thomas offer the best prices for duty-free shopping on a large scale.

WATCH OUT

U.S. citizens returning home must **consume tropical fruits and other produce, smoke those Cuban cigars,** and **(with rare exceptions) leave the bouquets of flowers behind** before heading home.

STUDENTS IN THE CARIBBEAN

Hiking in the rain forest, scuba diving, boating, and other Caribbean activities and adventures seem made-to-order for students—and the cultural enrichment and historical perspective add depth to all that book learning. The Caribbean isn't as far out of a student's budget as you might expect. Summer, when most students have free time, is the least expensive time to travel to the Caribbean. All but the toniest islands, such as St. Barths, have inexpensive guest houses and small, no-frills hotels. Tourist boards provide listings of these alternative lodgings on request. You're most likely to meet students from other countries in the French and Dutch West Indies, where many go for vacations or sabbaticals. Puerto Rico, Jamaica, Grenada, and Dominica, among others, have large resident international student populations at their universities. In many cases, your student I.D. card may provide access to their facilities, from the library to the cafeteria.

An alternative to individual travel is an educational program or expedition. Colleges and universities often sponsor programs that coincide with spring or summer breaks, as do independent—usually nonprofit—organizations.

➤ I.D.s AND SERVICES: **Council Travel** (✉ 205 E. 42nd St., 15th floor, New York, NY 10017, ☎ 212/822–2700 or 888/226–8624, FAX 212/822–2719, WEB www.counciltravel.com). **Travel Cuts** (✉ 187 College St., Toronto, Ontario M5T 1P7, Canada, ☎ 416/979–2406 or 888/838–2887, FAX 416/979–8167, WEB www.travelcuts.com).

TELEPHONES

Phone and fax service to and from the Caribbean is up-to-date and efficient. Phone cards are used throughout the islands; you can buy them (in various denominations) at many retail shops and convenience stores. Some must be used in special card phones, which are also widely available.

AREA AND COUNTRY CODES

For island area and country codes, *see* the A to Z sections *in* individual island chapters. When calling home, the country code is 1 for the United States and Canada, 61 for Australia, 64 for New Zealand, and 44 for the United Kingdom.

LONG-DISTANCE SERVICES

AT&T, MCI, and Sprint access codes make calling long distance relatively convenient, but you may find the local access number blocked by individual hotels or throughout the entire island by the local telephone company. On some islands, you can dial a toll-free number and use a major credit card to call overseas. Although that may cost slightly more than using a calling card, you can avoid paying a hotel surcharge.

TIME

The Caribbean islands fall into two time zones. The Cayman Islands, Cuba, Haiti, Jamaica, and the Turks and Caicos Islands are all in the Eastern Standard Time zone, which is five hours earlier than Greenwich Mean Time (GMT). All other Caribbean islands are in the Atlantic Standard Time zone, which is one hour later than Eastern Standard or four hours earlier than GMT. During Daylight Savings Time, between April and October, Atlantic Standard is the same time as Eastern Daylight Time.

TOURS AND PACKAGES

Because everything is prearranged on a prepackaged tour or independent vacation, you spend less time planning—and often get it all at a good price.

BOOKING WITH AN AGENT

Travel agents are excellent resources. But it's a good idea to collect brochures from several agencies, as some agents' suggestions may be influenced by relationships with tour and package firms that reward them for volume sales. If you have a special interest, **find an agent with expertise in that area**; the American Society of Travel Agents (ASTA; ☞ Travel Agencies) has a database of specialists worldwide.

Make sure your travel agent knows the accommodations and other services of the place being recommended. Ask about the hotel's location, room size, beds, and whether it has a pool, room service, or programs for children, if you care about these. Has your agent been there in person or sent others whom you can contact?

Do some homework on your own, too: local tourism boards can provide information about lesser-known and small-niche operators, some of which may sell only direct.

BUYER BEWARE

Each year consumers are stranded or lose their money when tour operators—even large ones with excellent reputations—go out of business. So **check out the operator.** Ask several travel agents about its reputation, and try to **book with a company that has a consumer-protection program.** (Look for information in the company's brochure.) In the United States, members of the National Tour Association and the United States Tour Operators Association are required to set aside funds to cover your payments and travel arrangements in the event that the company defaults. It's also a good idea to choose a company that participates in the American Society of Travel Agents' Tour Operator Program (TOP); ASTA will act as mediator in any disputes between you and your tour operator.

Remember that the more your package or tour includes the better you can predict the ultimate cost of your vacation. Make sure you know exactly what is covered, and **beware of hidden costs.** Are taxes, tips, and transfers included? Entertainment and excursions? These can add up.

➤ TOUR-OPERATOR RECOMMENDATIONS: **American Society of Travel Agents** (☞ Travel Agencies). **National Tour Association** (NTA; ✉ 546 E. Main St., Lexington, KY 40508, ☎ 859/226–4444 or 800/682–8886, WEB www.ntaonline.com). **United States Tour Operators Association** (USTOA; ✉ 275 Madison Ave., Suite 2014, New York, NY 10016, ☎ 212/599–6599 or 800/468–7862, FAX 212/599–6744, WEB www.ustoa.com).

TRAVEL AGENCIES

A good travel agent puts your needs first. Look for an agency that has been in business at least five years, emphasizes customer service, and has someone on staff who specializes in your destination. In addition, **make sure the agency belongs to a professional trade organization.** The American Society of Travel Agents (ASTA)—the largest and most influential in the field with more than 26,000 members in some 170 countries—maintains and enforces a strict code of ethics and will step in to help mediate any agent-client disputes involving ASTA members if necessary. ASTA (whose motto is "Without a travel agent, you're on your own") also maintains a Web site that includes a directory of agents. (If a travel agency is also acting as your tour operator, *see* Buyer Beware *in* Tours and Packages.)

➤ LOCAL AGENT REFERRALS: **American Society of Travel Agents** (ASTA; ✉ 1101 King St., Suite 200, Alexandria, VA 22314, ☎ 800/965–2782 24-hr hot line, FAX 703/739–7642, WEB www.astanet.com). **Association of British Travel Agents** (✉ 68–71 Newman St., London W1T 3AH, ☎ 020/7637–2444, FAX 020/7637–0713, WEB www.abtanet.com). **Association of Canadian Travel Agents** (✉ 130 Albert St., Suite 1705, Ottawa, Ontario K1P 5G4, ☎ 613/237–3657, FAX 613/237–7052, WEB www.acta.ca). **Australian Federation of Travel Agents** (✉ Level 3, 309 Pitt St., Sydney, NSW 2000, ☎ 02/9264–3299, FAX 02/9264–1085, WEB www.afta.com.au). **Travel Agents' Association of New Zealand** (✉ Level 5, Tourism and Travel House, 79 Boulcott St., Box 1888, Wellington 6001, ☎ 04/499–0104, FAX 04/499–0827, WEB www.taanz.org.nz).

VISITOR INFORMATION

Many islands have tourist board offices in Canada, the United Kingdom, and the United States. Such boards can be good sources of general information, up-to-date calendars of events, and listings of hotels, restaurants, sights, and shops. The Caribbean Tourism Organization (CTO) is another resource, especially for information on the islands that have limited representation overseas.

➤ CARIBBEAN-WIDE INFORMATION: **CTO** (✉ 80 Broad St., New York, NY 10004, ☎ 212/635–9530, FAX 212/635–9511; in Canada: ✉ 512 Duplex Ave., Toronto, Ontario M4R 2E3, ☎ 416/485–8724, FAX 416/485–8256; in the U.K.: ✉ 42 Westminster Palace Gardens Artillery Row, London SW1P 1RR, ☎ 0207/222–4335, FAX 0207/222–4325, WEB www.doitcaribbean.com).

➤ U.S. GOVERNMENT ADVISORIES: **U.S. Department of State** (✉ Overseas Citizens Services Office, Room 4811, 2201 C St. NW, Washington, DC 20520, ☎ 202/647–5225 interactive hot line or 888/407–4747, WEB www.travel.state.gov); enclose a business-size SASE.

WEB SITES

Do check out the World Wide Web when planning your trip. You'll find everything from weather forecasts to virtual tours of famous cities. Be sure to **visit Fodors.com** (www.fodors.com), a complete travel-planning site. You can research prices and book plane tickets, hotel rooms, rental cars, vacation packages, and more. In addition, you can post your pressing questions in the Travel Talk section. Other planning tools include a currency converter and weather reports, and there are loads of links to travel resources.

For island-specific sites, *see* Visitor Information *in* the A to Z section at the end of each chapter.

➤ CARIBBEAN WEB SITES: **Caribbean Aviation Page** (WEB www.caribbeanaviation.com). **Caribbean Home Page** (WEB www.caribinfo.com). **Caribbean Hotel Association** (WEB www.caribbeantravel.com). **Caribbean news** (www.cananews.com or WEB www.cweek.com). **Caribbean newspaper links** (WEB www.caribbeannewspapers.com). **Caribbean Tourism Organization** (WEB www.doitcaribbean.com). **Cruise Lines International Association** (WEB www.cruising.org).

WHEN TO GO

The Caribbean high season is traditionally winter—from December 15 to April 14—when northern weather is at its worst. During this season, you're guaranteed the most entertainment at resorts and the most people with whom to enjoy it. It's also the most fashionable, the most expensive, and the most popular time to visit—and most hotels are heavily booked. You must make reservations at least two or three months in advance for the very best places (sometimes a year in advance for the most exclusive spots). Hotel prices drop 20%–50% after April 15; airfares and cruise prices also fall. Saving money isn't the only reason to visit the Caribbean during the off-season. Temperatures are only a few degrees warmer than at other times of the year, and many islands now schedule their carnivals, music festivals, and other events during the off-season. Late August, September, October, and early November are least crowded.

In summer, the flamboyant trees are at their peak, as are most of the flowers and shrubs of the West Indies. The water is clearer for snorkeling and smoother for sailing in the Virgin Islands and the Grenadines in May, June, and July. The peak of local excitement on many islands, most notably Trinidad, St. Vincent, Dominica, and the French West Indies, is Carnival—traditionally held in February, the weekend before Ash Wednesday.

CLIMATE

The Caribbean climate is fairly constant. The average year-round temperatures for the region are 78°F–88°F. The temperature extremes are 65°F low, 95°F high; but, as everyone knows, it's the humidity, not the heat, that makes you suffer, especially when the two go hand in hand. You can count on downtown shopping areas being hot at midday any time of the year, but air-conditioning provides some respite. Spend the day near beaches, where water and trade winds can keep you cool, and shop early or late in the day.

As part of the fall rainy season, hurricanes occasionally sweep through the Caribbean. Check the news daily and keep abreast of brewing tropical storms. The southernmost Caribbean islands (from St. Vincent to Trinidad, along with Aruba, Bonaire, and Curaçao) are generally spared the threat of hurricanes. The rainy season consists mostly of brief showers interspersed with sunshine. You can watch the clouds thicken, feel the rain, then have brilliant sunshine dry you off, all while remaining on your lounge chair. A spell of overcast days or heavy rainfall is unusual, as everyone will tell you.

High altitudes can be cool, particularly when winter winds hit Caribbean peaks (late November through January). Since many Caribbean islands are mountainous or at least hilly (notable exceptions are the Cayman Islands, Anguilla, Antigua, Aruba, Bonaire, and Curaçao), the altitude always offers an escape from the latitude. Kingston (Jamaica), Port-of-Spain (Trinidad), and Fort-de-France (Martinique) swelter in summer; climb 1,000 ft (305 m) or so and everything is cool.

➤ FORECASTS: **Weather Channel Connection** (☎ 900/932–8437), 95¢ per minute from a Touch-Tone phone.

1 DESTINATION: CARIBBEAN

The Many Faces of the Islands

A Sampling of Island Culture

What's Where

Pleasures and Pastimes

Fodor's Choice

THE MANY FACES OF THE ISLANDS

I F YOU HAVE SEEN ONE ISLAND you have by no means seen them all. Tiny 5-square-mi (13-square-km) Saba has less in common with the vast 19,000-square-mi (49,000-square-km) Dominican Republic than Butte, Montana, has with Biloxi, Mississippi. Butte and Biloxi, however different in terrain and traits, sit in the same country and the citizenry speak more or less the same language. Saba, which is Dutch, and the Dominican Republic, whose roots are in Spain, simply sit in the same sea.

The Caribbean has towering volcanic islands, such as Saba; islands with lush rain forests, such as Dominica, St. Lucia, Martinique, and Guadeloupe; and some islands, notably Puerto Rico, that have both jungles and deserts. You'll find glittering discos, casinos, and dazzling nightlife on such islands as Aruba and the Dominican Republic, and throughout the region there are isolated cays with only sand, sea, sun, lizards, and mosquitoes. Some islands—Puerto Rico and St. Kitts among them—have ancient forts to view, while Barbados and the Caicos Islands have caverns and caves to explore. There are also places like Grand Turk and Little Cayman, where the only notable sights to see are beneath the translucent sea.

Different though they are in many ways, the islands are stylistically similar. The style setter is the tropical climate. Year-round summertime temperatures and a plethora of beaches produce a pace that's known as "island time." Only the trade winds move swiftly. Operating on island time means, "I'll get to it when the spirit moves me."

Similarities are also attributable to the history of the region. The agrarian Arawaks paddled up from South America and populated the islands more than 1,000 years ago. In the early 14th century, the mighty Caribs, who gave the area its name, arrived, probably from Brazil or Venezuela, gradually pushing the Arawaks up the spine of the Caribbean. (The original name of the Caribs was Galibi, a word the Spanish corrupted to *Canibal*—the origin of the word "cannibal.") Both tribes (as well as the peaceful Taíno people of Puerto Rico, Hispaniola, Cuba, and Jamaica) had remarkably sophisticated cultures and elaborate sociological systems.

Christopher Columbus made four voyages through the region between 1492 and 1504, christening the islands while dodging the Carib arrows. He landed on or sailed past all of the Greater Antilles and virtually all of the eastern Caribbean islands. From the 16th century until the early 19th century, the Dutch, Danes, Swedes, English, French, Irish, and Spanish fought bitterly for control of the islands. Some islands have almost as many battle sites as sand flies. After gaining control of the islands and annihilating the remaining Arawaks (mostly through diseases brought from Europe) and Caribs (mostly by sword and musket), the Europeans established vast sugar plantations and brought in Africans to work the fields. With the abolition of slavery in the mid-19th century, Asians were imported as indentured laborers. Today, the Caribbean population is a rich gumbo of nationalities, including Americans and Canadians who have retired to and invested in the islands. Although little remains of the indigenous populations (there's a Carib reservation on Dominica and a community of Caribs on St. Vincent, as well as tantalizing, if sparse, archaeological remains), each colonial power left its own cultural imprint on the Caribbean.

It must be remembered that the Caribbean, like the European continent, is made up of individual countries, each with customs, immigration officials, and, in some instances, political difficulties. Most of the islands have opted for independence; others retain their ties to the mother country. They are developing nations, and many have severe economic and unemployment problems. Virtually all of the islands depend upon tourism. And, human nature being what it is, many islanders resent their dependency on tourist dollars. Like as not, the person who serves you has stood in a long line, vying with other anxious applicants for the few available jobs. After serving your meals or cleaning your luxurious room, he or she returns to a tiny shack knowing full well that in less than a week you will have shelled out more than an islander makes in a month.

Some visitors object to encountering resentment when all they seek is a pleasant vacation and they've paid dearly for it. Some feel rather keenly that they'd always like hot water—or at least *some* water—when they turn on the shower; in even the most luxurious resorts there are times when things simply don't work; it's a fact of Caribbean life. No matter how diligent the upkeep, humidity and salt air take their toll, and cracked tiles and chipped paint are common everywhere. Many first-time visitors also forget that they're in the tropics, and find it hard to get used to some of the fauna (a lizard scurrying away at the opening of a door is a common sight). Still other visitors simply have no patience with island time. There are those, however, who travel to the Caribbean year after year. Some return to the same hotel on the same beach on the same island, while others try to sample as much as this smorgasbord has to offer.

A SAMPLING OF ISLAND CULTURE

The Caribbean population is a rich gumbo of nationalities, including Americans, British, and Canadians who have retired to and invested in the islands. Little remains of the indigenous populations (there are Carib communities on Dominica and St. Vincent, as well as tantalizing, if sparse, archaeological remains), and many other groups have left their cultural imprint on the Caribbean.

Nowhere is **African** culture more noticeable than in island music. Calypso was born in Trinidad, and its catchy rhythms veil the barbed political satire of many of the lyrics. The island is also the stomping ground of a flat-out, freewheeling Carnival that rivals the pre-Lenten celebrations in Rio de Janeiro and New Orleans. Jamaica is the home of reggae, the Rastafarian sound that has racial, political, and religious undertones. The pulsating merengue, born in the Dominican Republic, is danced exuberantly everywhere

on the island. On Puerto Rico you'll find the salsa, whose range encompasses unabashed hip-swiveling tunes and wailing ballads lamenting lost love. Martinique and Guadeloupe claim to be the cradle of the sinuous beguine, whose lilting rhythm sways like the palm trees. The music that animates Barbados ranges from *soca* (a catchy mix of soul and calypso) and calypso to the hottest jazz. St. Lucia is also proud of its annual jazz festival (held in May). On many islands with a French heritage, *zouk* (a syncopated beat, akin to Caribbean house) is now the rage.

It was from St. Kitts, known as the Mother Colony of the West Indies, that **British** colonists were dispatched in the 17th century to settle Antigua, Barbuda, Tortola, and Montserrat. If you're a history buff, you won't want to miss the beautifully restored Nelson's Dockyard (as in Horatio, Lord), at Antigua's English Harbour; Port Royal, outside Kingston, Jamaica, a pirate stronghold until an earthquake shook things up in 1692; or the hunkering fortress of Brimstone Hill on St. Kitts. Fans who understand the intricacies of cricket can watch matches between Nevis and St. Kitts teams. And the waters around Antigua and the BVI are a mecca for serious sailors. Barbados, which flew the British flag without interruption for 350 years, has cricket, horse racing at Garrison Savannah, polo, and rugby.

Saba, St. Eustatius, St. Maarten, Bonaire, and Curaçao all fly the **Dutch** flag, but they're laced with subtle differences. Saba is a tiny volcanic island known for its beauty, its friendly inhabitants, and its gingerbread-trim houses. Curaçao's colorful waterfront shops and restaurants are reminiscent of Amsterdam. Quiet St. Eustatius—affectionately called Statia—has well-preserved historical sites and is famed for being the first foreign nation to salute the new American flag in 1776. The streets of Philipsburg, the capital of St. Maarten, are lined with colorful Dutch colonial buildings replete with fretwork and verandas. Bonaire is best known for its excellent scuba diving.

Martinique, Guadeloupe, St. Martin, and St. Barthélemy (often called St. Barths or St. Barts) compose the **French** West Indies—actual *départements* (administrative regions) of France. The language, the currency, the culture, and the style are *très* French.

St. Barths is the quietest (and chicest), Martinique the liveliest, St. Martin the friendliest, and Guadeloupe the lushest.

In the Dominican Republic, which occupies the eastern two-thirds of the island of Hispaniola, the language and culture are decidedly **Spanish.** The Colonial Zone of Santo Domingo is the site of the oldest city in the western hemisphere; its restored buildings reflect the 15th-century Columbus period. You also get a sense of the past in Puerto Rico's Old San Juan, with its narrow cobblestone streets and filigreed iron balconies.

WHAT'S WHERE

Finding Your Own Place in the Sun

The Caribbean Sea, an area of more than a million square miles, stretches south of Florida down to the coast of Venezuela. The **Greater Antilles**—the islands closest to the United States—are composed of Cuba, Jamaica, Hispaniola (divided into Haiti and the Dominican Republic), and Puerto Rico. (Haiti and Cuba are not included in this book.) The **Cayman Islands** lie south of Cuba, while the **Turks and Caicos Islands,** in the Atlantic Ocean north of Hispaniola and technically part of the Bahamas, are included in this book because of their proximity to and affinity with the Caribbean islands. The **Lesser Antilles**—greater in number but smaller in size than the Greater Antilles—are divided into three groups: the **Leewards** and the **Windwards** in the eastern Caribbean, and the islands in the **southern Caribbean.** Islands in the Leeward chain are the U.S. Virgin Islands (USVI), the British Virgin Islands (BVI), Anguilla, St. Martin/St. Maarten, St. Barthélemy, Saba, St. Eustatius, St. Kitts, Nevis, Barbuda, Antigua, Montserrat, and Guadeloupe; the Windwards are composed of Dominica, Martinique, St. Lucia, St. Vincent & the Grenadines, and Grenada. Barbados is just east of this group. In the southern Caribbean, off the coast of Venezuela, Trinidad and Tobago are anchored in the east, while Aruba, Bonaire, and Curaçao (known as the ABC Islands) bathe in western waters.

PLEASURES AND PASTIMES

Arts and Nightlife

CASINOS➤ You can flirt with Lady Luck until the wee hours on several islands. San Juan, **Puerto Rico,** arguably offers the most elegant, Old World–style casinos, in the suave Bondian tradition, followed by Santo Domingo, **Dominican Republic. Aruba** and **St. Maarten** have equally spacious casinos, but the ambience is distinctly more American (and, yes, that does mean tour groups at the one-armed bandits). **Curaçao,** a quieter island in general, has a few more restrained casinos, while **Antigua** has perhaps the gaudiest establishment—King's Casino—as well as three small hotel casinos and a few tiny slots saloons. With casino-building on the upswing, you will also now find gambling establishing a foothold on other islands. For example, there is now a casino on **St. Croix,** the only gambling establishment in the U.S. Virgin Islands. And in addition to **Guadeloupe** and **Martinique,** which each have several small casinos, **St. Kitts, St. Vincent,** and Providenciales in the **Turks & Caicos** have one each.

MUSIC➤ Calypso was born in **Trinidad,** its catchy rhythms veiling the barbed working-class satire of many of the lyrics. **Jamaica** is the home of reggae, the Rastafarian sound that has racial, political, and religious undertones; its annual Sunsplash Festival (mid-July–August) is world-renowned. The wild, pulsating merengue, born in the **Dominican Republic,** is exuberantly danced everywhere on the island. On Puerto Rico, you'll find the slightly less frenzied salsa, whose range encompasses unabashed hip-swiveling tunes and wailing ballads lamenting lost love. Both **Martinique** and **Guadeloupe** claim to be the cradle of the sinuous beguine, whose lilting rhythm sways like the palm trees. The music that animates **Barbados** ranges from *soca* (a mix of soul and calypso) and calypso to the hottest jazz. **St. Lucia** is also proud of its annual Jazz Festival (held each May). On many islands *zouk* (a syncopated beat, almost akin to Caribbean house) is now the rage.

NIGHTLIFE➤ Steel drums, limbo dancers, and jump-ups are ubiquitous in the Caribbean. Jump-up? Simple. You hear the music, jump up, and dance. Or just indulge the art of "liming" (we call it "hanging out"), which can mean anything from playing pool or dominoes to engaging in heated political debate to dancing. Bridgetown in **Barbados, Jamaica**'s Montego Bay, and **Trinidad**'s Port-of-Spain are loaded with lively night places, and in **Puerto Rico**, San Juan's glittering Vegas-style floor shows are legendary. But each island also takes great pride in its rich heritage. Many major resorts host local floor shows, a riot of song, dance, and color, incorporating such uniquely Caribbean folkloric traditions as *mocko jumbies* (evil spirits) on stilts and re-creations of Carnival costumes and masks. San Juan, Puerto Rico's year-round Le Lai Lo Festival is perhaps the most successful attempt to introduce visitors to local music and dance.

Cuisine

Caribbean food is a complex blend of indigenous, African, and colonial influences. The Arawaks, Caribs, and Taíno contributed native tubers (also called "provisions" in the islands) such as yuca (also known as cassava) and *tania* (also known as taro), leafy vegetables like callaloo (similar to spinach—though slightly bitter—it also doubles as the name of the soup made from it throughout the Lesser Antilles), and such spices as cilantro and *achiote*. From Africa came plantains, yams, green pigeon peas, and assorted peppers. The Spaniards brought rice, while the British imported such plants as breadfruit from the Pacific.

Don't shy away from such classic dishes as goat water (**Dominica**, among others), pepper pot (**Grenada, St. Lucia**, and most of the Windwards), and *sancocho* (the **Dominican Republic** and **Puerto Rico**), all thick, sultry stews made with various meats and vegetables. Sample johnnycakes (Caribbean muffins) with breakfast, *fungi* (cornmeal) at lunch, local vegetables like christophene with dinner. Then try tangy soursop ice cream or passion fruit sorbet for dessert.

The national dish of **Jamaica** is salt fish and ackee: salted cod and a plant that, when boiled, tastes remarkably like scrambled eggs. You can still find such exotica as *crapaud* or "mountain chicken" (actually enormous frogs' legs) or agouti (a large rodent delicious when roasted or smoked)

on Dominica. And you must try flying fish, the national dish of **Barbados. Grenada**, the spice island (it produces much of the world's supply of nutmeg and cloves), has an abundance of seafood and an incredible variety of fruits and vegetables. On **St. Lucia**, where countless banana plantations cover the mountainsides, you'll find many varieties of banana prepared in dozens of ways. The cuisine on **Martinique** and **Guadeloupe** is a marvelous marriage of Creole cooking and classic French dishes; you'll find much of the same on the other French islands of **St. Martin** and **St. Barths.** You'll also find a fine selection of French wines in the French West Indies. Anegada, in the **British West Indies,** is, arguably, where you'll find the Caribbean's best lobster. You can even find *roti* (a pancake stuffed with chicken or pork and rice) and curries, East Indian legacies that have gradually spread north from **Trinidad.**

Foreign Culture and History

AFRICAN➤ **Trinidad** moves with the rhythm of calypso and is the stomping ground of a flat-out, freewheeling Carnival that rivals the pre-Lenten celebrations in Rio de Janeiro and New Orleans. The Trinidadians have built up one of the most prosperous commercial centers in the Caribbean. Haiti was once another option. (It's now politically volatile and is not covered in this book.)

BRITISH➤ It was from **St. Kitts,** known as the Mother Colony of the West Indies, that British colonists were dispatched in the 17th century to settle Antigua, Barbuda, Tortola, and Montserrat. If you're a history buff, you won't want to miss the beautifully restored Nelson's Dockyard (as in Horatio, Lord) at **Antigua**'s English Harbour; Port Royal, outside Kingston, **Jamaica,** a pirates' stronghold until an earthquake shook things up in 1692; or the hunkering fortress of Brimstone Hill on St. Kitts. Sports fans who understand the intricacies of cricket can watch matches between **Nevis** and St. Kitts teams. And the waters around Antigua and the **BVI** are a mecca for serious sailors. **Barbados,** with its lovely trade winds, has cricket, horse racing at Garrison Savannah, and rugby.

DUTCH➤ **Saba, St. Eustatius, St. Maarten, Bonaire,** and **Curaçao** all fly the Dutch flag, but there the similarity ends. Saba is a tiny volcanic island known for its beauty, its friendly inhabitants, and its gingerbread trimmed houses. Curaçao's colorful waterfront shops and restaurants are reminiscent of Amsterdam. Quiet St. Eustatius—affectionately called Statia—has well-preserved historical sites and is famed for being the first foreign nation to salute the new American flag in 1776. The main streets of Philipsburg, the capital of St. Maarten, are lined with colorful Dutch colonial buildings replete with fretwork and verandas. Bonaire is best known for its excellent scuba diving.

FRENCH➤ **Martinique, Guadeloupe, St. Martin,** and **St. Barthélemy** (often called St. Barths or St. Barts) compose the French West Indies. The language, the currency, the culture, and the style are très French. St. Barths is the quietest (and chicest), Martinique the liveliest, St. Martin the friendliest, and Guadeloupe the lushest.

SPANISH➤ In the **Dominican Republic,** which occupies the eastern two-thirds of the island of Hispaniola, the language and culture are decidedly Spanish. The Zona Colonial of Santo Domingo is the site of the oldest city in the Western Hemisphere; its restored buildings reflect the 15th-century Columbus period. You also get a sense of the past in **Puerto Rico**'s Old San Juan, with its narrow cobblestone streets and filigreed iron balconies.

Getting Away from It All

If you're looking to back out of the fast lane, you can park at a secluded, spartan mountain lodge on **Dominica,** a ruggedly beautiful island laced with rivers and waterfalls and embroidered with untamed vegetation. **Puerto Rico**'s luxuriant 28,000-acre El Yunque is the only rain forest in the U.S. Forestry system. Or opt for the quiet grandeur of a renovated sugar plantation on **Nevis** or **St. Kitts,** where you can feast in an elegant dining room or enjoy a barbecue on the beach. Tranquil **Anguilla,** with soft white beaches nudged by incredibly clear water, offers posh resorts as well as small, inexpensive, locally owned lodgings. From the low-key **Turks and Caicos Islands,** which lie in stunning blue-green waters, you can boat to more than a score of cays so isolated that even the term "low-key" would imply too fast a pace.

On tiny **Saba** there's little to do but tuck into a small guest house, admire the lush beauty of the island (hiking the aptly named Mt. Scenery), and chat with the friendly Sabans. Nearby **St. Eustatius,** where adventurers can crawl down into a jungle cradled within a crater, is another friendly, laid-back island. On **St. Lucia,** you can drive right into a volcano. **St. Vincent and the Grenadines** offer three tiny, private-island luxury resorts: Young Island, Palm Island, and Petit St. Vincent. Or you can opt for sleepy islands off islands, such as Vieques and Culebra (off **Puerto Rico**), or Marie Galante, Les Saintes, and La Désirade (off **Guadeloupe**)—all with practically deserted pristine beaches, true local color, and charming guest houses. Guadeloupe also has a 74,000-acre nature park with dramatic waterfalls, cool pools, and miles of hiking trails. Majestic Mount Pelée, a not entirely dormant volcano, towers over **Martinique**'s rain forest.

Golf

According to those who have played it, the course at Casa de Campo on the **Dominican Republic** is one of the best in the Caribbean, and there is a brand-new seaside course at the Punta Cana Resort & Club. The course at the Four Seasons Resort on **Nevis** is also challenging (and breathtaking). Golfers on St. Thomas, **USVI** play the Mahogany Run. There are superb courses in **Puerto Rico,** including four shared by the Hyatt Dorado Beach and the Hyatt Regency Cerromar Beach. Among the courses on **Jamaica** are the top-rated Tryall near Montego Bay, and the new Negril Hills Golf Club. Golf is second only to cricket in **Barbados**; the Royal Westmoreland Golf Club opened its first 18 holes for the 1996 season; another 9 holes are under way. The **Cayman Islands** have an 18-hole championship course, the Links at Safehaven, and **Aruba** has the 18-hole, Robert Trent Jones–designed Tierra del Sol.

Water Sports

BOATING AND SAILING➤ Whether you charter a boat with a crew or captain a vessel yourself, the waters of the Caribbean are excellent for boating and sailing, and the many secluded bays and inlets provide ideal spots to drop anchor and picnic or explore. The marinas on Tortola in the **BVI,** at Rodney Bay and Marigot in **St. Lucia,** throughout **St. Vincent and the Grenadines,** St. Thomas in the **USVI,** and Port la Royale and Oyster Pond in **St. Martin** are the starting points for some of the Caribbean's finest sailing. Yachtspeople also favor the waters around **Antigua** and put in regularly at Nelson's Dockyard, which hosts a colorful regatta in late April or early May.

DIVING➤ Although **scuba** (the word is derived from what was once an acronym for "self-contained underwater breathing apparatus") diving is surprisingly simple, *call your physician before your vacation, and make sure that you have no condition that should prevent you from diving!* A full checkup is an excellent idea, especially if you're over 30. Since it can be dangerous to travel on a plane after diving, you should schedule both your diving courses and travel plans accordingly.

Learning to dive with a reputable instructor is a must. In addition to teaching you how to resurface properly, a qualified instructor can train you to read "dive tables," the charts that calculate how long you can safely stay at certain depths. Many resorts offer courses consisting of two to three hours of instruction on land and time in a swimming pool or waist-deep water to get used to the mouthpiece and hose (the regulator) and the mask. A shallow (20-ft), supervised dive from a boat or beach follows.

Successful completion of an introductory course may prompt you to earn a certification card—often called a C-card—from an accredited diving organization: NAUI (National Association of Underwater Instructors), CMAS (Confederation Mondiale des Activités Subaquatiques, which translates into World Underwater Activities Federation), NASE (National Association of Scuba Educators), or PADI (Professional Association of Diving Instructors). PADI offers a free list of training facilities.

Jacques Cousteau, who invented scuba diving, named Pigeon Island, off the west coast of **Guadeloupe,** one of the 10 best dive sites in the world. The Wall off Grand Turk in the **Turks and Caicos Islands** is a sheer drop of 7,000 ft (2,100 m); more than 200 mi (323 km) of reef surround the chain. The eruption of **Martinique**'s Mt. Pelée at 8 AM on May 8, 1902, resulted in the sinking of several ships that are now great sites. **St. Eustatius** also has an undersea "supermarket" of ships, as well as entire 18th-century warehouses below the surface of Oranjestad Bay. The waters surrounding all three of the **Cayman Islands** are acclaimed by experts; even novices adore Stingray City on Grand Cayman, where dozens of unusually tame stingrays swim and twist around divers in the shallow waters. **Bonaire**'s 86 spectacular sites, all protected as part of the Bonaire Marine Park, make that island a diving mecca. **Tortola** is famous in diving circles for the wreck of the RMS *Rhone,* a mail ship sunk by a hurricane in 1867. **Tobago** has a great array of unspoiled coral reefs, and it's the only place in the Caribbean where divers regularly see huge manta rays. **Saba** has some of the best advanced diving with its marine park and deep dive sites. **Dominica** offers dramatic underwater walls and sudden drops, as well as unusual volcanic vents (like diving in warm champagne), off Scott's Head.

SNORKELING➤ Snorkeling requires no special skills, and many establishments that rent equipment have a staff member to teach you the basics. As with any water sport, it's never a good idea to snorkel alone. You don't have to be a great swimmer to snorkel, but occasionally currents come up that require stamina. Time seems to slow down underwater, so wear a water-resistant watch and let someone on land know when to expect you back. Remember that taking souvenirs—shells, pieces of coral, interesting rocks—is forbidden. Many reefs are legally protected marine parks, where removal of living shells is prohibited because it upsets the ecology.

WATERSKIING➤ Some large hotels have their own concessions, with special boats, equipment, and instructors. Many beaches (especially those in Barbados), however, are patrolled by individuals who own boats and several sizes of skis; they offer their services through a hotel or directly to you or can be hailed like taxis. Ask your hotel staff or other guests about their experiences with these entrepreneurs. Be *sure* they provide life vests and at least two people in the boat: one to drive and one to watch the skier at all times.

WINDSURFING➤ Windsurfing is as strenuous as it is exciting, so it may not be the sport to try on your first day out, unless you're already in excellent shape. Always windsurf with someone else around who can go for help if necessary.

Weddings

More and more couples are tying the knot in the sunny Caribbean. Recognizing this trend, many islands have relaxed their marriage requirements with shortened (or no) residency periods and simplified paperwork. In addition, many no longer require blood tests. To marry on most islands, you must submit the necessary paperwork before your stay. Ship your documents by courier or, if acceptable, fax them. Keep copies of all papers, and carry them with you on your trip. If this isn't your first marriage, you'll need to present a certified divorce decree or, if you're widowed, the death certificate of your previous spouse. (If this documentation is not in the island's official language, you may be required to supply a certified translation of it.) You'll also need to provide proof of your identity and citizenship (documentation requirements for this vary slightly). Wedding fees range from about $40 to $200, including a marriage license.

The easiest and most efficient way to arrange an island wedding is through a resort. Many of them not only have wedding packages but also staff members who can help you with all the pre-wedding paperwork as well as with the ceremony itself. (Some resorts, such as SuperClubs and Sandals, even offer free weddings—including paperwork and a marriage official.) As soon as your reservations are confirmed, speak with the hotel's wedding coordinator.

FODOR'S CHOICE

Beaches

Bahoruco Beach, Dominican Republic. Eight miles (13 km) from the town of Barahona, on the isolated south coast, this gorgeous stretch of virgin beach goes on for miles in either direction, with rugged cliffs dropping to golden sand and gin-clear water.
Baie Oriental, St. Martin. This lively strand with lots of beach bars is best known as the Caribbean's premier clothing optional beach. The sight of cruise ship passengers gawking is alone worth a visit.
Grande Anse Beach, Grenada. Gentle surf laps the gleaming sand of this 2-mi (3-km) beach. To the north, you can see the narrow mouth of St. George's Harbour and the pastel houses, with their fish-scale tile rooftops, that climb the surrounding hills.

Grande Saline, St. Barthélemy. This beautiful, secluded beach is just about everyone's favorite place for swimming.
Macaroni Beach, Mustique, St. Vincent and the Grenadines. Surfy swimming, powdery white sand, a few palm huts and picnic tables, and very few people are the draws here.
Seven Mile Beach, Grand Cayman, Cayman Islands. It's actually 5½ mi (9 km) of powdery white sand, litter- and peddler-free, and headquarters for the island's water sports outfitters.
Shoal Bay, Anguilla. This 2-mi (3-km), L-shape beach of talcum-powder-soft white sand may get crowded, but that's only because it's one of the prettiest in the Caribbean.
Trunk Bay, St. John, USVI. You'll find sensational snorkeling on this perfect scimitar, one of many such sandy stretches on an island that's 66% protected national park.

Caribbean Classics
Gambling in a Casino in Aruba. The casinos all along L. G. Smith and J. E. Irausquin boulevards have something for the high roller, the curious novice, and those who simply want to see a show.
Visiting Bonaire Marine Park. The current is mild, the reefs often begin just offshore, visibility is generally 60 ft–100 ft, and the marine life is magnificent.
Barhopping on Jost Van Dyke, British Virgin Islands. You can't go wrong at any bar on this island, which does its best to entertain the charter-yacht crowd.
Hiking on Dominica. The island's lush forests are scored by ancient footpaths (some made by escaped slaves and Carib Indians).
Strolling through Santo Domingo's Colonial Zone, Dominican Republic. Wandering the narrow cobbled streets, it's easy to imagine what the city was like in the days of Columbus, Cortés, and Ponce de León. Now that the zone is well-lit by antique lanterns, the bustling area is the happening place in the capital.
Buying Spices in Grenada. For nutmeg, cinnamon sticks, cocoa, cloves, and more, visit a historic spice plantation, tour a nutmeg-processing plant, and replenish your spice rack at an outdoor market.
Playing Golf on Puerto Rico. The island has acres of golf greens. Check out Palmas del Mar's Flamboyant course, with its 18 elegant Rees Jones–designed holes and a

Gary Player course as well. The Westin Río Mar's Ocean and River courses have challenging bunkers and fairways as well as views of El Yunque and the Atlantic.

Shopping for Lace on Saba. On weekdays Saban ladies sell their lace creations—collars, tea towels, napkins, tablecloths—at the community center in Hell's Gate. Many also sell their wares from their homes; just follow the signs.

Visiting Diamond Botanical Gardens, St. Lucia. Shady pathways meander through 2,000 privately owned acres of dense tropical foliage bursting with flowers and lead to a picturesque waterfall and curative mineral baths.

Duty-free Shopping on St. Maarten/St. Martin or St. Thomas. Hundreds of duty-free shops make these islands the best in the Caribbean for bargain-hunters.

Bird-watching in Trinidad and Tobago. You might spot blue-backed manakin, yellow oriole, scarlet ibis, or another of the more than 200 varieties of birds at the Asa Wright Nature Centre.

Hotels

Anse Chastanet Hotel, St. Lucia. Rooms were designed to meld with the mountainside; louvered wooden walls open to stunning Piton and Caribbean vistas or to the deep-green forest. $$$$

Biras Creek, Virgin Gorda, BVI. A former guest bought this resort and completely renovated it, from building a new kitchen to lining the beach with palm trees; it's now a spectacular hideaway. $$$$

Caneel Bay Resort, St. John, USVI. With seven beaches spread out over 170 acres, this open-air resort is a sun worshiper's paradise. Numerous tennis courts, myriad water sports, and good restaurants make it hard to stir from this luxury property. $$$$

Cap Juluca, Anguilla. This spectacular 179-acre resort wraps around the edge of Maunday's Bay and almost 2 mi (3 km) of sugary white-sand beach. $$$$

Cobblers Cove, Barbados. Pretty in pink, this intimate resort on a picturesque cove blends English country-house elegance with casual Caribbean style—the epitome of a perfect Bajan holiday. $$$$

Cotton House, Mustique, St. Vincent and the Grenadines. Whoever coined the term "lap of luxury" must have had in mind this exquisite resort on Mustique. Hobnob with the rich and famous on their private-island playground. $$$$

Curtain Bluff, Antigua. The setting, book-ended by two exquisite beaches, is breathtaking. The ambience is pure country-club elegance—and a surprisingly good value. $$$$

Franklyn D. Resort (FDR), Jamaica. On arrival, each family is assigned a girl Friday, who works with the children throughout their stay. The children's miniclub includes computer training, a satellite TV room, video games, donkey rides, picnics, arts and crafts, children's slides and pools, and a kiddies' disco. $$$$

Grand Lido Sans Souci, Jamaica. As if the decorative luxury of this pastel cliffside palace weren't enough, a free spa session is also offered. $$$$

Horned Dorset Primavera, Puerto Rico. The emphasis here is on privacy and relaxation. The pounding of the surf and the squawk of the resident parrot are the only sounds you'll hear as you lounge on the beach. $$$$

Hôtel Isle de France, St. Barthélemy. An intimate resort on a beautiful beach, it's a Caribbean dream come true. If you want to join the lucky few, book your room far, far in advance. $$$$

Ottley's Plantation Inn, St. Kitts. This great house inn with ravishing gardens epitomizes low-key, worldly sophistication and down-home Caribbean hospitality. $$$$

Parrot Cay, Providenciales, Turks & Caicos. Natural beauty and tranquillity attract jet setters to this resort. $$$$

Ritz-Carlton, St. Thomas, U.S. Virgin Islands. Built like a palatial Italian villa, there's elegance everywhere, from the marbled-floor reception area to a pool that seems to flow right into the sea. $$$$

Spice Island Beach Resort, Grenada. The spacious suites, fabulous bathrooms, and private plunge pools or in-room whirlpools are great, but it's the location on beautiful Grande Anse Beach that steals the show. $$$$

Young Island Resort, Young Island, St. Vincent and the Grenadines. On its own private island a stone's throw from St. Vincent's shore, these luxury cottages fall somewhere between the Swiss Family Robinson's tree house and the Ritz. $$$$

Bucuti Beach Resort, Aruba. Popular with honeymooners (who receive champagne and other goodies upon arrival), the hacienda-style buildings here house sunny rooms with ocean-view terraces. The resort has an enviable location on the widest, most secluded section of Eagle Beach. $$$

Avila Beach Hotel, Curaçao. Dutch royals and government VIPs have given this 200-year-old mansion the nod for the peace, privacy, and service it offers. Still, you don't need a royal bank account to stay here. *$$*

Hotel 1829, St. Thomas, U.S. Virgin Islands. It's all romance and classic elegance at this historic Spanish-style inn. *$$*

Le Plein Soleil, Martinique. This small resort is chic, contemporary creole at its unexpected best. As appealing as the gingerbread guest cottages are, it is the inn's great house that captivates. Très chic, it is a study in white, with classy tropical furnishings, art, and objets d'nature. *$*

Papillote Wilderness Retreat, Dominica. The owners and staff have infused this mountain getaway with their charm and warmth—from the gorgeous botanical gardens to the homey rooms. *$*

Restaurants

Anacaona, Providenciales, Turks and Caicos. This is a true gourmet dining experience, minus the attitude. Traditional French recipes are combined with Caribbean fruits, vegetables, and spices. *$$$*

Auberge de la Vielle Tour, Guadeloupe. This inviting restaurant within a historic sugar mill serves some of the island's best contemporary cuisine. Dessert presentations are dazzling. *$$$*

Carambola, Barbados. Barbados can legitimately claim sophisticated cuisine that rivals the world's best. Romantic Carambola, on a cliff overlooking the sea, stands out as one of the island's finest. *$$$*

Caribbean Blue, Dominican Republic. Exquisite taste permeates this multistory, 16th-century restoration in Santo Domingo's Zona Colonial, but new-world cuisine is the ticket here. Up the circular staircase is Aqua Lounge, the Zone's hottest dance club. *$$$*

Chez Pascal, Antigua. Perched on a cliff overlooking the ocean, this restaurant is an authentic piece of sunny, southern France transplanted to the Caribbean. Melt-in-your-mouth seafood specialities particularly shine, as do the silken sauces. *$$$*

Dasheene, St. Lucia. The exquisite cuisine at the Ladera Resort's restaurant, perched high on a hill between The Pitons, is upstaged only by the view. Whether the panorama is more spectacular at midday or at sunset is a toss-up. *$$$*

Fatzo, Martinique. This grande dame in the village of Anse d'Arlet has it all: contemporary cuisine, ambience, service, history, and an interesting crowd from fun locals to yachtsmen. *$$$*

Hemingway's, Grand Cayman, Cayman Islands. Enjoy the breezes on Seven Mile Beach while sipping a Seven Mile Meltdown (dark rum, peach schnapps, pineapple juice, and fresh coconut) and savoring grouper stuffed with sweet corn and crab. *$$$*

Madame Janette's, Aruba. The Carribean-influenced French fare here has set romantics abuzz. Start with delicious shellfish or sirloin steak, then finish with crème brûlée or stuffed crepes. *$$$*

Rijsttafel Indonesia Restaurant, Curaçao. Walls hung with batik, handwoven baskets, and shadow puppets set the stage for a traditional Indonesian rijsttafel banquet, with as many as 25 dishes served buffet-style. *$$$*

Top Hat, St. Croix, USVI. Both the wonderful Danish menu and the Danish owners are reminders of St. Croix's colonial past. Try the *frikadeller* (meatballs in a tangy sauce) and fried Camembert with lingonberries. *$$$*

Virgilio's, St. Thomas, USVI. Come here for some of the best northern Italian cuisine in the islands, and don't leave without having a Virgilio's cappuccino, a chocolate-and-coffee drink so rich, it's dessert. *$$$*

Veni Mangé, Trinidad. Cordon Bleu–trained Allyson Hennessey cooks up the best creole lunches in town. *$$*

Skinny Legs Bar and Restaurant, St. John, USVI. Exuding scads of island charm, here is a place where you can gather with the locals for lunch, supper, or just drinks. The owners, Doug and Moe, are characters, as are some of those who frequent the place. *$*

2 ANGUILLA

Updated by
Michael de
Zayas

"But I arranged for lobster in advance," snarled the man at the beachfront table. "That was the whole point of coming here." The waitress tried to soothe him: "I'm sorry; we ran out of lobsters, but it's really no problem—I've talked to the manager." But her gracious assurances and charming West Indian accent had no effect. The man's face reddened until it seemed he would explode. Just then, a handsome, wiry Anguillan man approached from the beach, a bag over his shoulder. "Ah, yes. Here's the manager with fresh lobster now," said the waitress with a smile. "I told you it was no problem."

Peace, pampering, fine dining, and beaches are among the star attractions on Anguilla (pronounced ang-gwill-a). If you're a beach lover, you may become giddy when you first spot the island from the air; its blindingly white sand and lustrous blue and aquamarine waters are intoxicating sights. If you like shopping and late-night action, you won't find a lot to do here. There are no glittering casinos or nightclubs, no duty-free shops stuffed with irresistible buys (although you're only about 30 watery minutes from St. Maarten/St. Martin's bustling resorts and casinos). However, if you like sophisticated cuisine served in stunning open-air settings, this may be your culinary Shangri-La. Despite being one of the smaller Caribbean islands, Anguilla has nearly 70 restaurants. Some serve up the latest culinary trends in atmospheres that range from casual to fancy, and others stick to the simple fare you'd expect to find at a barefoot-friendly, beachfront bar.

This dry, limestone isle is the most northerly of the Leeward Islands, lying between the Caribbean Sea and the Atlantic Ocean. It stretches, from northeast to southwest, about 16 mi (26 km) and is only 3 mi (5 km) across at its widest point. The highest spot is 213 ft (65 m) above sea level, and there are neither streams nor rivers, only saline ponds used for salt production. The island's name, a reflection of its shape, is most likely a derivative of *anguille,* which is French for "eel." (French explorer Pierre Laudonnaire is credited with having given the island this name when he sailed past it in 1556.)

In 1631 the Dutch built a fort here, but no one has been able to locate its site. English settlers from St. Kitts colonized the island in 1650, and except for a brief period of independence with St. Kitts–Nevis in the 1960s, Anguilla has remained a British colony ever since.

From the early 1800s various island units and federations were formed and disbanded, with Anguilla all the while simmering over its subordinate status and enforced union with St. Kitts. Anguillans twice petitioned for direct rule from Britain and twice were ignored. In 1967, when St. Kitts, Nevis, and Anguilla became an associated state, the mouse roared; citizens kicked out St. Kitts' policemen, held a self-rule referendum, and for two years conducted their own affairs. A British "peacekeeping force" then parachuted down onto the island, squelching Anguilla's designs for autonomy but helping a team of royal engineers stationed there to improve the port and build roads and schools. Today Anguilla elects a House of Assembly and its own leader to handle internal affairs, while a British governor is responsible for public service, the police, judiciary, and external affairs.

The territory of Anguilla includes a few islets (or cays), such as Scrub Island, Dog Island, Prickly Pear Cays, Sandy Island, and Sombrero Island. The 10,000 or so residents are predominantly of African descent, but there are also many of Irish background, whose ancestors came over from St. Kitts in the 1600s. Historically, because the limestone land was hardly fit for agriculture, attempts at enslavement and colonization never lasted long; consequently, Anguilla doesn't bear the scars of slavery found on so many other Caribbean islands. Because the island couldn't be farmed successfully (although cotton was produced here for a while), Anguillans became experts at making a living from the sea and are known for their boatbuilding and fishing skills. Tourism is the growth industry of the island's stable economy, but the government is determined to keep expansion at a slow and cautious pace to protect the island's natural resources and beauty. New hotels are built small, select, and definitely casino free. The island has chosen to emphasize its high-quality service, serene surroundings, and friendly people.

Lodging

Anguilla accommodations range from grand, sumptuous resorts to apartments and villas—deluxe or simple—to small, locally owned guest houses. Because the island has so many beautiful and uncrowded beaches, it's not necessary (the way it is on some other islands) for beach lovers to choose a particular property because of its beach. If calling to reserve a room in a resort, inquire about special packages and meal plans.

CATEGORY	COST EP/CP*	COST A.I.**
$$$$	over $350	over $375
$$$	$250–$350	$275–$375
$$	$150–$250	$175–$275
$	under $150	under $175

*EP/CP prices are per night for a standard double room in high season, excluding taxes, service charges, and meal plans**A.I. (all-inclusive) prices are per person, per night based on double-occupancy during high season, excluding taxes and service charges

Hotels

$$$$ 🏨 **Cap Juluca.** Isolated, cool, and serene, this 179-acre resort wraps around
★ the edge of Maundays Bay on a breathtaking 2-mi (3-km) stretch of sugary sand. The white, Moorish-style, two-story villas are luxurious; the stylish rooms have Moroccan fabrics, Brazilian hardwood furniture, and built-in seating areas. Diners can choose from casual George's on the Beach, the elegant Pimms restaurant, and Kemia, a tapas bar. An appealing activity program in July and August includes visits to local boatbuilders. However, variable standards of service and a sometimes boisterous atmosphere make this a resort more for those who can go

with the flow of life on the island. ⊠ *Maundays Bay (Box 240),* ☎ *264/497–6666 or 888/858–5822,* FAX *264/497–6617,* WEB *www.capjuluca.com. 98 rooms, 18 villas. 3 restaurants, bar, room service, 3 tennis courts, pool, club, spa, beach, snorkeling, windsurfing, boating, croquet, shops, library, baby-sitting, children's programs (ages 3–14), laundry service, Internet. AE, MC, V. EP, FAP, MAP. Closed Sept.–Oct.*

\$\$\$\$
★ 🏨 **Cuisinart Resort & Spa.** The stark white architecture of the Greek island of Mykonos is the inspiration for this luxurious beachfront resort. Rooms, suites, and penthouses, in a cluster of stucco villas on stunning Rendezvous Bay, are white inside and out. Units are decorated in Haitian cottons, and all have marble bathrooms. The resort is a development of the Cuisinart company, so one distinctive amenity is a demonstration kitchen with complimentary cooking classes. The spa offers massages and body treatments, a state-of-the-art, 24-hour fitness center, and an art gallery designed for relaxation and meditation. ⊠ *Rendezvous Bay (Box 2000),* ☎ *264/498–2000 or 800/943–3210,* FAX *264/498–2010,* WEB *www.cuisinart-resort.com. 93 rooms, 2 penthouses. 3 restaurants, 2 bars, 3 tennis courts, pool, hot tub, health club, beach, snorkeling, windsurfing, boating, billiards, shops, baby-sitting, laundry service, Internet. AE, MC, V. EP, MAP. Closed Sept.–Oct.*

\$\$\$\$
☾ ★ 🏨 **Malliouhana.** Anguilla's classiest resort sits on 25 tropical acres along a promontory between two exquisite beaches. Its success can be attributed to charming, hands-on owner Leon Roydon, who founded Malliouhana in 1983 as one of the Caribbean's first luxury resorts. Moorish-style buildings have white interiors decorated with Haitian art—one of the largest collections in the Caribbean; marble bathrooms have oversize tubs. The Malliouhana restaurant is the most elegant on the island. Kids will love the winding water slides and pirate ship–playground that sits in a pool lagoon beside the beach. Adults will enjoy the new state-of-the-art spa. All activities, even waterskiing, are included. ⊠ *Meads Bay (Box 173),* ☎ *264/497–6111 or 800/835–0796,* FAX *264/497–6011,* WEB *www.malliouhana.com. 34 rooms, 19 suites. 2 restaurants, 2 bars, no room TVs, 4 tennis courts, 3 pools, aerobics, hair salon, hot tub, health club, massage, spa, beach, snorkeling, windsurfing, boating, waterskiing, basketball, playground, Internet, business services, meeting room. No credit cards. EP, MAP. Closed Sept.–Oct.*

\$\$\$\$ 🏨 **Sonesta Beach Resort & Villas Anguilla.** This pink-and-green Moorish fantasia is right on the beach, and many rooms have grand views of St. Martin. The route to reception, the restaurants, and the pool may take your breath away: you pass through a long, open-air arcade with authentic Moroccan mosaics and by a long reflecting pool. In the rooms, bold prints hang on the walls, and Moroccan throw rugs are scattered hither and yon. Marble bathrooms have spacious tubs. The four-bedroom Oleander villa has Italian marble floors, mahogany furniture and accents, luxury kitchen appliances, ceiling fans, and spacious baths with whirlpool tubs. ⊠ *Rendezvous Bay West (Box 444),* ☎ *264/497–6999,* FAX *264/497–6899,* WEB *www.sonesta.com. 79 rooms, 5 suites, 3 villas. 2 restaurants, bar, 2 tennis courts, pool, gym, hair salon, beach, snorkeling, windsurfing, bicycles, shops, library. AE, MC, V. BP, FAP, MAP.*

\$\$\$–\$\$\$\$ 🏨 **Cinnamon Reef Beach Club.** Low-key luxury sets the tone at this small, appealing place. There are three types of casual accommodations, all decorated with Mexican tile, floral prints, and colorful paintings. Villa Suites are unattached and have a living room, raised bedroom, dressing room, sunken shower, patio with a hammock, and stunning views of the Caribbean. Beach Suites are nestled among palm trees on the beach. Garden Suites are smaller and have a combined living-bedroom area. This is a friendly place with a gracious staff and lots of regulars. Several chefs at the Palm Court restaurant have been Anguilla

14

Anguilla

0 | 4 miles
0 | 6 km

N

Katouche Bay

Ram's Head

Masara

Flat Cap Point

Little Bay

5

The Valley

8

Sandy Island

①-④

Road Bay

North Hill

7

Sandy Ground

Wallblake Airport

Sandy Ground

1
2 **3**

6

4

South Hill

5

15

Little Harbour

Long Bay

②⑧ - ③①

⑦

Meads Bay

⑲ ⑱ ⑰

Blowing Point Harbour

Barnes Bay

Rendezvous Bay

West End

②④

Maunday's Bay

②①

②⓪

16

②⑥

②⑤

Shoal Bay West

②③

②②

Cove Bay

Anguillita Island

Lodging

Allamanda Beach Club **10**
Altamer **24**
Anguilla Great House Beach Resort **19**
Arawak Beach Inn . .**12**
Blue Waters **23**
Cap Juluca **22**
Carimar Beach Club **29**

Cinnamon Reef Beach Club **15**
Covecastles Villa Resort **26**
Cuisinart Resort & Spa **18**
Easy Corner Villas . . .**7**
Ferryboat Inn **16**
Frangipani Beach Club **27**
Malliouhana **31**

Paradise Cove **21**
Rendezvous Bay Hotel **17**
Shoal Bay Villas . . .**11**
La Sirena **30**
Sonesta Beach Resort & Villas Anguilla **20**
Syd-An's **3**

Dining

Altamer **24**
Le Bistro Phil **5**
Blanchard's **28**
Casablanca **20**
Covecastles **26**
Ferryboat Inn **16**
Hibernia **13**

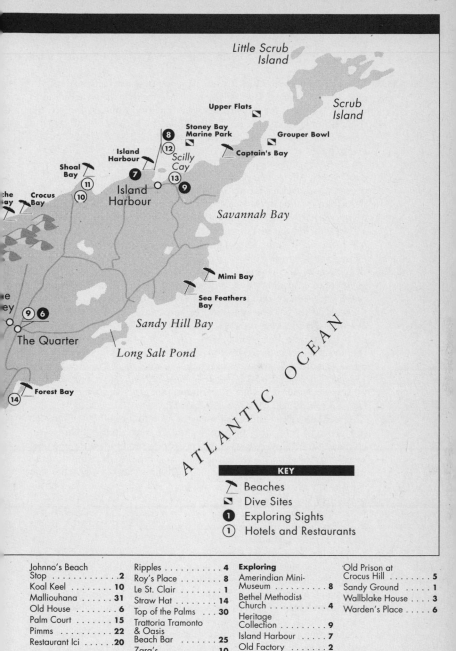

Little Scrub
Island

Upper Flats

Scrub
Island

Stoney Bay
Marine Park

Grouper Bowl

8

12

Island
Harbour

Captain's Bay

Scilly
Cay

Shoal
Bay

7

11

13

10

Island
Harbour

9

:he
:ay

Crocus
Bay

Savannah Bay

Mimi Bay

Sea Feathers
Bay

e
ey

9 **6**

Sandy Hill Bay

The Quarter

Long Salt Pond

ATLANTIC OCEAN

Forest Bay

14

KEY

Beaches

Dive Sites

1 Exploring Sights

(1) Hotels and Restaurants

Chef of the Year. ✉ *Little Harbour (Box 141)*, ☎ 264/497–2727 or 800/223–1108, FAX 264/497–3727, WEB *www.cinnamon-reef.com. 8 studios, 14 1-bedroom suites. Restaurant, bar, 2 tennis courts, pool, hot tub, beach, snorkeling, windsurfing. AE, MC, V. CP, EP, MAP. Closed Aug.–mid-Dec.*

$$$–$$$$ 🛏 **Frangipani Beach Club.** The splashy, inviting hotel sits on 1 mi (1½
    ★   km) of sandy beach. The pink Spanish Mediterranean-style buildings with archways, stone balustrades, wrought-iron railings, and red-tile roofs sit on grounds that are lushly landscaped with colorful tropical flowers. Each one-, two-, or three-bedroom suite has arched windows and exposed beam ceilings and is tastefully decorated with blond rattan furniture and fabrics in a mix of blue-and-white stripes and colorful prints. All units have marble and tiled bathrooms and doors that open onto a spacious terrace or balcony; many have full kitchens. The restaurant overlooks the ocean and has a French-influenced menu. ✉ *Meads Bay (Box 328)*, ☎ 264/497–6442 or 800/892–4564, FAX 264/ 497–6440, WEB *www.frangipani.ai. 17 rooms, 8 suites. Restaurant, bar, tennis court, pool, beach, snorkeling, windsurfing. AE, MC, V. EP. Closed Sept.–mid-Oct.*

$$$ 🛏 **La Sirena.** At this small, well-run resort, you can opt for a regular guest room, a spacious villa, or a suite with its own hot tub. The complex's white-stucco buildings, all set amid tropical greenery, have red-tile roofs, lots of balconies and terraces, and interesting angles and circular openings. Interiors are typical Caribbean: rattan furniture, pastel-print fabrics, and, of course, ceiling fans. The second-floor Top of the Palms restaurant serves Italian, Mexican, vegetarian, and Caribbean items. It's a four-minute walk from the beach. ✉ *Meads Bay (Box 200)*, ☎ 264/ 497–6827 or 800/223–9815, FAX 264/497–6829, WEB *www.la-sirena.com. 20 rooms, 3 suites, 5 villas. Restaurant, bar, 2 pools, dive shop, bicycles, car rental. AE, MC, V. CP, EP, MAP.*

$$$ 🛏 **Shoal Bay Villas.** This small two-story condominium hotel is tucked in a grove of palm trees on 2 mi (3 km) of splendid sand. Units—including two studios, two with two bedrooms, and nine with one bedroom—are brightly decorated in pink and blue, with painted rattan furniture and fully equipped kitchens. All have patios or porches that open to the beach or the courtyard pool. All water sports can be arranged. ✉ *Shoal Bay (Box 81)*, ☎ 264/497–2051, FAX 264/497–3631, WEB *www.sbvillas.ai. 2 studios, 3 2-bedroom condos, 10 1-bedroom condos. Restaurant, bar, pool, beach, snorkeling. AE, D, MC, V. EP. Closed Sept.–mid-Oct.*

$$–$$$ 🛏 **Anguilla Great House Beach Resort.** Rooms here are in white West Indian–style bungalows strung along one of Anguilla's longest 2½ mi (4 km) beaches. From a chaise on your charming veranda, the view of the ocean is framed by vine-covered trellises and gingerbread trim. Most bungalows have five rooms, and each has mahogany furnishings, tropical-print fabrics, a huge tile shower, and ceiling fans. Most rooms have air-conditioning. The restaurant serves a mix of West Indian, French, and Continental cuisines. ✉ *Rendezvous Bay (Box 157)*, ☎ 264/497– 6061; 800/583–9247 direct to hotel, FAX 264/497–6019. *27 rooms. Restaurant, no air-conditioning in some rooms, pool, gym, beach, snorkeling, windsurfing. AE, D, MC, V. EP.*

$$ 🛏 **Arawak Beach Inn.** Built on the site of an ancient Arawak village at the east end of the island, this resort consists of breezy, two-story pastel villas along a narrow curve of beach overlooking Island Harbour. Cheerful rooms are painted white and decorated with colorful floral prints. Restaurant Caribe's menu is Continental but incorporates Caribbean ingredients and fresh local fish. The casual Arawak Beach Bar and Cafe serves up barbecues and live music on weekends. A small museum displays artifacts uncovered during construction. Canoeing is available. Scilly Cay and its beautiful beaches are just a minute away by launch. ✉ *Island Harbour (Box 114)*, ☎ *264/497–4888*, FAX *264/ 497–4889*, WEB *www.arawakresort.com. 13 rooms, 4 suites. 2 restaurants, bar, pool, beach, boating, snorkeling, windsurfing, shops. AE, MC, V. EP.*

$$ 🔲 **Ferryboat Inn.** The spacious one-bedroom apartments at this small family-run complex are a bargain. Each is simply decorated with white or pastel fabrics and has a full kitchen, dining area, cable TV, and ceiling fans (two have air-conditioning). It's on a small beach and just a short walk from the ferry dock. The two-bedroom beach house is air-conditioned. All rooms and the open-air restaurant look out across the water toward St. Martin. ✉ *Blowing Point (Box 189)*, ☎ *264/497– 6613*, FAX *264/497–6713*, WEB *www.ai/ferryboatinn. 6 apartments, 1 beach house. Restaurant, bar, no air-conditioning in some rooms, fans, beach, snorkeling, windsurfing. AE, MC, V. EP.*

$$ 🔲 **Rendezvous Bay Hotel.** Opened in 1972, Anguilla's first resort sits amid 60 acres of coconut groves on the fine white sand of Rendezvous Bay, just 1 mi (1½ km) from the ferry dock. The original guest rooms are 100 yards (91 m) from the beach and are quite spare, with one double and one single bed, a private shower-bath, Haitian art on the walls, and ceiling fans. Newer, connected, two-story villas along the shore have spacious one-bedroom suites with refrigerators or kitchenettes. For larger groups, entire villas can be rented. There's a wide beach and a rocky stretch of coast that's great for snorkeling. ✉ *Rendezvous Bay (Box 31)*, ☎ *264/497–6549, 732/738–0246, or 800/274–4893*, FAX *264/ 497–6026*, WEB *www.rendezvousbay.com. 20 rooms, 16 1-bedroom villa suites, 8 studios. Restaurant, lounge, no air-conditioning in some rooms, fans, in-room data ports, some kitchenettes, some refrigerators, 2 tennis courts, windsurfing, recreation room, car rental. AE, D, MC, V. EP, MAP. Closed Sept.–Oct.*

$ 🔲 **Syd-An's.** These very basic efficiencies are a bargain for those looking to trade luxury for an entertaining location. A terrific beach is across the street, and you're steps from the bustling activity of Road Bay, including island classics Johnno's and Ripples, as well as the nightclub Pumphouse. Eight of the nine rooms have kitchenettes, shower-bath, basic furnishings, and ample room, but they're old and it's time for a renovation. ✉ *Sandy Ground*, ☎ *264/497–3180*, FAX *264/497–5381*, WEB *www.inns.ai/sydans. 9 studios. Kitchenettes, shops. AE, MC, V.*

Villas and Condominiums

The tourist office has a complete listing of the plentiful vacation apartment rentals. You can contact the **Anguilla Connection** (✉ Box 1369, South Hill, ☎ 264/497–4403, FAX 264/497–4402, WEB www. luxuryvillas.com) for condo and villa listings. **Sunshine Villas** (✉ Box 142, Blowing Point, ☎ 264/497–6149, FAX 264/497–6021) offers a wide array of different island properties.

$$$$ 🔲 **Altamer.** It's easy to imagine celebrities and corporate execs indulging for a week at this stunningly expensive, state-of-the-art beachfront villa designed by architect Myron Goldfinger, who also built neighboring Covecastles. American owner Rebecca Eggleton oversees a private staff of nine, including three butlers and a private chef, dedicated to that week's 10 guests. The striking, decidedly un-Caribbean mansion is peppered with colorful *objets d'art* from around the world, the newest stereo systems, wireless Internet, and such indulgences as a rooftop viewfinder. Two more villas (each must be rented in its entirety) are slated to open in early 2003. ✉ *Shoal Bay West (Box 3001)*, ☎ *264/498–4000*, FAX *264/498–4010*, WEB *www.altamer.com. 3 5-bedroom villas. Dining room, tennis court, pool, gym, hot tub, beach,*

snorkeling, windsurfing, boating, recreation room, laundry service, Internet, business services. AE, D, DC, MC, V. All-inclusive.

$$$$ ★ 🏨 **Covecastles Villa Resort.** What look like glistening white pieces of modern sculpture are actually elegant, comfortable, and very private villas—eight with two bedrooms and four with three bedrooms. Each is decorated with custom-made wicker furniture, raw-silk cushions, and hand-embroidered linens. Balconies are wide and secluded, kitchens are state of the art, and you can't beat the location on one of Anguilla's prettiest beaches. Two four-bedroom "supervillas" are also superluxurious, with a grand atrium entrance, a contemporary kitchen, and a 75-ft (23-m) veranda overlooking the ocean. The restaurant is elegant and intimate. ✉ *Shoal Bay West (Box 248),* ☎ *264/497–6801 or 800/348–4716,* FAX *264/497–6051,* WEB *www.covecastles.com. 13 apartments. Restaurant, tennis court, beach, snorkeling, shops. AE, MC, V.*

$$$–$$$$ ★ 🏨 **Blue Waters.** These Moorish-style buildings sit at one end of a spectacular ½-mi (1-km) beach and are within walking distance of excellent restaurants. Sunny one- and two-bedroom units are decorated with pastel fabrics and have white-tile floors, separate dining areas, full kitchens, and comfortable balconies or terraces. ✉ *Shoal Bay West (Box 69),* ☎ *264/497–6292,* FAX *264/497–3309. 9 apartments. Kitchens, beach, snorkeling. AE, MC, V.*

$$$–$$$$ 🏨 **Carimar Beach Club.** This horseshoe-shape complex on the beach at beautiful Meads Bay has seven two-story buildings capped by orange-tile roofs. Although only two are on the water's edge, all have ocean views from balconies or patios. Bright white apartments have one or two bedrooms, a living-dining area, and fully equipped kitchens. There's no restaurant, but several are within walking distance. ✉ *Meads Bay (Box 327),* ☎ *264/497–6881 or 800/235–8667,* FAX *264/497–6071,* WEB *www.carimar.com. 24 apartments. Kitchens, 2 tennis courts, beach, snorkeling. AE, D, MC, V.*

$$$–$$$$ 🏨 **Paradise Cove.** This pretty complex of luxury one- and two-bedroom apartments is arranged around a courtyard with two whirlpools, a large pool, and beautiful tropical landscaping. This place is for those who prefer independence and slight savings over a beachfront spot— beautiful Cove Beach, where you'll find the Sonesta, is 100 yards away, as is another smaller, private beach, in the opposite direction. White rattan and wicker furniture, colorful tropical-print fabrics, fully equipped kitchens (efficiencies come with kitchenettes), and private laundry facilities are standard. Second-floor units have high ceilings. Maid service and private cooks are available. ✉ *Cove Beach (Box 135),* ☎ *264/497–6959 or 364/497–6603,* FAX *264/497–6927,* WEB *www. paradise.ai. 12 efficiencies, 14 apartments, 3 suites. Restaurant, bar, in-room data ports, some kitchens, some kitchenettes, pool, croquet, shops, playground, laundry facilities. AE, MC, V.*

$–$$ 🏨 **Allamanda Beach Club.** Enjoy an ocean view from your balcony at this casual resort. One-bedroom suites and studios fill the three-story, white-stucco building just off the beach. Views are better from the higher floors. All units have tile floors. The restaurant, Zara's, is a popular draw. ✉ *Upper Shoal Bay Beach (Box 662),* ☎ *264/497–5217,* FAX *264/497–5216,* WEB *www.allamanda.ai. 16 units. Restaurant, kitchens, pool, gym, dive shop. AE, D, MC, V.*

$–$$ 🏨 **Easy Corner Villas.** The villas, on a bluff overlooking Road Bay, are a five-minute walk from the beach, with spectacular hilltop views of Salt Pond and the ocean beyond. The price is right at these modest two- and three-bedroom villas, which can be broken down to accommodate couples in one-bedroom units or studios. All are adequately furnished and have well-equipped kitchens with microwaves. ✉ *South Hill (Box 65),* ☎ *264/497–6433 or 264/497–6541,* FAX *264/497–6410. 10 villas. Kitchens, car rental. AE, MC, V.*

Dining

Anguilla has an extraordinary number of excellent restaurants—from elegant establishments to down-home seaside shacks. Most restaurants are open to the breezes, and many have terraces where you can dine under the stars. Call ahead—in winter to make a reservation and in late summer and fall to confirm if the place you've chosen is open. Restaurants not affiliated with a hotel often tack on an additional 5% to the service charge if you pay by credit card.

What to Wear

During the day, casual clothes are widely accepted: shorts will be fine, but don't wear bathing suits and cover-ups unless you're at a beach bar. In the evening, shorts are okay at the extremely casual eateries. Elsewhere, women should wear sundresses or nice casual slacks; men will be fine in shirt sleeves and casual pants. Some hotel restaurants are more formal and may have a jacket requirement in high season; ask when you make your reservation.

CATEGORY	COST*
$$$$	over $30
$$$	$20–$30
$$	$11–$20
$	under $10

per person for a main course at dinner

West End

CONTEMPORARY

$$$$ ✕ **Pimms.** Local chef George Reid oversees this elegant restaurant at the Cap Juluca resort, and he's receiving accolades for his culinary magic. The innovative menu is Caribbean at heart, but globally inspired. Chef Reid's cuisine uses fresh local ingredients but hints at Asian and European influences. Look for pan-seared tuna with risotto, grilled Anguillan lobster, mustard-encrusted grouper, and filet mignon. At the water's edge on a half-moon bay, the dining room is open to soft evening breezes, and some tables are so close to the water that you can actually look down and see fish swimming about. ⊠ *Cap Juluca, Maundays Bay,* ☎ *264/497–6666. Reservations essential. AE, MC, V.*

ECLECTIC

$$$$ ✕ **Blanchard's.** Bob and Melinda Blanchard's popular waterfront spot
★ has floor-to-ceiling shutters that fold back to let in the breezes. Dishes show Cajun, Caribbean, and Asian influences, including fresh crab and noodle corn cakes for starters, and swordfish with a Thai citrus sauce for an entrée. Desserts are tempting, especially the cappuccino brownies and the remarkable gingerbread box filled with warm bananas and cinnamon cream. There's also a 2,000-bottle wine cellar and a selection of fine Armagnacs and cognacs. While here, peruse a copy of the Blanchards' book *A Trip to the Beach,* which recounts the experience of opening this restaurant. ⊠ *Meads Bay,* ☎ *264/497–6100. Reservations essential. AE, MC, V. Closed Sun. and Aug.–Sept. No lunch.*

$$$$ ✕ **Malliouhana.** Sparkling crystal and fine china, exquisite service,
★ and a spectacularly romantic candlelit, open-air room complement exceptional haute French cuisine at this restaurant in the Malliouhana resort. Consulting chef Michel Rostang, renowned for his Paris boîte, and chef Alain Laurent create a new menu each season. Past choices have included conch chowder with fennel, lobster and crab pancake, crayfish brochette, braised mahimahi with sweet-potato puree, and grilled snapper with pumpkin. Don't pass up dessert, which might include a creamy raspberry cheesecake. The wine cellar has nearly 25,000 bot-

tles. ⊠ *Meads Bay,* ☎ *264/497–6111. Reservations essential. AE, MC, V. Closed Sept.–Oct.*

$$$–$$$$ ✕ **Altamer.** From its stark white geometric architecture to its stainless steel wine storage units, this formal beachfront restaurant seems custommade to reflect an austere chicness. It delivers via fine service and Chef Maurice Leduc's cooking. Start with his wonderful white gazpacho soup. The culinary prize is *Navarin de Fruits de Mer Carib* (lobster, scallops, shrimp, clams, and fish in a spiced saffron broth), which is nothing short of a feast. Some of the table settings are over-the-top; but the rattan chairs lessen the pretense. A special chef's table, set to the side of the kitchen, is available, as is an impressive wine list. ⊠ *Shoal Bay West,* ☎ *264/498–4040. Reservations essential. AE, D, DC, MC, V.*

$$$–$$$$ ✕ **Covecastles.** Elegant, intimate dinners are served here in a garden overlooking beautiful Shoal Bay. Each season a new menu of excellent dishes combines the best of Caribbean and French cooking. Past favorites include West Indian chicken stew, lobster medallions with ginger sauce, roasted vegetable lasagna, balsamic-marinated tuna with sautéed spinach, and veal chops in truffle cream sauce. There are only seven tables here, so call for reservations well in advance. ⊠ *Shoal Bay West,* ☎ *264/497–6801. Reservations essential. AE. Closed Sept.– Nov. No lunch.*

$$$ ✕ **Top of the Palms.** This indoor-outdoor eatery overlooking the pool on the second floor of La Sirena hotel may feel laid-back, but the chefs are definitely on their toes. Anguillan fish soup or crispy conch fritters are good starters. Then move on to seafood quesadillas, tagliatelle with fresh garden vegetables, steamed grouper on a bed of lemongrass, or thyme-crusted fillet of snapper. ⊠ *La Sirena, Meads Bay,* ☎ *264/ 497–6827. AE, MC, V.*

ITALIAN

$$$–$$$$ ✕ **Trattoria Tramonto & Oasis Beach Bar.** Listen to the waves lapping softly a few feet away and feel the soft ocean breezes as you dine by candlelight in the island's only Italian restaurant. Try the lobster ravioli in a truffle sauce, and for dessert don't miss the tiramisu. Although you might wander in here for lunch after a swim, when casual dress is accepted, you'll still be treated to the same impressive menu, and a good selection of champagne fruit drinks. ⊠ *Shoal Bay West,* ☎ *264/ 497–8819. Reservations essential. MC, V. Closed Mon. and Sept.–Oct.*

Sandy Ground, South Hill, and Rendezvous Bay

CARIBBEAN

$$–$$$ ✕ **Johnno's Beach Stop.** Performances by island bands make this *the* place to be on Friday night and Sunday afternoon, but the grilled or barbecued lobster, kingfish, snapper (some caught by Johnno himself), and chicken are good any time. This is a classic Caribbean beach bar, attracting a funky eclectic mix, from locals to movie stars. You can also take Johnno's boat from this spot to his lunch restaurant on Prickly Pear isle. ⊠ *Sandy Ground,* ☎ *264/497–2728. MC, V. Closed Mon.*

CONTEMPORARY

$$–$$$$ ✕ **Restaurant Ici.** Tables right at the edge of the beach show off a romantic night sky at this popular eatery at the Sonesta Beach Resort & Villas Anguilla. Specialties are grilled lobster with lemon butter and firecracker sauce, beef tenderloin with roasted-garlic potato pillows, and tomato gnocchi. The lunch menu has salads, sandwiches, pizzas, and burgers. ⊠ *Sonesta Beach Resort & Villas, Rendezvous Bay,* ☎ *264/497–6999. AE, MC, V. Closed Sept.–Oct.*

ECLECTIC

$$$–$$$$ ✕ **Le St. Clair.** People flock to sample chef Franck Duval's blend of French favorites and Vietnamese specialties. Menu standouts include homemade pâté and pastas, steaks, seafood, fresh spring rolls, local tuna sashimi, and sushi. If you want Vietnamese, call Franck the day before dining to ensure fresh ingredients and adequate preparation time. This is an informal beachside place, and tables are on a huge deck overlooking the water. There's a happy hour every Thursday and Friday from 5 to 7. ✉ *Sandy Ground,* ☎ *264/497–2833. AE, MC, V.*

$$–$$$$ ✕ **Ferryboat Inn.** This charming waterside restaurant at the Ferryboat
★ Inn is a short walk from the Blowing Point ferry dock. Tables are open to the breezes, and the twinkling lights of St. Martin make it even more romantic. The French onion and black-bean soups, grilled lobster, lobster thermidor (the specialty), and entrecôte *du vin au poivre* (a version of steak au poivre with a red wine sauce) are all delicious. There are also veal and chicken dishes, hamburgers, and omelets. ✉ *Ferryboad Inn, Cul de Sac Rd., Blowing Point,* ☎ *264/497–6613. AE, MC, V. No lunch Sun.*

$$–$$$ ✕ **Casablanca.** Multiarched ceilings with Moroccan mosaics and evening views of St. Martin's twinkling lights lend a dramatic air to this favored dining spot in the Sonesta Beach Resort & Villas Anguilla. The menu offers light selections that are frequently grilled, such as local lobster, skewered shrimp, free-range chicken, filet mignon, and fresh grouper. ✉ *Sonesta Beach Resort & Villas Anguilla, Rendezvous Bay,* ☎ *264/497–6999. AE, MC, V.*

$$–$$$ ✕ **Ripples.** The eclectic menu at this popular eatery a block from the beach has Mexican, West Indian, Asian, Italian, and vegetarian items. Try the coconut fried shrimp or the garlic-crusted snapper. Ripples is an especially happening scene from 5 to 7 Saturday during happy hour (ask for a Bailey's colada). ✉ *Sandy Ground,* ☎ *264/497–3380. MC, V.*

FRENCH

$$$ ✕ **Le Bistro Phil.** This casual Parisian-style bistro offers French-influenced and créole-style seafood, and pastas. Creative dishes include pan-seared tuna steak in an herb reduction, or sautéed medallions of lobster in a crayfish sauce. ✉ *South Hill,* ☎ *264/497–6810. MC, V. Closed Sun. and Aug.–Sept. No lunch.*

The Valley, George Hill, and the Forest

CARIBBEAN

$$–$$$ ✕ **Old House.** This lovely, relaxed restaurant on a hill near the airport
★ has great local cuisine. Tables are decorated with fresh flowers, even at breakfast, when regulars know to order the island fruit pancakes. For lunch or dinner try the conch simmered in lime juice and wine, curried local lamb with pigeon peas and rice, or Anguillan pot fish cooked in a sauce of limes, garlic, and tomatoes. The daily happy hour, 5–7, is popular. ✉ *George Hill,* ☎ *264/497–2228. MC, V.*

CONTEMPORARY

$$$–$$$$ ✕ **Palm Court.** This stylish eatery in the Cinnamon Reef Beach Club
★ is a long, palm-lined, open-air corridor with terra-cotta tile floors, Haitian furniture, a beautiful mural of local fish, and arches that frame the twinkling lights of St. Martin. Anguillan chef Vernon Hughes's exciting nouvelle Caribbean menu includes specialties of creamless spiny lobster, pumpkin, and corn bisque, pan-seared tuna in a sweet-potato wrap, and a Caribbean jerk veal chop. The mango puffs in caramel sauce are famous. ✉ *Cinnamon Reef Beach Club, Little Harbour,* ☎ *264/497–2727. AE, MC, V. Closed mid-Sept.–mid-Oct.*

ECLECTIC

$$$–$$$$ ✕ **Koal Keel.** This restaurant, in a restored 18th-century great house
★ that was once part of a sugar and cotton plantation, is a nice alternative to the island's beachfront eateries. A replica rock oven is used to bake fresh breads and to roast chickens and racks of lamb. Chef Smoke

makes abundant use of local ingredients. Try the outstanding pea soup, a smooth blend of pigeon peas and Caribbean sweet potatoes, then move on to the succulent goatfish with snow peas and ginger, or the fish ravioli with garlic and rosemary. More than 20,000 bottles of wine are stored in the cellar. ⊠ *The Valley,* ☏ *264/497–2930. Reservations essential. AE, MC, V. Closed Sept.–mid-Oct.*

$$–$$$$ ✕ **Straw Hat.** If you pick a table along the edge of this remarkable restaurant, you can peer right into the sea: the open-air structure is built over the water and gentle waves roll in beneath it. The menu combines French and Caribbean ingredients and cooking styles. For appetizers, start with Caribbean fish chowder, pork with chestnut dumplings, or sautéed shrimp. Grilled New York strip steak, conch cakes, Jamaican jerk pork or chicken, and grouper with citrus sauce are specialties. ⊠ *Forest Bay,* ☏ *264/497–8300. AE, MC, V. No lunch.*

ENGLISH

$$ ✕ **Roy's Place.** The dainty pink-and-white-covered deck belies the rowdy reputation of Roy and Mandy Bosson's pub, an Anguillan mainstay with some of the island's best buys. The menu's most popular items are Roy's fish-and-chips, cold English beer, pork fricassee, and a wonderful chocolate rum cake. Sunday's lunch special is roast beef and Yorkshire pudding. A faithful clientele gathers in the lively bar. ⊠ *Crocus Bay,* ☏ *264/497–2470. MC, V. Closed Mon. No lunch Sat.*

East End

ECLECTIC

$$–$$$$ ✕ **Hibernia.** Some of the island's most creative dishes are served in this wood-beamed cottage restaurant with water views. Unorthodox yet delectable culinary pairings—inspired by the chef's continued travels from France to the Far East—include Peking chicken pancakes, duck breast with grilled almonds and passion-fruit sauce, fricassee of lobster in mustard-cinnamon sauce, spicy lobster soufflé, and an unusual Thai-inspired bouillabaisse of assorted local seafood. ⊠ *Island Harbour,* ☏ *264/497–4290. AE, MC, V. Closed Mon.*

$$–$$$ ✕ **Zara's.** Chef Shamash presides at this cozy indoor restaurant at the Allamanda Beach Club, where the cuisine is a mix of Italian and Caribbean. Try the lobster pasta in a white-wine sauce, the garlic-crusted snapper, or the very popular seafood platter, which has a bit of everything from conch to calamari. Grilled chicken, steaks, and veal are also available. ⊠ *Allamanda Beach Club, Upper Shoal Bay,* ☏ *264/497–3229. AE, MC, V.*

Beaches

Renowned for their beauty, the dazzling white-sand beaches are the best reason to come to Anguilla, and each one is different. You'll find deserted sands, long stretches that are great for walking, and beaches lined with bars and restaurants—all accompanied by surf that ranges from wild to super calm.

NORTHEAST COAST

Captain's Bay. If you make the grueling four-wheel-drive-only trip along the inhospitable dirt road that leads to the northeastern end of the island toward Junk's Hole, you will be rewarded with peaceful isolation. The surf here slaps the sands with a vengeance, and the undertow is strong—wading is the safest water sport.

Island Harbour. These mostly calm waters are surrounded by a slender beach. For centuries Anguillans have ventured from these sands in colorful handmade fishing boats. There are several bars and restaurants, and this is the departure point for the three-minute boat ride to **Scilly Cay,** where a beach bar serves seafood.

NORTHWEST COAST

Barnes Bay. This is a superb spot for windsurfing and snorkeling. In high season this beach can get a bit crowded with day-trippers from St. Martin.

Little Bay. Sheer cliffs embroidered with agave and creeping vines rise behind a small gray-sand beach, usually accessible only by water (it's a favored spot for snorkeling and night dives). The hale and hearty can also clamber down the cliffs by rope to explore the caves and surrounding reef.

Road Bay. The clear blue waters of this beach are usually dotted with yachts. Several restaurants, a water-sports center, and lots of windsurfing and waterskiing activity make this area (often called Sandy Ground) a commercial one. The snorkeling isn't very good here, but the sunset vistas are glorious.

Sandy Island. From a distance, nestled in coral reefs about 2 mi (3 km) from Road Bay, it seems no more than a tiny speck of sand and a few spindly palm trees. Still, Sandy Island has the modern-day comforts of a beach boutique, a bar, and a restaurant. Use of snorkeling gear and underwater cameras is free. A ferry heads here every hour from Sandy Ground.

SOUTHEAST COAST

Mimi Bay. This isolated, half-mile-long, difficult-to-reach beach is east of Sea Feathers Bay. The trip is worth it. When the surf is down, the reef makes for great snorkeling.

Sandy Hill. Not far from Sea Feathers Bay is this base for fishermen. Here you can buy fish and lobster right off the boats and snorkel in the warm waters. Don't plan to sunbathe—the beach is narrow.

Shoal Bay. Unfortunately, it's no longer a secret that Shoal Bay—not to be confused with Shoal Bay West—has one of the Caribbean's prettiest beaches. There are beach chairs, umbrellas, and a backdrop of sea-grape and coconut trees. Restaurants offer seafood and tropical drinks, shops sell T-shirts and sunscreen, and the water-sports center arranges diving, sailing, and fishing trips.

SOUTHWEST COAST

Cove Bay. Lined with coconut palms, this is a quiet spot. There's a little bar and a place where you can rent floats, umbrellas, and mats.

Maundays Bay. The dazzling, 1-mi-long (1½-km-long) beach is known for good swimming and snorkeling. You can also rent water-sports gear.

Rendezvous Bay. Here you'll find 1½ mi (2½ km) of pearl-white sand. The water is calm, and there's a great view of St. Martin. The open-air bar of the Anguilla Great House Beach Resort is handy for snacks and frosty island drinks.

Shoal Bay West. This 1-mi-long (1½-km-long) sweep of sand is rimmed with mangroves; there are coral reefs not too far from shore. It can be crowded with day-trippers from St. Martin.

Outdoor Activities and Sports

BOATING AND SAILING

Anguilla is the perfect place to try all kinds of boating and sailing activities. The major resorts offer complimentary Windsurfers, paddleboats, and water skis to their guests. If your hotel has no water-sports facilities, you can get in gear at the **Dive Shop** (⊠ Sandy Ground, ☎ 264/497–2020) or charter its *Sundancer,* a 30-ft powerboat. **Tropical Watersports** (⊠ Sandy Ground, ☎ 264/497–6666) rents Sunfish and Hobie Cats. You can rent sailboats and speedboats from **Sandy Island Enterprises** (⊠ Sandy Ground, ☎ 264/497–5643).

FISHING

Albacore and kingfish are among the sea creatures angled after off Anguilla's shores. **Johnno's** in Sandy Ground (☎ 264/497–2728) has a boat and can help you plan a trip.

HORSEBACK RIDING

Scenic nature trails and miles of beaches are the perfect places to ride, even if you're a novice. Ride English or Western at **El Rancho Del Blues** (☎ 264/497–6164). Prices start at $25 per hour.

SCUBA DIVING

Sunken wrecks, a long barrier reef, and exceptionally clear water make for excellent diving. **Stoney Bay Marine Park,** off the northeast end of Anguilla, showcases the late-18th-century *El Buen Consejo,* a Spanish vessel that sank here in 1772. Other good dive sites include **Grouper Bowl,** with exceptional hard-coral formations; **Ram's Head,** with caves, chutes, and tunnels; and **Upper Flats,** where you are sure to see stingrays. The **Dive Shop** (☎ 264/497–2020) is a full-service dive operator with a PADI 5-Star training center. Two guided dives are offered daily; a single tank dive costs $60. At Shoal Bay, contact **Shoal Bay Scuba and Watersports** (☎ 264/497–4371).

SEA EXCURSIONS

Anguilla Sails Ltd. (✉ Sandy Ground, ☎ 264/497–2253) offers day sails, sunset sails, and moonlight cruises. *Chocolat* (✉ Sandy Ground, ☎ 264/497–3394) is a 35-ft catamaran available for private charter or scheduled excursions to nearby cays. Rates for day sails start at $30 per person. For a look at what goes on underwater without getting wet, catch a ride ($15 per person) on **Junior's Glass Bottom Boat** (✉ Sandy Ground, ☎ 264/497–4456). Snorkel trips and instruction are available, too.

Picnic, swimming, and diving excursions to Prickly Pear, Sandy Island, and Scilly Cay are available through **Sandy Island Enterprises** (☎ 264/497–5643).

TENNIS

You'll find tennis courts (some lighted) at several resorts. Simply call ahead and make a reservation. Fees range $15–$20 per hour. **Carimar Beach Club** (☎ 264/497–6881) has two hard courts. **Rendezvous Bay Hotel** (☎ 264/497–6549) has two hard courts. The **Mariners Cliffside Beach Resort** (☎ 264/497–2671) has one hard court. **Ronald Webster Park** (✉ The Valley, no phone) has one public hard court.

Shopping

The free *Anguilla Life* and *What We Do in Anguilla,* available at the airport and in shops and hotel lobbies, have shopping tips. Outstanding local artists sell their work in galleries. For upscale designer sportswear, check out the little shops (most are branches of larger stores in Marigot on St. Martin). For a better selection catch the ferry to St. Martin and spend a day browsing in chic boutiques that carry the latest European fashions.

CLOTHES

Azemmour Boutique (✉ Cap Juluca resort, Maundays Bay, ☎ 264/497–6666) specializes in European swimwear and also carries fine jewelry. **Beach Stuff** (✉ Back St., South Hill, ☎ 264/497–6814), in its brightly painted building, attracts the younger crowd looking for bathing suits, sunglasses, T-shirts, and other sportswear. **Boutique at Malliouhana** (✉ Malliouhana, Meads Bay, ☎ 264/497–6111) is the most upscale shop on Anguilla, selling such designer specialties as jewelry by Oro De Sol,

Gottex swimwear, and Robert LaRoche sunglasses. **Caribbean Fancy** (✉ George Hill, ☎ 264/497–3133) sells Ta-Tee's line of crinkle-cotton resort wear, plus books, spices, and gift items. **Caribbean Silkscreen** (✉ South Hill, ☎ 264/497–2272) creates designs and prints them on golf shirts, hats, sweatshirts, and jackets. **Java Wraps** (✉ George Hill, ☎ 264/497–5497) has superb batik clothing for the whole family. **La Romana** (✉ Meads Bay, ☎ 264/497–6181), an international specialty boutique, is the place to go for swimwear, Fendi fashions, and fine luggage. **Objets D'Art Collectibles** (✉ Warden's Place, The Valley, ☎ 264/497–2787) sells "wearable art" as well as sandals and jewelry. **Oluwakemi's Afrocentric Boutique** (✉ Lansome Rd., The Valley, ☎ 264/497–5411) sells books, sandals, umbrellas, jewelry, T-shirts, and hats. You can also have apparel custom-made. **Sunshine Shop** (✉ South Hill, ☎ 264/497–6964) stocks cotton *pareus* (saronglike beach cover-ups), silkscreen items, cotton resort wear, and hand-painted Haitian wood items. **Tradewinds Boutique** (✉ Sonesta Beach Resort & Villas Anguilla, Meads Bay, ☎ 264/497–6999) carries Tommy Bahama, Anne Cole, Sloop Jones, and other designer fashions. **Whispers** (✉ Cap Juluca, Maundays Bay, ☎ 264/497–6666) has Caribbean handicrafts and stylish resort wear for men and women.

FOODSTUFFS

Try **Fat Cat Gourmet** (✉ George Hill, ☎ 264/497–2307) for escargots to go plus take-out quiche, soups, chili, chicken, and conch dishes.

HANDICRAFTS

Alicea's Place (✉ The Quarter, ☎ 264/497–3540) sells locally made ceramics and pottery and Balinese wooden flowers. **Anguilla Arts & Crafts Center** (✉ The Valley, ☎ 264/497–2200) carries island crafts. **Cheddie's Carving Studios** (✉ The Cove, ☎ 264/497–6027) showcases Cheddie's creations crafted out of mahogany, walnut, and driftwood. **Devonish Art Gallery** (✉ George Hill, ☎ 264/497–2949) purveys the wood, stone, and clay creations of Courtney Devonish, an internationally known potter and sculptor, as well as works by other local artists. **Michele R. Lavalette Art Studio** (✉ North Hill, ☎ 264/497–5668) displays the appealing watercolors and oil paintings of French artist Michele Lavalette, an Anguilla resident since 1985. **Mother Weme** (✉ The Valley, ☎ 264/497–4504) paints charming montages of Anguillan and general Caribbean life, incorporating homes, churches, marketplaces, and people. Call for an appointment. **New World Gallery** (✉ The Valley, ☎ 264/407–5950) exhibits local art and sells jewelry, textiles, and antiquities. **Savannah Gallery** (✉ Lower Valley, ☎ 264/497–2263) specializes in Caribbean art, including watercolors, oil paintings, and brightly painted metal work. **Scruples Gift Shop** (✉ Social Security Bldg., The Valley, ☎ 264/497–2800) offers simple gift items, such as shells, handmade baskets, wooden dolls, and hand-crocheted mats and bedspreads.

Nightlife and the Arts

Nightlife

A Calypso combo plays most nights in season at **Cinnamon Reef Beach Club** (✉ Little Harbour, ☎ 264/497–2727). The **Dune Preserve** (✉ Rendezvous Bay, ☎ 264/497–2660) is the home of Bankie Banx, Anguilla's famous recording star, who performs here weekends and during the full moon. Things are lively at **Johnno's Beach Stop** (✉ Sandy Ground, ☎ 264/497–2728), with live music and alfresco dancing nightly and also on Sunday afternoons, when just about everybody drops by. There's live music nightly in season at the **Malliouhana** (✉ Meads Bay, ☎ 264/497–6111) during cocktail hours. During high season, **Pimms**

(✉ Cap Juluca, ☎ 264/497–6666) entertains with live music at dinner. At the **Pumphouse** (✉ Sandy Ground, ☎ 264/497–5154), in the old Rock Salt factory, you'll find live music on weekends and a minimuseum displaying artifacts and equipment from salt factories of the 19th century. **Rafe's Back Street** (✉ Sandy Ground, ☎ 264/497–3918) is the spot to go for late-night—even all-night on weekends—food, music, and dance. At the **Red Dragon Disco** (✉ The Valley, ☎ 264/497–2687) a DJ plays music Friday, Saturday, and Sunday nights. **Uncle Ernie's** (✉ Shoal Bay, ☎ 264/497–3907) often has live music, and a spirited crowd heads here almost every night.

The Arts

The **Mayoumba Folkloric Theater** performs song-and-dance skits depicting Antillean and Caribbean culture with African drums and a string band. They appear every Thursday night at **La Sirena Hotel** (✉ Meads Bay, ☎ 264/497–6827).

Exploring Anguilla

Exploring on Anguilla is mostly about checking out the spectacular beaches and classy resorts. Though the island has only a few roads, some are in bad condition and unmarked. Locals are happy to provide directions, but having a good map—and using it—is the best strategy. Get one at the airport, the ferry dock, your hotel, or the tourist office in The Valley.

Numbers in the margin correspond to points of interest on the Anguilla map.

SIGHTS TO SEE

❽ Amerindian Mini-Museum. A small display of Arawak Indian objects is showcased here. There's also a 4×8-ft oil painting that shows what Big Springs, a nearby ceremonial ground, might have looked like when Amerindians lived there. ✉ *Arawak Beach Resort, Island Harbour,* ☎ *264/497–4888,* WEB *www.arawakresort.com.* ▣ *Free.* ☉ *Daily 10–4.*

❹ Bethel Methodist Church. Not far from Sandy Ground, this charming little church is an excellent example of skillful island stonework. It also has some colorful stained-glass windows. ✉ *South Hill,* ☎ *no phone.*

❾ Heritage Collection. Anguillan artifacts, old photographs, and records trace the island's history from the days of the Arawaks to the present at this inviting museum. You can see examples of ancient pottery shards and stone tools along with fascinating photographs of the island in the early 20th century, including many photos that depict the heaping and exporting of salt and the christening of schooners. Also on display is a complete set of beautiful postage stamps issued by Anguilla since 1967. ✉ *East End, at Pond Ground,* ☎ *264/497–4440,* WEB *www.offshore.com.ai/heritage.* ▣ *$5.* ☉ *Mon.–Sat. 9–5.*

❼ Island Harbour. Anguillans have been fishing for centuries in the brightly painted, simple handcrafted fishing boats that line the shore of the harbor. It's hard to believe, but skillful pilots take these little boats out to sea as far as 50 or 60 mi (80 or 100 km). Late afternoon is the best time to see the day's catch. ✉ *Island Harbour, at northwest end of island, facing Island Harbour Bay.*

❷ Old Factory. For many years the cotton that was grown on Anguilla and exported to England was ginned in this beautiful historic building. Some of the original ginning machinery is intact and on display here, and this is also the home of the **Anguilla Tourist Office.** ✉ *The Valley,* ☎ *264/497–2759.* ▣ *Free.* ☉ *Weekdays 10–noon, 1–4.*

⑤ Old Prison at Crocus Hill. On the highest point in Anguilla—213 ft (65 m) above sea level—the historic prison is pretty much in ruin, but the view is outstanding. ⊠ *Valley Rd. at Crocus Hill.*

❶ Sandy Ground. This is by far the most active and most developed of the island's beaches, and almost everyone who comes to Anguilla stops by here at least once. Little open-air bars and restaurants line the shore, and there are several boutiques, a dive shop, and a small commercial pier. This is where you catch the ferry for tiny **Sandy Island,** just 2 mi (3 km) offshore.

❸ Wallblake House. On Wallblake Road, just north of the traffic circle, is a plantation house with spacious rooms and handsome woodwork that was built in 1787 by Will Blake (Wallblake is probably a corruption of his name). The place is associated with many a tale involving murder, high living, and the French invasion in 1796. Its days of debauchery are over, though; today it's owned and actively used by the Catholic Church. On the grounds are an ancient vaulted stone cistern and an outbuilding called the Bakery (which wasn't used for making bread at all but for baking turkeys and hams). Call Father John to make an appointment to tour the plantation. ⊠ *Wallblake Rd., The Valley,* ☎ *264/497–2405.*

❻ Warden's Place. This former sugar-plantation great house was built in the 1790s and is a fine example of island stonework. It's now the site of the Koal Keel restaurant, but for many years it served as the residence of the island's chief administrator, who also doubled as the only medical practitioner. ⊠ *The Valley.*

ANGUILLA A TO Z

To research prices, get advice from other travelers, and book travel arrangements, visit www.fodors.com.

AIR TRAVEL

American Airlines is the major airline, with nonstop flights from the continental United States to its hub in San Juan, from which the airline's American Eagle flies three times daily (twice daily off-season) to Anguilla's Wallblake Airport. Windward Islands Airways (Winair) wings in daily from St. Thomas and at least three times a day from St. Maarten's Juliana Airport. LIAT comes in from Antigua, Nevis, St. Kitts, St. Martin, St. Thomas, and Tortola. Air Anguilla offers several flights daily from St. Martin and the U.S. Virgin Islands and provides air-taxi service on request from neighboring islands. Tyden Air has scheduled daily flights from St. Maarten and several weekly flights to and from St. Kitts and St. Thomas; the airline also offers charter day trips to many neighboring islands.

➤ AIRLINES AND CONTACTS: **Air Anguilla** (☎ 264/497–3643). **American Airlines** (☎ 264/497–3131). **LIAT** (☎ 264/497–2748 or 264/497–5002). **Tyden Air** (☎ 264/497–2719 or 800/842–0261). **Windward Islands Airways** (☎ 264/497–2238).

AIRPORTS

Wallblake Airport is the hub on Anguilla. A taxi ride to Sandy Ground is about $10; to West End resorts it's $16–$22.
➤ AIRPORT INFORMATION: **Wallblake Airport** (☎ 264/497–2719).

BIKE AND MOPED TRAVEL

Motorcycles and scooters run about $30 per day from Boo's Cycle Rental, which also rents bicycles.
➤ CONTACTS: **Boo's Cycle Rental** (⊠ Water Swamp, ☎ 264/497–2323).

BOAT AND FERRY TRAVEL
FARES AND SCHEDULES

Ferries run frequently between Anguilla and St. Martin. Boats leave from Blowing Point on Anguilla every half hour from 7:30 to 5 and from Marigot on St. Martin every half hour from 8 to 5:30. Evening ferries leave Blowing Point at 6 and 9:15 and Marigot at 7 and 10:45. You pay a $4 departure tax before boarding and the $15 one-way fare ($17 evenings) on board. Don't buy a round-trip ticket because it restricts you to the boat for which it is purchased. On very windy days the 20-minute trip can be bouncy, and if you suffer from motion sickness, you may want medication. An information booth outside the customs shed in Blowing Point is usually open daily from 8:30 to 5, but sometimes the attendant wanders off. It's also possible to travel directly by ferry from Julianna Airport on St. Maarten to Anguilla (for $5 extra, by reservation only). For schedule information, and info on special boat charters, contact Link Ferries.

➤ BOAT AND FERRY INFORMATION: **Link Ferries** (☎ 264/497–2231, WEB www.link.ai).

BUSINESS HOURS
BANKS

Banks are open Monday–Thursday 8–3 and Friday 8–5.

POST OFFICES

The post office is open weekdays 10–noon and 1–4.

SHOPS

Most shops are open 10–4 on weekdays, but call first, or ask the tourist office for opening and closing times. Or adopt the island way of doing things: If it's not open when you stop by, try again.

CAR RENTALS

This is your best bet for maximum mobility if you're comfortable driving on the left and don't mind some jostling. To rent a car, you'll need a temporary local license, which you can obtain for $10 at any of the car-rental agencies; you'll need your valid driver's license from home.

Apex (Avis), Budget, and Connors (National) rent four-wheel-drive vehicles and sedans. You can also head to Triple K Car Rental for car rentals, including four-wheel-drive vehicles. Rates are $45 to $55 per day, plus insurance.

➤ MAJOR AGENCIES: **Apex (Avis)** (✉ Airport Rd., ☎ 264/497–2642). **Budget** (✉ Airport Rd., ☎ 264/497–5871). **Connors (National)** (✉ Blowing Point, ☎ 264/497–6433). **Triple K Car Rental** (✉ Airport Rd., ☎ 264/497–5934).

CAR TRAVEL
GASOLINE

There are several gas stations on the island, and they are generally open from 7 AM to 11 PM. Gasoline is expensive; expect to pay about EC$7.55 per gallon (about US$2.82 per gallon).

ROAD CONDITIONS

Anguilla's roads are generally paved, but those that are not can be incredibly rutted.

RULES OF THE ROAD

Driving is on the left. Observe the 30-mph speed limit and watch out for livestock that amble across the road.

ELECTRICITY

The current is 110 volts, the same as in North America; U.S.-standard two-prong plugs will work just fine.

EMERGENCIES

➤ AMBULANCE AND FIRE: **Ambulance** (☎ 264/497–2551). **Fire** (☎ 911).
➤ HOSPITALS: **Princess Alexandra Hospital** (✉ Sandy Ground, ☎ 264/497–2551).
➤ PHARMACIES: **Government Pharmacy** (✉ Princess Alexandria Hospital, The Valley, ☎ 264/497–2551, ⊙ daily 8:30–4). **Paramount Pharmacy** (✉ Water Swamp, ☎ 264/497–2366, ⊙ Mon.–Sat. 8:30–7).
➤ POLICE: ☎ 911 emergencies; 264/497–2333 nonemergencies.

ETIQUETTE AND BEHAVIOR

It's an Anguillan custom to greet people and exchange polite comments about the day or the weather before getting down to business. It's considered quite rude to skip this step, so join in, even if you're in a hurry.

FESTIVALS AND SEASONAL EVENTS

In February the National Cultural & Educational Festival celebrates Anguilla's traditional cultures through dance, storytelling, games, and music programs. March brings Moonsplash, a three-day music festival that showcases local talent and begins on the night of the full moon. The Anguilla Culinary Competition is held the last week of May. At the end of July is the International Arts Festival, which hosts artists from around the world. The first two weeks of August is Carnival, which includes parades, street dancing, boat racing, and lots of general merrymaking.

HOLIDAYS

Public holidays are: New Year's Day, Easter (varies, usually Apr. or May), Easter Monday (the day after Easter), Labour Day (May 7), Anguilla Day (May 28), Whit Monday (1st Monday in May), Queen's Birthday (June 11), August Monday (1st Monday in Aug.), Constitution Day (Aug. 8), Separation Day (Dec. 19), Christmas (Dec. 25), Boxing Day (Dec. 26).

LANGUAGE

English, with a strong West Indian lilt, is spoken here.

MAIL AND SHIPPING

Airmail postcards and letters cost EC$1.50 (for the first ½ ounce) to the United States and Canada, EC$1.90 to the United Kingdom, and EC$2.50 to Australia and New Zealand. The only post office is in The Valley; it's open weekdays 8–3:30. When writing to the island, you don't need a postal code; just include the name of the establishment, address (location or post-office box), and "Anguilla, British West Indies."
➤ CONTACTS: **Post Office** (✉ Wallblake Rd., The Valley, ☎ 264/497–2528).

MONEY MATTERS

Prices quoted throughout this chapter are in U.S. dollars unless otherwise indicated.

ATMS

Don't count on ATMs, which are often on the blink. Remember, ATMs will dispense money in EC dollars.

CREDIT CARDS

Credit cards are not always accepted; some resorts will only settle in cash, but a few accept personal checks. Some restaurants add a charge if you pay with a credit card.

CURRENCY

Though the legal tender here is the Eastern Caribbean (EC) dollar, U.S. dollars are widely accepted. (You'll often get change in EC dollars.) The exchange rate between U.S. and EC dollars is set at EC$2.68 to the U.S. dollar. Be sure to carry lots of small bills; change for a $20 is often difficult to obtain.

➤ CONTACTS: **Scotiabank** (☎ 264/497–3333, WEB www.scotiabank.ca).

PASSPORTS AND VISAS

U.S. and Canadian citizens need proof of identity. A passport is preferred (even one that has expired within the past five years). Also acceptable is a government-issued photo ID, such as a driver's license, *along with* a birth certificate (with raised seal) or naturalization papers. Citizens of the United Kingdom, Australia, and New Zealand must have passports. Everyone must also have a return or ongoing ticket. Visitor's passes are valid for stays of up to three months.

SAFETY

Anguilla is a quiet, relatively safe island, but there's no point in tempting fate by leaving your valuables unattended in your hotel room, on the beach, or in your car.

SIGHTSEEING TOURS

A round-the-island tour by taxi takes about 2½ hours and costs $40 for one or two people, $5 for each additional passenger. Bennie's Tours is one of the island's more reliable tour operators. Malliouhana Travel and Tours create personalized package tours of the island.

➤ CONTACTS: **Bennie's Tours** (✉ Blowing Point, ☎ 264/497–2788). **Malliouhana Travel and Tours** (✉ The Valley, ☎ 264/497–2431).

TAXES

DEPARTURE TAX

The departure tax is $15 at the airport, $4 if you leave by boat.

OTHER TAXES

A 10% accommodations tax is added to hotel bills.

TAXIS

Taxi rates are regulated by the government, and there are fixed fares from point to point (listed in brochures the drivers should have). Posted rates are for one or two people; each additional passenger adds $3 to the total.

Taxis are always waiting to pick up passengers at the Blowing Point landing docks. It costs $14 to get to Malliouhana, $17 to Cap Juluca, and $20 to most hotels farther afield.

TELEPHONES

Cable & Wireless is open weekdays 8–6, Saturday 9–1, and Sunday 10–2; it sells Caribbean phone cards for use in specially marked phone booths. The cards can be used for local calls, calls to other islands, and calls to the United States. Inside the departure lounge at the Blowing Point ferry dock and at the airport there's an AT&T USADirect access phone for collect or credit-card calls to the United States.

➤ CONTACTS: **Cable & Wireless** (✉ Wallblake Rd., ☎ 264/497–3100).

COUNTRY AND AREA CODES

To call Anguilla from the United States, dial 1 plus the area code 264, then the local seven-digit number. From the United Kingdom dial 001 and then the area code and the number. From Australia and New Zealand dial 0011, then 1, then the area code and the number.

INTERNATIONAL CALLS

International direct dial is available on the island. To call internationally, dial 1, the area code, and the seven-digit number to reach the United States and Canada; dial 011, 44, and the local number for the United Kingdom; dial 011, 61, and the local number for Australia; and dial 011, 64, and the local number for New Zealand. Although you can dial direct from your hotel room, it's cheaper to dial 800/877–8000 and charge your call to a major credit card.

LOCAL CALLS

To make a local call, dial the seven-digit number.

TIPPING

A 10% service charge is added to all hotel bills; sometimes it covers all staff members, sometimes not. If you're unsure whether to tip hotel staff, ask the hotel management. Tip wait staff as you would at home — 15% to 18%. Tip taxi drivers 10% of the fare.

VISITOR INFORMATION

➤ BEFORE YOU LEAVE: **Anguilla Tourist Office/River Communications** (✉ Box 2119 Woodford Green, London 1G8 0GC, ☎ 0208/505–6614, FAX 0208/505–8974).

➤ IN ANGUILLA: **Anguilla Tourist Office** (✉ Old Factory Plaza, Box 1388, The Valley, ☎ 264/497–2759; 800/553–4939 from the U.S., FAX 264/497–2710, WEB www.anguilla-vacation.com).

3 ANTIGUA

Updated by
Jordan Simon

It's Antigua Sailing Week, the island's version of the
Henley Regatta. Seasoned sea salts claim prized seats
on the flagstone terrace of the 18th-century Admiral's
Inn in English Harbour. Some boats are docked so
close that you can almost eavesdrop from shore. Competitors trade stories (tall and otherwise) of sailing—
and drinking—two sheets to the wind, while eyeing
the yachts. Blazered bluebloods mingle with lobster-
hue tourists; it's Cannes in the Caribbean.

Antigua (an-*tee*-ga), which at 108 square mi (280 square km) is the
largest of the British Leeward Islands, is renowned among sailors for
its incomparable air of nautical history. For Anglophiles and history
buffs, English Harbour and the surrounding villages and sites are also
immensely rewarding. And Antigua seduces landlubbers and sailors alike
with its sensuous beaches, 366 in all—one for every day of the year
and one left over, as locals like to boast. All are public, some are absolutely deserted, and others, particularly in the northwest, are lined
with resorts that offer dining, nightlife, shopping, sailing, diving, windsurfing, and snorkeling.

The original inhabitants of Antigua were the Ciboney. They lived here
4,000 years ago and disappeared mysteriously, leaving the island un-
populated for about 1,000 years. When Columbus arrived in 1493, the
Arawaks had set up housekeeping. The English took up residence in
1632. After 30-odd years of bloody battles involving the Caribs, the
Dutch, the French, and the English, the French ceded Antigua to the
English in 1667. Antigua remained under English control until achiev-
ing full independence on November 1, 1981, along with its sister island, Barbuda, 26 mi (42 km) to the north.

Tourism is the leading industry here, but Antigua maintains a strong
sense of national identity to match its rich historic inheritance. Its cricketers, like the legendary Viv Richards (arguably the greatest batsman
the game has ever seen), are famous throughout the world. Its people
are known for their sharp commercial spirit (a typically revealing—
and disarming—sign reads DIANE'S BOUTIQUE AND CAR PARTS); their
wit; and unfortunately, at the government level, their corruption.

Lodging

Scattered along Antigua's beaches and hillsides are exclusive, elegant
hideaways; romantic restored inns; go-barefoot-everywhere places;
and, increasingly, all-inclusive hot spots for couples. Choose accom-

modations near St. John's—anywhere between Dickenson Bay and Five
Islands Peninsula—if you want to be close to the action. English Harbour, far from St. John's, has the best inns and several excellent restaurants; it's also the hangout for the yachting crowd. Elsewhere on the
island, resorts cater more to those people who want to stay put or are
seeking seclusion. Be sure to ask about specials: the larger properties
often host tour groups who are paying as little as ⅓ the rack rate usually quoted. Many of the smaller establishments have become all-inclusive to survive the fierce competition; some are so remote that trying
to arrange an EP rate makes no sense unless you have a car. Another
similar trend: restaurants adding a clutch of charming, affordable cottages. Redevelopment of formerly closed or damaged properties continues, most notably Carlisle Bay on the southwest coast, where an
upscale resort will rise from the ruins of a previous incarnation in 2003,
and the expanded, renovated Jolly Harbour Villa Resort on the 500-
acre, Mediterranean-style complex of the same name, which includes
a marina, retail center, casino, and 18-hole golf course.

CATEGORY	COST EP/CP*	COST A.I.**
$$$$	over $350	over $375
$$$	$250–$350	$275–$375
$$	$150–$250	$175–$275
$	under $150	under $175

*EP/CP prices are per night for a standard double room in high season, ex-
cluding taxes, service charges, and meal plans**A.I. (all-inclusive) prices are
per person, per night based on double-occupancy during high season, excluding taxes and service charges*

$$$$ ⊞ **Jumby Bay.** At this writing, the ultra-swank 330-acre Long Island
resort remains in management limbo following ongoing ownership feuds
worthy of primetime soaps. *Rondavels* (round cottages) and regular
cottages hold junior suites whose dark furnishings, including hand-carved
mahogany four-poster beds, play up vibrant throw rugs, fabrics, and
local crafts. Luxe, individually decorated villas have pools and favor
Laura Ashley–style florals, wicker, Asian bibelots, and handpainted tile-
work. Villa owners—such as Robin Leach and Ken Follett—mingle at
the 250-year-old stone-and-mahogany Estate House dining room and
its sybaritic, whimsical, jungle-theme lounge. But if you need to get away,
you can bike along nature trails and luxuriate on secluded beaches anywhere on the island. Airport transfers and ferry service are free. ⊠ *Long
Island (Box 243, St. John's),* ☎ *268/462–6000 or 800/237–3237,* FAX
268/462–6020, WEB *www.elegantresorts.com. 38 rooms, 13 villas. 2
restaurants, fans, minibars, no rooms TVs, putting green, 3 tennis
courts, gym, 3 beaches, snorkeling, windsurfing, waterskiing, bicycles,
croquet, 2 bars, shops. AE, MC, V. All-inclusive.*

$$$$ ⊞ **K Club.** The *K* is famed Italian designer Krizia, whose dramatic style
★   animates this superdeluxe Barbuda hideaway. Public spaces have gleaming white tiles and columns, natural-wicker furnishings with plush cushions, and cloth-and-bronze sculptures. Beachfront units are equally chic:
white wicker and tile, cool, ocean-hued fabrics, wooden chairs whimsically carved with pineapples, bamboo mats, showers submerged in
vegetation, wittily provocative paintings (blood red stilettos sitting on
a beach). The kitchen innovatively fuses Tuscan grilling and Caribbean
ingredients. Rates are princely, but what price privacy and style if you
have the ducats? ⊠ *Spanish Wells Point (Box 2288, St. John's),* ☎ *268/
460–0300,* FAX *268/460–0305,* WEB *www.lhw.com. 35 units. Restaurant,
grill, fans, some kitchenettes, no room TVs, 2 tennis courts, pool, hot
tub, beach, snorkeling, windsurfing, boating, waterskiing, fishing, bar,
recreation room. AE, MC, V. FAP.*

34

Goat Pt.

Hog Pt.

BARBUDA

Cedar-Tree Pt.

11

Two Foot Bay

Bird Sanctuary

Codrington Lagoon

N

Low Bay

Codrington

Palmetto Pt.

Martello Tower

0   5 miles

0   5 km

Pink Beach

19

Spanish Pt.

ly Pear Island

eggar's t.

Long Island

20

V.C. Bird Int'l. Airport

North Sound

Bird Island

Guiana Island

Crump Island

Long Bay

ATLANTIC

18   9

10 Parham

Rd.

Pares

8

Willikies

Nonsuch Bay

7

Green Island

Freetown

OCEAN

Liberta

3

Half Moon Bay

4

Falmouth

Falmouth Bay

English Harbour

17

16

Willoughby Bay

5

Mamora Bay

10 12

15

13 14

6

Shirley Heights

oint

Guadeloupe Passage

KEY

Beaches

Cruise Ship Terminal

Dive Sites

1 Exploring Sights

1 Hotels and Restaurants

$$$–$$$$ 🏨 **Blue Waters Hotel.** Despite its small twin beaches, the hotel's loca-
tion—amid 14 acres of tropical gardens—is splendid, luring a soigné
British crowd. The colonnaded lobby has sweeping sea views, mosaic
tile lamps, peacock wicker chairs, and fountains. Rooms are stark but
sparkling in white with teal accents, rattan furnishings and glazed tile
bathrooms. The four villas and two enormous suites are exquisite, but
the ultimate in hedonism is the separate, fully equipped three-bedroom
Rock Cottage. Afternoon tea and one sauna per week are included.
The casual Palm Restaurant serves Italian cuisine, while Vyvien's has
a Continental menu that changes daily. ⊠ *Boon Point (Box 256, St.
John's)*, ☎ *268/462–0290 or 800/557–6536*, FAX *268/462–0293*, WEB
*www.bluewaters.net. 73 rooms, 4 villas, 1 2-bedroom cottage. 2 restau-
rants, fans, in-room safes, minibars, cable TV, tennis court, 2 pools,
gym, hair salon, spa, 2 beaches, snorkeling, windsurfing, boating, 2
bars, shops. AE, D, DC, MC, V. All-inclusive, BP, FAP.*

$$$–$$$$ 🏨 **Curtain Bluff.** Howard Hulford continually reinvigorates his 41-year
★   old beachfront grande dame, but it remains devoted to life's (and
Howard's) pleasures: lavish gardens, Cubanos, fine food, and finer wine
(the resort's 25,000-bottle cellar is legendary). Spacious junior suites
are stunning, with marble bathrooms, stylish local artworks, Mexican
earthenware, and coffered raw wood ceilings. Ravishing duplex suites
zigzag up the bluff. The open-air restaurant (jackets required in-sea-
son except Sunday and Wednesday) provides sterling Continental din-
ing, followed by dancing to live bands. The unparalleled setting,
exceptional service, extras (free scuba and deep-sea fishing), and qui-
etly posh country-club feel make Curtain Bluff that rare world-class
resort that's a bargain in its class. ⊠ *Morris Bay (Box 288, St. John's)*,
☎ *268/462–8400; 212/289–8888 or 888/289–9898 outside NY for
reservations*, FAX *268/462–8409*, WEB *www.curtainbluff.com. 64 rooms,
9 suites. 2 restaurants, no air-conditioning, fans, in-room safes, no room
TVs, putting green, 4 tennis courts, pool, gym, hair salon, massage, 2
beaches, dive shop, snorkeling, windsurfing, boating, fishing, croquet,
squash, bar, shops. AE. All-inclusive. Closed mid-May–mid-Oct.*

$$$–$$$$ 🏨 **Galley Bay.** This tony all-inclusive appeals to couples and corpo-
rate honchos. Showy features include a man-made pool grotto and a
bleached-wood boardwalk along the champagne-hued beach. A blue
lagoon, manicured gardens, and bird sanctuary with trails surround
the enclave. African carvings and Caribbean art naïf fill the thatch-roofed
public spaces and sinuous stucco walls of the Gauguin Village's wat-
tle-and-daub cottages, whose bathrooms are connected via private
walkways. Airy beachfront rooms have terra-cotta tiles, island art, and
custom-made rattan and bamboo furnishings; deluxe suites have nat-
ural wicker furnishings, huge patios, and Italian marble bathrooms.
Afternoon tea and lilting live nightly entertainment are pleasant ex-
tras. ⊠ *Five Islands (Box 305, St. John's)*, ☎ *268/462–0302 or 800/
345–0271*, FAX *268/462–4551*, WEB *www.antigua-resorts.com. 70 rooms.
2 restaurants, grill, fans, in-room safes, refrigerators, no room TVs,
tennis court, pool, gym, beach, snorkeling, windsurfing, boating, bi-
cycles, croquet, horseshoes, bar, shops, no children under 16. AE, D,
DC, MC, V. All-inclusive.*

$$$–$$$$ 🏨 **Inn at English Harbour.** A complete 2002 overhaul left only this gen-
teel resort's original buildings: the hilltop reception area, bar-dining
room, and six guest rooms, all with majestic views of English Harbour,
plus the four original beachfront rooms and the funky-elegant beach
bar. Three new whitewashed gray-shingled buildings inexplicably sit
behind the horizon pool far from the beach in a breezeless area. Huge,
handsome units are regrettably dark, featuring louvers, hand-painted
armoires, white rattan furnishings, four-poster beds, candelabra sconces,
and porphyry bathrooms. The flagstone-terrace dining room, a romantic

place, serves Continental fare. The beach isn't great, but water taxis within the harbor are free, as are nonmotorized water sports. ⊠ *English Harbour (Box 187, St. John's),* ☎ *268/460–1014or 800/223–6510; 800/424–5500 in Canada,* FAX *268/460–1603,* WEB *www.theinn.ag. 36 units. Restaurant, grill, no air-conditioning, fans, in-room safes, refrigerators, no room TVs, 4 tennis courts, pool, gym, beach, snorkeling, windsurfing, boating, 2 bars. AE, D, DC, MC, V. EP, MAP. Closed mid-Aug.–Oct.*

\$\$\$–\$\$\$\$ ⊞ **Sandals Antigua Resort and Spa.** This superior resort exclusively for male-female couples percolates with activity, from vigorous volleyball competitions to relaxing karaoke at the swank piano bar. Almost everything—including tennis coaching and scuba diving—is included (spa treatments and weddings are extra). The reception area opens onto a courtyard with painted tile stairways, stained-glass panels, and an unimpeded sea view. The spacious, fresh guest quarters (most refurbished in 2001 and 2002) include ocean- or garden-view rooms, beachfront suites, and rondavels, many with four poster beds. A separate 100-room complex is planned. Four restaurants prepare superlative Continental, Italian, Japanese, and southwestern fare. There's a three-night minimum. ⊠ *Dickenson Bay (Box 147, St. John's),* ☎ *268/ 462–0267 or 888/726–3257,* FAX *268/462–4135,* WEB *www.sandals.com. 100 rooms, 77 suites, 16 rondavels. 4 restaurants, grill, fans, in-room safes, 2 tennis courts, 5 pools, hair salon, 5 hot tubs, gym, spa, beach, dive shop, snorkeling, windsurfing, boating, waterskiing, 4 bars, shops, nightclub. AE, D, DC, MC, V. All-inclusive.*

\$\$–\$\$\$\$ ⊞ **Rex Halcyon Cove Beach Resort.** This lively large, somewhat impersonal hotel on beautiful Dickenson Bay is typically crowded with European and American tour groups. The institutional concrete buildings, softened by coral or lavender paint jobs, terra-cotta tile walkways, and luxuriant gardens, sit around a courtyard and along the beach. Size, view, and amenities vary widely (poolside rooms with limited sea views are best buys), but most units favor white tile, blond woods, rattan beds and mirrors, and delicate pastel fabrics. A water-sports center is on the busy beach. The Warri Pier restaurant, perched dramatically on stilts over the ocean, serves superior seafood and grilled items. ⊠ *Dickenson Bay (Box 251, St. John's),* ☎ *268/462–0256 or 800/255– 5859,* FAX *268/462–0271,* WEB *www.rexresorts.com. 193 rooms, 17 suites. 2 restaurants, grill, ice cream parlor, room service, in-room safes, some refrigerators, 4 tennis courts, pool, hair salon, massage, beach, dive shop, windsurfing, boating, waterskiing, 4 bars, shops, children's programs (ages 3 to 12), business services, car rental. AE, D, DC, MC, V. All-inclusive, EP, FAP, MAP.*

\$\$\$ ⊞ **Hawksbill Beach Hotel.** This refined resort straddles 37 lavishly landscaped acres, including five beaches (one clothing-optional). The reception area, and main dining room rest on a small bluff with panoramic vistas of the restored sugar mill, classy three-bedroom West Indian great house, the sea, and Montserrat. The secluded Club rooms have tile floors, light rattan furnishings, hand-painted bathroom tiles, vaulted ceilings, and the most spectacular views (especially numbers 138–142). Gingerbread-trim cottages have smallish deluxe and garden-view rooms (the latter usually have restricted water views and represent better value). Most water sports are free. Hawksbill primarily attracts a mix of mature couples and honeymooners. ⊠ *Five Islands (Box 108, St. John's),* ☎ *268/462–0301 or 800/223–6510; 416/622–8813 in Canada,* FAX *268/462–1515,* WEB *www.hawksbill.com. 111 rooms, 1 3-bedroom villa. 2 restaurants, fans, refrigerators, no room TVs, tennis court, pool, 5 beaches, snorkeling, windsurfing, boating, 2 bars, shops, Internet, meeting rooms. AE, DC, MC, V. EP, FAP, MAP.*

$$–$$$ 🏨 **Dickenson Bay Cottages.** This small development perches on Marble Hill, just above Dickenson Bay. Gardens surround the two-story villa-style buildings; units are attractively appointed with high-quality painted rattan furnishings, blond woods, and vivid abstract and floral fabrics. Larger units have two bedrooms upstairs and large verandas overlooking the ocean. Resort guests have privileges at Halcyon Cove's active beach, a five-minute walk; you can also use the tennis and water-sports facilities there at a 20% discount. Entertainment and restaurants are available at nearby resorts. This appealing complex is often inexplicably deserted, so ask about last-minute discounts. ✉ *Marble Hill (Box 1376, St. John's),* ☎ *268/462–4940,* FAX *268/462–4941,* WEB *www.dickensonbaycottages.com. 11 units. Fans, kitchens, some in-room VCRs, pool. AE, DC, MC, V. EP.*

$$–$$$ 🏨 **Siboney Beach Club.** Aussie Tony Johnson arrived in Antigua in the
★   late 1950s on a yacht crew but ended up building some of the island's finest resorts and eventually opening his own small gem on Dickenson Bay. Each suite has a small bedroom, cleverly designed Pullman-style kitchen, living room, and cozy garden-view patio or balcony. Rooms vary slightly, but they all have bright splashes of color, rattan furnishings, and knickknacks from Tony's travels. Room 9 overlooks the sea, but the soothing sound of the surf permeates even those with partial views. Tony and his staff cordially dispense advice like a de facto tourist board. TVs can be provided on request. ✉ *Dickenson Bay (Box 222, St. John's),* ☎ *268/462–0806 or 800/533–0234,* FAX *268/462–3356,* WEB *www.siboneybeachclub.com. 12 suites. Restaurant, fans, in-room safes, kitchenettes, no room TVs, pool, beach, bar. AE, MC, V. EP, MAP.*

$$–$$$ 🏨 **St. James's Club.** This out-of-the-way hotel occupies a prime 100-acre spit of land at Mamora Bay. Good-size rooms have fresh, vibrant color schemes, though discolored concrete terraces and soiled carpets undermine the luxe image. A cluster of two-bedroom villas spills down hills toward the main buildings. The oceanfront Beach Club offers the best value: larger, more distinctive rooms at a lower price. The accommodations, top-notch restaurants, lovely setting, and extensive facilities (from helicopter sightseeing charters to full-scale marina) make this a popular resort; though nonmotorized water sports and afternoon tea are complimentary, most people opt for the more reasonable all-inclusive package. ✉ *Mamora Bay (Box 54, St. John's),* ☎ *268/460–5000 or 800/345–0271,* FAX *268/460–3215,* WEB *www.antigua-resorts.com. 187 rooms, 72 villas. 5 restaurants, snack bar, room service, fans, 6 tennis courts, 3 pools, gym, hair salon, hot tub, massage, spa, 2 beaches, dive shop, dock, snorkeling, windsurfing, boating, croquet, 5 bars, casino, nightclub, helipad. AE, D, DC, MC, V. All-inclusive.*

$$ 🏨 **Allegro Resort Pineapple Beach.** Buildings at this bustling all-inclusive are painted in fun gumball colors; public spaces and facilities, including a pool with bridges and waterfall, brim with local charm. The most stylish units cling to a hill, featuring marble tables, natural-wicker armoires and beds, and terra-cotta floors. The buffet-style main restaurant and the intimate Pineapple Grill serve worthy Caribbean and Continental dishes. The latter, a split-level riot of lime, mango, and peach, becomes a late-night disco. The shack-chic hilltop Outhouse Bar is the perfect sunset perch. Despite its remote location, the range of activities entices families and honeymooners alike. ✉ *Long Bay (Box 2000, St. John's),* ☎ *268/463–2006 or 800/858–2258,* FAX *268/463–2452,* WEB *www.allegroresorts.com. 180 rooms. 3 restaurants, fans, no TVs in some rooms, 4 tennis courts, 2 pools, gym, beach, snorkeling, windsurfing, boating, waterskiing, fishing, croquet, horseshoes, volleyball, 3 bars, shops, nightclub, children's programs (ages 4 to 12). AE, MC, V. All-inclusive.*

$$ ⊡ **CocoBay.** This restful hillside retreat occupies 10 secluded acres on the west coast. Creole-style cottages in luscious pastels (powder blue, lilac, coral) with corrugated iron roofs are staggered amid fragrant tropical gardens. The understated decor stresses natural beauty: bleached wood louvers, stained pine floors, mosquito netting, and sisal rugs. The blue-and-white tile bathrooms open onto terraces with marvelous bay views (wattle-and-daub walls ensure privacy between adjoining units). A "wellness center" offers massages, facials, scrubs, and aromatherapy. Complimentary cell phones are available, though you pay for calls. CocoBay aims to "eliminate all potential worries." ⊠ *Valley Church (Box 431, St. John's),* ☎ *268/562–2400,* FAX *268/562–2424,* WEB *www. cocobayresort.com. 42 rooms, 4 2-bedroom houses. Restaurant, no air-conditioning, fans, in-room safes, refrigerators, no room TVs, pool, spa, gym, 2 beaches, snorkeling, bar, shops. AE, MC, V. All-inclusive.*

$$ ⊡ **Rex Blue Heron.** This cozy, welcoming resort sits on a magnificent sweep of sand. Don't be misled by the mousy faux-stucco buildings; each room—save for a few standard units—has hardwood or gleaming white tile floors, powder-blue and tropical-print fabrics, stylish ceramic lamps, and an oceanview patio or terrace. It's extremely difficult to get a reservation here, because discerning European tour operators keep it booked. The reasonable prices, intimacy, and secluded location lure a young, hip clientele. ⊠ *Johnson's Point (Box 1715, St. John's),* ☎ *268/462–8565 or 800/255–5859,* FAX *268/462–8005,* WEB *www.rexresorts.com. 64 rooms. Restaurant, no air-conditioning in some rooms, fans, no TVs in some rooms, pool, beach, snorkeling, windsurfing, boating, bar, shops. AE, D, MC, V. All-inclusive.*

$–$$ ⊡ **Admiral's Inn.** Once the engineers' office and warehouse at what is
★ now Nelson's Dockyard, the lovingly restored, 18th-century Ads (as yachtspeople call it) reverberates with history. Its best rooms, upstairs in the main building have the original timbered ceilings—complete with iron braces—hardwood floors, and brick walls. Straw mats from Dominica, four-poster beds, and sunny harbor views through wispy Australian pines complete the effect. The gigantic, fully equipped, two-bedroom Loft (once the dockyard's joinery) has a magnificent harbor view from its timbered living room. Avoid the hordes descending on the Dockyard (and the Ads' terrace for lunch) by taking advantage of the complimentary shuttle to nearby beaches. ⊠ *English Harbour (Box 713, St. John's),* ☎ *268/460–1027 or 800/223–5695,* FAX *268/460–1534,* WEB *www.antiguanice.com. 14 rooms, 1 2-bedroom apartment. Restaurant, no air-conditioning in some rooms, fans, no TVs in some rooms, pub. AE, MC, V. EP, MAP.*

$–$$ ⊡ **Jolly Beach Resort** Colorful splashes and fancy touches like the free-form pool, faux sugar mills, and a charming re-creation of an old-style Creole village to gather the pesky beach vendors can't disguise this hotel's origin as the gimcrack Club Antigua. Its horrid cinderblock structures still have rusting rails and peeling paint. Many of the original rooms are the size of monks' cells with bizarre, built-in concrete shelves and tables. Still, the grounds are lovely, the long beach strewn with inviting palapas, the restaurant's good, and even the smallest quarters have ocean views. The resort is remarkable value for budget-minded honeymooners and singles (the rate in lower categories is half that for couples). ⊠ *Jolly Harbour (Box 2009, St. John's),* ☎ *268/462–0061,* FAX *268/562–2302,* WEB *www.jollybeachresort.com. 462 units. 4 restaurants, grill, in-room safes, some refrigerators, 4 tennis courts, 2 pools, aerobics, gym, beach, snorkeling, windsurfing, boating, water-skiing, 4 bars, nightclub, recreation room, shops, Internet, meeting rooms. AE, D, MC, V. All-inclusive.*

$–$$ 🏨 **Royal Antiguan Resort.** Though sterile, this ugly high-rise has all
the amenities and facilities of a moderate American chain. Fortunately,
island flair includes spectacular large murals in the restaurants, plus
fountains, hand-painted columns, local pottery, and Carnival costume
displays in the lobby. Unusual extras range from dialect classes to
palm readings. There's a lagoon pool with swim-up bar, three restaurants serving Italian to Caribbean cuisine, 150 slot and video poker
machines, and hiking trails and guided nature walks to Ft. Barrington
with its stunning views of St. John's Harbour. This resort is popular
with singles, honeymooners, groups, and families on a budget. ⊠
Deep Bay (Box 1322, St. John's), ☎ *268/462–3733 or 800/345–0271,*
FAX *268/462–3732,* WEB *www.antigua-resorts.com. 266 rooms, 12 suites.
3 restaurants, refrigerators, some in-room VCRs, golf course, 8 tennis courts, pool, gym, hair salon, beach, dive shop, snorkeling, windsurfing, boating, waterskiing, fishing, croquet, horseshoes, 4 bars,
shops. AE, D, MC, V. All-inclusive.*

$–$$ 🏨 **Sunsail Club Colonna.** The British Sunsail outfit is renowned world-
wide for its superior, affordable sailing and windsurfing schools, and
attentiveness to families. Red-tile and stucco buildings charmingly surround a faux sugar mill. The free-form pool, said to be the largest in
the Lesser Antilles, compensates for the smallish man-made beaches.
Public areas are a tad dilapidated, but rooms have immaculate tile floors,
Italian striped fabrics, and wicker and rattan furnishings. Use of the
superb state-of-the-art sailing and windsurfing equipment and group
instruction are free. Most meals, usually buffet or barbecue, are included.
Avid sailors should inquire about weekly discounts and land/sail packages. ⊠ *Hodges Bay (Box 591, St. John's),* ☎ *268/462–6263 or 800/
327–2276,* FAX *268/462–6430,* WEB *www.sunsail.com. 102 rooms, 15
villas. 2 restaurants, in-room safes, minibars, pool, hair salon, 3
beaches, snorkeling, windsurfing, boating, 2 bars, shops, children's programs (ages 3 to 12). AE, D, MC, V. MAP.*

$ 🏨 **Ocean Inn.** This convivial property with scintillating harbor views
is composed of a private home that's been converted into six guest rooms,
and four hillside cottages. Simple, slightly frilly decor favors florals and
pink fabrics. Informal parties are often thrown by the small, mural-
adorned pool, while Thursday Steak Nights lure local characters,
yachties, and eccentric expats to the Tree Trunk Bar. A separate four-
bedroom house, replete with kitchen, hot tub, washer-dryer, and private jetty rents for an astounding $600 a night; when not taken over
by groups, rooms are let individually—and those lucky enough to stay
there have the run of the joint. The nearest beach is a five-minute drive.
⊠ *English Harbour (Box 838, St. John's),* ☎ *268/463–7950,* FAX *268/
460–1263,* WEB *www.theoceaninn.com. 6 rooms, 4 cottages, 1 4-bed-
room house. Grill, fans, pool, bar. AE, MC, V. CP.*

Dining

Antigua's restaurants are varied, and you can find excellent food
whether you feel like dressing up or dressing down. Virtually every chef
incorporates local ingredients and elements of West Indian cuisine.

Most menus list prices in EC dollars, but you should verify in which
currency the prices are listed. It's also a good idea to ask if credit cards
are accepted. Dinner reservations are needed during high season.

What to Wear
Perhaps because of the island's British heritage, Antiguans tend to
dress more formally for dinner than on many other Caribbean islands.
Wraps and shorts (no beach attire) are de rigueur for lunch, except at
local hangouts.

CATEGORY	COST*
$$$$	over $30
$$$	$20–$30
$$	$10–$20
$	under $10

per person for a main course at dinner

CARIBBEAN

$$–$$$ ✕ **Commissioner Grill.** The gaudy raspberry, mango, lime, and blueberry exterior of this 19th-century tamarind warehouse seems edible itself. The interior is more restrained, with white tile floors, powder-blue chairs, floral tablecloths, glass buoys, Antiguan pottery, conch shells, and historic maps. Specials might include whelks in garlic butter, bacon-wrapped plantains in mustard sauce, snapper in lobster sauce, or mahimahi creole. Local seafood is the obvious choice, although beef and poultry are also reliable. ⊠ *Commissioner Alley and Redcliffe St., St. John's,* ☎ *268/462–1883. AE, DC, MC, V.*

CONTEMPORARY

$$–$$$$ ✕ **Coconut Grove.** Coconut palms grow through the roof of this open-
★ air thatched restaurant, part of the Siboney Beach Club. Flickering candlelight illuminates colorful local murals, waves lap the white sand, and the waitstaff is warm and unpretentious. Although the signature item is beer-battered shrimp with coconut cream sauce, try Jean-Franĉois Bellanger's other superbly presented, imaginative dishes, perhaps seared salmon with asparagus over sorrel Sancerre sauce or lobster and arugula salad with passionfruit dressing served in a coconut shell. Cap a memorable meal with an old rum or a Cuban cigar. ⊠ *Siboney Beach Club, Dickenson Bay,* ☎ *268/462–1538. AE, MC, V.*

$$–$$$ ✕ **Bay House.** This romantic hilltop, alfresco eatery (request Table 10 for the best views) is in the estimable Tradewinds Hotel above Dickenson Bay. Dishes run the culinary gamut from Thailand to Tuscany, with a healthy dollop of West Indian spice. Excellent starters range from deep-fried pork and prawn *gow gees* (wontons) in sweet-and-sour chile peanut sauce to seafood boudin on leeks edged with lobster sauce. Main dishes are just as eclectic. After your meal, head to the hip, hopping, happening bar for a cordial. ⊠ *Tradewinds Hotel, Dickenson Bay,* ☎ *268/462–1223. AE, MC, V.*

$$–$$$ ✕ **Coco's.** Overlooking the headlands of Five Islands Bay, Coco's could
★ be recommended simply for ravishing sunsets followed by moonlight spectacularly dappling the bay as if with silver doubloons. But its cheerful aquamarine trim, bougainvillea-draped bleached-wood deck, gingerbread fretwork, and blue tile tables also handsomely replicate an old chattel house. Although part of the small all-inclusive resort of the same name, the restaurant welcomes outside diners. Globetrotting chef Nigel Martin presents a virtual United Nations of influences with such offerings as air-dried duck breast with chili jam and avocado or plantain-crusted grouper over sundried tomatoes, snowpeas, and shitakes in lime-ginger beurre blanc. ⊠ *Coco's Resort, Mt. Prospect, Jolly Bay,* ☎ *268/462–9700. Reservations essential. AE, MC, V.*

$$–$$$ ✕ **HQ.** At this restaurant occupying part of the Officers' Quarters build-
★ ing in Nelson's Dockyard, adventuresome, typically peripatetic Aussie chef Darryn Pitman excitingly blends indigenous Caribbean ingredients with preparations—tempura to tandoori—from his Asian postings. Polished hardwood floors, brickwork, and beamed ceilings make an effective contrast to the vivid Creole artworks and the contemporary open kitchen, with a vast colonnaded terrace overlooking the water. The canny, fairly priced wine list offers more than 150 selections. Impeccably balanced dishes trigger all sets of taste buds, from lamb marinated in *harissa* (Moroccan tomato garlic preparation) with smoked eggplant

and pumpkin puree to pear-frangipani tart. ⊠ *Nelson's Dockyard, English Harbour,* ☎ *268/562–2563. Reservations essential. AE, MC, V.*

ECLECTIC

\$\$–\$\$\$
★ ✕ **Admiral's Inn.** This English Harbour tavern in the Admiral's Inn hotel is a must for Anglophiles and mariners. Soak up the centuries at the inside bar under dark timbers (sailors from Nelson's fleet even carved their names into the bar top), but most diners sit on the terrace under shady Australian gums to enjoy the views of the harbor complex. Specialties include curried conch, fresh snapper with equally fresh limes, and lobster thermidor. The pumpkin soup is not to be missed. ⊠ *Admiral's Inn, Nelson's Dockyard, English Harbour,* ☎ *268/460–1027. Reservations essential. AE, MC, V.*

\$\$–\$\$\$ ✕ **Jimmy's.** You'll find all the essential elements of a casual marina eatery here: sleek yachts moored at the deck, fresh sea breezes, exuberant boating barflies, and simple yet scrumptious food. Fresh seafood dishes include lobster in garlic cream or dolphinfish in shrimp sauce. Chicken in orange ginger sauce is another worthy choice. It's particularly fun and raucous on Monday (roast pork barbecue night). ⊠ *Catamaran Marina, Falmouth Harbour,* ☎ *268/463–8866. AE, MC, V. Closed June–Sept.*

\$\$–\$\$\$ ✕ **Redcliffe Tavern.** The split-level dining room in a beamed colonial warehouse at Redcliffe Quay sports brick-and-stone walls; salvaged antique water-pumping equipment, replete with flywheels and pistons, has been imaginatively integrated—one pump supports the buffet bar. Dinner appetizers include creole crab puffs with cucumber, onion, and sesame relish; for a main course try plantain-stuffed chicken in mild curry cream or entrecôte in rum and green peppercorn sauce. The lunch menu also lists salads, sandwiches, and burgers. ⊠ *Redcliffe Quay, St. John's,* ☎ *268/461–4557. AE, MC, V.*

FRENCH

\$\$\$–\$\$\$\$
★ ✕ **Chez Pascal.** Pascal and Florence Milliat built this hilltop charmer themselves. The flagstone terrace overlooks a tinkling fountain and lighted pool (there are also four guest rooms, with whirlpool baths and splendid sea views); the tasteful elevated dining room is furnished in dark rattan, with ceramics, local paintings, and copper pots. Pascal's classic Lyonnaise cuisine with tropical touches exhibits his remarkably deft hand with subtle sauces. Witness the gossamer chicken-liver mousse in thyme sauce and sublime steamed grouper in beurre blanc. Finish with a heavenly flourless chocolate cake with strawberry coulis (sauce) or a classic tarte Tatin. ⊠ *Galley Bay Hill, Five Islands,* ☎ *268/462–3232. Reservations essential. AE, D, MC, V. Closed Aug.*

\$\$\$–\$\$\$\$ ✕ **Le Bistro.** This Antiguan institution's peach and pistachio accents subtly match the tile work, jade chairs, and painted lighting fixtures. Trellises cannily divide the large space into intimate sections. Chef Patrick Gaducheau delights in blending regional fare with indigenous ingredients. You might start with salmon and scallop carpaccio in passionfruit-lime vinaigrette, then drift into sterling snapper in mustard tarragon white wine sauce or veal medallions with caramelized onions, prunes, bacon and Beaujolais sauce. As for dessert, the exquisite Death by Chocolate teasingly tortures the taste buds. ⊠ *Hodges Bay,* ☎ *268/462–3881. Reservations essential. AE, MC, V. Closed Mon. No lunch.*

\$–\$\$ ✕ **Catherine's Café.** This little deck café overlooking English Harbour marina brims with Gallic brio thanks to ebullient hostess, Catherine Ricard. The food is simple: ham-and-leek quiche, a proper *salade niçoise,* and crepes even airier than Catherine herself. Evening delights might include *moules mariniéres* (marinated mussels) or *gratin de cèpes* (wild mushrooms in a cheese sauce). The fairly priced, extensive wine list offers Catherine's pert comments (for Solaia, she writes, "Just to show we're not narrow-minded Frogs, here is the top from Italy . . ."). This delightful place always percolates with life and good strong espresso. ⊠ *English Harbour,* ☎ *268/460–5050. MC, V. Closed Tues. and Sept.–Oct. No dinner Mon.*

ITALIAN

$$–$$$ ✕ **Abracadabra.** It's always a party at this busy, bright trattoria. The courtyard is strung with lights; R&B and 1980s dance music play in the background; and the cheery rooms are daubed in sea-foam green and full of hand-painted tables and murals of jamming jazz musicians. The food sings with flavor and color. Specialties include an amazing antipasto, bonito marinated in sweet onions and capers, and homemade crab ravioli in pesto. The wine list has some real finds from lesserknown areas of Italy (the owners confide—or rather joke—"We smuggle them in"). ⊠ *English Harbour,* ☎ *268/460–1732. AE, MC, V. Closed July–Sept.*

$$–$$$ ✕ **Alberto's.** Despite its somewhat remote southeastern location, this
★ sensational Italian restaurant is wildly popular. The vivacious owner, Alberto, taught his culinary secrets to his English wife, Vanessa; she now bests her mentor with her Italian and French inspirations. Try leek and Parmesan soufflé; melting sushi; veal medallions in mushroom crust; or yummy, traditional linguine with clams. The homemade, lusciously textured sorbets are a must: tangy passion fruit, creamy coconut, lipsmacking lemon. Tables line a trellised balcony open to the breezes and hung with bougainvillea, and painted china graces the walls (check out the octopi and squid on the plates by the bar). ⊠ *Willoughby Bay,* ☎ *268/460–3007. Reservations essential. AE, D, MC, V. Closed Mon. and May–Oct. No lunch.*

$–$$ ✕ **Big Banana–Pizzas in Paradise.** This tiny, often crowded spot is tucked into one side of a restored warehouse with broad plank floors, wood beams, and stone archways. Cool Benetton-style photos of locals and jamming musicians adorn the brick walls. It serves some of the island's best pizza (try the lobster or the seafood variety) as well as such tasty specials as conch salad. There's live entertainment some nights and sports nuts congregate at the bar's huge satellite TV. ⊠ *Redcliffe Quay, St. John's,* ☎ *268/480–6985. AE, MC, V. Closed Sun.*

Beaches

Antigua's beaches are public, and many are dotted with resorts that have water-sports outfitters and beach bars. Sunbathing topless or in the buff is strictly illegal except on one of the small beaches at Hawksbill Beach Hotel. Beware that when cruise ships dock in St. John's, buses drop off loads of passengers on most of the west-coast beaches. Choose such a time to tour the island by car, visit one of the more remote eastend beaches, or take a day trip to Barbuda.

ANTIGUA

Darkwood Beach. This delightful taupe ribbon on the southwest coast has views of Montserrat.

Dickenson Bay. With a lengthy stretch of powder-soft white sand and exceptionally calm water, you'll find small and large hotels, water sports, concessions, and beachfront restaurants.

Five Islands Peninsula. Five secluded beaches (including one nude) are of fine tan sand; there are coral reefs for snorkeling at the Hawksbill Beach Hotel, as well as a good surfing beach at Galley Bay.

Half Moon Bay. A ¼-mi (1-km) crescent, it's a prime snorkeling and windsurfing area. On the Atlantic side of the island the water can be quite rough at times. The eastern end is much calmer.

Johnson's Point. This series of connected, deliciously deserted beaches of bleached white sand is on the southwest coast overlooking Montserrat. You can explore a ruined fort at one end; notable beach bars include OJ's (try the snapper) and Turner's.

Long Bay. On the far-eastern coast, you'll find coral reefs in water so shallow that you can actually walk out to them. Along the beach are the Long Bay Hotel and the rambling Allegro Resort Pineapple Beach.

Pigeon Point. Near Falmouth Harbour are these two fine white-sand beaches; the leeward side is calmer, while the windward side is rockier, with sensational views and snorkeling around the point. Several restaurants and bars are nearby.

Runaway Beach. Where you will find the Barrymore Beach Hotel, Lashings, and the Runaway Beach Hotel, this stretch of white sand can get crowded.

BARBUDA

Pink Beach. On Barbuda you'll find an uncrowded 8-mi (13-km) stretch of white sand that reaches from Coco Point to Palmetto Point. The island, encircled by reefs and shipwrecks, is great for scuba diving.

Outdoor Activities and Sports

Participant Sports

Several all-inclusives offer day passes that permit use of all sporting facilities from tennis courts to water-sports concessions, as well as free drinks and meals. They start around $40 for singles, $150 for couples (at Sandals), and generally run from 8AM to 6PM, with extensions available until 2 AM.

BICYCLING

Bicycling isn't terribly arduous on Antigua, except in the southernmost region, where the roads soar, dip, and corkscrew. Try **Bike Plus** (⊠ Camacho's Ave., St. John's, ☎ 268/462–2453) for rentals, which run about $30 a day. Everything from racing models to mountain bikes is available.

BOATING

Experienced boaters will particularly enjoy Antigua's east coast, which is far more rugged and has several offshore islets; be sure to get a good nautical map as there are numerous minireefs that can be treacherous. If you're just looking for a couple of hours of wave hopping, stick to the Dickenson Bay/Runaway or Jolly Harbour area.

Nicholson Yacht Charters (☎ 800/662–6066 and 268/460–1530) are real professionals. A long-established island family, they can charter you anything from a 20-ft ketch to a giant schooner. **Sea Sports** (☎ 268/462–3355) in Dickenson Bay rents Jet Skis and Sunfish and offers parasailing and waterskiing trips. This can be a hectic operation. **Sunsail Club Colonna** (☎ 268/462–6263 or 800/327–2276) has an extensive modern fleet of dinghies and 32-ft day sailers available for $25 per half day, $50 per full day.

FISHING

Antigua's waters teem with such game fish as marlin, wahoo, and tuna. Most boats include equipment, lunch, and drinks. Figure at least $400 for a half-day, $600 for a full day, for up to six people. The 45-ft Hatteras Sportfisherman *Obsession* (☎ 268/462–2824) has top-of-the-line equipment, including an international standard fighting chair, outriggers, and handcrafted rods. *Overdraft* (☎ 268/464–4954 or 268/462–1961) is a sleek, spacious fiberglass 40-footer operated by a knowledgeable professional fisherman.

GOLF

Cedar Valley Golf Club (✉ Friar's Hill, ☎ 268/462–0161), northeast of St. John's, has a 6,100-yard, 18-hole course. The bland, not terribly well-maintained terrain offers some challenge with tight hilly fairways and numerous doglegs. Greens fees are $35, including cart. **Jolly Harbour Golf Course** (✉ Jolly Harbour, ☎ 268/480–6950) is a par-71, 6,001-yard, 18-hole course designed by Karl Litten. The layout is hilly and lushly tropical, with seven lakes adding to the challenge. Greens fees are $60 (including cart).

HORSEBACK RIDING

Comparatively dry Antigua is best for beach rides, though you won't find anything wildly romantic and deserted à la *The Black Stallion*. **Spring Hill Riding Club** (✉ Falmouth, ☎ 268/460–7787) really specializes in equestrian lessons in showjumping and dressage, but also offers $40 trail rides on the beach or through the bush; half-hour private lessons are $25.

SAILING AND SNORKELING TRIPS

Not a sailor yourself? Consider signing up for one of the following boat tours. Each provides a great opportunity to enjoy the seafaring life while someone else captains the ship.

Jolly Roger cruises (☎ 268/462–2064), on a true-to-life replica of a pirate ship, come complete with "pirate" crew, limbo dancing, plank walking, and other pranks. Their Saturday night boozecruises with open bar and live bands are legendary for their frat party feel. They also offer Barbuda day trips on their catamaran, *Excellence*. **Kokomo Cats** (☎ 268/462–7245) runs several cruises, including one to deserted beaches and islets, one to English Harbour, and one to sunset-gazing spots. **Miguel's Holiday Adventures** (☎ 268/460–9978; 268/723–7418 for cellular) leaves every Tuesday, Thursday, and Saturday morning at 10 AM from the Hodges Bay jetty for snorkeling, rum punches, and lunch at Prickley Pear Island. The glass-bottom *Shorty's* (☎ 268/462–6326) offers various snorkeling trips to Bird Island, as well as sunset cruises and lobster picnics. **Wadadli Cats** (☎ 268/462–4792) offers several cruises, including a circumnavigation of the island and snorkeling at Bird Island, on its four sleek catamarans, including the handsome *Spirit of Antigua*.

SCUBA DIVING

With all the wrecks and reefs, there are lots of undersea sights to explore, from coral canyons to sea caves. The most accessible wreck is the schooner *Andes,* not far out in Deep Bay, off Five Islands Peninsula. Among the favorite sites are **Green Island, Cades Reef,** and **Bird Island** (a national park).

Big John's Dive Antigua (✉ Rex Halcyon Cove Beach Resort, Dickenson Bay, ☎ 268/462–3483) offers certification courses and day and night dives. **Dockyard Divers** (✉ Nelson's Dockyard, English Harbour, ☎ 268/460–1178), owned by British ex-merchant seaman Captain A. G. Fincham, is one of the island's most established outfits and offers diving and snorkeling trips, PADI courses, and dive packages with accommodations. Another top option is **Octopus Divers** (✉ English Harbour, ☎ 268/460–6286), which provides PADI certification and snorkeling trips.

TENNIS AND SQUASH

Many of the larger resorts have their own tennis courts. Guests at the various hotels have top priority. There is also one public court on the island. The only hotel that allows nonguests to play on a regular basis is the **Royal Antiguan Resort** (✉ Deep Bay, ☎ 268/462–3733), which has eight lighted courts. **Rex Halcyon Cove Beach Resort** (✉ Dickenson Bay, ☎ 268/462–0256) has four lighted courts, but they are not always available for nonguests to use. The **Temo Sports Complex** (✉ Falmouth Bay, ☎ 268/463–6376) has four floodlit synthetic grass tennis courts, two glass-backed squash courts, showers, a sports shop, and snack bars, including a wonderful kebab stand. Court time is generally $25 per hour.

WINDSURFING

Most major hotels offer windsurfing equipment. The best areas are Nonsuch Bay and the east coast (notably Half Moon and Willoughby bays), which is slightly less protected and has a challenging juxtaposition of sudden calms and gusts. **Sea Sports** (☎ 268/462–3355), at Dickenson Bay, rents top-quality boards for $25 per hour. **Sunsail Club Colonna** (☎ 268/462–6263 or 800/327–2276) allows use of its top-of-the-line equipment for $50 a day and $25 a half-day.

Spectator Sports

CRICKET

Practically the only thing most Americans know about this game is that there's something called a sticky wicket. Here, as in Britain and all the West Indies, the game is a national passion. Youngsters play on makeshift pitches, which are comparable to sandlots, and international matches are usually contested in the stadium on Independence Avenue in St. John's. For information on top matches and their venues, call the **Antigua Cricket Association** (✉ Newgate St., St. John's, ☎ 268/ 462–9089 or 268/460–9966).

Shopping

Antigua's duty-free shops are at Heritage Quay; they're the reason so many cruise ships call here. Bargains can be found on perfumes, liqueurs and liquor (including, of course, Antiguan rum), jewelry, china, and crystal. As for other local items, look for straw hats, baskets, batik, pottery, and hand-printed cotton clothing.

Areas

Redcliffe Quay, on the waterfront at the south edge of St. John's, is by far the most appealing shopping area. Several restaurants and more than 30 boutiques, many with one-of-a-kind items, are set around landscaped courtyards shaded by colorful trees. **Heritage Quay,** in St. John's, has 35 shops—including many that are duty-free—that cater to the cruise-ship crowd, which docks almost at its doorstep. Outlets here include Benetton, the Body Shop, Sunglass Hut, Dolce and Gabbana, and Oshkosh B'Gosh. There are also shops along **St. John's, St. Mary's, High,** and **Long Streets.** The tangerine-and-lilac-hued four-story **Vendor's Mall** at the intersection of Redcliffe and Thames streets gathers the pushy, pesky vendors that clogged the narrow streets. It's jammed with stalls; air-conditioned indoor shops sell some higher-priced, if not higher-quality merchandise. On the west coast, the Mediterranean-style, arcaded **Jolly Harbour Villa Resort and Marina** holds some interesting galleries and shops.

Specialty Items

ART

At **Harmony Hall** (✉ Brown's Bay Mill, Brown's Bay, ☎ 268/460–4120), near Freetown, you'll find hand-painted Annabella boxes, books and cards, pottery, carved wooden birds, Jennifer Meranto's incomparable hand-colored black-and-white photos of Caribbean scenes, Heather Doram's exquisite, intricately woven "collage" wall-hangings, and ever-changing exhibits. There's also a marvelous Italian restaurant that's open for lunch and on weekends for dinner. **Island Arts Galleries** (✉ Alton Pl., Sandy La., behind Hodges Bay Club, Hodges Bay, ☏ 268/461–6324; ✉ Heritage Quay, St. John's, ☏ 268/462–2787), run by artist-filmmaker Nick Maley, showcases artists from throughout the Caribbean. Some of the art naïf pieces are stunning, and the genre paintings of local life often have a raw elemental power. Call first to ensure that Nick is around so he can tell fascinating anecdotes of helping create Yoda from *Star Wars* and other famed film characters. **Lydia Llewellyn Art** (✉ Fort Rd., inside Chutney's Restaurant, St. John's, ☏ 268/560–0062) carries Lydia's striking marine art, where the iridescent fish actually extend onto the frames; avid celeb collectors include Robin Leach, Eric Clapton, and Viscount Portman.

BOOKS AND MAGAZINES

Map Shop (✉ St. Mary's St., St. John's, ☏ 268/462–3993) has a "must" buy for those interested in Antiguan life: the paperback *To Shoot Hard Labour: The Life and Times of Samuel Smith, an Antiguan Workingman.* Also check out any of the books of Jamaica Kincaid, whose works on her native Antigua have won international acclaim. The shop also offers a fine assortment of books on Caribbean cuisine, flora, fauna, and history.

CIGARS, LIQUOR, AND LIQUEURS

La Casa Habana (✉ Heritage Quay, St. John's, ☏ 268/462–2677) sells Cuban cigars (just remember that it's illegal to take them into the United States). **Manuel Dias Liquor Store** (✉ Long and Market Sts., St. John's, ☏ 268/462–0490) has a wide selection of Caribbean rums and liqueurs. **Quin Farara** (✉ Long St., St. John's, ☏ 268/462–0463; ✉ Heritage Quay, St. John's, ☏ 268/462–1737; ✉ Jolly Harbour, ☏ 268/462–6245) has terrific deals on both hard liquor and wines, as well as cigars.

CLOTHING

The hand-dyed clothing and scarves of the famed **Caribelle Batik** (✉ St. Mary's St., St. John's, ☏ 268/462–2972) are done in the festive colors of a Caribbean Carnival. **Exotic Antigua** (✉ Redcliffe Quay, St. John's, ☏ 268/562–1288) sells everything from antique Indonesian *ikat* throws to crepe de chine caftans to Tommy Bahama resort wear. At **Galley Boutique** (✉ Nelson's Dockyard, English Harbour, ☏ 268/460–1525), Janey Easton personally seeks out exclusive creations from both international couturiers (Calvin Klein, Adrienne Vittadini) to local Caribbean designers, ranging from swimwear to evening garb. She also sells handicrafts and lovely hammocks. **Jacaranda** (✉ Redcliffe Quay, St. John's, ☏ 268/462–1888) sells batik, sarongs, and swimwear, as well as Caribbean food and local artwork. **New Gates** (✉ Redcliffe Quay, St. John's, ☏ 268/562–1627) is a duty-free authorized dealer for such name brands as Ralph Lauren, Calvin Klein, and Tommy Hilfiger. **Noreen Phillips** (✉ Redcliffe Quay, St. John's, ☏ 268/462–3127) creates glitzy appliquéd and beaded evening wear—inspired by the colors of the sea and sunset—in sensuous fabrics ranging from chiffon and silk to Italian lace and Indian brocade. **Sunseakers** (✉ Heritage Quay, St. John's, ☏ 268/462–3618) racks up every conceivable bathing suit and cover-up—from bikini thongs to sarongs—by top designers. **A Thousand Flowers** (✉ Redcliffe Quay, St. John's, ☏ 268/462–4264) carries resort wear made of comfortable silks, linens, and batiks from all over the world.

DUTY-FREE GOODS

Abbott's (✉ Heritage Quay, St. John's, ☏ 268/462–3108 or 268/462–3073) sells pricey items from Baume and Mercier watches to Belleek china to Kosta Boda art glass in a luxurious, air-conditioned showroom. **Lipstick** (✉ Heritage Quay, St. John's, ☏ 268/562–1130) imports high-priced scents and cosmetics, from Clarins to Clinique and Givenchy to Guerlain. The **Scent Shop** (⊠ High St., St. John's, ☎ 268/462–0303) offers scent-sational buys in perfumes and cosmetics.

HANDICRAFTS

Cedars Pottery (⊠ Buckleys, ☎ 268/460–5293) is the airy studio of Michael and Imogen Hunt. Michael produces a vivid line of domestic ware and Zen-simple teapots, vases, and water fountains featuring rich earth hues and sensuous lines. Imogen fashions ethereal paper clay fish sculptures and mask-shaped, intricately laced light fixtures and candelabras. **Ego** (⊠ Redcliffe Quay, St. John's, ☎ 268/562–1591) is a veritable United Nations of *objets*, including Thai Sa paper notebooks (pounded from mulberry bark), Ethiopian bread baskets, appliquéd Indian purses, even Japanese metalwork. The **Gazebo** (⊠ Redcliffe Quay, St. John's, ☎ 268/460–2776) is a vast, bilevel jumble of Mexican pottery and ceramics, Indonesian furnishings, gorgeous blue-glaze plates that rival delftware in both beauty and craftsmanship, hand-painted rocking horses, basketry, hammocks, and more. **Isis** (⊠ Redcliffe Quay, St. John's, ☎ 268/462–4602) sells island and international bric-a-brac, such as antique jewelry, hand-carved walking sticks, and glazed pottery. **Kate Designs** (⊠ Redcliffe Quay, St. John's, ☎ 268/460–5971) sells acclaimed artist Kate Spencer's distinctive work—lovely silk-screened scarves and sarongs, vividly colored place mats, paintings, prints, note cards—from neighboring St. Kitts as well as Liza Kirwan's delicate hand-painted silk scarves and former fashion designer Heike Petersen's whimsical "ethnic dolls." **Mimosa** (⊠ Heritage Quay, St. John's, ☎ 268/462–2923) sells hand-painted wind chimes and porcelain clowns in island dress. The **New Pottery** (⊠ Coolidge, ☎ 268/562–1264) gallery sells the work of gifted potter Sarah Fuller, whose hand-painted tiles, wind chimes, and plates and cobalt-blue glazes are striking. **Pigeon Point Pottery** (⊠ Pigeon Point, ☎ 268/460–1614) is the atelier of Nancy Nicholson, who's renowned for her exquisite glazed and matte finished ceramics, featuring Caribbean-pure shades, as well as her black-and-white yachting photos. The delightfully whimsical **Sofa** (⊠ English Harbour, ☎ 268/463–0610) carries some of the quirkier creations of island artisans, including hand-painted furniture, mosaic vases, and recycled paper books—justifying the name (an acronym for Sculpture, Objects, Functional Art). Owner Fiona Jade will happily direct you to the studios of such intriguing Antiguan artists as Gilly Gobinet, Gramma Aki, and Yolanda Woodberry. **Things Local** (⊠ Nelson's Dockyard, English Harbour, no phone) is the bailiwick of local woodcarver, Carl Henry, who recycles dead trees into figurative yet intriguingly gnarled sculpture. He also makes splendid warri boards (an ancient African game played with large pods) and painted gourds.

JEWELRY

Colombian Emeralds (⊠ Heritage Quay, St. John's, ☎ 268/462–3462) is the largest retailer of Colombian emeralds in the world. The **Goldsmitty** (⊠ Redcliffe Quay, St. John's, ☎ 268/462–4601) is Hans Smit, an expert goldsmith who turns gold, black coral, and precious and semiprecious stones into one-of-a-kind works of art.

Nightlife and the Arts

Most of Antigua's evening entertainment takes place at the resorts, which regularly present calypso singers, steel bands, limbo dancers, and folkloric groups. Check with the tourist office for up-to-date information.

Nightlife

BARS

The Beach (⊠ Dickenson Bay, ☎ 268/460–6940) is a sophisticated-funky combination of casual beach bar, lounge (with pianist or jazz trios playing nightly), and bistro (with Asian-Euro fusion cuisine), all daubed in sexy reds. **Colombo's** (⌧ Galleon Beach Club, English Harbour, ☎ 268/460–1452) is the place to be on Wednesday night for live reggae. It's also a yachty hangout, with pennants of various boats hanging from the rafters. Beware: the once-fine Italian fare is overrated. **The Inn at English Harbour Bar** (⌧ English Harbour, ☎ 268/460–1014) with its green leather and petit-point chairs, wood beams, fieldstone walls, copper pots and warming pans, wagon wheel chandelier, 19th-century maps, and maritime prints, is uncommonly refined. **Trappa's** (⌧ Main Rd., English Harbour, ☎ 268/562–3534) is a hipster hangout set in a bamboo-walled courtyard amid a virtual jungle of greenery, with everything from columns to booths in blue hues. It serves delectable, sizable tapas (fried mushrooms, Brie dip, Thai mango chicken curry, seafood pizzetta) into the wee hours for just EC$20. Live music is often on the menu. **Hype** (⌧ Nelson's Dockyard, English Harbour, ☎ 268/562–2353), right outside the entrance to Nelson's Dockyard, is a semi-enclosed wooden pier that groans under the weight of yachties and their groupies during the 2-for-1 happy hours and Caribbean party nights with live bands. **Lashings** (⌧ Runaway Bay, ☎ 268/462–4438) is a funky place that attracts world-renowned cricketers, as well as a jovial crowd for liberal happy hours, dirt-cheap Tex-Mex and local cuisine, and dirty dancing on the sand.

The **Mad Mongoose** (⌧ Falmouth Harbour, ☎ 268/463–7900) is a wildly popular yachty (and singles) joint, splashed in vivid Rasta colors, with a game room and satellite TV. Right inside Nelson's Dockyard and part of the restored Copper and Lumber Store Hotel, the lively **Mainbrace Pub** (⌧ English Harbour, ☎ 268/460–1058) offers proper fish-and-chips, darts, Bass on tap, and occasional live jazz. The crowd at **Millers by the Sea** (⌧ Fort James Beach, ☎ 268/462–9414) spills over onto the beach during the ever-popular happy hour and live nightly entertainment. It's packed with cruise-ship passengers tanning and noshing on barbecue and burgers during the day. You can hike to the 18th-century ruins of Fort James at the other end of the beach for stunning views of St. John's. **Dickenson Park Leisure Center** (⌧ Dickenson Bay Rd., Dickenson Bay, ☎ 268/463–4653) is wildly popular with Brits, even though it's essentially just an open deck overlooking a lagoon that's really a swamp. There are also a playground, video arcade, disco, Internet café, and a lighted miniature golf course where you can access your inner child between brews. **Shirley Heights Lookout** (⌧ Shirley Heights, ☎ 268/460–1785) hosts Sunday-afternoon barbecues that continue into the night with reggae and steel-band music and dancing. On Sunday afternoon and Thursday evening, residents and visitors gather for boisterous fun, the latest gossip, and great sunsets. **Southern Cross** (⌧ English Harbour Yacht Club Marina, English Harbour, ☎ 268/460–1797) is an overpriced Italian eatery, but its brick-and-mahogany bar, vaulted ceilings, stylish scrap-metal artworks, and phenomenal location make it a primo yachty hangout. Owner Flavio Scala has been a helmsman on several Italian entries in the America's Cup.

CASINOS

There are four true casinos on Antigua, as well as several holes-in-the-wall that have mostly one-armed bandits. Hours depend on the season, so it's best to inquire upon your arrival. **Coral Reef Casino** (⌧ Jolly Harbour Marina, Jolly Harbour, ☎ 268/++CE: number TK++) moved into slick, new three-story digs in 2002; management plans to add dining and entertainment. You'll find abundant slots and gaming tables at the somewhat dilapidated, unintentionally retro (icicle chandeliers, naugahyde seats, and 1970s soul crooners on the sound system), smoky **King's Casino** (⌧ Heritage Quay, St. John's, ☎ 268/462–1727). **Riv-**

iera Casino (✉ Runaway Bay, ☎ 268/562–6262) has pretensions to elegance (Palladian doorways, a spiral staircase leading to a cozier bar, a nice restaurant undercut by blue neon and early bird dinner specials. Galoots in suits scan the room as if it were Vegas. Still, you can indulge in blackjack, roulette, Caribbean stud poker, slots, and the sport book, for placing bets on international events. The **St. James's Club** (✉ Mamora Bay, ☎ 268/463–1113) has an elegant, almost Bondian casino and looks as if it came straight out of the Côte d'Azur.

DANCE CLUBS

The Outback (✉ Dickenson Park Leisure Center, Dickenson Bay Rd., Dickenson Bay, ☎ 268/463–4653) is Antigua's only indoor, air-conditioned disco. The DJs spin house, reggae, hip-hop, and jungle. The **Web** (✉ Old Parham Rd., St. John's, ☎ 268/462–3186) attracts a somewhat rowdy local crowd and spins ethnic sounds such as reggae, soca, and salsa.

Exploring Antigua

Major hotels provide free maps but you should get your bearings before heading out on the road. Street names aren't posted, so orient yourself in advance; look to see if a popular restaurant is near your destination, because easy-to-spot signs leading the way to restaurants are posted all over the island. Locals generally give directions in terms of landmarks (turn left at the yellow house, or right at the big tree). Wear a swimsuit under your clothes—one of the sights to strike your fancy might be a secluded beach.

Numbers in the margin correspond to points of interest on the Antigua and Barbuda map.

SIGHTS TO SEE

⓫ **Barbuda.** This flat 62-square-mi (161-square-km) coral atoll—with 17 mi (27 km) of pinkish white-sand beaches—is 26 mi (42 km) north of Antigua. Most of the island's 1,500 people live in Codrington. Pink Beach lures beachcombers, a bird sanctuary attracts ornithologists, caves and sinkholes filled with rainforest or underground pools attract spelunkers, and offshore wrecks and reefs draw divers and snorkelers. **Carib Aviation** flies to Barbuda daily from Antigua, and air and boat charters are available if you want to make a day-trip. The sole historic ruin on Barbuda is the 18th-century, cylindrical, 56-ft-tall **Martello Tower,** which is believed to have been a lighthouse built by the Spaniards before the English occupied the island. The **Bird Sanctuary,** a wide mangrove-filled lagoon, is home to an estimated 400 species of birds, including frigate birds with 8-ft (2½-m) wingspans. Tours commonly take you here and to a beach for snorkeling.

⓼ **Betty's Hope.** Just outside the village of Pares, a marked dirt road leads to Betty's Hope, Antigua's first sugar plantation, founded in 1650. You can tour the twin windmills, and the visitor center has exhibits on the island's sugar era. The village isn't much now, but the private trust overseeing its restoration has ambitious plans. ✉ *Pares,* ☎ *268/462–1469.* 🎫 *Free.* ☉ *Tues.–Sat. 9–4.*

⓽ **Devil's Bridge.** This limestone arch formation, sculpted by the crashing breakers of the Atlantic at Indian Town, is a national park. Blowholes have been carved by the hissing, spitting surf. They may be hard to spot at first, but just wait until a wave bursts through. The park also encompasses some archeological excavations of Carib artifacts.

⓹ **English Harbour.** The most famous of Antigua's attractions lies on the coast, just south of Falmouth. In 1671 the governor of the Leeward Islands wrote to the Council for Foreign Plantations in London, pointing out the advantages of this landlocked harbor. By 1704 English Harbour was in regular use as a garrisoned station.

In 1784, 26-year-old Horatio Nelson sailed in on the HMS *Boreas* to serve as captain and second-in-command of the Leeward Island Station. Under him was the captain of the HMS *Pegasus*, Prince William Henry, duke of Clarence, who was to ascend the throne of England as William IV. The prince was Nelson's close friend and acted as best man when Nelson married Fannie Nisbet on Nevis in 1787.

When the Royal Navy abandoned the station at English Harbour in 1889, it fell into a state of decay. The Society of the Friends of English Harbour began restoring it in 1951, and on Dockyard Day, November 14, 1961, Nelson's Dockyard was re-opened with much fanfare. Today it's reminiscent, albeit on a much smaller scale, of Williamsburg, Virginia. Within the compound are crafts shops, restaurants, and two splendidly restored 18th-century hotels, the Admiral's Inn and The Copper and Lumber Store Hotel, worth peeking into. (The latter, occupying a supply store for Nelson's Caribbean fleet, is a particularly fine example of Georgian architecture, with warm brick, hardwood floors, timber ceilings, sailing prints, nautical maps, burgundy leather armchairs and sofas, and an interior courtyard evoking Old England in the public spaces.) The Dockyard is a hub for oceangoing yachts and serves as headquarters for the annual Sailing Week Regatta. Beach lovers tend to stay elsewhere, but those who love history and the nautical scene often choose one of the nearby hotels. Water taxis will ferry you between points for EC$5. The Dockyard National Park also includes serene nature trails accessing beaches, rock pools, and crumbling plantation ruins and hilltop forts.

The **Admiral's House Museum** displays ship models, a model of English Harbour, silver regatta trophies, maps, prints, and Nelson's very own telescope and tea caddy. ⊠ *Nelson's Dockyard,* ☎ *268/463–1053 or 268/463–1379.* ☞ *$2, suggested donation.* ☉ *Daily 8–6.*

④ Falmouth. This town sits on a lovely bay backed by former sugar plantations and sugar mills. The most important historic site here is St. Paul's Church, which was rebuilt on the site of a church once used by troops during the Nelson period.

Fig Tree Drive. This often muddy, rutted, steep road takes you through the rain forest, which is rich in mangoes, pineapples, and banana trees (*fig* is the Antiguan word for "banana"). The rain-forest area is the hilliest part of the island—Boggy Peak, to the west, is the highest point, at 1,319 ft (439 m). You'll also pass through several tranquil villages with charming churches.

③ Ft. George. East of Liberta—one of the first settlements founded by freed slaves—on Monk's Hill, this fort was built from 1689 to 1720. Among the ruins are the sites for 32 cannons, water cisterns, the base of the old flagstaff, and some of the original buildings.

⑦ Harmony Hall. Northeast of Freetown (follow the signs) is this interesting art gallery built on the foundation of a 17th-century sugar-plantation great house. Artists Graham Davis and Peter and Annabella Proudlock, who founded the sister gallery in Jamaica, teamed up with local entrepreneur Geoffrey Pidduck to create this Antiguan establishment, which specializes in high-quality West Indian art. A large exhibit space is used for one-person shows; another space displays watercolors. A small bar in a sugar mill and a superlative Italian restaurant occupying the courtyard are open in season. Both are run by the enterprising Italians who operate the top-notch Abracadabra restaurant. There's also a pool, the beach is a five-minute walk down the hill, and you can arrange boat rides to nearby Green Island. You can also spend the night in one of the six comfortable, spacious cottages, which rent for $160 (CP); the owners will graciously deliver dinner to your patio at 6 PM during the week. ⊠ *Brown's Mill Bay, Brown's Mill,* ☎ *268/463–8657 or 268/460–4120.* ⊙ *Daily 10–6.*

② **Megaliths of Greencastle Hill.** It's an arduous climb to these eerie rock slabs in the south-central part of the island. Some say the megaliths were set up by early inhabitants for their worship of the sun and moon; others believe they're nothing more than unusual geological formations.

⑩ **Parham.** This tiny village is a splendid, sleepy example of a traditional colonial settlement. St. Peter's Church, built in 1840 by Thomas Weekes, an English architect, is an octagonal Italianate building with unusual ribbed wooden ceiling, whose facade is richly decorated with stucco and keystone work, though it suffered considerable damage during the earthquake of 1843.

① **St. John's.** Antigua's capital, with some 45,000 inhabitants (approximately half the island's population), lies at sea level at the inland end of a sheltered northwestern bay. Although it has seen better days, a couple of notable historic sights and some good waterfront shopping areas and restaurants make it worth a visit. Signs at the **Museum of Antigua and Barbuda** say PLEASE TOUCH, encouraging you to explore Antigua's past. Try your hand at the educational video games or squeeze a cassava through a *matapi* (a grass sieve). Exhibits interpret the nation's history, from its geological birth to its political independence in 1981. There are fossil and coral remains from some 34 million years ago; models of a sugar plantation and a wattle-and-daub house; an Arawak canoe; a wildly eclectic assortment of objects from cannonballs to 1920s telephone exchanges; and a small shop with handicrafts, books, prints, and paintings. The colonial building that houses the museum is the former courthouse, which dates from 1750. The museum gift shop carries such unusual items as calabash purses, seed earrings, and lignum vitae pipes. ⊠ *Church and Market Sts.,* ☎ *268/462–1469.* ☞ *$2 suggested donation.* ⊙ *Weekdays 8:30–4, Sat. 10–1.* At the south gate of the **Anglican Cathedral of St. John the Divine** are figures of St. John the Baptist and St. John the Divine said to have been taken from one of Napoléon's ships and brought to Antigua. The original church was built in 1681, replaced by a stone building in 1745, and destroyed by an earthquake in 1843. The present building dates from 1845. With an eye to future earthquakes, the parishioners had the interior completely encased in pitch pine, hoping to forestall heavy damage. The church was elevated to the status of cathedral in 1848. ⊠ *Between Long and Newgate Sts.,* ☎ *268/461–0082.* Shopaholics head directly for **Heritage Quay,** a continually expanding multimillion-dollar complex. The two-story buildings contain stores that sell duty-free goods, sportswear, T-shirts, imports from down-island (paintings, T-shirts, straw baskets), and local crafts. There are also several restaurants and a casino. Cruise-ship passengers disembark here from the 500-ft-long (153-m-long) pier. ⊠ *High and Thames Sts.*

Redcliffe Quay, set at the water's edge just south of Heritage Quay, is the most appealing part of St. John's. Attractively restored (and superbly re-created) buildings in a riot of cotton-candy colors house shops, restaurants, and boutiques and are linked by courtyards and landscaped walkways.

At the far south end of town, where Market Street forks into Valley Road and All Saints Road, a whole lot of haggling goes on every Friday and Saturday, when locals jam the public **marketplace** to buy and sell fruits, vegetables, fish, and spices. Be sure to ask before you aim a camera; expect your subject to ask for a tip. This is shopping the old-time Caribbean way, a jambalaya of sights, sounds, and smells.

❻ Shirley Heights. This bluff affords a spectacular view of English Harbour. The heights are named for Sir Thomas Shirley, the governor who fortified the harbor in 1787. At the top is Shirley Heights Lookout, a restaurant built into the remnants of the 18th-century fortifications. Most notable for its boisterous Sunday barbecues that often continue well into the night with live music and dancing; it serves dependable burgers, pumpkin soup, grilled items, and rum punches. Not far from Shirley Heights is the **Dows Hill Interpretation Centre,** where observation platforms provide still more sensational vistas of the whole English Harbour area. There's a multimedia sound-and-light presentation on the island's history and culture, in which illuminated displays, incorporating lifelike figures and colorful tableaux, are presented with running commentary and music—resulting in a cheery, if bland, portrait of Antiguan life from the days of the Amerindians to the present. ☎ *268/460–2777 (National Parks Authority).* ☒ *EC$15.* ☉ *Daily 9–5.*

ANTIGUA A TO Z

To research prices, get advice from other travelers, and book travel arrangements, visit www.fodors.com.

AIR TRAVEL
American Airlines has daily direct service from New York and Miami, and several flights from San Juan that connect with flights from more than 100 U.S. cities. Continental Airlines offers nonstop service from Newark and Miami. US Airways inaugurated direct service from Baltimore and Philadelphia in 2002. Air Canada has nonstop service from Toronto. Air France flies nonstop from Paris. British Airways has nonstop service from London. Virgin Atlantic also offers nonstop London flights. BWIA has nonstop service from New York, Miami, and Toronto. Carib Aviation flies daily to Barbuda, as well as neighboring islands. LIAT has daily flights to and from many other Caribbean islands.

➤ AIRLINES AND CONTACTS: **American Airlines** (☎ 268/462–0950). **Air Canada** (☎ 268/462–1147). **Air France** (☎ 268/462–1763). **British Airways** (☎ 268/462–0876). **BWIA** (☎ 268/480–2925 or 268/480–2942). **Carib Aviation** (☎ 268/462–3147, WEB www.candoo.com/carib). **Continental Airlines** (☎ 268/462–5355). **LIAT** (☎ 268/480–5600). **US Airways** (☎ 800/428–4322). **Virgin Atlantic** (☎ 268/560–2079).

AIRPORTS
Antigua's V. C. Bird International Airport, on the northeast coast, is a major hub for traffic between Caribbean islands and for international flights.

Taxis meet every flight, and drivers will offer to guide you around the island. The taxis are unmetered, but rates are posted at the airport, and drivers must carry a rate card with them. The fixed rate from the airport to St. John's is US$12 (although drivers have been known to *quote* in EC dollars); to English Harbour it's $21.

➤ AIRPORT INFORMATION: **V. C. Bird International Airport** (☎ 268/462–4672).

BIKE AND MOPED TRAVEL
You can rent Honda or Yamaha motorcycles for $35 per day ($150 per week) at J.T.'s Rent-A-Scoot.

➤ BIKE AND MOPED RENTALS: **J.T.'s Rent-A-Scoot** (✉ English Harbour, ☎ 268/463–3578).

BUSINESS HOURS

BANKS

Banks have varying hours but are generally open Monday–Thursday 8–2 and Friday 8–4.

POST OFFICES

Post offices are open Monday–Saturday 9–4.

SHOPS

Although some stores still follow the tradition of closing for lunch, most are open Monday–Saturday 9–5, especially in season; if a cruise ship is in port, shops in Heritage and Redcliffe Quays are likely to open Sunday.

CAR RENTALS

To rent a car, you need a valid driver's license and a temporary permit ($20), available through the rental agent. Costs average about $50 per day in season, with unlimited mileage, though you may get a better rate if you rent for several days. Most agencies offer automatic, stick-shift, and right- and left-hand-drive. Four-wheel-drive vehicles ($55 per day) will get you more places and are refreshingly open as many roads are full of potholes.

Among the agencies are Avis, Budget, Dollar, Hertz, National, and Thrifty.

➤ MAJOR AGENCIES: **Avis** (☎ 268/462–2840). **Budget** (☎ 268/462–3009). **Dollar** (☎ 268/462–0362). **Hertz** (☎ 268/462–6450). **National** (☎ 268/462–2113). **Thrifty** (☎ 268/462–8803).

CAR TRAVEL

GASOLINE

At press time, gasoline costs approximately $2.60 per gallon.

ROAD CONDITIONS

The main roads, by and large, are in good condition, although there are bronco-busting dirt stretches leading to some more remote locations and a few hilly areas that flood easily and become impassable for a day or two.

RULES OF THE ROAD

Driving is on the left, although many locals drive in the middle—or think nothing of stopping at roadside to chat. Don't be flustered by honking: it's the Caribbean version of hello.

ELECTRICITY

Antigua runs on 110 volts, allowing the use of most small North American appliances. Outlets are both two- and three-pronged, so bring an adapter.

EMBASSIES AND CONSULATES

➤ UNITED KINGDOM: **British High Commission** (✉ Old Parham Rd., St. John's, ☎ 268/462–0008 or 268/562–2124, WEB www.fco.gov.uk).
➤ UNITED STATES: The **United States Consulate** (✉ U.S. Consulate, Hospital Hill, English Harbour, ☎ 268/463–6531, FAX 268/460–1569, WEB usembassy.state.gov).

EMERGENCIES

➤ AMBULANCE AND FIRE: **Ambulance** (☎ 268/462–0251). **Fire** (☎ 268/462–0044).

➤ HOSPITALS: **Holberton Hospital** (✉ Hospital Rd., St. John's, ☎ 268/ 462–0251).

➤ PHARMACIES: **City Pharmacy** (✉ St. Mary's St., St. John's, ☎ 268/ 480–3314). **Woods Pharmacy** (✉ Woods Centre, Friar's Hill Rd., St. John's, ☎ 268/462–9287).

➤ POLICE: Police assistance (☎ 268/462–0125 or 268/460–7187/8/9).

ETIQUETTE AND BEHAVIOR

Antiguans are extremely proud and don't take kindly to strangers snapping photos without asking permission first.

FESTIVALS AND SEASONAL EVENTS

Antigua Sailing Week, which takes place at the end of April and in early May, draws more than 300 yachts for a series of races in several boat classes. The salt air crackles with excitement like a nautical Kentucky Derby. Late April sees the Antigua Classic Yacht Regatta, a five-day event including the Parade of Classics and Tall Ships race. Antigua Tennis Week, usually held the second week of May, has exhibitions by such masters as Billie Jean King, Kathy Rinaldi, Fred Stolle, and Bob Lutz, plus a pro-am tournament. Carnival runs from the end of July to early August and is one of the Caribbean's more elaborate, with eye-catching costumes, fiercely competitive bands, and the only Caribbean Queen show (a.k.a. the Miss Antigua Contest). Antigua International Hot Air Balloon Festival attracts dozens of fancifully shaped and colored hot air balloons in early January.

HOLIDAYS

Public holidays are: New Year's Day, Good Friday (usually late Mar. to Apr.), Easter Sunday and Monday (usually late Mar. to Apr.), Labour Day (1st Mon. in May), Whit Monday (2nd Mon. in June), Independence Day (Nov. 1), Christmas, and Boxing Day (Dec. 26).

LANGUAGE

Antigua's official language is English, and it's often spoken with a heavy West Indian lilt.

MAIL AND SHIPPING

Airmail letters to North America cost EC$1.50; postcards, EC75¢. Letters to the United Kingdom cost EC$1.20; postcards are EC60¢. Letters to Australia and New Zealand are EC$1.80, postcards EC90¢. The main post office is at the foot of High Street in St. John's. Note that when addressing letters to the island, there are no postal codes; you need only indicate the address and "Antigua, West Indies."

➤ CONTACTS: **Main Post Office** (☎ 268/462–0992).

MONEY MATTERS

Note: prices quoted throughout this chapter are in U.S. dollars unless otherwise indicated.

ATMS

ATMs are available at the island's banks (listed below) and at the airport.

CREDIT CARDS

Most hotels, restaurants, and duty-free shops take major credit cards; all accept traveler's checks.

CURRENCY

Local currency is the Eastern Caribbean dollar (EC$), which is tied to the U.S. dollar and fluctuates only slightly. At hotels, the rate is EC$2.60 to US$1; at banks, it's EC$2.68. American dollars are readily accepted, although you'll usually receive change in EC dollars.

➤ CONTACTS: **Bank of Antigua** (✉ High and Thames Sts., ☎ 268/480–5300). **Barclays Bank** (✉ High St., ☎ 268/480–5000).

PASSPORTS AND VISAS

U.S. and Canadian citizens need proof of identity. A valid passport is most desirable, but a birth certificate is acceptable provided it has a raised seal and has been issued by a county or state (not a hospital) and provided that you also have some type of photo identification, such as a driver's license. A driver's license by itself isn't sufficient. Citizens of Australia, New Zealand, and the United Kingdom need passports. All visitors must present a return or ongoing ticket.

SAFETY

Throughout the Caribbean, incidents of petty theft are increasing. Leave your valuables in the hotel safe-deposit box; don't leave them unattended in your room, on a beach, or in a rental car. Also, the streets of St. John's are fairly deserted at night, so it's not a good idea to wander about alone.

SIGHTSEEING TOURS

GUIDED TOURS

Virtually all taxi drivers double as guides, and you can arrange an island tour with one for about $25 an hour. Every major hotel has a cabbie on call and may be able to negotiate a discount, particularly off-season.

ORIENTATION

Antours, by far the most professional outfit on Antigua, gives half- and full-day island tours that focus on such highlights as Shirley Heights and English Harbour. Antours is also the island's American Express representative.
➤ CONTACTS: **Antours** (✉ Long and Thames Sts., St. John's, ☎ 268/462–4788).

SPECIAL-INTEREST

Estate Safari Adventure operates tours to the interior, where there are few marked trails and roads are rough. The cost (about $60 per person) includes lunch and snorkeling at a secluded beach. Tropikelly's four-wheel-drive off-road adventures enable you to fully appreciate the island's topography and rich history. Hiking is involved, though it's not strenuous. Four-wheel-drive tours with hikes are $65; bike tours cost $35; and hikes through the rain forest run $20.

Kayak Snorkel and Eco Tour takes you on a 3½-hour tour of serene mangroves and inlets, while explaining the fragile ecosystem of the swamp and reefs and the rich diversity of flora and fauna.

The adventuresome and morbidly curious may enjoy visiting neighboring Montserrat. Jenny's Tours arranges day trips—including the ferry ride from Antigua's Heritage Quay, an island tour, breakfast, and lunch—for $150 per person (departure taxes not included; weekend rate $130 per person).

Montserrat's Soufriere Hills Volcano still remains active, throwing the unfortunate island into the fire and wiping out much of its infrastructure. Though some residents have returned, the volcano often spews hot lava and plumes of ash visible from Antigua and other surrounding islands (plucky locals joke that new beachfront is being created; indeed a mountain is sprouting). The tourism industry is making a tentative comeback, with simple guest houses, inns, rental villas, restaurants, and water-sports concessions opening. The tour takes in some of Montserrat's lush green forests, often compared to those of Ireland;

the island's glistening, black-sand coast; lookout points showing the vast devastation, including the airport and Plymouth, the capital city buried under gray ash like a latter-day Pompeii; and the Montserrat Volcano Observatory to learn about volcanoes. Since the "safe zones" do change, it's strongly recommended that you go with a tour operator. However, hardy travelers do overnight and hike, kayak, and dive (check the Montserrat Tourist board Web site for information). The daily ferry (and occasionally, helicopter) from Antigua is met by island cabbies (the most reliable, friendly, and knowledgeable is Joe Phillips). ➤ CONTACTS: **Estate Safari Adventure** (☎ 268/463–4713). **Jenny's Tours** (✉ Box W471, St. John's, ☎ 268/461–9361). **Montserrat Tourist Board Web site** (WEB www.mrat.com).**Kayak & Snorkel Eco Tour** (✉ Seaton's Village, ☎ 268/560–3782). **Tropikelly** (☎ 268/461–0383).

TAXES AND SERVICE CHARGES

DEPARTURE TAX

The departure tax is $20, payable in cash only—either U.S. or EC currency.

SALES TAX

Hotels collect an 8½% government room tax; some restaurants will add a 7% tax.

SERVICE CHARGES

Hotels and restaurants usually add a 10% service charge to your bill.

TAXIS

Taxis are unmetered, and although fares mount up quickly, rates are fixed (your driver should have a rate card). Some cabbies may take you from St. John's to English Harbour and wait for a "reasonable" amount of time (about a half hour) while you look around, for about $40. You can always call a cab from the St. John's taxi stand.
➤ CONTACTS: **St. John's taxi stand** (☎ 268/462–5190; 268/460–5353 for 24-hour service).

TELEPHONES

Few hotels have direct-dial phones, but it's easy enough to make connections through the switchboard. You can use the Caribbean Phone Card (available in $5, $10, and $20 amounts in most hotels and post offices) for local and long-distance calls. Phone-card phones work much better than the regular pay phones.

COUNTRY AND AREA CODES

To call Antigua from the United States, dial 1, then area code 268, then the local seven-digit number.

INTERNATIONAL CALLS

To call the United States and Canada, dial 1, the area code, and the seven-digit number, or use the phone card or one of the USA Direct phones, which are available at several locations, including the airport departure lounge, the cruise terminal at St. John's, and the English Harbour Marina. These take credit cards and, supposedly, calling cards (though Cable & Wireless tacks on a fee).

LOCAL CALLS

To place a local call, simply dial the local seven-digit number.

TIPPING

In restaurants it's customary to leave 5% beyond the regular service charge added to your bill if you're pleased with the service. Taxi drivers expect a 10% tip, porters and bellmen about $1 per bag. Maids are rarely tipped, but if you think the service exemplary, figure $2–$3 per night. Staff at all-inclusives aren't supposed to be tipped unless they've truly gone out of their way.

TRANSPORTATION AROUND ANTIGUA

You'll see two bus stations in St. John's, near the Botanical Gardens and near Central Market, but don't expect to see many buses. Schedules follow "island time," which is to say that privately owned vehicles roll when the spirit (infrequently) moves them. Taxis are generally your best bet.

VISITOR INFORMATION

There is a tourist-information desk at the airport, just beyond the immigration checkpoint. The tourist office gives limited information. You may have more success with the Antigua Hotels and Tourist Association.

➤ BEFORE YOU LEAVE: **Antigua and Barbuda Tourist Offices** in the United States (✉ 610 5th Ave., Suite 311, New York, NY 10020, ☎ 212/541–4117 or 888/268–4227, WEB www.antiguanice.com; ✉ 25 S.E. 2nd Ave., Suite 300, Miami, FL 33131, ☎ 305/381–6762); in Canada (✉ 60 St. Clair Ave. E, Suite 304, Toronto, Ontario M4T 1N5, ☎ 416/961–3085); in the United Kingdom (✉ Antigua House, 15 Thayer St., London W1M 5LD, ☎ 0171/486–7073).

➤ IN ANTIGUA: **Antigua and Barbuda Department of Tourism** (✉ Nevis St., St. John's, ☎ 268/463–0125, FAX 268/462–2483). **Antigua Hotels and Tourist Association** (✉ Lower St. Mary's St., St. John's, ☎ 268/462–0374).

Updated by
Karen W.
Bressler

A natural coral limestone bridge, burnished beige in the golden sun, straddles a perfect crescent of ecru sand and sapphire surf. Terns and snowy egrets dive-bomb for their lunch. To one side, towering cacti and rock formations and boulders stretch as far as the eye can see. To the other side is a sea of wildly colored T-shirts (with even wilder slogans). Welcome to Aruba—an uneasy truce between natural beauty and tourism.

That delicate balance is the key to Aruba's undeniable success. Most of the island gleams with a fierce, extraterrestrial beauty, its battered coast defying development. But balmy sunshine, silky sand, aquamarine waters, and constant trade winds (so strong they've bent Aruba's trademark watapana tree—commonly known as the divi-divi tree—at a surreal 45-degree angle) have made the calmer southwest coast a tourist mecca. Most of its 28 major hotels sit side by side down a single strip of shore, with restaurants, exotic boutiques, fiery floor shows, and glitzy casinos on the premises. Nearly every night there are theme parties, treasure hunts, beachside barbecues, and fish fries with steel bands and limbo or Carnival dancers. Surround all this with warm blue-green waters whose visibility extends up to 100 ft (30 m), and you've got the perfect destination for anyone who wants sun salted with lots of activities.

The A in the ABC Islands (the other two being Bonaire and Curaçao), Aruba is small—only 19½ mi (31½ km) long and 6 mi (9½ km) across at its widest point. Once a member of the Netherlands Antilles, it became an independent entity within the Netherlands in 1986, with its own royally appointed governor and a 21-member elected parliament.

Aruba's economy was once based on oil. These days, education, housing, and health care are financed by tourism, and the island's population of 95,000 recognizes visitors as valued guests. The national anthem proclaims, "The greatness of our people is their great cordiality," and this is no exaggeration. Waiters serve you with smiles, English is spoken everywhere, and hotel hospitality directors appear delighted to fulfill your special needs.

The island's distinctive beauty lies in its countryside—full of rocky deserts, divi-divi trees, cactus jungles alive with the chattering of wild parakeets, secluded coves, and blue vistas with crashing waves. With its low humidity and average temperature of 82°F (28°C), Aruba has the climate of a paradise. Sun, cooling trade winds, friendly and courteous service, efficient amenities, golf and tennis clubs, modern casinos, glorious beaches, duty-free shopping, and remarkably varied cuisine help fill' Aruba's more than 7,500 hotel rooms.

Lodging

Most hotels are west of Oranjestad along L. G. Smith and J. E. Irausquin boulevards. These complexes have their own fitness centers, hair salons, casinos, restaurants, delis, drugstores, boutiques, and car-rental and travel desks. Room service, laundry and dry cleaning services, and baby-sitting are standard amenities at all but the smallest properties, and activities like water sports are usually part of the package. Children often get free accommodation in their parents' room; ask about age qualifications. Most hotels, unless specified, don't include meals in their room rates.

Hotels here are fairly expensive. To save money, take advantage of airline and hotel packages, which are plentiful. Rates are cheaper in summer, when rates are discounted by as much as 40%.

CATEGORY	COST EP/CP*	COST A.I.**
$$$$	Over $350	Over $375
$$$	$250–$350	$275–$375
$$	$150–$250	$175–$275
$	under $150	under $175

*EP/CP prices are per night for a standard double room in high season, excluding taxes, service charges, and meal plans**A.I. (all-inclusive) prices are per person, per night based on double-occupancy during high season, excluding taxes and service charges

$$$$ ★ 🏨 **Aruba Marriott Resort & Stellaris Casino.** You'll hear the sound of water everywhere at this high-rise hotel on Palm Beach, whether it's the beating of the surf below your balcony or the trickling of the waterfalls in the marble lobby and around the tropically landscaped pool. Spacious rooms have a distinctly Caribbean feeling. Most have ocean views, as well as walk-in closets, hair dryers, and irons. The path to the ocean from the garden-view rooms is longer than that from elsewhere in the complex, but the in-room hot tubs more than compensate for this. Tuscany offers superlative Italian cuisine, and Simply Fish serves up dishes fresh from the sea. Express checkout is available. ⊠ *L. G. Smith Blvd. 101, Palm Beach,* ☎ *297/8–69000 or 800/223–6388,* FAX *297/8–60649,* WEB *www.marriott.com. 413 rooms, 20 suites. 4 restaurants, 4 bars, café, in-room data ports, in-room safes, minibars, cable TV with movies, in-room VCRs, 2 tennis courts, pool, aerobics, hair salon, health club, massage, saunas, spa, beach, dive shop, windsurfing, boating, jet skiing, volleyball, casino, shops, concierge, Internet, meeting rooms, car rental. AE, D, DC, MC, V. EP, FAP, MAP.*

$$$$ ★ 🏨 **Hyatt Regency Aruba Beach Resort & Casino.** A favorite among honeymooners, this resort looks like a Spanish palace, with art deco–style flourishes and a multilevel pool with waterfalls, a two-story water slide, and a lagoon stocked with tropical fish and black swans. Rooms have slim balconies, but lots of extras; those on the Regency Club floor have such amenities as complimentary breakfast and concierge service. Relax on the beach, play tennis, or head out for a horseback ride before an afternoon hydrotherapy treatment and a stop at the juice bar. For a full meal choose from excellent restaurants, including Ruinas del Mar, where you'll find Continental fare, and Japengo, serving up seafood with an Asian flair. Parents appreciate the imaginative Camp Hyatt, which incorporates Aruban storytelling, cooking, and arts and crafts for kids ages 3–12. ⊠ *J. E. Irausquin Blvd. 85, Palm Beach,* ☎ *297/8–61234 or 800/ 554–9288,* FAX *297/8–61682,* WEB *www.hyatt.com. 342 rooms, 18 suites. 5 restaurants, 5 bars, snack bar, room service, fans, in-room safes, mini-*

bars, cable TV with movies, 2 tennis courts, pool, salon, health club, 2 outdoor hot tubs, massage, sauna, spa, steam room, beach, dive shop, dock, snorkeling, windsurfing, boating, jet skiing, waterskiing, basketball, horseback riding, volleyball, casino, shops, baby-sitting, children's programs, playground, concierge, business services, Internet, car rental, travel services, some pets allowed. AE, D, DC, MC, V. EP, MAP.

$$$$ ☆ 🏨 **Radisson Aruba Resort & Casino.** Aruba's newest and largest hotel reopened at the start of this century with a promise to pamper its guests. Exotic birds greet you in the expansive lobby. Colonial Caribbean–style guest rooms (each with a view of the ocean or the garden) have mahogany four-poster beds and such singular accents as hand-beaded lamp shades. The designers thought of everything: blue accent lighting, wood furniture on the balconies, and plantation shutters. In-room perks include minibars (careful, they're touch-sensored), coffeemakers, and hair dryers. Unwind in the fitness center and spa, and then enjoy a meal at one of the hotel's excellent restaurants. Try Gilligan's at the beach for simple fare, or the Sunset Grille for more elaborate dishes. ✉ *J. E. Irausquin Blvd. 81, Palm Beach,* ☎ *297/8–66555,* ℻ *297/8–63260,* 🌐 *www.radisson.com. 358 rooms, 32 suites. 4 restaurants, 3 bars, room service, in-room safes, minibars, cable TV with movies, golf privileges, 2 tennis courts, 2 pools, health club, spa, beach, dive shop, snorkeling, boating, jet skiing, video game rooms, baby-sitting, children's programs, dry cleaning, laundry service, business services, convention center, Internet, meeting rooms. AE, D, DC, MC, V. BP, FAP, MAP.*

$$$$ 🏨 **Tamarijn Aruba All Inclusive Beach Resort.** Low-rise buildings stretch along the shore at this all-inclusive resort catering to couples and families. The spacious oceanfront rooms, filled with light-wood furnishings, have private balconies. The rate covers food, beverages, entertainment, an array of activities, and even tickets to the weekly Bon Bini Festival. A bar at one end of the property serves food and drinks as a convenience for guests more removed from the main restaurants. Utilize the free shuttle that runs to the Alhambra Casino until 3 AM. ✉ *J. E. Irausquin Blvd. 41, Punta Brabo,* ☎ *297/8–24150 or 800/554–2008,* ℻ *297/8–31940,* 🌐 *www.tamarijnaruba.com. 236 rooms. 3 restaurants, 2 bars, snack bar, fans, cable TV, 2 tennis courts, 2 pools, health club, beach, snorkeling, windsurfing, boating, waterskiing, fishing, bicycles, Ping-Pong, shuffleboard, volleyball, shops, Internet, meeting rooms, car rental. AE, D, DC, MC, V. All-inclusive.*

$$$$ 🏨 **Wyndham Aruba Beach Resort & Casino.** From exciting windsurfing to sizzling nightlife, the Wyndham seems to have something for everyone. Grand public areas accommodate big groups from North and South America, which make up a good portion of the clientele. Rooms, which are oddly configured, have mustard-color stucco walls and handsome dark-wood furniture. All have ocean-view balconies and amenities like coffeemakers, refrigerators, and hair dryers. A day at the pool means more than swimming and sunning; a "pool concierge" makes the rounds, loaning out books, magazines, and CD players; pool attendants spritz you with Evian, offer chilled towels, and serve frozen drinks. If you still don't feel pampered, head to the health club for a massage, facial, or sauna. From there, you're only steps from the beach to dig your toes into the fine white sand. ✉ *J. E. Irausquin Blvd. 77, Palm Beach,* ☎ *297/8–64466 or 800/996–3426,* ℻ *297/8–68217,* 🌐 *www.wyndham.com. 481 rooms, 81 suites. 5 restaurants, 6 bars, in-room safes, cable TV, tennis court, pool, wading pool, 2 outdoor hot tubs, hair salon, health club, massage, sauna, steam room, beach, dive shop, snorkeling, windsurfing, boating, jet skiing, parasailing, waterskiing, Ping-Pong, shuffleboard, volleyball, casino, video game room,*

Lodging

Allegro Aruba
Resort & Casino ... **14**

Amsterdam
Manor Beach
Resort **22**

Aruba Grand Beach
Resort & Casino ... **16**

Aruba Marriott
Resort & Stellaris
Casino **11**

Aruba Sonesta
Resort **1**

Bucuti Beach
Resort **24**

Bushiri Beach
Resort **28**

Divi Aruba
Beach Resort Mega
All Inclusive **26**

Holiday Inn SunSpree
Aruba Resort
& Casino **12**

Hyatt Regency
Aruba Beach
Resort & Casino ... **13**

La Cabana All Suite
Beach Resort
& Casino **23**

Manchebo
Beach Resort **25**

Mill Resort
& Suites **20**

Radisson Aruba
Resort & Casino ... **15**

Tamarijn Aruba
All Inclusive
Beach Resort **27**

Vistalmar **5**

Wyndham Aruba
Beach Resort &
Casino **9**

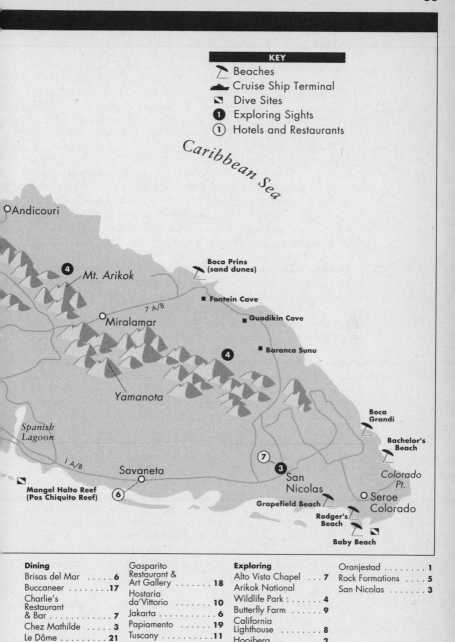

KEY

- ➤ Beaches
- 🚢 Cruise Ship Terminal
- ◣ Dive Sites
- **❶** Exploring Sights
- ⓵ Hotels and Restaurants

Caribbean Sea

○ Andicouri

❹ *Mt. Arikok*

Boca Prins
(sand dunes)

7 A/B

○ *Miralamar*

■ Fontein Cave

■ Guadikin Cave

❹

■ Baranca Sunu

Yamanota

Boca
Grandi

*Spanish
Lagoon*

Bachelor's
Beach

1 A/B

⓻

Savaneta

❸

Colorado
Pt.

San
Nicolas

◣

Mangel Halto Reef
(Pos Chiquito Reef)

⑥

Grapefield Beach

○ Seroe
Colorado

Rodger's
Beach

◣

Baby Beach

Dining		Exploring	
Brisas del Mar 6	Gasparito Restaurant & Art Gallery 18	Alto Vista Chapel . . . 7	Oranjestad 1
Buccaneer 17	Hostaria da'Vittorio 10	Arikok National Wildlife Park : 4	Rock Formations 5
Charlie's Restaurant & Bar 7	Jakarta 6	Butterfly Farm 9	San Nicolas 3
Chez Mathilde 3	Papiamento 19	California Lighthouse 8	
Le Dôme 21	Tuscany 11	Hooiberg 2	
L'Escale 1	Ventanas del Mar 10	Natural Bridge 6	
El Gaucho Argentine Grill 2			

shops, concierge, convention center, Internet. AE, D, DC, MC, V. All-inclusive, CP, EP, FAP, MAP.

$$$ ⊞ **La Cabana All Suite Beach Resort & Casino.** Across the road from Eagle Beach you'll find this self-contained resort. The original four-story building facing the beach surrounds two pools, a bar, and a restaurant. About a third of the studio and one-bedroom suites have ocean views. All have kitchenettes, balconies, and even hot tubs. Pricier villas are away from the main building near a parking lot. The hotel's "home food shopping program" means someone else does the legwork during your stay. You can order groceries on line up to two days prior to your vacation, and they'll be delivered when you arrive. ✉ *J. E. Irausquin Blvd. 250, Eagle Beach,* ☎ *297/8–79000; 212/251–1710 in NY; 800/835–7193;* FAX *297/8–70834,* WEB *www.lacabana.com. 803 suites. 3 restaurants, 5 bars, grocery, ice cream parlor, in-room safes, kitchenettes, microwaves, cable TV, 5 tennis courts, 3 pools, aerobics, health club, 3 outdoor hot tubs, massage, sauna, spa, dive shop, basketball, racquetball, shuffleboard, squash, volleyball, video game room, shops, playground, Internet, meeting rooms. AE, DC, MC, V. All-inclusive, EP, FAP, MAP.*

$$–$$$ ⊞ **Aruba Grand Beach Resort & Casino.** Regulars return again and again to this beachfront resort for its relaxed atmosphere. The yellow and white building, with its distinctive jade green roof, is accompanied by 55 thatched-roof beach huts. Large rooms and suites have such amenities as generous walk-in closets and balconies that overlook either the ocean, the pool, or the garden. The Seawatch restaurant offers international cuisine for breakfast, lunch, and dinner; the more casual Whale's Rib entices seafood lovers with its fresh fish. Ask about discount packages; discounts are available for children under 12. ✉ *J. E. Irausquin Blvd. 79, Palm Beach,* ☎ *297/8–63900 or 800/345–2782,* FAX *297/8–61941,* WEB *www.arubagrand.com. 130 rooms, 41 suites. 2 restaurants, 3 bars, ice cream parlor, snack bar, room service, in-room safes, refrigerators, cable TV, 2 tennis courts, pool, wading pool, beach, dive shop, snorkeling, windsurfing, boating, waterskiing, volleyball, casino, shops, baby-sitting, dry cleaning, laundry service, concierge, Internet, meeting rooms. AE, D, DC, MC, V. All-inclusive, EP, MAP.*

$$–$$$ ⊞ **Aruba Sonesta Resort.** For those who enjoy being in the thick of
★ things, this lively resort is surrounded by shops, restaurants, and casinos. It's a top choice for singles, yet also has plenty of activities for families. Seniors appreciate the discounted room rates. The newer building—whose roomy suites have kitchenettes—is near a private beach. The original high-rise has compact but attractive rooms; choose the quieter garden-view rooms. In the lobby, connected to the Seaport Mall, you can board a skiff for a day trip to the resort's 40-acre private island. The gourmet restaurant, L'Escale, is one of Aruba's best. ✉ *L. G. Smith Blvd. 9, Oranjestad,* ☎ *297/8–36000 or 800/766–3782,* FAX *297/8–25317,* WEB *www.arubasonesta.com. 300 rooms, 265 suites. 4 restaurants, 5 bars, room service, kitchenettes, minibars, some microwaves, cable TV with movies, golf privileges, tennis court, 3 pools, gym, massage, spa, beach, dive shop, snorkeling, marina, fishing, volleyball, 2 casinos, nightclub, video game room, shops, children's programs, playground, laundry facilities, concierge, convention center, Internet, meeting rooms; no-smoking rooms. AE, D, DC, MC, V. EP, FAP, MAP.*

$$–$$$ ⊞ **Bucuti Beach Resort.** Owner Ewald Biemans was named the island's
★ hotelier of the year for the second year in a row for his refreshingly peaceful European-style resort. Popular with honeymooners (who receive champagne and romantic goodies upon arrival), the hacienda-style buildings house sunny rooms with handsome cherrywood furnishings, sparkling tile floors, and ocean-view terraces. Extras in-

clude coffeemakers, microwaves, and hair dryers. The grounds are lushly landscaped, and the intimate resort has an enviable location on the widest, most secluded section of Eagle Beach. Work out in the open-air exercise pavilion and stay connected using the hotel's rare 24-hour access to the Internet. The resort also won an award in 2001 for being environmentally conscientious. ⊠ *L. G. Smith Blvd. 55-B, Eagle Beach,* ☎ *297/8–31100,* FAX *297/8–25272,* WEB *www.bucuti.com. 58 rooms, 5 suites. Restaurant, bar, grocery, fans, in-room safes, minibars, microwaves, refrigerators, cable TV, pool, beach, bicycles, shop, laundry facilities, business services, Internet, travel services. AE, D, DC, MC, V. CP, MAP.*

$$–$$$ ⊞ **Divi Aruba Beach Resort Mega All Inclusive.** At this Mediterranean-style resort, you have your choice of standard rooms, beachfront lanais, or casitas that overlook courtyards and are often only steps from the beach. The white-tile floors and mint and jade color schemes are soothing. Make your own daiquiri at the poolside Pelican Bar, where you can also enjoy pizza hot from the oven. In addition to the many on-site facilities, you can also use those at the adjacent Tamarijn Aruba. Despite the "mega all-inclusive" label, getting your laundry done, having your hair cut, or hiring a baby-sitter costs extra. ⊠ *L. G. Smith Blvd. 93, Manchebo Beach,* ☎ *297/8–23300 or 800/554–2008,* FAX *297/8–31940,* WEB *www.diviaruba.com. 203 rooms. 5 restaurants, 3 bars, fans, refrigerators, cable TV, tennis court, 2 pools, gym, hair salon, outdoor hot tub, beach, dive shop, snorkeling, windsurfing, boating, waterskiing, bicycles, shuffleboard, volleyball, shops, baby-sitting, laundry service, Internet. AE, D, DC, MC, V. All-inclusive.*

$$–$$$ ⊞ **Holiday Inn SunSpree Aruba Beach Resort & Casino.** Three seven-story buildings filled with spacious rooms are set apart from each other along a sugary, palm-dotted shore. The pool's cascades and sundeck draw as large a crowd as the wide beach, where you're invited to the Monday evening cocktail party. Enjoy live entertainment as you try your luck at the casino, or savor a beachfront meal at the Sea Breeze Grill. Get massaged and wrapped at the new Intermezzo Spa. At press time, plans were in the works to expand the fitness center—one of the final stages of a multimillion-dollar renovation that began at the turn of the millennium. The resort has a free club for kids ages 5 to 12. ⊠ *J. E. Irausquin Blvd. 230, Palm Beach,* ☎ *297/8–60236; 800/934–6750 direct to hotel,* FAX *297/8–60323,* WEB *www.holidayinn-aruba.com. 600 rooms, 15 suites. 3 restaurants, 3 bars, refrigerators, cable TV with movies, 4 tennis courts, 2 pools, gym, massage, beach, dive shop, dock, snorkeling, windsurfing, boating, waterskiing, basketball, Ping-Pong, volleyball, casino, video game room, shops, children's programs, concierge, Internet, meeting rooms. AE, DC, MC, V. All-inclusive, EP, FAP, MAP.*

$$ ⊞ **Allegro Aruba Resort & Casino.** Activity surrounds the cloverleaf-shape pool (with its waterfall and whirlpool tubs) at the heart of this resort. A popular place with tour groups, it has a buzzing atmosphere where you can enjoy everything from beer-drinking contests to bikini shows. The tropical-themed rooms have white-tile bathrooms that are snug and balconies that are narrow step-outs, but improvements include better air-conditioning. The Kids' Club, open from 9 to 5 daily, keeps children ages 4 to 12 busy with a wide range of activities. ⊠ *J. E. Irausquin Blvd. 83, Palm Beach,* ☎ *297/8–64500 or 800/447–7462,* FAX *297/8–63191,* WEB *www.allegroresorts.com. 403 rooms, 14 suites. 3 restaurants, 3 bars, in-room safes, cable TV with movies, 2 tennis courts, pool, gym, 2 outdoor hot tubs, beach, snorkeling, boating, waterskiing, basketball, Ping-Pong, volleyball, casino, dance club, shops, children's programs, Internet, meeting rooms. AE, D, DC, MC, V. All-inclusive.*

$$ 🖬 **Amsterdam Manor Beach Resort.** This mustard yellow hotel—all gables and turrets—looks like part of a Dutch colonial village. It's a cozy enclave surrounding a pool with a waterfall. Glorious Eagle Beach is just across the street. Rooms are furnished in either Dutch modern or provincial style and range from small studios—some with private balconies—to two-bedroom suites with peaked ceilings, full kitchens, and whirlpool tubs. Children under 12 stay free with their parents. Free diving lessons are available, and the hotel can arrange a variety of other activities. ✉ *J. E. Irausquin Blvd. 252, Eagle Beach,* ☎ *297/8–71492 or 800/932–6509,* ℻ *297/8–71463,* WEB *www.amsterdammanor.com. 70 units. Restaurant, bar, fans, in-room safes, kitchenettes, microwaves, cable TV with movies, pool, wading pool, snorkeling, playground, laundry facilities, Internet, car rental, some pets allowed. AE, DC, MC, V. CP, EP, MAP.*

$$ 🖬 **Bushiri Beach Resort.** A small, sandy cove that's a 20-minute walk from Oranjestad is the setting for this low-rise all-inclusive resort. There's plenty to do here, such as Papiamento language courses, arts-and-crafts classes, tennis clinics, scuba diving lessons, and nightly entertainment. One restaurant serves Italian fare; a more casual restaurant offers a breakfast buffet and lunch. Food, beverages, activities, airport transfers, and gratuities are included in the rate. ✉ *L. G. Smith Blvd. 35, Punta Brabo,* ☎ *297/8–25216,* ℻ *297/8–26789,* WEB *www. bushiri.com. 155 rooms. 2 restaurants, bar, fans, cable TV, 2 tennis courts, pool, wading pool, health club, 3 hot tubs, beach, dive shop, snorkeling, boating, 2 shops, video game room, baby-sitting, children's programs, laundry service, car rental, travel services. AE, D, DC, MC, V. All-inclusive.*

$$ 🖬 **Manchebo Beach Resort.** Set amid 100 acres of gardens, this resort feels away from it all. But it's just five minutes from town and right across from the Alhambra complex of shops, restaurants, and a casino. The international clientele appreciates a bargain (children under 12 stay free). Rooms are decorated with blond-wood furnishings and bright floral fabrics and equipped with amenities such as coffeemakers. Popular with diners from all over the island, the French Steakhouse is renowned for its *churrasco* (Argentine mixed grill). The chapel, on one of the prettiest stretches of Eagle Beach, is a charming spot for weddings. ✉ *J. E. Irausquin Blvd. 55, Eagle Beach,* ☎ *297/8–23444 or 800/528–1234,* ℻ *297/8–33667 or 297/8–32446,* WEB *aruba-manchebo.com. 71 rooms. 2 restaurants, 2 bars, snack bar, fans, in-room safes, refrigerators, cable TV, pool, beach, dive shop, snorkeling, shops, Internet, car rental. AE, D, DC, MC, V. EP, MAP.*

$$ 🖬 **Mill Resort & Suites.** With clean geometric lines, the architecture of this small resort is striking. The award-winning resort's whitewashed, red-roof buildings surround its open-air common areas. After a 2001 renovation, rooms are brighter and more attractive. Junior suites have a sitting area and kitchenette. Smaller studios have a full kitchen, a tiny bathroom, and no balcony. The beach is only a five-minute walk away; a morning coffee hour and a weekly scuba lesson are among the onsite amenities. At the Garden Café a special menu offers three courses at affordable prices. If you bring your pet you can board him overnight at the nearby vet. ✉ *J. E. Irausquin Blvd. 330, Oranjestad,* ☎ *297/ 8–67700,* ℻ *297/8–67271,* WEB *www.millresort.com. 64 studios, 128 suites. Restaurant, bar, grill, grocery, in-room safes, kitchenettes, microwaves, cable TV, 2 tennis courts, 2 pools, wading pool, gym, hair salon, massage, saunas, shops, laundry facilities, Internet, car rental, travel services, some pets. AE, D, DC, MC, V. EP.*

$ 🖬 **Vistalmar.** When Alby and Katy Yarzagary met at a Christmas party more than 20 years ago, they clicked. After they wed, they converted this property across the street from the fishing pier into a homey inn. Their hospitality infuses every part of the place. Simply furnished one-bedroom apartments each have a full kitchen, a living-dining room, and a sunny porch. The Yarzagarys provide snorkel gear and stock the refrigerator with breakfast fixings. There's no beach, but the sea is just across the street. One drawback is the distance from town, but you can ride the bus that departs from the hotel five times daily or rent a car. ⊠ *Bucutiweg 28, south of Oranjestad,* ☎ *297/8–28579,* ℻ *297/8–22200. 8 rooms. Kitchenettes, microwaves, cable TV with movies, laundry facilities, car rental. No credit cards. CP.*

Dining

Expect outstanding meals featuring cuisines from around the world. Although most resorts offer better-than-average dining, don't be afraid to try one of the many excellent, reasonably priced independent restaurants. Ask locals about their favorite spots; some of the lesser-known eateries offer food that's definitely worth sampling. Be sure to try such Aruban specialties as *pan bati* (a mildly sweet bread that resembles a pancake) and *keshi yena* (a baked concoction of Gouda cheese, spices, and meat or seafood in a rich brown sauce).

On Sunday you may have a hard time finding a restaurant outside a hotel that's open for lunch, and many restaurants are closed for dinner on Sunday or Monday. Reservations are essential for dinner in high season.

What to Wear

Even the finest restaurants require at most a jacket for men and a sundress for women. If you plan to eat in the open air, remember to bring along insect repellent—the mosquitoes sometimes get unruly.

CATEGORY	COST*
$$$$	over $30
$$$	$20–$30
$$	$10–$20
$	under $10

per person for a main course at dinner

ARGENTINE

$$–$$$ ✕ **El Gaucho Argentine Grill.** Faux-leather bound books, tulip-top lamps, wooden chairs, and tile floors decorate this Argentine steak house, which has been in business for more than 20 years. A bottle of rich red wine from the extensive cellar and the melt-in-your-mouth garlic bread will tantalize your taste buds as you await your meal. Main dishes include thick *churrasco* (Argentine steak) smothered in peppers and onions and served with corn on the cob, potatoes, and broccoli, or the catch of the day served with salad, rice, broccoli, and fried plantains. For dessert, go for the *helado argentino* (vanilla ice cream with sweet-potato marmalade and caramel) or the *torta de queso,* otherwise known as cheesecake. ⊠ *Wilhelminastraat 80, Oranjestad,* ☎ *297/8–23677. AE, D, MC, V. Closed Sun.*

ASIAN

$$–$$$ ✕ **Jakarta.** The abundant use of flavorful Indonesian spices brings this restaurant to life. The signature rijsttafel, which consists of 20 miniature meat, fish, vegetable, and fruit dishes, jumps off the page of the straw-faced, banana-leaf-covered menu. Another popular choice is Indonesian-style chicken soup, made with bean sprouts, hard-boiled eggs, and chicken liver. Vegetarians can order egg rolls, vegetable soup, or meat-free rijsttafel. Sample the java juice (blue Curaçao, vodka, Cointreau, banana liqueur, and orange and pineapple juice) at the bamboo bar on the back patio amid wind chimes, big clay pots, and tiki torches.

✉ *Wilhelminastraat 64, Oranjestad,* ☎ *297/8–38737. AE, D, DC, MC, V. Closed Tues.*

CARIBBEAN

$$–$$$ ✕ **Brisas del Mar.** Eating at this friendly place overlooking the sea (and
★ bus-accessible from hotels) is like dining in a private home. Old family recipes use such indigenous ingredients as the aromatic *yerbiholé*
leaf (with a minty basil flavor). Try the steamy fish soup, *keri keri* (shredded fish kissed with annatto), or some of the island's best pan bati.
The catch of the day cooked Aruban-style (panfried and covered with
creole sauce, or in garlic butter on request) has drawn a crowd for more
than 20 years. Reserve early for sunset gazing on the breezy terrace.
✉ *Savaneta 222A, Savaneta,* ☎ *297/8–47718. AE, D, MC, V, D.
Closed Mon.*

$$–$$$ ✕ **Gasparito Restaurant & Art Gallery.** You'll find this enchanting
★ hideaway in a *cunucu* (country house) in Noord, not far from the hotels. The works of local artists are showcased on its softly lit walls. The
Aruban specialties—pan bati, keshi yena, fish croquettes, conch stew—
are feasts for the eye as well as the palate. The standout dish is the Gasparito chicken; the sauce was passed down from the owner's ancestors
and features seven special ingredients including brandy, white wine,
and pineapple juice. (The rest, they say, are secret.). The service is excellent. ✉ *Gasparito 3, Noord,* ☎ *297/8–67044. AE, D, MC, V.
Closed Sun. No lunch.*

CONTEMPORARY

$$–$$$ ✕ **L'Escale.** You're missing out if you don't have at least one meal in
this upscale eatery, rated the island's best restaurant in 2001. Sip wine
as you gaze over bustling L. G. Smith Boulevard and watch the cruise
ships depart. Start with the sautéed baby snails, then move on to
Caribbean-style walnut-crusted snapper. For dessert try the rich chocolate soufflé. Sparkles and streamers decorate your table for a special
occasion, and the extensive cigar list can turn any night into a celebration. If time is short, opt for the pre-theater menu. ✉ *Aruba Sonesta Resort, L. G. Smith Blvd. 82, Oranjestad,* ☎ *297/8–36000.
Reservations essential. AE, D, MC, V. No lunch.*

CONTINENTAL

$$$ ✕ **Chez Mathilde.** This elegant restaurant occupies one of Aruba's last
★ surviving 19th-century houses. Ask to sit in the greenhouse atrium, which
some say has the ambience of Paris. The outstanding French-style
menu is constantly re-created by the Dutch chef, who has a deft touch
with sauces. Feast on baked escargots, roasted breast of duck with
tamarind sauce, ostrich fillet, or quail stuffed with calf's sweetbreads
in a bell pepper sauce. Crêpes suzette and chocolate layer cake with
ponche crema (Venezuelan brandied eggnog) sauce will also win you
over, as you listen to the tinkling ivories. ✉ *Havenstraat 23, Oran-
jestad,* ☎ *297/8–34968. Reservations essential. AE, DC, MC, V. No
lunch Sun.*

$$–$$$ ✕ **Le Dôme.** Belgian Peter Ballière and his partners imported 11,000
★ bricks from Antwerp to authenticate the Continental interior of this
fine dining spot. The service is polished, the decor is sumptuous, and
a local harpist and guitarist add considerable ambience. The Belgian
endive soup is delicious; the tournedos Rossini (prime-cut beef in a port
sauce with a goose-liver mousse), downright decadent. A seven-course
set menu is also available. Try one of the eight imported Belgian beers
or one of the wine list's 65 varieties. Savor champagne and a cup of
coffee with the prix-fixe Sunday brunch. Change for dinner, as shorts
are a no-no. ✉ *J. E. Irausquin Blvd. 224, Eagle Beach,* ☎ *297/8–71517.
Reservations essential. AE, D, DC, MC, V. Closed Mon. and Sept.*

ECLECTIC

$$–$$$ ✕ **Papiamento.** Longtime restaurateurs Lenie and Eduardo Ellis con-
★ verted their 130-year-old home into a bistro with an atmosphere that
is elegant, intimate, and always romantic. You can feast sumptuously
indoors surrounded by antiques or outdoors in a patio garden. The chefs
mix Continental and Caribbean cuisines to produce favorites that include seafood and meat dishes. You can't go wrong by sharing the "clay
pot" seafood medley for two. ⊠ *Washington 61, Noord,* ☎ *297/8–
64544. Reservations essential. AE, D, MC, V. No lunch. Closed Mon.*

$$–$$$ ✕ **Ventanas del Mar.** Floor-to-ceiling windows provide an ample view
across a golf course and beyond to rolling sand dunes and the sea off
the island's western tip. Dining on the intimate terrace amid flicker-
ing candles is especially romantic. Sandwiches, salads, conch fritters,
nachos, and quesadillas fill the midday menu; at night the emphasis is
on seafood and meat. Sea bass in orange sauce and the crab and corn
chowder are specialties. This restaurant participates in the AGA dine-
around program. ⊠ *Tierra del Sol Golf Course, Malmokweg,* ☎ *297/
8–67800. AE, D, DC, MC, V. Closed Mon. Apr.–Nov.*

$–$$ ✕ **Buccaneer.** Imagine you're in a sunken ship where sharks, barracu-
das, and groupers swim past the portholes. That's what you'll find at
Buccaneer, a restaurant with a fantastic 7,500-gallon saltwater aquarium. The chefs prepare surf-and-turf fare with European élan. Head
to this old stone building flanked by heavy black chains early (around
5:45 PM) to snag a booth beside the aquarium and order the catch of
the day, shrimp with Pernod, or smoked pork cutlets with sausage,
sauerkraut, and potatoes. The restaurant participates in the AGA's dine-
around program. ⊠ *Gasparito 11-C, Noord,* ☎ *297/8–66172. AE, MC,
V. No lunch. Closed Sun.*

$–$$ ✕ **Charlie's Restaurant & Bar.** Charlie's has been a San Nicolas hang-
out for more than 50 years. The walls and ceiling are *covered* with license plates, hard hats, sombreros, life preservers, baseball pennants,
intimate apparel—you name it. The draw here is the nonstop party atmosphere—somewhere between a frat house and a beach bar. Decent but
somewhat overpriced specialties are tenderloin and "shrimps jumbo
and dumbo" (dumb because they were caught). And don't leave before sampling Charlie's "honeymoon sauce" (so called because it's really
hot). ⊠ *Zeppenfeldstraat 56, San Nicolas,* ☎ *297/8–45086. AE, D,
MC, V. Closed Sun.*

ITALIAN

$$–$$$ ✕ **Tuscany.** Two chefs at this casually elegant restaurant won awards
in the Caribbean Culinary Competition, and when you sample the food
you'll know why. The *spannochie prima donna con capellini d'angelo*
(sautéed shrimp with prosciutto, shallots, wild mushrooms, and arti-
chokes in a light grappa cream sauce on angel hair pasta) is a delight.
Don't despair if the extensive menu doesn't feature your particular
fancy—the kitchen may be up for a challenge. The personalized service, excellent wine list, and soft piano music make for a special
evening. ⊠ *Aruba Marriott Resort & Stellaris Casino, L. G. Smith Blvd.
101, Palm Beach,* ☎ *297/8–69000. Reservations essential. AE, DC,
MC, V. No lunch.*

$$–$$$ ✕ **Hostaria Da' Vittorio.** Part of the fun at this family-oriented lunch
and dinner spot is watching chef Vittorio Muscariello prepare regional
specialties in the open kitchen. Rising above the decibel level of the
crowd, the staff helps you choose wines from the extensive list and share-
able portions of hot and cold antipasti, risottos, and pastas. Try the
branzino al sale (sea bass baked in a hard salt shell). Exciting presentations and warm service reflect the management's stated desire to honor
the essence of Italy: "ancient, but always young." As you leave, pick

up some limoncello liqueur or olive oil at the door. A 15% gratuity is automatically added to your bill. ☒ *L. G. Smith Blvd. 380, Palm Beach,* ☎ *297/8–63838. AE, MC, V.*

Beaches

Beaches in Aruba are legendary: white sand, turquoise waters, and virtually no litter—everyone takes the NO TIRA SUSHI (NO LITTERING) signs very seriously, especially with a $280 fine. The major beaches, which back up to the hotels along the southwestern strip, are public and crowded. You can make the hour-long hike from the Holiday Inn to the Tamarijn without ever leaving sand. Make sure you're well protected from the sun—it scorches fast despite the cooling trade winds. Luckily, there's at least one covered bar (and often an ice cream stand) at virtually every hotel. If you stroll at night, you can hotel-hop for dinner, dancing, gambling, and late-night entertainment. On the northeastern side, wind makes the waters too choppy for swimming, but the vistas are great, and the terrain is wonderful for exploring.

Baby Beach. On the island's eastern tip, this semicircular beach borders a bay that's as placid and just about as deep as a wading pool—perfect for tots and terrible swimmers. Thatched shaded areas are good for cooling off. Just down the road is the island's rather unusual pet cemetery. You may see some shore divers here. Stop by the nearby snack truck for chicken legs, burgers, hot dogs, beer, and soda.

Boca Grandi. Strong swimming skills are a must near Seagrape Grove and the Aruba Golf Club toward the island's eastern tip.

Boca Prins. You'll need a four-wheel-drive vehicle to make the trek here. Near the Fontein Cave and Blue Lagoon, this beach is about as large as a Brazilian bikini, but with two rocky cliffs and tumultuously crashing waves, it's as romantic as you get in Aruba. Boca Prins is famous for its backdrop of enormous vanilla sand dunes. This isn't a swimming beach, however. Bring a picnic, a beach blanket, and sturdy sneakers, and descend the rocks that form steps to the water's edge.

Eagle Beach. On the southwestern coast, across the highway from what is known as Time-Share Lane beach, which is more than a mile long, has been designated one of the 10 best in the world by *Travel & Leisure* magazine.

Fisherman's Hut. Next to the Holiday Inn is a windsurfer's haven. Swimming conditions are good, too. Take a picnic lunch (tables are available) and watch the elegant purple, aqua, and orange sails struggle in the wind.

Grapefield Beach. To the southeast of San Nicolas, a sweep of blinding white sand in the shadow of cliffs and boulders is marked by a statue of an anchor dedicated to all seamen. Pick sea grapes in high season (January–June). Swim at your own risk; the waves here can be rough.

Malmok Beach. On the northwestern shore, this small, nondescript beach (where some of Aruba's wealthiest families have built tony residences) borders shallow waters that stretch 300 yards from shore. It's the perfect place to learn to windsurf. Right off the coast here is a favorite haunt for divers and snorkelers—the wreck of the German ship *Antilla,* scuttled in 1940.

Manchebo Beach (Punta Brabo). Impressively wide, the shoreline in front of the Manchebo Beach Resort, is where officials turn a blind eye to the occasional top-free sunbathers.

Palm Beach. The center of Aruban tourism offers the best in swimming, sailing, and other water sports. It runs from the Wyndham Aruba Beach Resort to the Aruba Marriott Resort.

Rodger's Beach. Next to Baby Beach on the island's eastern tip, the beautiful curve of sand is only slightly marred by the view of the oil refinery at the far side of the bay. Swimming conditions are excellent, and there's live entertainment at the water's edge.

Outdoor Activities and Sports

On Aruba you can participate in every conceivable water sport as well as play tennis and golf or go on a fine hike through Arikok National Park. An up-and-coming sport popular with locals is bouldering. It's similar to mountain climbing and rappelling, only up and down the boulders of the Ayo rock formations or the eastern cliffs, which are more porous and can be dangerous. The Hyatt Regency Aruba Beach Resort & Casino can make arrangements for large groups to be guided, by sergeants of the Royal Dutch Marines, no less.

BIKING

Pedal pushing is a great way to get around the island; the climate is perfect, and the trade winds help to keep you cool. **Pablito's Bike Rental** (⊠ L. G. Smith Blvd. 234, Oranjestad, ☎ 297/8–78655) rents mountain bikes for about $15 per day.

FISHING

With catches including barracuda, kingfish, bonito, and black and yellow tuna, deep-sea fishing is great sport on Aruba. Many charter boats are available for half- or full-day sails. Prices range from $220 to $320 for a half-day charter and from $400 to $600 for a full day.

De Palm Tours (⊠ L. G. Smith Blvd. 142, Oranjestad, ☎ 297/8–24400 or 800/766–6016, WEB www.depalm.com) runs deep-sea fishing tours seven days a week. **Pelican Tours & Watersports** (⊠ J. E. Irausquin Blvd. 232, Palm Beach, ☎ 297/8–72302, WEB www.pelican-aruba.com) is not just for the surf and snorkel crowd; the company will help you catch one that didn't get away. **Red Sail Sports** (⊠ J. E. Irausquin Blvd. 83, Oranjestad, ☎ 297/8–61603 or 877/733–7245 in the U.S., WEB www.aruba-redsail.com) will arrange everything for your fishing trip.

GOLF

Aruba Golf Club (⊠ Golfweg 82, near San Nicolas, ☎ 297/8–42006) has a 9-hole course with 20 sand traps and five water traps, roaming goats, and lots of cacti. There are 11 greens covered with artificial turf, making 18-hole tournaments a possibility. The clubhouse has a bar and locker rooms. Greens fees are $10 for nine holes, $15 for 18 holes. Golf carts are available.

Tierra del Sol (⊠ Malmokweg, ☎ 297/8–60978) is on the northwest coast near the California Lighthouse. Designed by Robert Trent Jones Jr., this 18-hole championship course combines Aruba's native beauty—cacti and rock formations—with the lush greens of the world's best courses. The $130 greens fee includes a golf cart equipped with a communications system that allows you to order drinks that will be ready upon your return. Half-day golf clinics, a bargain at $45, include lunch in the clubhouse. The pro shop is one of the Caribbean's most elegant, with an extremely attentive staff.

Aruba Golf & Leisure (⊠ J. E. Irausquin Blvd. 326, Oranjestad, ☎ 297/8–64589) is the site of a 300-yard driving range, an 18-hole putting green, and a chipping area. Pay $3.50 for a basket of 35 balls and $10 for a half-set of rental clubs. It's open from 7:30 AM to 11 PM daily.

HIKING

Hiking in **Arikok National Wildlife Park** is generally not too strenuous, although you should exercise caution with the strong sun—bring plenty of water and wear sunscreen and a sun hat or visor. Sturdy, cleated shoes are a must to grip the granular, occasionally steep terrain. There are more than 20 mi (34 km) of trails, and it's important to stick to them. Look for different colors on signs to determine the degree of difficulty. The park is crowned by Aruba's second-highest mountain, the 577-ft (176-m) Mt. Arikok, so climbing is also a possibility.

De Palm Tours (⊠ L. G. Smith Blvd. 142, Oranjestad, ☎ 297/8–24400 or 800/766–6016, WEB www.depalm.com) offers a guided three-hour trip to sites of unusual natural beauty that are accessible only on foot. The fee is $25 per person, including refreshments and transportation.

HORSEBACK RIDING

Four ranches offer short jaunts along the beach or longer trail rides through countryside flanked by cacti, divi-divi trees, and aloe vera plants. Ask if you can stop off at Conchi, a natural pool that's reputed to have restorative powers. Rides are also possible in the Arikok National Wildlife Park. Rates run from $25 for an hour-long trip to $65 for a 3½-hour tour. Private rides cost slightly more.

Rancho el Paso (⊠ Washington 44, ☎ 297/8–73310 or 297/8–67165, WEB ranchoelpaso.bizland.com) has seasoned guides that show you Malmok's beautiful beach and the surrounding countryside. Tours, costing $45 per person, head out daily at 9 AM. **Rancho del Campo** (⊠ Sombre 22E, Santa Cruz, ☎ 297/8–50290, WEB www.ranchodelcampo.com), the first to offer rides to the Natural Pool almost 11 years ago, offers that excursion for $50 per person. **Rancho Daimari** (⊠ Plantage Daimari, ☎ 297/8–60239, WEB www.visitaruba.com/ranchodaimari) will lead your horse to water—either at Natural Bridge or Natural Pool—in the morning or afternoon for $55 per person. **Rancho Notorious** (⊠ Boroncana, Noord, ☎ 297/8–60508, WEB www.ranchonotorious.com) will take you to the beach to snorkel for $55, on a tour of the countryside for $50, or on a three-hour ride up to the California Lighthouse for $65.

KAYAKING

Kayaking is a popular sport on Aruba's calm waters. Every day except Sunday, **De Palm Tours** (⊠ L. G. Smith Blvd. 142, Oranjestad, ☎ 297/8–24400 or 800/766–6016, WEB www.depalm.com) offers a four-hour guided kayaking tour that also includes some snorkeling. The cost, including lunch, is $65.

SCUBA DIVING AND SNORKELING

With visibility of up to 90 ft (27 m), Aruban waters are excellent for snorkeling and diving. Certified divers can go wall or reef diving or explore wrecks sunk during World War II. All sites have several varieties of coral, fish ranging in size from grunts to groupers, sensuously waving sea fans, giant sponge tubes, gliding manta rays, sea turtles, lobsters, octopuses, and green moray eels.

Expect snorkel gear to rent for about $15 per day and trips to cost around $40. Scuba rates are around $50 for a one-tank reef or wreck dive, $65 for a two-tank dive, and $45 for a night dive. Resort courses, which offer an introduction to scuba diving, average $65 to $70. If you want to go all the way, complete open-water certification costs around $300.

The more seasoned diving crowd might check with **Aruba Pro Dive** (⊠ Ponton 88, Noord, ☎ 297/8–25520, WEB www.arubaprodive.com) for special deals. **Dax Divers** (⊠ Kibaima 7, Santa Cruz, ☎ 297/8–51270) is the operator that boasts an instructor training course. Some dives are less expensive, at $35 for 40 minutes with one tank. **De Palm Tours** (⊠ L. G. Smith Blvd. 142, Oranjestad, ☎ 297/8–24400 or 800/766–6016) is one of the best options for your undersea experience. Don a helmet and walk along the ocean floor near De Palm Island, home of huge blue parrot fish. Have your picture taken at an underwater table loaded with champagne and roses. Try Snuba—like scuba diving but without the heavy air tanks—either from a boat or from an island. Rates are $79 to $99, including meals. **Dive Aruba** (✉ Williamstraat 8, Oranjestad, ☎ 297/8–25216, WEB www.divearuba.com) offers resort courses, certification courses, and dives to interesting shipwrecks. **Mermaid Sport Divers** (✉ Manchebo Beach Resort, J. E. Irausquin Blvd. 55A, Eagle Beach, ☎ 297/8–35546, WEB www.scubadivers-aruba.com) offers full dive packages with PADI-certified instructors.

Native Divers Aruba (✉ Koyari 1, Noord, ☎ 297/8–64763, WEB www.nativedivers.com) offers all types of dives. Courses in specialties such as underwater naturalist are taught by PADI-certified instructors.At **Pelican Tours & Watersports** (✉ J. E. Irausquin Blvd. 232, Palm Beach, ☎ 297/8–72302, WEB www.pelican-aruba.com) there are options for divers of all levels. Novices start with mid-morning classes and then move to the pool to practice what they've learned; by afternoon they put their new skills to use at a shipwreck off the coast. **Red Sail Sports** (✉ J. E. Irausquin Blvd. 83, Oranjestad, ☎ 297/8–61603; 877/733–7245 in the U.S., WEB www.aruba-redsail.com) has courses for children and others new to scuba diving. An introductory class costs about $80. **Unique Sports of Aruba** (✉ L. G. Smith Blvd. 79, Oranjestad, ☎ 297/8–60096 or 297/8–63900, WEB www.visitaruba.com/uniquesports) lives up to its name, providing dive master, rescue, and certification courses.

TENNIS

Aruba's winds make tennis a challenge even if you have the best of backhands. Although visitors can make arrangements to play at the resorts, priority goes to guests. Some private tennis clubs can also accommodate you. Try the world-class facilities at the **Aruba Racquet Club** (✉ Rooisanto 21, Palm Beach, ☎ 297/8–60215). Host to a variety of international tournaments, the club has eight courts (six lighted), as well as a swimming pool, an aerobics center, and a restaurant. Fees are $10 per hour; a lesson with a pro costs $20 for a half hour, $35 for one hour.

WINDSURFING

The southwestern coast's tranquil waters make it ideal for both beginners and intermediates, as the winds are steady but sudden gusts rare. Experts will find the Atlantic coast, especially around Grapefield and Boca Grandi beaches, more challenging; winds are fierce and often shift course without warning. Most operators also offer complete windsurfing vacation packages.

Fisherman's Huts Windsurf Center (✉ Aruba Marriott Resort, L. G. Smith Blvd. 101, Palm Beach, ☎ 297/8–69898) is a popular spot among wanna-be and expert windsurfers alike. **Pelican Tours & Watersports** (✉ J. E. Irausquin Blvd. 232, Palm Beach, ☎ 297/8–72302, WEB www.pelican-aruba.com) usually has boards and sails on hand. **Roger's Windsurf Place** (✉ L. G. Smith Blvd. 472, Malmok Beach, ☎ 297/8–61918, WEB www.rogerswindsurf.com) is located where the winds carry fastest over calmer waters.The day will fly by when you windsurf with **Sailboard Vacations** (✉ L. G. Smith Blvd. 462, Malmok Beach, ☎ 297/8–61072, WEB www.sailboardvacations.com).Trade jokes and snap photos with your fellow windsurfers at **Vela Aruba** (✉ Palm Beach, ☎ 297/8–69000 Ext. 6430, WEB www.velawindsurf.com). This is *the* place to make friends on the water.

Shopping

"Duty free" *is* a magical term here. Major credit cards are welcome virtually everywhere, U.S. dollars are accepted almost as readily as local currency, and traveler's checks can be cashed with proof of identity.

Aruba's souvenir and crafts stores are full of Dutch porcelains and figurines, as befits the island's heritage. Dutch cheese is a good buy
(you're allowed to bring up to 10 pounds of hard cheese through U.S.
customs), as are hand-embroidered linens and any products made
from the native aloe vera plant—sunburn cream, face masks, skin re-
freshers. Local arts and crafts run toward wood carvings and earthenware emblazoned with ARUBA: ONE HAPPY ISLAND and the like. Since
there's no sales tax, the price you see on the tag is what you pay. (Note
that although large stores in town and at hotels are duty free, in tiny
shops and studios, you may have to pay the value-added tax of 6.5%.)
Don't try to bargain. Arubans consider it rude to haggle, despite what
you may hear to the contrary.

Areas and Malls

Oranjestad's **Caya G. F. Betico Croes** is Aruba's chief shopping street,
lined with several duty-free boutiques and jewelry stores noted for the
aggressiveness of their vendors on cruise-ship days.

For late-night shopping, head to the **Alhambra Casino Shopping Arcade**
(⊠ L. G. Smith Blvd. 47, ☎ 297/8–35000), open 5 PM–11 PM. Souvenir
shops, art boutiques, and fast-food outlets fill the arcade, which is attached to the busy casino. The **Aquarius Mall** (⊠ Elleboogstraat 1) is a
small but relatively upscale shopping center. The **Holland Aruba Mall**
(⊠ Havenstraat 6) houses a collection of smart shops and eateries.

Port of Call Marketplace (⊠ L. G. Smith Blvd. 17, ☎ 297/8–36706)
sells fine jewelry, perfumes, duty-free liquors, batik, crystal, leather goods,
and fashionable clothing. At **Royal Plaza Mall** (⊠ L. G. Smith Blvd.
94), across from the cruise-ship terminal, you'll find cafés, a post office branch (open Monday–Saturday 7 AM–6:45 PM), and such stores
as Nautica, Benetton, Tommy Hilfiger, and Gandelman Jewelers.
There's also the Internet Café, where you can send e-mail home and
get your caffeine fix all in one stop. **Seaport Village Mall** (⊠ L. G. Smith
Blvd. 82, across from harbor, ☎ 297/8–36000) is five minutes from
the cruise-ship terminal. It includes the Crystal Casino and more than
120 stores, with merchandise to meet every taste and budget.

Specialty Items

CLOTHES

Confetti (⊠ Seaport Village Mall, L. G. Smith Blvd. 82, Oranjestad,
☎ 297/8–38614) has the hottest European and American swimsuits,
cover-ups, and other beach essentials.

J. L. Penha & Sons (⊠ Caya G. F. Betico Croes 11/13, Oranjestad, ☎
297/8–24160), a venerated name in Aruba, sells perfumes and cosmetics.
It stocks such brands as Boucheron, Swiss Army, Dior, Cartier, and
Givenchy. **Wulfsen & Wulfsen** (⊠ Caya G. F. Betico Croes 52, Oranjestad, ☎ 297/8–23823) has been one of the most highly regarded clothing stores in the Netherlands Antilles for three decades.

DUTY-FREE GOODS

For perfumes, cosmetics, men's and women's clothing, and leather goods,
stop in at **Aruba Trading Company** (⊠ Caya G. F. Betico Croes 12, Oranjestad, ☎ 297/8–22602), which has been in business more than 70 years.
Little Switzerland (⊠ Caya G. F. Betico Croes 14, Oranjestad, ☎ 297/
8–21192; Royal Plaza Mall, L. G. Smith Blvd. 94, Oranjestad, ☎ 297/
8–34057) is the place to go for china, crystal, and fine tableware.
You'll also find good buys on Omega and Rado watches, Swarovski
and Baccarat crystal, and Lladro figurines. At **Weitnauer** (⊠ Caya G.
F. Betico Croes 29, Oranjestad, ☎ 297/8–22790) you'll find a wide
range of fragrances.

HANDICRAFTS

Art and Tradition Handicrafts (✉ Caya G. F. Betico Croes 30, Oranjestad, ☎ 297/8–36534; Royal Plaza Mall, L. G. Smith Blvd. 94, Oranjestad, ☎ 297/8–27862) sells intriguing items that look hand-painted. Buds from the *mopa mopa* tree are boiled to form a resin colored by vegetable dyes. Artists then stretch the resin by hand and mouth. Tiny pieces are cut and layered to form intricate designs—truly unusual gifts.

The **Artistic Boutique** (✉ Caya G. F. Betico Croes 25, Oranjestad, ☎ 297/8–23142; Wyndham Aruba Beach Resort and Casino, J. E. Irausquin Blvd. 77, ☎ 297/8–64466 Ext. 3508; Seaport Village Mall, L. G. Smith Blvd. 82, Oranjestad, ☎ 297/8–32567; Holiday Inn Aruba Beach Resort & Casino, J. E. Irausquin Blvd. 230, ☎ 297/8–33383) has been in business for 30 years. It's known for its Giuseppe Armani figurines from Italy, usually sold at a 20% discount; Aruban hand-embroidered linens; gold and silver jewelry; and porcelain and pottery from Spain.

Creative Hands (✉ Socotorolaan 5, Oranjestad, ☎ 297/8–35665) sells porcelain and ceramic miniatures of *cunucu* (country) houses and divi-divi trees, but the store's real draw is its exquisite Japanese dolls.

JEWELRY

In business for more than 25 years, **Boolchand's** (✉ Seaport Village Mall, L. G. Smith Blvd. 82, Oranjestad, ☎ 297/8–30147) sells jewelry and watches. It also fills its 6,000-square-ft space with leather goods, cameras, and electronics. If green fire is your passion, **Colombian Emeralds** (✉ Seaport Village Mall, L. G. Smith Blvd. 82, Oranjestad, ☎ 297/8–36238) has a dazzling array of emeralds. There's also a fine array of watches by Breitling, Baume & Mercier, Jaeger-Le Coultre, Ebel, Seiko, Citizen, and Tissot. **Gandelman Jewelers** (✉ Royal Plaza Mall, L. G. Smith Blvd. 94, Oranjestad, ☎ 297/8–34433) sells Gucci and Rolex watches at reasonable prices, as well as gold bracelets, and a full line of Lladro figurines. **Kenro Jewelers** (✉ Seaport Village Mall, L. G. Smith Blvd. 82, Oranjestad, ☎ 297/8–34847 or 297/8–33171) has two stores in the same mall, attesting to the popularity of its stock of bracelets and necklaces from the Ramon Leopard collection; jewelry by Arando, Micheletto, and Blumei; and various brands of watches.

Nightlife and the Arts

Nightlife

Unlike on many islands, nightlife isn't confined to the touristic folkloric shows at the hotels. Arubans like to party, and the more the merrier. They usually start celebrating late; the action doesn't pick up 'til around midnight. One uniquely Aruban institution is a psychedelically painted '57 Chevy bus called the **Kukoo Kunuku** (☎ 297/8–62010). Weeknights you'll find as many as 40 passengers traveling between six bars from sundown to around midnight. The $55 fee per passenger includes dinner, drinks, and picking you up (and pouring you off) at your hotel.

BARS

At **Carlos & Charlie's** (✉ Weststraat 3A, Oranjestad, ☎ 297/8–20355), you'll find Mexican fare; American music from the '60s, '70s, and '80s; and a mike-toting emcee. In business since 1948, **Cheta's Bar** (✉ Paradera 119, Paradera, ☎ 297/8–23689) is a local joint that holds no more than four customers at a time. There aren't any bar stools, either, which is why most patrons gather out front.

Iguana Joe's (✉ Royal Plaza Mall, L. G. Smith Blvd. 94, Oranjestad, ☎ 297/8–39373) has a creative reptilian-theme decor and a color scheme featuring such planter's-punch colors as lime and grape. With parrots painted on the ceiling, **Mambo Jambo** (✉ Royal Plaza Mall,

2nd floor, L. G. Smith Blvd. 94, Oranjestad, ☏ 297/8–33632) is daubed in sunset colors. Sip one of the special libations sold nowhere else. With front-row seats to view the green flash—that ray of light that flicks through the sky as the sun sinks into the ocean—the **Palms Bar** (✉ Hyatt Regency Aruba Beach Resort & Casino, J. E. Irausquin Blvd. 85, Palm Beach, ☏ 297/8–61234) is the perfect spot to enjoy the sunset.

CASINOS

Aruban casinos offer something for both high rollers and low-stakes types, as well as live, nightly entertainment in their lounges. Diehard gamblers might look for the largest or the most active casinos, but many simply visit the casino closest to their hotel.

In the casual **Alhambra Casino** (✉ L. G. Smith Blvd. 47, Oranjestad, ☏ 297/8–35000 Ext. 480/482), a "Moorish slave" named Roger gives every gambler a hearty handshake upon entering. Smart money is on the Wyndham's **Casablanca Casino** (✉ J. E. Irausquin Blvd. 77, Palm Beach, ☏ 297/8–64466). It's quietly elegant and has a Bogart theme. The **Centurion Casino** (✉ J. E. Irausquin Blvd. 79, Palm Beach, ☏ 297/8–63900 Ext. 149) at the Aruba Grand Beach Resort is decorated with musical instruments. It opens at 10 AM for slots, 6 PM for all games. The Hyatt Regency's ultramodern **Copacabana Casino** (✉ J. E. Irausquin Blvd. 85, Palm Beach, ☏ 297/8–61234) is an enormous complex with a Carnival in Rio theme and live entertainment. The Aruba Sonesta's **Crystal Casino** (✉ L. G. Smith Blvd. 82, Oranjestad, ☏ 297/8–36000) is open 24 hours. The **Excelsior Casino** (✉ J. E. Irausquin Blvd. 230, Palm Beach, ☏ 297/8–67777) has sports betting in addition to the usual slots and table games.

Overhead at the **Radisson Aruba Resort & Casino** (✉ J. E. Irausquin Blvd. 81, Palm Beach, ☏ 297/8–64045), thousands of lights simulate shooting stars that seem destined to carry out your wishes for riches. The slots here open at 10 AM, and table action begins at 4 PM. The **Royal Cabana Casino** (✉ J. E. Irausquin Blvd. 250, ☏ 297/8–77000) is the largest in the Caribbean. It has an expansive, sleek interior, 400 slot machines, no-smoking gaming tables and slot room, and the Tropicana nightclub. In the Allegro Aruba Resort & Casino, the **Royal Palm Casino** (✉ J. E. Irausquin Blvd. 250, Eagle Beach, ☏ 297/8–74665) opens daily at noon for slots, 5 PM for all games. Low-key gambling can be found at the waterside **Seaport Casino** (✉ L. G. Smith Blvd. 9, Oranjestad, ☏ 297/8–35027 Ext. 4212). The Aruba Marriott Resort's **Stellaris Casino** (✉ L. G. Smith Blvd. 101, Palm Beach, ☏ 297/8–69000) is one of the island's most popular.

DANCE AND MUSIC CLUBS

At **Café Bahia** (✉ Weststraat 7, Oranjestad, ☏ 297/8–89982) an elegant spiral staircase leads up to a bar and dance floor backed by a mural of colorful cacti against a cloud-smattered Aruban sky. Locals and tourists drink cocktails and sashay to salsa music provided by island bands. Live bands perform at the **Cellar** (✉ Klipstraat 2, Oranjestad, ☏ 297/8–26490) on weekends. The music might be blues, jazz, funk, reggae, or rock. Bartenders in hard hats serve up drinks at the exotic **E-Zone** (✉ Bayside Mall, Westraat 5, Oranjestad, ☏ 297/8–87474) where the walls are decorated with hair-dryer tubes and other oddities. The huge stainless-steel dance floor doesn't fill up 'til after 1 AM.

For jazz and other types of music, try **Garufa Cigar & Cocktail Lounge** (✉ Wilhelminastraat 63, Oranjestad, ☏ 297/8–27205). Stop by for a drink before dining at the nearby El Gaucho Argentine Grill. The laid-back atmosphere may draw you back for an after-dinner cognac. Stop by the cozy **Sirocco Lounge** (✉ Wyndham Aruba Beach Resort &

Casino, L. G. Smith Blvd. 77, Palm Beach, ☎ 297/8–64466) for jazz performances Thursday through Saturday.

The Arts

At **Galeria Eterno** (✉ *Emanstraat 92, Oranjestad,* ☎ 297/8–39607) you'll find local and international artists at work. Be sure to stop by for concerts by classical guitarists, dance performances, visual-arts shows, and plays. **Galeria Harmonia** (✉ Zeppenfeldstraat 10, San Nicolas, ☎ 297/8–42969), the island's largest exhibition space, has a permanent collection of works by local and international artists. **Gasparito Restaurant and Art Gallery** (✉ Gasparito 3, Noord, ☎ 297/8–67044) features an ongoing exhibition of Aruban artists.

ISLAND CULTURE

The **Bon Bini Festival,** a year-round folkloric event, is held every Tuesday from 6:30 PM to 8:30 PM at the historic Fort Zoutman in Oranjestad. Stop by to check out the local arts and crafts, food, drink, music, and dance. The entrance fee is $3. At the **Watapana Food & Art Festival,** listen to live music, enjoy local art, and indulge in authentic Aruban foods and beverages at the festival grounds between the Hyatt Regency Aruba Beach Resort & Casino and the Allegro Aruba Beach Resort & Casino. Held from April to October, the event takes place every Wednesday from 6 PM to 8 PM. Admission is free.

Exploring Aruba

Aruba's wildly sculpted landscape is replete with rocky deserts, cactus clusters, secluded coves, blue vistas, and the trademark divi-divi tree. To see the island's wild, untamed beauty, you can rent a car, take a sightseeing tour, or hire a cab for $30 an hour (for up to four people). The main highways are well paved, but on the windward side (the north- and east-facing side) some roads are still a mixture of compacted dirt and stones. Although a car is fine, a four-wheel-drive vehicle will allow you to explore the unpaved interior.

Traffic is sparse, but signs leading to sights are often small and hand-lettered (this is slowly changing as the government puts up official road signs), so watch closely. Route 1A travels southbound along the western coast, and 1B is simply northbound along the same road. If you lose your way, just follow the divi-divi trees.

Numbers in the margin correspond to points of interest on the Aruba map.

SIGHTS TO SEE

❼ **Alto Vista Chapel.** Alone near the island's northwest corner sits the scenic little Alto Vista Chapel. The wind whistles through the simple mustard-color walls, eerie boulders, and looming cacti. Along the side of the road back to civilization are miniature crosses with depictions of the stations of the cross and hand-lettered signs exhorting PRAY FOR US, SINNERS and the like—a simple yet powerful evocation of faith. To get here, follow the rough, winding dirt road that loops around the island's northern tip, or, from the hotel strip, take Palm Beach Road through three intersections and watch for the asphalt road to the left just past the Alto Vista Rum Shop.

❹ **Arikok National Wildlife Park.** Nearly 20% of Aruba has been designated part of this national park, which sprawls across the eastern interior and the northeast coast. The park is the keystone of the government's long-term ecotourism plan to preserve resources, and showcases the island's flora and fauna as well as ancient Arawak petroglyphs, the ruins of a gold mining operation at Miralmar, and the remnants of Dutch peasant settlements at Masiduri. At the park's main entrance, Arikok Center houses offices, rest rooms, and food facilities. All visitors must stop here upon entering so that officials can manage the traffic flow and hand out information on park rules and features. Within the confines of the park is Mt. Arikok, as well as the 620-ft (188-m) Mt. Yamanota, Aruba's highest peak.

Anyone looking for geological exotica should head for the park's caves, found on the northeastern coast. Baranca Sunu, the so-called Tunnel of Love, has a heart-shape entrance and naturally sculpted rocks farther inside that look like the Madonna, Abe Lincoln, and even a jaguar. Guadirikiri Cave and Fontein Cave are marked with ancient drawings (rangers are on hand to offer explanations), as both were used by indigenous people centuries ago. Bats are known to make appearances—don't worry, they won't bother you. Although you don't need a flashlight because the paths are well lighted, it's best to wear sneakers.

❾ Butterfly Farm. Hundreds of butterflies from around the world flutter about this spectacular garden. Guided 20- to 30-minute tours (included in the price of admission) provide an entertaining look into how these creatures complete their life cycle: from egg to caterpillar to chrysalis to butterfly. There's a special deal offered here: after your initial visit, you can return as often as you like for free. ⊠ *J. E. Irausquin Blvd., Palm Beach,* ☎ *297/8–63656,* WEB *www.thebutterflyfarm.com.* 🎫 *$10.* ⊗ *Daily 9–4:30;last tour at 4.*

❽ California Lighthouse. The lighthouse, built by a French architect in 1910, stands at the island's far northern end. Although the interior is closed to the public, you can ascend the hill to its base for some great views. In this stark landscape you'll feel as though you've just landed on the moon. The lighthouse is surrounded by huge boulders that look like extraterrestrial monsters and sand dunes embroidered with scrub that resemble undulating sea serpents.

❷ Hooiberg. Named for its shape (*hooiberg* means "haystack" in Dutch), this 541-ft (165-m) peak lies inland just past the airport. If you have the energy, climb the 562 steps to the top for an impressive view of the city.

❻ Natural Bridge. Centuries of raging wind and sea sculpted this coral rock bridge in the center of the windward coast. To reach it, drive inland along Hospitalstraat and then follow the signs. Just before you reach the geological wonder you'll pass the massive stone ruins of the Bushiribana Gold Smelter, an intriguing structure that resembles a crumbling fortress, and a section of surf-pounded coastline called Boca Mahos. Near Natural Bridge are a souvenir shop and a café overlooking the water.

❶ Oranjestad. Aruba's charming capital is best explored on foot. The palm-lined thoroughfare in the center of town runs between pastel-painted buildings, old and new, of typical Dutch design. There are many malls with boutiques and shops.

At the **Archaeological Museum of Aruba** you'll find two rooms chockfull of fascinating Indian artifacts, farm and domestic utensils, and skeletons. ⊠ *J. E. Irausquinplein 2A,* ☎ *297/8–28979.* 🎫 *Free.* ⊗ *Weekdays 8–noon and 1–4.*

One of the island's oldest edifices, **Fort Zoutman** was built in 1796 and played an important role in skirmishes between British and Curaçao troops in 1803. The Willem III Tower, named for the Dutch monarch of that time, was added in 1868 to serve as a lighthouse. Over time, the fort has been put to use as a government office building, a police station, and a prison. Now its historical museum displays Aruban artifacts in an 18th-century house. ⊠ *Zoutmanstraat*, ☎ *297/8–26099.* 🖃 *Free.* ⊙ *Weekdays 8–noon and 1–4.*

The tiny **Numismatic Museum of Aruba,** next to St. Francis Roman Catholic Church, displays coins and currencies—including a few salvaged from shipwrecks in the region. Some of the coins on display circulated during the Roman Empire, the Byzantine Empire, and the ancient Chinese dynasties; a few date as far back as the 5th century BC. The museum had its start as one Aruban's private collection and is now run by a family. ⊠ *Zuidstraat 7*, ☎ *297/8–28831.* 🖃 *Free.* ⊙ *Weekdays 7:30–noon and 1–4:30.*

❺ Rock Formations. The massive boulders at Ayo and Casibari are a mystery, as they don't match the island's geological makeup. You can climb to the top for fine views of the arid countryside. On the way you'll doubtless pass Aruba whip-tail lizards—the males are cobalt blue, the females blue with dots. The main path to Casibari has steps and handrails (except on one side), and you must move through tunnels and along narrow steps and ledges to reach the top. At Ayo you'll find ancient pictographs in a small cave (the entrance has iron bars to protect the drawings from vandalism). You may also encounter a boulder climber, one of many who are increasingly drawn to Ayo's smooth surfaces. Access to Casibari is via Tanki Highway 4A to Ayo via Route 6A; watch carefully for the turnoff signs near the center of the island on the way to the windward side.

❸ San Nicolas. During the heyday of the oil refineries, Aruba's oldest village was a bustling port; now it's primary purpose is tourism. The main promenade is full of interesting kiosks, and the whole district is undergoing a revitalization project that will bring parks, a cultural center, a central market, a public swimming pool, and an arts promenade.

ARUBA A TO Z

To research prices, get advice from other travelers, and book travel arrangements, visit www.fodors.com.

AIR TRAVEL
Aruba is 2½ hours from Miami and 4½ hours from New York. Flights leave daily to Aruba's Reina Beatrix International Airport from New York area airports and Miami International Airport, with easy connections from most American cities.

Air ALM flies daily from Miami via Curaçao, twice a week nonstop from Atlanta, and twice a week from San Juan, Puerto Rico, through Curaçao. The airline also has connecting flights to Caracas, Bonaire, Curaçao, St. Maarten, and other islands, and it offers the Visit Caribbean Pass for travel between islands.

American Airlines offers daily nonstop service from New York and twice daily from San Juan. From Toronto and Montréal the flights are via San Juan. Continental Airlines has nonstop service twice a week from Houston. Delta flies nonstop daily from Atlanta. KLM offers regular service from Amsterdam. TWA has flights daily from San Juan.
➤ AIRLINES & CONTACTS: **Air ALM** (☎ 297/8–23546 on Aruba or 800/327–7230 in North America). **American** (☎ 297/8–22700 on Aruba; 800/433–7300 in North America). **Continental** (☎ 800/525–0280 in North America). **Delta** (☎ 297/8–80044 on Aruba; 800/241–4141 in

North America). **KLM** (☎ 297/8–23546 on Aruba; 31/20–4–747–747 in Amsterdam). **TWA** (☎ 800/221–2000 in North America).

AIRPORTS

The island's state-of-the-art Reina Beatrix International Airport reopened in 2001 after a multimillion-dollar expansion. The three-level concourse is triple the size of the previous airport, and is equipped with security, flight display, and baggage handling systems.

A taxi from the airport to most hotels takes about 20 minutes. It will cost about $16 to get to the hotels along Eagle Beach; $18 to the high-rise hotels on Palm Beach; and $9 to the hotels downtown. You'll find a taxi stand right outside the baggage claim area.

➤ AIRPORT INFORMATION: **Reina Beatrix International Airport** (☎ 297/ 8–24800).

BUSINESS HOURS

BANKS

Bank hours are weekdays 8:15–5:45; some close from noon to 1. The Caribbean Mercantile Bank at the airport is open Saturday 9–4 and Sunday 9–1.

POST OFFICES

The central post office in Oranjestad is across from the San Francisco Church and is open weekdays 7:30–noon and 1–4:30. The post office in the Royal Plaza mall is open Monday–Saturday, 7–6:45.

SHOPS

Shops are generally open Monday–Saturday 8:30–6. Some stores stay open through the lunch hour, noon–2, and many open when cruise ships are in port on Sunday and holidays.

BUS TRAVEL

Buses run hourly trips between the beach hotels and Oranjestad. The one-way fare is $1.15 ($2 round-trip), and exact change is preferred. Buses also run down the coast from Oranjestad to San Nicolas for the same fare.

CAR RENTALS

You'll need a valid driver's license to rent a car, and you must meet the minimum age requirements of each rental service (Budget, for example, requires drivers to be over 25; Avis, between the ages of 23 and 70; and Hertz, over 21). A deposit of $500 (or a signed credit-card slip) is required. Rates are between $35 and $65 a day (local agencies generally have lower rates). Insurance is available starting at $10 per day, and all companies offer unlimited mileage. Try to make reservations before arriving, and opt for a four-wheel-drive vehicle if you plan to explore the island's natural sights.

➤ AGENCIES: **Avis** (⊠ Kolibristraat 14, Oranjestad, ☎ 297/8–28787; Airport, ☎ 297/8–25496). **Budget** (⊠ Kolibristraat 1, Oranjestad, ☎ 297/8–28600 or 800/472–3325). **Dollar** (⊠ Grendeaweg 15, Oranjestad, ☎ 297/8–22783; Airport, ☎ 297/8–25651; Manchebo Beach Resort, J. E. Irausquin Blvd. 55, ☎ 297/8–26696). **Economy** (⊠ Kolibristraat 5, ☎ 297/8–25176). **Hedwina Car Rental** (⊠ Bubali 93A, Noord, ☎ 297/8–76442; Airport, ☎ 297/8–30880). **Hertz** (⊠ Sabana Blanco 35, near the airport, ☎ 297/8–21845; Airport, ☎ 297/8–29112). **National** (⊠ Tanki Leendert 170, Noord, ☎ 297/8–71967; Airport, ☎ 297/8–25451). **Thrifty** (⊠ Balashi 65, Santa Cruz, ☎ 297/8–55300; Airport, ☎ 297/8–35335).

CAR TRAVEL

Most of Aruba's major attractions are fairly easy to find; others you'll happen upon only by sheer luck. Aside from the major highways, the island's winding roads are poorly marked. International traffic signs and Dutch-style traffic signals (with an extra light for a turning lane) can be misleading if you're not used to them; use extreme caution, especially at intersections, until you grasp the rules of the road. Speed limits are rarely posted but are usually 80 kph (50 mph) in the countryside.

Gas prices average $1 a liter (roughly ⅓ gallon), which is reasonable by Caribbean standards.

ELECTRICITY

Aruba runs on a 110-volt cycle, the same as in the United States; outlets are usually the two-prong variety. Total blackouts are rare, and most large hotels have backup generators.

EMERGENCIES

➤ AMBULANCE AND FIRE: **Ambulance and Fire emergencies** (☏ 115).
➤ HOSPITALS: **Dr. Horacio Oduber Hospital** (⊠ L. G. Smith Blvd., across from Costa Linda Beach Resort and the Alhambra Bazaar and Casino, ☏ 297/8–74300).
➤ PHARMACIES: **Botica Eagle** (⊠ L. G. Smith Blvd., ☏ 297/8–76103).
➤ POLICE: **Police emergencies** (☏ 111000).

LANGUAGE

Everyone on the island speaks English, but the official language is Dutch. Most locals, however, speak Papiamento—a fascinating, rapid-fire mix of Spanish, Dutch, English, French, and Portuguese—in normal conversation. Here are a few helpful phrases: *bon dia* (good day), *bon nochi* (good night), *masha danki* (thank you very much).

MAIL AND SHIPPING

You can send an airmail letter from Aruba to the United States or Canada (it will take 7–14 days) for AFl2 and a postcard for AFl1.15; a letter to Europe (2–3 weeks) is AFl1.75, a postcard AFl1. Prices to Australia and New Zealand (3–4 weeks) may be slightly higher. When addressing letters to Aruba, don't worry about the lack of formal addresses or postal codes; the island's postal service knows where to go.

MONEY MATTERS

Arubans happily accept U.S. dollars virtually everywhere. That said, there's no real need to exchange money, except for necessary pocket change (for soda machines or pay phones). The official currency is the Aruban florin (AFl), also called the guilder, which is made up of 100 cents. Silver coins come in denominations of 1, 2½, 5, 10, 25, and 50 (the square one) cents. Paper currency comes in denominations of 5, 10, 25, 50, and 100 florins.

If you need fast cash, you'll find ATMs that accept international cards at banks in Oranjestad, at the major malls, and along the roads leading to the hotel strip.
➤ BANKS: **ABN/Amro Bank** (⊠ Caya G. F. Betico Croes 89, Oranjestad, ☏ 297/8–21515). **Caribbean Mercantile Bank** (⊠ Caya G. F. Betico Croes 5, Oranjestad, ☏ 297/8–23118).

PASSPORTS AND VISAS

U.S. and Canadian citizens need a valid passport or a birth certificate with a raised seal and a government-issued photo I.D. Visitors from the member countries of the European Union must carry their European Union Travel Card as well as a passport. All other nationalities must have a valid passport.

SAFETY

Arubans are very friendly, so you needn't be afraid to stop and ask anyone for directions. It's a relatively safe island, but common sense rules still apply. Lock your rental car and leave valuables in your hotel safe. Don't leave bags unattended in the airport, on the beach, or on tour transports.

Mosquitoes and flies can be bothersome during the odd rain shower, so pack some repellent. The strong trade winds are a relief in the subtropical climate, but don't hang your bathing suit on a balcony—it will probably blow away. Help Arubans conserve water and energy: turn off air-conditioning when you leave your room, and don't let water run unnecessarily. Tap water is okay to drink.

SIGHTSEEING TOURS

BOATS

If you try a cruise around the island, know that the choppy waters are stirred up by trade winds and that catamarans are much smoother than single-hulled boats. Sucking on a peppermint or lemon candy may help a queasy stomach; avoid boating with an empty or overly full stomach. Moonlight cruises cost about $25 per person. There are also a variety of snorkeling, dinner and dancing, and sunset party cruises to choose from, priced from $25 to $60 per person. Many of the smaller operators work out of their homes; they often offer to pick you up (and drop you off) at your hotel or meet you at particular hotel pier.

➤ CONTACTS: **De Palm Tours** (⊠ L. G. Smith Blvd. 142, Oranjestad, ☎ 297/8–24400 or 800/766–6016, WEB www.depalm.com). **Pelican Tours & Watersports** (⊠ J. E. Irausquin Blvd. 232, Oranjestad, ☎ 297/8–72302, WEB www.pelican-aruba.com). **Red Sail Sports** (⊠ Seaport Village Mall, L. G. Smith Blvd. 82, Oranjestad, ☎ 297/8–61603; 877/733–7245 in the U.S., WEB www.aruba-redsail.com).

ORIENTATION

You can see the main sights in one day, but set aside two days to really meander. Guided tours are your best option if you have only a short time. Aruba's Transfer Tour & Taxi C.A. takes you to the main sights on personalized tours that cost $30 per hour.

De Palm Tours has a near monopoly on Aruban sightseeing; you can make reservations through its general office or at hotel tour-desk branches. The basic 3½-hour tour hits such highlights as the Santa Anna Church, the Casibari Rock Formation, the Natural Bridge, and the Gold Smelter Ruins. Wear tennis or hiking shoes, and bring a lightweight jacket or wrap, as the air-conditioned bus gets cold.

➤ CONTACTS: **Aruba's Transfer Tour & Taxi C.A.** (⊠ Pos Abao 41, Oranjestad, ☎ 297/8–22116).**De Palm Tours** (⊠ L. G. Smith Blvd. 142, Oranjestad, ☎ 297/8–24400 or 800/766–6016, WEB www.depalm.com).

SPECIAL-INTEREST

Explore an underwater reef teeming with marine life without getting wet. Atlantis Submarines operates a 65-ft air-conditioned sub that takes 48 passengers 95–150 ft (29–46 m) below the surface along Barcadera Reef. Make reservations one day in advance. Another option is the *Seaworld Explorer,* a semisubmersible that allows you to sit and view Aruba's marine habitat from 5 ft (1½ m) below the surface.

Romantic horse-drawn-carriage rides through the city streets of Oranjestad run $30 for a 30-minute tour; hours of operation are 7 PM–11 PM, and carriages depart from the clock tower at the Royal Plaza Mall.

➤ CONTACTS: **Atlantis Submarines** (✉ Seaport Village Marina, ☎ 297/8–36090). *Seaworld Explorer* (☎ 297/8–62416).

TAXES

DEPARTURE TAX
The airport departure tax is a whopping $34.50, but the fee is usually included in your ticket price.

SALES TAX
Hotels usually add an 11% service charge to the bill and collect a 6% government tax.

VALUE-ADDED TAX (V.A.T.)
For purchases you'll pay a 6.5% ABB tax (value-added tax) in all but the duty-free shops.

TAXIS
There's a dispatch office at the airport; you can also flag down taxis on the street (look for license plates with a "TX" tag). Rates are fixed (i.e., there are no meters; the rates are set by the government and displayed on a chart), though you and the driver should agree on the fare before your ride begins. Add $1 to the fare after midnight and $1–$3 on Sunday and holidays. An hour-long island tour costs about $30, with up to four people. Rides into town from Eagle Beach run about $5; from Palm Beach, about $8.

➤ TAXI SERVICE: **Airport Taxi Dispatch** (☎ 297/8–22116).

TELEPHONES
When making calls to anywhere in Aruba, simply dial the five-digit number. AT&T customers can dial 800–8000 from special phones at the cruise dock and in the airport's arrival and departure halls. Otherwise dial 121 to contact the international operator to place a call.

COUNTRY AND AREA CODES
To call Aruba direct from the United States, dial 011–297–8, followed by the five-digit number in Aruba. (To call from elsewhere abroad, substitute 011 with the country of origin's international access code.)

LOCAL CALLS
Local calls from pay phones, which accept both local currency and phone cards, cost 25¢.

TIPPING
Restaurants generally include a 10%–15% service charge on the bill; when in doubt, ask. If service isn't included, a 10% tip is standard; if it is included, it's still customary to add something extra, usually small change, at your discretion. Taxi drivers expect a 10%–15% tip, but it isn't mandatory. Porters and bellhops should receive about $2 per bag; chambermaids about $2 a day.

VISITOR INFORMATION
➤ ARUBA INFORMATION: **Aruba Tourism Authority** (☎ 800/862–7822, WEB www.arubatourism.com; ✉ L. G. Smith Blvd. 172, Eagle Beach, Aruba, ☎ 297/8–23777; ✉ 1 Financial Plaza, Suite 136, Fort Lauderdale, FL 33394, ☎ 954/767–6477; ✉ 3455 Peach Tree Rd. NE, Suite 500, Atlanta, GA 30326, ☎ 404/892–7822; ✉ 5901 N. Cicero, Suite 301, Chicago, IL, 60646, ☎ 773/202–5054; ✉ 1000 Harbor Blvd., Ground Level, Weehawken, NJ 07087, ☎ 201/330–0800; ✉ 12707 North Freeway, Suite 138, Houston, TX 77060-1234, ☎ 281/872–7822; ✉ Business Centre 5875, Suite 201, Hwy. 7, Vaughan, Ontario, L4L 8Z7, ☎ 905/264–3434).

5 BARBADOS

Updated by
Jane E. Zarem

Head wrapped neatly in a kerchief and her skirt sweeping the sand, the doll lady trudges along the beach to the shade of a mahogany tree and settles in for the day. Her bag is full of unfinished poppets and bits of cloth. Today she's making eyes. Using oversize shears with one tip broken off, she deftly cuts white and black snippets that give expression to blank faces. "Doll, lady?" she beckons to passersby. Surrounded by a sea of luxury, the doll lady and her work are the cultural anchors.

Barbadians (Bajans) are a warm, friendly, and hospitable people who are genuinely proud of their country and culture. Tourism is the island's number one industry, but with a sophisticated business community and stable government, life here doesn't skip a beat after visitors pack up their sunscreen and return home. Financial services, agriculture (sugar), and light manufacturing (rum, chemicals, and electrical components) are predominant industries.

About 85% of the 268,000 Bajans live in the urban area around the capital city of Bridgetown, along the west coast north to Speightstown, and along the south coast down to Oistins. Others reside inland, in tiny hamlets scattered throughout the island's 11 parishes.

Barbados stands apart both physically and geographically from its Caribbean neighbors; it's a full 100 mi (161 km) east of the Lesser Antilles chain that arcs from the Virgin Islands to Trinidad. Although many neighboring islands are the peaks of a volcanic mountain range, Barbados is the top of a single mountain of coral and limestone, sources of building blocks for many a plantation manor. Barbados is 21 mi (34 km) long, 14 mi (22½ km) wide, and relatively flat; the highest point, Mt. Hillaby, is in the north and has an elevation of 1,115 ft (341 m). The interior hills and valleys are covered by impenetrable acres of sugarcane, punctuated only by the sugar factories and great houses that the crop has sustained for centuries.

Besides picturesque rolling hills, a perimeter of white-sand beaches, a central flatland, and even deposits of underground oil (providing 60% of the island's petroleum requirements), Barbados's unique geology has created its most popular attraction, Harrison's Cave. This natural phenomenon has bubbling underground streams, cascading waterfalls, and stalactites and stalagmites created through the millennia by the constant drip of calcite-laden water.

Actually, it was during a search for fresh water that Barbados was "discovered" by the Portuguese in 1536. They didn't stay but did give the island its name: Barbados, or "the bearded ones," after native fig trees with beardlike roots. A century later—and quite by accident—the British landed on the west coast at what is now Holetown. The first British settlement was established two years later, in 1627. Unlike the turbulent history of most of the Caribbean islands, British rule sustained uninterrupted until 1966, when Barbados became independent. The island has since had an elected prime minister and membership in the British Commonwealth of Nations.

Facilities here are top-notch. Beaches along the tranquil west coast, facing the Caribbean, are lined with posh resorts and residences that are virtually enveloped in lush foliage and a healthy dose of peace and quiet. This luxurious area, appropriately called the Platinum Coast, is a favorite destination of British vacationers. North Americans tend to prefer the hotels and resorts stretched along the beaches of the trendier south coast, which has good shopping, countless restaurants, and an active nightlife. Bajans, however, spend their holidays along the rugged east coast, where the Atlantic surf pounds the dramatic shoreline with unrelenting force.

Barbados retains a noticeable British feel. Most islanders are members of the Anglican church, afternoon tea is a ritual, polo ("the sport of kings") is played all winter, and cricket is the national passion—Barbados has produced some of the world's top cricketers. The tradition of dressing for dinner is firmly entrenched, yet the island is hardly stuffy. You can dine by candlelight facing the sea, in festive company at a sumptuous Bajan buffet, or casually with a burger at the beach. This is still the Caribbean, after all.

Lodging

Most people stay on either the fashionable west coast, north of Bridgetown, or the action-packed south coast. The west coast beachfront resorts in the parishes of St. Peter, St. James, and St. Michael are mostly self-contained enclaves. Highway 1, a two-lane road with considerable traffic, runs past these resorts, which makes strolling to a nearby bar or restaurant difficult. Along the south coast, in Christ Church Parish, many hotels are clustered near the busy strip known as the St. Lawrence Gap, with its dozens of small restaurants, bars, and nightclubs. On the much more remote east coast, a couple of small inns offer oceanfront views, cool breezes, and get-away-from-it-all tranquillity. Accommodations range from elegant resorts and private villas to modest but comfortable small hotels and inns. Another popular option is renting a time-share condominium, apartment, or private home. Hotels usually operate on the EP but also offer CP or MAP if you wish; some require MAP in winter, and others offer all-inclusive packages. The hotels below all have air-conditioning, telephones, and TVs in guest rooms unless otherwise noted.

CATEGORY	COST EP/CP*	COST A.I.**
$$$$	over $350	over $375
$$$	$250–$350	$275–$375
$$	$150–$250	$175–$275
$	under $150	under $175

*EP/CP prices are per night for a standard double room in high season, excluding taxes, service charges, and meal plans. **A.I. (all-inclusive) prices are per person, per night based on double-occupancy during high season, excluding taxes and service charges.*

86

Barbados

KEY

- ⛵ Beaches
- 🚢 Cruise Ship Terminal
- ◧ Dive Sites
- ❶ Exploring Sights
- ① Hotels and Restaurants

ATLANTIC OCEAN

N

Barclays Park
Beach

⑱ Cattlewash
Bathsheba
Bathsheba
Soup Bowl

JOSEPH

Consett
Bay

⑮ Four
Crossroads

Ragged
Pt.

❶⑯⑰⑰

ST. JOHN

❶⑯

Marley
Vale

Hill

4

❶⑪
⑫

4B

❶⑬

GEORGE

Edgecumbe

ST. PHILIP

Bottom
Bay

⑭⑮

❶⑭

The Crane

❶⑬ Crane Beach

Crane
Bay

COBBLER'S REEF

CHURCH

ce

⑫

7

Oistins

Grantley Adams
International
Airport

Long
Bay

Silver Sands
Beach

South Pt.

0   3 miles

0   3 km

Hotels
EAST COAST

$$$$ 🏨 **Villa Nova.** Formerly a historic great house, Villa Nova is an ele-
★ gant, all-suites hotel surrounded by 15 acres of gardens and woodland.
Exquisitely decorated throughout with antiques and works of art,
rooms and suites have king-size beds, comfortable sitting areas, and
bathrooms with Victorian claw-foot tubs. If you like, the butler serves
breakfast on your wraparound terrace. Relax in the lounge or on the
verandah, swim in the pool, choose a book from the extensive library,
picnic at the hotel's beach club at Cattlewash, and enjoy fine dining
in the Plantation Room. The pampering begins with limousine service
from the airport. ✉ *Villa Nova, St. John,* ☎ *246/433–1524,* FAX *246/*
433-6363, WEB *www.villa-nova.com. 17 rooms, 11 suites. Restaurant,*
3 bars, room service, fans, in-room data ports, in-room safes, golf priv-
ileges, 2 tennis courts, pool, gym, spa, hiking, billiards, library, piano,
shop, laundry service, concierge, Internet, meeting room, airport shut-
tle, no kids under 12. AE, MC, V. BP.

$–$$ 🏨 **The Edgewater Inn.** Most appealing to nature lovers or surfers, this
rustic, cliffside hideaway—originally a 1760 beach house—overlooks
the pounding Atlantic surf and unusual rock formations of Bathsheba
Beach. The inn resembles a mountain lodge. Heavy, hand-hewn mahogany furniture and woodwork add a rugged quality; beveled-glass
windows and parquet *ceilings* are truly unique. Rooms are otherwise
basic, but the friendly staff, spectacular views, low prices, and good
food easily make up for that. The property backs up to an 85-acre rain
forest, providing a serene natural environment—perfect for relaxation
and reflection. ✉ *Bathsheba Beach, Bathsheba, St. Joseph,* ☎ *246/433–*
9900, FAX *246/433–9902,* WEB *www.edgewaterinn.com. 16 rooms, 4*
suites. Restaurant, bar, no air-conditioning in some rooms, fans, no room
phones, refrigerators, no room TVs, pool, beach, hiking. AE, MC, V.
CP, FAP, MAP.

$ 🏨 **Atlantis Hotel.** The Atlantis has a spectacular cliffside location over-
looking the rocky Atlantic coast, where the sea views are mesmerizing. A modest guest house for more than a century, most of the activity
happens around midday, when folks touring the east coast stop for a
traditional Bajan buffet lunch at the Atlantis Hotel restaurant. Rooms
are simply furnished, and some have balconies overlooking that great
view. You won't find a TV, and there's no air-conditioning—although
the fresh Atlantic breeze that usually wafts through the open windows
makes that no problem. Bathsheba Beach—the island's premier surfing spot—is next door. ✉ *Tent Bay, Bathsheba, St. Joseph,* ☎ *246/433–*
9445, FAX *246/433–7180,* WEB *www.atlantisbarbados.com. 10 rooms.*
Restaurant, bar, beach. AE. EP, MAP.

SOUTH COAST

$$$$ 🏨 **Turtle Beach Resort.** Named for the sea turtles that lay their eggs on
★ the beach, visible from the three-story open-air lobby, everything a family could wish for is here to enjoy—all the time, all included. Boats and
boogie boards are fun at the beach; golfers get special privileges at the
nearby Barbados Golf Club; and the Kids Club has daily activities for
children 3–11. Suites are large and attractively decorated with wicker
furniture and tropical colors; all have ocean views. With two restaurants, a snack/sports bar (or dining at four sister hotels), and nightly
entertainment, you won't want to go home. ✉ *St. Lawrence Gap, Dover,*
Christ Church, ☎ *246/428–7131,* FAX *246/428–6089,* WEB *www.*
eleganthotels.com. 166 suites. 2 restaurants, 2 bars, snack bar, sports
bar, cabaret, room service, fans, in-room safes, refrigerators, golf priv-
ileges, 2 tennis courts, 3 pools, aerobics, gym, hair salon, hot tub, mas-
sage, beach, snorkeling, windsurfing, boating, waterskiing, shops,

baby-sitting, children's programs (ages 3–11), playground, dry cleaning, laundry service, Internet, business services. AE, DC, MC, V. All-inclusive.

$$$–$$$$ ⊡ **Crane Beach Hotel.** In its refurbished (2001) original building, high on a seaside cliff, Barbados's first resort hotel has 18 large suites decorated with antiques. Corner suites have walls of windows and broad patios with panoramic views. Two modern buildings are built in corresponding style, with coral-stone walls; suites have an Oriental touch, hardwood floors, hand-carved four-poster beds, spectacular bathrooms, fully equipped kitchens, and washer/dryer; some have private plunge pools. A crescent of pink-sand beach, with rolling waves, is 200 steps down the cliff. A testament to the beautiful location, The Crane's signature pool has been the backdrop for numerous photo shoots. ✉ *Crane, Crane Bay, St. Philip,* ☎ *246/423–6220,* FAX *246/423–5343,* WEB *www.thecrane.com. 4 rooms, 64 suites. Restaurant, bar, no air-conditioning in some rooms, fans, in-room data ports, in-room safes, kitchenettes, microwaves, refrigerators, no room TVs, 2 pools, 4 tennis courts, beach, laundry facilities, meeting room. AE, DC, MC, V. EP, MAP.*

$$$–$$$$ ⊡ **Sam Lord's Castle.** About 14 mi (22½ km) east of Bridgetown, this former pirate's lair is surrounded by 72 acres of grounds, gardens, and beach. Seven rooms in the great house have canopied beds; downstairs, the public rooms have furniture by Sheraton, Hepplewhite, and Chippendale—for admiring, not for sitting. Guest rooms in surrounding cottages have conventional hotel furnishings, and some have kitchenettes. The beach is 1 mi (1½ km) long, the Wanderer Restaurant offers Continental cuisine, and there are even a few slot machines. Rates include unlimited daytime tennis, all meals and beverages, airport transfers, and a Thursday Shipwreck party. ✉ *Long Bay, St. Philip,* ☎ *246/423–7350,* FAX *246/423–6361,* WEB *www.samlordscastle.com. 236 rooms, 12 suites. 3 restaurants, bar, 3 pools, 7 tennis courts, exercise equipment, hair salon, beach, shops, meeting room. AE, D, DC, MC, V. All-inclusive.*

$$$ ⊡ **Club Rockley Barbados.** On 65 acres near one of the island's most popular beach areas, this all-inclusive resort offers extensive amenities. The resort's 9-hole, par-36 golf course is challenging, attractive, and open to the public. The one- and two-bedroom accommodations are former time-share condominiums, and those time-shares that remain are set apart from the hotel. Each room has a balcony or patio. There's free shuttle service to the beach, just five minutes away. ✉ *Golf Club Rd., Rockley, Christ Church,* ☎ *246/435–7880,* FAX *246/435–8015,* WEB *www.clubrockley.com. 152 rooms. 2 restaurants, 3 bars, some kitchenettes, 9-hole golf course, 5 tennis courts, 7 pools, gym, hair salon, squash, shops, baby-sitting, children's programs (ages 3–12), Internet, meeting room. AE, DC, MC, V. All-inclusive.*

$$–$$$ ⊡ **Divi Southwinds Beach Resort.** The toss-up here is whether to take one of the larger rooms—with a kitchenette and a balcony that overlooks the gardens and pool—or one of the smaller, older rooms just steps from the sandy, white beach. Though all the rooms are pleasant, the buildings themselves are rather plain. Most come for the action, and that includes making full use of the water-sports facilities and 20 lush acres. ✉ *St. Lawrence Main Rd., Dover, Christ Church,* ☎ *246/ 428–7181,* FAX *246/428–4674,* WEB *www.diviresorts.com. 150 rooms. 2 restaurants, 2 bars, kitchenettes, putting green, 2 pools, 2 tennis courts, hair salon, beach, dive shop, basketball, volleyball, shops, meeting room. AE, DC, MC, V. CP, EP, FAP, MAP.*

$$–$$$ ⊡ **The Savannah.** The Savannah comprises the completely renovated, historic Sea View Hotel as its main building, along with two additional wings that extend to the sea. Waterfalls from the main building spill into a lagoon-style pool, which separates the two wings. Rooms are

beautifully appointed with antique-style furniture, including carved mahogany four-poster beds. French doors open to a patio or balcony. All
rooms have state-of-the-art TVs, DVDs, and CD players; duplex suites
have large sitting rooms, bars, fax machines, and printers. The restaurant is a popular luncheon spot for local businesspeople. ✉ *Garrison
Main Rd., Hastings, Christ Church,* ☎ *246/228–3800,* 𝔽𝔸𝕏 *246/228–
4385,* 𝖶𝖤𝖡 *www.gemsbarbados.com/savannah. 92 rooms, 8 suites. 2
restaurants, 2 bars, in-room data ports, in-room safes, minibars, in-
room VCRs, pool, saltwater pool, gym, hair salon, spa, beach, shop,
Internet, business services, meeting room. AE, DC, MC, V. EP, MAP.*

\$\$ 🖬 **Accra Beach Hotel & Resort.** The beautifully appointed rooms in the
four-story Accra have balconies facing sandy, white Accra Beach. Six
duplex penthouse suites have ocean-view sitting rooms downstairs, and
spacious bedrooms and huge baths with whirlpools upstairs. All rooms
have handcrafted furniture. Between the hotel and its beach are a large
cloverleaf-shape pool, a snack bar, and a poolside bar. In the evening,
after sumptuous dining in Wytukai (pronounced Y2K)—the island's
first Polynesian restaurant—take a turn on a dance floor that's open
to the stars. ✉ *Hwy. 7, Rockley, Christ Church (Box 73W),* ☎ *246/
435–8920,* 𝔽𝔸𝕏 *246/435–6794. 122 rooms, 6 suites. Restaurant, 2 bars,
snack bar, fans, pool, gym, hair salon, squash, beach, meeting rooms.
AE, MC, V. CP, EP, MAP.*

\$\$ 🖬 **Casuarina Beach Club.** Popular with those who prefer self-catering
vacations, this is a peaceful place—unique among south coast resorts—but you're within walking distance of restaurants, nightlife,
and shopping. The luxury four-story apartment hotel consists of five
clusters of Spanish-style buildings in 8 acres of gardens and casuarina
pines. The restaurant and a mobile bar are on the beach—1,500 ft (930
m) of soft, fine sand. All rooms and one- or two-bedroom suites are
colorfully decorated; each has a fully equipped kitchenette and a large
balcony. ✉ *St. Lawrence Gap, Dover, Christ Church,* ☎ *246/428–3600,*
𝔽𝔸𝕏 *246/428–1970,* 𝖶𝖤𝖡 *www.casuarina.com. 124 rooms, 34 suites.
Restaurant, 3 bars, piano bar, grocery, fans, kitchenettes, microwaves,
2 tennis courts, pool, wading pool, hair salon, beach, snorkeling, billiards, boccie, shuffleboard, squash, volleyball, library, shops, baby-
sitting, children's programs (ages 3–6), playground, laundry facilities,
Internet, business services, meeting room. AE, D, MC, V. CP, EP,
MAP.*

WEST COAST

\$\$\$\$ 🖬 **Almond Beach Club & Spa.** A sister property to Almond Beach Village, this convenient all-inclusive resort within strolling distance of Holetown's shops and activities is perfect for couples, honeymooners, or
singles. A horseshoe of rooms and junior suites overlooks the sea or
the pool and garden. Lavish breakfast buffets, four-course lunches, afternoon tea, and intimate dinners are served in the main dining room.
Enjoy West Indian cuisine for dinner at Enid's, the colorful Bajan
restaurant, which also offers free cooking classes. Water sports are included; spa and salon services are extra. ✉ *Hwy. 1, Vauxhall, St. James,*
☎ *246/432–7840,* 𝔽𝔸𝕏 *246/432–2115,* 𝖶𝖤𝖡 *www.almondresorts.com.
133 rooms, 28 junior suites. 2 restaurants, 4 bars, nightclub, room service, in-room safes, tennis court, 3 pools, aerobics, health club, hair
salon, massage, sauna, spa, beach, snorkeling, windsurfing, boating,
waterskiing, squash, shop, laundry service, Internet, airport shuttle.
AE, MC, V. All-inclusive.*

\$\$\$\$ 🖬 **Almond Beach Village.** A premier family resort on 30 acres, with a
1-mi-long (1½-km-long) beach, the Village has a separate adults-only
area—and plenty for all to do. Seven buildings house the guest rooms;
the family section has junior and one-bedroom suites, a nursery, play

area, wading pool, and supervised Kid's Klub with programs for infants–age 12. A historic sugar mill is a lovely spot for weddings. Restaurants serve Continental, Italian, and Bajan cuisine. Shopping excursions, island tours, nightly entertainment, cooking classes, and a dine-around program are included. Need more? Hop the shuttle to Almond Beach Club and enjoy more facilities there. ☒ *Hwy. 1B, Heywoods, St. Peter,* ☎ *246/422–4900,* FAX *246/422–0617,* WEB *www.almondresorts.com. 289 rooms, 41 suites. 4 restaurants, 5 bars, dance club, room service, in-room safes, 9-hole golf course, 4 tennis courts, 10 pools, wading pool, health club, 2 hot tubs, beach, snorkeling, windsurfing, boating, waterskiing, fishing, billiards, racquetball, squash, shops, children's programs (ages infant–12), playground, business servcies, Internet, meeting room, airport shuttle. AE, MC, V. All-inclusive.*

$$$$ ★ 🖬 **Cobblers Cove Hotel.** In the style of an elegant English country house, Cobblers Cove is surrounded by tropical gardens on one side and the sea on the other. Each suite has a comfortable sitting room with a wet bar and a wall of louvered shutters that opens onto a patio or balcony. Only bedrooms are air-conditioned. For all-out luxury, the Colleton and Camelot suites have richly decorated sitting rooms, king-size four-poster beds, dressing rooms, whirlpool baths, private sundecks, and plunge pools. Enjoy the bar, the lounge-library, and fine seaside dining—plus special rates and guaranteed tee times at the Royal Westmoreland Golf Club. Children aren't allowed to stay at the hotel from January through March. ☒ *Road View, Speightstown, St. Peter,* ☎ *246/422–2291,* FAX *246/422–1460,* WEB *www.cobblerscove.com. 40 suites. Restaurant, bar, room service, fans, in-room safes, minibars, no room TVs, golf privileges, tennis court, pool, gym, beach, snorkeling, windsurfing, boating, waterskiing, library, shop, baby-sitting, meeting room. AE, MC, V. CP, EP, FAP, MAP. Closed Sept.–Oct.*

$$$$ 🖬 **Coconut Creek Hotel.** Quiet and secluded, this small, picturesque resort is set on handsomely landscaped grounds. From a low bluff, steps lead down to two tiny coves and a sandy beach. Rooms have rattan furnishings with tropical accents. Some have spectacular ocean views; others overlook the garden or pool. TV is available in the lounge. Sunfish, kayaks, and other nonmotorized water-sports equipment are available. Meals are served at the open-air Pavilion restaurant, with nightly entertainment and dancing at the Cricketers Bar. A free water taxi provides transportation to the sister Elegant hotels on the west coast. ☒ *Hwy. 1, Derricks, St. James (Box 249, Bridgetown),* ☎ *246/432–0803,* FAX *246/432–0272,* WEB *www.eleganthotels.com. 41 rooms, 12 suites. Dining room, bar, in-room safes, refrigerators, pool, golf privileges, beach, snorkeling, windsurfing, boating, waterskiing, baby-sitting, dry cleaning, laundry service. AE, DC, MC, V. All-inclusive.*

$$$$ ★ 🖬 **Colony Club Hotel.** Once a gentlemen's private club, the stylish, colonial feeling suits the adult clientele. Rooms are spacious, with white-washed wood and rattan furniture and neutral fabrics. Twenty rooms have private access to lagoon pools, which flow through the garden. Relax on the beach, soak in one of four pools, and enjoy an exquisite meal in the Orchid Room or a more informal repast at the open-air Laguna Restaurant. Nonmotorized water sports, an in-pool scuba-diving lesson, tennis, and golf privileges at Royal Westmoreland Golf Course are all included. A free water taxi provides transportation among four sister hotels along the west coast. ☒ *Hwy. 1, Porters, St. James,* ☎ *246/422–2335,* FAX *246/422–0667,* WEB *www.eleganthotels.com. 64 rooms, 34 junior suites. 2 restaurants, 3 bars, room service, fans, in-room safes, minibars, golf privileges, 2 tennis courts, 4 pools, hair salon, beach, snorkeling, windsurfing, boating, waterskiing, shops, dry cleaning, laundry service, Internet, meeting room, no kids under 16. AE, D, DC, MC, V. CP, EP, FAP, MAP.*

$$$$ 🛏 **Coral Reef Club.** Spend your days relaxing on the white-sand beach
or around the pool, taking time out for the hotel's superb afternoon
tea. Small coral-stone cottages are scattered over 12 flower-filled acres;
the public areas ramble along the beach. Each spacious room has a small
patio. Junior suites have sitting areas and larger patios or private balconies. Cottage-style suites have an additional single bed and dressing
room. TV is available by request at an extra charge. Those on MAP
have dining and golf privileges at Royal Westmoreland Golf Club. ✉
Hwy. 1, Holetown, St. James, ☎ *246/422–2372,* 🖷 *246/422–1776,*
🌐 *www.coralreefbarbados.com. 34 rooms, 30 suites. Restaurant,
bar, room service, fans, in-room safes, refrigerators, no room TVs, golf
privileges, 3 tennis courts, 2 pools, gym, hair salon, massage, beach,
dive shop, snorkeling, windsurfing, boating, waterskiing, billiards,
shops, baby-sitting. AE, MC, V. EP, FAP, MAP.*

$$$$ 🛏 **Crystal Cove Hotel.** White duplex cottages, trimmed in the perky
pastels typical of the Caribbean and connected by garden paths, spill
down a hillside to the beach. Rooms are bright and spacious, with
bleached wood and rattan furniture. During the day, sail on a Hobie
Cat, have a scuba lesson, or water-ski, windsurf, or kayak to your heart's
content. For a change of scene, a free water taxi serves four west-coast
Elegant Hotels properties. Luncheon is generally a beachside buffet;
the table d'hôte dinner at Reflections Restaurant is superb, followed
by steel band or other live music. You can also dine around at sister
resorts. ✉ *Hwy. 1, Appleby, St. James,* ☎ *246/432–2683,* 🖷 *246/432–
8290,* 🌐 *www.eleganthotels.com. 88 rooms. Restaurant, grill, 2 bars,
room service, fans, in-room safes, refrigerators, golf privileges, 2 tennis courts, 3 pools, gym, beach, snorkeling, windsurfing, boating, waterskiing, shop, baby-sitting, children's programs (ages 3–11), laundry
service. AE, D, DC, MC, V. All-inclusive.*

$$$$ 🛏 **Glitter Bay.** Shipping magnate Sir Edward Cunard built this estate
in the 1930s to resemble his palazzo in Venice. Newer buildings have
one- and two-bedroom suites and duplex penthouses, all with private
balconies or terraces; some have full kitchens. Manicured gardens separate the reception area and lounge from an alfresco dining room
(with evening entertainment), pools with a waterfall and footbridge,
and ½ mi (1 km) of beach. It's more casual and family-oriented than
the Royal Pavilion, its sister property next door; the resorts share facilities, including water sports and dining privileges. Guests at Glitter
Bay also enjoy privileges at Royal Westmoreland Golf Club. ✉ *Hwy.
1, Porters, St. James,* ☎ *246/422–5555,* 🖷 *246/422–1367,* 🌐 *www.
fairmont.com. 69 suites. Restaurant, room service, fans, in-room safes,
minibars, golf privileges, 2 tennis courts, 2 pools, gym, hair salon, massage, beach, snorkeling, windsurfing, boating, waterskiing, shops,
baby-sitting, meeting room. AE, D, DC, MC, V. CP, EP, MAP.*

$$$$ 🛏 **Lone Star Garage Motel.** For something completely different, this
renovated 1940s-era service station is now a four-suite motel. Two suites
are at beach level; two are upstairs. The Lincoln Bedroom is named
for the car; others are appropriately dubbed Buick, Cord, and Stude-
baker. All are large and beautifully furnished in Bajan mahogany and
Italian-designed upholstered furniture. Each suite has its own communications center. Upon arrival you receive personalized stationery,
business cards, and an assistant. The beach is at the door; golf, tennis,
fishing, snorkeling, scuba diving, and horseback riding are available
nearby. The Lone Star restaurant is extraordinary. ✉ *Hwy. 1, Mount
Standfast, St. James,* ☎ *246/419–0599,* 🖷 *246/419–0597,* 🌐 *www.
thelonestar.com. 4 suites. Restaurant, bar, room service, fans, in-room
data ports, in-room fax, refrigerators, golf privileges, beach, Internet.
AE, D, DC, MC, V. CP, EP, MAP.*

$$$$ ⊡ **Royal Pavilion.** Those who want serenity enjoy the oceanfront suites here; only three suites are nestled in a two-story garden villa. Ground-floor rooms allow you to simply step through sliding doors, cross your private patio, and walk onto the sand. Breakfast and lunch are served alfresco at the edge of the beach; afternoon tea and dinner are in the Palm Terrace. Recreational facilities and dining privileges are shared with the adjoining and more informal sister hotel, Glitter Bay. ⊠ *Hwy. 1, Porters, St. James,* ☎ *246/422–4444,* FAX *246/422–3940,* WEB *www.fairmont.com. 75 suites. 2 restaurants, 2 bars, room service, golf privileges, 2 tennis courts, pool, hair salon, beach, snorkeling, windsurfing, boating, waterskiing, shops, laundry service, concierge, meeting room. AE, D, DC, MC, V. CP, EP, MAP.*

$$$$ ⊡ **Sandy Lane Hotel.** The spectacular Sandy Lane Hotel, a coral-stone,
★ Palladian-style mansion, overlooks a sweeping stretch of beach shaded by mature trees. Exquisite guest suites, sumptuous in every detail, have remote-controlled lighting, sound, draperies, fans, and temperature; three flat-screen plasma TVs with DVD and Internet access; Quadriga communication system for E-mail, wake-up calls, and room service; a private bar; luxurious bathrooms; and a personal butler. The 45,000-square-ft spa is a vacation in itself. Elegant dining, 45 holes of championship-level golf, a tennis center, a full complement of water sports, a special lounge for teenagers, and incomparable style complete the extraordinary picture. ⊠ *Hwy. 1, Paynes Bay, St. James,* ☎ *246/444–2000,* FAX *246/444–2222,* WEB *www.sandylane.com. 102 rooms, 10 suites. 4 restaurants, 5 bars, room service, fans, in-room data ports, in-room fax, in-room safes, minibars, 1 9-hole golf course, 2 18-hole golf courses, 9 tennis courts, pool, hair salon, massage, spa, steam room, beach, snorkeling, windsurfing, boating, shops, children's programs (ages 3–12), cleaning, laundry service, concierge, business services, Internet, meeting rooms AE, DC, MC, V. EP.*

$$$$ ⊡ **Tamarind Cove Hotel.** This large, Mediterranean-style hotel rambles along 750 ft (229 m) of prime beachfront. Rooms, either close to the action or in cozy privacy, are spacious and attractively decorated with rattan furnishings and subdued colors. Ten luxury ocean-view suites have four-poster beds, marble floors, and coral-stone walls. Four suites have private Jacuzzis. Tangiers serves all meals daily; Sasso and Daphne's Barbados both offer fine dining at dinner. The resort offers a full complement of water sports as well as golf privileges at the Royal Westmoreland Golf Club. A free water taxi operates between the four Elegant hotels on the west coast. ⊠ *Hwy. 1, Paynes Bay, St. James,* ☎ *246/432–1332,* FAX *246/432–6317,* WEB *www.eleganthotels.com. 58 rooms, 108 suites. 3 restaurants, 4 bars, snack bar, room service, in-room safes, refrigerators, golf privileges, 2 tennis courts, 4 pools, gym, hair salon, beach, snorkeling, windsurfing, boating, waterskiing, shops, baby-sitting, dry cleaning, laundry service, concierge, Internet, meeting room. AE, D, DC, MC, V. EP, MAP.*

$$$$ ⊡ **Treasure Beach.** Quiet, upscale, and friendly, this resort feels almost residential. Most guests are British, often staying two or three weeks, year after year. Two floors of one-bedroom suites form a horseshoe around a small garden and pool. Most have sea views, but all are just steps from the beach. The super-deluxe Hemmingway Suite blends antiques with modern luxury, an enormous terrace, and special amenities. All others have comfortable sitting rooms, with full kitchenettes, a shelf of books, and an open fourth wall that can be shuttered at night for privacy. Bedrooms are air-conditioned. The restaurant enjoys a well-deserved reputation for fine dining. ⊠ *Hwy. 1, Paynes Bay, St. James,* ☎ *246/432–1346,* FAX *246/432–1094,* WEB *www.barbados.org/hotels/treasure.htm. 29 suites. Restaurant, bar, room service, fans, in-room data ports, in-room safes, kitchenettes, refrigerators, pool, gym, beach,* snorkeling, library, dry cleaning, laundry service, Internet. AE, D, DC, MC, V. CP, EP, MAP.

$$$-$$$$ ⛱ **Mango Bay Hotel & Beach Club.** Within walking distance of Hole-town's shops and historic sights, each room in Mango Bay's whitewashed buildings has a private terrace or balcony and a picturesque view of the garden, pool, or beach. All are decorated in bright colors and have wicker furniture. The all-inclusive price extends to beverages and a dine-around program at two local restaurants for those staying a week or more. Activities include water sports, scuba instruction in the pool, aquacise classes, a catamaran cruise, glass-bottom boat rides, snorkeling trips, walking tours, and a shopping excursion to Bridgetown. Enjoy a nightcap and after-dinner entertainment at the piano bar. ✉ *2nd St., Holetown, St. James,* ☎ *246/432–1384,* ℻ *246/432–5297,* 🌐 *www.mangobaybarbados.com. 64 rooms. Restaurant, bar, piano bar, in-room safes, 2 pools, beach, snorkeling, windsurfing, boating, waterskiing. AE, MC, V. All-inclusive.*

Villas, Apartments, and Condominiums

Villas, private homes, and condos are available south of Bridgetown, in the Hastings-Worthing area, and along the west coast in St. James and in St. Peter. Most include maid service, and the owner or manager can arrange for a cook.

A handful of time-share resorts have cropped up along the south and west coasts. Nonowner vacationers can rent the units by the week from the property managers. Two- and three-bedroom condos run $800–$1,400 per week in the summer—double that in winter. This is an economical option for family groups or couples vacationing together.

On the south coast, the seaside villas at **Bougainvillea Beach Resort** (✉ Maxwell Coast Rd., Maxwell, Christ Church, ☎ 246/418–0990, 🌐 www.bougainvillearesort.com) are appropriate for families, couples, or honeymooners. Farther east, but also on the south coast, the up-scale private residences at **The Crane** (✉ Crane Beach, St. Philip, ☎ 246/423–6220, 🌐 www.thecrane.com) overlook the ocean at Crane Beach and are perfect for anyone seeking peace, tranquillity, and natural beauty.

On the west coast, **Royal Westmoreland Villas** (✉ Hwy. 2A, Westmoreland, St. James, ☎ 246/422–4653, 🌐 www.royal-westmoreland. com) overlook the Royal Westmoreland Golf Club's championship course and, therefore, are an ideal base for golfers. Just beyond Speightstown, the luxurious town homes at **Port St. Charles** (✉ Hwy. 1B, Heywoods, St. Peter, ☎ 246/419–1000, 🌐 www.portstcharles.com) are the best choice for boating enthusiasts.

The **Barbados Tourism Authority** (☎ 246/427–2623) on Harbour Road in Bridgetown has a listing of apartments in prime resort areas on both the south and west coasts, along with the facilities offered and the rates. Some apartment complexes are small, with only three or four units; others range up to 30 units or more.

Dining

First-class restaurants and hotel dining rooms serve quite sophisticated cuisine—prepared by chefs with international experience—to rival that served in the world's best restaurants. Most menus include seafood; dorado, kingfish, snapper, and flying fish are prepared every way imaginable. Flying fish is so popular a delicacy that it has become a national symbol. Shellfish abounds; on the other hand, so do steak, local black-belly lamb, and fresh fruits and vegetables.

Local specialty dishes include *buljol* (a cold salad of pickled codfish, tomatoes, onions, sweet peppers, and celery) and *conkies* (cornmeal, coconut, pumpkin, raisins, sweet potatoes, and spices, mixed together, wrapped in a banana leaf, and steamed). *Cou-cou*, often served with steamed flying fish, is a mixture of cornmeal and okra topped with a spicy creole sauce made from tomatoes, onions, and sweet peppers. Bajan-style pepper-pot is a hearty stew of oxtail, beef chunks, and "any other meat" in a rich, spicy gravy and simmered overnight.

For lunch, restaurants often offer a traditional Bajan buffet of fried fish, baked chicken, salads, and a selection of local roots and vegetables. Be cautious with the West Indian condiments; like the sun, they're hotter than you think. Typical Bajan drinks, besides Banks beer and Mount Gay rum, are *falernum* (a liqueur concocted of rum, sugar, lime juice, and almond essence) and *mauby* (a nonalcoholic drink made by boiling bitter bark and spices, straining the mixture, and sweetening it). You're sure to enjoy the fresh fruit punch, with or without the rum.

What to Wear

Barbados's dress code is conservative and, on occasion, formal—a jacket and tie for gentlemen and a cocktail dress for ladies in the fanciest restaurants, particularly in winter. Other places are more casual, although jeans and shorts are always frowned upon at dinner. Beach attire should be worn only at the beach.

CATEGORY	COST*
$$$$	over $30
$$$	$20–$30
$$	$10–$20
$	under $10

*£pcfn:*per person for a main course at dinner*

Bridgetown
CARIBBEAN/CREOLE

$$ ✕ **Waterfront Cafe.** This friendly bistro facing the Careenage is the perfect place to enjoy a drink, snack, or meal—and to people-watch. Locals and tourists gather at outdoor tables for all-day dining on sandwiches, salads, fish, pasta, pepper-pot stew, and tasty Bajan snacks such as buljol, fish cakes, or plantation pork (plantains stuffed with spicy minced pork). The panfried flying-fish sandwich is especially popular. In the evening you can gaze through the arched windows while savoring nouvelle creole cuisine, enjoying cool trade winds, and listening to live jazz. There's a special Carib Buffet and steel-pan music on Tuesday night from 7 to 9. ⊠ *Bridge House, The Careenage, Bridgetown, St. Michael,* ☎ *246/427–0093. AE, DC, MC, V. Closed Sun.*

East Coast
CARIBBEAN

$$ ✕ **Atlantis Hotel.** People have enjoyed lunch with a view at this hotel's restaurant for more than 40 years. An enormous Bajan buffet is served daily, with pumpkin fritters, spinach cake, pickled breadfruit, fried flying fish, roast chicken, pepper-pot stew, and fried okra and eggplant. Homemade coconut pie tops the dessert list. The Atlantis is a lunch stop for many organized day tours. ⊠ *Atlantis Hotel, Tent Bay, Bathsheba, St. Joseph,* ☎ *246/433–9445. AE.*

$$ ✕ **Bonito Beach Bar & Restaurant.** Enid Worrell's wholesome West Indian home cooking has soothed the hunger pangs of many folks who find themselves on the east coast at lunchtime. The view of the Atlantic from the second-floor dining room is striking, and the Bajan buffet lunch includes fried fish and baked chicken accompanied by salads and vegetables fresh from the family garden. If your timing is right, Mrs. Wor-

rell might have homemade cheesecake for dessert. The fresh fruit punch—with or without rum—is great. ⊠ *Coast Rd., Bathsheba, St. Joseph,* ☎ *246/433–9034. No credit cards.*

South Coast

CARIBBEAN

$$$ ✕ **David's Place.** Come here for sophisticated Bajan cuisine in a prime waterfront location on St. Lawrence Bay. Waves slap against the pilings of the open-air deck—a rhythmic accompaniment to the soft classical background music. To start, the pumpkin soup is divine. Specialties such as flying fish, pepper-pot stew, curried shrimp, and vegetarian dishes come with homemade cheddar-cheese bread. Dessert might be bread pudding, carrot cake with rum sauce, or coconut cream pie. David's has an extensive wine list. ⊠ *St. Lawrence Main Rd., Worthing, Christ Church,* ☎ *246/435–9755. Reservations essential. AE, MC, V. Closed Mon. No lunch.*

ITALIAN

$$–$$$ ✕ **Bellini's Trattoria.** Soft Italian music and waves gently lapping beneath the Mediterranean-style veranda set the stage for informal yet romantic dining. The cuisine at Bellini's is classic northern Italian with a contemporary flair. Toast the evening with a Bellini cocktail (sparkling wine with a splash of fruit nectar), and start your meal with antipasto, an individual pizza, or a tasty homemade pasta dish. Move on to the signature shrimp, veal, steak, or seafood dishes, and top it all off with excellent tiramisu. ⊠ *Little Bay Hotel, St. Lawrence Gap, Dover, Christ Church,* ☎ *246/435–7246. AE, DC, MC, V.*

SEAFOOD

$$$–$$$$ ✕ **Josef's Restaurant.** The signature restaurant of Austrian restaurateur Josef Schwaiger is, perhaps, the most upscale seaside dining spot
★   on the south coast. Fruits of the sea—fillet of dolphin with pawpaw and pineapple salsa or red snapper with sun-dried tomato crust—are prominent on the menu, and the wine list is extensive. Try tuna and salmon tartar with wasabi Dijon dressing as an innovative starter, and free-range chicken teriyaki with stir-fry noodles will tingle your taste buds. Pasta dishes assuage the vegetarian palate. ⊠ *St. Lawrence Gap, Dover, Christ Church,* ☎ *246/435–8245. Reservations essential. AE, DC, MC, V. No lunch.*

$$–$$$ ✕ **The Crane.** Perched on a oceanfront cliff, The Crane in the Crane Beach Hotel is an informal luncheon spot by day. Enjoy seafood chowder—prepared with lobster, shrimp, dolphin, local vegetables, and a dash of sherry—or a light salad or sandwich while absorbing the breathtaking view. In the evening, candlelight and a soft guitar enhance fabulous grilled Caribbean lobster seasoned with herbs, lime juice, and garlic butter and served in its shell. Landlubbers can order a perfect filet mignon, too. Sundays are really special, with a Gospel Brunch at 10 AM and a Bajan Buffet at 12:30 PM. ⊠ *Crane Beach Hotel, Crane Bay, St. Philip,* ☎ *246/423–6220. Reservations essential. AE, D, DC, MC, V.*

$$–$$$ ✕ **Pisces.** Seafood is prepared here in every way—from charbroiled to sautéed. Specialties include conch strips in tempura, rich fish chowder, panfried fillets of flying fish with a toasted almond crust and a light mango-citrus sauce, and seared prawns in a fragrant curry sauce. There are also some chicken, beef, and pasta dishes. Whatever your selection, the herbs that flavor it and the accompanying vegetables will have come from the chef's garden. Save room for the bread pudding, yogurt lime cheesecake, or homemade rum-raisin ice cream. Twinkling white lights reflect on the water as you dine. ⊠ *St. Lawrence Gap, Dover, Christ Church,* ☎ *246/435–6564. AE, DC, MC, V. No lunch.*

West Coast
CONTEMPORARY

$$$$ ✕ **The Cliff.** The mastery of Chef Paul Owens is the foundation of one
★ of the finest dining establishments in Barbados. Every candlelit table
has a sea view. In fact, steep steps hug the cliff to which the restaurant
clings and reach down to the sea to accommodate those arriving by
yacht. Imaginative art accents the tiered dining terrace. The artistry extends to the innovative menu, which offers excellent cuts of prime meat
and fresh fish, creatively presented with nouvelle accents and accompanied by fresh local vegetables. Don't skip dessert, which falls in the
sinful category. Service is impeccable, of course. ⌧ *Hwy. 1, Derricks,
St. James,* ☎ *246/432–1922. AE, DC, MC, V. No lunch.*

$$$$ ✕ **Orchid Room.** Hotel restaurants on Barbados generally offer excel-
★ lent cuisine, but enjoying a special dinner at the Colony Club's intimate Orchid Room is nothing short of extraordinary. Chef Philippe's
haute cuisine appeals to the eye as well as the palate. The à la carte
menu changes nightly but might include chateaubriand for two with
sauce bordelaise, veal scallops with mushrooms and escargot, or
poached salmon with dill. Dessert is also perfect—perhaps a rich
chocolate mousse cake, passion fruit brûlée, or banana tartlet with crème
anglaise. ⌧ *Colony Club Hotel, Hwy. 1, Porters, St. James,* ☎ *246/
422–2335. Reservations essential. AE, DC, MC, V. Closed weekends.
No lunch.*

$$$–$$$$ ✕ **La Mer.** Chef Hans Schweitzer, who earned a reputation in Barba-
★ dos for elegant cuisine, works his magic in a more relaxed—but still
stylish—way. His restaurant hugs the lagoon at Port St. Charles, an
exclusive waterfront community. Fresh fish from Six Men's Bay, just
up the road, and tender cuts of meat are seared on either of two grills,
wood or lava rock, while vegetarian dishes might be stirred up at the
wok station. This is a perfect place for a light meal at the bar, just steps
from the dock, or a romantic dinner, with moonlight reflecting on the
lagoon. ⌧ *Port St. Charles, Speightstown, St. Peter,* ☎ *246/429–2000.
Reservations essential. AE, DC, MC, V.*

$$$–$$$$ ✕ **Carambola.** Dramatic lighting, alfresco dining, and a cliffside location
★ make this one of the island's most romantic restaurants. The menu is
a mix of classic French and Caribbean cuisines—with Asian touches
for good measure. Start with a spicy crab tart, served with hollandaise
sauce on a bed of sweet red peppers. For an entrée, try fillet of mahimahi
broiled with Dijon mustard sauce, or sliced duck breast with a wild
mushroom fumet served with stuffed tomatoes and *gratin dauphi-
noise* (potatoes au gratin). For dessert, the *citron gâteau* (lime mousse
on a pool of lemon coulis) is a wonderfully light finish. ⌧ *Hwy. 1, Der-
ricks, St. James,* ☎ *246/432–0832. Reservations essential. AE, MC,
V. Closed Sun. No lunch.*

ECLECTIC

$$–$$$$ ✕ **The Lone Star.** In the 1940s this was the only garage on the west
coast; today it's the snazzy restaurant in the chic Lone Star Garage Motel,
where top chefs turn the finest raw ingredients into gastronomic delights. In the Oriental Room (upstairs), dishes are influenced by Chinese, Thai, and Vietnamese cuisines. In the main dining room
(downstairs), the menu emphasizes Mediterranean, Modern European, and Caribbean cuisines. The extensive à la carte choices will please
any palate. ⌧ *Lone Star Garage Motel, Hwy. 1, Mount Standfast, St.
James,* ☎ *246/419–0598. AE, MC, V.*

$$–$$$$ ✕ **Olives Bar & Bistro.** Owner-chef Larry Rogers and his wife, Michelle,
have turned a quaint Bajan house in the center of Holetown into an
intimate restaurant. Mediterranean and Caribbean flavors enliven in-
ventive pizzas and tasty salads at lunch or dinner; special dishes on the

menu might include fresh seafood, such as seared yellowfin tuna with ratatouille, and tasty Swiss-style *rösti* potatoes (shredded and fried like a pancake) with smoked salmon and sour cream. Dine inside or on the courtyard; the popular upstairs bar is a great spot to mingle over coffee, refreshing drinks, or snacks (pizza, pastas, salads). ⌧ *2nd St., Holetown, St. James,* ☎ *246/432–2112. AE, MC, V.*

$$–$$$ ✕ **Angry Annie's.** You can't miss this place. Outside and inside, everything's painted in bright Caribbean pinks, blues, greens, and yellows—and it's just steps from the main road. The food is just as lively: great barbecued "jump-up" ribs and chicken, grilled fresh fish or juicy steaks, "Rasta pasta" for vegetarians, and several spicy curries. Eat inside on gaily colored furniture or outside under the stars—or take it away with you. ⌧ *1st St., Holetown, St. James,* ☎ *246/432–2119. AE, DC, MC, V.*

$–$$ ✕ **Baku Beach Bar.** Going to the beach, coming from the beach, or just wanting to be near the beach, this is a great place for lunch or an informal dinner. Tables spill onto the courtyard, through tropical gardens, and onto a boardwalk by the sea. Try a Caesar salad, burger, spareribs, or grilled fish served with the salsa of your choice: fruit, pesto, herb lemon, ginger soy, and more. On the side, have garlic bread, sautéed onions, rice pilaf, or spicy potato wedges. Got room for crème brûlée, lemon tart, or a brownie with ice cream? Maybe dawdling over cappuccino is enough. ⌧ *Hwy. 1, Holetown, St. James,* ☎ *246/432–2258. AE, MC, V.*

$$–$$$ ✕ **Ragamuffins.** The only restaurant on Barbados in an authentic chattel house, Ragamuffins is tiny, funky, lively, and informal. The menu offers seafood, perfectly broiled T-bone steaks, West Indian curries, and vegetarian dishes such as Bajan stir-fried vegetables with noodles. Dine inside or out. The kitchen is within sight of the bar—which is a popular meeting spot most evenings. ⌧ *1st St., Holetown, St. James,* ☎ *246/432–1295. Reservations essential. AE, MC, V. No lunch.*

Beaches

Bajan beaches have fine, white sand, and all are open to the public. Most have access from the road, so nonguest bathers don't have to pass through hotel properties.

EAST COAST

With long stretches of open beach, crashing ocean surf, rocky cliffs, and verdant hills, the windward side of Barbados is full of dramatic views. This is also where many Barbadians have second homes and spend their holidays. But be cautioned: swimming at east coast beaches is treacherous, even for strong swimmers, and *not* recommended. Waves are high, the bottom tends to be rocky, the currents are unpredictable, and the undertow is strong.

Barclays Park. Serious swimming is unwise at this beach along the Ermy Bourne Highway, but there are tide pools where you can take a dip, wade, and play—and a lovely shaded picnic area across the road.

Bathsheba Soup Bowl. The rolling surf attracts surfers from around the world to the site of the Independence Classic Surfing Championships each November.

Cattlewash. Just north of Bathsheba, there is this long stretch of untouched, windswept sand that's great for beachcombing, wading, and expert-only surfing.

SOUTH COAST

A young, energetic crowd favors the south coast beaches, which are broad, blessed with white, powdery sand, and dotted with tall palms. The reef-protected waters are crystal clear and safe for swimming and snorkeling. The surf is medium to high, and the waves get bigger and the winds stronger (windsurfers take note) the farther southeast you go.

Accra Beach. The popular beach in Rockley has gentle surf and a lifeguard. There are plenty of places for a meal or drink and to rent equipment for snorkeling and other water sports. There's also a convenient parking lot.

Bottom Bay. The cove north of Sam Lord's Castle is mesmerizing. Follow the steps down the cliff to a strip of white sand lined by coconut palms and washed by an aquamarine sea. There's even a cave to explore. It's out of the way and not near restaurants, so bring a picnic lunch.

Carlisle Bay Beach. This beach at Needham's Point is one of the island's best and gets crowded with locals on weekends and holidays. The Carlisle Bay Centre has changing rooms and showers to accommodate cruiseship passengers spending a day at the beach.

Casuarina Beach. At the east end of the St. Lawrence Gap area you'll always get a nice breeze and a fair amount of surf. Public access is from Maxwell Coast Road. Refreshments are available at the Casuarina Beach Hotel.

Crane Beach. This exquisite crescent of pink sand is protected by steep cliffs. As attractive as this location is now, it was named not for the elegant long-legged wading birds but for the crane used for hauling and loading cargo when this area was a busy port. Protected by a reef, the rolling surf is great for bodysurfing. A lifeguard is on duty. Changing rooms are available at Crane Beach Hotel for a small fee (which you can apply toward drinks or a meal at the restaurant). Beach access is through the hotel and down about 200 steps.

Sandy Beach. In Worthing, next to the Sandy Beach Island Resort, this beach has shallow, calm waters and a picturesque lagoon, making it an ideal location for families. There's parking on the main road, and plenty of places nearby sell food and drink.

Silver Sands Beach. Close to the southernmost tip of the island, Silver Sands is a beautiful strand of white sand that always has a stiff breeze, which attracts intermediate and advanced windsurfers.

WEST COAST

Gentle Caribbean waves lap the west coast, and the stunning coves and sandy beaches are shaded by leafy mahogany trees. The water is perfect for swimming and water sports. An almost unbroken chain of beaches runs between Bridgetown and Speightstown. Elegant homes and luxury hotels take up most of the beachfront property in this area, Barbados's Platinum Coast.

Although west coast beaches are seldom crowded, they aren't isolated. Vendors stroll by, selling handmade baskets, hats, dolls, jewelry—even original watercolors; owners of private boats offer waterskiing, parasailing, and snorkeling excursions. There are no concession stands, but hotels welcome nonguests for terrace lunches (wear a cover-up), and you can buy picnic items at supermarkets in Holetown.

Brighton Beach. Just north of Bridgetown and convenient to the port, Brighton is as calm as a lake. Locals often take quick swims here on hot days.

Mullins Beach. This picturesque beach just south of Speightstown is a perfect place to spend the day. The water is safe for swimming and snorkeling, there's easy parking on the main road, and Mullins Beach Bar serves snacks, meals, and drinks.

Paynes Bay. South of Holetown, this beach is lined with luxury hotels. It's a very pretty area, with plenty of beach to go around and good snorkeling. Parking areas and public access are available opposite the

Coach House. Grab a bite to eat and liquid refreshments at Bomba's Beach Bar.

Outdoor Activities and Sports

Participant Sports

FISHING

Fishing is great year-round—but ideal from January to April. Half- or full-day charter trips are available for serious deep-sea fishers looking for billfish or for those who prefer angling in calm coastal waters where wahoo, barracuda, and other small fish reside. Charters depart from the Careenage, in Bridgetown. Expect to pay $60–$120 per person, depending on the length of time, size of the boat, and whether it's a shared or private charter.

Billfisher II (☎ 246/431–0741) is a 40-ft Pacemaker that can accommodate up to six people; trips include drinks and transportation to and from the boat. Full-day charters include a full lunch and guaranteed fish. *Blue Jay* (☎ 246/429–2326) is a fully equipped 45-ft Sport Fisherman, with a crew that knows where blue marlin, sailfish, barracuda, and kingfish play. Four people can be accommodated; each is guaranteed his or her own rod and chair and can invite, free of charge, a spouse or guest. Drinks and snacks are provided. *Cannon II* (☎ 246/424–6107), a 42-ft Hatteras Sport Fisherman, accommodates six fishing passengers; drinks and snacks are complimentary, and lunch is served on full-day charters.

GOLF

Barbadians love golf, and golfers love Barbados. Learn to play or improve your game at the **Barbados Academy of Golf & Public Driving Range** (⊠ ABC Hwy., Balls Complex, Balls, Christ Church, ☎ 246/420–7405). It has a chipping and putting green, with sand bunkers and 48 hitting bays. The adjacent 18-hole miniature golf course is fun for the whole family. Both are open daily 8 AM–11 PM, and snacks are available.

Almond Beach Village (⊠ Hwy. 1B, Heywoods, St. Peter, ☎ 246/422–4900), on the island's northwest corner, has a 9-hole, par-3 executive course for hotel guest–use only; there's no fee, and clubs are provided. **Barbados Golf Club** (⊠ Hwy. 7, Durants, Christ Church, ☎ 246/426–8463), the first public golf course on Barbados, is a par-72, 18-hole championship course redesigned and reconstructed in 2000 by noted golf architect Ron Kirby. Greens fees are $115 for 18 holes, $70 for 9 holes. Several hotels offer golf privileges, with preferential tee-time reservations and reduced rates. Club and shoe rentals are available. **Club Rockley Barbados** (⊠ Golf Club Rd., Rockley, Christ Church, ☎ 246/435–7873), on the southeast coast near Sam Lord's Castle, has a challenging 9-hole course that can be played as 18 from varying tee positions. It's open to the public daily, and club rentals are available. Greens fees are $37.50 for 9 holes in season; $27.50, off-season. The **Royal Westmoreland Golf Club** (⊠ Hwy. 2A, Westmoreland, St. James, ☎ 246/422–4653) has a world-class Robert Trent Jones, Jr., 18-hole championship course that meanders through the former 500-acre Westmoreland Sugar Estate. Greens fees ($92 for 9 holes or $150 for 18 holes) include use of an electric cart; equipment rental is available. Access is limited to villa residents or guests of hotels with golf privileges. **Sandy Lane Golf Club** (⊠ Hwy. 1, Paynes Bay, St. James, ☎ 246/432–2829) has undergone a dramatic redesign by renowned architect Tom Fazio. Golfers can play on the bottom 9 or on either of two 18-hole championship courses. Greens fees are $60 for 9 holes or $100 for 18 holes.

HIKING

Hilly but not mountainous, the northern interior and the east coast are ideal for hiking. The **Arbib Heritage and Nature Trail** (✉ Speightstown, St. Peter, ☏ 246/426–2421), maintained by the Barbados National Trust, is actually two trails—one offers a rigorous hike through gullies and plantations to old ruins and remote north-country areas; the other is a shorter, easier walk through Speightstown's side streets and past an ancient church and chattel houses. Guided hikes take place on Wednesday, Thursday, and Saturday 9–2:30 (book by 3 PM the day before) and cost $7.50. The **Barbados National Trust** (✉ Wildey House, Wildey, St. Michael, ☏ 246/426–2421) sponsors free 5-mi (8-km) walks year-round on Sunday from 6 AM to about 9 AM and from 3:30 PM to 6 PM, as well as monthly moonlight hikes. Experienced guides group you with others of similar levels of ability. Wear sensible shoes and a hat, and bring your camera. Hikes start and finish at the same location. Check newspapers or call the trust for the meeting place.

HORSEBACK RIDING

A ride through the hilly north country or along the beach is exhilarating, and equestrian tours can accommodate any level of experience. The **Caribbean International Riding Center** (✉ Auburn, St. Joseph, ☏ 246/422–7433 or 246/420–1246) offers one- and two-hour rides through the Scotland District and longer treks that continue on to Morgan Lewis Beach, on the Atlantic coast. Prices range from $40 for a one-hour trail ride to $82.50 for a 2½-hour trek; transportation to and from your hotel is included.

PARASAILING

Parasailing is available, wind conditions permitting, on the beaches of St. James and Christ Church. The chute is attached to a speedboat with a launching and landing platform; a hydraulic winch system hauls you in simply and safely. You don't even have to get wet! *The Falcon* **Parasail** (☏ 246/419–0579) picks people up all along the beach on either coast, or you can book ahead. Rates are $45 per flight.

SCUBA DIVING AND SNORKELING

More than two dozen dive sites lie along the west coast between Maycocks Bay and Bridgetown and off the south coast as far as the St. Lawrence Gap. Certified divers can explore flat coral reefs and see sea fans and corals, huge barrel sponges, and more than 50 varieties of fish. Nine sunken wrecks are dived regularly, and at least 10 more are accessible to experts. Underwater visibility is generally 80–90 ft (24–28 m). The calm waters along the west coast are also ideal for snorkeling. The marine reserve, a stretch of protected reef between Sandy Lane and the Colony Club, contains beautiful coral formations accessible from the beach.

On the west coast, **Bell Buoy** is a large dome-shape reef where huge brown coral tree forests and schools of fish delight all categories of divers at depths ranging from 20 to 60 ft (6 to 18 m). At **Dottins Reef,** off Holetown, you can see schooling fish, barracudas, and turtles at depths of 40–60 ft (12–18 m). **Maycocks Bay,** on the northwest coast, is a particularly enticing site; large coral reefs are separated by corridors of white sand, and visibility is often 100 ft (30 m) or more. The 165-ft freighter *Pamir* lies in 60 ft of water off Six Men's Bay; still intact, you can peer through its portholes and view dozens of varieties of tropical fish. **Silver Bank** is a healthy coral reef with beautiful fish and sea fans; you may get a glimpse of the *Atlantis* submarine at 60–80 ft (18–24 m). Not to be missed is the *Stavronikita,* a scuttled Greek freighter at about 135 ft (41 m); hundreds of butterfly fish hang out around its mast, and the thin rays of sunlight filtering down through the water make fully exploring the huge ship a wonderfully eerie experience.

Farther south, **Carlisle Bay** is a natural harbor and marine park just below Bridgetown. Here you can retrieve empty bottles thrown overboard by generations of sailors and see cannons and cannonballs, anchors, and three unique shipwrecks (*Berwyn, Fox,* and *CTrek*) lying in 25–40 ft (8–12 m) of water, all close enough to visit on the same dive. The *Eilon,* a freighter confiscated for drug running, is the island's newest wreck. Sunk in 1996, it sits in 60 ft (18 m) of water in Carlisle Bay near three earlier wrecks.

Dive shops provide a two-hour beginner's "resort" course ($70–$75) or a weeklong certification course (about $350), followed by a shallow dive. Once you're certified, a one-tank dive runs about $50–$55; a two-tank dive is $70–$80. All equipment is supplied, and you can purchase multidive packages. Gear for snorkeling is available (free or for a small rental fee) from most hotels. Snorkelers can usually accompany dive trips for $20 for a one- or two-hour trip.

On the south coast, **Dive Boat Safari** (⊠ Grand Barbados Beach Resort, Aquatic Gap, St. Michael, ☎ 246/427–4350) offers three dives daily and full instruction. **Dive Shop, Ltd.** (⊠ Aquatic Gap, St. Michael, ☎ 246/426–9947; 800/693–3483 in the U.S.; 888/575–3483 in Canada), the island's oldest dive shop, offers three dives daily, beginner dives, and certification. Underwater camera rentals are available.

On the west coast, **Dive Blue Reef** (⊠ Mount Standfast, St. James, ☎ 246/422–3133) offers all levels of PADI instruction, reef and wreck dives, underwater video and camera rental, and free transportation. **Hightide Watersports** (⊠ Coral Reef Club, Holetown, St. James, ☎ 246/432–0931 or 800/513–5763) offers one- and two-tank dives, night reef/wreck/drift dives, PADI instruction, and free transportation.

SEA EXCURSIONS

Minisubmarine voyages are enormously popular with families and those who enjoy watching fish but can't snorkel or dive. Party boats depart from Bridgetown's harbor, near the Careenage, for lunchtime snorkeling or sunset cruises. Prices are $65 per person and include transportation to and from the dock.

The 48-passenger *Atlantis III* (⊠ The Shallow Draught, Bridgetown, ☎ 246/436–8929) turns the Caribbean into a giant aquarium. The 45-minute trip aboard the 50-ft submarine takes you to wrecks and reefs as deep as 150 ft (46 m). Special nighttime trips, using high-power searchlights, are spectacular. Cost for the trip is $80 per person.

A five-hour cruise on the 54-ft catamaran *Cool Runnings* (☎ 246/436–0911) includes stops along the coast for snorkeling on a coral reef, exploring a shallow shipwreck, and visiting sea turtles in a quiet bay; lunch is served on board. The 44-ft CSY sailing yacht *Limbo Lady* (☎ 246/420–5418) sails along the captivating west coast, stopping for a swim, snorkeling, and a Bajan buffet lunch. Sunset cruises are another option. *Secret Love* (☎ 246/432–1972), a 41-ft Morgan sailboat, offers daily lunchtime or evening snorkeling cruises for no more than 14 people. The 53-ft catamaran *Tiami* (☎ 246/430–0900) offers an early morning breakfast cruise, a luncheon cruise to a secluded bay, or a romantic sunset and moonlight cruise with special catering and live music; all cruises last four hours. Four- and five-hour daytime cruises along the west coast on the 100-ft MV *Harbour Master* (☎ 246/430–0900) stop in Holetown and land at beaches along the way; evening cruises are shorter but add a buffet dinner and entertainment. Day or night you can view the briny deep from the ship's onboard 34-seat semisubmersible. Either cruise runs about $65 per person. The red-sail *Jolly Roger* (☎ 246/430–0900) "pirate" ship runs lunch-and-snorkeling sails along the south or west coasts. Be prepared for a rather raucous time, with rope swinging, plank walking, and other games—and plenty of calypso music. The cruise costs about $65 per person, with complimentary drinks.

SURFING

The best surfing is on the east coast, at Bathsheba Soup Bowl, where the Independence Classic Surfing Championship (an international competition) is held every November—when the surf is at its peak. For information, call the **Barbados Surfing Association** (☎ 246/228–5117).

TENNIS AND SQUASH

On the west coast, public tennis courts are available for free on a first-come, first-served basis at **Folkestone Park** (✉ Holetown, ☎ 246/422–2314). On the south coast, the **National Tennis Centre** (✉ Sir Garfield Sobers Sports Complex, Wildey, St. Michael, ☎ 246/437–6010) charges $12 per hour and requires reservations. At the **Barbados Squash Club** (✉ Marine House, Hastings, Christ Church, ☎ 246/427–7913), court fees run $9 for 45 minutes; matches with players of similar ability can be arranged. At **Club Rockley Barbados** (✉ Golf Club Rd., Rockley, Christ Church, ☎ 246/435–7880) nonguests can reserve courts for $10 per hour.

WINDSURFING

Barbados is part of the World Cup Windsurfing Circuit and one of the best locations in the world for windsurfing. Winds are strongest November through April at the island's southern tip, which is where the Barbados Windsurfing Championships are held in mid-January. Use of boards and equipment is often among the amenities included at larger hotels; equipment can usually be rented by nonguests.

Club Mistral (✉ Oistins, Christ Church, ☎ 246/428–7277) is a great place to learn to windsurf, because the waves here are usually flat. More experienced windsurfers congregate at **Silver Rock Windsurfing Club** (✉ Silver Rock Hotel, Silver Sands Beach, Christ Church, ☎ 246/428–2866), where the surf ranges from 3 to 15 ft (1 to 5 m) and provides an exhilarating windsurfing experience.

Spectator Sports

CRICKET

Barbados is mad for cricket. Although the season is from May to late December, international test matches are usually played from January to April. The Sandy Lane Gold Cup is held in March. Tickets to cricket matches at Kensington Oval, Bridgetown, range from $7.50 to $30. For information about upcoming cricket matches, call the **Barbados Cricket Association** (☎ 246/436–1397).

HORSE RACING

Horse racing is administered by the **Barbados Turf Club** (☎ 246/426–3980) and takes place on alternate Saturdays most of the year at the Garrison Savannah, a six-furlong grass oval in Christ Church, about 3 mi (5 km) south of Bridgetown. The important races are the 5,000 meters run in February, the Sandy Lane Gold Cup in May, the United Barbados Derby Day in August, and the Heineken Stakes on Boxing Day (day after Christmas). Post time is 12:30 PM, and general admission is $1 (grandstand seats are $5; those in the Club House are $12.50).

POLO

Polo matches are inexpensive (about $2.50) and are played at the **Barbados Polo Club** (⊠ Holder's Hill, St. James, ☎ 246/432–1802) on Wednesday and Saturday from October through April.

RUGBY

The rough-and-tumble game of rugby is played Tuesday and Thursday evenings at the Garrison Savannah, 3 mi (5 km) south of Bridgetown. Touring teams are always welcome to visit the clubhouse and join in the customary social activity. For schedules, call the **Barbados Rugby Football Union** (☎ 246/437–3836).

SOCCER

The football (soccer) season runs January–June at the National Stadium. For game information contact the **Barbados Football Association** (☎ 246/228–1707).

Shopping

Areas and Malls

Bridgetown's **Broad Street** is the downtown shopping area. At the **Cruise Ship Terminal** shopping arcade, passengers can buy both duty-free goods and Barbadian-made merchandise at more than 30 boutiques and a dozen vendor carts and stalls. **DaCostas Mall,** in the historic Colonnade Building on Broad Street, has more than 25 shops that sell everything from Piaget to postcards. Across the street from the DaCostas Mall, **Mall 34** has 22 shops where you can buy duty-free goods, souvenirs, and snacks.

Holetown and St. Lawrence Gap each have a **Chattel House Village,** a cluster of brightly colored shops selling local products, fashions, beachwear, and souvenirs. **Sunset Crest,** in Holetown, has a branch of the Cave Shepherd department store, a bank, a pharmacy, and several small shops. In Holetown's **West Coast Mall,** you can find duty-free goods, island wear, services, and groceries. The **Quayside Shopping Center,** in Rockley, Christ Church, houses a small group of boutiques.

Department Stores

Cave Shepherd (⊠ Broad St., Bridgetown, ☎ 246/431–2121) offers a wide selection of clothing and luxury goods; branch stores are in Holetown, at the airport, and in the Cruise Ship Terminal. **Harrison's** (⊠ Broad St., Bridgetown, ☎ 246/431–5500) has 11 locations—including its two large stores on Broad Street and one each at the airport and the Cruise Ship Terminal—offering luxury name-brand goods from the fashion corners of the world.

Specialty Items

ANTIQUES

In Barbados you can find British antiques as well as wonderful local pieces—particularly mahogany furniture. Look for planters' chairs and the classic Barbadian rocking chair, as well as old prints and paintings. **Greenwich House Antiques** (⊠ Greenwich Village, Trents Hill, St. James, ☎ 246/432–1169) fills an entire plantation house with Barbadian mahogany furniture, crystal, silver, china, books, and pictures; it's open daily 10:30–5:30.

CLOTHES

Dresses and resort wear are often handmade of hand-printed fabrics. **Del Sol** (⊠ Galleria Mall, Broad St., Bridgetown, ☎ 246/431–0678) has unique shirts, hats, other apparel, and accessories. The designs appear black and white indoors but change to bright colors when exposed to the sun. **Dingolay** (⊠ Bay St., Bridgetown, St. Michael, ☎ 246/436–

2157; ⊠ Hwy. 1, Holetown, St. James, ☎ 246/432–8709) sells tropical clothing designed and made in Barbados for ladies and girls, as well as shoes, handbags, and accessories from around the world. Check out the colorful T-shirts from **Irie Blue** (⊠ DaCostas Mall, Broad St., Bridgetown, St. Michael,☎ 246/431–0017; ⊠ Worthing, Christ Church, ☎ 246/435–7699), which are designed and made in Barbados. You can find them in many gift shops as well. **Sandbox & Co.** (⊠ Bell House, Sunbury Plantation, St. Philip, ☎ 246/423–0888) offers original designs of swimwear, resort wear, children's clothing, and home furnishings all made and hand-painted in Barbados.

DUTY-FREE GOODS

Duty-free luxury goods—china, crystal, cameras, porcelain, leather items, electronics, jewelry, perfume, and clothing—are found in Bridgetown's Broad Street department stores and their branches, at the Cruise Ship Terminal shops (for passengers only), and in the departure lounge shops at Grantley Adams International Airport. Prices are often 30% to 40% less than at home. To buy items at duty-free prices, you must produce your outbound travel ticket and passport at the time of purchase—or you can have your purchases delivered free to the airport or harbor for pickup. Duty-free alcohol, tobacco products, and some electronic equipment *must* be delivered to you at the airport or harbor.

Little Switzerland (☎ 246/431–0030) is the anchor shop at DaCostas Mall on Broad Street in Bridgetown and has a branch at the Cruise Ship Terminal. Here you can find perfume, jewelry, cameras, audio equipment, Swarovski and Waterford crystal, and Wedgwood china. The **Royal Shop** (⊠ 32 Broad St., Bridgetown, ☎ 246/429–7072) carries fine watches and jewelry fashioned in Italian gold, Caribbean silver, diamonds, and other gems.

HANDICRAFTS

Typical crafts include pottery, shell and glass art, hand-printed fabrics, handmade dolls; and watercolors and other paintings (originals and prints).The **Best of Barbados** (⊠ Worthing, Christ Church, ☎ 246/421–6900), which has a total of seven locations, offers high-quality artwork and crafts, in both "native style" and modern designs; everything is made or designed on Barbados. **Earthworks Pottery** (⊠ Edghill Heights, No. 2, Edghill Heights, St. Thomas, ☎ 246/425–0223) is a family-owned and -operated pottery where you can purchase anything from a dish or knick-knack to a complete dinner service or one-of-a-kind art piece. The products are sold in gift shops throughout the island, but the biggest selection is at the pottery, where you also can watch the potters work. **Island Crafts** (⊠ 5 Pelican Craft Centre, Bridgetown, St. Michael, ☎ 246/426–4391) offers locally made pottery, wood carvings, straw items, glass art, batik, and wire sculptures. Additional shops are at Harrison's Cave, the airport courtyard, and the airport departure lounge. **Pelican Craft Centre** (⊠ Harbour Rd., Bridgetown, ☎ 246/427–5350) is a cluster of workshops halfway between the Cruise Ship Terminal and downtown Bridgetown, where craftspeople create and sell "100% Barbadian-made" leather goods, batik, basketry, carvings, jewelry, glass art, paintings, pottery, and other items. It's open weekdays 9–6 and Saturday 9–2, with extended hours during holidays or to accommodate cruise-ship arrivals. **Redclay Pottery** (⊠ Fairfield Cross Rd., Fairfield, St. Michael, ☎ 246/426–3800) is in an old syrup boiling house 2 mi (3 km) from Bridgetown. Each piece here is handcrafted of local clay and individually painted; call for a tour of the works. Items are for sale on-site and in island gift shops. In the chattel houses at **Tyrol Cot Heritage Village** (⊠ Codrington Hill, St. Michael, ☎ 246/424–2074), you can watch local artisans make hand-painted figurines, straw baskets, clothing, paintings, pottery, etc.—and, of course, buy their wares.

Nightlife and the Arts

Nightlife

When the sun goes down, the musicians come out and folks in Barbados "lime" (which can be anything from a "chat-up" to a fullblown "jump-up"). Performances by reggae groups and calypso singers are major events, and tickets can be hard to come by—but give it a try. Most large resorts have nightly entertainment in season, and nightclubs often have live bands for listening and dancing. The busiest bars and dance clubs rage until 3 AM. On Saturday nights, some clubs—especially those with live music—charge a cover of about $10.

The **Oistins Fish Fry** is the place to be on weekend evenings, when the south coast fishing village becomes an outdoor street fair. Barbecued chicken and flying fish are served right from the coal pot; servings are huge and inexpensive. Drinks, music, and dancing add to the fun.

BARS

Barbados supports the rum industry with more than 1,200 "rum shops," simple bars where men (mostly) congregate to discuss the world's ills, and in more sophisticated inns, where you find world-class rum drinks made with the island's renowned Mount Gay and Cockspur brands.

The **Boatyard** (✉ Bay St., Bridgetown, ☎ 246/436–2622) is a pub with both a DJ and live bands; from happy hour until the wee hours, the patrons are mostly local and visiting professionals. **Waterfront Cafe** (✉ The Careenage, Bridgetown, ☎ 246/427–0093) has live jazz in the evening, with a small dance floor for dancing. The wharf-side location is also a draw.

On the south coast, **Café Sol** (✉ St. Lawrence Gap, Dover, Christ Church, ☎ 246/435–9531) has a wraparound terrace with a great view of the St. Lawrence Gap strip. Margaritas (rubbed with sugar not salt) will fortify you for the late-night complimentary Spanish dance lessons. **Champers** (✉ Hwy. 1, Hastings, Christ Church, ☎ 246/435–6644) is a waterfront wine bar, where folks gather for good conversation, a great view, snacks, and a selection from the extensive wine list.

On the west coast, **Coach House** (✉ Hwy. 1, Paynes Bay, St. James, ☎ 246/432–1163) has live entertainment nightly and live sports via satellite TV. **Upstairs at Olives** (✉ 2nd St., Holetown, St. James, ☎ 246/432–2112) is a sophisticated watering hole. Enjoy cocktails and conversation seated amid potted palms and cooled by ceiling fans—either before or after dinner downstairs.

DANCE CLUBS

After Dark (✉ St. Lawrence Gap, Dover, Christ Church, ☎ 246/435–6547) attracts mostly young people to live appearances of reggae, calypso, and *soca* (an upbeat, sexy variation of calypso) headliners such as Krosfyah and Red Plastic Bag. **Harbour Lights** (✉ Marine Villa, Bay St., Bridgetown, St. Michael, ☎ 246/436–7225) claims to be the "home of the party animal" and, most any night, there is dancing under the stars to live reggae and soca music. The **Ship Inn** (✉ St. Lawrence Gap, Dover, Christ Church, ☎ 246/435–6961) is a large, friendly pub with local band music every night for dancing.

THEME NIGHTS

On Wednesday and Friday evenings at the **Plantation Restaurant and Garden Theater** (✉ St. Lawrence Rd., Dover, Christ Church, ☎ 246/

428–5048), the Tropical Spectacular calypso cabaret with dancing, fire eating, limbo, steel-band music, and the sounds of a top reggae and soca band. The fun begins at 6:30 PM. A Barbadian buffet dinner, unlimited drinks, transportation, and the show cost $75; for the show and drinks only, it's $37.50.

The Arts

GALLERIES

The **Barbados Gallery of Art** (⊠ The Garrison, Bush Hill, St. Michael, ☎ 246/228–0149) is the only museum on Barbados dedicated to the visual arts. Its permanent collection includes artwork from the Caribbean, South America, and the United States. Admission is $2.50 weekdays and $1 on Saturday. The gallery is closed Sunday and Monday. The Cunard Gallery at the **Barbados Museum** (⊠ The Garrison, Bush Hill, St. Michael, ☎ 246/427–0201 or 246/436–1956) has a permanent collection of 20th-century Barbadian and Caribbean paintings and engravings; the Connell Gallery houses European decorative arts. The galleries are closed on Sunday and Monday, and there's an entrance fee of $5. **Queen's Park Art Gallery** (⊠ Queen's Park, Bridgetown, St. Michael, ☎ 246/427–2345), managed by the National Culture Foundation, is the island's largest gallery. It's open daily, and exhibits change monthly.

THEATER

Every Thursday and Sunday night, 6:30–10, the folkloric show *1627 and All That* (⊠ Barbados Museum, Hwy. 7, Garrison, St. Michael, ☎ 246/428–1627) traces island culture from colonization through slavery and emancipation to the present time. It's performed by energetic dancers dressed in period costumes and accompanied by lively steel-band music. Unlimited complimentary drinks are included; pay more for a Bajan buffet dinner and transportation. Admission is $27.50 for the show and drinks; $60 for the show, drinks, dinner, and transportation. Major credit cards are accepted.

Exploring Barbados

The terrain of the island's 11 parishes changes dramatically from one to the next, and so does the pace and ambience. Bridgetown, the capital, is a rather sophisticated city. West coast resorts and private estates ooze luxury, whereas the small villages and vast sugar plantations found throughout central Barbados mark the island's history. The relentless Atlantic surf designed the cliffs of the dramatic east coast, and the northeast is called Scotland because of its hilly landscape. Along the lively south coast a palpable energy continues day and night.

The **Barbados National Trust** (⊠ Wildey House, Wildey, St. Michael, ☎ 246/426–2421) has designed a Heritage Passport for some of Barbados's most popular attractions. When the holder pays full admission to visit some attractions, the passport will be stamped to validate free admission to other sights. Passports are free, and you can pick them up at displays in shops, hotels, and restaurants.

Bridgetown

This bustling capital city is a major duty-free port, with a compact shopping area. The principal thoroughfare is Broad Street, which leads west from National Heroes Square. The busy capital has both rush hours and traffic congestion.

Numbers in the margin correspond to points of interest on the Bridgetown map.

SIGHTS TO SEE

❶ Barbados Synagogue. Representing one of the oldest Jewish congregations in the Western Hemisphere, this synagogue was formed by Jews who left Brazil in the 1620s and introduced sugarcane to Barbados. The adjoining cemetery has tombstones dating from the 1630s. The original house of worship, built in 1654, was destroyed in an 1831 hurricane. The building was rebuilt in 1833 and restored by the Barbados National Trust in 1992. Services are held, and the building is open to the public. ⊠ *Synagogue La., St. Michael,* ☎ *246/426–5792.* ⊠ *Donation requested.* ⊙ *Weekdays 9–4.*

❷ The Careenage. Bridgetown's natural harbor and gathering place is where, in the early days, schooners were careened (turned on their sides) to be scraped of barnacles and repainted. Today the Careenage serves as a marina for pleasure yachts and excursion boats. The Chamberlain Bridge and the Charles O'Neal Bridge cross the Careenage.

❸ National Heroes Square. Across Broad Street from the Parliament Buildings and bordered by High and Trafalgar streets, this triangular "square" (formerly called Trafalgar Square) marks the center of town. Its monument to Lord Horatio Nelson (although Nelson was in Barbados only briefly in 1777, when he was a 19-year-old navy lieutenant) predates Nelson's Column in London's Trafalgar Square by 27 years. Also here are a war memorial and a fountain that commemorates the 1865 advent of running water on Barbados.

❹ Parliament Buildings. Overlooking National Heroes Square in the center of town, these Victorian buildings were built around 1870 to house the British Commonwealth's third-oldest parliament. A series of stained-glass windows depicts British monarchs from James I to Victoria. There are twice-daily tours when sessions are not in progress (call ahead to confirm). ⊠ *Broad St., St. Michael,* ☎ *246/427–2019.* ⊠ *Donations welcome.* ⊙ *Tours weekdays (when parliament isn't in session) at 11 and 2.*

❻ Queen's Park. Northeast of Bridgetown, Queen's Park contains one of the island's largest trees, an immense baobab more than 10 centuries old. Queen's Park House, the historic home of the British troop commander, has been converted into a theater with an exhibition room on the lower floor and a restaurant. ⊠ *Constitution Rd., St. Michael.* ⊠ *Free.* ⊙ *Daily 9–5.*

❺ St. Michael's Cathedral. Although no one has proved it conclusively, George Washington, on his only visit outside the United States, is said to have worshiped here in 1751. The original structure was nearly a century old by then. Destroyed twice by hurricanes, it was rebuilt in 1784 and again in 1831. ⊠ *Spry St., east of National Heroes Sq., St. Michael.*

Southern Barbados

In Christ Church, which is much busier and more developed than the west coast, there are condos, high-rise hotels, beach parks, and St. Lawrence Gap, with its many places to eat, drink, and shop. Moving southeast, the broad, flat terrain comprises acre upon acre of cane fields, interrupted only by an occasional oil rig and a few tiny villages hugging crossroads. Along the byways are colorful chattel houses, the property of tenant farmers. Historically, these typically Barbadian, ever-expandable houses were built to be dismantled and moved as required.

Numbers in the margin correspond to points of interest on the Barbados map.

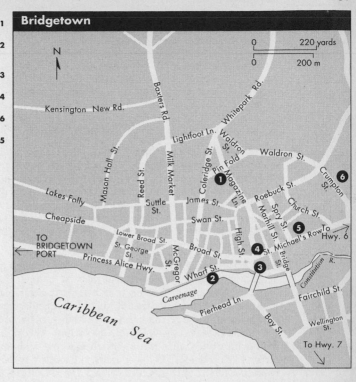

SIGHTS TO SEE

7 Barbados Museum. This intriguing museum, in the former British Military Prison (1815) in the historic Garrison area, has artifacts from Arawak days (around 400 BC) and galleries that depict 19th-century military history and everyday life. You can see cane-harvesting tools, wedding dresses, ancient (and frightening) dentistry instruments, and slave sale accounts kept in a spidery copperplate handwriting. There are also wildlife and natural history exhibits, an art gallery, a children's gallery, a gift shop, and a café. ⊠ *Hwy. 7, Garrison Savannah, St. Michael,* ☎ *246/427–0201 or 246/436–1956.* ⊠ *$5.* ☉ *Mon.–Sat. 9–5, Sun. 2–6.*

16 Codrington Theological College. An impressive stand of royal palms lines the road leading to the coral-stone buildings and serene grounds of Codrington College, an Anglican seminary founded in 1745 on a cliff overlooking Consett Bay. You're welcome to tour the buildings and walk the nature trails. Keep in mind, though, that beachwear isn't appropriate here. ⊠ *Sargeant St., Consett Bay, St. John,* ☎ *246/433–1274.* ⊠ *$2.50.* ☉ *Daily 10–4.*

10 Emancipation Statue. This larger-than-life statue of a slave—with raised hands, evoking both contempt and victory, and broken chains hanging from each wrist—is commonly referred to as the Bussa Statue. Bussa was the man who, in the early part of the 19th century, led the first slave rebellion in Barbados. The statue overlooks a broad cane field just outside Bridgetown, making the monument all the more poignant. ⊠ *St. Barnabas Roundabout (intersection of ABC Hwy. and Hwy. 5), Haggatt Hall, St. Michael.*

8 Harry Bayley Observatory. Built in 1963, this is the headquarters of the Barbados Astronomical Society. The observatory, equipped with a

14-inch reflector telescope, is the only one in the Eastern Caribbean. ✉ *Off Hwy. 6, Clapham, St. Michael,* ☎ *246/426–1317 or 246/422–2394.* 🎫 *$4.* ⊘ *Fri. 8:30 AM–11:30 PM.*

㉘ Malibu Visitor Centre. Located just north of Bridgetown, the fun-loving Malibu Rum people encourage those taking the distillery tour to make a day of it. The beach and water sports are adjacent to the Visitor Centre. Lunch and drinks are served at the beachside grill. ✉ *Black Rock, Brighton, St. Michael,* ☎ *246/425–9393.* 🎫 *$7.50; $27.50 with lunch; $37.50 day pass.* ⊘ *Weekdays 9–5.*

㉙ Mount Gay Rum Visitors Centre. On this popular 45-minute tour, you learn the colorful story behind the world's oldest rum. Although the distillery is elsewhere, tour guides explain the rum-making procedure. Historic and modern equipment are on display, and rows and rows of barrels are stored in this location. The tour concludes with a tasting and an opportunity to buy bottles of rum and gift items. ✉ *Spring Garden Hwy., Brandons, St. Michael,* ☎ *246/425–8757.* 🎫 *$6; $27.50 with lunch.* ⊘ *Weekdays 9–4.*

☝ ⑭ Rum Factory and Heritage Park. A long road through acres of cane fields brings you to the first rum distillery to be built in Barbados in the 20th century. Situated on a 350-year-old sugar plantation, the spotless, environmentally friendly, high-tech distillery produces ESA Field white rum and premium Alleyne Arthur varieties. Adjacent is the 7-acre Heritage Park, which showcases Bajan skills and talents in its Art Foundry and Cane Pit Amphitheatre; a row of shops and vendor carts is filled with local products, crafts, and foods. ✉ *Foursquare Plantation, St. Philip,* ☎ *246/420–1977.* 🎫 *$5.* ⊘ *Daily 9–5.*

⑮ Sam Lord's Castle. The Regency house built in 1820 by the buccaneer Sam Lord is considered one of the island's finest mansions. Now the centerpiece of a resort, the opulent estate has double verandas on all sides and magnificent plaster ceilings created by Charles Rutter, who also crafted some of the ceilings in England's Windsor Castle. Rooms are furnished with fine mahogany furniture and gilt mirrors that Sam Lord is reputed to have pillaged from passing ships. It's said he lured them onto treacherous reefs just offshore by hanging lanterns in palm trees to simulate harbor lights. ✉ *Long Bay, St. Philip,* ☎ *246/423–7350.* 🎫 *$5; hotel guests free.* ⊘ *Daily 10–4.*

⑬ Sunbury Plantation House & Museum. Lovingly rebuilt after a 1995 fire destroyed everything but the thick flint-and-stone walls of this 300-year-old plantation house, Sunbury offers an elegant glimpse of the 18th and 19th centuries on a Barbadian sugar estate. Period furniture, old prints, and a collection of horse-drawn carriages have been donated to lend an air of authenticity. Luncheon is served in the back garden. ✉ *Off Hwy. 5, Six Cross Roads, St. Philip,* ☎ *246/423–6270.* 🎫 *$6.* ⊘ *Daily 10–5.*

☝ ⑨ Tyrol Cot Heritage Village. This interesting coral-stone cottage just south of Bridgetown was constructed in 1854 and has been preserved as an example of period architecture. In 1929 it became home of Sir Grantley Adams, the first premier of Barbados. Part of the Barbados National Trust, the cottage is now filled with antiques and memorabilia that belonged to the late Sir Grantley and Lady Adams. It's the centerpiece of an outdoor "living" museum of colorful chattel houses, each with a traditional artisan or craftsman at work inside. The crafts are for sale, and refreshments are available at the "rum shop." ✉ *Rte. 2, Codrington Hill, St. Michael,* ☎ *246/424–2074 or 246/436–9033.* 🎫 *$6.* ⊘ *Weekdays 9–5.*

Northern Barbados

Speightstown, the north's commercial center and once a thriving port city, now relies economically on quaint local shops and informal restaurants. Many of Speightstown's 19th-century buildings, with typical overhanging balconies, have been or are being restored. The island's northernmost reaches, St. Peter and St. Lucy parishes, are varied and lovely. Between the tiny fishing towns along the northwestern coast and the sweeping views out over the Atlantic to the east are forest and farm, moor and mountain. Most guides include a loop through this area on a daylong island tour—it's a beautiful drive.

SIGHTS TO SEE

(☺ ㉓) **Animal Flower Cave.** Small sea anemones, or sea worms, resemble jewel-like flowers when they open their tiny tentacles. They live in small pools—some large enough to swim in—in this cave at the island's very northern tip. The view of breaking waves from inside the cave is magnificent. ⊠ *North Point, St. Lucy,* ☎ *246/439–8797.* ⌦ *$1.50.* ☉ *Daily 9–4.*

(☺ ㉑) **Barbados Wildlife Reserve.** The reserve is the habitat of herons, innumerable land turtles, screeching peacocks, shy deer, sometimes elusive green monkeys, brilliantly colored parrots (in a large walk-in aviary), a snake, and a caiman. The animals run or fly freely, except for the snake and caiman, so step carefully and keep your hands to yourself. Late afternoon is your best chance to catch a glimpse of a green monkey. ⊠ *Farley Hill, St. Peter,* ☎ *246/422–8826.* ⌦ *$11.50.* ☉ *Daily 10–5.*

㉐ **Farley Hill.** At this national park in northern St. Peter, across the road from the Barbados Wildlife Reserve, the imposing ruins of a plantation great house are surrounded by gardens and lawns, along with an avenue of towering royal palms and gigantic mahogany, whitewood, and casuarina trees. Partially rebuilt for the filming of *Island in the Sun,* the classic 1957 film starring Harry Belafonte and Dorothy Dandridge, the structure was later destroyed by fire. Behind the estate, there's a sweeping view of the region called Scotland for its rugged landscape. ⊠ *Farley Hill, St. Peter,* ☎ *246/422–3555.* ⌦ *$1.50 per car; walkers free.* ☉ *Daily 8:30–6.*

★ ㉒ **St. Nicholas Abbey.** With no religious connection at all, the name of the island's oldest great house (circa 1650) is an amalgamation of the owners' ancestral British home, St. Nicholas parish near Bristol, and Bath Abbey nearby. Its stone-and-wood architecture makes it one of only three original Jacobean-style houses still standing in the Western Hemisphere. It has Dutch gables, finials of coral stone, and beautiful grounds. The first floor, fully furnished with period furniture and portraits of family members, is open to the public. Fascinating home movies, shot by the current owner's father, record Bajan life in the 1930s. The Calabash Café, in the rear, serves snacks, lunch, and afternoon tea. ⊠ *Cherry Tree Hill, St. Lucy,* ☎ *246/422–8725.* ⌦ *$5.* ☉ *Weekdays 10–3:30.*

Central Barbados

On the west coast, Holetown, in St. James Parish, is the center of the Platinum Coast—so called for the vast number of luxurious resorts and mansions that face the sea. Holetown is also where British captain John Powell landed in 1625 to claim the island for King James. On the east coast the crashing Atlantic surf has eroded the shoreline, forming steep cliffs and rocks that look like giant mushrooms. Bathsheba and Cattlewash are favorite local seacoast destinations on weekends and holidays. In the interior, narrow roads weave through tiny villages and along and between the ridges. The landscape is covered with tropical vegetation and riddled with fascinating caves and gullies.

SIGHTS TO SEE

★ ⑰ **Andromeda Gardens.** An intriguing collection of unusual and beautiful plant specimens from around the world is cultivated in 6 acres of gardens nestled among streams, ponds, and rocky outcroppings overlooking the sea above the Bathsheba coastline. The gardens were created in 1954 with flowering plants collected by the late horticulturist Iris Bannochie. They're now administered by the Barbados National Trust. The Hibiscus Café serves snacks and drinks. ⊠ *Bathsheba, St. Joseph,* ☎ *246/433–9261.* ⌑ *$6.* ☉ *Daily 9–5.*

⑱ **Barclays Park.** Straddling the Ermy Bourne Highway, just north of Bathsheba, this public park was donated by Barclays Bank. Pack a picnic or stop at the popular bar-restaurant and enjoy lunch with a gorgeous ocean view.

⑲ **Chalky Mount.** A handful of potters has workshops in this tiny east coast village, high in the hills that produce the clay that has supplied generations of potters for 300 years. The potteries are open daily to visitors. You can watch as artisans create bowls, vases, candleholders, and decorative objects that they, of course, offer for sale.

㉕ **Flower Forest.** It's a treat to meander among fragrant flowering bushes, canna and ginger lilies, puffball trees, and more than 100 other species of tropical flora in a cool, tranquil forest of flowers and other plants. A ½-mi-long (1-km-long) path winds through the 50 acres of grounds, a former sugar plantation; it takes about 30–45 minutes to follow the path—or you can wander freely for as long as you wish. Seats, where you can pause and reflect, are located throughout the forest. There are also a snack bar, gift shop, and beautiful view of Mt. Hillaby. ⊠ *Hwy. 2, Richmond Plantation, St. Joseph,* ☎ *246/433–8152.* ⌑ *$7.* ☉ *Daily 9–5.*

Ⓒ ㉔ **Folkestone Marine Park & Visitor Centre.** At this park north of Holetown there's a lot for the whole family to enjoy—both on land and offshore. A museum illuminates some of the island's marine life; and for some firsthand viewing, there's an underwater snorkeling trail around Dottin's Reef (glass-bottom boats are available for nonswimmers). A barge sunk in shallow water is home to myriad fish, making it a popular dive site. ⊠ *Church Point, Holetown, St. James,* ☎ *246/422–2314.* ⌑ *Free.* ☉ *Weekdays 9–5.*

⑪ **Francia Plantation House.** Built of large coral-stone blocks in 1913, the architecture of this great house blends French, Brazilian, and Caribbean influences. You can tour the house (descendents of the original owner still live here) and gardens. Most of the antique furniture was made in Barbados of local mahogany; 17th- and 18th-century maps, watercolors, and prints grace the walls. ⊠ *Gun Hill, St. George,* ☎ *246/429–0474.* ⌑ *$4.50.* ☉ *Weekdays 10–4.*

Ⓒ ⑫ **Gun Hill Signal Station.** The 360° view from Gun Hill, 700 ft (215 m) above sea level, was what made this location of strategic importance to the 18th-century British army. Using lanterns and semaphore, soldiers based here could communicate with their counterparts at the south coast garrison and at Grenade Hill in the north. Time moved slowly in 1868, and Captain Henry Wilkinson whiled away his off-duty time by carving a huge lion from a single rock—which is on the hillside just below the tower. Come for a short history lesson but mainly for the view; it's so gorgeous, military invalids were once sent here to convalesce. ⊠ *Gun Hill, St. George,* ☎ *246/429–1358.* ⌑ *$5.* ☉ *Weekdays 9–5.*

Ⓒ ㉗ **Harrison's Cave.** This limestone cavern, complete with stalactites, stalagmites, subterranean streams, and a 40-ft (12-m) waterfall, is a rare find in the Caribbean—and one of Barbados's most popular attractions. The one-hour tours are on electric trams, which fill up fast; reserve ahead of time. Hard hats are required and provided, but all that may fall on you is a little dripping water. ⊠ *Hwy. 2, Welchman Hall, St. Thomas,* ☎ *246/438–6640.* ☞ *$12.50.* ⊘ *Daily 9–6; last tour at 4.*

㉖ **Welchman Hall Gully.** This 1-mi-long (2-km-long) natural gully is really a collapsed limestone cavern, once part of the same underground network as Harrison's Cave. The national trust protects the peace and quiet here, making it a beautiful place to hike among acres of labeled flowers and stands of trees. You can see and hear some interesting birds and, with luck, a native green monkey. ⊠ *Welchman Hall, St. Thomas,* ☎ *246/438–6671.* ☞ *$6.* ⊘ *Daily 9–5.*

BARBADOS A TO Z

To research prices, get advice from other travelers, and book travel arrangements, visit www.fodors.com.

AIR TRAVEL

Several international carriers serve Barbados from North America and Europe. Air Canada flies nonstop from Toronto and Montréal. Air Jamaica has nonstop service from New York and from other cities through its Montego Bay hub. American Airlines has nonstop service from New York and Miami and direct service from other U.S. cities, connecting with American Eagle in San Juan. British Airways offers daily service from London, as well as limited Concorde service. BWIA flies nonstop from New York and Miami and from Washington Dulles several times a week; the airline also has weekly flights from Toronto and thrice-weekly flights from the United Kingdom through Trinidad. US Airways has daily nonstop service from Philadelphia. Virgin Atlantic flies nonstop from London Gatwick.

Barbados is also well connected to other Caribbean destinations. BWIA Express flies from Antigua, Grenada, Guyana, Jamaica, St. Lucia, St. Maarten, St. Vincent, and Trinidad and Tobago. Caribbean Star flies three times daily between Barbados and Antigua via Dominica. HelenAir flies regional charters between Barbados and St. Lucia. LIAT connects Barbados with Anguilla, Antigua, Dominica, Grenada, Guadeloupe, Guyana, Martinique, Nevis, Puerto Rico, St. Croix, St. Kitts and Nevis, St. Lucia, St. Maarten, St. Thomas, Trinidad and Tobago, and St. Vincent and the Grenadines. Mustique Airways links Barbados with St. Vincent and the Grenadines (Bequia, Canouan, Carriacou, Mustique, and Union) on scheduled charter flights. SVG Air flies between Barbados and St. Vincent and the Grenadines. Trans Island Air flies regional charters between Barbados and the Grenadines.

➤ AIRLINES AND CONTACTS: **Air Canada** (☎ 246/428–5077). **Air Jamaica** (☎ 246/420–1956 or 800/523–5585). **American Airlines** (☎ 246/428–4170). **British Airways** (☎ 246/436–6413). **BWIA/BWIA Express** (☎ 246/426–2111 or 800/538–2942). **Caribbean Star** (☎ 268/431–0540). **HelenAir** (☎ 758/452–7196). **LIAT** (☎ 246/434–5428). **Mustique Airways** (☎ 246/428–1638). **SVG Air** (☎ 784/457–5124). **Trans Island Air** (☎ 246/418–1654). **US Airways** (☎ 800/622–1015). **Virgin Atlantic** (☎ 246/228–4886 or 800/744–7477).

AIRPORTS

Grantley Adams International Airport, a major hub for airlines serving Eastern Caribbean destinations, is situated in Christ Church Parish, on the south coast. It's a large, modern facility; taxis and other ground transportation (such as vans from hotels that provide airport transfers) are available immediately upon exiting the customs area. The airport is about 15 minutes from hotels situated along the south coast, 45 minutes from the west coast, and about 30 minutes from Bridgetown.

Note that airport taxis aren't metered, but fares are regulated (about $28 to Speightstown, $20–$22 to west coast hotels, $10–$13 to south coast ones). Be sure, however, to establish the fare before getting into the cab and that you understand whether the price quoted is in U.S. or Barbadian dollars.

➤ AIRPORT INFORMATION: **Grantley Adams International Airport** (☎ 246/428–7101).

BOAT AND FERRY TRAVEL
Half the annual visitors to Barbados are cruise passengers. Bridgetown's Deep Water Harbour is on the northwest side of Carlisle Bay, and up to eight cruise ships can dock at the Cruise Ship Terminal. Downtown Bridgetown is a ½-mi (1-km) walk from the pier; a taxi costs about $3 each way.

BUSINESS HOURS
BANKS
Banks are open Monday–Thursday 8–3, Friday 8–5 (some branches in supermarkets are open Saturday morning 9–noon), and at the airport the Barbados National Bank is open from 8 AM until the last plane leaves or arrives, seven days a week (including holidays).

POST OFFICES
The general post office, in Cheapside, Bridgetown, is open weekdays 7:30–5; the Sherbourne Conference Center branch is open weekdays 8:15–4:30 during conferences; and branches in each parish are open weekdays 8–3:15.

SHOPS
Most stores in Bridgetown are open weekdays 8:30–5, Saturday 8:30–1. Out-of-town locations may stay open later. Some supermarkets are open daily 8–6 or later.

BUS TRAVEL
Bus service is efficient, inexpensive, and plentiful. Blue buses with a yellow stripe are public, yellow buses with a blue stripe are private, and private "zed-R" vans (so called for their ZR license plate designation) are white with a maroon stripe. All travel frequently along Highway 1 (St. James Road) and Highway 7 (South Coast Main Road), as well as inland routes. The fare is Bds$1.50 (75¢) for any one destination; exact change in either currency is appreciated. Buses pass along main roads about every 20 minutes. Stops are marked by small signs on roadside poles that say TO CITY or OUT OF CITY, meaning the direction relative to Bridgetown. Flag down the bus with your hand, even if you're standing at the stop. Bridgetown terminals are at Fairchild Street for buses to the south and east and at Lower Green for buses to Speightstown via the west coast.

CAR RENTALS
To rent a car in Barbados, you must have a valid driver's license and major credit card. More than 60 agencies rent cars, Jeeps, or minimokes (small, open-air vehicles) for an average $105 a day (or $400 a week), depending on the vehicle and whether it has air-conditioning. Most firms also offer discounted three-day rates. The rental generally includes insurance, pickup and delivery service, maps, 24-hour emergency service, and unlimited mileage. Baby seats are usually available upon request.

➤ MAJOR AGENCIES: **Coconut Car Rentals** (✉ Bay St., Bridgetown, ☎ 246/437–0297). **Corbins Car Rentals** (✉ Upper Collymore Rock, Bridgetown, ☎ 246/427–9531). **Courtesy Rent-A-Car** (✉ Grantley Adams International Airport, ☎ 246/418–2500). **Drive-a-Matic** (✉ Lower Carlton, St. James, ☎ 246/422–3000). **National Car Rentals** (✉ Lower Carlton, St. James, ☎ 246/426–0603). **Sunny Isle Sixt Car Rentals** (✉ Worthing, Christ Church, ☎ 246/435–7979). **Sunset Crest Car Rental** (✉ Sunset Crest, Holetown, St. James, ☎ 246/432–2222).

CAR TRAVEL

If you are staying in a remote location, such as the east coast, you will find it practical to rent a car for the duration of their stay. Folks staying in more populated areas, where taxis and public transportation are available at the door, might rent a car or minimoke for a day or two of exploring on their own. Bathing suits and beach towels—and a map— are requisite gear for such an adventure; hotels can supply a picnic lunch.

GASOLINE

Gas costs about 80¢ per liter (approximately $3 per gallon), and there are stations in Bridgetown, on the main highways along the west and south coasts, and in most inland parishes. Although times vary, you'll find most open daily with hours that extend into the evening; some are open 24 hours a day.

ROAD CONDITIONS

Barbados has nearly 975 mi (1,570 km) of paved roads that follow the coastline and meander through the countryside. A network of main highways facilitates traffic flow into and out of Bridgetown; the Adams-Barrow-Cummins (ABC) Highway bypasses Bridgetown, which saves time getting from coast to coast. Small signs tacked to trees and poles at intersections point the way to most attractions, and local people are helpful if you become lost. Remote roads are in fairly good repair, yet few are well lighted at night—and night falls quickly at about 6 PM year-round. Even in full daylight, the tall sugarcane fields lining both sides of the road in interior sections can make visibility difficult.

RULES OF THE ROAD

Drive on the left, British-style. Be mindful of pedestrians and occasional livestock walking on country roads. When someone flashes headlights at you at an intersection, it means "after you." Be especially careful negotiating roundabouts (traffic circles). The speed limit, in keeping with the pace of life and the narrow roads, is 30 mph in the country, 20 mph in town. Bridgetown actually has rush hours: 7–9 and 4–6. Park only in approved parking areas; downtown parking costs Bds75¢– Bds$1 per hour.

ELECTRICITY

Electric current on Barbados is 110 volts/50 cycles, U.S. standard. Hotels generally have adapters/transformers for appliances made in countries that operate on 220-volt current.

EMBASSIES

➤ AUSTRALIA: **Australian High Commission** (✉ Bishop's Court Hill, Pine Rd., Bridgetown, St. Michael, ☎ 246/435–2834).
➤ CANADA: **Canadian High Commission** (✉ Bishop's Court Hill, Pine Rd., Bridgetown, St. Michael, ☎ 246/429–3550).
➤ UNITED KINGDOM: **British High Commission** (✉ Lower Collymore Rock, Bridgetown, St. Michael, ☎ 246/430–7800).
➤ UNITED STATES: **Embassy of the United States** (✉ Broad St., Bridgetown, St. Michael, ☎ 246/436–4950).

EMERGENCIES

➤ AMBULANCE: **Ambulance** (☎ 511).

➤ FIRE: **Fire emergencies** (☎ 311).

➤ HOSPITALS: **Bayview Hospital** (✉ St. Paul's Ave., south of Bridgetown, Bayville, St. Michael, ☎ 246/436–5446); **Queen Elizabeth Hospital** (✉ Martindales Rd., Bridgetown, east of the Careenage, St. Michael, ☎ 246/436–6450)

➤ PHARMACIES: **Collins Ltd.** (✉ Broad St., ☎ 246/426–4515). **Grant's** (✉ Fairchild St., Bridgetown, ☎ 246/436–6120; ✉ Main Rd., Oistins, ☎ 246/428–9481). **Knight's** (✉ Lower Broad St., Bridgetown, ☎ 246/426–5196; ✉ Super Centre Shopping Center, Main Rd., Oistins, ☎ 246/428–6057; ✉ Suncrest Mall, Hwy. 1, Holetown, ☎ 246/432–1290; and ✉ Hwy. 1, Speightstown, ☎ 246/422–0048).

➤ POLICE: **Police** (☎ 211 for emergencies; 242/430–7100 for nonemergencies).

➤ SCUBA-DIVING EMERGENCIES: **Coast Guard Defence Force (24-hour hyperbaric chamber)** (✉ St. Ann's Fort, Garrison, St. Michael, ☎ 246/427–8819; 246/436–6185 for nonemergencies). **Divers' Alert Network** (☎ 246/684–8111 or 246/684–2948).

ETIQUETTE AND BEHAVIOR

The British influence remains strong, in part because Barbados is the favorite island retreat of most Brits and the retirement choice of many. Most hotels serve afternoon tea, cricket is the national pastime, and patrons at some bars are as likely to order a Pimm's Cup as a rum and Coke. British-style manners combine with a Caribbean friendliness and openness to give Bajans their special charm. Dress appropriately and discreetly, saving swimwear for the beach. Shorts and T-shirts are fine for sightseeing and shopping but frowned upon in restaurants in the evening.

FESTIVALS AND SEASONAL EVENTS

In mid-January, the Barbados Jazz Festival is a weekend event jammed with performances by international artists, jazz legends, and local talent. In February the weeklong Holetown Festival is held at the fairgrounds to commemorate the date in 1627 when the first European settlers arrived in Barbados.

Three weeks of opera, concerts, and theatrical performances are presented each March during Holder's Opera Season. The open-air theater at Holder's House, St. James, seats 600, and the program has won acclaim for its productions. Around Easter weekend, Oistins Fish Festival celebrates the rich history of this south coast fishing village. Dubbed the "world's greatest street party," the Congaline Street Festival is a festive celebration of music, dance, and local arts and crafts; held at the end of April.

Gospelfest occurs in May and has performances by gospel headliners from around the world. Dating from the 19th century, the Crop Over Festival, a monthlong event beginning in July and ending on Kadooment Day (a national holiday), marks the end of the sugarcane harvest.

HEALTH

Insects aren't much of a problem, but if you plan to hike or spend time on secluded beaches in late afternoon, use insect repellent. Tap water on the island is plentiful and pure. It's naturally filtered through 1,000 ft (305 m) of pervious coral and safe to drink.

HOLIDAYS

Public holidays are: New Year's Day (Jan. 1), Errol Barrow Day (Jan. 21), Good Friday (Fri. before Easter), Easter Monday (day after Easter),

National Heroes Day (Apr. 28), Labour Day (May 1), Whit Monday (7th Mon. after Easter), Emancipation Day (Aug. 1), Kadooment Day (first Mon. in Aug.), Independence Day (Nov. 30), Christmas (Dec. 25), and Boxing Day (Dec. 26).

LANGUAGE

English, the official language, is spoken by everyone, everywhere. The Bajan dialect is based on Afro-Caribbean rhythms, but you may notice a distinctly Irish lilt that differentiates the Bajan accent from its Caribbean neighbors. As for the African influence, you can see it in names of typical Bajan foods, such as cou-cou and buljol.

MAIL AND SHIPPING

An airmail letter from Barbados to the United States or Canada costs Bds$1.15 per half ounce; an airmail postcard, Bds45¢. Letters to the United Kingdom cost Bds$1.40; postcards, Bds75¢. Letters to Australia and New Zealand cost Bds$2.75; postcards, Bds$1.75. When sending mail to Barbados, be sure to include the parish name in the address.

MONEY MATTERS

Prices quoted throughout this chapter are in U.S. dollars unless otherwise noted.

The local Barbados National Bank has a branch at Grantley Adams International Airport that is open every day from 8 AM until the last plane lands or arrives. Barclays Bank is an international bank with several branches in Barbados. The Bank of Nova Scotia, or Scotiabank, is a major Canadian bank that is represented throughout the Caribbean. Caribbean Commercial Bank has convenient Saturday morning hours at its branch at Sunset Crest Mall, in Holetown. CIBC, also a Canadian bank with a network of operations on Caribbean islands, has several branches and ATM machines in Barbados.

➤ CONTACTS: **Barbados National Bank** (✉ Broad St., Bridgetown, St. Michael, ☎ 246/431–5800; ✉ Grantley Adams International Airport, Christ Church, ☎ 246/428–0921). **Barclays Bank** (✉ Broad St., Bridgetown, St. Michael, ☎ 246/431–5151; ✉ Sunset Crest, Holetown, St. James, ☎ 246/419–8413; ✉ Speightstown, St. Peter, ☎ 246/419–8422; ✉ Oistins, Christ Church, ☎ 246/418–8712). **Bank of Nova Scotia** (✉ Broad St., Bridgetown, St. Michael, ☎ 246/431–3000; ✉ Holetown, St. James, ☎ 246/419–1600; ✉ Worthing, Christ Church, ☎ 246/431–3170). **Caribbean Commercial Bank** (✉ Lower Broad St., Bridgetown, St. Michael, ☎ 246/431–2500; ✉ Sunset Crest, Holetown, St. James, ☎ 246/419–8530; ✉ Hastings Plaza, Christ Church, ☎ 246/431–2450). **CIBC** (✉ Broad St., Bridgetown, St. Michael, ☎ 246/431–3700; ✉ Sunset Crest, Holetown, St. James, ☎ 246/432–1678; ✉ Speightstown, St. Peter, ☎ 246/422–2429; ✉ Oistins, Christ Church, ☎ 246/428–6184).

ATMS

Automated teller machines (ATMs) are available 24 hours a day at bank branches, transportation centers, shopping centers, gas stations, and other convenient spots throughout the island.

CREDIT CARDS

Major credit cards readily accepted throughout Barbados include American Express, BarclayCard, Carte Blanche, Diners Club, EnRoute, Eurocard, MasterCard, and Visa. You can use major credit cards, if you have a PIN, to obtain cash advances (in Barbadian dollars) from most ATM machines.

CURRENCY

The Barbados dollar is tied to the U.S. dollar at the rate of Bds$1.98 to $1. U.S. paper currency, major credit cards, and traveler's checks are all accepted islandwide. Be sure you know which currency is being quoted when making a purchase.

PASSPORTS AND VISAS

U.S. and Canadian citizens can enter Barbados for visits of up to three months with proof of citizenship and a return or ongoing ticket. Acceptable proof is a valid passport or a birth certificate with a raised seal and a government-issued photo ID; no other documents, including voter registration cards or baptismal certificates, are acceptable. British subjects and citizens of countries that are members of the British Commonwealth must present a valid passport and ongoing ticket.

SAFETY

Crime isn't a major problem, but take normal precautions. Lock your room, and don't leave valuables in plain sight or unattended on the beach. Lock your rental car, and don't pick up hitchhikers.

SIGHTSEEING TOURS

A half- or full-day bus or taxi tour is a good way to get your bearings and can be arranged by your hotel. The price varies according to the number of attractions included; an average full-day tour (five to six hours) costs about $50–$60 per person and generally includes lunch and admissions. **Bajan Helicopters** offers an eagle's-eye view of the island for $75 to $125. Family-run **Bajan Tours** offers eight coach or minivan tours, including cultural, historic, ecological, and general sightseeing routings for $40 to $56 per person. Every Wednesday afternoon from mid-January through mid-April, the **Barbados National Trust** offers a bus tour that stops at historic great houses and private homes. The cost is $18 per person, which includes transportation to and from your hotel. **Island Safari** will take you to all the popular spots and some that are out-of-the-way and inaccessible by buses or normal vehicles, but you'll be riding in a 4x4 Land Rover. The cost is $40 to $60 per person. **L. E. Williams Tour Co.** offers island bus tours, which cost $30–$85 per person. Sally Shearn operates **VIP Tour Services.** Up to four people are picked up in an air-conditioned Mercedes-Benz and charged $40 per hour for a minimum of four hours. Your choice of tours (coastal, inland, cultural, naturalist, architectural, or customized) includes refreshment stops.

➤ CONTACTS: **Bajan Helicopters** (✉ Bridgetown Heliport, Bridgetown, St. Michael, ☎ 246/431–0069). **Bajan Tours** (✉ Bishop's Court Hill, St. Michael, ☎ 246/437–9389). **Barbados National Trust** (✉ Wildey House, Wildey, St. Michael, ☎ 246/426–2421). **Island Safari** (✉ Main Rd., Bush Hall, St. Michael, ☎ 246/429–5337). **L. E. Williams Tour Co.** (Hastings, Christ Church, ☎ 246/427–1043). **VIP Tour Services** (✉ Hillcrest Villa, Upton, St. Michael, ☎ 246/429–4617).

TAXES & SERVICE CHARGES

DEPARTURE TAX

At the airport, each adult passenger leaving Barbados must pay a departure tax of $12.50 (Bds$25), payable in either Barbadian or U.S. currency; children 12 and under are exempt.

SALES TAX

A 7½% government tax is added to all hotel bills. A 10% service charge is usually added to hotel bills and restaurant checks in lieu of tipping. At your discretion, tip beyond the service charge to recognize extraordinary service.

VALUE ADDED TAX (V.A.T.)

A 15% VAT is imposed on restaurant meals, admissions to attractions, and merchandise sales (other than duty-free). Prices are often tax inclusive; if not, the VAT will be added to your bill.

TAXIS

Taxis operate 24 hours a day. They aren't metered but charge according to fixed rates set by the government. They carry up to four passengers, and the fare may be shared. For short trips, the rate per mile (or part thereof) should not exceed $1.50. Drivers are courteous and knowledgeable; most will narrate a tour at an hourly rate of $20 for up to three people. Be sure to settle the price before you start off and agree on whether it's in U.S. or Barbados dollars.

TELEPHONES

COUNTRY AND AREA CODES

The area code for Barbados is 246.

INTERNATIONAL CALLS

Direct-dialing to the United States, Canada, and other countries is efficient and reasonable, but always check with your hotel to see if a surcharge is added. Some toll-free numbers cannot be accessed in Barbados. To charge your overseas call on a major credit card without incurring a surcharge, dial 800/744–2000 from any phone.

LOCAL CALLS

Local calls are free from private phones; some hotels charge a small fee. For directory assistance dial 411. Calls from pay phones cost Bds25¢ for five minutes. Prepaid phone cards, which can be used throughout Barbados and other Caribbean islands, are sold at shops, attractions, transportation centers, and other convenient outlets.

TIPPING

If no service charge is added to your bill, tip waiters 10%–15% and maids $1 per room per day. Tip bellhops and airport porters $1 per bag. Taxi drivers also appreciate a 10% tip.

VISITOR INFORMATION

➤ Before you leave: **Barbados Tourism Authority** (✉ 800 2nd Ave., 2nd floor, New York, NY 10017, ☎ 212/986–6516 or 800/221–9831, FAX 212/573–9850, WEB www.barbados.org; ✉ 150 Alhambra Circle, Suite 1000, Coral Gables, FL 33134, ☎ 305/442–7471, FAX 305/567–2844; ✉ 3440 Wilshire Blvd., Suite 1215, Los Angeles, CA 90010, ☎ 213/380–2198, FAX 213/384–2763; in Canada: ✉ 4800 de Maisonneuve West, Suite 532, Montreal, Ontario H3Z 1M2, ☎ 514/932–3206 or 800/268–9122, FAX 514/932–3775; ✉ 105 Adelaide St. W, Suite 1010, Toronto, Ontario M5H 1P9, ☎ 416/214–9880 or 800/268–9122, FAX 416/214–9882; in the U.K.: ✉ 263 Tottenham Court Rd., London W1T 7LA, ☎ 44–20/7636–9448, FAX 44–20/7637–1496; in Australia: ✉ 456 Kent St., 17th floor, Sydney 2000, ☎ 61–2/9285–6850, FAX 61–2/9267–4600).

➤ In Barbados: **Barbados Tourism Authority** (✉ Harbour Road, Bridgetown, ☎ 246/427–2623, FAX 246/426–4080, WEB www.barbados.org; ✉ Grantley Adams International Airport, ☎ 246/428–5570; ✉ Cruise Ship Terminal, ☎ 246/426–1718).

6   BONAIRE

Updated by
Vernon
O'Reilly-
Ramesar

It is 6 PM on Sunday and hundreds gather for the weekly party at Lac Bay—a normally peaceful peninsula. "It is not showtime yet ladies and gentlemen," the bandleader says in halting English, "but we want you to have fun so we will play." As waves break a few feet away and spill onto the floor of the outdoor bar the crowd dances and laughs, illuminated by the coral light of another perfect Bonaire sunset.

For years Bonaire was regarded simply as one of the top diving destinations in the Caribbean, with most divers practically oblivious to the equally rich beauty on land. But the government embarked on a program to expand its ecotourism base without succumbing to overdevelopment. Now there are facilities and tours geared toward snorkelers, hikers, bikers, and kayakers, as well as luxury resorts that offer pampering, fine dining, and solitude.

Bonaire, on land, is a stark arid island, perfect for those who are turned off by the overcommercialized high life of the other Antillean islands. While the island does not have a tremendous diversity of flora and fauna, there are still many sights to occupy the ecotourist. You will find it worth your while to rent a vehicle to go flamingo watching or exploring Washington National Park. Bolstering efforts to preserve the region's natural wonders, Bonaire purchased the neighboring deserted island of Klein Bonaire from its private owner, protecting it against development.

Divers still come to Bonaire as pilgrims to a holy land. Here diving is learned and perfected. Even Bonaire license plates tout the island as "Divers' Paradise." But the residents have worked hard to preserve the pristine conditions (any diver with a reckless streak should go elsewhere). Back in 1979 the government made all the waters surrounding Bonaire part of a marine park. These areas are designated a National Park, meaning that anyone who disobeys the area's regulations could face legal action. The entire coastline—from the high-water tidemark to a depth of 200 ft (61 m)—is protected by strict regulations including mandatory orientation classes, warm-up dives with a local instructor, and bans on spearfishing and coral collecting. But certain hazards can't be avoided, Hurricane Lenny wreaked havoc on some of the island's coastal reefs in 1999. Conditions for divers, who typically descend below 30 ft, have not been significantly affected, but snorkelers who seek out the sea's wonders in the shallow waters will likely notice the damage: while the coral reefs are naturally regenerating (which could take several years), the views in some areas may be disappointing.

Most Bonaireans live on the west coast, an area that's also where you will find the capital city, Kralendijk, as well as many hotels, dive sites, and beaches. In the southeast you'll find mangrove swamps, windsurfing schools, and two small resorts in the Lac Bay area; south of here are a rocky, windswept coast, the magnificent salt ponds, and a flamingo sanctuary. The highest elevation is Brandaris Hill (784 ft [239 m]) in the north. With just over 14,000 inhabitants, this little (116-square-mi [290-square-km]) island has the feeling of a small community with a gentle pace. As the locals say, folks come here to dive, eat, dive, sleep, and dive. But they also come to kayak, mountain bike, hike, snorkel, and simply soak in the sunshine and natural beauty.

Lodging

Hotels on Bonaire—with several exceptions—cater primarily to avid divers who spend their days underwater and come up for air only for evening festivities. Hence, facilities tend to be modest, with clean but unadorned rooms, pools, a restaurant, and perhaps a bar. Amenities are often limited to laundry, baby-sitting, car rental, and travel services; unless noted below, room service is usually unavailable. Groomed sandy beaches aren't a requisite for a hotel, but an efficient dive shop is. Many resort rooms have fully equipped kitchens and in-room safes. Although the larger hotels offer meal plans, most are on the EP; and as a rule, hotel restaurants are more expensive than restaurants in town. Many properties offer all-inclusive packages for an extra per-day charge.

Rental Apartments

If you prefer do-it-yourself homestyle comfort over the pampering and services offered by a hotel, rental apartments are also available.
➤ RENTAL AGENCIES: **Black Durgon Inn Properties** (☎ 599/717–5736; 800/526–2370 in the U.S., WEB www.blackdurgon.com) is a small, non-commercial community with its own pier on the water, though no beach. **Bonaire Intimate Stays** (☎ 800/388–5951, WEB www.bonairestays.com) manages 13 small, non-resort-style budget properties (only one is on the water), all with 12 rooms or less. **Sun Rentals** (☎ 599/717–6130, WEB www.sunrentals.an) offers quite a range of accommodations. You can choose from private ocean view villas in luxurious areas like Sabadeco, furnished oceanfront apartments with a pool in town, or bungalows in Lagoenhill, set inland.

CATEGORY	COST EP/CP*	COST A.I.**
$$$$	over $350	over $375
$$$	$250–$350	$275–$375
$$	$150–$250	$175–$275
$	under $150	under $175

*EP/CP prices are per night for a standard double room in high season, excluding taxes, service charges, and meal plans**A.I. (all-inclusive) prices are per person, per night based on double-occupancy during high season, excluding taxes and service charges

HOTELS

$$–$$$$ 🏨 **Plaza Resort Bonaire.** At this flagship property of the Dutch Van der Valk chain, lush landscaped grounds surround a man-made lagoon with bridges. You can also enjoy a gorgeous beach (open to nonguests for $6 per day), loads of amenities, an activities program, and very large guest rooms. Each has terra-cotta tile floors, green rattan furnishings, pastel floral bedspreads, coffeemakers, big TVs, and enormous bathrooms. One- and two-bedroom villas have full kitchens. Thursday is Bonairean folklore night, with live island music, dancing, and typical local foods. ✉ J. A. Abraham Blvd. 80, Kralendijk, ☎ 599/717–2500

or 800/766–6016, FAX 599/717–7133. *200 rooms, 48 villas. 3 restaurants, 4 bars, grocery, room service, fans, in-room safes, refrigerators, 4 tennis courts, 2 pools, aerobics, gym, hair salon, massage, beach, dive shop, dock, windsurfing, boating, bicycles, shops, children's programs (ages 5–15), business services, convention center, meeting rooms. AE, DC, MC, V. EP, FAP, MAP.*

$$–$$$ 🛏 **Port Bonaire Resort.** Adjacent to the airport, Port Bonaire has 26 luxury apartments and penthouses with sea-view patios or balconies (though no beach). The Dutch Mediterranean design is evident in the tile roofs and pastel exteriors. Inside, florals and a powder-blue color scheme complement cream tile floors and blond-wood furnishings. Kitchens are well equipped with microwaves, dishwashers, and washing machines. Daily maid service is another welcome convenience. There are few on-site facilities, but you can use the facilities at the Plaza Resort Bonaire, its sister property, which is a short walk away. ✉ *J. A. Abraham Blvd. 80, Kralendijk,* ☎ *599/717–2500 or 800/766–6016,* FAX *599/717–7133.* WEB *www.plazavillas.com. 10 2-bedroom apartments, 8 1-bedroom apartments, 4 beach houses, 4 penthouses. Kitchens, pool, dock, laundry facilities. AE, D, DC, MC, V. EP.*

$–$$$ 🛏 **Buddy Dive Resort.** Reasonable rates and cozy, well-equipped accommodations keep divers coming back. The small, raised beach and its superb shore snorkeling is a major draw, as well. The dive shop has a drive-through air-fill station for Nitrox or compressed air tanks. Each apartment has a phone and a balcony or patio with an ocean or garden view. Rooms in the original building are small, but they're clean and offer the same amenities as newer units, including telephones. If you are staying for a week the "Drive and Dive" package, which includes a room, a vehicle, and diving, may be cheaper than simply renting a room. ✉ *Kaya Gobernador N. Debrot 85, Kralendijk (Box 231),* ☎ *599/717–5080,* FAX *599/717–8647,* WEB *www.buddydive.com. 6 rooms, 40 apartments. Restaurant, bar, kitchenettes, 2 pools, beach, dive shop, laundry facilities, car rental. AE, D, MC, V. CP, EP, FAP, MAP.*

$$ 🛏 **Captain Don's Habitat.** Captain Don Stewart's Habitat is no longer
★   merely a guest house for divers. Its upscale rooms are really junior suites, and its spacious Mediterranean-style villas (the Hamlet section) have ocean-view verandas, full kitchens, and stylish appointments. The garden cottages are nicely secluded and have full kitchens as well. This is a laid-back place, where the emphasis is on round-the-clock diving—PADI 5-Star training, SSI referral, Nitrox diving, and more than 20 specialty courses are at your fingertips. There are charges for using the in-room safes. The Rum Runners restaurant offers breakfast, lunch, and dinner, and a pizza oven serves up sizzling slices from 3 PM until 10. The beach is postage-stamp size but fine for shore dives or snorkeling, with mesmerizing reef formations just 90 ft from shore. ✉ *Kaya Gobernador N. Debrot 103, Kralendijk (Box 88),* ☎ *599/717–8290 or 800/327–6709,* FAX *599/717–8240,* WEB *www.habitatdiveresorts.com. 24 suites, 9 villas, 20 cottages. Restaurant, 2 bars, fans, in-room safes, kitchens, pool, beach, dive shop, 2 docks, snorkeling, bicycles, volleyball, meeting room, business services. AE, D, DC, MC, V. EP, FAP, MAP.*

$$ 🛏 **Caribbean Court Bonaire.** This apartment complex has first-class accommodations in a Netherlands Antilles–style village along a canal dotted with colorful boats. The back of the complex faces a lagoon with access to the ocean; at the front a pool sits in a lovely courtyard. All units have balconies and top-rate amenities. Although most Bonaire hotels cater to divers, here business travelers will feel comfortable, too, as rooms have phones and free Internet access. Of course, divers' needs aren't ignored: you'll find a program that gives those of all levels individualized attention. There is a charming café serving delicious and really inexpensive meals on the dock. ✉ *J. A. Abraham Blvd., Kral-*

endijk, ☎ *599/717–5353,* FAX *599/717–5363,* WEB *caribbeancourt.com.*
26 units. Fans, kitchens, 2 pools, dive shop, snorkeling, boating, mountain bikes. MC, V. EP, MAP.

$$
★ 🖬 **Deep Blue View Bed & Breakfast.** Pete and Shannon Connely have created a near perfect getaway in their charming four-room B&B in Santa Barbara Heights. Guest rooms have high ceilings, crisp white walls, Italian tile floors, cozy wooden furnishings, fish motifs, and a choice of king- or twin-size beds. Two of the rooms share a bathroom. Shannon serves a delicious homemade breakfast on the terrace around the pool, allowing you to nibble on your granola while enjoying a spectacular view of the island. Be sure to join the couple for nighttime stargazing using their 8-inch Meade telescope. A communal refrigerator is stocked with beverages, and box lunches are available for day trips. ⊠ *Kaya Diamanta 50, Santa Barbara Heights,* ☎ *599/717–8073,* FAX *599/717–7826,* WEB *www.deepblueview.com. 4 rooms. Fans, pool, laundry service. AE, DC, MC, V. BP.*

$$ 🖬 **Sand Dollar Condominium Resort.** These spacious time-share apartments combine a European design with tropical rattan furnishings, though this varies according to the individual owner's taste. Studio, one-, two-, and three-bedroom units are available. Each has a patio or terrace that looks out to the sea. The minuscule beach disappears at high tide, but this doesn't faze the serious divers and their families. The Sand Dollar Terrace Sports Bar & Restaurant serves three meals a day. A grocery store and bank are located next door. ⊠ *Kaya Gobernador N. Debrot 79, Kralendijk (Box 262),* ☎ *599/717–8738 or 800/288–4773,* FAX *599/717–8760,* WEB *www.sanddollarbonaire.com. 85 condos. Restaurant, bar, grocery, ice cream parlor, kitchens, 2 tennis courts, pool, beach, dive shop, children's programs (ages 5–15). AE, D, DC, MC, V. EP, FAP, MAP.*

$$ 🖬 **Sorobon Beach Naturist Resort.** At this secluded southeast-shore cluster of chalets, you must bare all at the beach (the beach is open to the public durng the day for $15), but you can wear clothing throughout the rest of the premises. Be aware that sunbathers can be seen by windsurfers from the public beach next door. Room furnishings are as minimalist as the dress code verging on spartan. The shallow water in the crystal-clear bay is perfect for snorkeling. Yoga classes, kayaking, and nude cruises are available, and you can get a manicure and/or pedicure by appointment. ⊠ *Sorobon Beach (Box 14, Kralendijk),* ☎ *599/717–8080 or 800/828–9356,* FAX *599/717–6080,* WEB *sorobonbeachresort.com. 30 1-bedroom units. Restaurant, bar, fans, in-room safes, kitchenettes, hair salon, massage, beach, snorkeling, boating, Ping-Pong, library, laundry service, airport shuttle. AE, MC, V. EP, MAP.*

$–$$ 🖬 **Divi Flamingo Resort.** The brightly colored buildings of this resort are nestled in beautifully landscaped grounds featuring some of the sparse grass you will see on the island. Rooms are immaculate and have balconies or terraces. If you ask for a ground-floor ocean-view room, the waves will be lapping at your terrace. The bi-level waterfront Chibi Chibi Restaurant offers Caribbean fare. You can munch on your blackened shrimp while watching the dazzling nightly underwater light show. The first-rate dive facility here offers instruction, certification, and excursions to meet your needs. You can also try your luck at Bonaire's only casino. ⊠ *J. A. Abraham Blvd. 40, Kralendijk (Box 143),* ☎ *599/717–8285,* FAX *599/717–8238,* WEB *www.divibonaire.com. 89 rooms, 40 time-share units. 2 restaurants, bar, grocery, in-room safes, tennis court, 2 pools, outdoor hot tub, spa, dive shop, dock, snorkeling, volleyball, shops, casino, meeting rooms, car rental. AE, MC, V. BP, CP, EP, FAP, MAP.*

Caribbean Sea

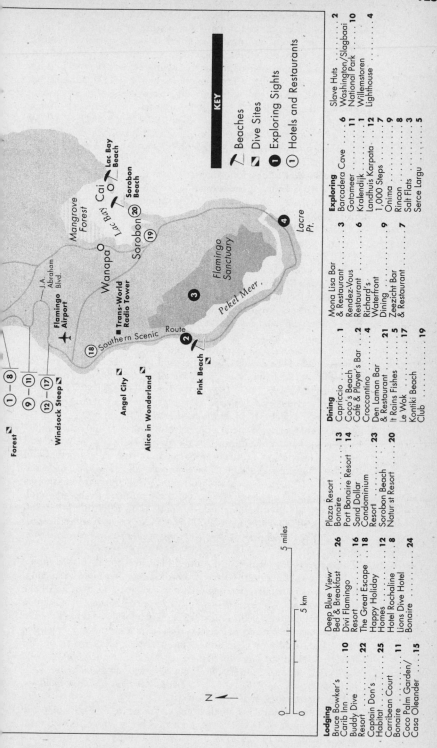

KEY

⊿ Beaches

◪ Dive Sites

❶ Exploring Sights

① Hotels and Restaurants

Exploring

Barcadera Cave	6	Slave Huts	2
Gotomeer	11	Washington/Slagbaai National Park	10
Kralendijk	1	Willemstoren Lighthouse	4
Landhuis Karpata	12		
1,000 Steps	7		
Onima	9		
Rincon	8		
Salt Flats	3		
Serce Largu	5		

Dining

Capriccio	1
Coco's Beach	2
Café & Player's Bar	2
Croccantino	4
Den Laman Bar & Restaurant	21
It Rains Fishes	5
Kontiki Beach Club	19
Le Wok	17
Mona Lisa Bar & Restaurant	3
Rendez-Vous Restaurant	6
Richard's Waterfront Dining	9
Zeezicht Bar & Restaurant	7

Lodging

Bruce Bowker's Carib Inn	10
Buddy Dive Resort	22
Captain Don's Habitat	25
Carribean Court Bonaire	11
Coco Palm Garden/Casa Oleander	15
Deep Blue View Bed & Breakfast	26
Divi Flamingo Resort	16
The Great Escape	18
Happy Holiday Homes	12
Hotel Rochaline	8
Lions Dive Hotel Bonaire	24
Plaza Resort Bonaire	13
Port Bonaire Resort	14
Sand Dollar Condominium Resort	23
Soroban Beach Resort	20

5 miles

5 km

$–$$ 🏨 **Lions Dive Hotel Bonaire.** Pastels, florals, and wicker furnishings set
   👐 the tone of the rooms in this hotel's two-story, soft-yellow buildings.
Second-floor rooms are more private than those on the first floor,
which are set around a quadrangle with a small, busy pool and sunbathing area. Studios have kitchenettes, while suites have spacious living rooms with sofa beds, large balconies looking out to sea, and full
kitchens. All units are ideal for families. There is a sandy recreational
area near the dive shop that is great for socializing. ✉ *Kaya Gobernador N. Debrot 91, Kralendijk (Box 380),* ☎ *599/717–5580,* FAX
599/717–5680, WEB *lionsdivebonaire.com. 32 rooms. Restaurant, bar,
fans, some kitchenettes, some kitchens, pool, dive shop, dock, snorkeling. AE, MC, V. CP, FAP, MAP.*

$ 🏨 **Bruce Bowker's Carib Inn.** American diver Bruce Bowker started this
   ★ small PADI 5-Star diving lodge out of a private home about a mile from
the airport. Rooms are clean and cozy and many have kitchens. Novice
divers will enjoy his very small scuba classes, and PADI certification
is available. The beach is just a sliver but is fine for shore entries. ✉
J. A. Abraham Blvd. 46, Kralendijk (Box 68), ☎ *599/717–8819,* FAX
*599/717–5295. 10 units. Kitchenettes, fans, refrigerators, pool, beach,
dive shop, snorkeling. MC, V. EP.*

$ 🏨 **Coco Palm Garden/Casa Oleander.** Neighbors Marion and Brigitte
decided that they would both open small guest houses and manage them
together. The result is one of the best valued surprises on the island.
Each unit is completely self-sufficient and has its own garden complete
with hammock. A short walk will take you to the common area, with
a pool, sunbathing deck, restaurant and bar. Need to send an e-mail?
Just ask one of the owners, and they will take care of it for you for
free—almost like being home. ✉ *Kaya van Eps 9, Belnem (Box 216,
Kralendijk),* ☎ *599/717–2108 or 599/790–9080,* FAX *599/717–8193,*
WEB *www.cocopalmgarden.com. 10 rooms (6 in Coco Palm, 4 in Casa
Oleander). Kitchens, pool, laundry facilities. MC, V. EP.*

$ 🏨 **The Great Escape.** Honeymooners from Venezuela and others in the
know come here, a few minutes' walk from Pink Beach, for peace and
privacy. The spotless rooms have pastel and beige color schemes and
overlook flowers and foliage. Superior rooms have king-size beds and
cost only $10 more than standard rooms. The courtyard contains a
small waterfall, an open-air bar and grill restaurant, a freshwater pool,
and a kids' pool with a small playground. ✉ *E. E. G. Blvd. 97, Belnem,* ☎ *599/717–7488,* FAX *599/717–7412. 8 rooms, 2 suites. Restaurant, bar, fans, refrigerators, pool, wading pool, shop, playground. AE,
MC, V. CP.*

$ 🏨 **Happy Holiday Homes.** Just south of the airport, this small complex
of bungalows is across the street from the ocean in a quiet residential
area. The comfortable accommodations are spic-and-span and have
wooden ceilings, white tile floors, fully equipped kitchens, living/dining
areas, air-conditioned bedrooms, a selection of books, and cable TV. Each
unit also has a barbecue and deck furniture on a sun terrace or garden
patio. The friendly owners, Louise and Mel Villanueva, go all out for
their guests. ✉ *Punt Vierkant 9, Belnem (Box 216, Kralendijk),* ☎ *599/
717–8405,* FAX *599/717–8605,* WEB *www.happyholidayhomes.com. 12 1-
and 2-bedroom bungalows. In-room safes, kitchens, laundry facilities,
airport shuttle. MC, V. EP.*

$ 🏨 **Hotel Rochaline.** This small hotel in the heart of Kralendijk and
above the popular City Café is a good bet for budget travelers who want
to be downtown. The clean rooms have single beds, TVs, shower-only
baths, and small balconies overlooking the harbor. A change of management started major renovations in Fall 2001, and a superbudget wing
has been added, although even these 10 rooms have a shower, television, and air-conditioning. ✉ *Kaya Grandi 7, Kralendijk,* ☎ *599/717–*

*8286, FAX 599/717–8258, WEB mainstreetbonaire.com. 35 rooms. 2
restaurants, bar, meeting rooms. AE, MC, V. EP, FAP, MAP.*

Dining

Dining on Bonaire is far less expensive than on neighboring islands,
and you'll find everything from Continental to Mexican to Asian fare.
Most restaurants offer seafood fresh from the surrounding waters; in
season try the snapper, wahoo, or dorado (a mild white fish). Meat
lovers will appreciate the availability of Argentinian beef, and vegetarians will be pleased by the abundance of fresh Venezuelan produce.
Many restaurants only serve dinner—only a few establishments not affiliated with hotels are open for breakfast, so check ahead.

What to Wear

Dress on the island is casual but conservative. Most places don't allow
beachwear; even casual poolside restaurants prefer a cover-up.

CATEGORY	COST*
$$$$	over $30
$$$	$20–$30
$$	$10–$20
$	under $10

per person for a main course at dinner

CONTINENTAL

$$$ ★ ✕ Rendez-Vous Restaurant. People (Queen Beatrix among them) come
to Rendez-Vous for the hearty, consistently well-prepared food: warm
French bread with garlic butter, conch chowder, creole-style fresh fish,
and seafood, steak, and vegetarian entrées. Enjoy your meal indoors—
the dining room showcases works by a local artist—or on the outdoor
patio. Also marvel at the collection of hundreds of cigarette lighters
from around the world on display in the bar area. ⊠ *Kaya L. D. Ger-
harts 3, Kralendijk,* ☎ *599/717–8454. AE, MC, V. Closed Sun.*

ECLECTIC

$$–$$$$ ✕ Zeezicht Bar & Restaurant. Zeezicht (pronounced *zay-zeekt* and
meaning "sea view") serves three meals a day. At breakfast and lunch
you'll get basic American fare with an Antillean touch, such as a fish
omelet; dinner is more Caribbean and mostly seafood. Dinner is either
on the terrace overlooking the harbor or in the nautically themed
homey, rough-hewn main room. Locals are dedicated to this hangout,
especially for the ceviche, conch sandwiches, and the Zeezicht special
soup with conch, fish, shrimp, and oysters. ⊠ *Kaya J. N. E. Craane
12, Kralendijk,* ☎ *599/717–8434. AE, MC, V.*

$$$ ✕ Mona Lisa Bar & Restaurant. Here you'll find Continental, Caribbean,
and Indonesian fare. Popular bar dishes include Wiener schnitzel and
fresh fish with curry sauce. The intimate stucco-and-brick dining room,
presided over by a copy of the famous painting of the eponymous lady,
is decorated with Dutch artwork, lace curtains, and whirring ceiling
fans. The colorful bar adorned with baseball-style caps is a great place
for late-night schmoozing and noshing on light snacks or the catch of
the day, served until 10 PM. ⊠ *Kaya Grandi 15, Kralendijk,* ☎ *599/
717–8718. AE, MC, V. No lunch. Closed Sun.*

$$–$$$ ✕ Le Wok. This popular newcomer serves satisfying French, Thai,
and Indian fusion dishes and is open for dinner only. Be sure to try Lu-
cille's seafood gumbo. The restaurant is housed in an early 20th-cen-
tury building featuring typical Bonairean architecture. ⊠ *Kaya C. E.
B. Hellmund 19, Kralendijk,* ☎ *599/717–7884. D, MC, V. Closed Tues.*

$$ ✕ **Kontiki Beach Club.** The dining room is a harmonious blend of terra-cotta tile floors and rattan furnishings, set around the limestone half-moon bar. There's also a brick terrace for alfresco dining. Dutch chef-owners Miriam and Martin serve dishes such as a delicious creamy curry soup, and "Catch Original" (pan-fried local fish in red pepper sauce). There are frequent live jazz performances on the outdoor stage. Seven studio apartments on premises rent for a very reasonable $73 per night. ⊠ *Kaminda Sorobon 64, Lac Bay,* ☎ *599/717–5369. AE, MC, V. Closed Mon.*

$–$$ ✕ **Coco's Beach Café and Players Bar.** This outdoor waterfront eatery with umbrella-shaded tables is a colorful, fun place to grab a bite any time of day. For breakfast, enjoy bagels, croissants, muffins, and pastries. The lunch and dinner menus include grilled options like fish, chorizo, chicken, and ribs. Banana and strawberry smoothies are popular heat-beaters. Open until 2 AM, the indoor bar has four pool tables (where any sharks you might encounter are not the underwater kind). ⊠ *Kaya Jan Craane 12, Kralendijk,* ☎ *599/717–8434. AE, D, MC, V.*

ITALIAN

$$–$$$$ ✕ **Croccantino.** At this casual restaurant decorated in splashes of purple and green, you can indulge in authentic Italian food on the large outdoor terrace or in the air-conditioned indoor smoking or non-smoking rooms. For an appetizer try *funghi gratinati* (mushrooms smothered in a creamy cheese sauce), and follow it up with lobster fetuccine. ⊠ *Kaya Grandi 48, Kralendijk,* ☎ *599/717–5025. MC, V. Closed Sun. No lunch Sat.*

$–$$ ✕ **Capriccio.** This splendid, family-run Italian eatery has plenty to
★ boast about. The pastas are handmade daily, fresh mozzarella is imported from Italy once a week, and there's a true climate-controlled wine cellar. You can opt for casual à la carte dining on the terrace or a romantic meal in the tonier air-conditioned dining room. If your appetite is hearty, go for the six-course prix-fixe "Menu' del buon appetito." Otherwise choose from the numerous pasta, meat, and fish dishes or thin-crust pizza. ⊠ *Kaya Isla Riba 1, Kralendijk,* ☎ *599/717–7230. AE, MC, V. Closed Tues. No lunch Sun.*

SEAFOOD

$$$–$$$$ ✕ **It Rains Fishes.** The mood is vivacious at this popular eatery on the terrace of a converted mansion overlooking the water. There is an interesting mural of colorful underwater creatures near the bar, each uniquely conceived and hand-painted by a member of the staff or one of the owners. Fish dominate the menu, but tapas and satays are also available. The signature dish is fresh fish in a mustard sauce. ⊠ *Kaya Jan N. E. Craane 24, Kralendijk,* ☎ *599/717–8780. MC, V.*

$$–$$$ ✕ **Den Laman Bar & Restaurant.** A 6,000-gallon aquarium and a nautical theme are the backdrop at this casual restaurant. Eat indoors next to the glass-enclosed "ocean show" (request a table in advance) or outdoors on the noisier patio overlooking the sea. Pick a fresh Caribbean lobster from the tank or order red snapper creole, a hands-down winner. Homemade cheesecake is a draw, as is the live entertainment each Saturday night. ⊠ *Kaya Gobernador N. Debrot 77, Kralendijk,* ☎ *599/ 717–8955. AE, MC, V. No lunch. Closed Tues.*

$$–$$$ ✕ **Richard's Waterfront Dining.** Animated, congenial Richard Beady
★ and his partner Mario own this casually romantic waterfront eatery. It has become the island's most recommended restaurant—a reputation that's well deserved. The daily menu is listed on large blackboards, and the food is consistently excellent. The fish soup is sure to please, as is the grilled wahoo. ⊠ *J. A. Abraham Blvd. 60, Kralendijk,* ☎ *599/717–5263. DC, MC, V. No lunch. Closed Mon.*

Beaches

Don't expect long stretches of glorious powdery sand. Bonaire's beaches are small, and though the water is blue (several shades of it, in fact), the sand isn't always white. You have your pick of beaches according to color: pink, black, or white. The best public beach is "Pink Beach," and for those who prefer a more complete tan, Sorobon is the island's only nude beach (open to nonguests for $15).

Boca Cocolishi. You'll find hermit crabs along the shore of this black-sand beach in Washington/Slagbaai National Park, on the northeast coast. The term *windswept* has true meaning here: cooling breezes whip the water into a frenzy as the color of the sea changes from midnight blue to aquamarine. The water is too rough for anything more than wading, but the spot is perfect for an intimate picnic *à deux*. To get here, take the Northern Scenic Route to the park; ask for directions at the gate.

Boca Slagbaai. Inside Washington/Slagbaai Park is this beach of coral fossils and rocks with interesting offshore coral gardens that are good for snorkeling. Bring scuba boots or canvas sandals to walk into the water because the beach is rough on bare feet. The gentle surf makes it an ideal place for swimming and picnicking.

Lac Bay Beach. Known for its festive music on Sunday nights, this open bay area with pink-tinted sand is equally dazzling by day. It's a bumpy drive (10–15 minutes on a dirt road) to get here, but you'll be glad when you arrive. It's a good spot for diving, snorkeling, and kayaking (bring your own), and there are public rest rooms and a restaurant for your convenience.

Pink Beach. As the name suggests, the sand here has a pinkish hue that takes on a magical shimmer in the late afternoon sun. The water is suitable for swimming, snorkeling, and scuba diving. Take the Southern Scenic Route on the island's western side; the beach is close to the slave huts. It's a favorite Bonairean hangout on the weekend, but it's almost deserted during the week. Because of the coral that is thrown up on the beach sandals are recommended.

Playa Funchi. This Washington Park beach is notable for the lagoon on one side, where flamingos nest, and the superb snorkeling on the other, where iridescent green parrot fish swim right up to shore.

Sorobon Beach. Adjacent to the Sorobon Beach Resort's private stretch of sand, this is *the* windsurfing beach. You'll find a restaurant/bar next to the resort and a couple of windsurfing outfitters on the beach. The public beach area has rest rooms and huts for shade.

Windsock Beach. Near the airport, this pretty little spot, also known as Mangrove Beach, looks out toward the north side of the island and has about 200 m of white sand along a rocky shoreline. It's a popular dive site and swimming conditions are good.

Outdoor Activities and Sports

Cycling

Twenty-one-speed mountain bikes are the perfect way to travel Bonaire's more than 180 mi (290 km) of unpaved routes (as well as the many paved roads). For mountain bikes try **Captain Don's Habitat** (☒ Kaya Gobernador N. Debrot 103, Kralendijk, ☎ 599/717–8290 or 599/717–8913). Rates average around $15–$20 per day, and a credit card or cash deposit is usually required. **Cycle Bonaire** (☒ Kaya L. D. Gerharts 11D, next to Cultimara Supermarket, Kralendijk, ☎ 599/717–7558) rents mountain bikes and gear (trail maps, water bottles, helmets, locks, repair and first-aid kits) for $15 a day or $75 a week; half-day and full-day guided excursions start at $40, not including bike rental.

Hot Shot Rentals (⊠ Kaya Bonaire 4-C, Kralendijk, ☎ 599/717–7166) rents regular, hybrid, and Dutch touring bikes for $10 a day.

Fishing

Captain Cornelis of **Big Game Sportfishing** (⊠ Kaya Warawara 3, Kralendijk, ☎ FAX 599/717–6500) offers deep-sea charters for those in search of wahoo, marlin, tuna, swordfish, and sailfish. His rates—which cover bait, tackle, and refreshments—average $350 for a half-day, $500 for a full day for as many as four people. **Multifish Charters** (☎ 599/717–7033) has day or night reef fishing on a 32-ft Permacraft twin diesel; the cost for six hours is $300 (four-person maximum). A nine-hour day of deep-sea fishing costs $450 (six-person maximum). **Piscatur Charters** (⊠ Kaya H. J. Pop 4, Kralendijk, ☎ 599/717–8774) offers light-tackle angler reef fishing for jacks, barracuda, and snapper from a 15-ft skiff. Rates are $225 for a half-day, $300 for a full day. You can charter the 42-ft Sport Fisherman *Piscatur*, which carries up to six people, for $350 for a half-day; $500 for a full day. Bonefishing runs $200 for a half-day.

Horseback Riding

You can take hour-long trail rides at the 166-acre **Kunuku Warahama Ranch** (⊠ Kaya Guanare 11, east of Kralendijk (off road to Cai), ☎ 599/717–6786, FAX 599/717–6796) for $20. Guides take you through groves of cacti where iguanas, wild goats, donkeys, and flamingos reside. Reserve one of the gentle pintos or palominos a day in advance, and try to go early in the morning, when it's cool. The ranch, open Tuesday–Sunday 10–6, also has an alfresco restaurant, a golf driving range, and two playgrounds.

Kayaking

Divers and snorkelers use the kayak to reach inaccessible dive sites and simply tow the craft along during their dive. Nondivers use kayaks to explore the flora and fauna of the island's rich mangrove forests (apply plenty of insect repellent before touring).

At **Jibe City** (⊠ Sorobon Beach, ☎ 599/717–5233; 800/748–8733 for a U.S. representative) kayaks go for $10 (single) and $15 (double) per hour; $25 and $30, respectively, per half-day (closed in October). Guided trips and kayak rentals are available from **Sand Dollar Dive and Photo** (⊠ Kaya Gobernador N. Debrot 79, Kralendijk, ☎ 599/717–8738 or 800/288–4773. **Discover Bonaire** (⊠ Box 361, ☎ 599/717–5433 or 599/717–5252) offers kayaking trips (beginning at $45 for a half-day, single kayak trip), nature tours to explore Bonaire's unique flora and fauna (led by biologist Jerry Ligon are $50 per person), snorkeling adventures, special children's programs, and mountain biking trips. Guided tours are available.

Sailing

Bonaire Boating (⊠ At Divi Flamingo Resort, ☎ 599/790–5353), offers half- or full-day charters aboard a luxury 56-ft sailing yacht ($395 and $695, respectively), a 57-ft motor yacht ($455 for four hours), or the private charter of a 26-ft Bayliner day cruiser for $295 for three hours.

Scuba Diving

Bonaire has some of the best reef diving this side of Australia's Great Barrier Reef. It takes only 5–25 minutes to reach many sites, the current is usually mild, and although some reefs have sudden, steep drops, most begin just offshore and slope gently downward at a 45° angle. General visibility runs 60–100 ft (18–30 m), except during surges in October and November. You can see several varieties of coral: knobby-brain, giant-brain, elkhorn, staghorn, mountainous star, gorgonian, and black. You'll also encounter schools of parrot fish, surgeonfish, angelfish, eels, snappers, and groupers. Beach diving is excellent just about everywhere on the leeward side, so night diving is popular. There are sites here suitable for every skill level; they're clearly marked by yellow stones on the roadside.

In the well-policed Bonaire Marine Park, which encompasses the entire coastline around Bonaire and Klein Bonaire, divers take the rules seriously. Don't even *think* about (1) spearfishing; (2) dropping anchor; or (3) touching, stepping on, or collecting coral. You must pay an admission of $10 (used to maintain the park), for which you receive a colored plastic tag (to attach to an item of scuba gear) entitling you to one calendar year of unlimited diving. Checkout dives—diving first with a master before going out on your own—are required, and you can arrange them through any dive shop. All dive operations offer classes in free buoyancy control, advanced buoyancy control, and photographic buoyancy control. Tags are available at all scuba facilities and from the **Marine Park Headquarters** (☎ 599/717–8444) at Karpata.

DIVE SITES

The *Guide to the Bonaire Marine Park* lists 86 dive sites (including 16 shore-dive-only and 35 boat-dive-only sites). Another fine reference book is the *Diving and Snorkeling Guide to Bonaire,* by Jerry Schnabel and Suzi Swygert. Guides associated with the various dive centers can give you more complete directions. It's difficult to recommend one site over another; to whet your appetite, here are a few of the popular sites.

Angel City. Take the trail down to the shore adjacent to the Trans-World Radio station; dive in and swim south to Angel City, one of the shallowest and most popular sites in a two-reef complex that includes Alice in Wonderland. The boulder-size green-and-tan coral heads are home to black margates, Spanish hogfish, gray snappers, and large purple tube sponges.

Bari Reef. Go to the free slide show on Tuesday at the Sand Dollar Condominium Resort to catch a glimpse of the elkhorn and fire coral, queen angelfish, and other wonders of Bari Reef, just off the resort's pier.

Calabas Reef. Off the coast from the Divi Flamingo Resort, this is the island's busiest dive site. It's replete with Christmas-tree worms, sponges, and fire coral adhering to a ship's hull. Fish life is frenzied, with the occasional octopus putting in an appearance.

Forest. You'll need to catch a boat to reach Forest, a dive site off the southwest coast of Klein Bonaire. Named for the abundant black-coral forests found in it, the site gets a lot of fish action, including a resident spotted eel that lives in a cave.

Rappel. This spectacular site is near the Karpata Ecological Center. The shore is a sheer cliff, and the lush coral growth is the habitat of some unusual varieties of marine life, including occasional orange sea horses, squid, spiny lobsters, and spotted trunkfish.

Small Wall. One of Bonaire's three complete vertical wall dives (and one of its most popular night-diving spots), Small Wall is offshore from the road north of Captain Don's Habitat, near Barcadera Beach. The 60-ft (18-m) wall is frequented by squid, turtles, tarpon, and barracudas, and has dense hard and soft coral formations; it also allows for excellent snorkeling.

Something Special. South of the marina entrance at Harbour Village Beach Resort, this spot is famous for its garden eels. They wave about from the relatively shallow sand terrace looking like long grass in a breeze.

Windsock Steep. This excellent shore-dive site (from 20 to 80 ft [6 to 24 m]) is in front of the small beach opposite the airport runway. It's a popular place for snorkeling. The current is moderate, the elkhorn coral profuse; you may also see angelfish and rays.

DIVE CENTERS

Many of the dive shops listed below offer PADI and NAUI certification courses and SSI, as well as underwater photography and videography courses. Some shops are also qualified to certify dive instructors. Full certification courses cost approximately $370; open-water refresher courses run about $185; a one-tank boat dive with unlimited shore diving costs about $37; a two-tank boat dive with unlimited shore diving is about $55. As for equipment, renting a mask, fin, and snorkel costs about $8.50 all together; for a BC and regulator, expect to pay about $16.

Bon Bini Divers. ⊠ *Lions Dive Hotel Bonaire, Kaya Gobernador N. Debrot 91, Kralendijk,* ☎ *599/717–5425.*

Bonaire Scuba Center. ⊠ *Black Durgon Inn, Kaya Gobernador N. Debrot 145, Kralendijk,* ☎ *599/717–5736 (Box 775, Morgan, NJ 08879),* ☎ *908/566–8866 or 800/526–2370.*

Bruce Bowker's Carib Inn Dive Center. ⊠ *J. A. Abraham Blvd. 46, Airport Rd., Kralendijk,* ☎ *599/717–8819.*

Buddy Dive Resort. ⊠ *Kaya Gobernador N. Debrot 85, Kralendijk,* ☎ *599/717–5080.*

Captain Don's Habitat Dive Shop. ⊠ *Kaya Gobernador N. Debrot 103, Kralendijk,* ☎ *599/717–8290.*

Dee Scarr's "Touch the Sea." ⊠ *Box 369, Kralendijk,* ☎ *599/717–8529.*

Dive Inn. ⊠ *Kaya C. E. B. Hellmund, Kralendijk, close to South Pier,* ☎ *599/717–8761.*

Photo Tours Divers. ⊠ *Caribbean Court Bonaire, J. A. Abraham Blvd., Kralendijk,* ☎ *599/717–5353 Ext. 328.*

Sand Dollar Dive and Photo. ⊠ *Sand Dollar Condominium Resort, Kaya Gobernador N. Debrot 79, Kralendijk,* ☎ *599/717–8738.*

Toucan Diving. ⊠ *Plaza Resort Bonaire, J. A. Abraham Blvd. 80, Kralendijk,* ☎ *599/717–2500.*

SNORKELING

Bonaire, in conjunction with *Skin Diver Magazine*, developed the **Guided Snorkeling Program.** The highly educational and entertaining program begins with a slide show on the topics, from a beginner's look at reef fish, coral, and sponges to advanced fish identification and night snorkeling. Guided snorkeling for all skill levels can be arranged through most resort dive shops; the cost is $25 (discounts available for more than one session) and includes slide presentations, transportation to the site, and a guided tour. Gear is an additional $9 per 24-hour period. The best snorkeling spots are on the island's leeward side, where you have shore access to the reefs, and along the west side of Klein Bonaire, where the reef is better developed.

In addition to the dive shops, **SeaCow WaterTaxi** (⊠ Club Karel's Bar, at the waterfront, Kralendijk, ☎ 599/780–7126) has snorkel trips (day and night) and daily excursions to Klein Bonaire.

TENNIS

Tennis isn't a common activity on tiny Bonaire, but you do have a few options to volley about. Court prices generally run about $20 per hour for nonguests (free for guests), but pros aren't available. **Plaza Resort Bonaire** (⊠ J. A. Abraham Blvd. 80, Kralendijk, ☎ 599/717–2500) has four tennis courts. The **Sand Dollar Condominium Resort** (⊠ Kaya Gobernador N. Debrot 79, Kralendijk, ☎ 599/717–8738) has two courts.

WINDSURFING

Lac Bay, a protected cove on the east coast, is ideal for windsurfing. Novices will find it especially comforting since there's no way to be blown out to sea. The **Bonaire Windsurf Place** (✉ Lac Bay, ☎ 599/ 717–2288), commonly referred to as "the place," rents the latest Mistral, ProTech, and Naish equipment for $35–$60 per hour. A two-hour group lesson costs $35. Private lessons are $45 per hour (rates include equipment for beginners only). The three-day lesson package is a real bargain at $120 per individual, $95 per group.

Jibe City (✉ Sorobon Beach, ☎ 599/717–5233; 800/748–8733 for a U.S. representative) offers lessons for $45 (includes board and sail for beginners only); board rentals start at $20 an hour, $45 for a half-day. There are pickups at all the hotels at 9 AM and 1 PM; ask your hotel to make arrangements.

Shopping

You can get to know all the shops in Kralendijk in an hour or so. But sometimes there's no better way to enjoy some time out of the sun and sea than to go shopping (particularly if your companion is a dive fanatic and you're not). Almost all the shops are on the Kaya Grandi and adjacent streets and in tiny malls. Harborside Mall is a pleasant, airy, air-conditioned mall with several fine shops. The most distinctive local crafts are fanciful painted pieces of driftwood and hand-painted *kunuku,* or little wilderness houses. One word of caution: buy as many flamingo T-shirts as you want, but don't take home items made of goatskin or tortoiseshell; they aren't allowed into the United States. Remember, too, that it's forbidden to take sea fans, coral, conch shells, and *all* forms of marine life off the island.

Specialty Items

CLOTHES

Benetton (✉ Kaya Grandi 49, Kralendijk, ☎ 599/717–5107) claims that its prices for men's, women's, and children's clothes are 30% lower than in New York. **Best Buddies** (✉ Kaya Grandi 32, Kralendijk, ☎ 599/717–7570) stocks a selection of Indonesian batik shirts, *pareus* (beach wraps), and T-shirts. Colorful cotton resort wear and T-shirts are available at **Bye-Bye Bonaire** (✉ Harborside Mall, Kaya Gobernador, Kralendijk, ☎ 599/717–7578). At **Island Fashions** (✉ Kaya Grandi 5, Kralendijk, ☎ 599/717–7565) you can buy swimsuits, sunglasses, T-shirts, and costume jewelry.

DUTY-FREE GOODS

Flamingo Airport Duty Free (✉ Flamingo Airport, ☎ 599/717–5563) sells perfumes and cigarettes. Cigar smokers will find friends at **Little Holland** (✉ Harborside Mall, Kaya Gobernador, ☎ 599/717–5670) as they breathe in the smoky splendor of Havanas. Montecristo, H. Upmann, Romeo & Juliet, and Cohiba are all here. Far from being banished to the porch, smokers are welcomed into the acclimatized Cedar Cigar Room. **Perfume Palace** (✉ Harborside Mall, Kaya Gobernador, ☎ 599/717–5288) sells perfumes and makeup from Lancôme, Estée Lauder, Chanel, Ralph Lauren, and Clinique.

HANDICRAFTS

Bon Tiki (✉ Kaya C. E. B. Hellmund 3, Kralendijk, ☎ 599/717–6877) sells unique works from Bonaire's finest artists. The **Harmony Art Gallery** (✉ Kaya L. D. Gerharts 10, Kralendijk, ☎ 599/717–8539) showcases the works of local, Dutch, and American artists and will ship artwork (shrink-wrapped but unframed) to the United States. Whatever you do, make a point of visiting **Jenny's Art** (✉ Kaya Betico Croes #6,

Kralendijk, near the post office, ☎ 599/717–5004). Roam around her house, which is a replica of a traditional Bonaire town complete with her handmade lifesize dolls and the skeletons of all her dead pets! Lots of fun (and sometimes kitschy) souvenirs made out of driftwood, clay, and shells are all handmade by Jenny. **Roselord Souvenir & Gift Shop** (⊠ Kaya Kanari 42, North Nikiboko, ☎ 599/717–6765), outside Kralendijk, sells plates and woodwork painted by local artists. **Things Bonaire** (⊠ Kaya Grandi 38C, Kralendijk, ☎ 599/717–8423) purveys T-shirts, earrings, batik dresses, souvenirs, and guidebooks.

JEWELRY

Littman's (⊠ Kaya Grandi 33, Kralendijk, ☎ 599/717–8160; ⊠ Harborside Mall, Kaya Gobernador, Kralendijk, ☎ 599/717–2130) is an upscale jewelry and gift shop where many items are handpicked by owner Steven Littman on his regular trips to Europe. Look for Rolex, Omega, Cartier, and Tag Heuer watches, fine gold jewelry, antique coins, nautical sculptures, resort clothing, and accessories.

Nightlife and the Arts

Nightlife

Most divers are exhausted after they finish their third, fourth, or fifth dive of the day, which may explain why there are so few discos. Indeed, many people's idea of nightlife is looking for the elusive "green flash" just before sunset, a harbinger of luck (some swear it exists, others say that it can only be seen after several daiquiris), or else they go diving, snorkeling, windsurfing by the light of the moon. Most of the time nightlife consists of sitting on a quiet beach sipping a local Amstel Bright beer.

On Sunday afternoon at Lac Cai enjoy the festive Sunday Party, where locals celebrate the day with music, dancing, and food from 3 to 11. Take a taxi, especially if you plan to imbibe a few rum punches. Top island performers, including the Kunuku Band and Fomayan Boys, migrate from one resort to another throughout the week. You'll find information in the free magazines (published once a year) *Bonaire Holiday, Bonaire Affair,* and *Bonaire Nights.* The twice-monthly *Bonaire Update Events & Activities* pamphlet is available at most restaurants.

BARS

Amadeus (⊠ Kaya Bonaire 4, Kralendijk, ☎ 599/717–2888), a lively outdoor bar across the street from the waterfront, draws throngs of young partiers. The Thursday night happy hour at **Captain Don's Habitat** (⊠ Kaya Gobernador N. Debrot 85, Kralendijk, ☎ 599/717–8286) is very popular. Downtown, **City Cafe** (⊠ Hotel Rochaline, Kaya Grandi #7, Kralendijk, ☎ 599/717–8286) is a wacky hangout splashed in magenta, banana, and electric blue. Here you'll find cocktails, snack food, and live music on weekends. **Karel's** (⊠ Kaya J. N. E. Craane 12, Kralendijk, ☎ 599/717–8434) sits on stilts above the sea and is *the* place for mingling—especially Friday and Saturday nights, when there's live island and pop music.

CASINOS

At the **Divi Flamingo Resort**'s casino (⊠ J. A. Abraham Blvd., Kralendijk, ☎ 599/717–8285), you can try your hand at blackjack, roulette, and slot machines until 4 AM.

DANCE CLUBS

City Cafe (⊠ Kaya Grandi #7, Kralendijk, ☎ 599/717–8286) is the island's closest thing to a dance club. On weekend nights the restaurant moves the tables aside and it becomes an instant dance floor.

MOVIES

The **Bonaire Twin Cinema** (⊠ Kaya Prinses Marie, Kralendijk, ☎ 599/ 717–2400) has four to six daily showings of popular American movies. Tickets are about $6.

The Arts

Nature's artistry earns top billing on Bonaire. Slide shows of under- water and above-water scenes fascinate both divers and nondivers. Dee Scarr, a dive guide, presents the fascinating Touch the Sea show Mon- day night at 8:45, November–June, at **Captain Don's Habitat** (⊠ Kaya Gobernador N. Debrot 85, Kralendijk, ☎ 599/717–8290). Flora and fauna of the Caribbean are the focus of the slide show presented by naturalist Jerry Ligon on Thursday night at 8:15 at the **Sand Dollar Condominium Resort** (⊠ Kaya Gobernador N. Debrot 79, Kralendijk, ☎ 599/717–8738).

Exploring Bonaire

Two routes, north and south from Kralendijk, the island's small cap- ital, are possible on the 24-mi-long (39-km-long) island; either route will take from a few hours to a full day, depending on whether you stop to snorkel, swim, dive, or lounge.

Numbers in the margin correspond to points of interest on the Bonaire map.

Kralendijk

① Bonaire's small, tidy capital city (population 3,000) is five minutes from the airport. The main drag, J. A. Abraham Boulevard, turns into **Kaya Grandi** in the center of town. Along it are most of the island's major stores, boutiques, and restaurants. Across Kaya Grandi, opposite the Littman jewelry store, is Kaya L. D. Gerharts, with several small su- permarkets, a handful of snack shops, and some of the better restau- rants. Walk down the narrow waterfront avenue called Kaya C. E. B. Hellmund, which leads straight to the **North and South piers.** In the center of town, the Harborside Mall has chic boutiques. Along this route is **Ft. Oranje,** with its cannons. From December through April, cruise ships dock in the harbor once or twice a week. The elegant white struc- ture that looks like a tiny Greek temple is the **fish market**; local fish- ermen no longer bring their catches here (they sell out of their homes these days), but you'll find plenty of fresh produce. Pick up the brochure *Walking and Shopping in Kralendijk* from the tourist office to get a map and full listing of all the monuments and sights in the town.

South Bonaire

The trail south from Kralendijk is chock-full of icons—both natural and man-made—that tell Bonaire's minisaga. Rent a four-wheel-drive vehicle (a car will do, but during the rainy season of October–Novem- ber the roads can become muddy) and head out along the Southern Scenic Route. The roads wind through dramatic desert terrain, full of organ-pipe cacti and spiny-trunk mangroves—huge stumps of saltwater trees that rise from the marshes like witches. Watch for long-haired goats, wild donkeys, and lizards of all sizes.

SIGHTS TO SEE

③ **Salt Flats.** You can't miss the salt flats—voluptuous white drifts that look something like mountains of snow. Harvested once a year, the "ponds" are owned by Cargill, Inc., which has reactivated the 19th- century salt industry with great success (one reason for that success is that the ocean on this part of the island is higher than the land—which makes irrigation a snap). Keep a lookout for the three 30-ft (9-m) obelisks—white, blue, and red—that were used to guide the trade boats coming to pick up the salt. Look also in the distance across the pans to the abandoned solar salt works that's now a designated **flamingo sanctuary.** With the naked eye you might be able to make out a pink-orange haze just on the horizon; with binoculars you will see a sea of bobbing pink bodies. The sanctuary is completely protected, and no entrance is allowed (flamingos are extremely sensitive to disturbances of any kind).

❷ **Slave Huts.** The salt industry's gritty history is revealed in Rode Pan, the site of two groups of tiny slave huts. The white grouping is on the right side of the road, opposite the salt flats; the second grouping, called the red slave huts (though they appear yellow), stretches across the road toward the island's southern tip. During the 19th century slaves worked the salt pans by day, then crawled into these huts at night. Each Friday afternoon they walked seven hours to Rincon to weekend with their families, returning each Sunday. Only very small people will be able to enter, but walk around and poke your head in for a look.

❹ **Willemstoren Lighthouse.** Bonaire's first lighthouse was built in 1837 and is now automated (but closed to visitors). Take some time to explore the beach and notice how the waves, driven by the trade winds, play a crashing symphony against the rocks. Locals stop here to collect pieces of driftwood in spectacular shapes and to build fanciful pyramids from objects that have washed ashore.

North Bonaire

The Northern Scenic Route takes you into the heart of Bonaire's natural wonders—desert gardens of towering cacti (*kadushi,* used to prepare soup, and the thornier *yatu,* used to build cactus fencing), tiny coastal coves, and plenty of fantastic panoramas. The road also weaves between eroded pink-and-black limestone walls and eerie rock formations with fanciful names like the Devil's Mouth and Iguana Head (you'll need a vivid imagination and sharp eye to recognize them). Brazil trees growing along the route were used by Indians to make dye (pressed from a red ring in the trunk). Inscriptions still visible in several island caves were made with this dye.

A snappy excursion with the requisite photo stops will take about 2½ hours, but if you pack your swimsuit and a hefty picnic basket (forget about finding a Burger King), you could spend the entire day exploring this northern sector. Head out from Kralendijk on the Kaya Gobernador N. Debrot until it turns into the Northern Scenic Route. Once you pass the Radio Nederland towers you cannot turn back to Kralendijk. The narrow road becomes one-way until you get to Landhuis Karpata, and you have to follow the cross-island road to Rincon and return via the main road through the center of the island.

SIGHTS TO SEE

❻ **Barcadera Cave.** Once used to trap goats, this cave is one of the oldest in Bonaire; there's even a tunnel that looks intriguingly spooky. It's the first sight along the northern route; watch closely for a yellow marker on your left before you reach the towering Radio Nederland antennas. Pull off across from the entrance to the Bonaire Caribbean Club, and you'll discover some stone steps that lead down into a cave full of stalactites and vegetation.

⓫ **Gotomeer.** This saltwater lagoon near the island's northern end is a popular flamingo hangout. Bonaire is one of the few places in the world where pink flamingos nest. The shy, spindly legged creatures—affectionately called "pink clouds"—are magnificent birds to observe, and there are about 15,000 of them in Bonaire (the same as the number of permanent island residents). The best time to catch them at home is

January to June, when they tend to their gray-plumed young. For the best view take the newly paved access road alongside the lagoon through the jungle of cacti to the parking and observation area on the rise overlooking the lagoon and Washington/Slagbaai Park beyond.

⑫ Landhuis Karpata. This mustard-color building was the manor house of an aloe plantation more than 100 years ago. The site was named for the *karpata* (castor oil) plants that are abundant in the area—you'll see them along the sides of the road as you approach. Notice the rounded outdoor oven where aloe was boiled down before exporting the juice. Although the government has built a shaded rest stop at Karpata, there's still no drink stand.

❼ 1,000 Steps. Directly across the road from the Radio Nederland towers on the main road north, watch closely for a short yellow marker on the opposite side of the road to locate these limestone stairs carved right out of the cliff. If you trek down the stairs, you'll discover a lovely coral beach and protected cove where you can snorkel and scuba dive. Actually, you'll count only 67 steps, but it feels like 1,000 when you walk back up carrying scuba gear.

❾ Onima. Small signposts direct the way to the Indian inscriptions found on a 3-ft (1-m) limestone ledge that juts out like a partially formed cave entrance. Look up to see the red-stained designs and symbols inscribed on the limestone, said to have been the handiwork of the Arawak Indians when they inhabited the island centuries ago. The pictographs are at least 500 years old, and nobody has a clue what they mean. To reach Onima, pass through Rincon on the road that heads back to Kralendijk, but take the left-hand turn before Fontein.

❽ Rincon. The island's original Spanish settlement, Rincon is where the slaves, who were brought from Africa to work the plantations and salt fields, lived. Superstition and voodoo lore still have a powerful impact here, more so than in Kralendijk, where the townspeople work hard at suppressing old ways. Rincon is now a well-kept cluster of pastel cottages and century-old buildings that constitute Bonaire's oldest village. Watch your driving here—goats and dogs often sit right in the middle of the main drag. There are a couple of local eateries, but the real temptation is **Prisca's Ice Cream** (☎ 599/717–6334), to be found at Prisca's house, on Kaya Komkomber (watch for the hand-lettered sign).

❺ Seroe Largu. Just off the main road, this spot, at 394 ft (120 m), is one of the highest on the island. A paved but narrow and twisting road leads to a magnificent daytime view of Kralendijk's rooftops and the island of Klein Bonaire. A large cross and figure of Christ stand guard at the peak, with an inscription reading: *ayera* (past), *awe* (present), and *semper* (future).

☝ ❿ Washington/Slagbaai National Park. Once a plantation producing divi-divi trees (the pods were used for tanning animal skins), aloe (used for medicinal lotions), charcoal, and goats, the park is now a model of conservation. It's easy to tour the 13,500-acre tropical desert terrain on the dirt roads. As befits a wilderness sanctuary, the well-marked, rugged routes force you to drive slowly enough to appreciate the animal life and the terrain. (Think twice about coming here if it rained the day before—the mud you may encounter will be more than inconvenient.) If you're planning to hike, bring a picnic lunch, camera, sunscreen, and plenty of water. There are two routes: the long one (22 mi [35½ km]) is marked by yellow arrows, the short one (15 mi [24 km])—by green arrows. Goats and donkeys may dart across the road, and if you keep your eyes peeled, you may catch sight of large iguanas camouflaged in the shrubbery.

Bird-watchers are really in their element here. Right inside the park's gate, flamingos roost on the salt pad known as **Salina Mathijs**, and exotic parakeets dot the foot of **Mt. Brandaris**, Bonaire's highest peak, at 784 ft (239 m). Some 130 species of birds fly in and out of the shrubbery in the park. Keep your eyes open and your binoculars at hand. Swimming, snorkeling, and scuba diving are permitted, but you're requested not to frighten the animals or remove anything from the grounds. Absolutely no hunting, fishing, or camping is allowed. A useful guide to the park is available at the entrance for about $6. To get there, take the secondary road north from the town of Rincon. ☎ 599/717–8444. 🎫 $10. ⊙ *Daily 8–5, but you must enter before 3.*

BONAIRE A TO Z

To research prices, get advice from other travelers, and book travel arrangements, visit www.fodors.com.

AIR TRAVEL

Air DCE has daily flights via Curaçao from Miami. It also has flights to Aruba, Caracas, Venezuela, St. Maarten, Trinidad, and other Caribbean islands—using Curaçao as its hub. The airline's Visit Caribbean Pass allows easy interisland travel. American Eagle flies direct to Bonaire from San Juan four times a week. Air Jamaica flies to Bonaire on Wednesday, Saturday, and Sunday from its hub in Montego Bay. Travelers can also connect to the nonstop flight from Montego Bay from the airline's U.S. gateways. KLM flies direct to Bonaire from Amsterdam twice a week in low season and daily in high season. ➤ AIRLINES AND CONTACTS: **Air DCE** (☎ 599/717–8500). **Air Jamaica** (☎ 800/523–5585). **American Airlines/American Eagle** (☎ 599/717–7400). **KLM** (☎ 599/717–5352; 800/374–7747 in the U.S.; 3120/4747747 in the Netherlands).

AIRPORTS

Bonaire's Flamingo Airport is tiny but welcoming (the KLM 747 almost dwarfs the airport when it lands). Rental cars and taxis are available, but try to arrange for pickup through your hotel. A taxi will run between $9 and $12 (for up to four people) to most hotels; $16 to the Lac Bay Resort or Sorobon Beach Resort. Fares are 25% extra from 7 PM to midnight and 50% extra from midnight to 6 AM. ➤ CONTACTS: **Flamingo Airport** (☎ 599/717–3800).

BIKE AND MOPED TRAVEL

Scooters are a great way to zip around the island. Rates are about $18 per day for a one-seater, and up to $38 for a deluxe two-seater. A valid driver's license and cash deposit or credit card are required. ➤ BIKE AND MOPED RENTALS: **Hot Shot Rentals** (✉ Kaya Bonaire 4-C, Kralendijk, ☎ 599/717–7166). **Macho!Scooter Rentals** (✉ J.A. Abraham Blvd. 80, Kralendijk, ☎ 599/717–2500).

BUSINESS HOURS

BANKS

Banks are generally open weekdays 8:30–noon and 1:15–3:30. The bank at the airport has extended hours: weekdays 6:30 AM–11:30 PM and weekends 6 AM–11:30 PM.

POST OFFICES

Post offices are open weekdays 7:30–noon and 1:30–4.

SHOPS

Stores in the Kralendijk area are generally open Monday–Saturday 8–noon and 2–6.

CAR RENTALS

You'll need a valid U.S., Canadian, or international driver's license to rent a car, and you must meet the minimum and maximum age requirements (usually 21 and 70) of each rental company. There's a government tax of $3.50 per day per car rental; no cash deposit is needed if you pay by credit card.

➤ MAJOR AGENCIES: **Avis** (✉ Kaya Betico Croes 1, Kralendijk, ☎ 599/717–5795). **Budget** (✉ Flamingo Airport, ☎ 599/717–7424). **Flamingo Car Rental** (✉ Kaya Grandi 86, Kralendijk, ☎ 599/717–8888; 599/717–5588 at the airport). **Hertz** (✉ Flamingo Airport, ☎ 599/717–7221). **Island Rentals** (✉ Kaya Industria 31, Kralendijk, ☎ 599/717–2100). **National** (✉ Kaya Nikiboko Zuid 114, Kralendijk, ☎ 599/717–7940 or 599/717–7907).

CAR TRAVEL

GASOLINE

Gas costs $3.00–$3.50 per gallon (NAf 1.50 per liter), and you'll find stations in Kralendijk, Rincon, and Antriol.

ROAD CONDITIONS

Main roads are very well paved, but remember that there are also many miles of unpaved road; the roller-coaster hills at the national park require a strong stomach, and during the rainy season (October–November) mud—called Bonairean snow—can be difficult to navigate.

RULES OF THE ROAD

All traffic stays to the right, and there's not a single traffic light. Signs or green arrows are usually posted to leading attractions; if you stick to the paved roads and marked turnoffs, you won't get lost.

ELECTRICITY

Bonaire runs on 120 AC/50 cycles. A transformer and occasionally a two-prong adapter are required. Note that some appliances may work slowly (60 cycles are typical in North America), hairdryers may overheat, and sensitive equipment may be damaged.

EMERGENCIES

➤ AMBULANCE AND FIRE: **Ambulance** (☎ 599/717–8900). **Fire** (☎ 599/717–8000). **Police** (☎ 599/717–8000). **Scuba-Diving Emergencies** (☎ 599/717–8187); the hyperbaric chamber is next to the hospital in Kralendijk.

➤ HOSPITALS: **St. Franciscus Hospital** (✉ Kaya Soeur Bartola 2, Kralendijk, ☎ 599/717–8900).

➤ PHARMACIES: **Botika Bonaire** (✉ Kaya Grandi 27, Kralendijk, by Harborside Mall, ☎ 599/717–8905).

FESTIVALS AND SEASONAL EVENTS

Carnival, generally held in February, is the usual nonstop parade of steel bands, floats, and wild costumes, albeit on a much smaller scale than on some other islands. It culminates in the ceremonial burning in effigy of King Momo, representing the spirit of debauchery. April ushers in the festival of Simadan, a celebration of the corn harvest, with special songs paying tribute to the farmers. The week-long Bonaire Dive Festival is held in June, filled with educational and fun activities to raise people's awareness of the importance of the world's coral reefs. Early October sees the well-attended International Sailing Regatta. December marks the beginning of the Bari (Drum) Festival, for which local bands write and play songs about events of the past year.

HOLIDAYS

Public holidays are: New Year's Day, Carnival Monday (the Monday before Ash Wednesday), Good Friday (the Friday before Easter), Rincon Day and Queen's Birthday (Apr. 30), Labor Day (May 1), Bonaire Day (Sept. 6), Antilles Day (Oct. 21), Christmas and the day after (Dec. 25–26).

LANGUAGE

The official language is Dutch, but the everyday language is Papiamento, a mix of Spanish, Portuguese, Dutch, English, and French as well as African tongues. You'll light up your waiter's eyes if you can say *masha danki* (thank you very much) and *pasa un bon dia* (have a nice day). English is spoken by almost everyone on the island.

MAIL AND SHIPPING

Airmail postage to North America and Europe is Naf 2.25 and Naf 1.10 for postcards. The main post office is at the southeast corner of Kaya Grandi and Kaya Libertador S. Bolivar in Kralendijk.

MONEY MATTERS

Prices quoted in this chapter are in U.S. dollars unless otherwise noted.

ATMS

You'll find ATMs at the airport, Kralendijk, and Hato branches of MCB, as well as at the Sand Dollar Resort and the Plaza Resort; at the Kaya Grandi branch of the ABN-AMRO; at Banco di Caribe on Kaya Grandi.

BANKS

R.B.T.T Bank (⊠ Kaya Corona 15, Kralendijk, ☎ 599/717–8417; ⊠ Kaya Grandi 22, Kralendijk, ☎ 599/717–7595; ⊠ Kaya Grandi 49, Kralendijk, ☎ 599/717–7660). **Maduro & Curiel's Bank Bonaire N. V.** (MCB; ⊠ Flamingo Airport, ☎ 599/717–5522; ⊠ Kaya L. D. Gerharts, Kralendijk, ☎ 599/717–5520; ⊠ Rincon, ☎ 599/717–6266; ⊠ Hato, ☎ 599/717–5520).

CURRENCY

There's no real need to convert your American dollars into the local currency, the NAf guilder. U.S. currency and traveler's checks are accepted everywhere, and the difference in exchange rates is negligible. Banks accept U.S. dollar banknotes at the official rate of NAf 1.78 to the U.S. dollar, traveler's checks at NAf 1.80. This rate is practically fixed. The rate of exchange at shops and hotels ranges from NAf 1.75 to NAf 1.80. The guilder is divided into 100 cents.

PASSPORTS AND VISAS

U.S. and Canadian citizens need proof of identity (a valid passport or an original birth certificate with a raised seal along with a photo ID). All others must carry valid passports. In addition, everyone must have a return or ongoing ticket and is advised to confirm reservations 48 hours before departure. The maximum stay is 90 days.

SAFETY

Because of strong trade winds pounding against the rocks, the windward (eastern) side of Bonaire is much too rough for diving. The *Guide to the Bonaire Marine Park* (available at dive shops around the island) specifies the level of diving skill required for 44 sites and knows what it's talking about. No matter how beautiful a beach may look, heed all warning signs regarding the rough undertow. Also get an orientation on what stings underwater and what doesn't.

During Bonaire's rainy season (October–November), mosquitoes can be a minor nuisance. Open-air restaurants usually have a can of repellent handy.

Bonaire has a reputation for being friendly and safe, but lately people have taken to locking their car doors, especially in the heart of town. Don't leave your camera in an open car, and keep your money, credit cards, jewelry, and other valuables in your hotel's safety-deposit box.

SIGHTSEEING TOURS
BOAT TOURS AND CRUISES
On Bonaire, the myriad of choices for getting out and enjoying the deep blue sea seems as limitless as the ocean itself. Among them: snorkeling, picnicking, and sunset cruises (prices range from $25 to $50 per person), and private or group sails (expect to pay about $425 per day for a party of four). Glass-bottom boat trips are another highlight: the 1½-hour trip costs $23 per person and leaves twice daily, except Sunday, from the Harbour Village Marina.

➤ DAY-SAIL CONTACTS: *Sea Witch* (☎ 599/9–560–7449) is a 56-ft ketch. *Woodwind* (☎ 599/9–560–7055) is a 37-ft trimaran. *Oscarina* ☎ 599/9–560–7674) is a 42-ft sloop.

➤ GLASS-BOTTOM BOAT TRIPS: *Bonaire Dream* (✉ Harbour Village Marina, Kaya Gobernador N. Debrot, ☎ 599/717–8239 or 599/717–4514, WEB http://bonairenet.an/bonairedream).

ORIENTATION TOURS
➤ CONTACTS: **Achie Tours** (✉ Kaya Nikiboko Noord 33, ☎ 599/717–8630) has several half- and full-day island tours. **Baranka Tours** (✉ Kaya Gobernador N. Debrot 79A, ☎ 599/717–2200, WEB www.barankabonaire.com) offers several island tours at reasonable prices. **Bonaire Sightseeing Tours** (✉ Kaya General Manuel Piar, next to the main Air ALM office, Kralendijk, ☎ 599/717–8778) will chauffeur you around on two-hour tours of either the island's north or south or on a half-day city-and-country tour ($25), which visits sights in both regions.

TAXES
DEPARTURE TAX
The departure tax when going to Curaçao is $5.75. For all other destinations it's $20. This tax must be paid in cash at the airport prior to departure. U.S. currency is accepted but paying in guilders is usually faster.

HOTEL TAXES AND SERVICE CHARGES
Hotels charge a room tax of $6.50 per person, per night in addition to the V.A.T. Many hotels add a 10%–15% service charge to your bill.

VALUE ADDED TAX (V.A.T.)
A V.A.T (value-added tax) of 6% is tacked on to dining and lodging costs.

TAXIS
Taxis are unmetered; they have fixed rates controlled by the government. A trip from the airport to your hotel will cost between $9 and $12 for up to four passengers. A taxi from most hotels into town costs between $5 and $8. Fares increase from 7 PM to midnight by 25% and from midnight to 6 AM by 50%. Drivers are usually knowledgeable enough about the island to conduct half-day tours; they charge about $30 for up to four passengers for half-day northern- or southern-route tours.

➤ CONTACTS: **Taxi Central Dispatch** (☎ 599/717–8100).

TELEPHONES

It's difficult for visitors to Bonaire to get involved in dramatic, heart-wrenching phone conversations or *any* phone discussions requiring a degree of privacy. You can make calls from hotel front desks or from the Telbo central phone company office (located next to the tourism office in Kralendijk), which is open 24 hours a day. Telephone connections have improved, but static is still common. You can rent a cell phone from CellularOne Bonaire. The phone will cost you $1.40 rental a day (plus a deposit) and you can buy prepaid phone cards—cell call costs are about 75% cheaper than a hotel call.

➤ CONTACTS: **CellularOne Bonaire** (Kaya Grandi 26, Kralendijk, ☎ 599/717–8787).

COUNTRY AND AREA CODES

The area code is 599; 717 is the exchange for every four-digit telephone number on Bonaire.

INTERNATIONAL CALLS

Forget about trying to use your own phone cards; it's theoretically possible but utterly maddening trying to get connected to the right operator. You can try AT&T by dialing 001–800/872–2881 from public phones, but there are no guarantees. To call Bonaire from the United States, dial 011–599/717 + the local four-digit number.

LOCAL CALLS

When making interisland calls, dial 717 + the local four-digit number. Local phone calls cost NAf 50¢.

TIPPING

Most restaurants add a 10%–12% service charge. Taxi drivers like a 10% tip, but it isn't mandatory. Bellhops should receive $1 per bag.

VISITOR INFORMATION

➤ BEFORE YOU LEAVE: **Bonaire Government Tourist Office** (✉ 10 Rockefeller Plaza, Suite 900, New York, NY 10020, ☎ 212/956–5913 or 800/266–2473, WEB www.infobonaire.com).

➤ IN BONAIRE: Stop by the **Tourism Corporation Bonaire** office (✉ Kaya Grandi 2, Kralendijk, ☎ 599/717–8322 or 599/717–8649).

7 BRITISH VIRGIN ISLANDS

Updated by
Pamela
Acheson and
Richard B.
Myers

The eight-seater Cessna took off smoothly and on schedule for the 20-minute flight from St. Thomas. As it flew up the Sir Francis Drake Channel to the Beef Island/Tortola Airport, passengers gazed out at stunning views of island and channel. Suddenly everyone turned from the windows and looked at each other quizzically. They sat in stunned silence as the plane flew past the airport and headed to the little runway on nearby Virgin Gorda. After this unscheduled landing, the pilot turned around nervously and said, "Sorry. I'm late for my wedding. Nelson, my copilot, will fly you back to Tortola."

The British Virgin Islands (BVI) consist of about 50 islands, islets, and cays. Most are remarkably hilly, and all but Anegada are volcanic, having exploded from the depths of the sea some 25 million years ago. The BVI are serene, seductive, spectacularly beautiful, and still remarkably laid-back. At some points they lie only a mile or so from the U.S. Virgin Islands (USVI), but they remain unique and have maintained their quiet, friendly, casual character.

The pleasures here are understated: sailing around the multitude of tiny nearby islands; diving to the wreck of the RMS *Rhone*, sunk off Salt Island in 1867; snorkeling in one of hundreds of wonderful spots; walking empty beaches; taking in spectacular views from the island peaks; and settling in on a breeze-swept terrace to admire the sunset.

Several factors have enabled the BVI to retain the qualities of yesteryear's Caribbean: no building can rise higher than the surrounding palms, and there are no direct flights from the mainland United States, so the tourism tide is held back. Many visitors travel here by water, aboard their own ketches and yawls or on one of the ferries that cross the waters between St. Thomas and Tortola. Such a passage is a fine prelude to a stay in these unhurried havens.

Tortola, about 10 square mi (26 square km), is the largest and most populated of the islands; Virgin Gorda, with 8 square mi (21 square km), ranks second. The islands scattered around them include Jost Van Dyke, Great Camanoe, Norman, Peter, Salt, Cooper, Ginger, Dead Chest, and Anegada. Tortola has the most hotels, restaurants, and shops. Virgin Gorda offers a few restaurants, shops, and resorts (many are self-contained). Jost Van Dyke is a major charter-boat anchorage; little bars line the beach at Great Harbour, but there are few places to stay. The

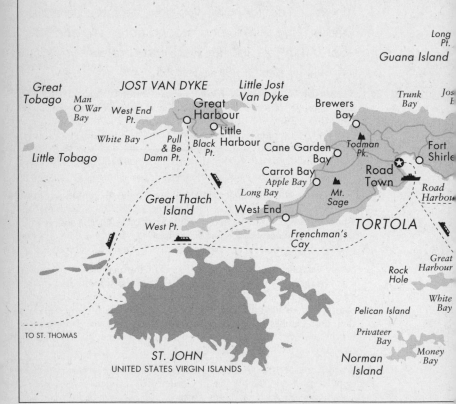

ATLANTIC

Long
Pt.

Guana Island

Great
Tobago

JOST VAN DYKE

Little Jost
Van Dyke

Trunk
Bay

Jos
E

Man
O War
Bay

West End
Pt.

Great
Harbour

Brewers
Bay

Fort
Shirle

White Bay

Pull
& Be
Damn Pt.

Black
Pt.

Little
Harbour

Cane Garden
Bay

Todman
Pk.

Road
Town

Little Tobago

Carrot Bay

Apple Bay

Mt.
Sage

Road
Harbou

Great Thatch
Island

Long Bay

West End

West Pt.

Frenchman's
Cay

TORTOLA

Great
Harbour

Rock
Hole

White
Bay

Pelican Island

TO ST. THOMAS

ST. JOHN
UNITED STATES VIRGIN ISLANDS

Privateer
Bay

Norman
Island

Money
Bay

West End
Pt.

Bones
Bight

Flamingo
Pond

Red
Pond

Loblolly
Bay

Table Bay

Pomato
Pt.

Saltheap
Pt.

The
Settlement

ANEGADA

(15 miles north of Necker Is.)

Lower
Bay

Budrock
Pond

Horse
Shoe
Reef

White
Bay

OCEAN

Necker
Island

Prickly Pear
Island

Mosquito Island

Eustatia Island

Great
Camanoe

Towing
Pt.

Cockroach
Island

George
Dog

Long
Bay

North
Sound

North
Bay

North Bay

West
Dog

Virgin
Gorda
Peak

Gun
Creek

Berchers
Bay

Kitto
Ghut

Great
Dog

Pond
Bay

South Sound

Monkey
Pt.

Scrub Island

VIRGIN
GORDA

uh's
y

Pusser's Marina

Little
Camanoe

Cay

Spanish
Town

Handsome
Bay

East End

Beef Island
International Airport

Virgin Gorda
Airport

Anegada Passage

Fat Hogs
Bay

Beef Island

Copper Mine
Pt.

Buck
Island

Fallen Jerusalem

Sir Francis Drake Channel

Broken Jerusalem

Quart-a-Nancy
Pt.

Round Rock

Manchioneel Bay

N

Dead
Chest

South
Bay

Ginger Island

Markoe Pt.

Salt
Island

Salt
Island
Bluff

Cooper
Island

Big Reef
Bay

KEY

Peter Island

Cruise Ship
Anchorage/Terminal

Ferry

Peter Island
Bluff

0   6 miles

0   9 km

other islands are either uninhabited or have a single hotel or resort—or even just a restaurant. Many of these, such as Peter Island, offer excellent anchorages, and their bays and harbors are popular with overnighting boaters.

Sailing has always been a popular activity in the BVI. The first arrivals here were a romantic seafaring tribe, the Ciboney Indians. They were followed (circa AD 900) by the Arawaks, who sailed from South America, established settlements, and farmed and fished. Still later came the mighty Caribs.

In 1493 Christopher Columbus was the first European visitor. Impressed by the number of islands dotting the horizon, he named them *Las Once Mil Virgines*—the 11,000 Virgins—in honor of the 11,000 virgin companions of St. Ursula, martyred in the 4th century. In the ensuing years, the Spaniards passed through, fruitlessly seeking gold. Then came pirates and buccaneers, who found the islands' hidden coves and treacherous reefs ideal bases from which to prey on passing galleons crammed with gold, silver, and spices. Among the most notorious of these fellows were Blackbeard Teach, Bluebeard, Captain Kidd, and Sir Francis Drake, who lent his name to the channel that sweeps through the BVI's two main clusters. In the 17th century the colorful cutthroats were replaced by the Dutch, who, in turn, were sent packing by the British. It was the British who established a plantation economy and for the next 150 years developed the sugar industry. When slavery was abolished in 1838, the plantation economy faltered, and the majority of the white population left for Europe.

The islands still are politically tied to Britain. The governor, appointed by the queen of England, has limited powers, and these are concentrated on external affairs and local security. The local legislative council, with representatives from nine districts, administers all other matters. General elections are held every four years and the political mood is serene.

Although offshore banking is currently the BVI's number one industry, tourism is the second major source of income, and the majority of the islands' jobs are tourism-related. The Beef Island airport has been recently expanded and the enlarged runway accommodates larger prop planes and small regional jets but is still too small for full-size jets, so there's no doubt that BVIers—who so love their unspoiled tropical home—will maintain their islands' easygoing charms for both themselves and their guests.

TORTOLA

Unwinding can easily become a full-time occupation on Tortola. Though the island offers a wealth of things to see and do, many visitors prefer just to loll about on its deserted sands or linger over lunch at one of its many delightful restaurants. Beaches are never more than a few minutes away, and the steep green hills that form Tortola's spine are fanned by gentle trade winds. The neighboring islands glimmer like emeralds in a sea of sapphire. It's a world far removed from the hustle of modern life.

Lodging

Luxury on Tortola is more a state of mind—serenity, seclusion, gentility—than state-of-the-art amenities and facilities. Hotels in Road Town don't have beaches, but they do have pools and are within walking distance of restaurants, nightspots, and shops. Accommodations outside

Road Town are relatively isolated but are on beaches (some of them are exquisite; others are small or have been enlarged by bringing in sand). The BVI resorts are intimate: none is large—only four have more than 50 rooms. You will likely spend most of your time outside, so the location, size, or price of a hotel are more important than the decor of its rooms. Guests are treated as more than just room numbers, however, and many return year after year. This can make booking a room at popular resorts difficult, even off-season, despite the fact that more than half the island's visitors stay aboard their own or chartered boats.

Throughout the BVI a few hotels lack air-conditioning, relying instead on ceiling fans to capture the almost constant trade winds. Nights are cool and breezy, even in midsummer, and never reach the temperatures or humidity levels that are common in much of the United States during the summer.

CATEGORY	COST EP/CP*	COST A.I.**
$$$$	over $350	over $375
$$$	$250–$350	$275–$375
$$	$150–$250	$175–$275
$	under $150	under $175

£pcfn:*EP/CP prices are per night for a standard double room in high season, excluding taxes, service charges, and meal plans**A.I. (all-inclusive) prices are per person, per night based on double-occupancy during high season, excluding taxes and service charges

Hotels and Inns

ROAD TOWN

$$–$$$ ⊡ **Moorings-Mariner Inn.** This two-story inn is also the headquarters for the Moorings Charter operation. It's popular with both yachting folk and landlubbers who are happy with simple furnishings. It's a laid-back *and* lively place. The pale peach color scheme is picked up in the floor tiles, and tropical-print fabrics add splashes of contrasting color. All units are on the large side and have small kitchenettes and balconies. ⊠ *Waterfront Dr. (Box 139),* ☎ *284/494–2332 or 800/535–7289,* FAX *284/494–2226. 38 rooms, 4 suites. Kitchenettes, tennis court, pool, dive shop, dock, marina, volleyball, shops. AE, MC, V. EP.*

$–$$$ ⊡ **Pusser's Fort Burt Hotel.** Originally a Dutch fort, this hillside landmark is at the edge of town and overlooks the harbor. Rooms are painted in pale pastels; cushions and bedspread fabrics are floral prints; and balconies are private. Two suites have private pools. This hotel is close to town. Two-line data port telephones and printer/fax machines in every room make it Tortola's only true business hotel. ⊠ *Waterfront Dr. (Box 3380),* ☎ *284/494–2587,* FAX *284/494–2002,* WEB *www.pussers.com. 12 rooms, 5 suites. Restaurant, bar, in-room data ports, in-room fax, pool. AE, MC, V. EP.*

$$ ⊡ **Maria's Hotel by the Sea.** Perched on the edge of Road Harbour, next to a large government building and the cruise ship dock, this simple hotel is an easy walk from restaurants in town. The small rooms are minimally decorated, with white rattan furniture, floral-print spreads, and murals by local artists. All rooms have balconies, some with harbor views. ⊠ *Waterfront Dr. (Box 206),* ☎ *284/494–2595,* FAX *284/494–2420. 38 rooms. Restaurant, bar, kitchenettes, pool. AE, MC, V. EP.*

$–$$ ⊡ **Village Cay Resort and Marina.** Right in town, this pleasant, compact hotel looks out on Road Harbour and several marinas. It's popular with yachters and those who love to shop and dine. Rooms have natural rattan furniture and pastel prints. Some units have cathedral ceilings and harbor views; others are quite small. After shopping in town,

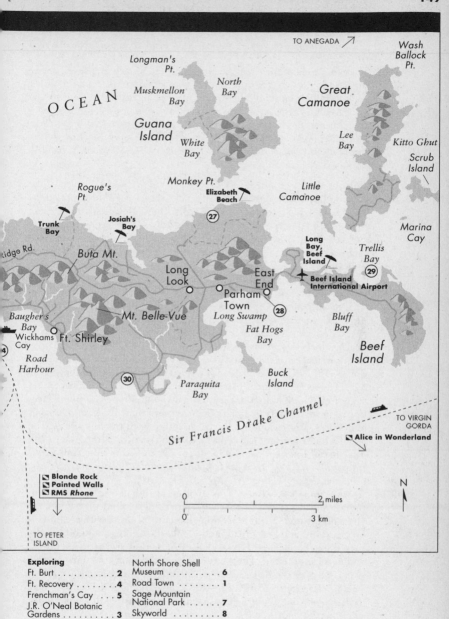

TO ANEGADA ↗

Wash
Ballock
Pt.

Longman's
Pt.

North
Bay

Great
Camanoe

Muskmellon
Bay

O C E A N

Guana
Island

White
Bay

Lee
Bay

Kitto Ghut

Scrub
Island

Monkey Pt.

Rogue's
Pt.

Elizabeth
Beach

Little
Camanoe

Marina
Cay

㉗

Trunk
Bay

Josiah's
Bay

Long
Bay,
Beef
Island

Trellis
Bay

Ridge Rd.

Buta Mt.

Long
Look

East
End

Beef Island
International Airport

㉙

Parham
Town

Baugher's
Bay

Mt. Belle-Vue

Long Swamp

㉘

Bluff
Bay

Wickhams
Cay

Ft. Shirley

Fat Hogs
Bay

Beef
Island

Road
Harbour

㉚

Paraquita
Bay

Buck
Island

Sir Francis Drake Channel

TO VIRGIN
GORDA

◣ **Alice in Wonderland**

◣ **Blonde Rock**
◣ **Painted Walls**
◣ **RMS** *Rhone*

0 ————————— 2 miles
0 ————————— 3 km

N
↑

TO PETER
ISLAND

you can have a swim in the tiny pool and then head for the bar. ✉ *Wickham's Cay 1 (Box 145),* ☎ *284/494–2771,* FAX *284/494–2773,* WEB *www.villagecay.com. 19 rooms. Restaurant, bar, pool, marina. AE, MC, V. EP.*

$ 🖾 **Hotel Castle Maria.** You can spend all the money you save here at the nearby in-town attractions. And these very simple accommodations have everything most folks need: a refrigerator and cable TV; some rooms also have full kitchenettes, balconies, and air-conditioning. Refresh yourself either in the bar or the freshwater pool. ✉ *Waterfront Dr. (Box 206),* ☎ *284/494–2553,* FAX *284/494–2111. 30 rooms. Bar, no air-conditioning in some rooms, some kitchenettes, refrigerators, cable TV, pool. AE, MC, V. EP.*

OUTSIDE ROAD TOWN

$$$–$$$$ 🖾 **Long Bay Beach Resort.** Spectacularly set on a 1-mi-long (1½-km-long) beach, this resort is one of Tortola's best, despite sometimes less than stellar service. Some beachfront hideaways are set on stilts; hillside rooms with dramatic views. In addition, spacious one- and two-bedroom hillside villas are available. The casual Beach restaurant offers all-day dining. The Garden Restaurant serves romantic dinners. A full-service spa and fitness center, tennis courts, and a 9-hole, par-3 pitch-and-putt golf course complete the complex. ✉ *Long Bay (Box 433, Road Town),* ☎ *284/495–4252 or 800/729–9599,* FAX *284/495–4677,* WEB *www.longbay.com. 78 rooms, 12 suites, 26 villas. 2 restaurants, 2 bars, kitchenettes, 3 tennis courts, 2 pools, gym, massage, spa, beach, snorkeling, shops, meeting rooms. AE, MC, V. EP, MAP.*

$$$–$$$$ 🖾 **Sugar Mill Hotel.** The owners of this small hotel know what they're
★   doing—they were food and travel writers before they opened the Sugar Mill. The reception area, bar, and restaurant are in the ruins of an old sugar mill. Guest houses are scattered up a hill; rooms are simply decorated in soft pastels. A small pool is set into the hillside, and lunches and dinners (in season) are served on a terrace at the tiny beach. The Sugar Mill Restaurant is well known on the island. ✉ *Apple Bay (Box 425, Road Town),* ☎ *284/495–4355,* FAX *284/495–4696,* WEB *www.sugarmillhotel.com. 16 rooms, 4 suites, 2 villas. 2 restaurants, 2 bars, pool, beach, snorkeling. AE, MC, V. EP, MAP.*

$$–$$$$ 🖾 **Frenchman's Cay Hotel.** This small collection of one- and two-bedroom condos overlooks Drake's Channel. Each includes a full kitchen and a dining area. Rooms are done in neutral colors, with cream-colored curtains and bedspreads and tile floors. Ceiling fans and breezes keep things cool. There is a small pool, a modest-size artificial beach, and good snorkeling. The alfresco bar and dining room are breeze-swept and offer simple fare. ✉ *Frenchman's Cay, West End (Box 1054),* ☎ *284/495–4844 or 800/235–4077,* FAX *284/495–4056,* WEB *www.frenchmans.com. 9 units. Restaurant, bar, no air-conditioning, fans, kitchenettes, tennis court, pool, beach, snorkeling. AE, MC, V. EP.*

$$–$$$$ 🖾 **The Villas of Fort Recovery Estates.** This complex has all the ingre-
★   dients for a good Caribbean vacation: grounds full of flowers; a remote beachside location includes the remnants of a Dutch fort; and friendly, helpful management. All the suites and the four-bedroom villa have excellent views and fully equipped kitchens. The kitchen provides room-service dinners. There are exercise and yoga classes. ✉ *Waterfront Dr., Pockwood Pond (Box 239),* ☎ *284/495–4354 or 800/367–8455,* FAX *284/495–4036,* WEB *www.fortrecovery.com. 14 suites, 1 villa. Kitchens, pool, massage, beach, snorkeling, baby-sitting. AE, MC, V. EP.*

$–$$$ 🖾 **Lambert Beach Resort.** On the remote north shore, this Mediterranean-style cottage complex has rooms in eight one-story buildings with red-tile roofs and white stucco exteriors. Two two-bedroom villas on a hillside have full kitchens. Rooms face the beach or look out on tropical gardens. It's a very short walk to the stunning beach or the remarkably large pool. The restaurant offers alfresco breakfasts, lunches, and dinners. ⊠ *Lambert Bay, East End (Box 534),* ☎ *284/495–2877,* ℻ *284/495–2876,* WEB *www.lambertbeachresort.com. 34 rooms, 2 villas. Restaurant, bar, pool, tennis court, beach, snorkeling, windsurfing, shop. AE, MC, V. EP.*

$–$$$ ⌂ **Sebastian's on the Beach.** The best rooms here are the eight small rooms that open onto the beach. They're airy, white, and have terraces or balconies so you can catch the great breezes and views (the ocean lulls you to sleep). Tiny bathrooms have only stall showers. The other 18 rooms are very basic, lack views, and can be noisy, but are all air-conditioned. The casual restaurant looks out over the water; at lunch you can order fresh salads, grilled vegetables, or soups and sandwiches; the dinner menu includes grilled fish, lobster, and steak. ⊠ *Apple Bay (Box 441, Road Town),* ☎ *284/495–4212 or 800/336–4870,* ℻ *284/495–4466,* WEB *www.sebastiansbvi.com. 26 rooms. Restaurant, bar, no air-conditioning in some rooms, fans, refrigerators, no room TVs, beach. AE. EP.*

$–$$ ⌂ **Ole Works Inn.** Tucked against a hill and across the road from a beautiful beach is this rustic, appealing inn—owned by local recording star Quito Rhymer. A steeply pitched roof along with wood and stonework add contemporary flair to what was once an old sugar mill. Rooms are simply decorated, but some have private balconies and kitchenettes, and you can't beat the Cane Garden Bay location. The Honeymoon Suite has an indoor swing for two. ⊠ *Cane Garden Bay (Box 560, Road Town),* ☎ *284/495–4837,* ℻ *284/495–9618. 15 rooms, 3 suites. Refrigerators, no room TVs. MC, V. EP.*

Private Homes and Villas

Areana Villas (⊠ Box 263, Road Town, ☎ 284/494–5864, ℻ 284/494–7626, WEB www.areanavillas.com) represents top-of-the-line properties. Homes offer accommodations for 2 to 10 people in one- to five-bedroom villas decorated in soothing pastels. Many have pools, Jacuzzis, and glazed terra-cotta courtyards. On Long Bay, Areana represents Sunset House and Villas, an exquisite hideaway whose first guest was Britain's Princess Alexandra (but you needn't be royalty to receive the royal treatment here). The company also works with Equinox House, also on Long Bay, a handsome three-bedroom estate set amid lavish tumbling gardens. Rates range from expensive ($$$) to very expensive ($$$$) in season. **Lambert Beach Villas** (⊠ Lambert Estate, Box 534, East End, ☎ 284/495–2877, ℻ 284/495–2876) rents two- and three-bedroom villas on the hills overlooking Elizabeth Beach.

Campground

$ ⚠ **Brewers Bay Campground.** Both prepared and bare sites are on Brewers Bay, one of Tortola's prime snorkeling spots. Check out the ruins of the distillery that gave the bay its name. You'll find a small commissary and public bathrooms but no showers. ⊠ *Brewers Bay (Box 185, Road Town),* ☎ *284/494–3463. 28 sites. Restaurant, bar, beach, windsurfing, baby-sitting. No credit cards.*

Dining

On Tortola local seafood is plentiful, and although other fresh ingredients are scarce, the island's chefs are a creative lot, who apply genius to whatever the weekly supply boat delivers. Contemporary American dishes prepared with a Caribbean influence are very popular. The fancier, more expensive restaurants have dress codes: long pants and collared shirts for men, and elegant, casual resort wear for women.

CATEGORY	COST*
$$$$	over $30
$$$	$20–$30
$$	$10–$20
$	under $10

per person for a main course at dinner

Road Town

AMERICAN/CASUAL

$–$$$ ✕ **The Pub.** At this lively waterfront spot, tables are arranged along a terrace facing a small marina and the Road Town harbor. Hamburgers, salads, and sandwiches are typical lunch offerings. In the evening you can also choose grilled fish, steak, chicken, sautéed conch, or barbecued ribs. In fact, head here on Saturday night for all-you-can-eat ribs. There's entertainment on weekends, and locals gather here nightly for spirited dart games. ⊠ *Waterfront Dr.,* ☎ *284/494–2608. Reservations not accepted. AE, DC, MC, V. No lunch Sun.*

$–$$ ✕ **Pusser's Road Town Pub.** Almost everyone who visits Tortola stops here at least once to have a bite to eat and to sample the famous Pusser's Rum Painkiller (fruit juices and rum). The menu includes cheesy pizza, shepherd's pie, fish-and-chips, and hamburgers. Dine inside in air-conditioned comfort or outside on the veranda, which looks out on the harbor. Stop by on Wednesdays and Fridays for nickel beer night. ⊠ *Waterfront Dr.,* ☎ *284/494–3897. AE, MC, V.*

CARIBBEAN

$$–$$$ ✕ **C and F Restaurant.** Crowds head to this casual spot for the best
★   barbecue in town (chicken, fish, and ribs), fresh local fish prepared your way, and excellent curries. Sometimes there's a wait for a table, but it's worth it. The restaurant is just outside Road Town, on a side street past the Moorings and Riteway. ⊠ *Purcell Estate,* ☎ *284/494–4941. Reservations not accepted. AE, MC, V. No lunch.*

ECLECTIC

$$–$$$ ✕ **Virgin Queen.** The sailing and rugby crowds head here to play darts,
★   drink beer, and eat Queen's Pizza—a crusty, cheesy pie topped with sausage, onions, green peppers, and mushrooms. Also on the menu is excellent West Indian and English fare: salt fish, barbecued ribs with beans and rice, bangers and mash, shepherd's pie, chili, and grilled sirloin steak. ⊠ *Fleming St.,* ☎ *284/494–2310. Reservations not accepted. No credit cards. Closed Sept. and Sun.*

FRENCH

$$–$$$$ ✕ **Le Cabanon.** Birds and bougainvillea brighten the patio of this breezy French restaurant and bar, a popular gathering place for locals and visitors alike. Caesar salad or the French onion soup are good appetizer choices. Then move on to the rack of lamb, the grilled salmon, or the rib-eye steak. Or try the shepherd's pie made with a French twist—duck instead of ground beef. Save room for such tasty dessert offerings as chocolate mousse, coconut mousse, cherry cheesecake, and a platter of French cheeses. ⊠ *Waterfront Dr.,* ☎ *284/494–8660. MC, V. Closed Sun.*

ITALIAN

$–$$$ ✕ **Spaghetti Junction.** Popular with the boating crowd, this well-
★   known island favorite is right near the cruise ship dock. Join the crowd outside on the deck overlooking the marina or inside, where it's bustling. The menu includes fresh seafood and many nightly specials but also house specialties such as penne with a spicy tomato sauce, spinach-mushroom lasagna, *cappellini* (very thin spaghetti) with shell-

fish, and spicy jambalaya pasta. ⊠ *Inner Harbour Marina,* ☎ *284/494–4880. MC, V. Closed Sun. No lunch.*

$–$$ ✕ **Capriccio di Mare.** The owners of the well-known Brandywine Bay
★ restaurant also run this authentic little Italian outdoor café. Stop by
for an espresso, fresh pastry, toast Italiano (a grilled ham and Swiss
cheese sandwich), a bowl of perfectly cooked linguine, or a crispy tomato
and mozzarella pizza. Drink specialties include the Mango Bellini, an
adaptation of the famous Bellini cocktail served by Harry's Bar in Venice.
⊠ *Waterfront Dr.,* ☎ *284/494–5369. Reservations not accepted. No
credit cards. Closed Sun.*

MEXICAN

$$–$$$ ✕ **Lime 'n' Mango.** The menu at this popular restaurant includes local
specialties and authentic Mexican cuisine. Try the conch fritters, salt
fish cakes, or Jamaican calamari for an appetizer. The fajitas—chicken,
beef, or vegetarian arrive at your table sizzling in a hot iron frying pan,
with a side of warm tortillas. The coconut shrimp is also popular. Saturday night crowds form here to enjoy the popular West Indian barbecue. ⊠ *Waterfront Dr.,* ☎ *284/494–2501. AE, MC, V.*

SEAFOOD

$$–$$$$ ✕ **The Captain's Table.** Select the lobster you want from the pool here,
and be careful not to fall in—it's in the floor right in the middle of the
dining room. The menu also includes traditional escargots, fresh local
fish, filet mignon with béarnaise sauce, duckling with berry sauce, and
creative daily specials. Ceiling fans keep the dining room cool, but there
are also tables on a breezy terrace overlooking the harbor. ⊠ *Colum-
bus Centre, Wickham's Cay 1,* ☎ *284/494–3885. AE, MC, V. No lunch
Sat.*

Outside Road Town
AMERICAN/CASUAL

$–$$$ ✕ **Pusser's Landing.** Yachters flock to this waterfront restaurant.
Downstairs, from late morning to well into the evening, belly up to
the outdoor mahogany bar or choose a waterside table for drinks, sandwiches, rotis, fish and chips, and pizzas. At dinnertime head upstairs
for a harbor view and a quiet alfresco meal of grilled steak or local
fish. ⊠ *Soper's Hole,* ☎ *284/495–4554. AE, MC, V.*

CARIBBEAN

$$–$$$ ✕ **Mrs. Scatliffe's.** The island's best West Indian cooking is served on
the upstairs terrace of Mrs. Scatliffe's home. The food is freshly prepared; the baked chicken in coconut is meltingly tender. If you're lucky,
after dinner you'll be treated to a lively *fungi* (bands that make music
using household items—washboards, spoons, and the like—as instruments) performance by members of Mrs. Scatliffe's family. ⊠ *Carrot
Bay,* ☎ *284/495–4556. Reservations essential. No credit cards.*

$$–$$$ ✕ **Gazebo.** This rustic beachside bar and restaurant is owned and op-
erated by Quito Rhymer, a multitalented BVI recording star who plays
the guitar and sings on Tuesday, Thursday, Friday, and Sunday; a reggae band performs Saturday. The menu is Caribbean with an emphasis on fresh fish. Try the conch stew or the curried chicken. A Caribbean
buffet is featured on Sunday night, and Friday is fish-fry night. ⊠ *Cane
Garden Bay,* ☎ *284/495–4837. MC, V. Closed Mon.*

$$–$$$ ✕ **Myett's.** Right on the beach, this bi-level restaurant-bar is hopping
★ day and night. Chowder made with fresh Anegada lobsters is the specialty, though the menu includes everything from hamburgers to fruit
platters and vegetarian dishes to grilled shrimp, steak, and tuna. There's
live entertainment on Saturday and Sunday nights. ⊠ *Cane Garden
Bay,* ☎ *284/495–9649. Reservations not accepted. AE, MC, V.*

$$–$$$$ ✕ **Garden Restaurant.** Relax over dinner in this open-air restaurant
★ at Long Bay Beach Resort. Tables are well-spaced, offering enough pri-
vacy for intimate conversations. The menu changes daily. Appetizers
might include garlicky escargots in pastry, creamy leek soup, or shrimp
fritters; the list of entrées could include grilled Anegada swordfish
steak with avocado hollandaise, pan-roasted duck with Portobello
mushrooms, or a filet mignon served with artichoke duxelle. There are
always at least five desserts to choose from, such as Belgian chocolate
mousse, strawberry cheesecake, and carrot cake. ⊠ *Long Bay Beach
Resort, Long Bay,* ☎ *284/495–4252. AE, MC, V. No lunch.*

$$–$$$$ ✕ **Skyworld.** The top of a mountain is the location for this casually
★ elegant dining room. The filet mignon with port wine and mushroom
sauce is truly exceptional. Other specialties include chicken stuffed with
sausage, grilled local fish, roast duck, cinnamon roast pork loin with
pears and rosemary, and key lime pie. The very simple lunch menu is
mostly hamburgers and sandwiches, though the restaurant can be
crowded at this time when a cruise ship docks. ⊠ *Ridge Rd., Joe's Hill,*
☎ *284/494–3567. AE, MC, V.*

$$–$$$$ ✕ **Sugar Mill Restaurant.** Candles gleam, and the background music
is peaceful in this romantic restaurant that is inside a 360-year-old
mill. Well-prepared selections on the à la carte menu, which changes
nightly, include pasta and vegetarian entrées. Crab bisque with crab
rolls or Caribbean sweet-potato soup are good starters. House fa-
vorite entrées include the Jamaican jerk pork roast, the beef curry
with *poppadoms* (Indian popovers), marinated roast duck, and fresh
fish with spicy creole sauce. ⊠ *Apple Bay,* ☎ *284/495–4355. AE,
MC, V. No lunch.*

$$–$$$ ✕ **Eclipse.** Dine by the waterfront caressed by soft ocean breezes at this
★ popular spot that isn't much more than a terrace filled with tables. The
menu is a mixture of fusion and Caribbean cuisine. Spend the evening
sampling one dish after another—cracked conch, baked chevre, tuna
carpaccio—as you order off the two-page grazing menu, or dig into
the spicy curries, fusion chicken, fresh grilled Anegada swordfish, and
vegetarian dishes on the regular menu. ⊠ *Fat Hog's Bay, East End,*
☎ *284/495–1646. AE, MC, V. No lunch Aug.*

$$–$$$ ✕ **The Last Resort.** Actually on an island just off Beef Island (free ferry
service is provided to and from Trellis Bay/Beef Island), this spot has
an English buffet, complete with pumpkin soup, prime rib, and York-
shire pudding, as well as vegetarian selections. This is also the site of
the longest-running show in the BVI. For over 30 years, people have
been laughing at the inimitable cabaret humor and ribald ditties of owner
Tony Snell, the BVI's answer to Benny Hill. He performs nightly at 9:30.
⊠ *Bellamy Cay,* ☎ *284/495–2520. AE, MC, V.*

$$–$$$$ ✕ **Brandywine Bay.** Here, candlelit outdoor tables have sweeping
★ views of neighboring islands, and owner-chef Davide Pugliese pre-
pares foods the Tuscan way: grilled with lots of fresh herbs. The remarkable menu can include homemade mozzarella, foie gras, grilled
local swordfish, and grilled veal chop with ricotta and sun-dried tomatoes; it always includes duck with a berry sauce. The wine list is excellent, and the lemon tart and the tiramisu are irresistible. ⊠ *Sir
Francis Drake Hwy., east of Road Town, Brandywine Bay,* ☎ *284/495–
2301. Reservations essential. AE, MC, V. Closed Sun. No lunch.*

Beaches

Beaches in the BVI are less developed than those on St. Thomas or St. Croix. Try to get out on a dive-snorkeling boat or a day-trip sailing vessel at least once. This is often the best way to reach the most virgin Virgin beaches, which are on deserted islands. Tortola's north side has several perfect palm-fringed white-sand beaches that curl around turquoise bays and coves. Nearly all are accessible by car (preferably one with four-wheel-drive), albeit down bumpy roads that corkscrew precipitously. Facilities run the gamut, from absolutely none to a number of beachside bars and restaurants as well as places to rent water-sports equipment.

Apple Bay. If you want to surf, the area including Little Apple Bay and Capoon's Bay, is the spot—although the beach itself is pretty narrow. Sebastian's, the very casual hotel here, caters to those in search of the perfect wave. Good surf is never a sure thing, but you're more apt to find it in January and February. ⊠ *North Shore Rd.*

Brewers Bay. The water is good for snorkeling, and there are a campground and beach bar here. The beach and its old sugar mill and rum-distillery ruins are just north of Cane Garden Bay, just past Luck Hill. There's another entrance just east of the Skyworld restaurant. ⊠ *Brewers Bay Rd. W or Brewers Bay Rd. E.*

Cane Garden Bay. This enticing beach has exceptionally calm, crystalline waters and a silky stretch of sand. It's the closest beach to Road Town—one steep uphill and downhill drive—and is one of the BVI's best-known anchorages (unfortunately, it can be very crowded when cruise ships are in town). You can rent sailboards and such, stargaze from the bow of a boat, and nosh or sip at several beach-side restaurants, including Gazebo. ⊠ *Cane Garden Bay Rd.*

Elizabeth Beach. Lined with palm trees, wide, and sandy, the beach is accessible by walking down a private road. However, the undertow can be severe here in winter. ⊠ *Ridge Rd.*

Josiah's Bay. The oft-deserted Josiah's Bay is a favored place to picnic or to hang ten, although in winter the undertow is often strong. ⊠ *Ridge Rd.*

Long Bay, Beef Island. The scenery here draws superlatives: you can catch a glimpse of Little Camanoe and Great Camanoe islands, and if you walk around the bend to the right, you can see little Marina Cay and Scrub Island. Long Bay is also a good place to find seashells. ⊠ *Beef Island Rd., Beef Island.*

Long Bay West. Have your camera ready for snapping the breathtaking approach to this stunning 1-mi (1½-km) stretch of white sand. Although Long Bay Resort sprawls along part of it, the entire beach is open to the public. The water isn't as calm here as at Cane Garden or Brewers Bay, but it's still swimmable. ⊠ *Long Bay Rd.*

Smuggler's Cove. After bouncing your way to this beautiful beach, you'll feel as if you've found a hidden piece of the island, although you probably won't be alone on weekends. There's a fine view of Jost Van Dyke Island, and the snorkeling is good. ⊠ *Belmont Rd.*

Trunk Bay. About the only thing you'll find moving is the surf. The beach is directly north of Road Town, midway between Cane Garden Bay and Beef Island, and to reach it you have to hike down a *ghut* (gully) from Ridge Road. ⊠ *Ridge Rd.*

Outdoor Activities and Sports

Participant Sports

FISHING

The deep-sea fishing here is so good that tournaments draw competitors from around the world for the largest bluefish, wahoo, swordfish, and shark. You can bring a catch back to your hotel's restaurant, and the staff will prepare it for you for dinner. A half-day of deep-sea fishing runs $300–$350, a full day $500–$600. For a few hours of reel fun, try **Persistence** (⊠ Towers, West End, ☎ 284/495–4122). If bonefishing is your cup of tea, call **Caribbean Fly Fishing** (⊠ Nanny Cay, ☎ 284/499–1590).

HORSEBACK RIDING

If you've ever wanted to ride a horse along a deserted beach, now's your chance. Or you can head up to Tortola's ridges for spectacular views. **Shadow Stables** (⊠ Ridge Rd., Todman Peak, ☎ 284/494–2262) offers small group rides for $25 per person per hour.

SAILING

The BVI are among the world's most popular sailing destinations. They're close together and surrounded by calm waters, so it's fairly easy to sail from one anchorage to the next. If you know how to sail, you can charter a bare boat (perhaps for your entire vacation); if you're unschooled, you can hire a boat with a captain or learn to sail. Prices vary quite broadly depending on the type and size of the boat you wish to charter. In season, a weekly charter runs $1,500–$35,000.

BVI Yacht Charters (⊠ Inner Harbour Marina, Road Town, ☎ 284/ 494–4289) offers 38-ft to 51-ft sailboats for charter—with or without a captain, whichever you prefer. **Catamaran Charters** (⊠ Nanny Cay Marina, Nanny Cay, ☎ 284/495–6661) charters catamarans with or without captains. **The Moorings** (⊠ Wickham's Cay II, Road Town, ☎ 284/494–2501 or 800/535–7289), considered one of the best bareboat operations in the world, has a large fleet of well-maintained, mostly Beneteau yachts. Hire a captain or sail the boat yourself. If you prefer a powerboat, call **Regency Yacht Vacations** (⊠ Inner Harbour Marina, Road Town, ☎ 284/495–1970) for both bareboat and captained charters. **Sunsail** (⊠ Hodge's Creek Marina, West End, ☎ 284/495–4740) offers a full fleet of boats to charter with or without a captain.

SCUBA DIVING AND SNORKELING

Clear waters and numerous reefs afford some wonderful opportunities for underwater exploration. There are several popular dive spots around the islands. **Alice in Wonderland** is a deep dive south of Ginger Island with a wall that slopes gently from 15 ft (5 m) to 100 ft (30 m). It's an area overrun with huge mushroom-shape coral, hence its name. Crabs, lobsters, and shimmering fan corals make their home in the tunnels, ledges, and overhangs of **Blonde Rock,** a pinnacle that goes from just 15 ft (5 m) below the surface to 60 ft (18 m) deep. It's between Dead Chest and Salt Island. When the currents aren't too strong, **Brewer's Bay Pinnacle** (20–90 ft [6–27 m] down) teems with sea life. At **The Indians,** near Pelican Island, colorful corals decorate canyons and grottoes created by four large, jagged pinnacles that rise 50 ft (15 m) from the ocean floor. The **Painted Walls** is a shallow dive site where corals and sponges create a kaleidoscope of colors on the walls of four long gullies. It's northeast of Dead Chest.

The *Chikuzen,* sunk northwest of Brewer's Bay in 1981, is a 246-ft vessel in 75 ft (23 m) of water; it's home to thousands of fish, colorful corals, and big rays. In 1867 the RMS *Rhone,* a 310-ft-long royal mail steamer, split in two when it sank in a devastating hurricane. It's so well preserved that it was used in the movie *The Deep.* You can see the crow's nest and bowsprit, the cargo hold in the bow, and the engine and enormous propeller shaft in the stern. Its four parts are at various depths from 30 to 80 ft (9 to 24 m; nearby Rhone Reef is only

20–50 ft [6–15 m] down). Get yourself some snorkeling gear and hop a dive boat to this wreck, off Salt Island (across the channel from Road Town) and part of the BVI National Parks Trust. Every dive outfit in the BVI runs superlative scuba and snorkel tours here.

Baskin' in the Sun (⊠ Prospect Reef, ☏ 284/494–2858) offers beginner and advanced diving courses and daily trips. Trainers teach open-water, rescue, advanced diving, and resort courses. The resort course costs $96; a one-tank dive is $85 and a two-tank dive is $95, including equipment. **Blue Waters Divers** (⊠ Nanny Cay, ☏ 284/494–2847) teaches resort, open-water, rescue, and advanced diving courses and also makes daily trips. Resort courses cost $90, one-tank dives run $80, two-tank dives cost $90, including equipment. **Underwater Safaris** (⊠ The Moorings, Wickham's Cay 2, Road Town, ☏ 284/494–3235) has resort and advanced diving courses, including rescue and open water, and scheduled day and night dives. The resort course fee is $80; one-tank dives are $68 with your own equipment, $80 including equipment. Two-tank dives cost $83 with your own equipment, $95 including equipment.

TENNIS

Tortola's tennis options range from simple, untended, concrete courts to professionally maintained facilities that host organized tournaments. The courts listed below are all open to the public; some have restrictions for nonguests.

Frenchman's Cay Hotel (⊠ West End, ☏ 284/495–4844) has an artificial-grass court with a pretty view of Sir Francis Drake Channel. Patrons of the hotel or restaurant can use the court free of charge; for others there's an hourly fee of $5. Although the court is night-lit, there's no pro available to be your guiding light, so to speak. **Long Bay Beach Resort** (⊠ Long Bay, ☏ 284/495–4252) has three courts and a tennis program run by Peter Burwash International. Private lessons are $55 per hour. Nonguests may rent a court for $10 an hour. Tennis rackets can be rented for $7 an hour. **Moorings-Mariner Inn** (⊠ Waterfront Dr., Road Town, ☏ 284/494–2332) has one all-weather hard court to which inn, marina, and Treasure Isle Hotel guests have free access; if it's empty, nonguests can use it at no charge. The lack of lights and a pro staffer may leave you in the dark, though. At **Prospect Reef Resort** (⊠ Waterfront Dr., Road Town, ☏ 284/494–3311) guests of the resort can play free by day (there's a fee for lights) on any of six hard-surface courts; nonguests pay $7 an hour. Lessons are $40 an hour.

WINDSURFING

The winds are so steady here that some locals use sailboards to get from island to island. Three of the best spots for sailboarding are Nanny Cay, Slaney Point, and Trellis Bay on Beef Island.

Boardsailing BVI (⊠ Trellis Bay, Beef Island, ☏ 284/495–2447) rents equipment for $35 a half-day and offers private and group lessons. With **HIHO** (⊠ Prospect Reef Resort, Waterfront Dr., Road Town, ☏ 284/494–0337) you can take private or group lessons or rent equipment for $35 a half-day.

Spectator Sports

BASKETBALL

The NBA games are a national passion and folks also play pretty good basketball here. Diehard fans can catch games at the New Recreation Grounds on Monday, Wednesday, Friday, or Saturday between May and August.

CRICKET

Fans of this sport are fiercely loyal and exuberant. Matches are held at the New Recreation Grounds, next to the J. R. O'Neal Botanic Gardens weekends February–April.

SOFTBALL

If you enjoy watching softball, you can catch local games on weekend evenings at the Old Recreation Grounds between Long Bush Road and Lower Estate Road. The season runs February–August.

Shopping

The BVI aren't really a shopper's delight, but there are many shops showcasing original items—from jams and spices to resort wear to excellent artwork. Don't be put off by an informal shop entrance; some of the best finds in the BVI lie behind shabby doors.

Areas

Many shops and boutiques are clustered along and just off Road Town's **Main Street.** You can shop in Road Town's **Wickham's Cay** area adjacent to the marina. There's an ever-growing number of art and clothing stores at **Soper's Hole,** in West End.

Specialty Items

ART

Caribbean Fine Arts Ltd. (✉ Main St., Road Town, ☎ 284/494–4240) carries Caribbean art, including original watercolors, oils, and acrylics, as well as signed prints, limited-edition serigraphs, and turn-of-the-century sepia photographs. **Sunny Caribbee Art Gallery** (✉ Main St., Road Town, ☎ 284/494–2178) has many paintings, prints, and watercolors by artists from throughout the Caribbean.

CLOTHES AND TEXTILES

Arawak (✉ On the dock, Nanny Cay, ☎ 284/494–5240) carries gifts, batik sundresses, sportswear and resort wear for men and women, sandals, accessories, and children's clothing. **Caribbean Handprints** (✉ Main St., Road Town, ☎ 284/494–3717) creates Caribbean-theme silk-screened fabric and sells it by the yard or in all forms of clothing and beach bags. **Latitude 18°** (✉ Main St., Road Town, ☎ 284/494–7807; ✉ Soper's Hole Marina, West End, ☎ 284/495–4347) sells Maui Jim, Smith, Oakley, and Revo sunglasses; Freestyle, Quiksilver, and Roxy watches; and a fine collection of sandals, beach towels, sundresses, and sarongs. **Pusser's Company Store** (✉ Main St. at Waterfront Rd., Road Town, ☎ 284/494–2467; ✉ Soper's Hole Marina, West End, ☎ 284/495–4603) sells nautical memorabilia, ship models, marine paintings, an entire line of clothes (for both men and women) and gift items bearing the Pusser's logo, handsome decorator bottles of Pusser's rum, Caribbean books, and luggage. **Sea Urchin** (✉ Waterfront, Columbus Centre, Road Town, ☎ 284/494–2044; ✉ Mill Mall, Road Town, ☎ 284/494–4108; ✉ Soper's Hole Marina, West End, ☎ 284/495–4850) is the source for local books, island jewelry, sunglasses, and resort wear— print shirts and shorts, colorful swimsuits, cover-ups, sandals, T-shirts—for the whole family. **Serendipity** (✉ Main St., Road Town, ☎ 284/494–5879) showcases a colorful collection of comfortable, light cotton clothing—including selections from Indonesia—as well as island jewelry and gift items. **Turtle Dove Boutique** (✉ Flemming St., Road Town, ☎ 284/494–3611) is one of the best shops in the BVI for designer swimwear, silk and linen dresses, and gifts and accessories for the home. **Zenaida's of West End** (✉ Soper's Hole Marina, West End, ☎ 284/495–4867) displays the fabric finds of Argentine Vivian Jenik Helm, who travels through South America, Africa, and India in search of batiks, hand-painted and hand-blocked fabrics, and interesting weaves that can be made into pareus (women's wraps) or wall hangings. The shop also sells unusual bags, belts, sarongs, scarves, and ethnic jewelry.

FOODSTUFFS

Ample Hamper (✉ Village Cay Marina, Wickham's Cay I, Road Town, ☎ 284/494–2494; ✉ Soper's Hole Marina, West End, ☎ 284/495–4684) has an outstanding collection of cheeses, wines, fresh fruits, and canned goods from the United Kingdom and the United States. You can have the management here provision your yacht or rental villa.

GIFTS

Buccaneer's Bounty (✉ Main St., Road Town, ☎ 284/494–7510) purveys greeting cards, pirate memorabilia, nautical and tropical artwork, books on seashells and the islands, and Christmas ornaments. **Caribbean Corner Spice House** (✉ Soper's Hole, West End, ☎ 284/495–4498) sells exotic herbs and spices and homemade jams, jellies, hot sauces, and natural soaps. You'll find Cuban cigars here, too. **J. R. O'Neal, Ltd.** (✉ Main St., Road Town, ☎ 284/494–2292) stocks the shelves of its somewhat hidden shop with fine crystal, Royal Worcester china, hand-painted Italian dishes, handblown Mexican glassware, Spanish ceramics, and Indian woven rugs and tablecloths. **Sunny Caribbee Herb and Spice Company** (✉ Main St., Road Town, ☎ 284/494–2178), in a brightly painted West Indian house, packages its own herbs, teas, coffees, vinegars, hot sauces, soaps, skin and suntan lotions, and exotic concoctions—Arawak Love Potion and Island Hangover Cure, for example. You'll also find Caribbean books and art and hand-painted decorative accessories.

JEWELRY

Columbian Emeralds International (✉ Wickham's Cay I, Road Town, ☎ 284/494–7477), a Caribbean chain catering to the cruise-ship crowd, is the source for duty-free emeralds plus other gems, gold jewelry, crystal, and china. **Samarkand** (✉ Main St., Road Town, ☎ 284/494–6415) crafts charming gold and silver pendants, earrings, bracelets, and pins—many with an island theme: seashells, lizards, pelicans, palm trees. You'll also find genuine Spanish pieces of eight (coins—old Spanish pesos worth eight reals—from sunken galleons).

PERFUMES AND COSMETICS

Flamboyance (✉ Main St., Road Town, ☎ 284/494–4099; ✉ Soper's Hole Marina, ☎ 284/495–5946) carries designer fragrances and upscale cosmetics.

Nightlife and the Arts

Nightlife

Like any good sailing destination, Tortola has watering holes that are popular with salty and not-so-salty dogs. Many offer entertainment; check the weekly *Limin' Times* for schedules. The local beverage is the painkiller, an innocent-tasting mixture of fruit juices and rums. It goes down smoothly but packs quite a punch, so give yourself a moment before you order another.

Bing's Drop In Bar (✉ Fat Hog's Bay, East End, ☎ 284/495–2627) is a rollicking local hangout that has a DJ nightly in season. By day **Bomba's Surfside Shack** (✉ Apple Bay, ☎ 284/495–4148)—covered with everything from crepe-paper leis to license plates to colorful graffiti—looks like a pile of junk; by night it's one of Tortola's liveliest spots and one of the Caribbean's most famous beach bars. Sunday at 4 there's always some sort of live music, and Wednesday at 8 the locally famous Blue

Haze Combo shows up to play everything from reggae to Top 40 tunes. Every full moon, bands play all night long and people flock here from all over. There's a fish fry and a live band every Thursday night at the informal **Ceta's Place** (✉ Capoon's Bay, no phone). BVI recording star Quito Rhymer sings island ballads and love songs, accompanied by the guitar at **Gazebo** (✉ Cane Garden Bay, ☎ 284/495–4837), a rustic beachside bar-restaurant. Solo shows are on Sunday, Tuesday, Thursday, and Friday nights at 8:30; Saturday night a reggae band performs. At the **Jolly Roger** (✉ West End, ☎ 284/495–4559). an ever-changing roster of local, U.S., and down-island bands plays everything from rhythm and blues to reggae to country to good old rock and roll Friday and Saturday—and sometimes Sunday—starting at 8. Local bands play at **Myett's** (✉ Cane Garden Bay, ☎ 284/495–9543) on Saturday and Sunday evenings, and there's usually a lively dance crowd. Wednesdays and Fridays are nickel-beer nights at **Pusser's Deli** (✉ Waterfront St., Road Town, ☎ 284/494–4199), and crowds gather here for courage (John Courage, that is) by the pint. Other nights try Pusser's famous mixed drinks—painkillers—and snack on the excellent pizza. At **The Pub** (✉ Waterfront St., Road Town, ☎ 284/494–2608) you'll find an all-day happy hour on Friday, and Ruben Chinnery on the guitar Friday evenings from 6 to 9. There's often live music at **Sebastian's** (✉ Apple Bay, ☎ 284/495–4214) on Saturday evenings, and you can dance under the stars.

The Arts

Musicians from around the world perform in the **Classics in the Atrium** (✉ The Atrium at the H. Lavity Stoutt Community College, Paraquita Bay, ☎ 284/494–4994) series from October to February each year. Past artists have included Britain's premier a cappella group, Black Voices; New Orleans jazz pianist Ellis Marsalis; and Keith Lockhart and the Serenac Quartet (from the Boston Pops Symphony).

Exploring Tortola

Tortola doesn't have many historical sights, but it does have lots of beautiful natural scenery. Although you could explore the island's 10 square mi (26 square km) in a few hours, opting for such a whirlwind tour would be a mistake. Life in the fast lane has no place amid some of the Caribbean's most breathtaking panoramas and beaches. Also the roads are extraordinarily steep and twisting, making driving demanding. The best strategy is to explore a bit of the island at a time. For example, you might try Road Town (the island's main town) one morning and a drive to Cane Garden Bay and West End (a little town on, of course, the island's west end) the next afternoon. Or consider a visit to East End, a *very* tiny town located exactly where its name suggests. The north shore is where you'll find all the best beaches.

Numbers in the margin correspond to points of interest on the Tortola map.

Sights to See

❷ **Ft. Burt.** The most intact historic ruin on Tortola was built by the Dutch in the early 17th century to safeguard Road Harbour. It sits on a hill at the western edge of Road Town and is now the site of a small hotel and restaurant. The foundations and magazine remain, and the structure offers a commanding view of the harbor. ✉ *Waterfront Dr., Road Town, no phone.* ▨ *Free.* ☉ *Daily dawn–dusk.*

❹ **Ft. Recovery.** The unrestored ruins of a 17th-century Dutch fort, 30 ft in diameter, sit amid a profusion of tropical greenery on the Villas of

Fort Recovery Estates grounds. There's not much to see here, and there are no guided tours, but you're welcome to stop by and poke around. ✉ *Waterfront Dr., Road Town,* ☏ *284/485–4467.* 🎫 *Free.*

❺ **Frenchman's Cay.** On this little island connected by a causeway to Tortola's western end, there are a marina and a captivating complex of pastel West Indian–style buildings with shady balconies, shuttered windows, and gingerbread trim that house art galleries, boutiques, and restaurants. Pusser's Landing here is a lively place to stop for a cold drink (many are made with Pusser's famous rum) and a sandwich and watch the boats in harbor.

❸ **J. R. O'Neal Botanic Gardens.** Take a walk through this 4-acre showcase of lush plant life. There are sections devoted to prickly cacti and succulents, hothouses for ferns and orchids, gardens of medicinal herbs, and plants and trees indigenous to the seashore. From the tourist board office in Road Town, cross Waterfront Drive and walk one block over to Main Street and turn right. Keep walking until you see the high school. The gardens are on your left. ✉ *Botanic Station, Road Town, no phone.* 🎫 *Free.* ☉ *Mon.–Sat. 9–4:30.*

❾ **Mt. Healthy National Park.** The remains of an 18th-century sugar plantation are here. The windmill structure has been restored, and you can see the ruins of a mill, a factory with boiling houses, storage areas, stables, a hospital, and many dwellings. This is a nice place to picnic. ✉ *Ridge Rd., Todman Peak, no phone.* 🎫 *Free.* ☉ *Daily dawn–dusk.*

❻ **North Shore Shell Museum.** On Tortola's north shore, this casual museum has a very informal exhibit of shells, unusually shaped driftwood, fish traps, and traditional wooden boats. ✉ *North Shore Rd., Carrot Bay,* ☏ *284/495–4714.* 🎫 *Free.* ☉ *Daily dawn–dusk.*

❶ **Road Town.** The laid-back capital of the BVI looks out over Road Harbour. It takes only an hour or so to stroll down Main Street and along the waterfront, checking out the traditional West Indian buildings, painted in pastel colors and with high-pitched, corrugated-tin roofs; bright shutters; and delicate fretwork trim. For hotel and sightseeing brochures and the latest information on everything from taxi rates to ferry-boat schedules, stop in the BVI Tourist Board office. Or just choose a seat on one of the benches in Sir Olva Georges Square, on Waterfront Drive, and watch the people come and go from the ferry dock and customs office across the street.

❼ **Sage Mountain National Park.** At 1,716 ft (525 m) Sage Mountain is the highest peak in the BVI. From the parking area a trail leads you in a loop not only to the peak itself (and extraordinary views) but also to a small rain forest, sometimes shrouded in mist. Most of the forest was cut down over the centuries to clear land for sugarcane, cotton, and other crops; to create pastureland; or to simply utilize the stands of timber; in 1964 this park was established to preserve what rain forest remained. Up here you can see mahogany trees, white cedars, mountain guavas, elephant-ear vines, mamey trees, and giant bullet woods, to say nothing of such birds as mountain doves and thrushes. Take a taxi from Road Town or drive up Joe's Hill Road and make a left onto Ridge Road toward Chalwell and Doty villages. The road deadends at the park. ✉ *Ridge Rd. Sage Mountain, no phone.* 🎫 *Free.*

★ ❽ **Skyworld.** Drive up here and climb the observation tower for a stunning, 360° view of numerous islands and cays. On a clear day you can even see St. Croix (40 mi [64½ km] away) and Anegada (20 mi [32 km] away). ✉ *Ridge Rd., Joe's Hill, no phone.* 🎫 *Free.*

VIRGIN GORDA

Virgin Gorda, with its mountainous central portion connected by skinny necks of land to southern and northern appendages—on a map it looks like the slightest breeze would cause the whole island to splinter apart—is quite different from Tortola. The pace is even slower here, and Virgin Gorda receives less rain, so some areas are more arid; much of the landscape is covered by scrub brush and cactus. Goats and cattle own the right of way, and the unpretentious friendliness of the people is winning.

Lodging

Virgin Gorda's charming hostelries appeal to a select, appreciative clientele; repeat business is extremely high. Those who prefer Sheratons, Marriotts, and the like may feel they get more for their money on other islands, but the peace and pampering offered on Virgin Gorda are priceless to the discriminating traveler.

For approximate costs, *see* the lodging price chart *in* Tortola.

Hotels and Inns

$$$$ 🏨 **Biras Creek Hotel.** This resort is so classy that it's a member of the
★ exclusive Relais & Chateaux family of hotels. Units, decorated in soft, Caribbean colors, are in duplex cottages, and each has a separate bedroom and a living room. Although entrances are hidden among the trees, many cottages are feet from the water's edge. Bike paths and trails lead to the beaches and the outstanding Biras Creek restaurant. On a hilltop is the open-air stonework bar-restaurant area. A sailaway package includes two nights on a private yacht. Rates are per couple, per night and include everything but beverages. ⊠ *North Sound (Box 54),* ☎ *284/494–3555 or 800/223–1108,* 🟥 *284/494–3557,* 🌐 *www. biras.com. 33 suites, 2 villas. 3 restaurants, bar, 2 tennis courts, pool, beach, snorkeling, windsurfing, boating, bicycles, hiking, shop. AE, MC, V. All-inclusive.*

$$$$ 🏨 **Bitter End Yacht Club and Marina.** This family-oriented, convivial resort-cum-marina is accessible only by boat. Accommodations range from comfortable hillside or beachfront rooms with spacious balconies to live-aboard yachts. Your day can include snorkeling and diving trips to nearby reefs, cruises, windsurfing lessons, excursions to local attractions, and lessons at the well-regarded Nick Trotter Sailing School. When the sun goes down, the festivities continue at The Clubhouse, an open-air restaurant-bar overlooking North Sound. ⊠ *North Sound (Box 46),* ☎ *284/494–2746 or 800/872–2392,* 🟥 *284/494–4756,* 🌐 *www.beyc.com. 95 rooms. 2 restaurants, bar, no air-conditioning in some rooms, pool, beach, dive shop, snorkeling, windsurfing, boating, waterskiing. AE, MC, V. EP, FAP.*

$$$$ 🏨 **Drake's Anchorage Resort Inn.** Set on the edge of its own 125-acre
★ island, this tiny and secluded getaway provides the utmost in privacy. Dinner attire here means changing from bathing suit to comfortable cottons. Three West Indian–style waterfront bungalows contain four rooms and five suites that are simply furnished. Three villas with full kitchens are also available. The appealing restaurant is an elegant stop for all meals. Hiking trails, water-sports facilities, four delightful beaches, and hammocks here and there make this a place you never want to leave. ⊠ *North Sound (Box 2510),* ☎ *284/494–2254 or 800/ 624–6651,* 🟥 *284/495–2254,* 🌐 *www.drakesanchorage.com. 4 rooms, 5 suites, 3 villas. Restaurant, bar, beach, snorkeling, boating, hiking. AE, MC, V. MAP.*

$$$$ ⊡ **Little Dix Bay.** Relaxed elegance is the hallmark here. The resort sits
★ along a curving beach. Duplexes with hexagonal units and quadruplex
cottages are tucked among the trees and on a little hill. About half the
rooms are air-conditioned. Lawns are beautifully manicured; the reef-
protected beach is long and silken; and the candlelight dining is memorable. This resort is popular with honeymooners and older couples
who have been coming for years. ⊠ *Little Dix Bay (Box 70),* ☎ *284/
495–5555,* FAX *284/495–5661,* WEB *www.littledixbay.com. 94 rooms, 4
suites. 3 restaurants, 2 bars, 7 tennis courts, beach, snorkeling, windsurfing, library, children's programs (ages 3–16). AE, MC, V. EP, MAP.*

$–$$$ ⊡ **Nail Bay Resort.** On 147 acres that stretch from three beaches up
★ into the hills, this remarkable complex, though small, has a surprising
variety of accommodations. There are rooms, one- and two-bedroom
units with kitchens, and elegant villas. Villas are scattered around the
property, but most rooms and apartment-style units are clustered to-
gether halfway up the hilllside, with beautiful views of the Sir Francis
Drake Channel. The alfresco restaurant and bar overlooks the free-
form pool. ⊠ *Nail Bay (Box 69),* ☎ *284/494–8000,* FAX *284/495–5875,*
WEB *www.nailbay.com. 16 rooms, 8 1- and 2-bedroom units, 14 villas.
Restaurant, bar, tennis court, beach, snorkeling, windsurfing, boccie,
croquet. AE, MC, V. EP.*

$–$$$ ⊡ **Olde Yard Inn.** Owners Charlie Williams and Carol Kaufman have
★ cultivated a friendly, refreshing atmosphere here. Rooms are cozy and
simply furnished. You can make arrangements for day sails and scuba
excursions, and you can swim in the large pool, work out, or get a massage. There are two excellent restaurants: the Olde Yard Inn, for
French-accented dinners, and the Sip and Dip Grill, for poolside
lunches. ⊠ *The Valley (Box 26),* ☎ *284/495–5544 or 800/653–9273,*
FAX *284/495–5986,* WEB *www.oldeyardinn.com. 14 rooms, 1 suite. 2
restaurants, bar, pool, health club, croquet, library, shops. AE, MC,
V. EP.*

$ ⊡ **Leverick Bay Hotel.** The small hillside rooms at this hotel are dec-
orated in pastels and original artwork. All have refrigerators, balconies, and views of North Sound; four two-bedroom condos are also
available. Down the hill, a Spanish colonial-style main building houses
the Lighthouse restaurant and a store (operated by Pusser's of Tortola).
The resort's office has games that you can borrow. Several shops, a
pool, a beauty salon, a tiny beach, a dive shop, a coin-operated laundry, and a market are just down the hill. ⊠ *Leverick Bay (Box 63),* ☎
284/495–7421, FAX *284/495–7367,* WEB *www.virgingordabvi.com. 16
rooms, 4 condos. Fans, refrigerators. AE, D, MC, V. EP.*

Private Homes and Villas

Those craving seclusion would do well at a villa or even a private home.
Both offer comfortable lodgings with full kitchens and maid service.
Virgin Gorda Villa Rentals (⊠ Box 63, Leverick Bay, ☎ 284/495–7421,
WEB www.virgingordabvi.com) manages over 20 properties that are near
Leverick Bay Hotel, so it's perfect for those who want to be close to
some activity. Many villas—ranging from studios to 3-bedroom houses—
have private swimming pools and air-conditioning, at least in the bedrooms; all have full kitchens, are well maintained, and have spectacular
views. Prices run from $120 to $700 per night, and major credit cards
are accepted.

$$–$$$$ ⊡ **Mango Bay Resort.** Sparkling white villas framed by morning glo-
ries and frangipanis, handsome contemporary Italian furnishings, and
a gorgeous ribbon of golden sand that all but vanishes at high tide make
this an idyllic family retreat. Even for Virgin Gorda it's a study in iso-
lation. ⊠ *Mahoe Bay (Box 1062),* ☎ *284/495–5672,* FAX *284/495–5674,*

Mountain Pt.

Long Bay ⑫

George Dog

Cockroach Island ⑥

Great Dog

Mango Bay

⑪

Mahoe Bay ⑩

West Dog

⑤

Pond Bay ⑨

Sir Francis Drake Channel

Little Dix Bay

Savannah Bay

Colison Pt.

⑧

TO TORTOLA

St. Thomas Bay

⑦

Handsome Bay

Spanish Town

Fort Pt.

① ②
② ❶
❷

Virgin Gorda Airport

③

The Valley

Copper Mine Bay

Devil's Bay

④
❸ ⑤ ④
⑥

Crook's Bay

Stoney Bay

Fallen Jerusalem

❻

Lodging		Dining	
Biras Creek Hotel . . .**15**	Little Dix Bay **8**	The Bath and Turtle . . .**1**	Lighthouse **14**
Bitter End Yacht Club and Marina **16**	Mango Bay Resort **10**	Biras Creek **15**	Little Dix Bay Pavilion **8**
Drake's Anchorage Resort Inn **17**	Nail Bay Resort **12**	Chez Bamboo **2**	Mad Dog's **5**
Guavaberry Spring Bay Vacation Homes **4**	Olde Yard Inn **7**	The Clubhouse **16**	Olde Yard Inn **7**
	Paradise Beach Resort **11**	Drake's Anchorage . **17**	Sip and Dip Grill **7**
Leverick Bay Hotel **13**	Virgin Gorda Villa Rentals **14**	The Flying Iguana . . . **3**	Top of the Baths **6**
		Giorgio's Table **9**	

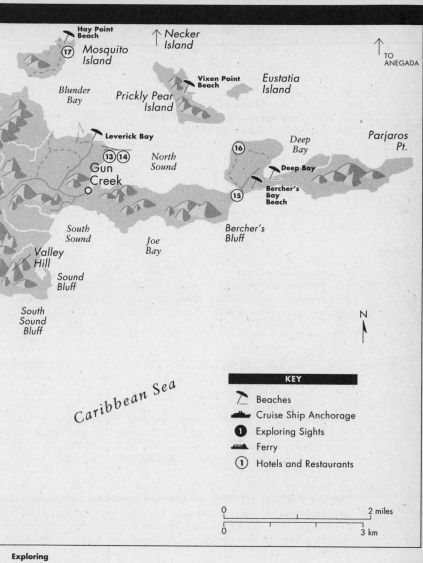

Hay Point
Beach

↑ Necker
Island

⑰ Mosquito
Island

↑
TO
ANEGADA

Blunder
Bay

Vixen Point
Beach

Eustatia
Island

Prickly Pear
Island

Leverick Bay

Deep
Bay

Parjaros
Pt.

⑯

⑬⑭

North
Sound

Gun
Creek
○

Deep Bay

Bercher's
Bay
Beach

⑮

South
Sound

Joe
Bay

Bercher's
Bluff

Valley
Hill

Sound
Bluff

South
Sound
Bluff

N

Caribbean Sea

KEY

Beaches

Cruise Ship Anchorage

❶ Exploring Sights

Ferry

① Hotels and Restaurants

0 _____ 2 miles
0 _____ 3 km

WEB *www.mangobayresort.com. 5 villas. Grocery, no air-conditioning, no room phones, kitchens, no room TVs, beach. No credit cards.*

$$–$$$$ 🏠 **Paradise Beach Resort.** These one-, two-, and three-bedroom beach-front suites and villas have handsome, Caribbean-style furnishings, pastel color schemes, and outdoor showers. Four-wheel-drive vehicles are included in the daily rate. ✉ *Mahoe Bay (Box 534),* ☎ *284/495–5871,* FAX *284/495–5872,* WEB *www.paradisebeachresort.com. 9 units. Some kitchenettes, some kitchens, beach. No credit cards.*

$$ 🏠 **Guavaberry Spring Bay Vacation Homes.** These hexagonal one- and two-bedroom units are scattered about a hillside and you hear chirping birds and feel ocean breezes. It's just a short walk from the cottages down to the tamarind-shaded beach and not far from the mammoth boulders and cool basins of the famed Baths, which adjoin this property. Eleven private houses are also available. ✉ *The Valley (Box 20),* ☎ *284/495–5227,* WEB *www.guavaberryspringbay.com. 12 1-bedroom units, 9 2-bedroom units. Fans, kitchens, beach. No credit cards.*

Dining

Restaurants range from simple to elegant. Hotels that are accessible only by boat will arrange transport in advance upon request for nonguests who wish to dine at their restaurants. It's wise to make dinner reservations almost everywhere except really casual spots.

For approximate costs, *see* the dining price chart *in* Tortola.

AMERICAN/CASUAL

$$–$$$$ ✕ **Top of The Baths.** At the entrance to The Baths, this popular restaurant starts serving at 8 AM. Tables are outside on a terrace or in an open-air pavilion; all have stunning views of the Sir Francis Drake Channel. Hamburgers, salads, and sandwiches are offered at lunch. Conch fritters and pumpkin soup are among the dinner appetizers. Entrées include Cornish hen with wild rice, grilled wahoo with lime butter, and local lobster. For dessert you can choose from such delectables as chocolate cheesecake or pecan pie. ✉ *The Valley,* ☎ *284/495–5497. AE, MC, V.*

$$–$$$ ✕ **The Flying Iguana.** Local artwork is displayed in this charming restaurant's comfortable lounge. The open-air dining room looks out over Virgin Gorda's tiny airport to the sea. Sandwiches and thick, juicy hamburgers are served for lunch. The dinner menu includes a pasta special, grilled chicken, and steaks. ✉ *Virgin Gorda Airport, The Valley,* ☎ *284/495–5277. AE, MC, V.*

$$–$$$ ✕ **Lighthouse.** This bi-level restaurant at the Leverick Bay Hotel looks out over North Sound. The upstairs is slightly less casual but definitely more expensive, with a menu that includes grilled steak, chops, and chicken dishes. Below, the Beach Bar offers light fare all day—starting with breakfast and moving on to hamburgers, salads, and pizzas until well into the evening. ✉ *Leverick Bay Hotel, Leverick Bay,* ☎ *284/495–7369. AE, MC, V.*

$–$$ ✕ **The Bath and Turtle.** You can really sit back and relax at this infor-
★   mal patio tavern with a friendly staff—although the TV noise can be a bit much. Burgers, well-stuffed sandwiches, pizzas, pasta dishes, and daily specials round out the casual menu. Live entertainers perform Saturday nights. ✉ *Virgin Gorda Yacht Harbour, Spanish Town,* ☎ *284/495–5239. MC, V.*

$–$$ ✕ **Sip and Dip Grill.** At the pool at the Olde Yard Inn you'll find this
★   pleasant, informal lunch spot. Come for the grilled fish, pasta salads, spicy chili, chilled soups, and ice cream. Sunday evening there's a bar-

becue with live entertainment. ⊠ *The Valley,* ☎ *284/495–5544. Reservations not accepted. AE, MC, V. No dinner Mon.–Sat.*

$ ✕ **Mad Dog's.** Piña coladas are *the* thing at this breezy bar just outside The Baths. The menu includes great BLTs, hot dogs, and burgers. ⊠ *The Valley, at the entrance to The Baths,* ☎ *284/495–5830. Reservations not accepted. MC, V. No dinner.*

CAJUN/CREOLE

$$–$$$$ ✕ **Chez Bamboo.** This pleasant little hideaway isn't really that hard to find: look for the building with the purple and green latticework. Candles on the dining room tables and the patio help make this a mellow place where you can enjoy such dishes as conch gumbo, Chez B's bouillabaisse, and steak New Orleans. For dessert try the chocolate bourbon mint cake. Stop by Friday night for live jazz. ⊠ *Across from and a little north of Virgin Gorda Yacht Harbour, Spanish Town,* ☎ *284/ 495–5752. Reservations not accepted. AE, MC, V. Closed Mon. No lunch.*

CONTEMPORARY

$$$$ ✕ **Biras Creek.** This hilltop restaurant at the Biras Creek Hotel has stun-
★ ning views of North Sound. The four-course prix-fixe menu changes daily and includes several choices per course. Roast duck breast with plum sauce, grilled swordfish with bacon and caper sauce, pan-seared snapper with a ginger beurre blanc, and a roast breast of pheasant are some of the enticing entrées. Dinner ends with Biras Creek's signature offering of Stilton and port. ⊠ *North Sound,* ☎ *284/494–3555. Reservations essential. AE, MC, V.*

$$$$ ✕ **Drake's Anchorage.** Waves lap almost within reach at the tables of
★ this waterside, open-air restaurant, where you can watch the twinkling lights of neighboring resorts. Dinner is an elegant four-course affair. The evening begins with a soup of the evening. Next comes a salad, then the entrée you chose, such as boneless breast of duck with orange-pineapple sauce, roasted rack of lamb, or a fillet of local red snapper. ⊠ *Drake's Anchorage Resort Inn, North Sound,* ☎ *284/494–3555. Reservations essential. AE, MC, V. No lunch.*

$$$–$$$$ ✕ **Little Dix Bay Pavilion.** For an elegant evening, you can't do better
★ than this—the candlelight in the main open-air pavilion is enchanting, the menu sophisticated, the service attentive. The dinner menu changes daily, but there's always a fine selection of superbly prepared seafood, meat, and vegetarian entrées—gingered duck breast with Pacific Rim vegetables, black Angus rib eye with horseradish and mustard sauce, pan-seared snapper with christophene ratatouille. The breakfast and lunch buffets shine. ⊠ *Little Dix Bay Resort, Spanish Town,* ☎ *284/ 495–5555 Ext. 174. AE, MC, V.*

$$$–$$$$ ✕ **Olde Yard Inn.** The intimate dining room is suffused with gentle,
★ classical melodies and the scent of herbs; a cedar roof covers the breezy space, which is decorated with old-style Caribbean charm. The French-accented cuisine includes lamb chops with mango chutney, chicken breast in a rum cream sauce, grilled fish, steaks, and lobster. Chocolate mousse, cheesecake, and Key lime pie are sweet endings. ⊠ *The Valley, north of the marina,* ☎ *284/495–5544. AE, MC, V.*

ITALIAN

$$–$$$$ ✕ **Giorgio's Table.** Gaze out at the stars and the lights of Tortola and listen to the water lap against the shore while dining on veal scallopini, filet mignon with mushrooms, fresh local fish, or penne with garlic and tomatoes. Lunch fare at this casual establishment includes pizzas and sandwiches. ⊠ *Mahoe Bay,* ☎ *284/495–5684. MC, V.*

SEAFOOD

$$–$$$$ ✕ **The Clubhouse.** The Bitter End Yacht Club's open-air waterfront restaurant is a favorite rendezvous for the sailing set—busy day and

night. At the lavish buffets you get your choice of an entrée for break-fast, lunch, and dinner. Dinner selections include grilled swordfish or tuna, chopped sirloin, scallops, and shrimp. ⊠ *Bitter End Yacht Club, North Sound,* ☎ *284/494–2746. AE, MC, V.*

Beaches

The best beaches are easily reached by water, although they're also accessible on foot, usually after a moderately strenuous 10- to 15-minute hike. Either way, your persistence is rewarded. Anybody going to Virgin Gorda must experience swimming or snorkeling among its unique boulder formations, which can be visited at several beaches along Lee Road. The most popular of these spots is The Baths, but there are several others nearby that are easily reached.

The Baths. Featuring the most outstanding grouping of boulders on Virgin Gorda, this beach is usually quite crowded.

Bercher's Bay Beach. From Biras Creek or Bitter End on the north shore, you can walk to Bercher's Bay and along the windswept surf.

The Crawl. Swim or walk north from Spring Bay Beach to reach this small and appealing bounder-strewn beach.

Deep Bay. Footpaths from Bitter End and foot and bike paths from Biras Creek also lead to the calm, well-protected swimming beach.

Hay Point Beach. Mosquito Island's best beach is a broad band of white sand accessible only by boat or by a path from a little dock on the island's east side.

Leverick Bay. You'll find a tiny, busy beach-cum-marina that fronts a resort restaurant and pool. Come here if you want a break from the island's serenity. The view of Prickly Pear Island is a plus, and the dive facility here can arrange to motor you out to beautiful Eustatia Reef, just across North Sound.

Nail Bay. It's worth heading out to here near Virgin Gorda's northern tip, in the Nail Bay Resort complex, for the snorkeling. The drive takes about half an hour after the turnoff from North Sound Road, and a dirt road makes up part of the route.

Savannah Bay. For a wonderfully private beach close to Spanish Town, try Savannah Bay. It may not always be completely deserted, but it's a lovely, long stretch of white sand.

Spring Bay Beach. From The Baths you can walk on Lee Road or swim north to this less-populated beach, which is a gem.

Vixen Point Beach. Prickly Pear Island has this calm swimming beach.

Outdoor Activities and Sports

Participant Sports

FISHING

The sportfishing here is so good that anglers from around the world fly in for the annual tournaments. **Walford Ferrington** (⊠ Leverick Bay, North Sound, ☎ 284/495–7612) will pick you up almost anywhere on Virgin Gorda and take you out on his 24-ft speedboat for half- or full-day fishing jaunts. Plan to spend $250–$600.

SAILING

The BVI waters are calm and, hence, terrific places to learn to sail. The **Nick Trotter Sailing School** (⊠ Bitter End Yacht Club, North Sound, ☎ 284/494–2745) offers beginner and advanced courses. Private lessons are $40 per hour.

SCUBA DIVING AND SNORKELING

Many of the breathtaking sites off Tortola can also be reached easily from Virgin Gorda. Also, note that the North Sound has some terrific snorkeling spots. The **Bitter End Yacht Club** (⊠ North Sound, ☎ 284/494–2746) offers a number of snorkeling trips day and night. Costs range from $5 per person to $60 per person depending on the length and type of trip. Contact **Dive BVI** (⊠ Virgin Gorda Yacht Harbour, Spanish Town, ☎ 284/495–5513) for expert instruction, certification, and day trips. It costs $100 for a resort course, $85 for a two-tank dive, and $65 for a one-tank dive; equipment rental is an additional $15. **Kilbride's** (⊠ Bitter End Yacht Harbor, North Sound, ☎ 284/495–9638) offers resort, advanced, and rescue courses. The fee for a resort course is $95. One-tank dives run $60; two-tank dives, $85. Equipment rental is an additional $15.

WINDSURFING

The North Sound is a good place to learn to windsurf: it's protected, so you can't be easily blown out to sea. The **Bitter End Yacht Club** (⊠ North Sound, ☎ 284/494–2746) gives lessons and rents equipment for $20 per hour.

Spectator Sports

CRICKET

You can catch a match at the **Recreation Grounds** in Spanish Town February–April. The Virgin Gorda BVI Tourist Board office can give you information on game dates and times.

Shopping

Most boutiques are within hotel complexes. Two of the best are at Biras Creek and Little Dix Bay. Other properties—the Bitter End, Leverick Bay, and the Olde Yard Inn—have small but equally select boutiques, and there's a respectable and diverse scattering of shops in the bustling yacht harbor complex in Spanish Town.

CLOTHING

Dive BVI (⊠ Virgin Gorda Yacht Harbour, Spanish Town, ☎ 284/495–5513) sells books about the islands as well as snorkeling equipment, sportswear, sunglasses, and beach bags. **Next Wave** (⊠ Virgin Gorda Yacht Harbour, Spanish Town, ☎ 284/495–5623) offers bathing suits, T-shirts, canvas tote bags, and locally made jewelry. **Pavilion Gift Shop** (⊠ Little Dix Bay Hotel, Little Dix Bay, ☎ 284/495–5555) has the latest in resort wear for men and women, as well as jewelry, books, housewares, and expensive T-shirts. **Pelican's Pouch Boutique** (⊠ Virgin Gorda Yacht Harbour, Spanish Town, ☎ 284/495–5477) is where you'll find a large selection of swimsuits plus cover-ups, T-shirts, and accessories. **Pusser's Company Store** (⊠ Leverick Bay, ☎ 284/495–7369) has a trademark line of sportswear, rum products, and gift items.

FOODSTUFFS

Bitter End's Emporium (⊠ North Sound, ☎ 284/494–2745) is the place for such edible treats as local fruits, cheeses, and baked goods. **Commissary and Ship Store** (⊠ The Valley, ☎ 284/495–5555) offers daily specials prepared by Little Dix Resort chefs, as well as assorted cheeses, canned goods, wines, and fancy foods. **Wine Cellar and Bakery** (⊠ Virgin Gorda Yacht Harbour, Spanish Town, ☎ 284/495–5250) bakes bread, rolls, muffins, and cookies and has sandwiches and sodas to go.

GIFTS

Palm Tree Gallery (⊠ Leverick Bay, ☎ 284/495–7479) sells attractive handcrafted jewelry, paintings, and one-of-a-kind gift items, as well as games and books about the Caribbean. **Thee Artistic Gallery** (⊠ Virgin Gorda Yacht Harbour, Spanish Town, ☎ 284/495–5104) sells Caribbean jewelry, 14-karat-gold nautical jewelry, maps, collectible coins, and crystal. **The Reeftique** (⊠ Bitter End Yacht Harbor, North Sound, ☎ 284/494–2745) carries island crafts and jewelry, clothing, and nautical odds and ends with the Bitter End logo.

HANDICRAFTS

Virgin Gorda Craft Shop (⊠ Virgin Gorda Yacht Harbour, Spanish Town, ☎ 284/495–5137) sells the work of island artisans, and carries West Indian jewelry and crafts styled from straw, shells, and other local materials. It also stocks clothing and paintings by Caribbean artists.

Nightlife

The Bath and Turtle (⊠ Virgin Gorda Yacht Harbour, Spanish Town, ☎ 284/495–5239), one of the liveliest spots on Virgin Gorda, hosts island bands on Saturday nights from 8 PM until midnight. Local bands play at **Bitter End Yacht Club** (⊠ North Sound, ☎ 284/494–2746) on weekends in season. Call for schedules. **Chez Bamboo** (⊠ across from Virgin Gorda Yacht Harbour, Spanish Town, ☎ 284/495–5752) is the place for jazz on Friday nights and a live band Sunday nights. The **Lighthouse** (⊠ Leverick Bay, ☎ 284/495–7370) has live bands on Saturday night and Sunday afternoon in season. **Little Dix Bay** (⊠ Little Dix Bay, ☎ 284/495–5555) presents elegant live entertainment several nights a week in season. **Rock Café** (⊠ The Valley, ☎ 284/495–5672) has live bands Friday, Saturday, and Sunday nights. **Sip and Dip Grill** (⊠ Olde Yard Inn, The Valley, ☎ 284/495–5544) has a live local band at their Sunday night barbecue.

Exploring Virgin Gorda

One of the most efficient ways to see Virgin Gorda is by sailboat. There are few roads, and most byways don't follow the scalloped shoreline. The main route sticks resolutely to the center of the island, linking The Baths at the tip of the southern extremity with Gun Creek and Leverick Bay at North Sound and providing exhilarating views. The craggy coast, scissored with grottoes and fringed by palms and boulders, has a primitive beauty. If you drive, you can hit all the sights in one day. The best plan is to explore the area near your hotel (either The Valley or North Sound) first, then take a day to drive to the other end. Stop to climb Gorda Peak, in the island's center.

Numbers in the margin correspond to points of interest on the Virgin Gorda map.

Sights to See

❸ The Baths. At Virgin Gorda's most celebrated sight, giant boulders are scattered about the beach and in the water. Some are almost as large as houses and form remarkable grottoes. Climb between these rocks to swim in the many pools. Early morning and late afternoon are the best times to visit if you want to avoid crowds. (If it's privacy you crave, follow the shore northward to quieter bays—Spring, the Crawl, Little Trunk, and Valley Trunk—or head south to Devil's Bay.) ⊠ *Lee Rd., The Baths,* ☎ *no phone.* ⌷ *Free.*

❻ Coastal Islands. You can easily reach the quaintly named Fallen Jerusalem Island and the Dog Islands by boat. They're all part of the BVI National Parks Trust, and their seductive beaches and unparalleled snorkeling display the BVI at their beachcombing, hedonistic best. ☎ *No phone.* ⌷ *Free.*

❹ Copper Mine Point. Here you'll see a tall, stone shaft silhouetted against the sky and a small stone structure that overlooks the sea. These are the ruins of a copper mine established 400 years ago and worked first by the Spanish, then by the English, until the early 20th century. ⊠ *Copper Mine Rd.,* ☎ *no phone.* ☞ *Free.*

➋ Little Fort National Park. This 36-acre wildlife sanctuary has the ruins of an old fort. Giant boulders like those at The Baths are scattered throughout the park. ⊠ *Spanish Town Rd.,* ☎ *no phone.* ☞ *Free.*

➊ Spanish Town. Virgin Gorda's peaceful main settlement, on the island's southern wing, is so tiny that it barely qualifies as a town at all. Also known as The Valley, Spanish Town has a marina, some shops, and a couple of car-rental agencies. Just north of town is the ferry slip. At the Virgin Gorda Yacht Harbour you can stroll along the dock and do a little shopping.

➎ Virgin Gorda Peak National Park. There are two trails at this 265-acre park, which contains the island's highest point, at 1,359 ft (414 m). Small signs on North Sound Road mark both entrances; sometimes, however, the signs are missing, so keep your eyes open for a set of stairs that disappears into the trees. It's about a 15-minute hike from either entrance up to a small clearing, where you can climb a ladder to the platform of a wooden observation tower and a spectacular 360° view. ⊠ *North Sound Rd., Gorda Peak,* ☎ *no phone.* ☞ *Free.*

JOST VAN DYKE

Named after an early Dutch settler, Jost Van Dyke is a small island northwest of Tortola and is *truly* a place to get away from it all. Mountainous and lush, the 4-mi-long (6½-km-long) island—with only about 136 full-time residents—has one tiny resort, some rental houses, a campground, a handful of cars, and a single road. This is one of the Caribbean's most popular anchorages, and there's a disproportionately large number of informal bars and restaurants, which have helped earn Jost its reputation as the "party island" of the BVI.

Lodging

For approximate costs, *see* the lodging price chart *in* Tortola.

$$ $$$ 🏠 **Sandy Ground Estates.** The eight privately owned one- and two-bedroom houses here are tucked into the foliage along the edge of a beach at the island's east end. Each house is architecturally different, and interiors range from spartan to stylish. The fully equipped kitchens can be pre-stocked if you supply a list of groceries (a good idea, as supplies are limited on the island), and there are three very casual restaurants on the other side of the hill—a long walk away. ⊠ *Sandy Ground,* ☎ *284/494–3391,* WEB *www.sandyground.com. 8 houses. Kitchens, no air-conditioning, fans, microwaves, no room TVs, beach. AE, MC, V. EP.*

$$ 🏠 **Sandcastle.** This six-cottage hideaway is on a ½-mi (¾-km) stretch of white-sand beach at remote White Bay. There's "nothing" to do here, except relax in a hammock, read, walk, swim, and enjoy sophisticated cuisine by candlelight in the Sandcastle restaurant. You can also make arrangements for diving, sailing, and sportfishing trips. ⊠ *White Bay,* ☎ *284/495–9888,* FAX *284/495–9999,* WEB *www.sandcastle-bvi.com. 6 cottages. Restaurant, bar, beach, shops. MC, V. EP.*

$ ⚠ **White Bay Campground.** On the east end of White Bay Beach, this simple campground has bare sites, equipped tent sites (with electricity and a lamp), and screened cabins. The owners will take you on nature walks and can arrange island tours and sailing and diving trips. ⊠ *White Bay,* ☎ *284/495–9312. 12 sites, 4 cabins. Restaurant, bar, beach. No credit cards.*

Dining

Restaurants on Jost Van Dyke are informal (some serve meals family style at long tables), but charming. The island is a favorite charter stop, and you're bound to hear people exchanging stories about the previous night's anchoring adventures. Most restaurants don't take reservations, and in all cases dress is casual.

For approximate costs, *see* the dining price chart *in* Tortola.

ECLECTIC

$$$$ ✕ **Sandcastle.** Candlelit dinners in the tiny beachfront dining room of the sandcastle cottage complex are four-course prix-fixe affairs with seating at 7 PM. The menu changes but can include a West Indian pumpkin or curried-apple soup; curried shrimp or three-mustard chicken; and for dessert, rum bananas or Key lime pie. Reservations are requested by 4 PM. Sandwiches are served at lunch at the Soggy Dollar Bar, famous as the purported birthplace of the lethal painkiller drink. ⊠ *White Bay,* ☎ *284/495–9888. Reservations essential. MC, V.*

$$–$$$ ✕ **Club Paradise.** The dinner menu at this casual beachfront establishment includes grilled local fish such as mahimahi, red snapper, and grouper, grilled steak, and barbecued chicken and ribs. Hamburgers, West Indian conch stew, and curried chicken are the luncheon fare. ⊠ *Great Harbour,* ☎ *284/495–9267. No credit cards.*

$$–$$$ ✕ **Harris' Place.** Owner Harris Jones is famous for his pig-roast buffets and Monday night Lobstermania. Harris' Place is a great spot to rub elbows with locals and the charter-boat crowd. ⊠ *Little Harbour,* ☎ *284/495–9302. AE, MC, V.*

$$–$$$ ✕ **Sydney's Peace and Love.** Here you'll find great lobster, barbecue, and a sensational (for the BVI) jukebox. The cognoscenti sail here for dinner since there's no beach—meaning no irksome sand fleas. ⊠ *Little Harbour,* ☎ *284/495–9271. No credit cards.*

$–$$$ ✕ **Abe's Little Harbour.** Specialties at this informal, popular spot include fresh lobster, conch, and spareribs. During most of the winter season there's a pig roast every Wednesday night. ⊠ *Little Harbour,* ☎ *no phone (boaters can use VHF Channel 16). No credit cards.*

$–$$ ✕ **Foxy's Tamarind.** One of the true hot spots in the BVI—and a must-
★ stop for yachters from the world over—Foxy's hosts the madcap Wooden Boat Race every May and throws big parties on New Year's Eve, April Fools' Day, and Halloween. This lively place serves local dishes and terrific barbecue, and it makes a rum punch that's all its own. Foxy plays the guitar and creates calypso ditties about diners. Next door is Foxy's Store, which sells clothing, sundries, souvenirs, and cassettes of Foxy performing. ⊠ *Great Harbour,* ☎ *284/495–9258. AE, MC, V. No lunch weekends.*

$–$$ ✕ **Happy Laury's.** Hamburgers, cheeseburgers, and honey-dipped fried chicken are the specialties at this beachfront spot. ⊠ *Great Harbour,* ☎ *284/495–9259. No credit cards.*

Beaches

Sandy Cay. Just offshore, the little islet known as Sandy Cay is a gleaming scimitar of white sand, with marvelous snorkeling.
White Bay. On the south shore, west of Great Harbour, you'll find this long stretch of white sand.

ANEGADA

Anegada lies low on the horizon about 14 mi (22½ km) north of Virgin Gorda. Unlike the hilly volcanic islands in the chain, this is a flat coral and limestone atoll. Nine miles (14 km) long and 2 mi (3 km) wide, the island rises no more than 28 ft (9 m) above sea level. In fact, by the time you're able to see it, you may have run your boat onto a reef. (More than 300 captains unfamiliar with the waters have done so since exploration days; note that bareboat charters don't allow their vessels to head here without a trained skipper.) Although the reefs are a sailor's nightmare, they (and the shipwrecks they've caused) are a scuba diver's dream. Snorkeling, especially in the waters around Loblolly Bay on the north shore, is also a transcendent experience. You can float in shallow, calm, reef-protected water just a few feet from shore and see one coral formation after another, each shimmering with a rainbow of colorful fish. Such watery pleasures are complemented by ever-so-fine, ever-so-white sand (the northern and western shores have long stretches of the stuff) and the occasional beach bar (stop in for burgers, Anegada lobster, or a frosty beer). The island's population of about 150 lives primarily in a small south-side village called The Settlement. Many local fisherfolk are happy to take visitors out bonefishing.

Lodging

For approximate costs, *see* the lodging price chart *in* Tortola.

$$$ 🏨 **Anegada Reef Hotel.** If you favor laid-back living, this is the spot for you. Pack a bathing suit and a few warmer garments for the evening, and you're good to go. The hotel's simply furnished rooms are laid out in motel fashion. It has its own narrow strip of beach, but beach lovers will want to spend their days on the deserted strands at the other side of the island. Cool down at the outdoor bar, and be sure to try the island's famous lobster—freshly grilled in the Anegada Reef restaurant. ✉ *Setting Point,* ☎ *284/495–8002,* FAX *284/495–9362,* WEB *www. anegadareef.com. 16 rooms. Restaurant, bar, beach. MC, V. FAP.*

$ 🏨 **Neptune's Treasure.** This little guest house offers simple double and single rooms that are very basically furnished. However, all have private baths. You'll find a restaurant, Neptune's Treasure, and a little gift shop on the premises. ✉ *Between Pomato and Saltheap points,* ☎ *284/495–9439. 4 rooms. Restaurant, beach. AE, MC, V. EP.*

$ ⛺ **Anegada Beach Campground.** The tents (8×10 ft [2×3 m] or 10×12 ft [3×4 m]) here are pitched in a marvelously serene setting. Bare sites cost $7 per person, per night; equipped sites are $20 per person. ✉ *The Settlement,* ☎ *284/495–9466. 18 sites. Restaurant, bar, beach. No credit cards.*

Dining

There are between 6 and 10 restaurants open at any one time, depending on the season and also on whim. Check when you're on the island.

For approximate costs, *see* the dining price chart *in* Tortola.

SEAFOOD

$$–$$$$ ✕ **Anegada Reef Hotel.** Seasoned yachters gather nightly at the Anegada Reef Hotel's bar-restaurant to converse and dine with hotel guests. Dinner is by candlelight and always includes famous Anegada lobster, steaks, and chicken—all prepared on the large grill by the little open-air bar. ✉ *Setting Point,* ☎ *284/495–8002. Reservations essential. No credit cards.*

$$–$$$$ ✕ **Neptune's Treasure.** The owners catch, cook, and serve the seafood (lobster is a specialty) at this casual bar and restaurant in the Neptune's Treasure guest house. ✉ *Between Pomato and Saltheap points,* ☎ *284/ 495–9439. AE.*

$$–$$$$ ✕ **Pomato Point.** This relaxed restaurant-bar is on a narrow beach, a short walk from the Anegada Reef Hotel. Entrées include steak, chicken, lobster, and fresh-caught seafood. Owner Wilfred Creque displays various island artifacts, including shards of Arawak pottery and 17th-century coins, cannonballs, and bottles. ✉ *Pomato Point,* ☎ *284/495–8038. Reservations essential. No credit cards.*

$–$$$ ✕ **Big Bamboo.** Ice-cold beer, island drinks, burgers, and grilled lobster entice a steady stream of barefoot diners to this beach bar for lunch. Dinner is by request. ✉ *Loblolly Bay,* ☎ *284/495–2019. AE.*

Shopping

Anegada Reef Hotel Boutique (✉ Setting Point, ☎ 284/495–8002) has a bit of everything: resort wear, hand-painted T-shirts, locally made jewelry, books, and one-of-a-kind gifts. **Pat's Pottery** (✉ Nutmeg Point, ☎ 284/495–8031) sells bowls, plates, cups, candlestick holders, original watercolors, and more.

OTHER BRITISH VIRGIN ISLANDS

Cooper Island

This small, hilly island on the south side of the Sir Francis Drake Channel, about 8 mi (13 km) from Road Town, Tortola, is popular with the charter-boat crowd. There are no roads (which doesn't really matter because there aren't any cars), but you will find a beach restaurant, a casual little hotel, a few houses (some are available for rent), and great snorkeling at the south end of Manchioneel Bay.

Dining and Lodging

For approximate costs, *see* the dining and lodging price charts *in* Tortola.

$$ ✕☉ **Cooper Island Beach Club.** Six West Indian–style cottages—set back from the beach among the palm trees—house 12 no-frills units, each with a living area, a small but complete kitchen, and a balcony. A stay here takes you back to the basics: you use rainwater that has been collected in a cistern, and you can't use any appliances because electricity is so limited (who needs pressed clothes and blow-dried hair anyway?). The restaurant, popular with yachties, serves great ratatouille, grilled fish, chicken and vegetable rotis, penne pasta, steak, and conch creole. For lunch there are hamburgers, conch fritters, sandwiches, and pasta salad. Reservations are essential. ✉ *Manchioneel Bay (Box 859, Road Town, Tortola),* ☎ *Hotel 413/659–2602 or 800/542–4624; restaurant 284/494–3111,* ⓦⒺⒷ *www.cooper-island.com. 12 rooms. Restaurant, bar, no air-conditioning, no room phones, fans, kitchens, no room TVs, beach, dive shop. AE, MC, V. EP.*

Guana Island

Guana Island is very quiet and, because the whole island is owned by the resort, *very* private. There are *no* public amenities, and access is limited (the hotel sends a private launch to pick up its guests on Beef Island). If you arrive on your own boat, the only place you're allowed is on the beach.

Dining and Lodging

For approximate costs, *see* the dining and lodging price charts *in* Tortola.

$$$$ ✕☉ **Guana Island.** The hotel complex, atop a hill, is a 10-minute walk from the beach and has stunning views. The 15 comfortable rooms are

in seven houses, each with its own porch, scattered throughout the grounds. You can observe more than 50 species of birds on this island, and the terrain is a verdant collection of plants ringed by six deserted beaches. Guests mingle during cocktail hour and often dine together at several large tables in the main house, but there are small tables if you prefer a more intimate meal. Daily rates include three meals, afternoon tea, and house wine with lunch and dinner. ⊠ *Hilltop (Box 32, Road Town, Tortola),* ☏ *284/494–2354 or 914/967–6050,* FAX *284/495–2900,* WEB *www.guana.com. 15 rooms. Restaurant, fans, no room TVs, tennis court, croquet, hiking, laundry service. No credit cards. All-inclusive.*

Necker Island

Necker Island, just north of Virgin Gorda, is yet another private isle. Accommodations here are luxurious, but you can stay only if you rent the whole island.

Dining and Lodging

For approximate costs, *see* the lodging price chart *in* Tortola.

$$$$ ⊞ **Necker Island.** You and as many as 25 friends can lease the whole island, including its five beaches, many walks, tennis courts, luxurious villa with 10 spacious guest rooms, and two Balinese cottages. The common living area is anything but common: the huge room is lined with doors that open to the breezes. Here and there are oversize couches and chairs, surrounded by potted plants, artwork, and sculptures. Bedrooms have slate floors, stonework walls, and stunning views. A chef prepares meals for you in the state-of-the-art kitchen; a full staff takes care of everything else. ⊠ *Box 1091, The Valley, Virgin Gorda,* ☏ *284/494–2757,* FAX *284/494–4396,* WEB *www.virgin.com/limitededition. 2 pools, 2 tennis courts, gym, beach, windsurfing, boating. AE, MC, V. All-inclusive.*

Marina Cay

Beautiful little Marina Cay is in Trellis Bay, not far from Beef Island. Sometimes you can see it and its large J-shape coral reefs—a most dramatic sight—from the air soon after takeoff from the airport on Beef Island. With only 6 acres, this islet is considered small even by BVI standards. You'll find a restaurant, Pusser's Store, and a six-unit hotel here. Ferry service is free from the dock on Beef Island.

Dining and Lodging

For approximate costs, *see* the lodging price chart *in* Tortola.

$$ ⊞ **Pusser's Marina Cay Hotel and Restaurant.** The tiny island's only hotel has four rooms and two villas, all with lovely views of the water and neighboring islands. Each has its own porch. The restaurant's menu ranges from fish and lobster to steak, chicken, and barbecued ribs. Pusser's Painkiller Punch is the house specialty. There's free ferry service from the Beef Island dock for anyone visiting the island (call for ferry times, which vary with the season). ⊠ *West side of Marina Cay (Box 76, Road Town, Tortola),* ☏ *284/494–2174,* FAX *284/494–4775,* WEB *www.pussers.com. 4 rooms, 2 villas. Restaurant, bar, no air-conditioning, no room TVs, beach. AE, DC, MC, V. EP.*

Peter Island

Dramatic, hilly, and with wonderful anchorages and beautiful beaches, privately owned Peter Island is about 5 mi (8 km) directly south across the Sir Francis Drake Channel from Road Town, Tortola. Amid the string of islets that stream from the southern tip of Virgin Gorda, the island is an idyllic hideaway replete with white sand beaches, stunning views, and the Peter Island Resort. You can sail here on your own craft or take a launch from the Peter Island dock east of Road Town, Tortola ($15 each way or free if you're coming for dinner; just mention that you have a reservation). Note that the resort discourages nonguests from using hotel facilities other than the restaurants.

Dining and Lodging

For approximate costs, *see* the dining and lodging price charts *in* Tortola.

$$$$ ✕🏠 **Peter Island Resort and Yacht Harbour.** Guest rooms are in four-
★   unit cottages. The more luxurious Beachfront Junior Suites are clustered at one end of a lovely main beach. Over the hill and near the main building are the second-floor Ocean View units and more spacious first-floor Garden Terrace rooms, both of which face the pool and gardens. There's lots to do here: facilities include a Peter Burwash tennis program, a water sports center, a fitness trail, and a 5-Star PADI dive facility. The air-conditioned Tradewinds Restaurant overlooks the Sir Francis Drake Channel. The à la carte menu offers mostly Continental selections with subtle Caribbean touches. A more casual restaurant is down by the beach. ✉ *Sprat Bay (Box 211, Road Town, Tortola),* ☎ *284/495–2000 or 800/346–4451,* ⨍ᴀˣ *284/495–2500,* ᴡᴇʙ *www. peterisland.com. 52 rooms, 3 villas. 2 restaurants, 2 bars, 4 tennis courts, pool, gym, spa, beach, dive shop, windsurfing, basketball, mountain bikes, laundry service, helipad. AE, MC, V. All-inclusive.*

BRITISH VIRGIN ISLANDS A TO Z

To research prices, get advice from other travelers, and book travel arrangements, visit www.fodors.com.

AIR TRAVEL

Both the Beef Island/Tortola and Virgin Gorda airports are classic Caribbean—almost always sleepy. However, the Beef Island terminal can get crowded when several departures are scheduled close together, and lines at service desks move slowly when this happens; give yourself at least an hour. There's no nonstop service from the continental United States to the BVI; connections are usually made through San Juan, Puerto Rico, or St. Thomas, USVI. Several airlines serve either San Juan or St. Thomas or both. Air St. Thomas flies between St. Thomas and San Juan and Virgin Gorda. Air Sunshine flies back and forth from St. Thomas and San Juan to Beef Island/Tortola and Virgin Gorda. American Eagle flies between St. Thomas and Beef Island/Tortola, and between San Juan and Beef Island/Tortola. Cape Air flies to both San Juan and St. Thomas from Beef Island/Tortola. Clair Aero Services flies back and forth to St. Thomas from Beef Island/Tortola. Continental flies between San Juan and Beef Island/Tortola.

Regularly scheduled flights between the BVI and most other Caribbean islands are provided by LIAT. Many Caribbean islands can also be reached through Fly BVI, a charter service on Virgin Gorda.
➤ AIRLINES AND CONTACTS: **Air St. Thomas** (☎ 284/495–5935). **Air Sunshine** (☎ 284/495–8900, ᴡᴇʙ www.airsunshine.com). **American Eagle** (☎ 284/495–1122). **Cape Air** (☎ 284/495–2100, ᴡᴇʙ www.flycapeair.com). **Clair Aero Services** (☎ 284/495–2271). **Continental** (☎ 340/777–8190). **Fly BVI** (☎ 284/495–1747, ᴡᴇʙ www.fly-bvi.com). **LIAT** (☎ 284/495–2577).

AIRPORTS

At the Beef Island/Tortola Airport, taxis hover at the exit from customs. Fares are officially set; they're not negotiable and are lower per person when there are several passengers. Figure about $15 for up to three people and $5 for each additional passenger for the 20-minute ride to Road Town and about $20–$30 for the 45-minute ride to West End. Expect to share your taxi, and be patient if your driver searches for people to fill his cab—only a few flights land each day, and this could be your driver's only run. You can also call the BVI Taxi Association.

On Virgin Gorda call Mahogany Rentals and Taxi Service. If you are staying on North Sound, a taxi will take you from the airport to the dock, where your hotel launch will meet you, but be sure to make launch arrangements with your hotel before your arrival. If your destination is Leverick Bay, your land taxi will take you there directly. Note that if your destination is Virgin Gorda, you can also fly to Beef Island/Tortola and catch the nearby North Sound Express, which will take you to Spanish Town or North Sound.

➤ AIRPORT INFORMATION: **BVI Taxi Association** (☎ 284/495–1982). **Mahogany Rentals and Taxi Service** (✉ The Valley, ☎ 284/495–5469).

BOAT AND FERRY TRAVEL
FARES AND SCHEDULES
Ferries connect St. Thomas, USVI, with Tortola and Virgin Gorda. Inter-Island Boat Services' *Sundance II* connects St. John and West End, Tortola, daily. Native Son, Inc. operates three ferries (*Native Son, Oriole,* and *Voyager Eagle*) and has daily service between St. Thomas and Tortola (West End and Road Town). The *Nubian Princess* operates between Red Hook, St. Thomas; Cruz Bay, St. John; and West End, Tortola, daily. Smiths Ferry Services operates between downtown St. Thomas and Road Town and West End daily. Speedy's Ferries runs between Virgin Gorda, Tortola, and St. Thomas on Tuesday, Thursday, and Saturday, and its *Speedy's Fantasy* runs between Road Town, Tortola, and Spanish Town, Virgin Gorda, daily.

North Sound Express boats run daily between Virgin Gorda's North Sound and Spanish Town and Beef Island/Tortola. The Peter Island Ferry runs daily between Peter Island's private dock on Tortola (just east of Road Town) and Peter Island. Jost Van Dyke Ferry Service makes the Jost Van Dyke–Tortola run several times daily. New Horizon Ferry Service makes the Jost Van Dyke–Tortola trip a number of times each day.
➤ BOAT AND FERRY INFORMATION: **Inter-Island Boat Services** (☎ 284/495–4166). **Jost Van Dyke Ferry Service** (☎ 284/494–2997). **Native Son, Inc.** (☎ 284/495–4617). **New Horizon Ferry Service** (☎ 284/495–9477). **North Sound Express** (☎ 284/495–2271). *Nubian Princess* (☎ 284/495–4999). **Peter Island Ferry** (☎ 284/495–2000). **Smiths Ferry Services** (☎ 284/495–4495). **Speedy's Ferries** (☎ 284/495–5240).

BUSINESS HOURS
BANKS
Banks usually have hours Monday–Thursday 9–2:30 and Friday 9–2:30 and 4:30–6.

POST OFFICES
Post offices are open weekdays 9–5 and Saturday 9–noon.

SHOPS
Stores are generally open Monday–Saturday 9–5. You may find some open on Sunday.

CAR RENTALS
Both Tortola and Virgin Gorda have a number of car rental agencies. Although taxi service is good on these two islands, many people who want to explore the islands and try a different beach every day opt for renting a vehicle. On Anegada it is possible to rent a car, but most peo-

ple rely on taxis for transportation. Jost Van Dyke has a single road, and visitors travel by foot or local taxi. On the other islands there are no roads.

You'll need a temporary BVI license, available at the rental car company for $10 with a valid license from another country. Most agencies offer both four-wheel-drive vehicles and cars (often compacts).

On Tortola try Avis, Hertz, or Itgo Car Rental. On Virgin Gorda contact Mahogany Rentals and Taxi Service or L&S Jeep Rental.
➤ MAJOR AGENCIES: **Avis** (⊠ Botanic Gardens, Road Town, Tortola, ☎ 284/494–3322). **Hertz** (⊠ West End, Tortola, ☎ 284/495–4405). **Itgo Car Rental** (⊠ Wickham's Cay I, Road Town, Tortola, ☎ 284/494–2639, WEB www.itgosurfbvi.com). **L&S Jeep Rental** (⊠ Spanish Town, Virgin Gorda, ☎ 284/495–5297). **Mahogany Rentals and Taxi Service** (⊠ Spanish Town, Virgin Gorda, ☎ 284/495–5469).

CAR TRAVEL
GASOLINE
Gas costs about $2.50 a gallon.

ROAD CONDITIONS
Tortola's main roads are, for the most part, well paved, but there are exceptionally steep hills and sharp curves; driving demands your complete attention. A main road encircles the island and several roads cross it, almost always through mountainous terrain. Virgin Gorda has a smaller road system, and a single, very steep road links the north and south ends of the island.

RULES OF THE ROAD
Driving in the BVI is on the left side of the road, British-style. Speed limits (rarely enforced) are 20 mph in town and 35 mph outside town.

ELECTRICITY
Electricity is 110 volts, the same as in North America, so European appliances will require adaptors. The electricity is quite reliable.

EMERGENCIES
➤ AMBULANCE AND FIRE: **General emergencies** (☎ 999).
➤ HOSPITALS: **Medicure Health Center** (⊠ Spanish Town, Virgin Gorda, ☎ 284/495–5479). **Peebles Hospital** (⊠ Road Town, Tortola, ☎ 284/494–3497).
➤ PHARMACIES: In Road Town, Tortola: **Cay Pharmacy** (⊠ Road Town, Tortola, ☎ 284/494–8128). **J. R. O'Neal Drug Store** (⊠ Road Town, Tortola, ☎ 284/494–2292). **Island Drug Centre** (⊠ Spanish Town, Virgin Gorda, ☎ 284/495–5449). **Medicure** (⊠ Spanish Town, Virgin Gorda, ☎ 284/495–5479).
➤ POLICE: **General emergencies** (☎ 999).

ETIQUETTE AND BEHAVIOR
Islanders are religious, and churches fill up on Sunday. You're welcome to attend services, but be sure to dress up. If you encounter any rudeness, you probably didn't begin the conversation properly: only after courteous exchanges ("Hello, how are you today?" and "Not too bad, and how are you?") should you get down to the business of buying groceries, ordering lunch, or hiring a taxi.

FESTIVALS AND SEASONAL EVENTS
In March catch the breathtaking displays of local foliage at the Horticultural Society Show at the botanical gardens; also in March, gather together with locals and yachties at Foxy's Annual St. Patrick's Celebration on Jost Van Dyke. In April, join the fun at the Virgin Gorda Festival, which culminates with a parade on Easter Sunday; also in April,

glimpse the colorful spinnakers as sailing enthusiasts gather for the internationally known BVI Spring Regatta. May is the time for partying at Foxy's Wooden Boat Regatta, on Jost Van Dyke. In August try your hand at sportfishing as anglers compete to land the largest catch at the BVI Sportfishing Tournament; August sees two weeks of joyful revelry during Tortola's BVI Emancipation Festival Celebrations. If you've always wanted to escape to the islands and live on a boat, then the November BVI Boat Show is for you. To compete in sailing races and games, drop in on Virgin Gorda's North Sound during the last six weeks of the year for the Bitter End Yacht Club's Competition Series, including the Invitational Regatta. For the best in local *fungi* bands (bands that make music using household items as instruments), stop by the Scratch/Fungi Band Fiesta in December.

HOLIDAYS

The following public holidays are celebrated in the BVI: New Year's Day, Commonwealth Day (Mar. 14), Good Friday (the Fri. before Easter), Easter (the first Sunday after the first full moon after the vernal equinox, Easter Monday (the Mon. after Easter), Whit Monday (the first Mon. in May), Sovereign's Birthday (June 16), Territory Day (July 1), BVI August Festival Days (usually the first two weeks Aug.), St. Ursula's Day (Oct. 21), Christmas, and Boxing Day (the day after Christmas).

LANGUAGE

English is the official language, and it's often spoken with a West Indian accent and with a few idiomatic expressions. If someone says he's just limin', it means he's hanging out. If you ask for an item in a store, and the shopkeeper replies, "It's finished," then the shop has temporarily run out.

MAIL AND SHIPPING

There are post offices in Road Town on Tortola and in Spanish Town on Virgin Gorda (note that postal service in the BVI isn't very efficient). Postage for a first-class letter to the United States, Canada, Australia, New Zealand, or the United Kingdom is 55¢; for a postcard, 35¢. For a small fee Rush It, in Road Town and in Spanish Town, offers most U.S. mail and UPS services (via St. Thomas the next day). If you wish to write to an establishment in the BVI, be sure to include the specific island in the address; there are no postal codes.
➤ CONTACTS: **Rush It** (⊠ Road Town, Tortola, ☎ 284/494–4421; ⊠ Spanish Town, Virgin Gorda, ☎ 284/495–5822).

MONEY MATTERS

BANKS AND ATMS

On Tortola you'll find a Barclays Bank near the waterfront in Road Town; Chase Manhattan Bank is also near Road Town's waterfront and has an ATM machine. On Virgin Gorda, Barclays Bank isn't far from the ferry dock in Spanish Town.
➤ CONTACTS: **Barclays Bank** (⊠ Wickham's Cay I, Road Town, Tortola, ☎ 284/494–2171; ⊠ Virgin Gorda Yacht Harbour, Spanish Town, Virgin Gorda, ☎ 284/495–5271). **Chase Manhattan Bank** (⊠ Wickham's Cay I, Road Town, Tortola, ☎ 284/494–2662).

CREDIT CARDS

Most hotels and restaurants in the BVI accept MasterCard and Visa, and some also accept American Express, Diners Club, and Discover. Beware that a few accept only cash or traveler's checks.

CURRENCY

The currency is the U.S. dollar. Any other currency must be exchanged at a bank.

PASSPORTS AND VISAS

U.S. and Canadian citizens need a valid passport, or an original birth certificate with a raised seal along with a government-issued photo ID. Citizens of all other countries need a valid passport.

SAFETY

Although crime is rare, use common sense: don't leave your camera on the beach while you take a dip or your wallet on a hotel dresser when you go for a walk.

SIGHTSEEING TOURS

Travel Plan Tours can arrange island tours, boat tours, and yacht charters from its Tortola base. Or you can just rent a taxi (minimum of three people) on either Tortola or Virgin Gorda.
➤ CONTACTS: **Travel Plan Tours** (☎ 284/494–2872).

TAXES & SERVICE CHARGES

DEPARTURE TAX

The departure tax is $5 per person by boat and $10 per person by plane. There is a separate booth at the airport to collect this tax, which must be paid in cash.

SERVICE CHARGES

Most hotels add a service charge ranging from 5% to 18% to the bill. A few restaurants and some shops tack on an additional 10% charge if you use a credit card.

TAXES

There's no sales tax in the BVI. However, there's a 7% government tax on hotel rooms.

TAXIS

Your hotel staff will be happy to summon a taxi for you. Rates aren't published, so you should negotiate the fare with your driver before you start your trip. It's cheaper to travel in groups because there's a minimum fare to each destination, which is the same whether you are one, two, or three people. The taxi number is also the license plate number. On Tortola, there are BVI Taxi Association stands in Road Town near the ferry dock, at Wickham's Cay I, and at the Beef Island/Tortola airport. You can also usually find a taxi at the ferry dock at Soper's Hole, West End, where ferries arrive from St. Thomas.

Andy's Taxi and Jeep Rental offers service from one end of Virgin Gorda to the other. Mahogany Rentals and Taxi Service provides taxi service all over Virgin Gorda.
➤ CONTACTS: **Andy's Taxi and Jeep Rental** (✉ The Valley, Tortola, ☎ 284/495–5511). **BVI Taxi Association** (✉ Near the ferry dock, Road Town, Tortola, ☎ 284/494–7519; ✉ Wickham's Cay I, Road Town, Tortola, ☎ 284/494–2322; ✉ Beef Island Airport, Tortola, ☎ 284/495–1982). **Mahogany Rentals and Taxi Service** (✉ The Valley, Virgin Gorda, ☎ 284/495–5469).

TELEPHONES

COUNTRY AND AREA CODES

The area code for the BVI is 284; when you make calls from North America, you need only dial the area code and the number. From the United Kingdom you must dial 001 and then the area code and the number. From Australia and New Zealand you must dial 0011 followed by 1, the area code, and the number.

INTERNATIONAL CALLS

For credit card or collect long-distance calls to the United States, use a phone-card telephone or look for special USADirect phones, which are linked directly to an AT&T operator. For access dial 800/872–2881, or dial 111 from a pay phone and charge the call to your MasterCard or Visa. USADirect and pay phones can be found at most hotels and in towns.

LOCAL CALLS

To call anywhere in the BVI once you've arrived, dial all seven digits. A local call from a pay phone costs 25¢, but such phones are sometimes on the blink. An alternative is a Caribbean phone card, available in $5, $10, and $20 denominations. It's sold at most major hotels and many stores and can be used to call within the BVI as well as all over the Caribbean and to access USADirect from special phone-card phones.

TIPPING

Tip porters and bellhops $1 per bag. Sometimes a service charge (10%) is included on restaurant bills; it's customary to leave another 5% if you liked the service. If no charge is added, 15% is the norm. Cabbies normally aren't tipped because most own their cabs; add 10%–15% if they exceed their duties.

**TRANSPORTATION AROUND
THE BRITISH VIRGIN ISLANDS**

There's limited bus service on Tortola. For information about schedules, call Wheatley's Bus Service. The bus runs in a loop from East End on Beef Island to Road Town along Blackburn Highway and then back to East End via Ridge Road. The fare is $1.

Speedy's Ferries runs between Road Town, Tortola, and Spanish Town, Virgin Gorda, daily. North Sound Express boats run daily between Virgin Gorda's North Sound and Spanish Town and Beef Island/Tortola. The Peter Island Ferry runs daily between Peter Island's private dock on Tortola (just east of Road Town) and Peter Island. Jost Van Dyke Ferry Service makes the Jost Van Dyke–Tortola run several times daily. New Horizon Ferry Service makes the Jost Van Dyke–Tortola trip a number of times each day.

Clair Aero Services flies between Tortola and Anegada on Monday, Wednesday, Friday, and Sunday.
➤ CONTACTS: **Clair Aero Services** (☎ 284/495–2271). **Jost Van Dyke Ferry Service** (☎ 284/494–2997). **New Horizon Ferry Service** (☎ 284/495–9477). **North Sound Express** (☎ 284/495–2271). **Peter Island Ferry** (☎ 284/495–2000). **Speedy's Ferries** (☎ 284/495–5240). **Wheatley's Bus Service** (☎ 284/495–2421).

VISITOR INFORMATION

➤ BEFORE YOU LEAVE: **BVI Tourist Board (U.S.)** (✉ 370 Lexington Ave., Suite 1605, New York, NY 10017, ☎ 212/696–0400 or 800/835–8530, WEB www.bvitouristboard.com; ✉ 3450 Wilshire Blvd., Suite 1202 Los Angeles, CA 90010, ☎ 213/736–8931; ✉ 3390 Peachtree Rd. NE, Suite 1000, Atlanta, GA 30326, ☎ 404/240–8018). **BVI Tourist Board (U.K.)** (✉ 55 Newman St., London W1P 3PG, U.K., ☎ 011–44–207–947–8200).
➤ IN THE BRITISH VIRGIN ISLANDS: **BVI Tourist Board** (✉ Cruise Ship Dock, Road Town, Tortola, ☎ 284/494–3134). **Virgin Gorda BVI Tourist Board** (✉ Virgin Gorda Yacht Harbor, Spanish Town, Virgin Gorda, ☎ 284/495–5181).

8 CAYMAN ISLANDS

Updated by
JoAnn
Milivojevic

The signpost just past the airport/post office/fire station reads, "Iguanas have the right of way." Many of these prehistoric-looking lizards lurk about Little Cayman, the smallest of the Cayman Islands' trio. According to Gladys of Pirates Point, iguanas love grapes. She keeps extras on hand just so her guests can feed them to the iguanas. That kind of hospitality is the norm on an island where the repeat guest list is high and the island's police officer has yet to use his siren. Each of the three Cayman Islands has its own rhythm from Grand Cayman to the Brac to Little Cayman, it's slow, slower, slowest.

This British colony, which consists of Grand Cayman, smaller Cayman Brac, and Little Cayman, is one of the Caribbean's most popular destinations. Columbus is said to have sighted the islands in 1503, but he didn't stop off to explore. He did note that the surrounding sea was alive with turtles, so the islands were named Las Tortugas. The name was later changed to Cayman, referring to the caiman crocodiles that once roamed the islands. The Cayman Islands remained largely uninhabited until the late 1600s, when England took them and Jamaica from Spain under the Treaty of Madrid. Emigrants from England, Holland, Spain, and France then arrived, as did refugees from the Spanish Inquisition and deserters from Oliver Cromwell's army in Jamaica; many brought slaves with them as well. The Caymans' caves and coves were also perfect hideouts for the likes of Blackbeard, Sir Henry Morgan, and other pirates out to plunder Spanish galleons. Many ships fell afoul of the reefs surrounding the islands, often with the help of Caymanians who lured vessels to shore with beacon fires.

The legend of one wreck in particular—the Wreck of the Ten Sails—has remained popular with Caymanians through the years. In 1794 a convoy of 10 Jamaican ships bound for England foundered on the reefs. The islanders saved everyone, including, it was said, a few members of royalty. The tale has it that a grateful King George III decreed that Caymanians would forever be exempt from conscription and would never have to pay taxes. However, though Caymanians don't pay taxes, this tale has been proven pure fiction.

As for current politics, this British colony has a governor, who appoints three official members to the Legislative Assembly. He must also accept the advice of the Executive Council in all matters except foreign affairs, defense, internal security, and civil-service appointments. Though the governor is appointed from England, locally elected Caymanians greatly influence how their islands are run.

Today's Caymans may be seasoned with suburban prosperity, particularly Grand Cayman (residents joke that the national flower is the satellite dish), and stuffed with crowds (the hotels that line the famed Seven Mile Beach are often full, even in the slow summer season), but the 31,000 Cayman Islanders—most of whom live on Grand Cayman—add considerable flavor with their renowned courtesy and civility. The cost of living may be about 20% higher here than in the United States (one U.S. dollar is worth only about 80 Cayman cents), but you won't be hassled by panhandlers or feel afraid to walk around on a dark evening (the crime rate is very low). Add political and economic stability to the mix, and you have a fine island recipe indeed.

GRAND CAYMAN

Grand Cayman is world-renowned for two offshore activities: banking and scuba diving. The former pays dividends in the manicured capital of George Town, which bulges with some 554 banks. The latter offers its rewards in translucent waters that are full of colorful and varied life—much of it protected by a marine parks system. Although about a third of Grand Cayman's visitors come for the diving, a growing number are young honeymooners. The island offers many additional pleasures, from shopping for jewelry to fine dining to simply strolling hand-in-hand on a powder-soft beach.

Lodging

In the off-season (summer) it's easy to find lodgings, even on short notice, but for peak-season and holiday visits book well in advance. Note that most hotels require a 7- or 14-day minimum stay at Christmas time, though condominiums will let you book on a day-to-day basis for stays of any length.

Brace yourself for resort prices—there are few accommodations in the economy range. Most of the larger hotels along Seven Mile Beach don't offer meal plans. Smaller properties that are farther from restaurants usually offer MAP or FAP (to estimate rates for hotels offering MAP or FAP, add about $40 per person, per day to the average EP price ranges below).

CATEGORY	COST EP/CP*	COST A.I.**
$$$$	over $350	over $375
$$$	$250–$350	$275–$375
$$	$150–$250	$175–$275
$	under $150	under $175

*EP/CP prices are per night for a standard double room in high season, excluding taxes, service charges, and meal plans**A.I. (all-inclusive) prices are per person, per night based on double-occupancy during high season, excluding taxes and service charges*

Hotels

$$$$ ☆ **Hyatt Regency Grand Cayman.** For a plush albeit it pricey stay, the ★ one-bedroom ocean-view suites sleep up to four and have teak furnishings, marble baths, and formal entryways. The main resort, adjacent to Britannia Golf Course, has gorgeously landscaped grounds. Moderate-size standard rooms have marble entranceways, oversize bathtubs, French doors, and verandas; 44 Regency Club rooms include concierge services and complimentary Continental breakfast, early evening hors d'oeuvres,

Grand Cayman

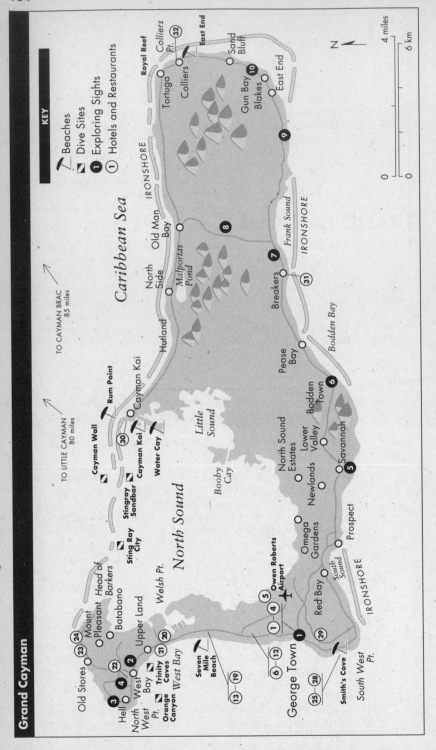

TO CAYMAN BRAC
85 miles

TO LITTLE CAYMAN
80 miles

Caribbean Sea

North Sound

Little Sound

Booby Cay

IRONSHORE

IRONSHORE

IRONSHORE

IRONSHORE

KEY

Beaches
Dive Sites
Exploring Sights ①
Hotels and Restaurants ①

N

0 — 4 miles
0 — 6 km

Old Stores
Hell
North West Pt.
West Bay
Mount Pleasant
Batabano
Upper Land
Welsh Pt.
Head of Barkers
Sting Ray City
Stingray Sandbar
Rum Point
Cayman Wall
Cayman Kai
Water Cay
Royal Reef
Colliers
Tortuga
Colliers Pt.
East End
Sand Bluff
East End
Gun Bay
Blakes
Old Man Bay
North Side
Hutland
Malportas Pond
Breakers
Frank Sound
Bodden Bay
Pease Bay
Bodden Town
Lower Valley
Savannah
Newlands
North Sound Estates
Omega Gardens
Prospect
Red Bay
South Sound
South West Pt.
Smith's Cove
George Town
Owen Roberts Airport
Seven Mile Beach
Orange Canyon
Trinity Caves
West Bay

Orange Canyon
Trinity Caves

Cayman Brac and Little Cayman

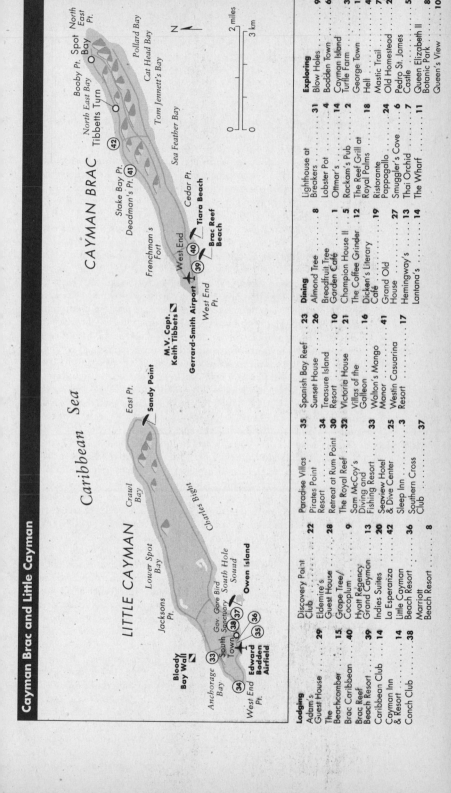

Lodging

Adam's Guest House	29
The Beachcomber	15
Brac Caribbean	40
Brac Reef Beach Resort	39
Caribbean Club	14
Cayman Inn & Resort	14
Conch Club	38
Discovery Point Club	22
Eldemire's Guest House	28
Grape Tree/Cocoplum	9
Hyatt Regency Grand Cayman	13
Indies Suites	20
La Esperanza	42
Little Cayman Beach Resort	36
Marriott Beach Resort	8
Paradise Villas	35
Pirates Point Resort	34
Retreat at Rum Point	30
The Royal Reef	32
Sam McCoy's Diving and Fishing Resort	33
Seaview Hotel & Dive Center	25
Sleep Inn	3
Southern Cross Club	37
Spanish Bay Reef	23
Sunset House	26
Treasure Island Resort	10
Victoria House	21
Villas of the Galleon	16
Walton's Mango Manor	41
Westin Casuarina Resort	17

Dining

Almond Tree	8
Breadfruit Tree Garden Café	1
Champion House II	5
The Coffee Grinder	12
Dicken's Literary Café	19
Grand Old House	27
Hemingway's	13
Lantana's	14
Lighthouse at Breakers	31
Lobster Pot	4
Ottmar's	14
Rackam's Pub	2
The Reef Grill at Royal Palms	18
Ristorante Pappagallo	24
Smuggler's Cove	6
Thai Orchid	7
The Wharf	11

Exploring

Blow Holes	9
Bodden Town	6
Cayman Island Turtle Farm	3
George Town	1
Hell	4
Mastic Trail	7
Old Homestead	2
Pedro St. James Castle	5
Queen Elizabeth II Botanic Park	8
Queen's View	10

and cocktails. Some balconies are small "step outs," while others have a table and chairs—inquire carefully as there's no price difference. ⊠ *West Bay Rd., Seven Mile Beach (Box 1698)*, ☎ *345/949–1234 or 800/233–1234*, ℻ *345/949–8528*, WEB *grandcayman.hyatt.com. 112 rooms, 63 suites, 70 villas. 3 restaurants, 4 bars, minibars, 9-hole golf course, 4 tennis courts, 7 pools, gym, hair salon, outdoor hot tub, massage, spa, beach, dive shop, snorkeling, windsurfing, boating, parasailing, waterskiing, croquet, shops, children's programs (ages 3–12), concierge, car rental. AE, D, DC, MC, V. CP, EP, MAP.*

$$$$ 🏨 **Marriott Beach Resort.** A popular choice for families and couples, this five-story luxury property is designed in colonial style with arched doorways and an airy marble lobby that opens onto a plant-filled courtyard. Large adjoining rooms are ideal for families, and all have balconies. Price varies according to the view—ocean or garden courtyard. There's a nearby reef with good snorkeling and a beach bar near the pool. The Marriott is popular for conventions. ⊠ *West Bay Rd., Seven Mile Beach (Box 30371)*, ☎ *345/949–0088 or 800/228–9290*, ℻ *345/949–0288*, WEB *www.marriott.com. 309 rooms, 4 suites. Restaurant, bar, snack bar, air-conditioning, pool, hair salon, hot tub, spa, beach, dive shop, snorkeling, windsurfing, shops, dry cleaning, laundry service, meeting rooms, car rental. AE, DC, MC, V. EP.*

$$$$ 🏨 **Westin Casuarina Resort.** Though the surroundings are elegant, be sure to ask for rooms that have at least partial ocean views, (standards have an "island" view, which translates into the parking lot and main drag.) The lobby spills out onto the waterfront, where tall royal palms shade the elegant walkway. Rooms have bleached-wood furniture and stucco ceilings. The suites aren't much different from regular rooms, so they're hardly worth the extra money. Havana, the Westin's high-end restaurant, deserves praise for its excellent Cuban/Caribbean fare. ⊠ *West Bay Rd., Seven Mile Beach (Box 30620)*, ☎ *345/945–3800 or 800/228–3000*, ℻ *345/949–5825*, WEB *www.westin.com. 339 rooms, 2 suites. 2 restaurants, 3 bars, grill, 2 tennis courts, pool, gym, hair salon, 2 hot tubs, beach, dive shop, shops, meeting rooms. AE, MC, V. EP.*

$$$–$$$$ 🏨 **Indies Suites.** For a more peaceful and affordable stay, this prop-
★   erty is across the road from and on the quieter north end of Seven Mile Beach. One- and two-bedroom suites have a dining-living room (with a sleeper sofa), a terrace, and a storeroom for dive gear and are furnished with contemporary wood furniture. Continental buffet breakfast, maid service, and a free sunset cruise once a week are nice extras. The lobby is spectacular, with vintage 1930s Fords on display. ⊠ *West Bay Rd., Seven Mile Beach (Box 2070 GT)*, ☎ *345/945–5025 or 800/654–3130*, ℻ *345/945–5024. 38 suites. Bar, snack bar, kitchens, pool, hot tub, dive shop, snorkeling, laundry facilities. AE, MC, V. CP.*

$$–$$$ 🏨 **Spanish Bay Reef.** Flowering trees and bushes surround pale pink two-story stucco units at this resort on a small, sandy beach at the northwest tip of the island near 27 spectacular north-wall scuba diving sites. Boardwalks connect simple, comfortable guest rooms. The outdoor bar–dining area surrounds the pool and has views of the ocean; the indoor bar–dining area is spacious and made of coral stone. Spanish Bay Reef is a deep drop-off, which means superior diving and snorkeling. Rates include round-trip transfers, taxes and gratuities, shore diving, boat dives, and use of bicycles (not in mint condition). ⊠ *167 Conch Point Rd., George Town (Box 903)*, ☎ *345/949–3765*, ℻ *345/949–1842. 67 rooms. Restaurant, bar, pool, hot tub, beach, dive shop, snorkeling. AE, MC, V. All-inclusive.*

$$–$$$ 🏨 **Treasure Island Resort.** There's plenty of room to roam at this sprawling complex, which has a huge pool with adjacent bar and encompasses a section of Seven Mile Beach for sunbathing and lounging. Rooms here are functional, with tile floors, stucco walls, rattan furniture, and watercolor prints. ⊠ *West Bay Rd., Seven Mile Beach (Box 1817),* ☎ *345/949–7777 or 800/203–0775,* FAX *345/949–8672. 278 rooms. Restaurant, bar, 2 tennis courts, 2 pools, beach, snorkeling, windsurfing. AE, DC, MC, V. EP.*

$$
★ 🖭 **Sunset House.** Low-key and laid-back describe this motel-style resort on the ironshore. A congenial staff, a happening bar, and a seafood restaurant are pluses, but the diving (and the dive packages) is the star attraction here. Full dive services include free waterside lockers, two- and three-tank dives at the better reefs around the island, Cathy Church's U/W Photo Centre, and a made-to-order full hot breakfast. The latest dive attraction is a newly sunk 9-ft bronze mermaid sculpture dubbed Aphrodite. It's a five-minute walk to a sandy beach. ⊠ *S. Church St., George Town (Box 479),* ☎ *345/949–7111 or 800/854–4767,* FAX *345/ 949–7101,* WEB *www.sunsethouse.com. 58 rooms, 2 suites. Restaurant, bar, pool, hot tub, dive shop. AE, MC, V. CP, EP, MAP.*

$–$$ 🖭 **Cayman Inn & Resort.** This two-story hotel is a quick stroll from Seven Mile Beach, close to the airport, and a mile from George Town's shops. Rooms are motel-modern, with maroon, mauve, and beige color schemes and contemporary wood furnishings. All superior rooms and junior suites have mini-refrigerators and microwaves, a nice extra. The Diver's Down dive shop is here, as are tour agencies, and car and motorcycle rental offices. Full American breakfast is included in the rates. ⊠ *West Bay Rd., Seven Mile Beach (Box 30111),* ☎ *345/949–9111 or 800/720–9626,* FAX *345/949–6699. 115 rooms.* WEB *www.caymaninn-resort.com. Bar, grill, microwaves, refrigerators, pool, hot tub, dive shop, laundry service, meeting rooms, travel services, car rental. AE, D, DC, MC, V. BP.*

$ 🖭 **Seaview Hotel & Dive Center.** South of George Town, this perfectly pleasant and affordable hotel is good for tight budgets. The staff is friendly, and the amenities are quite adequate. It's a perfect place to go if you're interested in a hotel from which to base yourself for a diving vacation. It's on the water, so the best rooms have ocean views; most are decorated with tropical-pattern bedspreads and pale blue walls. However, the closest beach is at Smith Cove, about a mile away. ⊠ *S. Church St., George Town (Box. 260),* ☎ *345/945–0558 or 945–0577,* FAX *345/945–0559. 18 rooms. Restaurant, bar, pool, snorkeling. AE, MC, V.*

Guest Houses

They may be some distance from the beach and short on style and facilities, but these lodgings offer rock-bottom prices (all fall below the $ category), a friendly atmosphere, and your best shot at getting to know the locals. Rooms are clean and simple, often with cooking facilities, and most have private bathrooms. These establishments do not accept personal checks or credit cards, but do take reservations.

$ 🖭 **Adam's Guest House.** This economic choice near the Seaview Hotel is 1 mi (1½ km) south of downtown George Town and 4 mi (6½ km) from the beach. ⊠ *Melnac Ave., George Town (Box 312),* ☎ *345/949–2512,* ☎ FAX *345/949–0919,* WEB *www.adamsguesthouse.ky. 6 rooms. Some kitchenettes, no room phones, laundry facilities. MC, V. EP.*

$ 🖭 **Eldemire's Guest House.** Grand Cayman's first guest house has standard rooms, studio apartments, and a one-bedroom apartment. It's a 15-minute drive to Seven Mile Beach, but less than 1 mi (1½ km) south of pretty Smith Cove Bay. Continental breakfast comes only with the rooms. ⊠ *S. Church St. (Box 482),* ☎ *345/949–5387,* FAX *345/949–6987,* WEB *www.eldemire.com. 6 rooms, 4 studios, 1 1-bedroom apartment. Fans, some kitchenettes, some kitchens, no room phones. MC, V. EP, CP.*

Villas and Condominiums

Rates are higher in winter, and there may be a three- or seven-night minimum. These complexes are all similar, with telephones, satellite

TV, air-conditioning, living and dining areas, and patios. Differences arise in property amenities and proximity to town. The **Cayman Islands Department of Tourism** (WEB www.caymanislands.ky) provides a list of condominiums and small rental apartments.

$$$$ 🏨 **The Beachcomber.** Each of the simply furnished two-bedroom apartments in this older condo community has a view of the ocean from a private screened patio. When the sun gets too warm, you can retreat to the shade of the palabas on Seven Mile Beach or go snorkeling in the reef offshore. A grocery store is across the street, and there are places to shop and dine within walking distance, so you don't really need a car. ⊠ *West Bay Rd., Seven Mile Beach (Box 1799),* ☎ *345/945–4470,* FAX *345/945–5019,* WEB *www.beachcomber1.com. 23 condos. Grill, kitchens, pool, beach, laundry facilities. AE, MC, V. EP.*

$$$$ 🏨 **Discovery Point Club.** This secluded complex—all ocean-front suites— is at the far north end of Seven Mile Beach in West Bay, 6 mi (9½ km) from George Town. It has a lovely beach and great snorkeling in the protected waters of nearby Cemetery Reef. Tennis courts, a hot tub, a pool, and screened-in private porches add to the appeal here. Kids 6 and under stay free April–December. ⊠ *West Bay Rd., West Bay (Box 439),* ☎ *345/945–4724,* FAX *345/945–5051,* WEB *www.cayman.org/ discoverypoint. 45 units. Grill, pool, hot tub, 2 tennis courts, beach, laundry facilities. AE, MC, V. EP.*

$$$–$$$$ 🏨 **Caribbean Club.** For a quiet condo getaway, these 18 one- and two-bedroom villas (six on the beach) are a good choice. Although these units are not necessarily deluxe, they are secluded and have tidy tiled baths and simple wicker furniture. There's also maid service—always a plus. In the same complex, Lantana's restaurant serves Caribbean and American fare. ⊠ *West Bay Rd., Seven Mile Beach (Box 30499),* ☎ *345/945–4099,* FAX *345/945–4443,* WEB *www.caribclub.com. 18 villas. Restaurant, bar, kitchens, tennis court, beach, dry cleaning, laundry facilities, laundry service. AE, MC, V. EP, MAP.*

$$$–$$$$ 🏨 **Grape Tree/Cocoplum.** A half-mile (¾ km) from George Town on Seven Mile Beach, these sister condos are adjacent to one another. Grapetree's units are carpeted and have traditional wicker furnishings and a beige-and-brown color scheme. Cocoplum's units are similar, though they're decorated with Caribbean pastel prints, and their grounds have more plants and trees. ⊠ *West Bay Rd., Seven Mile Beach (Box 1802),* ☎ *345/949–5640,* FAX *345/949–0150,* WEB *www.grapetree.ky. 51 units. Kitchens, 2 pools, tennis court, beach. AE, MC, V. EP.*

$$$–$$$$ 🏨 **Villas of the Galleon.** Beach and golf are steps away from this property. The exteriors of these deluxe stucco cottages look shabby, but the interiors are attractive and beautifully maintained, and their location—on the widest section of Seven Mile Beach, just across from the Jack Nicklaus–designed Links Golf Club—couldn't be better. Each one- or two-bedroom unit has a terrace and enormous closets (a big plus for families); decor varies, though such tasteful touches as eggshell-tile floors, pastel finishes, and rattan furnishings are common. ⊠ *West Bay Rd., Seven Mile Beach (Box 1797),* ☎ *345/945–4433,* FAX *345/945– 4705,* WEB *www.villasofthegalleon.com. 74 units. Grill, kitchens, beach, laundry facilities. AE, D, MC, V. EP.*

$$–$$$$ 🏨 **Victoria House.** On a quiet stretch of beach 3 mi north of George Town, these simple one-, two-, and three-bedroom condos are decorated with muted Caribbean prints and rattan furniture. Choose from activities including tennis and water sports. If you're an early riser, you may catch a glimpse of giant sea turtles on the sand. ⊠ *West Bay Rd., Seven Mile Beach, near West Bay (Box 30571),* ☎ *345/945–4233,* FAX *345/945–5328,* WEB *www.victoriahouse.com. 25 units. Kitchens, tennis court, beach, snorkeling, laundry facilities. AE, MC, V. EP.*

$$$ ☷ **Retreat at Rum Point.** The resort has its own narrow beach with casuarina trees, far from the crowd. Up to six people can rent a two-bedroom villa here, and two or three people will be comfortable in a one-bedroom unit. These privately owned condos are individually decorated, but for the most part you'll find tropical motifs and wicker furniture. All units are spacious and have a washer and dryer. Take advantage of superb offshore diving (there are dive facilities nearby), including the famed North Wall. You'll be stranded without a car; it's a 35-minute drive to George Town or the airport. ✉ *North Side (Box 46),* ☎ *345/947–9135,* FAX *345/947–9058,* WEB *www.retreatcondos.com. 23 units. Restaurant, bar, kitchens, tennis court, pool, gym, sauna, beach, racquetball. AE, MC, V. EP.*

$$–$$$ ☷ **The Royal Reef.** This small, well-run timeshare property on the less hectic east end of Grand Cayman offers good value for the price. Consider renting a car as it's a 45-minute drive back to George Town. Each of the tile-floored villas has a roomy terrace facing the sea and can be divided into a large one-bedroom and studio for weekly rental throughout the year; the entire unit can sleep up to six. All have satellite TV; the larger ones have separate dining areas and stereos. ✉ *Queen's Hwy., East End (Box 20865 SMB),* ☎ *345/345–3100 or 800/221–8090; 954/485–5412 (reservations),* FAX *345/947–3191,* WEB *www.royalreef.com. 32 villas. Restaurant, bar, grocery, fans, some kitchens, kitchenettes, tennis court, pool, gym, hair salon, outdoor hot tub, massage, spa, beach, dive shop, dock, snorkeling, boating, bicycles, laundry facilities, concierge. AE, MC, V. EP.*

Dining

Grand Cayman's restaurants satisfy every palate. There are extravagant and expensive establishments and moderately priced ethnic eateries. Local hangouts that serve West Indian fare offer both flavor and value. Fish—including grouper, snapper, tuna, wahoo, and marlin—is served either simply baked, broiled, steamed, or Cayman style (with peppers, onions, and tomatoes). Conch, the meat of a large pink mollusk, is ubiquitous in stews and chowders and as fritters or panfried (cracked). Caribbean lobster is available but is often quite expensive, and other shellfish are in short supply in local waters. The only traditional culinary treat of the islands is turtle—served in soup or stew or as a steak—though fewer restaurants offer it these days.

Dining out here can be expensive, so replenish your cash reserves because some places do not accept plastic. Many restaurants add a 10%–15% service charge to the bill, so check before leaving a tip.

What to Wear

Smart casual wear (slacks and sundresses) is acceptable for dinner in all but a few places. The nicer resorts and more expensive restaurants may require a jacket, especially in high season; ask when making reservations. Shorts are usually acceptable during the day, but unless you're going to an ultracasual beach bar, beachwear (bathing suits, cover-ups, tank tops, etc.) is a no-no. Most restaurants have an alfresco dining section, and if you plan to dine under the stars, you may need a spritz of bug spray (mosquitoes can be pesky, especially at sunset), which most places provide.

CATEGORY	COST*
$$$$	over $30
$$$	$20–$30
$$	$10–$20
$	under $10

*per person for a main course at dinner

ASIAN

$$–$$$ ✕ **Thai Orchid.** It looks like a typical Thai restaurant, but the food more than makes up for the ordinary decor. Try the delicious *pad thai, ped phad khing* (crispy duck stir-fried with ginger and vegetables), or Thai spring rolls with marinated pork. Many vegetarian dishes are offered as well. The main difference between the lunch and dinner menus is the price. ⊠ *Queens Court Shopping Plaza, West Bay Rd., George Town,* ☎ *345/949–7955. AE, MC, V. No lunch Sun.*

CAFÉS

$ ✕ **The Coffee Grinder.** For breakfast or lunch that's tasty and light on your wallet, this bakery and deli serves wraps with ingredients like black beans, seasoned rice, and cheese; sandwich choices include Italian subs, Reubens, and roast turkey Waldorf on a sourdough walnut roll. For breakfast it's bagels, rolls, sweet pastries, and excellent coffees. Dine indoors or out on the sidewalk. ⊠ *Seven Mile Shops, West Bay Rd., George Town,* ☎ *345/949–6294. AE, MC, V. No dinner.*

$ ✕ **Dicken's Literary Cafe.** Located across the street from the popular Royal Palms beach area, this café provides a cool respite from the heat as well as the chance to check your e-mail on one of the four high-speed-Internet–connected computers. Food choices includes made-to-order sandwiches, quiches, pasteries, and desserts. Coffee refills are free, and several international newspapers are available for all to read. ⊠ *Galleria Plaza, West Bay Rd., George Town,* ☎ *345/945–9195. No credit cards. No dinner.*

CARIBBEAN

$$$–$$$$ ✕ **Hemingway's.** Sea views and breezes attract diners to this elegant
★   open-air restaurant in the Hyatt Regency Grand Cayman. Nouvelle Caribbean and seafood dishes include lemongrass-crusted grouper with *udon* noodles and baby Portobello mushrooms in a coconut sauce, and sugarcane-skewered tempura lobster with basil mashed potatoes and *ponzu* butter. Portions are large, and service is superb. ⊠ *Hyatt Regency Grand Cayman, West Bay Rd., Seven Mile Beach,* ☎ *345/945–5700. AE, D, DC, MC, V.*

$$–$$$$ ✕ **Almond Tree.** The large patio dining area combines architecture from the South Seas isle of Yap with bones, skulls, and bric-a-brac from Africa, South America, and the Pacific. Good-value seafood entrées include turtle steak and fresh snapper breaded with crushed almonds. For an after-dinner drink or a late dinner menu (served until 1 AM most nights) try their neighboring beach-side bar and grill, the Tree House Beach Bar. ⊠ *N. Church St., West Bay Rd., George Town,* ☎ *345/949–2893 Almond Tree; 345/945–0155 Tree House. AE, D, MC, V.*

$$ ✕ **Breadfruit Tree Garden Cafe.** Favored by locals, the jerk chicken rivals any on the island. Also on the menu are curry chicken and stewed pork, oxtail, rice and beans, and homemade soups. Drinks include breadfruit, mango, passion fruit, and carrot juices. The interior is kitschy, with silk roses, white porch swings, straw hats, empty birdcages, and fake ivy crawling along the ceiling. It's open until the wee hours, which makes it a good midnight munchie stop. ⊠ *58 Eastern Ave., George Town,* ☎ *345/945–2124. No credit cards.*

$–$$ ✕ **Champion House II.** Tucked back behind the original Champion House restaurant is this eatery serving tasty traditional island dishes, including marinated conch, curried goat, turtle stew, ackee, and cod fish—all served with rice and beans, plantains, and veggies. Try one of the fruit juices like tamarind, Irish moss, or soursop, or a spicy, homemade ginger beer. The entrées are large, and half portions are available. The breakfast and lunch buffets are quite popular and reasonably priced. ⊠ *43 Eastern Ave., George Town,* ☎ *345/949–7882. AE, MC, V.*

CONTEMPORARY

$$$–$$$$ ✗ **Lantana's.** The restaurant—on the edge of the Caribbean Club villa complex in the heart of Seven Mile Beach—creates excellent American-Caribbean dinners. Enjoy lobster quesadillas, homemade lamb sausage, or Cayman mahimahi with cardamom-scented tabbouleh and cassava fritters. *Don't* miss the incredible roasted garlic soup and the apple pie. The bi-level restaurant's simple décor—potted plants, teak furniture, painted wooden fish—places you in the perfectly serene island state of mind. ✉ *Caribbean Club, West Bay Rd., Seven Mile Beach,* ☎ *345/945–5595. AE, D, MC, V.*

CONTINENTAL

$$$–$$$$ ✗ **Grand Old House.** The menu here consists of Continental entrées and a few local specialties. Among the spicier appetizers is fried coconut shrimp with mustard apricot sauce. On the milder side are lobster served "the chef's way" (dipped in egg batter and sautéed with shallots, mushrooms, and white wine) and duck with fresh pear chutney. The ocean-side gazebos are surrounded by palms and cooled by ceiling fans; service is stellar. ✉ *S. Church St., George Town,* ☎ *345/949–9333. Reservations essential. DC, MC, V. Closed Sun. May–Nov. No lunch weekends.*

$$$–$$$$ ✗ **Ottmar's.** This quietly elegant restaurant is styled after a West Indian great house: jade carpeting, peach walls, mahogany furniture, glass
★   chandeliers, and a trickling fountain. Service is excellent. Favorites on the international menu include bouillabaisse, the Indonesian rijsttafel, and French pepper steak (flamed in cognac and doused with green peppercorn sauce and crème fraîche). ✉ *Grand Pavillion Commercial Centre, West Bay Rd., Seven Mile Beach,* ☎ *345/945–5879 or 345/945–5882. Reservations essential. AE, MC, V.*

ECLECTIC

$$–$$$$ ✗ **Rackam's Pub.** North of George Town, jutting out onto a jetty, is this low-key bar and grill popular for drinks and terrific sunset views. The young, friendly staff serves good jerk burgers (basted with Jamaican jerk sauce), grouper fish-and-chips, and tasty chiles rellenos. ✉ *N. Church St., George Town,* ☎ *345/945–3860. AE, MC, V.*

ITALIAN

$$–$$$$ ✗ **Lighthouse at Breakers.** About a 25-minute drive from Seven Mile Beach, this restaurant offers seaside dining with good food, a well-chosen wine list (with an especially good selection of wines by the glass), and stellar desserts. Start with the salad of green asparagus points and baby field greens or flash-fried calamari; pastas are all a good bet as are yellowfin tuna with a brandy peppercorn sauce or the char-grilled veal chop. Save room for dessert, especially the hot chocolate soufflé or some of the homemade ice creams. Reservations are essential for dinner. ✉ *Breakers,* ☎ *345/947–2047. AE, MC, V.*

$$–$$$$ ✗ **Ristorante Papagallo.** If you're not taking a cab, be sure to pack a map for the journey down twisted, unmarked roads to this oversize Polynesian hut at the northernmost tip of the island. Try the arugula salad with mango vinaigrette, followed by the blackened yellowtail or the snapper fillet with pineapple salsa. Caymanians and tourists alike say it's worth the trip for the island's best Italian-Caribbean fusion cuisine. ✉ *Conch Point Rd., West Bay,* ☎ *345/949–1119,* FAX *345/949–1114. Reservations essential. AE, MC, V. No lunch.*

SEAFOOD

$$$–$$$$ ✗ **The Reef Grill at Royal Palms.** The impeccable service by the knowledgeable wait staff is only surpassed by the divine food served in an elegant dining room or on the more casual garden patio. Try the signature honey-soy glazed sea bass in a mild Thai curry sauce; it's ten-

der, succulent, and served with coconut rice and a spicy sautéed red cabbage. Other creative dishes include pepper-crusted yellowfin tuna and plank-roasted barbecue salmon. Desserts include fresh sorbets, crème brûlée, and chocolate almond mousse. The adjoining beach bar is a popular night spot with live bands most evenings. ⊠ *West Bay Rd., Seven Mile Beach,* ☎ *345/945–6358. Reservations essential. AE, D, MC, V. No lunch.*

$$$–$$$$ ✕ **The Wharf.** Managed by Austrians, this tidy blue-and-white restaurant overlooks the sea. On the surf-and-turf menu are conch fritters, home-smoked salmon, turtle steak, broiled lobster, and steak fillet béarnaise; anything on the fresh daily menu is also recommended. A harpist entertains after a lively happy hour band. The Ports of Call bar is a perfect spot from which to watch the sun set, and tarpon feeding off the deck is a nightly (9 PM) spectacle here. ⊠ *West Bay Rd., George Town,* ☎ *345/949–2231. AE, MC, V.*

$$$–$$$$ ✕ **Smuggler's Cove.** The comfortable, candlelit dining room and lovely
  ★   deck overlooking the ocean are perfect spots to bring someone for a special or romantic dinner. Excellent appetizers include tuna carpaccio marinated in basil and dill, and jerk duck seasoned with pimiento and scotch bonnet peppers. The best entrées are those with Caribbean lobster—particularly the Smuggler's Fillet (a lobster-stuffed beef tenderloin seared in rosemary butter and glazed with port). ⊠ *N. Church St., George Town,* ☎ *345/949–6003. Reservations essential. AE, D, MC, V. No lunch weekends.*

$$–$$$$ ✕ **Lobster Pot.** The second-floor terrace of this cozy restaurant overlooks the bay downtown, offering a perfect sunset view. The menu includes Continental dishes and such Caribbean specialties as conch chowder, seafood curry, shrimp Diane, and, of course, lobster. This place is popular, and the constant turnover makes it feel a little frenzied at times. If you can't make it for dinner, drop by the pub and have a frozen banana daiquiri. ⊠ *N. Church St., George Town,* ☎ *345/949–2736. AE, D, MC, V.*

Beaches

Cayman Kai. This favored hideaway is on the north side of the island.
East End. The best windsurfing is just off the beaches of Grand Cayman's East End, at Colliers, by Morritt's Tortuga Club.
Rum Point. This North Sound beach is convenient for snorkeling and has a bar and grill especially popular on Sundays.
Seven Mile Beach. Although Grand Cayman has several smaller beaches, Grand Cayman's west coast, the most developed area of the entire colony, is where you'll find the famous Seven Mile Beach—5½ mi (9 km) long—and its expanses of powdery white sand. The beach is litter-free and sans peddlers, so you can relax in an unspoiled and almost hassle-free (if somewhat crowded) environment. This is also Grand Cayman's busiest vacation center, and most of the island's accommodations, restaurants, and shopping centers are on this strip. You'll also find headquarters for the island's aquatic activities.
Smith's Cove. Off South Church Street and south of the Grand Old House, this is a popular local bathing spot on weekends.
Water Cay. If you seek a little more privacy than you can find on Seven Mile Beach, head to a more isolated, unspoiled beach.

Outdoor Activities and Sports

Participant Sports

FISHING
If you enjoy action fishing, Cayman waters have plenty to offer. Some 25 boats are available for charter, offering fishing options that include

deep-sea, reef, bone, tarpon, light-tackle, and fly-fishing. **Bayside Watersports** (☎ 345/949–3200) offers half-day snorkeling trips, North Sound Beach lunch excursions, and full-day deep-sea fishing and dinner cruises. **Burton's Tourist Information & Activity Services** (☎ 345/949–6598) can hook you up with a number of different charters and tours. **Captain Alphonso Ebanks** (☎ 345/949–1012) specializes in fishing and snorkeling tours to Stingray City and has half- and full-day tours. **Island Girl** (☎ 345/947–3029) offers customized private fishing and snorkeling charters; deep-sea fishing excursions include trolling, live bait, and drift fishing for yellowfin tuna and marlin; night fishing trips are also available.

GOLF

The **Grand Cayman–Britannia** golf course (West Bay Rd., Seven Mile Beach, ☎ 345/949–8020), next to the Hyatt Regency, was designed by Jack Nicklaus. The course is really three in one—a 9-hole, par-70 regulation course, an 18-hole, par-57 executive course, and a Cayman course (played with a Cayman ball that goes about half the distance of a regulation ball). Greens fees run $40–$90, and golf carts ($15–$25) are mandatory. Windier, and therefore more challenging, than most courses is the **Links at Safe Haven** (off West Bay Rd., Seven Mile Beach, ☎ 345/949–5988), Cayman's first 18-hole championship golf course, which is a botanical garden of indigenous trees, plants, and flowering shrubs. The Roy Case–designed, par-71, 6,605-yard course also has an aqua driving range (the distance markers and balls float), a clubhouse, pro shop, and restaurant. Greens fees run to $60. Golf carts ($15–$20 per person) are mandatory.

HORSEBACK RIDING

Nicki's Beach Rides (✉ Box 482, ☎ 345/945–5839) offers 1½-hour leisurely family horseback rides along one of the many white-sand beaches; the guides provide bits of island history and lore as you ride. **Pampered Ponies** (✉ Box 455, ☎ 345/945–2262 or 345/916–2540) has horses trained to walk, trot, and canter along the beaches and beach trails. Private rides, early mornings, sunsets, and evenings under the moonlight available.

HIKING

Guided nature walks are available at the National Trust's **Mastic Trail** (✉ Off Frank Sound Rd., Breakers, ☎ 345/945–6588), a rugged 2-mi (3-km) slash through pristine woodlands, mangrove swamps, and ancient rock formations. There is no entry fee; guided hikes are $45 and run daily 9–5 by appointment only.

SCUBA DIVING AND SNORKELING

Pristine water (visibility often exceeding 100 ft [30 m]), breathtaking coral formations, and plentiful and exotic marine life mark the **Great Wall**—a world-renowned dive site just off the north side of Grand Cayman. A must-see for adventurous souls is **Stingray City** in the North Sound, noted as the best 12-ft (3½-m) dive in the world, where dozens of stingrays congregate, tame enough to suction squid from your outstretched palm. Nondivers gravitate to **Stingray Sandbar,** a shallower part of the North Sound, which has become a popular snorkeling spot, which is also a popular spot for the stingrays. **Trinity Caves** in West Bay is a deep dive with numerous canyons starting at about 60 ft (18½ m). **Orange Canyon** starts at the edge of a wall at about 40 ft (12 m) and is an easy shallow dive. The best shore-entry snorkeling spots are off the ironshore south of George Town, at **Eden Rock**; north of town, at the reef off the West Bay Cemetery on Grand Cayman's **west coast**; and in the reef-protected shallows of the island's **north and south coasts,** where coral and fish life are much more varied and abundant.

Since Grand Cayman is one of the Caribbean's top diving destinations, you will find many top-notch dive operations offering instruction and equipment. Divers are required to be certified and possess a "C" card. Otherwise, you can take a full certification course, which costs $350–$400, lasts four to six days, and includes classroom, pool, boat sessions, and checkout dives. A short resort course lasts a day, costs about $80–$100, and introduces novices to the sport and teaches the rudimentary skills needed to make a shallow, instructor-monitored dive. A single-tank dive averages $50; a two-tank dive, about $75. Snorkel-equipment rental runs $5–$15 a day. Most operations rent gear and underwater photography equipment.

There are many dive operators in Grand Cayman. Call the **Cayman Islands Watersports Operators Association** (☎ 345/949–8522) for details on local providers. **Aquanauts** (☎ 345/945–1990 or 888/786–6887) is at Morgans Harbour just minutes from spectacular North and West Walls; complimentary shuttle service is available. **Bob Soto's** (☎ 345/949–2871 or 800/262–7686) was the first dive operation in Cayman and now has several island locations; it has film-processing facilities and underwater photo courses. One-week live-aboard dive cruises are available on the 110-ft **Cayman Aggressor III** (☎ 800/348–2628), which cruises around all three of the Cayman Islands. **Don Foster's** (☎ 345/949–5679 or 800/833–4837) is headquartered in George Town and offers both film processing and underwater photo courses. **Eden Rock** (☎ 345/949–7243) provides easy access to excellent George Town shore diving at Eden Rocks and Devil's Grotto; both reefs are a short swim from shore. **Red Sail Sports** (☎ 345/949–8745 or 800/255–6425) offers daily trips to Stingray City and has locations at many Grand Cayman hotels along Seven Mile Beach. **Sunset Divers** (☎ 345/949–7111 or 800/854–4767) has six dive boats, great shore diving, Nitrox tanks, and rebreathers. **Turtle Reef Divers** (☎ 345/949–1700) offers Nitrox dives and certification; it is next to the Turtle Farm, where there are some excellent shore dives.

TENNIS AND SQUASH

The **South Sound Squash Club** (⊠ S. Sound Rd., George Town, ☎ 345/949–9469) has courts available to the general public. Call the resident pro, John McCrury, for a court or game.

WINDSURFING

Cayman Windsurf (☎ 345/947–7492) offers lessons and rentals on the east end of the island at Morritt's Tortuga Beach Club and on North Sound by Safe Haven. **Sailboards Caribbean** (⊠ West Bay Rd., West Bay, ☎ 345/949–1068) offers windsurfing rentals and lessons for everyone.

Shopping

On Grand Cayman the good news is that there's no sales tax *and* there's plenty of duty-free merchandise. The bad news is that prices on imported merchandise—English china, Swiss watches, French perfumes, and Japanese cameras and electronic goods—are not always lower than elsewhere. Locally made items to watch for include woven mats, baskets, jewelry made of a marblelike stone called caymanite (from the cliffs of Cayman Brac), and authentic sunken treasure. Cigar lovers take note: some shops carry Cohiba and Partagas brands (but enjoy them on the island, as bringing them back to the United States is illegal).

Although you'll find black coral products in Grand Cayman, they're controversial. Most of the coral used to make items sold here comes from Belize and Honduras because Cayman Islands marine law prohibits the removal of live coral from its own sea. Black coral grows at a very slow rate (3 inches every 10 years), it is often designated as an endangered species, and reefs are not always harvested carefully. Environmental groups generally discourage people from purchasing coral products.

Areas and Malls

The main shopping areas are **Elizabethan Square, Cardinal Avenue,** and the chic **Kirk Freeport Plaza,** known for its fine jewelry, plus duty-free china, crystal, Gucci items, perfumes, and fine cosmetics. The **Queen's Court Shopping Centre,** on Seven Mile Beach close to town, has shops that sell souvenirs, crafts, and gifts. At the **West Shore Shopping Centre** or the **Galleria Shopping Plaza,** both on Seven Mile Beach, you'll find good-quality island art, beachwear, and more.

Specialty Items

ART

The waterfront **Artifacts** gallery (Harbour Dr., George Town, ☎ 345/949–2442) sells Spanish pieces of eight, doubloons, and Halcyon Days' enamels, which are handpainted collectible pillboxes made in England. **Cathy Church's Underwater Photo Centre and Gallery** (⊠ S. Church St., George Town, ☎ 345/949–7415) has a collection of spectacular underwater photos by the famed photographer Cathy Church. At **Cayman Glassblowing Studio** (⊠ N. Church St., George Town, ☎ 345/949–7020) you can watch artisans create vibrantly colored glass sculptures, vases, and more. You'll find original prints, paintings, and sculpture with a tropical theme at **Island Art Gallery** (⊠ Anchorage Shopping Centre, George Town, ☎ 345/949–9861). The **Kennedy Gallery** (⊠ West Shore Centre, West Bay Rd., George Town, ☎ 345/949–8077) sells lithographs and prints depicting the Cayman Islands by local artists. Debbie van der Bol runs the arts-and-crafts shop **Pure Art** (⊠ S. Church St., George Town, ☎ 345/949–9133; ⊠ Hyatt Regency, West Bay Rd., Seven Mile Beach, ☎ 345/945–5633), which sells watercolors, wood carvings, and lacework by local artists, as well as her own sketches and cards.

CLOTHES

Calico Jack's (⊠ West Bay Rd., George Town, ☎ 345/949–4373) is a good source for T-shirts, casual resort wear, and dive gear. **St. Michael** (⊠ Galleria Plaza, off West Bay Rd., George Town, ☎ 345/945–5165) sells clothes and other items.

FOODSTUFFS

For groceries and pharmaceutical needs, try **Foster's Food Fair** (⊠ Strand Shopping Center, George Town, ☎ 345/945–4748 store; 345/945–7759 pharmacy), a huge modern supermarket just off Seven Mile Beach. The **Tortuga Rum Company** (⊠ N. Sound Rd., George Town, ☎ 345/949–7701 or 345/949–7867) has scrumptious rum cake (sealed fresh) that's sweet and moist and makes a great souvenir.

HANDICRAFTS

The coral creations of **Bernard Passman** (⊠ Fort St., George Town, ☎ 345/949–0123) have won the approval of the British royal family, and the pope even owns a piece of Passman's work. **Carey Cayman Coral** (⊠ S. Sound Rd., George Town, no phone) is a workshop run by Carey Hurlstone, who carves glass and makes black coral jewelry and figurines. The **Heritage Crafts Shop** (George Town, ☎ 345/945–6041), near the harbor, sells local crafts and gifts. You'll find beautiful coral pieces at **Richard's Fine Jewelry** (⊠ Harbour Dr., George Town, ☎ 345/949–7156), where designers Richard and Rafaela Barile attract a share of celebrities.

Nightlife

Look at the free *What's Hot* or check the Friday edition of the *Caymanian Compass* for listings of music, movies, theater, and other entertainment.

On Tuesdays and Wednesdays locals go to **Legendz** (⊠ West Bay Rd., George Town, ☎ 345/945–1950) for the live bands and comedy night, respectively. The **Cracked Conch** (⊠ West Bay Rd., West Bay, near the Turtle Farm, ☎ 345/945–5217) is where islanders congregate on Thursday night for karaoke, classic dive films, and happy hour. On Friday nights the locals head to **Bed** (⊠ Harquail Bypass, George Town, ☎ 345/949–7199), a popular bar and restaurant with a comfortable lounge and servers in pajamas. **Royal Palms** (⊠ West Bay Rd., George Town, ☎ 345/945–6358) is where local bands play Wednesday through Saturday nights; it's an outdoor beach bar with plenty of room for dancing under the stars. If you are dying to see a film, **Cinema 1 & 2** (⊠ Harquail Bypass, George Town, ☎ 345/949–4011 for show times) is across from Bed.

Exploring Grand Cayman

The historic capital of George Town, which is at one end of Seven Mile Beach, is easy to explore on foot. If you're a shopper, you can spend days here; otherwise, you can tour downtown in an hour. To see the rest of the island, rent a car or scooter or take a guided tour. The portion of the island called West Bay is noted for its jumble of affluent colonial neighborhoods and rather tawdry tourist attractions. A drive along West Bay Road will take you past the dense Seven Mile Beach area and into a less congested scene. It's about a half hour to West Bay from George Town. The less developed East End has natural attractions, from blowholes to botanical gardens, as well as the remains of the original settlements. Plan on at least 45 minutes for the drive out from George Town. You need a day to circle and explore the entire island—including a stop at a beach for a picnic or swim.

Numbers in the margin correspond to points of interest on the Grand Cayman map.

Sights to See

⑨ Blow Holes. These make the ultimate photo opportunity as crashing waves force water into caverns and send geysers shooting up through the ironshore. Frank Sound Rd., near East End.

⑥ Bodden Town. In the island's original south-shore capital you'll find an old cemetery on the shore side of the road. Graves with A-frame structures are said to contain the remains of pirates. There are also the ruins of a fort and a wall erected by slaves in the 19th century. A curio shop serves as the entrance to what's called the Pirate's Caves, partially underground natural formations that are more hokey (decked out with fake treasure chests and mannequins in pirate garb) than spooky.

☝ ③ Cayman Island Turtle Farm. Hurricane Michelle devastated Grand Cayman's most popular tourist attraction in 2001. The most extensive damage was to the breeding ponds, display tanks, and snack bar/gift shop. Though only about a third of the turtles were washed out to sea, most of these were the breeders. You can still see thousands of turtles displayed in holding tanks across the street from the original location. Rebuilding is in progress. ⊠ *West Bay Rd.,* ☎ *345/949-3893.* ➲ *$6.* ☉ *Mon.–Sat. 8:30–5.*

① George Town. Begin exploring the capital by strolling along the waterfront, Harbour Drive. The circular gazebo is where passengers from the cruise ships disembark. Diagonally across the street from the cruise ship dock is the **Elmslie Memorial United Church,** named after Scotsman James Elmslie, the first Presbyterian missionary to serve in the Caymans. The church was the first concrete-block building built in the Cayman Islands. Its vaulted ceiling, wooden arches, and sedate nave reflect the quietly religious nature of island residents. Along your rambles in George Town you'll easily come across **Fort Street,** a main shopping street where you'll also notice the small clock tower dedicated to Britain's King George V and the huge fig tree manicured into an umbrella shape. Here, too, is a statue of national hero James Bodden, the father of Cayman tourism. Across the street is the Cayman Islands Legislative Assembly Building, next door to the 1919 Peace Memorial Building. That the Caymanians built a memorial to peace rather than war speaks to their character.

On **Edward Street** you'll find the charming library, built in 1939; it has English novels, current newspapers from the United States, and a small reference section. It's worth a visit just for its old-fashioned charms and a look at the shields with insignias of Britain's prominent institutions of learning; they decorate the ceiling beams. Across the street is the courthouse. Down the next block is the financial district, where banks from all over the world have offices.

Down from the financial district is the **General Post Office,** also built in 1939, with its strands of decorative colored lights and some 2,000 private mailboxes on the outside (mail is not delivered on the island). Behind the post office is **Elizabethan Square,** a shopping and office complex on Shedden Road with food, clothing, and souvenir establishments. The courtyard has benches placed around a garden and a fountain; it's a pleasant place to rest your feet.

Built in 1833, the home of the **Cayman Islands National Museum** has had several different incarnations over the years, including that of courthouse, jail (now the gift shop), post office, and dance hall. It's small but fascinating, with excellent displays and videos that illustrate local geology, flora, fauna, and island history. Pick up a walking-tour map of George Town at the museum gift shop before leaving. ✉ *Harbour Dr., George Town,* ☏ *345/949–8368.* ✉ *$5.* ⊙ *Weekdays 9–5, Sat. 10–2.*

❹ **Hell.** This tiny village is little more than a patch of incredibly jagged rock formations called ironshore. The big attraction here is the small post office and a nearby gift shop, where you can get cards and letters postmarked from Hell (a postcard of bikini-clad beauties emblazoned with WHEN HELL FREEZES OVER gives you a picture of what this place is like).

❼ **Mastic Trail.** In the 1800s this woodland trail was often used as a shortcut to and from the North Side. The low-lying area was full of hardwood trees, including mahogany, West Indian cedar, and the mastic that early settlers used in building their homes. Along the trail you'll see an abundance of trees, birds, and plants unique to this old-growth forest. Walk it on your own (about two hours round trip) or call the National Trust to book a guide. ✉ *Frank Sound Rd., entrance by the fire station and across from the Botanic Park,* ☏ *345/949–0121 for guide reservations.*

❷ **Old Homestead.** Formerly known as the West Bay Pink House, this is probably the most photographed home in Grand Cayman. The pink-and-white Caymanian cottage was built in 1912 of wattle and daub around an ironwood frame. Cheery Mac Bothwell, who grew up in the house, takes you on tours that present a nostalgic and touching look at life in Grand Cayman before the tourism and banking booms. ⊠ *West Bay Rd., West Bay,* ☎ *345/949–7639.* ⊡ *$5.* ☉ *Mon.–Sat. 8–5.*

☺ ❺ **Pedro St. James Castle.** Built in 1780, the great house is Cayman's oldest stone structure and the only remaining late-18th-century residence on the island. The buildings are surrounded by 8 acres of natural parks and woodlands. You can stroll through landscaping of native Caymanian flora and experience one of the most spectacular views on the island from atop the dramatic Great Pedro Bluff. Don't miss the impressive multimedia theater show complete with smoking pots, misting rains, and two film screens where the story of Pedro's Castle is presented. The show plays on the hour; see it before you tour the site. ⊠ *S. Sound Rd., Savannah,* ☎ *345/947–3329.* ⊡ *$8.*

❽ **Queen Elizabeth II Botanic Park.** This 65-acre wilderness preserve showcases a wide range of indigenous and nonindigenous tropical vegetation. Interpretive signs identify the flora along the walking trail. Rare blue iguanas are bred and released in the gardens; there's usually one named Charlie hanging around the entrance gate. You can also see native orchids and, if you're lucky, the brilliant green Cayman parrot. ⊠ *Frank Sound Rd., Frank Sound,* ☎ *345/947–9462; 345/947–3558 (info line),* ⫽ *345/947–7873.* ⊡ *$3.* ☉ *Daily 9–6:30 (last admission at 5:30).*

❿ **Queen's View.** This functions as both an eastern lookout point and has a monument that commemorates the legendary Wreck of the Ten Sails, which took place just offshore. ⊠ *Queens Hwy., East End.*

CAYMAN BRAC

Brac, the Gaelic word for "bluff," aptly identifies this island's most distinctive feature, a rugged limestone cliff that runs down the center of the 12-mi (19-km) island and soars to 140 ft (43 m) at its eastern end. Lying 89 mi (143 km) northeast of Grand Cayman, Brac is accessible via Cayman Airways and Island Air. Only 1,200 people live on the island, in communities such as Watering Place and Spot Bay. Residents are very friendly, so it's easy to strike up conversation; in fact, you'll often have to be the one to end the chat if you expect to do anything else that day.

Lodging

Hotels here are usually a better value than their prices indicate at first glance. Rates often include meals, if not drinks and diving. In addition, lodgings are much cozier and more intimate than their Grand Cayman counterparts, and hoteliers often treat their guests like family. Most hotels give you the option of including all meals in your stay, but there are a few restaurants on the island. To reach them, however, you'll need a taxi or a bike (most hotels have these for guest use). Most restaurants serve island fare (stewed fish, conch fritters, curries), and portions are generally large.

For approximate costs, *see* the lodging price chart *in* Grand Cayman.

Hotels

$$ 🏨 **Brac Caribbean.** This condo complex offers all the comforts of
★   home in one- to four-bedroom units. Each unit has white tile floors, light peach stucco walls, and a private balcony overlooking the sea. ⊠ *Stake Bay (Box 4),* ☎ *345/948–2265 or 800/791–7911,* ⫽ *345/948–2206. 14 condos. Restaurant, bar, pool, hot tub, dive shop, fishing, bicycles. AE, MC, V. CP.*

$ 🏨 **Brac Reef Beach Resort.** Popular with divers, this well-run resort sits on a large stretch of beach with plenty of shade trees and hammocks strung about. The large dock is illuminated nightly and attracts everything from stingrays to squid to tarpon, a great place to hang out after dinner. The modest all-inclusive package rates include three buffet meals daily, all drinks, airport transfers, and taxes and service charges for two persons; dive packages cost a little more. ✉ *Brac Reef Beach (Box 56),* ☎ *345/948–1323; 800/327–3835; 727/323–8727 in FL;* FAX *727/323–8827,* WEB *www.bracreef.com. 40 rooms. Restaurant, bar, tennis court, pool, gym, hot tub, massage, spa, beach, dive shop, dock, snorkeling, bicycles, meeting rooms. AE, D, MC, V. All-inclusive, EP, FAP, MAP.*

$ 🏨 **La Esperanza.** This modest, family-run property on the north side of the island offers four two-bedroom apartments with fully equipped kitchens and a three-bedroom house with two baths. Guest quarters have white tile floors and simple furnishings. The seaside restaurant terrace offers breathtaking Cayman Brac sunsets—and the owner's famous jerk chicken, which he prepares by the side of the road every Friday and Saturday night. ✉ *Stake Bay (Box 28),* ☎ *345/948–0531 or 345/948–0591,* FAX *345/948–0525,* WEB *www.candw.ky/users/cay06865. 11 rooms. Restaurant, bar, kitchens, shop, laundry facilities. AE, MC, V. MAP.*

$ 🏨 **Walton's Mango Manor.** This tranquil, two-story traditional West
★ Indian home has five rooms (with bath). Beautiful antique furnishings and architectural details abound. The nearby ironshore beach is the perfect place for a sunrise walk. The proprietors love to relate Brac history and help you make arrangements for game-fishing trips, scuba-diving excursions, and other activities. As only breakfast is included, you'll need a car so you can get out for other meals and exploring the island. The newly built seaside cottage is spacious and private. ✉ *Stake Bay (Box 56),* ☎ FAX *345/948–0518. 5 rooms, 1 cottage. Fans. AE, MC, V. CP.*

Beaches

Southwest Coast. The accommodations on the southwest coast have fine small beaches, better for sunning than for snorkeling because of the abundance of turtle grass in the water. Everyone is welcome on hotel beaches.

Outdoor Activities and Sports

HIKING

Nature trails abound on the Brac. Get nature tourism maps at the airport or your hotel. To encourage more hikers, free guides are available from **Brac Tourism Office** (✉ Stake Bay [near the airport], ☎ 345/948–1849). It's easy to hike on your own (look for white heritage markers along the way), though some trails could be better maintained.

SCUBA DIVING AND SNORKELING

The waters off Cayman Brac are more pristine than those off Grand Cayman, so you'll see more (and larger) critters. The snorkeling is excellent off the **north coast.** Many fish have taken to the Russian warship that was scuttled offshore from the now-defunct Buccaneer's Inn. (Look for the beautiful queen angelfish that makes its home between two of the guns.) All the ship's doors have been removed, so you can swim through it—not for the faint of heart as it's pitch black in some spaces.

Two-tank dives cost $60–$70 at **Brac Aquatics** (☎ 345/948–1429 or 800/544–2722), a full-service dive operation that offers courses in addition to daily and packaged dive rates. **Brac Reef Divers** (☎ 345/948–

1323) offers scuba and snorkeling gear and courses, with two-tank dives priced around $60–$70.

SPELUNKING

If you plan to explore any of Cayman Brac's caves, wear sneakers as some of the paths are steep and rocky. **Peter's Cave** is a great place to view the south side bluffs. **Great Cave** is near the old lighthouse and has numerous stalagmites and stalactites. **Bat Cave** is well lighted and where you'll most likely see bats hanging from the ceiling. **Rebecca's Cave** has a grave site where a Cayman Brac family buried baby Rebeka who lost her life during a hurricane in 1932.

Exploring Cayman Brac

Cayman Brac Museum. In addition to displaying implements used in the daily lives of Bracers in the 1920s and '30s, this two-room museum exhibits a few oddities, such as a 4,000-year-old axe. Examples of Brac flora on the property include unusual orchids, mangoes, papaya, agave, and cacti. ⊠ *Old Government Administration Bldg., Stake Bay,* ☎ *345/948–2622.* ☞ *Free.* ☉ *Weekdays 9–noon and 1–4, Sat. 9–noon. Closed Sun.*

Parrot Preserve. The easiest place to spot the endangered Cayman Brac parrot is in this preserve on Major Donald Drive (also known as Lighthouse Road). This 6-mi (9½-km) dirt road also leads to ironshore cliffs that offer the best panoramic view of North East Point and the open ocean, it's the best place to view sunrise.

LITTLE CAYMAN

Only 7 mi (11 km) from Cayman Brac, Little Cayman has a population of about 100 on its 12 square mi (31 square km). This is a true hideaway: few phones, fewer shops, no man-made sights or nightlife to speak of—just spectacular diving, great fishing, fantastic bird-watching, placid beaches, and laid-back camaraderie. The newest attraction is a luxurious nature spa, which offers pampering services such as full-body massages, body wraps, and facials; it's fast becoming a popular indulgence for locals and visitors.

Lodging

Accommodations are mostly in small lodges, many of which offer meal and dive packages. The meal packages are a good idea; the chefs in most places are impeccably trained.

For approximate costs, *see* the lodging price chart *in* Grand Cayman.

Hotels

$$$ ⊞ **Pirates Point Resort.** The guest-house feel of this informal resort generates almost instant camaraderie among those who stay here—and many return. Owner Gladys Howard's down-home welcome (she's originally from Texas) belies her upscale meals (she trained at Cordon Bleu with Julia Child, James Beard, and Jacques Pepin). The main building and the rooms have tile floors, ceiling fans, and white rattan and wicker furnishings. All-inclusive rates include mouthwatering meals, alcoholic beverages, and two daily boat dives; nondiver packages available. ⊠ *Preston Bay (Box 43),* ☎ *345/948–1010,* ᖴᐱᕽ *345/948–1011. 10 rooms. Restaurant, bar, no air-conditioning in some rooms, gym, dive shop, bicycles, airport shuttle. MC, V. All-inclusive, FAP.*

$$$ ⊞ **Southern Cross Club.** The stunning beach is dotted with brightly colored cottages, all with fabulous sea views. Pastel colors and wicker furniture keep you comfortable, while tile floors and swirling fans keep you cool. Service and meals are impeccable, though diving and fish-

ing are the true draws here. Wading through seagrass is the norm on all resort beaches. But this resort is near secluded Owen Island, which has a lovely sandy beach; it's a short kayak away. ⊠ *South Hole Sound (Box 44),* ☎ *345/948–1099 or 800/899–2582,* FAX *317/636–9503,* WEB *www.southerncrossclub.com. 11 rooms. Restaurant, bar, dive shop, snorkeling, fishing, bicycles, airport shuttle. AE, MC, V. FAP.*

$$–$$$ 🏨 **Little Cayman Beach Resort.** The rooms in this two-story property have contemporary furnishings and tropical, jewel-tone color schemes. Some rooms have water views and will be quieter than those facing the bar. The resort offers fishing and diving packages and also caters to bird-watchers and soft-adventure ecotourists. Check out the affiliated Nature Spa for pampering treatments like marine algae body masks, sea salt body polishes, and relaxing massages. All-inclusive packages (for spa goers, divers, and nondivers). ⊠ *Blossom Village (Box 51),* ☎ *345/948–1033 or 800/327 3835,* FAX *345/948–1040,* WEB *www. littlecayman.com. 40 rooms. Restaurant, bar, tennis court, pool, gym, hot tub, spa, dive shop, fishing, bicycles, shops, meeting rooms. AE, MC, V. All-inclusive, EP, FAP, MAP.*

$$ 🏨 **Sam McCoy's Diving and Fishing Resort.** Stays here are ultracasual. Bedrooms (all with bath) are simple but cheerful and are done in royal and powder blues. You eat at beachside barbecues or with Sam, the good-natured owner, and his family. "Relaxing" rates (for nondivers) include three meals a day and airport transfers; all-inclusive rates also include beach and boat diving. Sam is a *very* experienced fishing guide; his bonefishing trips cost around $45 an hour for two (slightly less for one). ⊠ *North Side (Box 12),* ☎ *345/948–0026 or 800/626–0496,* FAX *345/948–0057,* WEB *mccoyslodge.com.ky. 8 rooms. Fans, pool. AE, MC, V. All-inclusive, FAP.*

Villas

$$$$ 🏨 **Conch Club.** These two- to three-bedroom town homes can sleep four
★ to six people, are well appointed, and have pretty aqua floor tiles, vaulted ceilings, fully equipped kitchens, decks, and patios overlooking the sea. As a guest here, you can use all the facilities of the Little Cayman Beach Resort less than ¼ mi away. These spacious units are a good option for families and couples traveling together. There are also a dock and huts for dive gear. ⊠ *Blossom Village (Box 51),* ☎ *345/948–1033 or 800/327–3835. 15 condos. Kitchens, pool, hot tub, spa, dive shop, bicycles, gift shop. AE, MC, V. All-inclusive, FAP, MAP.*

$$ 🏨 **Paradise Villas.** The cozy one-bedroom units have terraces that
★ open onto the beach. Your quarters are simply but immaculately appointed with rattan furnishings and muted abstract fabrics. Each cottage has a few hammocks for those lazy days when you don't want to go on a dive. If you get tired of cooking for yourself in the well-equipped kitchens, delicious island-style food (not to mention the island's only bar) is just steps away at the Hungry Iguana restaurant. ⊠ *Southern Hole Sound (Box 48),* ☎ *345/948–0001,* FAX *345/948–0002. 12 units. Kitchens, pool, dive shop, bicycles, gift shop. AE, MC, V.*

Beaches

Sandy Point. This beach, at the eastern tip of Little Cayman, is an isolated patch of powder and worth every effort to reach by boat, car, or bike.

Owen Island. Rowboating distance (200 yards [183 m]) from the south coast, this island has a sandy beach. You can pack a picnic lunch and spend the day.

Outdoor Activities and Sports

BIRD-WATCHING

Governor Gore Bird Sanctuary is home for 5,000 pairs of red-footed boobies (the largest colony in the western hemisphere) and 1,000 magnificent frigate birds. You may catch black frigates and snowy egrets competing for lunch in dramatic dive-bombing battles. The sanctuary is near the airport.

FISHING

Bloody Bay, off the north coast, has spectacular fishing, including angling for tarpon and bonefish. Sam McCoy, of **Sam McCoy's Fishing & Diving** (☎ 345/948–0026 or 800/626–0496), is among the premier fishermen on the island. The **Southern Cross Club** (☎ 800/899–2582), a resort near South Hole Sound, also offers deep-sea fishing trips for nonguests.

SCUBA DIVING AND SNORKELING

Jacques Cousteau considered **Bloody Bay Wall,** just 15 minutes from Little Cayman by boat, one of the world's top dives. The drop begins at a mere 18 ft (6 m) and plunges to more than 1,000 ft (306 m), with visibility often reaching 150 ft (46 m)—diving doesn't get much better than this. Expect to pay $60–$75 for a two-tank boat dive. Most hotels have diving instructors and equipment.

Kirk Sea Tours (☎ 345/949–6986) runs frequent snorkel and scuba diving excursions. The luxury yacht *Little Cayman Diver II* (☎ 800/458–2722) offers one-week dive cruises focusing on the pristine dive sites around Little Cayman. **Paradise Divers** (☎ 345/948–0001) runs a 46-ft pontoon boat from the North Coast of Little Cayman to Bloody Bay and Jackson Bay. **Reef Divers** (☎ 345/948–1033) has its own dock and a full-service photo and video center. **Sam McCoy's Fishing & Diving** (☎ 345/948–0026 or 800/626–0496) is run by a Little Cayman family that will transport you to dive boats and shore locations. The **Southern Cross Club** (☎ 800/899–2582) limits each of its boats to 12 divers and has its own dock.

CAYMAN ISLANDS A TO Z

To research prices, get advice from other travelers, and book travel arrangements, visit www.fodors.com.

AIR TRAVEL

American Airlines has daily nonstop flights from Miami and twice-weekly flights from New York (JFK). British Airways offers twice-weekly service from London (Gatwick) to Grand Cayman with an intermediate stop in Nassau, Bahamas. Cayman Airways flies nonstop to Grand Cayman from Miami two or three times daily, from Tampa four times a week, from Orlando three times a week, and from Houston and Atlanta three times a week. Continental flies nonstop to Grand Cayman from Newark, New Jersey, three times a week. Delta has daily nonstops from Atlanta and New York (JFK) to Grand Cayman. Northwest has nonstops from Minneapolis and Detroit to Grand Cayman. USAirways flies nonstop daily to Grand Cayman from Charlotte, North Carolina, and Philadelphia. Air service from Grand Cayman to Cayman Brac and Little Cayman is offered by two airlines: Cayman Airways has daily morning and evening service to both Cayman Brac and Little Cayman, and Island Air offers morning and afternoon service from Grand Cayman to both Cayman Brac and Little Cayman.

➤ AIRLINES AND CONTACTS: **American Airlines** (☎ 345/949–8799 or 800/433–7300). **Cayman Airways** (☎ 345/949–2311 or 800/422–

9626, WEB www.caymanairways.com). **Continental** (☎ 345/916–5545 or 800/231–0856). **Delta** (☎ 800/221–1212). **Island Air** (☎ 345/949–5252, WEB www.islandaircayman.com). **Northwest** (☎ 345/949–2956 or 800/447–4747). **US Airways** (☎ 800/428–4322).

AIRPORTS

Flights land at Owen Roberts Airport (Grand Cayman), Gerrard-Smith Airport (Cayman Brac), or Edward Bodden Airstrip (Little Cayman). Upon arrival some hotels offer free pickup at the airport, particularly on Cayman Brac and Little Cayman. Taxi service and car rentals are also available.

➤ Airport Information: **Owen Roberts Airport** (☎ 345/949–5252 or 345/949-7811). **Gerrard Smith International Airport** (☎ 345/948–1222). **Edward Bodden Airstrip** (☎ 345/948–0021).

BIKE AND MOPED TRAVEL

When renting a motor scooter or bicycle, remember to drive on the left—and wear sunblock. Bicycles ($10–$15 a day) and scooters ($30–$35 a day) can be rented from several outlets on Grand Cayman. Since the island is fairly flat, riding is generally not a problem. On Cayman Brac or Little Cayman, your hotel can make arrangements for you. Many resorts also offer bicycles for local sightseeing. Eagles Nest specializes in renting Harley-Davidson motorcycles.

➤ Bike and Moped Rentals: **Bicycles Cayman** (☎ 345/949–0608). **Cayman Cycle** (☎ 345/945–4021). **Eagles Nest** (☎ 345/949–4866). **Soto Scooters** (☎ 345/945–4652).

BUSINESS HOURS

BANKS

Banks are open Monday–Thursday 9–2:30 and Friday 9–1 and 2:30–4:30.

POST OFFICES

Post offices are generally open weekdays from 8:30 to 3:30 and Saturday from 8:30 to 11:30.

SHOPS

Shops are open weekdays 9–5, and Saturday in George Town from 10 to 2; in outer shopping plazas they are open from 10 to 5. Shops are usually closed Sunday except in hotels.

CAR RENTALS

To rent a car, bring your current driver's license, and the car-rental firm will issue you a temporary permit ($7.50). Most firms offer everything from compacts to jeeps to minibuses. Rates range from $35 to $65 a day. The major agencies have offices in a plaza across from the airport terminal in Grand Cayman, where you can pick up and drop off vehicles. You can rent a car from Ace Hertz, Budget, Coconut, Economy, Soto's, and Thrifty on Grand Cayman. Ace Hertz also has an office on Cayman Brac. McLaughlin operates on Little Cayman, though you probably won't need to rent a car there.

➤ Major agencies: **Ace Hertz** (☎ 345/949–2280 or 800/654–3131). **Budget** (☎ 345/949–5605 or 800/472–3325). **Coconut Car Rentals** (☎ 345/949–4377 or 800/941–4562, WEB www.coconutcarrentals.com). **Economy** (☎ 345/949–9550). **McLaughlin Rentals** (☎ 345/948–1000). **Soto's 4X4** (☎ 345/945–2424 or 800/625–6174, WEB www.sotos4x4.ky). **Thrifty** (☎ 345/949–6640 or 800/367–2277).

CAR TRAVEL

Traffic on West Bay Road in Grand Cayman can be congested, especially during high season as it's the only thoroughfare on the Seven Mile

Beach strip. Head out of the strip and get beyond George Town, and traffic will be sparse. Exploring Cayman Brac on a scooter is easy and fun. You won't really need a car on Little Cayman, though there are a limited number of jeeps for rent.

GASOLINE

Gas prices at press time were about $3 for an imperial gallon, slightly more than a U.S. gallon.

ROAD CONDITIONS

If you're touring Grand Cayman by car, there's a well-maintained road that circles the island; it's hard to get lost. Grand Cayman is relatively flat and fairly easy to negotiate if you're careful in traffic. Roads are well-marked and in decent condition on all three islands.

RULES OF THE ROAD

Remember—driving in the Cayman Islands is on the left, so when pulling out into traffic, look to your right.

ELECTRICITY

Electricity is the same in the Caymans as it is in the United States (110 volts, 60 cycles); it's reliable throughout the islands.

EMBASSIES AND CONSULATES

➤ CONTACTS: **U.S. Consular Representative** is Mrs. Gail Duquesney at Adventure Travel (☎ 345/945–1511).

EMERGENCIES

George Town Hospital has a 24-hour two-person double-lock hyperbaric chamber.

➤ AMBULANCE AND FIRE: **Medical and Fire emergencies** (☎ 911).

➤ DENTISTS: **David Godfrey** (☎ 345/949–7623). **David Wolfe** (☎ 345/945–4388).

➤ HOSPITALS: **George Town Hospital** (⊠ Hospital Rd., George Town, ☎ 345/949–4234).

➤ PHARMACIES: **Island Pharmacy** (⊠ West Shore Centre, West Bay Rd., George Town, ☎ 345/949–8987).

➤ POLICE: **Police emergencies** (☎ 911).

ETIQUETTE

You'll hear first names preceded by "Mr." or "Miss" (e.g., Mr. Sam)—these are terms of respect generally used for Caymanian senior citizens.

FESTIVALS AND SEASONAL EVENTS

During April's colorful Batabano Carnival, revelers dress up as dancing flowers and swimming stingrays. If you want to see an utterly British parade spiced with island-style panache, check out the Queen's Birthday bash in June. During Million Dollar Month in June, you'll find fishing tournaments on all three islands (five tournaments in all), each with its own rules, records, and entrance fees; huge cash prizes are awarded, including one for a quarter of a million dollars that's given to the angler who breaks the existing Blue Marlin record (currently 584 pounds). October sees the carnival-like atmosphere of Pirates Week (which really lasts 10 days and includes a mock invasion of Hog Sty Bay by a mock Blackbeard and company). Visitors and locals dress up like pirates and wenches; music, fireworks, and competitions take place island-wide.

HOLIDAYS

Public holidays include New Year's Day, Ash Wednesday (46 days before Easter), Good Friday (Friday before Easter), Easter Sunday (usually April or May), Discovery Day (May 19), Queen's Birthday (June 16), Constitution Day (July 7), Christmas, and Boxing Day (Dec. 26).

LANGUAGE

English is the official language in the Cayman Islands, and it is spoken with a distinctive brogue that reflects Caymanians' Welsh, Scottish, and English heritage. For example, *three* is pronounced "tree"; *pepper* is "pep-ah"; and *Cayman* is "K-man." The number of Jamaican residents in the workforce means the Jamaican patois and heavier accent are also common (other Jamaican influences are tales about the *duppy*—pronounced like "puppy"—a scary night creature that haunts the Caymans).

MAIL AND SHIPPING

Beautiful stamps are available at the General Post Office in downtown George Town and at the philatelic office in West Shore Plaza. Sending a postcard to the United States, Canada, the Caribbean, or Central America costs CI20¢. An airmail letter is CI30¢ per half ounce. To Europe and South America, rates are CI25¢ for a postcard and CI40¢ per half ounce for airmail letters. When addressing letters to the Cayman Islands, be sure to include "BWI" (British West Indies) at the bottom of the envelope. Note that the islands don't use postal codes, but don't let this worry you; your letter should arrive fine without one.

MONEY MATTERS

All prices quoted in this book are in U.S. dollars unless otherwise noted.

ATMS

ATMs are readily available, particularly on Grand Cayman; they usually give the option of U.S. or Cayman dollars.

CREDIT CARDS

Major credit cards are widely accepted, except for Discover.

CURRENCY

The Cayman dollar is divided into a hundred cents with coins of 1¢, 5¢, 10¢, and 25¢ and notes of $1, $5, $10, $25, $50, and $100. There is no $20 bill. Although the American dollar is accepted everywhere, you'll often get your change in Cayman dollars. A Cayman Dollar is worth about 20% more than a U.S. dollar, so keep this in mind when looking at menu and other prices.

PASSPORTS AND VISAS

It is always best when traveling abroad to carry a valid passport. However, U.S., U.K., and Canadian citizens, as well as citizens of Commonwealth countries, may carry an original birth certificate (with a raised seal) and a valid picture ID. A voter registration card is no longer acceptable identification. Citizens of all other countries need a valid passport, and everyone must have a valid return ticket.

SAFETY

Theft is not widespread, but be smart: lock your room and car and secure valuables as you would at home. Outdoors, marauding blackbirds called ching chings have been known to carry off jewelry if it is left out in the open.

SIGHTSEEING TOURS

Half-day tours average $30–$50 a person and generally include a visit to the Turtle Farm and Hell in West Bay, drives along Seven Mile Beach and through George Town, and time for shopping downtown. In addition to those stops, full-day tours, which average $55–$75 per person and include lunch, also visit Bodden Town to see pirate caves

and graves and the East End, where you visit blowholes on the ironshore and the site of the famous Wreck of the Ten Sails.
➤ CONTACTS: **A. A. Transportation Services** (☎ 345/949–7222; ask for Burton Ebanks). **Majestic Tours** (☎ 345/949–7773). **Reid's Premier Tours** (☎ 345/949–3345). **Rudy's Travellers Transport** (☎ 345/949–3208). **Tropicana Tours** (☎ 345/949–0944).

BOAT TOURS

The most impressive sights in the Cayman Islands are underwater, and several submarine trips will allow you to see these wonders. On Grand Cayman don't miss a trip on the *Atlantis* submarine, which takes 48 passengers, a driver, and two guides down along the Cayman Wall to depths of up to 100 ft (31 m). Through its large windows you can see huge barrel sponges, corals in extraterrestrial-like configurations, strange eels, and schools of beautiful and beastly fish. Costs range around $72–$85 per person for trips lasting 1–1½ hours. The *Nautilus* is a semisubmersible (part of the craft remains above water). You can catch some sun on the deck or venture to the cabin below, where windows allow you to see the reefs and marine life. A one-hour undersea tour is $35. In the semisubmersible *Seaworld Explorer,* you sit before windows in the hull of the boat just 5 ft (1½ m) below the surface, observing divers who swim around with food, attracting fish to the craft. The cost of this hour-long trip is $38.

Glass-bottom-boat trips cost around $25 and are available through several companies, including Acqua Delights, the *Cayman Mermaid,* and Kirk Sea Tours.

Sunset sails, dinner cruises, and other theme (dance, booze, pirate, etc.) cruises are available aboard several vessels. Party cruises typically run $20–$50 per person. The *Jolly Roger* is a replica of a 17th-century Spanish galleon offering afternoon, sunset, and dinner cruises. *Blackbeard's Nancy* is a 1912 topsail schooner, offering dinner cruises among others. The *Spirit of Ppalu* is a 65-ft glass-bottom catamaran offering dinner cruises.
➤ CONTACTS: **Aqua Delights** (☎ 345/945–4786). **Atlantis** (☎ 345/949–7700 or 800/877–8571, WEB www.goatlantis.com/cayman). **Blackbeard's Nancy** (☎ 345/949–8988). **Cayman Mermaid** (☎ 345/949–8100). **Jolly Roger** (☎ 345/949–8534). **Kirk Sea Tours** (☎ 345/949–6986). **Nautilus** (☎ 345/945–1355, WEB www.nautilus.ky). **Seaworld Explorer** (☎ 345/949–8534). **Spirit of Ppalu** (☎ 345/949–1234).

TAXES

A 10% government tax is added at all accommodations. Otherwise, there is no tax on goods or services.

TAXIS

Taxis offer 24-hour island-wide service. Fares are determined by an elaborate rate structure set by the government, and although it may seem pricey for a short ride (the fare from Seven Mile Beach for four people to the airport is $15 to $25), cabbies rarely try to rip off tourists. Ask to see the chart if you want to double-check the quoted fare.
➤ CONTACTS: **A. A. Transportation** (☎ 345/949–7222). **Cayman Cab Team** (☎ 345/945–1173).

TELEPHONES

COUNTRY AND AREA CODES

For international dialing to the Cayman Islands, the area code is 345.

INTERNATIONAL CALLS

To call outside the Caymans, dial 0 + 1 + area code and number. You can call anywhere, anytime through the cable and wireless system and

local operators. To place credit-card calls, dial 110; credit card and calling card calls can be made from any public phone and most hotels. Beware though, most hotels add huge surcharges to all calls local and international, even to toll-free access numbers for prepaid phone cards.
➤ ACCESS NUMBERS: **AT&T USADirect** (☎ 800/872–2881). **MCI Direct** (☎ 800/888–8000). **Sprint Direct** (☎ 800/366–4663).

LOCAL CALLS
To make local calls (on or between any of the three islands), dial the seven-digit number.

TIPPING
At large hotels a service charge is generally included and can be anywhere from 6% to 10%; smaller establishments and some villas and condos leave tipping up to you. Although tipping is customary at restaurants, note that some automatically include 15% on the bill—so check the tab carefully. Taxi drivers expect a 10%–15% tip.

TRANSPORTATION AROUND THE CAYMAN ISLANDS
If your accommodations are along Grand Cayman's Seven Mile Beach, you can walk or bike to the shopping centers, restaurants, and entertainment spots along West Bay Road. George Town is small enough to see on foot. If you want to see Grand Cayman, renting a car for a day is an option. You can also take a taxi, though the cost might be substantial. On Cayman Brac and Little Cayman, renting a car, bike, or moped is a must if you want to see more of the islands. There is no ferry service between any of the islands; you must fly.

VISITOR INFORMATION
➤ BEFORE YOU LEAVE: **Cayman Islands Department of Tourism** (✉ 6100 Blue Lagoon Dr., Suite 150, Miami, FL 33126-2085, ☎ 305/266–2300; ✉ 2 Memorial City Plaza, 820 Gessner, Suite 170, Houston, TX 77024, ☎ 713/461–1317; ✉ 420 Lexington Ave., Suite 2733, New York, NY 10170, ☎ 212/682–5582; ✉ 9525 W. Bryn Mawr Ave., Suite 160, Rosemont, IL 60018, ☎ 847/678–6446; ✉ 3440 Wilshire Blvd., Suite 1202, Los Angeles, CA 90010, ☎ 213/738–1968; ✉ 234 Eglinton Ave. E, Suite 306, Toronto, Ontario M4P 1K5, ☎ 416/485–1550; and ✉ Trevor House, 100 Brompton Rd., Knightsbridge, London SW3 1EX, ☎ 0171/491–7771; WEB www.caymanislands.ky).
➤ IN THE CAYMAN ISLANDS: **Department of Tourism** (✉ Cricket Sq. and Elgin Ave., George Town, ☎ 345/949–0623; ✉ Grand Cayman Airport, ☎ 345/949–2635; ✉ George Town Craft Market, Cardinal Ave., George Town, ☎ 345/949–8342 [open when cruise ships are in port]; ✉ kiosk at the cruise-ship dock, George Town, no phone). **Islands-wide tourist hot line** (☎ 345/949–8989). **Tourist Information and Activities Service** (☎ 345/949–6598, FAX 345/945–6222).

Updated by
Vernon
O'Reilly-
Ramesar

Noontime pedestrians go about their business as the jewel-colored buildings of Punda blaze in the Caribbean sun. People make their way home for lunch across the Queen Emma bridge, which connects the two sides of the city. Suddenly the blare of a ship's horn pierces the air. Within seconds the bridge separates itself from the Punda side and swings away. The crowd crossing the bridge is unconcerned as their pathway moves under their feet. Moments later a giant tanker sails into the city—within feet of a sidewalk café. The bridge leisurely swings back into its original position. Just another magic moment in Willemstad.

Curaçao—the largest island of the Netherlands Antilles (38 mi [61 km] long and 2–7½ mi [3–12 km] wide)—is also the most staunchly Dutch in its culture and its architecture. Although Dutch is the official language, Papiamento is the tongue common to all the Netherland Antilles and spoken most often by locals. Curaçao's charming capital of Willemstad, its underwater park, and its dozens of little cove beaches make it ideal for exploring. Willemstad's historic city center and the island's natural harbor (Schottegat) are inscribed on UNESCO's World Heritage List, a coveted distinction reserved for the likes of the Palace of Versailles and the Taj Mahal.

Thirty-five miles (56 km) north of Venezuela and 42 mi (68 km) east of Aruba, Curaçao sits below the so-called hurricane belt. The sun smiles down on the island, but it's never stiflingly hot, thanks to the gentle trade winds. Water sports—including outstanding reef diving—attract enthusiasts from all over the world. Curaçao claims 38 beaches, though only a handful are long strips of silky sand; most are stretches of washed-up coral that have broken down into white or pink sand, to varying degrees of smoothness. The island is dominated by arid countryside, rocky coves, and a sprawling capital built around a natural harbor. The economy is based primarily on oil refining and offshore banking; however, tourism is becoming increasingly important, and over the years the government has invested millions of dollars to restore colonial buildings to their original stature.

In Willemstad, Curaçao's "face" is a surprise—spiffy rows of brightly colored town houses that look transplanted from Holland. Although the gabled roofs and red tiles show a Dutch influence, the gay colors of the facades are peculiar to Curaçao. It's said that a popular governor suffered from migraines, a condition irritated by the color white, so all the houses were painted in colors. In the countryside, the doll-house look of the plantation houses, or *landhuizen* (literally, "land houses"), makes a cheerful contrast to the stark cacti and the austere shrubbery.

Curaçao was discovered by Alonzo de Ojeda (one of Columbus's lieu-tenants) in 1499. The first Spanish settlers arrived in 1527. In 1634 the Dutch came via the Netherlands West India Company. They promptly shipped off the Spaniards and the few remaining Indians—survivors of the battles for ownership of the island—to Venezuela. Eight years later Peter Stuyvesant began his rule as governor, which lasted until he left for New York around 1645. Twelve Jewish families ar-rived from Amsterdam in 1651, and by 1732 there was a synagogue; the present structure is the oldest synagogue still in use in the western hemisphere. Over the years the city built fortresses to defend against French and British invasions—many of those ramparts now house restaurants and hotels. The Dutch claim to Curaçao was recognized in 1815 by the Treaty of Paris. In 1954 Curaçao became an autonomous part of the Kingdom of the Netherlands, with a governor appointed by the queen, an elected parliament, and an island council.

Today Curaçao's population is derived from more than 50 nationali-ties in an exuberant mix of Latin, European, and African roots and with a Babel of tongues, resulting in superb restaurants and an active cultural scene. The island, like its Dutch settlers, is known for its reli-gious tolerance, and tourists are warmly welcomed.

Lodging

Beach hotels on the island's southwestern end tend to be small, secluded, and peaceful, but are a 30- to 45-minute drive from town. Those east and west of Willemstad proper tend to be large-scale luxury resorts. In town you can find places that cater to budget and business travel-ers. Most hotels provide beach or shopping shuttles. The larger ones provide kids' programs and allow children to stay in their parents' room for free or at a discounted rate. These hotels also include a Continen-tal breakfast or a large buffet breakfast. Full American Plans aren't pop-ular because of the abundance of good restaurants.

The Curaçao Apartments and Small Hotels Association, in conjunc-tion with the CTDB, publishes a brochure on quality accommodations. Rentals are popular with European visitors. Contact the **Curaçao Tourism Development Bureau** (✉ Pietermaai 19, Willemstad, ☎ 5999/461–6000 Ext. 117 or 112) at least two months in advance for a list of available properties.

CATEGORY	COST EP/CP*	COST A.I.**
$$$$	over $350	over $375
$$$	$250–$350	$275–$375
$$	$150–$250	$175–$275
$	under $150	under $175

*EP/CP prices are per night for a standard double room in high season, ex-cluding taxes, service charges, and meal plans**A.I. (all-inclusive) prices are per person, per night based on double-occupancy during high season, exclud-ing taxes and service charges*

$$$–$$$$ 🔲 **Hotel Kurá Hulanda.** This is more than a mere hotel; it's an 18th century village within Willemstad. Lovingly restored by Dutch millionaire and philanthropist Jacob Dekker and partner John Padget, this com-plex includes a boutique hotel, an amazing museum of African history, and a business center. Rooms are large, with high ceilings; each one is

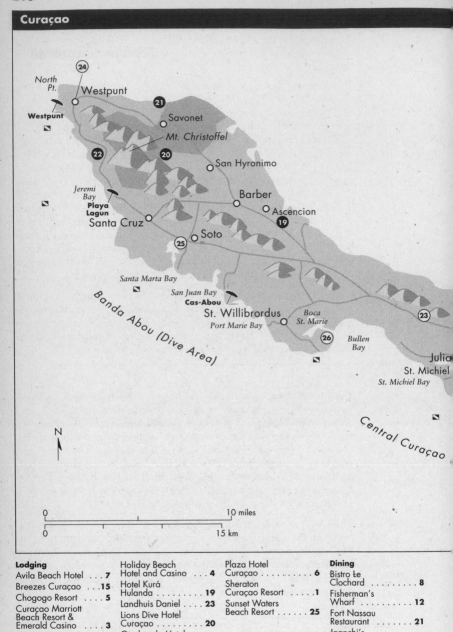

N

0   10 miles

0   15 km

Lodging

Avila Beach Hotel . . . **7**

Breezes Curaçao . . .**15**

Chogogo Resort **5**

Curaçao Marriott
Beach Resort &
Emerald Casino **3**

Floris Suite Hotel **2**

Habitat Curaçao . . .**26**

Holiday Beach
Hotel and Casino . . . **4**

Hotel Kurá
Hulanda **19**

Landhuis Daniel **23**

Lions Dive Hotel
Curaçao **20**

Otrobanda Hotel
& Casino **9**

Plaza Hotel
Curaçao **6**

Sheraton
Curaçao Resort **1**

Sunset Waters
Beach Resort **25**

Dining

Bistro Le
Clochard **8**

Fisherman's
Wharf **12**

Fort Nassau
Restaurant **21**

Jaanchi's
Restaurant **24**

The Living Room **17**

Beaches

Cruise Ship Terminal

Dive Sites

1 Exploring Sights

① Hotels and Restaurants

Caribbean Sea

Curaçao
International
Airport
18

Brievengat **17**

Santa
Catarina

St. Joris Bay

16 Great St. Joris

Little St. Joris

Willemstad
1 – 11
SEE DETAIL
MAP

dorp

Santa Rosa

Mt. Tafelberg

Bottelier

Brakkeput

Ostpunt

*St. Anna
Bay* **21** **22**

12

Bapor
Kibra

*Spanish
Water*

15

2

① Nieuwpoort

① **3** **4**

*Piscadera
Bay*

18 – 20
Seaquarium
Beach

13

*Caracas
Bay*

Santa
Barbara
Beach

14

5 – 17

Curaçao Underwater Marine Park

(Dive Area)

ve Area)

Mambo Beach **18**	Small World	**Exploring**	Den Paradera **15**
Otrobanda Bay	International	Boka Tabla **21**	Hato Caves **18**
Sight Terrace **9**	Cuisine **13**	Christoffel Park **20**	Landhuis
La Pergola **14**	Time Out Café **11**	Country House	Brievengat . . . . / . . . **17**
Rijsttafel Indonesia	The Wine Cellar **16**	Museum **19**	Landhuis Knip **22**
Restaurant **22**		Curaçao	Ostrich Farm **16**
Rodeo House of		Seaquarium **13**	Senior Curaçao
Ribs **10**		Curaçao	Liqueur Distillery . . . **12**
		Underwater	
		Marine Park **14**	

uniquely decorated with Indian and Indonesian furnishings. The safety
conscious will take consolation from the high-tech security system. ✉
Langestraat 8, Willemstad, ☎ *5999/434–7700,* FAX *5999/434–7701,*
WEB *www.kurahulanda.com. 100 rooms, 12 suites. 4 restaurants, coffee shop, 2 bars, room service, fans, in-room safe, minibars, 2 pools,
health club, shops, business services, meeting room. AE, MC, V. EP.*

$$$ 🏨 **Curaçao Marriott Beach Resort & Emerald Casino.** One of the island's
★   most elegant resorts, the Marriott lies on landscaped grounds brim-
ming with oleander, hibiscus, and palms. Its beach is beautiful; facili-
ties include a lively pool with a swim-up bar, tennis courts, a fitness
center, an alluring albeit small casino, and a 3,000-square-ft (279-square-
m) ballroom. Rooms are well equipped, with hair dryers, irons and iron-
ing boards, and balconies or patios. The Curaçao World Trade Center
is a stone's throw away, and the hotel's conference service staff will
help you coordinate business engagements. For upscale Northern Ital-
ian cuisine, try the pleasing Portofino restaurant. ✉ *Piscadera Bay (Box
6003),* ☎ *5999/736–8800,* FAX *5999/462–7502,* WEB *www.marriott.com.
237 rooms, 10 suites. 3 restaurants, 2 bars, room service, minibars,
golf privileges, 2 tennis courts, pool, health club, hair salon, hot tub,
sauna, steam room, beach, dive shop, dock, snorkeling, windsurfing,
business services, convention center, meeting rooms, car rental, no-smok-
ing rooms. AE, D, DC, MC, V. EP, FAP, MAP.*

$–$$$ 🏨 **Avila Beach Hotel.** Dignitaries and celebrities often choose to stay
★   at this 200-year-old mansion overlooking the ocean. The lobby, with
gilt mirrors, Asian rugs, porcelain figurines, and gas lamps, evokes a
more genteel era. Rooms range from the budget-priced and basic to
the luxurious (with whirlpool tubs) in the Blues Wing. The Belle Terrace restaurant, shaded by an enormous tree, serves imaginative international dishes. Saturday is Caribbean grill night, with music by
mariachi or steel bands. At the Blues Seafood Restaurant and Cocktail Bar, live jazz takes center stage Thursday and Saturday evenings,
and there's a terrific tapas buffet on Friday night. ✉ *Penstraat 130,
Willemstad (Box 791),* ☎ *5999/461–4377,* FAX *5999/461–1493,* WEB
*www.avilahotel.com. 100 rooms, 8 suites. 3 restaurants, 2 bars, in-room
data ports, in-room safes, kitchenettes, refrigerators, tennis court,
beach, business services, convention center, meeting rooms. AE, DC,
MC, V. EP, MAP.*

$–$$$ 🏨 **Floris Suite Hotel.** Dutch architect Jan des Bouvrie designed this won-
derfully minimalist boutique hotel near the Curaçao World Trade Cen-
ter. Here the rich glow of mahogany is juxtaposed with the cool
starkness of stainless steel. Spacious suites equipped with full kitchens
have made this a popular choice for visiting business travelers. Start
your morning sipping a cappuccino at the coffee bar in the airy lobby
before heading out to face the world. A lush tropical garden surrounds
the pool and restaurant, and the beach is just across the street. ✉ *J. F.
Kennedy Blvd., Piscadera Bay (Box 6246),* ☎ *5999/462–6111,* FAX *5999/
462–6211. 72 suites. Restaurant, in-room data ports, golf privileges,
tennis court, pool, beach, dive shop, business services, meeting room.
AE, MC, V. EP.*

$$ 🏨 **Breezes Curaçao.** The former Princess Beach Resort has been reborn
as the newest Breezes property. This family resort has a large private
beach, lushly landscaped grounds, and spacious rooms. Although it is
all-inclusive, you will, however, have to spend money if you choose to
test your luck in the large casino on the property. At press time, the
hotel was undergoing large-scale renovations as it completes its transformation into a Breezes property. ✉ *Martin Luther King Blvd. 8,
Willemstad,* ☎ *5999/736–7888 or 800/467–8737,* FAX *5999/461–4131,*
WEB *www.superclubs.com. 339 rooms, 54 suites. 3 restaurants, bar, snack
bar, room service, in-room data ports, in-room safes, refrigerator, 2 ten-*

nis courts, 2 pools, hair salon, gym, beach, dive shop, dock, snorkeling, volleyball, shops, casino, baby-sitting, children's programs (ages 0–16), dry cleaning, laundry service, car rental, no-smoking rooms. AE, DC, MC, V. All-inclusive.

$$ 🏨 **Habitat Curaçao.** The sprawling, beachfront Habitat is a diver's dream, with top-notch facilities and 24-hour diving. Clusters of canary yellow and red buildings are surrounded by tropical foliage and connected by stairways and winding paths. The raised pool affords grand vistas. Rooms are brightly outfitted with marine-life fabrics specially commissioned from local artist Nena Sanchez. Each room has a furnished terrace or balcony and a fully equipped kitchenette. The rooms with new lanai additions are excellent for accommodating families. Request an ocean view (the price is the same). ✉ Coral Estates, Rif St. Marie, ☎ 5999/864–8800 or 800/327–6709, FAX 5999/864–8464, WEB www.habitatdiveresorts.com. 56 suites, 14 lanai rooms. Restaurant, bar, in-room safes, pool, beach, dive shop, dock, shops, meeting room. AE, DC, MC, V. CP, EP.

$$ 🏨 **Holiday Beach Hotel and Casino.** This older hotel remains popular with Americans. The lobby is spacious, and one of the island's largest casinos, Casino Royale, is right next door. There's also a video arcade for the kids. The crescent beach is quite large for Curaçao and dotted with palm trees. Rooms are airy, bright, and clean, but much of the hotel has a dated motel feel. There's a 24-hour Denny's on-site, and the shops of Willemstad are within walking distance. There's also a free shuttle to and from town. ✉ Pater Euwensweg 31, Otrobanda, Willemstad (Box 2178), ☎ 5999/462–5400 or 800/444–5244, FAX 5999/462–4397, WEB www.hol-beach.com. 200 rooms, 1 suite. 2 restaurants, 2 bars, in-room safes, 2 tennis courts, pool, health club, beach, dive shop, Ping-Pong, volleyball, casino, laundry facilities, playground, meeting rooms. AE, D, DC, MC, V. EP.

$$ 🏨 **Lions Dive Hotel Curaçao.** This yellow-and-blue caravansary is a hop, skip, and plunge away from the Seaquarium (complimentary admission is given to guests), on ¼ mi (½ km) of private beach. Most guests are dive enthusiasts satisfied by the top-notch scuba center and the young, helpful staff. Rooms are airy, modern, and light-filled, with tile floors, wicker furnishings, and large bathrooms (showers only). French doors open onto a spacious balcony or terrace, and every room has a sea view. The Sunday-night happy hour is especially festive, with a merengue band playing poolside. ✉ Bapor Kibra, ☎ 5999/434–8888, FAX 5999/434–8889, WEB www.lionsdive.com. 72 rooms. Restaurant, bar, fans, in-room safes, pool, health club, beach, dive shop, dock, windsurfing, boating. AE, DC, MC, V. EP.

$$ 🏨 **Sheraton Curaçao Resort.** You may have a hard time choosing be-
★ tween the two fine beaches or the huge, free-form pool, which seems to merge with the ocean. Rooms have many creature comforts; those on the fifth (executive) floor include in-room fax machines. Staff are polite and knowledgeable. The West Indies Spa offers everything from massage to aromatherapy. The hotel is five minutes from the shops, sights, and eateries of Willemstad; a free shuttle takes you there twice a day. Savor a meal at the hotel's Yellow Bird Restaurant (international cuisine) or La Piazzetta (Italian). There's also a large casino just off the lobby. ✉ J. F. Kennedy Blvd., Piscadera Bay (Box 2133), ☎ 5999/462–5000, FAX 5999/462–5846, WEB curacaosheraton.com. 197 rooms, 13 suites. 3 restaurants, 3 bars, room service, in-room safes, golf privileges, miniature golf, 2 tennis courts, 2 pools, health club, hair salon, outdoor hot tub, spa, beach, dive shop, dock, snorkeling, windsurfing, boating, jet skiing, waterskiing, fishing, volleyball, casino, shops, baby-sitting, laundry service, business services, meeting rooms, car

rental, travel services, free parking, no-smoking rooms. AE, DC, MC, V. EP, FAP, MAP.

$$ 🏨 **Sunset Waters Beach Resort.** Curaçao's first all-inclusive hotel is removed from the bustle of downtown, set in a remote area on a luscious stretch of beach. Rooms are bright and airy, with white tile floors, a terrace or patio, and sleeping sofas in blue and mauve. All rooms have an ocean or garden view. One area of the beach is designated for nude sunbathing, and some of the rooms afford a full view, so request a room elsewhere if you'd prefer less exposure. The casino offers slots, blackjack, and roulette. Complimentary shuttles run to and from town. Kids under 12 stay free. ✉ *Santa Marta Bay,* ☎ *5999/864–1233,* FAX *5999/864–1237,* WEB *www.sunsetwaters.com. 70 rooms. 2 restaurants, 3 bars, refrigerators, miniature golf, tennis court, pool, gym, outdoor hot tub, beach, dive shop, snorkeling, boating, casino, shop, children's programs (ages 6 and up), meeting rooms, car rental, travel services. AE, D, MC, V. All-inclusive.*

$–$$ 🏨 **Plaza Hotel Curaçao.** This pink landmark at the entrance to Willemstad's harbor is the only hotel in the world with marine collision insurance. The lobby is laden with antiques, and a winding lagoon and waterfall give the hotel the air of an elegant colonial outpost. Rooms are elegantly appointed and most offer excellent views of either the city or the ocean. You give up beachfront (but you have beach privileges at Seaquarium, and there's a shuttle) for walking access to the city's center. The hotel is popular with business travelers and has a fully equipped business center in the lobby. ✉ *Plaza Piar, Willemstad (Box 813),* ☎ *5999/461–2500,* FAX *5999/461–6543,* WEB *www.plazahotelcuracao.com. 205 rooms, 27 suites. 2 restaurants, 3 bars, room service, in-room safes, pool, dive shop, casino, shops, business services, meeting rooms, car rental, no-smoking rooms. AE, MC, V. All-inclusive, CP, MAP.*

$ 🏨 **Chogogo Resort.** Vacationers who prefer bungalows over hotel rooms will appreciate Chogogo, on the island's eastern end and a two-minute walk from Jan Thiel Beach. All the rooms are spotless and have fully equipped kitchens, TVs, CD players, and balconies or patios. It's a quiet, relaxing place catering mainly to Dutch tourists. There's an excellent outside restaurant near the lovely pool. ✉ *Jan Thiel Beach,* ☎ *5999/747–2844,* FAX *5999/747–2424,* WEB *www.chogogo.com. 26 bungalows, 16 apartments, 18 studios. Restaurant, fans, kitchenettes, refrigerators, pool, beach, laundry service. AE, D, MC, V. EP.*

$ 🏨 **Landhuis Daniel.** Dating from 1711, this mustard plantation house with white colonnades and red-tile roof always served as an inn. The property, near the narrow center of the island, has a pool, dive shop, and a French-Caribbean restaurant, serving dishes made with organic fruits, vegetables, and herbs grown right on the plantation. The intriguing menu varies according to the seasonal crop yield. Rooms are tiny but clean, with basic furnishings; choose one of the larger rooms in the main house. Join in the fun at the poolside barbecue on Fridays, Saturdays, and Sundays. ✉ *Weg Naar, Westpunt,* ☎ FAX *5999/864–8400,* WEB *www.best-caribbean.com/landhuisdaniel. 8 rooms. Restaurant, bar, fans, pool, dive shop. AE, MC, V. EP, MAP.*

$ 🏨 **Otrobanda Hotel & Casino.** In the heart of historic Otrobanda, this little hotel offers superior value for the money. Standard rooms are cramped but appealing, with terrific harbor views, rattan furnishings, and paintings of country scenes. The most attractive and roomiest are those tucked under the peaked roof. For a good meal and a good view, stop by the Otrobanda Bay Sight Terrace. The hotel's location puts you right in the middle of all the downtown action. ✉ *Breedestraat, Otrobanda, Willemstad,* ☎ *5999/462–7400,* FAX *5999/462–7299. 42 rooms, 3 suites. Restaurant, bar, pool, casino, shops, baby-sitting. AE, DC, MC, V. CP.*

Dining

Dine beneath the boughs of magnificent old trees, in the romantic gloom of wine cellars in renovated plantation houses, or on the ramparts of 18th-century forts. Curaçaoans partake of some of the best Indonesian food in the Caribbean; you can also find fine French, Swiss, Dutch, and Swedish fare.

What to Wear

Dress in restaurants is almost always casual (though beachwear isn't acceptable). Some of the resort dining rooms and nicer restaurants require that men wear jackets, especially in high season; ask when you make reservations.

CATEGORY	COST*
$$$$	over $30
$$$	$20–$30
$$	$10–$20
$	under $10

per person for a main course at dinner

AMERICAN

$$ ✕ **Rodeo House of Ribs.** This family-owned restaurant has been in business for more than 20 years. The staff (dressed in the requisite cowboy outfits) keeps the place lively all night long. Other than a couple of fish offerings, everything else is strictly red meat. The ribs and steaks are all imported from the United States. Try the charcoal broiled tenderloin in pepper sauce. ⊠ *Fokkerweg 3, Saliña, Willemstad,* ☎ *5999/ 465–9465. AE, MC, V. Closed Mon.*

ASIAN

$$–$$$$ ✕ **Rijsttafel Indonesia Restaurant.** An antique rickshaw at the entrance
★ sets the mood. Exotic delicacies make up the traditional Indonesian banquet called *rijsttafel*, where some 16 to 25 dishes are set buffet style around you. Smaller appetites should opt for the *nasi rames,* with only eight dishes. A vegetarian rijsttafel is also available. An à la carte menu includes fried noodles and combination meat-and-fish platters. ⊠ *Mercurriusstraat 13–15, Saliña, Willemstad,* ☎ *5999/461–2606. AE, DC, MC, V. No lunch Sun.*

CARIBBEAN

$$–$$$ ✕ **Jaanchi's Restaurant.** This sheltered, open-air restaurant has lunches of mouth-watering Curaçaoan dishes. The specialty is a hefty platter of fresh wahoo with sides of potatoes or *funchi* (a cornmeal dish similar to polenta) and vegetables. Jaanchi's iguana soup is famous on the island. The place usually closes at 6:30 PM but will stay open later if you call ahead. ⊠ *Westpunt 15, Westpunt,* ☎ *5999/864–0126. AE, DC, MC, V.*

CONTINENTAL

$$–$$$$ ✕ **The Wine Cellar.** Master Dutch chef Nico Cornelisse serves consis-
★ tently excellent meals in his Victorian-style dining room. The *Menu Romantique* offers a complete meal, which includes smoked salmon, creamy pumpkin soup, leg of lamb, and banana fritters. The restaurant is wheelchair accessible. ⊠ *Kaya Zusternan Di Schyndel, Willemstad,* ☎ *5999/461–2178 or 5999/767–4909. Reservations essential. AE, DC, MC, V. No lunch weekends. Closed Sun.*

$$$ ✕ **Bistro Le Clochard.** This romantic gem is built into the 19th-century
★ Riffort—an oasis of arched entryways, exposed brickwork, wood beams, and lace curtains. The waterside terrace has a beautiful view of the floating bridge and harbor. The Swiss chefs prepare exquisite French and Swiss dishes. Try the broiled salmon steak in a creamy lob-

ster sauce, and make sure to leave room for the delicious homemade Swiss Toblerone chocolate mousse. The restaurant is fully wheelchair accessible. ⊠ *Harbourside Terrace, Riffort, Otrobanda, Willemstad,* ☎ *5999/462–5666,* WEB *bistroleclochard.com. Reservations essential. AE, DC, MC, V. No lunch Sat. Closed Sun.*

$$$ ✕ **Fort Nassau Restaurant.** On a hill above Willemstad, this restaurant
★   is built into an 18th-century fort with a 360° view. Go for a drink in the breezy Battery Terrace bar or dine in air-conditioned comfort beside huge bay windows. Delicious highlights of the diverse menu include Dover sole topped with calvados and fruit and oven-baked shrimp in hollandaise sauce. Desserts here are delectable. ⊠ *Schottengatweg 82, near Juliana Bridge, Willemstad,* ☎ *5999/461–3450 or 5999/461– 3086. Reservations essential. AE, MC, V. No lunch weekends.*

ECLECTIC

$$$–$$$$ ✕ **The Living Room.** The deep red interior of this cavernous establishment has become the island's trendiest eatery and nightspot. Sofas are strewn around the lounge, creating a surprisingly intimate feel. The woodburning oven turns out tasty pizzas. If pizza doesn't suit your taste-buds, there are many other imaginative items on the menu, such as braised leg of duck in an apricot and rosemary sauce. Vegetarians should try the delicious vegetarian wrap, which consists of caramelized nuts and goat cheese on a bed of ratatouille. ⊠ *Saliña 129, Saliña, Willemstad,* ☎ *5999/461–4443. AE, MC, V. No lunch Sun.*

$$–$$$ ✕ **Mambo Beach.** On the west end of Seaquarium Beach, this hip, open-air bar and grill, spread over the sand, serves good food for breakfast, lunch, and dinner. Hearty sandwiches on baguette bread dominate the lunch menu; steaks, fresh seafood, and pasta fill the dinner menu. There is an excellent fish buffet on Fridays. This is a fantastic place to watch the sun set, but don't forget your insect repellent. ⊠ *Seaquarium Beach, Bapor Kibra,* ☎ *5999/461–8999. MC, V.*

$$–$$$ ✕ **Otrobanda Bay Sight Terrace.** The best thing about this low-key eatery in the Otrobanda Hotel & Casino is its remarkable view of Santa Anna Bay and the colorful town-house facades. As you dine, you're so close to the passing ships, it seems you can almost touch them. Meals are reasonably priced. The Gouda cheese stuffed with spicy shredded chicken is a good choice. ⊠ *Otrobanda Hotel & Casino, Breedestraat, Otrobanda, Willemstad,* ☎ *5999/462–7400. AE, MC, V.*

$$–$$$ ✕ **Small World International Cuisine.** For a tasty, pleasant dining ex-
★   perience, try this eclectic eatery, whose outdoor deck juts out over the Caribbean. The menu is broken down into French, Spanish, Creole, and Chinese sections. *Gambas al ajillo* (shrimp in garlic sauce served with flavorful veggies and rice) is a savory choice, as is the salmon fillet papillote (cooked in its own juices and wrapped in a foil pouch with carrots and onions). If you prefer indoor seating, request the nifty glass-top table with the built-in terrarium. ⊠ *Waterfort Boogjes 18–19, Willemstad,* ☎ *5999/465–5575. AE, DC, MC, V.*

$ ✕ **Time Out Café.** Tucked into an alley in the shopping heartland of Punda, this outdoor eatery serves up light bites like tuna sandwiches and *tostis* (toasted cheese), as well as the omnipresent "catch of the day" option. Drop by for a beer and a game of billiards before venturing out. There are live rock performances on Thursday nights. ⊠ *Keukenplein 8, Punda, WIllemstad,* ☎ *5999/667–2455. No credit cards.*

ITALIAN

$$–$$$$ ✕ **La Pergola.** Built into the stuccoed walls of the Waterfort Arches, with huge picture windows fronting the rambunctious sea, copper pots hanging everywhere, and a pretty pink-and-white arbor wound with bunches of grapes, La Pergola offers creative variations on Italian standards and has no fewer than 14 pastas and 11 pizza options.

✉ *Waterfort Archesboog 12, Willemstad,* ☎ *5999/461–3482. AE, DC, MC, V. No lunch Sun.*

SEAFOOD

$$–$$$ ✗ **Fisherman's Wharf.** A terrific outdoor terrace and a comprehensive menu make this eatery a good choice. Fish lovers will enjoy the *Barracuda Picasso* (barracuda served under flambéed fruit and cashews). The more adventurous meatlovers can have a go at the ostrich loin served on a bed of green peppers and stir-fried shrimp. ✉ *Martin Luther King Blvd. 93, Willemstad,* ☎ *5999/465–7558. AE, MC, V.*

Beaches

Curaçao has some 38 beaches, many of them quite striking. Those along the southeast coast are often rocky (wear your flip-flops or reef shoes into the water), but in the west you'll find stretches of smooth sand at the shoreline. Rent a Jeep, motor scooter, or heavy-treaded car, ask your hotel to pack a picnic basket, and go exploring. You can discover the joy of inlets: tiny bays marked by craggy cliffs, exotic trees, and small pebbly or sandy beaches. There are snack bars and rest rooms on many of the larger beaches.

Among the hotels with the best beaches are the Sheraton Curaçao, the Curaçao Marriott Beach Resort, Sunset Waters Beach Resort, and the Lions Dive Hotel Curaçao.

Barbara Beach. To reach this popular family beach on the eastern tip, you can drive through one of Curaçao's toniest neighborhoods, Spanish Water, where gleaming white yachts replace humble fishing fleets. The beach has changing facilities and a snack bar but charges an admission fee, usually around $2.25 per person, but up to $7 per person on weekends. Around the bend, Caracas Bay is a popular dive site, with a sunken ship so close to the surface that snorkelers can view it clearly.

Cas Abou. This white sand gem has the brightest blue water in Curaçao. Divers and snorkelers will appreciate the on-site dive shop and sunbathers can make use of the small snack bar. The rest rooms and showers are immaculate.

Playa Lagun. This northwestern cove is caught between gunmetal gray cliffs, which beautifully frame the Caribbean blue. Couples can steal quiet moments here on weekday mornings, but locals flock here on weekends. Canoe trips, dive sessions, and swimming lessons are available through the dive shop on the beach. Cognoscenti know this is one of the best places to snorkel.

Seaquarium Beach. You'll pay a fee ($2.25 per person) to enter here, but the amenities (rest rooms, showers, boutiques, water-sports center, snack bar, restaurants with beach bars, thatched shelters and palm trees for shade, security patrols) on this 1,600-ft (490-m) man-made sandy beach and the calm waters protected by a carefully placed breakwater are well worth it.

Westpunt. On the northwest tip of the island, Westpunt is shady in the morning. It doesn't have much sand; but you can sit on a shaded rock ledge. The Playa Forti Bar & Restaurant offers refreshing soft drinks and beer and an exquisite fish soup. Take in the view of the boats in the marina and watch the divers jump from the high cliff. Water-sports enthusiasts, take note: the All West Dive Shop is on the beach here.

Outdoor Activities and Sports

Participant Sports

For the full gamut of activities in one spot, nature buffs (especially birdwatchers), families, and adventure-seekers may want to visit **Caracas**

Bay Island (☎ 5999/747–0777). Things to do here include hiking, mountain biking, canoeing, kayaking, windsurfing, jetskiing, and snorkeling. There's a fully equipped dive shop, a restaurant, and a bar on premises. Admission to the scenic area is $3; activities cost extra.

BOATING, SAILING, AND WINDSURFING

Top Watersports Curaçao (⊠ Seaquarium Beach, Bapor Kibra, ☎ 5999/461–7343) rents smaller craft like Sunfish, as well as canoes, snorkel gear, and floating mats. This section of coast tends to be calmer than most, making it ideal for beginners, although the breezes are sufficiently steady to keep experienced windsurfers on their toes.

FISHING

There are surprisingly few charter boats available for deep-sea fishing, but the small 18-ft *Hemingway* (☎ 5999/888–8086) offers Penn International, senator, and spinning reels as well as an experienced guide. It can accommodate no more than two people (one person $45, two $70) but can negotiate fairly deep water where shark, wahoo, tuna, barracuda, sailfish, and marlin are abundant. They'll pick up at your hotel. For tarpon fishing closer to shore, the **Plaza Hotel Curaçao** (Plaza Piar, Willemstad, ☎ 5999/461–2500) offers fishing outings in the 13-ft *Boston Whalers*. If you're in search of marlin, book the 54-ft yacht *War Eagle* (☎ 5999/461–2500).

GOLF

In the mood to hit the green? Try the **Blue Bay Curaçao Golf and Beach Resort** (⊠ Landhuis Blauw, ☎ 5999/868–1755). This 18-hole, par-72 course beckons experts and novices alike. Facilities include a golf shop, locker rooms, and a snack bar. Greens fees range $65–$105 per person, and you can rent carts, clubs, and shoes. If you'd like to drive your game to a new level, take a lesson from the house pro ($30 for a half hour) or head for the driving range and putting green ($10 per person for unlimited range balls). The 9-hole course at the **Curaçao Golf and Squash Club** (⊠ Wilhelmenalaan, Emmastad, ☎ 5999/737–3590) is a challenge because of the stiff trade winds and the sand greens. Greens fees are $20 for 18 holes.

SCUBA DIVING AND SNORKELING

The **Curaçao Underwater Marine Park** includes almost a third of the island's southern diving waters. Scuba divers and snorkelers can enjoy more than 12½ mi (20 km) of protected reefs and shores, with normal visibility from 60 to 150 ft (18 to 45 m). With water temperatures ranging from 75°F to 82°F (24°C to 28°C), wet suits are generally unnecessary. No coral collecting, spearfishing, or littering is allowed. An exciting wreck to explore is the SS *Oranje Nassau*, which ran aground more than 90 years ago. The other two main diving areas are **Banda Abou,** along the southwest coast between West Point and St. Marie, and along **central Curaçao,** which stretches between Bullen Bay to the Breezes Curaçao resort. The north coast is not recommended for diving because of the dangerously rough conditions found there.

Introductory scuba resort courses run about $60–$75. Full certification courses average $200 for three days and $325 for the advanced five-day version. Virtually every operator below charges $33–$35 for a single-tank dive and $55–$60 for a two-tank dive. Snorkel gear commonly rents for $12–$15 per day. For detailed information on dive sites and operators, call 800/328–7222 and ask for the brochure, "Take the Plunge in Curaçao," or pick up the *DIP–Curaçao's Official Dive Guide* for a nominal cost from the CTDB.

The following operators can help get you started: **Caribbean Sea Sports** at the Curaçao Marriott Beach Resort (⊠ Piscadera Bay, ☎ 5999/462–

2620) takes divers to popular nearby sites including the *Superior Producer* wreck. **Curaçao Seascape** (✉ John F. Kennedy Blvd., Piscadera Bay, ☎ 5999/462–5000) offers shore dives and open water certification programs. The closest operation to the famous Mushroom Forest dive site, **Easy Divers Curaçao** (✉ Sunset Waters Beach Resort, Santa Marta Bay, ☎ 5999/864–2822), will customize dive trips for you, or you can take part in one of the daily two-tank dives from their 38-ft boat. PADI instruction is available. The dive center of **Habitat Curaçao** (✉ Coral Estates, Rif St. Marie, ☎ 5999/864–8800) offers everything from a two-day, three-dive introductory course to underwater video and photography courses ($275–$400). **Underwater Curaçao** (✉ Lions Dive Hotel Curaçao, Bapor Kibra, ☎ 5999/461–8100) offers shore and boat dives and packages, as well as certified PADI instruction.

TENNIS

If you're not staying at a hotel with a tennis court, try the **Santa Catherina Sports Complex** (✉ Club Seru Coral, Koraal Partier 10, Santa Barbara, ☎ 5999/767–7028). Court time costs $20 an hour.

Spectator Sports

Centro Deportivo Curaçao (✉ Bonamweg 49, Willemstad, ☎ 5999/737–6620), a modern and comfortable stadium about 10 minutes from town, hosts soccer matches and baseball games March–October. It's open daily 9:30–12:30 and 1–6.

Shopping

Curaçao offers a number of exciting buys, from Dutch classics like embroidered linens, blue delft china, cheeses, and clogs to local crafts (you can find some marvelous ceramic work). There are also fine local painters, most of whom work in the landscape mode. If you're looking for bargains on Swiss watches, cosmetics, cameras, crystal, perfumes, Nike or Reebok sneakers, or electronic equipment, do some comparison shopping back home and come armed with a list of prices. Willemstad is no longer a free port: there's now a tax, so prices are higher.

Areas

Most shops are concentrated in **Willemstad**'s Punda within about a six-block area. The main shopping streets are Heerenstraat, Breedestraat, and Madurostraat. Heerenstraat and Gomezplein are pedestrian malls, closed to traffic, and their roadbeds have been raised to sidewalk level and covered with pink inlaid tiles. **Otrobanda** can also be a shopping adventure, though it's not as picturesque as Punda. A walk up Breedestraat, starting at the Otrobanda Hotel & Casino on the waterfront, takes you past colorful variety stores and food shops.

Specialty Items

ART

Gallery Eighty Six (✉ Trompstraat, Punda, Willemstad, ☎ 5999/461–3417) represents the work of local artists and occasionally those of South Americans and Africans. **Kas di Alma Blou** (✉ De Rouvilleweg 67, Otrobanda, Willemstad, ☎ 5999/462–8896) is in a gorgeous 19th-century indigo town house and presents the top local artists; you can find shimmering landscapes, dazzling photographs, ceramics, even African-inspired Carnival masks. **Open Ateliér** (✉ F. D. Rooseveltweg 443, Willemstad, ☎ 5999/868–6027), just past Santa Maria on the way to the airport, is a very special gallery featuring work by children and handicapped local artists. Proceeds from the gallery help community organizations. The gallery is open 9–2 daily.

CIGARS

The sweet smell of success permeates **Cigar Emporium** (✉ Gomezplein, Willemstad, ☎ 5999/465–3955), where you'll find the largest selection of cigars on the island, including H. Upmann, Romeo & Julietta, and Montecristo. Visit the climate-controlled cedar cigar room.

CLOTHES

Left your gym shoes at home? Step into **Athlete's Foot** (✉ Heerenstraat 10, Willemstad, ☎ 5999/461–3239) and you'll be up and running in no time. At the Willemstad branch of **Batik Exclusive** (✉ Handelskade 6, Willemstad, ☎ 5999/461–0262), you can outfit yourself in vibrant Caribbean colors. The shop sells batik sarongs for adults and kids ($21), knapsacks, bathing suits, dresses, halter tops, and gift items, including mobiles with aquatic designs and hand puppets. **Benetton** (✉ Madurostraat 4, Willemstad, ☎ 5999/461–4619; ✉ Curaçao International Airport, ☎ 5999/869–6054) has winter stock in July and summer stock in December, all of it 20% off the retail price. At **Big Low Center** (✉ Heerenstraat 6, Willemstad, ☎ 5999/461–1680) there are T-shirts galore. Special deals include three regular tees or two embroidered tees for $15. **Clog Dance** (✉ De Rouvilleweg 9B, Willemstad, ☎ 5999/462–3280) has Dutch clogs and fashions, cheeses, tulips, delftware, and chocolate. **Fendi** (✉ Breedestraat 9, Willemstad, ☎ 5999/461–2618) sells its merchandise for 25% less than in the United States.

FOODSTUFFS

Toko Zuikertuintje (✉ Zuikertuintjeweg, Willemstad, ☎ 5999/737–0188), a supermarket built on the site of the original 17th-century Zuikertuintje Landhuis, is where most of the local elite shop for all sorts of European and Dutch delicacies. Perfect on a sunny day or on an evening harbor-front stroll, **Vienna Ice Café** (✉ Handelskade 14, Punda, Willemstad, ☎ 5999/736–1086) serves up scrumptious homemade ice cream. Indulge your sweet tooth with such flavors as green apple, mango, and rum plum.

GIFTS

Boolchand's (✉ Heerenstraat 4B, Willemstad, ☎ 5999/461–6233) handles an interesting combination of merchandise behind a facade of red-and-white-checkered tiles. Stock up here on electronics, jewelry, Swarovski crystal, Swiss watches, and cameras. **Julius L. Penha & Sons** (✉ Heerenstraat 1, Willemstad, ☎ 5999/461–2266), in front of the Pontoon Bridge, sells French perfumes and cosmetics. At **Little Switzerland** (✉ Breedestraat 44, Willemstad, ☎ 5999/461–2111) you can find jewelry, watches, crystal, china, and leather goods at significant savings. The very first gift shop to open on Curaçao more than 60 years ago, **Warenhaus Van Der Ree** (✉ Breedestraat 5, Willemstad, ☎ 5999/461–1645), offers quite a selection of novelties. Look for stainless-steel wind chimes, dolls, frames, hammocks, Dutch cheese, and hand-painted whistles.

HANDICRAFTS

Arawak Craft Factory (✉ Cruise Terminal, Otrobanda, Willemstad, ☎ 5999/462–7249) has a factory showroom of locally made crafts. You can purchase tiles, plates, pots, and tiny replicas of land houses. A special walkway allows you to watch the artisans at work and ask questions. **Bamali** (✉ Breedestraat, Punda, Willemstad, ☎ 5999/461–2258) sells Indonesian batik clothing, leather bags, and charming handicrafts. **Caribbean Handcraft Inc.** (✉ Kaya Kakina 8, Jan Thiel, ☎ 5999/767–1171) offers an elaborate assortment of locally handcrafted souvenirs. It's worth visiting just for the spectacular hilltop view. **Landhuis Groot Santa Martha** (✉ Santa Martha, ☎ 5999/864–1559) is where artisans with disabilities fashion handicrafts. An open house is held every last Sunday of the month, when visitors can browse and buy. **Open Atelier** (✉ F. D. Rooseveltweg 443, Willemstad, ☎ 5999/868–6027), just past Santa Maria on the road to the airport, promotes Curaçaoan artists' work, with an emphasis on watercolors.

JEWELRY

Freeport (✉ Heerenstraat 13, Willemstad, ☎ 5999/461–9500) has a fine selection of duty-free watches and jewelry (lines include David Yurman, Christofle, Movado, and Maurice Lacroix), attracting shoppers who pour in from the cruise ships that dock nearby. **Gandelman** (✉ Breedestraat 35, Willemstad, ☎ 5999/461–1854; ✉ Curaçao Marriott Beach Resort, Piscadera Bay, ☎ 5999/462–8386) has watches by Cartier and Rolex, leather goods by Prima Classe, and Baccarat and Daum crystal.

LINENS

New Amsterdam (✉ Gomezplein 14, Willemstad, ☎ 5999/461–2437; ✉ Breedestraat 29, Willemstad, ☎ 5999/461–3239) is the place to price hand-embroidered tablecloths, napkins, and pillowcases, as well as Italian gold and Hummel figurines.

PERFUMES AND COSMETICS

Perfume Palace (✉ Braastraat 23, Willemstad, ☎ 5999/461–7462) carries all the major brands of cosmetics and perfume. **The Yellow House** (✉ Breedestraat 23, Willemstad, ☎ 5999/461–3222) offers an amazing selection of perfumes at low prices.

Nightlife

Friday is a big night out, with rollicking happy hours—most with live music—at several hotels, most notably the Plaza Hotel Curaçao and the Avila Beach Hotel. And while it might surprise you, Sunday night revelry into the wee hours is an island tradition. A museum by day, Landhuis Brievengat turns into a party house after dark—the night owls flock here Wednesday through Sunday for live music in the outdoor courtyard from 8 PM until dawn. The hippest hangout is The Living Room, where well-heeled partiers dance the night away on weekends. Check with the tourist board for the schedule of events or pick up a copy of the weekly free entertainment listings, *K-Pasa,* available at most restaurants and hotels.

BARS

Live jazz electrifies the pier at the **Blues Bar & Restaurant** (✉ Avila Beach Hotel, Penstraat 130, Willemstad, ☎ 5999/461–4377) Thursdays (*the* night to go) and Saturdays. **De Heeren** (✉ Suikertuintjeweg [Shopping Center], Suikertuintjeweg, ☎ 5999/736–0491) is a great spot to grab a locally brewed Amstel Bright and meet a happy blend of tourists and transplanted Dutch locals. Meaning "Fort Alertness," **Fort Waakzaamheid Tavern & Restaurant** (✉ Seru Domi, Willemstad, ☎ 5999/462–3633) is a pleasant place for a cocktail day or night, complete with a panoramic view of the island. By day **Hook's Hut** (✉ Next to the Sheraton Curaçao Resort, Piscadera Bay, ☎ 5999/462–6575) is a local beach hangout. The daily happy hour from 5 to 6 kicks off a lively nighttime scene. The outdoor pool table is in terrible shape, but it's one of the few bar tables around. There's a $3 flat fee per half hour; pay the bartender.

Anchor yourself at a dockside table at the **International Café** (✉ Handelskade 13, Willemstad, ☎ 5999/465–1056), and sip frozen cappuccinos as the ships pass by in Santa Anna Bay. Or, loosen up with a cocktail—specialties include the Blue Curaçao Margarita and the Pink Panther (Baileys, Amaretto, coconut liqueur, grenadine, Ponche Crema, coconut cream, and pineapple juice). **Keizershof,** a complex of reno vated heritage buildings, has two restaurants and a café, in addition to dancing under the stars at **Keizershof Terrace** (Hoogstraat at Rouvilleweg, Otrobanda, Willemstad, ☎ 5999/462–3493) and sing-alongs at **Pianobar Kalimba** (☎ 5999/462–3583). Sunday Happy Hours are hot at **Rumors** (✉ Lions Dive Hotel, Bapor Kibra, ☎ 5999/461–7555), featuring some of the best rock and reggae bands.

CASINOS

Gambling seems almost an afterthought on Curaçao. Although casinos are a staple at most hotels, even the biggest have only a few card tables, and some are limited to slot machines. The following hotels have casinos that are open daily 1 PM–4 AM: the Curaçao Marriott Beach Resort & Emerald Casino, the Sheraton Curaçao, the Plaza Hotel Curaçao, Holiday Beach Hotel and Casino, and the Breezes Curaçao. Of these, only the Marriott and Sheraton casinos even approach a small Vegas hotel in terms of the number of games and Bond-like elegance.

DANCE AND MUSIC CLUBS

Baya Beach (✉ Caracas Bay Island Park, Caracas Bay Island, ☎ 5999/747–0777) is a festive place that lures dancers with its pulsating blend of salsa, merengue, and hip-hop. Saturday nights are the liveliest. **Club Facade** (✉ Lindberghweg 32, Willemstad, ☎ 5999/461–4640) seems to be as popular with locals as it is with visitors. **The Living Room** (✉ Saliña 129, Saliña, Willemstad, ☎ 5999/461–4443) is the hippest place to be on weekends. Dance into the wee hours in the chic, burnished-red interior. **Mambo Beach Club** (Seaquarium Beach, Bapor Kibra, ☎ 5999/461–8999), an open-air bar, draws a hip, young crowd that flocks here to dance the night away under the stars. Popular with tourists and locals throughout the week, insiders know this as *the* place to be on Sunday night; come in time for happy hour and warm up for the nightlong party with some beach volleyball.

Exploring Curaçao

Willemstad

What does the capital of Curaçao have in common with New York City? Broadway, for one thing. Here it's called Breedestraat, but the origin is the same. Dutch settlers came here in the 1630s, the same period when they sailed through the Narrows to Manhattan, bringing with them original red-tile roofs, first used on the trade ships as ballast and later incorporated into the architecture of Willemstad.

The city is cut in two by Santa Anna Bay. On one side is the Punda—crammed with shops, restaurants, monuments, and markets—and on the other is the less touristy Otrobanda (literally, the "other side"), with lots of narrow, winding streets full of private homes notable for their picturesque gables and Dutch-influenced designs. There are three ways to cross the bay: drive or take a taxi over the Juliana Bridge; traverse the Queen Emma Pontoon Bridge on foot; or ride the free ferry, which runs when the Pontoon Bridge is open for passing ships. All the major hotels outside town offer free shuttle service to town once or twice daily. Shuttles coming from the Otrobanda side leave you at Riffort. From here it's a short walk north to the foot of the pontoon bridge. Shuttles coming from the Punda side leave you near the main entrance to Ft. Amsterdam.

Numbers in the margin correspond to points of interest on the Willemstad map.

SIGHTS TO SEE

⓫ **Curaçao Museum.** Housed in an 1853 plantation house, this small museum is filled with artifacts, paintings, and antiques that trace the is-

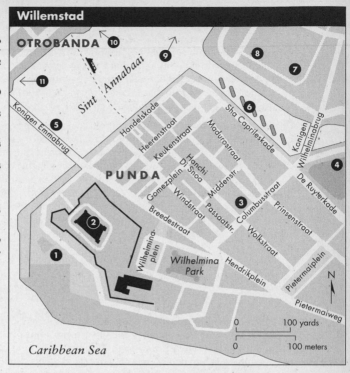

land's history. This is also the venue for art exhibitions that visit the island. ✉ *V. Leeuwenhoekstraat, Otrobanda,* ☎ *5999/462–3873.* ✆ *$2.50.* ☉ *Weekdays 9–noon and 2–5, Sun. 10–4.*

❻ Floating Market. Each morning dozens of Venezuelan schooners laden with tropical fruits and vegetables arrive at this bustling market on the Punda side of the city. Mangoes, papayas, and exotic vegetables vie for space with freshly caught fish and herbs and spices. The buying is best at 6:30 AM—too early for many people on vacation—but there's plenty of action throughout the afternoon. Any produce bought here, however, should be thoroughly washed or peeled before eating. ✉ *Sha Caprileskade.*

❷ Ft. Amsterdam. Step through the archway and enter another century. The entire structure dates from the 1700s, when it was the center of the city and the island's most important fort. Now it houses the governor's residence, the Fort Church, the Council of Ministers, and government offices. Outside the entrance a series of majestic gnarled *wayaka* trees are fancifully carved with human forms—the work of local artist Mac Alberto. ✉ *Foot of Queen Emma Bridge,* ☎ *5999/461–1139.* ✆ *$1.75 (to church museum only).* ☉ *Weekdays 9–noon and 2–5, Sun. service, 10.*

★ ❿ Kurá Hulanda Museum. This fascinating museum is housed within the confines of a restored 18th century village in Otrobanda. The museum is built around the square (Kurá Hulanda means "Holland courtyard"), where slaves were sold by the Dutch to be resold throughout the Caribbean. The museum's huge collection is divided into variously themed buildings and covers all aspects of world African history. The most disturbing and profound collection is in the "Black Holocaust" section, which illustrates all aspects of the transatlantic slave trade. It's impossible to enter the replica of a slave ship hold without feeling a shiver. The museum and complex are the brainchild of Dutch millionaire philanthropist Jacob Gelt Dekker. The on-site Kurá Hulanda Conference Center has state-of-the-art facilities for lectures, seminars, and tutorials. The Jacob Gelt Dekker Institute for Advanced Cultural Studies is an international think tank and learning exchange center dedicated to the people and ideas of the Atlantic Rim, with an emphasis on African studies and the African diaspora. ⊠ *Klipstraat 9, Otrobanda,* ☎ *5999/ 462–1400,* WEB *www.kurahulanda.com.* 🎟 *$5.* ⊙ *Daily 10–5.*

★ ⑧ **Maritime Museum.** The 40-odd chronological exhibits at this museum truly give you a sense of Curaçao's maritime history, using ship models, maps, nautical charts, navigational equipment, and audiovisual displays. Topics explored along the way include the development of Willemstad as a trading city, Curaçao's role as a contraband hub, the explosion of the *De Alphen* in 1778, the slave trade, the development of steam navigation, the rise of cruise tourism, and the role of the Dutch navy on the island. The third floor hosts temporary exhibits, and the museum also offers a two-hour guided tour on its "water bus" through Curaçao's harbor—a route familiar to traders, smugglers, and pirates. When you're ready for a break, drop anchor at the Harbor Café or browse through the souvenir shop. ⊠ *Van der Brandhofstraat 7, Scharloo,* ☎ *5999/465–2327.* 🎟 *$6 museum only; $12 museum and harbor tour.* ⊙ *Tue.–Sat. 10–5.*

③ **Mikveh Israel-Emanuel Synagogue.** The temple, the oldest still in use in the western hemisphere, is one of Curaçao's most important sights and draws 20,000 visitors a year. Brilliant white sand covers the synagogue floor, a remembrance of Moses leading his people through the desert and of the diaspora. The synagogue was dedicated in 1732 by the Jewish community, which originally came from Amsterdam in 1651 to establish a new congregation and to seize freedoms that weren't generally afforded them in Europe at that time. They were later joined by Jews from Portugal and Spain (via Amsterdam) fleeing persecution from the Inquisition. A number of Jews also came from Brazil, after the Portuguese reconquest of Recife—a Dutch trading post—raised fears that the Inquisition would be introduced there, too. By the early 1700s, more than 2,000 Jews resided on Curaçao. The fascinating **Jewish Cultural Museum** (☎ 5999/461–1633), in the back, displays Jewish antiques (including a set of circumcision instruments) and artifacts collected from all over the world. English and Hebrew services are held Friday at 6:30 PM and Saturday at 10 AM. Men who attend should wear a jacket and tie. ⊠ *Hanchi Snoa 29, Punda,* ☎ *5999/461–1633.* 🎟 *Small donation expected in synagogue; $2 Jewish Cultural Museum.* ⊙ *Weekdays 9–11:45 and 2:30–4:45.*

④ **Old Market (Marche).** Local women prepare hearty Antillean lunches at the Old Market behind the post office. Enjoy such Curaçaoan specialties as funchi (a cornmeal dish), *keshi yena* (gouda cheese stuffed with a seasoned chicken mixture), goat stew, fried fish, peas and rice, and fried plantains. Small portions cost $2.50; large plates for $7 are a feast for two. ⊠ *De Ruyterkade.*

① **Plaza Piar.** This plaza is dedicated to Manuel Piar, a native Curaçaoan who fought for the independence of Venezuela under the liberator Simón Bolívar. On one side of the plaza is the Waterfort, a bastion dating from 1634. The original cannons are still positioned in the battlements. The foundation, however, now forms the walls of the Plaza Hotel Curaçao.

⑤ **Queen Emma Bridge.** This bridge is affectionately called the Swinging Old Lady by the locals. If you're standing on the Otrobanda side, take a few moments to scan Curaçao's multicolor face, on the other side of

Santa Anna Bay. If you wait long enough, the bridge will swing open (at least 30 times a day) to let seagoing ships pass through. The original bridge, built in 1888, was the brainchild of the American consul Leonard Burlington Smith, who made a mint off the tolls he charged for using it: 2¢ per person for those wearing shoes, free to those crossing barefoot. Today it's free to everyone.

⑨ Queen Juliana Bridge. This 1,625-ft-long (497-m-long) bridge was completed in 1974 and stands 200 ft (61 m) above water—a great vantage point for photos of the city. It's the bridge you drive over to cross to the other side of the city, and although the route is time-consuming (and more expensive if you're going by taxi), the view is worth it. At every hour of the day, the sun casts a different tint, creating an ever-changing panorama; the nighttime view is breathtaking.

⑦ Scharloo. The Wilhelmina Drawbridge connects Punda with the once-flourishing district of Scharloo, where the early Jewish merchants first built stately homes. The end of the district closest to Kleine Werf is now a red-light district and is pretty run-down, but the rest of the area is well worth a visit. The architecture along Scharlooweg (much of it from the 17th century) is intriguing, and, happily, many of the structures that had become dilapidated have been meticulously renovated.

The Rest of the Island

The Weg Maar Santa Cruz road through the village of Soto winds to the island's northwest tip through landscape that Georgia O'Keeffe might have painted—towering cacti, flamboyant dried shrubbery, and aluminum-roof houses. Throughout this *kunuku,* or countryside, you can see fishermen hauling nets, women pounding cornmeal, and an occasional donkey blocking traffic. Land houses, large plantation houses from centuries past, dot the countryside, though most are closed to the public. To explore the island's eastern side, take the coastal road— Martin Luther King Boulevard—from Willemstad about 2 mi (3 km) to Bapor Kibra. This is where the Seaquarium and the Underwater Park are located.

Numbers in the margin correspond to points of interest on the Curaçao map.

SIGHTS TO SEE

㉑ Boka Tabla. At Boka Tabla, the sea has carved a magnificent grotto. Safely tucked in the back, you can watch and listen to the waves crashing against the rocks. Several of the surrounding minicaverns serve as nesting places; watch flocks of parakeets emerge in formation, magnificent hawks soar and dip, and gulls dive-bomb for lunch. Steer clear of the many manchineel trees near the cave. ⊠ *Westpunt Hwy., just past village center, Soto.*

★ ⑳ Christoffel Park. This fantastic 4,450-acre garden and wildlife preserve centers on the towering Mt. Christoffel. There are eight hiking trails in the park, which take anywhere from 20 minutes to 2½ hours to complete. You can drive your own car (if it has heavy-treaded tires) or rent a four-wheel-drive vehicle with an accompanying guide (NAf 150 for up to five passengers). Start out early (by 10 AM the park starts to feel like a sauna), and if you're going solo, first study the *Excursion Guide to Christoffel Park,* sold at the front desk of the Savonet Museum. It outlines the various routes and identifies the flora and fauna found here. There's a 20-mi (32-km) network of roads, and no matter what route you take, you'll be treated to views of hilly fields full of prickly pear cacti, divi-divi trees, bushy-haired palms, and exotic flowers that bloom unpredictably after November showers. There are also caves—the strong at heart will revel in the rustling of bat wings and the sight of

scuttling scorpion spiders (not poisonous)—and ancient Indian drawings. Spectacular bird-watching is abundant, and experts lead the way
twice daily.

Watch for goats and small wildlife that might cross your path or dart
in front of your car, and consider yourself lucky if you see any of the
elusive, protected white-tail deer. The whip snakes and minute silver
snakes you may encounter aren't poisonous. White-tail hawks may be
seen on the green route, white orchids and crownlike passionflowers
on the yellow route. Climbing the 1,239-ft (379-m) **Mt. Christoffel** on
foot is an exhilarating challenge to anyone who hasn't grown up scal-
ing the Alps. The park's guidebook claims the round trip will take an
hour, and Curaçaoan adolescent boys do make a sport of racing up
and down, but it's really more like two (sweaty) hours from the mountain's base for a reasonably fit person who's not an expert hiker. The
view from the peak, however, *is* thrilling—a panorama that includes
Santa Marta Bay and the tabletop mountain of St. Hironimus. On a
clear day you can even see the mountain ranges of Venezuela, Bonaire,
and Aruba.

You might also enjoy one of the park's fascinating tours. Every Friday
morning at 10, park rangers lead a 2½-mi (4-km) nature hike, discoursing
on the indigenous flora and fauna. The fee ($9) includes an iguana pre-
sentation and a soft drink. Jeep tours ($100 for one to five people) go
off the beaten track, raising plenty of dust. The 15-minute deer-watch-
ing expeditions (with no more than eight people to prevent startling
the skittish creatures) track the herd of 150–200 small white-tail deer
in the park for $6 per person (Saturdays and Sundays, beginning at
4:30 PM). ⊠ *Savonet,* ☎ *5999/864–0363.* 🎫 *Park and museum $13.50.*
🕐 *Mon.–Sat. 8–4, Sun. 6–3; last admission 1 hr before closing.*

⑲ **Country House Museum.** The thatched-roof cottage is a living museum
demonstrating country life as it was in the 19th century. It's filled with
antique furniture, farm implements, and clothing typical of colonial
life. Out back is a minifarm with a vegetable garden, penned donkeys,
and caged parrots, eagles, and iguanas. Look closely at the fence—it's
made of living cacti. There's also a snack bar. A festival featuring live
music and local crafts takes place here on the first Sunday of each month.
⊠ *Dokterstuin 27 (on road to Westpunt from Willemstad), Westpunt,*
☎ *5999/864–2742.* 🎫 *$1.50.* 🕐 *Tues.–Fri. 9–4, weekends 9–5.*

★ 🖑 ⑬ **Curaçao Seaquarium.** The Seaquarium is *the* place to see the island's
underwater treasures without getting your feet wet. It's the world's only
public aquarium where sea creatures are raised and cultivated naturally. Where else can you hand-feed a shark (or watch a diver do it)?
The **Animal Encounters** section consists of a broad, 12-ft-deep (4-m-
deep) open-water enclosure that brings you face to face with several
different species. Snorkelers and divers are welcome to swim freely with
stingrays, tarpon, groupers, and such. Diving instruction and equipment are part of the package; it's a thrilling introduction to the sport
in a controlled environment, and, in fact, up to 75% of participants
have never tried diving before. If shark feeding isn't your cup of tea,
there's an underwater observatory. The cost is $55 for divers, $35 for
snorkelers, which includes admission to the Seaquarium, training, use
of equipment, and food for the fish, turtles, and sharks. Reservations
for Animal Encounters must be made 24 hours in advance.

You can spend several hours mesmerized by the 46 freshwater tanks
full of more than 400 varieties of fish and vegetation found in the waters around Curaçao. The Maritime Awareness Center offers hands-
on discovery of the underworld wonders of coral reefs. In the minitheater,

a high-tech, three-dimensional slide show makes you feel as if you're actually in the ocean. There are also glass-bottom-boat tours, feeding shows, and a viewing platform overlooking the wreck of the steamship SS *Oranje Nassau,* which sank in 1906. You can stop by the on-site snack bar and restaurant or browse in the souvenir shop. A nearby beach is well suited to novice swimmers and children. ⊠ *Bapor Kibra,* ☎ *5999/461–6666.* 🖀 *$13.25, or $24 for six-week pass.* ⊘ *Daily 8–5.*

⑭ Curaçao Underwater Marine Park. About 12½ mi (20 km) of untouched coral reefs off the southeast shore have been granted the status of a national park. Mooring buoys placed at the most interesting dive sites provide safe anchoring and prevent damage to the reef. Several sunken ships lie quietly in the deep. The park stretches along the south shore from the Breezes Curaçao resort in Willemstad to the island's eastern tip.

⑮ Den Paradera. Dazzle your senses at this organic herb garden, where local plants are cataloged according to their traditional use in folk medicine. As part of owner Dinah Veeris's research, she interviewed dozens of older islanders about the plants and their use in treating everything from diabetes to stomach ulcers. A reconstructed settlement at the rear of the property consists of small huts with life-size rag dolls depicting traditional folkloric scenes. Top off your visit with a special refreshing beverage (made of aloe, ginger, and lemon). A shop sells natural perfumes and potpourri. ⊠ *Seru Grandi Kavel 105A, Banda Riba,* ☎ *5999/767–5608.* 🖀 *$5.65 with guided tour, $4.25 without guided tour.* ⊘ *By appointment only.*

⑱ Hato Caves. Hour-long guided tours wind down into various chambers to the water pools, a "voodoo" chamber, a wishing well, fruit bats' sleeping quarters, and Curaçao Falls, guarded by a limestone "dragon." Hidden lights illuminate the limestone formations (use your imagination and you might see such fantastic shapes as the Sleeping Giant, the Madonna, and the Woolly Mammoth) and gravel walkways. This is one of the better Caribbean caves open to the public, but keep in mind that there are 49 steep steps to reach the entrance, and the cave itself is dank and hot (though they've put electric fans in some areas to provide relief). To reach the caves, head northwest toward airport, take right onto Gosieweg, follow loop right onto Schottegatweg, take another right onto Jan Norduynweg, a final right onto Rooseveltweg, and follow signs. ⊠ *Rooseveltweg, Hato,* ☎ *5999/868–0379.* 🖀 *$6.50.* ⊘ *Daily 10–5.*

⑰ Landhuis Brievengat. This mustard-color plantation house is a fine example of a home from the island's past. You can see the original kitchen still intact, the 18-inch-thick walls, fine antiques, and the watchtowers once used for lovers' trysts. The restaurant, open only on Wednesday and Friday, serves a tasty Indonesian rijsttafel. Friday night a party is held on the wide wraparound terrace, with bands and plenty to drink ($6 cover charge). On the last Sunday of the month (6 PM–7:30 PM), this estate holds an open house with crafts demonstrations and folkloric shows. It's a 15-minute drive northeast of Willemstad, near Centro Deportivo stadium. ⊠ *Brievengat,* ☎ *5999/737–8344.* 🖀 *$1.* ⊘ *Mon.–Sat. 9:15–12:15 and 3–6.*

㉒ Landhuis Knip. In terms of slave population, this was once the island's largest plantation. It therefore comes as no surprise that the slave revolt took place here in 1795. The renovated plantation house near the island's western tip is filled with period furnishings, clothing, and household items. ⊠ *Weg Naar Santa Cruz, Knip,* ☎ *5999/864–0244.* 🖀 *$2.* ⊘ *Weekdays 9–4, weekends 10–4.*

🐦 ⑯ **Ostrich Farm.** If you (and the kids) are ready to stick your neck out for an adventure, visit one of the largest ostrich breeding farms outside Africa and the only one in the Caribbean. Every hour guided tours (reservations are essential) show the creatures' complete development from egg to mature bird. At the Restaurant Zambezi you can sample local ostrich specialties and other African dishes (reservations are suggested). Be sure to visit the Art of Africa shop, featuring crafts from Zimbabwe and South Africa including handmade wall hangings, exotic leather products, and wood carvings. ⊠ *Groot St. Joris,* ☎ *5999/747–2777,* WEB *www.ostrichfarm.net.* 🎫 *$10 (includes tour).* ⊙ *Tues.–Sun. 9–4.*

⑫ **Senior Curaçao Liqueur Distillery.** The charming 17th-century Landhuis Chobolobo (just outside Willemstad) is where the famed Curaçao liqueur, made from the peels of the bitter Iranha orange, is produced. Don't expect a massive factory—it's just a small showroom in an open-air foyer. There are no guides, but delightful old hand-painted posters explain the distillation process, and you'll be graciously offered samples in assorted flavors. If you're interested in buying—the orange-flavored chocolate liqueur is delicious over ice cream—you can choose from a complete selection in equally enticing bottles, including those shaped like Dutch ceramic houses. ⊠ *Landhuis Chobolobo, Saliña Arriba,* ☎ *5999/461–3526.* 🎫 *Free.* ⊙ *Weekdays 8–noon and 1–5.*

CURAÇAO A TO Z

To research prices, get advice from other travelers, and book travel arrangements, visit www.fodors.com.

AIR TRAVEL

Air DCE (formerly Air ALM) offers frequent service from Miami and Atlanta and interisland service to Aruba and Bonaire. For Atlanta departures Air DCE has connecting service to most U.S. gateways with Delta. Aeropostal has nonstop service from Caracas. American Airlines flies direct daily from Miami. E-Liner Airways has interisland service, including sightseeing and beach tours of Aruba and Bonaire. KLM flies direct from Amsterdam (to fly from Australia, New Zealand, or the United Kingdom, consider flying to Amsterdam for this flight to Curaçao). SLM (Suriname Airways) flies direct from Paramaibo, Suriname.

➤ AIRLINES AND CONTACTS: **Air DCE** (☎ 5999/869–5533). **Aeropostal** (☎ 5999/888–2818). **American Airlines** (☎ 5999/869–5701). **E-Liner Airways** (☎ 5999/465–8099). **KLM** (☎ 5999/465–2747). **SLM** (☎ 5999/868–4360).

AIRPORTS

The airport has car rental facilities, duty-free shops, and a restaurant. It takes about 20 minutes to get to the hotels in Willemstad by taxi.
➤ AIRPORT INFORMATION: **Curaçao International Airport** (no phone).

BUSINESS HOURS

BANKS

Banks are open weekdays 8–3:30 or 8–11:30 and 1:30–4; the airport branch has extended hours: 8–8 Monday–Saturday and 9–4 on Sunday.

POST OFFICES

Post office hours are 7:30–noon and 1:30–5 weekdays. The Groot Kwartier branch is open 7–7 on weekdays and 7–3 on Saturday.

SHOPS

Some shops remain closed on Monday. Many are open Monday–Saturday 8–noon and 2–6. Some stay open during the lunch hour and on Sunday and holidays when cruise ships are in port.

CAR RENTALS

You can rent a car from any of the major car agencies at the airport or have one delivered free to your hotel. Rates range from about $60 a day for a Toyota Tercel to about $75 for a four-door sedan or four-wheel-drive vehicle; add 6% tax and required $10 daily insurance.
➤ MAJOR AGENCIES: **Avis** (☎ 5999/461–1255 or 800/331–1212). **Budget** (☎ 5999/868–3466 or 800/472–3325). **Dollar** (☎ 5999/461–3144). **Hertz** (☎ 5999/888–0088). **National Car Rental** (☎ 5999/864–4433).

CAR TRAVEL

If you're planning to do country driving or rough it through Christoffel Park, a four-wheel-drive vehicle is best. All you need is a valid U.S., Canadian, or British driver's license.

GASOLINE

Gas prices in Curaçao are about NAf 1.56 per liter for unleaded; NAf 1.48 for regular; and NAf 1.50 for diesel. There are many gas stations in the Willemstad area as well as in the suburban areas, including two on the main road as you head to the western tip of the island.

RULES OF THE ROAD

Driving in the Netherlands Antilles is the same as in the U.S., on the right-hand side of the road. Right turns on red are prohibited. Local laws require drivers and passengers to wear seat belts and motorcyclists to wear helmets. Children under 4 years of age should be in child safety seats; if older they should ride in the back seat.

ELECTRICITY

The current is 110–130 volts/50 cycles, which is compatible with such small North American appliances as electric razors and blow dryers. Some electrical items may overheat, and internal timers in devices such as clock radios and camcorders won't keep the correct time.

EMBASSIES

➤ CANADA: **Consulate of Canada** (✉ Plaza Jojo Correa 2–4, Willemstad, ☎ 5999/461–3515).
➤ UNITED KINGDOM: **British Consulate** (✉ Jan Sofat 38, Willemstad, ☎ 5999/747–3322).
➤ UNITED STATES: **United States Consulate** (✉ Roosevelthouse, J. B. Gorsira 1, Willemstad, ☎ 5999/461–3066).

EMERGENCIES

➤ HEALTH & SAFETY: **Ambulance and fire** (☎ 912). **On-call dentists** (☎ 8888). **On-call doctors** (☎ 1111).
➤ HOSPITALS: **St. Elisabeth's Hospital** (✉ Breedestraat 193, Willemstad, ☎ 5999/462–4900 or 5999/462–5100).
➤ PHARMACIES: **Botica Popular** (✉ Madurostraat 15, Willemstad, ☎ 5999/461–1269).
➤ POLICE: **Police emergencies** (☎ 911).
➤ SCUBA-DIVING EMERGENCIES: **St. Elisabeth's Hospital** (✉ Breedestraat 193, ☎ 5999/462–4900 or 5999/462–5100) is equipped with a hyperbaric chamber.
➤ SEA EMERGENCIES: **Coast Guard** (☎ 113).

ETIQUETTE AND BEHAVIOR

To guarantee a smile, wish someone *bon dia* (good day) or offer a warm *masha danki* (thank you very much) after someone has performed a service. Dutch culture is stronger on Curaçao than on many Antillean islands, so the island has a European flavor (note that topless sunbathing is tolerated at some hotels).

FESTIVALS AND SEASONAL EVENTS

Carnival lasts longer on Curaçao than on many islands: the revelries begin at New Year's and continue until midnight the day before Ash Wednesday. The highlight is the Tumba Festival (dates vary), a four-day musical event featuring fierce competition between local musicians for the honor of having their piece selected as the official road march during parades. Easter Monday's Seú Folklore Parade is made up of groups celebrating the harvest in traditional costumes. May is when the Curaçao International Jazz Festival is held. The Curaçao Salsa Festival is held in June, July, or August and attracts international performers and audiences.

HEALTH

Mosquitoes are a presence on Curaçao, at least during the rainy season. The bad news is that the rainy season falls between October and February, coinciding with the tourist high season. To be safe, keep perfume to a minimum, use insect repellent before dining alfresco, and spray your hotel room at night—especially if you've opened a window. If you plan to go into the water, beware of long-spine sea urchins, which can be painful if you come in contact with them.

Don't eat any of the little green applelike fruits (they even smell like apples) of the manchineel tree: they're poisonous. In fact, steer clear of the trees altogether; raindrops or dewdrops dripping off the leaves can blister your skin. If contact does occur, rinse the affected area with water and, in extreme cases, get medical attention. Usually the burning sensation won't last longer than two hours.

HOLIDAYS

Public holidays are: New Year's Day, Good Friday (Apr. 13), Easter Monday (Apr. 16), the Queen's Birthday (not Beatrix, but rather her mother, Juliana; Apr. 30), Labor Day (May 1), Curaçao Flag Day (July 2), Antilles Day (Oct. 21), and Christmas holiday (Dec. 25 and 26).

LANGUAGE

Dutch is the official language, but the vernacular is Papiamento—a mixture of Dutch, African, French, Portuguese, Spanish, and English. One theory holds that the language developed during the 18th century as a mode of communication between land owners and their slaves. These days English is studied by schoolchildren as well as Spanish and, of course, Dutch. Anyone involved with tourism generally speaks English.

MAIL AND SHIPPING

There are post offices in Punda, Otrobanda, and Groot Kwartier on Schottegatweg (Ring Road), as well as small branches at the Curaçao World Trade Center and the airport. Some hotels sell stamps and have letter drops; you can also buy stamps at some bookstores. An airmail letter to the United States, Canada, or Europe costs NAf 2.25, a postcard NAf.90.

MONEY MATTERS

Prices quoted throughout this chapter are in U.S. dollars unless otherwise indicated.

ATMS

There are over 50 ATM locations on the island that dispense money in the local currency. The airport has an ATM (it dispenses U.S. dollars) as do many bank branches.

CURRENCY

U.S. dollars—in cash or traveler's checks—are accepted nearly everywhere, so there's no need to worry about exchanging money. However, you may need small change for pay phones, cigarettes, or soda machines. The currency in the Netherlands Antilles is the florin (also called the guilder) and is indicated by fl or NAf on price tags. The florin is very stable against the U.S. dollar; the official rate of exchange at press time was NAf 1.80 to US$1.

➤ BANKS: **ABN-AMRO Bank** (☎ 5999/763–8000). **Antilles Banking Corporation** (☎ 5999/461–2822). **Maduro & Curiel's Bank** (☎ 5999/466–1100).

PASSPORTS AND VISAS

U.S. and Canadian citizens need either a valid passport or a birth certificate with a raised seal along with a government-authorized photo ID. Citizens of Australia, New Zealand, and the United Kingdom must produce a passport. Everyone must show an ongoing or return ticket.

SAFETY

Crime is on the increase (but not rampant) in Curaçao, so common-sense rules apply. Lock rental cars, and don't leave valuables in the car. Use in-room safes or leave valuables at the front desk of your hotel, and never leave bags unattended at the airport, on tours, or on the beach.

SIGHTSEEING TOURS

BOAT TOURS

Many sailboats and motorboats offer sunset cruises and daylong snorkel and picnic trips to Klein Curaçao, the "clothes-optional" island between Curaçao and Bonaire. Prices run $50–$65. Or for a unique vantage point, soak up the local marine life from one of Seaworld Explorer/Atlantis Adventures' semi-submersibles. An hour-long tour of the beautiful coral reefs is $40. The *Bounty* is a 90-ft shooner, the *Insulinde* is a 120-ft Dutch sailing ketch, and the *Mermaid* is a 66-ft motor yacht, all of which offer boat tours.

➤ CONTACTS: *Atlantis Adventures* (☎ 5999/462–8833). *Bounty* (☎ 5999/560–1887). *Insulinde* (☎ 5999/560–1340). *Mermaid* (☎ 5999/560–1530).

ORIENTATION

Does Travel & Kadushi Tours takes you around in an air-conditioned coach with a knowledgeable guide. They can also arrange short hops to Aruba and Bonaire. Peter Trips offers full-day island tours ($37, meal not included) departing from the hotels Friday, Saturday, and Sunday at 9 AM, with visits to many points of interest, including Scharloo, Slavebridge, Jan Thiel, Fort Nassau, and Knip Bay. Or you can opt for 3½-hour tours of the island's east (Monday at 3 PM, $19) or west side (Tuesday and Thursday at 3 PM, $21). Taber Tours offers a three-hour East Tour ($13) that includes the Curaçao Liqueur Factory at Landhuis Chobolobo, the Curaçao Museum, and the Bloempot shopping center. Day trips to Aruba ($175) and Bonaire ($165) are also available.

➤ CONTACTS: **Does Travel & Kadushi Tours** (✉ Caracasbaaiweg 164, ☎ 5999/461–1626). **Peter Trips** (☎ 5999/561–5368). **Taber Tours** (✉ Dokway, ☎ 5999/737–6637).

SPECIAL INTEREST

For personalized history and nature tours contact Dornasol Tours; half-day tours run $25, and full-day tours are $40 per person. Dutch Dream Adventures targets the action-seeker with canoe safaris, mountain biking, and jeep tours. The Ostrich Express visits one of the largest ostrich farms outside Africa and gives you a 60-minute guided tour. Kids enjoy the chance to hold an egg, stroke a fluffy day-old chick, and sit atop a fully grown ostrich for an unusual photo op. The price is $8.50 for adults, $5.60 for children 2–14, with pick-up at your hotel. Animal lovers can take an escorted deer watching tour at Christoffel National Park at a cost of $9 for adults and $5 for children under 15 (reservations required). Wild Curaçao offers expertly guided ecotourism adventures highlighting the island's flora and fauna, with stops at nature preserves, caves, salt lakes, and more. Or keep track of your surroundings as you visit key historic sites aboard the Willemstad Trolley Train ($16 for a 1½-hour tour).

➤ CONTACTS: **Christoffel National Park** (☎ 5999/864–0363). **Dornasol Tours** (☎ 5999/468–2735). **Dutch Dream Adventures** (☎ 5999/461–2500). **Ostrich Express** (☎ 5999/560–1276). **Willemstad Trolley Train** (☎ 5999/462–8833). **Wild Curaçao** (☎ 5999/561–0027).

WALKING TOURS

Walking tours of historic Otrobanda, focusing on the unique architecture of this old section of town, are led by architect Anko van der Woude every Thursday (reservations are suggested), leaving from the central clock at Brionplein at 5:15 PM. Jopie Hart offers a walking tour that emphasizes the sociocultural aspects of Otrobanda; it begins at 5:15 PM on Wednesday and departs from the clock at Brionplein. Mention ahead to your tour leader that you speak English.

➤ CONTACTS: **Anko van der Woude/Jenny Smit** (☎ 5999/461–3554). **Jopie Hart** (☎ 5999/767–3798).

TAXES & SERVICE CHARGES

DEPARTURE TAX

The airport international departure tax is NAf 35 (or $20), and the interisland departure tax is NAf 10 (about $5.65).

SALES TAX

Hotels add a 12% service charge to the bill and collect a 7% government room tax; restaurants add 10%–15%.

VALUE ADDED TAX (V.A.T.)

Most goods and services purchased on the island will also have a 5% OB tax (a goods and services tax) added to the purchase price.

TAXIS

Drivers have an official tariff chart, with fares from the airport to Willemstad and the nearby beach hotels running about $10–$15 and those to hotels at the island's western end about $25–$40. Since there are no meters, you should confirm the fare with the driver before departure. There's an additional 25% surcharge after 11 PM. Taxis are readily available at hotels; in other cases, call Central Dispatch.

➤ CONTACTS: **Central Dispatch** (☎ 5999/869–0752).

TELEPHONES

Phone service through the hotel operators in Curaçao is slow, but direct-dial service, both on-island and to elsewhere in the world, is fast and clear. Hotel operators will put the call through for you, but if you make a collect call, do check to make sure the hotel does not charge you as well.

COUNTRY AND AREA CODES

To call Curaçao direct from the United States, dial 011–5999 plus the number in Curaçao.

INTERNATIONAL CALLS

AT&T Direct service is available by calling 001/800/872–2881, which connects you with an AT&T International operator, but it's impossible from pay phones, and your hotel will likely add a surcharge.

LOCAL CALLS

To place a local call on the island, dial the seven-digit local number. Pay phones charge NAf.50 for a local call—far cheaper than what a hotel will charge you.

TIPPING

As service is usually included, tipping at restaurants isn't expected, though if you found the staff exemplary, you can add another 5%–10% to the bill. Taxi drivers normally receive a 10% gratuity, but this is at your discretion. Tip porters and bellmen about $1 a bag, the hotel house-keeping staff $2–$3 per day.

VISITOR INFORMATION

➤ In CURAÇAO: **Curaçao Tourism Development Bureau** (✉ Pieter-maai 19, Willemstad, ☎ 5999/461–6000 Ext. 117, WEB www.curacao-tourism.com; ✉ Curaçao International Airport, ☎ 5999/868–6789).

Updated by
Carla Armour

In the early hours of the morning—after the day's first rainfall has seemingly washed the whole world clean—the sun slides up into the sky over the mountains and under the arch of a faint rainbow. Aroused by the light, birds begin their wildly orchestrated chorus—nature's alarm clock. In breezes heavy with the scents of damp earth and lemongrass and not yet fully warmed by the sun, leaves quiver and sparkle with raindrops and dew and the promise of another beautiful day.

"Isle of beauty, isle of splendor," rings the first line of the national anthem of the Commonwealth of Dominica. Indeed, the intensity of the unspoiled beauty and splendor of this isle, dubbed "the nature island of the Caribbean," is truly inspiring as it turns and twists, towers to mountain crests, then tumbles to falls and valleys. The weather is equally dramatic: torrential rains, dazzling sunshine, and, above all, rainbows are likely to greet you in the course of a day.

Wedged between the two French islands of Guadeloupe to the north and Martinique to the south, Dominica (pronounced dom-in-*ee*-ka) is a wild place. Wild orchids, anthurium lilies, ferns, heliconias, and myriad fruit trees sprout profusely. Much of the interior is still covered by luxuriant rain forest and remains inaccessible by road. Here everything grows more intensely: greener, brighter, and bigger. The ideal environment that gave the early Caribs (the region's original inhabitants) a natural fortress against the European settlers also kept Dominica from being colonized like other Caribbean islands. Today the rugged northeast is reserved as home to the last survivors of the Caribs, along with their traditions and mythology.

Dominica—29 mi (47 km) long and 16 mi (26 km) wide, with a population of just 71,000—is a former British colony; having attained its independence in November 1978, it now has a seat in the United Nations as the central Caribbean's only Natural World Heritage Site. Its capital is Roseau (pronounced rose-*oh*); the official language is English, although most locals communicate with each other in Creole; roads are driven on the left; family and place names are a melange of English, Carib, and French; and the religion is predominantly Catholic. The economy is still heavily dependent on agriculture.

With under 70,000 overnight travellers, she is a little-known destination; there are no major hotel chains, but her National Forestry Division has spent the last 50 years preserving and designating more national forests, and marine reserves, and parks, per capita, than almost anywhere on earth, Dominica is a popular "alternative" Caribbean experience.

It's an ideal place to go if you want to really get away—hike, bike, trek, spot birds and butterflies in the rain forest; explore waterfalls and discover the world's largest boiling lake; experience a vibrant culture in Dominica's traditions; kayak, dive, snorkel, or sail in marine reserves; or go out in search of the many resident whale and dolphin species. From the Elfin Woodlands and dense rain forest to the therapeutic geothermal springs and world-class dive sites that mirror her terrestrial terrain, to experience Dominica is really to know the earth as it was created.

Lodging

Places to stay, amenities offered, and prices asked are as varied as the island's landscapes. Here you'll find intimate city hotels, mountain retreats, secluded bungalows, plantation houses, and seaside cottages. Most properties offer packages with dives, hikes, tours, and/or meal plans included, along with all the usual amenities. Many properties advertise winter rates with either a discount for summer or longer stays.

CATEGORY	COST EP/CP*	COST A.I.**
$$$$	over $350	over $375
$$$	$250–$350	$275–$375
$$	$150–$250	$175–$275
$	under $150	under $175

*EP/CP prices are per night for a standard double room in high season, excluding taxes, service charges, and meal plans**A.I. (all-inclusive) prices are per person, per night based on double-occupancy during high season, excluding taxes and service charges*

$$ ⊞ **Castaways Beach Hotel.** An eclectic crowd: hikers, divers, athletes, and leisure seekers are drawn to this beachfront hotel 20 minutes north of Roseau. Ten of the spacious rooms, having been totally remodeled in 2001, have refrigerators, hair dryers, coffeemakers, and wood and rattan furnishings. All rooms have balconies with views of the Caribbean through tropical gardens; all rooms have ceiling fans and are open, comfortable, and cool. Guests gather at the Almond Tree Restaurant and Bar. On Sunday there's a beach barbecue with drinks and live music. ✉ *Mero (Box 5, Roseau)*, ☎ *767/449-6244*, ℻ *767/449-6216*, WEB *www.castaways.dm. 26 rooms. Restaurant, no air-conditioning in some rooms, fans, tennis court, beach, dive shop, snorkeling, boating, fishing, 2 bars. Closed Sept.–mid-Oct. MC, V. CP, EP, MAP.*

$$ ⊞ **Castle Comfort Lodge.** Past the wrought iron gates and within the
★ lush gardens of this dedicated dive lodge 1 mi south of Roseau you are confronted with the tranquil Caribbean Sea. The boats anchored just off the pier, the telltale dive log, and the divers in the hot tub with mask imprints on their foreheads give it all away. This Lodge offers dive packages with everything included: dives, transfers, meals, accommodation, taxes. The brightly decorated rooms with verandas are in two buildings: one directly on the sea. Bountiful meals are served on a large terrace. Nondivers can enjoy the property's pool, kayaking, and a multitude of island adventures. ✉ *Castle Comfort (Box 2253, Roseau)*, ☎ *767/448-2188*, ℻ *767/448-6088*, WEB *www.divedominica.com. 15 rooms. Restaurant, fans, pool, hot tub, dive shop, boating. Closed Sept. AE, MC, V. MAP.*

$$ ⊞ **Picard Beach Cottages.** Eighteen hardwood cottages on Dominica's
★ longest golden sand beach fringe the remnants of an old coconut plantation and its lushly landscaped gardens. The cottages are only steps away from the sea; a white picket fence with private gates allows you access to the beach. Each cottage accommodates two adults with two

Dominica

ATLANTIC OCEAN

Dominica Passage

Capucin Pt.

Vieille Case

11 Morne Aux Diables

Toucari Beach and Reef

Douglas Bay

Purple Beach

Cabrits Drop-off

10

9 **8** Portsmouth

Prince Rupert Bay

Picard Beach

21 **22**

Picard R.

Pt. Ronde

Indian Rd.

Indian R.

Hampstead **6**

Bense

Hodges

19 **20**

Calibishie

L'Anse Tortue

Woodford Hill Bay

6 Marigot

Londonderry Bay

6

Melville Hall Airport

18

5

Castle Bruce

4

River

Layou

Syndicate Rd.

Dublanc

Colihaut

Nose Reef

Brain Coral Garden

Salisbury Falls

23 **24**

Salisbury

25 Mero

Castaways

7

children or three adults and has a kitchenette, a living and dining area, and a veranda; most have tubs. The casual Le Flambeau Restaurant next door serves creole food, and you are a 15-minute walk from Portsmouth's stores and a 15-minute drive from the areas' key nature attractions. Taxis cost $50 from Roseau. ✉ *Prince Rupert Bay (Box 34, Roseau),* ☎ *767/445–5131,* FAX *767/445–5599,* WEB *www.delphis. dm/picard.htm. 18 cottages. Restaurant, fans, kitchenettes, beach, bar. AE, MC, V. CP, EP, MAP.*

$–$$ ⊡ **Pointe Baptiste.** Set above the windblown Atlantic coast with two secluded white sand beaches, this weathered plantation house with a large dining and sitting room, four bedrooms, kitchen, and a sprawling veranda with an inspiring view is ideal for families or groups of friends. For a romantic getaway, a separate whitewashed cottage in the garden has a bedroom, kitchenette, and bathroom. The house and the cottage can be rented separately. A cleaner and cook will come daily to the main house, but otherwise you're on your own. Miles from any of the popular nature attractions, you'll need a car—this can be arranged. ✉ *Calibishie (c/o Annick Giraud, Calibishie),* ☎ *767/445–8495 or 767/245– 2460,* WEB *www.delphis.dm/pointeb.htm. 1 4-bedroom house, 1 1-bedroom cottage. No air-conditioning, fans, kitchens, beach. D, MC, V.*

$ ⊡ **Anchorage Hotel.** A favorite nesting ground for adventure-seekers of every age who come to use the dive and whale-watching center or take advantage of the in-house tour company. A comfortable, inexpensive option for those wishing to stay close to Roseau and enjoy being on the ocean. Brightly decorated rooms have all modern conveniences plus balconies. Twenty oceanfront rooms have two double beds; 12 poolside rooms have twin beds or one double. The Ocean Terrace Restaurant and Bar are open to dramatic sunsets with visiting yachts in the foreground. Both locals and visitors frequent the weekly buffet dinners with live music. ✉ *Castle Comfort (Box 34, Roseau),* ☎ *767/448– 2638,* FAX *767/448–5680,* WEB *www.anchoragehotel.dm. 32 rooms. Restaurant, pool, dive shop, bar. AE, D, MC, V. CP, EP, FAP, MAP.*

$ ⊡ **Anse–A–Liane Lodge & Dive Center.** Developing a reputation for its quality service, this lodge tumbles down a cliff face on the west coast. The dive center is a big draw. Ten soothingly furnished, spacious rooms have tile floors and balconies and are housed in various buildings along a staircase that descends down the hillside. Although it is a 10-minute hike to the beach, the lodge is strategically located for hiking into the interior and convenient to some of the island's best dive sites. The restaurant serves continental fare with a twist. ✉ *Coulibistrie (Box 2180, Roseau),* ☎ *767/446–6652,* FAX *767/446–6651,* WEB *www. ansealianedive.com. 10 rooms. Restaurant, dive shop, bar, shop. AE, MC, V. EP, MAP.*

$ ⊡ **Calibishie Lodges.** Just turning east out of the beautiful seaside village of Calibishie, on the Northeast coast, you are struck by the bright bamboo- and melon-colored buildings emerging from behind the terraced lemon grass. Six one-bedroom self-contained units offer all the comforts of home, with Scandinavian furnishings throughout. It's a five-minute walk down to the beach, which is in one of Dominica's most picturesque villages. Chef Patrick Borre migrated to this spot, but his feasts utilize all local produce from the earth and the sea with his European flare. A small swimming pool and sun deck lead off from the bar where Dominican Clem is right at home with a passion for potent punches. ✉ *Calibishie Main Rd., Calibishie,* ☎ FAX *767/445–8537,* WEB *www.calibishie-lodges.com. 6 apartments. Restaurant, no air-conditioning, fans, kitchenettes, pool, bar. D, MC, V.*

$ ⊡ **D'Auchamps Cottages.** Just outside Roseau en route to Trafalgar are these three cottages amid lush gardens. You'll find a studio with rustic fixtures, an outdoor bathroom (no hot water), and a garden view;

the two-bedroom and one-bedroom bungalows are closer to the main estate home and are simple but cozy, with modern fixtures, kitchens, and covered patios. The gardens have marked walkways through exotic anthuriums and ferns. No meals are provided here, but it's not far from Roseau and shops where you can purchase basic supplies. ⊠ *Trafalgar (Box 1889, Roseau),* ☎ *767/448–3346,* FAX *767/449–9637,* WEB *www.delphis.dm/dauchamps. 3 cottages. No air-conditioning, kitchens. No credit cards. EP.*

$ ☎ **Evergreen Hotel.** Just 1 mi (1½ km) south of Roseau on the water's edge, Jenny and her family ensure your stay within these beautiful gardens will be a pleasant one. Spacious rooms in the waterfront annex are decorated with bright floral prints and rattan furniture, large showers, and balconies. The original stone building houses a meeting room and more guest rooms. Wooden furnishings and needlepoint hangings give these a quaint feel; modern facilities make up for the lack of sea views. A Honeymoon Hut is set off in a foliage-filled nook. The Crystal Terrace, just off the pool, has a creative creole menu. ⊠ *Castle Comfort (Box 309, Roseau),* ☎ *767/448–3288,* FAX *767/448–6800,* WEB *www.delphis.dm/evergreen.htm. 16 rooms, 1 cottage. Restaurant, pool, bar, meeting rooms. AE, MC, V. CP, MAP.*

$ ☎ **Exotica.** After winding your way up the mountain through lush veg-
★   etation, you arrive at this sanctuary at 1,600 ft (485 m). Wooden bungalows have red roofs with solar panels; rooms with bright interiors furnished with rattan and floral fabrics, a bedroom with two (extra-long) double beds, and a large living room with trundle beds. If you don't want to cook, Fae serves delicious creole food at the Sugar Apple Café, including produce from her organic garden; it's a great place to bird-watch. The view of the distant ocean from your bungalow is stunning. You may need to rent a jeep to get around. ⊠ *Gommier (Box 109, Roseau),* ☎ *767/448–8839,* FAX *767/448–8829,* WEB *www.exotica-cottages.com. 8 bungalows. Restaurant, no air-conditioning, fans, kitchens. AE, MC, V. CP, EP, MAP.*

$ ☎ **Fort Young Hotel.** Originally built in the 1700s, Fort Young was once
★   the island's main military installation; now it's the island's leading business hotel. Massive walls encircle the original part of the hotel. The cannons guarding the entrances and flagstone floors convey a real sense of history throughout the property. Below, at the edge of the tranquil Caribbean, are an additional 21 guest rooms and suites, along with a waterfall, shops, and a spa; the hotel has no swimming beach. Guest rooms have modern furnishings, private baths, balconies, and spectacular views. The Waterfront Restaurant and Boardwalk Café and Bar offer excellent cuisine and a repose within the hustle of Roseau. ⊠ *Victoria St., Roseau (Box 519),* ☎ *767/448–5000,* FAX *767/448–5006,* WEB *www.fortyounghotel.com. 53 rooms. 2 restaurants, fans, some in-room hot tubs, some kitchens, pool, gym; outdoor hot tub, spa, dive shop, dock, 2 bars, shops, business services, meeting rooms. AE, MC, V. CP, EP, MAP.*

$ ☎ **Garraway Hotel.** Towering plants, fresh flowers, and original paintings adorn public spaces. The guest rooms and suites are decorated in bright fabrics and cool colors; some suites have in-room faxes. Views from the higher floors of the hotel, on the western edge of Roseau, survey the town's quaint architecture, a nostalgic foreground for the imposing mountains. The second-floor Balizier Restaurant specializes in creole cuisine, with a daily lunch buffet. At the Ole Jetty Bar and its sidewalk café you can share the sunset with the cocktail. ⊠ *Bayfront, Roseau (Box 789),* ☎ *767/449–8800,* FAX *767/449–8807,* WEB *www.delphis.dm/garraway.htm. 20 rooms, 11 suites. Restaurant, fans, bar, meeting rooms. AE, DC, MC, V. CP, EP, FAP, MAP.*

$ · ⊞ **Hummingbird Inn.** Dominican Jeane James Finucane, who has a passion for hummingbirds, is queen bee at this lush hillside retreat 2 mi north of Roseau. Ten rooms with white walls, terra-cotta floors, wooden ceilings, and verandas have outstanding Caribbean views. Beds are dressed with handmade quilts. There is no air-conditioning, but shutters can be left open all night to let in breezes and the sound of the ocean while a ceiling fan turns overhead. The Honeymoon Suite has a stately mahogany four-poster bed, a kitchen, and a patio. The reception area, lounge, and dining terrace are all in the main house. ⊠ *Morne Daniel (Box 1901, Roseau)*, ☎ FAX *767/449–1042*, WEB *www.thehummingbirdinn.com. 9 rooms, 1 suite. Restaurant, no air-conditioning, no room phones, no room TVs, fans, some kitchens, bar. AE, MC, V. CP, EP, MAP.*

$ ⊞ **Itassi Cottages.** These three cottages are set amid beautifully landscaped grounds. The two-bedroom, two-bath cottage can house as many as six people; the one-bedroom, one-bath cottage accommodates up to four; and the studio cottage comfortably sleeps two. Each has a full kitchen and cable TV, and there's a shared laundry facility. They are furnished with mix of antiques, straw mats, handmade floral bedspreads, and calabash lamps. Spacious porches with hammocks and sweeping views of the west coast make for an ideal hideaway five minutes southeast of the city. ⊠ *Morne Bruce (Box 2333, Roseau)*, ☎ *767/448–7247*, FAX *767/448–3045*, WEB *www.delphis.dm/itassi.htm. 3 cottages. Fans, kitchens, cable TV, laundry facilities. AE, MC, V. EP.*

$ ⊞ **Papillote Wilderness Retreat.** Luxuriant vegetation abounds, the river ★ beckons you to take a dip, and the 200-ft (61-m) Trafalgar Falls are a short hike from your room. Owner Anne Jean-Baptiste's botanical garden is a mind-boggling collection of rare and indigenous plants and flowers—all planted around secluded mineral pools and stone sculptures. Anne's walking tours of the garden end at the bird-watching station at the top of the property. The charming rooms are decorated with local handicrafts: quilts, grass rugs, prints, and pottery. The terrace-style Papillote restaurant, which has spectacular mountain and valley views, serves excellent local cuisine. ⊠ *Trafalgar Falls Rd., Trafalgar (Box 2287, Roseau)*, ☎ *767/448–2287*, FAX *767/448–2285*, WEB *www.papillote.dm. 4 rooms, 3 suites. Restaurant, no phones, bar, shop. Closed Sept.–mid-Oct. AE, D, MC, V. EP, MAP.*

$ ⊞ **Roxy's Mountain Lodge.** This mountain retreat 4 mi north of Roseau is popular with nature enthusiasts as a gateway to the Morne Trois Pitons World Heritage Site. Regular rooms are clean and comfy with local furnishings. A second, self-contained building offers a suite. The restaurant, which serves traditional Dominican cuisine, opens onto a huge terrace that overlooks the gardens. Bottles containing herbs steeped in rum line the shelves of the tiny bar, a watering hole frequented by hikers fresh from the nearby trails. Laudat can get chilly during winter months, so be sure to pack something warm. ⊠ *Laudat (Box 265, Roseau)*, ☎ FAX *767/448–4845*, WEB *www.delphis.dm/eiroxys.htm. 10 rooms, 1 suite. Restaurant, bar, hiking. AE, MC, V. CP, EP, MAP.*

$ ⊞ **Sunset Bay Club.** Lush gardens filled with scurrying wildlife are crisscrossed by pathways that meander from rooms to garden benches, to the pool, the sauna hut, and back to the beach and restaurant. This is Dominica's only all-inclusive resort, and it's on a stretch of west coast beach. The rooms are all simply furnished but maintain a crisp feeling with ceiling fans and bright colors throughout. Cable TV is available for an additional charge. The restaurant is renowned for its seafood and wide selection of cocktails. ⊠ *Batalie Beach, Coulibistrie*, ☎ *767/446–6522*, FAX *767/446–6523*, WEB *www.sunsetbayclub.com. 12 rooms, 1 honeymoon suite. Restaurant, no air-conditioning, fans, in-room safes, no room phones, pool, beach, sauna, bar. AE, MC, V. All-inclusive, CP.*

$ ★ 🏨 **Sutton Place Hotel.** In the heart of Roseau, large wrought-iron gates lead up from the street into a cool foyer, reception area, and restaurant, which serves scrumptious contemporary creole cuisine. Up a few more hardwood stairs are the five standard rooms, superbly decorated with imported fabrics and fittings. Hotel guests share a lounge and a kitchenette, where a complimentary Continental breakfast is served overlooking the courtyard. Three spacious top-floor suites with their own kitchens have restored antiques and replicas, teak-louvered windows, and polished wood floors. The structure's original 18th-century stonework can be seen in the cozy, air-conditioned Cellars Bar, a popular local hangout. ⊠ *25 Old St., Roseau (Box 2333),* ☎ *767/449–8700,* FAX *767/448–3045,* WEB *www.delphis.dm/sutton.htm. 5 rooms, 3 suites. Restaurant, fans, some kitchens, bar. AE, D, MC, V. CP.*

$ 🏨 **Wesleeann Apartel.** It's hard to miss the red Spanish-tile roof of this five-story building, which stands out against the nearby suburban development. Guest quarters include rooms, suites, and two- and three-bedroom apartments. Each unit has a small balcony, a dining area, a small kitchen, and rattan furnishings. The restaurant and bar serves cocktails as well as contemporary and creole cuisine; the hotel also has a small breakfast room and meeting room, all on the top floor. ⊠ *Between 8th and 9th Sts., Canefield (Box 1764, Roseau),* ☎ *767/449–0419,* FAX *767/449–2473,* WEB *www.wesleeann.com. 3 rooms, 4 suites, 5 apartments. Restaurant, kitchenettes, refrigerators, cable TV, bar, meeting rooms. AE, MC, V. CP, EP, MAP.*

$ ★ 🏨 **Zandoli Inn.** Perched on an 80-ft (24-m) cliff overlooking the southeast Atlantic coast, this five-room inn has several amazing views from its 6-acre gardens. Rooms are elegant and comfortable with bathrooms, locally made furnishings, and imported fabrics, though no air-conditioning, phones, or TV. Downstairs in the dining room and bar, where hotel guests join Linda for scrumptious organic meals and interesting rum-laced concoctions. Further down the cliff is the plunge pool—under a canopy of orchids; or you can go for a more adventurous swim among huge boulders in the aqua-blue Atlantic. Car rentals and excursions can be arranged. ⊠ *Roche Cassée (Box 2099, Roseau),* ☎ *767/446–3161,* FAX *767/446–3344,* WEB *www.zandoli.com. 5 rooms. Dining room, no air-conditioning, fans, no room phones, no room TVs, pool, hiking, bar, no kids under 12. AE, D, MC, V. EP, CP, MAP.*

Dining

You can expect an abundance of vegetables, fruits, and root crops to appear on menus around the island, Dominica's economy, after all, is based on agriculture. Sweet ripe plantains, *kushkush* yams, breadfruit, dasheen (a tuber similar to the potato, called "taro" elsewhere), fresh fish, and chicken prepared in at least a dozen different ways are among the staples. The locals drink a spiced rum—steeped with herbs such as anisette (called "nanny") and *pweve* (lemongrass). And be sure that when you ask for a glass of juice it's going to come directly from the fruit and not a box.

Dominican cuisine is also famous for its use of local game, such as the "mountain chicken"—a euphemism for a large frog called *crapaud*—and for more intrepid diners, the *manicou* (a small opossum) and the *agouti* (a large indigenous rodent).

In and around Roseau and all over the island, throughout villages and hamlets you can find myriad tiny food shops, where the food is local, plentiful, and highly seasoned. So if what you are looking for is a quick bite to sample Dominica's local cuisine, make your way in and ask for the day's special. Otherwise, you could try roadside vendors making breakfasts of bakes and accras for the passersby.

What to Wear

Most Dominicans dress elegantly but practically when eating out—for dinner it's shirt and trousers for men and modest dresses for women. During the day, nice shorts are acceptable at most places; beach attire is frowned upon, unless of course you're eating on the beach.

CATEGORY	COST*
$$$$	over $30
$$$	$20–$30
$$	$10–$20
$	under $10

per person for a main course at dinner

CARIBBEAN

$$–$$$ ✕ **Crystal Terrace Restaurant and Bar.** You'll find classic local food with a very elegant twist at this restaurant in the Evergreen Hotel. Dine on a large, airy terrace perched right over the sea, or relax at the bar while sipping a tropical cocktail. Dinners are usually prix fixe, with a choice of appetizer such as crab back, soup, or salad; entrées of chicken, fish, or other meats served with local produce; and a dessert of fresh fruit or homemade cake and ice cream. Breakfast and lunch are also served here, and reservations are advised. ✉ *Evergreen Hotel, Castle Comfort, Roseau,* ☎ 767/448–3288. *AE, MC, V.*

$$–$$$ ✕ **La Salle JoJo.** This air-conditioned beachfront bar and restaurant at the Coconut Beach Hotel is popular with visiting yachtsmen, students from the nearby medical school, and anyone interested in an afternoon or evening on a stretch of golden-sand beach. Fresh tropical drinks and local seafood dishes are the specialties; sandwiches, burgers, and rotis, and even a children's menu are offered here. On weekends this place really comes alive when the DJs crank up the latest hits at the Palladium Nightclub. ✉ *Coconut Beach Hotel, Picard Beach,* ☎ 767/445–5393. *AE, D, MC, V.*

$$–$$$ ✕ **Papillote.** Savor a lethal rum punch while lounging in a hot mineral
  ★   bath in the Papillote Wilderness Retreat gardens. Then try the bracing callaloo soup, dasheen puffs, fish "rain forest" (marinated with papaya and wrapped in banana leaves), or the succulent freshwater shrimp. This handsome Caribbean restaurant has quite possibly one of the best views in the region. Dine at an altitude cool enough to need a throw and watch the glimmer of the moonlight on the Caribbean Sea in the distance. ✉ *Papillote Wilderness Retreat, Trafalgar Falls Rd., Trafalgar,* ☎ 767/448–2287. *Reservations essential. AE, D, MC, V.*

$$–$$$ ✕ **Pearl's Cuisine.** From her base in a creole town house in central Roseau, chef Pearl, with her robust and infectious character, prepares some of the island's best local cuisine. She offers everything—including *sousse* (pickled pigs' feet), blood pudding, and rotis—in typical Dominican style. When sitting down to lunch or dinner, ask for a table on the open-air gallery that overlooks Roseau, prepare for an abundant portion, but make sure you leave space for dessert. If you're on the go, enjoy a quick meal from the daily varied menu in the ground-floor snackette. You're spoiled for choice when it comes to the fresh fruit juices. ✉ *50 King George V St., Roseau,* ☎ 767/448–8707. *AE, D, MC, V.*

$$–$$$ ✕ **Port of Call Restaurant and Bar.** A haunt of middle-aged barristers and laid-back locals is ideally just around the corner from the bayfront in downtown Roseau. The interior of this breezy restaurant is a traditional stone building with a soothing gray-and-white color scheme. The layout is such that you can have your privacy or just a laid-back meal. Management here is always ready to meet your needs for home-style local cuisine or a selection of à la carte items such as a hamburger with french fries or maybe just an exotic cocktail from the bar. ✉ *3 Kennedy Ave., Roseau*, ☎ *767/448–2910. AE, D, MC, V.*

$$ ✕ **Callaloo Restaurant.** On one of the busiest streets in Roseau you can escape the bustle and step into a quaint informal eatery where the effervescent Marge Peters is Queen. Taking pride in age-old cooking traditions, she uses only the freshest local produce. Changing lunch and dinner specials might include curried conch, mountain chicken, or callaloo (fragrant with cumin, coconut cream, lime, clove, and garlic). Don't miss the fresh fruit juices, ice creams, and desserts. ✉ *66 King George V St., Roseau,* ☎ *767/448–3386. AE, D, MC, V.*

$$ ✕ **Floral Gardens.** The sound of water falling in the background, rough-hewn timber beams, and vertivert mats help create the rustic setting for this restaurant. Dinner is served in the main building, but there are more tables in a building across the road overlooking the river. The home-style creole fare includes fresh fish and beef stews, fruits and vegetables, and tropical-flavored pies and tarts. ✉ *Concord,* ☎ *767/445–7636. AE, D, MC, V.*

$$ ✕ **La Robe Creole.** A cut-stone building only steps away from the Old
★ Market Plaza houses one of Dominica's best restaurants. In a cozy dining room with wood rafters, ladder-back chairs, and colorful madras tablecloths, you can dine on a meal selected from an eclectic à la carte menu. Callaloo soup is one specialty, lobster crepes and salads are others. The downstairs takeout annex, Mouse Hole, is an inexpensive and tasty place to snack when you're on the run. The restaurant makes its own delicious mango chutney and plantain chips, which you can buy in local shops. ✉ *3 Victoria St., Roseau,* ☎ *767/448–2896. D, MC, V. Closed Sun.*

$–$$ ✕ **Guiyave.** This popular lunchtime restaurant in a quaint Caribbean town house also has a pastry shop downstairs serving a scrumptious selection of sweet and savory pastries, tarts, and cakes. These can also be ordered from upstairs, along with more elaborate fare such as fish court bouillon or chicken in a sweet-and-sour sauce. Choose to dine either in the airy dining room or on the sunny balcony perched above Roseau's colorful streets—the perfect spot to indulge in one of the fresh-squeezed tropical juices. ✉ *15 Cork St., Roseau,* ☎ *767/448–2930. AE, MC, V. Closed Sun. No dinner.*

$–$$ ✕ **Miranda's Corner.** Just past Springfield on the way to Pont Casse, you'll begin to see hills full of flowers. At a big bend, a sign on a tree reads MIRANDA'S CORNER, referring to a bar, rum shop, and diner all in one. Here Miranda Alfred is at home, serving everyone from Italian tourists to banana farmers. The specialties are numerous—all prepared with a potion of passion and a fistful of flavor. It's open for breakfast, lunch, and dinner, and if you want something specially prepared, just call ahead and Miranda will help you out. ✉ *Mount Joy, Springfield,* ☎ *767/449–2509. Reservations essential. No credit cards.*

$ ✕ **Back-A-Yard.** Talk about down-home cooking. At the back ("in de yard") of a beautifully restored creole town house is this mouthwatering vegetarian restaurant. Seated on iron garden chairs, you are served vegetable, pasta, and grain dishes. This is a cool, cheap hangout with great people, food, and drinks. ✉ *19 Castle St., Roseau,* ☎ *767/449–9736. No credit cards. Closed Sun. No dinner.*

CHINESE

$–$$ ✕ **Taiwanese Delicacies.** Keeping up with their industrious reputation, the Chinese emigrants (from both Taiwan and mainland China) are the newest ethnic group to be added to Dominica's melting-pot culture. Taiwanese Dominicans are opening businesses including, of course, restaurants. This spot in Castle Comfort has drawn the biggest crowds for hot and spicy dishes, crispy vegetable and tofu selections, tender meats, elegant understated dining, and takeaway service. If you enjoy Chinese, you have to try it Dominican (Taiwanese) style. ⊠ *Castle Comfort,* ☎ 767/448–3497. *No credit cards.*

ECLECTIC

$$–$$$$ ✕ **Waterfront Restaurant.** From upstairs in the Fort Young Hotel, at
★ the southern end of Roseau's bayfront, this very elegant restaurant sur-
veys the tranquil Caribbean coastline. The large veranda wraps around
the air-conditioned formal dining room. The à la carte menu choices
range from appetizers of smoked salmon and roasted vegetable que-
sadillas to mains of orange duck and rack of lamb. Tropical desserts
include cheesecake and guava tart. ⊠ *Fort Young Hotel, Victoria St.,
Roseau,* ☎ 767/448–5000. *AE, MC, V.*

$–$$ ✕ **Cornerhouse Café.** Just off the Old Market Plaza in a historic three-
story stone and wooden town house is Dominica's only true Internet
café; the sign on the lattice veranda reads DOMINICA'S INFORMATION CAFÉ.
Here an eclectic menu of meals and other treats are on offer: bagels
with an assortment of toppings, delicious soups, sandwiches, salads,
cakes, and coffee. Computers are rented in 30-minute intervals; relax
on soft chairs and flip through books and magazines while you wait.
Wednesday is quiz night, and every night is game night—but arrive early,
as there's always a full house. ⊠ *Corner of Old and King George V
Sts., Roseau,* ☎ 767/449–9000. *No credit cards. Closed Sun.*

FRENCH

$–$$ ✕ **Ti Caz Café.** It's hard to miss the umbrella-covered chairs and ta-
bles at this Parisian café–style restaurant on a prominent Bayfront corner in Roseau. From 8:30 breakfast crepes, croissants, baguette
sandwiches, and piping hot café au lait are available. Throughout the
day you can relax indoors or out and enjoy any of the extensive menu's
selections with the perfect glass of wine. In the Cellar downstairs, the
Cocorico wine store houses reasonably priced selection from more than
eight countries. You can also choose from a wide assortment of pâtés
and cheeses, sausages, cigars, French breads, and chocolates. ⊠ *Corner of Bayfront and Kennedy Aves., Roseau,* ☎ 767/449–8686 *or
767/449–9774. MC, V. Closed Sun. No dinner.*

Beaches

As a volcanic island, Dominica offers many powder-fine black-sand
beaches. Found mostly in the north and east, they are windswept, dramatic, and uncrowded, lending themselves more to relaxation than swimming because many have undercurrents. However, slightly further
north there are beautiful secluded white- or brown-sand beaches and
coves. Although northeast coast beaches offer excellent shallow swimming, their wind-tossed beauty can be dangerous; there are sometimes
strong currents with the whipped-cream waves. From these beaches
you can see the islands of Marie Galante, Les Saintes, and parts of Guadeloupe. On the southwest coast, beaches are fewer and mostly made of
black sand and rounded volcanic rocks. Swimming off these rocky shores
has its pleasures, too: the water is usually as flat as a lake, deep and
blue, and is especially good for snorkeling.

Castaways. A short stone staircase leads down from the Castaways
Beach Hotel's bar to this popular hang-out spot just halfway along Dominica's west coast. It's both convenient and accessible.

Champagne. On the west coast, just south of the village of Pointe Michel,
this stony beach is hailed as one of the best sports for swimming, snorkel-

ing, and diving. It gets its name from volcanic vents that constantly puff steam into the sea, which makes you feel as if you are swimming in warm champagne.

Hampstead Beach. This beach on the northeast coast actually encompasses three bays (one of which is sheltered and calm) and is a bit off the beaten path.

Hodges Beach. If you're looking for a secluded spot, this beach is just a bit further along the northeast coast past Woodford Hill Beach. There is also a slow-flowing river here for a refreshing rinse after a hot day at the beach. It's easy to miss this one as it is accessed through an estate road and private lands, so keep on the look out.

L'Anse Tortue. This beach on the northeast coast is also a favorite for the more adventurous; it sits on a cove just past Woodford Hill, and some days the odd surfer finds just the right wave.

Mero Beach. A silver-grey stretch of beach is on the west coast, just outside of the village of Mero, where the entire community comes to party on Sunday.

Picard Beach. The golden stretch of sand is the longest on the island and is a favorite of both locals and visitors. You'll find many restaurants and hotels along this part of the coast.

Purple Beach. Fringed by sea-almond trees and tucked under the bay of the Cabrits, this wide silver-grey stretch of sand is a popular haunt for weekend partiers; during the week, you will often have the whole beach to yourself.

Scotts Head. At the southernmost tip of the island, a small landmass is connected to the mainland by a narrow stretch of stony beach separating the Atlantic and the Caribbean. It's a fantastic spot for snorkeling, and you can have lunch at one of the village restaurants.

Soufrière Beach. By the laid-back village of the same name and in the center of the Soufrière Scotts Head Marine Reserve, this beach serves as an ideal spot to enjoy the healthy underwater life.

Toucari Beach. On the extreme northwest coast, this little secret is tucked away in one of the island's most picturesque spots. A long stretch of golden grey sand is spotted with colorful fishing boats and the tangle of nets left to dry after a morning out at sea. From here, you can enjoy views of neighboring Guadeloupe and Les Saintes.

Woodford Hill Beach. If you are adventuring out on your own, ask locals for directions to hidden spots like this one on the northeast coast, a favorite just past the village of Woodford Hill, though on holidays it can be crowded.

Outdoor Activities and Sports

BOATING AND SAILING

Motorboat and sailing excursions to neighboring islands like Guadeloupe, Martinique, and Les Saintes can be an exciting add-on to a vacation on Dominica. If the channel crossing is not your thing, a morning at a secluded spot on Dominica's west coast with picnic and rum punch might be more appealing. A couple of companies organize trips either on an hourly or a daily basis, with costs ranging from $80 per hour to $750 for a full day. You can arrange trips through **Anchorage Dive & Whale Watch Center** (⊠ Anchorage Hotel, Castle Comfort, ☎ 767/448–2638 or 767/448–2639). **Castaways Beach Hotel** (⊠ Mero, ☎ 767/449–6245) organizes day-sails.

CYCLING

Cyclists find Dominica's rugged terrain to be an exhilarating challenge, but there are routes suitable for all levels of bikers. **Nature Island Dive** has a fleet of bikes in good condition. Knowledgeable guides lead tours through specific areas for $30–$65.

FISHING

Anglers will delight in the numerous banks and drop-offs, as well as in the year-round fair weather. **Game Fishing Dominica** (✉ Box 2077, St. Joseph, Roseau, ☎ FAX 767/449–6638, ☎ 767/235–6638) works off the Castaways dock in Mero. Eight years ago they started the Annual International Sportfishing Tournament in Dominica. Francis Cambran will take you out for between $450 and $700 for five to eight hours, providing all equipment, bait, and refreshments.

HIKING

Dominica's majestic mountains, clear rivers, and lush vegetation conspire to create adventurous hiking trails. The island is crisscrossed by ancient footpaths of the Arawak and Carib Indians and the Nègres Maroons, escaped slaves who established camps in the mountains. Existing trails range from easygoing to arduous. To make the most of your excursion, you'll need sturdy hiking boots, insect repellent, a change of clothes (kept dry), and a guide. Hikes and tours run $25 to $50 per person, depending on destinations and duration. Some of the natural attractions within the island's National Parks require visitors to purchase a site pass. These are sold for varying numbers of visits. A Site Pass costs $2; a day pass; $5, and a week's pass, $10. Hiking guides can be arranged through the **Dominican Tourist Office** (✉ Valley Rd., Roseau, ☎ 767/448–2045). The **Forestry Division** (☎ 767/448–2401) is responsible for the management of forests and wildlife and have numerous publications on Dominica as well as a wealth of information on reputable guides. Their offices are in the Botanical Gardens in Roseau. Local bird and forestry expert **Betrand Jno Baptiste** (☎ 767/446–6358) leads hikes up Morne Diablotin and along the Syndicate Nature Trail; if he's not available, ask him to recommend another guide.

SCUBA DIVING AND SNORKELING

Voted one of the top 10 dive destinations in the world by *Skin Diver* and *Rodale's Scuba Diving* magazines, Dominica's dive sites are truly awesome. There are numerous highlights all along the west coast of the island, but the best are those in the southwest—within and around **Soufrière Scottshead Marine Reserve.** This bay is the site of a submerged volcanic crater; the Dominica Watersports Association has worked along with the Fisheries Division for years establishing this reserve and have set stringent regulations to prevent the degradation of the ecosystem. Within a half mile (¾ km) of the shore, there are vertical drops from 800 ft (240 m) to more than 1,500 ft (450 m), with visibility frequently extending to 100 ft (30 m). Shoals of boga fish, Creole wrasse, and blue cromis are common, and you might even see a spotted moray eel or a honeycomb cowfish. Crinoids (rare elsewhere) are also abundant here, as are giant barrel sponges. Other noteworthy dive sites outside this reserve are **Salisbury Falls, Nose Reef, Brain Coral Garden,** and—even farther north—**Cabrits Drop-Off** and **Toucari Reef.** The conditions for underwater photography, particularly macrophotography, are unparalleled. The going rate is between $65 and $75 for a two-tank dive or $100 for a resort course with an open-water dive. All scuba-diving operators also offer snorkeling; equipment rents for $10–$20 a day.

The **Anchorage Dive & Whale Watch Center** (✉ Anchorage Hotel, Castle Comfort, ☎ 767/448–2638) has two dive boats that can take you out day or night. They also offer PADI instruction (all skill levels), snorkeling and whale-watching trips, and shore diving. **Dive Castaways** (✉ Castaways Beach Hotel, Mero, ☎ 767/449–6244), a PADI dive shop 11 mi (18 km) north of Roseau, offers diving, courses, snorkeling, and other water and beach activities. **Dive Dominica** (⊠ Castle Comfort Lodge, Castle Comfort, ☎ 767/448–2188) conducts NAUI, PADI, and SSI courses as well as Nitrox certification. They offer diving, snorkeling, and whale-watching trips and packages including accommodation at the Castle Comfort Lodge. **Nature Island Dive** (⊠ Soufrière, ☎ 767/449–8181) is run by an enthusiastic crew. Some of the island's best dive sites are right outside their door, and they offer diving, snorkeling, kayaking, and mountain biking as well as resort and full PADI courses.

SWIMMING

Locals boast of having a river for every day of the year. Some are better for swimming than others, but all guarantee a pick-me-up during a hot day. As an extra treat, you can often find hot springs among the boulders; look for the telltale orange sulfur stains. Any tour guide or taxi can take you to one but it's really more fun to go off discovering the perfect river pool on your own.

WHALE AND DOLPHIN WATCHING

Dominica records the highest species counts of resident cetacea in the region, so it's not surprising that tours claim 90% sighting success for their excursions. Humpback whales, false killer whales, minke, and orcas are all occasionally seen, as are several species of dolphin. But the resident sperm whales (they calve in Dominica's 3,000-ft-deep [900-m-deep] waters) are truly the stars of the show. During your 3½-hour expedition you may be asked to assist in recording sightings, which aid operators in collecting data that can be shared with local and international organizations. Although there are resident whales and dolphins and therefore year-round sightings, there are more species to be observed in November through February. The **Anchorage Dive & Whale Watch Center** (⊠ Anchorage Hotel, Castle Comfort, ☎ 767/448–2638) offers whale-watching trips. **Dive Dominica** (⊠ Castle Comfort Lodge, Castle Comfort, ☎ 767/448–2188) is a major whale-watching operator.

WINDSURFING

Although windsurfing isn't a very widely practiced sport in Dominica, there are a few individuals who will swear that the conditions are right for an exhilarating experience. You will need to bring your own gear with you and wait out the weather at beaches like Turtle Beach in the northeast or down at Scottshead, where chances for waves on the Atlantic side can be mixed with the winds within the Soufrière Bay. For windsurfing information contact **Andrew Armour** at the **Anchorage Dive & Whale Watch Center** (⊠ Anchorage Hotel, Castle Comfort, ☎ 767/ 448–2638).

Shopping

Dominicans produce distinctive handicrafts, with various communities specializing in their specific products. The crafts of the Carib Indians include traditional baskets made of dyed *larouma* reeds and waterproofed with tightly woven *balizier* leaves. These are sold in the Carib Indian Territory as well as in Roseau's shops. Vertivert straw rugs, screwpine tableware, fwije (the trunk of the forest tree fern), and wood carvings are just some examples. Also notable are local herbs, spices, condiments, and herb teas. Café Dominique, the local equivalent of Jamaican Blue Mountain coffee, is an excellent buy, as are the Dominican rums Macoucherie and Soca. Proof that the old ways live on in Dominica can be found in the number of herbal remedies available. One stimulating memento of your visit is rum steeped with *bois bandé* (scientific name *Richeria grandis*), a tree whose bark is reputed to have aphrodisiacal properties. These are sold at shops, vendor's stalls, and supermarkets all over the island. The charismatic roadside vendors can be found all over the island bearing trays laden with local and imported souvenirs, T-shirts, and trinkets. Duty-free shopping is also available in specific stores around Roseau.

Stores are generally open from 8 until 4 or 5 on weekdays and from 8 to 1 on Saturdays. Most are closed on Sundays. Vendors are usually out on roadsides when there are French groups in for the day or on weekend excursions or when there are cruise ships in port.

Major Shopping Areas

One of the easiest places to pick up a souvenir is the Old Market Plaza, just behind the Dominica Museum, in Roseau. Slaves were once sold here, but today handcrafted jewelry, T-shirts, spices, souvenirs, and batik are available from a group of vendors in open-air booths set up on the cobblestones. These are usually busiest when there is a cruise ship berthed across the street. On these days you can also find a vast number of vendors along the bay front.

Specialty Items

ART

Most artists work from their home studios and it often takes the right contact to find them. Contact the Old Mill Cultural Center or Earl Etienne, a Cultural Officer and himself Dominica's most sought after painter. He will be able to put you on the right path to find exactly what you are looking for. Works by Dominican artists can be seen at the Old Mill as well as at Earl's home Studio. Hilroy Fingol, a young artist specializing in airbrush painting, has his little studio cum gallery in the heart of Roseau called **Balisier** (⊠ 35 Great George St., Roseau, ☎ no phone); it's a real treasure.

Block 44 Arts & Crafts (⊠ Main St., Grand Bay, ☎ 767/446–3737 or 767/446–3731) is the contact spot for the artisans of the southeast community. These guys create souvenirs, furniture, and musical instruments, primarily in wood. It's a trip out of town, but taking time to talk with Hilroy George, who runs the place and directs the creation of most of the pieces, is enlightening.

CLOTHING

There is such a wide selection of price and value when it comes to clothing stores in Roseau that it really is best to walk around and explore for yourself. However, for classic Caribbean and International designer clothing, there are several reliable boutiques to try. **Ego Boutique** (⊠ 9 Hillsborough St., Roseau, ☎ 767/448–2336) carries an extensive selection of designer clothing and exquisite crafts and home accessories from around the world. At **Desiderata** (⊠ 65 King George V St., 1st floor of J. Astaphans & Co. Ltd., Roseau, ☎ 767/448–6522), a little boutique that carries clothing and accessories from Caribbean and American designers, many pieces are made specifically for her boutique. It's really difficult to leave without picking up at least one thing. **Mango Tango** (⊠ Fort Young Hotel, Victoria St., Roseau, ☎ 767/448–0342) is an exquisite store selling international fashions, including fine Indian silks, linens, beaded evening gowns, and a well-chosen selection of shoes. Be prepared to spend, though. A beautiful but limited selection of men's clothing is available as well.

GIFTS AND SOUVENIRS

With tourism development comes the added benefits of increasing commerce; duty-free shops are cropping up in Roseau. Some name-brand stores carry jewelry, perfumes, crystals, and leather goods; several of these are within Roseau's bay front. **Ashbury's and Colombian Emeralds** (⊠ Fort Young Hotel, Victoria St., Roseau) carries perfumes, crystals, emerald, diamond, gemstone, gold and silver jewelry, liquor, and other gift items. **Baroon International** (✉ Kennedy Ave., Roseau) sells unique jewelry from Asia, the United States, and other Caribbean islands; there are also pieces that are assembled in the store, as well as personal accessories, souvenirs, and special gifts. **Booze & Smoke** (✉ Cork St., Roseau) has exactly what its name implied: a large selection of duty-free cigarettes, cigars, and alcohol. **Island Stuff** (✉ 25 Hanover St., ☎ 767/449–9969), just a couple of blocks east of the ferry terminal, is a tiny Pandora's box, where you can find fine art, souvenirs, or the perfect hand-carved piece of furniture among the numerous items on sale. For quality leather goods and other personal accessories, try **Land** (✉ Castle St., Roseau). **Rare Earth Treasures** (✉ Fort Lane, Roseau) is where you will find exactly what the name says, uniquely fashioned fine jewelry. Their collection of gemstones and crystals is a treat not to be missed, even when you can't afford to buy.

HANDICRAFTS

The Crazy Banana (✉ 17 Castle St., ☎ 767/449–8091) purveys everything from earthenware to doorstops, as well as other Caribbean-made crafts, rums, cigars, jewelry, and local art. **Dominica Pottery** (✉ Bayfront St. and Kennedy Ave., Roseau, ☎ no phone) is run by a local priest, whose products are fashioned with various local clays and glazes. **Papillote Wilderness Retreat** (✉ Trafalgar, ☎ 767/448–2287) has an intimate gift shop with an excellent selection of local handcrafted goods and particularly outstanding wood carvings by Louis Desire. **Tropicrafts** (✉ corner of Queen Mary St. and Turkey La., Roseau, ☎ 767/448–2747) has a back room where you can watch local ladies weave grass mats. You'll also find arts and crafts from around the Caribbean, local wood carvings, rum, hot sauces, perfumes, and traditional Carib baskets, hats, and woven mats.

Nightlife and the Arts

The friendly, intimate atmosphere and colorful patrons at the numerous bars and hangouts will keep you entertained for hours. If you're looking for jazz, calypso, reggae, steel-band, *soca* (a variation of calypso), cadence/zouk, or jing ping—a type of folk music featuring the accordion, the *quage* (a kind of washboard instrument), drums, and a "boom boom" (a percussive instrument)—you're guaranteed to find it. Wednesday through Saturday nights are really lively, and during Carnival, Independence, and the summer celebrations, things can be intense. Indeed, Dominica's Carnival, the pre-Lenten festival, is the most spontaneous in the Caribbean. The annual World Creole Music Festival in late October also packs in the action, with three days and nights of pulsating rhythm and music. Creole Music enthusiasts come from all over the world. Throughout the year, however, most larger hotels have some form of live evening entertainment.

Nightlife

Once Friday afternoon rolls around you can sense the mood change. Local bars crank up the music, and each village and community has its own particular nightly entertainment. If by this point in your trip you have made friends with some locals, they will be only too happy to take you to the current hot spot.

At **Cellars Bar** (✉ Sutton Place Hotel, Old St., Roseau, ☎ 767/449–8700), Wednesday night is Amateur Bartenders Soca Rum Night. Volunteer to be the bartender; taste tests of the featured cocktails are free. Friday is Kubuli Karaoke Night, with patrons competing for prize drinks; it's a real blast and perfect way to totally kick back. There is a $4 minimum on both nights. **Symes Zee's** (✉ 34 King George V St., Roseau,

☎ 767/448–2494) draws a crowd on Thursday night from 10 until the wee hours of the morning, when there is a jazz/blues/reggae band. There's no cover, and the food, drinks, and cigars are reasonably priced. **Warehouse** (⊠ Canefield, ☎ 767/449–1303), outside Roseau just past the airport, is *the* place to dance on Saturday night. DJs are brought in from other islands to ensure there's variety to all the vibrations. The entrance fee is $5.

The Arts

Arawak House of Culture (⊠ Kennedy Ave. near Government Headquarters, Roseau, ☎ 767/449–1804), managed by Aileen Burton at the Cultural Division, is Dominica's performing-arts theater. A number of productions are staged here throughout the year, including plays, recitals, and dance performances. **Old Mill Cultural Center** (⊠ Canefield, ☎ 767/449–1804) is one of Dominica's historic landmarks. The Old Mill was once the home of the island's first sugarcane-processing mill and rum distillery. This is the place to learn about Dominica's traditions. Performances and events take place here throughout the year.

Exploring Dominica

Despite the small size of this almond-shaped island, it can take a couple of hours to travel between the popular destinations. Many sights are isolated and difficult to find; you may be better off taking an organized excursion. If you do go it alone, drive carefully: the roads can be narrow and winding. Plan on eight hours to see the highlights; to fully experience the island, set aside a couple of days and work in some hikes.

Numbers in the margin correspond to points of interest on the Dominica map.

SIGHTS TO SEE

⑩ **Cabrits National Park.** Along with Brimstone Hill in St. Kitts, Shirley Heights in Antigua, and Ft. Charlotte in St. Vincent, the Cabrits' Fort Shirley ruins are among the most significant historic sites in the Caribbean. Just north of the town of Portsmouth, this 1,300-acre park includes a marine park and herbaceous swamps, which are an important environment for several species of rare birds and plants. At the heart of the park is the Ft. Shirley military complex. Built by the British between 1770 and 1815, it once comprised 50 major structures, including storehouses that were also quarters for 700 men. With the help of the Royal Navy (which sends sailors ashore to work on the site each time a ship is in port) and local volunteers, historian Dr. Lennox Honychurch restored the fort and its surroundings, incorporating a small museum that highlights the natural and historic aspects of the park, and an open canteen-style restaurant.

⑤ **Carib Indian Territory.** In 1903, after centuries of conflict, the Caribbean's first settlers, the Kalinago, were granted a portion of land (approximately 3,700 acres) on the island's northeast coast to establish a reservation with their own chief. Today it's known as Carib Territory, clinging to the northeasterly corner of Dominica, where a group of just over 3,000 Caribs, who resemble native South Americans, live like most other people in rural Caribbean communities. Many are farmers and fishermen; others are entrepreneurs who have opened restaurants, guest houses, and little shops where you can buy exquisite Carib baskets and other handcrafted items. The craftspeople retain knowledge of basket weaving, wood carving, and canoe building, which has been passed down from one generation to the next.

The Caribs' long, elegant canoes are created from the trunk of a single *Gommier* tree. If you're lucky, you may catch canoe builders at work.

The reservation's Catholic church in Salybia has a canoe as its unique altar, which was designed by Dr. Lennox Honychurch, a local historian, author, and artist.

L'Escalier Tête Chien (literally "Snake's Staircase," it's the name of a snake whose head resembles that of a dog), a hardened lava formation that runs down into the Atlantic. The ocean here is particularly fierce, and the shore is full of countless coves and inlets. According to Carib legend, at night the nearby Londonderry Islets metamorphose into grand canoes to take the spirits of the dead out to sea.

Though there's not currently much in the territory that demonstrates the Caribs' ancient culture and customs, plans for a museum showing early Carib life are in the works. In addition, the territory's Karifuna Cultural Group travels nationally and internationally, performing traditional dance and wearing traditional costumes—their bodies painted and adorned with feathers and beads.

❹ Emerald Pool. Quite possibly the most-visited nature attraction on the island, this emerald green pool fed by a 50-ft (15-m) waterfall is an easy trip to make. To reach this spot in the Morne Trois Pitons National Park, you follow a trail that starts at the side of the road near the reception center (it's an easy 20-minute walk). Along the way you'll pass lookout points with views of the windward (Atlantic) coast and the forested interior. If you don't want a crowd, check whether there are cruise ships in port before going out, as this spot is popular with cruise-ship tour groups.

❽ Indian River. Indian River, in Portsmouth, was once a Carib Indian settlement. A gentle rowboat ride for wildlife spotting along this river, lined with *terra carpus officinalis* trees, whose buttress roots spread up to 20 ft (6 m), is not only a relaxing treat but educational and most times entertaining. To arrange such a trip, stop by the Visitor Center at the mouth of the river and ask for one of the "Indian River Boys." These young, knowledgeable men are members of the Portsmouth Indian River Tour Guides Association (PIRTGA) and have for years protected and promoted one of Dominica's special areas. Most boat trips take you up as far as Rahjah's Jungle Bar. You can usually do an optional guided walking tour of the swamplands and the remnants of one of Dominica's oldest plantations. Tours last one to three hours and cost $15 to $30 per person. .

⓫ Morne Aux Diables. In the far north of Dominica, this peak soars 2,826 ft (848 m) above sea level and slopes down to Toucari and Douglas bays and long stretches of dark-sand beach. To reach the mountain, take the road along the Caribbean coast. It twists by coconut, cocoa, and banana groves, past fern-festooned embankments, over rivers, and into villages where brightly painted shanties are almost as colorful as all the flora and fauna.

❼ Morne Diablotin National Park. Named after one of the regions highest mountains, Morne Diablotin—at 4,747 ft (1,424 m), Dominica's highest peak—takes its name from a bird, known in English as the black-capped petrel, which was prized by hunters in the 18th century. Though there aren't any of these birds left today, Dominica is still a major birding destination, whose aviary crown jewels are the green-and-purple Sisserou parrot (*Amazona imperialis*) and the Jaco, or red-neck, parrot (*Amazona arausiaca*), found here in greater numbers than in other parts of the island, but still Dominica's endemic endangered species. Before the establishment of the national park, the 200-acre site of Project Sisserou was the protected area, including the Syndicate Nature Trail, set aside with the help of some 6,000 schoolchildren, each of whom donated 25¢ to protect the habitat of the flying pride of Dominica, as well as countless other species of birds and other wildlife. The west-coast road (at the bend near Dublanc) runs through three types of forests and leads into the park. The trail offers a casual walk; just bring a sweater and binoculars. The five- to eight-hour hike up Morne Diablotin isn't for everyone. You need a guide, sturdy hiking shoes, warm clothing, and a backpack with refreshments and a change of clothes (including socks) that are wrapped in plastic to keep them dry. A good guide for Morne Diablotin is local ornithology expert **Betrand Jno Baptiste** (☎ 767/446–6358).

❸ Morne Trois Pitons National Park. Dedicated a national park in 1975 and named a UNESCO World Heritage Site in 1998, this 17,000-acre (covering 9% of Dominica) swath of lush, mountainous land in the south-central interior is the nature island's crown jewel. Named after one of the highest 4,600 ft (1,380 m) mountains on the island, it contains the world's largest boiling lake, majestic waterfalls, and cool mountain lakes. There are four types of vegetation zones here. Ferns grow 30-ft (9-m) tall and wild orchids sprout from trees, sunlight leaks through green canopies, and a gentle mist rises over the jungle floor. A system of trails has been developed in the park, and the Division of Forestry and Wildlife works hard to maintain it—with no help from the excessive rainfall and the profusion of vegetation that seems to grow right before your eyes. Access to the park is possible from most points of the compass, though the easiest approaches are via the small mountaintop villages of Laudat (pronounced low-*dah*) and Cochrane.

About 5 mi (8 km) out of Roseau, the Wotton Waven Road branches off toward Sulphur Springs, where you'll see the belching, sputtering, and gurgling releases of volcanic hot springs. At the base of Morne Micotrin, you'll find two crater lakes: the first, at 2,500 ft (750 m) above sea level, is **Freshwater Lake.** According to a local legend, it's haunted by a vindictive mermaid and a monstrous serpent. Farther on is **Boeri Lake,** fringed with greenery and with purple hyacinths floating on its surface. The undisputed highlight of the park is **Boiling Lake.** The world's largest such lake, it is a cauldron of gurgling gray-blue water, 70 yards wide and of unknown depth, with water temperatures from 180°F to 197°F. Although generally believed to be a volcanic crater, the lake is actually a flooded fumarole—a crack through which gases escape from the molten lava below. The two- to four-hour (one-way) hike up to the lake is challenging (on a very rainy day, be prepared to slip and slide the whole way up and back). You'll need attire appropriate for a strenuous hike, and a guide is a must. Most guided trips start early (no later than 8:30 AM) for this all-day, 7-mi (11-km) round-trip trek. On your way to Boiling Lake, you'll pass through the **Valley of Desolation,** a sight that definitely lives up to its name. Harsh sulfuric fumes have destroyed virtually all the vegetation in what must have once been a lush forested area. Small hot and cold streams with water of various colors—black, purple, red, orange—web the valley. Stay on the trail to avoid breaking through the crust that covers the hot lava. During this hike you'll pass rivers where you can refresh yourself with a dip (a particular treat is a soak in a hot-water stream on the way back). At the beginning of the Valley of Desolation trail is the **TiTou Gorge,** where you can swim in the pool or relax in the hot-water springs along one side. If you're a strong swimmer, you can head up the gorge to a cave (it's about a five-minute swim) that has a magnificent waterfall; a crack in the cave about 50 ft (15 m) above permits a stream of sunlight to penetrate the cavern.

Also in the national park are some of the island's most spectacular waterfalls. The 45-minute hike to **Sari Sari Falls,** accessible through the east-coast village of La Plaine, can be hair-raising. But the sight of water

cascading some 150 ft (45 m) into a large pool is awesome. So large
are these falls that you feel the spray from hundreds of yards away.
Just beyond the village of Trafalgar and up a short hill, there's the reception facility, where you can purchase passes to the national park
and find guides to take you on a rain-forest trek to the twin **Trafalgar
Falls.** If you like a little challenge, let your guide take you up the
riverbed to the cool pools at the base of the falls (check whether there's
a cruise ship in port before setting out; this sight is popular with the
tour operators). You need a guide for the arduous 75-minute hike to
Middleham Falls. The turnoff for the trailhead is just before the village of Laudat. The trail takes you to another spectacular waterfall,
where water cascades 100 ft (30 m) over boulders and vegetation and
then into an ice-cold pool (a swim here is absolutely exhilarating). Guides
for these hikes are available at the trailheads; still, it's best to arrange
a tour before even setting out.

6 **Northeast Coast.** Steep cliffs, dramatic reefs, and rivers that swirl down
through forests of mangroves and fields of coconut define this section
of Dominica. The road along the Atlantic, with its red cliffs, whipped
cream waves and windswept trees, crosses the Hatton Garden River
before entering the village of Marigot. In the northeastern region there
are numerous estates—old family holdings planted with fruit trees. Beyond Marigot and the Melville Hall Airport is the beautiful Londonderry Estate. The beach here is inspiring, with driftwood strewn about
its velvety black sands, which part halfway—where the Londonderry
River spills into the Atlantic (swimming isn't advised because of strong
currents, but a river bath here is a memorable treat). Farther along the
coast, beyond the village of Wesley (which has a gas station and a shop
that sells wonderful bread) and past Eden Estate, there are still more
beautiful beaches and coves. The swimming is excellent at Woodford
Hill Bay, Hodges Beach, Hampstead Estate, Batibou Bay, and L'Anse
Tortue. A stop in the charming community of Calibishie is a must; here
you'll find bars and restaurants right on the beach, as well as laid back
villas and guest houses. At Bense, a village in the interior just past Calibishie, you can take a connector road to Chaud Dwe (pronounced show-
dweh), a beautiful bathing spot in a valley; the only crowd you're likely
to encounter is a group of young villagers frolicking in the 15-ft-deep
(4½-m-deep) pool and diving off the 25-ft-high (7½ m high) rocks.

9 **Portsmouth.** In 1782 Portsmouth was the site of the Battle of Les
Saintes, a naval engagement between the French and the English. The
English won the battle but lost the much tougher fight against malaria-
carrying mosquitoes that bred in the nearby swamps. Once intended
to be the capital of Dominica, thanks to its superb harbor on Prince
Rupert Bay, in its heyday as many as 400 ships docked here at one time,
but on account of those swamps, Roseau, not Portsmouth, is the capital today. Maritime traditions are continued here by the yachting set,
and a 2-mi (3-km) stretch of sandy beach fringed with coconut trees
runs to the Picard Estate area.

1 **Roseau.** Although it is one of the smallest capitals in the Caribbean,
Roseau has the highest concentration of inhabitants of any town in the
eastern Caribbean. Caribbean vernacular architecture and a bustling
marketplace transport visitors back in time. Although you can walk
the entire town in about an hour, you'll get a much better feel for the
place on a leisurely stroll.

For some years now, the Society for Historical Architectural Preservation & Enhancement (SHAPE) has organized programs and projects
to preserve the city's architectural heritage. Several interesting buildings have already been restored. **Lilac House** (⊠ Kennedy Ave.) has

three types of gingerbread fretwork, latticed veranda railings, and heavy hurricane shutters. The **J. W. Edwards Building** (✉ corner of Old and King George V Sts.) has a stone base and a wooden second-floor gallery and is also where you will find the cozy Cornerhouse Cafe. **The old market Plaza,** the center of the historic district of Roseau, was first established by the French on a radial plan rather than a grid, so streets such as Hanover, King George V, and Old radiate from this area. South of the marketplace is the Fort Young Hotel, built as a British fort in the 18th century; the nearby state house, public library, and Anglican cathedral are also worth a visit.

The 40-acre **Botanical Gardens,** founded in 1891 as an annex of London's Kew Gardens, is a great place to relax, stroll, or watch a cricket match. In addition to the extensive collection of tropical plants and trees, there's also a parrot aviary. At the Forestry Division office, which is also on the garden grounds, you'll find numerous publications on the island's flora, fauna, and national parks. The forestry officers are particularly knowledgeable on these subjects and can also recommend good hiking guides. ✉ *Between Bath Rd. and Valley Rd.,* ☎ 767/448–2401 Ext. 3417. ⊘ *Mon. 8–1 and 2–5, Tues.–Fri. 8–1 and 2–4.*

New developments at Bayfront on the Dame M. E. Charles Boulevard have brightened up the waterfront. The old post office now houses the **Dominica Museum.** This labor of love by local writer and historian Dr. Lennox Honychurch contains furnishings, documents, prints, and maps that date back hundreds of years; you'll also find an entire Carib hut as well as Carib canoes, baskets, and other artifacts. The museum is open. ✉ *Dame M. E. Charles Blvd., opposite the cruise ship berth,* ☎ 767/448–8923. ⊘ *Weekdays 9–4 and Saturday 9–noon.* 🎫 *$2.*

❷ **Soufrière.** Tourism is quietly mingling with the laid-back lifestyle of the residents of this gently sunbaked village in the southwest, near one of the island's two marine reserves. Although first settled by French lumbermen in the 17th century, today, it's mainly fishermen you'll find here. In the village you'll find a historic 18th-century Catholic church built of volcanic stone, one of the island's prettiest churches; the ruins of the L. Rose Lime Oil factory; Sulfur Springs, with its hot mineral baths to the east; and the best diving and snorkeling on the island within the **Soufrière Scottshead Marine Reserve.** To the west you'll find Bois Cotlette (a historic plantation house), and to the south the Scotts Head Peninsula—at the island's southern tip—which separates the Caribbean from the Atlantic. So if there isn't enough treasure here to satisfy you, there's always the rain forest waiting to be challenged.

DOMINICA A TO Z

To research prices, get advice from other travelers, and book travel arrangements, visit www.fodors.com.

AIR TRAVEL
American Eagle flies into Melville Hall Airport every afternoon from San Juan—during peak seasons twice a day. LIAT, Air Caraïbes, and Caribbean Star all bring a number of regional airlines together into Dominica from various hubs, including Martinique, St. Lucia, and Antigua, into Canefield Airport and Melville Hall Airport on scheduled flights throughout the day. These flights also connect out of other countries in the region, including Guyana.

➤ AIRLINES AND CONTACTS: **American/American Eagle** (☎ 767/448–6680). **Air Caraïbes** (☎ 767/448–2181). **LIAT** (☎ 767/448–2421). **Whitchurch Travel (for Caribbean Star Airlines)** (☎ 767/448–2181 or 767/445–8841).

AIRPORTS

Canefield Airport, about 3 mi (5 km) north of Roseau, handles only small aircraft and daytime flights; landing here can be a hair-raising experience for those uneasy about flying. Melville Hall Airport is on the northeast coast, 75 minutes from Roseau, and handles larger planes.

Cab fare from Canefield Airport to Roseau is about $15. The 75-minute drive from Melville Hall Airport to Roseau takes you through the island's Central Forest Reserve and is a tour in itself. The trip costs about $55 by private taxi or $20 per person by co-op cab.

➤ AIRPORT INFORMATION: **Canefield Airport** (☎ 767/449–1199). **Melville Hall Airport** (☎ 767/445–7101).

BOAT AND FERRY TRAVEL
FARES AND SCHEDULES

Express des Isles has scheduled inter-island Jet Catamaran Ferry service, which runs according to a printed schedule; during peak seasons additional arrivals and departures are added. Generally, though, the ferry arrives and departs at the Roseau Ferry Terminal on Monday, Wednesday, and Friday–Sunday from Guadeloupe; it continues south to Martinique, as well as St. Lucia, on specific days. The crossing costs $90–$110, takes approximately 90 minutes, and offers superb views of the other islands.

➤ BOAT AND FERRY INFORMATION: **Express des Isles** (☎ 767/448–2181).

BUSINESS HOURS
BANKS

Banks are open Monday–Thursday 8–3, Friday 8–5.

POST OFFICES

Post offices are open Monday 8–5, Tuesday–Friday 8–4, Saturday 8–1.

SHOPS

Generally businesses are open Monday 8–5, Tuesday–Friday 8–4, Saturday 8–1. Some stores have longer hours, but you should call ahead to confirm them.

CAR RENTALS

Daily car-rental rates begin at $50 (weekly and long-term rates can be negotiated). Expect to add approximately another $7–$17 a day for optional collision damage insurance; otherwise, you will be asked to leave a credit card number or cash deposit. You'll need to buy a visitor's driving permit (EC$20) at one of the airports or at the Traffic Division office on High Street in Roseau. Most rental car companies offer airport and hotel pick-up and drop-off.

➤ MAJOR AGENCIES: **Best Deal Car Rental** (✉ 15 Hanover St., Roseau, ☎ 767/449–9204 or 767/235–3325). **Island Car Rentals** (✉ Goodwill Rd., Goodwill, ☎ 767/448–2886 or 767/445–8789). **Wide Range Car Rentals** (✉ 79 Bath Rd., Roseau, ☎ 767/448–2198).

CAR TRAVEL
GASOLINE

Gasoline stations can be found all over the island; gas costs approximately $2.70 per gallon.

ROAD CONDITIONS

The roads can be narrow in places, and they meander around the coast and through mountainous terrain.

RULES OF THE ROAD

Driving in Dominica is on the left side, though you can rent vehicles with a steering wheel on either the left or right.

ELECTRICITY

Electric voltage is 220/240 AC, 50 cycles. North American appliances require an adapter and transformer; however, many establishments provide these and often have dual voltage fittings (110/120 and 220/240 volts).

EMBASSIES

➤ UNITED KINGDOM: **Honorary Consul** (☎ 767/448–7655).

EMERGENCIES

➤ AMBULANCE AND FIRE: **Ambulance and fire emergencies** (☎ 999).
➤ HOSPITALS: **Princess Margaret Hospital** (✉ Federation Dr., Goodwill, ☎ 767/448–2231 or 767/448–2233).
➤ PHARMACIES: **Jolly's Pharmacy** (✉ 12 King George V St., Roseau, ☎ 767/448–3388).
➤ POLICE: **Police emergencies** (☎ 999).

ETIQUETTE AND BEHAVIOR

Unlike neighboring Martinique and Guadeloupe, topless bathing is frowned upon in Dominica. In addition, swimsuits should not be worn on the street. Dominicans, on the whole, are laid-back and polite. You will no doubt be greeted with a warm "good morning" or "good night" by anyone you pass on the street. Yet the people here are very private; it's better to ask permission before photographing someone. Note also that bargaining is not generally appreciated in Dominican shops.

FESTIVALS AND SEASONAL EVENTS

Dominicans boast that they have the most spontaneous carnival in the region, Mas Domnik. It's great to join a band and get all costumed and painted. Revelling in the streets during Carnival Monday and Tuesday, it's one big family. Celebrations usually heat up the last 10 days or so before Ash Wednesday. The National Cultural Council hosts the Emancipation Celebrations in August. September and October see Independence celebrations, culminating on Independence Day on November 3. Another major event is the Annual World Creole Music Festival, held the last weekend in October. This three-day music and cultural festival draws performers and Creole music enthusiasts from around the globe. Community Day of Service is November 4. In addition to these major Festivals there are a number of Village Feasts which take place all over the island from month to month.

HOLIDAYS

Public holidays are: New Year's (Jan. 1), Merchant's Holiday (Jan. 2), Carnival Jump-Up Days (two days before Ash Wednesday each year), Ash Wednesday, Labour Day (May 1), Whit Monday (May 24), Emancipation Day (Aug. 5), Independence Day (Nov. 3), Community Service Day (Nov. 4), Christmas Day (Dec. 25), and Boxing Day (Dec. 26).

LANGUAGE

The official language is English. Most Dominicans also speak Creole, a language based primarily on a French vocabulary with indigenous Carib loan words and traces of West African syntax.

MAIL AND SHIPPING

First-class letters to North America cost EC95¢ and those to the United Kingdom cost EC90¢; postcards are EC55¢ to just about anywhere in the world. The general post office is opposite the ferry terminal in Roseau. Dominica is often confused with the Dominican Republic, so when addressing letters to the island, be sure to write: The Commonwealth of Dominica, Eastern Caribbean. Islands in this part of the Caribbean do not use postal codes.

MONEY MATTERS

Prices throughout this chapter are quoted in U.S. dollars, unless indicated otherwise.

ATMS

You'll find ATMs in all the banks in Roseau—including Barclays Bank on Old Street, the Royal Bank of Canada near the cruise-ship berth, Banque Française Commerciale on Queen Mary Street, and the Bank of Nova Scotia on Hillsborough Street—as well as some in larger villages such as Portsmouth. They dispense EC dollars only and accept international bank cards.

CREDIT CARDS

Major credit cards are widely accepted, as are traveler's checks.

CURRENCY

The official currency is the Eastern Caribbean dollar (EC$) but U.S. dollars are readily accepted. The exchange rate will be EC$2.67 to the US$1, but you'll usually get change in EC dollars.

PASSPORTS AND VISAS

U.S. citizens need a valid passport or an original birth certificate along with a government-issued photo I.D. Citizens of other countries must have a valid passport. Citizens from Cuba, Haiti, Russia, The People's Republic of China, and Eastern European countries who wish to stay in Dominica for longer than 21 days are require to obtain a Visitors' Visa. Everyone needs a return or ongoing ticket.

SAFETY

As with all destinations in the world, crime has been known to rear its ugly head on Dominica. It's always wise to secure valuables in hotel safe and not carry too much money or many valuables around. Remember that if you rent a car to tour the island, you may have to park it in a remote area, so don't leave valuables in your vehicle while you're off on a hike or a tour.

SIGHTSEEING TOURS

Since Dominica is such a nature-centered destination, there is no shortage of tour certified guides. There are also numerous tour and taxi companies. Ask the staff at your hotel for a recommendation. Ken's Hinterland Adventure Tours & Taxi Service, Dominica Tours, and Whitchurch Tours are among the most reputable operators specializing in ornithological, botanical, or more intense adventure tours, and any of the three will be able to arrange an excursion to suit your desires. Generally tours start off in the Roseau area, but most operators will arrange convenient pick-ups. Prices range between $30 and $75 per person depending on the duration, amenities provided and number of persons on the excursion.
➤ CONTACTS: **Ken's Hinterland Adventure Tours & Taxi Service** (✉ Fort Young Hotel, Victoria St., Roseau, ☎ 767/448–4850 or 767/235–3517). **Dominica Tours** (✉ Anchorage Hotel, Castle Comfort, ☎ 767/448–2638 or 767/448–0990). **Whitchurch Tours** (✉ Old St., Roseau, ☎ 767/448–2181).

TAXES AND SERVICE CHARGES

DEPARTURE TAX
The departure/embarkation tax is US$20 or EC$50, payable in cash only at the airport at the time of departure from the island.

SALES TAX
Hotels collect a 5% government hotel occupancy tax, restaurants a 5% government sales tax.

TAXIS
Taxis and minibuses are available at the airports and in Roseau, as well as at most hotels and guest houses. Rates are fixed by the government, but if you opt for a co-op—sharing a taxi (and the fare) with other passengers going in the same direction—you will be able to negotiate a special price. Drivers also offer their services for tours anywhere on the island for beginning at $20 an hour for up to four persons; a 3½-hour island tour will cost approximately $80. It's best to get a recommendation from your hotel. You can recognize a taxi and/or minibus by the HA plates; simply flag them down or make your way to the nearest bus stop. For more information on reputable taxi companies contact the Dominica Taxi Association or Nature Island Taxi Association.
➤ CONTACTS: **Dominica Taxi Association** (☎ 767/449–8533). **Nature Island Taxi Association** (☎ 767/448–1679).

TELEPHONES

COUNTRY AND AREA CODES
To call Dominica from the United States, dial the area code (767) and the local access code (44), followed by the five-digit local number.

INTERNATIONAL CALLS
The island has a very advanced telecommunication system and accordingly efficient direct-dial international service. All pay phones are equipped for local, overseas dialing, and credit card calling, accepting either EC coins or phone cards, which you can buy at many island stores and at the airports.

LOCAL CALLS
On the island, dial only the seven-digit number that follows the area code.

TIPPING
Most hotels and restaurants add a 10% service charge to your bill. A 5% tip for exceptionally good service on top of the service charge is always welcome; otherwise just tip accordingly.

VISITOR INFORMATION
➤ BEFORE YOU LEAVE: **Dominican Tourist Office** (⊠ 800 2nd Ave., Suite 1802, New York, NY 10017, ☎ 212/949–1711, FAX 212/949–1714, WEB www.dominica.dm). **The Dominica Tourist Office–UK** (⊠ MKI Ltd., Mitre House, 66 Abbey Rd., Bush Hill Park, Enfield, Middlesex EN1 2QE, U.K., ☎ 44–208/350–1004, FAX 44–208/350–1011). **Office of the Dominica High Commission, London** (⊠ 1 Collingham Gardens, London SW5 0HW, U.K., ☎ 44–207/370–5194, FAX 44–207/373–8743).
➤ IN DOMINICA: **Division of Tourism** (⊠ Valley Rd., Roseau, ☎ 767/448–2045; Old Post Office branch, ⊠ Dame M. E. Charles Blvd., Roseau, ☎ 767/448–2045 Ext. 118; Canefield Airport branch, ⊠ Canefield, ☎ 767/449–1242; Melville Hall Airport branch, ⊠ Marigot, ☎ 767/445–7051).

11 DOMINICAN REPUBLIC

Updated by
Eileen Robinson
Smith

It was electricity in the air, like Paris on an evening in early spring. Love was in the air as well as the sizzle of creativity and talent. The intelligent conversation that it generates, when global types converge at sidewalk cafés, could be overheard. After dusk, in Santo Domingo's Colonial Zone, the Spanish gas lights illuminate the extraordinary cityscape of buildings dating back to the 1500s. Small Euro-hotels and scores of cafés and bars stand behind centuries-old facades. They come alive as intimate, informal rendezvous. One group moved their party down the cobblestone street to a trendy, two-story restaurant that is a young visionary's restoration of a 16th-century building. The first European city in the Western Hemisphere has finally come of age. It has "it" going on.

Sprawling over two thirds of the island of Hispaniola, the Dominican Republic is a delightful, almost magical place. Its people are friendly and hospitable by nature; if you return their courtesy, they'll do their best to ensure that your vacation is memorable. The D.R. also happens to be one of the least expensive Caribbean destinations.

The island has had a stormy history replete with revolutions, military coups, invasions, epidemics, and bankruptcy. Columbus happened upon this island on December 5, 1492, and on Christmas Eve his ship, the *Santa María,* was wrecked on its Atlantic shore. He named it La Isla Española (the Spanish Island), established a small colony, and sailed back to Spain on the *Pinta.* His brother Bartholomeo, along with Nicolás de Ovando, founded Santo Domingo in 1496, making it the oldest continuously inhabited city in this hemisphere. During the 16th century it became the bustling New World hub of Spanish commerce and culture.

The continued restoration of its Colonial Zone, under the auspices of the Office de Cultural Patrimonio, includes the renovation of the Parque de Colón and the construction of underground parking garages and a new, large hotel. A new security force, trained especially for the Zone, more frequent garbage pick-ups, and improvements in lighting, have made this a desirable neighborhood once again. Clearly the D.R. is realizing more of its vast potential.

Still, most Dominican towns and cities are generally not quaint, neat, or particularly pretty, and poverty is everywhere. However, the ever-increasing role of tourism in the economy is bringing about changes that benefit residents and visitors alike: major highways have been repaved; sidewalks, lighting, and signage in urban areas are being improved.

American influence looms large in Dominican life. Major thoroughfares in the capital, Santo Domingo, are named after American presidents; many Dominicans speak at least rudimentary English and have relatives living in the States; and baseball is a national passion. Still, this is a vibrantly Latin country—at times cool, collected, and laid-back; at times fiery hot, frenetic, and chaotic.

The country has several areas with all the attractions and amenities necessary for the perfect island vacation. Sun-worshipers head to one of the many beach resort areas. The highest peak in the West Indies, Pico Duarte, lures hikers to the central mountain range. Ancient sunken galleons and coral reefs divert divers and snorkelers. And everywhere there's the breathtaking scenery, the land ever turning and twisting and towering into mountains before tumbling into the sea.

Lodging

The D.R. has the largest hotel inventory (at this writing 52,000 rooms with 3,000 more under construction) in the Caribbean, though many Americans are still unfamiliar with the country. The options range from rustic country inns to posh beach resorts to chic Santo Domingo hotels.

Santo Domingo hotels generally base their tariffs on the EP plan and maintain the same room rates year-round. Beach resorts have high winter and low summer rates—with prices reduced by as much as 50%. Along the north coast you'll find many all-inclusive properties. Although it wasn't long ago that most people wanted all-inclusive packages, the trend now is toward flexibility. Many Punta Cana resorts are once again offering the EP and MAP (occasionally, you'll also find the FAP). Sosua and Cabarete are strongholds of the small inn, but that does not mean that larger, strictly all-inclusive resorts don't exist there. They do.

Most tourists traveling to the D.R. take advantage of the many charter air-hotel packages available through travel agents and tour operators, particularly in winter. You can get a direct flight to Punta Cana from, say, Connecticut or Missouri and pay $700 for a week's vacation including airfare and a stay at a new, all-inclusive property.

CATEGORY	COST EP/CP*	COST A.I.**
$$$$	over $350	over $375
$$$	$250–$350	$275–$375
$$	$150–$250	$175–$275
$	under $150	under $175

*EP/CP prices are per night for a standard double room in high season, excluding taxes, service charges, and meal plans.**A.I. (all-inclusive) prices are per person, per night based on double-occupancy during high season, excluding taxes and service charges

Santo Domingo

The seaside capital of the country is in the middle of the island's south coast. In Santo Domingo, most of the better hotels are on the Malecón, or in neighborhoods near to it.

$$ ⊞ **Barceló Gran Hotel Lina Spa & Casino.** A steadfast city landmark for decades, now painted in bold Caribbean colors (from mango to hot pink), this hotel is near the Malecón and the Presidential Palace. Busi-

ness and conventions are a large part of their repeat clientele because of the professional and helpful staff. Both hotel guests and the capital's movers and shakers still frequent the Restaurante Lina, with its classic continental dishes and piano bar. The rooftop pool area has been beautified, with the white tenting giving it a resort appeal. ✉ *Av. Maximo Gomez and av. 27 de Febrero, Gazcue (Box 1915),* ☎ *809/563–5000,* FAX *809/686–5521,* WEB *www.barcelo-hotels.com. 202 rooms, 15 suites. 2 restaurants, coffee shop, minibars, 2 pools, health club, hot tub, casino, piano bar, concierge, Internet, business services, meeting rooms. AE, DC, MC, V. EP, FAP, MAP.*

$$ ⊞ **Hotel Santo Domingo.** Surrounded by walled gardens and over-
★ looking the sea, this in-town getaway is favored by diplomats (many VIPs check into one of the Excel Club's eight business rooms with king-size beds and offices with 4-line speaker phones). A sophisticated after-work crowd gathers at the Marrakesh Café & Bar, with its American music (jazz on Mondays) and Casablanca-style decor that complements the lobby's mahogany arches and potted palms. A trellised arcade leads to a large, peaceful pool that's beautifully landscaped. Business people favor this hotel for its professionalism; tourists love the pampering service. ✉ *Avs. Independencia and Abraham Lincoln, El Malecón (Box 2112),* ☎ *809/221–1511 or 800/877–3643,* FAX *809/533–8898,* WEB *www.hotel.stodgo.com.do. 215 rooms. 3 restaurants, some in-room data ports, 3 tennis courts, pool, hair salon, health club, sauna, 2 bars, concierge, concierge floor, business services, meeting rooms, car rental, helipad, travel services. AE, MC, V. EP.*

$$ ⊞ **Melia Santo Domingo Hotel and Casino.** The lavish lobby, restau-
★ rants, and rooms of this Malecón hotel are contemporary yet classic. Wonderful ocean views are found throughout. Those on the Royal Service Level stay in the lap of luxury, with such special amenities as a full breakfast, complementary premium liquors, and hors d'oeuvres in the lounge. Your butler will even have your clothes pressed for free. Casabe serves noteworthy buffets and is open 24 hours; the impressive Da Vinci restaurant faces the ocean. A full-service spa and fitness center look out to the glorious rooftop pool. A piano bar, disco, and an adjacent casino provide the fun. ✉ *Av. George Washington 365, El Malecón (Box 8326),* ☎ *809/221–6666,* FAX *809/687–8150,* WEB *www.solmelia.es. 245 rooms, 17 suites. 2 restaurants, minibars, no-smoking rooms, 2 tennis courts, pool, health club, spa, shops, 2 bars, piano bar, casino, dance club, concierge, concierge floor, business services, meeting rooms, travel services. AE, DC, MC, V. EP, FAP, MAP.*

$$ ⊞ **Occidental El Embajador and Casino.** Although this landmark hotel isn't on the Malecón, its multinational flags wave a welcome from a safe residential neighborhood close by. The spacious lobby is a social hub; orchestras perform near its fountain. Executive rooms on the fifth and sixth floors have extra amenities and comprise the Occidental Club; there's also an upscale concierge level, the Miguel Angel Club. Standard guest rooms are spacious and quiet; bathrooms are exceptional. The appealing pool complex is a popular weekend gathering place. ✉ *Av. Sarasota 65, Bella Vista,* ☎ *809/221–2131,* FAX *809/532–4494.* WEB *www.occidental-hoteles.com. 291 rooms, 14 suites. 2 restaurants, 4 tennis courts, pool, gym, sauna, shops, 3 bars, casino, concierge floor, business services, meeting rooms. AE, DC, MC, V. CP, MAP.*

$$ ⊞ **Renaissance Jaragua Hotel and Casino.** Gardens, waterfalls, and foun-
★ tains surround this luxurious urban oasis. You'll find Champions, a sports bar, serving all-American burgers within the huge casino; local and big-name performers play the 1,000-seat La Fiesta Showroom. Cascade, a glass-enclosed bar, looks out to a waterfall. Rates are based on a view of the ocean, garden, or of the huge, free-form pool. The expanded Renaissance Club—accessed by 53 rooms on the concierge

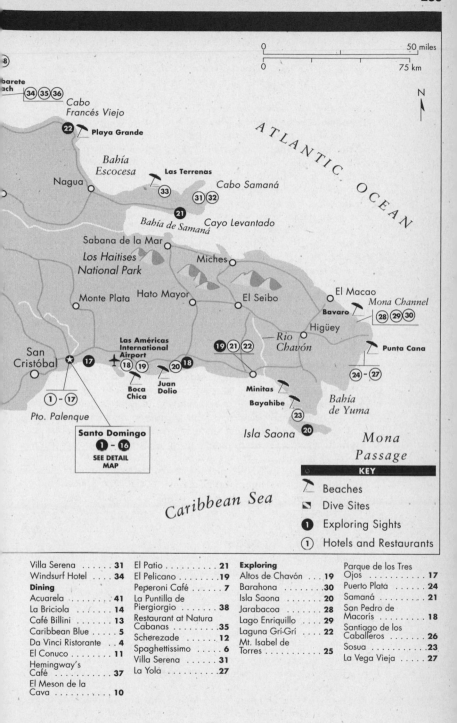

0   50 miles
0   75 km

N

barete
ach   ㉞ ㉟ ㊱

Cabo Francés Viejo

㉒   **Playa Grande**

Bahía Escocesa

Nagua

Las Terrenas

㉝   *Cabo Samaná*

㉛ ㉜

㉑

Bahía de Samaná   *Cayo Levantado*

A T L A N T I C   O C E A N

Sabana de la Mar

Los Haitises National Park

Miches

El Macao

Mona Channel

Bavaro   ㉘ ㉙ ㉚

Monte Plata   Hato Mayor   El Seibo

Higüey

Río Chavón

Punta Cana

San Cristóbal   ★   ⑰

Las Américas International Airport

⑲ ㉑ ㉒

⑱   ⑲   ⑳ ⑱

Boca Chica   **Juan Dolio**

㉔ - ㉗

①-⑰

Pto. Palenque

Minitas

Bayahibe

㉓

⑳

Isla Saona

Bahía de Yuma

Mona Passage

Santo Domingo
❶ - ⓰
SEE DETAIL MAP

Caribbean Sea

KEY

⌇ Beaches

◥ Dive Sites

❶ Exploring Sights

① Hotels and Restaurants

floors—has its lounge and terrace that affords ocean vistas. Suites have Club privileges, data ports, and larger desks. The presidential suite is vast, with its own hot tub. The fitness center is the largest in the city. ✉ *Av. George Washington 367, El Malecón,* ☎ *809/221–2222,* FAX *809/686–0528,* WEB *www.renaissancehotels.com. 292 rooms, 8 suites. 4 restaurants, some in-room data ports, minibars, pool, hot tub, sauna, spa, golf course, 4 tennis courts, 5 bars, casino, dance club, concierge, concierge floor, business services. AE, MC, V. EP, FAP, MAP.*

$ 🏨 **Hodelpa Caribe Colonial.** This new boutique hotel provides yet another option in the burgeoning Colonial Zone. With superior sophistication for the price, and a friendly, accommodating staff, the hotel is wooing business people and tourists away from more established properties. The feel is European, the furnishings art deco with white gauze canopies draped over king-size beds. Rooms come in standard and superior; suites offer more space and amenities. Go up to the rooftop sundeck or sit out on your balcony and wave to the neighbors. ✉ *Isabel La Catolica, #59, Zona Colonial,* ☎ *809/683–1000 or 888/403–2603,* FAX *809/683–2303.. 52 rooms, 2 suites. Restaurant, room service, minibars, bar. AE, MC, V. EP.*

$ 🏨 **Hotel Mercure Commercial.** Less than five years old and in the Colonial Zone, the Mercure was designed as a businessmen's hotel, yet is attracting tourists because of its location and moderate price tag. It has the characteristic French élan of the Accor Group, from the music to the yellow leather couches in the small lobby and the French cuisine at El Colonial Brasserie. Rooms in this renovated 1940s building are cramped but attractive, with decorative tile work. ✉ *El Conde at Hostos, Zona Colonial,* ☎ *809/688–5500,* FAX *809/688–5522,* WEB *www.mercure.com. 96 rooms. Restaurant, minibars. AE, MC, V. EP.*

$ 🏨 **Hotel Sofitel Frances.** The facade of this two-story, 16th-century structure has handsome native stonework; the interior is done in pink stucco. Columned arches open to a European-style fountain and a courtyard furnished with teak and shaded by white umbrellas. Thanks to rattan furniture and potted plants, second-floor patios have a tropical, colonial feel. Guest rooms and baths are minimalistic, with rugs on tiled floors and stylish French bedspreads. The lobby restaurant specializes in French and international cuisine. ✉ *Calle Las Mercedes and Arzobispo Merino, Zona Colonial,* ☎ *809/685–9331,* FAX *809/685–1289,* WEB *www.sofitel.com. 19 rooms. Restaurant, cable TV, minibars, bar. AE, MC, V. EP.*

Boca Chica/Juan Dolio

The Boca Chica/Juan Dolio resort area is the area immediately east of Las Americas airport, where you would fly in.

$ 🏨 **Barceló Capella Beach Resort.** This grand resort's 17 acres are punc-
★ tuated with benches and manicured shrubbery. An eclectic mix of architectural styles—from Victorian to Moorish—the yellow-stucco exterior is accented by white latticework and columns, and a red-tile roof. The large, quiet rooms have a civilized, almost British colonial air; some have balconies and sea views; 200 of the newest are on the beach. There's entertainment at the theater or the bar, and a tri-level, palapa disco on the beach near the water sports club. Barceló is dominating Juan Dolio and now has Colonia Tropical, Talanquera, and the Decameron Beach Resort & Casino. ✉ *Juan Dolio (Box 4750, Villas Del Mar, Santo Domingo),* ☎ *809/526–1080,* FAX *809/526–1088,* WEB *www.barcelo-hotels.com. 271 rooms, 22 suites. 3 restaurants, minibars, 2 tennis courts, 2 pools, health club, massage, sauna, beach, snorkeling, boating, windsurfing, 3 bars, dance club, recreation room, theater, shops, children's programs (ages 4–12), concierge, concierge floor, meeting rooms. AE, MC, V. All-inclusive.*

$ ⌂ **Coral Hamaca Beach Hotel and Casino.** Hamaca has a large fun quo-
☺ tient; its sweet, friendly staffers make you feel a part of the whole. East
of Santo Domingo and close to Las Américas Airport, this all-inclusive offers around-the-clock services. Opt for one of the 247 newer rooms.
A lovely champagne-color beach has two bars, a juice bar, and an á la
carte *palapa* (thatch-roof, open-air) restaurant. Many business people
who choose to headquarter here for an overnight or a week pay $25
to upgrade, which includes many perks, including a massage. For fun
head to the casino, amphitheater, or disco. ⊠ *Boca Chica Beach, ☎ 809/
523–4611 or 888/942–6725,* FAX *809/523–6767,* WEB *www.coralhotels.
com.do. 630 rooms. 5 restaurants, grill, 3 tennis courts, 2 pools, gym,
massage, sauna, beach, dive shop, snorkeling, windsurfing, boating,
bicycles, 6 bars, casino, dance club, theater, children's programs (ages
4–12), playground, laundry service, Internet, meeting rooms. AE, DC,
MC, V. All inclusive.*

La Romana

La Romana is on the southeast coast of the Dominican Republic,
about a two-hour drive from Santo Domingo, southwest of the Punta
Cana area, which is on the easternmost end of the island. There is a
new international airport here now, so you can often fly direct from
the United States or Canada.

$$$ **Casa de Campo.** A truly world-class property, always evolving, it has
★ ☺ the best equestrian center in the islands and even a trap-shooting sa-
fari club. But golf is the big draw. Players can fly into its airport and
an hour later be teeing off on one of three courses. With sea and river
views, the newest Pete Dye course was designed around the artisan vil-
lage of Altos de Chavon. The specialty restaurants at Chavon and El
Patio, which has a new, authentically Dominican menu, are fine op-
tions to the great buffets. A luxurious yacht marina and villa complex
has opened. Excellent recreation programs make this perfect for fam-
ilies. It's just a five-minute cab ride from La Romana/Casa de Campo
International Airport. ⊠ *La Romana (Box 140), ☎ 809/523–3333 or
305/856–7083,* FAX *809/523–8548,* WEB *www.casadecampo.cc. 350
rooms, 150 villas. 9 restaurants, 3 18-hole golf courses, 13 tennis
courts, 16 pools, health club, sauna, dive shop, snorkeling, windsurf-
ing, fishing, bicycles, horseback riding, 4 bars, shops, theater, children's
programs (ages 4–18). AE, MC, V. All-inclusive, EP, FAP, MAP.*

$ ⌂ **Casa del Mar.** This deluxe property, its whimsical gingerbread fret-
work awash in Caribbean colors, is on an exceptional palm-fringed
ribbon of white sand close Casa de Campo. An Amhsa Marina Hotel
& Resort, most of the attractive guest rooms have views of the sea,
the spectacular pool, or both. In the Bayahibe Restaurant, buffets of
fresh, tasty dishes are served beneath stunning handcrafted chandeliers.
There's more fine dining to be found in the on-site Asian and Italian
restaurants. The free half-day excursion to pristine Saona Island is a
photo opportunity. ⊠ *Bayahibe Bay, La Romana, ☎ 809/221–8880,*
FAX *809/221–8881,* WEB *www.AMHSAmarina.com. 568 rooms. 4 restau-
rants, minibars, 4 tennis courts, 2 pools, gym, hot tub, beach, dive shop,
snorkeling, windsurfing, boating, bicycles, archery, horseback riding,
volleyball, 4 bars, dance club, children's program (ages 5–12), meet-
ing rooms. AE, MC, V. All-inclusive.*

Punta Cana

On the easternmost coast, Punta Cana is a 20-mi strand of incredible
beach punctuated by coco palms. The area includes Bávaro Beach. You
will fly into the Punta Cana International Airport. The capital, Santo
Domingo, is about a three-hour trip by car.

$$ 🖭 **Meliá Caribe Tropical.** This is an American-friendly resort, designed
★ ☾ for both couples and families. The lobby has fountains, lagoons, board-
walks, pillars, and sculptures. The sprawling complex is beautified by
waterscapes and mangroves. Hot-pink flamingos aren't plastic, and the
pond's white rotunda is the site of many a wedding. Surrounded by
palms, the pool has a Jacuzzi at its center and a kids' pool. At the his-
and-her spa, with its Grecian-style white columns, you can relax in a
whirlpool surrounded by classical sculptures. Gourmet Boulevard,
lined with specialty restaurants, helps you beat the buffet blues. Golf,
all 27 holes, is at the adjacent Cocotal Golf Club. ⊠ *Punta Cana,* ☎
809/221–1290, FAX *809/221–4595,* WEB *www.solmelia.es. 1,044 junior
suites. 15 restaurants, 1 18-hole golf course, 1 9-hole golf course, 8
tennis courts, 2 pools, health club, spa, beach, boating, snorkeling, wind-
surfing, 6 bars, casino, dance club, showroom, children's programs (ages
4–11), business services, convention center. AE, DC, MC, V. All-in-
clusive.*

$$ 🖭 **Paradisus Punta Cana All-Inclusive Exclusive Beach Resort.** Par-
★ ☾ adisus has an open-air lobby of lagoons and rock gardens. The path
to the elegant casino is punctuated by sculptures. Bi-level suites have
tropical motifs and brightly painted wooden furnishings. From the simple grilled seafood and meats at the beach palapa to the sophisticated
international fare (and complimentary cognacs and liqueurs) at the à
la carte Romantico restaurant, the cuisine here is exceptional. You'll
find everything from aquaerobics (often followed by cocktails at the
swim-up bar) to spa services, painting lessons and PADI dive instruction. Honeymoon packages are exceptional, and weddings are blissful. (Love that white, horse-drawn marriage carriage.) ⊠ *Bávaro
Beach,* ☎ *809/687–9923,* FAX *809/687–0752. 527 suites. 8 restaurants, minibars, 4 tennis courts, golf privileges, pool, health club, spa,
beach, dive shop, boating, snorkeling, windsurfing, bicycles, archery,
4 bars, casino, children's programs (ages 4–12). AE, DC, MC, V. All-
inclusive.*

$ 🖭 **Barceló Bávaro Palace.** The Barceló Bávaro complex is nearly a mini-
city with decidedly more restaurants and shops than most towns, with
tennis and golf complexes, a lakefront church, Vegas-quality reviews,
a shuttle train, a dazzling new convention center (considered the finest
in the Caribbean), villas, and four other hotels (Bávaro Golf, Beach,
Garden, and Casino) plus the five-star Palace. The showplace, its serpentine pools with swim-up bar, borders one of the world's best
beaches. Gastronomy is a main attraction, noise levels are lower, and
the clientele more upscale than the other resorts. Those staying at the
Palace can use the facilities at all five properties, but the Palace's are
exclusively theirs. ⊠ *Bávaro Beach,* ☎ *809/686–5797,* FAX *809/788–
7723.* WEB *www.barcelo.com, 594 rooms. 5 restaurants, minibars,18-
hole golf course, 3 tennis courts, 2 pools, health club, beach, snorkeling, boating, volleyball, 5 bars, dance club, theater. AE, MC, V.
All-Inclusive.*

$ 🖭 **Catalonia Beach, Golf & Casino Resort.** This handsome property is
☾ punctuated with fountains and sculptures, lagoons, and garden areas.
The beach, with no property visible on either side, offers a roster of
aquatic sports. The tour desk offers a good mix of excursions, many
in English. It's big fun at the disco, what with the international music,
mystery night, perfect couple night, and the Mr. & Mrs. Catalonia
pageant. The Gran Caribe buffet has a theme night cycle—one night
is the Dominican feast for a taste of local cuisine—and there are Japanese, Brazilian, Italian, and French restaurants. The mix of patrons
is equally international. The noise level is acceptable, despite the high
occupancy, which is the catalyst for a planned expansion. ⊠ *Cabeza
de Toros, Báevaro Beach (Box N8, Higuey),* ☎ *809/412–0000,* FAX *809/*

412–0001, WEB *www.cataloniabavaro.com. 704 junior suites, 1 presidential suite. 8 restaurants, minibars, 18-hole golf course, 2 tennis courts, 2 pools, gym, hair salon, beach, boating, water skiing, bicycling, billiards, 5 bars, casino, dance club, showroom, shops, children's programs (ages 4–12), Internet, convention center. AE, MC, V. All-Inclusive.*

$ 🖳 **Club Med Punta Cana.** This renovated "village" is looking fine, with the sleeping rooms particularly attractive. Set on one of the island's best beaches, it is a great for families, what with two different kids' clubs (one for toddlers, the other for older kids). Though the resort is American-friendly, there is a lot that happens here in Spanish—and French. Ask about frequent specials, and try for a package that comes with airfare. And have fun. Nonguests can pay for a day-pass, which includes lunch with complimentary beer and wine service. For everyone, cocktails and any beverages (even coffee) consumed between meals cost extra. ⊠ *Punta Cana,* ☎ *809/686–5500,* FAX *809/685–5287. 522 rooms. 3 restaurants, pool, aerobics, beach, boating, windsurfing, archery, volleyball, 2 bars, nightclub, children's programs (ages 2–13). AE, MC, V. All-inclusive.*

$ 🖳 **Natura Park.** Squeaky clean and environmentally correct, this resort's furniture is handcrafted from the coco palms that were cut down to make room for the gardens, walkways, and man-made lakes. On the grounds, are the remains of a coconut plantation as well as a mangrove forest and a natural lake. Guest rooms are in 13 buildings that put stone, wood, and cane to use in an ecosensitive way. The outdoor à la carte restaurant, where meals are made from wholesome, all-natural ingredients, looks onto a spectacular lagoon-style pool (with a swim-up bar) and beyond to Bávaro Beach. The luxurious spa is a relaxing place for a physical renewal. ⊠ *Bávaro Beach,* ☎ *809/538–3111 or 888/628–8727,* FAX *809/221–6060. 518 rooms, 6 suites. 3 restaurants, 3 tennis courts, 2 pools, spa, beach, windsurfing, boating, 4 bars, dance club, children's programs (ages 4–11). MC, V. All-inclusive.*

$ 🖳 **Punta Cana Resort & Club.** A charismatic resort appreciated by die-
★ ☼ hard Caribophiles, it has reinvented itself. On an incredible 6-mi beach, studded with seaswept, coco palms, the original hotel is transformed, the new beach wing upscale with hardwoods, marble, and chic tropical furnishings. Luxury, beachfront golf villas, decorated by investor Oscar de La Renta, overlook a spectacular P. B. Dye golf course. The La Yola restaurant stars at the new Marina. In Corales, an exclusive, residential development, the oceanfront mansions of de la Renta and Julio Iglesias are flanked by those of other VIPs. The golf clubhouse, facing the ocean and its own pool, opened with raves. ⊠ *Playa Punta Cana,* ☎ *809/221–2262 or 888/442–2262,* FAX *809/687–8745,* WEB *www.puntacana.com. 418 rooms. 5 restaurants, minibars, 18-hole golf course, 4 tennis courts, 2 pools, hair salon, health club, beach, dive shop, snorkeling, windsurfing, boating, fishing, horseback riding, 5 bars, dance club, theater, children's programs (ages 5–12), playground, laundry service, business services, meeting rooms.. AE, MC, V. All-Inclusive, EP, MAP.*

Samaná

Samaná is both the name of the peninsula that curves around the bay of the same name and juts out into the Atlantic. The nearest major international airport is Puerto Plata International Gregorio Luperon.

$ 🖳 **Occidental Gran Bahía.** This seaside, Victorian-style hotel is all turrets, gables, and fretwork; it also has graceful verandas that overlook the pool. Rooms are very large and have cheerful floral prints, tile floors, and watercolor paintings. The grand yet welcoming reception area and three-story white, colonnaded atrium surround a spectacular fountain flanked by cozy nooks. The superb views make breakfast on your private balcony a treat. Dining in the alfresco restaurant, overlooking the pool and the sea, is a pleasure. Horseback riding is a popular Samaná excursion as is whale watching in season. It's just 10 minutes from Samaná. ⊠ *Las Cacao (Box 2024, Santo Domingo),* ☎ *809/538–3111,* FAX *809/538–2764,* WEB *www.occidental-hoteles.com. 110 rooms. 2 restaurants, golf privileges, 2 tennis courts, pool, gym, hair salon, archery, bar. AE, MC, V. All-inclusive.*

$ ⊞ **Playa Colibri.** The location is splendid, right on a beautiful beach
☺   and close to the center of the village. The apartments are new and commodious, and all have an ocean and garden view from a spacious terrace. The oval swimming pool is in the center of the garden. Rates depend on the size of apartment, the number of persons, and the number of nights; this hotel/residence is available for daily, weekly, or monthly rentals. You may find that you want to stay forever. If that's the case, the apartments are for sale. ⊠ *Avenida de la Mar, Las Terrenas,* ☎ *809/240–6434,* FAX *809/240–6917,* WEB *www.playacolibri.com. 45 apartments. Restaurant, kitchens, pool, outdoor hot tub, beach, bar, baby-sitting. MC, V. EP.*

$ ⊞ **Villa Serena.** This little-known gem is down the beach from the fishing village of Las Galeras and at the end of the long, scenic road from Puerto Plata. Each room is individually decorated and has a lanai overlooking the Bahía de Rincón. The Villa Serena restaurant serves some of the best food on the peninsula. Horses can be hired nearby. ⊠ *Las Galeras (Box 51–1),* ☎ *809/538–0000,* FAX *809/538–0009. 11 rooms. Restaurant, pool, beach, dive shop, snorkeling, bicycles, bar. AE, MC, V. CP.*

The Amber Coast

Named for the large quantities of amber ore found in the area, the sands on its 75 mi of beach are also golden. In the northern part of the island, with mountains on one side, the resort area with the major hotels is called Playa Dorada. Plan to fly into Puerto Plata International Gregorio Luperon Airport.

$$–$$$$ ⊞ **Sea Horse Ranch.** Internationally known celebrities frequent this luxury residential resort. Formerly a dairy farm—with more than 5,000 acres that include preserved eco-areas—it was mentioned in *British Vogue* as one young celebrity's favorite get-away. Local businesspeople and an international community of vacationers and part-time residents hang their hats here. All of the villas have three or four bedrooms— about 4,000 square ft, a pool, and are on sites from half an acre upwards to four acres (the latter has a private beach). An exclusive beach club is nestled amongst coves with mountain views. Prices decrease dramatically when rented by the month. ⊠ *Cabarete,* ☎ *809/571–3880,* FAX *809/571–2374,* WEB *www.sea-horse-ranch.com. 75 villas. Dining room, kitchens, 5 tennis courts, beach, horseback riding, snorkeling, bar, baby-sitting. AE, MC, V. EP.*

$ ⊞ **Gran Ventana.** This hotel is characterized by style and pizzazz. The
★   lobby has a central fountain surrounded by commodious white sofas. The main buffet dining area is within a gazebo. Rooms are in two handsome buildings with canopied entrances, ocher stucco facades, and red-tile roofs. Most rooms have sea views obstructed by only a few palms and a picket fence that keeps the beach private and tranquil. The 141 oversize rooms in the newer building do not face the water, but you'll have a lap pool and peace and quiet. Packages are popular with those renewing vows or getting married. A new roof-top bar serves premium liquors. ⊠ *Playa Dorada, Puerto Plata (Box 22),* ☎ *809/320–2111,* FAX *809/320–2112,* WEB *www.victoriahoteles.com.do. 504 rooms, 2 suites. 5 restaurants, tennis court, 3 pools, gym, hair salon, 2 hot tubs, sauna, beach, snorkeling, windsurfing, boating, bicycles, 6 bars, dance*

club, recreation room, theater, shops, meeting rooms, car rental. AE, DC, MC, V. All-inclusive.

$ ⊞ **Iberostar Costa Dorada.** You will be dazzled when you view the sprawling lobby with its hardwood benches and sculptures. The curvaceous pool is known for its central Jacuzzi encircled by Roman pillars, which appears in many wedding photos. The pool action begins with aqua-aerobics, and the animated, sometimes over-zealous staff keeps the games and music going. Those seeking quiet head for the delightful stretch of undeveloped beach. Other all-inclusives could learn from the buffeteria, which offers a surprising variety and quality of international and Dominican dishes. Rodizio, the authentic Brazilian restaurant, is a must-do. You can get a massage outdoors or at the spa. ✉ *Playa Dorada, Puerto Plata,* ☎ *809/320–1000,* 𝖥𝖠𝖷 *809/320–2023,* 𝖶𝖤𝖡 *www.iberostar.com. 498 rooms, 16 junior suites. 3 restaurants, minibars, pool, health club, spa, snorkeling, boating, billiards, 3 bars, dance club, showroom, shops, Internet, business services, meeting rooms. AE, MC, V. All-Inclusive.*

$ ⊞ **Natura Cabanas.** This spa getaway is paradisiacal. No phones or TVs in the simple, criollo-style, thatched-roof bungalows, each with a fully equipped kitchen, which can accommodate from two to six people. The secluded pool is separated by exuberant vegetation from the private beach. The owners' mantra is "peace, quiet, and health." There are yoga lessons, deep massages, mud baths, salt scrubs, facials, and a sauna. Rates include airport transfers from the Puerto Plata airport. You can rent mountain bikes, horses, or four-wheel-drive vehicles. Afterward refresh yourself with fresh juices and head to the alfresco dining room for a candlelight dinner with a sea view. Day guests to the spa are welcome. ✉ *Playa Perla Marina, Cabarete,* ☎ *809/571–1507 or 809/571–9902, 809/844–6881,* 𝖥𝖠𝖷 *809/571–1507,* 𝖶𝖤𝖡 *www. naturacabana.com. 5 bungalows. Restaurant, kitchenettes, pool, spa, massage, sauna, beach, bar. MC, V. CP.*

$ ⊞ **Occidental Gran Hotel Playa Dorada.** Anyone who saw this property before the millennium—that is, before it's face-lift (one total renovation)—literally would not recognize it now. It's fine. The European tiles in the lobby bar and the gas lamps give public spaces a colonial feel. Dark ceiling beams and exposed brick and stucco walls continue the theme in the specialty restaurants. The huge buffet area is enclosed with glass and air-conditioned. Two pools (one for kids) look out to a quiet stretch of Las Papas Beach. A 150-room addition overlooks another huge pool. You can try to hit pay dirt at the striking El Dorado Casino. ✉ *Playa Dorada, Puerto Plata,* ☎ *809/320–3988,* 𝖥𝖠𝖷 *809/320– 1190,* 𝖶𝖤𝖡 *www.occidental-hoteles.com. 501 rooms. 5 restaurants, golf privileges, 2 tennis courts, 3 pools, beach, dive shop, snorkeling, windsurfing, boating, 4 bars, casino, theater, shops. AE, DC, MC, V. All-inclusive.*

$ ⊞ **Piergiorgio Palace Hotel.** The dream of an Italian fashion designer, this white-clapboard inn has a sweeping veranda and intricate fretwork. It replicates the Victorian splendor for which early Sosua was known. A gazebo is integrated into the front entrance, and a staircase rises from the marble-tiled lobby. Romantics take to the pink-and-white floral guest rooms; half have ocean views; the rest overlook the kidney-shape pool and gardens. Piergiorgio's stretch limo whisks you from the Puerto Plata Airport to the inn, and the moderate rates include breakfast (and for $20 more, dinner) at the cliff-side La Puntilla de Piergiorgio restaurant. ✉ *Calle La Puntilla 1, El Batey, Sosua,* ☎ *809/571–2626,* 𝖥𝖠𝖷 *809/ 571–2786,* 𝖶𝖤𝖡 *www.piergiorgiohotel.com. 51 rooms. Restaurant, 2 pools, hot tub, 2 bars. AE, MC, V. CP, MAP.*

$ ⊞ **Victoria Resort.** This study in pastels and gingerbread fretwork is
★ smack in the middle of the Playa Dorada golf course with a view of
Isabel de Torres Mountain. The public areas have such touches as marble floors and carnival masks hung on mint green walls. Deluxe accommodations, set apart for quiet, have plantation-style wicker furniture
and terraces. The clubhouse looks onto a lake, a pool, and hot tub.
The alfresco café has fine buffets; you can now opt for à la carte service as well. Jardin Victoria offers Continental cuisine, professional service, and strolling musicians. The Victoria Beach Club is just five
minutes away. ✉ *Playa Dorada, Puerto Plata (Box 22, Puerto Plata),*
☎ *809/320–1200,* FAX *809/320–4862,* WEB *www.victoriahoteles.com.do.
190 rooms. 4 restaurants, minibars, 18-hole golf course, tennis court,
2 pools, outdoor hot tub, gym, dive shop, snorkeling, windsurfing, boating, jet skiing, parasailing, 2 bars, nightclub. AE, MC, V. All-inclusive.*

$ ⊞ **Windsurf Hotel.** Loyal repeat visitors to this young and fun, mod-
☺ est hotel may soon be saying, "I knew it when." The Canadian owners have some big plans. In 2002 they acquired the property next door,
which more than doubled their capacity. A full face lift is in the making. A palapa-roofed barbecue area has already been built, and a beach
club with showers, lockers, towel service and bar is underway. Windsurf is a great value for the peso, with hotel rooms on a par with the
full-service resorts and a kicked-back atmosphere, where American
surfers dance with Scandinavian beauties at the welcome mixer. Those
staying at the hotel can use CaribBic Center, Cabarete's famous watersports school, on the beach across the street. ✉ *Carretera Principal,
Cabarete,* ☎ *809/571–0718,* FAX *809/571–0710,* WEB *www.sunsetresorts.
com. 48 rooms, 38 1-bedroom condos, 12 2-bedroom condos,. Restaurant, picnic area, room service, kitchenettes, pool, boccie, volleyball,
2 bars, shop, playground. MC, V. EP.*

Barahona

The least developed and perhaps the most ruggedly beautiful region
in the Dominican Republic, Barahona is in the far southwest of the island.

$ ⊞ **Barceló Bahoruco Beach Resort.** "Maravilloso!" best describes this
★ resort on a gorgeous stretch of virgin beach staggered with rugged cliffs,
that goes for miles. The tri-level lobby is an artistic mix of West Indian, African colonial, and contemporary style. Classical music plays,
but it's Dominican dance music at the pool complex with its Jacuzzi
and swim-up bar, all traversed by wooden bridges. The alfresco buffet restaurant, which, like the lobby, is topped by a huge palapa, serves
exceptional food. Tasteful guest rooms with balconies face the sea. Eco-
tours visit national parks and flamingo refuges. Nonguests can buy day
passes. ✉ *Carretera de la Costa, Km 17, Bahoruco, Barahona.* ☎ *809/
524–1111,* FAX *809/524–6060,* WEB *www.barcelo-hotels.com. 105 rooms.
2 restaurants, tennis court, 2 pools, beach, snorkeling, 3 bars, shop,
meeting room. AE, MC, V. All-inclusive.*

$ ⊞ **Casa Bonita.** In the scenic southwest, this gentrified country inn in
the foothills outside Baharona is a charming alternative to high-rise
hotels and busy all-inclusives. Julio and Virginia Schiffino expanded
their vacation home and added 12 criollo-style cottages with roofs of
thatched *cana* palm, rough-hewn walls. Now all have air-conditioning and are handsomely redecorated in 2001; they face the sea or the
verdant forest of the Sierra de Bahoruco and two mountain rivers. The
open-air gallery—adjacent sitting areas—and restaurant overlook the
pool area and are tastefully appointed with comfortable sofas and scads
of colorful throw pillows. ✉ *Baharona,* ☎ *809/696–0215,* FAX *809/223–
0548, 12 cottages. Restaurant, pool, bar. AE, MC, V. MAP.*

Dining

The island's culinary repertoire includes Spanish, Latin American, Italian, Middle Eastern, Indian, Japanese, and Chinese cuisines. The latest trend at the larger, all-inclusive resorts, particularly in Punta Cana, is to offer numerous specialty restaurants, in addition to their buffeteria, to avoid the buffet blues. One mega resort even has a Gourmet Boulevard, with 11 ethnic options, from *haute* French to a Japanese steakhouse. Another has an authentic Brazilian Rodizio, where seven different meats, including sweetbreads, are carved tableside.

The dining scene in Santo Domingo rivals that of any cosmopolitan city and probably has the largest and finest selection of restaurants of any Caribbean city. *Capitalenos* dress for dinner, and dine late. The crowds pick up after 9 PM, when the Americans are just finishing dessert.

Every year, there are more establishments serving contemporary Caribbean dishes as well as places specializing in *nueva cocina Dominicana* (contemporary Dominican cuisine). If seafood is on the menu, it's bound to be fresh.

Among the best Dominican specialties are *sancocho* (a thick stew usually made with five meats and served with rice and avocado slices), *arroz con pollo* (rice with chicken), and *plátanos* (plantains) in all their tasty varieties. Many meals are finished with *majarete*, a cornmeal custard. Shacks and stands that serve cheap eats are an integral part of the culture and landscape. They might offer johnny cakes (fried dough stuffed with everything from chicken to seafood) or pork sandwiches laden with onions, tomatoes, pickles, and seasonings. Presidente is the best local beer; Barceló *anejo* (aged) rum is as smooth as cognac.

What to Wear

In resort areas shorts and bathing suits under beach wraps are usually (but not always) acceptable at breakfast and lunch. For dinner, long pants, skirts, and collared shirts are the norm. Restaurants tend to be more formal in Santo Domingo, both at lunch and at dinner, with trousers required for men and dresses suggested for women. Ties aren't required anywhere but jackets are (even at the midday meal) in some of the finer establishments.

CATEGORY	COST*
$$$$	over $30
$$$	$20–$30
$$	$10–$20
$	under $10

*per person for a main course at dinner

Santo Domingo

CARIBBEAN

$$ ✕ **El Conuco.** The name means "the countryside," and it *is* hard to believe that this thatched-roof patio—alive with hanging plants, hibiscus, and frangipani—is right in Santo Domingo. The Dominican dishes on the single prix-fixe menu here are superb, from *la bandera* (white rice, kidney beans, and stewed beef duplicating the colors of the flag) to a magnificent, delicately flaky *bacalao de la comai* (cod in white cream sauce with garlic and onions). A celebration always seems to be going on; costumed waiters dance with you or take to makeshift drums, all in time with the merengue music. ✉ *Calle Casimiro de Moya 152, Gazcue,* ☎ *809/686–0129 or 809/689–4290. MC, V.*

CONTEMPORARY

$$–$$$ ✕ **Caribbean Blue.** Just being in this ultra-chic, 16th-century restora-
★   tion is a celebratory occasion. Exquisite taste permeates the multistory
        renovation: steel shelves, amber tiles, mirrors, circular staircases of cor-
        dova hardwood, bamboo plants, and oversize vases set in recessed arches;
        colonial artifacts are juxtaposed with contemporary artwork. It is an-
        other indicator of what's so hot about the Colonial Zone. New World
        Cuisine is the ticket here. As an appetizer or a main course, grilled shrimp
        on skewers form a pyramid over arugula and rounds of papaya, dressed
        with a tamarind vinaigrette. Or go for the all-crabmeat cakes. The *magic*
        chocolate truffles pair beautifully with Armagnac. ✉ *Calle Hostos 205,
        Zona Colonial,* ☎ *809/682–1238. AE, MC, V. Closed Mon.*

$$–$$$ ✕ **Peperoni Café.** This is one that has *capitalenos* talking—a salute to
        cuisine from around the world. Fusion food—Thai beef salad, crab-
        encrusted Chilean sea bass, calamari salad, Szechuan steak, and things
        as "American pie" as hamburgers—but with unusual add-ons like
        pancetta and barbecue sauce, as in the Wyoming burger. It has an ad-
        mirable *carta de vinos*—with French, Spanish, Californian, Argentine,
        and Italian selections—up to Dom Perignon. Finish with pecan pie or
        tiramisu and a piping hot Irish coffee, café latte, or chocolate Peper-
        oni. In a commercial neighborhood, this is a place well worth finding.
        Most taxi drivers know of it. ✉ *Plaza Universitaria Mall, Sarasota,
        #25, La Julia,* ☎ *809/508–1330. AE, MC, V.*

CONTINENTAL

$$$ ✕ **El Meson de la Cava.** A capital landmark since 1969, this cave, which
        has served as a hideaway for pirates, continues to draw a crowd of loyal
        locals and tourists. Thanks to the hospitality, it's one warm cavern.
        Leave the high heels off, for descending the circular staircase is tougher
        than a field sobriety test. The original owner's daughter, Laura Ricart,
        is contemporizing the classic, continental menu with such dishes as
        chicken roulade stuffed with almonds, mushrooms, mozzarella, and
        prosciutto, finished with a roasted red pepper sauce. The aged Black
        Angus sirloins and Omaha steaks are better yet with Roquefort sauce.
        Finish with a cappuccino meringue. ✉ *Av. Mirador del Sur, #1, Bella
        Vista,* ☎ *809/532–2615 or 809/533–2818. Reservations essential. AE,
        MC, V.*

ITALIAN

$$$–$$$$ ✕ **Da Vinci Restorante.** At the glamorous Meliá Hotel, but with its own
        entrance, this Italian restaurant is accented with burnished hardwood,
        and is a tribute to the fabled painter. Table settings are elegantly sim-
        ple. All of the traditional classics from carpaccio to risottos and tortelli-
        nis are here, but they are given a contemporary twist, as in the veal
        scallopine with black truffle sauce. Presentation is contemporary and
        the plates are artfully painted, particularly for the outstanding desserts.
        Lunch and dinner share the same menu, which is now a series of four-
        and five-course prix-fixes. The wine list is admirable, the personalized
        service totally professional and very caring. ✉ *Meliá Hotel, Av. George
        Washington, #365, El Malecón,* ☎ *809/221–6666 Ext. 2510. AE, MC.*

$$$–$$$$ ✕ **La Briciola.** This restaurant is the result of an exemplary combina-
        tion and renovation of the interiors of two adjoining 16th-century colo-
        nial buildings. The vaulted-ceiling, stone-and-brick main dining room
        and the piano bar overlook a courtyard with trees romantically lit at
        night. Mahogany furnishings and Italian tile work are elegant. Celebrity
        sightings are frequent. Excellent homemade pastas include a velvety
        gnocchi *fume*. The meat falls away from the bone on the osso buco.
        Owner Franco Riccobono can help you select from the all-Italian wine
        list; son Alessandro will choose a grappa to complement your delicious
        tiramisu. ✉ *Calle Arzobispo Merino 152-A (at Padre Bellini), Zona*

Colonial, ☎ 809/688–5055. *Jacket required. Reservations essential. AE, DC, MC, V. Closed Sun.*

$$–$$$ ✕ **Café Billini.** Filled with contemporary Italian furniture (your seat is for sale as are the books, Venetian vases, grappa in frosted bottles and Marchessi chocolates), this started out as a place where the ladies who come to shop 'til they drop at Nuovo Rinascimento could lunch. Then a stellar Italian chef came on the scene. Now the same ladies go on the wait-list at dinner. Carpaccios are big, from the beef and fresh salmon to illiput, a local fish. You'll find main courses such as veal scaloppine with port, fish, and lobster on the menu, but fresh-made pastas dominate. Finish with a grappa, cappuccino, and tiramisu with mango. ✉ *Design Plazoleta Padre Billini, Zona Colonial,* ☎ 809/686–3387. *AE, MC, V. Closed Sun.*

$$–$$$ ✕ **Spaghettissimo.** This contemporary Italian spot has earned plaudit
★ for its food, wine, and service. Owner Frederic Gollong will charm you with his dry wit and welcoming ways. Starting with the antipasto buffet, the quality and freshness of the food are apparent. Savor the veal rack with wild mushroom sauce or shrimp and lobster flambéed tableside, with your choice of rum, cognac, or Pernod. And don't overlook the specials. On Tuesdays and Thursday nights, live Italian and Brazilian music in the candlelit garden captures a devoted crowd. Brunch is *the* thing on Sunday. ✉ *Paseo de los Locubres 13, Piantini,* ☎ 809/565–3708 *or* 809/547–2650. *AE, DC, MC, V.*

MIDDLE EASTERN

$$$ ✕ **Scherezade.** The exotic decor—Moorish arches, tile work, a terrace with orchids—is just one of the reasons why this restaurant is so popular. The excellent service is provided by waiters who wear embroidered vests and fez hats. Hummus, not butter, comes with the pita bread. Try the velvety cream of asparagus and watercress or the tabbouleh. Superb entrées include the Madagascar shrimp in green pepper and spinach sauce or the Arabian lobster, grilled simply with oil, garlic, and lemon. Desserts include baklava, orange soufflé, and ginger flan. On some nights flamenco dancers perform to live music. ✉ *Av. Roberto Pastoriza 226, Naco,* ☎ 809/227–2323. *AE, DC, MC. Closed Mon.*

Boca Chica/Juan Dolio

SEAFOOD

$$–$$$ ✕ **El Pelicano.** Begin with a perfect, hazelnut piña colada and watch the sun drop behind the pier that extends into gin-clear water. The seafood is as fresh as it gets. Professional waiters pamper diners as they set down shellfish salads dressed with vinaigrette followed by red snapper in lemon sauce or a pound of broiled Spiny Lobsters. Although within an all-inclusive resort, it is open to the public for lunch and dinner. Ten minutes from Las Americas Airport, it's an ideal for spending a long layover if you are in transit; use the beach and hot tubs, then rinse off with a shower. ✉ *Coral Hamaca Beach Hotel & Casino, Boca Chica,* ☎ 809/523–6506 *or* 809/523–4611 *Ext. 830. AE, MC, V.*

La Romana

CARIBBEAN

$$–$$$ ✕ **El Patio.** In 2001, two talented Dominican chefs, Andres Rijo and Domingo Castillo, who are dedicated to their culture, revised the menu, while interior designers added color and authenticity to the decorations. An oversize *yucca empanada,* stuffed with conch meat, is served with a tomato and basil concasse. Cod fish croquettes come with a sauce of ginger and *viga* (a colorful, indigenous spice). There is a lamb stew with red wine, and *locrio de cerdo*; the innovation of this traditional Dominican dish is that it is cooked with smoked ham hock and served with fresh avocado. Imagine the combination of flavors. ✉ *Casa de*

Campo, La Romana, ☎ *809/523–8548. Reservations essential. AE, MC, V.*

Samaná
SEAFOOD

$$ ✕ **Villa Serena.** At the very end of the long road from Puerto Plata, and on the beach of the Villa Serena Hotel, the restaurant's specialties include fresh fish and delicious homemade desserts. ⊠ *Samaná,* ☎ *809/ 696–0065. MC, V.*

The Amber Coast
CONTEMPORARY

$$$ ✕ **Acuarela.** Named for the watercolors that adorn its walls, the
★ Acuarela café is in a 120-year-old home surrounded by a garden. The talented chef-owner, Rafael Vasquez, creates a contemporary menu, and the dishes are artistically presented. Local ingredients like goat, plantains, *auyama* (Dominican squash) are incorporated imaginatively in his Caribbean nuevo cuisine. The clientele—well-heeled expats and Dominicans—is partial to such appetizers as Thai carpaccio (beef) with peanut sauce, and lobster medallions with a Pernod cream served over fried polenta. Certified Angus beef is served. The grand finale might be coconut crepes with Grand Marnier, coconut ice cream, and caramel sauce. ⊠ *Calle Prof. Certad 3, at Calle Presidente Vasquez, Puerto Plata,* ☎ *809/261–1000. MC, V. Closed Mon.*

ECLECTIC

$$ ✕ **Hemingway's Café.** As much a meeting place as a memorial to the late great writer, this café is full of old photos that chronicle his life with dishes whose names bring to mind his work. Everyone, from long-haired expats to government VIPs, comes to savor For Whom the Bell Tolls fajitas (in chicken, shrimp, or beef versions) and drink sangria. More upscale items have been added, from shrimp to Angus beef steaks. It's a fun place with a young crowd. ⊠ *Playa Dorada Plaza, Puerto Plata,* ☎ *809/320–2230. AE, MC, V.*

ITALIAN

$$$–$$$$ ✕ **La Puntilla de Piergiorgio.** Atop a seaside cliff, this restaurant has waiters who will pamper you as you sit overlooking the precipice to the sea below. Aperitifs and appetizers make the setting of the sun a true occasion rather than just a nightly occurrence. Cascades of pink bougainvillea rustle about you in the cooling breeze. The pasta dishes or a simple grilled lobster are among the best choices. Live bands often play in the bandstand, and if you don't have a car, the restaurant will pick you up and drop you off in a festive horse-drawn wagon. ⊠ *Piergiorgio Palace Hotel, Calle La Puntilla 1, El Batey, Sosua,* ☎ *809/571– 2215. AE, MC, V.*

SEAFOOD

$$ ✕ **Restaurant at Natura Cabanas.** The waves breaking on the coral rock that frames the virgin beach is reason enough to be here. This alfresco restaurant—new in 2001—has a palapa roof and the unexpected artistry characteristic of architect/owner Pablo Garmimani. Open for breakfast (with fresh juices and fruit), lunch, and dinner, it is the seafood for which they come: the ceviche, octopus salad with avocado puree, the day's catch with pistachio butter, and shrimp grilled with garlic and olive oil. As the sun goes down, horse riders go loping past, while "Lole," Pablo's wife and *duena* of the spa, welcomes patrons in her charismatic way. ⊠ *Natura Cabanas, Perla Marina, Cabarete,* ☎ *809/571–1507, 809/571–9902, or 809/787–8614. Reservations essential. MC, V.*

Punta Cana
SEAFOOD

$$$ ✗ **La Yola.** The *yola* in the name of this restaurant is a colorful, wooden boat small enough to be placed in the dining room. Rustic, open-air, and on the water, this restaurant's "bow" points out to sea, and the choice tables are there. The food is simple and simply delicious. Think fresh fish. Go right to the grilled squid salad with arugula. There's steamed red snapper for purists; shrimp in garlic sauce is hard to resist, unless you cannot say "no" to the grilled lobster with butter, garlic, and lime. Have a side of perfect yucca fries. Finish with a coffee tiramisu. ✉ *La Marina, Punta Cana Resort & Club, Punta Cana,* ☎ *809/221–2262 Ext. 7124. Reservations essential. AE, MC, V.*

Beaches

The Dominican Republic has more than 1,000 miles (1,600 km) of beaches, including the Caribbean's longest stretch of white sand: Punta Cana/Bávaro. Many beaches are accessible to the public and may tempt you to stop for a swim. That's part of the uninhibited joy of this country. Do be careful, though: some have dangerously strong currents, which may be the reason why they are undeveloped.

Boca Chica. The beach closest to Santo Domingo (2 mi [3 km] east of Las Américas Airport, 21 mi [34 km] from the capital) is crowded with city folks on weekends. In the 1900s, it was developed by wealthy industrialist Juan Vicini. Entire families moved their households here for the summer. The beach was an immaculate stretch of fine sand, and you could (and still can) walk far out into the gin-clear waters protected by coral reefs. Alas, progress has made its mark; areas are cluttered with plastic furniture, pizza stands, and cottages. The strip with the mid-rise resorts is well kept but busy. The old Hamaca Hotel was the place to see and be seen; dictator Trujillo kept quarters here, and former President Lionel Fernández stayed (appropriately), in the Presidential Suite.

Cabarete Beach. On the north coast, this beach has ideal wind and surf conditions. It's an integral part of the international windsurfing circuit. Segments of it are strips of golden sand punctuated only by palm trees. In the most commercial area, restaurants and bars are back-to-back. Moderately priced, the scene is young and fun, with expats and tourists from every imaginable country.

Juan Dolio. A narrow beach of fine white sand, Juan Dolio is a 20-minute drive east of Boca Chica, some 40 minutes from the capital and has a long row of all-inclusive resorts.

La Romana. This is the site of the 7,000-acre Casa de Campo resort, so you're not likely to find any private place in the sun. The miniature Minitas Beach and lagoon are also here.

Las Terrenas. On the north coast of the Samaná Peninsula, tall palms list toward the sea, the beach is narrow but sandy, and there's plenty of color—vivid blues, greens, and yellows. Two hotels are on the beach at Punta Bonita.

Luperón Beach. About an hour's drive west of Puerto Plata, this wide white-sand beach is fit for snorkeling, windsurfing, and scuba diving. The Luperón Beach Resort is handy for rentals and refreshments.

Playa Grande. On the north coast, this long stretch of powdery sand is slated for development (the Playa Grande Hotel has already disturbed the solitude). For now the entire northeast coast still seems like one unbroken golden stretch, littered only with kelp, driftwood, and the occasional beer bottle. If you don't mind the lack of facilities, you have your pick of deserted patches.

Puerto Plata. On the north's Amber Coast (so called because of its un-usual—and large—deposits of amber) this is one of the D.R.'s most established resort areas, especially along Playa Dorada. The beaches are of soft beige or white sand, with lots of reefs for snorkeling. The Atlantic waters are great for windsurfing, waterskiing, and fishing. The substantial city of Puerto Plata, with its Victorian vestiges, is a 10-minute cab ride away.

Punta Cana. The gem of the Caribbean is a 20-mi (32-km) strand of pearl white sand shaded by swaying coconut palms. It's on the east-ernmost coast, which includes Bávaro Beach, and it's the home of nu-merous all-inclusive resorts. There's no major town close to this resort area, though.

Sosua. Here calm waters gently lap a shore of soft white sand. Un-fortunately, the backdrop is a string of tents where hawkers push sou-venirs, snacks, and rental of water-sports equipment from the vendors.

Outdoor Activities and Sports

Although there's hardly a shortage of activities here, the resorts have virtually cornered the market on sports, including every conceivable water sport. In some cases facilities may be available only to guests of the resorts.

Participant Sports

BOATING

Sailing conditions are ideal, with a constant trade wind. Favorite ex-cursions include day-trips to Catalina Island and sunset cruises on the Caribbean. Prices for crewed sailboats of 26 ft and longer with a ca-pacity from 4 to 12 people range from $120 to $700 a day. The **Carib BIC Center** (⊠ Cabarate, ☎ 809/571–0640) is a renowned windsurf-ing center that also rents Lasers, 17-ft catamarans, boogie boards, and sea kayaks. The private marina at **Casa de Campo** (⊠ La Romana, ☎ 809/523–3333) has charter sailing vessels. Check with **Club Med Punta Cana** (⊠ Punta Cana, ☎ 809/686–5500) about its boating options. Hobie Cats and pedal boats are available at **Heavens** (⊠ Playa Do-rada, Puerto Plata, ☎ 809/586–5250). The full-service marina, **La Ma-rina Punta Cana** (⊠ Punta Cana Resort & Club, Punta Cana, ☎ 221–2262), rents small boats by the half or full day.

CYCLING

Pedaling is easy on pancake-flat beaches, but there are also some steep hills in the D.R. Several resorts rent bikes. **Dorado Naco** (⊠ Playa Do-rada Beach, Puerto Plata, ☎ 809/320–2019) has bicycle rentals. **Hotel Cofresi** (⊠ Puerto Plata, ☎ 809/586–2898) rents bikes by the day. **Iguana Mama, Mountain Bike, Hiking & Cultural Vacations** (⊠ Cabarete, ☎ 800/571–0908) has traditional and mountain bikes and will take you on bike hikes on the flats or test your mettle on the steep grades of the mountain areas. **Jack Tar Village** (⊠ Puerto Plata, ☎ 809/586–3800) will rent bicycles by the day or week. **Villas Doradas** (⊠ Playa Dorada, Puerto Plata, ☎ 809/320–3000) has a bike rental center that is con-veniently located within the Playa Dorada strip.

FISHING

Marlin and wahoo are among the fish that folks angle for here (note that fishing is best between January and June). Costs to charter a boat—with a crew, refreshments, bait, and tackle—generally range from $300 to $500 for a half-day and from $400 to $700 for a full day. You can arrange fishing trips through **Actividas Acuaticás** (⊠ Playa Dorada, Puerto Plata, ☎ 809/586–3988). The marina at **Casa de Campo** (⊠ La Ro-mana, ☎ 809/523–3333) arranges fishing charters. There are more fish-ing options now that the new marina complex opened in 2001. At **La**

Marina Punta Cana (Punta Cana Resort & Club, ☎ 809/221–2262), which is on the southern end of the resort, half-day fishing excursions are available for $75 per person, with a minimum of 2 people.

GOLF

The **Barceló Bávaro Beach Golf and Casino Resort** (⊠ Bávaro Beach, near Higüey, ☎ 809/686–5797) has an 18-hole course, open to its own guests and those of other hotels. The greens fee for those not staying at Bávaro is $32; golf carts rent for $50. *Golf* magazine has called **Casa de Campo** (⊠ La Romana, ☎ 809/523–3333) "the finest golf resort in the Caribbean." Greens fees range from $125 to $175; if you're an avid golfer, though, inquire about the resort's multiday passes and golf packages. Pete Dye has designed a third 18-hole course close to Altos de Chavón. It hugs a cliff that overlooks the ocean as well as Río Chávon and its palm groves. The **Metro Country Club** (⊠ Juan Dolio, ☎ 809/526–3315), east of Santo Domingo on the road to La Romana, has an 18-hole public course designed by Charles Ankrom. Greens fees run $35 to $50, and a cart costs $16 to $20. **Playa Dorada**'s 18-hole Robert Trent Jones–designed course, adjacent to the Victoria Resort (⊠ Puerto Plata, ☎ 809/320–3344) is open to guests staying at all the hotels in the complex. Greens fees range from $15 (9 holes) to $27. **Playa Grande Golf Course** (⊠ Carretera Rio San-Juan-Cabrera, Km 9, Maria Trinidad Sanchez, ☎ 809/582–0860), on the north coast, is described as the "Pebble Beach" of the Caribbean, with 10 holes interacting with the Atlantic Ocean. Greens fees to play the 18-hole, par 72 are $57, $32 for nine holes, which includes carts, which are mandatory, as are caddies. Caddies are $10 for 18 holes, $5 for nine, and most players double that figure for a tip. **Punta Cana Resort & Club** (⊠ Punta Cana, ☎ 809/688–1561 Exts. 101/111) has an 18-hole course by P. B. Dye, with spectacular views of the Caribbean. Rates (including golf carts) for resort guests are $40 for 9 holes, $65 for 18 holes; for non-guests, 9 holes are $70, 18 holes $100. The mandatory fees for caddies are: $5 for 9 holes, $10 for 18. The resort offers great golf packages. Guests in Santo Domingo hotels are usually allowed to use the 18-hole course at the **Santo Domingo Country Club** (⊠ Av. Isabella Guiar, in front of El Club del Banco Reservo, 40 mins south of Santo Domingo, ☎ 809/530–6606) on weekdays—*after* members have teed off—for $35 (9 or 18 holes).

HIKING

At 10,370 ft (3,171 m), Pico Duarte is the highest peak in the West Indies and a favorite for serious hikers and mountain climbers. Hire a guide in La Ciénaga, one hour (8½ mi [14 km]) west of Jarabacoa, if you're prepared and equipped for an arduous 12-mi (19-km) two-day climb; you can also rent a mule here. The **park service** (☎ 809/472–4204) can assist you in obtaining a guide to lead you up Pico Duarte.

HORSEBACK RIDING

Alonzo Horse Ranch (⊠ Bávaro-Cabeza de Toro, ☎ 809/523–3503) has both morning and afternoon rides in the country or on the beach, for one or two hours, with or without a barbecue. Sunset rides go out daily (though never on Sundays, the horses' day of rest). On Monday, Wednesday, and Friday, the ride is followed by a barbecue. Prices range from $20 for an hour, to nearly $45 for two hours with a barbecue. The 250-acre Equestrian Center at **Casa de Campo** (⊠ La Romana, ☎ 809/523–3333) has something for both Western and English riders—a dude ranch, a rodeo arena, guided trail rides, and jumping and riding lessons. Guided rides run about $25 an hour; lessons cost $40 an hour. Handsome, old-fashioned carriages are available for hire, too. **The Equestrian Center** (⊠ Punta Cana Resort & Club, Punta

Cana, ☎ 809/688–1561 Ext. 7124) is across from the main entrance of the resort. The rate for a three-hour trail ride is $24 per person, and it goes along the beach and through tropical forests. A crash course on how to handle your horse precedes the outing. **Sea Horse Ranch** (✉ Cabarete, ☎ 809/571–3880) has an upscale equestrian center featuring both *paso fino* and dressage instruction for a moderate $10 per hour. Trail riding and endurance riding start at $15 per hour, and reservations are required. The most popular ride is one that includes stretches of beach and a bridle path across a neighboring farm's pasture, replete with wild flowers and butterflies, but tours are custom-designed.

SCUBA DIVING

Ancient sunken galleons, undersea gardens, and offshore reefs are among the lures here. In the waters off **Sosua** alone you'll find a dozen dive sites (for all levels of ability) with such catchy names as 3 Rocks (a deep, 163-ft [50-m] dive), Airport Wall (98 ft [30 m]), and Pyramids. Some 10 dive schools are represented on Sosua Beach. Most resorts have dive shops on the premises or can arrange trips for you. **Northern Coast Aquasports** (✉ Sosua, ☎ 809/571–3883) is a five-star PADI instruction center and resort.

TENNIS

There must be a million nets around the island, and most of them can be found at the large resorts. **La Terraza Tennis Club** (✉ Casa de Campo, La Romana, ☎ 809/523–8548) has been called the "Wimbledon of the Caribbean." This 12-acre facility, perched on a hill with sea views, has 13 Har-Tru courts. Nonguests are welcome (just call in advance); court time costs $20 an hour; lessons are $45 an hour with an assistant pro, $50 with a pro. The **Playa Naco Golf & Tennis Resort** (✉ Playa Dorada, La Romana, ☎ 809/320–6226 Ext. 2568) allows nonguests to play on its four clay courts for $4 an hour—day or night. Lessons from a pro cost $14 an hour.

WINDSURFING

Between June and October, Cabarete Beach has what many consider to be optimal windsurfing conditions: wind speeds at 20–25 knots and 3- to 15-ft (1- to 5-m) waves. The Professional Boardsurfers Association has included Cabarete in its international windsurfing slalom competition. The novice is also welcome to learn and train on modified boards stabilized by flotation devices. **Carib BIC Center** (✉ Cabarete, ☎ 809/571–0640, FAX 809/571–0649) offers equipment and instruction. Lessons are generally $30–$35 an hour; boards rent for $20 an hour. A gem of a windsurfing club, this family-owned business has many repeat clients, who made their expansion possible.

Spectator Sports

BASEBALL

Baseball is a national passion, and Sammy Sosa is still a legend in his own time. But he is just the latest in a string of baseball heroes. Triple-A Dominican and Puerto Rican players and some American major leaguers hone their skills in the D.R.'s Professional Winter League, which plays from October through January. Some games are played in the Tetelo Vargas Stadium, in the town of San Pedro de Macorís. As many as 20,000 fans often crowd the **Liga de Béisbol** stadium (☎ 809/567–6371) in Santo Domingo. If your Spanish is good, you can call the stadium or consult local newspaper listings for details on the five teams and game schedules; otherwise, you may want to ask staff at your hotel to arrange tickets for you.

There are races (flats) year-round at the **Hipódromo V Centenario** (✉ Av. Las Américas, Santo Domingo, ☎ 809/687–6060), daily 8–2:45.

POLO

Casa de Campo is a key place to play or watch the fabled sport of kings. The resort has always prided itself on the polo traditions it has kept alive since its opening some 20 years ago. (For many years a nephew of the Maharajah of Jodhpur, Jaber Singh, was an instructor. His pupils included Ramfis Trujillo, son of the former dictator.) Matches are scheduled from October to June, with high-goal players flying in from France and Argentina. Private polo lessons and clinics are available for those who always wanted to give it a shot. There is also a polo field in Santo Domingo.

Shopping

The hottest items continue to be cigars. Many exquisite hand-wrapped smokes come from the island's rich Ciabo Valley, and Fuente Cigars—handmade in Santiago—are highly prized, but beware of anyone selling cigars on the street. Only reputable cigar shops sell the real thing. Dominican rum and coffee are also good buys. *Mama juana,* an herbal potion, is the Dominican answer to Viagra. The D.R. is the homeland of designer Oscar de la Renta, and you may want to stop at the chic shops that carry his creations. La Vega is famous for its *diablos cajuelos* (devil masks), which are worn during Carnival. Look also for the delicate, faceless ceramic figurines that symbolize the Dominican culture.

Though locally crafted products are often of a high caliber (and often very affordable), expect to pay hundreds of dollars for designer jewelry made of amber and larimar. Larimar—a semiprecious stone that's the color of the Caribbean sea—is found on the D.R.'s south coast. Prices vary according to the stone's hue; the rarest and most expensive gems have a milky haze, and the less expensive are solid blue. Amber has been mined extensively between Puerto Plata and Santiago. A fossilization of resin from a prehistoric pine tree, it often encases ancient animal and plant life from leaves to spiders to tiny lizards. Beware of fakes, which are especially prevalent in street stalls. Visit a reputable dealer or store and ask how to tell the difference between real larimar and amber and imitations.

Bargaining is both a game and a social activity in the D.R., especially with street vendors and at the stalls in El Mercado Modelo. Vendors are disappointed and perplexed if you don't haggle. They're also tenacious, so unless you really plan to buy, don't even stop to look.

Areas and Malls

SANTO DOMINGO

The restored buildings of **La Atarazana,** which is across from Alcazar in the Colonial Zone, are filled with shops, art galleries, restaurants, and bars. One of the main shopping streets in the Colonial Zone is **Calle El Conde,** a pedestrian thoroughfare. With the advent of so many restorations and upscale businesses coming aboard, the dull and dusty stores with dated merchandise are giving way to hip, new shops. Some of the best shops on **Calle Duarte** are north of the Colonial Zone, between Calle Mella and Avenida de Las Américas. **El Mercado Modelo,** a covered market, borders Calle Mella in the Colonial Zone. Vendors here sell a dizzying selection of Dominican crafts. **Plaza Criolla,** on av. Maximo Gomez, is filled with shops that sell everything from scents to nonsense. **Plaza Central,** between avs. Winston Churchill and 27 de

Febrero, has many top international boutiques. **Unicentro,** on av. Abraham Lincoln, is a major Santo Domingo mall.

A popular shopping street for costume jewelry and souvenirs is **Calle Beller. Playa Dorada Plaza,** on Calle Duarte at av. 30 de Marzo, is a shopping center in the American tradition. Stores here sell everything from cigars, rum, coffee, and herbal remedies to ceramics, hand-carved wooden items, and T-shirts; there are Nautica, Guess, and Bennetton stores. The seven showrooms of the **Tourist Bazaar,** on Calle Duarte, are in an old mansion with a patio bar.

Altos de Chavón is a re-creation of a Mediterranean village on the grounds of the Casa de Campo resort, where you'll find art galleries, boutiques, and souvenir shops grouped around a cobbled square. Extra special are: El Club de Cigaro and the rotating art exhibits at the Museo Arqueológico Regional.

Specialty Items

Arawak Gallery (⊠ Av. Pasteur 104, Gazcue, Santo Domingo, ☎ 809/685–1661) specializes in pre-Columbian artifacts and contemporary pottery and paintings. **Casa Jardin** (⊠ Balacer Gustavo Medjia Ricart 15, Naco, Santo Domingo, ☎ 809/565–7978) is the garden studio of abstract painter Ada Balacer. Works by other women artists are also shown; look for pieces by Yolarda Naranjo, known for her modern work that integrates everything from fiberglass, hair, rocks, and wood to baby dresses. **Galería de Arte Mariano Eckert** (⊠ Av. Winston Churchill and Calle Luis F. Tomen, 3rd floor, Evaristo Morales, Santo Domingo, ☎ 809/541–7109) focuses on the work of Eckert, an older Dominican artist who's known for his still lifes. **Galería de Arte Nader** (⊠ Rafael Augusto Sanchez 22, Ensanche Piantini and Plaza Andalucia II, Piantini, Santo Domingo, ☎ 809/687–6674 or 809/544–0878) showcases top Dominican artists in various media. The gallery staff is well known in Miami and New York and works with Sotheby's. **Lyle O. Reitzel Art Contemporaneo** (⊠ Plaza Andalucia II, Piantini, Santo Domingo, ☎ 809/227–8361) specializes in very contemporary art, such as the very dark paintings of José Garcia Cordero, a Dominican living in Paris. **Mi Pais** (⊠ Calle Villanueva at Antera Mota, Puerto Plata, no phone) is an innovative gallery that showcases paintings and sculptures by such Dominican artists as Orlando Menicucci, Servio Certad, Pedro Terrero, and Celia Vargas Nadel.

Plaza Central (⊠ Avs. Winston Churchill and 27 de Febrero, Piantini, Santo Domingo, ☎ 809/541–5929) is a major shopping center with a Jenny Polanco shop (an upscale Dominican designer) and other high-end stores.

Centro de los Héroes (⊠ Av. George Washington, EL Malecon, Santo Domingo) sells liquor, cameras, and the like.

Artesanía Lime (⊠ Autopista Duarte, 1½ mi [2½ km] from Santiago, Santiago, ☎ 809/582–3754) is worth a visit for its mahogany carvings and Carnival masks. **Collector's Corner Gallery and Gift Shop** (⊠ Plaza Shopping Center, Calle Duarte at Av. 30 de Marzo, Puerto Plata, no phone) has souvenirs, including many made of amber. **Felipe & Co.** (⊠ El Conde, #105, Zona Colonial, Santo Domingo, ☎ 809/689–581) has a fascinating assortment of Dominican crafts and artwork, coffee, inexpensive "free spirit" jewelry, and some tropical clothing. **Taimas-caros** (✉ Camino Libre 70, Sosua, ☎ 809/571–3138) is a group of artists and carnival goers organized by artist Jacinto Manuel Beard Gomez, to preserve both the event and Dominican culture. They make their own masks and costumes, and Jacinto's striking artwork incorporates carnival elements.

HOME FURNISHINGS

Nuovo Rinascimento (✉ Plazoleta Padre Billini, Zona Colonial, Santo Domingo, ☎ 809/686–3387) is in the grandiose space formerly occupied by Italian designer Versace. This exquisite emporium, replete with contemporary furniture, like leather sofas by Ferrari and antiques such as iron canopied beds, has a room with a treasure full of Venetian linens and towels. Shipping can be arranged. The wooden, hacienda doors open to a world of white sculptures and an inner courtyard with a pool dotted with lily pads. It is surrounded by megacandles, for sale at the retail shop within their Café Bellini.

JEWELRY

Ambar Tres (✉ La Atarazana 3, Zona Colonial, Santo Domingo, ☎ 809/688–0474) carries a wide selection of items made with amber, including high-end jewelry. If you tour the in-house museum, you'll have an even deeper appreciation of the gem.

TOBACCO

Cigar King (✉ Calle Conde 208, Baguero Bldg., Zona Colonial, Santo Domingo, ☎ 809/686–4987) keeps Dominican and Cuban cigars in a temperature-controlled cedar room (note that Cuban stogies can't be brought through U.S. customs legally). **Santo Domingo Cigar Club** (✉ Av. George Washington 367, El Malecón, Santo Domingo, ☎ 809/221–1483), in the lobby of the Renaissance Jaragua Hotel and Casino, is a great place to find yourself a good smoke.

Nightlife

Get a copy of the *Vacation Guide* and the newspaper, *Touring*—both available free at the tourist office and at hotels—to find out what's happening around. Look in the *Santo Domingo News* and the *Puerto Plata News* for listings of events and the monthly *Dominican and Fiesta.*

CAFÉS

Cigarro Café (✉ Av. Maximo Gomez and av. 27 de Febrero, Gazcue, Santo Domingo, ☎ 809/688–7038) in the Grand Hotel Lina is the place to go for high-quality cigars and coffee, with an appealing assortment of gadgets for the smoker. Cigar brands include the country's best—Aurturo Fuente and Fuente Fuente Opus X. **Doubles** (✉ Calle Arzobispo Merino 54, Zona Colonial, Santo Domingo, ☎ 809/688–3833) looks like a friend's place—that is, if you have a friend who has a hip sense of interior design and would mix rattan furniture, antiques, subdued lighting, and candles in a space that's centuries old. Spanish tiles add interest to this atmospheric piano bar. Don't think of the sandwich when you visit **Monté Cristo** (✉ Av. Jose Armado Soler at av. Abraham Lincoln, Serralles, Santo Domingo, ☎ 809/542–5000), although the crowds can sandwich you in at this pub. The clientele spans the decades, music crosses the Americas, and there is a small dance floor. Both hot and cold tapas and sandwiches are served. Open after work until whenever, usually 4 AM, and there's no cover. At **Punto Y Corcho** (✉ Av. Abraham Lincoln at Gustavo Mejía Ricart, Piantini, Santo Domingo, ☎ 809/683–0533), on Plaza Andalucia, wine (by the glass and bottle) and local and international liquors are the order of the night.

This is a great date and late-night spot, and tends to appeal to an older crowd.

CASINOS

Well into the wee small hours, casinos keep the action hot. Gambling here is more a sideline than a raison d'être. Most casinos are in the larger hotels of Santo Domingo, a couple in Playa Dorada, and more now in Punta Cana. All offer blackjack, craps, and roulette and are generally open daily 3 PM–4 AM. You must be 18 to enter, and jackets are required.

Barceló Gran Hotel Lina (⊠ Av. Máximo Gomez and av. 27 de Febrero, Gazcue, Santo Domingo, ☎ 809/563–5000) is a stalwart landmark drawing from its business and convention trade. **Hispaniola** (⊠ Av. Independencia and av. Abraham Lincoln, University Zone, Santo Domingo, ☎ 809/221–7111) attracts a younger crowd, which goes back and forth between the tables and the Neon Disco. The casino at the **Occidental El Embajador** (⊠ Av. Sarasota 65, Bella Vista, Santo Domingo, ☎ 809/533–2131) is an aside, but can heat up late. The **Renaissance Jaragua Hotel** (⊠ Av. George Washington 367, El Malecón, Santo Domingo, ☎ 809/686–2222) has one of the largest and busiest gaming operations, and its live entertainment and restaurants have added to its popularity.

The **American Casino** (⊠ Jack Tar Village, Playa Dorada, Puerto Plata, ☎ 809/320–6014) wants your pesos and will pay for your taxi, give you complimentary lessons to learn or perfect your game, and then give you free drinks and snacks. The casino at the **Hotel Occidental Playa Dorada** (⊠ Playa Dorada, Puerto Plata, ☎ 809/320–3988) is *the* most appealing gambling option, with a pleasing mix of CDs and live music that won't damage your eardrums.

DANCE CLUBS

Santo Domingo has more than its fair share of hot spots. As in other Latin countries, after dinner it's not a question of *whether* people will go dancing but *where* they'll go. Move with the rhythm of the merengue and the pulsing beat of salsa (adopted from neighboring Puerto Rico). Just about every resort in Puerto Plata and Punta Cana has live entertainment, dancing, or both. Many clubs stay open until dawn or until the last couple gives it up.

Aqua Lounge (⊠ Calle Hostos, #205, Zona Colonial, Santo Domingo, ☎ 809/682–1238) is the new "in" place, on the second level of Caribbean Blue, *the* spot for dinner in the Colonial Zone. Among the five rooms, there are cozy nooks for those young and in love and a V.I.P lounge. Movies play on a large video screen. **Bachata Rosa** (⊠ La Atarazana 9, Colonial Zone, Santo Domingo, ☎ 809/688–0969 or 809/682–7726) is named after a popular song by the Dominican merengue megastar Juan Luís Guerra (he's a part owner). It has three floors and includes a stage, a dance floor, a Caribbean restaurant, and often live music. Guerra has his videos going on three wide screens. Free transportation is available to and from hotels. **Bella Bleus** (⊠ George Washington Ave., El Malecón, Santo Domingo, ☎ 809/622–5452) is on the Malecón, next to Vesuvio. This disco, owned by baseball star Jose Rio, attracts players, business types, and tourists. A study in blue, its walls are adorned with paintings of ballerinas (the bellas). It has an aquarium and a water view, particularly from its open-air terrace. This is one spot that draws an older crowd, not that they don't have some twentysomethings. Closed Mondays. **The Monaco Disco Club** (⊠ John F. Kennedy Ave. at Horacio Blanco Fonbona, La Agustina, Santo Domingo, ☎ 809/562–6613) is off the tourist path and populated primarily with young, upscale Dominicans. Large, yet still crowded on weekends, it has a sense of humor. For example, on Halloween, you could find mummies rising out of their coffins and crypts near the parking lot. Contemporary Latin music dominates. Older couples head to the VIP area. The room is closed on Tuesdays. **Neon Lounge & Discotheque** (✉ Hotel Hispaniola, Av. Abraham Lincoln at av. Independencia, University Zone, Santo Domingo, ☎ 809/532–0054 or 809/532–0172) has been perennially popular for over 25 years. On Fat Tuesdays (à la New Orleans), live jazz bands play from 7:00 PM. You must be 22 years old to enter, and a strict dress code of no caps, T-shirts, or sneakers is enforced. Closed Mondays. **Zanzibars** (✉ the waterfront at Av. del Puerto, Zona Colonial, Santo Domingo, ☎ 809/930–7343), a tri-level entertainment "yacht," is a creative concept, with a different theme working on each level. You'll find everything from African to Cuban to techno. The music is tasteful, danceable, and Dominican-loud, but the river water absorbs noise. The boat faces the night-lit Casa Colón, which looks like a colonial stage set.

Andromeda (✉ Playa Dorada, Puerto Plata, ☎ 809/586–5250) is a happening dance club–video bar with frenetic energy and a high-decibel Latin/Afro beat. Dominicans come here from town to "work out" and show the tourists how dancing is done. **Crazy Moon** (✉ Paradise Beach Club and Casino, Playa Dorada, Puerto Plata, ☎ 809/320–3663) is a megaspace that's often back-to-back, wall-to-wall. Latin music and hip-hop mixed with Euro sounds are popular. Rest up from time to time at the horseshoe bar so that you can keep the pace until the wee small hours of the *mañana*.

Exploring the Dominican Republic

Santo Domingo

Spanish civilization in the New World began in Santo Domingo's 12-block Zona Colonial. With narrow cobbled streets, it's easy to imagine this old city as it was when the likes of Columbus, Cortés, Ponce de León, and pirates sailed in and out and colonists were settling themselves. Tourist brochures tout that "history comes alive here"—a surprisingly truthful statement.

A quick taxi tour of the old section takes about an hour; if you're interested in history, you'll want to spend a day or two exploring the many old "firsts," and you'll want to do it in the most comfortable shoes you own. Buy a walking tour map in English. Or you can jump on one of the green, open-air trolleys that pass the Parque Colón every hour; a 45-minute tour costs about $7, a full-blown two-hour excursion $20. Multilingual guides hit the highlights, and you can hop out to take photos.

Parque Independencia separates the old city from the modern Santo Domingo, a sprawling, noisy city with a population of close to 2 million. (Note: hours and admission charges to sights are erratic.)

Numbers in the margin correspond to points of interest on the Santo Domingo map.

SIGHTS TO SEE

☝ ❹ **Alcazar de Colón.** The castle of Don Diego Colón, built in 1517, has 40-inch-thick coral-limestone walls. The Renaissance-style structure, with its balustrade and double row of arches, has strong Moorish, Gothic, and Isabelline influences. The 22 rooms are furnished in a style to which the viceroy of the island would have been accustomed—right down to the dishes and the viceregal shaving mug. ✉ *Plaza de España, off Calle*

Santo Domingo

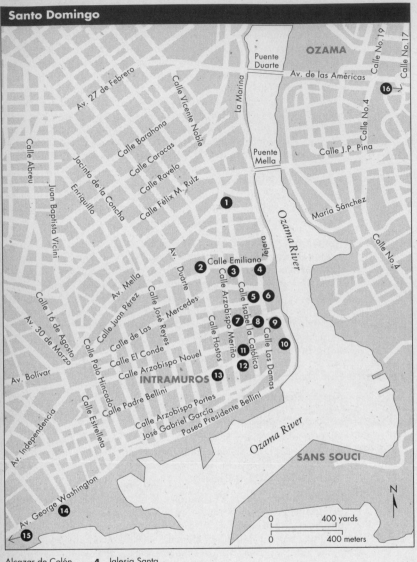

Emiliano Tejera at ft of Calle Las Damas, Zona Colonial, ☎ *809/687–5361.* 🎟 *RD$10.* ☉ *Mon. and Wed.–Fri. 9–5, Sat. 9–4, Sun. 9–1.*

⑧ Calle Las Damas. The Street of the Ladies was named after the elegant ladies of the court who, in the Spanish tradition, promenaded in the evening. Here you'll see a sundial dating from 1753 and the Casa de los Jesuitas, which houses a fine research library for colonial history as well as the Institute for Hispanic Culture; admission is free, and it's open weekdays 8–4:30.

⑨ Casa de Bastidas. There's a lovely inner courtyard here with tropical plants and temporary exhibition galleries. ⊠ *Calle Las Damas, off Calle El Conde, Zona Colonial,* ☎ *no phone.* 🎟 *Free.* ☉ *Tues.–Sun. 9–5.*

❸ Casa del Cordón. This structure, built in 1503, is the western hemisphere's oldest surviving stone house. Columbus's son, Diego Colón, viceroy of the colony, and his wife lived here until the Alcazar was finished. It was in this house, too, that Sir Francis Drake was paid a ransom to prevent him from totally destroying the city. ⊠ *Corner of Calle Emiliano Tejera and Calle Isabel la Católica, Zona Colonial,* ☎ *no phone.* 🎟 *Free.* ☉ *Weekdays 8:30–4:30.*

⑫ Casa de Tostado. The house was built in the early 16th century and was the residence of writer Don Francisco Tostado. Note its unique twin Gothic windows. It now houses the Museo de la Familia Dominicana (Museum of the Dominican Family), which has exhibits on the well-heeled 19th-century Dominican family. ⊠ *Calle Padre Bellini, near Calle Arzobispo Meriño, Zona Colonial,* ☎ *809/689–5057.* 🎟 *RD$10.* ☉ *Thurs.–Tues. 9–2.*

⑪ Catedral Santa María la Menor. The coral-limestone facade of the first cathedral in the New World towers over the south side of the Parque Colón. Spanish workmen began building the cathedral in 1514 but left to search for gold in Mexico. The church was finally finished in 1540. Its facade is composed of architectural elements from the late Gothic to the lavish plateresque styles. Inside, the high altar is made of hammered silver. ⊠ *Calle Arzobispo Meriño, Zona Colonial,* ☎ *809/689–1920.* 🎟 *Free.* ☉ *Mon.–Sat. 9–4; Sun. masses begin at 6 AM.*

🖐 ⑯ El Faro a Colón. This striking, laser-powered, lighthouse and monument, dedicated to Christopher Columbus, is shaped like a pyramid cross (although from ground level it looks like a giant concrete casket). Its inauguration coincided with the 500th anniversary (1992) of the great navigator's landing on the island. The complex holds the tomb of Columbus and six museums. ⊠ *Av. España, El Faro,* ☎ *809/591–1492.* 🎟 *RD$10.* ☉ *Tues.–Sun. 10–5.*

⑥ Hostal Palacio Nicolás de Ovando. This was once the residence of Nicolás de Ovando, one of the principal organizers of the colonial city. It was later transformed into a hotel. There are still plans to restore this historic landmark into a boutique hotel, but the going has been slow. ⊠ *Calle Las Mercedes 44, Zona Colonial.*

⑬ Iglesia y Convento Domínico. This graceful building with the rose window is the Dominican Church and Convent, founded in 1510. In 1538 Pope Paul III visited here and was so impressed with the lectures on theology that he granted the church and convent the title of university, making it the oldest institution of higher learning in the New World. ⊠ *Calle Padre Bellini and Av. Duarte, Zona Colonial,* ☎ *809/682–3780.* 🎟 *Free.* ☉ *Tues.–Sun. 9–6.*

❶ Iglesia Santa Bárbara. This combination church and fortress, the only one of its kind in Santo Domingo, was completed in 1562. ⊠ *Av. Mella,* between Calle Isabel la Católica and Calle Arzobispo Meriño, Zona Colonial, ☎ no phone. 🎫 Free. ⊙ Weekdays 8–noon; Sun. masses begin at 6 AM.

⑭ **El Malecón.** Avenida George Washington, better known as the Malecón, runs along the Caribbean and has tall palms, cafés, hotels, and sea breezes.

② **Monasterio de San Francisco.** Constructed between 1512 and 1544, the San Francisco Monastery contained the church, chapel, and convent of the Franciscan order. Sir Francis Drake's demolition squad significantly damaged the building in 1586, and in 1673 an earthquake nearly finished the job, but when it's floodlighted at night, the eerie ruins are dramatic, indeed. ⊠ Calle Hostos at Calle Emiliano, Zona Colonial.

⑤ **Pantheon Nacional.** The National Pantheon (circa 1714) was once a Jesuit monastery and later a theater. ⊠ Calle Las Damas, near corner of Calle de Las Mercedes, Zona Colonial, ☎ no phone. 🎫 Free. ⊙ Mon.–Sat. 10–5.

⑦ **Parque Colón.** The huge statue of Christopher Columbus in the park named after him dates from 1897 and is the work of French sculptor Gilbert. ⊠ El Conde at Arzobispo Meriño, Zona Colonial.

⑮ **Plaza de la Cultura.** Landscaped lawns, modern sculptures, and sleek buildings make up the Plaza de la Cultura. There are several museums and a theater here. The works of 20th-century Dominican and foreign artists are displayed in the **Museo de Arte Moderno** (Museum of Modern Art; ☎ 809/682–8260). Native sons include Elvis Aviles, an abstract painter whose works have a lot of texture. His art has obvious Spanish influences with Dominican symbols, such as those from the Taíno Indians. Tony Capellan is one of the best-known artists, representing the D.R. in major international exhibitions. The **Museo de Historia Natural** (Museum of Natural History; ☎ 809/689–0106) examines the flora and fauna of the island. The **Museo del Hombre Dominicano** (Museum of Dominican Man; ☎ 809/687–3623) traces the migrations of Indians from South America through the Caribbean islands. The **Teatro Nacional** (National Theater; ☎ 809/687–3191) stages performances in Spanish. 🎫 Museums RD$10 each. ⊙ Tues.–Sat. 10–5.

⑩ **Torre del Homenaje.** You won't have any trouble spotting the Tower of Homage in Ft. Ozama. The fort has a brooding crenellated tower that still guards the Ozama River. ⊠ Paseo Presidente Bellini, ☎ no phone. 🎫 RD$10. ⊙ Tues.–Sun. 8–7.

The East Coast

Las Américas Highway (built by the dictator Trujillo as a place for his son to race his sports cars) runs east along the coast from Santo Domingo to La Romana—a two-hour drive. Midway are the well-established resort area of Juan Dolio and Sammy Sosa's hometown, San Pedro de Macoris. East of La Romana are Punta Cana and Bávaro, glorious beaches on the sunrise side of the island. Along the way is Higüey, an undistinguished collection of ramshackle buildings notable only for its controversial church and shrine (someone had a vision of the Virgin Mary here), which resembles a pinched, concrete McDonald's arch.

Numbers in the margin correspond to points of interest on the Dominican Republic map.

SIGHTS TO SEE

⑲ **Altos de Chavón.** Cattle and sugarcane used to be the two big mainstays around La Romana. That was before Gulf & Western created (and then sold) the Casa de Campo resort, which is a very big business, indeed. Altos de Chavón, a re-creation of a 16th-century Mediterranean village and an artists' colony, is on the resort grounds. It sits on a bluff overlooking the Río Chavón, about 3 mi (5 km) east of the main facility of Casa de Campo. There are cobblestone streets lined with lanterns, wrought-iron balconies, wooden shutters, and courtyards swathed with bougainvillea. More than a museum piece, this village is a place where artists live, work, and play. Dominican and international painters, sculptors, and artisans come here to teach sculpture, pottery, silk-screen printing, weaving, dance, and music at the art school, which is affiliated with New York's Parsons School of Design. They work in their studios and crafts shops and sell their finished wares. The village also has an archaeological museum, five restaurants, and a 5,000-seat amphitheater where Julio Iglesias has entertained. The focal point of Altos de Chavón is **Iglesia St. Stanislaus,** which is named after the patron saint of Poland in tribute to Polish pope John Paul II, who visited the D.R. in 1979 and left some of the ashes of St. Stanislaus behind. The charmed chapel is the romantic setting of many a wedding, with honeymoons at the resort.

20 **Isla Saona.** Off the east coast of Hispaniola lies this island, now a national park inhabited by sea turtles, pigeons, and other wildlife. Caves here were once used by Indians. The beaches are beautiful, and legend has it that Columbus once strayed ashore here. Getting there, on the catamarans and other excursion boats, is half the fun.

17 **Parque de los Tres Ojos.** About 1½ mi (2½ km) outside the capital is the Park of the Three Eyes. The "eyes" are cool blue pools peering out of deep limestone caves.

18 **San Pedro de Macorís.** The national sport and the national drink are both well represented in this city, an hour or so east of Santo Domingo. Some of the country's best baseball games are played in Tetelo Vargas Stadium. Many major-league baseball players in the States have roots here. Many Dominican baseball stars have their roots here, including George Bell, Tony Fernandez, Jose Río, and Sammy Sosa. The Macorís Rum distillery is on the eastern edge of the city. During the 1920s it was a very important town, and mansions from that era are being restored by the Office of Cultural Patrimony, as are some remaining vestiges of 16th-century architecture. Outside town is Juan Dolio, a beach and resort area popular with Dominicans and foreign visitors.

The Amber Coast

The Autopista Duarte ultimately leads (a three- to four-hour drive) from Santo Domingo to the Amber Coast, so called because of its large, rich amber deposits. The coastal area around Puerto Plata is a region of splashy resorts and megadevelopments; the north coast has more than 70 mi (110 km) of beaches, with condominiums and villas going up fast. The farther east from Puerto Plata and its little sister, Sosua, you get, the prettier and less spoiled the scenery becomes. The autopista runs past Cabarete, a village that's a popular windsurfing haunt, and Playa Grande. Its white-sand beach is miraculously unspoiled.

SIGHTS TO SEE

22 **Laguna Grí-Grí.** This swampland looks as if it's smack out of Louisiana bayou country. It also has a cool blue grotto that almost outdoes the Blue Grotto of Capri. Laguna Grí-Grí is only about 90 minutes west of Puerto Plata, in Río San Juan (ask your hotel concierge for directions off the autopista).

25 **Mt. Isabel de Torres.** Southwest of Puerto Plata, this mountain soars 2,600 ft (795 m) above sea level. On it there are botanical gardens and a huge statue of Christ. Cable cars take you to the top for a spectacular view. ⊠ *Off Autopista Duarte, follow the signs,* ☎ *no phone.* ⌨ *Cable car $6.50.* ⊙ *Cable car: Mon.–Tues. and Thurs.–Sun. 9–5.*

24 **Puerto Plata.** Although now quiet and almost sleepy, this was a dynamic city in its heyday. You can get a feeling for this past in the magnificent Victorian gazebo in the central Parque Independencia. On Puerto Plata's own Malecón, the Fortaleza de San Felipe protected the city from many a pirate attack and was later used as a political prison. Big changes are afoot in this town, which is just realizing what it needs to do to become a tourist destination. The Office of Cultural Partrimony, which has done an admirable job of pulling the Zona Colonial from the darkness to the place to be seen, has set its sights on Puerto Plata. Simultaneously, a group of private business owners and investors have been conferencing to come up with a long-term plan for beautifying this city, which has a wonderful town square and hundreds of classic, wooden gingerbread buildings. Mansions are to be restored and opened for tours, as is the lighthouse. Puerto Plata is the home of the **Museo de Ambar Dominicano** (Dominican Amber Museum), which is in a lovely old galleried mansion. The museum displays and sells the D.R.'s national stone. Semiprecious, translucent amber is actually fossilized pine resin that dates from about 50 million years ago, give or take a few millennia. Shops on the museum's first floor sell amber, souvenirs, and ceramics. ⊠ *Calle Duarte 61,* ☎ *809/586–2848.* ⌨ *RD$15.* ⊙ *Mon.–Sat. 9–5.*

21 **Samaná.** Back in 1824, a sailing vessel called the *Turtle Dove,* carrying several hundred escaped American slaves from the Freeman sisters' underground railway, was blown ashore in Samaná. The escapees settled and prospered, and today their descendants number several thousand. The churches here are Protestant; the worshippers live in villages called Bethesda, Northeast, and Philadelphia; and the language spoken is an odd 19th-century form of English mixed with Spanish.

Sportfishing at Samaná is considered to be among the best in the world. In addition, about 3,000 humpback whales winter off the coast of Samaná from December to March. Major whale-watching expeditions are being organized and should boost the region's economy without scaring away the world's largest mammals.

Samaná makes a fine base for exploring the area's natural splendors. Most hotels on the peninsula arrange tours to Los Haitises National Park, a remote, unspoiled rain forest with limestone knolls, crystal lakes, mangrove swamps teeming with aquatic birds, and caves stippled with Taíno petroglyphs. Las Terrenas, a remote stretch of beautiful, nearly deserted beaches on the north coast of the Samaná peninsula, attracts surfers and windsurfers. There are several modest seafood restaurants, a dusty main street in the town of Las Terrenas, a small airfield, an all-inclusive resort, and several congenial hotels right on the beach. If you're happy just hanging out, drinking rum, and soaking up the sun, this is the place, one that is really catching on. A new highway is in the planning that would connect Samana to Santo Domingo in a record two hours.

23 **Sosua.** This small community was settled during World War II by 600 Austrian and German Jews. After the war many of them returned to Europe or went to the United States, and most who remained married Dominicans. Only a few Jewish families reside in the community today, and there's only the original one-room, wooden synagogue.

Sosua, called Puerto Plata's little sister, has become one of the country's most popular destinations. Hotels and condos are going up at breakneck speed. It actually consists of two communities—El Batey, the modern hotel development, and Los Charamicos, the old quarter—separated by a cove and one of the island's prettiest beaches. The sand is soft and white, the water crystal clear and calm. The walkway above the beach is packed with tents filled with souvenirs, pizzas, and even clothing for sale—a jarring note in this otherwise idyllic place.

The Cibao Valley

The heavily trafficked, four-lane, divided highway north from Santo Domingo, known as the Autopista Duarte, cuts through the lush banana plantations, rice and tobacco fields, and royal poinciana trees of the Cibao Valley. Along the road are stands where, for a few pesos, you can buy pineapples, mangoes, avocados, *chicharrones* (fried pork rinds), and fresh fruit drinks.

㉘ **Jarabacoa.** Nature lovers should consider a trip to Jarabacoa, in the mountainous region known rather wistfully as the Dominican Alps. There's little to do in the town itself but eat and rest up for excursions on foot, horseback, or by motorbike taxi to the surrounding waterfalls and forests—quite incongruous in such a tropical country. Other activities include adventure tours, particularly white-water raft or canoe trips, jeep safaris, and paragliding. Accommodations in the area are rustic, but comfortable.

㉗ **La Vega Vieja.** Founded in 1495 by Columbus, La Vega is the site of one of the oldest settlements in the New World. You may find the tour of the ruins of the original settlement, the Old La Vega, rewarding. About 3 mi (5 km) north of La Vega is Santo Cerro (Holy Mount), site of a miraculous apparition of the Virgin and therefore many local pilgrimages. The Convent of La Merced is here, and the views of the Cibao Valley are breathtaking. The town's remarkable Concepción de la Vega Church was constructed in 1992 to commemorate the 500th anniversary of the discovery of America. The unusual modern Gothic style—all curvaceous concrete columns, arches, and buttresses—is striking.

La Vega is also celebrated for its Carnival, featuring haunting devil masks. These papier-mâché creations are intricate, fanciful gargoyles painted in surreal colors; spiked horns and real cow's teeth lend an eerie authenticity. Several artisans work in dark, cramped studios throughout the area; their skills have been passed down for generations. Closest to downtown is the art studio of José Luís Gomez. Ask any local (tip 10–20 pesos) to guide you to his atelier (☏ no phone). José speaks no English but will show you the stages of a mask's development. He sells the masks for $50–$60, a great buy, considering the craftsmanship.

㉖ **Santiago de los Caballeros.** The second city of the D.R., where many past presidents were born, sits about 90 mi (145 km) northwest of Santo Domingo. This industrial center has a surprisingly charming, provincial feel. A massive monument honoring the restoration of the republic guards the entrance to the city. Traditional yet progressive, Santiago is still relatively new to the tourist scene, but new restaurants are popping up, and an extravagant hotel is under construction. It's worth setting aside a day or two to explore this city, which dates from the 1500s. There are colonial-style buildings with wrought-iron details and tiled porticos as well as many homes reflecting a Victorian influence, with the requisite gingerbread latticework and fanciful colors. An original route from centuries past, the highway between Santiago and Puerto Plata, is dotted with sugar mills. The Office of Cultural Patrimony will be overseeing their restoration.

Santiago is a center for processing tobacco leaf. The Fuente factory is here, the family-owned cigar company that enjoys an enviable reputation worldwide for quality. Arturo Fuente, the founder, was born in Cuba. His background and knowledge has played a part in Fuente cigars being able to out-distance Cuba's *Habanos* in popularity. His son, Carlos Fuente, Jr. has brought them to international attention by his contemporary thinking and skill in marketing. Of course, the fact that Dominican stogies can legally be bought or brought into the states, has helped considerably. You can gain an appreciation of the art and skill of Dominican (similar to Cuban) cigar making with a tour of **E. Leon Jiménez Tabacalera** (☎ 809/563–1111 or 809/535–5555).

The Southwest

③⓪ **Barahona.** Here mountains, carpeted with rain forests and laced with streams, slope down into white stretches of sand and into the Caribbean. You can bathe in the cascades of icy mountain rivers or in hot thermal springs surrounded by dense foliage, *llanai* vines, and fruit trees. Barahona is a tropical Garden of Eden. Be tempted to come while you and yours can still have it to yourself. With the new, daily American Eagle flight (64-seat planes) from San Juan, it won't be long now that it will be a true touristic destination.

② ⑨ **Lago Enriquillo.** The largest lake in the Antilles is near the Haitian border. The salt lake is also the lowest point in the Antilles: 114 ft (35 m) below sea level. It encircles wild, arid, and thorny islands that serve as sanctuary to such exotic birds and reptiles as flamingoes, iguanas, and caimans—the indigenous crocodile. The area is targeted by the government for improvements and infrastructure designed for ecotourists.

DOMINICAN REPUBLIC A TO Z

To research prices, get advice from other travelers, and book travel arrangements, visit www.fodors.com.

AIR TRAVEL

Aeromar flies nonstop from Miami to Santo Domingo daily. Air DCE (formerly Air ALM) connects Santo Domingo to St. Martin and Curaçao. Air Atlantic has service from Miami and San Juan into Las Américas on Monday, Wednesday, and Friday. Air Caraïbes services Santo Domingo, connecting it with the French West Indies–Guadeloupe, Les Saintes, Marie-Galante, La Désirade, Martinique, St. Martin, St. Barth's, and the Caribbean "down" islands of Dominica and St. Lucia. Air Transat serves Santo Domingo from Montréal, Toronto, Vancouver, Victoria, and the maritime provinces; it now has three weekly flights into La Romana/Casa de Campo Airport. American Airlines has the most extensive service to the D.R. It flies nonstop from New York and Miami to Santo Domingo, Puerto Plata, and La Romana/Casa de Campo Airport and offers connections to both Santo Domingo and Puerto Plata from San Juan, Puerto Rico. From San Juan, American Eagle has six daily flights to Santo Domingo, two daily flights to La Romana/Casa de Campo Airport, two flights daily to Santiago, and several flights weekly to Punta Cana. Continental flies nonstop from Newark to Puerto Plata and Santo Domingo. Queen Air flies from New York to Santo Domingo four times a week. US Airways offers daily service into Santo Domingo directly from Philadelphia; flights from other U.S. cities must connect in Philadelphia. US Airways also has frequent service to San Juan, from Philadelphia, Pittsburgh, and Charlotte, where you can connect for flights to Santo Domingo, Punta Cana, Puerto Plata, Barahona, and Santiago.

➤ AIRLINES AND CONTACTS: **Aeromar** (☎ 877/237–6672). **Air DCE** (☎ 809/687–4569). **Air Atlantic** (☎ 809/687–4569). **Air Caraïbes**

(☎ 011–590–590–21–11–99 [in Guadeloupe]). **Air Transat** (☎ 416/259–1118). **American Airlines/American Eagle** (☎ 809/542–5151). **Continental** (☎ 809/562–6688). **Queen Air** (☎ 809/565–4041). **US Airways** (☎ 809/540–0505).

AIRPORTS

The Barahona International Airport on the southwest coast now has daily, direct service from San Juan on American Eagle; you can also fly there on a private charter and soon regularly scheduled charter. Flights from the United States and Canada generally arrive at Las Américas International Airport, about 20 mi (32 km) outside Santo Domingo, and Puerto Plata International Gregorio Luperon Airport, about 15 mi (24 km) east of Puerto Plata on the north coast, the latter benefiting from a much needed, multiphase renovation project. The Punta Cana International Airport is a unique experience; the terminal building is a thatched-roof structure with cane partitions; it covers several acres and is surrounded by gardens. The La Romana/Casa de Campo International Airport has a creative design that replicates a sugar mill factory—the area was originally a sugar cane plantation.

Anticipate long lines and allow 2–3 hours for checking in for an international flight, especially at Las Américas. Due to major renovation efforts, this airport is significantly better than in past years; still it can be daunting for the uninitiated. Do confirm your flight two days in advance. Keep a sharp eye on your luggage; almost everyone checks black luggage, and between that and the many huge boxes that the Dominicans bring in from the states, the carousels are chaotic. If you fly out of a U.S. airport such as Miami—where a shrink-wrap service is offered—avail yourself of it (plastic-wrap your bag like meat in a supermarket, and no one is likely to tamper with it).

Choose wisely in order to fly into the airport closest to where you will be staying. It may also be possible to book an inbound flight into one airport and an outbound flight from another airport, in order to see more of the D.R. This country is larger than most Caribbean islands, and a logistical mistake could place you a four-hour bus ride away (which translates into a $100 taxi), when there is very likely an airport only a 30-minute drive from your hotel.

Taxis are available at the airports, and the 25-minute ride into Santo Domingo averages about $30. Some order has been imposed outside the airport—taxis line up and, for the most part, charge official, established rates. If you've arranged for a hotel transfer (a good idea), a representative should be waiting for you in the immigration hall. Fares from the Puerto Plata airport average $16 to Playa Dorada; expect to pay about $30 from Punta Cana airport to the hotels.

➤ AIRPORT INFORMATION: **Barahona International Airport** (Barahona, ☎ 809/524–4109). **Las Américas International Airport** (Santo Domingo, ☎ 809/549–0450). **Puerto Plata International Gregorio Luperon Airport** (Puerto Plata, ☎ 809/586–0107 or 809/586–0219). **Punta Cana International Airport** (☎ 809/668–4749). **La Romana/Casa de Campo International Airport** (☎ 809/556–5565).

BUSINESS HOURS
BANKS
Banks are open weekdays 8:30–4:30.

POST OFFICES
Post offices are open weekdays 7:30–2:30.

Offices and shops are open weekdays 8–noon and 2–6, Saturday 8–
noon. About 50% of the stores stay open all day, no longer closing for
a midday siesta.

CAR RENTALS
If you are staying at one of the all-inclusive resorts, which are self-contained compounds, you will probably not need a car. But if you travel
around the D.R., you'll need a valid driver's license from your own
country and a major credit card (or cash deposit) to rent a car. Your
credit card will be used to secure a deposit of some $200. This should
be "torn up" upon safe return of the vehicle. Make certain that it is.
Both international and local companies rent cars in the D.R. Rates average $70 and more per day, and the asking rate is seldom negotiable,
and lower rates usually entail renting a car for a week or more.

Some local agencies give better rates than the "big guys." However,
you may feel more confident in going with one of the name brands—
there is more recourse, for example, in case of an accident. If you do
not receive insurance from your credit card, you will need to buy insurance, which is expensive.
➤ MAJOR AGENCIES: **Avis** (☎ 809/535–7191). **Budget** (☎ 809/562–
6812). **Hertz** (☎ 809/221–5333). **McBeal** (☎ 809/688–6518). **National**
(☎ 809/562–1444). **Nelly Rent-a-Car** (☎ 809/544–1800; 800/526–
6684 in the U.S.).

CAR TRAVEL
GASOLINE
Fill up—and keep an eye on—the tank; gas stations are few and far
between in rural areas. Gas prices are high by U.S. standards, approximately $2.60–$2.70 a gallon. Make certain that attendants don't
reach for the super pump. You don't need to be putting that expensive liquid in a rent-a-car.

ROAD CONDITIONS
Many Dominicans drive recklessly, and their cars are often in bad shape
(missing headlights, taillights, etc.). It's strongly suggested that you don't
drive outside the major cities at night. If you must, use extreme caution, especially on the narrow, unlighted mountain roads. Watch out
for pedestrians, bicycles, motorbikes, and the occasional stray cow or
goat.

Before setting out, consult with your hotel concierge about routes and
obtain a good road map. Although some roads are still full of potholes,
the route between Santo Domingo and Santiago is now a four-lane divided highway, and the road between Santiago and Puerto Plata is a
smooth blacktop. The highway from Casa de Campo to Punta Cana
is also a smooth ride—not too long ago it was like a lunar moonscape.
Surprisingly, many of the scenic secondary roads, such as the "high road"
between Playa Dorada and Santiago, are in good shape.

RULES OF THE ROAD
Driving is on the right. The 80-kph (50-mph) speed limit is strictly enforced: there is even radar in areas like Punta Cana. The "old days"
of getting stopped for speeding, even if you weren't, and handing the
cop the equivalent of $3, are slowly coming to an end. Now you really
will get a ticket and have to pay a much higher fine.

ELECTRICITY
The current is 110 volts, 60 cycles—just like in North America. Electrical blackouts occur less frequently and tend to last only one to two

minutes (when they're over, everyone claps). Hotels and most restaurants have generators.

EMBASSIES

➤ CANADA: **Canadian Embassy** (✉ Capitan Eugenia de Marchena, No. 39, La Esperilla, Santo Domingo [Box 2054], ☎ 809/685–1136). **Canadian Consulate** (✉ Edificio Isabel de Torres, Suite 311C, Puerto Plata, ☎ 809/586–5761).

➤ UNITED KINGDOM: **British Embassy** (✉ Edificio Corominas Pepin, Ave. 27 de Febrero No 233, Naco, Santo Domingo, ☎ 809/472–7671 or 809/472–7373).

➤ UNITED STATES: **United States Embassy** (✉ Leopoldo Navarro esq. Cesar Nicolas Penson, Naco, Santo Domingo, ☎ 809/221–5511).

EMERGENCIES

➤ AMBULANCE AND FIRE: **Ambulance and fire emergencies** (☎ 911).

➤ HOSPITALS: **Centro Médico Sosua** (✉ Av. Martinez, Sosua, ☎ 809/571–3949). **Centro Médico Universidad Central del Este** (✉ Av. Máximo Gómez 68, La Esperilla, Santo Domingo, ☎ 809/221–0171). **Clínica Abreu** (✉ Calle Beller 42, Gazcue, Santo Domingo, ☎ 809/688–4411). **Clínica Dr. Brugal** (✉ Calle José del Carmen Ariza 15, Puerto Plata, ☎ 809/586–2519). **Clínica Gómez Patino** (✉ Av. Independencia 701, Gazcue, Santo Domingo, ☎ 809/685–9131). **Hospiten Hospital Bávaro** (✉ Bávaro, ☎ 809/686–1414). **Servimed** (✉ Plaza La Criolla, Sosua, ☎ 809/571–0964).

➤ PHARMACIES: **Farmacia Deleyte** (✉ Av. John F. Kennedy 89, Puerto Plata, ☎ 809/586–2583). **San Judas Tadeo** (✉ Av. Independencia 57, Gazcue, Santo Domingo, ☎ 809/689–6664).

➤ POLICE: **Police Emergencies** (☎ 809/586–2804 in Puerto Plata; 711 in Santo Domingo; 809/571–2233 in Sosua).

ETIQUETTE AND BEHAVIOR

Wearing shorts, miniskirts, and halter tops in churches is considered inappropriate. Men in Santo Domingo never wear shorts.

FESTIVALS AND SEASONAL EVENTS

Santo Domingo hosts a day-long Carnival in late February, coinciding with Dominican Independence Day. Pre-Lenten carnivals are held several Sundays prior to Ash Wednesday in Santiago and La Vega, which is renowned for its papier-mâché carnival masks. The renowned Festival del Merengue is held in late July and early August in Santo Domingo and showcases name entertainers, bands, and orchestras. During the last week in August the island's top restaurants compete in the capital city's Gastronomic Festival. The Jazz Festival is an impressive line up of international and Latino jazz stars that runs for three days during the first week of October, with venues in Cabarete, Sosúa and Puerto Plata. The "Bienal del Caribe" occurs every two years in Santo Domingo at the Museum of Modern Art, when four artists are chosen to represent each of 80 Caribbean islands and countries in this major festival; artists' works are exhibited at the museum and some 50 other venues included on walking circuits in the Colonial Zone, in art galleries, and public spaces throughout the city.

HEALTH

Though it's reasonably safe to drink water from the tap (especially in the better resorts), you're better off playing it safe with bottled water. Many resorts have adopted the Crystal Program, which sets strict guidelines for food service, particularly for hot and cold buffets. Still, try to arrive at the very start of a buffet meal, before the food has sat out for a while in the tropical heat.

HOLIDAYS

Public holidays are: New Year's Day, Our Lady of La Altagracia Day (Jan. 21), Duarte's Birthday (Jan. 26), Independence Day (last Mon. in Feb.), Good Friday (Fri. before Easter), Labor Day (1st Mon. in May), Corpus Christi (June 14), Restoration Day (Aug. 16), Our Lady of Las Mercedes Day (Sept. 24), Columbus Day (Oct. 26), Discovery of Hispaniola Day (Dec. 5), and Christmas.

LANGUAGE

Spanish is spoken in the D.R. Staff at major tourist attractions and front-desk personnel in most major hotels, speak a fascinating form of English, and you may have difficulty making yourself understood. Outside the popular tourist establishments, restaurant menus are in Spanish, as are traffic signs everywhere. Using smiles and gestures will help, and though you can manage with just English, people are even more courteous if you try to speak their language.

MAIL AND SHIPPING

Airmail postage to North America for a letter or postcard is RD$2, to Europe RD$4; letters may take up to three weeks to reach their destination. Or you can pay almost US$1.45 to buy a pale green stamp for "fast mail" in a gift shop (outside Santo Domingo, post offices aren't easy to find). The main branch of the post office in Santo Domingo is on Calle Heroes del Luperon at Rafael Damiron La Ferla.

MONEY MATTERS

Prices quoted in this chapter are in U.S. dollars unless noted otherwise.

ATMS

Banco Popular has many locations throughout the country; many have ATMs that accept international cards.

CREDIT CARDS

Major credit cards are accepted at most hotels, large stores, and restaurants.

CURRENCY

The coin of the realm is the Dominican peso (written RD$). At this writing, RD$16.16 was equivalent to US$1. Sometimes, independent merchants will accept U.S. dollars, but don't count on it. Always make certain you know in which currency any transaction is taking place. Carry a pocket calculator to make conversions easier. You'll find *cambios* (currency exchange offices) at the airports as well as in major shopping areas throughout the island. At times, they offer better rates than the banks and at others, *el banco* is best. Check the posted rates for any given day. In addition, some hotels provide exchange services, but, as a general rule, hotels and restaurants will not give you as much for your money as cambios and banks.

PASSPORTS AND VISAS

U.S. and Canadian citizens must have either a valid passport or proof of citizenship, such as an original birth certificate with a raised seal. Legal U.S. residents must have an alien registration card (green card) and a valid passport from their home country. Citizens of Australia, New Zealand, and the United Kingdom need a valid passport. Additionally, upon arrival, all U.S., U.K., Australian, Canadian, and Irish citizens must purchase a tourist card, which costs $10.

SAFETY

In general, the island is very safe—even for women traveling alone—and you rarely hear about violent crime against tourists. Theft, however, is prevalent. In Santo Domingo in particular be conscious of your wallet or pocketbook, especially around the Malecón. At night you may see men in civies with shoulder rifles standing outside businesses or homes. Don't be unnerved by this. These men are the Dominican equivalents of private security guards. Always lock your car and never leave valuables in it even if it is locked. If you have a safe in your hotel room, use it.

SIGHTSEEING TOURS

Apolo Tours, which is based in Playa Dorada, offers a full-day tour of Playa Grande and tours to Santiago (including a casino excursion) and Sosua; all cost $35; the company will also arrange transfers between your hotel and the airport, day-trips, and custom and small group tours along the north coast, which include stops for swimming and a trip to Samaná ($49). Cabemba Tours, which operates in Playa Dorada, runs various tours of the Cibao Valley and the Amber Coast, including Puerto Plata, Sosua, and Río San Juan. Caribbean Jeep Safaris is an English-speaking outfit in Playa Dorada that runs jeep tours in the mountains behind Puerto Plata and Sosua, ending up at the Cabarete Adventure Park, where you can swim in an underground pool and explore caves with Taíno rock paintings; buffet lunch and drinks are included in the $40. Go Dominican Tours in Playa Dorada has tours to Jarabacoa for $85, which include lunch, drinks, and 3½ hours of river rafting; jumping off cliffs is optional. Jeep safaris trek to flower, fruit, and coffee plantations. Horseback riding in the Puerto Plata area is another option.

Iguana Mama, Mountain Bike, Hiking & Cultural Vacations, a company based in Cabarete, offers adventure tours with an ecological conscience: 20% of their profits are donated to local environmental projects and education; a well-established company, safety is a major consideration for them.

Winchester Tours, a Massachusetts-based company, specializes in wildlife and bird-watching tours of Barahona for groups of 6–10 nature lovers. The company's president, Fred Sladen, also acts as tour leader. Having lived in the Caribbean for 15 years, he's a recognized authority on tropical birds and ecosystems and is a very personable host as well. He, too, donates to conservation organizations.

Prieto Tours, which is in Santo Domingo and operates Gray Line of the D.R., has half-day bus tours of Santo Domingo, nightclub tours, beach tours, trips to Cibao Valley and the Amber Coast, and other excursions; prices start at $30. Turinter offers a six-hour trip to Altos de Chavón ($45); a full day of swimming and boating on Saona Island ($78); and specialty trips (museum, shopping, fishing), all from Santo Domingo.

➤ CONTACTS: **Apolo Tours** (☎ 809/586–5329). **Cabemba Tours** (☎ 809/586–2177). **Caribbean Jeep Safaris** (☎ 809/571–1924). **Go Dominican Tours** (☎ 809/586–5969). **Iguana Mama, Mountain Bike, Hiking & Cultural Vacations** (☎ 800/571–0908). **Prieto Tours** (☎ 809/685–0102). **Turinter** (☎ 809/685–4020). **Winchester Tours** (☎ 800/391–2473).

TAXES AND SERVICE CHARGES
DEPARTURE TAX
The D.R. has a $10 departure tax, often included in ticket prices. You need to ask.

SALES TAX AND SERVICE CHARGE
A 10% service charge is usually added to restaurant checks and hotel bills, as is a 12% government tax.

TAXIS

Taxis, which are government-regulated, line up outside hotels and restaurants. They're unmetered, and the minimum fare within Santo Domingo is about $4, but you can bargain for less if you order a taxi away from the major hotels. Some taxis aren't allowed to pick up from hotels, so they hang out on the street in front of them. On the average, they're $1 cheaper per ride. Avoid unmarked street taxis, particularly in Santo Domingo—they're a little risky.

Hiring a taxi by the hour—with unlimited stops—is $10 per hour with a minimum of two hours. Be sure to establish the time that you start; drivers like to advance the time a little. Always carry small denominations, like 5-, 10-, and 20-peso notes, because drivers rarely seem to have change. Taxis can also drive you to destinations outside the city. Rates are posted in hotels and at the airport. Sample fares from Santo Domingo are $80 to La Romana and $150 to Puerto Plata. If you're negotiating, the going rate is RD$5 per kilometer. Round-trips are considerably less than twice the one-way fare. Two good cab companies are El Conde Taxi and Tecni-Taxi.

Radio taxis are not only convenient but also a wise choice if you don't speak Spanish. The fare is negotiated over the phone when you make the appointment. The most reliable company is Apolo Taxi. The standard charge is about $7 per hour during the day and $8 at night, no minimum, and with as many stops as you like. Call P. Green Taxi for a courteous, English-speaking driver. Another option is to go in high-Dominican style and hire a limo, even if it's just for a night. Call The Limousine Connection, whose rates run around $50 per hour.
➤ CONTACTS: **Apolo Taxi** (☎ 809/541–9595). **El Conde Taxi** (☎ 809/563–6131). **P. Green Taxi** (☎ 809/251–0571). **Limousine Connection** (☎ 809/540–5304 or 809/567–3435). **Tecni-Taxi** (☎ 809/567–2010 in Santo Domingo; 809/320–7621 in Puerto Plata).

TELEPHONES

COUNTRY AND AREA CODES

To call the D.R. from the United States, dial 1 and then the area code 809 and the local number. From the D.R. there's also direct-dial service.

INTERNATIONAL CALLS

To reach the United States and Canada, dial 1, followed by the area code and number; to the United Kingdom dial 011, the country and city codes, and the number.

LOCAL CALLS

To make a local call, dial the 7-digit number.

TIPPING

Generally, a 10% service charge is included. The bill will say, *propino incluido*. When in doubt ask. If you found the service to your liking, tip an extra 5%–10%. It's customary to leave a dollar per day for the hotel maid. Taxi drivers expect a 10% tip, especially if they've had to lift luggage or to wait for you. Skycaps and hotel porters expect at least RD$10 per bag.

TRANSPORTATION AROUND THE DOMINICAN REPUBLIC

AIRPLANES

Air Century, flying out of Herrara Airport and La Romana/Casa de Campo Airport, offers charters, transfers, excursions, and sightseeing. Air Santo Domingo offers service between the capital (Las Americas and Herrera Airports) and Puerto Plata, Punta Cana, La Romana/Casa de Campo, El Portillo, and Santiago. Each hop is about $60. Jimmy and Irene Butler of Air Taxi charter planes for trips around the island or to neighboring islands. Caribar has both planes and helicopters and offers general air service, ambulance service, and aerial photography trips.

➤ CONTACTS: **Air Century** (✉ Herrara Airport, Santo Domingo, ☎ 809/566–0888 or 809/567–6778; ✉ La Romana/Casa de Campo Airport, La Romana, ☎ 809/550–6636 or 809/550–8201; ✉ Casa de Campo, La Romana, ☎ 809/523–3333 Ext. 8351). **Air Santo Domingo** (✉ Herrara Airport, Santo Domingo, ☎ 809/683–8020). **Air Taxi** (✉ Herrera Airport, Núñez de Cáceres 2, Santo Domingo, ☎ 809/227–8333 or 809/567–1555). **Caribar** (✉ Herrara Airport, av. Luperon, Santo Domingo, ☎ 809/542–6688; ✉ La Romana/Casa de Campo Airport, La Romana, ☎ 809/550–2585).

BUSES

Privately owned air-conditioned buses make regular runs to Santiago, Puerto Plata, and other destinations from Santo Domingo. You should make reservations by calling Metro Buses or Caribe Tours. One-way bus fare from Santo Domingo to Puerto Plata is about $6, and it takes four hours. Metro's buses have more of an upscale clientele. Although the coffee and cookies are complimentary, there are no movies. Caribe, which shows bilingual movies, is favored by locals and families; buses are often filled to capacity, especially on weekends.

Frequent service from Santo Domingo to the town of La Romana is provided by Express Bus. Buses depart from Revelos Street in front of Enriquillo Park every hour on the hour from 5 AM to 9 PM; the schedule is exactly the same from Romana, where they leave from Camino Avenue. There is no office and no phone, but a ticket-taker will take your $3 just before departure. There is general chaos, a crazy kind of congestion (allow time in a taxi), horns blowing, diesel fumes, but it all comes together. Don't be dismayed, remember that you are spending $3 instead of $80 or $100 by taxi, which might be an aging vehicle without A/C. Travel time is about 1¼ hours, and if luck is with you, you'll get the larger bus, which will show a first-rate American movie. Once in town you can take a taxi from the bus stop to Casa de Campo ($7) or Casa del Mar ($10).

➤ CONTACTS: **Metro Buses** (☎ 809/566–7126 in Santo Domingo; 809/586–6062 in Puerto Plata; 809/587–4711 in Santiago). **Caribe Tours** (☎ 809/221–4422).

OTHER OPTIONS

Traditionally, *públicos* or *conchos* are small blue-and-white or blue-and-red cars that run regular routes, stopping to let passengers on and off. But now everyone is getting into the act. Anyone who owns a car can operate it as a *público* and after 5 PM many do. The fare is RD$2. Competing with the públicos are the *colectivos* (privately owned vans), whose drivers coast around the major thoroughfares, leaning out of the window or jumping out to try to persuade you to climb aboard. It's a colorful if cramped way to get around. The fare is about RD$1.

Voladoras (fliers) are vans that run from Puerto Plata's Central Park to Sosua and Cabarete a couple of times each hour for RD$10. They have a reliable schedule, but aren't always labeled with their destination.

Motoconchos are a popular, inexpensive mode of transportation in such areas as Puerto Plata, Sosua, and Jarabacoa. You can flag one of these bikes down along rural roads and in town; rates vary from RD$3 to RD$20 per person, depending upon distance. You can find a pair of them, one to take you, the other your luggage. Be careful and good luck: no helmets are provided, and the Dominicans drive like they are possessed.

VISITOR INFORMATION

➤ BEFORE YOU LEAVE: **Dominican Republic Tourist Office** (✉ 136 E. 57th St., Suite 803, New York, NY 10022, ☎ 212/575–4966 or 888/374–6361, WEB www.dr1.com/travel.shtml; ✉ 248 W. Le Jeune Rd., Miami, FL 33126, ☎ 305/444–4592 or 888/358–9594; ✉ 1464 Crescent St., Montréal, Québec H3A 2B6, Canada, ☎ 514/933–6126; ✉ 20 Hand Court, High Holborn, London WC1, U.K., ☎ 0171/723–1552).

➤ IN THE DOMINICAN REPUBLIC: **Secretary of Tourism** (✉ Secretaria de Estado de Turismo, Edificios Guberbamentales, Av. México, corner of av. 30 de Marzo, Gazcue Santo Domingo, ☎ 809/221–4660). **Ministry of Tourism** (✉ Av. Mexico, Gazcue, Santo Domingo, ☎ 809/221–4660). **Puerto Plata tourist office** (✉ Playa Long Beach, Puerto Plata, ☎ 809/586–3676).

12 GRENADA

By Jane E.
Zarem

It's cool, dark, and pungent inside the nutmeg co-op. In loose floral skirts and cotton shirts, bandanas around their heads, the ladies of Gouyave work hard for their money. Perched on stools, facing huge wooden chutes, they sort nutmegs all day. Fingers move like lightning, sorting thousands per hour. When sunlight briefly brightens the room, the chute wall reveals someone's handwritten message: GOD LOOKED AT MY WORK AND WAS PLEASED. THEN HE LOOKED AT MY SALARY, BOWED HIS HEAD, AND SADLY WALKED AWAY.

Grenada, just 21 mi (34 km) long and 12 mi (19 km) wide, has 45 beaches and countless secluded coves. Crisscrossed by nature trails and laced with spice plantations, its mountainous interior is lush rain forest. Select hotels cling to hillsides or skirt the sea; a mellow island spirit juxtaposes nicely with top facilities and sensible development. St. George's is one of the most picturesque capital cities in the Caribbean, and Grand Anse is one of the finest beaches. Nicknamed Isle of Spice, Grenada is a major producer of nutmeg, cinnamon, mace, cocoa, and other spices and flavorings. The aroma of spices fills the air in markets, in restaurants, and throughout the countryside.

Grenada lies in the eastern Caribbean, 12 degrees north of the equator, and is the southernmost of the Windward Islands. The nation of Grenada consists of three islands: Grenada, the largest, with 120 square mi (311 square km) and a population of just over 90,000; Carriacou (*car*-ree-a-coo), 23 mi (37 km) north of Grenada, with 13 square mi (34 square km) and a population of about 5,000; and Petite Martinique, 2 mi (3 km) northeast of Carriacou, with just 486 acres and a population of only 700. Carriacou and Petite Martinique are popular for day-trips, fishing, or snorkeling excursions, but most of the tourist activity is on Grenada.

Although he never set foot on the island, Christopher Columbus sighted Grenada in 1498 and named it Concepción. Spanish sailors following in his wake renamed it Granada, after the city in the hills of their homeland. Adapted to Grenade by French colonists, the transformation to Grenada was completed by the British in the 18th century.

Throughout the 17th century, Grenada was the scene of many bloody battles between indigenous Carib Indians and the French. Rather than surrender upon losing their last battle in 1651, the Caribs committed mass suicide by leaping off a cliff in Sauteurs, at the island's northern tip. The French were later overwhelmed by the British in 1762, thus beginning a seesaw of power between the two nations. By the Treaty of Versailles in 1783, Grenada was granted to the British and, almost immediately, African slaves were brought in to work the sugar plantations. Slavery continued for 50 years until it was abolished in 1834.

On February 7, 1974, Grenada was granted total independence within the British Commonwealth. The socialist New Jewel Movement (NJM) party seized power in 1979, formed the People's Revolutionary Government, and named Maurice Bishop prime minister. A division within the party led to the murder of Bishop and many of his supporters, after which NJM deputy prime minister Bernard Coard and Army Commander Hudson Austin took over the government. Days later, on October 25, 1983, at the request of Grenada's governor general and the heads of state of neighboring islands, U.S. troops intervened. American students attending St. George's University Medical School were evacuated, and the revolution was quickly quelled. Coard and Austin (and others) were arrested, found guilty of murder, and are currently serving life sentences in prison, high on a hill overlooking St. George's Harbour and the scene of the crime.

With U.S. and Canadian aid, government officials elected in 1984 reorganized Grenada's economy to emphasize agriculture, light manufacturing, and tourism. The country rebuilt roads and installed a direct-dial phone system. Grenada's modern Point Salines International Airport, which was begun with Cuban assistance prior to the intervention, was completed and opened in 1984.

Grenada's popularity as a vacation destination increases each year as travelers seek friendly, exotic islands to visit. Hotels continue to renovate, improve, and expand, but all expansion of the tourism industry is carefully controlled: no building can stand taller than a coconut palm. Many hotels, resorts, and restaurants are family-owned, run by people whose guests often become their friends. Grenadians have a well-deserved reputation for their friendliness, hospitality, and entrepreneurial spirit.

Lodging

Grenada's tourist accommodations are almost all in the southwest part of the island, primarily on or near Grand Anse Beach. Lodging options range from simply furnished, inexpensive apartments to elegant suites just steps from the sea. Hotels tend to be small and intimate, with friendly management and attentive staff. All guest rooms are equipped with air-conditioning, an in-room TV, and telephone unless indicated otherwise. During the off-season (April 15–December 15), prices may be discounted up to 40%.

CATEGORY	COST EP/CP*	COST A.I.**
$$$$	over $350	over $375
$$$	$250–$350	$275–$375
$$	$150–$250	$175–$275
$	under $150	under $175

*EP/CP prices are per night for a standard double room in high season, excluding taxes, service charges, and meal plans**A.I. (all-inclusive) prices are per person, per night based on double-occupancy during high season, excluding taxes and service charges*

Hotels

GRENADA

$$$$ **Calabash Hotel.** Elegant suites are in two-story cottages, distributed
★   around 8 acres of garden that hug a curved beach. Each suite has a spacious bedroom and sitting area, with rattan and wicker furniture,

and a veranda where breakfast is freshly prepared and served by your maid. Twenty-two suites have whirlpool baths; eight have private plunge pools. Each room has a CD player, but you'll have to go to the library to watch TV. Complimentary fruit is served on the beach each morning; tea is served in the restaurant each afternoon; and canapés are delivered to your suite in the evening. Cicely's restaurant serves memorable cuisine. ⊠ *L'Anse aux Épines (Box 382, St. George's),* ☎ *473/444–4334,* FAX *473/444–5050,* WEB *www.calabashhotel.com. 30 suites. Restaurant, 2 bars, room service, fans, no room TVs, golf privileges, tennis court, pool, gym, spa, beach, snorkeling, boating, billiards, shuffleboard, shops, library, baby-sitting, dry cleaning, laundry service, concierge, car rental. AE, MC, V. CP, MAP.*

$$$$ 🖼 **Laluna.** Laluna is a quiet, upscale cottage enclave hidden away on a remote, pristine beach near Grenada's Quarantine Point. Sixteen large cottages with thatched roofs—each with its own plunge pool—line the beachfront, with the wooded hillside as a backdrop. Bedrooms, with king-size beds, open onto large verandas that serve as indoor-outdoor sitting areas. Each room has a stereo CD player and coffeemaker. Bathrooms have custom-made tubs and showers that partially open to the natural environment. The restaurant, bar with weekly entertainment, a small CD and video library, and other services are in the main "club house." Nightly sunset meditation and yoga classes set the mood. ⊠ *Morne Rouge (Box 1500, St. George's),* ☎ *473/439–0001,* FAX *473/439–0600,* WEB *www.laluna.com. 16 cottages. Restaurant, bar, fans, in-room data ports, in-room safes, minibars, in-room VCRs, pool, massage, beach, snorkeling, windsurfing, boating, bicycles, shops, library, concierge, car rental. AE, DC, MC, V. BP, MAP.*

$$$–$$$$ 🖼 **LaSOURCE.** Minutes from the airport, LaSOURCE unfolds on 40
★ acres facing Pink Gin Beach. A breezy courtyard leads to the Oasis spa, the Great House restaurant with its colonnaded terrace, a piano bar, and a two-level swimming pool. Guest quarters are in four-story buildings (lots of stairs) facing the beach. Bedrooms have Oriental-design rugs on Italian marble floors, Jamaican mahogany furniture and woodwork, four-poster king-size beds, balconies, and marble bathrooms. There's plenty to do, day or night. The cuisine is memorable, with light and vegetarian choices always available. Best of all, rates include daily spa treatments—massages, wraps, aromatherapy, and more. ⊠ *Pink Gin Beach (Box 852, St. George's),* ☎ *473/444–2556,* FAX *473/444–2561,* WEB *www.lasourcegrenada.com. 91 rooms, 9 suites. 2 restaurants, 2 bars, fans, in-room safes, refrigerators, 9-hole golf course, 2 tennis courts, pool, aerobics, health club, hair salon, sauna, spa, beach, dive shop, snorkeling, windsurfing, boating, waterskiing, archery, badminton, Ping-Pong, volleyball, piano, shops, laundry service, concierge, travel services, no kids under 16. AE, D, MC, V. All-inclusive.*

$$$–$$$$ 🖼 **Spice Island Beach Resort.** The grand entrance and reception area
★ of Grenada's premier resort lead straight to Grand Anse Beach, with exquisite suites in dozens of peach-colored buildings extending along 1,600 ft of beachfront. Guest rooms have dark rattan furniture and stylish fabrics; huge bathrooms have double-size whirlpool tubs, hair dryers, ironing equipment, and plenty of plush towels. Beachfront suites are steps from the sand, and 13 oceanview suites have private gardens, patios, and plunge pools. Four Royal suites offer the ultimate luxury: private pool and garden, sitting room, and in-room sauna. Oliver's Restaurant, overlooking the beach, serves contemporary cuisine. The Sea & Surf lounge and free-form pool are friendly gathering places, day or night. No kids under 5 in high season. ⊠ *Grand Anse (Box 6, St. George's),* ☎ *473/444–4258,* FAX *473/444–4807,* WEB *www.spicebeachresort.com. 66 suites. Restaurant, room service, fans, in-room safes, minibars, golf privileges, tennis court, pool, outdoor hot*

302

Grenada and Carriacou

tub, gym, hair salon, spa, beach, dive shop, snorkeling, boating, bicycles, shops, recreation room, laundry service, concierge, business services, meeting room. AE, D, DC, MC, V. All-inclusive.

$$-$$$ ▥ **Grenada Grand Beach Resort.** The location (across from the Grand Anse Shopping Centre) is convenient, the 20 acres of grounds are lush, the rooms are comfortable, and the amenities are extensive. Best of all, this appealing resort complex also fronts on a broad section of Grand Anse Beach. Fresh-water lovers can swim in the 300-ft pool with waterfalls. Groups are attracted to this resort, which has Grenada's largest convention center. Guest rooms have attractive mahogany furniture, king-size or twin beds, and a balcony or patio. The restaurant offers table d'hôte and à la carte menus—you can even get a good New York–style steak. ⊠ *Grand Anse (Box 441, St. George's),* ☏ *473/444–4371,* FAX *473/444–4800,* WEB *www.grandbeach.net. 234 rooms, 2 suites. Restaurant, snack bar, 2 bars, room service, 9-hole golf course, 2 tennis courts, 2 pools, gym, hair salon, beach, dive shop, snorkeling, boating, shops, laundry service, business services, convention center, car rental, travel services. AE, DC, MC, V. CP, EP, MAP.*

$$-$$$ ▥ **Rex Grenadian.** This massive resort on Tamarind Bay is minutes from the airport. Guests, many of whom are European, are welcomed into a glistening reception area with lofty ceilings, vast arched doorways, trellised walkways, and tiled terraces. Most rooms are in eight two-story buildings on a bluff overlooking the sea. Rooms have simple rattan furniture and balconies. The pool, casual restaurant, and bar are near the beach but separated from the guest rooms by a large lawn and lake. Activities abound—water sports, nature walks, dance classes, dive lessons, evening shows in the lounge, and happy hours. Buffet breakfast and dinner are served at the International restaurant. ⊠ *Point Salines (Box 893, St. George's),* ☏ *473/444–3333,* FAX *473/444–1111,* WEB *www.rexcaribbean.com. 191 rooms, 21 suites. 3 restaurants, café, 4 bars, no air-conditioning in some rooms, fans, 2 tennis courts, pool, health club, sauna, 2 beaches, dive shop, snorkeling, windsurfing, boating, waterskiing, piano, shops, baby-sitting, business services, meeting rooms. AE, D, DC, MC, V. All-inclusive, CP, EP, MAP.*

$$ ▥ **Allamanda Beach Resort.** Right on Grand Anse beach, this small hotel has some rooms with whirlpool baths; many also have connecting doors, making it a good choice for families. All rooms have tile floors and a balcony or patio. The restaurant serves international cuisine, and a poolside snack bar has great fresh-fruit smoothies. At the water-sports center, you'll find Sunfish, snorkeling equipment, and Dive Grenada, a private scuba operation. Shopping, restaurants, nightlife, and the minibus to town are right at the doorstep. An all-inclusive option is available, which also includes a massage. ⊠ *Grand Anse (Box 1025, St. George's),* ☏ *473/444–0095,* FAX *473/444–0126,* WEB *www.allamandaresort.com. 50 suites. 2 restaurants, snack bar, fans, in-room safes, refrigerators, tennis court, pool, gym, massage, beach, dive shop, snorkeling, boating, volleyball, meeting room. AE, MC, V. EP.*

$$ ▥ **Blue Horizons Cottage Hotel.** An especially good value, the regular
★ suites and studios here have kitchenettes and private terraces. Deluxe suites have separate sitting-dining rooms and one king- or two queen-size beds; studios have dining alcoves and king-size beds. Handsome mahogany furniture is set off by white walls, floral prints, and white-tile floors with grass mats. Palm trees and tropical plants stud the 6 acres of grounds, where 21 species of birds can be found. Lunch is served poolside and dinner at La Belle Creole—renowned for its contemporary West Indian cuisine. It's a short walk from Grand Anse Beach, where Blue Horizons guests use sister hotel Spice Island's beach chairs, tennis court, fitness center, and water-sports equipment. ⊠ *Grand Anse (Box 41, St. George's),* ☏ *473/444–4316 or 473/444–4592,*

FAX *473/444–2815*, WEB *www.bluegrenada.com. 26 suites, 6 studios. Restaurant, 2 bars, fans, kitchenettes, golf privileges, pool, outdoor hot tub, recreation room, baby-sitting, laundry service, car rental. AE, MC, V. CP, EP, MAP.*

$$ 🏨 **Coyaba Beach Resort.** Family-run Coyaba (Arawak for "heaven")
★ is a remarkable value, particularly considering the location directly on Grand Anse Beach. Rooms, decorated with natural wood and Arawak-inspired folk art, are in eight two-story buildings surrounding 5½ acres of lawn and gardens. Nonmotorized water-sports equipment is complimentary; you can also play tennis and volleyball, and enjoy pool with a swim-up bar. Excellent West Indian cuisine is served at the bamboo-walled Arawakabana restaurant or on the poolside terrace, with musical entertainment several nights a week. Each room has a king-size or two double beds, a balcony or patio, and most have a water view. ⊠ *Grand Anse (Box 336, St. George's),* ☎ *473/444–4129 or 473/444–2011,* FAX *473/444–4808,* WEB *www.coyaba.com. 70 rooms. 2 restaurants, 2 bars, room service, golf privileges, tennis court, pool, beach, dive shop, snorkeling, shuffleboard, volleyball, shops, baby-sitting, laundry service, meeting room. AE, D, DC, MC, V. CP, EP, FAP, MAP.*

$$ 🏨 **Flamboyant Hotel & Cottages.** Built into a steep hillside, each room in this friendly Grenadian-owned hotel has a private veranda with a fabulous panoramic view of Grand Anse Bay. Self-catering one-bedroom suites and two-bedroom, two-bath cottages each have a fully equipped kitchen and sitting room with sofa bed, making this an excellent value for families. Be prepared for lots of stairs—about 100 to get to Grand Anse Beach. But halfway down—or on the way back up—you can stop for a dip in the pool or grab a bite at the Beachside Terrace restaurant. ⊠ *Grand Anse (Box 214, St. George's),* ☎ *473/444–4247,* FAX *473/444–1234,* WEB *www.flamboyant.com. 38 rooms, 20 suites, 2 cottages. Restaurant, bar, room service, grocery, in-room safes, kitchenettes, minibars, golf privileges, pool, beach, snorkeling, billiards, recreation room, shop, baby-sitting, laundry service, meeting room, car rental. AE, D, DC, MC, V. CP, EP, MAP.*

$$ 🏨 **Secret Harbour Resort.** Perched on a cliff above Mount Hartman Bay (and away from the throng on the south coast), this resort attracts a yachting crowd. The on-site Moorings' Club Mariner Water-sports Centre has a fleet of sailboats and yachts available for day or long-term charters. But this is also a small, romantic retreat. The 20 suites are beautifully decorated, with two antique, full-size four-poster beds and an Italian-tile bath. Water-sports equipment, including Windsurfers, Sunfish, and sailboats, can be used without charge. Just offshore, Calvigny Island is a 10-minute ride by speedboat; bring a picnic and spend the afternoon on your own deserted isle. ⊠ *Mount Hartman Bay (Box 11, St. George's),* ☎ *473/444–4439,* FAX *473/444–4819,* WEB *www.secretharbour.com. 20 suites. 2 restaurants, bar, room service, tennis court, pool, beach, dock, snorkeling, windsurfing, boating, waterskiing, no kids under 12. AE, D, DC, MC, V. EP, MAP.*

$$ 🏨 **Twelve Degrees North.** Named for the latitude on which it sits, this small secluded inn's one- and two-bedroom suites all face the sea. Accommodations come with a personal housekeeper, who cooks breakfast and lunch, cleans, and tends to your laundry. Groceries are stocked for your arrival, along with flowers, rum punch, and a spice basket. Apartments are bright and airy, with modern furniture and woven-grass rugs on the tile floors. The balcony or patio is perfect for breakfast (in the terry cloth robes provided), a quiet lunch, sunset drinks, or a romantic dinner for two. Activities center on the private beach, pool, and tennis court. ⊠ *L'Anse aux Épines (Box 241, St. George's),* ☎ FAX *473/444–4580,* WEB *www.twelvedegreesnorth.com. 8 suites. No air-condi-*

tioning, tennis court, pool, beach, snorkeling, boating, library, laundry service, no kids. AE, V. EP.

$–$$ ⊞ **True Blue Bay Resort.** On a former indigo plantation, this family-run resort is on several acres of lawn and gardens that slope down to True Blue Bay. Three cottages are near the pool, and four spacious apartments are perched on a cliff. Each has a dining area, a living room with sofa bed, and a fully equipped kitchen. Other attractive rooms, decorated in Caribbean colors, overlook the bay. The restaurant specializes in Mexican and Caribbean cuisine. Though a five-minute drive from Grand Anse Beach, the bay has a beach, and there is a larger beach 100 yards away. Arrange yacht charters at the marina or dive excursions at the on-site dive center. ⊠ *Old Mill Ave., True Blue Bay (Box 1414, St. George's),* ☏ *473/443–8783 or 888/550-8783,* FAX *473/444–5929,* WEB *www.truebluebay.com. 28 rooms, 4 1-bedroom apartments, 3 2-bedroom cottages. Restaurant, bar, fans, kitchens, pool, gym, 2 beaches, dive shop, snorkeling, boating, marina, fishing, shop, baby-sitting, laundry service, meeting room, car rental. AE, MC, V. EP.*

$ ⊞ **Gem Holiday Beach Resort.** Owner Miriam Bedeau and her family operate this friendly apartment hotel on Morne Rouge Beach. One- and two-bedroom self-catering apartments are small and simple, with a kitchenette, dining-living room with mahogany furniture, and private veranda overlooking the sea. If you don't want to cook, Sur La Mer beachside restaurant specializes in seafood and West Indian dishes for lunch and dinner. And for later, Fantazia, one of Grenada's premier dance clubs, is also on the property (and soundproof). ⊠ *Morne Rouge Bay (Box 58, St. George's),* ☏ *473/444–2288,* FAX *473/444–1189,* WEB *www.gembeachresort.com. 15 one-bedroom apartments, 4 two-bedroom apartments. Restaurant, bar, grocery, fans, kitchenettes, beach, snorkeling, dance club, baby-sitting, laundry service, car rental. AE, D, DC, MC, V. EP.*

$ ⊞ **La Sagesse.** In a nature reserve on La Sagesse bay 10 mi (16 km) east of the airport (about a 30-minute drive), the grounds of this secluded, rustic inn include a salt-pond bird sanctuary, thick mangroves, nature trails, and ½ mi (¾ km) of tree-shaded beach. Guest rooms are in the manor house and a beach cottage; two tiny rooms are located behind La Sagesse restaurant. Rooms, just 30 ft from the beach, have screened-in patios. Be content to relax and enjoy the natural surroundings or rent a car if you stay this far out; although the owner will usually run you into town. ⊠ *La Sagesse Nature Center, St. David's (Box 44),* ☏ *473/444–6458,* FAX *473/444–6458,* WEB *www.lasagesse.com. 8 rooms. Restaurant, no air-conditioning in some rooms, fans, kitchenettes, beach, snorkeling, hiking, laundry service. MC, V. EP.*

$ ⊞ **Mariposa Beach Resort.** Over the hill from Grand Anse Beach, this colony of Mediterranean-style, coral-colored villas covers the side of a hill overlooking Morne Rouge Bay. Each stylishly decorated room and self-catering apartment has a water view, a covered veranda or garden, and an Italian-tile bathroom. It's a short walk downhill to Morne Rouge Beach or a water-taxi ride to the beach club. The restaurant specializes in seafood and international dishes. ⊠ *Morne Rouge Bay (Box 857, St. George's),* ☏ *473/444–3171,* FAX *473/444–3172,* WEB *www.mariposaresort.com. 30 rooms, 15 apartments. Restaurant, bar, room service, fans, in-room safes, kitchenettes, pool, beach, laundry service. AE, MC, V. MAP.*

CARRIACOU

$$ ⊞ **Caribbee Inn.** The views from this rambling country house, high on a promontory overlooking the sea in northwest Carriacou, are magnificent, particularly at sunset. Hillside suites are decorated by theme

(Colonial, South American, West Indian) and have four-poster beds draped with netting, soft-pastel color schemes, and Italian-tile floors. One suite has a step-up shower with an open-air view of the bay; another has its own beach. Breakfast and dinner (French creole cuisine) are served in the dining room—and don't be surprised if a macaw joins you, looking for a treat. The inn is isolated, perfect if you like nature walks, meditation, romance, and total relaxation. ✉ *Prospect,* ☎ *473/ 443-7380,* FAX *473/443-8142,* WEB *www.caribbeeinn.com. 6 rooms, 3 suites. Dining room, no air-conditioning, beach, snorkeling, hiking, library, laundry service, airport shuttle, no kids. No credit cards. CP, EP, MAP.*

$ 🏠 **Ade's Dream Guest House.** Adjacent to the jetty in Hillsborough, this small guest house is a convenient place to rest your weary head after a day touring Carriacou, snorkeling at Sandy Island, or scuba diving at some of Grenada's best dive spots. Enjoy a good meal at Sea Wave, the owner's restaurant across the street; next day, fall out of bed at your leisure to catch the boat back. Or hey, stay longer! The accommodations (7 of the 23 rooms have shared baths) are simple, with queen-size or twin beds and writing table, but the view of the mountains, sea, neighboring islands, and all the harbor activity is great— and it's certainly priced right. ✉ *The Esplanade, Hillsborough,* ☎ *473/ 443-7317,* FAX *473/443-8435. 23 rooms.* WEB *grenadines.net/carriacou/ade.htm, Restaurant, grocery, fans, kitchenettes, beach, laundry facilities, car rental. AE, MC, V. BP.*

$ 🏠 **Silver Beach Resort.** Choose between a self-catering cottage, with sitting room and kitchenette, or an oceanfront double room at this laidback beachfront resort, a short walk from the jetty in Hillsborough. All quarters have a patio or balcony; most have an ocean view. You can arrange fishing or spearfishing excursions on the resort's 30-ft Chris-Craft. From the dock you can see Sandy Island, a deserted islet a stone's throw from shore, where you can picnic and snorkel. The open-air Shipwreck Restaurant serves hearty breakfasts and Caribbean and seafood dinners. Those who purchase MAP may dine around at other local restaurants. ✉ *Beausejour Bay, Hillsborough,* ☎ *473/443– 7337,* FAX *473/443–7165,* WEB *www.silverbeachhotel.com. 10 rooms, 6 cottages. Restaurant, bar, no air-conditioning, fans; kitchenettes, tennis court, dive shop, dock, snorkeling, windsurfing, boating, fishing, shops, laundry service, travel services, airport shuttle, car rental. AE, MC, V. CP, EP, MAP.*

Villa and Private-Home Rentals

For Grenada rental information contact **Villas of Grenada** (✉ Box 218, St. George's, ☎ 473/444–1896, FAX 473/444–4529, WEB www. grenadaexplorer.com/villa). In-season rates range from about $600 a week for a two-bedroom home with a pool to about $3,500 for a six-bedroom home on the beach.

For Carriacou rental information contact **Down Island Villa Rentals, Ltd.** (✉ Craigston, ☎ 473/443–8182, FAX 473/443–8290, WEB www. islandvillas.com). In-season rates range from about $50 per day for a small cottage or in-town apartment suitable for two people to $215 per day for a villa with panoramic views and a swimming pool that accommodates up to six people.

Dining

Grenada grows everything from lettuce and tomatoes to plantains, mangoes, papaya (called *pawpaw*), callaloo (similar to spinach), citrus, yams, christophenes (like squash), breadfruit—the list is endless. And all restaurants prepare dishes with local produce and season them with the many spices grown here. Be sure to try the local flavors of ice cream: mango, soursop, guava, rum raisin, coconut (the best), or nutmeg.

Soups—especially pumpkin and callaloo—are divine and often start a meal. Pepper pot is a savory stew of pork, oxtail, vegetables, and spices simmered for hours. Oildown, the national dish, is salted meat, breadfruit, onion, carrot, celery, dasheen (a root vegetable), and dumplings all boiled in coconut milk until the liquid is absorbed and the savory mixture becomes "oily."

Fresh seafood of all kinds, including lobster, is plentiful. Conch, known here as *lambi,* is popular and often appears curried or in a stew. Crab back, though, is not seafood—it's land crab. Most Grenadian restaurants serve seafood and at least some native dishes.

Rum punches are ubiquitous and always topped with grated nutmeg. Clarke's Court and Westerhall are locally produced and marketed rums. Carib, the local beer, is refreshing, light, and quite good.

What to Wear
Dining in Grenada is casual. Collared shirts and long pants for men (even the fanciest restaurants don't require jacket and tie) and sundresses or slacks for women are appropriate. Beachwear, of course, should be reserved for the beach.

CATEGORY	COST*
$$$$	over $30
$$$	$20–$30
$$	$10–$20
$	under $10

per person for a main course at dinner

Grenada
CAFÉS

$ ✕ **La Boulangerie.** This French bakery and coffee shop, convenient to the Grand Anse hotels, is a great place for breakfast or a light meal—to eat in, take out, or have delivered. You'll find croissants and other special breads and pastries, espresso, juices, baguette sandwiches, focaccia, roasted chicken, and homemade gelati. ⊠ *Le Marquis Complex, Grand Anse,* ☎ *473/444–1131. AE, MC, V.*

CARIBBEAN

$$ ✕ **Brown Sugar.** Tucked on a terrace overlooking Grand Anse, this popular restaurant has contemporized Grenadian recipes handed down over the generations. Thick, rich callaloo soup is a perfect starter, perhaps followed by fish fillet wrapped in callaloo leaves and steamed in coconut milk and local seasonings, oildown (the Grenadian national dish), Caribbean shrimp dredged in shredded coconut and deep-fried, creole chicken, or a simple steak—all accompanied by local vegetables and warm fresh-baked bread. Vegetarian choices and a children's menu are always available. Dining is accompanied by steel-pan music on Tuesday, Friday, and Sunday evenings. Complimentary transportation is provided. ⊠ *Main Rd., Grand Anse,* ☎ *473/444–2374. Reservations essential. AE, D, DC, MC, V.*

$$ ✕ **Coconut Beach, the French Creole Restaurant.** Take local seafood,
★ add butter, wine, and Grenadian spices, and you have excellent French creole cuisine. Throw in a beautiful location at the northern end of Grand Anse Beach, and this West Indian cottage becomes an even more delightful spot. Lobster is a specialty, perhaps wrapped in a crepe, dipped in garlic butter, or added to pasta. There are also the seafood platter, lambi Calypso, and T-bone steak. Homemade coconut pie is a winner for dessert. Wander down the beach and stop by for an alfresco lunch.

In season, there's a beach barbecue with live music Wednesday and Sunday nights. ⊠ *Grand Anse,* ☎ *473/444–4644. AE, D, MC, V. Closed Tues.*

$–$$ ✕ **The Nutmeg.** Fresh seafood, homemade West Indian dishes, great hamburgers, and the waterfront view make this a favorite with locals and visitors alike. It's upstairs on the Carenage (above Sea Change bookstore), with large open windows from which you can watch the harbor activity as you eat. Try the callaloo soup, curried lambi, lobster, shrimp—or just stop by for a rum punch and a roti, a fish sandwich and a Carib, or a hamburger and a Coke. ⊠ *The Carenage, St. George's,* ☎ *473/440–2539. AE, D, MC, V.*

CHINESE

$–$$ ✕ **Tropicana.** The chef-owner here hails from Trinidad and specializes in both Chinese and West Indian cuisine. Local businesspeople seem to be the best customers for the extensive menu of Chinese food, the tantalizing aroma of barbecued chicken notwithstanding. Eat in or take out—it's open from 7:30 AM until midnight. Tropicana is right at the Lagoon Road traffic circle, overlooking the marina. ⊠ *Lagoon Rd., St. George's,* ☎ *473/440–1586. AE, DC, MC, V.*

CONTEMPORARY

$$$ ✕ **La Belle Creole.** The marriage of Continental and West Indian ★ cuisines and a splendid view of distant St. George's are the hallmarks of this romantic hillside restaurant at the Blue Horizons Cottage Hotel. The always-changing five-course table d'hôte menu is based on original recipes of the owner's mother, a pioneer in incorporating local products into "foreign" cuisines. Try, for instance, Grenadian caviar (roe of the white sea urchin), cream of bread-nut soup, lobster-egg flan, or callaloo quiche, followed by lobster à la creole or ginger pork chops. The inspired cuisine, intimate dining room, and gracious service are impressive. ⊠ *Blue Horizons Cottage Hotel, Grand Anse,* ☎ *473/444–4316 or 473/444–4592. Reservations essential. AE, D, MC, V.*

$$–$$$ ✕ **Cicely's.** The small, open-air restaurant at the Calabash Hotel, ★ named for chef Cicely Roberts, is surrounded by palms, flowers, and twinkling lights. Cicely's culinary skills are complemented by those of Graham Newbould, former chef to the British royal family; the result is international cuisine with a Caribbean flair. The five-course table d'hôte dinner is a good bet; past menus have included chilled lobster mousse, cream of tannia (similar to potato) soup or christophene vichyssoise, followed by baked stuffed rainbow runner or charcoal-grilled pork fillet with piquant guava, garlic, and ginger sauce. Fresh-fruit sorbet or cheese and English biscuits top off your meal. ⊠ *Calabash Hotel, L'Anse aux Épines,* ☎ *473/444–4334. Reservations essential. AE, MC, V. No lunch.*

$$–$$$ ✕ **Oliver's Restaurant.** Diners tend to dress up for the five-course prix-fixe evening meal at the open-air, beachfront dining room of the Spice Island Beach Resort, where dozens of ceiling fans stir the sultry air. The menu combines international cuisine with local specialties. Roast beef or grilled pork are as likely to appear on the menu as, for instance, chicken stuffed with bread nuts or grapefruit consommé. You'll always find seafood and a vegetarian choice. On Friday nights, steel pan music accompanies dinner. ⊠ *Spice Island Beach Resort, Grand Anse,* ☎ *473/444–4258 or 473/444–4423. Reservations essential. AE, D, DC, MC, V.*

$$–$$$ ✕ **The Beach House.** At this restaurant, next door to the Laluna resort, a gleaming white-sand and sea view is the perfect backdrop for a salad or pasta luncheon on the deck. At dinner excellent steak and seafood, sashimi tuna, rack of lamb, blackened fish, or prime rib of beef—accompanied by a superb wine—give "beach party" new mean-

ing. A kids' menu is available, too. ✉ *Airport Rd., Point Salines,* ☎
473/444–4455. Reservations essential. AE, MC, V. Closed Sun.

ECLECTIC

$$–$$$ ✕ **Tout Bagay Restaurant & Bar.** Its name means "everything is possi-
ble," and the eclectic menu proves the point. At lunch, for example,
you might select a salad (lobster, shrimp, Caesar) or try a local specialty, such as a roti, flying fish sandwich, or creole-style fish. At dinner, the menu is equally broad—lobster Thermidor, cappellini with red
pepper pesto and shrimp, curry goat, or sweet and sour lambi. On the
water at the northern end of The Carenage, the view (day or night) is
spectacular. It's a popular lunch choice for businesspeople, as well as
those touring the capital or shopping on adjacent streets. ✉ *The Carenage, St. George's,* ☎ *473/440–3000. AE, DC, MC, V.*

$$ ✕ **Rudolf's.** This busy, English-style waterfront pub offers West Indian
fare, as well as fish-and-chips, sandwiches, and burgers. Skip the at-
tempts at haute cuisine and enjoy the crab back, lambi, steak, and
delectable nutmeg ice cream. The rum punches are lethal—even for
Grenada. Rudolf's is a popular luncheon spot for local businesspeo-
ple, as well as visitors. On the canopied terrace, patrons enjoy alfresco
drinks or meals with a full view of the harbor. ✉ *The Carenage, St.
George's,* ☎ *473/440–2241. MC, V. Closed Sun.*

$–$$ ✕ **The Boatyard.** As its name implies, boaters frequent this lively
restaurant and its Tiki Bar, located at the Spice Island Marina. Burg-
ers, fish-and-chips, and deep-fried shrimp are served at lunchtime. At
dinner you can order charcoal-grilled club steaks, lobster, and meat or
seafood brochettes. The menu always includes pasta, a vegetarian
plate, West Indian dishes—and even some Mexican snacks. In season
there's music and dancing on weekend nights. For quieter nights,
there's a book-exchange library. ✉ *L'Anse aux Épines,* ☎ *473/444–
4662. MC, V.*

FAST FOOD

$ ✕ **Fish 'n' Chick.** All day and most of the night, this fast-food restau-
rant serves up snacks, sandwiches, burgers, salads, rotis, stewed or curried lambi—and, of course, fish or chicken (barbecued, baked, or jerk)
and chips. Local folks and visitors alike drop by during the day for a
bite to eat in or take away; after dancing and mingling next door at
the Sugar Mill nightclub, it's a popular place for a midnight snack. ✉
Old Sugar Mill, Grand Anse, ☎ *473/444–4132. No credit cards.*

ITALIAN

$$$ ✕ **La Dolce Vita.** Hidden away at the southern end of Grand Anse Beach,
★ overlooking the sea and the twinkling lights of St. George's in the dis-
tance, this is *the* place to come for fine dining and delicious Italian cui-
sine. The chef is noted for his homemade pasta, prepared fresh daily.
Start with a selection of cold and hot antipasti, then try lobster spaghetti,
gnocchi, or fresh seafood. The restaurant is at the bottom of the 100-
step beach access at the Flamboyant Hotel. ✉ *Grand Anse Beach,* ☎
*473/444–3456. Reservations essential. D, MC, V. No lunch. Closed
Mon.*

SEAFOOD

$$–$$$$ ✕ **The Red Crab.** Locals and expats love to gather at this pub, especially on Saturday night. The curried lambi and garlic shrimp keep the
regulars coming back. Seafood, particularly lobster, and steak (imported
from the U.S.) are staples of the menu; hot garlic bread comes with all
orders. Eat inside or under the stars, and enjoy live music Monday and
Friday in season. ✉ *L'Anse aux Épines, near the Calabash,* ☎ *473/
444–4424. Reservations essential. AE, MC, V. Closed Sun.*

$–$$ ✕ **Aquarium Beach Club and Restaurant.** The beach club rents ocean kayaks and snorkeling equipment. When you come up for air, enjoy fresh seafood or luncheon salads and a cool drink at the restaurant. On Friday, happy hour at the Bamboo Bar is from 4:30 to 6:30; then dinner is served. Besides fresh fish and lobster, the menu might include callaloo cannelloni or pepper steak. Saturday is volleyball day, and on Sunday there's a lobster barbecue. It's a very congenial spot. ⊠ *La-Source Rd., Point Salines,* ☎ *473/444–1410. Reservations essential. AE, D, DC, MC, V. Closed Mon.*

$–$$ ✕ **La Sagesse.** The perfect spot to soothe a frazzled soul, La Sagesse resort's open-air, mostly seafood restaurant and beach bar is on a se-cluded cove in a nature preserve about 30 minutes from Grand Anse. You can combine your lunch or dinner with a hike or a day at the beach. Select from sandwiches, salads, or lobster for lunch. Lambi, smoked marlin, dolphinfish, and tuna steak may be joined on the dinner menu by chicken française and a daily vegetarian special. Wash down your meal with a cold beer or a fresh-fruit smoothie. Transportation is available. ⊠ *La Sagesse Nature Center, St. David's,* ☎ *473/444–6458. Reservations essential. AE, MC, V.*

Carriacou

CARIBBEAN

$–$$ ✕ **Callaloo by the Sea Restaurant & Bar.** On the main road, south of town, diners enjoy extraordinary views of Sandy Island and Hillsbor-ough Bay. The emphasis is on West Indian dishes and excellent seafood, including lobster thermidor. The callaloo soup, of course, is out-standing. Don't miss it! ⊠ *Hillsborough,* ☎ *473/443–8004. AE, MC, V. Closed Sept.*

SEAFOOD

$ ✕ **Scraper's.** Scraper's serves up lobster, conch, and the fresh catch of the day. It's a simple spot seasoned with occasional calypsonian ser-enades (by owner Steven Gay "Scraper," who's a pro). Order a rum punch and just enjoy yourself. ⊠ *Tyrrel Bay,* ☎ *473/443–7403. AE, D, MC, V.*

Beaches

Grenada

Grenada has some 80 mi (130 km) of coastline, 65 bays, and 45 white-sand (and a few black-sand) beaches—many in little coves. The best beaches face the Caribbean, south of St. George's, where the resorts are also clustered.

Bathway Beach. A beautiful strip of sand with a natural reef that pro-tects swimmers from the rough Atlantic surf on Grenada's north shore, this Levera National Park beach has changing rooms at the park head-quarters.

Grand Anse Beach. In the southwest, about 3 mi (5 km) south of St. George's is Grenada's loveliest and most popular beach. It's a gleam-ing 2-mi (3-km) semicircle of white sand, lapped by clear, gentle surf. Seagrape trees and coconut palms provide shady escapes from the sun. Brilliant rainbows frequently spill into the sea from the high green moun-tains that frame St. George's Harbour to the north. The Grand Anse Craft & Spice Market is at the midpoint of the beach.

La Sagesse Beach. Along the southeast coast, at La Sagesse Nature Cen-ter, is this lovely, quiet refuge with a strip of powdery white sand. Plan a full day of nature walks, with lunch at the small inn adjacent to the beach.

Levera Beach. This beach in Levera National Park at the north end of the island is pretty and remote but too rough for more than wading (note that it's closed from April to June, when turtle eggs are hatching).
Morne Rouge Beach. Just 1 mi (1½ km) south of Grand Anse Bay, this ½-mi-long (¾-km-long) crescent has a gentle surf that is excellent for swimming. Light meals are available nearby.
Pink Gin Beach. This beach is at Point Salines, near the airport.

Carriacou

Anse La Roche. Like all the beaches on Carriacou, this one—about a 15-minute hike from the village of Prospect, in the north—has pure white sand, sparkling clear water, and abundant marine life for snorkelers. It's never crowded here.
Hillsborough. Day-trippers can take a dip at this beach adjacent to the jetty. The beach stretches for quite a distance in each direction, so there is plenty of room to swim without interference from the boat traffic.
Paradise Beach. This long, narrow stretch of sand between Hillsborough and Tyrrel Bay has calm, clear, inviting water, but there are no changing facilities.
Sandy Island. This is a truly deserted island off Hillsborough—just a strip of white sand, with a few palm trees, surrounded by a reef and crystal-clear waters. Anyone hanging around the jetty with a motorboat will provide transportation for a few dollars.
Tyrrel Bay. This swath of sand follows the coastline. But beware the manchineel trees here; they drop poisonous green "apples," and their foliage can burn your skin.

Outdoor Activities and Sports

BOATING AND SAILING

As the "Gateway to the Grenadines," Grenada attracts significant numbers of seasoned sailors to its waters. Large marinas are in the lagoon area of St. George's, at Prickly Bay on Grenada's south coast, and at Tyrrel Bay in Carriacou. You can charter a yacht, with or without crew, for weeklong sailing vacations through the Grenadines or along the coast of Venezuela. Scenic half- or full-day sails along Grenada's coast cost $30–$60 per person (with a minimum of four passengers), including lunch or snacks and open bar; a full-day cruise from Grenada to Carriacou may cost $350–$700, depending on the boat, for one to six people.

On Grenada: **Carib Cats** (☎ 473/444–3222) departs from the Tropicana jetty in the lagoon area of St. George's for either a full-day sail along the southwest coast, a half-day snorkel cruise to Molinière Bay, or a two-hour sunset cruise along the west coast. **Footloose Yacht Charters** (☎ 473/440–7949) has both sailing or motoring yachts available for day trips around Grenada or longer charters to the Grenadines. **Horizon Yacht Charters** (☎ 473/443–8783), at True Blue Bay Resort, will arrange bareboat or crewed charters, as well as day sails or three-day trips to the Grenadines. **Island Dreams** (☎ 473/443–3603) has a 45-ft sailing yacht available for private half- or full-day charters for up to 10 passengers or overnight sails around Grenada or to the Grenadines for two people. **Moorings "Club Mariner" Watersports Center** (☎ 473/444–4439 or 473/444–4549), at the Secret Harbour Resort, in L'Anse aux Épines, has half- and full-day skippered charters, rental sailboats, and a several sailing programs for beginning and experienced sailors. **Starwind Enterprise** (☎ 473/440–3678) offers day, half-day, and sunset sailing trips along Grenada's southwest coast aboard *Starwind II*, a 43-ft sailing yacht, or the 42-ft catamaran *Starwind III*. **Tradewind Yacht Charters** (☎ 473/444–4924), at the Spice Island Marina on

Prickly Bay, rents sailing or power yachts, with or without crew, by the day or week.

On Carriacou: **Carriacou Yacht Charters** (☎ 473/443–8599) has a 76-ft ketch, *Suvetar,* which cruises the Grenadines on either long- or short-term charters or for day trips.

CYCLING

Level ground is rare in Grenada, but that doesn't stop the aerobically primed. Roads are narrow and winding, however, and sharing lanes with fast-moving vehicles can be hazardous. You can rent bikes at **Ride Grenada** (✉ L'Anse aux Épines, ☎ 473/444–1157).

FISHING

Deep-sea fishing around Grenada is excellent, with marlin, sailfish, yellowfin tuna, and dolphin topping the list of good catches. You can arrange half- or full-day sportfishing trips for $250–$500, depending on the type of boat, number of people, and length of trip. **Bezo Charters** (☎ 473/443–5477 or 473/443–5021) has a tournament-equipped Bertram 31 Flybridge Sport Fisherman, called *Bezo,* with air-conditioned cabin, fighting chair, and an experienced crew just waiting to take you blue-water fishing. Charters can be customized; equipment and beverages are included. **Evans Fishing Charters** (☎ 473/444–4422 or 473/444–4217) has a Bertram 35 Sport Fisherman, *Xiphias Seeker,* with an air-conditioned cabin; equipment includes Penn International and Shimano reels. **True Blue Sportfishing** (☎ 473/444–2048) offers big-game charters on its "purpose-built" 31-ft Sport Fisherman, *Yes Aye.* It has an enclosed cabin, fighting chair, and professional tackle. Refreshments and courtesy transport are included.

GOLF

Determined golfers might want to try the 9-hole course at the **Grenada Golf and Country Club** (☎ 473/444–4128), about halfway between St. George's and Grand Anse. Greens fees are EC$7, and club rental is available; your hotel can make arrangements for you. It's the only truly public course on the island. **Grenada Grand Beach Resort** (☎ 473/444–4371) in Grand Anse has a 9-hole, par-3 course. **LaSOURCE** (☎ 473/444–2556), in Point Salines, has a 9-hole, par-3 course.

HIKING

Mountain trails wind through **Grand Étang National Park and Forest Preserve** (☎ 473/440–6160); if you're lucky, you may spot a Mona monkey or some exotic birds on your hike. There are trails for all levels—from a self-guided nature trail around Grand Étang Lake to a demanding one through the bush to the peak of Mount Qua Qua (2,373 ft [724 m]) or a real trek up Mount St. Catherine (2,757 ft [841 m]). Long pants and hiking shoes are recommended. The cost is $25 per person for a four-hour guided hike up Mount Qua Qua, $20 each for two or more, or $15 each for three or more; the Mount St. Catherine hike starts at $35 per person. **EcoTrek** (☎ 473/444–7777) takes small groups on day-trips to the heart of the rain forest, where you'll find hidden waterfalls and hot spring pools. **Henry's Safari Tours** (☎ 473/444–5313) offers hiking excursions through rich agricultural land and rain forest to Upper Concord Falls and other fascinating locations. **Telfor Bedeau, Hiking Guide** (☎ 473/442–6200) is a Grenadian treasure. Over the years, he has walked up, down, or across nearly every mountain, trail, and pathway on the island. His experience and knowledge make him an excellent guide, whether it's an easy walk with novices or the most strenuous hike with experts.

RUNNING

At 4 PM on alternate Saturdays throughout the year, **Hash House Harriers** (☎ 473/440–3343) welcomes not-so-serious runners and walkers to join them for exercise and fun in the countryside.

SCUBA DIVING AND SNORKELING

You can see hundreds of varieties of fish and more than 40 species of coral at more than a dozen sites off Grenada's southwest coast, only 15 to 20 minutes by boat, and another couple of dozen sites around Carriacou's reefs and neighboring islets.

Off Grenada: A spectacular dive is *Bianca C,* a 600-ft cruise ship that caught fire in 1961, sank to 100 ft (30½ m), and is now encrusted with coral and a habitat for giant turtles, spotted eagle rays, barracuda, and jacks. **Boss Reef** extends 5 mi (8 km) from St. George's Harbour to Point Salines, with a depth ranging from 20 to 90 ft (6 to 27½ m). **Flamingo Bay** has a wall that drops to 90 ft (27½ m) and is teeming with fish, sponges, seahorses, sea fans, and coral. **Molinère Reef** slopes from about 20 ft (6 m) below the surface to a wall that drops to 65 ft (20 m). It's a good dive for beginners, and advanced divers can continue farther out to view the wreck of the *Buccaneer,* a 42-ft sloop.

Off Carriacou: **Kick-em Jenny** is an active underwater volcano, with plentiful coral and marine life and visibility up to 100 ft (31 m). **Sandy Island,** in Hillsborough Bay, is especially good for night diving and has fish that feed off its extensive reefs 70 ft (21 m) deep. For experienced divers, **Twin Sisters of Isle de Rhonde** is one of the most spectacular dives in the Grenadines, with walls and drop-offs of up to 185 ft (56½ m) and an underwater cave.

Most dive operators take snorkelers along on dive trips or have special snorkeling adventures. The best snorkeling in Grenada is at Molinère Point, north of St. George's; in Carriacou, Sandy Island is magnificent and just a few hundred yards offshore.

The PADI-certified dive operators listed below offer scuba and snorkeling trips to reefs and wrecks, including night dives and special excursions to the *Bianca C.* They also offer resort courses for beginning divers and certification instruction for more experienced divers. It costs about $40–$45 for a one-tank dive, $70–$75 for a two-tank dive, $50 for *Bianca C,* $75–$80 to dive Isle De Rhonde, and $50–$55 for night dives. Discounted 5- and 10-dive packages are also offered. Resort courses cost about $70, lifetime open-water certification about $350, and snorkeling trips about $15.

Aquanauts Grenada (✉ Rendezvous Hotel, L'Anse aux Épines, ☎ 473/444–1126) has a multilingual staff, so instruction is available in English, German, Dutch, French, and Spanish. Two-tank dive trips, accommodating no more than eight divers, are offered each morning to both the Caribbean and Atlantic sides of Grenada. **Dive Grenada** (✉ Allamanda Beach Resort, Grand Anse, ☎ 473/444–1092) offers dive trips twice daily (at 10 AM and 2 PM), specializing in diving the *Bianca C.* **EcoDive** (✉ Coyaba Beach Resort, Grand Anse, ☎ 473/444–7777) offers two dive trips daily, both drift and wreck dives, as well as weekly day trips to dive Isle de Rhonde. The company also runs Grenada's marine conservation and education center that conducts coral-reef monitoring and turtle projects. **EcoDive True Blue** (✉ True Blue Bay Resort, True Blue, ☎ 473/444–2133) offers trips to Atlantic sites. **Sanvics Scuba** (✉ Grenada Grand Beach Resort, Grand Anse, ☎ 473/444–4753) offers daily one- and two-tank dive trips to coral reefs, walls, and wreck sites. **Scuba World** (✉ Rex Grenadian Resort, Point Salines, ☎ 473/444–3684) offers daily trips to the *Bianca C.* **Spice Island Div-**

ing (✉ Spice Island Beach Resort, Grand Anse, ☎ 473/444–3483) offers single- and two-tank dives to reefs and wrecks, the *Bianca C.*, night dives, and two-tank dives to Isle de Rhonde.

Arawak Divers (✉ Tyrrel Bay, Carriacou, ☎ 473/443–6906) has its own jetty at Tyrrel Bay; it takes small groups on daily dive trips and night dives, offers courses in German and English, and provides pick-up service from yachts. **Carriacou Silver Diving** (✉ Main St., Hillsborough, Carriacou, ☎ 473/443–7882) accommodates up to 12 divers on one of its dive boats and up to six on another. The center operates two guided single-tank dives daily, as well as individually scheduled excursions. **Tanki's Watersport Paradise Ltd.** (✉ Paradise Beach, Carriacou, ☎ 473/443–8406) offers dive trips to nearby reefs and snorkeling trips to Sandy Island.

TENNIS

Those staying at a hotel without tennis on-site may play on the unattended, first come–first "serve" public courts in Grand Anse and in Tanteen, St. George's.

Shopping

The best souvenirs of Grenada are little spice baskets filled with cinnamon, nutmeg, mace, bay leaves, cloves, turmeric, and ginger. You can buy them for as little as $2 in practically every shop, at the open-air produce market at Market Square in St. George's, at the vendor stalls near the pier, and at the Craft & Spice Market on Grand Anse Beach. Vendors also sell inexpensive handmade fabric dolls, coral jewelry, seashells, and hats and baskets handwoven from green palm fronds. Bargaining is not appropriate in the shops, and it isn't customary with vendors—although most will offer you "a good price."

Areas and Malls

In St. George's, vendor stalls and gift shops along **The Carenage** are particularly convenient for cruise-ship passengers. On the north side of the harbor, **Young Street** is a main shopping thoroughfare; it rises steeply from the Carenage, then descends just as steeply to the market area.

In Grand Anse, a short walk from the resorts, the **Excel Mall** has numerous shops and services to interest locals and tourists alike. **Grand Anse Shopping Centre** offers a supermarket-liquor store, a clothing store, a bank, a fast-food restaurant, a pharmacy, an art gallery, and several small gift shops. **Le Marquis Complex,** diagonally across the street, has restaurants, shops, an art gallery, and tourist services. **Spiceland Mall** has a modern supermarket (with a liquor section), clothing and shoe boutiques for men and women, housewares, a wine shop, gift shops, a food court, bank, and a video-game arcade.

Specialty Items

DUTY-FREE GOODS

Duty-free shops at the airport sell liquor at impressive discounts of up to 50%, as well as perfumes, gifts, and crafts. You can shop duty free at some shops in town, but you must show your passport and outbound ticket to benefit from the duty-free prices. **Colombian Emeralds** has a large selection of fine jewelry, watches, and gift items at its two shops (The Carenage, St. George's, ☎ 473/440–1746; ✉ Point Salines International Airport, ☎ 473/444–1047). **The Gift Shop** sells crystal, china, watches, and leather goods at its shop at the Grand Anse Shopping Centre (☎ 473/444–4408). **Gitten's** carries perfume and cosmetics at its three shops (✉ The Carenage, St. George's, ☎ 473/440–3174;

✉ Spiceland Mall, ☎ 473/439–0860; ✉ Point Salines International Airport, ☎ 473/444–2549).

FOODSTUFFS

Marketing & National Importing Board (✉ Young St., St. George's, ☎ 473/440–1791) stocks fresh fruits and vegetables, spices, hot sauces, and local syrups and jams at lower prices than you'll find in gift shops. **Market Square** (✉ foot of Young St., St. George's) is a bustling, open-air produce market that's open mornings; Saturday is the best—and busiest—time to stock up on fresh fruit to enjoy during your stay and spices to take home. Crafts, leather goods, and decorative items are also for sale.

GIFTS

Arawak Islands (✉ Upper Belmont Rd., St. George's, ☎ 473/444–3577) blends island perfumes, colognes, body oils, soaps, and herbal teas—all packaged for gift-giving. The workshop is on-site. **Figleaf** (✉ The Carenage, St. George's, ☎ 473/440–9771) is a small gift shop where you'll find an interesting selection of Caribbean arts and crafts, aromatherapy and herbal bath products, and resort wear. **Gifts Remembered** (✉ Cross St., St. George's, ☎ 473/440–2482; ✉ Coyaba Beach Resort, Grand Anse, ☎ 473/444–4129) is crammed with wonderful, inexpensive things, including hammocks, scrimshaw, wood carvings, beachwear, sundries, and hand-painted masks made from calabashes. **Pssst Boutique** (✉ Spiceland Mall, Grand Anse, ☎ 473/443–8783) will catch your eye; it's chock full of unusual costume jewelry, colorful island clothing, and fascinating gift items for the home.

HANDICRAFTS

Art Fabrik (✉ 9 Young St., St. George's, ☎ 473/440–0568) is a studio where you can watch artisans create batik before turning it into clothing or accessories. In the shop you'll find fabric by the yard or fashioned into dresses, shirts, shorts, hats, and scarves. The **Grand Anse Craft & Spice Market** (✉ Grand Anse, ☎ 473/444–3780), managed by the Grenada Board of Tourism, is between the main road and the beach. The facility has 82 booths for vendors who sell arts, crafts, spices, music tapes, clothing, produce, and refreshments. It's open daily 7–7. **La Sagesse Arts & Crafts Market** (✉ La Sagesse Natural Works, St. David's, ☎ 473/443–1695), in an 18th-century sugar factory, is a showcase for Grenadian arts and craftspeople to display and sell their work. **Imagine** (✉ Grand Anse Shopping Centre, Grand Anse, ☎ 473/444–4028) specializes in island handicrafts, including straw work, ceramics, island fashions, and batik fabrics. **Tikal** (✉ Young St., St. George's, ☎ 473/440–2310) is known for its exquisite baskets, artwork, jewelry, batik items, and fashions, both locally made and imported from Africa and Latin America.

RECORDS

Turbo Charge Records & Tapes (✉ St. John's St., St. George's, ☎ 473/440–0586) is the place to buy the latest reggae, calypso, soca, and steel-band music.

Nightlife and the Arts

Nightlife

Grenada's nightlife is centered on the resort hotels and a handful of nightspots in the Grand Anse area. During the winter season many hotels have a steel band or other local entertainment several nights a week.

BARS

Boatyard (✉ L'Anse aux Épines, ☎ 473/444–4662), at the Spice Island Marina, is the place to be on Friday from 11 PM 'til sunup, when there's a steel band and international discs are spun by a smooth-talkin' local DJ; on Saturday, there's dancing to live band music. **Casablanca** (⌧ Grand Anse, ☎ 473/444–1631) is a sports bar, upstairs above the banks, where you can play chess, cards, dominoes, darts, pool, or snooker, and watch games on a big-screen TV while having a drink and a snack; Monday to Saturday, from 5 PM to 3 AM, you can listen and dance to a DJ or live music. **Castaways** (⌧ L'Anse aux Épines, ☎ 473/444–1250) is a friendly spot, with a DJ and dancing most nights, live music on Friday and Saturday in season, and snacks and meals served indoors or out, if you wish.

DANCE CLUBS
Dynamite Disco (⌧ The Limes, Grand Anse, ☎ 473/444–4056) has a party every weekend, with disco, reggae, and calypso music. **Fantazia** (⌧ Morne Rouge, ☎ 473/444–2288) is a popular nightspot; disco, soca, reggae, and international pop music are played from 9:30 PM until the wee hours on Thursday, Friday, and Saturday nights. Wednesday is oldies night, and Friday night is a Cultural Cabaret designed to give visitors a taste of local folklore and traditional dances. There's a small cover charge of EC$10–EC$20 on weekends. **Le Sucrier** (⌧ Grand Anse Roundabout, Grand Anse, ☎ 473/444–1068) is lively Wednesday–Saturday 9:30 PM–3 AM. Wednesday is oldies night, there's live jazz on Thursday, and a mostly young crowd gathers for dancing on Friday and Saturday.

THÈME NIGHTS
Rhum Runner (⌧ The Carenage, St. George's, ☎ 473/440–4386), a 60-ft twin-deck catamaran, leaves from the Carenage at 7:30 PM each Friday and Saturday for a moonlight cruise in the waters around St. George's and Grand Anse, returning about midnight. Tickets are $8 (EC$20), and reservations are recommended. On Wednesday from 6 to 9 there's a sunset dinner cruise for $40 (EC$107) per person; reservations must be made by 4:30 the day before. *Rhum Runner II*, a 72-ft sister ship, operates monthly moonlight cruises the Friday and Saturday nights nearest the full moon for $11 (EC$30) per person— add $3 (EC$6) for a barbecue dinner.

The Arts
GALLERIES
Art Grenada (⌧ Suite 7, Grand Anse Shopping Centre, Grand Anse, ☎ 473/444–2317) displays and sells works exclusively by Grenadian artists. Exhibitions change monthly, and you can have your purchases shipped. At **United Artists Art Gallery** (⌧ No. 15, Le Marquis Complex, Grand Anse, ☎ 473/444–5022), you'll find wood and stone carvings, painted masks, paintings, furniture, and other objets d'art created by artists from Grenada, Carriacou, and Petite Martinique. **Yellow Poui Art Gallery** (⌧ Cross St., St. George's, ☎ 473/440–3001) displays and sells original paintings, sculpture, photography, lithographs, and antique engravings by artists from Grenada and elsewhere in the Caribbean.

ISLAND CULTURE
Marryshow Folk Theatre (⌧ Herbert Blaize St., St. George's, ☎ 473/440–2451) presents concerts, plays, and special cultural events. Call for a schedule.

Exploring Grenada

Numbers in the margin correspond to points of interest on the Grenada (and Carriacou) map.

Grenada

It may be hard to pull yourself away from the beach, but a day or more of exploring is time well spent: the scenery is stunning, and the scent of nutmeg fills the air. St. George's has a busy harbor, interesting shops, and several historic sites. Visit a spice plantation and a nutmeg processing plant, or if you're adventurous, take guided hikes into the rain forest, up a mountainside, or to hidden waterfalls.

SIGHTS TO SEE

⑤ Annandale Falls. A mountain stream cascades 40 ft into a pool surrounded by exotic vines, such as liana and elephant ears. This is a lovely, cool spot for swimming and picnicking. ⊠ *Main interior road, 15 mins northeast of St. George's,* ☎ *473/440–2452.* ☜ *$1.* ⊙ *Daily 9–5.*

③ Bay Gardens. Fifteen minutes from St. George's, on what was once a sugar plantation, some 450 species of flowers and plants have been cultivated in patterns mimicking their growth in the wild. Eight acres of paths are open to visitors. ⊠ *Morne Delice, St. Paul's,* ☎ *473/440–5291.* ☜ *$1.* ⊙ *Daily 7–6.*

⑪ Carib's Leap. At Sauteurs (the French word for "leapers"), on the island's northernmost tip, Carib's Leap (or Leapers Hill) is the 100-ft vertical cliff from which the last of the indigenous Carib Indians flung themselves into the sea in 1651. After losing several bloody battles with European colonists, they chose to exterminate their race rather than surrender to the French. A commemorative display recounts the historical event.

⑦ Concord Falls. About 8 mi (13 km) north of St. George's, a turnoff from the west coast road leads to Concord Falls—actually three separate waterfalls. The first is at the end of the road; during the dry months (January–May) when the currents aren't too strong, you can take a dip under the cascade. Reaching the two other waterfalls requires an hour's hike into the forest reserve. The third and most spectacular waterfall, at Fountainbleu, thunders 65 ft over huge boulders and creates a small pool where you can cool off before hiking back down the trail. It's smart to hire a guide. The path is clear, but slippery boulders toward the end can be treacherous without assistance. ⊠ *West Coast Rd.* ☜ *$1 for changing room.*

☙ ⑧ Dougaldston Spice Estate. Just south of Gouyave, this historic plantation, now primarily a living museum, still grows and processes spices the old-fashioned way. You can see cocoa, nutmeg, mace, cloves, and other spices laid out on giant racks to dry in the sun. A worker will be glad to explain the process (and will appreciate a small donation). You can buy spices for about $2 a bag. ⊠ *Gouyave,* ☎ *no phone.* ☜ *$1.* ⊙ *Weekdays 9–4.*

☙ ⑨ Gouyave Nutmeg Processing Cooperative, in the center of the west-coast fishing village of Gouyave (pronounced *gwahve*), is a fragrant, fascinating way to spend a half-hour. Workers in the three-story plant, which turns out 3 million pounds per year of Grenada's most famous export, sort nutmegs by hand and pack them in burlap bags for shipping worldwide. ⊠ *Gouyave,* ☎ *473/444–8337.* ☜ *$1.* ⊙ *Weekdays 10–1 and 2–4.*

② Grand Anse. A residential and commercial area about 5 mi (8 km) south of downtown St. George's, Grand Anse is named for the world-renowned beach it surrounds. Most of Grenada's tourist facilities—resorts, restaurants, some shopping, and most nightlife—are in this general area. **Grand Anse Beach** is a 2-mi (3-km) crescent of sand, shaded by coconut palms and seagrape trees, with gentle turquoise surf. A handful of resort hotels line the beachfront, and there's a public entrance at Camerhogne Park, just a few steps from the main road. **St. George's University**, which for years held classes at its enviable beachfront location in Grand Anse, has a sprawling campus in True Blue, a nearby residential community. The university's Grand Anse property, from which the evacuation of U.S. medical students was a high priority of U.S. forces during the 1983 intervention, is currently used only for administrative purposes.

👋 **6** **Grand Étang National Park and Forest Reserve.** Deep in the interior of lush, mountainous Grenada is a bird sanctuary and forest reserve, with miles of hiking trails, lookouts, and fishing streams. **Grand Étang Lake** is a 36-acre expanse of cobalt-blue water that fills the crater of an extinct volcano 1,740 ft (530 m) above sea level. Although legend has it the lake is bottomless, maximum soundings are recorded at 18 ft (5½ m). The informative **Grand Étang Forest Center** has displays on the local wildlife and vegetation. A forest manager is on hand to answer questions. A small snack bar and souvenir stands are nearby. ⊠ *Main interior road, between Grenville and St. George's,* ☎ *473/440–6160.* 🎟 *$1.* ⊙ *Daily 8:30–4.*

👋 **15** **Grenville Cooperative Nutmeg Association** is open to the public for guided tours. You can see and learn about the entire process of receiving, drying, sorting, and packing nutmegs. ⊠ *Grenville,* ☎ *473/442–7241.* 🎟 *$1.* ⊙ *Weekdays 10–1 and 2–4.*

👋 **4** **Laura Herb and Spice Garden.** The 6½-acre gardens are part of an old plantation in the village of Laura, in St. David's, just 6 mi (10 km) east of Grand Anse. On the 45-minute tour, you'll learn all about Grenada's indigenous spices and herbs, including cocoa, clove, nutmeg, pimiento, cinnamon, turmeric, and tonka beans (vanilla). ⊠ *St. David's,* ☎ *473/443–2604.* 🎟 *$2.* ⊙ *Weekdays 8–4.*

12 **Levera National Park and Bird Sanctuary.** This portion of Grenada's protected parkland encompasses 450 acres at the northeastern tip of the island, where the Caribbean Sea meets the Atlantic Ocean. Facilities include a visitor center, changing rooms, a small amphitheater, and a gift shop. A natural reef protects swimmers from the rough Atlantic surf at Bathway Beach. Thick mangroves provide food and protection for nesting seabirds and seldom-seen parrots. Some fine Arawak ruins and petroglyphs are on display, and the first islets of the Grenadines are visible from the beach. Admittance and use of the beaches and grounds are free; there's a small charge to view the displays in the visitor center. ⊠ *Levera,* ☎ *473/442–1018.* 🎟 *$1.* ⊙ *Daily 8:30–4.*

10 **Mt. Rodney Estate.** When touring northern Grenada, plan to have lunch in Sauteurs. A road winds up a mountainside to an 1880s plantation house, lovingly restored by Lin and Norris Nelson. Sugar, coffee, and cocoa grew on the plantation in its heyday, and the fabulous views north to the Grenadines remain. Buffet luncheon is served from noon to 2 on the dining terrace. (This lunch stop is often included on a guided island tour; or call 473/442–9420 for reservations.) ⊠ *Sauteurs.*

14 **Pearl's Airport.** Just north of Grenville, on the east coast, is the island's original airport, which was replaced in 1984 by Point Salines International Airport. Deteriorating Cuban and Soviet planes sit at the end of the old runway, abandoned after the 1983 intervention, when Cuban "advisors" helping to construct the airport at Point Salines were summarily removed from the island. There's a good view north to the Grenadines and a small beach nearby. ⊠ *Grenville.*

⑬ **River Antoine Rum Distillery.** At this rustic operation, kept open primarily as a museum, Rivers rum is produced by the same methods used since the distillery opened in 1785. The process begins with the crushing of sugarcane from adjacent fields in the River Antoine (pronounced an-*twine*) Estate. The result is a potent overproof rum that will knock your socks off. ✉ *River Antoine Estate, St. Patrick's,* ☎ *473/442–7109.* 📷 *$1.* ⊘ *Guided tours daily 9–4.*

❶ **St. George's.** Grenada's capital is a busy West Indian city, most of which remains unchanged from colonial days. Narrow streets lined with shops wind up, down, and across steep hills. Pastel-painted warehouses with roofs covered in orange tiles (brought over from Europe as ballast in 18th-century ships) cling to the waterfront. Small rainbow-hue houses rise from the waterfront and disappear into steep green hills.

St. George's Harbour is the center of town. Schooners, ferries, and tour boats tie up along the seawall or at the small dinghy dock. Cruise ships dock at the large pier at the harbor entrance or anchor just outside and transport passengers ashore by tender. On weekends, a tall ship is likely to be anchored in the middle of the harbor, giving the scene a 19th-century appearance. **The Carenage** (pronounced car-a-*nahzh*), which surrounds horseshoe-shape St. George's Harbour, is the capital's main thoroughfare. Warehouses, shops, and restaurants line the waterfront. Near the cruise-ship welcome center, at the south end of The Carenage, the Grenada Board of Tourism has its offices, and you can buy inexpensive spices and crafts at vendor stalls nearby. At the center of The Carenage, on the pedestrian plaza, sits the ***Christ of the Deep*** statue. It was presented to Grenada by Costa Cruise Line in remembrance of its ship *Bianca C,* which burned and sank in the harbor in 1961 and

۞ is now a favorite dive site. The **Grenada National Museum,** a block from The Carenage, is set in the foundation of a French army barracks and prison that was built in 1704. The small museum has exhibitions of news items, photos, and proclamations regarding the 1983 intervention, along with Empress Josephine's childhood bathtub and other memorabilia from earlier historical periods. ✉ *Young and Monckton Sts.,* ☎ *473/440–3725.* 📷 *$1.* ⊘ *Weekdays 9–4:30, Sat. 10–1.* An engineering feat for its time, the 340-ft-long (103-m-long) **Sendall Tunnel** was built in 1895 and named for an early governor. It separates the harborside of St. George's from the Esplanade on the bay side of town, where you'll find the open-air meat, fish, and produce markets. The Esplanade is also the terminus of the minibus route. Don't miss picturesque **Market Square,** a block from The Esplanade at Granby Street. It's open every weekday morning but really comes alive on Saturday from 8 to noon. Vendors sell baskets, spices, brooms, clothing, knickknacks, coconut water, and heaps of fresh produce. Market Square is historically where parades and political rallies take place—and the beginning of the minibus routes to all areas of the island. **St. Andrew's Presbyterian Church,** built in 1830, is at the intersection of Halifax and Church streets. Also known as Scots' Kirk, it was constructed with the help of the Freemasons. Built in 1825, the beautiful stone and pink stucco **St. George's Anglican Church,** on Church Street, is filled with statues and plaques depicting Grenada in the 18th and 19th centuries. **St. George's Methodist Church,** on Green Street near Herbert Blaize Street, was built in 1820 and is the oldest original church in the city. The Gothic tower of **St. George's Roman Catholic Church** dates from 1818, but the current structure was built in 1884; the tower is the city's most visible landmark. On Church Street, **York House** (1801) is home to Grenada's Houses of Parliament and Supreme Court. It, the neighboring

Registry Building (1780), and Government House (1802) are fine examples of early Georgian architecture.

Ⓢ **Ft. George** is high on the hill at the southern tip of Church Street. The fort, which rises above the entrance to St. George's Harbour, is Grenada's oldest—built by the French in 1705 to protect the harbor. No shots were fired here until October 1983, when Prime Minister Bishop and some of his followers were assassinated in the courtyard. The fort now houses police headquarters but is open to the public daily; admission is free. The 360° view of the capital city, St. George's Harbour, and the open sea is spectacular.

Ⓢ On Richmond Hill, high above the city of St. George's and the inland side of the harbor, historic **Ft. Frederick** provides a panoramic view of two-thirds of Grenada. The fort was completed in 1791; it was also the headquarters of the People's Revolutionary Government during the 1983 coup. Today, you can get a bird's-eye view of the prison, on top of an adjacent hill, where the rebels remain incarcerated—and have, by all accounts, one of the most picturesque views in all of Grenada.

In St. Paul's, five minutes outside St. George's, **de la Grenade Industries** produces syrups, jams, jellies, and liqueurs made from nutmeg and other homegrown fruits and spices. It began in 1960 as a cottage industry. You're welcome to watch the process and purchase gift items from the retail operation on-site. ☎ *473/440–3241.* ▱ *Free.* ☉ *Weekdays 8–5, Sat. 9–12:30.*

Carriacou

Carriacou, the land of many reefs, is a hilly island and (unlike its lush sister island of Grenada) has neither lakes nor rivers—only rainwater, caught in cisterns and purified with bleach. It gets arid during the dry season (January–May). Nevertheless, plenty of fruit is grown here, and the climate seems to suit the mahogany trees used for furniture-making and the white cedar critical to the boatbuilding that has made Carriacou famous.

Hillsborough is Carriacou's main town. Rolling hills cut a wide swath through the island's center, from Gun Point in the north to Tyrrel Bay in the south. The small town of Windward, on the northeast coast, is a boatbuilding community. You'll likely encounter half-finished hulls on the roadside. Originally constructed for interisland commerce, the boats are now built for fishing and pleasure sailing.

Interestingly, tiny Carriacou has several distinct cultures. Hillsborough is decidedly English; the southern region, around L'Esterre, reflects French roots; and the northern town of Windward has Scottish ties. African culture, of course, is the overarching influence.

SIGHTS TO SEE

⑱ **Belair.** For a wonderful bird's-eye view of Carriacou's west coast, drive to Belair, 700 ft (213½ m) above sea level, in the north-central part of the island. On the way you'll pass the photogenic ruins of an old sugar mill. The Belair lookout is adjacent to Princess Royal Hospital, where patients surely find the view of Hillsborough, the harbor, and endless sea to be restorative.

⑯ **Historical Museum.** Housed in a building that once held a cotton gin, one block from the waterfront, the museum has exhibitions of Amerindian, European, and African artifacts, a collection of watercolors by native artist Canute Caliste, and a gift shop loaded with local items. ✉ *Paterson St., Hillsborough,* ☎ *no phone.* ▱ *$2.* ☉ *Weekdays 9:30–4, Sat. 10–4.*

⑰ Sandy Island. Just off Hillsborough Harbour, tiny Sandy Island is a gorgeous islet, lapped by crystal-clear water, with nothing more on it than powdery white sand and some palm trees. For a few dollars, any local fellow with a motorboat will transport you back and forth. Bring your snorkeling gear and, if you want, a picnic—and leave all your cares behind.

⑲ Tyrrel Bay. Picturesque Tyrrel Bay is a large protected harbor in southwest Carriacou. The bay is almost always full of sailboats, powerboats, and working boats—coming, going, or bobbing at their moorings. Edging the bay is a beach with pure white sand; bars, restaurants, a guest house, and a few shops face the waterfront.

Petite Martinique

Petite Martinique (pronounced *pit*-ty mar-ti-*neek*), 10 minutes north of Carriacou by boat, is tiny and residential, with a guest house or two but no tourist facilities or attractions—just peace and quiet. Meander along the beachfront and watch the boatbuilders at work. And if by chance there's a boat launch, sailboat race, wedding, or cultural festival while you're there, you're in for a treat. The music is infectious, the food bountiful, the spirit lively.

GRENADA A TO Z

To research prices, get advice from other travelers, and book travel arrangements, visit www.fodors.com.

AIR TRAVEL

Air Jamaica has twice-weekly nonstop flights into Grenada's Point Salines International Airport from New York and connecting flights from its other gateway cities via Montego Bay, Jamaica, with a stop in St. Lucia. American Airlines/American Eagle has daily flights from major U.S. and Canadian cities via San Juan. BWIA flies to Grenada from New York, Miami, Washington, D.C., and Toronto via Trinidad. British Airways flies from London/Gatwick twice a week. From other parts of the world, connections must be made through U.S. cities, San Juan, Toronto, or London.

Caribbean Star flies daily to Grenada from its Antigua hub, via Dominica, St. Lucia, St. Vincent, and Trinidad. LIAT has scheduled service between Grenada and several neighboring islands. SVG Air flies from Grenada and Carriacou to St. Vincent and the Grenadines (St. Vincent, Union, Canouan, and Bequia).

➤ AIRLINES AND CONTACTS: **Air Jamaica** (☎ 473/444–5975). **American Airlines/American Eagle** (☎ 473/444–2222). **BWIA** (☎ 473/444–1221). **British Airways** (☎ 473/444–1664). **Caribbean Star** (☎ 268/480–2561). **LIAT** (☎ 473/440–2796 or 473/440–4121). **SVG Air** (☎ 473/444–0328).

AIRPORTS

Point Salines International Airport, at the southwestern tip of Grenada, is a modern facility suitable for the largest jets. The departure lounge and gate areas were renovated and enlarged in 2001 to accommodate increased traffic. Passenger amenities include a restaurant, snack bar, and several shops (including duty-free shopping in the departure lounge).

On Carriacou, five minutes south of Hillsborough, Lauriston Airport is a lighted landing strip suitable only for light planes, with a small building for ticket sales and shelter. What's particularly fascinating about this airport is that the main road between Hillsborough and Tyrrel Bay crosses the live runway at its midpoint. Look both ways before crossing!

There is no bus service between the Point Salines Airport and hotels, but taxis are always available. Fares to St. George's are $15; to the hotels of Grand Anse and L'Anse aux Épines, $10. Rides taken between 6 PM and 6 AM incur a $4 surcharge. From Carriacou's Lauriston Airport to Hillsborough, the taxi fare is $4.

➤ AIRPORT INFORMATION: **Lauriston Airport** (☎ 473/443–6306). **Point Salines Airport** (☎ 473/444–4101).

BOAT AND FERRY TRAVEL

Approximately two-thirds of the annual visitors to Grenada arrive on cruise ships. Small ships, including tall ships, tie up at the pier or anchor in St. George's Harbour. Cruise ships generally anchor offshore and bring passengers by launch to the welcome center on The Carenage. From there, they can easily explore the capital city on foot, take a taxi (land or water) or bus to Grand Anse Beach, or join a sightseeing tour of the island.

Passenger ferries and cargo schooners (that also take passengers) to Grenada's other islands, Carriacou and Petite Martinique, depart from The Carenage.

FARES AND SCHEDULES

Two high-speed power catamarans—*Lexianna Jet* and *Osprey Express*—each make two round-trip voyages daily (except Wednesday) from Grenada to Carriacou and on to Petite Martinique. The fare for the 90-minute one-way trip is $18 per person; round-trip, $35. For the 15-minute trip between Carriacou and Petite Martinique, the fare is $4 each way. The boat leaves from The Carenage in St. George's.

The schooners *Alexia II*, *Alexia III*, and *Adelaide B.* leave from The Carenage in St. George's in the morning (except Monday and Thursday), ferrying cargo and passengers on the four-hour voyage to Carriacou; they return to Grenada daily (except Tuesday and Friday). The *Adelaide B* continues on from Carriacou to Petite Martinique (about a 1½-hour trip) on Wednesday and Saturday afternoons, returning early on Monday and Thursday mornings. The fare between Grenada and Carriacou is $7.50 one-way, $12 round-trip; between Carriacou and Petite Martinique, it's about $5 each way. Reservations aren't necessary.

The mail boat between Carriacou and Petite Martinique makes one round-trip on Monday, Wednesday, and Friday, leaving Petite Martinique at 8 AM and returning from Windward, Carriacou, at noon. The fare is about $5 each way.

BUSINESS HOURS

BANKS

Banks are open Monday–Thursday 8–3, Friday 8–5.

POST OFFICES

The main post office, at Burns Point by the port in St. George's, is open weekdays 8–3:30. Each town or village has a post office branch.

SHOPS

Stores are generally open weekdays 8–4 or 4:30 and Saturday 8–1; some close from noon to 1 during the week. Most are closed Sunday, although tourist shops usually open if a cruise ship is in port.

CAR RENTALS

To rent a car, you need a valid driver's license and a local permit (available at the Central Police Station on The Carenage and at some car-rental firms), which costs $12 (EC$30). Some rental agencies impose a minimum age of 25 and a maximum age of 65 to rent a car. Rental cars (including four-wheel-drive vehicles) cost $60–$75 a day or $300–$370 a week with unlimited mileage. In high season there may be a three-day minimum rental.

On Grenada, Avis is at Spice Island Rentals, on Paddock and Lagoon roads in St. George's. David's has offices at Point Salines International Airport, The Grenada Grand Beach Resort, Rex Grenadian Hotel, and the Limes in Grand Anse. Dollar Rent-a-Car is at Point Salines Airport. In the True Blue area, call McIntyre Bros. Ltd. On Carriacou, Barba's Auto Rentals, at Tyrrel Bay, will meet you at the airport.
➤ MAJOR AGENCIES: **Avis** (☎ 473/440–3936; 473/440–2624; 473/444–5480 after hrs). **Barba's Auto Rentals** (☎ 473/443–7454). **David's** (☎ 473/444–3399 or 473/444–3038). **Dollar Rent-a-Car** (☎ 473/444–4786; 473/443–2330 after hrs). **McIntyre Bros. Ltd.** (☎ 473/444–3944; 473/443–5319 after hrs).

CAR TRAVEL
Having a car or jeep is a convenience—particularly for those people staying at resorts in locations other than Grand Anse, which has frequent minibus service. Otherwise, round-trip taxi rides can get expensive if you plan to leave the resort frequently for shopping, meals, or visiting other beaches. Driving is also a reasonable option if you want to explore the island on your own.

GASOLINE
Gasoline costs about $2.80 per gallon, and filling stations are in St. George's, Grand Anse, Grenville, Gouyave, and Sauteurs.

ROAD CONDITIONS
Driving is a constant challenge in the tropics, but most of Grenada's 650 mi (1,050 km) of paved roads are kept in fairly good condition—albeit steep and narrow beyond the Grand Anse area. The main road between St. George's and Grand Anse winds along the coast and is heavily traveled—and kept in good condition. Directions are clearly posted, but having a map on hand is certainly a good idea when traveling in the countryside.

RULES OF THE ROAD
Driving is on the left, British-style.

ELECTRICITY
Electric current on Grenada is 220 volts/50 cycles. Appliances rated at 110 volts (U.S. standard) will work only with a transformer and adapter plug. For dual-voltage computers or appliances, you'll still need an adapter plug; some hotels will loan adapters. Most hotels have 110 outlets for shavers.

EMBASSIES
➤ UNITED KINGDOM: **British High Commission** (✉ The Netherlands Building, St. George's, ☎ 473/440–3536 or 473/440–3222).
➤ UNITED STATES: **Embassy of the United States** (✉ L'Anse Aux Épines Stretch, St. George's, ☎ 473/444–1173 or 473/444–1177).

EMERGENCIES
➤ AMBULANCE: **St. George's, Grand Anse, and L'Anse aux Épines Ambulance** (☎ 434). **St. Andrew's Ambulance** (☎ 724). **Carriacou Ambulance** (☎ 774).➤ COAST GUARD: **Coast Guard** (☎ 399 emergencies; 473/444–1931 for nonemergencies).
➤ FIRE: **Fire emergencies** (☎ 911).

> HOSPITALS: **Princess Alice Hospital** (Grenville, ☎ 473/442–7251).
St. George's General Hospital (St. George's, ☎ 473/440–2051),
Grenada's main hospital. **St. Augustine's Medical Services, Inc.** (Grand
Anse, ☎ 473/440–6173) is a private hospital. On Carriacou, **Princess
Royal Hospital** (Hillsborough, ☎ 473/443–7400).

> PHARMACIES: **Gitten's** (✉ Halifax St., St. George's, ☎ 473/440–2165;
473/440–2340 after hrs). **Gitten's Drugmart** (✉ Main Rd., Grand
Anse, ☎ 473/444–4954; 473/440–2340 after hrs). **Mitchell's Pharmacy**
(✉ Grand Anse Shopping Centre, Grand Anse, ☎ 473/444–3845). **Par-
ris' Pharmacy Ltd.** (✉ Victoria St., Grenville, ☎ 473/442–7330). On
Carriacou: **Charles Pharmacy** (✉ Sea View, ☎ 473/443–7933).

> POLICE: **Police emergencies** (☎ 911).

ETIQUETTE AND BEHAVIOR

A Grenadian will always greet you with a friendly "good morning,"
"good afternoon," or "good evening" and will be disappointed if the
courtesy isn't returned. That's true whether it's a perfect stranger or
someone you've met before. Though such greetings are common
throughout the Caribbean, in Grenada they will often be followed by,
"Are you enjoyin' it?" It seems everyone wants to make sure you're
having a good time in Grenada.

Taking photos of local people, their boats, homes, or children isn't appreciated without first asking permission and offering a tip for the favor.

Dress appropriately and discreetly, saving swimwear for the beach. Shorts
and T-shirts are fine for sightseeing and shopping but frowned upon
in restaurants in the evening.

FESTIVALS AND SEASONAL EVENTS
GRENADA

In late January, during the Spice Island Billfish Tournament, sportfishermen vie for cash prizes for the biggest game fish (marlin, sailfish,
yellowfin tuna). The Grenada Sailing Festival, held at the end of January and early February, includes six days of races and regattas and a
daylong crafts market and street festival—all organized by the Grenada
Yacht Club.

February 7 is Independence Day. Watch the float parade and fireworks at Queen's Park, on the north side of St. George's. Beginning
around March 17 and lasting a week, the St. Patrick's Day Fiesta is
celebrated in Sauteurs (St. Patrick's Parish), in the north of Grenada,
with arts and crafts, agricultural exhibits, food and drink, and a cultural extravaganza with music and dancing.

Late April sees international triathletes compete in the annual Grenada
International Triathlon. The competition starts and finishes at Grand
Anse Beach. Participants swim 1½ km, cycle 25 km, and run 5 km on
the first day. A three-person relay takes place on the second day. Teams
must include at least one female and have a combined age of at least
100 years. Music lovers congregate at Grenada's Grenada Spice Jazz
Festival, a four-day event in late May that showcases regional and international jazz greats.

Each June 29 the Fisherman's Birthday Celebration is a sort of mini-
Carnival in villages on Grenada's west coast, particularly in Gouyave.
There are a blessing of the boats, boat racing, fishing contests, and music
and dancing in the street. In early August the Rainbow City Festival
is held in Grenville; it's primarily an agricultural fair, with local arts
and crafts and livestock.

The Grenada to Carriacou Yacht Race is a highlight of the Carriacou Regatta in August. A month of calypso road shows culminates in the Grenada Carnival the second week of August. It's the biggest celebration of the year, with a beauty pageant, a soca monarch competition, continuous steel-pan and calypso music, and a huge Parade of the Bands on the last Tuesday.

CARRIACOU

The biggest event of the year is the four-day Carriacou Carnival, held in mid-February. Revelers participate in parades, calypso contests, music and dancing, and general frivolity.

During the first weekend in August, the Carriacou Regatta attracts yachts and sailboats from throughout the Caribbean for three days of boat races. Festivities also include road relays, fashion shows, donkey rides, and greasy pole contests—and music and partying galore.

In December the week before Christmas, the Carriacou Parang Festival is a musical and cultural celebration. "Parang" is Spanish for ad-libbing. Costumed singers travel from village to village, creating spontaneous songs based on local gossip and accompanied by guitar, violin, and drums.

A highlight of most festivals on Carriacou is the Big Drum Dance, unique to this island (and neighboring Union Island). The term refers to the size of the gathering, not the drum. When the British took control of Carriacou in 1783, they banned the beating of drums for fear the former French slaves would use them to communicate and start a revolt. Despite the repression, the African tradition of drumming survived. Today on Carriacou, costumed dancers move to the rhythmic beat of pounding drums at social events, harvests, boat launches, weddings, and other happy occasions.

HEALTH

Insects can be a nuisance after heavy rains, when mosquitoes emerge, and on the beach after 4 PM, when tiny sand flies begin to bite. Use repellent, especially when hiking in the rain forest. Tap water in hotels and restaurants is perfectly safe to drink.

HOLIDAYS

New Year's Day (Jan. 1), Independence Day (Feb. 7), Good Friday (Fri. before Easter), Easter Monday (day after Easter), Labour Day (May 1), Whit Monday (7th Mon. after Easter), Corpus Christi (8th Thurs. after Easter), Emancipation Holidays (1st Mon. and Tues. in Aug.), Carnival (2nd Mon. in Aug.), Thanksgiving Day (Oct. 25), Christmas (Dec. 25), and Boxing Day (Dec. 26).

LANGUAGE

English—spoken with a fetching lilt with British intonations—is the official language here. Creole patois isn't commonly heard except, perhaps, among older folks in the countryside.

Here's some local terminology you should know: if you want a refreshing drink of coconut water at the market, for EC$1 or so the "jelly man" will hack off the top of a fresh green "jelly" (coconut) for you with one swipe of his machete. And if someone asks if you'd like a "sweetie," they're offering you a candy. When you're buying spices, you may be offered "saffron" and "vanilla." The saffron is really turmeric, a ground yellow root rather than the fragile pistils of crocus flowers; the vanilla is an essence made from locally grown tonka beans, a close substitute but not the real thing. No one is trying to pull the wool over your eyes; these are common local terms.

MAIL AND SHIPPING

Airmail rates for letters to the United States, Canada, and the United Kingdom are EC$1 for a half-ounce letter or postcard; airmail rates to Australia or New Zealand are EC$1.60 for a half-ounce letter or EC$1 for a postcard. When addressing a letter to Grenada, simply write "Grenada, West Indies" after the local address.

MONEY MATTERS

Prices quoted in this chapter are in U.S. dollars unless otherwise indicated.

Barclays Bank is a major international bank; its head office in Grenada is in downtown St. George's; branches are in Grand Anse, Grenville, and Carriacou. National Commercial Bank is a regional bank, with branches in St. George's, Grand Anse, Grenville, and Carriacou. Scotiabank (The Bank of Nova Scotia), an international bank, has its head office in Grenada in St. George's, with branches in Grand Anse and Grenville.

➤ CONTACTS: **Barclays Bank** (✉ Church and Halifax Sts., St. George's, ☎ 473/440–3232; ✉ Grand Anse, ☎ 473/444–3322; ✉ Grenville, ☎ 473/442–7733; ✉ Carriacou, ☎ 473/443–7232). **National Commercial Bank** (✉ True Blue, ☎ 473/444–2265; ✉ Halifax St., St. George's, ☎ 473/440–3566; ✉ Grand Anse, ☎ 473/444–2627; ✉ Grenville, ☎ 473/442–7532; ✉ Carriacou ☎ 473/443–7289). **Scotiabank** (✉ Halifax St., St. George's, ☎ 473/440–3274; ✉ Grand Anse, ☎ 473/444–1917; ✉ Grenville, ☎ 473/442–5507).

ATMS

ATMs are available 24 hours a day at bank branches, on The Carenage in St. George's, and at the airport.

CREDIT CARDS

Major credit cards—including Access, American Express, Diners Club, Discover, Eurocard, MasterCard, and Visa—are widely accepted.

CURRENCY

Grenada uses the Eastern Caribbean dollar (EC$). The official exchange rate is fixed at EC$2.67 to US$1; cabs, shops, and hotels sometimes have slightly lower rates (EC$2.50–EC$2.60). You can exchange money at banks and hotels, but U.S. and Canadian paper currency, traveler's checks, and major credit cards are widely accepted. You will usually receive change in EC$.

PASSPORTS AND VISAS

A valid passport and a return or ongoing ticket are required. An original birth certificate with raised seal and a valid, government-issued photo I.D. are also acceptable instead of a passport for U.S., Canadian, and British citizens only.

SAFETY

Crime isn't a big problem, but it's a good idea to secure your valuables in the hotel safe and not leave items unattended on the beach. Removing bark from trees, taking wildlife from the forest, and removing coral from the sea are all forbidden.

SIGHTSEEING TOURS

Guided tours offer the sights of St. George's, Grand Étang National Park, spice plantations and nutmeg processing centers, rain forest hikes, snorkeling trips to offshore islands, and day trips to Carriacou.

On Adventure Jeep Tours, you drive safari fashion along scenic coastal roads, trek in the rain forest, lunch at a plantation, take a swim, and skirt the capital. The full-day tour costs $65 for adults, $40 for children, and includes lunch. Caribbean Horizons offers a personalized tours of historic and natural island sites, market and garden tours, and excursions to Carriacou. EkoTrek, based at Grand Anse Beach, offers adventurous tours to the rain forest, snorkeling trips, and tours of Carib caves and plantation houses. Dennis Henry of Henry's Safari Tours knows Grenada like the back of his hand. He leads adventurous hikes and four-wheel-drive vehicle safaris, or you can design your own tour. A full-day island tour, including lunch, costs about $55 per person; a six-hour hike to Concord Falls is $30–$45 per person. Spiceland Tours has several five- and seven-hour island tours, from the Urban/Suburban tour of St. George's and the south coast to the Emerald Forest tour, highlighting Grenada's natural beauty. Sunsation Tours offers customized and private island tours to all the usual sites and "as far off the beaten track as you want to go." From garden tours or a challenging hike to a day sail on a catamaran, it's all possible. Tours Mandoo offers half- or full-day tours following northern, southern, or eastern routes, as well as hikes to Concord Falls and the mountains.

Grenada taxi drivers will conduct island sightseeing tours for $25 to $55 per person, depending on the destinations selected. Carriacou minibus drivers will take up to four people on a four-hour island tour for about $65; extra people, $15 each.

➤ CONTACTS: **Adventure Jeep Tours** (☎ 473/444–5337, FAX 473/444–5681, WEB www.grenadajeeptours.com). **Caribbean Horizons** (☎ 473/444–1550, FAX 473/444–2899, WEB www.caribbeanhorizons.com). **EkoTrek** (☎ 473/444–7777, FAX 473/444–4808, WEB www.scubadivegrenada.com). **Henry's Safari Tours** (☎ 473/444–5313, FAX 473/444–4460). **Spiceland Tours** (☎ 473/440–5127 or 473/440–5180, FAX 473/440–5466). **Sunsation Tours** (☎ 473/444–1594, FAX 473/444–1103, WEB www.grenadasunsation.com). **Mandoo Tours** (☎ FAX 473/440–1428, WEB www.grenadatours.com).

TAXES AND SERVICE CHARGES

DEPARTURE TAX

The departure tax, collected at the airport, is $19 (EC$50) for adults and $10 (EC$25) for children ages 5–11, payable in either currency. A $4 (EC$10) departure tax is collected when departing Carriacou.

SALES TAX

An 8% government tax is added to all hotel and restaurant bills.

SERVICE CHARGES

A 10% service charge is generally added to hotel and restaurant bills.

TAXIS

Taxis are plentiful, and rates are set by the government. The trip between Grand Anse and St. George's costs $8–$10; between Point Salines and St. George's, $15. A $4 surcharge is added for rides taken between 6 PM and 6 AM. Taxis often wait for fares at hotels, at the cruise-ship welcome center, and on the north side of The Carenage. They can be hired at an hourly rate of $20.

Water taxis are available along The Carenage. For $4 (EC$10) a motor boat will transport you on a lovely cruise between St. George's and the jetty at Grand Anse Beach. Water taxis are privately owned, unregulated, and don't follow any particular schedule—so make arrangements for a pickup time if you expect a return trip.

In Carriacou the taxi fare from Hillsborough to Belair is $4; to Prospect, $6; and to Tyrrel Bay or Windward, $8.

TELEPHONES

COUNTRY AND AREA CODES
The area code is 473.

INTERNATIONAL CALLS
Grenada has a fully digital telecommunications service. You can place direct-dial calls to anywhere in the world from pay phones, card phones, and most hotel room phones. For international calls using a major credit card, dial 111; there's no surcharge. Pay phones are available at the airport, the cruise-ship welcome center, or the Cable & Wireless office on The Carenage in St. George's, shopping centers, and other convenient locations. Pay phones accept EC25¢ and EC$1 coins, as well as U.S. quarters.

LOCAL CALLS
Local calls are free from most hotels; for directory assistance, dial 411. Prepaid phone cards, which can be used in special cardphones throughout the Caribbean for local or international calls, are sold at shops, attractions, transportation centers, and other convenient outlets.

TIPPING
If the usual 10% service charge is not added to your hotel or restaurant bill, a tip at that amount is appropriate. Additional tipping is discretionary.

VISITOR INFORMATION
➤ BEFORE YOU LEAVE: **Grenada Board of Tourism** in the U.S.: (✉ c/o Richartz Fliss Clark & Pope, 317 Madison Ave., New York, NY 10017, ☎ 212/687–9554, FAX 212/573–9731; ✉ 439 University Ave., Suite 930, Toronto, Ontario M5G 1Y8, Canada, ☎ 416/595–1343, FAX 416/595–8278; ✉ c/o CIB Communications, 1 Battersea Church Rd., London SW11 3LY, U.K., ☎ 020/7771–7016, FAX 020/7771–7181). **Grenada Hotel Association** (☎ 473/444–1353; 800/322–1753 in the U.S. and Canada, FAX 473/444–4847, WEB www.grenadahotelsinfo.com).
➤ IN GRENADA: **Grenada Board of Tourism** (✉ The Carenage, St. George's, ☎ 473/440–2001 or 473/440–2279, FAX 473/440–6637, WEB www.grenadagrenadines.com).

Updated by
Eileen
Robinson Smith

Shafts of sunlight break through the tree cover of the tropical forest. As you descend the river primeval, you enjoy a symbiotic relationship with nature. Walking, swimming, sliding, and jumping, you caress the water. In the hours it takes to slide your body, like a toboggan, into the last, deep pool, you learn the secrets of the river. Canyoning it's called. In Guadeloupe, the term is becoming common knowledge, like white-water rafting is in Colorado. The experience is rich in sensations. Adrenaline kicks in and jumpstarts your survival mechanisms. Wearing nothing but a swimsuit, sneakers, and a demi-wet suit, you need the same good humor as the river guide. It may be called ecotourism, but it's more like an early Tarzan movie. When it's over, a real camaraderie has been established.

Sprawling and changing by the mile—from jungle highlands to seaside resorts, from mall shopping to rustic dining—Guadeloupe is richly varied. At 629 square mi (1,629 square km), it looks like a giant butterfly resting on the sea between Antigua and Dominica. Its wings—Basse-Terre and Grande-Terre—are the two largest islands in the Guadeloupe archipelago. The Rivière Salée, a 4-mi (6½-km) channel flowing between the Caribbean and the Atlantic, forms the spine of the butterfly. Smaller, flatter Grande-Terre, at 218 square mi (565 square km), is dry and sandy. It has Guadeloupe's best beaches, restaurants, casinos, resorts, and clubs. Basse-Terre (Low Land) is wild, wet, and mountainous. It once lagged behind Grande-Terre, but today is popular with those who love hiking, whale-watching, diving, or deep-sea fishing. Its lush, west coast is as beautiful as any other place in the Caribbean. On Les Saintes, La Désirade, Marie-Galante, and the other islands of the archipelago, you'll find places have remained largely untouched by the world.

Guadeloupe was annexed by France in 1674. During the French Revolution, battles broke out between royalists and revolutionaries on the island. In 1794 Britain aided Guadeloupe royalists, and that same year France dispatched Victor Hugues to sort things out. (In virtually every town and village you'll run across a Victor Hugues street, boulevard, or park.) After his troops banished the British, Hugues abolished slavery and guillotined recalcitrant planters. Those who managed to keep their heads fled to Louisiana or hid in the hills of Grande-Terre, where their descendants now live. Hugues—"the Robespierre of the Isles"—was soon relieved of his command, slavery was reestablished by Napoléon, and the French and English continued to battle over the island. The 1815 Treaty of Paris restored Guadeloupe to France, and in 1848, thanks to Alsatian Victor Schoelcher, slavery was abolished. The island was made a *département* of France in 1946, and in 1974 was elevated to a *région,* administered by a prefect appointed from Paris. With Martinique, St. Barths, and St. Martin, it is *les Antilles Françaises,* the French West Indies.

An old saying of the French Caribbean refers to *les grands seigneurs de la Martinique et les bonnes gens de la Guadeloupe* (the lords of Martinique and the bourgeoisie of Guadeloupe). Though there are few aristocrats left on Martinique, the saying still holds some truth in Guadeloupe. Middle-class French tourists come (most on package tours) to swim and sunbathe, scuba dive, or hike. But sugar is still Guadeloupe's primary source of income. Only 10% of the workforce is employed in the tourism industry—which thrives from mid-November through May and is quiet the rest of the year. At harvest time, in February, the fields teem with workers cutting cane, and the roads are clogged with trucks taking the harvest to factories or distilleries.

Everything about Guadeloupe—from the *franglais* (*le topless, le snack-bar*) to the zippy little cars and ubiquitous *vendeuses de la plage* (women who model bathing suits on *le beach* and do a strip-tease show in the process)—is French. The prices, however, are Parisian, and unlike on St. Martin, there are stiff taxes on most goods. To really feel at home here, some *français* is indispensable, though you may receive a bewildering response in Creole patois. Still, you'll be welcomed in this land of volcanoes, French food, and 'ti punch (a heady concoction of white rum, sugarcane syrup, and lime juice).

Lodging

On Guadeloupe you can opt for a splashy hotel with a full complement of activities or a small *relais* (inn) for more personal attention or a more authentic island experience. Many of the island's chain hotels cater to French package groups. Gosier, St-François, and Bas-du-Fort are generally considered resort areas, as is Ste-Anne. First-time visitors often land in Gosier, but after touring the island, some decide to move over to St-François or St. Anne, or plan to next time. A smaller property, outside the large touristic areas, can offer a real island experience, and force your French. There are small hotels on Iles des Saintes and Marie-Galante. More, and better, hotels are opening in Basse-Terre. Most hotels include buffet breakfast in their rates. Prices decline 25%–40% in the off-season.

CATEGORY	COST EP/CP*	COST A.I.**
$$$$	over $350	over $375
$$$	$250–$350	$275–$375
$$	$150–$250	$175–$275
$	under $150	under $175

*EP/CP prices are per night for a standard double room in high season, excluding taxes, service charges, and meal plans**A.I. (all-inclusive) prices are per person, per night based on double-occupancy during high season, excluding taxes and service charges

Guadeloupe

KEY

Cruise Ship Terminal
Dive Sites
Exploring Sights
Ferry
Hotels and Restaurants

Anse Laborde, Anse Bertrand, Souffleur, Port Louis, Beauport, Anse du Canal, Petit-Canal, Ilet à Fajou, Guadeloupe Passage, Anse du Vieux Fort, Pte. Allègre, La Grande-Anse, Ste-Rose, Vieux-Bourg, Grand Cul-de-Sac Marin, Jabrun du Sud, Deshaies, Lamentin, Destrelan, Aéroport International Pôle Caraïbes, Abyn, Pointe-à-Pitre, Pointe-Noire, PARC NATIONAL DE LA GUADELOUPE, Anse Caraïbe, Bas-du-Fort, La Traversée, Mahaut, Petit Cul-de-Sac Marin, Petit-Bourg, Malendure, Vernou, Pigeon Island, Bouillante, Goyave, BASSE-TERRE, Marigot, Ste-Marie, Vieux-Habitants, La Soufrière, Capesterre-Belle-Eau, Matouba, Plage de Rocroy, St-Claude, Basse-Terre, Gourbeyre, St-Sauveur, Bananier, Caribbean Sea, Anse Turlet, Trois-Rivières, Vieux Fort, Iles des Saintes (Les Sainte, Terre-de-Haut, Plage Crawen, Terre-de-Bas, La Coche, Grand Ilet

Hotels
GRANDE-TERRE

$$$$ ★ ☺ 🔝 **La Cocoteraie.** Adjacent to and managed by Le Méridien, this classy, boutique hotel is its own entity. Twenty of the spacious suites are directly on the "private" beach. Suites have two bathrooms and Hermès octagonal tubs, set in the curve of bow windows. The pool is traversed by a white, covered footbridge and is adjacent to the circular Indigo Bar, where you can relive your day spent on the 18-hole Robert Trent Jones course, across from the hotel. La Varangue restaurant is renowned. A lobby and room renovation were completed in 2001. ✉ *Av. de l'Europe, St-François 97118,* ☎ *0590/88–79–81,* FAX *0590/88–78–33,* WEB *www.lemeridien.com. 50 suites. Restaurant, in-room safes, minibars, 2 tennis courts, pool, gym, beach, bar, baby-sitting, car rental. AE, DC, MC, V. CP, MAP.*

$$$–$$$$ ☺ 🔝 **Club Méditerranée La Caravelle.** This 1970s resort sits on 50 secluded acres on Caravelle beach, one of the island's best white-sand beaches. Regular rooms have twin beds and are acceptable to the clientele, which is 80% European. Americans may want to pay the 20% extra for the Marie Galante wing. Nonguests can call for day passes (about $60), which include all sports and lunch or dinner, with complimentary wine and beer. Bar bills are paid for with coupons. Soft, drinks, bottled water, and even coffee taken outside of meals, must be bought. The resort is great for children, who love the kids' club. ✉ *Quartier Caravelle, Ste-Anne 97180,* ☎ *0590/85–49–50,* FAX *0590/85–49–70,* WEB *www.clubmed.com. 340 rooms. 2 restaurants, 6 tennis courts, pool, aerobics, beach, windsurfing, boating, volleyball, archery, pub, nightclub, children's programs (ages 4–12). AE, MC, V. All-inclusive.*

$$–$$$$ ★ 🔝 **Auberge de la Vieille Tour.** One of the island's first, this resort has grown from six rooms fashioned around a 200-year-old stone sugar mill, to a luxury resort. Guests love it, from the time they are welcomed by pretty, local girls in white eyelet and madras, dispensing moist, scented towels and fresh juice, to each night when they return "home" to their split-level suite with a glass-walled bathroom looking out to a winking lighthouse. The restaurant is unquestionably one of the island's finest. A fabulous breakfast buffet is served poolside. Shuttles run to the Novotel, which has a long beach, and a host of water sports. ✉ *Rte. de Montauban, Gosier 97190,* ☎ *0590/84–23–23,* FAX *0590/84–33–43,* WEB *www.sofitel.com. 77 rooms, 102 suites. 2 restaurants, 2 tennis courts, pool, beach, shops, bar. AE, MC, V. EP, MAP.*

$$–$$$ 🔝 **Canella Beach Hotel-Residence.** Designed to look like a creole village, all fretwork and pastels, this is one resort where people actually do move in for a while because the monthly rates for the studios and duplex apartments are reasonable, particularly in low season. Weekly and daily rates are also available. The complex has its own semiprivate cove, a beach bar, and water-sports shack. The Veranda Restaurant, looking like a white gingerbread house serves creole, French, and lobster specialties and has a prix-fixe menu for $12. More important, it has personality. Live music, great bar concoctions, and a fun crowd make it a happening nightspot. ✉ *Pointe de la Verdure, Gosier 97190,* ☎ *0590/90–44–00,* FAX *0590/90–44–44. 86 studios, 59 suites. Restaurant, kitchenettes, 2 pools, beach, snorkeling, windsurfing, boating, jet skiing, waterskiing, fishing, bar. AE, DC, MC, V. EP, MAP.*

$$–$$$ ☺ 🔝 **Le Méridien St-François.** The emphasis at this resort is on the animation program and activities that might include a volleyball game, fashion show, circus, or Caribbean night on the beach with lobster and fireworks. By day, the beach restaurant serves grilled lobster and light salads. The hotel underwent a serious renovation in 2001 of the lobby and guest rooms, which have new tile floors and attractive mint and mango tropical fabrics. International movies are shown at night on wide-screen TV in the lounge. You can watch while taking a nocturnal swim in the delightful pool. A children's club opens during the French school holidays. ✉ *Av. de l'Europe, St-François 97118,* ☎ *0590/48–05–00,* FAX *0590/88–40–71,* WEB *www.lemeridien.com. 251 rooms, 12 suites. 2 restaurants, minibars, 2 tennis courts, pool, spa, beach, boating, snorkeling, windsurfing, waterskiing, jet skiing, 2 bars, shops, baby-sitting, car rental. AE, MC, V. CP, EP, MAP.*

$$ 🏨 **Novotel Coralia Bas du Fort.** This is a sprawling, water-sports–oriented resort, offering everything from kayaking to knee-boarding. The clientele is mostly French package tourists, but Americans can be found, too. Businessmen have also discovered it. Rooms are not luxurious but powder-blue fabrics and white tiles give them a pleasant, fresh look. All rooms have terraces, most with sea views. Six bungalows are smack on the beach. All bathrooms were renovated in 2001. The spacious grounds look magical when lit at night. Delightful full-day catamaran cruises to the Iles de Saintes are popular. Sundays there are beach barbecues and live bands. ✉ *Gosier 97190,* ☎ *0590/90–40–00,* FAX *0590/90–99–07. 385 rooms, 48 bungalows. 4 restaurants, minibars, 2 pools, health club, beach, snorkeling, boating, waterskiing, bar. AE, MC, V. CP, MAP.*

$–$$ 🏨 **La Créole Beach Hotel.** Part of a larger complex that includes a residential development and the upscale Mahogany Hotel, this resort spans 10 acres of tropical greenery and two beaches. The oversize rooms are akin to those on a fine wooden yacht. Palm fronds, painted blue, are under glass and hung over the beds. Expensive white bedspreads carry on the crisp, minimalistic look. An impressive, international buffeteria, Road of Spices, offers everything from curries to prime rib. La Créole Beach guests can sunbathe, topless or otherwise, on the expansive teak deck at the Mahogany. ✉ *Pointe de la Verdure, Gosier (Box 61, 97190),* ☎ *0590/90–46–46,* FAX *0590/90–46–66,* WEB *www.leader-hotels.gp. 156 rooms. 2 restaurants, some kitchenettes, pool, 2 beaches, snorkeling, boating, volleyball, bar, meeting rooms, car rental. AE, DC, MC, V. CP, EP, MAP.*

$–$$ 🏨 **Hôtel La Toubana.** Talk about a view: the solarium terrace, perched on a cliff that drops to the sea, has the kind of Caribbean views "that movies are made of." Adjacent to its fine restaurant, Le Grand Bleu, the magnificent infinity pool looks as if it flows into the sea below. Twelve bungalows have ocean views, 20 are amidst luxuriant gardens. All have terraces and are furnished with inexpensive, blond rattan pieces, including armoires. ✉ *Fonds Thezan, Ste-Anne 97180,* ☎ *0590/88–25–57,* FAX *0590/88–38–90,* WEB *www.leader-hotels.gp. 32 bungalows. 2 restaurants, kitchenettes, tennis court, pool, beach, snorkeling, jet skiing, bar. MC, V. CP, MAP, AP.*

$ 🏨 **Hotel Royal Caraïbes.** Le Moule, a major northern port on the Atlantic coast, was *the* seaside place to be 15 years ago, as was this hotel, located on its own peninsula. Both are making a comeback. Everything about the resort is spacious, from the 20 acres of landscaped grounds to the lobby and the bungalows—full-service, freestanding apartments. Many of the units have the tranquil view of the lagoon with no other development in sight. Fifty units are time shares in the RCI system. You'll find dual pools (one for children) raised on a teak deck, plus a lovely beach, and a creole restaurant. ✉ *La Baie, Le Moule 97160,* ☎ *0590/93–35–35,* FAX *0590/23–17–39.* WEB *www.royal-caraibes.com. 200 apartments. Restaurant, kitchenettes, 2 tennis courts, 3-hole golf course, 2 pools, beach, boating, billiards, Ping-Pong, bar, meeting rooms, car rental. AE, V. EP, MAP.*

$ 🏨 **Hôtel Saint-John.** This simple hotel next to the port is your best bet if you need to stay over in Pointe-à-Pitre. Small rooms are clean, comfortable, and decorated with Mediterranean colors—a number of them overlook the water. Popular with business travelers, the hotel lies within easy walking distance of the tourist office and is near the cruise-ship debarkation and the ferry to Les Saintes. Don't expect luxury—and be alert after dark—but this is the city's best option. ⊠ *Quai des Croisières, Pointe-à-Pitre 97110,* ☎ *0590/82–51–57,* FAX *0590/82–52–61. 44 rooms. Restaurant. AE, MC, V.*

$ ★ ☻ ⊞ **La Métisse.** On a hilltop, this resort, which is in an upscale residential neighborhood, arcs around a pool surrounded by acres of tropical gardens. A hot tub is in a central island. With pink stucco, white rattan furniture, and white and blue fretwork, it is one pretty picture and immaculately clean. The friendly owners give guests rides to and from town and the beach, which can eliminate the need to rent a car. Business travelers sometimes hide out here, loving the quiet and the free local calls. A lovely breakfast with house-made jam, is served poolside. Connecting rooms are ideal for families. ⊠ *66, les Hauts de St-François, St-François 97118,* ☎ *0590/88–70–00,* FAX *0590/88–59–08. 7 rooms, Minibars, pool, hot tub, playground. AE, MC, V. CP.*

$ ⊞ **Le Paradis Créole.** This is what the French call a *hôtel de charme.* It's certainly worth the long drive up the one-lane hill for the expansive views of the mountains, the sea, and Pigeon Island. The grounds are lush and green. Alas, most of the fun Europeans come on week-long trips to dive in the nearby Jacques Cousteau Reserve, so the hotel offers few other activities, and there is no beach. Happily, their famous restaurant, provides more than just fuel for the diving machines. The pool bar blends up some concoctions that make the crimson setting of the sun truly celebratory. ⊠ *Route de Poirier, Pigeon-Bouillante 97132,* ☎ *0590/98–71–62,* FAX *0590/98–77–76,* WEB *www.paradis-creole.gp. 10 rooms, 2 bungalows. Restaurant, pool, bar, dive shop. MC CP, MAP.*

BASSE-TERRE

$$–$$$ ★ ⊞ **Le Jardin de Malanga.** A hideaway for nature-lovers, this *hôtel de charme* is surrounded by tropical fruit and flower gardens. Accommodations are in traditional creole buildings of courbaril wood; the antiques-filled main house was built in 1927. A cliff-side pool looks to the sea, and the property, close to Guadeloupe's national park, faces Les Saintes. Each room's white-tile bathroom gleams and looks out to the lush surroundings. You'll find no TVs or radios here, so quiet is inevitable. French-creole meals with produce from the gardens are served for hotel guests only. You will need a car, especially since the closest beach, Grand Anse, is a 10-minute drive away. ⊠ *Hermitage, Trois-Rivières 97114,* ☎ *0590/92–67–57,* FAX *0590/92–67–58. 8 rooms, 1 suite. Dining room, fans, no room TVs, pool. AE, MC, V. CP, FAP, MAP.*

$–$$ ★ ⊞ **Habitation Grande Anse.** With beautiful views of Baie Anse and the surrounding hills, this lovely property offers a mix of bungalows, apartments, studios, and standard rooms. The quality of the accommodations and service is in striking contrast to that of similarly priced hotels on the island. Rooms have rattan furnishings; apartments house four to six people and share their own pools (apartments 16 and 17 have the best views). The youthful Italian owner, Fulvio, speaks English. Across the road, Grande Anse Beach is within a five-minute walk. The hotel will help arrange fishing and diving excursions and rents Citroëns at a reasonable price, full insurance included. ⊠ *Localité Ziotte 97126,* ☎ *0590/28–45–36,* FAX *0590/28–51–17,* WEB *www.grande-anse.com. 3 rooms, 20 studios, 6 apartments, 19 bungalows. Restaurant, kitchenettes, in-room safes, 3 pools, bar, car rental. AE, MC, V. EP, MAP.*

$ ☻ ⊞ **Domaine de Petite-Anse.** The ochre, red-roofed buildings of this complex spill down lushly landscaped hills above the ocean, and there's a terrific pool with adjacent bar overlooking the sea. Rustic accommodations are either in simple and small—though well-equipped—rooms (ask for one with a sea view, which costs the same as one without) or bungalows with full baths, kitchenettes, and terraces. The furnishings are dark rattan lightened by bright floral fabrics. The staff is friendly, but most speak only a little English. The resort is noted for its dive shop and nature tours of the national park. By night, guests gather around the piano bar or enjoy a folklorico show. ⊠ *Plage de Petite-Anse, Monchy, Bouillante 97125,* ☎ *0590/98–78–78,* FAX *0590/98–80–28. 135 rooms, 40 bungalows. Restaurant, in-room safes, some kitchenettes, refrigerators, pool, dive shop, boating, archery, hiking, volleyball, snorkeling, bar, shops. AE, DC, MC, V. EP.*

$ 🏨 **La Sucrerie du Comté.** The ruins of a 19th-century sugar factory punctuate the lawns and gardens; in fact, the historically significant grounds, along with the attractive public areas, are this resort's main attractions. The bar re-creates a plantation feel with wood beams and stone walls. The restaurant is built with a Brazilian wood roof and serves creole and international food. Small, simple rooms are in 26 bungalows that duplicate the gingerbread architecture of the turn of the 20th century. The nearest beach is a five-minute stroll through a tangle of greenery. Diving is nearby in "Grand Cul Sac Marin," and a free resort course is offered in the pool. ⊠ *Comté de Lohéac, Ste-Rose 97115,* ☎ *0590/ 28–60–17,* FAX *0590/28–65–63,* WEB *www.prime-invest-hotels.com. 52 rooms. Restaurant, fans, pool, bar. AE, DC, MC, V. CP, MAP.*

$ 🏨 **Les Pavillions Ti Ta'Anse.** This cluster of two-story bungalows makes its way up a verdant hillside, with the highest having views of the beach. The central complex houses a casual grill and small nightclub; a commendable creole restaurant is on the second floor. The facades and railed porches are of a beautiful hardwood. Buildings are capped with green copper roofs, detailed with fretwork. Interiors have the same dark, native mahogany and pine wood trim, beams, Dutch doors, and rustic floor tiles. Surrounded by frangipani trees, gardens with aromatic plants like citronella grass, and night-lit by lanterns, this is one nice place in the mountainous countryside. ⊠ *Baillargent, Pointe-Noire 97116,* ☎ *0590/99–97–51,* FAX *0590/99–97–57. 5 bungalows. 2 restaurants, kitchenettes, beach, dance club. AE, MC, V. EP, MAP.*

TERRE-DE-HAUT

$ 🏨 **Hôtel Cocoplaya.** It is rare when a new hotel opens in the heart of the village. And this renovation of a stark, two-story stucco on the main drag took time, but the result was worth the wait. Done with taste, each room has its own theme—Chinese, African, Romantic, Provençal. Sea views command the higher tariffs, but even the rooms facing the street are remarkably quiet. The soundproof double windows block out even the annoying drone of the motor scooters. The minimilistic, open lobby, its bar, and the restaurant (dinner only) on the beach have been designed with characteristic French élan. ⊠ *Terre-de-Haut 97137,* ☎ *0590/92– 40–00,* FAX *0590/99–50–41,* WEB *www.im-caraibes.com/cocoplaya. 10 rooms, 2 suites. Restaurant, cable TV, beach, bar. MC, V. CP, MAP.*

$ 🏨 **L'Auberge les Petits Saints aux Anarcadiers.** This distinctive inn is
★ trimmed with trellises and topped by dormers, but do not come expecting an American brand of luxury. A wild-looking clutter greets you in the reception area crammed with antiques, objets d'art, and attic treasures collected by owners. A separate guest house with five large rooms is suitable for families. Throughout the inn, windows open to a view of gardens, hills, and the bay. The pool area has an enviable hillside view of the bay. This is the island's *in* place, the one with charisma that attracts an interesting clientele. Rates include round-trip transfers to the ferry or the plane. ⊠ *La Savane, Terre-de-Haut 97137,*

☎ *0590/99–50–99,* FAX *0590/99–54–51,* WEB *www.petitssaints.com. 10 rooms, 2 bungalows. Restaurant, pool, sauna, bar. AE, MC, V. CP, MAP.*

$ ⊞ **Paradis Saintois.** These simple apartments are a superb value for the
★ money and a real find, just a 10-minute walk from the beach. Although not luxurious, each is spacious, with a terrace and hammock. Feel like king of the hill as you lull yourself into a *sieste,* above the village and the Caribbean blue. The newest units are embellished with native stonework and offer more privacy. Ceiling fans make up for the lack of air-conditioning, and you won't miss a TV or phone, whether you rent by the day, week, or month. A large barbecue grill is available to guests who want to do their own cooking. ⊠ *Route des Pres Cassin–B.P.I., Terre-de-Haut 97137,* ☎ *0590/99–56–16,* FAX *0590/99–56–11,* WEB *www.antilles-info-tourisme.com/guadeloupe/paradis.htm. 5 apartments, 3 studios, 1 room. Kitchens, fans, no air-conditioning, no room phones, no room TVs, 2 pools, bicycles, laundry service. MC, V. EP.*

MARIE-GALANTE

There are several small, simple lodgings on Marie-Galante. **Auberge de l'Arbre à Pain** (⊠ 32 Jeanne D'Arc du Docteur Marcel Enzol, ☎ 0590/97–73–69) has nine basic rooms in two stories surrounding a courtyard and a recommendable creole restaurant, where complimentary breakfast is served. Centrally located in the center of Grand-Bourg, it is an easy walk to any place in town, but a hike to the beach. **Hôtel Hajo** (⊠ Section Bernard, #140, Capesterre, ☎ 0590/97–32–76) has six rooms and is a good location if you want to be in the country yet near the beaches. **Le Touloulou** (⊠ Plage de Petite Anse, Capesterre, ☎ 0590/97–32–63) has four stucco bungalows with kitchenettes, which are simple but right there on the beach. The creole seafood restaurant is good and it's also a happening place, with atmospheric music from the beach bar vying with the slapping of the waves. The disco adjacent to the restaurant warms up to hot at night.

$ ⊞ **Au Village de Ménard.** Care has gone into the gardens of this hotel, which sits cliffside at the island's north end (the beach is 1 mi [1½ km] away). Inexpensive, this is for the independent traveler. Simple, Euro-style, the bungalows are situated around a central pool. The owner speaks English. ⊠ *Vieux Fort, St-Louis 97134,* ☎ *0590/97–09–45,* FAX *0590/97–15–40. 9 bungalows. Fans, kitchenettes, pool. MC, V. CP.*

$ ⊞ **Hôtel Cohoba.** Marie-Galante's only beach resort is named for a plant
☾ whose hallucinogenic red pods gave the earliest Caribbean peoples prophetic powers. Half of the basic suites are sky-blue and sea-green stucco bungalows; the rest are slightly larger studios. White walls and white tile floors lend an air of space; cool and warm fabrics add cheer. In the dining room you can contemplate the past while studying the painstakingly reproduced cave paintings that decorate the walls. Although the sandy beach is just two minutes from the delightful pool area, there are no sea views from the bungalows because of dense tree cover. ⊠ *Grand-Bourg 97112,* ☎ *0590/97–50–50,* FAX *0590/97–97–96,* WEB *www.cohoba.gp. 100 suites. Restaurant, pool, 2 tennis courts, beach, windsurfing, boating, waterskiing, volleyball, bar. AE, MC, V. CP, MAP.*

LA DÉSIRADE

An even more remote island than Marie-Galante or Isle des Saintes, La Désirade has few lodging options. There's **L'Oasis** (⊠ Grande-Anse, ☎ 0590/20–02–12), a six-room hotel whose simple restaurant serves excellent seafood. **Le Mirage** is a tiny, eight-room establishment (⊠ Grand-Anse, ☎ 0590/20–01–08, FAX 0590/20–07–45).

Villas

For information about villas and apartments contact one of the following agencies. **French Caribbean International** (☎ 800/322–22–23;

805/967–9850 in Santa Barbara, CA, FAX 805/967–7798, WEB
www.frenchcaribbean.com) handles private villa rentals, from charming cottages in Basse-Terre ($100 to $300 a night) to deluxe seaview
villas in Grand Terre ($1,650 to $7,000 per week), all with pools. With
more than 22 years of experience in the region and a reputation for
honesty and professionalism, the company provides travelers with
knowledgeable assistance and helpful, personal reservation services. The
Association des Villas et Meublés de Tourisme (⊠ 12 Faubourg Alexandre Issac, Pointe-a-Pitre 97171, ☎ 0590/82–02–62, FAX 0590/82–56–
65) is another reliable villa reservation service, but will respond to you
only if you speak French.

Dining

Guadeloupe's fine creole dishes are made up of primarily local seafood
and vegetables, such as christophenes (also known as chayote, like a
squash) and plantains, always with a healthy dose of pepper sauce. Favorite appetizers are *accras* (salted codfish fritters), *boudin* (highly seasoned blood sausage), and *crabes farcis* (stuffed land crabs). *Blaff* is a
spicy fish stew. *Langouste* (lobster) and *lambi* (conch) are widely available, as is *souchy,* a Tahitian version of sushi. You'll find a diverse selection of dining options—from pizza to grilled Caribbean lobster,
Vietnamese to contemporary *haute* French cuisine. And then there are
Italian, African, Indian, and South American establishments—which,
for the most part, aren't inexpensive. The local rum cocktail is 'ti
punch. (Now *that* you can find for three bucks.)

What to Wear
Dining is casual at lunch, but beach attire is a no-no, except at the more
laid-back marina and beach eateries. Dinner is slightly more formal.
Long pants, collared shirts, and skirts or dresses are appreciated, although not required.

CATEGORY	COST*
$$$$	over $30
$$$	$20–$30
$$	$10–$20
$	under $10

per person for a main course at dinner

Grande-Terre

CARIBBEAN

$$–$$$ ✕ **Le Bananier.** *Nouvelle cuisine creole*—creatively prepared food uti-
lizing local produce—is the specialty at this well-established Gosier restaurant. Try *les soupe aux crustacea* (bisque with lobster and fish with a
cheese-garlic crouton), or boiled red snapper with a passion-fruit banana sauce, and finish with a crepe of coconut flambéed with rum and
curaço. Jean Clarus is one of the island's most experienced chefs; however, this little wooden gingerbread "house" could use a serious spruc-
ing up. ⊠ *Montauban, Gosier,* ☎ *0590/84–34–85. MC, V. Closed Mon.*

CONTEMPORARY

$$–$$$$ ✕ **Auberge de la Vieille Tour Restaurant.** Tables are grouped around
★ a historic whitewashed sugar mill; the conservatory-style extension has
views up into lighted trees. Without a doubt, Chef George delivers some
of the best, most contemporary food on the island, like the starter of
smoked duck with a puree of asparagus, or the catch of the day with
sorrel cream sauce and a shallot preserve. Dessert presentations are daz-
zling with lots of puff pastry, Napoléon towers, sauces, and glacés. Con-
sider the imaginative, three-course, prix-fixe menus for $35. From *la
cave,* the selection includes muscadets, pinot noirs, Sancerres, pommerols,

and gewürztraminers. ✉ *Rte. de Montauban, Gosier,* ☎ *0590/84–23–23. AE, MC, V. No lunch.*

$$–$$$$ ✗ **Villa Fleur d'Epée.** The front-of-the-house man, humorless and snooty, will peer out from the locked iron door, and—with reservations confirmed— you will be allowed into this home in an upscale residential neighborhood. From the *amuse bouche* through the several courses, you'll have a global experience; you may have snapper in banana leaves or kangaroo steak with cèpe mushrooms. The chef/owner, Thierry Larade, is an *artiste* with food. Charming to boot, he visits each table. Although à la carte is best, the $27 discovery menu is a good value in an otherwise expensive restaurant. (Be certain to call for precise directions.) ✉ *Rue du Fort Fleur d'Epée, Bas du Fort,* ☎ *0590/90–86–59. Reservations essential. Jacket required. AE, MC, V. Closed Sun. No lunch.*

$$$ ✗ **Iguane Café.** Sylvan and Marie Seronait serve innovative food at this
★   excellent restaurant. Just beyond the bar, in an open kitchen, a group of chefs busily prepare such specialties as roasted duck with mangoes and cinnamon. The wine list is outstanding, populated with Margauxs, St. Juliens, and Sancerres. Iguanas are indeed the theme, and you will spy them in art forms in all the usual unsuspected places. Marie's *grandmere*'s portraits and antique French cherubs are juxtaposed with island artifacts, driftwood mirrors, and rotating shows of local artists. Cool music—jazz and French faves—set a mellow mood as you lovingly devour your dessert. ✉ *Rte. de La Pointe des Châteaux (½ mi [¼ km] from airport), St-François,* ☎ *0590/88–61–37. AE, MC. Closed Tues. No lunch Mon.–Sat.*

$$–$$$ ✗ **Château de Feuilles.** This relaxed but stylish country restaurant is 9 miles (14½ km) from Le Moule—on the Campêche road, past Gros-Cap—and it's worth a special trip. You'll be hard-pressed to find a finer luncheon than that served by Martine and Jean-Pierre Dubost. For an aperitif, you can choose from about 20 punch concoctions. The changing menu is an imaginative utilization of fresh produce and seafood. You can even take a dip in the pool or stroll around the 2-acre farm. ✉ *Rte. Campêche, Anse Bertrand,* ☎ *0590/22–30–30. V. Closed Mon. No dinner (except for groups of 10 or more by reservation).*

$$–$$$ ✗ **Les Oiseaux.** In a stucco-and-stone house amidst a tangle of gardens overlooking the sea, owner-chefs Claudette and Arthur Rolle prepare creative fish dishes—unlikely combinations with clever names. Ask Claudette to show you her book of local remedies. If your French is *very* good, she might even prepare a special infusion for your particular complaint, but it's best to stick to remedies for external illnesses only. If English is your only language, perhaps simply having a homemade *digestif* will be enough to cure what ails you. ✉ *Anse des Rochers,* ☎ *0590/88–56–92. Reservations essential. MC, V. Closed weekdays Sept.–Oct. No lunch.*

ECLECTIC

$–$$ ✗ **Cha Cha Café.** A minute from the Hotel St. John, two from the ferry docks, and next to KFC, this is a fun, hip hangout. A bar, a breakfast and lunch place, and an ice cream parlor, it's also a gift shop, with wares from exotic lands. This one-room emporium spills out to a terrace with umbrella tables. French belles sip espresso and tap their heels to the latest French, Latin, and American music, collected by the French owner, Ricard. It adds to the milieux of this meeting place. Richard's English is excellent and he will help you with your translations. ✉ *2 Quai Layrie, Pointe-à-Pitre,* ☎ *0590/89–61–94. No credit cards. No dinner.*

FRENCH

$$–$$$$ ✗ **La Mandarine.** In one of Gosier's original neighborhoods, this modest, unassuming spot is owned by a mature French couple—he's the chef, she's the hostess. Chef Alain's food is a pleasant gastronomic experience, with dishes like veal kidneys sautéed with port, which are impossible to find elsewhere. Tantalizing lobster profiteroles are one way to begin, as is the breast of duck and sautéed foie gras over greens with walnut oil and sherry vinegar. The wine list is intelligent. Desserts, a marriage of French classics and tropical fruit coulis, are luscious. You'll even find a cigar menu. ✉ *4 rue Simon, Gosier,* ☎ *0590/84–30–28. MC, V. Closed Mon.*

$$–$$$$ ✕ **La Varangue.** In the beautiful surroundings of La Cocoteraie, this
★ alfresco restaurant, overlooking the sea and the hotel's elegant pool, offers some of the island's most refined dining. Chef Menad Berkani incorporates top-quality imported meats, the freshest fish and lobster, and fresh island produce. An example is a fish cake with onion and apple compote and a vanilla sauce perfumed with citronella. The wine list is appropriately upscale. There are several prix-fixe menus: shrimp, lobster, and foie gras is $75, a four-course lobster menu is $68, and a plat du jour only $32. ✉ *La Cocoteraie, av. de l'Europe, St-François,* ☎ *0590/88–79–81. AE, MC, V.*

Basse-Terre

CARIBBEAN

$$$ ✕ **Le Karacoli.** With her flowing white dress and flamboyant style, Lucienne Salcede, the owner of this pleasant seaside restaurant, has her pictures hanging in the interior dining room, from when she began cooking decades ago. That's also when the place was decorated for the first and only time. Sit outside, instead, and listen to the waves splash. The food is solid (and expensive) creole fare like boudin noir with a piquante sauce. The prix-fixe menu is the best deal, but avoid the tough lambi. Do go with a fine French wine. Coconut flan with a rum digestif is a nice finale. Then stretch out on a chaise longue, and when you wake, take a swim. ✉ *La Grande-Anse, north of Deshaies,* ☎ *0590/28–41–17. MC, V. No dinner.*

$–$$$ ✕ **Chez Clara.** Clara Lesueur, who gave up a jazz-dancing career in Paris
★ to run her family's seaside restaurant with her mother, dishes out delicious creole meals. Seating is on the inviting terrace of a gorgeous house with lacy gingerbread trim. Clara takes the orders (her English is excellent), and the place is often so crowded with her friends and fans that you may have to wait at the octagonal wooden bar. Check the daily specials listed on the blackboard. ✉ *Bd. Maritime, Ste-Rose,* ☎ *0590/ 28–72–99. MC, V. Closed Wed. No dinner Sun.*

$$ ✕ **Les Pavillons Restaurant.** This restaurant is on a terrace with views
★ of Le Rouix beach. Traditional Antilles specialties like lambi in butter sauce are joined by innovations like avocado with hot Roquefort cream sauce and lamb with pine nuts. Finish with Tourment d'amour, Guadeloupe's famous coconut cake, and choose a homemade rum liqueur (punch) from the fascinating display (the best is aged with raisins, pistachios, or sea grapes). Downstairs a simple grill menu, from brochettes to lobster, is available for lunch. ✉ *Les Pavillons Ti Ta'Anse Hotel, Baillargent, Pointe-Noire 97116,* ☎ *0590/99–97–51. AE, MC, V.*

ECLECTIC

$–$$ ✕ **Chez Jackye.** Jacqueline Cabrion serves creole and African dishes in her cheerful, plant-filled seaside restaurant. Boudin is a house specialty, as are lobster (grilled, vinaigrette, or fricassee), fried crayfish, clam blaff, and goat in port sauce. There's also a wide selection of omelets, sandwiches, and salads. For dessert try the peach Melba or banana flambé. The menu will have you waddling out happily. ✉ *Anse Guyonneau, rue de la Bataille, Pointe-Noire,* ☎ *0590/98–06–98. DC, MC, V. Closed Sun.*

Terre-de-Haut

ECLECTIC

$$$ ✕ **L'Auberge les Petits Saints aux Anarcadiers.** Hotel guests and a few
★   visitors have the privilege of dining at this veranda restaurant. The set
    tableau de jour menu constantly changes, but what's certain is that meat
    is no longer served because proprietor Jean Paul Colas says he only
    wants what is fresh and available, i.e., seafood and produce. Dinner
    is consistently enjoyable, with the night sounds of the tropics and
    oldies like Bobby Darin's "Beyond the Sea." Didier Spindler, co-owner
    and pastry chef, makes a superb almond pastry with vanilla sauce with
    nuts from the overhanging trees. ⊠ *L'Auberge les Petits Saints aux An-
    arcadier, La Savane, Terre-de-Haut,* ☎ *0590/99–50–99. AE, MC, V.*

$$ ✕ **La Saladerie.** The menu here is a sophisticated mélange of light plates
★ and the freshest of fish. Perfect for light-appetites, you can make a meal
   of the assortment of smoked fish served cold and a refreshing bowl of
   gazpacho. Shrimp in coconut milk with rice, coupled with a salad that
   you compose, is another light dinner. The wine list is pleasantly varied, and this is one place where you can find calvados and Armagnac.
   Have a snifter full and just listen to the great French music and the
   waves lap the dock. Better yet, walk the pier and give in to the incli-
   nation to be romantic. ⊠ *Anse Mirre, Terre-de-Haut,* ☎ *0590/99–53–
   43. Closed Tues. No dinner Mon. MC, V.*

$$ ✕ **El Dorado.** This plant-filled creole-style house with a double veranda—
   on Bourg's delightful main square—is a good place to stop for tasty
   creole fare. Go with the cod fritters with *chien* (dog sauce), the warm
   goat cheese on toast with salad, the chicken columbo, and the fresh
   catch of the day, or lobster from the grill. The ice cream is the best—
   be it rum raisin or coffee. What makes this place special is that wife
   Roselle cooks and husband Guy is the very personable, English-speak-
   ing host. Breakfast, lunch, and dinner are available. ⊠ *Terre-de-Haut,*
   ☎ *0590/99–54–31. AE, MC, V. Closed Sun.*

FRENCH

$$ ✕ **Le Genois.** On the waterfront, this one has it all—location, creative
★ French-island cuisine, an exceptional wine list, and personality endowed
   by its owners Philip, an English-speaking French lawyer, and his beautiful wife (and chef) Chantal. Begin with a pâté, quiche, or a soufflé
   of lobster. Duck breast in a fruit and wine sauce with smashed green
   papaya might be one of the daily specials. Kids are welcome and go
   oo la la over Chantal's incredible desserts, like black chocolate pie. A
   fun place, it caters to yachties and sponsors the annual Genois regatta.
   Philip has the Havana Club for the celebration of fine Cuban cigars.
   ⊠ *Terre-de-Haut,* ☎ *0590/99–53–01. MC, V.*

Marie-Galante

SEAFOOD

$–$$ ✕ **Le Touloulou.** On the curve of Petite-Anse beach, with tables in the
      sand, this ultracasual eatery serves sumptuous seafood at down-to-earth
      prices. Chef José Viator's standouts include conch and lobster specialities.
      Set menus start at about $9 and go to $22. Jose plays DJ with his fine
      collection of French and international music. The circular bar in the
      gazebo is a great place to savor the best in rum cocktails while con-
      templating the sun's descent. ⊠ *Petite-Anse,* ☎ *0590/97–32–63. MC,
      V. Closed Mon. and mid-Sept.–mid-Oct.*

Beaches

Guadeloupe's beaches are generally narrow and tend to be cluttered
with cafés and cars (when the parking spots fill up, folks create impromptu lots in the sand). But all beaches are free and open to the pub-

lic; for a small fee, hotels allow nonguests to use changing facilities, towels, and beach chairs. On the southern coast of Grande-Terre, from Ste-Anne to Pointe des Châteaux, you'll find stretches of soft white sand. Along the western shore of Basse-Terre you'll see signposts to many small beaches. The sand starts turning gray as you reach Ilet de Pigeon (Pigeon Island); it becomes volcanic black farther south. There is one official nudist beach (noted below), and topless bathing is common. Note that the Atlantic waters on the northeast coast of Grande-Terre are too rough for swimming.

Grand-Terre Beaches

Anse de la Gourde. This beautiful stretch of sand is popular on weekends.

Ilet du Gosier. On this little speck off the shore of Gosier you can bathe in the buff. Take along a picnic for an all-day outing. The beach is closed on weekends.

Plage Caravelle. Southwest of Ste-Anne is one of Grande-Terre's longest and (the occasional dilapidated shack aside) prettiest stretches of sand. Protected by reefs, it's also a fine snorkeling spot. Club Med occupies one end of this beach; nude bathing is no longer permitted.

Pointe Tarare. This secluded, sandy strip just before the tip of Pointe des Châteaux is the island's only official nudist beach. There's a small bar-café in the parking area, a four-minute walk away.

Souffleur. On the west coast of Grande-Terre and north of Port-Louis, this beach has brilliant flamboyant trees that bloom in the summer. There are no facilities on the beach, but you can buy picnic supplies from nearby shops.

Basse-Terre Beaches

La Grande-Anse. North of Deshaies on Basse-Terre's northwest coast you'll find soft beige sand sheltered by palms; it's probably the best beach on the island. There's a large parking area, but no facilities other than those at a nearby restaurant.

Malendure. This beach lies on Basse-Terre's west coast, in Bouillante across from Pigeon Island.

Beaches on Other Islands

Anse Carot. Like all the beaches on Marie-Galante, this is longer, wider, and less crowded than other beaches in Guadeloupe.

Anse Crawen. A secluded ½-mi (¾-km) stretch of white sand on Terre-de-Haut (one of the Isles des Saintes) is popular with families on Sunday.

Anse de Vieux Fort. On Marie-Galante, this is known as a beach for lovers.

Les Pompierres. A palm-fringed stretch of tawny sand, this is a popular beach on Terre-de-Haut.

Petite-Anse. This long beach on Marie-Galante has golden sand that is crowded with locals on weekends. The only facilities are at the little seafood restaurant nearby.

Plage de Folle Anse This beach on Marie-Galante is perfect for a sunset walk.

Outdoor Activities and Sports

BICYCLING

The French are mad about *le cyclisme*, so if you want to feel like a native, take to two wheels. Pedal fever hits the island in August every year, when hundreds of cyclists converge here for the 10-day Tour de Guadeloupe, which covers more than 800 mi (1,290 km). On Grande-Terre you can rent bikes at **Eli Sport** (✉ Rond Point de Grand-Camp, Grand-Camp, Grande-Terre, ☎ 0590/90–37–50). In St-François you can rent from **Espace VTT** (⊠ St-François, Grand-Terre, ☎ 0590/88–79–91). On Iles des Saintes, try **Localizes** (⊠ Place des Débarcadere, Terre-de-Haut, Terre-de-Haut, ☎ 0590/99–51–99).

If you plan to sail these waters, you should be aware that the winds and currents tend to be strong. There are excellent, well-equipped marinas in Pointe-à-Pitre, Bas-du-Fort, Deshaies, St-François, and Gourbeyre. You can rent a yacht (bareboat or crewed) from the following companies: **Cap Sud** (⊠ 3 pl. Créole, Bas-du-Fort, Grande-Terre, ☎ 0590/90–76–70) has a fleet of 14 yachts, including both monohulls and catamarans. The sailboats are generally rented as bareboats and by the week. **Sunsail** (⊠ Bas du Fort Marina, Bas-du-Fort, Grande-Terre, ☎ 0590/90–92–02 or 800/889–2248; 866/644–2327 in the U.S., FAX 0590/90–97–99, WEB www.sunsail.com) has joined forces with Stardust Yacht Charters to form one of the largest charter companies in the world. Although it is primarily a bareboat operation, skippers can be hired by the week for those with limited experience, or they are available to instruct charterers in sailing skills and local waters. Ocean kayaks can be rented, too, and must be reserved in advance.

FISHING

You can fish for bonito, dolphinfish, captain fish, barracuda, kingfish, marlin, swordfish, and tuna. Expect to pay about $500 for a half-day boat charter and $645 for a full day ($115 per person). **Michel** (⊠ Plage de Malendure, Basse-Terre, Basse-Terre, ☎ 0590/85–42–17) is a reliable fishing charter company near Pigeon Island.

GOLF

Golf Municipal St-François (⊠ St-François, Grande-Terre, ☎ 0590/88–41–87), across from the Le Méridien and Cocoteraie hotels, is an 18-hole, par-71, Robert Trent Jones–designed course; it has an English-speaking pro, a clubhouse, a pro shop, and electric carts for rental. The greens fees are $30 for nine holes, $50 for the day; carts rent for $27 for nine holes and $40 for all day. Clubs can be rented, also.

HIKING

With hundreds of trails and countless rivers and waterfalls, the **Parc National de la Guadeloupe,** on Basse-Terre, is the main draw for hikers. Some of the trails should be attempted only with an experienced guide. All tend to be muddy, so wear a good pair of boots. Trips for as many as 12 people are arranged by **Organisation des Guides de Montagnes de la Caraïbe** (⊠ Maison Forestière, Matouba, Basse-Terre, ☎ 0590/99–28–92). A half-day guided tour costs $80, a full day $150. The acknowledged private-sector pros are at **Parfum d'Aventure** (⊠ Roche Blonval, St-François, Grande-Terre, ☎ 0590/88–47–62). They offer everything from hiking to four-wheel-drive safaris, sea kayaking, and white-water canoeing. The young and fun company has also become known for rappelling and canyoning. **Sport D'av** (⊠ La Marina, Gosier, Grande-Terre, ☎ 0590/32–58–41) is a reliable company that organizes both treks and canoe trips.

HORSEBACK RIDING

You can arrange lessons, beach rides, or trips with a picnic lunch through **Le Criolo** (⊠ Vieux Bourg, Morne-à-l'Eau, Grande-Terre, ☎ 0590/20–99–34). The half- or full-day excursions offered by **La Manade** (⊠ St-Claude, Basse-Terre, ☎ 0590/81–52–21) utilize trails through the rain forest and are an interesting place to ride.

SCUBA DIVING

The main diving area at the **Cousteau Underwater Park,** just off Basse-Terre near Pigeon Island, offers routine dives to 60 ft (18 m). But the numerous glass-bottom boats and day-trippers make the site feel like a crowded marine parking lot. That said, the underwater sights are spectacular. Guides and instructors here are certified under the French CMAS (and some have PADI, but none have NAUI). Most operators offer two-hour dives three times per day for about $40–$50 per dive. Hotels and dive operators usually rent snorkeling gear.

Caraïbes Plongées (✉ Gosier, Grande-Terre, ☎ 0509/90–44–90) is one of the best known dive operations in the area. **Centre Nautique des Saintes** (✉ Plage de la Coline, Terre-de-Haut, Terre-de-Haut, ☎ 590/99–54–25) prides itself on the quality of its instruction; some English is spoken. **Chez Guy et Christian** (✉ Plage de Malendure, Basse-Terre, ☎ 0590/98–82–43) has a good reputation and is well-established among those who dive Pigeon Island. After 10 years of experience, dive master Cedric Phalipon of **Club de Plongeé Des Saintes, Pisquettes** (✉ Le Mouillage, Terre-de-Haut, Terre-de-Haut, ☎ 0590/99–88–80) knows all the sites and islets and gives excellent lessons, in English. Equipment is new and of a high caliber. Small tanks are available for kids, who are taken buddy diving. An all-day scuba-diving cruise on a catamaran to Iles des Saintes is offered by **Croisieres sous le vent** (✉ Plage de Malendure, Basse-Terre, ☎ 0590/98–83–73). **Les Heures Saines** (✉ Plage de Malendure, Basse-Terre, ☎ 0590/98–86–63) is the premier operator for dives in the Cousteau Reserve. Trips to Les Saintes offer one or two dives, for medium and advanced card holders, and time for lunch and sightseeing. Wreck, night, and Nitrox diving are also available.

SEA EXCURSIONS
Coralia (✉ Novotel Coralia, Bas-du-Fort, Grande-Terre, ☎ 0590/90–40–00), a sleek, catamaran, sails to Marie Galante, where guests tour the island then come back aboard for rum cocktails and a barbecue lunch. A second sea voyage is to Les Saintes, with a shipboard luncheon, drinks, music, and snorkeling. *Nautilus* (✉ Plage de Malendure, Basse-Terre, ☎ 0590/98–89–08) offers (rather crowded) glass-bottom-boat tours and snorkeling. *Tip Top One* (✉ Section Leroux, Gosier, Grand-Terre, ☎ 0590/84–66–36) is a large, safe catamaran that flies through the water on its course to Les Saintes and other islands. It is a full day at sea, with snorkeling, lunch, rum libations, and shore excursions.

TENNIS
Many hotels have courts (most lighted); if you're not a guest of a hotel with tennis facilities, call ahead for more information and to reserve a court. The **Auberge de la Vieille Tour** (✉ Rte. de Montauban, Gosier, Grande-Terre, ☎ 0590/84–23–23) has two courts. **Club Méditerranée La Caravelle** (✉ Quart Carvelle, Ste-Anne, Grande-Terre, ☎ 0590/85–49–50) has six courts. **Le Méridien St-François** (✉ Av. de l'Europe, St-François, ☎ 0590/88–51–00) has two courts. **Marina Club** (✉ Point-à-Pitre, Grand-Terre, ☎ 0590/90–84–08) has seven courts. The **Tennis League of Guadeloupe** (✉ Centre Lamby-Lambert Stadium, Gosier, Grande-Terre, ☎ 0590/90–90–97) has six courts.

WINDSURFING
Most beachfront hotels can help you arrange lessons and rentals. Windsurfing buffs congregate at the **UCPA Hotel Club** (✉ St-François, Grande-Terre, ☎ 0590/88–64–80). You can rent a *planche-à-voile* (windsurfer) through **Callinago** (✉ Gosier, Grande-Terre, ☎ 0590/84–25–25).

Shopping

You can find good buys on anything French—perfume, crystal, china, cosmetics, fashions, scarves. Many stores offer a 20% discount on luxury items purchased with traveler's checks or, in some cases, major credit cards. As for local handicrafts, you'll find fine wood carvings, madras table linens, island dolls dressed in madras, woven straw baskets and hats, and *salako* hats made of split bamboo. Of course, there's the favorite Guadeloupean souvenir—rum—and, for foodies, great little baskets lined with madras and filled with aromatic, fresh spices.

Areas and Malls

Grande-Terre's largest shopping mall, **Destrelland,** has more than 70 stores and is just minutes from the Aéroport International Pôle Caraïbes, which, with its duty-free stores, is a shopping destination in its own right. In **Pointe-à-Pitre** you can enjoy browsing in the street stalls around the harbor quay and at the two markets (the best is the Marché de Frébault). The town's main shopping streets are rue Schoelcher, rue de Nozières, and the lively rue Frébault. At the St-John Perse Cruise Terminal there's an attractive mall with about two dozen shops. **Bas-du-Fort**'s two shopping areas are the Cora Shopping Center and the marina, where there are 20 or so boutiques and quite a few restaurants. In **St-François** there are more than a dozen shops surrounding the marina, some selling sensual French lingerie, swimsuits, and fashions. A supermarket has incredibly good prices on their French wines. Cheeses are many, and if you pick up some bread (fresh baquettes), you have a picnic. (Go get lost at a secluded beach.)

Specialty Items

ART

Brigitte Boesch (✉ St-François, Grande-Terre, ☎ 0590/88–48–94), a German-born painter who has exhibited all over the world, lives in St-François, and her studio is worth a visit. Call for directions. Guadeloupean painter **Joel Nankin** (✉ Baie Mahault, Basse-Terre, ☎ 0590/23–28–24) specializes in masks and acrylic and sand paintings.

CHINA, CRYSTAL, AND SILVER

Rosebleu (✉ 5 rue Frébault, Pointe-à-Pitre, Grande-Terre, ☎ 0590/82–93–43; ✉ Aéroport International Pôle Caraïbes, no phone) sells china, crystal, and silver by top manufacturers, including Christoffle.

COSMETICS, LINGERIE, AND PERFUME

L'Artisan Parfumeur (✉ Centre St-John Perse, Pointe-à-Pitre, Grande-Terre, ☎ 0590/83–80–25) sells top French and American brands as well as tropical scents. **Au Bonheur des Dames** (✉ 49 rue Frébault, Pointe-à-Pitre, Grande-Terre, ☎ 0590/82–00–30) sells several different lines of cosmetics and skin-care products in addition to its perfumes. **Phoenicia** (✉ Bas-du-Fort, Grande-Terre, ☎ 0590/90–85–56; ✉ 8 rue Frébault, Pointe-à-Pitre, Grande-Terre, ☎ 0590/83–50–36; ✉ 121 bis rue Frébault, Pointe-à-Pitre, Grande-Terre, ☎ 0590/82–25–75) sells various perfumes. **Vendôme** (✉ 8–10 rue Frébault, Pointe-à-Pitre, Grande-Terre, ☎ 0590/83–42–84) is Guadeloupe's exclusive purveyor of Stendhal and Germaine Monteil cosmetics.

HANDICRAFTS

Boutique de la Plage (✉ Bd. Général de Gaulle, Gosier, Grande-Terre, ☎ 0590/84–52–51) offers a mind-boggling jumble of items ranging from tacky tchotchkes ("fertility" sculptures, for example) to sublime art naïf canvases for as little as $20. **La Case à Soie** (✉ Ste-Anne, Grande-Terre, ☎ 0590/88–11–31) sells flowing silk dresses and scarves in Caribbean colors. The **Centre d'Art Haitien** (✉ 65 Montauban, Gosier, Grande-Terre, ☎ 0590/84–32–60) is the place to buy imaginative art. The **Centre Artisanat** (✉ Ste-Anne, Grande-Terre) offers a wide selection of local crafts.

The **Centre de Broderie** (✉ Vieux Fort, Basse-Terre, ☎ 0590/92–04–14) is renowned for its traditional lacework. The center is built into the ruins of Ft. l'Olive, and you can watch local ladies tat intricate tablecloths, napkins, and place mats. This kind of lacework is rare, so prices are *très cher* ($30 for a doily).

Didier Spindler (✉ Bourg, Terre-de-Haut,, ☎ 0590/99–50–99) has his second-floor art gallery in the row of shops between the dock and the church. His oils depict Caribbean life. On the first floor are objets d'art, mirrors, and lamps from around the world. At **Maogany Artisanat** (✉ Bourg, Terre-de-Haut, ☎ 0590/99–50–12) Yves Cohen, an artist and designer, creates batiks and hand-painted T-shirts in luminescent seashell shades. Hand-loomed silk fabrics are embellished with gold thread, others are translucent, like his sensual women's collection, 1000 & One Nights. Silk shawls and scarves, hand-embroidered with tropical birds, and his children's collection make great gifts. **Pascal Foy** (✉ Rte. à Pompierres, Bourg, Terre-de-Haut, ☎ 0590/99–52–29) produces stunning homages to traditional creole architecture: paintings of houses that incorporate collage and make marvelous wall hangings. Prices begin at $100.

LIQUOR AND TOBACCO

Aéroport International Pôle Caraïbes (✉ Grande-Terre, ☎ 0590/21–14–72) has a good selection of island rum and tobacco. **Délice Shop** (✉ 45 rue Achille René-Boisneuf, Pointe-à-Pitre, Grande-Terre, ☎ 0590/82–98–24) is the spot for island rum and items from France—from cheese to chocolate.

Nightlife

Cole Porter notwithstanding, Guadeloupeans maintain that the beguine began here (the Martinicans and St. Lucians make the same claim for their islands). Discos come, discos go, and the current music craze is zouk (music with an African-influenced Caribbean rhythm), but the beat of the beguine remains steady. Many resorts have dinner dancing, as well as entertainment by steel bands and folk groups.

BARS AND NIGHTCLUBS

Join Fidel Castro and Che Guevara, whose photos hang proudly on the walls of **Lollapalooza** (✉ 122 Montauban, Gosier, Grande-Terre, ☎ 0590/84–58–58) for hot Latin dancing and genuine Cuban rum. **Lele Bar** (✉ Le Méridien St-François, av. de l'Europe, St-François, Grande-Terre, ☎ 0590/88–51–00) draws locals and visitors alike. On Ile des Saintes, **Nilce's Bar** (✉ Bourg, Terre-de-Haut, ☎ 0590/99–56–80) at the pier still rocks, even though Nilce has sold out and gone to sing in the casino in Gosier. Next door to Nilce's and on the second floor, **Jardin Creole** (✉ Bourg, Terre-de-Haut, ☎ 0590/99–55–08) has live music five nights a week, with local bands playing blues and jazz. By day, its a kid-friendly *glacier*, with such adult ice cream dishes as vodka-laced lemon sorbet. Also, it is the island's hospitable Internet café.

CASINOS

Both of the island's two casinos are on Grande-Terre, and both have American-style roulette, blackjack, and chemin de fer. The legal age is 18, and you'll need a photo ID. Jacket and tie aren't required, but "proper attire" means no shorts. **Casino de Gosier** (✉ Gosier, Grande-Terre, ☎ 0590/84–79–69) has a bar, restaurant, and cinema. There are a number of well-priced packages, for dinner and a movie, for example. The higher stakes gambling is behind a closed door. You will have to pay $10 to be part of that action—or even to look on. It's open Monday to Saturday from 7:30 PM; slot machines open at 10 AM. **Casino de St-**

François (⊠ Marina, St-François, Grande-Terre, ☎ 0590/88–41–31) has a snack bar and nightclub and is open daily from 9 PM.

DISCOS

Night owls should note that carousing isn't cheap. Most discos charge a cover of at least $20, which includes one drink (drinks cost about $10 each). **Le Barracuda** (⊠ Rte. du Club Méditerranée, Ste-Anne, Grande-Terre, ☎ 0590/88–18–19) is really on fire with the hot dance rhythms of the tropics: zouk, funk, reggae, salsa, and soukouss. **Caraïbes 2** (⊠ Carrefour de Blanchard, Bas-du-Fort, Grande-Terre, ☎ 0590/90–85–27) plays Brazilian dance music and has erotic spectacles with charming girls from around the world; the ambience is like that of the Parisian music halls. **La Plantation** (⊠ Gourbeyre, Basse-Terre, ☎ 0590/81–23–37) is the top spot on Basse-Terre; couples dance to zouk, funk, and house on the immense mezzanine dance floor. Outside Gosier, there's **Shiva 1** (⊠ Le Moule, Grande-Terre, ☎ 0590/23–53–59) a tri-level club with the first floor like the loges in a theater; many local musicians perform here. **Le Sans Tabou** (⊠ 153, av. Charles de Gaulle, Gosier, Grande-Terre, ☎ 0590/84–31–15) is a high-tech, chrome-covered dance club that plays the music that's hot in New York, London, and Paris to a cosmopolitan clientele. **Zenith** (⊠ Rte. de la Riviera, Gosier, Grande-Terre, ☎ 0590/90–72–04) is one of the island's most exclusive clubs, featuring local creole salsa and remarkable service; there is a view of the sea and a terrace with a pool.

Exploring Guadeloupe

To see each "wing" of the butterfly, you'll need to budget at least one day. Grande-Terre has pretty villages along its south coast and the spectacular Pointe des Châteaux. You can see the main sights in Pointe-à-Pitre in about a half-day. Touring the rugged, mountainous Basse-Terre is a challenge. If time is a problem, head straight to the west coast; you could easily spend a day traveling its length, stopping for a bit of sightseeing, lunch, and a swim. It really isn't possible to visit the outlying islands unless you budget both the time and money, as you'll probably have to stay overnight.

Numbers in the margin correspond to points of interest on the Guadeloupe map.

Grande-Terre

SIGHTS TO SEE

❾ Anse Bertrand. The northernmost village in Guadeloupe lies 4 mi (6½ km) south of La Pointe de la Grande Vigie. It was the Caribs' last refuge and was prosperous in the days of sugar. Most excitement takes place in the St-Jacques Hippodrome, where horse races and cockfights are held. The beach at Anse Laborde is good for swimming.

❸ Aquarium de la Guadeloupe. The Caribbean's largest aquarium is a good place to spend an hour. The well-planned facility is in the marina near Pointe-à-Pitre and has an assortment of tropical fish, crabs, lobsters, moray eels, dorsal spines, trunkfish, and coral. ⊠ *Pl. Créole, off rte. N4, Point-à-Pitre,* ☎ *590/90–92–38.* 🎟 *€4.76.* ☾ *Daily 9–7.*

❷ Bas-du-Fort. The main attraction in this town is the Fort Fleur d'Épée, an 18th-century fortress that hunkers down on a hillside behind a deep moat. It was the scene of hard-fought battles between the French and the English in 1794. You can explore its well-preserved dungeons and battlements and take in a sweeping view of Iles des Saintes and Marie-Galante. The Other End of the World (☎ 0690/35–33–45 or 0690/55–38–52) is a 15-minute ferry ride from Bas-du-Fort Marina. This islet was a refuge from society for a French wine merchant and his bride,

When you pack your MCI Calling Card, it's like packing your loved ones along too.

Your MCI Calling Card is the easy way to stay in touch when you travel. Use it to call to and from over 125 countries. Plus, every time you call, you can earn frequent flier miles. So wherever your travels take you, call home with your MCI Calling Card. It's even easy to get one. Just visit **www.mci.com/worldphone** or **www.mci.com/partners**.

EASY TO CALL WORLDWIDE

1. Just enter the WorldPhone® access number of the country you're calling from.

2. Enter or give the operator your MCI Calling Card number.

3. Enter or give the number you're calling.

Aruba ❖	800-888-8
Bahamas ❖	1-800-888 8000

Barbados ❖	1-800-888-8000
Bermuda ❖	1-800-888-8000
British Virgin Islands ❖	1-800-888-8000
Canada	1-800-888-8000
Mexico	01-800-021-8000
Puerto Rico	1-800-888-8000
United States	1-800-888-8000
U.S. Virgin Islands	1-800-888-8000

❖ Limited availability.

EARN FREQUENT FLIER MILES

Find America *with a Compass*

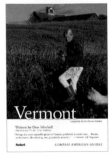

Written by local authors and illustrated throughout
with spectacular color images, Compass American
Guides reveal the character and culture of more than
40 of America's most fascinating destinations. Perfect
for residents who want to explore their own backyards
and for visitors who want an insider's perspective
on the history, heritage, and all there is to see and do.

Fodor's COMPASS AMERICAN GUIDES

At bookstores everywhere.

a Guadeloupean slave. Their lovely and talented granddaughter, the esteemed writer Simone Schwarz-Bart, has re-created their home that was destroyed in the hurricane of 1928. In addition to the museum, there is a vast, open-air restaurant with a buffet of authentic creole dishes, and rum libations. Dancing and card-playing follow lunch. The excursion costs €35.84, including the round-trip ferry ride.

4 **Gosier.** With its red-roofed villas perched above the sea, this could be a small town on the Côte d'Azur. People stroll about with baguettes under their arms or sit at sidewalk cafés reading *Le Monde* and drinking *planteurs,* the local rum punch. It's the island's major tourist center, with hotels and inns, nightclubs, shops, a casino, and a long stretch of sand.

11 **Morne-à-l'Eau.** This agricultural city of about 16,000 people has an amphitheater-shape cemetery, with black-and-white-checkerboard tombs, elaborate epitaphs, and multicolor (plastic) flowers. On All Saints' Day (November 1), it's the scene of a moving (and photogenic) candlelight service.

8 **Le Moule.** On the Atlantic coast, and once the capital city of Guadeloupe, this port city of about 24,000 has had more than its share of troubles: it was bombarded by the British in 1794 and 1809 and by a hurricane in 1928. Canopies of flamboyant trees hang over the narrow streets, where colorful vegetable and fish markets do a brisk business. The town hall, with graceful balustrades, and a small 19th-century neoclassical church are on the main square. Le Moule also has a beach protected by a reef, perfect for windsurfing.

7 **Pointe des Châteaux.** The island's easternmost point offers a breathtaking (though windy) view of the Atlantic crashing against huge rocks, carving them into pyramidlike shapes. The majestic cliffs are reminiscent of the headlands of Brittany. There are spectacular views of Guadeloupe's south and east coasts and the island of La Désirade. On weekends locals come in large numbers to walk their dogs, surf, or look for romance.

1 **Pointe-à-Pitre.** Although not the capital city, this is the largest commercial and industrial hub in the southwest of Grande-Terre. It's bustling, noisy, and hot—a place of honking horns and traffic jams and cars on sidewalks for want of a parking place. By day its pulse is fast, but at night, when its streets are almost deserted, you don't want to be there.

The city has suffered severe damage over the years from earthquakes, fires, and hurricanes. It took heavy hits by Hurricanes Frederick (1979), David (1980), and Hugo (1989). On one side of rue Frébault you can see the remaining French colonial structures; on the other, the modern city. Some of the downtown area has been rejuvenated. Completion of the Centre St-John Perse has transformed old warehouses into a cruise-terminal complex that consists of the Hotel St-John, restaurants, shops, ferry docks, and the port authority headquarters.

The heart of the old city is Place de la Victoire, surrounded by wooden buildings with balconies and shutters and many sidewalk cafés. Place de la Victoire was named in honor of Victor Hugues's 1794 victory over the British. The sandbox trees in the park are said to have been planted by Hugues the day after the victory. During the French Revolution Hugues ordered the guillotine to be set up in the square so the public could witness the bloody end of 300 recalcitrant royalists. Many were plantation owners, which put a fast end to the plantocracy.

Even more colorful is the bustling marketplace, between rues St-John Perse, Frébault, Schoelcher, and Peynier. It's a cacophonous place, where housewives bargain for spices, herbs (and herbal remedies), papayas, breadfruits, christophenes, tomatoes, and a bright assortment of other produce.

Anyone with an interest in French literature and culture won't want to miss the **Musée St-John Perse.** It's dedicated to Guadeloupe's most famous son and one of the giants of world literature, Alexis Léger, better known as St-John Perse, winner of the Nobel Prize for literature in 1960. Some of his finest poems are inspired by the history and landscape—particularly the sea—of his beloved Guadeloupe. The museum contains a complete collection of his poetry and some of his personal belongings. Before you go, look for his birthplace, at No. 54 rue Achille René-Boisneuf. ⊠ *Corner of rues Noizières and Achille René-Boisneuf,* ☎ *0590/90–01–92.* 🎟 *€1.25.* ⊙ *Thurs.–Tues. 8:30–12:30 and 2:30–5:30.* Guadeloupe's other famous son is celebrated at the **Musée Schoelcher.** Victor Schoelcher, a high-minded abolitionist from Alsace, fought against slavery in the French West Indies in the 19th century. The museum contains many of his personal effects, and exhibits trace his life and work. ⊠ *24 rue Peynier,* ☎ *0590/82–08–04.* 🎟 *€1.68.* ⊙ *Weekdays 8:30–11:30 and 2–5.* For fans of French ecclesiastical architecture, there's the imposing **Cathédrale de St-Pierre et St-Paul** (⊠ rue Alexandre Isaac at rue de l'Eglise), built in 1807. Although battered by hurricanes, it is reinforced with iron pillars and ribs that look like leftovers from the Eiffel Tower. The fine stained-glass windows and creole-style balconies make it worth a look.

⑩ **Port Louis.** This fishing village of about 7,000 is best known for the Souffleur Beach. It was once one of the island's prettiest, but it has become a little shabby. Still, the sand is fringed by flamboyant trees, and though the beach is crowded on weekends, it's blissfully quiet during the week. There are also spectacular views of Basse-Terre.

⑤ **Ste-Anne.** In the 18th century this town, 8 mi (13 km) east of Gosier, was a sugar-exporting center. Sand has replaced sugar as the town's most valuable asset. La Caravelle and the other beaches here are among the best in Guadeloupe. On a more spiritual note, Ste-Anne has a lovely cemetery with stark-white tombs.

⑥ **St-François.** This was once a simple little village primarily involved with fishing and harvesting tomatoes. Increasingly, though, St-François is overtaking Gosier as Guadeloupe's most fashionable tourist resort area (it also has a slightly better climate). The fish and tomatoes are still here, but so are some of the island's ritziest hotels. Avenue de l' Europe runs between the well-groomed 18-hole Robert Trent Jones–designed municipal golf course and the marina. On the marina side, a string of shops, hotels, and restaurants caters to tourists.

Basse-Terre

Yellow butterflies—clouds of them—are the first thing you see when you arrive on Basse-Terre. Rugged, green, and mysterious, this half of Guadeloupe is all mountain trails, lakes, waterfalls, and hot springs. It's the home of La Soufrière volcano, as well as of the capital city, also called Basse-Terre. The northwest coast, between Bouillante and Grande-Anse, is magnificent; the road twists and turns up steep hills smothered in vegetation and then drops down and skirts deep blue bays and colorful seaside towns. Constantly changing light, towering clouds, and frequent rainbows only add to the beauty. The Parc National de la Guadeloupe is crisscrossed by numerous trails, many following the old *traces,* routes that porters once took across the mountains.

SIGHTS TO SEE

㉓ Basse-Terre. Because Pointe-à-Pitre is so much bigger, few people suspect that this little town of 15,000 inhabitants is the capital and administrative center of Guadeloupe. But if you have any doubts, walk up the hill to the state-of-the-art Théâtre Nationale, where some of France's finest theater and opera companies perform. Paid for by the French government, it's a sign that Basse-Terre is reinventing itself. The town has had a lot to overcome. Founded in 1640, it has endured not only foreign attacks and hurricanes but sputtering threats from La Soufrière as well. The last major eruption was in the 16th century, though the volcano seemed active enough to warrant evacuating more than 70,000 people in 1975.

Start exploring the city at the imposing 17th-century Fort Louis Delgrès. Its small museum gives a good outline of Basse-Terre's history. The Cathedral of Our Lady of Guadeloupe, to the north across the Rivière aux Herbes, is also worth a look. On boulevard Félix Eboué you can see the impressive colonial buildings housing government offices. Two main squares, both with gardens, Jardin Pichon and Champ d'Arbaud, give you a feel for how the city used to be. Not far from Champ d'Arbaud are the botanical gardens.

For shopping, walk down rue Dr. Cabre, with its brightly painted creole houses and imposing church, Ste-Marie de Guadeloupe. For a flavor of local life, check out the daily vegetable and fruit market on boulevard Basse-Terre, which runs parallel to the ocean. The other main street is rue St-François. For a guided tour of Basse-Terre climb aboard the **Pom, Pom** (☎ 0590/81–24–83), a miniature train that does a circuit of the major sights. The ride costs €6.16 and lasts 2½ hours. **Jardin Botanique,** an exquisitely tasteful 10-acre park populated with parrots and flamingos, has a circuitous walking trail that takes you by ponds with floating lily pads, cacti gardens, and every kind of tropical flower and plant, including orchids galore. A restaurant and another snack bar are housed in terraced, gingerbread buildings, one overlooking a waterfall, the other the mountains. The garden has a kiddie park and nature-oriented playthings in the shop. ✉ *Deshaies,* ☎ *0590/28–43–02.* ⌨ *€8.50.* ☼ *Daily 7 AM–5:30 PM.*

㉑ Bouillante. The name means "boiling," and so it's no surprise that hot springs were discovered here. However, today the biggest attraction is scuba diving on nearby Pigeon Island, which is accessed by boat from Plage de Malendure. There's an information office on the beach that can help you with diving and snorkeling arrangements.

⑱ Cascade aux Ecrevisses. Part of the Parc National de la Guadeloupe, Crayfish Falls is one of the island's loveliest (and most popular) spots. There's a marked trail (walk carefully—the rocks can be slippery) leading to this splendid waterfall that dashes down into the Corossol River—a good place for a dip. Come early, though, otherwise you probably won't have it to yourself.

㉕ Centre de Broderie. Vieux Fort is renowned for its traditional lacework. In 1980, 40 local lace makers united to preserve—and display—the ancient tradition of lace-making. At the center, built into the ruins of Fort L'Olive, you can see these local ladies tat intricate handkerchiefs, tablecloths, and doilies. This kind of lacework is rare, so prices are *très cher* (about $30 for a doily). ✉ *Bourg, Vieux Fort,* ☎ *0590/92–04–14.* ⌨ *Free.* ☼ *8:30–6.*

㉖ Chutes du Carbet. You can reach three of the Carbet Falls (one drops from 65 ft [20 m], the second from 360 ft [110 m], the third from 410 ft [125 m]) via a long, steep path from the village of Habituée. On the way up you'll pass the Grand Étang (Great Pond), a volcanic lake surrounded by interesting plant life. For horror fans there's also the curiously named Étang Zombi, a pond believed to house evil spirits.

⑳ **Ilet de Pigeon.** This tiny, rocky island, a few hundred yards off the coast, is the site of the Jacques Cousteau Marine Reserve, the best scuba and snorkeling site on Guadeloupe. Les Heures Saines and Chez Guy et Christian, both on the attractive Malendure Beach, conduct diving trips, and the glass-bottom *Aquarium* and *Nautilus* make daily trips to this spectacular site.

⑰ **Maison de la Forêt.** This part of the Parc National de la Guadeloupe is where you can park and explore various nature trails. The Habitation Beausoleil has a variety of displays that describe (in French) the flora, fauna, and topography of the national park. It's open daily 9–4:30; admission is free. There are three marked botanical trails and picnic tables.

⑯ **Les Mamelles.** Two mountains—Mamelle de Petit-Bourg, at 2,350 ft (719 m), and Mamelle de Pigeon, at 2,500 ft (765 m)—rise in the Parc National de la Guadeloupe. *Mamelle* means "breast," and when you see the mountains, you'll understand why they are so named. Trails ranging from easy to arduous lace up into the surrounding mountains. There's a glorious view from the lookout point 1,969 ft (602 m) up Mamelle de Pigeon. If you're a climber, plan to spend several hours exploring this area.

㉔ **Le Musée Volcanologique.** Inland from Basse-Terre on the road to Matouba is the village of St-Claude, where you can see this museum that will tell you everything you need to know about volcanoes. ✉ *Rue Victor Hugo, St-Claude,* ☎ *0596/78–15–16.* 💷 *€2.65.* ⊙ *Daily 9–5.*

⑮ **Parc National de la Guadeloupe.** This 74,100-acre park has been recognized by UNESCO as a Biosphere Reserve. Before going, pick up a *Guide to the National Park* from the tourist office; it rates the hiking trails according to difficulty (note: most mountain trails are in the southern half of the park). The park is bisected by the Route de la Traversée, a 16-mi (26-km) paved road lined with masses of tree ferns, shrubs, flowers, tall trees, and green plantains. It's the ideal point of entry to the park. Wear rubber-soled shoes and take along a swimsuit, a sweater, and perhaps food for a picnic. Try to get an early start to stay ahead of the hordes of cruise-ship passengers who are making a day of it. ✉ *Administrative Headquarters, Rte. de la Traversée, Saint-Claude,* ☎ *0590/80–86–00.*

⑭ **Pointe-Noire.** This town has two small museums devoted to local products. **La Maison du Bois** (☎ 0590/98–17–09) offers a glimpse into the traditional use of wood on the island. Superbly crafted musical instruments and furnishings are on sale. It's open Tuesday to Sunday from 9:30 to 5:30 and charges a €.88 admission. Across the road from La Maison du Bois is **La Maison du Cacao** (☎ 0590/98–21–23), at which you can see a working cocoa plantation. It is open daily from 9 to 5 for a €3.52 admission fee. Pointe-Noire is a good jumping-off point from which to explore Basse-Terre's little-visited northwest coast. A road skirts magnificent cliffs and tiny coves, dances in and out of thick stands of mahogany and gommier trees, and weaves through unspoiled fishing villages with boats and ramshackled houses as brightly colored as a child's finger painting. One of the most attractive villages is Deshaies (pronounced "day").

⑬ **Ste-Rose.** In addition to a sulfur bath, there are two good beaches (Amandiers and Clugny) and several interesting small museums in Ste-

Rose. **Le Domaine de Séverin** (☎ 0590/28–91–86), free and open daily 8:30–12:30, is a historic rum distillery with a working waterwheel; the restaurant in a colonial house is known for its accras and colombos.

⑫ **Station Thermale de Ravine Chaude René Toribio.** It's not Vichy—nor tourist-oriented—but this spa is a good place to soak after tackling the trails. It draws upon the area's healthful geothermal waters. If you do nothing but bathe in the vast, warm pool you will feel healed. If time allows, have a sauna, massage, algae mask, or hydrotherapy. Almost no English is spoken here, but then it's all in the touch. The surrounding landscape in the foothills of Grosse Montagne—with its cane fields, country lanes, and colorful little villages—is very pleasant. However, do get specific directions from your hotel concierge or someone who speaks English. Finding it is not a day at the spa. ⊠ *Le Lamentin,* ☎ 0590/25–75–92. 🖾 €2.64. ☉ *Daily 8–8.*

⑲ **Vernou.** Many of the old mansions in this area remain in the hands of the original aristocratic families, the *bekés* (creole for "whites"), who trace their lineage to before the French Revolution. Traipsing along a path that leads beyond the village through the forest, you'll come to the waterfall at Saut de la Lézarde (Lizard's Leap).

㉒ **Vieux-Habitants.** This was the island's first colony, established in 1635. Beaches, a restored coffee plantation, and the oldest church on the island (1666) make this village worth a stop. From the new riverfront **Musée du Café** (☎ 0590/98–54–96), dedicated to the art of coffee-making, the tantalizing aroma of fresh ground beans reaches the highway. Plaques and photos tell of the island's coffee history. The shop sells excellent coffee and rum punches (liqueurs). Admission is €6.

Iles des Saintes

The eight-island archipelago of Iles des Saintes, usually referred to as Les Saintes, dots the waters off the south coast of Guadeloupe. The islands are Terre-de-Haut, Terre-de-Bas, Ilet à Cabrit, Grand Ilet, La Redonde, La Coche, Le Pâté, and Les Augustins. Columbus discovered them on November 4, 1493, and christened them Los Santos in honor of All Saints' Day.

Only Terre-de-Haut and Terre-de-Bas are inhabited, with a combined population of 3,260. Many of les Saintois, as the islanders are called, are fair-haired, blue-eyed descendants of Breton and Norman sailors. Fishing is their main source of income, and the shores are lined with their boats and *filets bleus* (blue nets dotted with burnt-orange buoys). The fishermen wear hats called *salakos*, which look like inverted saucers. They're patterned after a hat said to have been brought here by a seafarer from China or Indonesia.

㉗ **Terre-de-Haut.** With 5 square mi (13 square km) and a population of about 1,500, Terre-de-Haut is the largest and most developed of Les Saintes. Its "big city" is Bourg, with one street and a few bistros, cafés, and shops. Clutching the hillside are trim white houses with bright red or blue doors, balconies, and gingerbread frills.

Terre-de-Haut's ragged coastline is scalloped with lovely coves and beaches, including the semi-nudist beach at Anse Crawen. The beautiful bay, complete with a "sugarloaf" mountain, has been called a mini Rio. There are precious few vehicles on island, so to get around, you can get your exercise by walking. Terre-de-Haut is tiny, but it's also very hilly. Or you can add to the din and rent a motorbike. Take your time on these rutted roads. Around any bend there can be a herd of goats chomping on a fallen palm frond. This island makes a great day trip, but you'll really get a feel for Les Saintes if you stay over. It is much like St. Barths, but for a fraction of the prices.

Fort Napoléon. This gallery holds a collection of 250 modern paintings, influenced by cubism and surrealism. However, this museum is noted for its exhaustive exhibit of the greatest sea battles ever fought. You can also visit the well-preserved barracks and prison cells, or admire the botanical gardens, which specialize in cacti of all sizes and descriptions. ✉ *Bourg,* ☎ *0590/37–99–59.* ▧ *€2.64.* ⊘ *Daily 9–12:30.*

Other Islands

㉙ La Désirade. According to legend, this is the "desired land" of Columbus's second voyage. Along with Marie-Galante, it was spotted on November 3, 1493. The 8-square-mi (21-square-km) island, 5 mi (8 km) east of St-François, was a leper colony for many years. Most of today's 1,700 inhabitants are fishermen and boatbuilders. The main settlement is Grande-Anse, which has a pretty church and a couple of lodgings. There are good beaches here and there's little to do but loll around on them.

㉘ Marie-Galante. Columbus sighted this 60-square-mi (155-square-km) island on November 3, 1493, the day before he landed at Ste-Marie on Basse-Terre. He named it for his flagship, the *Maria Galanda,* and sailed on. It's dotted with ruined 19th-century sugar mills, and sugar is still its major product. With its rolling hills of green cane still worked by oxen and men with broad-brimmed straw hats, this island is a journey back to a time when all of Guadeloupe was an agrarian place. Only an hour by high-speed boat from Pointe-à-Pitre, this is where Guadeloupeans come for day trips; it has only just become a tourist destination. The country folk are still a bit shy and have a gentle sense of humor. You'll see yellow butterflies, pigs tethered by the side of the road, and some of the archipelago's best beaches. Ox-pulling contests, visits to distilleries, days at the beach, or country hikes await you. The main community on the island is Grand-Bourg; an entertainment complex here, called El Rancho, has a 400-seat movie theater, a restaurant, a terrace grill, a snack bar, a disco, and a few double rooms. The dramatic coast is also worth exploring. There are soaring cliffs—such as the Gueule Grand Gouffre (Mouth of the Giant Chasm) and Les Galeries (where the sea has sculpted a natural arcade)—and enormous sun-dappled grottoes, such as Le Trou à Diable, whose underground river can be explored with a guide. After sunset no-see-ums and mosquitoes can be a nuisance, especially near beaches. Always be armed with repellant. The **Château Murat** (✉ Grand-Bourg, Marie-Galante, ☎ 0590/ 97–94–41) is a restored 17th-century sugar plantation and rum distillery housing exhibits on the history of rum making and sugarcane production and an admirable *ecomusée,* whose displays celebrate local crafts and customs. The château is open daily 9:15–5; admission is €1.32. **Le Moulin de Bézard** (✉ Chemin de Nesmond, off D202, Marie-Galante) is the only rebuilt windmill in the Caribbean. There are two gift shops and a café here. They're housed in replicated slave quarters: tiny cabins (with wattle walls) of a type found only on this island. Admission is €1.25; it's open daily 10–2. You should make it a point to see the distilleries, especially **Père Labat** (✉ Grand Bourg, Section Poisson, Marie-Galante, ☎ 0590/97–03–79), whose rum is considered one of the finest in the Caribbean and whose atelier turns out lovely pottery; admission is free, and it's open daily 7–12.

GUADELOUPE A TO Z

To research prices, get advice from other travelers, and book travel arrangements, visit www.fodors.com.

AIR TRAVEL

American has many flights from U.S. cities direct to San Juan, Puerto Rico, with seasonal connections to Guadeloupe on American Eagle. Air Canada has direct flights from Montréal on Saturday. Air France flies nonstop from Paris to Guadeloupe and to Fort-de-France on Martinique and has direct service from Miami and San Juan. Air Caraïbes flies in daily from Martinique, St. Martin, St. Barths, and Santo Domingo in the Dominican Republic. LIAT flies from St. Croix, Antigua, and St. Maarten in the north and is your best bet from Dominica, Martinique, St. Lucia, Grenada, Barbados, and Trinidad. Air Tropical, with two twin-engine aircraft with five-passenger seating capacity, flies into Pointe-à-Pitre's Le Raizet Airport. An air-charter operator (English-speaking) based at the St. François Airport has day tours to the neighboring islands (☞ Sightseeing Tours) and provides air-taxi and ambulance services.

➤ AIRLINES AND CONTACTS: **Air Canada** (☎ 0590/21–12–77). **Air Caraïbes** (☎ 0590/82–47–00 or 590/21–12–88). **Air France** (☎ 0590/82–62–74). **Air Tropical** (☎ 0590/88–89–90 or 0690/35–05–15). **American/American Eagle** (☎ 0590/87–70–40 or 590/21–11–80). **LIAT** (☎ 0590/21–13–93).

AIRPORTS

Most airlines fly into Aéroport International Pôle Caraïbes. Cabs meet flights at the airport, 3 mi (5 km) from Pointe-à-Pitre. The metered fare is about $9 to Pointe-à-Pitre, $22 to Gosier, and $38 to St-François. Fares go up 40% on Sunday and holidays and from 9 PM to 7 AM. For $1 you can take a bus from the airport to downtown Pointe-à-Pitre. A local bus ($1) then runs from the capital to Gosier. If you have a lot of luggage, it's not advisable.

➤ AIRPORT INFORMATION: **Aéroport International Pôle Caraïbes** (☎ 0590/21–14–32).

BIKE AND MOPED RENTALS

You can rent a Vespa (motorbike) at Eli Sport and Equator Moto for about $29 per day, including insurance. You'll need to put down nearly $150 for a deposit. On Terre-de-Haut mopeds start at about $20 a day. There are numerous vendors by the ferry dock; shop around for the best price. On Marie-Galante try Loca Sol.

➤ BIKE AND MOPED RENTALS: **Eli Sport** (✉ Grand Camp, Grande-Terre, ☎ 0590/90–37–50). **Equator Moto** (✉ Gosier, Grande-Terre, ☎ 0590/90–36–77). **Loca Sol** (✉ Rue du Fort, Grand-Bourg, Marie-Galante, ☎ 0590/97–76–58).

BOAT AND FERRY TRAVEL

Express des Isles and Transport Maritime Brudey Frères provide ferry service to Les Saintes and Marie-Galante. Schedules often change, especially on weekends, so check them at the tourist or harbor offices.

FARES AND SCHEDULES

It's a choppy 45-minute crossing to Terre-de-Haut from Trois-Rivières on Basse-Terre; ferries leave at about 8:30 AM (7:30 AM on Sunday) and return about 3 PM. From Pointe-à-Pitre on Grande-Terre, it's a 60-minute ride. Departure time is 8 AM, with return at 4 PM; the round-trip fare is €22.

The ferry to Grand-Bourg on Marie-Galante departs from Pointe-à-Pitre at 8 AM, 2 PM, and 5 PM, with returns at 6 AM, 9 AM, and 3:45 PM. It takes one hour and costs about €22 round-trip. *Sotramade Bateau L'Impériale* runs between La Désirade and St-François on Grande-Terre, departing daily at 8 AM and 4 PM. Return ferries depart daily at 3:30 PM.

The *Express des Isles* has service to Dominica (about €59.84, 2½ hours) and Martinique (around €61.60, four hours) from Pointe-à-Pitre. The ferry departs at 8 AM four days a week; check schedules for changes. If you are not prone to seasickness, this can be the most direct and least costly way to get to Martinique.

➤ BOAT AND FERRY INFORMATION: *Express des Isles* (☎ 0590/83–12–45 or 0590/83–04–43). *Sotramade Bateau L'Impériale* (☎ 0590/88–58–06). **Transport Maritime Brudey Frères** (☎ 0590/90–04–48).

BUSINESS HOURS

BANKS

Banks are open weekdays 8–noon and 2–4. Crédit Agricole, Banque Populaire, and Société Générale de Banque aux Antilles have branches that are open Saturday. In summer most banks are open 8–3. Banks close at noon the day before a legal holiday that falls during the week.

POST OFFICES

Post offices are open weekdays 8–noon and 2–4.

SHOPS

Shops are open weekdays 8 or 8:30–noon and 2:30–6.

CAR RENTALS

There are rental offices at Aéroport International Pôle Caraïbes and the major resorts. Count on spending about $60 a day for a small car (usually Korean) with standard shift. Automatics are considerably more expensive, and normally (the beautiful Peugots) have to be reserved in advance. Try negotiating for better deals both on the phone and once again at the counters. Note: allow yourself an extra 30 minutes to drop off your car at the end of your stay—the rental return sites are still at the old airport, Le Raizet, 2 mi (3 km) away.

➤ MAJOR AGENCIES: **Avis** (☎ 0590/21–13–54 or 0590/85–00–11). **Budget** (☎ 0590/21–13–48). **Europcar** (☎ 0590/21–13–52). **Hertz** (☎ 0590/21–13–46). **Jumbo Car** (☎ 0590/91–42–17).

CAR TRAVEL

If you are based in Gosier or at a larger resort, you will probably not need a car for your entire stay. Most people rent a car for a day or two of sightseeing. But if driving isn't your forte, taxis are always available.

GASOLINE

Gas is expensive, at about $1 per liter (roughly $4 per gallon).

ROAD CONDITIONS

Guadeloupe has 1,225 mi (1,976 km) of roads (marked as in Europe), and driving around Grande-Terre is relatively easy. On Basse-Terre it will take more effort to navigate the hairpin bends on the mountains and around the eastern shore. At night these scenic roads are poorly lit and treacherous. Guadeloupeans are skillful, fast, and sometimes impatient drivers. Also avoid morning and evening rush hours, especially around Pointe-à-Pitre.

RULES OF THE ROAD

Driving is on the right, as in the U.S. and Europe. Your valid driver's license will suffice for up to 20 days, after which you'll need an international driver's permit.

ELECTRICITY

Electricity is 220 volts (though some hotels have 110 volts), so if you're visiting from North America, you'll need to pack an adapter and a converter to use any appliances you bring with you.

EMERGENCIES

Pharmacies alternate in staying open around the clock. The tourist offices or your hotel can help you locate a pharmacist who is on duty and/or find an English-speaking doctor. SAMU is a medical service, where you can get to see a doctor fast. However, the receptionists generally do not speak English. SOS Taxi Ambulance can get you to a hospital quickly, but you may need to have a French-speaking person make the call.

➤ AMBULANCE AND FIRE: **Ambulance** (☎ 15). **Fire** (☎ 18). **SAMU** (☎ 0590/89–11–00). **SOS Taxi Ambulance** (☎ 0590/82–89–33).

➤ HOSPITALS: **Centre Hôpitalier de Pointe-à-Pitre** (✉ Pointe-à-Pitre, Abymes, Grande-Terre, ☎ 0590/89–10–10).

➤ POLICE: **Police emergencies** (☎ 17). **Police non-emergencies on Basse-Terre** (☎ 590/81–11–55). **Police non-emergencies on Grande-Terre** (☎ 590/82–13–17).

ETIQUETTE AND BEHAVIOR

Ask permission before taking a picture of an islander, and don't be surprised if the answer is a firm "No." Guadeloupeans are also deeply religious and traditional. Don't offend them by wearing short-shorts or swimwear off the beach.

FESTIVALS AND SEASONAL EVENTS

Carnival starts in early January and continues until Lent, finishing with a parade of floats and costumes on Mardi Gras (Fat Tuesday) and a huge bash on Ash Wednesday. In October, the Union des Arts Culinaires sponsors an upscale food festival. On a Sunday in early August, Point-à-Pitre on Grande-Terre holds the Fête des Cuisinières, which celebrates the masters of creole cuisine with a five-hour banquet that's open to the public. The festival was started in 1916 by a guild of female cooks who wanted to honor the patron saint of cooks, St. Laurent. August also sees the Tour Cycliste de la Guadeloupe, a highly competitive bike race that begins in Point-à-Pitre and covers more than 800 mi (1,290 km) on both Grande-Terre and Basse-Terre.

HOLIDAYS

Public holidays are: New Year's Day, Ash Wednesday (beginning of Lent, usually Feb.), Good Friday (Fri. before Easter, usually Mar.–Apr.), Easter Monday (Mon. after Easter, usually Mar.–Apr.), Labor Day (May 1), Bastille Day (July 14), Assumption Day (August 15), All Saints' Day (Nov. 1), Armistice Day (Nov. 11), and Christmas (Dec. 25).

LANGUAGE

The official language is French. Everyone also speaks a Creole patois, which you won't be able to understand even if you're fluent in French. In the major hotels most of the staff knows some English, but communicating may be more difficult in the countryside and in stores. Some taxi drivers speak a little English. Arm yourself with a phrase book, a dictionary, patience, and a sense of humor.

MAIL AND SHIPPING

Postcards to the United States cost about €.44 and to Canada €.52; letters up to 20 grams, €.70. Postcards and letters to Europe cost around €.44. Stamps can be purchased at post offices, *café-tabacs,* hotel newsstands, and souvenir shops. When writing to Guadeloupe, be sure to include the name of the specific island in the archipelago (e.g., Grande-

Terre, Basse-Terre, etc.) as well as the postal code, Guadeloupe, and the French West Indies.

MONEY MATTERS
Prices quoted throughout the chapter are in U.S. dollars unless otherwise noted.

ATMS
There are ATMs that accept Visa and MasterCard at Aéroport International Pôle Caraïbes and at some banks—such as Crédit Agricole, Banque Populaire, and Société Générale de Banque aux Antilles, and BDAF; they dole out euros. However, they don't always work with foreign ATM cards, and don't always work, period (especially on Les Saintes, where the banks are not open every day). Do not *bank* on them. Have a back-up plan.

CURRENCY
In January 2002, The French West Indies, along with 12 nations and 300 million Europeans, adopted the euro (€) as legal tender. No more francs. At press time, the exchange rate was €.88 to US$1. Some places accept U.S. dollars, but it's best to change your money, which can be done at a bank or at your hotel (which will take a larger cut). You tend to get better rates at a bureau de change, such as Change Caraïbe, which is near both the tourist office and market in Point-à-Pitre. Sometimes the bank rate is the same, but they usually take a larger fee.
➤ CONTACTS: **Change Caraïbe** (⊠ 21 rue de Rene Frebault, Point-à-Pitre, Grande-Terre).

PASSPORTS AND VISAS
All citizens of the United States, Canada, and the United Kingdom need a passport and a return or ongoing ticket.

SAFETY
Put your valuables in the hotel safe. Don't leave them unattended in your room or on the beach. It isn't a good idea to walk around Pointe-à-Pitre at night, since it's almost deserted after dark. If you rent a car, always lock it, with luggage and valuables stashed out of sight.

SIGHTSEEING TOURS
Guadeloupe has the advantage of having a number of fun, professional tour operators. However, much happens in French. Air Tropical has two twin-engined planes (five-passenger capacity) and organizes day-trips to the neighboring islands; the most far-ranging is the Archipelago Air Cruise, which goes to Les Saintes in the morning and Marie Galante or Désirade in the afternoon. Guides de Montagne de la Caraïbe provides guides for hiking tours in the mountains. Emeraude Guadeloupe offers everything from hikes up the volcano to botanical tours and visits to creole homes; guides are certified by the state, but you'll probably need some French to understand them. Parfum d'Aventure is for those who really want a challenge; it offers adventure trips on Basse-Terre, including canoeing on the Lézarde, sea kayaking, four-wheel driving, hiking, rappelling, and canyoning; it has some English-speaking guides. Sport D'av can set you up with adventures on Basse-Terre, including mountain climbing, sea kayaking, hiking, and diving.
➤ CONTACTS: **Air Tropical** (⊠ St-François, Grande-Terre, ☎ 0590/88-89-90 or 0690/35-05-15). **Emeraude Guadeloupe** (⊠ St-Claude, ☎ 0590/81-98-28). **Guides de Montagne de la Caraïbe** (⊠ Maison Forestière, Matouba, Basse-Terre, ☎ 0590/99-28-92 or 590/92-06-10). **Parfum d'Aventure** (⊠ Roche Blonval, St-François, Grande-Terre, ☎ 0590/88-47-62). **Sport D'av** (⊠ Jarry, Basse-Terre, ☎ 0590/32-58-41).

TAXES AND SERVICE CHARGES

SALES TAX

The *taxe de séjour* (room tax) varies from hotel to hotel but never exceeds $1.80 per person, per day.

SERVICE CHARGES

Most hotel prices include a 10%–15% service charge; if not, it will be added to your bill. A 15% charge is included in all restaurant prices.

TAXIS

Taxis are metered and fairly pricey, and on Sunday, holidays, and between 9 PM and 7 AM, fares increase by 40%. Tourist offices or your hotel can arrange for an English-speaking taxi driver and even organize a small group for you to share the cost of a tour. Nicho—of Nicho's Reliable Taxi—speaks perfect English and knows every back way when the traffic backs up on the main highways. Call Narcisse Taxi for an English-speaking, professional taxi driver and tour guide. If your French is in order, you can call Radio Cabs.

➤ TAXI CONTACTS: Call **Narcisse Taxi** (on Grand-Terre, ☎ 0590/35–27–29 or 0590/83–24–79; on Basse-Terre, ☎ 0590/81–79–70). **Nicho's Reliable Taxi** (☎ 0590/74–86–85). **Radio Cabs** (☎ 0590/82–00–00, 0590/83–09–55, or 0590/20–74–74).

TELEPHONES

Coin-operated phones are rare. If you need to make many calls outside of your hotel, purchase a *télécarte* at the post office or other outlets marked TÉLÉCARTE EN VENTE ICI. Télécartes look like credit cards and are used in special booths labeled TÉLÉCOM. Local and international calls made with these cards are cheaper than operator-assisted calls. (Note: you can't place collect or credit-card calls to the United States from Guadeloupe.)

COUNTRY AND AREA CODES

The telephone number in Guadeloupe changed in 2001. To call direct from the United States, dial 011–590, another 590, and then the local number. If in one of the other French West Indies, you now must dial 0 then 590 and the six-digit local number.

LOCAL CALLS

To make on-island calls, simply dial the six-digit phone number.

TIPPING

Restaurants are legally required to include a 15% gratuity in the menu price, and no additional gratuity is necessary (although appreciated if service is particularly good). Tip skycaps and porters about €1 a bag. Many cab drivers own their own taxis and don't expect a tip. You won't have any trouble ascertaining if a 10% tip is expected. It's a look.

VISITOR INFORMATION

➤ BEFORE YOU LEAVE: **French Government Tourist Office.** In the U.S.: (✉ 9454 Wilshire Blvd., Beverly Hills, CA 90212, ☎ 310/276–2835; ✉ 645 N. Michigan Ave., Chicago, IL 60611, ☎ 312/337–6339, WEB www.francetourism.com). In Canada: (✉ 1981 McGill College Ave., Suite 490, Montréal, Québec H3A 2W9, Canada, ☎ 514/288–4264; ✉ 30 St. Patrick St., Suite 700, Toronto, Ontario M5T 3A3, Canada, ☎ 416/593–6427). In the U.K.: (✉ 178 Piccadilly, London W1V 0AL, U.K., ☎ 0171/499–6911).

➤ IN GUADELOUPE: **Office Départemental du Tourisme** (✉ 5 sq. de la Banque, Pointe-à-Pitre, ☎ 0590/82–09–30). **Syndicats d'Initiatives** (✉ Av. de l'Europe, St-François, ☎ 0590/88–48–74; ✉ Marie-Galante, ☎ 0590/97–56–51).

14 · JAMAICA

Updated by
Paris Permenter
and John Bigley

Around one bend of the winding North Coast Highway lies a palatial home; around another, a shanty
without doors or windows. The towns are frenetic centers of activity, filled with pedestrians, street vendors,
and neighbors visiting. Roads are crammed with vehicles and full of honking—not a chorus of hostility
but notes of greeting or of friendly caution or just for
the heck of it. Drivers wait patiently while groups of
uniformed schoolchildren and women bearing loads
on their heads cross the street, and a spirit of coop-
eration prevails amid chaos.

The cultural life of Jamaica is a wealthy one; its music, art, and cuisine
have a spirit that's as hard to describe as the rhythms of reggae or an
outburst of streetwise patois. Although 95% of the population traces
its bloodlines to Africa, Jamaica is a stockpot of cultures, including those
of other Caribbean islands, Great Britain, the Middle East, India, China,
Germany, Portugal, and South America. The third-largest island in the
Caribbean (after Cuba and Hispaniola), Jamaica enjoys a considerable
self-sufficiency based on tourism, agriculture, and mining.

The island's physical attractions include jungle mountaintops, clear
waterfalls, and unforgettable beaches, and its tourist areas are grouped
around the northern and western coastlines. Ocho Rios (often just
Ochi) is a major cruise port, resort center, and the home of Dunn's River
Falls, probably the most photographed spot in the nation. Montego Bay
(or MoBay, as it's affectionately known), destination of most tourist flights,
is a sprawling blend of opulent beach resorts and commerce. At the island's western tip lies Negril, once a sleepy hangout for bohemian travelers; though now bigger and glitzier, it's still a haven for the hip and
the hedonistic. In addition to these pleasure capitals, Jamaica has a real
capital in Kingston. For all its congestion—and for all the disparity between city life and the bikinis and parasails to the north—Kingston is
the true heart and head of the island. This is where politics, literature,
music, and art wrestle for acceptance in the largest (800,000 people)
English-speaking city in the Western hemisphere south of Miami.

The first group known to have reached Jamaica were the Arawak Indians, who paddled their canoes from the Orinoco region of South America around AD 1000. In 1494 Christopher Columbus stepped ashore
at what is now called Discovery Bay. Having spent four centuries on
the island, the Arawaks had little notion that his footsteps on their sand
would mean their extinction within 50 years thanks to overwork, cru-

elty, and European diseases. When the indigenous population died out, the Spanish brought African slaves to the island.

What is now St. Ann's Bay was established as New Seville in 1509 and served as the Spanish capital until the local government crossed the island to Santiago de la Vega (now Spanish Town). The Spaniards were never impressed with Jamaica; they found no precious metals, and they let the island fester in poverty for 161 years. When 5,000 British soldiers and sailors appeared in Kingston Harbor in 1655, the Spaniards didn't put up a fight.

The arrival of the English and the three centuries of rule that followed provided Jamaica with the genteel underpinnings of its present life—and a period of history enlivened by a rousing pirate tradition that was fueled by rum. The very British 18th century was a time of prosperity for Jamaican landholders. This was the age of the sugar baron, who ruled his plantation great house—and his slaves—and made the island the largest sugar-producing colony in the world.

The British were challenged soon after their arrival, however, by the Maroons, former slaves the Spanish had freed and armed to harass the island's new rulers. (Other accounts say the Maroons were actually escaped slaves, named for the Spanish word *cimarrón*: wild.) The Maroons took to the most rugged regions of the island, led by the runaway slave and head of an Ashanti freedom-fighting family, Cudjoe. The First Maroon War (1690–1739) was played out across the island using guerrilla warfare. The island then remained quiet until 1760, when a slave rebellion broke out; later that century the Second Maroon War began. Tensions reached a peak in 1832 with the hanging of a Baptist minister, Sam Sharpe, in Montego Bay—punishment for his role as ringleader in an island-wide slave rebellion. Three years later slavery was abolished. Today the hanging is remembered at Sam Sharpe Square in the midst of bustling MoBay with a statue of the fallen leader; nearby "the Cage," once used to imprison runaways, is another solemn reminder of this period in Jamaican history.

The second half of the 20th century brought independence to Jamaica. On August 6, 1962, the island became an independent nation, although still a member of the British Commonwealth. The government is headed by a freely elected prime minister. Two political parties, the People's National Party (PNP) and the Jamaica Labour Party (JLP), vie for this position, and elections can become heated, even violent, events. Elections in 1980 resulted in many deaths, mostly in Kingston's ghettos; seven more recent elections were carefully monitored by a contingent that included Jimmy Carter and Colin Powell and remained peaceful. But the 1990s brought high unemployment, low wages, and high interest rates as well as brief riots over an increase in the gasoline tax. Occasional rioting has continued to be a problem in Kingston, where gangs backing rival political parties have caused death.

Today's Jamaica is a place where poverty is rampant, and many citizens must work at the fringes of the tourist industry as unlicensed taxi drivers, hair braiders, and vendors who walk the beaches in search of a vacationer. Being hassled is one of the most common complaints by travelers to Jamaica, and the government has increased fines and even penalties of jail time for hassling tourists. Many problems involve attempts to sell marijuana, or *ganja,* an illegal product.

Smoking of sacramental ganja and flowing dreadlocks are the most recognized aspects of Rastafarianism, a religion that believes in the divinity of Haile Selassie, former emperor of Ethiopia. The Rastas gained strength in the 1960s, inspired in part by the 1930s movement led by

Jamaican Marcus Garvey, founder of the U.S.–based Universal Negro Improvement Association. Garvey advocated black pride, which, along with his "back to Africa" message, was picked up by the Rastas, who embraced Ethiopia as their homeland. Today the Rastas are a small sector of the Jamaican population, but they are known internationally because of prominent Rastas such as the late reggae singer Bob Marley.

The reggae rhythms and lyrics for which Marley is known provide a peek at the Jamaican culture, but music is just one aspect of this rich island. Travelers here find a multitude of melodies—from the sizzle of jerk pork on a roadside grill to the lap of waves on a sandy beach, the call of the magnificent doctor bird flitting through the trees, or the quiet whistle of a breeze through the Blue Mountains.

Lodging

Jamaica was the birthplace of the Caribbean all-inclusive resort, a concept that took the Club Med idea and gave it an excess-in-the-tropics spin. The all-inclusive is the most popular vacation option here, offering incredible values, with rates from $145 to $350 per person per night. Prices usually include airport transfers, accommodations, three meals a day plus snacks, all bar drinks (often including premium liquors) and soft drinks, a plethora of sports options (from scuba diving to golf), nightly entertainment, and all gratuities and taxes. Usually the only surcharges are for such luxuries as massages, tours, and weddings or vow-renewal ceremonies (though even these are often included at high-end establishments). The all-inclusives have branched out, some of them courting families, others going after an upper crust that wouldn't even have picked up a brochure a few years ago.

If you like to get out and explore, you may prefer an EP property. Many places offer MAP or FAP packages that include such extras as airport transfers and tours. Even if you don't want to be tied down to a meal plan, it pays to inquire because the savings can be considerable.

Jamaica's resorts and hotels have varying policies about children; some don't accept children under 16 or 18 years old, but those that do often allow up to two to stay in their parents' room at no additional charge. Others allow kids to stay free in the off-season or offer discounted meal plans. Baby-sitting is readily available at properties that accept children, and several offer fully supervised kids' programs. If you plan to bring the kids, ask lots of questions before making a reservation, or have your travel agent find the best deal. In addition, some resorts are for male-female couples only. If you're a same-sex couple or a single parent traveling with one child, you simply won't be allowed to book a room in a couples-only establishment like a Sandals resort.

As a rule, rates are reduced anywhere from 10% to 30% from April 30 to December 15. All price categories are based on standard double rooms at the most comprehensive (and most expensive) meal-plan rate. Opting for a less comprehensive plan (if it's available in winter) can save you 20%–40%. The **Jamaica Reservations Service** (☎ 800/526–2422 in the U.S. and Canada) can book resorts, hotels, villas, and guest houses throughout the country.

CATEGORY	COST EP/CP*	COST A.I.**
$$$$	over $350	over $375
$$$	$250–$350	$275–$375
$$	$150–$250	$175–$275
$	under $150	under $175

*EP/CP prices are per night for a standard double room in high season, excluding taxes, service charges, and meal plans**A.I. (all-inclusive) prices are per person, per night based on double-occupancy during high season, excluding taxes and service charges

Kingston

Some of the island's finest business hotels are in Kingston, and these high towers are filled with rooftop restaurants, English pubs, theater and dance presentations, art museums and galleries, jazz clubs, upscale supper clubs, and disco dives.

$$$–$$$$ ★ 🖬 **Strawberry Hill.** One of many island properties owned by Chris Blackwell, formerly the head of Island Records (the late Bob Marley's label), this Blue Mountains retreat 45 minutes north of Kingston offers refined luxury and absolute peace. Authors, musicians, and screenwriters come here to relax, rejuvenate the creative juices (perhaps in the Aveda spa), and work. The food is top-notch, as are the staff and the accommodations—elegant Georgian-style villas with mahogany furnishings and roomy balconies with grand vistas. ⊠ New Castle Rd., Irishtown, ☎ 876/944–8400, FAX 876/944–8408, WEB www.islandoutpost.com/ StrawberryHill. 12 1-, 2-, and 3-bedroom villas. Restaurant, room service, no air-conditioning, fans, refrigerators, pool, sauna, spa, croquet, bar, meeting rooms, airport shuttle. AE, MC, V. CP.

$–$$$ 🖬 **Hilton Kingston.** This high-rise is the best of Kingston's business hotels. The expansive marble lobby leads to attractive, well-appointed guest rooms. The concierge floors include complimentary cocktails, hors d'oeuvres, and Continental breakfast. Extras include secured-access elevators, an American Airlines service desk, and in-room coffee and tea setups. Rates include admission to Jonkanoo, the hotel's hot nightclub; there's also an art gallery. ⊠ 77 Knutsford Blvd. (Box 112), ☎ 876/ 926–5430, FAX 876/929–7439, WEB www.hilton.com. 284 rooms, 13 suites, 6 1- and 2-bedroom units. 2 restaurants, in-room data ports, in-room safes, 2 tennis courts, pool, health club, massage, sauna, 3 bars, shops, nightclub, recreation room, concierge. AE, DC, MC, V. EP, MAP.

$–$$ 🖬 **Le Méridien Pegasus.** You'll find an efficient, accommodating staff and modern furnishings at this 17-story complex near downtown. All rooms have balconies and large windows that face the Blue Mountains, the pool, or the Caribbean. There's also an excellent business center, duty-free shops, and 24-hour room service. ⊠ 81 Knutsford Blvd. (Box 333), ☎ 876/926–3690, FAX 876/929–5855, WEB www.meridienjamaica.com. 325 rooms, 16 suites. Restaurant, coffee shop, room service, in-room safes, minibars, 2 tennis courts, pool, gym, hair salon, basketball, 2 bars, playground, concierge, business services. AE, DC, MC, V. EP, MAP.

$$ 🖬 **Terra Nova.** This intimate hotel is in a quieter part of New Kingston, 1 mi (1½ km) from the commercial district and within walking distance of Devon House, a historic home surrounded by boutiques and fine restaurants. Rooms are decked out in classic mahogany furniture and fine art. The El Dorado restaurant offers international cuisine and reasonably priced buffets. You'll also find formal high-tea service here on Thursday. ⊠ 17 Waterloo Rd., ☎ 876/926–9334, FAX 876/929–2211. 35 rooms. Restaurant, coffee shop, grill, room service, in-room safes, pool, no-smoking rooms. AE, MC, V. EP.

Jamaica

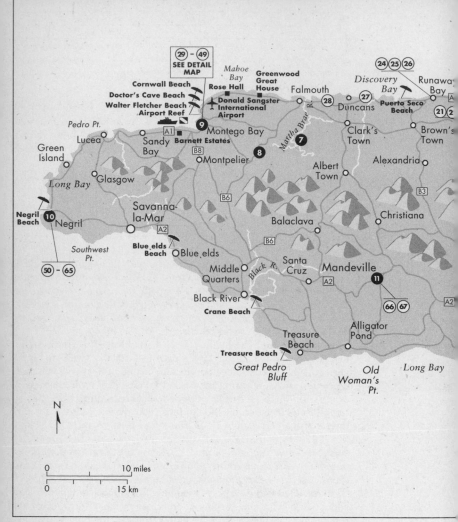

Lodging

Astra Country
Inn & Restaurant . . .**66**

Beaches Grande
Sport **21**

Beaches Royal
Plantation **22**

Breezes
Runaway Bay **24**

Charela Inn **52**

Coco La Palm **62**

Couples Negril **65**

Couples
Ocho Rios **19**

Couples Swept
Away Negril **56**

Crane Ridge
Resort **14**

Dragon Bay **11**

FDR, Franklyn
D. Resort **25**

Goblin Hill **7**

Grand Lido
Braco **27**

Grand Lido
Negril **57**

Grand Lido
Sans Souci **13**

Hedonism II **56**

Hedonism III **26**

Hilton Kingston **2**

Hotel Mocking
Bird Hill **8**

Jamaica Inn **12**

Jamaica Palace . . .**9**

Mandeville
Hotel **67**

Le Méridien
Pegasus **3**

Negril Cabins
Resort **61**

Point Village **62**

Renaissance
Jamaica
Grande **18**

Rockhouse **52**

Sandals Dunn's
River Golf Resort
and Spa **23**

Sandals Negril
Beach Resort
and Spa **60**

Starfish Trelawny . . .**28**

Strawberry Hill **6**

Terra Nova **5**

Trident Villas
and Hotel **10**

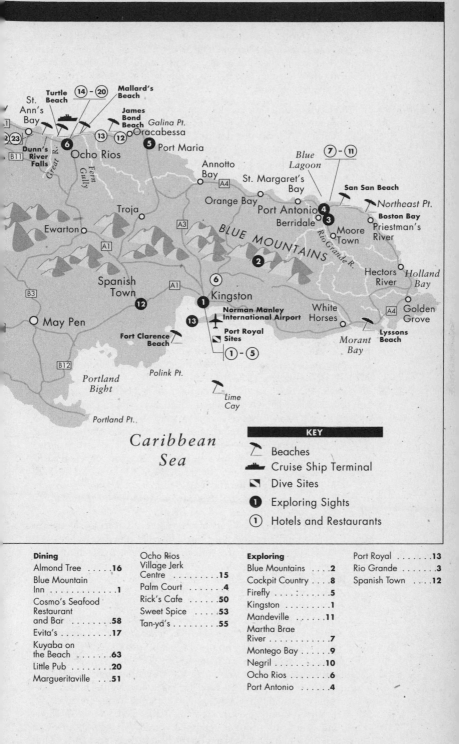

KEY

⚓ Beaches

🚢 Cruise Ship Terminal

◣ Dive Sites

1 Exploring Sights

① Hotels and Restaurants

Dining

Almond Tree **16**

Blue Mountain
Inn **1**

Cosmo's Seafood
Restaurant
and Bar **58**

Evita's **17**

Kuyaba on
the Beach **63**

Little Pub **20**

Margueritaville . . .**51**

Ocho Rios
Village Jerk
Centre **15**

Palm Court **4**

Rick's Cafe **50**

Sweet Spice **53**

Tan-ya's **55**

Exploring

Blue Mountains **2**

Cockpit Country **8**

Firefly . . . . : **5**

Kingston **1**

Mandeville **11**

Martha Brae
River **7**

Montego Bay **9**

Negril . . . . . . : . . .**10**

Ocho Rios **6**

Port Antonio **4**

Port Royal **13**

Rio Grande **3**

Spanish Town **12**

Port Antonio

Described by poet Ella Wheeler Wilcox as "the most exquisite port on earth," Port Antonio is a seaside town at the foot of verdant hills toward the east end of the north coast. The area's must-do activities include rafting the Rio Grande, snorkeling, or scuba diving in the Blue Lagoon, exploring the Nonsuch Caves, and stopping at the classy Trident resort for lunch or a drink.

$$$–$$$$ ⊞ **Trident Villas and Hotel.** The living here is truly gracious. Peacocks
★   strut the manicured lawns, colonnaded walkways wind through whimsically sculpted topiaries that dot the 14 acres, and the pool—on a rocky bit of land that juts out into crashing surf—is a memory unto itself. The luxurious Laura Ashley–style rooms, many with turrets, bay windows, and balconies or verandas, are awash in mahogany and local art; they do not have TVs or clocks. ⊠ *North Coast Hwy., Point Ann, Port Antonio (Box 119),* ☎ *876/993–2602,* FAX *876/993–2590,* WEB *www.tridentvillas.com. 8 rooms, 1 suite, 14 villas. Restaurant, in-room safes, minibars, 2 tennis courts, pool, aerobics, massage, beach, snorkeling, boating, croquet, bar, library, concierge. AE, MC, V. All-inclusive, CP, FAP, MAP.*

$$–$$$ ⊞ **Dragon Bay.** Set on a private cove, Dragon Bay is an idyllic grouping of individually decorated villas surrounded by tropical gardens. Villa 35 has a private pool, a large living room, and two bedrooms with separate sitting rooms that have sofa beds. This place is popular with German and Italian tour groups. ⊠ *Dragon Bay (Box 176),* ☎ *876/993–8751,* FAX *876/993–8971,* WEB *www.dragonbay.com. 30 1-, 2-, and 3-bedroom villas. 2 restaurants, room service, tennis court, pool, aerobics, gym, massage, beach, volleyball, beach, dive shop, snorkeling. AE, MC, V. All-inclusive, EP, FAP, MAP.*

$–$$ ⊞ **Goblin Hill.** This lush 12-acre estate is atop a hill overlooking San San Bay. Each attractively appointed villa comes with its own dramatic view, plus a staff member to do the grocery shopping, cleaning, and cooking for you. The rooms and villas aren't equipped with phones or TVs, but they do have ceiling fans, air-conditioning, and a tropical furnishings. The beach is a 10-minute walk away. Excellent car-rental packages are available. ⊠ *San San (Box 26),* ☎ *876/925–8108,* FAX *876/ 925–6248,* WEB *www.goblinhill.com. 12 rooms, 28 1- and 2-bedroom villas. No room phones, fans, kitchenettes, no room TVs, 2 tennis courts, pool, beach, bar, library. AE, MC, V. EP.*

$–$$ ⊞ **Hotel Mocking Bird Hill.** With only 10 rooms, all overlooking the sea and the Blue Mountains, Mocking Bird Hill feels more like a cozy B&B than a hotel. Owners Barbara Walker and Shireen Aga run an environmentally sensitive operation: you'll find bamboo instead of hardwood furniture, solar-heated water, meals made with local produce in the Mille Fleurs dining terrace, locally produced toiletries and stationery sets, and seven naturally landscaped acres. Wedding packages are available. ⊠ *North Coast Hwy., Point Ann, Port Antonio (Box 254),* ☎ *876/993–7267,* FAX *876/993–7133,* WEB *www.hotelmockingbirdhill. com. 10 rooms. Restaurant, no room phones, in-room safes, no room TVs, pool, massage, bar, no-smoking rooms. AE, MC, V. CP, EP, MAP.*

$–$$ ⊞ **Jamaica Palace.** Built to resemble a 17th-century Italian mansion, this imposing white-columned hotel has black lacquer and gilded oversize furniture throughout its common areas. Some rooms are more lavish than others, though each has a semicircular bed, European objets d'art, and Asian rugs; none is equipped with TV (you can, however, rent one). Although the hotel isn't on the beach, there's a 114-ft swimming pool that's shaped like Jamaica. ⊠ *Williamsfield (Box 277),* ☎ *876/993–7720,* FAX *876/993–7759,* WEB *www.in-site.com/jampal. 24 rooms, 56 suites. 2 restaurants, room service, in-room safes, pool, 2 bars, laundry service. AE, MC, V. CP, EP, MAP.*

Ocho Rios

On the northeast coast halfway between Port Antonio and MoBay, Ocho Rios is hilly and lush. Its resorts, hotels, and villas are all a short drive from a bustling crafts market, boutiques, duty-free shops, restaurants, and several scenic attractions.

$$$$ ☆ **Beaches Royal Plantation.** Formerly Plantation Inn, this resort has been transformed into an ultra-luxurious all-inclusive for those 16 and over. The all-suites property has the feel of a small, exclusive hotel; all rooms have ocean views. Built high atop a bluff, steps lead to the beach where the luxury continues with the services of a beach butler. Golf is available at the Sandals club. ✉ *North Coast Hwy. (Box 728),* ☎ *876/ 974–1027,* FAX *876/974–5838,* WEB *www.beaches.com. 80 suites. 3 restaurants, room service, in-room safes, golf privileges, 2 tennis courts, pool, health club, outdoor hot tub, spa, beach, dive shop, windsurfing, concierge, no kids under 16. AE, MC, V. All-inclusive.*

$$$$ ☆ **Grand Lido Sans Souci.** A stay at this pastel-pink cliff-side resort is a wonderfully luxurious experience. Romantic oceanfront suites have oversize whirlpool tubs. Throughout, blond-wood furniture, cool tile floors, and sheer curtains are accented by pastel watercolors and Jamaican prints on the walls. A highlight is Charlie's Spa, which offers complimentary pampering massages, body scrubs, reflexology sessions, facials, and manicures and pedicures (book treatments as soon as you arrive, if not before). ✉ *North Coast Hwy., Mammee Bay, 2 mi (3 km) east of Ocho Rios (Box 103),* ☎ *876/994–1353,* FAX *876/994–1544,* WEB *www.superclubs.com. 146 suites. 3 restaurants, 2 grills, room service, in-room safes, minibars, 2 tennis courts, 4 pools, outdoor hot tub, massage, spa, beach, 6 bars, complimentary weddings, concierge, airport shuttle. 2-night minimum. AE, D, DC, MC, V. All-inclusive.*

$$$$ ☆ **Jamaica Inn.** A combination of class and quiet attracts a discerning crowd, including such celebrities as Kate Moss and I. M. Pei, to this vintage property that was once a favorite of Winston Churchill. Each room has its own veranda (larger than most hotel rooms) on the private cove's powdery, champagne-colored beach. The dining room uses Wedgwood china; the inn has Jamaican antique furniture and terrazzo floors. Jackets in the evening are still de rigueur for men after 7 PM during high season (December–April), though off-season is a bit more relaxed. Note that the Full American Plan is available during summer months only. ✉ *North Coast Hwy., east of Ocho Rios (Box 1),* ☎ *876/ 974–2514,* FAX *876/974–2449,* WEB *www.jamaicainn.com. 49 rooms, 4 suites. Restaurant, room service, pool, gym, beach, boating, croquet, library, no kids under 12. AE, MC, V. FAP, MAP.*

$$$–$$$$ ☆ **Sandals Dunn's River Golf Resort and Spa.** This resort is exclusively for male-female couples. Twenty-five acres of lush, manicured grounds surround this luxury all-inclusive resort. Set on a wide, sugary beach, with courteous service and posh rooms, it's the finest of Sandals's Jamaican properties. Rooms are light pink, blue, turquoise, and cream, and most have a balcony or patio that overlooks the sea or the grounds. The resort prides itself on catering to guests' every whim. You have access to two nearby golf courses at other Sandals resorts, with a free shuttle service. ✉ *North Coast Hwy., Mammee Bay, 2 mi (3 km) east of Ocho Rios (Box 51),* ☎ *876/972–1610,* FAX *876/972–1611,* WEB *www.sandals.com. 256 rooms, 10 suites. 4 restaurants, in-room safes, putting green, 4 tennis courts, 2 pools, 3 outdoor hot tubs, spa, beach, 7 bars, concierge, no kids. AE, MC, V. All-inclusive.*

$$–$$$$ ☆ **Couples Ocho Rios.** This resort accepts reservations from only male-female couples. Each one-bedroom suite has a two-person hot tub in its bathroom that peeks through a window at the four-poster king-size bed. There's a lovely white beach for relaxation or water sports, and a private island where you can sunbathe in the buff. Weddings are included in the package as are five off-site excursions. If you plan to visit for seven nights, you can split your stay between this resort and Couples Negril. ⊠ *Tower Isle,* ☎ *876/975–4271,* FAX *876/975–4439,* WEB *www.couples.com. 201 rooms, 11 suites. 4 restaurants, room service, in-room safes, 5 tennis courts, pool, 5 outdoor hot tubs, massage, sauna, horseback riding, squash, beach, dive shop, snorkeling, windsurfing, 4 bars. 3-night minimum stay. AE, MC, V. All-inclusive.*

$$–$$$ **Beaches Grande Sport.** This expansive resort, formerly Ciboney, now welcomes those 16 and over in search of an active vacation. True to its sporty name, the resort offers a full menu of activities ranging from a rock-climbing wall to a running track to extensive watersports facilities. Accommodations here vary from traditional hotel rooms to expansive villas; 88 villas come with their own courtyard swimming pools. Some villa suites are a distance from the public facilities and the beach, so the resort offers transportation to your door. ⊠ *North Coast Hwy. (Box 2),* ☎ *876/974–5601,* FAX *876/974–5912,* WEB *www.beaches.com. 85 rooms, 200 suites. 4 restaurants, 3 grills, in-room safes, 4 tennis courts, 3 pools, spa, beach, concierge, no kids under 16. AE, MC, V. All-inclusive.*

$$–$$$ **Renaissance Jamaica Grande.** The Renaissance, one of the largest conference hotels in Jamaica, attracts all types of travelers: families, couples, singles (there are special singles activities and no supplementary fee for singles), and conference attendees. Even though it's a beachfront resort, the focal point is definitely the tiered and winding pool, which has a waterfall, a swaying bridge, and a swim-up bar. Rooms in the south building are the largest, but those in the north building have slightly better views. Kids are kept busy in the daily Club Mongoose activity program. The hotel's disco, Jamaic'N Me Crazy, is *very* popular. ⊠ *Main St. (Box 100),* ☎ *876/974–2201,* FAX *876/974–5378,* WEB *www.renaissancehotels. com. 706 rooms, 15 suites. 5 restaurants, in-room safes, 2 tennis courts, 3 pools, 2 outdoor hot tubs, massage, beach, dive shop, snorkeling, windsurfing, boating, 8 bars, children's programs (ages 4–12), playground, concierge, convention center. AE, DC, MC, V. All-inclusive, EP.*

$$ **The Crane Ridge Resort.** Families on a budget planning an extended stay should consider a suite here; the fully stocked kitchens can help keep the dining bills down. Each spacious, immaculate unit has white tile floors, rattan furniture, and tropical floral prints. The two-bedroom suite has an open bathroom (it's divided from the main room by only a screen), as well as a whirlpool tub in its master-bedroom loft. This hotel is not on the beach, although it's close enough to walk—and a shuttle is provided. ⊠ *17 Da Costa Dr.,* ☎ *876/974–8050,* FAX *876/974– 8070,* WEB *www.craneridge.net. 87 suites. Restaurant, room service, in-room safes, kitchenettes, refrigerators, tennis court, outdoor hot tub, bar, airport shuttle, no-smoking rooms. AE, MC, V. EP, FAP, MAP.*

Runaway Bay

The smallest of the resort areas, Runaway Bay, west of Ocho Rios, has a handful of modern hotels, a few all-inclusive resorts, and an 18-hole golf course.

$$$–$$$$ ★ ☺ **FDR, Franklyn D. Resort.** Upscale yet unpretentious, the beachside complex has spacious, well-planned one-, two-, and three-bedroom suites in pink villas set in a horseshoe around a pool. Best of all, a staff member is assigned to each suite, filling the role of nanny and housekeeper. Children and teens are kept busy with supervised activities and sports. Parents can join in or just lounge by the pool, play golf, or scuba dive. Children age 16 and under stay and eat free when staying in a room with their parents. ⊠ *Runaway Bay (Box 201),* ☎ *876/973–4591,* FAX *876/973–3071,* WEB *www.fdrholidays.com. 76 suites. 2 restaurants, kitchenettes, tennis court, pool, beach, dive shop, snorkeling, 3 bars, babysitting, children's programs (ages infant–16). AE, MC, V. All-inclusive.*

$$$–$$$$ 🏨 **Grand Lido Braco.** Just a 15-minute drive west of Runaway Bay, this
★ all-inclusive, adults-only, gingerbread- and Georgian-style village fo-
cuses on the culture, crafts, music, and food of Jamaica. Boutiques, an
art shop, and several restaurants—including a jerk grill and a sidewalk
café—fan out from a central fountain in the "town square." The pool
is one of the country's largest. Rooms, done in bright tropical colors,
are generous in size, and all but the garden-view rooms are steps from
the 2,000-ft (612-m) beach, including a nude beach and pool, or have
a great view of the ocean from a patio. ⊠ *Trelawny, between Dun-
cans and Rio Bueno,* ☎ *876/954–0000,* FAX *876/954–0020,* WEB *www.
superclubs.com. 232 rooms. 5 restaurants, café, in-room safes, driv-
ing range, 9-hole golf course, 3 tennis courts, 2 pools, health club, 4
hot tubs, spa, beach, dive shop, snorkeling, windsurfing, fishing, hik-
ing, soccer, 8 bars, shops, dance club, complimentary weddings,
concierge, meeting rooms, airport shuttle, no kids under 16. 2-night
minimum. AE, DC, MC, V. All-inclusive.*

$$$–$$$$ 🏨 **Hedonism III.** Like its more spartan cousin in Negril, Hedonism is an
★ adults-only, all-inclusive hotel for travelers looking for physical fun that
includes a circus clinic and waterslide (through the disco, no less). Un-
like its Negril equivalent, however, Hedonism III offers luxurious rooms
and Jamaica's first swim-up rooms. The guest rooms, each with mirrored
ceilings, have Jacuzzi tubs and CD players. The beach is divided into "nude"
and "prude" sides, although a quick look shows that most people choose
to leave the suits at home. Scheduled activities include nude body paint-
ing and volleyball; there's even shuffleboard in the buff as well as Ja-
maica's only nude weddings. ⊠ *Main Rd., Runaway Bay (Box 250),* ☎
876/973–5029, FAX *876/973–5402,* WEB *www.superclubs.com. 225 rooms.
4 restaurants, grill, in-room safes, 2 tennis courts, 3 pools, health club,
2 outdoor hot tubs, beach, dive shop, snorkeling, windsurfing, boating,
6 bars, dance club, complimentary weddings, airport shuttle, no kids under
18. 2-night minimum. AE, DC, MC, V. All-inclusive.*

$$–$$$$ 🏨 **Breezes Runaway Bay.** This moderately priced SuperClubs resort
★ emphasizes an active, sports-oriented vacation—from golf (at the re-
sort's own course), tennis, and horse and carriage rides to an array of
water sports. Expert instruction and top-rate equipment are part of the
package. Guests—often Germans, Italians, and Japanese—flock here
for the reef just off the beach, as well as for the superb golf school. ⊠
North Coast Hwy. (Box 58), ☎ *876/973–2436,* FAX *876/973–2352,* WEB
*www.superclubs.com. 234 rooms. 2 restaurants, 2 grills, in-room safes,
driving range, 18-hole golf course, 4 tennis courts, pool, 3 outdoor hot
tubs, beach, dive shop, snorkeling, windsurfing, 4 bars, complimentary weddings, airport shuttle, no kids under 17. 2-night minimum.
AE, DC, MC, V. All-inclusive.*

$$ 🏨 **Starfish Trelawny.** This moderately priced all-inclusive resort cater-
🐾 ing to all travelers, opened in December 2001 after a $5 million reno-
vation. Several cottages are especially popular with larger family groups.
Nightly entertainment is for the whole family; a late-night disco is aimed
at adults. Some motorized water sports, including waterskiing, the ba-
nana boat ride, and scuba diving, are not included in the all-inclusive
price. The resort has a rock-climbing wall, circus workshop, and "ice"
skating on a special plastic surface. ⊠ *North Coast Hwy., Falmouth,* ☎
876/954–2450, FAX *876/954–2173,* WEB *www.starfishresorts.com. 350
rooms. 4 restaurants, grill, 4 tennis courts, pool, beach, dive shop,
snorkeling, windsurfing, waterskiing, badminton, 6 bars, dance club, baby-
sitting, children's programs (ages 4 months–14), meeting rooms, airport
shuttle. 2-night minimum. AE, DC, MC, V. All-inclusive.*

Montego Bay

MoBay has miles of hotels, villas, apartments, and duty-free shops. Although lacking much in the way of cultural stimuli, it presents a comfortable island backdrop for the many conventions it hosts.

$$$$ 🖼 **Round Hill Hotel and Villas.** The Hollywood set frequents this peace-
★ ful resort, 8 mi (13 km) west of town on a hilly peninsula. Twenty-seven villas are set on 98 acres, and the Pineapple House, a building that overlooks the sea, houses 36 hotel rooms. Rooms are done in a refined Ralph Lauren style, with mahogany furnishings and terra-cotta floors. Villas are leased back to the resort by private owners and vary in decor, but jungle motifs are a favorite. All come with a personal maid and a cook to make your breakfast, and several have private pools. ⊠ *North Coast Hwy., Montego Bay (Box 64),* ☎ *876/956-70507,* FAX *876/956-7505,* WEB *www.roundhilljamaica.com. 36 rooms, 27 villas. Restaurant, room service, 5 tennis courts, pool, aerobics, gym, hair salon, beach, dive shop, windsurfing, bar, concierge, helipad. AE, DC, MC, V. All-inclusive, EP, FAP, MAP.*

$$$$ 🖼 **Tryall Golf, Tennis, and Beach Club.** Part of a posh residential de-velopment 15 mi (24 km) west of MoBay, Tryall clings to a hilltop that overlooks a golf course and the Caribbean. Here you'll stay in one of the many villas—each with its own pool, full staff (butler, cook, maid, and gardener), and golf cart—that dot the 2,200-acre island planta-tion. All accommodations are individually and plushly decorated. The elegant dining room in the great house serves Continental and Ja-maican cuisine. The beautiful seaside golf course is considered one of the meanest in the world and hosts big-money tournaments. ⊠ *North Coast Hwy., Sandy Bay (Box 1206),* ☎ *876/956-5660,* FAX *876/956-5673,* WEB *www.tryallclub.com. 57 villas. Restaurant, refrigerators, driving range, 18-hole golf course, 9 tennis courts, pool, massage, beach, dive shop, snorkeling, windsurfing, 4 bars, children's programs (ages 5-12). AE, DC, MC, V. EP.*

$$$-$$$$ 🖼 **Coyaba Beach Resort and Club.** Owners Joanne and Kevin Robert-
★ son live on the property, interacting with their guests and giving this oceanfront retreat the feel of an intimate country inn. The plantation-style great house, just east of MoBay, successfully blends modern amenities with antique charm. Rooms are decorated with lovely colo-nial prints and hand-carved mahogany furniture. A basket with bot-tled spring water and freshly baked banana bread greets you upon check-in; regular rates include afternoon tea and evening cocktail parties as well as tennis. It's a very family-friendly place. ⊠ *Mahoe Bay, Little River,* ☎ *876/953-91507,* FAX *876/953-2244,* WEB *www. coyabaresortjamaica.com. 50 rooms. 3 restaurants, tennis court, pool, gym, outdoor hot tub, massage, beach, dive shop, snorkeling, wind-surfing, volleyball, 3 bars, recreation room, library, playground, air-port shuttle. AE, MC, V. All-inclusive, EP, MAP.*

$$$-$$$$ 🖼 **Half Moon Golf, Tennis, and Beach Club.** Since 1962, this resort has been a destination unto itself. Although it has mushroomed from 30 to more than 400 units, it has maintained a luxurious feel with its black-and-white accents and such decorating touches as Asian rugs and an-tique radios. Several villas (which come with a cook, a butler, a housekeeper, and a golf cart) have private pools, and the 2-mi-long (3-km-long) stretch of beach is just steps from every room. On the grounds there's an upscale shopping mall as well as a nature reserve, a croquet lawn (considered one of the Caribbean's best), and a hospital. ⊠ *North Coast Hwy., Montego Bay, 7 mi (11 km) east of MoBay (Box 80),* ☎ *876/953-2211,* FAX *876/953-2731,* WEB *www.halfmoonclub.net. 245 rooms, 174 suites, 32 villas. 7 restaurants, 18-hole golf course, 13 tennis courts, 53 pools, aerobics, outdoor hot tub, sauna, spa,*

Montego Bay Lodging and Dining

beach, dive shop, snorkeling, windsurfing, bicycles, badminton, croquet, horseback riding, squash, 3 bars, theater, concierge, convention center. AE, DC, MC, V. All-inclusive, EP, FAP, MAP.

$$$–$$$$ ⊞ **Ritz-Carlton Rose Hall, Jamaica.** Across the road from the historic
★ Rose Hall estate, this expansive property is the newest addition to Jamaica's luxury hotels. The beige buildings span a large swath of beachfront east of Montego Bay, although most beach and water-sports action takes place at the nearby Rose Hall Beach Club (transportation is provided for guests). Rooms here are subtly Caribbean with understated tropical florals, plus mahogany and rattan furniture. Along with a full-service spa, the resort offers a fully supervised children's club, making it a popular choice for families. ⊠ 1 Ritz Carlton Dr., St. James, ☎ 876/953–2800, FAX 876/953–2501, WEB www.ritzcarlton. com. 427 rooms. 4 restaurants, in-room safes, 18-hole golf course, pool, health club, spa, beach, dive shop, snorkeling, windsurfing, 3 bars, children's programs (ages 5–12), concierge, meeting rooms. AE, DC, MC, V. EP, FAP, MAP.

$$–$$$ 🛏 **Breezes Montego Bay.** Like its cousin in Runaway Bay, this Super-
Clubs resort for adults emphasizes moderate prices and plenty of
around-the-clock activities. On the portion of Gloucester Avenue
known as the "Hip Strip," this small property's rooms have white tile
floors, cozy love seats, carved wooden headboards, and big marble bathrooms. The resort doesn't have its own private beach but uses the adjacent Doctor's Cave Beach. Free weddings are also part of the package.
⊠ *Gloucester Ave.,* ☎ *876/940–1150,* FAX *876/940–1160,* WEB *www.
superclubs.com. 124 rooms. 2 restaurants, grill, in-room safes, 2 tennis courts, pool, beach, dive shop, snorkeling, windsurfing, 4 bars, complimentary weddings, airport shuttle, no kids under 17. 2-night
minimum. AE, DC, MC, V. All-inclusive.*

$$–$$$ 🛏 **Sandals Montego Bay.** The largest private beach in MoBay is the spark
that lights this Sandals—one of the most popular upscale resorts in the
Caribbean, though restricted to male-female couples. Its all-inclusive
rate, nonstop activities, and rooms overlooking the bay make it a bit
like a cruise ship that remains in port. It certainly feels like a great big
party, despite the planes that zoom overhead (the airport is nearby). Rooms
are done in tropical colors and have four-poster beds. The Oleander Room
may well be the best fine-dining establishment in the Sandals chain. ⊠
Kent Ave. (Box 100), ☎ *876/952–5510,* FAX *876/952–0816,* WEB *www.
sandals.com. 245 rooms. 5 restaurants, snack bar, in-room safes, 4 tennis courts, 4 pools, 4 outdoor hot tubs, sauna, beach, boating, 4 bars,
concierge, no kids. 2-night minimum AE, MC, V. All-inclusive.*

$$–$$$ 🛏 **Sandals Royal Caribbean.** Formerly Sandals Royal Jamaican, this
upscale, all-inclusive resort is exclusively for male-female couples.
Rooms at the resort, which is 4 mi (6½ km) east of airport, are in Ja-
maican-style buildings arranged in a semicircle around attractive gardens. Although there are plenty of activities here, the resort is quieter
and more genteel than Sandals Montego Bay. Oceanfront rooms and
suites are elegant and inviting, with floral-print fabrics and mahogany
four-poster beds. A colorful "dragon boat" transports you to Sandals's
private island for meals at an Indonesian restaurant. ⊠ *North Coast
Hwy. (Box 167),* ☎ *876/953–2231,* FAX *876/953–2788,* WEB *www.
sandals.com. 176 rooms, 14 suites. 4 restaurants, in-room safes, 3 tennis courts, 4 pools, aerobics, hair salon, 5 outdoor hot tubs, sauna,
beach, dive shop, snorkeling, windsurfing, 5 bars, concierge, airport
shuttle, no kids. 2-night minimum. AE, MC, V. All-inclusive.*

$$ 🛏 **Sandals Inn.** If you can forgo a private beach (there's a public one
across the street), male-female couples can stay here for much less than
at the other Sandals resorts. Rooms are compact, and most have bal-
conies that face the pool. Dark carpet contrasts with white-lacquered
furniture and tropical-print fabrics. Free hourly shuttles hop to the two
other MoBay Sandals, but there's plenty to do here, too. The in-town
location puts you close to shops and sights. ⊠ *Gloucester Ave. (Box
412),* ☎ *876/952–4140,* FAX *876/952–6913,* WEB *www.sandals.com. 52
rooms. 2 restaurants, in-room safes, tennis court, pool, hair salon, out-
door hot tub, 2 bars, concierge, airport shuttle, no kids. 2-night min-
imum. AE, MC, V. All-inclusive.*

$$ 🛏 **Wyndham Rose Hall Beach Resort.** This self-contained resort 4 mi
♻ (6½ km) east of airport, on the 400-acre Rose Hall Plantation, is a bustling
business hotel that's popular with large groups. It has plenty of amenities, including a 110,000-square-ft (10,230-square-m) water complex,
Sugar Mill Falls, complete with lagoons and a towering water slide.
You can enjoy lazy river rafting among waterfalls scattered throughout the park. Rooms are comfortable if a bit sterile. The waters off the
thin crescent beach are good for sailing and snorkeling. ⊠ *North
Coast Hwy. (Box 999),* ☎ *876/953–2650,* FAX *876/953–2617,* WEB
www.wyndham.com. 470 rooms, 19 suites. 5 restaurants, in-room safes,

room service, 18-hole golf course, 6 tennis courts, 3 pools, aerobics, gym, massage, beach, dive shop, snorkeling, windsurfing, basketball, volleyball, 3 bars, nightclub, children's programs (ages 3–12), playground, meeting rooms. AE, DC, MC, V. All-inclusive, EP, MAP.

$–$$ ☷ **Lethe Estate.** Tucked on the bank of the Great River near the village of Lethe, 20 minutes west of Montego Bay, this quiet mountainside inn is a far cry from the bustling beach resorts for which MoBay is known. Interruptions come not from reggae music or dance contests but from the sounds of birds. You don't have the sea nearby, but you can take a dip in the river (or float down it on a bamboo raft), take a jitney through the nearby Lethe Estate plantation, or fish in freshwater ponds. ✉ *Reading Rd., Lethe (Box 23),* ☎ *876/956–4920,* 𝖥𝖠𝖷 *876/956–4963,* 𝖶𝖤𝖡 *www.lethe-jamaica.com. 15 rooms. Restaurant, tennis court, pool, fishing, horseback riding, airport shuttle. AE, MC, V. CP, FAP, MAP.*

$ ☷ **Holiday Inn Sunspree Resort.** There are activities day and night at this family-oriented resort 6 mi (9½ km) east of airport. Although the rooms—spread out in seven buildings—are cheerful enough, the hotel is big and can be noisy (rooms farthest from the pool and central dining entertainment area are the quietest). However, adults can take a break in the quiet pool with a swim-up bar on the resort's west side. On the east end, there is now a miniature golf course. Room service is available for breakfast only. ✉ *North Coast Hwy. (Box 480),* ☎ *876/953–2485,* 𝖥𝖠𝖷 *876/953–2840,* 𝖶𝖤𝖡 *www.holiday-inn.com. 521 rooms, 23 suites. 3 restaurants, 2 snack bars, room service, in-room safes, miniature golf, 4 tennis courts, 3 pools, beach, dive shop, snorkeling, windsurfing, 4 bars, children's programs (ages 3–17), playground, concierge, airport shuttle, no-smoking rooms. AE, DC, MC, V. All-inclusive, EP.*

$ ☷ **Richmond Hill Inn.** This hilltop inn—a quaint 200-year-old great house originally owned by the Dewars clan—has spectacular views of the Caribbean and a great deal of peace. Decor tends toward the dainty: frilly lace curtains and doilies, lots of lavenders and mauves, and crushed-velvet furniture here and there. A free shuttle will take you to shops and beaches, about 10 to 15 minutes away. ✉ *Union St. (Box 362),* ☎ *876/952–3859,* 𝖥𝖠𝖷 *876/952–6106,* 𝖶𝖤𝖡 *www.richmond-hill-inn.com. 15 rooms, 5 suites. Restaurant, pool, some microwaves, some refrigerators, cable TV, bar, laundry service, meeting rooms. AE, MC, V. EP, FAP, MAP.*

Negril

Some 50 mi (80 km) west of MoBay, Negril was long a sleepy bohemian retreat. In the last decade the town has blossomed and added a number of classy all-inclusive resorts, with several more on the drawing board for Bloody Bay (northeast of Negril Beach). Negril itself is only a small village with little of historic significance. But such sights are not what draws the sybaritic singles and couples. The young, hip crowd here comes for sun, sand, and sea.

$$$–$$$$ ☷ **Grand Lido Negril.** The dramatic entrance of marble floors and
★ columns, filled with Jamaican artwork, sets an elegant tone. The resort is geared to folks with some money in their pockets, attracting mostly mature couples and singles. The well-appointed split-level oceanfront and garden suites are spacious and stylish. For some, the pièce de résistance is a sunset cruise on the resort's 147-ft yacht, M/V *Zein,* a wedding gift from Aristotle Onassis to Prince Rainier and Princess Grace of Monaco. The Piacere restaurant is superb. The sprawling resort sits on one of Jamaica's top stretches of white-sand beach, including a clothing-optional beach. ✉ *Norman Manley Blvd. (Box 88),* ☎ *876/957–5010,* 𝖥𝖠𝖷 *876/957–5517,* 𝖶𝖤𝖡 *www.superclubs.com. 210 suites. 5 restaurants, room service, in-room safes, minibars, 4 tennis courts, 2 pools, health club, 5 outdoor hot tubs, massage, spa, beach, dive shop, snorkeling, windsurfing, 9 bars, complimentary weddings, concierge,*

convention center, airport shuttle, no kids under 16, no-smoking rooms. 2-night minimum. AE, DC, MC, V. All-inclusive.

$$$–$$$$ 🏨 **Sandals Negril Beach Resort and Spa.** Male-female couples looking for an upscale, sports-oriented getaway and a casual atmosphere (you can wear dressy shorts to dinner) flock to this resort on one of the best stretches of Negril Beach. Water sports, particularly scuba diving, are popular; the capable staff is happy to work with neophytes as well as certified veterans. There's a huge swim-up pool bar and a range of spacious accommodations. Both rooms and staff are sunny and appealing. ⊠ *Norman Manley Blvd. (Box 12),* ☎ *876/957–5216,* FAX *876/957–5338,* WEB *www.sandals.com. 137 rooms, 86 suites. 4 restaurants, in-room safes, 4 tennis courts, 2 pools, 2 outdoor hot tubs, sauna, spa, beach, dive shop, windsurfing, racquetball, squash, 4 bars, concierge, no kids. AE, MC, V. All-inclusive.*

$$–$$$ 🏨 **Couples Negril.** The emphasis at this resort exclusively for male-female couples is on romance and relaxation, and you will find neither hard to come by. The property's 18 acres are on Bloody Bay. Negril's bohemian nature is reflected throughout the nine low-rise buildings, where a rainbow of colors and lively art by local craftspeople pepper public spaces. All land and water activities, selected excursions, and weddings are included in the all-inclusive rates. ⊠ *Norman Manley Blvd.,* ☎ *876/ 957–5960,* FAX *876/957–5858,* WEB *www.couples.com. 216 rooms, 18 suites. 3 restaurants, room service, in-room safes, 4 tennis courts, 2 pools, aerobics, health club, 2 outdoor hot tubs, spa, beach, dive shop, snorkeling, windsurfing, 5 bars, complimentary weddings, concierge, airport shuttle, no kids. 3-night minimum. AE, MC, V. All-inclusive.*

$$–$$$ 🏨 **Couples Swept Away Negril.** This adults-only resort is exclusively
★   for male-female couples. With its emphasis on sports and healthful cuisine, it primarily attracts the fitness-minded. The suites are in 26 two-story, tropical villas—each with a private garden atrium—spread out along a ½-mi (¾-km) stretch of gorgeous beach. There's an outstanding 10-acre sports complex across the road. At the Feathers Continental restaurant, the chefs prepare dishes designed to keep you fit and trim, with lots of fish, white meat, fresh fruits, and vegetables. ⊠ *Norman Manley Blvd., Long Bay,* ☎ *876/957–4061,* FAX *876/957–4060,* WEB *www.sweptaway.com. 134 suites. 4 restaurants, in-room safes, 10 tennis courts, 2 pools, aerobics, health club, 2 outdoor hot tubs, massage, spa, beach, dive shop, snorkeling, windsurfing, racquetball, squash, 5 bars, complimentary weddings, concierge, airport shuttle, no kids. 3-night minimum. AE, DC, MC, V. All-inclusive.*

$$–$$$ 🏨 **Hedonism II.** Hedonism is best for uninhibited adults who like a robust mix of physical activities. The resort has a trampoline clinic, a rock climbing wall, gaming lounge with slots and table games, and an "ice" skating rink on a special surface. Handsome guest rooms, which do not include TVs, have mirrored ceilings above king or twin beds (those going solo either pay a hefty supplement or are assigned a roommate of the same sex). You'll find both "nude" and "prude" beaches. Most people prefer the nude beach, with its grill, pool, and swim-up bar plus activities ranging from nude body painting to volleyball to shuffleboard. ⊠ *Norman Manley Blvd., Ruthland Point (Box 25),* ☎ *876/957–5200,* FAX *876/957–5289,* WEB *www.superclubs.com. 280 rooms. 4 restaurants, 2 grills, in-room safes, no room TVs, 6 tennis courts, 2 pools, 4 outdoor hot tubs, beach, dive shop, windsurfing, squash, 6 bars, dance club, complimentary weddings, airport shuttle, no kids. 2-night minimum. AE, DC, MC, V. All-inclusive.*

$$–$$$ 🏨 **Negril Cabins Resort.** These elevated timber cottages are amid lush vegetation and towering royal palms. Rooms are open and airy, with floral bedspreads, gauzy curtains, natural-wood floors, and high ceilings. The most popular rooms have TVs and air-conditioning; others have no TV and are cooled by ceiling fans and breezes that come through slatted windows. The gleaming beach across the road is filled with sunbathers and water-sports enthusiasts; for shopping you can take the shuttle into town. A most convivial place, this property is popular with young Europeans. Children under 12 stay free in their parents' room. ⊠ *Norman Manley Blvd. (Box 118),* ☎ *876/957–5350,* FAX *876/957–5381,* WEB *www.negril-cabins.com. 82 rooms, 4 suites. 2 restaurants, room service, no air-conditioning in some rooms, in-room safes, no TV in some rooms, tennis court, pool, gym, outdoor hot tub, beach, dive shop, snorkeling, 2 bars, recreation room, baby-sitting, playground. AE, MC, V. All-inclusive, EP, MAP.*

$$ ⊡ **Charela Inn.** Each quiet, elegantly appointed room here has a private balcony or a covered patio. The owners' French-Jamaican roots find daily expression in La Vendôme restaurant, where you can dine on local produce and seafood dressed up with French sauces; there's also an excellent selection of wines. The small beach is part of the glorious 7-mi (11-km) Negril crescent. On Saturday night many guests staying at other resorts come here to watch a folkloric show. ⊠ *Norman Manley Blvd. (Box 3033),* ☎ *876/957–4277,* FAX *876/957–4414,* WEB *www.charela.com. 49 rooms. Restaurant, pool, beach, windsurfing, boating, bar, laundry service. 5-night minimum in high season, 3-night minimum summer. MC, V. EP, MAP.*

$$ ⊡ **Coco La Palm.** This quiet seaside hotel has oversized rooms (junior suites average 525 square ft [49 square m]) in octagonal buildings set in a U-shape around the pool. Amenities include direct-dial phones, color TVs, coffeemakers, and private patios or terraces—most overlooking gardens (only seven rooms have ocean views). On Negril Beach, the sandy shoreline of Coco La Palm is dotted with palm trees. The beachside restaurant is open-air and casual. ⊠ *Norman Manley Blvd.,* ☎ *876/957–4227,* FAX *876/957–3460,* WEB *www.cocolapalm.com. 41 rooms. Restaurant, bar, grill, air-conditioning, fans, refrigerators, pool, outdoor hot tub, beach. AE, DC, MC, V. EP, MAP.*

$$ ⊡ **Point Village.** This moderately priced resort is family friendly. Rooms have tile floors and basic furnishings, and each is individually decorated. Popular with tour groups, the sprawling complex has two small crescent beaches, rocky grottoes to explore, and fine snorkeling offshore. If you don't opt for the all-inclusive plan, the one- and two-bedroom suites with kitchens are a good choice. ⊠ *Norman Manley Blvd. (Box 105),* ☎ *876/957–5170,* FAX *876/957–5113,* WEB *www. pointvillage.com. 99 rooms; 66 1-, 2-, and 3-bedroom suites. 3 restaurants, 2 grills, tennis court, pool, outdoor hot tub, massage, beach, snorkeling, windsurfing, 4 bars, children's programs (ages infant–12), playground. AE, MC, V. All-inclusive, EP, MAP.*

$ ⊡ **Rockhouse.** You're side-by-side with nature at this stylish resort on Negril's rugged cliffs. Accommodations are built from rough-hewn timber, thatch, and stone, and are filled with furniture that echoes the nature theme. All rooms have private, indoor baths, but even these seem pleasantly rustic; villa rooms have private, enclosed, outdoor showers. There's a thatch-roofed Jamaican restaurant and a cliff-top pool and bar. ⊠ *West End Rd. (Box 24),* ☎ *876/957–4373,* FAX *876/957–0557,* WEB *www.rockhousehotel.com. 16 rooms, 12 villas. Restaurant, 2 bars, no air-conditioning, ceiling fans, in-room safes, minibars, pool, snorkeling, no kids under 12. AE, MC, V. EP.*

Mandeville

At 2,000 ft above the sea, Mandeville is noted for its cool climate and proximity to secluded south-coast beaches. Most accommodations don't have air-conditioning, but you really don't need it. Many are close to golf, tennis, horseback riding, and bird-watching areas.

$ 🖩 **Astra Country Inn & Restaurant.** "Country" is the key word in the name of this mountain retreat. The low price reflects the nature of the very basic rooms: they're spartan but immaculately clean. The small restaurant is open from 6:30 AM to 9 PM and serves snacks in addition to breakfast, lunch, and dinner. The food is billed as "home cooking" and emphasizes fresh produce—lots of vegetables and fruit juices. ⊠ *62 Ward Ave. (Box 60),* ☎ *876/962–3725. 20 rooms, 1 suite. Restaurant, no air-conditioning, kitchenettes, pool, sauna, bar, laundry service. MC, V. MAP.*

$ 🖩 **Mandeville Hotel.** Tropical gardens wrap around the building, and flowers spill onto the terrace restaurant, where breakfast and lunch are served. Rooms are simple and breeze-cooled; suites have full kitchens. You'll need a car to get around town, go out for dinner, and get to the beach, which is an hour away. ⊠ *4 Hotel St. (Box 78),* ☎ *876/962–2460,* FAX *876/962–0700,* WEB *www.mandevillehotel.com. 46 rooms; 17 1-, 2-, and 3-bedroom suites. Restaurant, coffee shop, no air-conditioning in some rooms, refrigerators, pool, bar, baby-sitting, laundry service, meeting rooms, travel services. AE, MC, V. EP.*

Dining

Although many cultures have contributed to Jamaica's cuisine, it has become a true cuisine in its own right. It would be a shame to travel to the heart of this complex culture without having at least one typical island meal.

Probably the most famous Jamaican dish is jerk pork—the ultimate island barbecue. The pork (purists cook a whole pig) is covered with a paste of Scotch bonnet peppers, pimento berries (also known as allspice), and other herbs and cooked slowly over a coal fire. Many aficionados believe the best jerk comes from Boston Beach, near Port Antonio. Jerk chicken and fish are also seen on many menus. The ever-so-traditional rice and peas, also known as "coat of arms," is similar to the *moros y christianos* of Spanish-speaking islands: white rice cooked with red kidney beans, coconut milk, scallions, and seasonings.

The island's most famous soup—the fiery pepper pot—is a spicy mixture of salt pork, salt beef, okra, and the island green known as callaloo. Patties (spicy meat pies) elevate street food to new heights. Although they actually originated in Haiti, Jamaicans excel at making them. Curry goat is another island standout: young goat is cooked with spices and is more tender and has a gentler flavor than the lamb for which it was substituted by immigrants from India. Salted fish was once the best that islanders could do between catches. Out of necessity, a breakfast staple (and the national dish of Jamaica) was invented. It joins seasonings with salt fish and ackee, a red fruit that grows on trees throughout the island. When cooked in this dish, ackee reminds most people of scrambled eggs.

Where restaurants are concerned, Kingston has the widest selection, with establishments that serve Italian, French, Cantonese, German, Thai, Indian, Korean, and Continental fare, as well as Rasta natural foods, also known as *I-tal.* There are also fine restaurants in all the resort areas, many in the resorts themselves. Most restaurants outside the hotels in MoBay and Ocho Rios will provide complimentary transportation.

What to Wear

Dress is usually casual chic (or just plain casual at many local hangouts). There are a few exceptions in Kingston and at the top resorts, some require semiformal wear in the evening during high season. People tend to dress up for dinner; men might be more comfortable in nice slacks, women in a sundress.

CATEGORY	COST*
$$$$	over $30
$$$	$20–$30
$$	$10–$20
$	under $10

per person for a main course at dinner

Kingston

CONTINENTAL

$$$–$$$$ ✕ **Blue Mountain Inn.** The elegant Blue Mountain Inn is a 30-minute
★ taxi ride from New Kingston and worth every penny of the fare. On
a former coffee plantation, the antiques-laden inn complements its En-
glish colonial atmosphere with Continental cuisine. All the classic beef
and seafood dishes are here, including chateaubriand béarnaise and lob-
ster thermidor. ⊠ *Gordon Town Rd., Gordon Town,* ☎ *876/927–1700
or 876/927–2606. Reservations essential. Jacket required. AE, MC, V.
Closed Sun. No lunch.*

$$–$$$ ✕ **Palm Court.** On the mezzanine floor of the Hilton Kingston, the el-
egant Palm Court is open for lunch and dinner. The menu is Conti-
nental; the rack of lamb, sautéed snapper almandine, and grilled
salmon are delicious. ⊠ *77 Knutsford Blvd.,* ☎ *876/926–5430. AE,
DC, MC, V.*

Ocho Rios

ECLECTIC

$–$$$ ✕ **Almond Tree.** One of the most popular restaurants in Ocho Rios,
★ the Almond Tree has a menu of Jamaican and Continental favorites:
pumpkin soup, pepper pot, and wonderful preparations of fresh fish,
veal *piccata,* and fondue. The swinging rope chairs of the terrace bar
and the tables perched above a Caribbean cove are great fun. ⊠ *83
Main St.,* ☎ *876/974–2813. Reservations essential. AE, DC, MC, V.*

$–$$$ ✕ **Evita's.** The large windows of this hilltop 1860s gingerbread house
★ open to cooling mountain breezes and stunning views of city and sea.
Over 30 kinds of pasta range from lasagna Rastafari (vegetarian) and
fiery jerk spaghetti to *rotelle colombo* (crabmeat with white sauce and
noodles). Other excellent choices include sautéed fillet of red snapper
with orange sauce, scampi and lobster in basil cream sauce, red snap-
per stuffed with crabmeat, and tasty grilled sirloin with mushroom sauce.
Kids under 12 eat for half price, and light eaters will appreciate half-
portion orders. ⊠ *Mantalent Inn, Eden Bower Rd.,* ☎ *876/974–2333.
AE, MC, V.*

$–$$ ✕ **Little Pub.** Relaxed alfresco dining awaits you at this charming
restaurant. It also has a bustling sports bar and an energetic Caribbean
revue several nights a week. Jamaican standards (jerk or curried
chicken, baked crab, sautéed snapper) accompany surf-and-turf, lobster thermidor, pasta primavera, seafood stir-fry, crêpes suzette, and
bananas flambé. Burgers and other standard pub fare are also available. ⊠ *59 Main St.,* ☎ *876/974–5826. AE, MC, V.*

JAMAICAN

$ ✕ **Ocho Rios Village Jerk Centre.** This blue-canopied, open-air eatery
★ is a good place to park yourself for frosty Red Stripe beer and fiery
jerk pork, chicken, or seafood. Milder barbecued meats, also sold by
weight (typically, ¼ or ½ pound makes a good serving), turn up on the
fresh daily chalkboard menu posted on the wall. It's lively at lunch,
especially when passengers from cruise ships swamp the place. ⊠ *Da-
Costa Dr.,* ☎ *876/974–2549. MC, V.*

Montego Bay

ECLECTIC

$$–$$$ ✕ **Sugar Mill.** Seafood is served with flair at this terrace restaurant on
★   the golf course of the Half Moon Golf, Tennis, and Beach Club.
Caribbean specialties, steak, and lobster are usually offered in a pungent sauce that blends Dijon mustard with Jamaica's own Pickapeppa
sauce. Otherwise, choices are the daily à la carte specials and anything
flame-grilled. Live music and a well-stocked wine cellar round out the
experience. ⊠ *Half Moon Golf, Tennis, and Beach Club, North Coast
Rd., Montego Bay, 7 mi (11 km) east of MoBay,* ☎ *876/953–2228.
Reservations essential. AE, MC, V.*

$$–$$$ ✕ **Town House.** Most of the rich and famous who have visited Jamaica
over the decades have eaten here. You'll find daily specials, delicious
variations of standard dishes (red snapper *papillote* is a specialty, with
lobster, cheese, and wine sauce), and many Jamaican favorites (curried
chicken with breadfruit and ackee). The 18th-century Georgian house
is adorned with original Jamaican and Haitian art. There's alfresco dining on the stone patio. ⊠ *16 Church St.,* ☎ *876/952–2660. Reservations essential. AE, DC, MC, V. No lunch Sun.*

$$ ✕ **Day-O Plantation Restaurant.** Transport yourself back in time with
a fine meal served on the garden terrace of this Georgian-style plan-
tation house. You might start with smoked marlin and then segue into
seafood ragout, broiled rock lobster with lemon butter, or beef fillet
with béarnaise sauce. Sweeten things up with one of the traditional Ja-
maican desserts (rum pudding, sweet cakes, or fruit salad). After din-
ner, tour the house. ⊠ *Next door to Barnett Estate Plantation, Fairfield,*
☎ *876/952–1825. AE, MC, V. Closed Mon.*

$–$$ ✕ **Le Chalet.** Don't let the French name fool you. This Denny's look-
★   alike, set in a nondescript shopping mall, serves heaping helpings of
some of the best Chinese and Jamaican food in MoBay. Tasty lobster
Cantonese costs only $15. ⊠ *32 Gloucester Ave.,* ☎ *876/952–6063.
AE, MC, V. No lunch Sun.*

$–$$ ✕ **Margueritaville Caribbean Bar and Grill.** This brightly painted bar-
restaurant is tough to miss: just look for the slide that connects it with
the water. You'll find plenty of casual dishes on the menu, including
burgers, chicken sandwiches, tuna melts, pizzas, and the like. ⊠
Gloucester Ave., ☎ *876/952–4777. AE, MC, V.*

$–$$ ✕ **The Native.** Shaded by a large poinciana tree and overlooking
Gloucester Avenue, this open-air stone terrace serves Jamaican and international dishes. To go native, start with smoked marlin, move on
to the *boonoonoonoos* platter (a sampler of local dishes), and round
out with coconut pie or *duckanoo* (a sweet dumpling of cornmeal, coconut, and banana wrapped in a banana leaf and steamed). Live entertainment and candlelit tables make this a romantic choice for dinner
on weekends. The popular afternoon buffets on Friday and Sunday are
family affairs. ⊠ *29 Gloucester Ave.,* ☎ *876/979–2769. Reservations
essential. AE, MC, V.*

ITALIAN

$$–$$$$ ✕ **Julia's Italian Restaurant.** Couples flock to this romantic Italian restau-
rant in the hills overlooking MoBay. You can choose from an à la carte
menu or order a five-course prix-fixe meal ($33–$45 per person) that
includes homemade soups and pastas, entrées of fish, chicken, and veal,
and scrumptious desserts. Don't expect the meal to equal the stupen-
dous view, and you won't be disappointed. ⊠ *Bogue Hill, Montego
Bay,* ☎ *876/952–1772. Reservations essential. AE, MC, V.*

SEAFOOD

$$–$$$ ✕ **Marguerites.** At this romantic pier-side dining room, "flambé" is the
operative word. Lobster, shrimp, fish, and several desserts are prepared

in dancing flames as you sip an exotic cocktail. The Caesar salad, prepared tableside, is also a treat. ⊠ *Gloucester Ave.,* ☎ *876/952–4777. Reservations essential. AE, MC, V. No lunch.*

$$–$$$ ✕ **Pier 1.** After tropical drinks at the deck bar, you'll be ready to dig into the international variations on fresh seafood; the best are the grilled lobster and any preparation of island snapper. Several party cruises leave from the marina here, and on Friday night the restaurant is mobbed by locals, who come to dance. ⊠ *Off Howard Cooke Blvd.,* ☎ *876/952–2452. AE, MC, V.*

Negril

CARIBBEAN

$ ✕ **Sweet Spice.** This mom-and-pop diner run by the Whytes serves inexpensive, generous plates of conch, fried or curried chicken, freshly caught fish, oxtail in brown stew sauce, and other down-home specialties. The fresh juices are quite satisfying. Drop by for breakfast, lunch, or dinner. ⊠ *1 White Hall Rd.,* ☎ *876/957–4621. MC, V.*

ECLECTIC

$–$$ ✕ **Margueritaville.** On a beautiful stretch of Negril Beach, this oper-
★ ation, a sibling of MoBay's wildly popular Margueritaville Caribbean Bar and Grill, is a sports bar, disco, beach club, and restaurant. You'll also find an art gallery, a gift shop, a five-star PADI dive shop, volleyball and basketball courts, and changing rooms. Lobster is the house specialty. Far less expensive are the fish, chicken, and sandwich platters. There are also more than 50 varieties of margaritas. ⊠ *Norman Manley Blvd.,* ☎ *876/957–9180. MC, V.*

$–$$ ✕ **Tan-ya's.** This alfresco restaurant overlooks the pool and hot tub at Sea Splash Resort, an intimate 15-suite property surrounded by palm trees on lovely Negril Beach. Jamaican delicacies with an international flavor are served for breakfast, lunch, and dinner. Try the excellent deviled crab backs or the smoked marlin. ⊠ *Sea Splash Resort, Norman Manley Blvd.,* ☎ *876/957–4041. AE, DC, MC, V.*

$–$$ ✕ **Rick's Café.** Here it is—the local landmark complete with cliffs, cliff divers, and powerful sunsets, all perfectly choreographed. Most folks come for the drinks and the renowned sunset party, since the standard pub menu is overpriced. In the sundown ritual the crowd toasts Mother Nature with rum drinks amid shouts, laughter, and ever-shifting meeting and greeting. When the sun slips below the horizon, there are more shouts, more cheers, and more rounds of rum. ⊠ *West End Rd.,* ☎ *876/957–0380. MC, V.*

$–$$ ✕ **Kuyaba on the Beach.** This charming thatch-roofed eatery has an international menu—including curried conch, kingfish steak, grilled lamb with sautéed mushrooms, and several pasta dishes—plus a lively ambience, especially at the bar. There's a crafts shop on the premises, and chaise longues line the beach; come prepared to spend some time, and don't forget a towel and bathing suit. ⊠ *Norman Manley Blvd.,* ☎ *876/957–4318. AE, MC, V.*

SEAFOOD

$–$$$ ✕ **Cosmo's Seafood Restaurant and Bar.** Owner Cosmo Brown has made
★ this seaside open-air bistro a pleasant place to spend the afternoon—and maybe stay on for dinner. Fish is the main attraction, and the conch soup—a house specialty—is a meal in itself. You'll also find lobster (grilled or curried), fish-and-chips, and the catch of the morning. Customers often drop cover-ups to take a dip before coffee and dessert and return to lounge in chairs scattered under almond and sea grape trees (there's a small entrance fee for the beach). ⊠ *Norman Manley Blvd.,* ☎ *876/957–4330. AE, MC, V.*

▼

Beaches

Jamaica has 200 mi (325 km) of beaches, some of them relatively deserted. Generally, the farther west you go, the lighter and finer the sand. The beaches listed below are public (though there's usually a small admission charge) and are among the best Jamaica has to offer. In addition, nearly every resort has its own private beach, complete with towels and water sports. Some of the larger resorts sell day passes to nonguests.

PORT ANTONIO

Boston Bay. Approximately 11 mi (18 km) east of Port Antonio, beyond the Blue Lagoon, is a small, intimate beach. It's a good place to buy the famous peppery delicacy jerk pork, available at any of the shacks spewing scented smoke along the beach.

San San Beach. About 5 mi (8 km) east of Port Antonio you'll find beautiful blue waters at this beach used mainly by area villa or hotel owners and their guests.

OCHO RIOS

Turtle Beach. Stretching behind the Renaissance Jamaica Grande is the busiest beach in Ocho Rios (where the islanders come to swim).

James Bond Beach. East of Ocho Rios in the quaint village of Oracabessa is this beach, which is popular because of the live reggae performances on its bandstand.

DISCOVERY BAY

Puerto Seco Beach. This stretch of sand is frequented primarily by locals. There's an admission charge of $5 for the beach, which is open daily 9–5. You'll find plenty of water-sports activities and some concessions that sell local foods.

MONTEGO BAY

Cornwall Beach. A lively beach with lots of places that sell food and drink, Cornwall also has a water-sports concession.

Doctor's Cave Beach. The 5-mi (8-km) beach has been spotlighted in so many travel articles and brochures that it often resembles Florida during spring break. On the bright side, it has much to offer admirers beyond just sugary sand, including changing rooms, colorful if overly insistent vendors, and plenty of places to grab a snack.

Walter Fletcher Beach. Near the center of town, there's protection from the surf on a windy day and therefore unusually fine swimming here; the calm waters make it a good bet for children.

NEGRIL

Negril Beach. Not too long ago, Negril was a beachcomber's Eden. Today much of its 7 mi of white sand is fronted by resorts, although some stretches along Bloody Bay remain relatively untouched. A few resorts have built accommodations overlooking their nude beaches, adding a new twist to the notion of "ocean view."

THE SOUTHWEST COAST

To find a beach off the main tourist routes, head for Jamaica's unexploited southwest coast. These isolated beaches are some of the island's safest because the population in this region is sparse, and hasslers are practically nonexistent. You should, however, use common sense; never leave valuables unattended on the beach.

Bluefields Beach. Near Savanna-La-Mar (or just Sav-La-Mar to locals), south of Negril, this is the south coast beach nearest to "civilization."

Crane Beach. At Black River, Crane Beach has retained its natural beauty and has—so far—remained undiscovered by most tourists.

Treasure Beach. This has to be the best that the south shore has to offer. By a quaint fishing village, this undeveloped beach has coves that are ideal for snorkeling explorations.

Outdoor Activities and Sports

The tourist board licenses all recreational activity operators and outfitters, which should ensure you of fair business practices as long as you deal with companies that display its decals.

BIRD-WATCHING

Many bird-watchers flock here for the chance to see the vervian hummingbird (the second-smallest bird in the world, larger only than Cuba's bee hummingbird), the Jamaican tody (which nests underground), or another of the island's 27 unique species. A great place to spot birds is the **Rocklands Feeding Station** (⌧ Anchovy, ☎ 876/952–2009), which is south of Montego Bay. It costs about $8 for an afternoon's visit. Tours of the bird sanctuary at **Marshall's Penn Great House** (Mandeville, ☎ 876/904–5451) are by appointment only and are led by owner Robert Sutton, one of Jamaica's leading ornithologists. A full-day of bird-watching costs $150 for as many as three people.

FISHING

Port Antonio makes deep-sea fishing headlines with its annual Blue Marlin Tournament, and MoBay and Ocho Rios have devotees who exchange tales (tall and otherwise) about sailfish, yellowfin tuna, wahoo, dolphinfish, and bonito. Licenses aren't required, and you can arrange to charter a boat at your hotel. A boat (with captain, crew, and equipment) that accommodates four to six passengers costs about $400 for a half-day.

GOLF

Golfers appreciate both the beauty and the challenges offered by Jamaica's courses. Caddies are almost always mandatory throughout the island, and rates are $5–$15. Cart rentals are available at all courses except Constant Spring and Manchester Country Club; costs are $20–$35. Some of the best courses in the country are found near MoBay.

The Runaway Bay golf course is found at **Breezes Runaway Bay** (⌧ North Coast Hwy., Runaway Bay, ☎ 876/973–7319). This 18-hole course has hosted many championship events (greens fee is $80 for nonguests; guests play for free). Near Kingston, **Caymanas** (⌧ Mandela Hwy., halfway between Kingston and Spanish Town, ☎ 876/922–3386, WEB www.caymanasgolfclub.com), actually 6 mi (9½ km) west of the city center, was Jamaica's first major championship 18-hole course (greens fee is $53).

The golf course adjacent to **Sandals Golf and Country Club** (⌧ Ocho Rios ☎ 876/975–0119), is 700 ft (214 m) above sea level (greens fee is $100 for nonguests). East of Falmouth, try **Grand Lido Braco Golf Club** (⌧ Trelawny, ☎ 876/954–0010), between Duncans and Rio Bueno, a 9-hole course with lush vegetation (nonguests should call for fee information). Caddies are not mandatory on this course.

Half Moon Golf, Tennis, and Beach Club (⌧ Montego Bay, ☎ 876/953–3105), a Robert Trent Jones–designed 18-hole course 7 mi (11 km) east of town, is the home of the Red Stripe Pro Am (greens fee is $90 for guests, $130 for nonguests). **Ironshore** (⌧ Montego Bay, ☎ 876/953–2800), 3 mi (5 km) east of the airport, is an 18-hole links-style course (the greens fee is $50). **Tryall Golf, Tennis, and Beach Club** (⌧ North Coast Hwy., Sandy Bay, ☎ 876/956–5681), 15 mi (24 km) west of Montego Bay, has an 18-hole championship course on the site of a 19th-century sugar plantation (greens fee is $40 for guests, $150 for nonguests). The **Wyndham Rose Hall** resort (⊠ North Coast Hwy., Montego Bay, ☎ 876/953–2650), 4 mi (6½ km) east of the airport, hosts several invitational tournaments (greens fee runs $115 for guests, $130 for nonguests). The newest course in Jamaica is the Ritz Carlton's **White Witch course** (⊠ 1 Ritz Carlton Dr., Rose Hall, St. James, ☎ 876/518–0174). The greens fee at this 18-hole championship course is $180 for guests of the resort, $225 for nonguests.

Great golf, rolling hills, and a "liquor mobile" go hand in hand at the 18-hole **Negril Hills Golf Club** (⊠ Sheffield Rd., Negril, ☎ 876/957–4638), which is east of town; the greens fee is $58. In the hills, the 9-hole **Manchester Club** (⊠ Caledonia Rd., Mandeville, ☎ 876/962–2403) is the Caribbean's oldest golf course and has a greens fee of about $35.

HORSEBACK RIDING

Jamaica is fortunate to have an outstanding equestrian facility in **Chukka Cove** (⊠ Ocho Rios, ☎ 876/972–2506). This resort offers riding, polo, and jumping (starting at $50), as well as hour-long trail rides ($30) and three-hour beach rides ($55). During in-season weekends this is the place for polo (and social) action. **Prospect Plantation** (⊠ Ocho Rios, ☎ 876/994–1373) offers horseback riding for $20 per hour, but advance reservations are required. You can saddle up at the **Rocky Point Riding Stables at Half Moon** (⊠ Montego Bay, ☎ 876/953–2286), which is east of the Half Moon Club.

SCUBA DIVING AND SNORKELING

You'll find good scuba diving off the the coasts of Ocho Rios, Port Antonio, and Negril. MoBay, known for its wall dives, has **Airport Reef** at its southwestern edge. The site is known for its coral caves, tunnels, and canyons. Near the Kingston airport is **Port Royal,** filled with sunken ships that are home to many different varieties of tropical fish. Prices on the island range from $30 to $60 for a single dive. All the large resorts rent equipment, and the all-inclusive places sometimes include scuba diving in their rates. To scuba dive, you need to show a certification card. Most dive operators licensed by the tourist board offer certification courses, dive trips, and snorkel gear rentals.

Dolphin Divers (⊠ Beach Rd., Negril, ☎ 876/957–4944) offers scuba facilities for sites in western Jamaica. **Garfield Diving Station** (⊠ Shop 13, Santa Maria, west of Renaissance Jamaica Grande, Ocho Rios, ☎ 876/974–5749) offers guided dives near Ocho Rios. **Negril Scuba Centre** (⊠ Negril Beach Club, Norman Manley Blvd., Negril, ☎ 876/957–4425) offers one-tank dives in the western end of Jamaica for $50. **North Coast Marine Sports** (⊠ Montego Bay, ☎ 876/953–2211) has several locations, one of which is at Half Moon, offering dives to numerous north coast sites. **Resort Divers** (⊠ Gloucester Ave., Montego Bay, ☎ 876/940–1183; ⊠ Island Plaza, Ocho Rios, ☎ 876/974–5338) offers dives from both Montego Bay and Ocho Rios.

TENNIS

Many hotels have tennis facilities that are free to their guests, but some will allow nonguests to play for a fee. Court fees generally run $5–$8 per hour for nonguests; lessons start at $12 an hour.

The **Hilton Kingston** (⊠ 77 Knutsford Blvd., Kingston, ☎ 876/926–5430) has two tennis courts for guest use only. **Le Méridien Pegasus** (⊠ 81 Knutsford Blvd., Kingston, ☎ 876/926–3690) has three courts for guest use only.

Grand Lido Sans Souci (⊠ North Coast Hwy., Ocho Rios,, ☎ 876/974–2353) has two lighted tennis courts and a pro. **Sandals Dunn's River**

Golf Resort and Spa (⊠ North Coast Hwy.,. Ocho Rios, ☎ 876/972–1610) has two courts lit for night play as well as the services of a pro. **Breezes Runaway Bay** (⊠ North Coast Hwy., Runaway Bay, ☎ 876/973–2436) has four tennis courts.

Half Moon Golf, Tennis, and Beach Club (⊠ Montego Bay, ☎ 876/953–2211) offers tennis buffs the use of 13 Laykold courts (7 lit for night play) along with a resident pro and a pro shop. Tennis is a highlight at **Sandals Montego Bay** (⊠ Kent Ave., Montego Bay, ☎ 876/952–5510), with four courts lit for night play and a tennis pro. **Tryall Golf, Tennis, and Beach Club** (⊠ North Coast Hwy., ☎ 876/956–5660), 15 mi (4 km) west of MoBay, has nine courts.

You'll find five hard courts and five clay courts, all lit for night play, at **Couples Swept Away Negril** (⊠ Norman Manley Blvd., Negril, ☎ 876/957–4061).

Shopping

Jamaican crafts are made with style and skill and take the form of resort wear, hand-loomed fabrics, silk-screened items, wood carvings, paintings, and other fine arts. Jamaican rum is a great take-home gift. So is Tia Maria, Jamaica's world-famous coffee liqueur. The same goes for the island's prized coffees (both Blue Mountain and High Mountain) and its jams, jellies, and marmalades. If you shop around, you'll find good deals on such duty-free luxury items as jewelry, cameras, china, Swiss watches, and Irish crystal. The top-selling French perfumes are sold alongside Jamaica's own fragrances.

Areas and Malls

A shopping tour of the **Kingston** area should begin at Constant Spring Road or King Street. The city's ever-growing roster of malls includes Twin Gates Plaza, New Lane Plaza, the New Kingston Shopping Centre, Tropical Plaza, Manor Park Plaza, the Village, the Springs, and the newest (and some say nicest), Sovereign Shopping Centre. Devon House is the place to find things old and new made in Jamaica. The great house is now a museum with antiques and furniture reproductions; boutiques and an ice cream shop—try one of the tropical flavors (mango, guava, pineapple, and passion fruit)—now fill what were once the stables.

The crafts markets in **Port Antonio** and—unless there's a cruise ship in port—**Ocho Rios** are less hectic than the one in MoBay. Ocho Rios shopping plazas are Pineapple Place, Ocean Village, the Taj Mahal, Coconut Grove, and Island Plaza.

In **MoBay** you should visit the crafts market on Market Street; just be prepared for haggling over prices in the midst of pandemonium. If you want to spend serious money, head for City Centre Plaza; Half Moon Village; Holiday Inn Shopping Centre; St. James's Place; Westgate Plaza; and Montego Bay Shopping Centre, a favorite with locals. At **Negril**'s Rutland Point crafts market you'll find a plethora of T-shirts, straw hats, baskets, and place mats, carved wood statues, colorful Rasta berets, and cheap jewelry. The most upscale shopping area in Negril is Time Square, filled with luxury items, from jewelry to watches to leather goods.

Specialty Items

COFFEE

Java lovers will find beans and ground coffee at **Hi-Lo Supermarket** (⊠ West End Rd., Negril, ☎ 876/957–4546). If the stores are out of Blue Mountain, you may have to settle for High Mountain coffee, the locals' second-favorite brand.

HANDICRAFTS

Gallery of West Indian Art (⊠ 11 Fairfield Rd., Montego Bay, ☎ 876/952–4547) is the place to find Jamaican and Haitian paintings. A corner of the gallery is devoted to hand-turned pottery (some painted) and beautifully carved and painted birds and animals. **Harmony Hall** (⊠ Hwy. A–1, Ocho Rios, ☎ 876/975–4222), an 8-minute drive east of the main part of town, is a restored great house where Annabella Proudlock sells her unique wooden boxes (their covers are decorated with reproductions of Jamaican paintings). Also on sale—and magnificently displayed—are larger reproductions of paintings, lithographs, and signed prints of Jamaican scenes and hand-carved wooden combs. In addition, Harmony Hall is well known for its shows by local artists. **Things Jamaican** (⊠ Devon House, 26 Hope Rd., Kingston, ☎ 876/929–6602; ⊠ Sangster International Airport, Montego Bay, ☎ 876/952–1936) sells some of the best Jamaican crafts—from carved wooden bowls and trays to reproductions of silver and brass period pieces.

LIQUOR AND TOBACCO

As a rule, only rum distilleries, such as Appleton's and Sangster's, have better deals than the airport stores. Best of all, if you buy your rum or Tia Maria at either the Kingston or the MoBay airport before you leave, you don't have to tote all those heavy, breakable bottles to your hotel and then to the airport. There are several good cigar shops in Negril. Fine handmade **Macanudo** (☎ 876/925–1082) cigars make great easy-to-pack gifts; why not pick some up at Montego Bay airport on your way home? If you get the urge to puff during your stay, call the company to find out where to buy them in Jamaica. **Cigar World** (⊠ 11 Time Square Mall, Negril, ☎ 876/957–3299) offers hand-made Jamaican cigars as well as Cubans. **Cigar King** (⊠ 7 Time Square Mall, Negril, ☎ 876/957–3315) has a wide selection of cigars along with a walk-in humidor.

RECORDS AND CDS

Kingston has several good music stores, but there are also good stores in both Port Antonio and Montego Bay. If you like reggae by world famous Jamaican artists—Bob Marley, Peter Tosh, and Third World, to name a few—a pilgrimage to **Randy's Record Mart** (⊠ 17 N. Parade, Kingston, ☎ 876/922–4859) is a must. **Record Plaza** (⊠ Tropical Plaza, Kingston, ☎ 876/926–7645) is a good place to stop for Jamaican tunes.

Record City (⊠ 1 William St., Port Antonio, ☎ 876/993–2836) has many new sounds as well as popular favorites. You'll find the works of Jamaican musical stars at **Top Ranking Records** (⊠ Westgate Plaza, Montego Bay, ☎ 876/952–1216).

SHOES

Cheap sandals are good buys in shopping centers throughout Jamaica. Although workmanship and leathers don't rival the craftsmanship of those found in Italy or Spain, neither do the prices (about $20 a pair). **Lee's Fifth Avenue Shoes** (⊠ Tropical Plaza, Kingston, ☎ 876/926–7486) is a good store in the capital. In Ocho Rios, the **Pretty Feet Shoe Shop** (⊠ Ocean Village Shopping Centre, Ocho Rios, ☎ 876/974–5040) is a good bet. In MoBay try **Best Ever Footwear** (⊠ 5 East St., Montego Bay, ☎ 876/979–5095) if you find yourself in need of footwear during your trip.

Nightlife and the Arts

Nightlife

Jamaica—especially Kingston—supports a lively community of musicians. For starters there's reggae, popularized by the late Bob Marley and the Wailers and performed today by son Ziggy Marley, Jimmy Tosh (the late Peter Tosh's son), Gregory Isaacs, Jimmy Cliff, and many others. If your experience of Caribbean music has been limited to steel drums and Harry Belafonte, then the political, racial, and religious messages of reggae may set you on your ear; listen closely and you just might hear the heartbeat of the people.

Those who know and love reggae should visit between mid-July and August for the Reggae Sunsplash. This four-night concert—at the Bob Marley Performing Center (a field set up with a temporary stage), in the Freeport area of MoBay—showcases local talent and attracts such big-name performers as Third World and Ziggy Marley and the Melody Makers.

DANCE AND MUSIC CLUBS

For the most part, the liveliest late-night happenings throughout Jamaica are in the major resort hotels, with the widest variety of spots probably in Montego Bay. Some of the all-inclusives offer a dinner and disco pass from about $50. Pick up a copy of the *Daily Gleaner,* the *Jamaica Observer,* or the *Star* (available at newsstands throughout the island) for listings on who's playing when and where.

Live jazz performances are offered on Saturday evenings at the **Blue Lagoon Restaurant** (⊠ San San Beach, Port Antonio, ☎ 876/993–7646). If you have but one night to dance, do it at the **Roof Club** (⊠ 11 West St., Port Antonio, ☎ 876/993–3817). On weekends from 11 PM on, this is where it's all happening. Dancers often head to **Shadows** (⊠ 40 West St., Port Antonio, ☎ 876/993–3823).

One of the top dance clubs is **Jamaic'N Me Crazy** (⊠ Renaissance Jamaica Grande, Main St., Ocho Rios, ☎ 876/974–2201); the popular club is a favorite with both locals and visitors who pay a hefty cover charge. The **Little Pub** (⊠ Main St., Ocho Rios, ☎ 876/974–5826) produces Caribbean revues several nights a week. **Silks** (⊠ Shaw Park Beach Hotel, Shaw Park Ridge Rd., Ocho Rios, ☎ 876/974–2552), 1½ mi (2½ km) south of town, has long been a favorite on the dance scene.

Brewery (⊠ Shop 4, Miranda Ridge, Gloucester Ave., Montego Bay, ☎ 876/940–2433) is a popular sports bar. With its location right on what's deemed the "Hip Strip," **Hurricanes Disco** (⊠ Breezes Montego Bay Resort, Gloucester Ave., Montego Bay, ☎ 876/940–1150) is packed with locals and visitors from other hotels willing to pay a hefty cover charge. The colorful **Margueritaville** (⊠ Gloucester Ave., Montego Bay, ☎ 876/952–4777; ⊠ Norman Manley Blvd., Negril, ☎ 876/952–4777) throbs with a spring-break crowd during the season and with a fun-loving atmosphere any night of the year. After 10 PM on Friday night, the crowd gathers at **Pier 1** (⊠ Howard Cooke Blvd., Montego Bay, ☎ 876/952–2452), opposite the straw market. **Walter's** (⊠ 39 Gloucester Ave., Montego Bay, ☎ 876/952–9391) is a downtown favorite. The **Witches Disco** (⊠ Holiday Inn Sunspree Resort, North Coast Hwy., Montego Bay, 6 mi [9½ km] east of airport, ☎ 876/953–2485) rocks with a Jamaican beat nightly.

You'll find the best live music at **Alfred's Ocean Palace** (⊠ Norman Manley Blvd., Negril, ☎ 876/957–4735), with live performances right on the beach. **De Buss** (⊠ Norman Manley Blvd., Negril, ☎ 876/957–4405) pulsates with a Jamaican sound, and it's impossible to miss; this joint is in a former double decker bus. The sexy, always packed disco at **Hedonism II** (⊠ Norman Manley Blvd., Negril, ☎ 876/957–5200) is the wildest dance spot on the island; Tuesday (pajama night) and Thursday (toga night) are tops.

Exploring Jamaica

Touring Jamaica can be both thrilling and frustrating. Rugged (albeit beautiful) terrain and winding—often potholed—roads make for slow going. (In the rainy season from June through October, roads can easily be washed out; *always* check conditions prior to heading out.) Primary roads that loop around and across the island are two-lane, and signs are not prevalent. Numbered addresses are seldom used outside major townships, locals drive aggressively, and people and animals seem to have a knack for appearing on the street out of nowhere. That said, Jamaica's scenery shouldn't be missed. The solution? Stick to guided tours and licensed taxis—to be safe and avoid frustration.

If you're staying in Kingston or Port Antonio, set aside at least one day for the capital's highlights and another for a guided excursion to the Blue Mountains. If you have more time, head for Mandeville. You'll find at least three days' worth of activity right along MoBay's boundaries; you should also consider a trip to Cockpit Country or Ocho Rios. If you're based in Ocho Rios, be sure to visit Dunn's River Falls; you may also want to stop by Firefly or Port Antonio. If Negril is your hub, take in the south shore, including Y. S. Falls and the Black River.

Numbers in the margin correspond to points of interest on the Jamaica map.

SIGHTS TO SEE

❷ Blue Mountains. These lush mountains rise to the north of Kingston. Unless you're traveling with a local, don't rent a car and go to the Blue Mountains on your own; the roads wind and dip, hand-lettered signs blow away, and you could easily get lost—not just for hours but for days. It's best to hire a taxi (look for red PPV license plates to identify a licensed taxi) or to take a guided tour. If you admire Jamaica's coffee, be sure to visit **Pine Grove** (☎ 876/977–8009), a working coffee farm that doubles as an inn. It also has a restaurant that serves owner Marcia Thwaites's Jamaican cuisine. Another place worth a visit is **Mavis Bank** (☎ 876/977–8005) and its Jablum coffee plant. A half-hour guided tour is available for $5; inquire when you arrive at the main office. **Appleton Rum Factory** (☎ 876/963–9215) is open Monday through Saturday from 9 to 3:30. You'll enjoy a tour of this expansive South Coast factory; samples are part of the tour.

❽ Cockpit Country. Fifteen miles (24 km) inland from MoBay is one of the most untouched areas in the West Indies: a terrain of pitfalls and potholes carved by nature in limestone. For nearly a century after 1655 it was known as the Land of Look Behind because British soldiers nervously rode their horses through here, on the lookout for the guerrilla freedom fighters known as Maroons. Former slaves who refused to surrender to the invading English, the Maroons eventually won their independence. Today their descendents live in this area, untaxed and virtually ungoverned by outside authorities. Most visitors to the area stop in Accompong, a small community in St. Elizabeth Parish. You can stroll through town, take in the historic structures, and learn more about the Maroons—considered Jamaica's greatest herbalists.

❺ Firefly. About 20 mi (32 km) east of Ocho Rios in Port Maria, Firefly was once Sir Noël Coward's vacation home and is now maintained by the Jamaican National Heritage Trust. Although the setting is Eden-like, the house is surprisingly spartan, considering that he often entertained jet-setters and royalty. He wrote *High Spirits, Quadrille,* and other plays here, and his simple grave is on the grounds next to a small stage where his works are occasionally performed. Recordings of Coward singing about mad dogs and Englishmen echo over the lawns. Tours include time in the photo gallery and a walk through the house and grounds, the viewing of a video on Coward, and a drink in the gift shop. ✉ *Port Maria*, ☎ *876/725–0920.* 💳 *$10.* ⊙ *Mon.–Sat. 8:30–5:00.*

❶ Kingston. The reaction of most newcomers to the capital is far from love at first sight. Yet the islanders themselves can't seem to let the city go. Everybody talks about it, about their homes or relatives there, about their childhood memories. Indeed, Kingston seems to reflect more of the true Jamaica—a wonderful cultural mix—than do the sunny havens of the north coast. As one Jamaican put it, "You don't really know Jamaica until you know Kingston." Parts of the city may be dirty, crowded, and raucous, yet it's still where international and local movers and shakers come to move and shake, where the arts flourish, and where the shopping is superb. It's also home to the University of the West Indies, one of the Caribbean's largest universities.

Sprawling Kingston spills over into communities in every direction. To the west, coming in from Spanish Town, lie some of the city's worst slums, in the neighborhoods of Six Miles and Riverton City. Farther south, Spanish Town Road skirts through a high-crime district that many Kingstonians avoid. In the heart of the business district, along the water, the pace is more peaceful, with a lovely walk and parks on Ocean Boulevard. Also here is the Jamaica Convention Centre, home of the UN body that creates all laws for the world's seas. From the waterfront you can look across Kingston Harbour to the Palisadoes Peninsula. This narrow strip is where you'll find Norman Manley International Airport and, farther west, Port Royal, the island's former capital, which was destroyed by an earthquake. Downtown Kingston is considered unsafe, particularly at night. Be careful.

New Kingston, north of downtown, is bordered by Old Hope Road on the east and Half Way Tree Road (which changes to Constant Spring Road) on the west. The area is sliced by Hope Road, a major thoroughfare that connects this region with the University of the West Indies, about 15 minutes east of New Kingston. You may feel most comfortable in New Kingston, which glistens with hotels, office towers, apartments, and boutiques. But don't let your trip to the capital end here; away from the high-rises of the new city, Kingston's colonial history is recalled at many well-preserved sites.

North of New Kingston, the city gives way to steep hills and magnificent homes. East of here, the views are even grander as the road winds into the Blue Mountains. Hope Road, just after the University of the West Indies, becomes Gordon Town Road and starts twisting up through the mountains—it's a route that leaves no room for error.

Devon House, built in 1881 and bought and restored by the government in the 1960s, is filled with period furnishings, such as Venetian crystal chandeliers, and period reproductions. You can see the inside of the two-story mansion (built with a South American gold miner's fortune) only on a guided tour. On the grounds you'll find some of the island's best crafts shops as well as one of the few mahogany trees to have survived Kingston's ambitious, but not always careful, development. ✉ *26 Hope Rd.,* ☎ *876/929–7029 or 876/929–6602.* 💳 *$3 for house tour.* ⊙ *Devon House Tues.–Sat. 9:30–5, shops Mon.–Sat. 10–6.*

The artists represented at the **National Gallery** may not be household names in other countries, but their paintings are sensitive and moving. You'll find works by such Jamaican masters as intuitive painter John Dunkley and Edna Manley, a sculptor who worked in a cubist style. Among other highlights from the 1920s through the 1980s are works by the artist Kapo, a self-taught painter whose creations portray religious images. Reggae fans should look for Christopher Gonzalez's controversial statue of Bob Marley (it was slated to be displayed near the National Arena but was placed here because many Jamaicans felt it didn't resemble Marley). ✉ *12 Ocean Blvd., Kingston Mall, near the waterfront,* ☎ *876/922–1561.* ⌨ *$1.* ◷ *Weekdays 10–4.*

At the height of his career, Bob Marley built a recording studio. Today the structure—painted Rastafarian red, yellow, and green—houses the **Bob Marley Museum.** The guided tour takes you through the medicinal herb garden, his bedroom, and other rooms wallpapered with magazine and newspaper articles that chronicle his rise to stardom. The tour includes a 20-minute biographical film on him; there's also a reference library if you want to learn more. Certainly there's much here that will help you to understand Marley, reggae, and Jamaica itself. A striking mural by Jah Bobby, *The Journey of Superstar Bob Marley,* depicts the hero's life from its beginnings, in a womb shaped like a coconut, to enshrinement in the hearts of the Jamaican people. ✉ *56 Hope Rd.,* ☎ *876/927–9152.* ⌨ *$8.* ◷ *Mon.–Sat. 9:30–4.*

⑪ **Mandeville.** At 2,000 ft (612 m) above sea level, Mandeville is considerably cooler than the coastal areas 25 mi (40 km) to the south. Its vegetation is also more lush, thanks to the mists that drift through the mountains. But climate and flora aren't all that separate it from the steamy coast: Mandeville seems a hilly tribute to all that is genteel in the British character. The people here live in tidy cottages with gardens around a village green; there's even a Georgian courthouse and a parish church. The entire scene could be set down in Devonshire, were it not for the occasional poinciana blossom or citrus grove.

The **Manchester Club** (☎ 876/962–2403) has tennis courts and a well-manicured 9-hole golf course, the first golf course in the Caribbean. At the **Bird Sanctuary** (☎ 876/975–7158), you may spot some of the more than 25 unique species of birds. Tours (by appointment only) are led by owner Robert Sutton, one of the island's leading ornithologists. At **Lovers' Leap,** legend has it that two slave lovers chose to jump off the 1,700-ft-high (520-m-high) cliff rather than be recaptured by their master. At the **High Mountain Coffee Plantation** (✉ Williamsfield, ☎ 876/963–4211) free tours (by appointment only) show how coffee beans are turned into one of the world's favorite morning drinks.

⑦ **Martha Brae River.** The gentle waterway takes its name from an Arawak Indian who killed herself because she refused to reveal the whereabouts of a local gold mine to the Spanish. According to legend, she agreed to take them there and, on reaching the river, used magic to change its course, drowning herself and the greedy Spaniards with her. Her *duppy* (ghost) is said to guard the mine's entrance. Rafting on this river is a very popular activity. Martha Brae River Rafting arranges trips downriver. Near the rafting company ticket office you'll find gift shops, a bar-restaurant, and a swimming pool.

⑨ **Montego Bay.** Today many explorations of MoBay are conducted from a reclining chair—frothy drink in hand—on Doctor's Cave Beach. Believe it or not, the area had a history before all the resorts went up. If you can pull yourself away from the water's edge and brush the sand off your toes, you'll find some very interesting colonial sights. The outstanding free tour of **Barnett Estates** is led by a charming guide in period costume who recites period poetry and sings period songs. The Kerr-Jarrett family has held the land here for 11 generations, and they still grow coconuts, mangoes, and sugarcane on 3,000 acres. ✉ *Granville Main Rd.,* ☎ *876/952–2382.* ⌨ *Free, but open only for diners at the Day-O Plantation Restaurant, next door.* ◷ *Great house 9:30*

AM–10 PM; *tours daily 6:30 PM–11 PM*. In the 1700s, **Rose Hall** may well have been the greatest of great houses in the West Indies. Today it's popular less for its architecture than for the legend surrounding its second mistress: Annie Palmer was credited with murdering three husbands and a *busha* (plantation overseer) who was her lover. The story is told in a novel that's sold everywhere in Jamaica: *The White Witch of Rose Hall*. There's a pub on-site. It's across the highway from the Wyndham Rose Hall resort. ✉ *North Coast Hwy.,* ☎ *876/953–2323.* 🎫 *$15.* ☉ *Daily 9–6.* The **Greenwood Great House** has no spooky legend to titillate, but it's much better than Rose Hall at evoking life on a sugar plantation. The Barrett family, from whom the English poet Elizabeth Barrett Browning descended, once owned all the land from Rose Hall to Falmouth; they built this and several other great houses on it. (The poet's father, Edward Moulton Barrett, "the Tyrant of Wimpole Street," was born at nearby Cinnamon Hill, currently the estate of country singer Johnny Cash.) Highlights of Greenwood include oil paintings of the Barretts, china made for the family by Wedgwood, a library filled with rare books from as early as 1697, fine antique furniture, and a collection of exotic musical instruments. There's a pub on-site as well. It's 15 mi (24km) east of Montego Bay. ✉ *Greenwood,* ☎ *876/953–1077.* 🎫 *$12.* ☉ *Daily 9–6.*

🔟 Negril. In the 18th century English ships assembled here in convoys for dangerous ocean crossings. The infamous pirate Calico Jack and his crew were captured right here while they guzzled rum. All but two of them were hanged on the spot; Mary Read and Anne Bonney were pregnant at the time, so their executions were delayed.

On the winding coast road 55 mi (89 km) southwest of MoBay, Negril was once Jamaica's best-kept secret. Recently, however, it has begun to shed some of its bohemian, ramshackle atmosphere for the attractions and activities traditionally associated with MoBay. One thing that hasn't changed around this west-coast center (whose only true claim to fame is a 7-mi [11-km] beach) is a casual approach to life. As you wander from lunch in the sun to shopping in the sun to sports in the sun, you'll find that swimsuits and cover-ups are common attire. Want to dress for a special meal? Slip on a caftan over your swimsuit.

Negril stretches along the coast south from horseshoe-shape Bloody Bay (named when it was a whale-processing center) along the calm waters of Long Bay to the Lighthouse section and landmark Rick's Café. Sunset at Rick's is a Negril tradition. Divers spiral downward off 50-ft-high cliffs into the deep green depths as the sun turns into a ball of fire and sets the clouds ablaze with color. Sunset is also the time when Norman Manley Boulevard, which intersects West End Road, comes to life with bustling bistros and ear-splitting discos.

Even nonguests can romp at **Hedonism II.** The resort beach is divided into "prude" and "nude" sides; a quick look around reveals where most guests pull their chaise longues. Nude volleyball, body-painting contests, and shuffleboard keep daytime hours lively; at night most action occurs in the high-tech disco or in the hot tub. Your day pass (10:30–5; $65) includes food and drink and participation in water sports, tennis, squash, and other activities. Night passes ($75) cover dinner, drinks, and entrance to the disco. Day or night, reservations are a must; bring a photo I.D. as well. West End Road leads to Negril's only structure of historical significance, the **Lighthouse,** which has guided ships past Jamaica's rocky western coast since 1895. You can stop by the adjacent caretaker's cottage 11–7 (except Tuesday) and, for the price of a tip, climb the spiral steps to the best view in town.

⑥ Ocho Rios. Although Ocho Rios isn't near eight rivers as its name would seem to indicate, it does have a seemingly endless series of cascades that sparkle from limestone rocks along the coast. (The name Ocho Rios came about because the English misunderstood the Spanish *laschorreras*—"the waterfalls.")

Today Ocho Rios can be a traffic-clogged community, but a visit is worthwhile, if only to enjoy its two chief attractions—Dunn's River Falls and Prospect Plantation. A few steps from the main road in Ocho Rios are some of the most charming inns and oceanfront restaurants in the Caribbean. Lying on the sand of what seems to be your very own cove or swinging gently in a hammock while sipping a tropical drink, you'll soon forget the traffic that's just a stroll away.

Dunn's River Falls is an eye-catching sight: 600 ft (184 m) of cold, clear mountain water splashing over a series of stone steps to the warm Caribbean. The best way to enjoy the falls is to climb the slippery steps: don a swimsuit, take the hand of the person ahead of you, and trust that the chain of hands and bodies leads to an experienced guide. The leaders of the climbs are personable fellows who reel off bits of local lore while telling you where to step; you can hire a guide's service for a tip of a few dollars. ⊠ *Off A–1, between St. Ann's and Ocho Rios,* ☎ *876/974–2857.* ⊠ *$6.* ⊙ *Daily 8:30–5.*

To learn about Jamaica's former agricultural lifestyle, a trip to **Prospect Plantation,** just west of town, is a must. But it's not just a place for history lovers or farming aficionados; everyone seems to enjoy the views over the White River Gorge and the tour by jitney (a canopied open-air cart pulled by a tractor). The grounds are full of exotic fruits and tropical trees, some planted over the years by such celebrities as Winston Churchill and Charlie Chaplin. You can also go horseback riding on the plantation's 900 acres or play miniature golf, grab a drink in the bar, or buy souvenirs in the gift shop. If you want more time to really explore, you can rent one of the on-site villas. ⊠ *Hwy. A–1,* ☎ *876/994–1058.* ⊠ *$12.* ⊙ *Daily 8–5; tours Mon.–Sat. 10:30, 2, and 3:30, Sun. 11, 1:30, and 3.*

Jamaica's national motto is "Out of Many, One People," and at the **Coyaba River Garden and Museum** you'll see exhibits on the many cultural influences that have contributed to the creation of the one. The museum covers the island's history from the time of the Arawak Indians up to the present day. A guided 45-minute tour through the lush 3-acre garden, which is 1½ mi (2½ km) south of Ocho Rios, introduces you to the flora and fauna of the island. The complex includes a crafts and gift shop and a snack bar. ⊠ *Shaw Park Estate, Shaw Park Ridge Rd.,* ☎ *876/974–6235.* ⊠ *$4.50.* ⊙ *Daily 8:30–5.*

The original "defenders" stationed at the Old Fort, built in 1777, spent much of their time sacking and plundering as far afield as St. Augustine, Florida, and sharing their booty with the local plantation owners who financed their missions. Fifteen miles (24 km) west is Discovery Bay, site of Columbus's landing, with a small museum of artifacts and such local memorabilia as ships' bells and cannons and iron pots used for boiling sugarcane. Other places nearby include Runaway Bay's Green Grotto Caves (and the boat ride on an underground lake); a ramble through the Shaw Park Botanical Gardens; a visit to Sun Valley, a working plantation with banana, coconut, and citrus trees; and a drive through Fern Gully, a natural canopy of vegetation filtered by sunlight. (Jamaica has the world's largest number of fern species, more than 570.)

④ Port Antonio. Early in the 20th century the first tourists seeking a respite from New York winters arrived on the northeast coast, drawn by the exoticism of the island's banana trade. In time the area became fashionable among a fast-moving crowd and has counted J. P. Morgan, Rudyard Kipling, William Randolph Hearst, Clara Bow, Bette Davis, and Ginger Rogers among its admirers. Its most passionate devotee was the actor Errol Flynn, whose spirit still seems to haunt the docks, and you can almost imagine him devouring raw dolphinfish and swigging gin at 10 AM. Although the action has moved elsewhere, the area can still weave a spell. Robin Moore wrote *The French Connection* here, and Broadway's tall and talented Tommy Tune found inspiration for the musical *Nine* while being pampered at Trident.

Port Antonio has also long been a center for some of the Caribbean's finest deep-sea fishing. Dolphins (the delectable fish, not the lovable mammal) are the likely catch here, along with tuna, kingfish, and wahoo. In October the weeklong Blue Marlin Tournament attracts anglers from around the world. By the time they've all had their fill of beer, it's the fish stories—rather than the fish—that carry the day.

A good way to spend a day in Port Antonio is to laze in the deep azure water of the **Blue Lagoon,** 1 mi (1½ km) east of San San Beach. Although there's not much beach to speak of, you'll find a water-sports center, changing rooms, and a soothing mineral pool. Good, inexpensive Jamaican fare is served at a charming waterside terrace restaurant; it's open daily for lunch and dinner and has live jazz music on Saturday night. **DeMontevin Lodge** (⊠ 21 Fort George St., ☎ 876/993–2604), on Titchfield Hill, is owned by the Mullings family. The late Gladys Mullings was Errol Flynn's cook, and you can still get great food here. The lodge, and a number of structures on nearby Musgrave Street (the crafts market is here), are built in a traditional seaside style that's reminiscent of New England. **Queen Street,** in the residential Titchfield area, a couple of miles north of downtown Port Antonio, has several fine examples of Georgian architecture.

A short drive east from Port Antonio puts you at Boston Bay, which is popular with swimmers and has been enshrined by lovers of jerk pork. The spicy barbecue was originated by the Arawaks and perfected by the Maroons. Eating almost nothing but wild hog preserved over smoking coals enabled them to survive years of fierce guerrilla warfare with the English.

Some 6 mi (9½ km) northeast of Port Antonio are the **Athenry Gardens,** a 3-acre tropical wonderland including the Nonsuch Caves, whose underground beauty has been made accessible by concrete walkways, railed stairways, and careful lighting. ⊠ *Nonsuch,* ☎ *876/993–3740.* ▨ *$6.* ☉ *Daily 10–4.*

❸ **Rio Grande.** The Rio Grande (yes, Jamaica has a Rio Grande, too) is a granddaddy of river-rafting attractions: an 8-mi-long (13-km-long) swift, green waterway from Berrydale to Rafter's Rest (it flows into the Caribbean at St. Margaret's Bay). The trip of about three hours is made on bamboo rafts pushed along by a raftsman who is likely to be a character. You can pack a picnic lunch and eat it on the raft or on the riverbank; wherever you lunch, a Red Stripe vendor will appear at your elbow. A restaurant, a bar, and souvenir shops are at Rafter's Rest. The trip costs about $40 per two-person raft.

❶❸ **Port Royal.** Just south of Kingston, Port Royal was called "the wickedest city in the world" until an earthquake tumbled much of it into the sea in 1692. The spirits of Henry Morgan and other buccaneers add energy to what remains. The proudest possession of St. Peter's Church, rebuilt in 1726 to replace Christ's Church, is a silver communion set said to have been donated by Morgan himself (who probably obtained it during a raid on Panama).

A ferry from the square in downtown Kingston goes to Port Royal at least twice a day, and the town is small enough to see on foot. If you drive out to Port Royal from Kingston, you'll pass several other sights, including remains of old forts virtually overgrown with vegetation, an old naval cemetery (which has some intriguing headstones), and a monument commemorating Jamaica's first coconut tree, planted in 1863 (there's no tree there now, just plenty of cactus and scrub brush).

You can no longer down rum in Port Royal's legendary 40 taverns, but two small pubs still remain in operation. You can explore the impressive remains of **Ft. Charles,** once the area's major garrison. Built in 1662, this is the oldest surviving monument from the British occupation of Jamaica. On the grounds are a maritime museum and the old artillery storehouse, Giddy House, that gained its name after being tilted by the earthquake of 1907: locals say its slant makes you giddy. ☎ 876/967–8438. ☞ $4. ☉ Daily 9–5.

⓬ **Spanish Town.** Twelve miles (19km) west of Kingston on A–1, Spanish Town was the island's capital when it was ruled by Spain. The town has a Georgian Antique Square, the Jamaican People's Museum of Crafts and Technology (in the Old King's House stables), and St. James, the oldest cathedral in the Western Hemisphere. Spanish Town's original name was Santiago de la Vega, meaning St. James of the Plains.

JAMAICA A TO Z

To research prices, get advice from other travelers, and book travel arrangements, visit www.fodors.com.

AIR TRAVEL

Air Canada offers daily service from Toronto, Halifax, Winnipeg, and Montréal in conjunction with Air Jamaica. Air Jamaica provides the most frequent service from U.S. cities, including Atlanta, Baltimore, Chicago, Fort Lauderdale, Houston, Los Angeles, Miami, New York, Orlando, Philadelphia, Phoenix, and San Francisco; flights are also available from London. American Airlines flies nonstop daily from New York and Miami. British Airways connects Kingston with London. Copa offers service between Miami and Kingston. Northwest Airlines offers service to MoBay from Minneapolis/St. Paul and Memphis. US Airways has service to Jamaica from Philadelphia.

➤ AIRLINES AND CONTACTS: **Air Canada** (☎ 876/952–5160 in Montego Bay; 876/942–8211 in Kingston). **Air Jamaica** (☎ 876/952–4300 in Montego Bay; 876/924–8331 in Kingston). **American Airlines** (☎ 876/952–5950 in Montego Bay; 876/924–8248 in Kingston). **British Airways** (☎ 876/924–8187 in Kingston). **Copa** (☎ 876/926–1762). **Northwest Airlines** (☎ 876/952–9740). **US Airways** (☎ 876/952–5532).

AIRPORTS

Donald Sangster International Airport, in MoBay, is the most efficient point of entry for travelers destined for MoBay, Ocho Rios, Runaway Bay, and Negril. Norman Manley International Airport, in Kingston, is the best arrival point for travelers headed to the capital or Port Antonio.

➤ AIRPORT INFORMATION: **Donald Sangster International Airport** (☎ 876/952–3124). **Norman Manley International Airport** (☎ 876/924–8452).

BIKE AND MOPED TRAVEL

Although the front desks of most major hotels can arrange the rental of bicycles, mopeds, and motorcycles, it isn't a very good idea. The strangeness of driving on the left, the less-than-cautious driving style that prevails on the island, the abundance of potholes, and the prevalence of vendors who will approach you at every traffic light are just a few reasons why.

BUSINESS HOURS

BANKS

Banks are generally open Monday–Thursday 9–2, Friday 9–4.

POST OFFICES

Post office hours are weekdays 9–5.

SHOPS

Normal business hours for stores are weekdays 8:30–4:30, Saturday 8–1.

CAR RENTALS

Although Jamaica has dozens of car-rental companies (you'll find branches at the airports and the resorts among other places), rentals can be difficult to arrange once you've arrived. Make reservations and send a deposit before your trip. (Cars are scarce, and without either a confirmation number or a receipt, you may have to walk.) You must be at least 25 years old, have a valid driver's license (from any country), and have a valid credit card. You may be required to post a security of several hundred dollars before taking possession of your car; ask about it when you make the reservation. Rates are quite expensive, averaging $65–$120 a day after the addition of the compulsory CDW coverage, which you must purchase even if your credit card offers it.

➤ MAJOR AGENCIES: **Budget** (☎ 876/952–3838 in Montego Bay; 876/924–8762 in Kingston). **Hertz** (☎ 876/979–0438 in Montego Bay; 876/924–8028 in Kingston). **Island Car Rentals** (☎ 876/952–5771 in Montego Bay; 876/926–5991 in Kingston). **Jamaica Car Rental** (☎ 876/952–5586 in Montego Bay; 876/974–2505 in Ocho Rios). **United Car Rentals** (☎ 876/952–3077 in Montego Bay).

CAR TRAVEL

GASOLINE

Gas stations are open daily but accept cash only. Gas costs roughly $1.35–$1.60 a gallon.

ROAD CONDITIONS

Driving is a chore and can be extremely frustrating. You must constantly be on guard—for enormous potholes, people, and animals darting out into the street, as well as aggressive drivers.

RULES OF THE ROAD

Traffic keeps to the left in Jamaica.

ELECTRICITY

Like the electrical current in North America, the current in Jamaica is 110 volts but only 50 cycles, with outlets that take two flat prongs. Some hotels provide 220-volt plugs as well as special shaver outlets. If you plan to bring electrical appliances with you, it's best to ask when making your reservation.

EMBASSIES

➤ CANADA: **Canadian High Commission** (✉ 3 West Kings House Rd., Kingston, ☎ 876/926–1500).

➤ UNITED KINGDOM: **British High Commission** (✉ Trafalgar Rd.,
Kingston, ☎ 876/926–9050).
➤ UNITED STATES: **U.S. Embassy** (✉ 32 Oxford Rd., Kingston, ☎ 876/
929–4850).

EMERGENCIES
➤ AIR RESCUE: **Air rescue** (☎ 119).
➤ AMBULANCE AND FIRE: **Ambulance and fire emergencies** (☎ 110).
➤ HOSPITALS: **Cornwall Regional Hospital** (✉ Mt. Salem, Montego Bay,
☎ 876/940–5297). **Mo Bay Hope** (✉ Half Moon Resort, Montego
Bay, ☎ 876/953–3981). **Port Antonio Hospital** (✉ Naylor's Hill, Port
Antonio, ☎ 876/993–2646). **St. Ann's Bay Hospital** (✉ St. Ann's Bay,
☎ 876/972–2272). **University Hospital** (✉ Mona, Kingston, ☎ 876/
927–1620).
➤ PHARMACIES: **Great House Pharmacy** (✉ Brown's Plaza, Ocho Rios,
☎ 876/974–2352). **Le Méridien Pegasus** (✉ 81 Knutsford Blvd.,
Kingston, ☎ 876/926–3690).
➤ POLICE: **Police emergencies** (☎ 119).
➤ SCUBA DIVING EMERGENCIES: **St. Ann's Bay Hospital** (✉ St. Ann's
Bay, ☎ 876/972–2272).

ETIQUETTE AND BEHAVIOR
As you travel the island, you'll see Rastafarians, with their flowing dreadlocks (although some prefer to wear their hair beneath knitted caps).
Rastas smoke marijuana as part of their religious rites, do not eat salt
or pork (many are vegetarians), and often sell crafts. Always ask for
permission before taking a photograph.

FESTIVALS AND SEASONAL EVENTS
The biggest festival is Carnival, an event filled with lots of music and
dancing in the streets. It's held in Kingston, Ocho Rios, and MoBay
every April and in Negril every May. Music lovers also fill the island
for the August Reggae Sunsplash International Music Festival, which
is getting hotter every year, because the best, brightest, and newest of
the reggae stars gather to perform in open-air concerts in MoBay. Anglers come to Port Antonio to compete in the annual Blue Marlin
Tournament, which is usually held in October.
➤ CONTACTS: **Reggae Sunsplash International Music Festival** (☎ 800/
526–2422).

HOLIDAYS
Public holidays include: New Year's Day, Ash Wednesday (beginning
of Lent, 6 weeks before Easter), Good Friday (Fri. before Easter),
Easter Monday (the day after Easter), Labor Day (May 23), Independence Day (1st Mon. in Aug.), National Heroes Day (Oct. 15), Christmas, and Boxing Day (Dec. 26).

LANGUAGE
The official language of Jamaica is English. Islanders usually speak a
patois among themselves, a lyrical mixture of English, Spanish, and
various African languages. Some examples of patois are *me diyah* (I'm
here; pronounced mee *de*-ya); *nyam* (eat; pronounced yam); and, if someone asks how your vacation is going, just say *irie* (pronounced *eye*-
ree), which means "great."

MAIL AND SHIPPING
Postcards may be mailed anywhere in the world for J$25. Letters to
the United States and Canada cost J$25, to Europe J$12.50, to Aus-
tralia J$40, and to New Zealand J$30.
➤ CONTACTS: **Kingston Post Office** (✉ 13 King St., ☎ 876/922–2120).
Montego Bay Post Office (✉ 122 Barnett St., ☎ 876/952–7389).

MONEY MATTERS

Note that prices quoted throughout this chapter are in U.S. dollars, unless otherwise noted.

ATMS

ATM machines do not accept American bank cards, although cash advances can be made using credit cards.

CREDIT CARDS

Major credit cards are widely accepted throughout the island, although cash is required at gas stations, in markets, and in many small stores. Discover and Diners Club are accepted at many resorts.

CURRENCY

The official currency is the Jamaican dollar. At press time the exchange rate was about J$45 to US$1. U.S. money (currency only, no coins) is accepted at most establishments, although you'll often be given change in Jamaican money.

CURRENCY EXCHANGE

Currency can be exchanged at airport bank counters, exchange bureaus, or commercial banks. Throughout the island you'll find branches of the Bank of Nova Scotia.

➤ CONTACTS: **Bank of Nova Scotia** (✉ Sam Sharpe Sq., Montego Bay, ☎ 876/952–4440; ✉ Main St., Ocho Rios, ☎ 876/974–2689; ✉ Negril Sq., Negril, ☎ 876/957–3040; ✉ 35 King St., Kingston, ☎ 876/922–1420).

PASSPORTS AND VISAS

U.S. and Canadian citizens must have a passport (not expired beyond one year). Or, to prove citizenship, bring an original birth certificate (with a raised seal) or a naturalization certificate along with a government-issued photo I.D. (all documents must bear exactly the same name). British, Australian, and New Zealand travelers must have passports. Everyone must have a return or ongoing ticket. Declaration forms are usually distributed in flight to keep customs formalities to a minimum.

SAFETY

Don't let the beauty of Jamaica cause you to abandon the caution you would practice in any unfamiliar place. Never leave valuables in your room; use the safe-deposit boxes that most hotels make available. Carry your funds in traveler's checks, and keep a record of the check numbers in a secure place. Never leave a rental car unlocked, and never leave valuables in a locked car. Ignore efforts, however persistent, to sell you *ganja* (marijuana). Independent travelers, especially those renting cars, need to take special precautions. Some travelers have been harassed by locals offering to "guard" cars and have experienced vandalism when requests for money were denied.

SIGHTSEEING TOURS

Half-day tours are offered by most tour operators in the important areas of Jamaica. The best great-house tours include Rose Hall, Greenwood, and Devon House. Plantations to tour are Prospect, Barnett Estates, and Sun Valley. The Appleton Estate Tour uses a bus to visit villages, plantations, and a rum distillery. The increasingly popular waterside folklore feasts are offered on the Dunn's, Great, and White rivers. The significant city tours are in Kingston, MoBay, and Ocho Rios. Caribic Tours offers tours of Jamaica, as well as to Cuba. Safari Tours offers guided jeep, bike, and horseback tours. Tourwise offers guided tours of top attractions including Dunn's River Falls, Black River Safari, Cockpit Country, Kingston, Mayfield Falls, Blue Lagoon, and more; tours are available in English, French, Spanish, German, Italian, and Dutch.

➤ CONTACTS: **Caribic Tours** (✉ 1310 Providence Dr., Montego Bay, ☎ 876/953–9878, WEB www.caribicvacations.com). **CS Tours** (✉ 66 Claude Clarke Ave., Montego Bay, ☎ 876/952–6260). **Glamour Tours** (✉ Montego Freeport, Montego Bay, ☎ 876/979–8207, WEB www. glamourtours.com). **Safari Tours** (✉ Mammee Bay, Montego Bay, ☎ 876/972–2639). **SunHoliday Tours** (✉ Donald Sangster International Airport, Montego Bay, ☎ 876/979–1061). **Tourwise** (✉ 103 Main St., Ocho Rios, ☎ 876/974–2323).

BOAT TOURS

Calico Sailing offers snorkeling trips and sunset cruises on the waters of MoBay; costs are $35 and $25, respectively. Martha Brae River Rafting leads trips down the Martha Brae River, about 25 mi (40 km) from most hotels in MoBay. The cost is just under $42 (two per raft) for the 1½-hour river run. Mountain Valley Rafting runs trips down the River Lethe, approximately 12 mi (19 km) (a 50-minute trip) southwest of MoBay; the excursion costs about $36 per raft (two per raft) and takes you through unspoiled hill country. Bookings can also be made through hotel tour desks. Rio Grande Attractions Ltd. guides raft trips down the Rio Grande; the cost is $45 per raft. South Coast Safaris Ltd. has guided excursions up the Black River for some 10 mi (16 km) (round-trip), into the mangroves and marshlands to see alligators, birds, and plant life. The trip on the 25-passenger *Safari Queen* or *Safari Princess* costs around $15.

➤ CONTACTS: **Calico Sailing** (✉ North Coast Hwy., Montego Bay, ☎ 876/952–5860). **Martha Brae River Rafting** (✉ Claude Clarke Ave., Montego Bay, ☎ 876/952–0889). **Mountain Valley Rafting** (✉ 31 Gloucester Ave., Montego Bay, ☎ 876/952–0527). **Rio Grande Attractions Ltd.** (✉ St. Margaret's Bay, ☎ 876/993–5778). **South Coast Safaris Ltd.** (✉ 1 Crane Rd., Black River, ☎ 876/965–2513).

HELICOPTER TOURS

Helitours Jamaica Ltd., 1 mi (1½ km) west of Ocho Rios, offers helicopter tours of Jamaica, ranging from 20 minutes to an hour, at prices from $65 to $225.

➤ CONTACTS: **Helitours Jamaica Ltd.** (✉ North Coast Hwy., Ocho Rios, ☎ 876/974–2265 or 876/974–1108).

SPECIAL-INTEREST TOURS

Countrystyle offers unique, personalized tours of island communities. You're linked with community residents based on your interests; there are tours that include anything from bird-watching in Mandeville to nightlife in Kingston. Maroon Attraction Tours leads full-day tours from MoBay to Maroon headquarters at Accompong, giving you a glimpse of the society of Maroons who live in Cockpit Country. The cost is $50 per person.

➤ CONTACTS: **Countrystyle** (✉ 62 Ward Ave., Mandeville, ☎ 876/962–7979). **Maroon Attraction Tours Co.** (✉ North Coast Hwy., Montego Bay, ☎ 876/952–4546).

TAXES

DEPARTURE TAX

The departure tax is $27, although many ticket prices now include the departure tax. Be sure to ask.

SALES TAX

Jamaica has replaced the room occupancy tax with a general consumption tax of 15% on most goods and services.

TAXIS

Some but not all of Jamaica's taxis are metered. If you accept a driver's offer of his services as a tour guide, be sure to agree on a price before

the vehicle is put into gear. (Note that a one-day tour should run about $100–$180, depending on distance traveled.) All licensed taxis display red Public Passenger Vehicle (PPV) plates. Cabs can be summoned by phone or flagged down on the street. Rates are per car, not per passenger, and 25% is added to the metered rate between midnight and 5 AM. Licensed minivans are also available and bear the red PPV plates. JUTA is the largest taxi franchise and has offices in all resort areas.
➤ CONTACTS: **JUTA** (☎ 876/974–2292 in Ocho Rios; 876/957–9197 in Negril; 876/952–0813 in Montego Bay).

TELEPHONES
Most hotels offer direct-dial telephone services; local businesses provide telegraph and fax services for a fee. Pay phones are available in most communities.

COUNTRY AND AREA CODES
To dial Jamaica from the United States, just dial 1 + the area code 876.

INTERNATIONAL CALLS
Some U.S. phone companies, such as MCI, won't permit credit-card calls to be placed from Jamaica because they have been victims of fraud. The best option is to purchase Jamaican phone cards, sold in most stores across the island.

LOCAL CALLS
While on the island, calls from town to town are long distance.

TIPPING
Most hotels and restaurants add a 10% service charge to your bill. When a service charge isn't included, a 10% to 20% tip is appreciated. Tips of 10% to 20% are customary for taxi drivers as well. However, many all-inclusives have a strict no-tipping policy.

TRANSPORTATION AROUND JAMAICA
Air Jamaica Express, a subsidiary of Air Jamaica, provides shuttle services on the island. Be sure to reconfirm your departing flight a full 72 hours in advance. Tropical Airlines offers service between Kingston and MoBay as well as flights to Cuba. Tim Air offers quick flights between resort areas as well as to Kingston.
➤ CONTACTS: **Air Jamaica Express** (☎ 876/952–5401 in Montego Bay; 876/923–8680 in Kingston, WEB www.airjamaica.com). **Tropical Airlines** (☎ 876/920–3770 in Kingston; 876/940–5917 in Montego Bay). **Tim Air** (☎ 876/952–2516 in Montego Bay).

VISITOR INFORMATION
➤ BEFORE YOU LEAVE: **Jamaica Tourist Board** (✉ 801 2nd Ave., 20th floor, New York, NY 10017, ☎ 212/856–9727 or 800/233–4582; ✉ 500 N. Michigan Ave., 10th Floor, Chicago, IL 60611, ☎ 312/527–1296; ✉ 1320 S. Dixie Hwy., Suite 1101, Coral Gables, FL 33146, ☎ 305/665–0557; ✉ 3440 Wilshire Blvd., Suite 805, Los Angeles, CA 90010, ☎ 213/384–1123; ✉ 303 Eglinton Ave. E, 2nd floor, Suite 616, Toronto, Ontario M4P 1L3, Canada, ☎ 416/482–7850; ✉ 1–2 Prince Consort Rd., London SW7 2BZ, U.K., ☎ 0441/207–224–0505; WEB www.jamaicatravel.com).
➤ IN JAMAICA: **Jamaica Tourist Board** (✉ 2 St. Lucia Ave., Kingston, ☎ 876/929–9200; 888/995–9999 for the on-island help line; ✉ Hendriks Bldg., 2 High St., Black River, ☎ 876/965–2074; ✉ Cornwall Beach, Montego Bay, ☎ 876/952–4425; ✉ Coral Seas Plaza, Negril, ☎ 876/957–4243; ✉ Ocean Village Shopping Centre, Ocho Rios, ☎ 876/974–2570; ✉ City Centre Plaza, Port Antonio, ☎ 876/993–3051).

15 MARTINIQUE

Updated by
Eileen Robinson
Smith

An idyllic drive of an hour north from Fort-de-France, along a staggered coastline, downshifting on the steep inclines of a sinuous highway, is exhilarating, especially when fueled by French Caribbean music on the car stereo. As you are en route to the infamous St. Pierre, everything you've heard about the once-beautiful seaport makes your head spin as much as the hairpin turns. Once called the "Paris of the Caribbean," the town was destroyed when Mont Pelée erupted and in two minutes solidified some 30,000 residents in molten lava. Foolishly, you wonder if, 100 years later, it is adventure travel to even ride into town? But curiosity gets the better of you, and the promise of museums with some fascinating and even gruesome relics, spurs you on.

The Arawak Indians named Martinique *Madinina* (Island of Flowers). Exotic wild orchids, frangipani, anthurium, jade vines, flamingo flowers, and hundreds of vivid varieties of hibiscus still grow on the island. But these days the scent of flowers competes with those of French perfume and espresso.

Martinique is like a tropical suburb of Paris; it has a definite sense of style that you first notice at the clean, contemporary airport. Fellow passengers, particularly *les femmes*, have that admirable chic, even the women at the airline and rental-car desks, manage to accessorize their uniforms so that they look like French designer ensembles.

In their dealings with foreigners, Martinicans are polite and self-assured—qualities anchored in the privileged position the island has enjoyed historically. Martinique was the administrative, social, and cultural center of the French Antilles. Guadeloupe was an island of merchants and shopkeepers. Martinique was a rich, aristocratic island, famous for its beautiful women and gracious living, which gave birth to an empress, Napoléon's Josephine, and saw the full flowering of plantocracy, with servants and soirees, wine cellars and snobbery. Today, the island has one of the highest standards of living in the Caribbean, and a fine educational system, with many young people going to study in France.

This 425-square-mi (1,101-square-km) island, the largest of the Windwards, has landscapes as varied as its culture and history. In the south, which holds most of the development and the best beaches, there are rolling hills and sugarcane fields. In the north look for lush, tropical vegetation, fields of bananas and pineapples, deep gorges, towering cliffs, and one of the Caribbean's most impressive volcanoes, Mont Pelée. Fort-de-France is the island's capital as well as its cultural and commercial hub. Most of the other towns—such as Ste-Anne and Vauclin, to the south, and Carbet and Marigot, to the north—are either small resorts or fishing villages.

Britain and France squabbled over Martinique until 1815, when the island was ceded by treaty to Paris. Today the French connection means French-influenced food from the motherland and wine, a wonderful elán, superb roads, Franco-Caribbean pop music, relatively high prices, and plenty of culture and arts (Martinique has one of the finest Caribbean jazz festivals). However, its tourism has suffered in recent decades. The chic upper-crust French, the women in long dresses and men in dinner jackets, are not prevalent as in the 1970s. French package tours attract a mass-market clientele and have reduced the high-end service and made it difficult for freestanding restaurants to remain in business. The upshot is prices have fallen and the island is generally more affordable than in years past. Most Americans who come are Francophiles.

You'll need some French to feel truly at home, though the locals are more forthcoming with English here than in other places in the French-speaking world. Franglais is universal. This island is not *like* France—it *is* France. Most everything shuts down at midday and reopens sometime after 2:30. Topless bathing is almost de rigueur, driving is frenetic, and poodles are the pedigree pooch of choice. High season runs mid-November through May, and the island can be very quiet the rest of the year, with some hotels closing down for months, particularly in September and October. Others discount tariffs significantly.

Lodging

Martinique's accommodations range from tiny inns called *relais créoles* to splashy tourist resorts—some all-inclusive—and restored plantation houses. The majority of hotels are clustered in Le Diamant, Ste-Anne, Pointe du Bout, and Anse-Mitan on Les Trois-Illets Peninsula, across the bay from Fort-de-France. There are only a few deluxe properties on the island. A number that lack mega-stellar ratings make up for it with charisma, hospitality, and French style. Most hotels have the busy, slightly frenetic feel that the French seem to like. The major establishments usually include a large buffet breakfast of fresh fruit, cheese, croissants, baguettes, jam, and café au lait. Many hotels can accommodate wheelchairs.

CATEGORY	COST EP/CP*	COST A.I.**
$$$$	over $350	over $375
$$$	$250–$350	$275–$375
$$	$150–$250	$175–$275
$	under $150	under $175

*EP/CP prices are per night for a standard double room in high season, excluding taxes, service charges, and meal plans **A.I. (all-inclusive) prices are per person, per night based on double-occupancy during high season, excluding taxes and service charges*

Hotels

BASSE-POINTE

$–$$ ★ ☎ **Leyritz Plantation.** Sleeping on a former sugar plantation in one of the antiques-furnished rooms of the manor house, cottages, or renovated slave cabins, is a novelty. The isolated Leyritz sits on 16 lush acres.

400

Martinique

KEY

☂ Beaches

1 Exploring Sights

① Hotels and Restaurants

ATLANTIC OCEAN

⑪

N1

⑫ Ste-Marie
⑬

Caravelle Peninsula ⑭ ⑭

Havre de la Trinité

Tartane ⑬

⑮ *Pointe Caracoli*

La Trinité

D2

N4

Baie du Galion

Gros-Morne

Le Robert

Havre du Robert

N1

Pte. Larose

Le Plein Soleil

⑬ ⑮ ⑯ ⑯

N1

⑰ Lamentin
Le François ⑰

Mt. Vauclin

Lamentin International Airport

N5 Ducos

N6

Le Vauclin ㉕

D7

Rivière-Salée
N5

⑳ ㉑

Rivière-Pilote

N6

D17
D18

Ste-Luce
D7 ㉒ ㉜

D18A

Le Marin
㉔
N5

Pte. Figuier ㉝ **Pointe Marin**

Cul-de-Sac du Marin D9

㉙-㉛ ㉞ ㉟ ㉓ **Ste-Anne**

Cap Chevalier

La Savane (Petrified Forest)

Les Salines **Baie des Anglais**

Grande Anse **Anse-Trabaud**

Pte. des Salines *Pte. d'Enfer*

St. Lucia Channel

Cottages have rough-wood beams, mahogany four-posters and secretaries. Ironically, it's the 20 newer bungalows that are smaller and lack individuality, but they do have sea views. Except when tours come through, it's very quiet here. A taxi will charge $70 from the airport, so most people pick up a rent-a-car. However, if the sun has set, stay closer to the airport and chart your course in the morning. ⊠ *Basse-Pointe 97218, ☎ 0596/78–53–92, FAX 0596/78–92–44. 72 rooms. Restaurant, tennis court, pool, bar. AE, DC, MC, V. CP, MAP.*

FORT-DE-FRANCE

$ 🏨 **Squash Hotel.** This accommodating hotel is a good base in the city for business or for touring the capital, especially if you need to stay the night after arriving at the airport (just 10 minutes away), before heading out to your hotel in the country. Its open-air restaurant and bar enjoy a panorama of the sea and Fort-de-France, as do some of the guest rooms. Rates are lower in the older building without elevators. Near the center of town, it is just a short walk from the Savannah (main park). A major renovation was completed in 2001. ⊠ *3 bd. de la Marne, 97200, ☎ 0596/72–80–80, FAX 0596/63–00–74, WEB www.karibea.com. 105 rooms, 3 suites. Restaurant, pool, health club, spa, squash, bar, business services, meeting rooms, car rental. AE, DC, MC, V. EP, CP.*

$ 🏨 **Valmenière.** The hotel closest to the airport, it is ideal for first-night stays, when your flight arrives too late to navigate a long drive to a remote hotel. Perched on a hilltop overlooking Fort-de-France, it has a high-tech elevator, and white tubular steel walkways, but no bell boys, nor airport shuttle. It is squeaky clean, efficient, and wired for work. Suites are large with desks and a separate entrance to the living room. Business rooms have beds you can fold up, turning the room into a flexible office space. The hotel offers most business services, including translation. A good restaurant, pool, and sun roof share the top floors. ⊠ *Av. des Arawaks, 97200, ☎ 0596/75–75–75, FAX 0596/75–69–70, WEB www.karibea.com. 116 rooms, 4 suites. Restaurant, pool, gym, bar, shop, business services, meeting rooms. AE, MC, V. CP.*

LA TRINITÉ

$ 🏨 **La Caravelle.** A simple hotel built in 1985, it is lovingly maintained by the Combaluziers, the hands-on owners, who will make you feel like family. Jean Luc, a Frenchman with the king's English, willingly helps you plot your course. The lack of a pool is compensated by extra special food at the restaurant and vistas of the sandy beach of L'Anse L'Etang, which is many steps down. Most guests rent a car, but Nicole can arrange a taxi for the initial transfer from the airport, a wise decision since first-day driving is intimidating, especially if arriving at night. ⊠ *L'Anse L'Etang, Trinité Route de Chateau Dubuc, 97220, ☎ 0596/58–07–32, FAX 0596/58–07–90. 14 studio apartments. Restaurant, kitchenettes. AE, MC, V. CP.*

$ 🏨 **Residence Oceane.** These fanciful creole bungalows overlook the Atlantic, with an unobstructed panorama of cliffs that meet blue ocean; some are many steps down a hillside. This patch of ocean is the wild side of the Caravelle peninsula; a professional surfing school is on-site. Each bungalow has five rooms, decorated with yellow and blue fabrics (there are a few bunk beds), and attractive tile in the bathrooms. Air-conditioning is extra, about $5 a day; televisions are available. English is spoken, and there is quiet. This place is an excellent value. Although the hotel is only 20 minutes from the airport, a taxi is $50. ⊠ *Anse Bonneville Trinité, 97220, ☎ 0596/25–85–93, FAX 0596/58–33–95. 24 bungalows. Fans, some kitchenettes, pool, beach. MC, V. EP.*

$$$ ⊡ **Diamant-Novotel.** This self-contained resort is in an ideal windsurfing location. A footbridge spans a pool on the way to spacious guest rooms, each with a balcony facing either the sea or the pool. The dining room is large and unromantic, set up to accommodate groups, but there's a pleasant terrace bar where local bands play. The three beaches on the 5-acres are small. The staff speaks English and maintains a surprising level of enthusiasm and efficiency, given the number of tour groups. ⊠ *Pointe de la Chery 97223,* ☎ *0596/76–42–42,* FAX *0596/76–22–87. 175 rooms, 6 suites. 2 restaurants, 2 tennis courts, pool, hair salon, beach, dive shop, snorkeling, windsurfing, 2 bars, shops, car rental. AE, DC, MC, V. CP, MAP.*

$ ⊡ **Diamant Les Bains.** For decades, Hubert Andrieu and his lovely, English-speaking wife, Marie-Yvonne, have been doing everything they can to make their guests feel at home at this intimate beachfront property. Their son, Herve, reigns over the creole kitchen. A few basic rooms are in the main house, above the restaurant and overlooking the pool, but opt for the beachfront chalets surrounded by flowers and palm trees. Simplistic, the tile floors, brightly painted furniture, white ceilings, and ocean breezes are like an old-fashioned seaside hotel. In fact, it was the first hotel in Diamant in the 1940s, but standards have been maintained. ⊠ *Bourg du Diamant 97223,* ☎ *0596/76–40–14,* FAX *0596/76–27–00. 7 rooms, 20 bungalows. Restaurant, refrigerators, pool, beach, bar. MC, V. CP, MAP. Closed Sept.*

$ ⊡ **Relais Caraïbes.** Twelve bungalows are spread over the manicured grounds, and each has a hammock, a bedroom, a small salon with a pull-out bed for two, and a bathroom; there are also three rooms in the main house. The pool is on the edge of a cliff that overlooks the sea and adjacent to the appealing terrace restaurant. Even nonguests come for the good French food, wine, and music. The present owner, Eric Bordiere, is maintaining the inn's charisma while sprucing it up. The tiny beach is a short walk, and there's scuba and boating instruction available at the nearby Diamant-Novotel. ⊠ *Pointe de la Chery 97223,* ☎ *0596/76–44–65,* FAX *0596/76–21–20. 3 rooms, 12 bungalows. Restaurant, some refrigerators, pool, bar. MC, V. CP, MAP. Closed Sept.–Oct.*

$$–$$$ ⊡ **L'Habitation de L'Ilet Thierry.** A dock with a palapa and a palm tree, attached to a pier, dead-ends at a steep, stone staircase. It goes up to a primitive hotel, the only edifice on this remote, windswept island. Rooms in the white, two-story, colonial-style stucco are large, but forget plush creature comforts. Although they have basic bathrooms, you must shower on the first floor due to lack of water pressure. The salon-dining room looks like it's from the movie *Key Largo.* Some come just for the prix-fixe lunch—$27 to $45 for lobster. Boat is not included (it is with room rates) and costs $43 round-trip and takes about 10 minutes. ⊠ *Ilet Thierry 97240,* ☎ *0596/65–88–54 or 0596/27–66–07. 5 rooms. Kitchenettes. No credit cards. MAP, FAP.*

$ ⊡ **Le Plein Soleil.** Chic, contemporary creole, the scattering of ginger-
★ bread cottages, with fretwork and facades painted in Caribbean pastels, clings to the hillside. As attractive as these terraced suites are, it is the inn's "great house" that captivates. It is a study in white, with classy, tropical furnishings, objets d' nature and art and up the wooden stairs, a loft—the designated TV room. Creative lighting plays up the artistic vignettes of pods, berries, and palm fronds in the terrace-restaurant. The pool is on its own plateau, with views down the coastline. The caring owner, Jean Christophe, is a former creative talent for a Parisian ad agency. ⊠ *Villa Lagon Sarc, Pointe Thalemont, Le*

François 97240, ☎ *0596/38–07–77,* ⦿ *0596/65–58–13. 12 bungalows. Restaurant, kitchenettes, pool. MC, V. EP, MAP.*

LES TROIS-ILETS

$$$–$$$$ 🏨 **Sofitel Bakoua Coralia.** Once a family estate overlooking the bay
★   of Fort-de-France, this is one of Martinique's finest hotels. Its impressive canopied entrance, with international flags hoisted, could be
an embassy's. Accommodations are in three hillside buildings, with a
fourth on the white-sand beach. Beach rooms, while small, are modern, light, quiet, and comfortable. All have a balcony or patio and a
bathroom with hand-painted tiles. The rooms in the original residence
are the largest and most charismatic. There is always an animated scene
at the circular bar near the gorgeous infinity pool. Entertainment consists of live music and nightly shows. ⊠ *Pointe du Bout, 97229,* ☎
0596/66–02–02, ⦿ *0596/66–00–41. 133 rooms, 6 suites. 2 restaurants,
minibars, 2 tennis courts, pool, beach, snorkeling, boating, 2 bars, shops,
Internet, business services, meeting rooms. AE, DC, MC, V. CP, MAP.*

$–$$ 🏨 **Hotel Amyris.** In the south, this resort from the Karibéa Group, is
☙   a stand out. The newest in this developing tourist area on the Caribbean
side, it has a panoramic view of a natural cove. Four three-story buildings (sans elevators), housing the guest rooms, are situated within the
parklike gardens and the beautifully designed pool. Each unit has two
bathrooms. There are convertible couches in the living rooms, balconies
and ceruse wood furniture. Garden rooms have full kitchenettes. The
food served is of a high caliber; the front-desk crew have young, smiling faces and are English-speaking. ⊠ *Ste-Luce 97228,* ☎ *0596/62–
12–00,* ⦿ *0596/62–12–10,* 🕸 *www.karibea.com. 110 junior suites.
Restaurant, in-room safes, some kitchenettes, refrigerators, tennis
court, pool, beach, snorkeling, children's programs (ages 4–12), meeting rooms, car rental. AE, MC, V. CP, MAP, All-Inclusive.*

$$ 🏨 **Le Méridien Trois-Ilets.** A great deal of the activity revolves around
the beautifully designed pool and man-made beach. Also, the jetty is
the delightful spot for special theme nights. The ferry to Fort-de-France
is just a walk-in-the-sand away. Soundproof guest rooms have been completely renovated, with tile floors. Some have balconies and a splendid view of the bay and the capital or the marina. Two luxury and four
one-bedroom suites are also available. The aerobic and aqua-aerobic
classes are exceptional, the 60-ft catamaran cruise with lobster lunch
a must-do. Most convivial, there's live entertainment nightly, including a folkloric ballet and a Dominican buffet. ⊠ *Pointe du Bout,
97229,* ☎ *0596/66–00–00,* ⦿ *0596/66–00–74,* 🕸 *www.lemeridien.
com. 295 rooms, 6 suites. 2 restaurants, minibars, 2 tennis courts, pool,
spa, beach, boating, dive shop, snorkeling, bar, casino, car rental. AE,
DC, MC, V. CP, MAP.*

$ 🏨 **La Résidence Village Créole.** Vacation rentals from studios to two-
☙   bedroom apartments are on the ground and second floors (no elevator) of this fun, attractive, nouveau creole complex. Most have French
doors that open onto the courtyard. Simple, modern, tropical furniture and bright, floral fabrics give these units a clean, uncluttered
look. Each has a fully equipped kitchen and TV. With convertible
couches, the units are ideal for families. Kids can maneuver safely within
the area. Laundry facilities are nearby. ⊠ *Pointe du Bout, 97229,* ☎
0596/66–03–19, ⦿ *0596/66–07–35,* 🕸 *www.villagecreole.com. 35
apartments. Kitchens. AE, DC, MC, V.*

$ 🏨 **Rivage Hotel.** You get good value for your money at Maryelle and
Jean Claude Riveti's small hotel. The place does have the air of a
motor inn of the 1950s, but it's immaculately maintained, and the studios are much larger than comparable rooms at neighboring hotels—
for about a third of the cost. Each pool-view unit has a private bath

and either a kitchenette or a mini-fridge. You should have no trouble communicating: English, Spanish, and French are spoken. The beach is across the road. ☒ *Anse Mitan 97229,* ☎ *0596/66–00–53,* 𝖥𝖠𝖷 *0596/ 66–06–56,* 𝖶𝖤𝖡 *pro.wanadoo.fr/rivagehotel/index.html. 4 rooms, 12 studios. Snack bar, some kitchenettes, refrigerators, pool, beach, car rental. MC, V. EP.*

$$$ 🏠 **Habitation Lagrange.** Nowhere on the island do you feel the style, romance, and elegance of the old plantation-house society more than in this 19th-century manor house, in a rain forest. (However, the "bush" and its critters threaten to take over.) Everything in the rooms in the main building—from the dual antique shaving mirrors to the flowered commodes in the "water closets"—bespeaks of another era. Lunch, like dinner, is served in the formal dining room. However, the food under the elegant silver domes is nothing exceptional, especially for the high prices. Serious capital is needed to return the property to its former glory. ☒ *Marigot 97225,* ☎ *0596/53–60–60 or 800/322-2223,* 𝖥𝖠𝖷 *0596/53–50–58,* 𝖶𝖤𝖡 *www.habitation-lagrange.com. 14 rooms, 1 suite. Dining room, tennis court, pool, bar, library. AE, DC, MC, V. CP, MAP.*

$$–$$$ 🏠 **Manoir de Beauregard.** Built in the 18th century, this plantation house became a hotel in 1928. Its 2-ft-thick stone walls and mullioned windows look like a medieval abbey church. Where the nave would be is a drawing room with bentwood rockers, chandeliers, and checkerboard marble floors. It is flanked by "aisles," one of which serves as the bar. The three rooms upstairs in the main building have wood-beam ceilings, antique furniture, and four-poster beds. Other rooms are in a modern annex. A circular tower room in the sugar mill is favored by honeymooners. This property has history and personality, but it would benefit greatly from a redecoration. ☒ *Chemin des Salines 97227,* ☎ *0596/76–73–40,* 𝖥𝖠𝖷 *0596/76–93–24. 11 rooms. Pool, bar. AE, MC, V. EP. Closed Sept.–Dec.*

$–$$ 🏠 **Anse Caritan.** This appealing property combines the amenities of a large hotel with the service of a more intimate one. It's amid exquisite gardens fronting a ribbon of champagne-colored sand. The restaurant is known for its innovative creole fare; the beachfront eatery serves everything from calzones to shrimp flambéed in aged rum. The staff is remarkably friendly. ☒ *Pointe des Salines, 97227,* ☎ *0596/76–74-12,* 𝖥𝖠𝖷 *0596/76–72–59. 228 rooms. 2 restaurants, snack bar, in-room safes, pool, beach, dive shop, snorkeling, boating, fishing, bar, dance club. AE, MC, V. CP, MAP.*

$ 🏠 **Club Med/Buccaneer's Creek.** Occupying 48 acres, this Club Med is a village with plazas, cafés, restaurants, a boutique, and marina. Pastel rooms contain twin beds and a shower. Excursions (in French) are not included, nor are bar drinks, soft drinks, bottled water, or even coffee—outside of meals. There's a white-sand beach, a plethora of water sports, and plenty of nightlife. It's one 24-hour-a-day party, appealing to singles, from their 20s to 40s, mainly French. Children are welcome, but there are no in-room TVs and no kids' club. The place is circa 1969, although well-maintained, but the club and rooms have never had a full renovation. Note: $50 per year for membership and $30 initiation fee is extra. ☒ *Pointe du Marin, 97227,* ☎ *0596/76–72–72 or 800/ 258-2633,* 𝖥𝖠𝖷 *0596/76–83–36,* 𝖶𝖤𝖡 *www.clubmed.com. 308 rooms. 2 restaurants, no room TVs, 7 tennis courts, pool, gym, beach, dock, dive shop, snorkeling, boating, basketball, volleyball, 2 bars, dance club, nightclub. AE, MC, V. All-inclusive.*

ST. MARIE

$ 🍴 **Le Primerêve.** This resort sprawls over acres of luxuriant, tropical parkland that borders the sea. The pool area is superb. Spacious accommodations in duplex bungalows—named after local flowers or fruits—are furnished modestly with rattan; you can have an en suite massage for one or two. English is spoken, but French tour groups make up most of the population. On certain nights musicians play zouk and the beguine; folkloric groups perform artistically. The idyllic beach town of Ste-Marie is 2 mi away. The resort's own beach is special, too, and very secluded. ✉ *Anse Azerot, Ste-Marie 97230,* ☎ *0596/69–40–40,* 🅵🅰🆇 *0596/69–09–37. 20 rooms, 87 suites, 1 villa. Restaurant, minibars, tennis court, pool, gym, beach, bar, shop, meeting rooms. MC, V. CP, MAP.*

Villas and Condominiums

French Caribbean (☎ 800/322–2223, 🆆🅴🅱 www.Frenchcaribbean.com), an English-speaking reservation service, represents many of the hotels in Martinique. It also handles villas for rent. The **Villa Rental Service** (☎ 0596/71–56–11, 🅵🅰🆇 0596/63–11–64) can help you find a home, a villa, or an apartment to rent. Most properties are in the south of the island near good beaches, and you can rent for a week or a month. **LocationSaisonnieres** (☎ 0596/78–05–72, 🅵🅰🆇 0596/78–09–43) has modest but spacious stucco duplexes near the beach at Carbet, available, primarily, by the week.

Dining

Martinique's restaurants serve classic French, contemporary, and creole cuisines, and their cellars are generally filled with fine French wines. You can find some great spots in the countryside that serve a savory combination of creole and French cuisines, using the local produce like breadfruit, yuccas, and christophine. The farther you venture from tourist hotels, the less likely you are to discover English-speaking islanders, but don't let that stop you.

The local creole specialties are *colombo* (curry), *accras* (cod or vegetable fritters), *crabes farcis* (stuffed land crab), *écrevisses* (freshwater crayfish), *boudin* (creole blood sausage), *lambi* (conch), *langouste* (clawless Caribbean lobster), *soudons* (sweet clams), *blaff* (fish or shellfish plunged into seasoned stock), and *oursin* (sea urchin). And, if you like your *poisson* (fish) or any other dish with a little tang, try the *chien* sauce; it literally means "dog" sauce. It's made from onions, shallots, peppers, oil, and vinegar. The favorite local libation is 'ti punch—four parts white rum and one part sugarcane syrup.

Most restaurants offer a prix-fixe menu, often with several choices of entrées and wine. Finding a cheap American-style bite at lunch is almost impossible. For additional savings pick up a copy *Ti Gourmet* at the tourist office and larger hotels; most restaurants listed in the booklet offer a free drink or discount upon presentation.

What to Wear

For dinner, casual resort wear is appropriate. Generally, men do not wear jackets and ties, as they did in decades past, but they do wear collared shirts. Women typically wear light cotton sundresses, short or long. At dinnertime, beach attire is too casual for most restaurants. Nice shorts are okay for lunch, depending on the venue. Keep in mind, in Martinque lunch is usually a wonderful three-course, two-hour affair.

CATEGORY	COST*
$$$$	over $30
$$$	$20–$30
$$	$10–$20
$	under $10

per person for a main course at dinner

Anse-d'Arlets

ECLECTIC

$–$$ ✕ **'Ti Plage.** This is one fun beach bar, from the continental "break-
★ fast club" attended by those about to go down deep with the nearby
dive center, to the monthly soirees, when the good-time sounds echo
across the quiet, mint green lagoon. (Swimming is paradisiacal.) "Beach
food" is taken to another level at this creole-style restaurant surrounded by coconut palms and tropical plants. Painted in colors
Caribbean—celery green, guava, and saffron, with a metal roof and a
wooden bar, it is *inches* from the water. Menu favorites are crepes, salads, chicken on the grill, and shish kebabs. It's tapas at sunset for Happy
Hour. ✉ *Anse-d'Artlets,* ☎ *0696/29–59–89. No credit cards.*

FRENCH

$$$–$$$$ ✕ **Fatzo.** Despite the connotations of its name, this former 1890 resi-
★ dence is one Grand Dame that has it all: food, service, hospitality, his-
tory, and a good crowd of interesting types, from fun locals to yachties.
For starters, consider raw mahimahi with fresh ginger mayonnaise, or
fried Camembert with gooseberry or black currant sauce. As a main course,
you can't beat the thick slab of grilled duck with two sauces—curry and
honey—and perfect pomme frites. Finish with a light coco mousse with
caramel sauce. Alain is a true mixologist and makes incredible daiquiris
with skewered fruit as a garnish. Fridays are celebratory Couscous Royal
nights. ✉ *11 Rue Felix Eboue,* ☎ *0596/68–62–79. V. Closed Mon.*

Basse-Pointe

CARIBBEAN

$$–$$$ ✕ **Le Ruisseau Restaurant.** Within the restored 17th century planta-
tion inn, Leyritz, this alfresco restaurant serves a full lunch and din-
ner, a pleasant respite after a walk-around. The dining room has stone
walls draped with luxuriant vines and hanging plants; the bar is crafted
from local stone. The servers are in creole costume and are pleasant
but stressed when large groups dominate the dining room. Calming
music helps drown the din. The fare is mostly creole: boudin, chicken
with coconut, curry dishes, stewed octopus, and steaks. Leyritz is an
ancient, rural estate, and a visit here is a must-do. ✉ *Leyritz Planta-
tion, Basse-Point,* ☎ *0596/78–53–92. MC, V.*

Carbet

CARIBBEAN

$$ ✕ **Couleurs Locales.** As the name suggests, this is a local restaurant, with
colorful food, plus views of a church and its steeple and in the distance
of the luxuriant mountains. Chef René may tell you that he doesn't speak
English, but he can definitely cook from the heart. Happily, someone
has translated the menu: shrimp fritters; callalou, pumpkin and shrimp
soups; smoked chicken with pineapple sauce, breadfruit patties, and
steamed pumpkin; stewed fish, crayfish, and lobster; duck fillet with
passion fruit sauce, and sautéed pork with dark rum and cinnamon. As
the bell tolls, a favorite American oldie plays "500 miles, 500 miles from
my home." ✉ *Morne-Vert,* ☎ *0596/55–59–12. AE, MC, V.*

SEAFOOD

$–$$ ✕ **Chez Les Pecheurs.** This is the kind of beach restaurant you expect
but seldom find anymore in the islands. It all began when the owner,

Palmont, who made his living fishing, would come back in and grill a
fish or two for his own lunch. He now devotes most of his energies to
raising crayfish. Thursdays and Fridays are crayfish nights. The fisherman's platter (which might be tuna, marlin, or loup) with two special sauces is served for lunch and dinner with red beans and rice for
about $9. On weekend nights, local bands play. The bar opens daily
at 10:30 AM. ⊠ *Grand Anse Beach,* ☎ *0596/78–05–72 or 0696/23–
95–59. MC, V.*

Fort-de-France
CAFÉS

$$ ✕ **Mille Et Une Brindilles.** Although a tea salon is not a new concept,
★ it is for Martinique. Aromatic pots of tea, in flavors like vanilla and
black current, as well as the Darjeeling and other favorites, comple-
ment some of the best-ever desserts, like the cocoa-dusted marquise
au chocolat. Lunch is also a possibility. Several *fraicheurs* offer a litany
of tapenades, olive cakes, flans, couscous, etc. Fred, the cute, bubbly
Parisian who is both chef and proprietress, is the queen of terrines and
can apparently make a paté out of anything—vegetable, fish or meat.
The decor is Morroccan à la Paris flea market. ⊠ *27 rue du Prof. R.
Garcin, rte. de Didier, Didier, Fort-de-France,* ☎ *596/71–75–61. No
credit cards. No dinner except on Fri.*

CARIBBEAN

$$–$$$ ✕ **La Canne á Sucre.** Three tiny rooms at this restaurant on the road
★ to Schoelcher seat only 40 people, but you are treated with a sincere,
personalized hospitality. Chef Gerard Virginus puts his heart into his
haute nouvelle Antilles gastronomy, which he presents at lunch and din-
ner with artistry. *Foie gras* is sautéed with tropical fruits, a fabulous
rabbit and prune terrine comes with an onion confit, duck breast with
rhum vieux sauce, local fish—a fillet of *vivaneau*—with vanilla sauce.
The wine list includes varietals from Sancerres, Graves, and St-Émil-
ions. The pastry chef turns out delicate creations, studies in flavors,
colors, and shapes. ⊠ *Patio de Cluny,* ☎ *0596/63–33–95. Reserva-
tions essential. AE, MC, V. Closed Sun.*

CONTEMPORARY

$$$ ✕ **La Belle Epoque.** Crystal glasses, proper silver cutlery, and white linens
★ adorn tables in the small antiques-filled dining room and on the gar-
den-view terrace of a century-old, white-pillared mansion in the upscale suburb of Didier. The food is divine—and French. You'll have
several prix-fixe menus to choose from, including one with lobster in
each course. Allow at least two hours for your meal. Owner, Martine,
a statuesque blonde, who interjects her Motown classics between the
romantic French ballads, makes this a personality palace. The wine selection is as good as any in Paris, and there you wouldn't get *vieux
rhum* from the 1930s, '50s and '90s. ⊠ *97 rte. de Didier, Didier, Fort-
de-France,* ☎ *0596/64–41–19. MC, V. Closed Sun.*

Lamentin
CONTEMPORARY

$$$–$$$$ ✕ **La Plantation Pays Mêlé.** Many of the businessmen take lunch on
the terrace of this restaurant on the grounds of the Martinique Cot-
tages hotel rather than in the dark, wood-paneled interior. The French
service is hospitable, the music inviting, the wine list excellent. Under
the silver domes is a composite of classical French fused with local créole
traditions and ingredients. *Foie gras* has myriad variations, from ravi-
olis to plaintains with muscat sauce. For decades, considered one of
Martinique's finest dining spots, it has changed hands, and the jury is
still out as to whether it will be able to maintain its reputation. ⊠ *Jeanne
d'Arc,* ☎ *0596/50–16–08. AE, MC, V. Closed Sun. No lunch Sat.*

La Trinité
FRENCH

\$–\$\$ ✕ **La Caravelle.** A gastronomic find in Tartane, a fishing village cum resort on the gorgeous peninsula, Caravelle. The amicable owner, Jean Luc, puts a French twist on local produce and dishes. Choose a wonderful roasted duck with tamarind sauce. Local callalou soup with crab could precede the freshest shrimp with aioli, followed by a frozen soufflé glacé with Schrubb, an orange-flavored rum. A creole *table d'hôte* is another option. Enjoy the panoramic sea view from the terrace or call for a take-out order. Lunch is served topside: simple and delicious crepes, pizza, and salads. ⊠ *Hotel La Caravelle, rte. du Château Dubuc, L'Anse L'Etang, Tartane,* ☎ *0596/58–07–32. MC, V.*

Le François
FRENCH

\$\$ ✕ **Le Plein Soleil.** Chef Eric creates one memorable meal after another,
★ all offered in a single prix-fixe menu. Fish is often a first course—like the carpaccio of Dorado or mussels Provençale, and then there is a luscious Camembert pâté with dried fruits, or a perfect red leaf lettuce salad with roasted yellow peppers, sun-dried tomatoes, avocados, herb-dusted mobellier cheese, croutons, and a vinaigrette. Laudable main courses include duck breast with Roquefort sauce or medallions of pork tenderloin unexpectedly coupled with prawns in a creamy saffron sauce. Dessert might be coconut flan or fondant chocolate. An aged rum and fruit digestive is the finale. ⊠ *Hotel Le Plein Soleil, Villa Lagon Sarc, Pointe Thalemont,* ☎ *596/38–07–77. Reservations essential. MC, V.*

SEAFOOD

\$\$\$\$ ✕ **La Maison de l'Ilet Oscar.** You must be fetched by yawl from Le François to land at this Robinson Crusoe bistro (included in the two prix-fixe menus). You choose between either grilled fish and lambi (conch) pie, or grilled lobster. Nice French wine is available. The vintage creole hotel was won by the owner's grand-uncle, circa 1935, in a poker game. Tables are laid out under shade palms at the water's edge. You will be taken to Joséphine's bath, a gorgeous shallow area with white sand, where Napoléon's wife would swim, and served 'ti punch and accras, in the emerald-color water. ⊠ *La Maison de l'Ilet Oscar, Baie de François, Ilet Oscar,* ☎ *0596/65–82–30. Reservations essential. AE, MC, V.*

Les Trois-Ilets
BARBECUE

\$\$ ✕ **Le Grange Inn.** Nearly every item is cooked over the open grill, top-quality meats, fish, and fresh jumbo crayfish, and served with two sauces, chien and *beurre blanc,* flanked by grilled okra and peppers and a breadfruit muffin. A fun starter is the chicken wings done in a Bacardi–brown sugar sauce. A kids' menu offers crispy fried fish or chicken tenders rub-a-dub style (that means with peanut sauce). You'll find large and good selection of French wines. The circular red-brick bar has promoted many friendships. Friday and Saturday nights a piano man performs. ⊠ *Village Créole, Pointe du Bout,* ☎ *0596/66–01–66. MC, V.*

ECLECTIC

\$\$–\$\$\$ ✕ **Les Passagers du Vent.** In a pretty brick building on the main street of the village, chef/owner Stephane Ourey and his wife, Aurelie, create superb Franco/Caribbean dishes: *filet de merou* (a local white fish) poached in coconut milk; fried breadfruit; sautéed lobster medallions with honey, lime, and herbs de Provence; duck breast in raspberry sauce; and bouillabaisse creole. Perfect profiteroles and premium ice creams in tropical flavors are dessert bests. Funky and fun—there's a fish skeleton encased in plexiglass on the wall—you'll also hear hip music, with jazz and blues performances on Saturday. ✉ *27 rue de l'Impératrice Joséphine*, ☎ *0596/68–42–11. MC, V. Closed Sun. and Sept. No lunch Sat.*

$$ ✕ **L'Abordage.** This is a fun, happening place, with a good bar scene downstairs in the tavern, which often has live entertainment. For lunch, you can have a couple of starters, such as a tropical fish tartar or an eggplant gratin. Or you can opt for the typical two-hour French lunch and go on to a breast of duck with pear sauce. Dinner could be something light, like grilled Dorado with honey sauce. Global specialities like Brazil's feijoada are offered. The wine list is laudatory, the music great. The waiters—friendly, professional, and English-speaking—wear French sailor jerseys. ✉ *Village Créole, Pointe du Bout*, ☎ *0596/66–64–40. Reservations not accepted. MC, V.*

ITALIAN

$$$ ✕ **Sapori d'Italia.** The Milanese owner of this outdoor terrace restaurant in Village Créole is confident that his Italian food is the island's most authentic. Pasta offerings include homemade gnocchi al Gorgonzola, ravioli stuffed with walnut cream sauce, and penne with broccoli, garlic, and anchovies. Shrimp with a white bean sauté is a laudable main course. The long wine list focuses on Italian vintages. Desserts are special, like the strawberry ice cream with a balsamic sauce. Finish with a perfect espresso and a grappa or a Barolo Chinato Cocchi. ✉ *Village Créole, Pointe du Bout*, ☎ *0596/66–15–85. AE, MC, V. Closed Wed. Apr. 15–May 31. Closed June–Oct.*

Macouba

SEAFOOD

$$–$$$ ✕ **Pointe-Norde.** If you're driving around the northern end of the island, this is one of the few watering holes in the area. Built among the ruins of the Perpigna distillery, with sea views and Dominica in the distance, it serves lunch daily. Seafood is special here, like the crab *étouffé* or fresh tuna with blonde lentils. The creole dishes are particularly interesting ones, like salted codfish mixed with farina and stuffed in avocado. *Prix fixe* menus offer good variety and value. Ask for the punch Paille, and find out what flavors of ice cream have just been made. Reservations are essential on weekends. ✉ *On road to Grand Rivière, between Macouba and Grand Rivière*, ☎ *0596/78–56–56. MC, V. No dinner.*

Precheur

ECLECTIC

$$$ ✕ **Habitation Céron.** In a tropical forest on the grounds of a 17th-century sugar plantation, this popular outdoor lunch spot serves a multi-course, prix-fixe creole menu. You may be served fresh crayfish from their crayfish farm and ground provisions grown on the estate. After eating, wander through the forest garden where you might find Madeira hummingbirds and red partridges, green and blue lizards, and trapdoor spiders. There's a river running through the property, with some of the island's oldest trees surrounding it. In the parish of Precheur, Saint-Pierre is a 15-minute drive away. ✉ *Anse Céron*, ☎ *0596/52–94–53. AE, MC, V. No dinner.*

Ste-Marie

CARIBBEAN

$$ ✕ **Le Colibri.** Gregarious Joel Paladino is lovingly continuing a family culinary tradition with this little local spot in the island's northeastern reaches. His beautiful twin sisters are the chefs. Begin with deep green, callalou soup with crab, conch pie, or avocado and crab salad, and go on to grilled lobster with a side of christophene gratin, or the rabbit blanquette. Some of the traditional creole dishes, like pigeon stuffed with pureed chicken and veal and *cochon au lait* (suckling pig), are favorites on Sundays. There's a good wine list. The view, across the ocean, is spectacular: if you're lucky, you'll see a rainbow. ⊠ *4 rue des Colibris, Morne-des-Esses,* ☎ *0596/69–91–95. AE, MC, V. Closed Mon.*

Beaches

All of Martinique's beaches are open to the public, but hotels charge a fee for nonguests to use changing rooms and facilities. There are no official nudist beaches, but topless bathing is prevalent. Unless you're an expert swimmer, steer clear of the Atlantic waters, except in the area of Cap Chevalier and the Caravelle Peninsula. The soft white-sand beaches are south of Fort-de-France; to the north, the beaches are hard-packed gray volcanic sand. Some of the most pleasant beaches are around Ste-Anne and Ste-Luce.

Anse-à-l'Ane. There are picnic tables and a nearby shell museum. Cool off in the bar of Le Calalou hotel.

Anse-Mitan. You'll find golden sand and excellent snorkeling. Small, family-owned bistros are half hidden among palm trees nearby.

Anse-Trabaud. On the Atlantic side, across the southern tip of the island from Ste-Anne, there's nothing here but white sand and the sea.

Baie des Anglais. Drive through a plantation in Ste-Anne and pay the owner two bucks to get to this huge, quiet, sandy beach with a bit of surf.

Diamant. The island's longest beach (2½ mi) has a splendid view of Diamond Rock, but the waters are rough.

Les Salines. A 1½-mi (2½-km) cove of soft white sand lined with coconut palms is a short drive south of Ste-Anne. Les Salines is awash with families and children during holidays and on weekends but quiet and uncrowded during the week—even at the height of the winter season. This beach, especially the far end, is the most beautiful.

Pointe du Bout. The beaches here are small, man-made, and lined with luxury resorts, among them the Méridien and the Bakoua.

Pointe Marin. Stretching north from Ste-Anne, this is a good windsurfing and waterskiing spot with restaurants, campsites, sanitary facilities, and a $3 charge. Club Med is on the northern edge.

Outdoor Activities and Sports

BOATING AND SAILING

Only people very familiar with handling marine craft should consider striking out on the rough Atlantic side. The Caribbean side is much calmer—more like a vast lagoon rather than an actual sea. If you are unsure of your nautical prowess, cruises can be arranged through several companies. You can rent Hobie Cats, Sunfish, and Sailfish by the hour from hotel beach shacks. As an example of bareboat prices, a Dufour 38-ft costs $3,480 in high season (winter) through Sunsail, $1,845 in low season (summer and early fall). A Sunodyssey 37.2-ft charters for $3,195 and $1,695, respectively. **Club Nautique du Marin** (⊠ Le François, ☎ 0596/74–92–48) rents Hobie Cats, windsurfers, small boats, and a large monohull, a 45-ft Gypsy. This yacht club has a sailing school as well, for both kids and adults; although most instruction is in French, the school will try to accommodate English-speakers. **Moorings Antilles Françaises** (⊠ Port de Plaisance du Marin, ☎ 0596/74–75–39, FAX 0596/74–76–44, WEB www.moorings.com), one of the largest bareboat operations in the world, has a fleet of some 30 boats in Martinique, including catamarans and monohulls. Boats can also be rented fully crewed, and provisioning is another option. **Sunsail** (⊠ Port de

Plaisance du Marin, ☎ 0596/74–77–61 or 800/889–2248; 866/644–2327 in the U.S., WEB www.sunsail.com) has joined with Stardust Yacht Charters to form one of the largest yacht-charter companies in the world. Although it's primarily a bareboat operation, skippers can be hired by the week by those with limited experience or are available to instruct charterers in sailing skills and local waters. Ocean kayaks can be rented, too, and must be reserved in advance.

CYCLING

Mountain biking is popular in mainland France, and now it has reached Martinique. You can rent a VTT (Vélo Tout Terrain), a bike specially designed with 18 speeds to handle all terrains, from **V.T.Tilt** (⊠ Les Trois-Ilets, ☎ 0596/66–01–01), which also does some fun day tours that include lunch.

FISHING

Fish cruising these waters include tuna, barracuda, dolphinfish, kingfish, and bonito. For a day's outing on the 37-ft *Egg Harbor,* with gear and breakfast included, contact **Bathy's Club** (⊠ Méridien, Pointe de Bout, ☎ 0596/66–00–00). **Bleu Marine Evasion** (⊠ Le Diamant, ☎ 0596/76–46–00) offers fishing excursions as well as day sails. Charters of up to five days can be arranged on Captain René Alaric's 37-ft *Rayon Vert* (⊠ Auberge du Vare, Case-Pilote, ☎ 0596/78–80–56).

GOLF

The **Golf Country Club de la Martinique** (⊠ Les Trois-Ilets, ☎ 0596/68–32–81) has a par-71, 18-hole Robert Trent Jones course with an English-speaking pro, a fully equipped pro shop, a bar, and a restaurant. A mile (1½ km) from Pointe du Bout, the club offers special greens fees to guests of some hotels as well as to cruise-ship passengers. Normal greens fees are $40; an electric cart costs another $40.

HIKING

The island has 31 marked hiking trails. At the beginning of each, a notice is posted advising on the level of difficulty, the duration of a hike, and any interesting points to note. The **Parc Naturel Régional de la Martinique** (⊠ 9 bd. Général de Gaulle, Fort-de-France, ☎ 0596/73–19–30) organizes inexpensive guided excursions year-round.

HORSEBACK RIDING

Excursions and lessons are available at several places on the island: at **Black Horse Ranch** (⊠ Les Trois-Ilets, ☎ 0596/68–37–80), trail rides of an hour's duration ($22) go into the countryside and across waving cane fields, two hours on the trail ($32) bring riders near the beach with beautiful sea views. Western saddles are used exclusively, even in the basic classes ($32 a person, semi-private lessons) where instruction is in French or English. Students are taught first how to stay in the saddle and then to walk, trot, and gallop. **Ranch Jack** (⊠ near Anse-d'Arlets, ☎ 0596/68–37–69) has trail rides (English saddle) across the countryside for $22 an hour; half-day excursions go through the country and forests to the beach. Beverages are included for $43. Little English is spoken at **Ranch de Trois Caps** (Ste-Anne, ☎ 0596/74–70–65), but for two hours you can ride (western) on the wild southern beaches and across the countryside for $36. Rides go out in the morning and afternoon, every day but Monday. Reserve in advance.

SCUBA DIVING AND SNORKELING

To explore the old shipwrecks, coral gardens, and other undersea sites, you must have a medical certificate and insurance papers. Martinique has several dive operators. At **Le Marine Hotel–Club Plongee** (⊠ Le Diamant, ☎ 0596/76–46–00 or 0596/76–41–06), all levels of divers are accommodated at the various beautiful Caribbean dive sites in the south of the island, including Anses-d'Arlets. Dive boats depart at 9 AM and 2 PM. A single dive costs $35, three cost $90, and six $163. Six dive classes are $258. At **Méridien Plongée** (⊠ Hotel Le Méridien Trois-Ilets, Pointe du Bout, ☎ 0596/66–00–00), you can take a three-hour dive at either 8:30 or 2; boats always head to the southwest side of the island, with Solomon's Gardens being a favorite spot. Packages for 3 and 10 dives drop the prices significantly. **Okeanos Club** (⊠ Village Pierre et Vacances, Ste-Luce, ☎ 0596/62–52–36) has a morning trip close to shore; in the afternoon dive boats go out to open water. A single dive is $37, a package of three dives is $99, six is $180, and eight $208.

SPORTS CENTERS

The **La Basse de Plein Air et Loisirs** (☎ 0596/58–24–32), on the Caravelle Peninsula, is an open-air sports and leisure center offering tennis, windsurfing, waterskiing, and other activities.

TENNIS AND SQUASH

There are two courts at **Le Bakoua** (⊠ Pointe du Bout, ☎ 0596/66–02–02). The **Diamant-Novotel** (⊠ Pointe de la Chery, Le Diamant, ☎ 0596/76–42–42) has two tennis courts. There are six excellent courts at **Framissima** (⊠ La Batelière, Schoelcher, ☎ 0596/61–64–52). In addition to its links, the **Golf Country Club de la Martinique** (⊠ Les Trois-Ilets, ☎ 0596/68–32–81) has three lighted tennis courts. **La Ligue Régionale de Tennis** (⊠ Petit Manoir, Lamentin, ☎ 0596/51–50–01) is a tennis club where an hour's court time averages $8 for nonmembers. **Le Mercure Diamant** (⊠ Pointe de la Chery, Le Diamant, ☎ 0596/76–46–00) has two tennis courts. **Le Méridien Trois-Ilets** (⊠ Pointe du Bout, Les Trois-Ilets, ☎ 0596/66–00–00) has two courts. There is one court at the **Leyritz Plantation** (⊠ Bourg, Basse-Pointe, ☎ 0596/78–53–92). **Primerêve Hotel** (⊠ Ste-Marie, ☎ 0596/69–40–40) has one court. There are three squash courts at the aptly named **Squash Hotel** (⊠ 3 bd. de la Marine, Fort-de-France, ☎ 0596/72–80–80).

Shopping

French fragrances and designer scarves, fine china and crystal, leather goods, and finally wine (amazingly inexpensive at supermarkets), liquors, and liqueurs are all good buys in Fort-de-France. Purchases are further sweetened by the 20% discount on luxury items when paid for with traveler's checks or certain major credit cards. Among local items, look for creole gold jewelry, such as hoop earrings and heavy bead necklaces; white and dark rum; and handcrafted straw goods, pottery, and tapestries.

Areas and Malls

The area around the cathedral in Fort-de-France has a number of small shops that carry luxury items. Of particular note are the shops on **rue Victor Hugo, rue Moreau de Jones, rue Antoine Siger,** and **rue Lamartine.** The **Galleries Lafayette** department store on rue Schoelcher in downtown Fort-de-France sells everything from perfume to crockery. On the outskirts of Fort-de-France, the **Centre Commercial de Cluny, Centre Commercial de Dillon, Centre Commercial de Bellevue, Centre Commercial la Rond Point,** and more than 100 boutiques at **La Galleria** in Le Lamentin are among the major shopping malls. In Pointe du Bout there are a number of appealing tourist shops, both in **Village Créole** and on the surrounding streets.

Specialty Items

CHINA AND CRYSTAL

Cadet Daniel (⊠ 72 rue Antoine Siger, Fort-de-France, ☎ 0596/71–41–48) sells Lalique, Limoges, and Baccarat. **Roger Albert** (⊠ 7 rue

Victor Hugo, Fort-de-France, ☎ 0596/71–71–71) carries designer crystal.

CLOTHING

Cannelle (✉ Pointe du Bout, LesTrois-Illets, ☎ 0596/66–05–33), across the street from the Village Créole, with smashing French maillots and bikinis, name-brand resort wear for women and men, sandals, watches, and backpacks, is a standout.

HANDICRAFTS

Following the roadside signs advertising ATELIERS ARTISANALES (art studios) can yield unexpected treasures, many of them reasonably priced. **Atelier Céramique** (✉ Le Diamant, ☎ 0596/76–42–65), which is just outside of the main part of town, displays the ceramics, paintings, and miscellaneous souvenirs of owners and talented artists David and Jeannine England, members of the island's small British expat community. **Art et Nature** (✉ Ste-Luce, ☎ 0596/62–59–19) carries Joel Gilbert's unique wood paintings, daubed with 20–30 shades of earth and sand. **Artisanat & Poterie des Trois-Ilets** (✉ Les Trois-Ilets, ☎ 0596/68–18–01) allows you to watch the creation of Arawak- and Carib-style pots, vases, and jars. **Bois Nature** (✉ La Semair, Le Robert, ☎ 0596/65–77–65) is all about mood—and mystique. The gift items begin with scented soap, massage oil, aromatherapy sprays, and perfumes. Then there are mosquito netting, windchimes, and sun hats made of coconut fiber. The big stuff includes natural wood-framed mirrors and furniture à la Louis XV. **Centre des Métiers d'Art** (✉ Rue Ernest Deproge, Fort-de-France, ☎ 0596/70–25–01) exhibits authentic local arts and crafts. **Galerie Arti-Bijoux** (✉ 89 rue Victor Hugo, Fort-de-France, ☎ 0596/63–10–62) has some unusual and excellent Haitian art—paintings, sculptures, ceramics, and intricate jewelry cases. **Galerie de Sophen** (✉ Pointe du Bout, Les Trois-Illets, ☎ 0596/66–13–64), across from the Village Créole, is a combination of Sophie and Henry, both in name and content. This art gallery showcases the work of a French husband and wife team, who live aboard their sailboat and paint the beauty of the sea and the island. At **Galerie du Village Créole** (✉ Village Créole, Pointe du Bout, Les Trois-Illets, ☎ 0596/66–15–75) water colors, oil paintings, and other works by local artists and the gallery owner—as well as reproductions—rotate weekly. **La Paille Caraibe** (✉ Morne des Esses, ☎ 0596/69–83–74) is where you can watch artisans weave straw baskets, mats, and hats. **L'Éclat de Verre** (✉ Hwy. N4, Gros Morne, ☎ 0596/58–34–03) specializes in all manner of glittering glasswork. **Victor Anicet** (✉ Monésie, ☎ 0596/68–25–42) fashions lovely ceramic masks and vases.

LIQUOR

One of the best rums on the island is the *vieux rhum* from **JM Distillery** (✉ Macouba, ☎ 0596/78–92–55). You can get some great rum and also tour the grounds of the bucolic 32-acre **Habitation Clément** (✉ Le François, ☎ 0596/54–62–07, FAX 0596/54–63–50). **Niesson Distillery** (✉ Carbet, ☎ 0596/78–07–90) is a "Mercedes"—a small, family-run, operation, whose rum is produced from pure sugar cane juice rather than molasses. It is open for tours and tastings, and the shop sells *vieux rhum* that truly rivals cognac. **St. James Distillery** (✉ Ste-Marie, ☎ 0596/69–30–02) is a somewhat wild scene when some dozen tour buses pull in, but the two-story, gingerbread mansion showcases some rum-related antiques, and like the others, the tasting is on the house.

PERFUMES

Roger Albert (✉ 7 rue Victor Hugo, Fort-de-France, ☎ 0596/71–71–71) stocks such popular scents as those by Dior, Chanel, and Guerlain.

Nightlife and the Arts

Although Martinique is dotted with lively discos and nightclubs, nightlife isn't confined to partying. Most leading hotels offer nightly entertainment in season, including the marvelous **Les Grands Ballets de Martinique,** one of the finest folkloric dance troupes in the Caribbean. Consisting of about 30 musicians and dancers dressed in traditional costume, the ballet revives the Martinique of yesteryear through dance rhythms such as the beguine or the mazurka. This folkloric group appears once a week at Le Méridien. In addition, many restaurants offer live entertainment, usually on weekends. The **Village Créole** complex itself has a good line-up of entertainment in season that includes music, theater, and art expos. Often the **Galerie du Village Créole** gives receptions when they rotate art on the weekends.

CASINOS

The **Casino Batelière Plaza,** (✉ Schoelcher, Fort-de-France, ☎ 596/61–91–51), on the outskirts of Fort-de-France, is divided into two areas: to the left are more than 100 slot machines; to the right you'll need $10, a passport (you must be 18 to play), and the proper attire (jacket and tie for men, dresses for women) to play blackjack, roulette, or baccarat. There are two restaurants; fine dining is offered in an area about the size of a boxing ring. Bands provide even more entertainment on weekends. The slots are open Monday–Saturday noon–3 AM; for the other games things start rolling at 8 PM and continue until 3 AM. You must be at least 18 (with a picture ID) to enter the **Casino Trois-Ilets** (✉ Le Méridien, Pointe du Bout, Les Trois- Ilets, ☎ 0596/66–00–30), where you can play American roulette or blackjack. Admission to the slot-machine room is free, but there is a $10 charge for the casino, which is open Monday to Saturday from 9 PM to 3 AM.

DANCE CLUBS

Your hotel or the tourist office can put you in touch with the current "in" places. It's also wise to check on opening and closing times and cover charges. For the most part, the discos draw a mixed crowd—Martinicans and tourists, and although predominately a younger crowd, all ages go dancing here. **Crazy Nights** (✉ Ste-Luce, ☎ 0596/68–56–68) remains popular because it is all about having one crazy night. With upward to 1,000 partying people, your chances are good here. **Las Tapas** (✉ 7 rue Garnier Pages, Fort-de-France, ☎ 0596/63–71–23) presents flamenco or salsa and merengue bands and attracts a mixed crowd. **Le Cheyenne** (✉ 6/8 rue Joseph Compere, Fort-de-France, ☎ 0596/70–31–19) is like a glittery Miami disco with international music and zouk—and dancing until the wee hours. **Le Top 50** (✉ Zone Artisanale, La Trinité, ☎ 0596/58–61–43) is one of the few night spots in the area where tourists, surfers, and locals all come together to party. **Yucca Bar** (✉ Zac de Rivière Roche, Fort-de-France, ☎ 0596/60–48–36), with a Mexican motif, is known for its piano bar and for the innovative local bands that perform, usually on Wednesdays.

MUSIC CLUBS

Jazz musicians, like their music, tend to be informal and independent. They rarely hold regular gigs. Zouk music mixes Caribbean rhythm and an Occidental tempo with Creole words. Jacob Devarieux is the leading exponent of this style and is occasionally on the island. You'll hear zouk played by one of his followers at the hotels and clubs.

At **La Case de Da Paulette** (✉ Village Créole, Pointe du Bout, Les Trois-Illets, ☎ 0596/66–15–15), with corrugated aluminum walls papered with vintage newspapers like an old criollo cottage, you might see anything from a ventriloquist to musicians playing limbo and samba to the crooner Alex Rosa. **Havana Café** (✉ Village Créole, Pointe du Bout, Les Trois-Illets, ☎ 0596/66–15–93) often has singing guitarists. **Le Molokoi** (✉ Le Diamant, ☎ 0596/76–48–63) is a hot spot for zouk and pop music. **Les Soirees de l'Amphore** (✉ Anse Mitan, ☎ 0596/66–03–03), a piano bar, is a mini-restaurant, too. You might hear anything from funk, soul, and disco, to international music from the 1970s and '80s. Wednesdays there are live soirees and Thursday is karaoke night. **La Villa Créole** (✉ Anse-Mitan, ☎ 0596/66–05–53) is a bistro whose owner, Guy Dawson, the man in black, strums nightly on the guitar—everything from Piaf to Sting, and some original ditties. For nearly 20 years, he has sung and his guests have danced in front of his gazebo stage. His understudy is a handsome Frenchman, who might first appear as your waiter. In season you'll find one or two combos playing at clubs and hotels, but it's only at **West Indies** (✉ Bd. Alfassa, Fort-de-France, ☎ 0596/63–63–77), next to the tourist office, that there are regular jazz sessions.

ISLAND CULTURE

L'Atrium (✉ Bd. Général de Gaulle, Fort-de-France, ☎ 0596/70–79–29 or 0596/60–78–78), Martinique's cultural center, is where large-scale theater, dance, and musical performances take place.

Exploring Martinique

The north of the island will appeal to nature lovers, hikers, and mountain climbers. The drive from Fort-de-France to St-Pierre is particularly impressive, as is the one across the island, via Morne Rouge, from the Caribbean to the Atlantic. This is Martinique's wild side—a place of waterfalls, rain forest, and mountains. The highlight is Mont Pelée. The south is the more developed half of the island, where the resorts and restaurants are, as well as the beaches.

Numbers in the margin correspond to points of interest on the Martinique map.

SIGHTS TO SEE

⑫ Ajoupa-Bouillon. This flower-filled 17th-century village amid pineapple fields is the jumping-off point for several sights. The Saut Babin is a 40-ft-high (12-m-high) waterfall, half an hour's walk from Ajoupa-Bouillon. The Gorges de la Falaise is a river gorge where you can swim. **Les Ombrages** botanical gardens has marked trails through the rain forest. ✉ *Ajoupa-Bouillon,* 🎟 €3.36. ☉ *Daily 9–5:30.*

④ Balata. This quiet little town has two sights worth visiting. Built in 1923 to commemorate those who died in World War I, **Balata Church** is an exact replica of Paris's Sacré-Coeur Basilica. The **Jardin de Balata** (Balata Gardens), created more than 20 years by Jean-Philippe Thoze, a professional landscaper and horticulturist, has thousands of varieties of tropical flowers and plants. There are shaded benches from which to take in the mountain view. You can order anthurium and other tropical flowers to be delivered to the airport. ✉ *Rte. de Balata,* ☎ 0596/64–48–73. 🎟 €6.72. ☉ *Daily 9–5.*

⑪ Basse-Pointe. On the route to this village on the Atlantic coast at the island's northern end, you pass many banana and pineapple plantations—agriculture for as far as the eye can see. Just south of Basse-Pointe is a **Hindu temple** built by descendants of the East Indians who settled in this area in the 19th century. The view of the eastern slope of Mont Pelée is terrific. The highlight of Basse-Pointe is the estimable **Leyritz Plantation,** which has been a hotel for several years. When tour groups aren't a-swarming, the rustic setting, complete with sugarcane factory and gardens, is delightful and includes Musée des Figurines Végétales. Local artisan Will Fenton has used bananas, *balisier* (a tall grass), and other local plants to make dolls of famous French women—from Marie Antoinette to Madame Curie—in period costumes. ⊠ *Leyritz Plantation, Basse Pointe,* ☎ *0596/78–53–92.* 🖾 *€3.36.* ⊗ *Daily 10–6.*

❸ **Bellefontaine.** This colorful fishing village has pastel houses on the hillsides and beautifully painted *gommiers* (fishing boats) bobbing in the water. Look for the restaurant built in the shape of a boat.

❷⓿ **Diamond Rock.** This volcanic mound is 1 mi (1½ km) offshore from the small, friendly village of Le Diamant and is one of the island's best diving spots. In 1804, during the squabbles over possession of the island between the French and the English, the latter commandeered the rock, armed it with cannons, and proceeded to use it as a warship. For almost 1½ years, the British held the rock, attacking any French ships that came along. The French got wind that the British were getting cabin fever on their isolated ship-island and arranged a supply of barrels of rum for those on the rock. The French easily overpowered the inebriated sailors, ending one of the most curious engagements in naval history.

❶⓹ **Dubuc Castle.** At the eastern tip of the Presqu'île du Caravelle are the ruins of this castle, once the home of the Dubuc de Rivery family, who owned the Caravelle Peninsula in the 18th century. According to legend, young Aimée Dubuc de Rivery was captured by Barbary pirates, sold to the Ottoman Empire, became a favorite of the sultan, and gave birth to Mahmud II.

❷❶ **Forêt de Montravail.** A few miles north of Ste-Luce, this tropical rain forest is ideal for a short hike. Look for the interesting group of Carib rock drawings.

❶ **Fort-de-France.** With its historic fort and superb location beneath the towering Pitons du Carbet on the Baie des Flamands, Martinique's capital—home to about one-third of the island's 360,000 inhabitants—should be a grand place. It isn't. The most pleasant districts, such as Didier, Bellevue, and Schoelcher, are on the hillside, and you need a car to reach them. But if you come here by car, you may find yourself trapped in gridlock in the warren of narrow streets in the center of town, especially on cruise ship days. Parking is difficult, and its best to try for one of the parking garages, second choice, outside public parking areas. A taxi is a good alternative.

There are some good shops with Parisian wares (at Parisian prices) and lively street markets that sell, among other things, human hair for wigs (starting price: €33.60). Town can be fun, and you probably should do it just to do it. But the heat, exhaust fumes, and litter tend to make exploring here a chore rather than a pleasure. At night, the city feels dark and gloomy, with little street life except for the extravagantly dressed prostitutes who openly parade the streets from 10 PM. If you plan to go out, it is best to go with a group.

The heart of Fort-de-France is **La Savane,** a 12½-acre park filled with trees, fountains, and benches. It's a popular gathering place and the scene of promenades, parades, and impromptu soccer matches. Along the east side are numerous snack wagons. A statue of Pierre Belain d'Esnambuc, leader of the island's first settlers, is unintentionally upstaged by Vital Dubray's vandalized white Carrara marble statue of the empress Joséphine, Napoléon's first wife. The most imposing historic site is **Fort St-Louis,** which runs along the east side of La Savane. It is open Monday–Saturday 9–3, and admission is €3.92. Near the harbor is a marketplace where local crafts and souvenirs are sold. Across from La Savane, you can catch the ferry *La Vedette* for the beaches at Anse-

Mitan and Anse-à-l'Âne and for the 20-minute run across the bay to the resort hotels of Pointe du Bout. It costs just €5.60 and is stress-free—much more safe, pleasant and faster than the journey round the bay by car.

The **Bibliothèque Schoelcher** is the wildly elaborate Romanesque public library. It was named after Victor Schoelcher, who led the fight to free the slaves in the French West Indies in the 19th century. The eye-popping structure was built for the 1889 Paris Exposition, after which it was dismantled, shipped to Martinique, and reassembled piece by ornate piece. ⊠ *Corner of rue de la Liberté (runs along west side of La Savane) and rue Perrinon,* ☎ *0596/70–26–67.* ⊠ *Free.* ☯ *Mon. 1–5:30, Tues.–Fri. 8:30–5:30, Sat. 8:30–noon.*

Le Musée Régional D' Histoire et D' Ethnographie is a learning experience that is best undertaken at the beginning of your vacation so as to better understand the history, background, and people of the island. Housed in an elaborate, former residence (circa 1888) with balconies and fretwork, it has everything from displays of the garish gold jewelry that prostitutes wore after emancipation, to reconstructed rooms of a home of proper, middle-class Martinicans. There is even a display of madras, creole headdresses with details of how they were tied to indicate if a woman was single, married, or otherwise occupied. ⊠ *10 bd. General de Gaulle,* ☎ *0596/72–81–87.* ⊠ *€3.36.* ☯ *Tues. 8–5, Mon.–Fri. 2–5, Sat. 8–noon.*

Rue Victor Schoelcher runs through the center of the capital's primary shopping district, a six-block area bounded by rue de la République, rue de la Liberté, rue de Victor Severe, and rue Victor Hugo. Stores sell Paris fashions and French perfume, china, crystal, and liqueurs, as well as local handicrafts. The Romanesque **St-Louis Cathedral** (⊠ Rue Victor Schoelcher) with its lovely stained-glass windows was the sixth to be built in 1878 on this site (the others were destroyed by fire, hurricane, and earthquake.The Galerie de Biologie et de Géologie at the **Parc Floral et Culturel,** in the northeastern corner of the city center, will acquaint you with the island's exotic flora. There's also an aquarium. The park contains the island's official cultural center, where there are sometimes free evening concerts. ⊠ *Pl. José-Marti, Sermac,* ☎ *0596/71–66–25.* ⊠ *Grounds free; aquarium €5.6; botanical and geological gallery €1.12.* ☯ *Park daily dawn–10 PM; aquarium daily 9–7; gallery Tues.–Fri. 9:30–12:30 and 3:30–5:30, Sat. 9–1 and 3–5.*

⑯ Le François. With some 16,000 inhabitants, this is the main city on the Atlantic coast. Sadly, the old wooden buildings are being replaced by concrete structures. But the classic West Indian cemetery, with its black-and-white tiles, is still here. The **Habitation Clément** is Martinique's version of colonial Williamsburg, complete with Créole ladies in traditional dresses moving about the grounds. It was built with the wealth generated by its rum distillery, and its 18th-century splendor has been lovingly preserved, providing a glimpse into the elegance and privilege of plantation society. Framed vintage labels from rum bottles track the changes in Martinique over the decades. The rum distillery is operational and offers free tastings. New is a top-of-the-line rum, Canne Bleu, made from a special cane. An antique carriage pulled by an impressive, black steed traverses the cane fields and returns through the tropical gardens and trees (call first to inquire if rides are being given). ⊠ *Domaine de l'Acajou,* ☎ *0596/54–62–07,* WEB *www.rhum-clement.com.* ⊠ *€8.96.* ☯ *Daily 9–6.*

Le François is also noted for its snorkeling. Offshore are the privately owned Les Ilets de l'Impératrice. The islands received that name because, according to legend, this is where Empress Joséphine came to bathe in the shallow basins known as *fonds blancs* because of their white-sand bottoms. Group boat tours leave from the harbor (€33.6) per person includes lunch and drinks). You can also haggle with a fisherman to take you out for a while on his boat to indulge in the uniquely Martinican custom of standing waist-deep in warm water, sipping a 'ti punch, eating accras, and smoking. There's a fine bay 6 mi (9½ km) farther along the coast at Le Robert, though the town is lackluster.

⑤ Habitation Anse Latouche. Tour the ruins of this former cane plantation, see its great house, distillery, and modern-day botanical gardens. ✉ *Carbet,* ☎ *0596/78–19–19.* ☞ *€3.36.* ⊙ *10–4. Closed Sun.*

⑰ Lamentin. There's nothing pretty about Lamentin; the multibillion-franc airport is its most notable landmark. The rest of the town is a sprawling industrial and commercial zone. But you come here for shopping in the big, fancy shopping mall Euromarché. La Galleria, a megamall of roughly 100 shops and boutiques, offers everything from pâté de foie gras and Camembert to CDs and sunglasses.

⑩ Macouba. Named after the Carib word for "fish," this village was a prosperous tobacco town in the 17th century. Today its cliff-top location affords magnificent views of the sea, the mountains, and—on clear days—the neighboring island of Dominica. The **JM Distillery** produces some of the best *rhum vieux* on the island here. A tour and samples are free. Macouba is the starting point for a spectacular drive, the 6-mi (9½-km) **route to Grand' Rivière** on the northernmost point. This is Martinique at its greenest: groves of giant bamboo, cliffs hung with curtains of vines, and 7-ft (2-m) tree ferns that seem to grow as you watch them. Literally, at the end of the road, is Grand' Rivière, a colorful sprawling fishing village at the foot of high cliffs.

㉔ Le Marin. The yachting capital of Martinique is also known for its colorful August carnival and its Jesuit church, circa 1766. From Le Marin a narrow road leads to picturesque Cap Chevalier (Cape Knight), about 1 mi (1½ km) from town.

⑧ Le Morne Rouge. This town sits on the southern slopes of the volcano that destroyed it in 1902. Today it's a popular resort spot and offers hikers some fantastic mountain scenery. From Le Morne Rouge you can start the climb up the 4,600-ft (1,406-m) **Mont Pelée** volcano. But don't try it without a guide unless you want to get buried alive under pumice stones. Instead, drive up to the Refuge de l'Aileron. From the parking lot it's a mile (1½ km) up a well-marked trail to the summit. Bring a sweatshirt because there's often a mist that makes the air damp and chilly. From the summit follow the route de la Trace (Route N3), which winds south of Le Morne Rouge to St-Pierre. It's steep and winding, but that didn't stop the *porteuses* of old: balancing a tray, these women would carry up to 100 pounds of provisions on their heads for the 15-hour trek to the Atlantic coast.

⑥ Musée Gauguin. Martinique was a brief station in Paul Gauguin's wanderings but a decisive moment in the evolution of his art. He arrived from Panama in 1887 with friend and fellow painter Charles Laval and, having pawned his watch at the docks, rented a wooden shack on a hill above the village of Carbet. Dazzled by the tropical colors and vegetation, Gauguin developed a style, his Martinique period, that directly anticipated his Tahitian paintings. Although this modest museum has no originals, it does have a set of reproductions. There are also interesting exhibits of letters and documents relating to the painter, and an exhibition of local costumes. Also remembered here is the Writer Lafcadio Hearn. In his endearing book *Two Years in the*

West Indies, he provides the most extensive description of the island before St-Pierre was buried in ash and lava. ⊠ *Anse-Turin, Carbet,* ☎ *0596/78–22–66.* ☺ *€3.36.* ☼ *Daily 9–5:30.*

⑲ **Pointe du Bout.** This touristic area has resort hotels, among them the Sofitel Bakoua and the Méridien, and a marina. The ferry to Fort-de-France leaves from here. A cluster of boutiques, ice-cream parlors, and rental-car agencies forms the hub from which restaurants and hotels of varying caliber radiate. The beach at Anse-Mitan is one of the best on the island. At Anse-à-l'Ane, a little to the west, is a pretty white-sand beach with picnic tables. There are also numerous small restaurants and inexpensive guest-house hotels here. Ten miles (16 kilometers) south is Anse-d'Arlets, a quiet, unspoiled fishing village.

⑨ **Le Prêcheur.** This quaint town, the last on the northern Caribbean coast, is surrounded by volcanic hot springs. The village itself was the childhood home of Françoise d'Aubigné, who later became the Marquise de Maintenon and the second wife of Louis XIV. At her request, the Sun King donated a handsome bronze bell, which still hangs outside the church, to the village. On the way from St-Pierre, The Tomb of the Carib Indians, commemorates a sadder event. Actually a formation of limestone cliffs, from which the last of the Caribs are said to have flung themselves, to avoid capture by the Marquise's forebears.

⑭ **Presqu'île du Caravelle.** Much of the Caravelle Peninsula, which juts 8 mi (13 km) into the Atlantic Ocean, is under the protection of the Regional Nature Reserve and offers places for trekking, swimming, and sailing. This is also the site of Anse-Spoutourne, an open-air sports and leisure center operated by the reserve. Tartane has a popular beach with cool Atlantic breezes.

㉓ **Ste-Anne.** A lovely white-sand beach and a Catholic church are the highlights of this town on the island's southern tip. To the south of Ste-Anne is Pointe des Salines, the southernmost tip of the island and site of Martinique's best beach. Near Ste-Anne is **La Savane des Pétrifications**, the Petrified Forest. This desertlike stretch was once swampland and is a veritable geological museum where a few specimens of petrified wood can still be found.

㉒ **Ste-Luce.** This quaint fishing village has a sleepy main street that's deserted at midday, panoramic views across to the island of St. Lucia, and excellent beaches. To the east is Pointe Figuier, an excellent spot for scuba diving. On the way from Ste-Luce to Pointe Figuier, is **Ecomusée de Martinique** (⊠ Anse Figuier, ☎ 0596/62–79–14), showcasing artifacts from Arawak and Carib settlements through the plantation years. Admission is €3.36, and it's open Tuesday through Sunday 9–1:30 and 2:30–5.

⑬ **Ste-Marie.** This town has a population of about 20,000 and is the commercial capital of the island's north. There's a lovely mid-19th-century church here. The **Musée du Rhum,** operated by the St. James Rum Distillery, is housed in a graceful, galleried creole house. Guided tours take in displays of the tools of the trade and include a visit and tasting at the distillery. ⊠ *Ste-Marie,* ☎ *0596/69–30–02.* ☺ *Free.* ☼ *Weekdays 9–5, weekends 9–1, except during the harvest period, Feb.–June (call first).* **Le Musée de la Banane.** You probably won't find more cordial hosts than those here. After navigating the extremely narrow road, you'll arrive at the compound. Four different stops with excellent graphics and beautiful prints tell the story of the banana (Martinique's primary export) as it makes its way from the fields to your table. ⊠ *Habitation Limbé,* ☎ *0596/69–45–52.* ☺ *€5.60.* ☼ *Daily 9–5.*

❼ St-Pierre. The rise and fall of St-Pierre is one of the most remarkable stories in the Caribbean. Martinique's modern history began here in 1635. By the turn of this century, St-Pierre was a flourishing city of 30,000, known as the Paris of the West Indies. As many as 30 ships at a time stood at anchor. By 1902 it was the most modern town in the Caribbean, with electricity, phones, and a tram. On May 8, 1902, two thunderous explosions rent the air. As the nearby volcano erupted, Mont Pelée split in half, belching forth a cloud of burning ash, poisonous gas, and lava that raced down the mountain at 250 mph. At 3,600°F, it instantly vaporized everything in its path; 30,000 people were killed in two minutes. One man survived. His name was Cyparis, and he was a prisoner in an underground cell in the town's jail. He was later pardoned and afterward was a sideshow attraction in the Barnum & Bailey Circus.

Today St-Pierre is trying to reinvent itself. An Office du Tourisme has been built, as well as a seafront promenade. There are plenty of sidewalk cafés, and you can stroll the main streets and check the blackboards before deciding where to lunch. At night, some places will have live music. Like stage sets for a dramatic opera, there are the ruins of the island's first church (built in 1640), the imposing theater, the toppled statues, and then there is Cyparis's cell. This city, situated on its naturally beautiful harbor, and with its narrow, winding streets has the feel of a European seaside, hill village. Although a lot of the oldest buildings need work, stark modernism has not invaded this burg. As much potential as it has, this is one town in Martinique where real estate is cheap—for obvious reasons. In 2002, and with the aid of the French government, St. Pierre honored those who died tragically in the volcano's eruption a hundred years before, with a series of programs and events.

For those interested in the eruption of 1902, the **Musée Vulcanologique Frank Perret** is a must. Established in 1932, it houses photographs of the old town, documents, and a number of relics—some gruesome—excavated from the ruins, including molten glass, melted iron, and contorted clocks stopped at 8 AM. ✉ *Rue de Victor Hugo*, ☎ *0596/78-15-16.* 🎫 *€2.24.* ◷ *Daily 9–5.* The *Cyparis Express* is a small tourist train that runs through the city, hitting the important sights with a running narrative (in French). ✉ *Pl. des Ruines du Figuier*, ☎ *0596/55-50-92.* 🎫 *€8.96.* ◷ *Departs hourly, weekdays 9:30–1 and 2:30–5:30.*

❷ Schoelcher. Pronounced "shell-*share*," this suburb of Fort-de-France is home of the University of the French West Indies and Guyana and the site of Martinique's largest convention center, Madiana.

⓲ Les Trois-Îlets. Named after the three rocky islands nearby, this lovely little village (population 3,000) has unusual brick and wood buildings roofed with antique tiles. It's known for its pottery, straw, and woodwork, but above all as the birthplace of Napoléon's empress Joséphine. In the square, where there's also a market and a fine *mairie* (town hall), you can visit the simple church where she was baptized Marie-Joseph Tascher de la Pagerie. The Martinicans have always been enormously proud of Joséphine, even though she reintroduced slavery on the island and most historians consider her to have been rather shallow. A stone building that held the kitchen of the estate where she grew up houses the **Musée de la Pagerie** (the main house blew down in the hurricane of 1766, when Joséphine was three). It contains an assortment of memorabilia pertaining to her life and rather unfortunate loves. At 16 she was wed (an arranged marriage) to Alexandre de Beauharnais. When he died, she married Napoléon, but he divorced her because she didn't produce any children. There are family portraits; documents, including a marriage certificate; a love letter written to her in 1796 by Napoléon; and various antiques. ⊠ *Les Trois-Ilets,* ☎ *0596/68–34–55.* ☜ *€3.36.* ☉ *Tues.–Fri. 9–5, weekends 9–1 and 1:30–5:30.* The **Maison de la Canne** will teach you everything you ever wanted to know about sugarcane. Exhibits take you through three centuries of cane production, with displays of tools, scale models, engravings, and photographs. ⊠ *Les Trois-Ilets,* ☎ *0596/68–32–04.* ☜ *€3.36.* ☉ *Tues.–Sun. 9–5.*

㉕ **Le Vauclin.** The return of the fishermen at noon is the big event in this important fishing port on the Atlantic. There's also the 18th-century Chapel of the Holy Virgin. Nearby is the highest point in the south, Mont Vauclin (1,654 ft). A hike to the top rewards you with one of the best views on the island.

MARTINIQUE A TO Z

To research prices, get advice from other travelers, and book travel arrangements, visit www.fodors.com.

AIR TRAVEL
Air France is the only airline with direct connections between the U.S. and Martinique (it flies daily from Miami), and you can purchase a code-share ticket with Delta or Continental Airlines to make the Miami connection. Alternatively, you can fly BWIA International Airways from Miami to Bridgetown, Barbados, and then take LIAT to Fort-de-France. LIAT flies in from Antigua, Barbados, Dominica, Grenada, Guadeloupe, St. Lucia, St. Maarten, and Trinidad and Tobago. Air Caraïbes offers interisland service to Guadeloupe and the Guadeloupean islands of Les Saintes, Marie-Galante, and La Desirade, St. Martin, St. Barths, Santo Domingo, Dominica, and St. Lucia. You can fly US Airways to San Juan and make connections or into Santo Domingo and connect with Air Caraïbes.
➤ AIRLINES AND CONTACTS: **Air France** (☎ 0596/55–33–33 or 800/237–2747). **BWIA International Airways** (☎ 800/538–2942; no local number). **LIAT** (☎ 0596/42–16–02). **Air Caraïbes** (☎ 0596/42–16–58). **US Airways** (☎ 800/428–4322; no local number).

AIRPORTS
There are no U.S. or Canadian airlines serving Martinique's contemporary Lamentin International Airport, so you will have to do some island-hopping. The airport is about a 15-minute taxi ride from Fort-de-France and about 40 minutes from Les Trois-Ilets peninsula.
➤ AIRPORT INFORMATION: **Lamentin International Airport** (☎ 0596/42–19–95 or 0596/42–19–96).

BIKE AND MOPED RENTALS
Bikes, scooters, and motorbikes are all popular, and you can rent them from Discount, Funny, or Grabin's Rental. In Ste-Anne try Huet, and in Ste-Luce check out Vespa Marquis.
➤ BIKE AND MOPED RENTALS: **Discount** (⊠ Pointe du Bout Marina, Les Trois-Ilets, ☎ 0596/66–05–34). **Funny** (⊠ 80 rue Ernest Deprage, Fort-de-France, ☎ 0596/63–33–05). **Grabin's Rental** (⊠ Morne Calbasse, Fort-de-France, ☎ 0596/71–51–61). **Huet** (☎ 0596/76–79–66). **Vespa Marquis** (☎ 0596/60–02–84).

BOAT AND FERRY TRAVEL
Weather permitting, *vedettes* (ferries) operate daily between Fort-de-France and the Marina Méridien, in Pointe du Bout, as well as between Fort-de-France and Anse-Mitan and Anse-à-l'Ane and take 15 minutes.

The Quai d'Esnambuc is the arrival and departure point in Fort-de-France.

The *Express des Isles* offers scheduled interisland service aboard a 128-ft, 227-passenger motorized catamaran, linking Martinique with Dominica, Guadeloupe, Les Saintes, and St. Lucia. For those who don't get seasick, it's an enormously pleasurable way to travel, with great views of the islands.

FARES AND SCHEDULES
The round-trip fare between Fort-de-France and the Marina Méridien, in Pointe du Bout, as well as between Fort-de-France and Anse-Mitan and Anse-à-l'Ane is about €5.6.

The *Express des Isles* fares run approximately 25% below economy airfares. Sailings are not every day of the week for all destinations; check the schedule.
➤ BOAT AND FERRY INFORMATION: *Express des Isles* (☎ 0596/63–12–11).

BUSINESS HOURS
BANKS
Banks are open weekdays 7:30–noon and 2:30–4.

POST OFFICES
Post offices are generally open Monday–Saturday 7 AM–6 PM, though many close on Wednesday at 1 PM.

SHOPS
Stores that cater to tourists are generally open weekdays 8:30–6, Saturday 8:30–1. Many stores in Fort de France close 12:30–2 for lunch.

CAR RENTALS
A valid U.S. driver's license is needed to rent a car for up to 20 days. After that, you'll need an International Driver's Permit. U.K. citizens can use their EU licenses (Martinique is still a part of France).

Rates are about $60 per day (unlimited mileage) in "season," but always question agents thoroughly about possible discounts. Although the rent-a-car companies have some automatics, they are substantially more expensive than the more common manuals. If you book from the U.S. at least 48 hours in advance, you can qualify for a hefty discount. If you wait until you arrive, you may be able to negotiate a weekly rate discount. A hefty deposit will be put on your credit card until the car is returned safely. If you have a gold or platinum credit card, which allows you to safely waive insurance, you can use it here. Insurance tariffs add substantially to your bill. Lowest prices are $225 per week in low season, $330 in high season. Among the many agencies in Fort-de-France are Avis, Budget, Hertz, Europcar, and Jumbo Car. You might want to start with the Jumbo, as far as cutting deals, they are among the most likely.
➤ MAJOR AGENCIES: **Avis** (☎ 0596/42–11–00 or 800/331–1212). **Budget** (☎ 0596/51–22–88 or 800/472–3325). **Hertz** (☎ 0596/42–16–90 or 800/654–3131). **JumboCar** (☎ 0596/42–22–22). **Europcar** (☎ 0596/42–42–42).

CAR TRAVEL
Unless you're at an all-inclusive resort, you may want a car. Almost everyone on the island drives a small car with a manual shift. Why? Because many of the roads are narrow in the small towns and in mountainous areas. It helps to have a stick shift to climb those hills. If you have questions, ask the rental agent to explain the gears and operation of the car to you. For those who haven't driven a stick in years, be aware that traffic jams often occur on steep inclines that will ne-

cessitate the deft use of clutch, gas pedal, and emergency brake. And then it will inevitably rain. It may be worth the additional cost to rent an automatic.

Martinique, especially around Fort-de-France and its environs, has become plagued with heavy traffic. Streets in the capital itself are narrow and choked with traffic during the day. It is wiser to tour it on the weekends, certainly not when on cruise ship days. Absolutely avoid the Lametin airport area and Fort-de-France during weekday rush hours, roughly 7–10 AM and 4–7:30 PM. Even the smaller towns like Trinité have rush hours that could cause you to spend two hours getting to Trois-des-Ilets instead of 30 minutes.

Watch out, too, for *dos d'ânes* (literally, donkey backs), speed bumps that are extremely hard to spot—particularly at night—though if you hit one, you'll know it. If you want a detailed map, the *Carte Routière et Touristique* is available at bookstores.

GASOLINE
Gas is costly, the equivalent of about $4 per gallon.

ROAD CONDITIONS
The main highways, about 175 mi (280 km) of well-paved and well-marked roads are excellent, but only in certain areas are they illuminated at night. Many of the hotels are off the beaten path on roads that should be condemned. Get wherever you are going by nightfall, or prepare to be lost.

RULES OF THE ROAD
Pay attention at the round-a-bouts, always a good source of collision possibilities. And drive defensively: Martinicans drive with aggressive abandon. Although they are polite on a one-to-one, its every man for himself when they hit the high-road.

ELECTRICITY
Most tourist locations are equipped with 220-volt electrical outlets. If you're coming from North America and plan to use your own appliances, bring a converter kit with adapters.

EMERGENCIES
➤ AMBULANCE AND FIRE: **Ambulance** (☎ 0596/70–36–48 or 0596/71–59–48). **Fire** (☎ 18).
➤ HOSPITALS: **Hôpital Pierre Zabla Quitman** (✉ Lamentin, ☎ 0596/55–20–00).
➤ PHARMACIES: **Pharmacie Cypria** (✉ Bd. Général de Gaulle, Fort-de-France, ☎ 0596/63–22–25). **Pharmacie de la Paix** (✉ Corner rue Victor Schoelcher and rue Perrinon, Fort-de-France, ☎ 0596/71–94–83).
➤ POLICE: **Police emergencies** (☎ 17).

FESTIVALS AND SEASONAL EVENTS
Martinique's Carnival begins in early January and runs through the first day of Lent. About 20 days into Lent, there's a mini-Carnival called Mi-carême. This one-day hiatus from what is traditionally 40 days of abstinence brings parties, dances, and the like; after it, however, everyone returns to the somber (and often sober) business of penance until Easter. Early August sees the Tour des Yoles Rondes point-to-point yawl race. In early December the island hosts the Caribbean's premier jazz festival, Jazz à la Martinique. In addition to showcasing the best musical talent of the islands, it has attracted such top American performers as Branford Marsalis.

HOLIDAYS

Public holidays are: New Year's Day, Ash Wednesday (6 weeks before Easter), Good Friday (Friday before Easter), Easter Monday (day after Easter), Labor Day (May 1), Bastille Day (July 14), Assumption Day (August 15), All Saints' Day (Nov. 1), Armistice Day (Nov. 11), and Christmas.

LANGUAGE

Many Martinicans speak Creole, a mixture of Spanish, French, and some African languages, all pronounced with a Caribbean accent. Even if you do speak fluent French, you may have a problem understanding the accent. Try *sa ou fe* for "hello" in creole. In major tourist areas you'll find someone who speaks English, but using a few French words—even if it's only to say, *"Parlez-vous anglais?"*—will be appreciated. Most menus are written in French. But rest assured that these people are typically courteous and will work with you on your French—or lack thereof.

MAIL AND SHIPPING

Airmail letters to the U.S. and Canada cost €.72 for up to 20 grams; postcards, about €.56. For Great Britain the costs are €.67 and €.50, respectively. Stamps may be purchased from post offices, café-tabacs, and hotel newsstands. Letters to Martinique should include the name of the business, street (if available), town, postal code, the island, and French West Indies. Be forewarned, however, that mail is extremely slow both coming and going.

MONEY MATTERS

Prices quoted here are in U.S. dollars, unless otherwise indicated.

ATMS

There are ATMs at the airport and at branches of the Crédit Agricole Bank, which is on the Cirrus system and also accepts Visa and MasterCard. If the change bureau at the airport is closed when you arrive, and you need Euros for a taxi, you can use the ATM machine and put in your American debit or credit card to withdraw and, *voila,* out will come euros.

CREDIT CARDS

Major credit cards are accepted in hotels and restaurants in Fort-de-France and the Pointe du Bout areas, and you will generally get a favorable exchange rate on purchases; few establishments in the countryside accept them. Many establishments are no longer accepting American Express because its fees are too high, so be certain not to leave home without it, but carry a second or third card, a MasterCard or Visa. There's generally a 20% discount on luxury items paid for with traveler's checks or with certain credit cards.

CURRENCY

The French franc is no longer. It has been replaced by the Euro, for which at press time the exchange is €1.12 to US$1. U.S. dollars are accepted in some hotels, but it's better to convert your money. Banks give a more favorable rate than hotels. A currency exchange service that also offers a favorable rate is Change Caraïbes. If you are cashing less than a $100, it is usually better to go to the exchange or to use your ATM card.

➤ CONTACTS: **Change Caraïbes** (✉ Lamentin International Airport, Lamentin, ☎ 0596/42–17–11; ✉ Rue Ernest Deproge, Fort-de-France, across from tourist office, ☎ 0596/60–28–40).

PASSPORTS AND VISAS

All visitors must have a valid passport and a return or ongoing ticket.

SAFETY

Exercise the same safety precautions you would in any large city. Don't leave jewelry or money unattended on the beach or in your car. Even a designer sunglass case on the dashboard might be the catalyst for a shattered window. Except for the area around Cap Chevalier and the Caravelle Peninsula, the Atlantic waters are rough and should be avoided by all but expert swimmers.

SIGHTSEEING TOURS

The terrific staff at the tourist office can help you arrange a personalized island tour with an English-speaking driver. There are set rates for certain tours, and if you share the ride with others, the per-person price will be whittled down.

Madinina Tours offers half- and full-day jaunts (lunch included). Boat tours are also available, as are air excursions to the Grenadines and St. Lucia. Madinina has tour desks in most of the major hotels. Parc Naturel Régional de la Martinique organizes inexpensive guided hiking tours. Descriptive folders are available at the tourist office.

The semi-submersible *Aquascape* conducts 45- to 60-minute excursions so that riders can see the flora and fauna beneath the sea.
➤ CONTACTS: **Aquascope** (✉ Pointe du Bout Marina, ☎ 0596/68–36–09; ✉ Ste-Anne, ☎ 0596/74–87–41). **Madinina Tours** (✉ 111–113 rue Ernest Deproge, Fort-de-France, ☎ 0596/70–65–25). **Parc Naturel Régional de la Martinique** (✉ 9 bd. Général de Gaulle, Fort-de-France, ☎ 0596/73–19–30).

TAXES AND SERVICE CHARGES

HOTEL TAX

A resort tax varies from city to city. Each has its own tax, with most between €.56 and €1.28 per person per day; the maximum is €2.24.

SERVICE CHARGES

Rates quoted by hotels usually include a 10% service charge; some hotels add 10% to your bill.

TAXIS

Taxis are expensive. From the airport to Fort-de-France is about €15.60; from the airport to Pointe du Bout, about €35.84, and to Trois Ilets, €31.36. A 40% surcharge is levied between 8 PM and 6 AM and on Sunday. This means that if you arrive at night, depending on where your hotel is, it may be cheaper (although not safer) to rent a car from the airport and keep it for 24 hours than to take a taxi to your hotel.
➤ CONTACTS: **Regular taxis** (☎ 0596/63–63–62 or 0596/63–10–10). **M. Morital Mercedes taxis** (☎ 0596/45–69–07; 0696/45–69–07 mobile).

TELEPHONES

There are no coin-operated phone booths. Public phones now use a *télécarte,* which you can buy at post offices, *café-tabacs,* hotels, and at *bureaux de change.*

COUNTRY AND AREA CODES

The telephone system in Martinique changed in 2001. To call Martinique from the United States, dial 011 + 596 + 596 + the local six-digit number (you must dial 596 *twice*). If calling from Guadeloupe you should dial the 0 then 596 and the six digits.

To call the United States from Martinique, dial 00 + 1, the area code, and the local number. You can now make collect calls to the states through the Bell operator; you can get the ATT or MCI operators from special service phones at the cruise ports and in town. These phones are blue, and one such is at the Super Sumo snack bar, on rue de la Liberté, near the library. To call Great Britain from Martinique, dial 00 + 44, the area code (without the first zero), and the number.
➤ CONTACTS: **AT&T** (☎ 0–800/99–00–11). **Bell** (☎ 0–800/99–00–16). **MCI** (☎ 0–800/99–00–19).

INTERNET SERVICE
In Fort-de-France there is the Cyber Café Blénac open Monday–Friday 10–1 and Saturday 6 PM–1 AM, and there is also Internet service at the main post office.
➤ CONTACTS: **Cyber Café Blénac** (✉ Rue Blénac, Fort-de-France, ☎ 0596/70–31–62).

LOCAL CALLS
Again, this is a new inconvenience beginning in 2001. To place a local or inter-island call you have to dial all 9 numbers, beginning with 596 and then the six-digit number.

TIPPING

All restaurants include a 15% service charge in their menu prices. You can always add to this if you feel that service was particularly good.

VISITOR INFORMATION

➤ BEFORE YOU LEAVE: **Martinique Promotion Bureau** (✉ 444 Madison Ave., New York, NY 10022, ☎ 800/391–4909; ✉ 9454 Wilshire Blvd., Beverly Hills, CA 90212, ☎ 310/271–6665; ✉ 676 N. Michigan Ave., Chicago, IL 60611, ☎ 312/751–7800; ✉ 1981 McGill College Ave., Suite 490, Montréal, Québec H3A 2W9, Canada, ☎ 514/288–4264; ✉ 1 Dundas St. W, Suite 2405, Toronto, Ontario M5G 1Z3, Canada, ☎ 416/593–4723 or 800/361–9099; ✉ 178 Piccadilly, London W1V 0AL, U.K., ☎ 0181/124–4123; WEB www.martinique.org).
➤ IN MARTINIQUE: **Martinique Tourist Office** (✉ Bd. Alfassa, Fort-de-France, ☎ 0596/63–79–60, FAX 0596/73–66–93).

16 PUERTO RICO

Updated by
Isabel
Abislaimán,
Cristina
Córdova
Suárez, Mary
Dempsey,
Delinda Karle,
John Marino,
Caryn Nesmith

The pigeons have made Old San Juan their own. They flutter through plazas, rushing for scraps dropped by office workers lunching on the run. Old men sit on shaded benches, enveloped by the scent of roasting coffee from a nearby kiosk, talking quietly about long lives, and holding crumbling paper bags of stale bread. The birds dance for that bread, their gray wings buffing arms and shoulders. It's an ancient, symbiotic moment—a gentle touch for morsels of food.

Few Caribbean cities are as steeped in Spanish tradition as Puerto Rico's Old San Juan. Originally built as a fortress, the old city's myriad attractions include restored 16th-century buildings and 200-year-old houses with balustraded balconies of filigreed wrought iron that overlook narrow cobblestone streets. Spanish traditions are also apparent in the countryside—from the festivals celebrated in honor of small-town patron saints to the *paradores*, inexpensive but accommodating inns whose concept originated in Spain.

Puerto Rico, 110 mi (177 km) long and 35 mi (56 km) wide, was populated by several tribes of Indians (primarily the Taíno) when Columbus landed during his second voyage in 1493. In 1508 Juan Ponce de León, the frustrated seeker of the Fountain of Youth, established a settlement on the island and became its first governor; in 1521 he founded what would become known as Old San Juan. For three centuries the French, Dutch, and English tried unsuccessfully to wrest the island from Spain. In 1897 Spain granted the island dominion status and a year later—as a result of the Spanish-American War—Spain ceded the island to the United States. In 1917 Puerto Ricans became U.S. citizens, and in 1952 Puerto Rico became a semiautonomous commonwealth.

The years since have brought several referenda to determine whether the island should remain a commonwealth, become a state, or gain independence. As recently as 1998, statehood received 47% of the vote. With such a narrow majority of voters choosing to remain a commonwealth, statehood advocates contend the tide is turning in their favor. Or perhaps not. It may be true that all the latest American TV programs are broadcast here, that *el béisbol* (baseball) is a major pastime, that San Juan has the trappings of any American city, and that many islanders have family stateside. But life *en la isla* (on the island) is far more traditional. A strong Latin sense of community and family prevails, and *puertorriqueños* are fiercely proud of both their Spanish and African heritages.

Music is another source of Puerto Rican pride, and increasingly it seems that everyone wants to live *la vida loca* espoused by Puerto Rican pop star Ricky Martin. The brash Latin sound is best characterized by the music–dance form salsa, which shares not only its name with the Spanish word for "sauce" but also has a zesty, hot flavor. This fusion of West African percussion, jazz (especially swing and big band) and other Latin beats (mambo, merengue, flamenco, cha-cha, rumba) is sexy and primal. Dancing to it is a chance to let go of inhibitions.

Moving to the beat of salsa isn't your only nightlife option here. In San Juan's sophisticated Condado and Isla Verde areas you'll find flashy cabaret shows and casinos. By day you can step into the Old World—in Old San Juan, in a quiet colonial town, or on a coffee plantation. If you're the athletic type, you'll appreciate the island's many acres of golf courses, its abundant tennis courts, and its hundreds of beaches that offer every imaginable water sport. In the extraordinary 28,000-acre Caribbean National Forest (known as El Yunque) you'll find 100-ft-high trees and dramatic mountain ranges. If all this isn't enough, you can head to the outlying islets of Culebra and Vieques where the snorkeling and scuba diving are fine.

Lodging

San Juan's high-rise beachfront hotels cater primarily to the cruise-ship and casino crowd, though several target business travelers. Outside San Juan, particularly on the east coast, you'll find self-contained luxury resorts that cover hundreds of acres. In the west, southwest, and south—as well as on the islands of Vieques and Culebra—smaller inns, villas, and condominiums for short-term rentals are the norm. Also look into government-sponsored paradores. Some of these are rural inns, some offer no-frills apartments, and some are large hotels, but all must meet certain standards, such as proximity to an attraction or beach.

Most hotels operate on the EP, although larger establishments often offer other meal plans or even all-inclusive packages. In the off-season, or summer months, rates at some hotels can drop 20% or more. For hotels outside of San Juan rates most often don't include airport transfers. Be sure to ask when you book.

For information on the paradores, contact the **Puerto Rico Tourism Company** (⊠ Box 902-3960, Old San Juan Station, San Juan 00902-3960, ☎ 787/721–2400, WEB www.gotopuertorico.com). **Small Inns of Puerto Rico** (⊠ 954 Av. Ponce de León, Suite 702, 00907, ☎ 787/725–2901, FAX 787/725–2913), a branch of the Puerto Rico Hotel and Tourism Association, is a marketing arm for some 25 small hotels island-wide.

For condos or villas on Vieques, contact **Connections** (⊠ Box 358, Esperanza, Vieques 00765, ☎ 787/741–0023). **Island West Properties & Beach Rentals** (⊠ Rte. 413, Km 1.3, Rincón [Box 700, 00677], ☎ 787/823–2323, FAX 787/823–3254) can you help you rent condos in Rincón by the week or the month. **Puerto Rico Vacation Apartments** (⊠ Marbella del Caribe Oeste S-5, Isla Verde, San Juan 00979, ☎ 787/727–1591 or 800/266–3639, FAX 787/268–3604) represents some 200 condo properties in San Juan's Condado and Isla Verde areas.

CATEGORY	COST EP/CP*	COST A.I.**
$$$$	over $350	over $375
$$$	$250–$350	$275–$375
$$	$150–$250	$175–$275
$	under $150	under $175

*EP/CP prices are per night for a standard double room in high season, excluding taxes, service charges, and meal plans**A.I. (all-inclusive) prices are *per person, per night based on double-occupancy during high season, excluding taxes and service charges*

Old San Juan

$$$–$$$$ ⊞ **El Convento Hotel.** Once a Carmelite convent, this 350-year-old
★ building is a prime example of the right way to blend Old World gentility with modern luxury. Much of the original architecture is intact, including a colonial interior courtyard. Rooms have a Spanish-deco look, with dark woods, wrought-iron lamps, and ornate furniture. Complimentary wine and hors d'oeuvres are served before dinner, and there's an honor bar that's open until 4 AM. The courtyard's Café de Nispero, street-side Café Bohemio, and the park-front tables of Agave Blue are among the dining choices. *100 Calle Cristo, Old San Juan, (Box 1048, 00902),* ☎ *787/723–9020 or 800/468–2779,* FAX *787/721–2877,* WEB *www.elconvento.com. 54 rooms, 4 suites. 4 restaurants, in-room safes, pool, gym, 2 bars, library, shops, meeting room, parking (fee). AE, D, DC, MC, V. CP.*

$$$ ⊞ **Wyndham Old San Juan Hotel & Casino.** The gleaming Wyndham blends classic Spanish colonial lines with a modern, triangular shape that subtly echoes the cruise ships docked nearby. The lobby, adjacent to the casino, shines with multihue tiles and mahogany. Each standard room—with honey-color rugs, floral prints, and light woods—has a two-line phone, a coffeemaker, and a hair dryer. Spacious suites also have sitting rooms and extra TVs. On the ninth floor you'll find a small patio pool and whirlpool bath; the seventh-floor concierge level provides hassle-free check-ins, Continental breakfasts, and evening hors d'oeuvres. ✉ *100 Calle Brumbaugh, Old San Juan 00901,* ☎ *787/721–5100 or 800/996–3426,* FAX *787/721–1111,* WEB *www.wyndham.com. 185 rooms, 55 suites. Restaurant, some minibars, cable TV, pool, gym, hot tub, massage, 2 bars, casino, concierge floor, business services, meeting rooms, parking (fee). AE, D, DC, MC, V. CP, EP.*

$–$$$ ⊞ **Gallery Inn.** Jan D'Esopo and Manuco Gandia transformed this rambling colonial house into an inn that's full of comforts and quirky details: winding, uneven stairs; a music room with a Steinway grand piano; courtyard gardens, where Jan's pet macaws and cockatoos hang out. Each room has a look all its own; several have whirlpool baths. From the rooftop deck there's a spectacular view of the forts and the Atlantic. The first-floor Galería San Juan displays artwork by Jan and others. There's no restaurant, but meals for groups can be prepared upon request. ✉ *204–206 Calle Norzagaray, Old San Juan 00901,* ☎ *787/722–1808,* FAX *787/724–7360,* WEB *www.thegalleryinn.com. 13 rooms, 10 suites. Dining room, some in-room hot tubs, piano; no room TVs. AE, DC, MC, V. CP.*

San Juan

$$$$ ⊞ **Ritz-Carlton San Juan Hotel, Spa & Casino.** The Ritz's signature el-
★ egance won't undermine the feeling that this is a true beach getaway. The hotel's sandy stretch is lovely, as is the free-form pool, which is surrounded by a garden overlooking the ocean. Works by local artists adorn the lobby lounge and the hallways leading to the well-equipped business center. A full-service spa begs to pamper you with aloe body wraps and *parcha* (passion-fruit juice) massages. Though most room windows are sealed shut to muffle airport noise, many suites open onto terraces. ✉ *Av. Las Gobernadores (Rte. 187), Isla Verde 00979,* ☎ *787/253–1700 or 800/241–3333,* FAX *787/253–0700,* WEB *www.ritzcarlton. com. 403 rooms, 11 suites. 3 restaurants, in-room data ports, cable TV, 2 tennis courts, pool, hair salon, health club, hot tub, massage, spa, beach, 3 bars, casino, nightclub, concierge floor, business services, meeting rooms, no-smoking floor. AE, D, DC, MC, V. EP.*

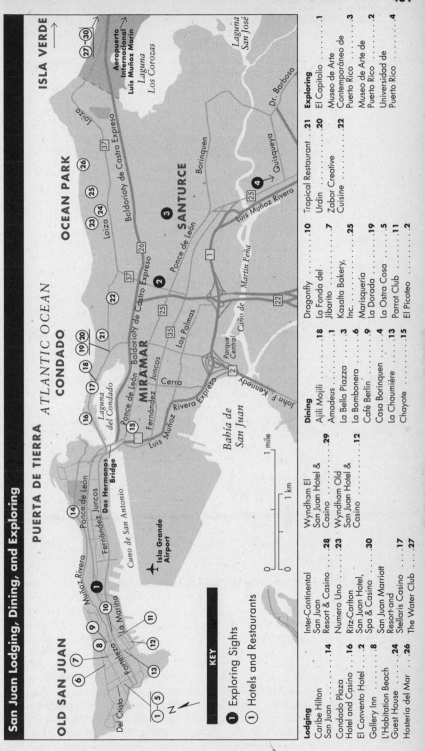

$$$$ ⊡ **The Water Club.** Every inch of this boutique hotel will soothe you. Aromatherapy scents waft through corridors, candles light your way, and water runs inside the glass walls of elevators that glow with blue neon. They seem the proper ride for trips to the rooftop pool or to the rooms, all of which have ocean views and such contemporary amenities as CD players. Four suites are equipped with telescopes for stargazing or people-watching along Isla Verde beach. The Tangerine Restaurant is sensuous; and water is again a literal and a decorative element in the lobby's Liquid lounge and the rooftop's Wet bar. ⊠ *2 Tartak St., Isla Verde, 00979,* ☎ *787/728–3666 or 888/265–6699,* FAX *787/728–3610,* WEB *www.waterclubsanjuan.com. 84 rooms. Restaurant, in-room data ports, cable TV, pool, gym, hot tub, massage, beach, 2 bars, Internet, parking (fee). AE, D, DC, MC, V. EP.*

$$$$ ⊡ **Wyndham El San Juan Hotel & Casino.** An immense antique chan-
★   delier illuminates the hand-carved mahogany paneling, Italian rose marble, and 250-year-old French tapestries in the huge lobby of this resort on Isla Verde beach. You'll be hard pressed to decide whether you want a main tower suite with a whirlpool bath and a wet bar; a garden room with a whirlpool bath and a patio; or a casita with a sunken Roman bath. All guest quarters have such amenities as walk-in closets, irons, and CD players. Relax at the lobby's Cigar Bar or take dinner at the Ranch, a rooftop country-western bar and grill. ⊠ *6063 Av. Isla Verde, Isla Verde 00902,* ☎ *787/791–1000, 800/468–2818, or 800/996–3426,* FAX *787/791–0390,* WEB *www.wyndham.com. 332 rooms, 57 suites. 8 restaurants, in-room data ports, in-room VCRs, 3 tennis courts, 2 pools, wading pool, health club, 5 hot tubs, beach, 14 bars, casino, nightclub, shops, children's programs, business services, no-smoking rooms. AE, DC, MC, V. EP, MAP.*

$$$–$$$$ ⊡ **Caribe Hilton San Juan.** In time for the new millennium, many amenities at the Caribe Hilton were refreshed so that you would be, too. The beach, the only private one in San Juan, has been expanded. The open-air lobby's sunken bar looks out over the gentle cascades of a trilevel pool, which is now adjacent to a wading pool and an area with whirlpool tubs. Rooms have ocean or lagoon views, and those on the executive floor include such services as private check-in and check-out and free Continental breakfasts and evening cocktails. Local businesspeople often frequent the on-site Morton's of Chicago restaurant. ⊠ *Calle Los Rosales, San Gerónimo Grounds, Puerta de Tierra, 00901,* ☎ *787/721–0303 or 800/468–8585,* FAX *787/725–8849,* WEB *www.caribehilton.com. 602 rooms, 44 suites. 3 restaurants, 3 tennis courts, pool, wading pool, hot tub, spa, beach, 2 bars, shops, children's programs, parking (fee). AE, D, DC, MC, V. CP, EP, MAP.*

$$$–$$$$ ⊡ **Inter-Continental San Juan Resort & Casino.** The spacious rooms in this 16-story hotel have pleasant views of the ocean, the San José Lagoon, or the city; suites overlook the pool. The jangling casino is just off the lobby, and on-site restaurants include the poolside Restaurant Ciao Mediterraneo; Ruth's Chris Steak House; and the Grand Market Café, with deli favorites you can eat on the spot or have packed up for a picnic on the beach. ⊠ *187 Av. Isla Verde, Isla Verde 00914,* ☎ *787/791–6100 or 800/443–2009,* FAX *787/253–2510,* WEB *www.intercontinental.com. 381 rooms, 19 suites. 6 restaurants, in-room safes, pool, gym, hot tub, spa, beach, boating, 3 bars, casino, nightclub, shops, children's programs, concierge floor, business services, meeting rooms, no-smoking rooms. AE, D, MC, V. EP.*

$$$–$$$$ ⊡ **San Juan Marriott Resort and Stellaris Casino.** The red neon sign atop the Marriott seems like a beacon, beckoning you to beautiful Condado beach. The hotel's soundproofed rooms have soothing pastel carpets, floral spreads, and attractive tropical art; balconies overlook the ocean, the pool, or both. Restaurants include the Tuscany, for northern Ital-

ian cuisine, and the casual La Vista, which is open 24 hours. On week-ends, there's live entertainment in the enormous lobby, which, combined with the ringing of slot machines from the adjoining casino, makes the area noisy. A large pool area and a gorgeous beach are right outside. ✉ *1309 Av. Ashford, Condado 00907,* ☎ *787/722–7000 or 800/228–9290,* FAX *787/722–6800,* WEB *www.marriott.com. 512 rooms, 17 suites. 3 restaurants, 2 tennis courts, pool, hair salon, health club, hot tub, beach, 2 lounges, casino, children's programs, business services, meeting rooms, no-smoking rooms. AE, D, DC, MC, V. EP, FAP, MAP.*

$$–$$$$ 🏨 **Condado Plaza Hotel and Casino.** The Atlantic and the Laguna del Condado border this high-rise, whose two wings—fittingly named Ocean and Lagoon—are connected by an enclosed, elevated walkway. Standard rooms have walk-in closets and dressing areas. There's a variety of suites, including those with oversize hot tubs. A stay on the Plaza Club floor entitles you to 24-hour concierge service, use of a private lounge, and complimentary Continental breakfasts and refreshments all day. Find your own place in the sun on the beach or beside one of four pools. Dining options include the poolside Tony Roma's as well as Max's Grill, which is open 24 hours. ✉ *999 Av. Ashford, Condado 00902,* ☎ *787/721–1000 or 800/624–0420,* FAX *787/722–7955,* WEB *www. condadoplaza.com. 570 rooms, 62 suites. 7 restaurants, some in-room hot tubs, 2 tennis courts, 3 pools, wading pool, health club, 3 hot tubs, beach, dock, boating, 2 bars, 2 lounges, casino, children's programs, concierge floor, business services. AE, D, DC, MC, V. CP, EP, MAP.*

$–$$ 🏨 **Numero Uno.** Former New Yorker Esther Feliciano bought this three-story, red-roof guest house, spruced it up, and made it a very pleasant place to stay. It's in a quiet residential area, and its rooms are simple and clean; three have ocean views. Two apartments come with kitchenettes. A walled-in patio provides privacy for sunning or hanging out by the small pool, the bar, and Pamela's restaurant. Beyond the wall, the wide, sandy beach beckons; if you're a guest here you're provided with beach chairs and towels. ✉ *1 Calle Santa Ana, Ocean Park 00911,* ☎ *787/726–5010,* FAX *787/727–5482. 11 rooms, 2 apartments. Restaurant, fans, pool, beach, bar. AE, MC, V. CP.*

$ 🏨 **L'Habitation Beach Guest House.** Alain Tasca—who is from Paris by way of Guadeloupe and Key West—has created a very relaxed and oh-so French ambience at this guest house, which has a primarily gay clientele. Rooms are simple and comfortable; numbers 8 and 9 are the largest and have ocean views. A combined bar-snack bar sits in the corner of a palm-shaded patio between the guest house and the sands of Ocean Park. Beach chairs and towels are provided: get your gear together before having one of Alain's margaritas, which will knock your sandals off. ✉ *1957 Calle Italia, Ocean Park 00911,* ☎ *787/727–2499,* FAX *787/727–2599. 10 rooms. Fans, beach, bar, free parking. AE, D, MC, V. CP.*

$ 🏨 **Hosteria del Mar.** Condado's high-rises are far to the west of this small,
★ white inn on the beach in Ocean Park. Rooms are attractive and simple, with tropical prints and rattan furniture. Many rooms have ocean views, and four apartments have kitchenettes. The staff is courteous and helpful, and the ground-floor restaurant, which serves many vegetarian dishes as well as seafood and steaks, faces the trade winds and has fabulous beach views. ✉ *1 Calle Tapia, Ocean Park 00911,* ☎ *787/727–3302 or 800/742–4276,* FAX *787/268–0772,* WEB *www.prhtasmallhotels. com. 8 rooms, 4 apartments, 1 suite. Restaurant, some kitchenettes, beach, free parking. AE, D, DC, MC, V. EP.*

Eastern Puerto Rico

$$$–$$$$ 🏨 **Wyndham El Conquistador Resort and Country Club.** What many
★ consider Puerto Rico's loveliest resort is on a bluff above the ocean. The colossal hotel and the villas in Las Casitas Village and Las Olas

Village have Moorish and Spanish colonial architectural details. Cobblestone streets and fountain-filled plazas enhance the feeling that this place is more like a community than a complex. The resort's beach is on Palomino Island just offshore; a free shuttle boat takes you there and back. The staff prides itself on its attentive service. If the place seems familiar, it may be because the James Bond movie *Goldfinger* was filmed here. ✉ *1000 Av. El Conquistador, Fajardo (Box 70001, 00738),* ☎ *787/863–1000, 800/996–3426, or 800/468–5228,* ℻ *787/253–0178,* WEB *www.wyndham.com. 750 rooms, 16 suites. 11 restaurants, cable TV with movies and video games, minibars, 18-hole golf course, 8 tennis courts, 5 pools, gym, spa, beach, dive shop, snorkeling, windsurfing, boating, jet skiing, marina, 4 bars, casino, nightclub, shop, children's programs, meeting rooms, airport shuttle. AE, MC, V. FAP.*

$$–$$$$ 🏨 **Westin Río Mar Beach Resort.** Golf, biking, tennis, and playing in the waters off a mile-long beach are just some of the attractions at this top-notch resort. Every room in the seven-story hotel, which anchors the complex, has a balcony that faces the sea or the golf courses and mountains. There are also one- and two-bedroom villas for guests who want more space and privacy. Tropical color schemes are used throughout as are such luxurious touches as natural woods, Italian tile, and marble accents. ✉ *6000 Río Mar Bul. (Rte. 968, Km 1.4), Río Mar (Box 2006, 00721),* ☎ *787/888–6000,* ℻ *787/888–6204,* WEB *www.westinriomar.com. 528 rooms, 72 suites. 7 restaurants, room service, in-room data ports, in-room safes, in-room VCRs, cable TV with movies and video games, 2 18-hole golf courses, 13 tennis courts, 3 pools, gym, spa, beach, dive shop, windsurfing, boating, fishing, bicycles, 4 lounges, casino, dance club, shop, children's programs, dry cleaning, laundry service, concierge, business services, meeting rooms, car rental, airport shuttle, no-smoking rooms. AE, MC, V. FAP.*

$$–$$$ 🏨 **Candelero Resort at Palmas del Mar.** Shuttle buses scoot you around, and parking attendants and other personnel are good about giving directions. You need such assistance: with 3,000 acres, the grounds are seemingly endless. Accommodations include a 100-room hotel with 110 villas. There are also 85 privately owned condos, a 106-unit time-share complex, myriad bars and restaurants, and a casino. The hotel's rooms and public spaces are open and airy; many have balconies. If you want more space, inquire about the villas, which can be rented by the day, the week, or longer. There's no shortage of activity, from water sports to tennis and golf. ✉ *Rte. 906 Humacao (Box 2020, 00792),* ☎ *787/852–6000,* ℻ *787/852–6320,* WEB *www.palmasdelmar.com. 100 rooms, 110 villas. 13 restaurants, room service, minibars, cable TV with movies, 2 18-hole golf courses, 20 tennis courts, pool, gym, beach, dive shop, dock, snorkeling, windsurfing, fishing, horseback riding, 15 bars, casino, shop, children's programs, airport shuttle. AE, MC, V. MAP.*

Vieques Island

$$–$$$ 🏨 **Inn on the Blue Horizon.** The island's most expensive hotel consists
★ of six villas and a main house near the sea on what used to be a plantation. You truly feel away from it all at this gorgeous 20-acre complex. None of the rooms has a phone, and even air-conditioning is rare (only two rooms have it), but with the breezy location you won't notice the absence. ✉ *Rte. 996, Km 4.2 (Box 1556, Esperanza, 00765),* ☎ *787/741–3318,* ℻ *787/741–0522,* WEB *www.innontheblushorizon.com. 9 rooms. Restaurant, fans, pool, massage, bicycles, bar, free parking; no air-conditioning in some rooms, no room TVs, no kids under 14. AE, MC, V. BP.*

$–$$ 🏨 **Hacienda Tamarindo.** Interior designer Linda Vail and her husband
★ Burr are the charming hosts at this hilltop guest house, which is named after the venerable tamarind tree that rises three stories in the lobby.

The panoramic views include grounds landscaped with coconut palms and mahogany trees as well as tropical flowers. Half the guest rooms—which have terra-cotta floors, light pastel color schemes, and antiques—are air-conditioned. The rest are cooled by overhead fans and trade winds. ⊠ *Rte. 996, Km 4.5 (Box 1569, Esperanza, 00765),* ☎ *787/741–8525,* FAX *787/741–3215,* WEB *www.enchanted-isle.com/ tamarindo. 16 rooms. Dining room, fans, pool; no kids under 15. AE, MC, V. BP.*

Southern Puerto Rico

$$$ ★ 🏨 **Hilton Ponce & Casino** Black-sand beaches border the south coast's biggest resort, a cream-and-turquoise complex on 80 acres 4 mi (6 km) outside of Ponce. Guest rooms have a tropical decor. The romantic, dark-paneled La Cava ($$–$$$) has a menu that blends different international cuisines—try the beef tenderloin with goose liver or the vegetable spring rolls. Near the lobby's spectacular waterfall is La Terraza ($$–$$$), a casual buffet serving breakfast and lunch. If the shopping arcade doesn't keep you busy, the many outdoor activities will. At this writing, plans for two golf courses were on the table. ⊠ *1150 Av. Caribe, La Guancha, Ponce (Box 7419, 00732),* ☎ *787/259–7676, 800/445– 8667, or 800/981–3232,* FAX *787/259–7674,* WEB *www.ponce-hilton.com. 148 rooms, 5 suites. 2 restaurants, in-room safes, minibars, cable TV with movies and video games, driving range, 4 tennis courts, pool, exercise equipment, hot tub, sauna, spa, beach, bicycles, basketball, Ping-Pong, volleyball, 3 bars, casino, dance club, video game room, shops, baby-sitting, children's programs, playground, business services, meeting rooms, parking (fee). AE, DC, MC, V. EP.*

$$ 🏨 **Copamarina Beach Resort.** To one side of the Copamarina's 16 acres of flowers and fruit trees is the Caribbean; to the other, is dry tropical forest. If the resort's beach is too crowded with other guests and their children, several equally beautiful stretches are minutes away. Rooms are basic but spacious; all have balconies or patios and at least partial ocean views. The red snapper is a must at the Coastal Cuisine restaurant ($$– $$$), but you'll need to rent a car for outings to other area eateries and nightspots. ⊠ *Rte. 333, Km 6.5, Guánica (Box 805, 00653),* ☎ *787/ 821–0505 or 800/468–4553,* FAX *787/821–0070,* WEB *www.copamarina. com. 106 rooms, 2 villas. Restaurant, refrigerators, cable TV, 2 tennis courts, 2 pools, 2 wading pools, gym, 2 hot tubs, massage, spa, beach, dive shop, snorkeling, windsurfing, boating, volleyball, bar, playground, meeting rooms. AE, DC, MC, V. CP, MAP, EP.*

$ 🏨 **Hotel Meliá.** In the heart of Ponce, near Plaza las Delicias, this family-owned hotel is a good, low-key base for exploring downtown's landmark buildings and museums. The lobby, with its high ceilings and blue-and-beige tile floors, is well-worn but charming. Rooms have a somewhat dated European feel. Breakfast is served on the rooftop terrace, which overlooks the city and mountains. Six suites have balconies with terrific views of Ponce's historic district. ⊠ *75 Calle Cristina, Ponce Centro, Ponce (Box 1431, 00733),* ☎ *787/842–0260 or 800/742–4276,* FAX *787/841–3602,* WEB *http://home.coqui.net/melia. 75 rooms. Restaurant, cable TV, bar, parking (fee). AE, MC, V. CP.*

$ ★ 🏨 **Parador Baños de Coamo.** On weekends musicians play in the interior patio of this rustic country inn, portions of which date from the 19th century. Rooms—in four modern two-story buildings—open onto latticed wooden verandas and have a cozy, lodgelike feel. Thermal water flows from sulfur springs into a swimming pool a few steps away from a cool-water pool, where you can still see walls dating from 1843. In the dining room ($–$$), portions of delicious *churrasco* (barbecued meats) with rice and beans are generous. ⊠ *Rte. 546, Km 1, Coamo (Box 540, 99769),* ☎ *787/825–2186 or 787/825–2239,* FAX *787/*

Pta.
Agujereada

⑳ Isabela

㉑ Hatillo

Puerto de
Tortuguero

Pta.
Borinquén

Bahía de
Aguadilla

Quebradillas Camuy

Arecibo

Vega
Baja

Playa Crashboat

Aguadilla

Bosque
Estatal
Guajataca

Manati

Maricao

Pta.
Gorda

Aguada

Rincón

San
Sebastián

129

⑭

⑰

22

2

⑱ ⑲ ⑬

⑮ ⑰

115

111

⑮

Bahía de
Añasco

⑯

Utuado

⑫

Jayuya

149

⑳

㉒

㉓

Mayagüez

⑫

102

105

Maricao

Bosque
Estatal
Maricao

Adjuntas

Bosque
Estatal
Toro Negro

**Cabo Rojo
Beaches**

⑭

Cabo
Rojo

2

102

⑪

⑬ San
Germán

Coamo

⑧

⑩

Juana Díaz

14

**Balneario
Boquerón**

101

La
Parguera

116

Yáuco

⑨

Guayanilla

52

⑧

Boquerón

Guánica

⑫

⑨

Santa
Isabel

Ponce

Bahía
Salinas

Bahía
Sucia

Bahía
Fosforescente

**Playa
Santa**

Ensenada
Las Pardas

**Playa
Ballena**

⑨ - ⑪

Bahía
de Rincón

Pta.
Jagüey

Caja de
Muertos

N

Caribbean Sea

0   20 miles
0   30 km

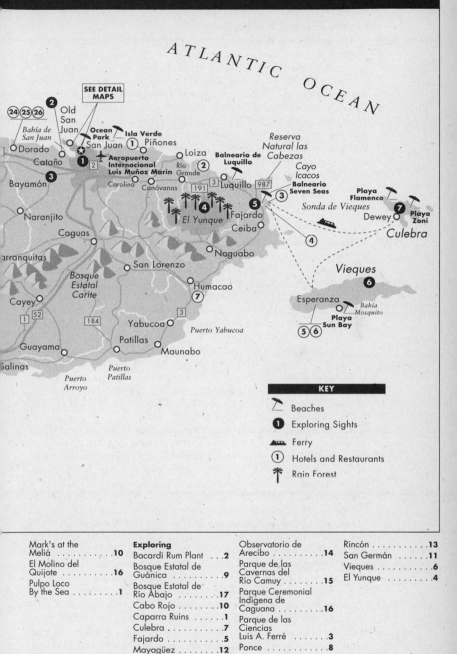

ATLANTIC OCEAN

SEE DETAIL MAPS

㉔㉕㉖ Old San Juan
②
Bahía de San Juan
◯ Dorado
Cataño
③
Bayamón
◯ Naranjito
Caguas
◯ arranquitas
★
Ocean Park Isla Verde
San Juan ① Piñones
①
Aeropuerto Internacional Luis Muñoz Marin
2
Carolina   Canóvanas
◯ Loíza
Río Grande
②
Balneario de Luquillo
3
191   Luquillo 987
El Yunque ④
Fajardo
Ceiba
⑤
③
Reserva Natural las Cabezas
Cayo Icacos
Balneario Seven Seas
Sonda de Vieques
Dewey
Playa Flamenco
⑦
Playa Zoni
Culebra
④
Bosque Estatal Carite
◯ San Lorenzo
◯ Naguabo
Cayey ◯
1 52
184
Yabucoa
3
Humacao
⑦
Patillas
◯ Maunabo
Guayama
alinas
Puerto Yabucoa
Puerto Arroyo
Puerto Patillas
Vieques
⑥
Esperanza
Bahía Mosquito
Playa Sun Bay
⑤⑥

KEY

⤵ Beaches

❶ Exploring Sights

🚢 Ferry

① Hotels and Restaurants

🌴 Rain Forest

825–4739. 48 rooms. Restaurant, cable TV, 2 pools, bar, video game room. AE, D, MC, V. EP.

Northwestern Puerto Rico

$$$$ **★**   ⊞ **Horned Dorset Primavera.** Each room at this secluded hotel is uniquely furnished with antiques, including four-poster beds. Some rooms have private plunge pools. There are no radios, TVs, or phones in the rooms, and no facilities for children. The main house has elegant West Indian plantation-style furniture and glistening chandeliers. The newer Casa Escondida is designed to resemble a turn-of-the-20th-century Puerto Rican hacienda. Dinner has tropical touches and a heavy Cordon Bleu influence. The menu changes daily but might include crab salad with cilantro and mango, and roasted duck with black cherries. Dress is formal by island standards—no shorts allowed—and reservations are required. Breakfast and lunch are more casual. ⊠ *Rte. 429, Km 3, Rincón (Box 1132, 00677),* ☎ *787/823–4030, 787/823–4050, or 800/ 633–1857,* ℻ *787/725–6068,* ⓦⓔⓑ *www.horneddorset.com. 31 rooms. Restaurant, fans, 2 pools, gym, beach, croquet, library; no room phones, no TVs. AE, MC, V. CP, EP, MAP.*

$$$$ ⊞ **Hyatt Dorado Beach Resort & Country Club.** Sprawling over 1,000 acres on a secluded white-sand beach, the Hyatt Dorado is a former plantation. Most rooms have four-poster beds, patios or balconies, and marble baths. For the requisite romantic dinner, ask for a table on the balcony at Su Casa ($$$–$$$$), one of the resort's five restaurants. Its creative cuisine includes such dishes as pork chops with *adobe* (a garlic-oregano marinade) and mahimahi in spicy corn sauce served with corn fritters. Free trolleys take you to the Dorado's sister property, the Regency Cerromar Beach, where you have access to all the facilities including the casino. ⊠ *Rte. 693, Km 10.8, Dorado, 00646,* ☎ *787/796–1234 or 800/233–1234,* ℻ *787/796–2022,* ⓦⓔⓑ *www.doradobeach.hyatt.com. 298 rooms. 5 restaurants, 2 18-hole golf courses, 7 tennis courts, 2 pools, spa, beach, bicycles, children's program. AE, D, DC, MC, V. EP, MAP (MAP compulsory Dec. 15–end of Feb.).*

$$$$ ⊞ **Hyatt Regency Cerromar Beach Resort & Casino.** Of the twin Hyatt resorts, this hotel is more lively, both night and day. The complex is very sports- and family-oriented and its famous river pool is one of the longest in the world, flowing some 1,776 ft under bridges and over waterfalls and waterslides. Most rooms have balconies with ocean views. The casino and Club Bacchus disco are centers of nightlife. At the Steak Co. ($$$–$$$$), try the pan-seared swordfish; the Zen Garden serves Japanese and Chinese cuisine and has a sushi bar. A trolley takes you next door to the Dorado Beach Resort. ⊠ *Rte. 693, Km 11.8, Dorado, 00646,* ☎ *787/796–1234 or 800/233–1234,* ℻ *787/796–4647,* ⓦⓔⓑ *www.cerromarbeach.hyatt.com. 506 rooms. 4 restaurants, 2 18-hole golf courses, 10 tennis courts, 3 pools, health club, spa, beach, bicycles, 6 bars, casino, children's program. AE, D, DC, MC, V. EP.*

$–$$ ⊞ **Lemontree Waterfront Cottages.** These large, sparkling-clean apartments sit right on the beach. Each unit is decorated with bright tropical colors and local artwork and has a deck with a wet bar and grill. Choose from one three-bedroom unit with two baths, one two-bedroom unit, two one-bedroom units, or two newer studios with kitchenettes. Maid service can be arranged. The beach here is small, but larger ones are nearby. ⊠ *Rte. 429, Km 4.1, Rincón (Box 200, 00677),* ☎ *787/823–6452,* ℻ *787/823–5821,* ⓦⓔⓑ *www.lemontreepr.com. 6 apartments. Cable TV, kitchenettes. AE, MC, V. EP.*

$–$$ ⊞ **Villas del Mar Hau.** The hub of the Villas del Mar Hau is a fanciful row of pastel one-, two-, and three bedroom cottages overlooking Montones Beach. They aren't luxurious, but if you're looking for comfort and seclusion in an unpretentious atmosphere, you'll have a hard time doing better. There are also 16 suites, some with kitchens. The popular restaurant, Olas y Arena ($–$$), is known for fish and shellfish; the paella is especially good. ⊠ *Rte. 4466, Km 8.3, Isabela (Box 510, 00662)*, ☎ *787/872–2045 or 787/872–2627*, ℻ *787/872–0273*, WEB *www.villahau.com. 40 rooms. Restaurant, fans, some kitchenettes, tennis court, pool, basketball, horseback riding, laundry facilities; no air-conditioning in some rooms, no TV in some rooms. AE, MC, V. Restaurant closed Mon. EP.*

$ ⊞ **Hotel La Casa Grande.** It's not hard to imagine Tarzan swinging in for dinner at this quaint inn. The main house contains a restaurant, bar, and reception area. The other five wooden buildings hold 20 guest rooms. There are no TVs, phones, or radios in the rooms, but a chorus of tiny tree frogs provides symphonies at night. Dining is on an outdoor patio at Jungle Jane's restaurant ($–$$); the menu features lemon-garlic chicken breast, and Puerto Rican specialties such as shrimp *asopao* (a soupy rice gumbo). ⊠ *Rte. 612, Km 0.3, Utuado (Box 1499, 00641)*, ☎ *787/894–3939 or 800/343–2272*, ℻ *787/894–3900*, WEB *www.hotelcasagrande.com. 20 rooms. Restaurant, fans, pool; no air-conditioning, no TVs. AE, MC, V. EP.*

$ ⊞ **Parador Hacienda Gripiñas.** Built on the grounds of a coffee planta-
★ tion, this elegant inn is surrounded by gardens and mountain peaks. Rooms have balconies overlooking lush scenery. Across from the house are a bar and a swimming pool filled with cool mountain water. One hiking trail near the property leads to Cerro de Punta, about a 2½-hour climb. The restaurant serves steaks, lobster, shrimp, and criollo fare such as chicken with rice and beans. For dessert, try the *tembleque*—a custard made from coconut milk and sugar. ⊠ *Rte. 527, Km 2.7, Jayuya (Box 387, 00664)*, ☎ *787/828–1717*, ℻ *787/828–1718*, WEB *www.haciendagripinas.com. 19 rooms. Restaurant, pool, hiking. AE, MC, V. MAP.*

Dining

In San Juan you'll find everything from Italian to Thai, as well as superb local eateries serving *comida criolla* (traditional Caribbean creole food). All of San Juan's large hotels have fine restaurants, but some of the city's best eateries are stand-alone, and smaller hotels also often present good options. There is also a mind-boggling array of U.S. chain restaurants. No matter your price range or taste, San Juan is a great place to eat.

Mesónes gastronómicos are restaurants recognized by the government for preserving culinary traditions. There are more than 40 island-wide. (Although there are fine restaurants in the system, the *mesón gastronómico* label is not an automatic symbol of quality.) Wherever you go, it's *always* good to make reservations in the busy season, mid-November–April, in restaurants where they are accepted.

Puerto Rican cooking uses a lot of local vegetables: plantains are cooked a hundred different ways—as *tostones* (fried green), *amarillos* (baked ripe), and chips. Rice and beans with tostones or amarillos are accompaniments to every dish. Locals cook white rice with *habichuelas* (red beans), *achiote* (annatto seeds), or saffron; brown rice with *gandules* (pigeon peas); and *morro* (black rice) with *frijoles negros* (black beans). Yams and other root vegetables, such as yucca and *yautía*, are served baked, fried, stuffed, boiled, and mashed. *Sofrito*—a garlic, onion, sweet pepper, coriander, oregano, and tomato puree—is used as a base for practically everything.

Beef, chicken, pork, and seafood are rubbed with *adobo*, a garlic-oregano marinade, before cooking. *Arroz con pollo* (chicken with rice), *sancocho* (beef or chicken and tuber soup), *asopao* (a soupy rice gumbo with chicken or seafood), and *encebollado* (steak smothered in onions) are all typical plates. Also look for fritters served along highways and beaches. You may find *empanadillas* (stuffed fried turnovers), *surrullitos* (cheese-stuffed corn sticks), *alcapurias* (stuffed green banana croquettes), and *bacalaitos* (codfish fritters). Caribbean lobster, available mainly at coastal restaurants, is sweeter and easier to eat than Maine lobster, and there is always plentiful fresh dolphinfish and red snapper. Conch is prepared in a chilled ceviche salad or stuffed with tomato sauce inside fritters.

Puerto Rican coffee is excellent black or cut *con leche* (with hot milk). The origin of the piña colada is attributed to numerous places, from the Caribe Hilton to a La Fortaleza Street bar. Puerto Rican rums range from light mixers to dark, aged liqueurs. Look for Bacardí, Don Q, Ron Rico, Palo Viejo, and Barrilito.

What to Wear

Dress codes vary greatly, though a restaurant's price category is a good indicator of its formality. For less expensive places, anything but beachwear is fine. Ritzier eateries will expect collared shirts for men (jacket and tie requirements are rare) and chic attire for women. When in doubt, do as the Puerto Ricans often do and dress up.

CATEGORY	COST*
$$$$	over $30
$$$	$20–$30
$$	$10–$20
$	under $10

per person for a main course at dinner

Old San Juan

CAFÉS

$–$$ ✕ **Café Berlin.** This casual café, bakery, and delicatessen overlooks the Plaza Colón. Tasty vegetarian fare prevails—try one of the creative salads—but nonvegetarian dishes are also available. The café's pastries, desserts, fresh juices, and Puerto Rican coffees are the perfect elixir after a day of touring Old San Juan. ✉ *407 Calle San Francisco,* ☎ *787/722–5205. AE, MC, V.*

$–$$ ✕ **La Bombonera.** Strong coffee and excellent pastries make this café, a landmark that was established in 1903, very popular in the morning—particularly on Sunday. All this despite the fact that the waiters are grumpy and give the appearance of having worked here since day one. It's open from 7:30 AM to early evening, and full breakfasts are served 'til 11 AM. ✉ *259 Calle San Francisco, Old San Juan,* ☎ *787/722–0658. AE, MC, V.*

CARIBBEAN

$$–$$$ ✕ **Casa Borinquen.** A portrait of independence leader Pedro Albizu Campos adorns the building's facade, a holdover from before restoration work, when a group of artists turned the crumbling walls into the "Museo sin Techo" ("Roofless Museum"). Today it's a bright, attractive restaurant serving radically delicious local cuisine. The vegetarian dishes are made with local produce, shrimp is served with *acerola* (a local fruit similar to a cherry but not as sweet) sauce and mashed casava, and pork loin comes with fresh corn relish. ✉ *109 Calle San Sebastián, Old San Juan,* ☎ *787/725–0888. AE, D, MC, V. Closed Mon.*

$–$$ ✕ **La Fonda del Jibarito.** Sanjuaneros have favored this casual, fam-
★   ily-run restaurant for years. The back porch is filled with plants, the dining room is filled with fanciful depictions of Calle Sol (the street outside), and the ever-present owner, Pedro J. Ruiz, is filled with the desire to ensure that everyone's happy. The conch ceviche and chicken

fricasse are among the specialties. ✉ *280 Calle Sol, Old San Juan,* ☎ *787/725–8375. Reservations not accepted. AE, MC, V.*

CONTEMPORARY

$$–$$$ ✕ **Amadeus.** A trendy crowd enjoys such nouvelle Caribbean appetizers as buffalo wings or plantain mousse with shrimp and entrées such as ravioli with a goat cheese-and-walnut sauce or Cajun-grilled mahimahi. The front dining room is attractive—whitewashed walls, dark wood, white tablecloths, ceiling fans—and an interior courtyard leads to a romantic back dining room with printed tablecloths, candles, and exposed brick. There's also a seating area on Plaza San José. ✉ *106 Calle San Sebastián, Old San Juan,* ☎ *787/722–8635. AE, MC, V. No lunch Mon.*

$$–$$$ ✕ **Parrot Club.** The cuisine is inventive, the decor is colorful, and the
★ staff is casual but efficient. Stop by the bar for the speciality passion-fruit drink before moving to the adjacent dining room or the back courtyard. The menu has contemporary variations of Cuban and Puerto Rican classics. You might start with mouthwatering crabcakes or tamarind-barbecued ribs, followed by blackened tuna in a dark rum sauce or churrasco with *chimichurri* (a green sauce made with herbs, garlic, and tomatoes). ✉ *363 Calle Fortaleza, Old San Juan,* ☎ *787/725–7370. Reservations not accepted. AE, DC, MC, V.*

$–$$$ ✕ **Dragonfly.** Don't leave town without eating here. With Chinese-red furnishings and a charming staff outfitted in kimonos and satin shirts, this hip little restaurant has the feel of an elegant opium den. Surely the frequent lines outside its door attest to the seductive power of chef Roberto Trevino's Latin-Asian cuisine. The *platos* (large appetizers) are meant to be shared and include pork-and-plantain dumplings with an orange dipping sauce; spicy, perfectly fried calimari; and Peking-duck nachos with wasabi sour cream. ✉ *364 Calle La Fortaleza, Old San Juan,* ☎ *787/977–3886. AE, MC, V. Reservations not accepted.*

ECLECTIC

$$ ✕ **La Ostra Cosa.** The menu here includes everything from oysters to burgers, but most people come for the large, succulent prawns, which are grilled and served with garlic butter. Opt for a seat in the back courtyard: with bougainvillea and moonlight, it's one of the city's prettiest alfresco dining spots. The gregarious owner, Alberto Nazario, brother of pop star Ednita Nazario, truly enjoys seeing his guests satisfied. ✉ *154 Calle Cristo, Old San Juan,* ☎ *787/722–2672. AE, MC, V.*

FRENCH

$$$–$$$$ ✕ **La Chaumière.** With black-and-white floor tiles, a beamed ceiling, and floral-print curtains, this two-story restaurant evokes rural France. It has been under the same management since 1969, and with all that experience the service is smooth. Daily specials augment a menu of stellar French classics, including onion soup, rack of lamb, scallops Provençale, and chateaubriand for two. ✉ *367 Calle Tetuan, Old San Juan,* ☎ *787/722–3330. AE, DC, MC, V. Closed Sun. No lunch.*

ITALIAN

$$–$$$ ✕ **La Bella Piazza.** The narrow dining room has Roman columns, gold-leaf flourishes, and arched doorways that lead to an interior terrace. You'll find such quintessentially Italian appetizers as calamari *in padella* (lightly breaded and sautéed in olive oil, parsley, and garlic) and such archetypal pasta dishes as fusilli *amatriciana* (in a crushed bacon, tomato, and red-pepper sauce). Main courses include *saltinbocca alla romana* (veal and prosciutto in a sage, white-wine, and butter sauce) and *medaglioni al Chianti* (beef medallions in a spicy Chianti sauce). ✉ *355 Calle San Francisco, Old San Juan,* ☎ *787/721–0396. AE, MC, V. Closed Wed.*

$–$$$ ✕ **El Picoteo.** Many patrons make a meal of the appetizers that dom-
★   inate the menu at this chic tapas bar. Entrées such as paella are also
        noteworthy. There's a long, lively bar inside; one dining area overlooks
        the hotel El Convento's courtyard, and the other takes in the action
        along Calle Cristo. Even if you have dinner plans elsewhere, consider
        stopping here for a cocktail or a nightcap. ⊠ *El Convento Hotel, 100
        Calle Cristo, Old San Juan,* ☎ *787/723–9621. AE, D, DC, MC, V.*

San Juan

$$ ✕ **Kasalta Bakery, Inc.** Make your selection from the display cases full
        of luscious pastries and other tempting treats. Walk up to the counter
        and order a sandwich (try the Cubano) or such items as the meltingly
        tender octopus salad and the savory *caldo gallego* (a soup of fresh veg-
        etables, sausage, and potatoes). Wash everything down with a cold drink
        or a café con leche that's guaranteed to be strong. ⊠ *1966 Calle
        McLeary, Ocean Park,* ☎ *787/727–7340. AE, MC, V.*

$$–$$$$ ✕ **Ajili Mojili.** The traditional Puerto Rican food is prepared with a flour-
★   ish and served in an attractive plantation-style setting. Sample the
         fried cheese and yautía dumplings with the house sauce, a tomato, herb,
         garlic, and shaved almond concoction. The *mofongo* (a mashed plan-
         tain casserole with seafood or meat), is wonderful, as is the plantain-
         crusted shrimp in a white-wine herb sauce. ⊠ *1052 Av. Ashford,
         Condado,* ☎ *787/725–9195. AE, DC, MC, V. No lunch Sat.*

$$–$$$ ✕ **Yerba Buena.** This "corner of South Beach in the Condado" serves
         Latin Caribbean food in contemporary trappings. The Cuban classic
         ropa vieja (meat cooked so slowly that it becomes tender shreds) comes
         in a stylish plantain nest. The shrimp has a coconut-and-ginger sauce,
         the halibut fillet one of mango and Grand Marnier. The restaurant claims
         to use the "original" recipe for its *mojito,* Cuba's tasty rum, lime, and
         mint drink. ⊠ *1350 Av. Ashford, Condado,* ☎ *787/721--5907. AE,
         MC, V. Closed Sun.*

$–$$$ ✕ **Tropical Restaurant.** For years, locals have favored this unpreten-
        tious Cuban restaurant for its reasonably priced, lovingly prepared Latin
        classics. Years of experience at preparing steak in brandy sauce, lob-
        ster stew, and chicken in rice shows up in the final product. For dessert,
        the *dulce de leche* (a sweet milk pudding) and the flan are good bets.
        ⊠ *1214 Av. Ashford, Condado,* ☎ *787/724–3760. AE, MC, V.*

$$–$$$ ✕ **Chayote.** Although it's slightly off the beaten path, this chic eatery—
        all earthtones and contemporary Puerto Rican art—is definitely an "in"
        spot. The chef gives haute international dishes tropical panache. Starters
        include *sopa del día* (soup of the day) made with local produce, chay-
        ote stuffed with prosciutto, and corn tamales with shrimp in a coconut
        sauce. Many of the entrées are seafood dishes, including an excellent
        pan-seared tuna with Asian ginger sauce. The ginger flan is a must for
        dessert. ⊠ *Hotel Olimpo Court, 603 Av. Miramar, Miramar,* ☎ *787/
        722–9385. AE, MC; V. Closed Sun. and Mon. No lunch Sat.*

$$–$$$ ✕ **Zabor Creative Cuisine.** In a restored plantation home with a pas-
        toral front yard, this inventive restaurant seems as if it's out on the is-
        land somewhere. One of the main pastimes here is grazing—that is,
        sharing such appetizers as breaded calamari in a tomato-basil sauce
        with your dinner companions. Of the notable main courses, try the veal
        chops stuffed with provolone, pancetta, and herbs and served with a
        garlic-merlot sauce or the catch of the day over yellow-raisin couscous
        in a mango-rosemary curry. ⊠ *14 Calle Candida, Condado,* ☎ *787/*

725–9494. *AE, D, DC, MC, V. Closed Sun.–Mon. No lunch Tues.–Thurs. and Sat.*

SEAFOOD

$$–$$$$ ✕ **Marisqueria La Dorada.** This fine seafood establishment on Condado's restaurant row is surprisingly affordable. The grilled seafood platter is the specialty, but there are also excellent pastas and other fish dinners, including mahimahi in caper sauce and codfish in green sauce. The friendly waitstaff makes you feel genuinely welcome. ✉ *1105 Av. Magdalena, Condado,* ☎ *787/722–9583. AE, D, MC, V.*

SPANISH

$$–$$$$ ✕ **Urdin.** The owners, who include Julían Gil, a well-known Puerto Rican model and actor, describe the menu here as Spanish with a Caribbean touch. The soup and seafood appetizers are particularly good, and a highly recommended entrée is *chillo urdin de lujo* (red snapper sautéed with clams, mussels, and shrimp in a tomato, herb, and wine sauce). The name of the restaurant comes from the Basque word for "blue," which is the dining room's dominant color. ✉ *1105 Av. Magdalena, Condado,* ☎ *787/724–0420. AE, MC, V.*

Eastern Puerto Rico

CONTEMPORARY

$$–$$$$ ✕ **Hermés Creative Cuisine.** The menu at this restaurant in the Palmas del Mar Country Club is distinctive. Chef Hermés Vargas, from the Condado restaurant that also bears his name, likes to experiment with game, including wild boar and venison. You can eat yours al fresco on the terrace or by candlelight in the dining room. ✉ *Rte. 906, Km 86.4, Palmas del Mar, Humacao,* ☎ *787/285–2277 or 787/285–2266. Reservations essential. AE, MC, V. No dinner Mon.*

SEAFOOD

$$–$$$ ✕ **Anchor's Inn.** Seafood is the specialty at this meson gastronómico. Clever maritime decor and superb cooking have made it a local favorite; the convenient location down the road from El Conquistador Resort lures visitors. Try the *chillo entero* (fried whole red snapper) or the paella. ✉ *Rte. 987, Km 2.7, Fajardo,* ☎ *787/863–7200. Reservations not accepted. AE, MC, V. Closed Tues.*

$–$$$ ✕ **Pulpo Loco By the Sea.** Octopus, oysters, mussels, and crab lead the lineup here, though many locals come for a beer or a cocktail as much as for the food. If your thirst is greater than your hunger, you can opt for a lighter snack. ✉ *Rte. 187, Km 4.5, Piñones,* ☎ *787/791–8382. Reservations not accepted. AE, MC, V.*

Southern Puerto Rico

CARIBBEAN

$–$$$ ✕ **Cilantro's.** In a 120-year-old mansion called Casa Real, chef Carlos Rosario serves new Puerto Rican cuisine in an intimate, second-floor dining room (reservations are a good idea). Surrounded by arched walls, stained-glass windows and decorative Spanish tiles, you can try dorado with a black bean sauce or squid stuffed with sausage and lobster. There are also vegetarian dishes, and on Tuesday nights sushi is added to the menu. ✉ *85 Calle Luna, San Germán,* ☎ *787/264–2735. D, MC, V. Closed Wed.*

ECLECTIC

$$–$$$ ✕ **Mark's at the Meliá.** One of the island's best restaurants is off
★ the lobby of the Meliá hotel. Chef Mark French has won praise from the Caribbean Chefs Association, and his menu lives up to that honor. The menu changes often, but you'll find a long list of appetizers that include a three-cheese onion soup or a bacon, lettuce, and tomato salad.

Entrées range from plantain-crusted dorado with congri to medallions of tenderloin with a shrimp and bearnaise sauce. The chocolate truffle cake draws diners all the way from San Juan. ⊠ *75 Calle Cristina, Ponce,* ☎ *787/284–6275. AE, MC, V. Closed Mon.–Tues.*

SEAFOOD

$–$$$ ✕ **El Ancla.** Families favor this restaurant at the edge of the sea. The kitchen serves generous and affordable plates of fish, crab, and other fresh seafood with tostones, *papas fritas* (french fries), and garlic bread. Try the shrimp in garlic sauce, the salmon fillet with capers, or the delectable mofongo. The piña coladas—with or without rum— and the flan are exceptional. There are two dining rooms—one for those who smoke and another for those who don't. ⊠ *9 Av. Hostos Final, Ponce Playa, Ponce,* ☎ *787/840–2450. AE, MC, V.*

$–$$$ ✕ **El Bohío.** Watch tarpon play in the water while you dine on the en-
★   closed deck at this informal restaurant. The long list of seafood is prepared in a variety of ways: shrimp comes breaded, stewed, or in a salad; conch is served as a salad or cooked in a butter and garlic sauce. ⊠ *Rte. 102, Km 9.7, Playa Joyuda, Cabo Rojo,* ☎ *787/851–2755. AE, DC, MC, V.*

Northwestern Puerto Rico

CARIBBEAN

$–$$ ✕ **El Buen Café.** Between Arecibo and the neighboring town of Hatillo, this diner attached to a parador is a local favorite and is often packed on the weekends. Favorites dishes include *carne mechada* (stuffed pot roast), chicken and rice soup, and seafood. Breakfast is also served. The restaurant opens at 5 AM and closes at 10:30 PM. ⊠ *381 Rte. 2, Km 84, Hatillo,* ☎ *787/898–3495. MC, V, AE.*

ECLECTIC

$$–$$$ ✕ **The Landing.** This spacious restaurant/bar/club has a large, beautiful wooden bar that's often filled with a mix of people, from surfers to retirees. You can dine on pasta, steaks, and burgers inside or on a back terrace overlooking the ocean. There's also a children's menu with junior burgers and chicken fingers. On weekend nights when live bands play, the place often fills with a younger crowd. ⊠ *Rte. 413, Km 4.7, Rincón,* ☎ *787/823–3112. AE, MC, V.*

$$–$$$ ✕ **Larry B's.** Tucked next to the bar at Beside the Point Inn is a wooden patio where you can watch the surf crash against the beach while dining on steaks, shrimp, pasta, salads, and fresh fish, all simply prepared and served in generous helpings. Larry himself serves up the food, and he's happy to regale guests with tales of his wave-seeking exploits. ⊠ *Rte. 413, Barrio Puntas, Rincón,* ☎ *787/823–3210. MC, V. Closed Mon.–Wed.*

ITALIAN

$$ ✕ **Mangére.** You'll find a long menu of Italian cuisine and 86 wines at this spacious restaurant decorated in pastel colors. Entrées include veal medallions with Portobello and porcini mushrooms, smoked Norwegian salmon with capers, and linguine carbonara. ⊠ *Rte. 693, Km 8.5, Dorado,* ☎ *787/796–4444. AE, D, MC, V.*

LATIN

$–$$$ ✕ **El Molino del Quijote.** Spanish and Puerto Rican cuisine are served here in a charming thatch-roof building. Additional tables in the garden overlook the water. The paella, mofongo, and sangría are superb, and so is the service. ⊠ *Rte. 429, Km 3.3, Rincón,* ☎ *787/823–4010. AE, MC, V. Closed Mon.–Thurs.*

Beaches

An island visit isn't complete without some time in the sand and sun. By law, everyone is welcome on Puerto Rico's *playas* (beaches), some of which—called *balnearios*—are maintained by the government. There are more than a dozen such beaches around the island, with dressing rooms; lifeguards; parking; and, in some cases, picnic tables, playgrounds, and camping facilities. Admission is free, parking is $2–$3. Hours vary, but most balnearios are open 9–5 daily in summer and Tuesday–Sunday the rest of the year.

SAN JUAN AREA

Playa de Isla Verde. Like Condado to its west, this beach is bordered by resorts and has plenty of places to rent chairs and sports equipment or grab a bite to eat. There aren't any lifeguards, but the sands are white, and the snorkeling is good.

Playa del Condado. West of Old San Juan and east of Ocean Park and Isla Verde, the long, wide Playa del Condado is often full of guests from the hotels that tower over it. Beach bars, sports outfitters, and chair-rental places abound, but there are no lifeguards.

Playa de Ocean Park. A residential neighborhood just east of Condado and west of Isla Verde is home to this wide, 1-mi-long (1½-km-long) stretch of golden sand. The waters are often choppy but still swimmable—take care, however, as there are no lifeguards.

EASTERN PUERTO RICO

Balneario de Luquillo. Coconut palms line crescent-shape Luquillo, and coral reefs protect its crystal-clear lagoon from Atlantic waters, making it an ideal place to swim. Amenities include changing rooms, lockers, showers, picnic tables, tent sites, and stands that sell cocktails and island savories. It also has a ramp that allows wheelchair users water access.

Balneario Seven Seas. Near the Reserva Natural Las Cabezas de San Juan, Seven Seas is a long stretch of powdery sand with a smattering of shade. Facilities include food kiosks, picnic and camping areas, changing rooms, bathrooms, and showers. On weekends, the beach attracts crowds keen on its calm, clear waters—perfect for swimming.

Playa Flamenco. On the north shore of Culebra Island, Flamenco has shade trees, clear, shallow water, picnic tables, and rest rooms. In winter, storms in the Atlantic often create great waves for bodysurfing.

Playa Sun Bay. Of Vieques's more than three dozen beaches, Sun Bay is one of the most popular. Its white sands skirt a mile-long, crescent-shape bay. You'll find food kiosks, picnic tables, camping areas, and a bathhouse; on weekdays, when the crowds are thin, you might also find wild horses grazing among the palm trees.

SOUTHERN PUERTO RICO

Balneario Boquerón. This broad beach of hard-packed sand is fringed with coconut palms. You'll find changing facilities, cabins, showers, rest rooms, and picnic tables. Nearby, Playa Santa and Ballena beaches are often deserted.

Cabo Rojo beaches. Of the beaches near Cabo Rojo, El Combate, Buyé, and the more secluded La Playuela are the most gorgeous.

NORTHWESTERN PUERTO RICO

Balneario de Rincón. Swimmers enjoy the tranquil waters of this beach, which has parking facilities and rest rooms. Surfers and snorkelers swear by the waters off the nearby beach, Tres Palmas.

Playa Crashboat. The beach near Aguadilla is famous for the colorful fishing boats docked on its shores; its long, beautiful stretch of sand; and its clear water, which often looks like glass. Named after rescue boats that were docked here when Ramey Air Force Base was in operation, the beach has picnic huts, showers, and rest rooms.

Outdoor Activities and Sports

Participant Sports

BOATING AND SAILING

The San Juan Marriott, Wyndham El San Juan, and Condado Plaza are just some of the resort hotels on the Condado and Isla Verde strips that have their own water-sports centers. **Eco Action Tours** (⌧ Condado Plaza Hotel, 999 Av. Ashford, Laguna Wing, Condado, San Juan, ☎ 787/791–7509 or 787/640–7385) rents kayaks, Sunfish, and jet skis; and offers kayaking trips to other parts of the island. In eastern Puerto Rico, **Puerto del Rey Marina** (⌧ Rte. 3, Km 51.2, Fajardo, ☎ 787/860–1000, WEB www.marinapuertodelrey.com), home to 750 ships, is one of the Caribbean's largest marinas. It's the place to arrange for a charter or find out about excursions to Vieques's bioluminescent Bahía Mosquito.

CYCLING

Selected areas lend themselves to bike travel. In general, however, the roads are congested and distances are vast. Avoid main thoroughfares in San Juan: the traffic is heavy and the fumes are thick. The Paseo Piñones is an 11-mi bike path that skirts the ocean east of San Juan. The entire southwest coast of Cabo Rojo also makes for good biking, particularly the broad beach at Boquerón. Road bike events are organized year-round by the **Federación Puertorriqueña de Ciclismo** (WEB www.federacionciclismopr.com). The **Puerto Rico Mountain Bike Association** (WEB www.prmtb.com) schedules mountain bike events from March to October.

Hot Dog Cycling (⌧ 5916 Av. Isla Verde, Isla Verde, San Juan, ☎ 787/982–5344, WEB www.hotdogcycling.com) rents Cannondale bicycles for $30 a day and organizes group excursions to El Yunque and other places out on the island. You can rent bikes for about $5 an hour from **Pulpo Loco By the Sea** (⌧ Rte. 187, Km 4.5, Piñones, ☎ 787/791–8382).

FISHING

Puerto Rico's waters are home to large game fish such as marlin, wahoo, dorado, tuna, and barracuda; as many as 30 world records for catches have been set off the island's shores. Half-day, full-day, split-charter, and big- and small-game fishing can be arranged through **Benitez Deep-Sea Fishing** (⌧ Club Náutico de San Juan, Miramar, San Juan, ☎ 787/723–2292). **Moondog Charters** (⌧ Black Eagle Marina off Rte. 413, Rincón, ☎ 787/823–7168) organizes fishing charters and whale-watching trips. **Shiraz Charters** (⌧ Rte. 906, Candelero Resort at Palmas del Mar, Site 6, Humacao, ☎ 787/285–5718, WEB www.charternet.com/fishers/shiraz) specializes in deep-sea fishing charters in search of tuna. **Tour Marine** (⌧ Rte. 101, Km 14.1, Joyuda Sector, Puerto Real, Cabo Rojo, ☎ 787/851–9259) takes anglers out to waters off Cabo Rojo's coast.

GOLF

For aficionados, Puerto Rico is known as the birthplace of golf legend Chi Chi Rodríguez—and he had to hone his craft somewhere. Currently, you'll find nearly 20 courses on the island, including many championship links. Be sure to call ahead for tee times; hours vary, and several hotel courses give preference to guests. Greens fees start at about $30 and go up as high as $150. The **Puerto Rican Golf Association** (⌧ 58 Calle Caribe, San Juan, ☎ 787/721–7742, WEB www.prga.org) is a good source for information on courses and tournaments.

Developed on what was once a coconut plantation, the public, 18-hole course at the **Bahía Beach Plantation** (✉ Rte. 187, Km 4.2, Río Grande, ☎ 787/256–5600) is an old-time favorite that skirts a slice of the east coast. **Candelero Resort at Palmas del Mar** (✉ Rte. 906, Humacao, ☎ 787/285–2256) has two courses: the Rees Jones–designed Flamboyán course, named for the flamboyant trees that pepper its fairway, winds around a lake, over a river, and to the sea before turning toward dunes and wetlands. The Gary Player–designed Palmas course has a challenging par 5 that scoots around wetlands. The 7,100-yard **Dorado Del Mar** golf course (✉ Rte. 693, Dorado, ☎ 787/796–3065) is a Chi Chi Rodríguez signature course with narrow fairways that can be a challenge to hit when the wind picks up.

The 18-hole Arthur Hills–designed course at **El Conquistador Country Club** (✉ 1000 Av. El Conquistador, Fajardo, ☎ 787/863–6784) is famous for its 200-ft changes in elevation. The trade winds make every shot challenging. There are four attractive Robert Trent Jones–designed 18-hole courses shared by the **Hyatt Dorado Beach Resort and the Hyatt Regency Cerromar Beach** hotels (✉ Rte. 693, Km 10.8 and Km 11.8, Dorado, ☎ 787/796–1234 Ext. 3238 or 3016). With El Yunque rain forest as a backdrop, the two 18-hole courses at the **Westin Río Mar Beach Resort and Country Club** (✉ 6000 Río Mar Blvd., Río Grande, ☎ 787/888–6000) are inspirational. The River Course was designed by Greg Norman, the Ocean course by George and Tom Fazio.

HORSEBACK RIDING

Campo Allegre (✉ Rte. 127, Km 5.1, Yauco, ☎ 787/856–2609) is a 204-acre horse ranch in southern Puerto Rico that conducts half-hour, one-hour, and two-hour rides through the hills surrounding Yauco. There are also pony rides for children. The family-run **Hacienda Carabali** (Rte. 992, Km 4, at Mameyes River Bridge, Barrio Mameyes, Río Grande, ☎ 787/889–5820 or 787/889–4954) in eastern Puerto Rico is a good place to see Puerto Rico's Paso Fino horses in action. You can even jump in the saddle yourself. Riding excursions ($45 an hour) include a one-hour jaunt along Río Mámeyes and the edge of El Yunque and a two-hour ride along Balneario de Luquillo. **Tropical Paradise Horse Back Riding** (✉ Off Rte. 690, west of Hyatt Regency Cerromar, Dorado, ☎ 787/720–5454) arranges rides along a north coast beach on Paso Fino horses.

SCUBA DIVING AND SNORKELING

The diving is excellent off Puerto Rico's south, east, and west coasts as well as its offshore islands. Particularly striking are dramatic walls created by a continental shelf off the south coast between La Parguera and Guánica. It's best to choose specific locations with the help of a guide or outfitter. Escorted half-day dives range from $45 to $95 for one or two tanks, including all equipment; in general, double those prices for night dives. Packages that include lunch and other extras start at $100; those that include accommodations are also available.

Snorkeling excursions, which include transportation equipment rental, and sometimes lunch, start at $50. Equipment rents at beaches for about $5–$7. (Caution: coral-reef waters and mangrove areas can be dangerous. Unless you're an expert or have an experienced guide, stay near the water-sports centers of hotels and avoid unsupervised areas.)

Aquatica Underwater Adventures (✉ Rte. 110, Km 10, Gate 5, Aguadilla, ☎ 787/890–6071) offers scuba diving certification courses and dives off Aguadilla and Isabela beaches. You can also rent snorkeling equipment. **Blue Caribe Dive Center** (✉ Calle Flamboyán, Esperanza, Vieques, ☎ 787/741–2522, WEB www.enchanted-isle.com/bluecaribe) offers scuba excursions to several sites and night dives in Bahía de Mosquito. **Divers' Outlet** (⊠ 38 Calle Fernández Garcia, Luquillo, ☎ 787/889–5721 or 888/746–3483) is a full-service dive shop. It offers PADI certification, rents equipment, and can arrange scuba outings.

Ocean Sports (⊠ 1035 Av. Ashford, Condado, San Juan, ☎ 787/723–8513, WEB www.osdivers.com) offers certified scuba dives; airtank fill-ups; and equipment repairs, sales and rentals. **Parguera Divers** (⊠ Posada Porlamar, Rte. 304, La Parguera, ☎ 787/899–4171) offers scuba and snorkeling expeditions and basic instruction. At **Sea Ventures Pro Dive Center** (⊠ Puerto del Rey Marina, Rte. 3, Km 51.4, Fajardo, ☎ 787/863–3483 or 800/739–3483, WEB www.divepuertorico.com) you can get PADI certified and arrange dive trips to 20 offshore sites.

SURFING

Although the west-coast beaches are considered *the* places to surf, San Juan was actually where the sport got its start on the island, back in 1958 thanks to legendary surfers Gary Hoyt and José Rodríguez Reyes. In San Juan many surfers head to La Punta, a reef break behind the Presbyterian Hospital, or the Sheraton, a break named after the hotel (it's now the Marriott) with either surf or boogie boards. In Isla Verde, white water on the horizon means that the waves are good at the beach break near the Ritz-Carlton known as Pine Grove.

East of the city, in Piñones, the Caballo has deep-to-shallow-water shelf waves that require a big-wave board known as a "gun." Playa La Pared, near Balneario de Luquillo is a surfer haunt with medium-range waves. Numerous local competitions are held here throughout the year. The very best surfing beaches are along the western coast from Isabela south to Rincón, which gained notoriety by hosting the World Surfing Championship in 1968. Today the town draws surfers from around the globe, especially in winter when the waves are at their best.

La Selva Surf (⊠ 250 Calle Fernández Garcia, Luquillo, ☎ 787/889–6205, WEB www.rainforestsafari.com/selva), near Playa La Pared, has anything a surfer could need, including news about current conditions. At Ocean Park beach, famous surfer Carlos Cabrero, proprietor of **Tres Palmas** (⊠ 1911 Av. McLeary, Ocean Park, San Juan, ☎ 787/728–3377), rents boards (daily rates are $25 for short boards, $30 for long boards), repairs equipment, and sells all sorts of hip beach and surfing gear. Pick up new and used surfboards, body boards, kayaks, and snorkeling gear, or rent equipment, at **West Coast Surf Shop** (⊠ 2E Calle Muñoz Rivera, Rincón, ☎ 787/823–3935).

TENNIS

If you'd like to use courts at a property where you aren't a guest, call in advance for information. Hotel guests usually get first priority, and you are likely to have to pay a fee. Courts at the following hotels are open to nonguests: Candelero Resort at Palmas del Mar, Caribe Hilton, Condado Plaza, Copamarina Beach Resort, Hilton Ponce, Hyatt Dorado Beach, Hyatt Regency Cerromar Beach, San Juan Marriott, Westin Río Mar Beach Resort, Wyndham El Conquistador, and Wyndham El San Juan. The four lighted courts of the **Isla Verde Tennis Club** (⊠ Calles Ema and Delta Rodriguez, Isla Verde, San Juan, ☎ 787/727–6490) are open for nonmember use at $4 per hour, daily 8 AM–10 PM. The **Parque Central Municipo de San Juan** (⊠ Calle Cerra, exit on Rte. 2, Santurce, San Juan, ☎ 787/722–1646) has 17 lighted courts. Fees are $3 per hour 8 AM–6 PM and $4 per hour 6 PM–10 PM.

WINDSURFING

You'll get the best windsurfing advice and equipment from Jaime Torres at **Velauno** (⊠ 2430 Calle Loíza, Punta Las Marías, San Juan,

☎ 787/728–8716, WEB www.velauno.com), the second-largest, full-service windsurfing center in the United States. Lisa Penfield, a former windsurfing competitor, teaches beginners at the **Watersports Center at the Dorado Beach Resort & Country Club** (⊠ Rte. 693, Km 10.8, Dorado, ☎ 787/796–2188).

Spectator Sports

BASEBALL

The late, great Roberto Clemente is just one of many Puerto Rican ballplayers to find success in the U.S. major leagues after honing their skills at home. The island's pro season runs from October to February. Santurce, Ponce, Carolina Caguas, Arecibo, and Mayagüez all have teams. Contact the tourist office for details on baseball games or call **Professional Baseball of Puerto Rico** (☎ 787/765–6285).

HORSE RACING

Thoroughbred races are run year-round at **Hípodromo El Comandante** (Av. 65th Infantry, Rte. 3, Km 15.3, Canóvanas, ☎ 787/724–6060, WEB www.comandantepr.com) a racetrack about 20 minutes east of San Juan. On race days the dining rooms open at 12:30 PM. Post time is 2:15 or 2:45 (depending on the season) Wednesday and Friday through Monday.

Shopping

San Juan, the island's shopping mecca, isn't a free port, so you won't find bargains on electronics and perfumes. You can, however, find excellent prices on china, crystal, fashions, and jewelry. Shopping for local crafts can also be gratifying: you'll run across a lot that's tacky, but you can also find treasures, and in many cases you can watch the artisans at work. For guidance on finding genuine craftspeople, contact the **Puerto Rico Tourism Company's Asuntos Culturales** (Cultural Affairs Office, ☎ 787/723–0692).

Popular items include *santos* (small carved figures of saints or religious scenes), hand-rolled cigars, handmade *mundillo* lace from Aguadilla, *vejigantes* (colorful masks used during Carnival and local festivals) from Loíza and Ponce, and fancy men's shirts called guayaberas.

Areas and Malls

In Old San Juan—especially on Calles Fortaleza and San Francisco—you'll find everything from T-shirt emporiums to selective crafts stores, bookshops, art galleries, jewelry boutiques, and even shops that specialize in made-to-order Panama hats. Calle Cristo is lined with factory-outlet stores, including Coach, Dooney & Bourke Factory Store, Polo/Ralph Lauren Factory Store, Guess Factory Story, and Tommy Hilfiger.

With many stores selling luxury items and designer fashions, the shopping spirit in the San Juan neighborhood of Condado is reminiscent of that in Miami. Avenida Condado is a good bet for souvenirs and curios as well as art and upscale jewelry or togs. Avenida Ashford is considered the heart of San Juan's fashion district. There's also a growing fashion scene in the business district of Hato Rey.

Look for vendors selling crafts from kiosks at the **Artesanía Puertorriqueña** (☎ 787/722–1709) in the tourism company's La Casita at Plaza Dársenas near Pier 1 in Old San Juan. Several vendors also set up shop to sell items such as belts, handbags, and toys along Calle San Justo in front of Plaza Dársenas. Right off the highway east of San Juan, the **Belz Factory Outlet World** (⊠ Rte. 3, Km 18.4, Canóvanas, ☎ 787/256–7040, WEB www.belz.com) has more than 75 stores, including Nike, Guess, Mikasa, The Gap, Levi's, Liz Claiborne, and Tommy Hilfiger. There's also a large food court.

Just outside of the southern city of Ponce, **Plaza del Caribe Mall** (✉ Rte. 2, Km 227.9, ☎ 787/259–8989), one of the island's largest malls, has stores such as Sears, JCPenney, and Gap. For a mundane albeit complete shopping experience, head to **Plaza Las Américas** (✉ 525 Av. Franklin Delano Roosevelt, Hato Rey, San Juan, ☎ 787/767–1525), which has 200 shops, including the world's largest JCPenney store, The Gap, Sears, Macy's, Godiva, and Armani Exchange as well as restaurants and movie theaters. About 20 minutes from Dorado via Highway 22 at Exit 55 is Puerto Rico's first factory outlet mall. **Prime Outlets Puerto Rico** (✉ Rte. 2, Km 54.8, Barceloneta, ☎ 787/846–9011) is a pastel village of more than 40 stores selling discounted merchandise from such familiar names as Liz Claiborne, Polo, Calvin Klein, Brooks Brothers, the Gap, Reebok, and Tommy Hilfiger.

Specialty Items

ART

Artists show and sell their work at **Casa Vieja Gallery** (✉ Rte. 996 outside Esperanza, Vieques, ☎ 787/741–3078), in a Caribbean-style building at the entrance to the grounds of Inn on the Blue Horizon. **Galería Botello** (✉ 314 Av. Franklin Delano Roosevelt, Hato Rey, San Juan, ☎ 787/250–8274, WEB www.botello.com) offers a broad range of works, from traditional santos to pieces by such up-and-coming Puerto Rican artists as María del Mater O'Neill, whose large formats and bold strokes and colors give familiar home-and-garden themes a twist.

Galería Raíces (✉ 314 Av. José de Diego, Santurce, San Juan, ☎ 787/ 723–8909) has works by such emerging Puerto Rican artists as Nayda Collazo Llorens, whose cerebral and sensitive multimedia installations examine connections and patterns in games, codes, and human memory. **OBRA** (✉ 301 Calle Tetuán, Old San Juan, ☎ 787/723–3206), is a visually pleasing space with museum-quality paintings, drawings, and sculptures by such Puerto Rican masters as Augusto Marín, Myrna Baez, and Rafael Tufiño. The picturesque **Treehouse Studio** (✉ Unmarked road off Rte. 3, Río Grande, ☎ 787/888–8062), not far from El Yunque, sells vibrant watercolors by Monica Laird, who also gives workshops. Call for an appointment and directions.

CLOTHES

After many years of catering to a primarily local clientele, **Clubman** (✉ 1351 Av. Ashford, Condado, San Juan, ☎ 787/722–1867) is the classic choice for gentlemen's clothing. **La Femme** (✉ 320 Av. Franklin Delano Roosevelt, Hato Rey, San Juan, ☎ 787/753–0915) also sells attractive (and sexy) women's clothes and accessories. **Matahari** (✉ 202 Calle San Justo, Old San Juan, San Juan, ☎ 787/724–5869) sells unusual clothes for men and women as well as accessories, jewelry, and trinkets that proprietor Fernando Sosa collects during his trips around the world.

Monsieur (✉ 1126 Av. Ashford, Condado, San Juan, ☎ 787/722–0918) has casual, contemporary designs for men. The window displays at **Nativa Boutique** (✉ 55 Calel Cervantes, Condado, San Juan, ☎ 787/724– 1396) are almost as daring as the clothes it sells. **Nono Maldonado** (✉ 1051 Av. Ashford, Condado, San Juan, ☎ 787/721–0456) is well-known for his high-end, elegant linen designs for men and women.

HANDICRAFTS

Among the offerings at **Artesanías Castor Ayala** (✉ Rte. 187, Km 6.6, Loíza, ☎ 787/876–1130), in eastern Puerto Rico, are the coconut-shell festival masks dubbed "Mona Lisas" because of their elongated smiles. Craftsman Raul Ayala Carrasquillo has been making these museum-quality pieces for more than 40 years, following in the footsteps of his late father, the esteemed craftsman for whom the store is named. Masks, priced from $50 to $350, are often snapped up by collectors.

At the **Convento de los Dominicos** (✉ 98 Calle Norzagaray, Old San Juan, San Juan, ☎ 787/721–6866)—the Dominican Convent on the north side of the old city that houses the offices of the Instituto de Cultura Puertorriqueña—you'll find baskets, masks, the famous *cuatro* guitars, santos, and reproductions of Taíno artifacts. At El Conquistador Resort, Maria Elba Torres runs the **Galería Arrecife** (✉ 1000 Av. El Conquistador, Fajardo, ☎ 787/863–3972), which shows only works by artists living in the Caribbean. Look for ceramics by Rafael de Olmo and jewelry made from fish scales.

JEWELRY

Aetna Gold (✉ 111 Calle Gilberto Concepción de Gracia, Old San Juan, San Juan, ☎ 787/721–4756), adjacent to the Wyndham Old San Juan Hotel, sells exquisite gold jewelry designed in Greece. For a wide array of watches and jewelry, visit the two floors of **Bared** (✉ Calle Fortaleza and Calle San Justo, Old San Juan, San Juan, ☎ 787/724–4811).

Diamonds and gold galore are found at **Joseph Manchini** (✉ 101 Calle Fortaleza, Old San Juan, San Juan, ☎ 787/722–7698). **Joyería Cátala** (✉ Plaza de Armas, Old San Juan, San Juan, ☎ 787/722–3231) is distinguished for its large selection of pearls. **Joyería Riviera** (✉ 205 Cruz St., Old San Juan, San Juan, ☎ 787/725–4000) sells fine jewelry by David Yurman, and Rolex watches.

SOUVENIRS

Carnival masks, hammocks, Puerto Rican coffee, and rum fill the shelves of **Mi Coquí** (✉ 9227 Calle Marina, Ponce Centro, Ponce, ☎ 787/841–0216). Chocolate-loving Laurie Humphrey had trouble finding a supplier for her sweet tooth, so she opened the **Paradise Store** (✉ Hwy. 194, Km 0.4, Fajardo, ☎ 787/863–8182). Lindt and other gourmet chocolates jam the shop, which also sells flowers and such gift items as Puerto Rican–made soaps. Buy a recording of the tree frog's song, pick up a coffee-table book about the rain forest, and check out the books for ecominded children at the large, lovely **El Yunque Gift Shop** (✉ Rte. 191, Km 4.3, ☎ 787/888–1880). Tucked among the rain-forest gifts are other Puerto Rican items, including note cards, maps, soaps, jams, and coffee.

Nightlife and the Arts

Qué Pasa, the official visitor's guide, has listings of events in San Juan and out on the island. For up-to-the-minute listings, pick up a copy of the English-language edition of the *San Juan Star*, the island's oldest daily. The Thursday edition's weekend section is especially useful. You can also check with the local tourist offices and the concierge at your hotel to find out what's doing.

Nightlife

From Thursday through Sunday, it's as if there's a celebration going on nearly everywhere in San Juan. In Old San Juan, Calle San Sebastián is lined with bars and restaurants. Salsa music blaring from jukeboxes in cut-rate pool halls competes with mellow Latin jazz in top-flight night spots. Well-dressed visitors and locals alike often mingle in the lobby bars of large hotels, many of which have bands in the evening. An eclectic crowd heads to the Plaza del Mercado off Avenida Ponce de León at Calle Canals after work to hang out in the plaza or enjoy drinks and food in one of the small establishments skirting the farmers market.

East of San Juan, funky Piñones has a collection of open-air, seaside eateries that are popular with locals. On weekend evenings, many places have merengue combos, Brazilian jazz trios, or reggae bands. In the southern city of Ponce, people embrace the Spanish tradition of the *paseo,* an evening stroll around the Plaza las Delicias. The boardwalk at La Guancha is also a lively scene. Live bands often play on weekends. Elsewhere en la isla, night-time activities center on the hotels and resorts.

Wherever you are, dress to party. Puerto Ricans have flair, and both men and women love getting dressed up to go out. Bars are usually casual, but if you have on jeans, sneakers, and a T-shirt, you may be refused entry at nightclubs and discos.

BARS AND MUSIC CLUBS

El Batey (✉ 101 Calle Cristo, Old San Juan, San Juan, ☎ 787/725–1787) is a hole-in-the-wall run by crusty New Yorker Davydd Gwilym Jones III; it looks like a military bunker, but it has the best oldies juke box in the city and is wildly popular. **Café Bohemio** (✉ El Convento Hotel, 100 Calle Cristo, Old San Juan, San Juan, ☎ 787/723–9200), a Latin restaurant, turns into a live jazz and Bohemian music club from 11 PM to 2 AM Tuesday through Friday (after the kitchen closes); Thursday night is best.

Power brokers indulge in fine smokes while mingling with local starlets and smartly attired visitors at the **Cigar Bar** (✉ 6063 Av. Isla Verde, Isla Verde, San Juan, ☎ 787/791–1000) in the Wyndham El San Juan. With a large dance and stage area and smokin' Afro-Cuban bands, **Rumba** (✉ 152 Calle San Sebastián, Old San Juan, San Juan, ☎ 787/725–4407) is one of the best parties in town.

CASINOS

By law, all casinos are in hotels, primarily in San Juan. The government keeps a close eye on them. Dress for the larger casinos is on the formal side, and the atmosphere is refined. Casinos set their own hours but are generally open from noon to 4 AM. In addition to slot machines, typical games include blackjack, roulette, craps, Caribbean stud (a five-card poker game), and *pai gow* poker (a combination of American poker and the Chinese game pai gow). Hotels with casinos have live entertainment most weekends, as well as restaurants and bars. The minimum age to gamble is 18.

Among the San Juan hotels that have casinos are the Condado Plaza Hotel, Ritz-Carlton San Juan, Inter-Continental San Juan Resort and Casino, San Juan Marriott, Wyndham El San Juan Hotel, and Wyndham Old San Juan Hotel. Elsewhere on the island, there are casinos at the Hyatt Regency Cerromar, the Candelero Resort at Palmas del Mar, Hilton Ponce and Casino, Westin Río Mar Beach Resort and Country Club, and Wyndham El Conquistador Resort & Country Club.

DANCE CLUBS

A long line of well-heeled patrons usually runs out the door of **Babylon** (Wyndham El San Juan Hotel, 6063 Av. Isla Verde, Isla Verde, San Juan, ☎ 787/791–1000). Those with the staying power to make it inside step out of the Caribbean and into the ancient Middle East. Those who tire of waiting often head to El Chico Lounge, a small room with live entertainment right off the hotel lobby.

The multilevel **Club Lazer** (251 Calle Cruz, Old San Juan, San Juan, ☎ 787/725–7581) has spots for quiet conversation, spaces for dancing to loud music, and a landscaped roof deck overlooking San Juan. An older, dressy crowd frequents the Inter-Continental's **Martini's** (187

Av. Isla Verde, Isla Verde, San Juan, ☎ 787/791–6100 Ext. 356). It's known for its Las Vegas–style reviews; acts have included celebrity impersonators and flamenco music and dance troupes. Record parties and fashion shows are also held here from time to time.

The oceanfront deck bar of the **Atlantic Beach** (1 Calle Vendig, Condado, San Juan, ☎ 787/721–6100) hotel is famed for its early evening happy hours, with pulsating tropical music, a wide selection of exotic drinks, and ever-pleasant ocean breezes. The music is terrific at **Eros** (1257 Av. Ponce de León, Santurce, San Juan, ☎ 787/722–1390), a club that's popular with the gay community but is just as welcoming to heterosexuals. The lighting is dim, the dance floor is large, and the balcony bar overlooks all the drama.

The Arts

The renaissance of the music and dance form known as *bomba* dates from 1961, when a TV producer showed up in the eastern town of Loíza searching for residents who remembered it. In response, mask-maker Castor Ayala put together the **Ballet Folklórico Hermanos Ayala** (⊠ Rte. 187, Km 6.6, Loíza, ☎ 787/876–1130), a folk group that performs around the island and elsewhere in Latin America. The group has no headquarters, but you can get its schedule at the mask-making shop, Artesanías Castor Ayala.

There's something going on nearly every night at the **Centro de Bellas Artes Luis A. Ferré** (Luis A. Ferré Center for the Performing Arts; ⊠ Av. José de Diego and Av. Ponce De León, Santurce, San Juan, ☎ 787/725–7334), from pop or jazz concerts to plays, opera, and ballet. It's also the home of the San Juan Symphony Orchestra. If you're in Old San Juan on the first Tuesday of the month (September–December and February–May) take advantage of **Gallery Night** (☎ 787/723–6286). Galleries and select museums open their doors after hours for viewings accompanied by refreshments and music.

The **Museo de Arte de Ponce** (⊠ 2325 Av. Las Américas, Sector Santa María, Ponce, ☎ 787/848–0505) occasionally sponsors chamber music concerts and recitals by members of the Puerto Rico Symphony Orchestra. Check for theater productions and concerts at the **Teatro La Perla** (⊠ Calle Mayor and Calle Cristina, Ponce Centro, Ponce ☎ 787/843–4322 information; 787/843–4080 ticket office). Named for Puerto Rican playwright Alejandro Tapia, **Teatro Tapia** (⊠ La Fortaleza at Plaza Colón, Old San Juan, San Juan, ☎ 787/722–0247) hosts theatrical and musical productions.

Exploring Puerto Rico

Old San Juan

Old San Juan, the original city, founded in 1521, contains carefully preserved examples of 16th- and 17th-century Spanish colonial architecture. More than 400 buildings have been beautifully restored. Graceful wrought-iron balconies with lush hanging plants extend over narrow streets paved with *adoquines* (blue-gray stones originally used as ballast for Spanish ships). The old city is partially enclosed by walls that date from 1633 and once completely surrounded it. Designated a U.S. National Historic Zone in 1950, Old San Juan is chockablock with shops, open-air cafés, homes, tree-shaded squares, monuments, pigeons, and people. You can get an overview on a morning's stroll (bear in mind that this "stroll" includes some steep climbs). However, if you plan to immerse yourself in history or to shop, you'll need two or three days.

SIGHTS TO SEE

Numbers in the margin correspond to points of interest on the Old San Juan Exploring map.

⓫ **Alcaldía.** The city hall was built between 1604 and 1789. In 1841 extensive renovations were done to make it resemble Madrid's city hall, with arcades, towers, balconies, and a lovely inner courtyard. A tourist information center and an art gallery are on the first floor. ⊠ *153 Calle San Francisco, Plaza de Armas, Old San Juan,* ☎ *787/724–7171 Ext. 2391.* ⌑ *Free.* ☉ *Weekdays 8–4.*

❽ **Capilla del Cristo.** According to legend, in 1753 a young horseman named Baltazar Montañez, got carried away during festivities in honor of San Juan Bautista (St. John the Baptist), raced down the street and plunged over the steep precipice. A witness to the tragedy promised to build a chapel if the young man's life could be saved. Historical records maintain the man died, though legend contends he lived. Regardless, this chapel was built, and inside it is a small silver altar dedicated to the Christ of Miracles. ⊠ *Calle Cristo, Old San Juan,* ☎ *no phone.* ⌑ *Free.* ☉ *Tues. 10–3:30.*

❺ **Casa Blanca.** The original structure on this site, not far from the ramparts of El Morro, was a frame house built in 1521 as a home for Ponce de León. But Ponce de León died in Cuba without ever having lived in it, and it was virtually destroyed by a hurricane in 1523, after which his son-in-law had the present masonry home built. His descendants occupied it for 250 years. From the end of the Spanish-American War in 1898 to 1966, it was the home of the U.S. Army commander in Puerto Rico. The home now contains several rooms decorated in colonial-era furnishings and an archaeology exhibit. The lush garden, cooled by spraying fountains, is a tranquil spot. ⊠ *1 Calle San Sebastián, Old San Juan,* ☎ *787/724–4102.* ⌑ *$2.* ☉ *Tues.–Sat. 9–noon and 1–4:30.*

❻ **Catedral de San Juan.** The Catholic shrine of Puerto Rico had humble beginnings in the early 1520s as a thatch-topped wooden structure. Hurricane winds tore off the thatch and destroyed the church. It was reconstructed in 1540, when the graceful circular staircase and vaulted Gothic ceilings were added, but most of the work was done in the 19th century. The remains of Ponce de León are in a marble tomb near the transept. ⊠ *153 Calle Cristo, Old San Juan,* ☎ *787/722–0861.* ⌑ *$1 donation suggested.* ☉ *Weekdays 8:30–4; masses Sat. at 7 PM, Sun. at 9 AM and 11 AM, weekdays at 12:15 PM.*

❸ **Convento de los Dominicos.** Built by Dominican friars in 1523, this convent often served as a shelter during Carib Indian attacks and, more recently, as headquarters for the Antilles command of the U.S. Army. Now home to some offices of the Institute of Puerto Rican Culture, the beautifully restored building contains religious manuscripts, artifacts, and art. The institute also maintains a craft store and bookstore here. ⊠ *98 Calle Norzagaray, Old San Juan,* ☎ *787/721–6866.* ⌑ *Free.* ☉ *Mon.–Sat. 9–5.*

❼ **La Fortaleza.** On a hill overlooking the harbor, La Fortaleza, the western hemisphere's oldest executive mansion in continuous use and official residence of Puerto Rico's governor, was built as a fortress. The original primitive structure, constructed in 1540, has seen numerous changes over the past four centuries, resulting in the present collection of marble and mahogany, medieval towers, and stained-glass galleries. Guided tours are conducted every hour on the hour in English, on the half hour in Spanish. ⊠ *Calle Recinto Oeste, Old San Juan,* ☎ *787/721–7000 Ext. 2211 or 2358.* ⌑ *Free.* ☉ *Weekdays 9–4.*

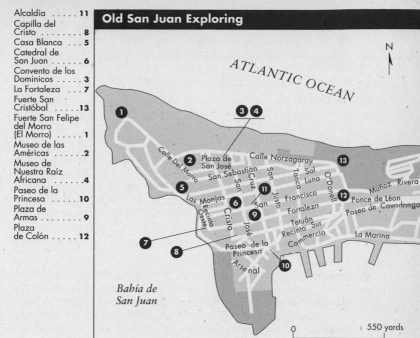

Old San Juan Exploring

🐾 ⑬ **Fuerte San Cristóbal.** This 18th-century fortress guarded the city from land attacks. Even larger than El Morro, San Cristóbal was known in its heyday as the Gibraltar of the West Indies. ⊠ *Calle Norzagaray, Old San Juan,* ☎ *787/729–6960,* WEB *www.nps.gov/saju/.* ⊠ *$2.* ☉ *Daily 9–5.*

🐾 ❶ **Fuerte San Felipe del Morro.** On a rocky promontory at the old city's northwestern tip is El Morro, which was built by the Spaniards between 1540 and 1783. Rising 140 ft above the sea, the massive six-level fortress covers enough territory to accommodate a 9-hole golf course. It's a labyrinth of dungeons, barracks, turrets, towers, and tunnels. Its small, air-conditioned museum traces the history of the fortress. Tours and a video show are available in English. ⊠ *Calle Norzagaray, Old San Juan,* ☎ *787/729–6960,* WEB *www.nps.gov/saju/.* ⊠ *$2.*

❷ **Museo de las Américas.** The Museum of the Americas is on the second floor of the imposing former military barracks, Cuartel de Ballajá. Most exhibits rotate, but the focus is on the popular and folk art of Latin America. The permanent exhibit, "Las Artes Populares en las Américas," has religious figures, musical instruments, basketwork, costumes, and farming and other implements of the Americas. ⊠ *Calle Norzagaray and Calle del Morro, Old San Juan,* ☎ *787/724–5052,* WEB *www.museolasamericas.org.* ⊠ *Free.* ☉ *Tues.–Fri. 10–4, weekends 11–5.*

❹ **Museo de Nuestra Raíz Africana.** The Institute of Puerto Rican Culture created this museum to help Puerto Ricans understand African influences in island culture. On display over two floors are African musical instruments, documents relating to the slave trade, and a list of African words that have made it into popular Puerto Rican culture. ⊠ *101 Calle San Sebastián, Plaza de San José, Old San Juan,* ☎ *787/724–0700 Ext. 4239,* WEB *www.icp.gobierno.org.* ⊠ *Free.* ☉ *Tues.– Sat. 9:30–5, Sun. 11–5.*

⑩ **Paseo de la Princesa.** This street down at the port is spruced up with flowers, trees, benches, street lamps, and a striking fountain depicting the various ethnic groups of Puerto Rico. Take a seat and watch the boats zip across the water. At the west end of the paseo, beyond the fountain, is the beginning of a shoreline path that hugs Old San Juan's walls and leads to the city gate at Calle San Juan.

⑨ **Plaza de Armas.** This is the original main square of Old San Juan. The plaza, bordered by Calles San Francisco, Fortaleza, San José, and Cruz, has a lovely fountain with 19th-century statues representing the four seasons.

⑫ **Plaza de Colón.** A statue of Christopher Columbus is atop a high pedestal in this bustling square. Originally called St. James Square, it was renamed in honor of Columbus on the 400th anniversary of the discovery of Puerto Rico. On the plaza's north side is a terminal for buses to and from San Juan. ⊠ *East of Calle O'Donell between calles San Francisco and Fortaleza.*

San Juan

You'll need to resort to taxis, buses, *públicos* (public cars), or a rental car to reach the points of interest in "new" San Juan. Avenida Muñoz Rivera, Avenida Ponce de León, and Avenida Fernández Juncos are the main thoroughfares that cross Puerta de Tierra, east of Old San Juan, to the business and tourist districts of Santurce, Condado, and Isla Verde. Dos Hermanos Bridge connects Puerta de Tierra with Miramar, Condado, and Isla Grande. Isla Grande Airport, from which you can take short hops, is on the bay side of the bridge. On the other side, the Condado Lagoon is bordered by Avenida Ashford, which threads past the high-rise Condado hotels and Avenida Baldorioty de Castro Expreso, which barrels east to the airport and beyond. Due south of the lagoon is Miramar, a residential area with fashionable turn-of-the-20th-century homes and a few hotels and restaurants. South of Santurce is the Golden Mile—Hato Rey, the financial hub. Isla Verde, with its glittering beachfront hotels, casinos, discos, and public beach, is to the east, near the airport.

Numbers in the margin correspond to points of interest on the San Juan Dining, Lodging, and Exploring map.

SIGHTS TO SEE

❶ **El Capitolio.** Puerto Rico's capitol is a white marble building that dates from the 1920s. The grand rotunda, with mosaics and friezes, was completed a few years ago. The seat of the island's bicameral legislature, the capitol contains Puerto Rico's constitution and is flanked by the modern buildings of the Senate and the House of Representatives. There are spectacular views from the observation plaza on the sea side of the capitol. Pick up a booklet about the building from the House Secretariat on the second floor. Guided tours are by appointment only. ⊠ *Av. Ponce de León, Puerta de Tierra,* ☎ 787/724–8979. ⊡ *Free.* ⊘ *Daily 8:30–5.*

❸ **Museo de Arte Contemporáneo de Puerto Rico.** The Universidad del Sagrado Corazón (Sacred Heart University) is the home of the Museum of Contemporary Puerto Rican Art, containing a wide range of painting, sculpture, photography, and new-media art by both established and up-and-coming Puerto Rican artists. Exhibits, in several rooms on the large second floor of the university's Barat Building, change once or twice per year. ⊠ *Calle San Antonio and Calle Rosales, Santurce,* ☎ 787/268–0049, WEB *museocontemporaneopr.org.* ⊡ *Free.* ⊘ *Mon.–Sat. 9–5.*

② **Museo de Arte de Puerto Rico.** The west wing of this ambitious 130,000-square-ft museum is the former San Juan Municipal Hospital, a 1920s neoclassical building that contains a permanent collection of Puerto Rican art dating from the 17th century to the present. The east wing is dominated by a five-story-tall stained-glass window, the work of local artist Eric Tabales, that towers over the museum's Grand Hall and faces a 5-acre garden. In the east wing there are galleries for changing exhibits, an interactive Family Gallery, and a 400-seat theater that's worth seeing for the stage's remarkable lace curtain alone. The garden has a sculpture trail, a pond, and a variety of native flora. ⊠ *300 Av. José de Diego, Santurce,* ☎ *787/977–6277,* WEB *www.mapr.org.* ✉ *$5.* ⊘ *Tues. and Thurs.–Sun. 10–5, Wed. 10–8.*

④ **Universidad de Puerto Rico.** The southern district of Río Piedras is home to the University of Puerto Rico, between Avenida Ponce de León and Avenida Barbosa. The campus is one of the two performance venues for the Puerto Rico Symphony Orchestra. (The other is the Centro de Bellas Artes Luis A. Ferré in Santurce.) Theatrical productions and other concerts are also scheduled here.

The university's **Museo de Historia, Antropología y Arte** (Museum of History, Anthropology, and Art) has archaeological and historical exhibits that deal with the Native American influence on the island and the Caribbean, the colonial era, and the history of slavery. Art displays are occasionally mounted; the museum's prize exhibit is the painting *El Velorio* (The Wake), by the 19th-century artist Francisco Oller. ⊠ *Next to main university entrance on Av. Ponce de León, Río Piedras,* ☎ *787/764–0000 Ext. 2452.* ✉ *Free.* ⊘ *Mon.–Wed. and Fri. 9–4:30, Thurs. 9–9, weekends 9–3.*

The university's main attraction is the **Jardín Botánico** (Botanical Garden), a 75-acre forest of more than 200 species of tropical and subtropical vegetation. Gravel footpaths lead to a graceful lotus lagoon, a bamboo promenade, an orchid garden with some 30,000 plants, and a palm garden. Signs are in Spanish and English. Trail maps are available at the entrance gate, and groups of 10 or more can arrange guided tours ($25). ⊠ *Intersection of Rtes. 1 and 847 at entrance to Barrio Venezuela, Río Piedras,* ☎ *787/767–1710.* ✉ *Free.* ⊘ *Daily 9–4:30.*

San Juan Environs

Numbers in the margin correspond to points of interest on the Puerto Rico map.

SIGHTS TO SEE

② **Bacardí Rum Plant.** The first Bacardí rum distillery was built in 1862 in Cuba, but it was confiscated by the Castro regime in 1960, and the Bacardí family was exiled. The Puerto Rico plant was built in the 1950s and is one of the world's largest, with the capacity to produce 100,000 gallons of spirits a day and 221 million cases a year. You can take a 45-minute tour of the bottling plant, museum (called the Cathedral of Rum), and distillery, and there's a gift shop. Yes, you'll be offered a sample. ⊠ *Bay View Industrial Park, Rte. 888, Km 2.6, Cataño,* ☎ *787/788–1500 or 787/788–8400.* ✉ *Free.* ⊘ *Tours every 30 mins Mon.–Sat. 9–10:30 and noon–4.*

① **Caparra Ruins.** In 1508 Ponce de León established the island's first settlement here. The ruins—a few crumbling walls—are what remains of an ancient fort, and the small Museo de la Conquista y Colonización de Puerto Rico (Museum of the Conquest and Colonization of Puerto Rico) contains historical documents, exhibits, and excavated artifacts, though you can see the museum's contents in less time than it takes to say the name. ⊠ *Rte. 2, Km 6.6, Guaynabo,* ☎ *787/781–4795,* 🆆🅴🅱 *www.icp.gobierno.pr.* 🖭 *Free.* ☉ *Tues.–Sat. 8:30–4:30.*

🖐 ❸ **Parque de las Ciencias Luis A. Ferré.** The 42-acre Luis A. Ferré Science Park contains a collection of intriguing activities and displays. The Transportation Museum has antique cars and the island's oldest bicycle. In the Rocket Plaza, children can experience a flight simulator, and in the planetarium, the solar system is projected on the ceiling. On site as well are a small zoo and a natural science exhibit. The park is popular with Puerto Rican schoolchildren, and, although it's a bit of a drive from central San Juan, it's a good activity for the family. ⊠ *Rte. 167, Bayamón,* ☎ *787/740–6878.* 🖭 *$5.* ☉ *Wed.–Fri. 9–4, weekends and holidays 10–6.*

Eastern Puerto Rico

❼ **Culebra.** There's archaeological evidence that small groups of pre-Columbian people lived on the islet of Culebra, and certainly pirates landed here from time to time. But Puerto Rico's Spanish rulers didn't bother laying claim to it until 1886; its dearth of freshwater made it unattractive for settlement. At one point it was controlled, like its neighbor Vieques, by the U.S. Navy. When the military withdrew, it turned much of the land into a wildlife reserve. Although the island now has modern conveniences, its pace seems little changed from a century ago. There's only one town, Dewey, named after U.S. Admiral George Dewey. When the sun goes down, Culebra winds down as well. But during the day it's a delightful place to stake out a spot on Playa Flamenco or Playa Zoni and read, swim, or search for shells. So what causes stress on the island? Nothing.

🖐 ❹ **El Yunque.** In the Luquillo mountain range, the 28,000-acre Caribbean National Forest (known popularly as El Yunque after the good Indian spirit Yuquiyu), didn't gain its "rain forest" designation for nothing. More than 100 billion gallons of precipitation fall over it annually, spawning rushing streams and cascades, 240 tree species, and oversized impatiens and ferns. In the evening, millions of inch-long *coquís* (tree frogs) begin their calls. El Yunque is also home to the *cotorra,* Puerto Rico's endangered green parrot, as well as 67 other types of birds.

Your best bet is to visit with a tour. If you'd rather drive here yourself, take Route 3 east from San Juan and turn right (south) on Route 191, about 25 mi (40 km) from the city. The forest's 13 hiking trails are well maintained; many of them are easy to walk and less than a mile long. Before you begin exploring, check out the high-tech, interactive displays—explaining forests in general and El Yunque in particular—at **Centro de Información El Portal** (⊠ Rte. 191, Km 4.3, off Hwy. 3, ☎ 787/888–1880, 🆆🅴🅱 www.southernregion.fs.fed.us/caribbean) the information center near the northern entrance. Test your sense of smell at an exhibit on forest products; inquire about the day's ranger-led activities; and pick up trail maps, souvenirs, film, water, and snacks. All exhibits and publications are in English and Spanish. The center is open daily 9–5; admission is $3.

❺ **Fajardo.** Founded in 1772, Fajardo has historical notoriety as a port where pirates stocked up on supplies. It later developed into a fishing community and an area where sugarcane flourished. (There are still cane fields on the city's fringes.) Today it's a hub for the yachts that use its marinas; the divers who head to its good offshore sites; and for the day-trippers who travel by catamaran, ferry, or plane to the off-islands of Culebra and Vieques. With the most significant docking facilities on the island's eastern side, Fajardo is a bustling city of 37,000—so bustling, in fact, that its unremarkable downtown is often congested and difficult to navigate.

6 **Vieques.** This island off Puerto Rico's east coast is famed for its Playa Sun Bay, a gorgeous stretch of sand with picnic facilities and shade trees. Bahía Mosquito (Mosquito Bay) is best experienced on moonless nights, when millions of bioluminescent organisms glow when disturbed—it's like swimming in a cloud of fireflies. The U.S. Navy controls two-thirds of Vieques, including some of the best beaches, and although Puerto Ricans have staged protests aimed at ousting the military from Vieques, they've made little headway. The 2001 terrorist attacks and the heightened concern over military preparedness decreased the likelihood that the military will cease exercises in the near future. Some 9,300 civilians call Vieques home, many of them expatriate artists and guest-house or vacation-villa owners from the mainland United States. Other islanders fish for a living or work in tourism-related fields. It has two communities—Isabel Segunda, where the ferries dock, and the smaller Esperanza.

Southern Puerto Rico

9 **Bosque Estatal de Guánica.** The 9,200-acre Guánica State Forest, a United Nations Biosphere Reserve, is a great place for hikes and bird-watching expeditions. It's an outstanding example of a tropical dry coastal forest, with some 700 species of plants and more than 100 types of birds. There are 12 major trails through the sun-bleached hills, from which you'll see towering cacti and gumbo limbo trees. There are also several caves to explore. You can enter on Route 333, which skirts the forest's southwestern portion, or at the end of Route 334, where there's a parks office. ⊠ *Rte. 333 or 334,* ☎ *787/821–5706.* ☞ *Free.* ⊙ *Daily 9–5.*

10 **Cabo Rojo.** Named for the pinkish cliffs that surround it, Cabo Rojo was founded in 1771 as a port for merchant vessels—and for the smugglers and pirates who inevitably accompanied ocean-going trade. Today it's known as a family resort destination, and many small, inexpensive hotels line its shores. Seaside settlements such as Puerto Real and Joyuda—the latter has a strip of more than 30 seafood restaurants overlooking the water—are found along the coast. Although you can hike in wildlife refuges at the outskirts of town, there aren't any area outfitters, so be sure to bring along water, sunscreen, and all other necessary supplies.

8 **Ponce.** Puerto Rico's second-largest urban area (population 194,000) shines in 19th-century style with pink-marble-bordered sidewalks, painted trolleys, and horse-drawn carriages. Stroll around the main square, Plaza las Delicias, with its perfectly pruned India-laurel fig trees, graceful fountains, gardens, and park benches. View the Catedral de Nuestra Señora de Guadalupe (Our Lady of Guadalupe Cathedral), perhaps even attend the 6 AM mass, and walk down calles Isabel and Cristina to see turn-of-the-20th-century wooden houses with wrought-iron balconies.

You haven't seen a firehouse until you've seen the **Parque de Bombas**, a structure built in 1882 for an exposition and converted to a firehouse the following year. Today it is a museum tracing the history—and glorious feats—of Ponce's fire brigade ⊠ *Plaza las Delicias, Ponce Centro,* ☎ *787/284–4141 Ext. 342.* ☞ *Free.* ⊙ *Wed.–Mon. 9:30–6.*

The neoclassical **Casa Armstrong-Poventud** houses the Ponce offices of the Institute of Puerto Rican Culture. You can walk through several rooms that display antique furnishings. ⊠ *Calle Union, across from Catedral, Ponce Centro,* ☎ *787/844–2540 or 787/840–7667.* ☞ *Free.* ⊙ *Weekdays 8–4:30.*

Two superlative examples of early 20th-century architecture house the **Museo de la Historia de Ponce** (Ponce History Museum), where 10 rooms of exhibits vividly re-create Ponce's golden years, providing fascinating glimpses into the worlds of culture, high finance, and journalism in the 19th century. Hour-long tours in English and Spanish are available, but there's no set time when they start. ⊠ *51–53 Calle Isabel, Ponce Centro,* ☎ *787/844–7071 or 787/843–4322.* ☞ *$3.* ☉ *Wed.–Mon. 9–5.*

Be sure to allow time to visit the **Museo de Arte de Ponce** (Ponce Museum of Art). The architecture alone is worth seeing: the modern two-story building designed by Edward Durrell Stone (one of the designers of New York's Museum of Modern Art) has seven interconnected hexagons, glass cupolas, and a pair of curved staircases. The collection includes late Renaissance and baroque works from Italy, France, and Spain, as well as contemporary art by Puerto Ricans. ⊠ *2325 Av. Las Américas, Sector Santa María,* ☎ *787/848–0505,* WEB *www. museoarteponce.org.* ☞ *$4.* ☉ *Daily 10–5.*

The **Castillo Serrallés** is a splendid Spanish Revival mansion on Vigía Hill. This former residence of the owners of the Don Q rum distillery has been restored with a mix of original furnishings and antiques that recall the era of the sugar barons. A short film details the history of the sugar and rum industries; tours are given every half hour in English and Spanish. The 100-ft-tall cross (La Cruceta del Vigía) behind the museum has a windowed elevator; you can ascend for views of Ponce and the coast for $1. ⊠ *17 El Vigía, El Vigía Hill,* ☎ *787/259–1774,* WEB *www.castilloserralles.com.* ☞ *$3.* ☉ *Tues.–Thurs. 9:30–5, Fri.–Sun. 10–5:30.*

Just outside the city, **Hacienda Buena Vista** is a 19th-century coffee plantation, restored by the Conservation Trust of Puerto Rico, with authentic machinery and furnishings intact. Reservations are required for the 90-minute Spanish-language tours (at 8:30, 10:30, 1:30, and 3:30). Tours in English are at 1:30, also by reservation only. ⊠ *Rte. 10, Km 16.8, Sector Corral Viejo,* ☎ *787/722–5882 weekdays; 787/284–7020 weekends,* WEB *www.fideicomiso.org/hacienda.htm.* ☞ *$5.* ☉ *Wed.–Fri. morning open to tour groups; Fri. afternoon–Sun. open to public.*

At the **Centro Ceremonial Indígena de Tibes** (Tibes Indian Ceremonial Center), you'll find pre-Taíno ruins and burials dating from AD 300 to AD 700. Some archaeologists, noting the symmetrical arrangement of stone pillars, surmise the cemetery may have been of great religious significance. The complex includes a detailed re-creation of a Taíno village and a museum. ⊠ *Rte. 503, Km 2.2, Barrio Tibes,* ☎ *787/840–2255 or 787/840–5685,* WEB *http://ponce.inter/edu/tibes/tibes.html.* ☞ *$2.* ☉ *Tues.–Sun. 9–4.*

⑪ **San Germán.** Around San Germán's (population 39,000) two main squares—Plazuela Santo Domingo and Plaza Francisco Mariano Quiñones (named for an abolitionist)—are buildings done in every conceivable style of architecture found on the island including mission, Victorian, creole, and Spanish colonial. The city's tourist office offers a free guided trolley tour. Students and professors from the Inter-American University often fill the center's bars and cafés.

The **Museo de Arte y Casa de Estudio** is an early 20th-century home that has been turned into a museum. Displays include colonial furnishings, religious art, and Taíno artifacts; there are also changing art exhibits. ⊠ *7 Calle Esperanza,* ☎ *787/892–8870.* ☞ *Free.* ☉ *Wed.–Sun. 10–noon and 1–3.*

One of the oldest Christian religious structures in the Americas, the **Capilla de Porta Coeli** (Heaven's Gate Chapel) overlooks the Plazuela de Santo Domingo. The original complex, which included a convent, was built in 1606; much of it was demolished in 1866, leaving only the chapel and a vestige of the convent's front wall. The chapel was restored and reopened for services in 1878. It functions as a museum of religious art, displaying painted wooden statuary by Latin American and Spanish artists. ⊠ *Plazuela Santo Domingo,* ☎ 787/892–5845. ⊞ *$1.* ⊙ *Wed.–Sun. 9–4:45.*

Northwestern Puerto Rico

⑰ **Bosque Estatal de Río Abajo.** In the middle of karst country, the Río Abajo State Forest spans some 5,000 acres and includes huge bamboo stands and silk-cotton trees. It also has several plantations of Asian teaks, Dominican and Honduran mahogany, and Australian pines, which are part of a government tree management program that supplies wood for the local economy (primarily for artisans and fence building). Walking trails wind through the forest, which is one of the habitats of the rare Puerto Rican parrot. An information office is near the entrance, and a recreation area with picnic tables is farther down the road. ⊠ *Rte. 621, Km 4.4,* ☎ 787/817–0984. ⊞ *Free.* ⊙ *Daily.*

⑫ **Mayagüez.** With a population of slightly more than 100,000, this is the largest city on Puerto Rico's west coast. Although bypassed by the mania for restoration that has spruced up Ponce and Old San Juan, Mayagüez is graced by some lovely turn-of-the-20th-century architecture, such as the landmark art deco Teatro Yagüez and the Plaza de Colón.

Just north of town, visit the **Tropical Research Station,** run by the U.S. Department of Agriculture, contains a plant collection that has been nurtured for more than half a century. More than 2,000 species from all over the tropical world are found here, including teak, mahogany, cinnamon, nutmeg, rubber, and numerous exotic flowers. Free maps are available for self-guided tours. ⊠ *Intersection of Rte. 2 and Rte. 108,* ☎ 787/831–3435. ⊞ *Free.* ⊙ *Weekdays 7–4.*

⑭ **Observatorio de Arecibo.** Hidden among fields and hills is the world's largest radar–radio telescope, operated by the National Astronomy and Ionosphere Center of Cornell University. A 20-acre dish, with a 600-ton suspended platform hovering eerily over it, lies in a 563-ft-deep sinkhole in the karst landscape. The observatory has been used to look for extraterrestrial life, and if it looks familiar it may be because scenes from the movie *Contact* were filmed here. You can walk around the platform and view the huge dish, and tour the visitor center, which has two levels of interactive exhibits on planetary systems, meteors, and weather phenomena. ⊠ *Rte. 625, Km 3.0,* ☎ 787/878–2612, WEB *www.naic.edu.* ⊞ *$4.* ⊙ *Wed.–Fri. noon–4, weekends 9–4.*

⑯ **Parque Ceremonial Indígena de Caguana.** The 13 acres of this park were used more than 800 years ago by the Taíno tribes for worship and recreation, including a game—thought to have religious significance—that resembled modern-day soccer. Today you can see 10 *bateyes* (courts) of various sizes, large stone monoliths (some with petroglyphs), and recreations of Taíno gardens. ⊠ *Rte. 111, Km 12.3,* ☎ 787/894–7325. ⊞ *$2.* ⊙ *Daily 8:30–4.*

⑮ **Parque de las Cavernas del Río Camuy.** This 268-acre park contains an enormous cave network and the third-longest underground river in the world. A tram takes you down a mountain covered with bamboo and banana trees to the entrance of Cueva Clara de Empalme. Hour-long guided tours in English and Spanish lead you on foot through the 180-ft-high cave, which has large stalactites and stalagmites and blind fish. The visit ends with a tram ride to Tres Pueblos sinkhole, where you can see the river passing from one cave to another, 400 ft below. Tours are first-come, first-served; plan to arrive early on holidays and weekends. ⊠ *Rte. 129, Km 18.9,* ☏ *787/898–3100.* ☐ *$10.* ☉ *Wed.– Sun. 8–4, last tour at 3:45.*

⓭ Rincón. Jutting out into the ocean along the rugged western coast, Rincón, meaning corner in Spanish, may have gotten its name because of how it is nestled in a "corner" of the coastline. Some, however, trace the town's name to Gonzalo Rincón, a 16th-century landowner who let poor families live on his land. Whatever the history, the name suits the town, which is like a little world unto itself.

The town jumped into the surfing spotlight after hosting the World Surfing Championship in 1968. Although the beat here picks up from October through April, when the waves are the best, Rincón is basically laid-back and unpretentious. If you visit between December and February, you might get a glimpse of the humpback whales that winter off the coast. Because of its unusual setting, Rincón's layout can be a little disconcerting. The main road, Route 413, loops around the coast, and many beaches and sights are on dirt roads intersecting with it. Most hotels and restaurants hand out detailed maps of the area.

PUERTO RICO A TO Z

To research prices, get advice from other travelers, and book travel arrangements, visit www.fodors.com.

AIR TRAVEL

San Juan is the regional hub of American Airlines, which flies nonstop from New York, Newark, Boston, Miami, Orlando, Fort Lauderdale, Los Angeles, and St. Louis. Other major U.S. carriers serving San Juan include Continental, with daily nonstop service from Newark, Houston, and Cleveland; Delta, with nonstop service from Atlanta; Northwest, offering daily nonstop flights from Detroit, Memphis, and Minneapolis; United, which flies nonstop daily from Chicago and has weekend flights from New York and Washington, DC; US Airways, flying nonstop daily from Pittsburgh, Philadelphia, and Charlotte; and Spirit Air, which has two daily nonstop flights from Fort Lauderdale with connections from New York, Atlantic City, and Detroit.

Air Canada has flights to San Juan from Montréal and Toronto, and Canadian Airlines has service—with a stop in Miami—from Toronto, Vancouver, and Calgary. British Airways serves San Juan from London, and Lufthansa's partner, Condor, flies out of Germany. LACSA connects San Juan to San José, Costa Rica. From Australia, you can take Qantas Airways from Sydney, Brisbane, Perth, Melbourne, and several other cities to Honolulu and Los Angeles for connections to Puerto Rico. Qantas also flies from Auckland, New Zealand, to Los Angeles.

Puerto Rico is also a good spot from which to hop to other Caribbean islands. American Airline's American Eagle serves many of the Lesser Antilles islands; Cape Air connects San Juan to St. Thomas and St. Croix; ALM travels to Jamaica, Aruba, Bonaire, and its base in Curaçao; and Leeward Islands Air Transport (LIAT), based in Antigua, flies to nearly all the Lesser Antilles islands. Vieques Air-Link connects San Juan with Vieques and Culebra.

➤ Major U.S. Airlines: **American Airlines** (☏ 800/433–7300). **Continental** (☏ 800/231–0856). **Delta** (☏ 800/241–4141). **Northwest** (☏ 800/447–4747). **Spirit Air** (☏ 800/756–7117). **United** (☏ 800/538–2929). **US Airways** (☏ 800/428–4322).

➤ SMALLER AIRLINES: **ALM** (☎ 800/327–7230). **American Eagle** (☎ 800/433–7300). **Cape Air** (☎ 800/352–0714). **LIAT** (☎ 800/468–0482; 787/791–0800 in Puerto Rico). **Vieques Air-Link** (☎ 888/901–9247; 787/723–9882 in Puerto Rico).

➤ FROM ELSEWHERE IN THE WORLD: **Air Canada Vacations** (☎ 800/774–8993 in North America). **British Airways** (☎ 0845/7222–111 in the U.K.; 800/247–9297 in the U.S). **Canadian Airlines** (☎ 800/426–7000 in North America). **Condor** (☎ 06107/939–229 in Germany). **LACSA–Group Taca** (☎ 506/231–0033 in Costa Rica). **Qantas** (☎ 800/062–241 in Australia; 09/357–8700 in Auckland; 0800/808–767 elsewhere in New Zealand; 800/227–4500 in the U.S.).

AIRPORTS

The Aeropuerto Internacional Luis Muñoz Marín (SJU) is minutes east of downtown San Juan in the coastal section of Isla Verde. San Juan's other airport is the small Fernando L. Rivas Dominici Airport in Isla Grande, near the city's Miramar section. From here you can catch Vieques Air-Link flights to Culebra, Vieques, and other destinations on Puerto Rico and throughout the Caribbean. (Note that although the Dominici airport was still operating at this writing, its future was uncertain.) Other Puerto Rican airports include Mercedita in the south coast town of Ponce, Eugenio María de Hostos in the west coast community of Mayagüez, Rafael Hernández in the northwestern town of Aguadilla, and Antonio Rivera Rodríguez on Vieques.

➤ AIRPORT INFORMATION: **Aeropuerto Antonio Rivera Rodríguez** (☎ 787/741–8358). **Aeropuerto Eugenio María de Hostos** (☎ 787/833–0148). **Aeropuerto Fernando L. Rivas Dominici** (☎ 787/729–8711). **Aeropuerto Mercedita** (☎ 787/842–6292). **Aeropuerto Internacional Luis Muñoz Marín** (☎ 787/791–3840). **Aeropuerto Rafael Hernández** (☎ 787/891–2286).

BOAT AND FERRY TRAVEL

The Autoridad de los Puertos (Port Authority) ferry between Old San Juan (Pier 2) and Cataño costs a mere 50¢ one-way. It runs every half hour from 6 AM to 10 PM, and every 15 minutes during peak hours. The Fajardo Port Authority's 400-passenger ferries run between that east coast town and the out islands of Vieques and Culebra; both trips take 90 minutes. The vessels carry cargo and passengers to Vieques three times daily ($2 one-way) and to Culebra twice a day Sunday through Friday and three times a day on Saturday ($2.25 one-way).

Get schedules for the Culebra and Vieques ferries by calling the port authority in Fajardo, Vieques, or Culebra. You buy tickets at the ferry dock. Reservations aren't necessary unless you're transporting a vehicle, in which case you should not only make a reservation but also arrive 1½ hours before the departure time.

➤ BOAT AND FERRY INFORMATION: **Autoridad de los Puertos** (☎ 787/788–1155 in San Juan; 787/863–4560 in Fajardo; 787/742–3161 in Culebra; 787/741–4761 in Vieques).

BUSINESS HOURS

BANKS AND OFFICES

Bank hours are generally weekdays 8–4 or 9–5, though a few branches are open Saturday 9–noon or 1. Post offices are open weekdays 7:30–4:30 and Saturday 8–noon. Government offices are open weekdays 9–5.

GAS STATIONS

Most stations are open daily from early in the morning until 10 PM or 11 PM. Numerous stations in urban areas are open 24 hours.

MUSEUMS AND SIGHTS

As a rule San Juan area museums are closed on Monday, and in some cases, Sunday. Hours otherwise are 9 or 10 AM to 5 PM, often with an hour off for lunch between noon and 2. Sights managed by the national parks service, such as Fuerte San Felipe del Morro and San Cristóbal, are open daily 9–5.

PHARMACIES

In cities, pharmacies are generally open 9–6 or 7 weekdays and on Saturday. Walgreens operates numerous pharmacies around the island; some are open 24 hours.

SHOPS

Street shops are open Monday through Saturday 9 to 6 (9–9 during Christmas holidays); mall stores tend to stay open to 9 or so. Count on convenience stores staying open late into the night, seven days a week. Supermarkets are often closed on Sunday, although some remain open 24-hours, seven days a week.

BUS TRAVEL

The Autoridad Metropolitana de Autobuses (AMA, or Metropolitan Bus Authority) operates *guaguas* (buses) that thread through San Juan, running in exclusive lanes on major thoroughfares and stopping at signs marked PARADA or PARADA DE GUAGUAS. The main terminals are at the Covadonga parking lot and Plaza de Colón in Old San Juan and the Capetillo Terminal in Río Piedras, next to the central business district. Most buses are air-conditioned and have wheelchair lifts and lock-downs.

Bus travel to outlying areas is less than comprehensive. Your best bet for travel to other parts of the island is by rental car or by *públicos*— "public cars," though most are actually 17-passenger vans. They have yellow license plates ending in "P" or "PD," and they scoot to towns throughout the island, stopping in each community's main plaza. They operate primarily during the day; routes and fares are fixed by the public service commission, but schedules aren't set, so you have to call ahead.

In San Juan, the main terminals are at the airport and at Plaza Colón on the waterfront in Old San Juan. San Juan–based público companies include Blue Line for trips to Aguadilla and the northwest coast, Choferes Unidos de Ponce for Ponce, Línea Caborrojeña for Cabo Rojo and the southwest coast, Línea Boricua for the interior and the southwest, Línea Sultana for Mayagüez and the west coast, and Terminal de Transportación Pública for Fajardo and the east.

FARES AND SCHEDULES

In San Juan, bus fares are 25¢ or 50¢, depending on the route, and are paid in exact change upon entering the bus. Buses adhere to their routes, but schedules are fluid, to say the least. Count on a bus passing your stop every 20–30 minutes, less frequently on Sunday and holidays. Service starts at around 6 AM and generally lasts until 9 PM. For more information, call the AMA or pick up a schedule at the nearest bus station.
➤ BUS INFORMATION: **AMA** (☎ 787/729–1512 or 787/767–7979). **Blue Line** (☎ 787/765–7733). **Choferes Unidos de Ponce** (☎ 787/764–0540). **Línea Boricua** (☎ 787/765–1908). **Línea Caborrojeña** (☎ 787/723–9155). **Línea Sultana** (☎ 787/765–9377). **Terminal de Transportación Pública** (☎ 787/250–0717).

CAR RENTALS

If you rent a car, a good road map will be helpful in remote areas. A valid driver's license from your country of origin can be used in Puerto Rico for three months. Rates start as low as $35 a day (plus insurance), with unlimited mileage. Discounts are often offered for long-term rentals and for cars that are booked more than 72 hours in advance. All major U.S. car-rental agencies are represented on the island, though many reliable local companies offer competitive rates.

You'll find offices for dozens of agencies at San Juan's airports, and a majority of them have shuttle service to and from the airport and the pickup point. Most rental cars are available with automatic or standard transmission. Four-wheel-drive vehicles aren't necessary unless you plan to go way off the beaten path or along the steep, rocky roads of Culebra or Vieques; in most cases a standard compact car will do the trick. Always opt for air-conditioning, though.

➤ MAJOR AGENCIES: **Avis** (☎ 787/721–4499). **Budget** (☎ 787/791–3685). **Hertz** (☎ 787/791–0840). **National** (☎ 787/791–1805). **Thrifty** (☎ 787/253–2525).

➤ LOCAL AGENCIES: **Charlie Car Rental** (☎ 787/791–1101 or 800/289–1227). **L & M Car Rental** (☎ 787/791–1160 or 800/666–0807). **Target** (☎ 787/728–1447 or 800/934–6457).

CAR TRAVEL

Several well-marked multilane highways link population centers. Route 26 is the main artery through San Juan, connecting Condado and Old San Juan to Isla Verde and the airport. Route 22, which runs east–west between San Juan and Camuy, and the Luis A. Ferré Expressway (Route 52), which runs north–south between San Juan and Ponce, are toll roads (35¢–50¢). Route 2, a smaller highway, travels along the west coast, and routes 3 and 53 traverse the east shore. Distances are posted in kilometers (1.6 km to 1 mi), whereas speed limits are posted in miles per hour. Speeding and drunk-driving penalties are much the same here as on the mainland.

GASOLINE

All types of fuel—unleaded regular, unleaded super-premium, diesel—are available by the litre. At this writing, the cost for regular gas was 32¢ a litre, which works out to roughly $1.22 a gallon. Most stations have both full- and self-service. Hours vary, but stations generally operate daily from early in the morning until 10 or 11 PM; in metro areas many are open 24 hours. Stations are few and far between in the central mountains and other rural areas; plan accordingly. In cities, you can pay with cash and bank or credit cards; in the hinterlands cash is often your only option.

ROAD CONDITIONS

Roads are in generally good condition although you may want to keep an eye out for potholes, especially after heavy rains. Some roads in the mountains are very curvy and take longer to cover than the distance on a map might suggest. Not every road is marked, but most Puerto Ricans are happy to help with directions.

ELECTRICITY

Puerto Rico uses the same electrical current as the U.S. mainland, namely 110 volts.

EMERGENCIES

➤ GENERAL CONTACTS: **Ambulance, police, and fire** (☎ 911). **Air Ambulance Service** (☎ 800/633–3590 or 787/756–3424). **Dental Emergencies** (☎ 787/722–2351 or 787/795–0320). **San Juan Tourist Zone Police** (☎ 787/726–7020; 787/726–7015 for Condado; 787/728–4770 or 787/726–2981 for Isla Verde). **Travelers' Aid** (☎ 787/791–1054 or 787/791–1034).

▶ HOSPITALS: **Ashford Presbyterian Memorial Community Hospital** (✉
1451 Av. Ashford, Condado, San Juan, ☎ 787/721–2160). **General Hospital Dr. Ramón Emeterio Betances** (✉ Rte. 2, Km 157, Mayagüez,
☎ 787/834–8686). **Hospital de la Concepción** (✉ 41 Calle Luna, San
Germán, ☎ 787/892–1860). **Hospital Damas** (✉ 2213 Ponce Bypass
Rd., Ponce, ☎ 787/840–8686). **Hospital Dr. Dominguez** (✉ 300 Font
Martello, Humacao, ☎ 787/852–0505). **Hospital Gubern** (✉ 110
Antonio R. Barcelo, Fajardo, ☎ 787/863–0294).

ETIQUETTE AND BEHAVIOR

Puerto Ricans have, in general, a strong sense of religion—as evidenced by the numerous Catholic patron-saint festivals held throughout the year. Many islanders are somewhat conservative in dress and manners despite a penchant for frenetic music and sexually charged dance. There's also a strong sense of island identity, marked by often-ferocious debates over Puerto Rico's political destiny.

FESTIVALS AND SEASONAL EVENTS

Puerto Rico's festivals are colorful and inclined toward lots of music and feasting. The towns and villages are particularly fond of their patron saints, and every year each of the island's 78 municipalities celebrate *fiestas patronales* (patron saints' festivals). The festivities are religious in origin and feature processions, sports events, folklore shows, feasts, music, and dance. They last about 10 days, with more activities on weekends than on weekdays. San Juan's *fiesta patronal* honors San Juan Bautista in late June; Ponce honors Nuestra Señora de la Guadalupe in mid-December. Several towns and regions also have pre-Lenten Carnivales, complete with parades, folk music, local dishes, a Carnival Queen pageant, and music competitions. Ponce's carnival, celebrated the week before Ash Wednesday, is the most famous. Contact the tourist office for a complete list of fiestas patronales and other events.

In addition to the patron saints' festivals, Old San Juan holds an annual San Sebastián Street Festival in January. Emancipation Day on March 22 honors the abolition of slavery. Mid-April's Sugar Harvest Festival, in San Germán, celebrates the crop with exhibitions, music, and feasts. The Casals Festival, held at the Luis A. Ferré Performing Arts Center in San Juan in early June, honors the late, great cellist with 10 days of classical music. In mid-November you can find the annual Festival of Puerto Rican Music in San Juan and other venues, celebrating the vibrancy of Puerto Rico's *plena* and *bomba* folk music, highlighted by a contest featuring the cuatro, a traditional guitar. During Christmas week you can join the residents of Hatillo for the Hatillo Masks Festival, when they retell the Biblical tale of King Herod's attempt to find and kill the infant Jesus. Men in masks move about town all day, representing Herod's soldiers, and the town brings out music and crafts.

HOLIDAYS

Public holidays in Puerto Rico include: New Year's Day, Three Kings Day (Jan. 6), Eugenio María de Hostos Day (Jan. 8), Dr. Martin Luther King Jr. Day (3rd Mon. in Jan.), Presidents' Day (3rd Mon. in Feb.), Palm Sunday, Good Friday, Easter Sunday, Memorial Day (last Mon. in May), Independence Day (July 4), Luis Muñoz Rivera Day (July 16), Constitution Day (July 25), José Celso Barbosa Day (July 27), Labor Day (1st Mon. in Sept.), Columbus Day (2nd Mon. in Oct.), Veteran's Day (Nov. 11), Puerto Rico Discovery Day (Nov. 19), Thanksgiving Day, and Christmas.

LANGUAGE

Puerto Rico is officially bilingual, but Spanish predominates. Although English is widely spoken, you'll probably want to take a Spanish phrase book along on your travels about the island.

MAIL AND SHIPPING

Puerto Rico uses the U.S. postal system, and all addresses on the island carry Zip codes. You can buy stamps and aerograms and send letters and parcels in post offices. Stamp-dispensing machines can occasionally be found in airports, office buildings, and drugstores. Major post office branches are at 153 Calle Fortaleza in Old San Juan, 163 Avenida Fernández Juncos in San Juan, 102 Calle Garrido Morales in Fajardo, 94 Calle Atocha in Ponce, and 60 Calle McKinley in Mayagüez.
➤ GENERAL INFORMATION: **Postal Services** (☎ 787/622–1756).

MONEY MATTERS

ATMS

Automated Teller Machines (ATMs; known as ATHs here), are readily available and reliable in the cities; many are attached to banks, but you can also find them on the streets and in supermarkets. Just about every casino has one—the better to keep people in the game—as do many of the larger hotels. ATMs are found less frequently in rural areas. Look to local banks such as Banco Popular.

CREDIT CARDS

Credit cards, including Diner's Club and Discover, are widely accepted, especially in tourist areas. Some stateside gasoline credit cards may not be accepted at gas stations here.

CURRENCY

Puerto Rico, as a commonwealth of the United States, uses the U.S. dollar as its official currency.
➤ CONTACTS: **Banco Popular de Puerto Rico** (✉ 206 Calle Tetuán, Old San Juan, San Juan, ☎ 787/725–2636; ✉ 1060 Av. Ashford, Condado, San Juan, ☎ 787/725–4197; ✉ 115 Muñoz Rivera, Isabel Segunda, Vieques, ☎ 787/741–2071; ✉ Rte. 3, Km 42.4, Fajardo, ☎ 787/860–1570; Plaza las Delicias, Ponce, ☎ 787/843–8000 or 787/848–2410; ✉ Mayagüez Mall, Rte. 2; Km 159.4, Mayagüez, ☎ 787/834–4750).

PASSPORTS AND VISAS

Puerto Rico is a commonwealth of the United States, so U.S. citizens don't need passports to visit the island (they must have a valid photo I.D., however). Canadians need proof of citizenship (preferably a valid passport; otherwise bring a birth certificate with a raised seal along with a government-issued photo I.D.). Citizens of Australia, New Zealand, and the United Kingdom must have passports.

SAFETY

San Juan, like any other big city, has its share of crime, so guard your wallet or purse on the city streets. Puerto Rico's beaches are open to the public, and muggings can occur at night even on the beaches of the posh Condado and Isla Verde tourist hotels. Although you certainly can, and should, explore the city and its beaches, use common sense. Don't leave anything unattended on the beach. Leave your valuables in the hotel safe, and stick to the fenced-in beach areas of your hotel. Always lock your car and stash valuables and luggage out of sight. Avoid deserted beaches at night.

SIGHTSEEING TOURS

In Old San Juan, free trolleys can take you around, and the tourist board can provide you with a copy of *Qué Pasa,* which contains a self-guided walking tour. The Caribbean Carriage Company gives old city tours in horse-drawn carriages. Look for these buggies at Plaza Dársenas near Pier 1; the cost is $30–$60 per couple. If you'd like to explore other parts of the island, several companies offer tours. Leading San Juan operators include Cordero Caribbean Tours, Normandie Tours, Rico Suntours, Tropix Wellness Outings, and United Tour Guides.

➤ CONTACTS: **Caribbean Carriage Company** (☎ 787/797–8063). **Cordero Caribbean Tours** (☎ 787/786–9114; 787/780–2442 evenings). **Normandie Tours, Inc.** (☎ 787/722–6308). **Rico Suntours** (☎ 787/722–2080 or 787/722–6090). **Tropix Wellness Outings** (☎ 787/268–2173). **United Tour Guides** (☎ 787/725–7605 or 787/723–5578).

TAXES
SALES TAX
Accommodations incur a tax: for hotels with casinos it's 11%, for other hotels it's 9%, and for government-approved paradores it's 7%. Ask your hotel before booking. The tax, in addition to the standard 5%–12% service charge applied by most hotels, can add a hefty 20% or more to your bill. There's no sales tax on Puerto Rico. Airport departure taxes are usually included in the cost of your plane ticket rather than being collected at the airport.

TAXIS
The Puerto Rico Tourism Company has instituted a well-organized taxi program. Taxis painted white and sporting the *garita* (sentry box) logo and TAXI TURISTICO label charge set rates depending on the destination; they run from the airport or the cruise-ship piers to Isla Verde, Condado/Ocean Park, and Old San Juan, with rates ranging from $6 to $16. City tours start at $30 per hour. Metered cabs authorized by the Public Service Commission start at $1 and charge 10¢ for every additional ⅓ mi, 50¢ for every suitcase. Waiting time is 10¢ for each 45 seconds. The minimum charge is $3 and there is an extra $1 night charge between 10 PM and 6 AM.In other Puerto Rican towns, you can flag cabs down on the street, but it's easier to have your hotel call one for you. Either way, make sure the driver is clear on whether he or she will charge a flat rate or use a meter to determine the fare. In most places, the cabs are metered.

LINÉAS
Linéas are private taxis you share with three to five other passengers. There are more than 20 companies, each usually specializing in a certain region. Most will arrange door-to-door service. Check local Yellow Pages listings under *Linéas de Carros*. They're affordable and are a great way to meet people, but be prepared to wait: they usually don't leave until they have a full load.

➤ CONTACTS: **Atlantic City Taxi** (☎ 787/268–5050 in San Juan). **Fajardo Taxi Service** (☎ 787/860–1112). **Lolo Felix Tours** (☎ 787/485–5447 on Vieques). **Major Taxicabs** (☎ 787/723–2460 in San Juan). **Ponce Taxi Association** (☎ 787/842–3370). **Public Service Commission** (☎ 787/751–5050). **Ruben's Taxi** (☎ 787/405–1209 on Culebra). **White Taxi** (☎ 787/832–1115 in Mayagüez).

TELEPHONES
COUNTRY AND AREA CODES
Puerto Rico's area codes are 787 and 939. Toll-free numbers (prefix 800, 888, or 877) are widely used in Puerto Rico, and many can be accessed from North America (and vice versa). For North Americans, dialing Puerto Rico is the same as dialing another U.S. state or a Canadian province.

Dial 011, the country code, the city code, and the number. Dial 00 for an international long-distance operator. Phone cards are not required, but can be useful and are widely available (most drug stores carry them). The Puerto Rico Telephone Company sells its "Ring Cards" in various denominations.

LOCAL CALLS
To make a local call in Puerto Rico you must dial 1, the area code, and the seven-digit number.

TIPPING
Tips are expected, and appreciated, by restaurant waitstaff (15%–20% if a service charge isn't included), hotel porters ($1 per bag), maids ($1–$2 a day), and taxi drivers (15%–18%).

TROLLEYS
If your feet fail you in Old San Juan, climb aboard the free open-air trolleys that rumble and coast through the narrow streets. Departures are from La Puntilla and from the marina, but you can board anywhere along the route. Ponce has free trolleys that leave from Plaza las Delicias and stop at major tourist attractions.

VISITOR INFORMATION
➤ Before You Leave: **Puerto Rico Tourism Company** (✉ Box 902-3960, Old San Juan Station, San Juan, PR 00902-3960, ☎ 787/721-2400, WEB www.gotopuertorico.com). From the States, you can call the New York office toll-free at ☎ 800/223–6530. Other branches: ✉ 3575 W. Cahuenga Blvd., Suite 560, Los Angeles, CA 90068, ☎ 213/874-5991; ✉ 901 Ponce de León Blvd., Suite 101, Coral Gables, FL 33134, ☎ 305/445–9112.
➤ In Puerto Rico: **Culebra Tourism Office** (✉ 250 Calle Pedro Marquez, Dewey, ☎ 787/742–3521). **Fajardo Tourism Office** (✉ 6 Av. Munoz Rivera, ☎ 787/863–4013 Ext. 274). **Mayagüez City Hall** (☎ 787/834–8585). **Ponce Municipal Tourist Office** (✉ 2nd floor of Citibank, Plaza las Delicias [Box 1709], Ponce 00733, ☎ 787/841–8160 or 787/841–8044). **Puerto Rico Tourism Company** (✉ Box 902-3960, Old San Juan Station, San Juan 00902-3960, ☎ 787/721–2400; ✉ Plaza Dársenas, near Pier 1, Old San Juan, ☎ 787/722–1709; ✉ Aeropuerto Internacional Luis Muñoz Marín, ☎ 787/791–1014 or 787/791–2551; ✉ Rte. 101, Km 13.7, Cabo Riojo, ☎ 787/851–7070; 291 Vallas Torres, Ponce, ☎ 787/843–0465). **Rincón Tourism Office** (☎ 787/823–5024). **Vieques Tourism Office** (✉ 449 Calle Carlos Lebrón St., Isabel Segunda, ☎ 787/741–5000 Ext. 26).

17 SABA

Updated by
Suzanne
Gordon

Just after daybreak, the street sweepers begin their task, brooms in hand, up and down the winding roads that zigzag around the mountains—steep and dramatic. Every day they follow these concrete ribbons that twist and turn—connecting the villages on the island—sweeping them all by hand until no dirt or litter remains. This tradition of cleanliness makes Saba special, and by nightfall the streets are pristine again, a testimony to what makes the islanders proud.

Tiny Saba (pronounced *say*-ba) has some of the Caribbean's most dramatic scenery, with sweeping, steep mountainsides and sheer cliffs. The breeze is always pleasant, the 1,200 friendly Sabans more so. Everyone knows everyone—indeed, there are fewer than a dozen family names on the island, so many people are also related—and unemployment and crime are virtually nonexistent. The island is a perfect hideaway, a challenge for hikers (Mt. Scenery rises to 2,855 ft [871 m]), a haven for seasoned divers, and heaven on water. It's no wonder Sabans call their island "the unspoiled queen."

Despite all its glories, however, this 5-square-mi (13-square-km) fairy-tale isle isn't for everybody. If you want exciting nightlife or lots of shopping, forget Saba (or make it a one-day excursion from St. Maarten). There are only a handful of shops, a few inns and eateries, and cable TV has replaced the movie theater. Sun worshipers should note that Saba is an essentially beachless volcanic island: steep cliffs ring the island and plummet sharply to the sea. Saba's famous disappearing black-sand beach at Well's Bay, on the northwestern coast, is usually only around for a few months in summer (the sand is washed in and out by rough winter surf). And because of precarious overhanging rocks above, it's no longer recommended as a place to swim.

The capital of Saba is The Bottom, which sits at the bottom of an extinct volcano. In Windwardside, the island's second-largest village, the streets have no names. On the Road (and there's really only one), meandering goats have right of way, though chickens cross at their own risk. In toylike villages, flower-draped walls and neat picket fences border narrow paths. Tidy, sturdy white houses with gingerbread trim, green shutters, and red roofs are planted on the mountainsides among the bromeliads, palms, hibiscus, orchids, and Norwegian pines. Despite such modern additions as TVs (since 1965) and electricity (since 1970), this immaculate, picturesque island's uncomplicated lifestyle has persevered, giving it a make-believe air. Saban ladies still produce handmade lace—a genteel art that has flourished since the 1870s—and brew a potent rum-based liquor, Saba Spice, that's flavored with herbs and spices. Families still follow the generations-old tradition of burying their dead in their neatly tended gardens.

Saba is part of the Netherlands Antilles' Windward Islands and is 28 mi (45 km)—a 12-minute flight with a hair-raising landing on a teeny airstrip (with a 100% safety record)—from St. Maarten. The island is a volcano that has been extinct for 5,000 years. Columbus spotted the little speck in 1493, but except for the Carib Indians who may have lived here around AD 800, Saba remained uninhabited until Dutch settlers arrived from St. Eustatius (Statia) in 1640. From that time on, until the early 19th century, the French, Dutch, English, and Spanish vied for control, and Saba changed hands 12 times before permanently raising the Dutch flag in 1816. Today the Kingdom of the Netherlands comprises three entities: Holland, the Netherlands Antilles (Saba, St. Maarten, St. Eustatius, Bonaire, and Curaçao), and Aruba. Saba's local administration supervises internal affairs, and the island elects representatives and sends them to the capital of the Netherlands Antilles, Willemstad in Curaçao, to attend to regional issues.

Sabans are a hardy lot. To get from Fort Bay to The Bottom, early settlers carved 900 steps out of the mountainside. Everything that arrived on the island, from a pin to a piano, had to be hauled up. Those rugged steps were the only way to travel until the Road was built by Josephus Lambert Hassell (a carpenter who took correspondence courses in engineering) in the 1940s. An extraordinary feat, the Road—known as the "road that couldn't be built"—took 25 years to construct. If you like roller coasters, you'll love the 9-mi (14½-km) white-knuckle route, which begins at sea level in Fort Bay, zigs up to 1,968 ft (600 m), and zags down to 131 ft (40 m) above sea level at the airport, constructed on the island's only flat point, called (what else?) Flat Point.

Lodging

Saba's stock of hotel rooms are in tidy inns or guest houses perched on ledges or tucked into tropical gardens. There are also more than a dozen apartments, cottages, and villas—all with hot water and modern conveniences—for daily, weekly, and monthly rental.

For a list of properties contact the **Saba Tourist Office. WIMCO** (⊠ Box 1461, Newport, RI 02840, ☎ 800/932–3222) rents the fabulous and palatial Haiku House ($2,000–$4,500 a week) and other villas.

CATEGORY	COST EP/CP*	COST A.I.**
$$$$	over $350	over $375
$$$	$250–$350	$275–$375
$$	$150–$250	$175–$275
$	under $150	under $175

*EP/CP prices are per night for a standard double room in high season, excluding taxes, service charges, and meal plans**A.I. (all-inclusive) prices are per person, per night based on double-occupancy during high season, excluding taxes and service charges*

$$$$
★ 🏨 **Willard's of Saba.** From this luxury hotel's cliff-side perch at 2,000 ft (610 m), you can see the faint profiles of neighboring isles. It also has a large solar-heated pool and the island's only tennis court. Rooms have tile floors, ceiling fans, rattan furniture, and balconies. Though isolated from town, this hotel offers privacy and tranquillity. The onsite Willard's of Saba restaurant is good. (Note: because of its location, this hotel isn't recommended for families with children under 12

Saba

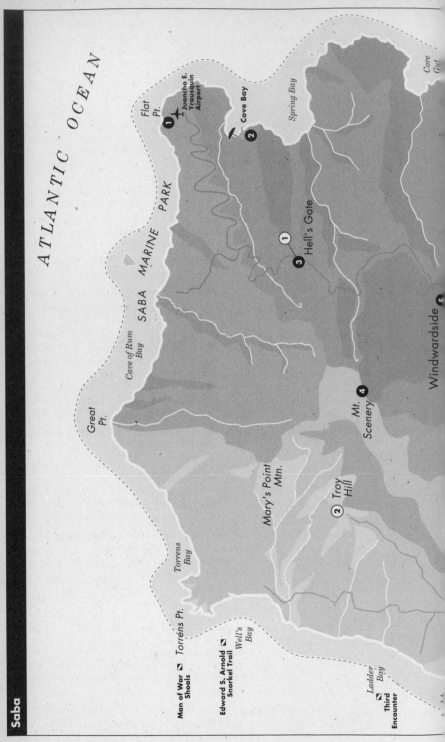

ATLANTIC OCEAN

Flat Pt.

Juancho E. Yrausquin Airport

Cove Bay

Spring Bay

Core Gut

SABA MARINE PARK

Cave of Rum Bay

Great Pt.

Hell's Gate

Mary's Point Mtn.

Mt. Scenery

Troy Hill

Windwardside

Torrens Bay

Man of War Shoals

Torrens Pt.

Edward S. Arnold Snorkel Trail

Well's Bay

Ladder Bay

Third Encounter

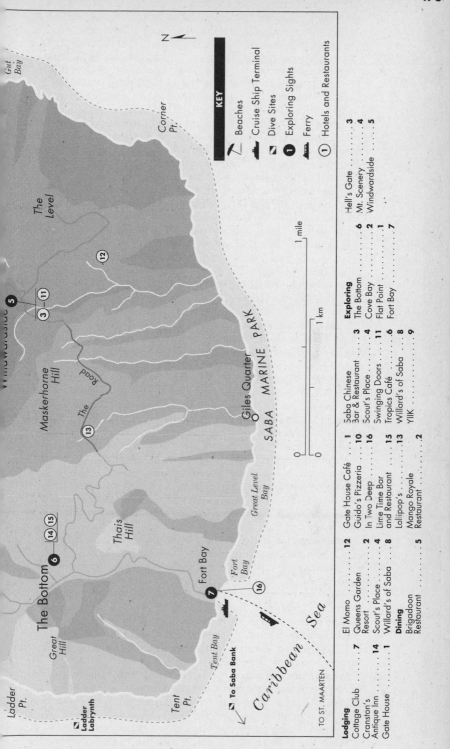

years old.) ✉ *Windwardside (Box 515)*, ☎ *599/416–2498*, FAX *599/ 416–2482*, WEB *www.willardsofsaba.com. 7 rooms. Restaurant, bar, fans, tennis court, pool, exercise equipment, hot tub. AE, D, MC, V. EP, MAP.*

$$$–$$$$ ⊡ **Queens Garden Resort.** This classy resort is an elegant addition to
★ Saba's collection of intimate inns. Three four-story buildings hug the mountain and house 12 suites with antique Dutch colonial and Indonesian furnishings, four-poster beds, TVs, kitchens, and verandas that have breathtaking ocean views. Sit inside the Mango Royale Restaurant or on the patio beside the island's largest pool—which is particularly nice when the torches are lighted and soft music plays in the background. ✉ *1 Troy Hill Dr., Troy Hill (Box 4)*, ☎ *599/416–3494*, FAX *599/416–3495*, WEB *www.queenssaba.com. 12 suites. Restaurant, bar, fans, kitchenettes, pool. AE, D, MC, V. EP.*

$ ⊡ **Cottage Club.** These 10 gingerbread bungalows overlooking the sea or the village of English Quarter (Numbers 1, 2, and 6 have the best views) are owned by the Johnson brothers. Spacious and breezy, rooms are furnished in a basic style and have beamed ceilings, cable TV, and kitchens that the Johnsons will stock for you. Below the stone colonial-style main house, there's a lovely secluded pool area, where you can just catch the edge of the runway and see planes landing and taking off. ✉ *Windwardside*, ☎ *599/416–2486 or 599/416–2386*, FAX *599/ 416–2476*, WEB *www.cottage-club.com. 10 units. Kitchenettes, pool. MC, V. EP.*

$ ⊡ **Cranston's Antique Inn.** Recent renovations have made the five rooms of this reasonably priced inn good values indeed. They have mahogany four-poster beds and other antiques, baths (one even has an original stone oven in it), cable TV, air-conditioning, and fans. ✉ *The Bottom*, ☎ *599/416–3203*, FAX *599/416–3469. 5 rooms. Restaurant, bar. D, MC, V. EP.*

$ ⊡ **El Momo.** This funky inn amid tropical gardens is about 1,500 ft (458 m) up Jimmy's Hill, near Windwardside, and is a 70-step climb— a good reason to pack light. But the views from the gingerbread cottages are well worth the trek. Rooms use solar power and a new eco-toilet has been added to the new unit. Claim a hammock or chair in the snack bar (with honor bar) in the main house to watch the sunset. The property has the only bridge on Saba—a footbridge across its pool. Breakfast is available for about $6. ✉ *Jimmy's Hill (Box 542, Windwardside)*, ☎ FAX *599/416–2265*, WEB *www.elmomo.com. 6 cottages. Snack bar, pool, shop. D, MC, V. EP.*

$ ⊡ **Gate House.** Lillian and Michel Job, formerly of France and Boston, are the new owners of this whimsical hideaway in the tiny village of Hell's Gate. They kept the colorful color schemes created by former owner, artist Jim Siegel. The cheery rooms are decorated with tile floors and crisp pinstripe or checked fabrics. Two units have kitchenettes, and there is a villa and cottage available. The pool is a great place to relax as the sun goes down. You can eat indoors or out at the Gate House Café, which overlooks the sea. ✉ *Hell's Gate*, ☎ *599/416–2416*, FAX *599/416–2550*, WEB *www.sabagatehouse.com. 5 rooms, 1 villa, 1 cottage. Restaurant, pool. MC, V. CP.*

$ ⊡ **Scout's Place.** German dive masters Wolfgang Tooten and Barbara Schafer have created the first dive operation with its own accommodations. You can take initial dive instruction at the property's pool and take advantage of special dive packages through Saba Divers, which Wolfgang and Barbara operate here. All rooms have private baths; 11 rooms have four-poster beds as well as balconies and refrigerators. The Scout's Place restaurant serves three meals daily. ✉ *Windwardside*, ☎ *599/416–2740*, FAX *599/416–2741. 13 rooms. Restaurant, bar, dive shop, pool, shop. MC, V. BP.*

Dining

The caliber of Saban restaurants is definitely improving, so it's easy to find an appealing meal every night of a weeklong stay. Several restaurants serve wonderfully fresh seafood and such Caribbean dishes as stuffed crabs, goat stew, and grilled lobster. A decent selection of wines is available at the better restaurants. Reservations aren't usually necessary, but it wouldn't hurt to call ahead to confirm hours and stake your claim to a table (some of the restaurants are quite small). In addition, some places provide transportation.

What to Wear

Restaurants are informal. Shorts are fine during the day, but for dinner you may want to put on pants or a casual sundress. Just remember that nights in Windwardside can be cool due to the elevation.

CATEGORY	COST*
$$$$	over $30
$$$	$20–$30
$$	$10–$20
$	under $10

*per person for a main course at dinner

ASIAN

$$ ✕ **Saba Chinese Bar & Restaurant.** In this plain little house with plastic cloths on its tables you can get, among other things, sweet-and-sour pork or chicken, cashew chicken, and curried dishes. ⊠ *Windwardside,* ☎ *599/416–2268. MC, V. Closed Mon.*

CARIBBEAN

$$–$$$ ✕ **Gate House Café.** Slightly out of the way, on the road to the airport, this delightful restaurant in the Gate House hotel offers French cuisine prepared by owner Michel Job. Choose from the extensive wine list to round out the meal, be it seafood, chicken, or beef. Don't miss the tantalizing "Queen of Saba" chocolate cake. Both lunch and dinner are served seven days a week. ⊠ *Gate House Hotel, Hell's Gate,* ☎ *599/416–2416. MC, V.*

$$–$$$ ✕ **Lollipop's.** Owner Carmen Caines was nicknamed Lollipop in honor
★ of her sweet disposition. She and her husband, Will, prepare land crab, goat, and fresh grilled fish. Meals are served in a down-home–style dining room overlooking the sea, and there's a room for shooting pool as well. No reservations are necessary, but if you call, Lollipop will pick you up and drop you off after dinner—a sweet touch, indeed. ⊠ *St. John's,* ☎ *599/416–3330. MC, V.*

$$ ✕ **Lime Time Bar and Restaurant.** A Saban house has been spruced up to create this lively bar-eatery. You can eat on the front porch with a view of the Governor's House. Sample such local favorites as spare ribs, burgers, garlic shrimp, and conch chowder. The music here is lively and modern. ⊠ *The Bottom,* ☎ *599/416–3351. AE, MC, V.*

CONTEMPORARY

$$$–$$$$ ✕ **Willard's of Saba.** On a cliff high above Windwardside, Saba's most expensive restaurant in the Willard's of Saba hotel has views of the sea at a dizzying 2,000 ft (610 m) below. Chef Corazon de Johnson, an enthusiastic, charming cook, fuses international and Asian cuisine to offer such dishes as drunken pork loin, Shanghai rolls, and fresh lobster; Corazon also prepares kosher and vegetarian, and will fill requests to fit most any dietary need. Access to the restaurant is up a steep drive; only a few taxis will make the climb, but you can call the restaurant to arrange transport. ⊠ *Willard's of Saba hotel, Windwardside,* ☎ *599/416–2498. AE, D, MC, V.*

$$$–$$$$ ✕ **YIIK.** Latticework, plants, tiny lights, and wind chimes add consid-
★   erable charm to this rooftop restaurant in the heart of town. During
the day folks are drawn to this relaxed café for the pastries and the
coffee. Local chefs Rudolph Hassell and Carl Buncamper also offer tasty
shrimp and lobster dishes for dinner and lunch specialties such as cur-
ried goat. ⊠ *Windwardside,* ☎ *599/416–2539. MC, V. Closed Sun.*

$$ ✕ **Tropics Cafe.** A black-and-white-checked tile floor, crisp black-and-
white napery, and gleaming silver flatware contribute to the chic look
of this poolside restaurant of Juliana's hotel. Run by British-trained
chef Caroline Willcock, the restaurant has a menu of contemporary
bistro-style dishes such as penne with crab in a mango sauce. The restaurant serves three meals most days. ⊠ *Windwardside,* ☎ *599/416–2469.
MC, V. No dinner Mon.*

ECLECTIC

$$–$$$ ✕ **Brigadoon Restaurant.** A local favorite, this restaurant on the first
★   floor of a colonial house lets you take in the passing action on the street—
which may not mean a whole lot on Saba, but it's still a nice thought.
Fresh fish grilled and served with a light creole sauce is the specialty,
but there are also chicken and steak dishes, lobster, and flavorful creations such as shrimp encrusted with salt and pepper. ⊠ *Windwardside,* ☎ *599/416–2380. AE, DC, MC, V. No lunch. Closed Tues.*

$–$$ ✕ **Scout's Place.** At this restaurant in the Scout's Place hotel, chef/dive
master Wolfgang Tooten is in charge of the kitchen. Tables on the porch
offer stunning views of the water and on the outdoor veranda overlooking the tiny houses and lush forest that create this fairyland Saba.
Cuisine runs the gamut from local goat stew to Italian pasta dishes to
German specialties as well as fresh lobster and catch of the day. Wednesday breakfast is when many American expatriates gather for their un-
official town meeting. ⊠ *Scout's Place hotel, Windwardside,* ☎ *599/
416–2740. Reservations essential. MC, V.*

$ ✕ **In Two Deep.** The owners of the Saba Deep dive shop run this lively
harborside spot, with its stained-glass window and mahogany bar. The
soups and sandwiches (especially the Reuben) are excellent, and the
customers are usually high-spirited—most have just come from a
dive. ⊠ *Fort Bay,* ☎ *599/416–3438. MC, V. No dinner, except on some
holidays.*

$ ✕ **Swinging Doors.** A cross between an English pub and an Old West
saloon (yes, there are swinging doors), this lively watering hole serves
good, ample burgers, jalapeño poppers (a deep-fried flour puff ball seasoned with hot peppers), parrotfish sandwiches, and plenty of brew
daily from 9 AM until late at night. There's also plenty of conversation, including some local gossip. ⊠ *Windwardside,* ☎ *599/416–
2506. No credit cards.*

FRENCH

$$–$$$ ✕ **Mango Royale Restaurant.** This elegant spot in the Queens Garden
★   Resort serves the creative cuisine of chef Martin Laurent, who specializes
in Creole and French seafood dishes. Try lobster thermidor or seafood
chowder, or—if you're not in a seafood mood—chicken scallopini in
a delicate basil cream sauce. In these magical hillside surroundings you
can dine inside or out. After dinner, you can dance under the stars; poolside barbecues, musical events, and theme nights with international flavors are also on offer. And it's a popular spot for weddings. ⊠ *Queens
Garden Resort, 1 Troy Hill Dr., Troy Hill,* ☎ *599/416–3494. AE, D,
MC, V.*

ITALIAN

$–$$ ✕ **Guido's Pizzeria.** Students at the Saba University School of Medicine
love this place. And what's not to love? In addition to pizza and

lasagna, there are a pool table, a few rooms to rent, and a fitness center. ✉ *Windwardside,* ☎ *599/416–2230. No credit cards. Closed Sun.*

Outdoor Activities and Sports

FISHING

This island isn't a big fishing destination, but a few Sabans will take you out on their boats. Keep in mind that these are not big, fancy vessels. **Saba Deep** (☎ 599/416–3347 or 888/348–3722) can take people fishing, or ask the tourist office or your hotel to arrange it for you.

HIKING

On Saba you can't avoid some hiking, even if you just go to mail a postcard. The big deal, of course, is Mt. Scenery, with 1,064 steps leading to its top. Many of the trails, including the Mt. Scenery trail, have signs that describe the flora. For information about Saba's 18 recommended botanical hikes, check with the **Saba Conservation Foundation** (✉ behind tourist office, Windwardside, ☎ 599/416–2630), which maintains trails, or the foundation's **trail shop** (☎ 599/416–2630 or 599/416–3307) across the street. Botanical tours are available upon request. A guided, strenuous full-day hike through the undeveloped back side of Mt. Scenery costs about $50. At the shop you can book a hike with island native Crocodile James (James Johnson), who will explain the local flora and fauna.

SCUBA DIVING AND SNORKELING

Saba has long been recognized as one of the world's premier scuba-diving destinations. Within ½ mi (¾ km) from shore, sea walls drop to depths of more than 1,000 ft (305 m). Visibility is extraordinary, and the dive sites administered by the Saba Marine Park include shoals, reefs, and sea walls, alive with corals and other sea creatures. As other islands become "dived out," Saba is dedicated to preserving its marine life, despite hosting 22,000 dives each year.

Divers have a pick of 26 sites, including **Third Encounter,** a top-rated pinnacle dive (usually to about 110 ft [34 m]) for advanced divers, with plentiful fish and spectacular coral; **Man of War Shoals,** another hot pinnacle dive (70 ft [21 m]), with outstanding fish and coral varieties; and **Ladder Labyrinth,** a formation of ridges and alleys (down to 80 ft [24 m]), where likely sightings include groupers, sea turtles, and sharks. **Saba Bank** is a fertile fishing ground 3 mi (5 km) southwest of Saba. It's also an excellent dive spot because of its coral gardens and undersea mountains.

Snorkelers need not feel left out: the marine park has several marked spots where reefs or rocks sit in shallow water. Among these sites are **Torrens Point,** on the northwest side of the island, and the **Edward S. Arnold Snorkel Trail**—a self-guided underwater tour (off the northwest coast near Well's Bay) with 11 numbered and marked sites. Waterproof maps are available from the marine park, the Saba Conservation Foundation, or dive shops.

Expect to pay about $50 for a one-tank dive, and around $90 for a two-tank dive. Here are some dive operators that can help get you started: **Caradonna Caribbean Tours** (✉ 435 Douglas Ave., Suite 2205, Altamonte Springs, FL 32714, ☎ 407/774–9000 or 800/328–2288, WEB www.caradonna.com) puts together packages at the hotel of your choice. **Saba Deep** (✉ Fort Bay, ☎ 599/416–3347 or 888/348–3722, WEB www.sabadeep.com) offers both PADI- and/or NAUI-certified instructors, directed by owner Mike Myers. **Saba Divers** (✉ Windwardside, ☎ 599/416–2740, WEB www.sabadivers.com) is founded by a German-state registered instructor and offers multilingual instruction.

Sea Saba (⊠ Windwardside, ☎ 599/416–2246) takes you to all of Saba's dive sites. Packages that include accommodations anywhere on the island are available. **Unique Destinations** (⊠ 120 Elmdale Rd., North Scituate, RI 02857, ☎ FAX 401/934–3398, WEB www.unique-destinations. com) can make arrangements and recommend activities for your trip.

Shopping

Lace is one of the island's most popular purchases. The history of Saba lace goes back more than a century to Saban Gertrude Johnson, who attended a Caracas convent school where she learned the arts of drawing and tying threads to adorn fine linens. When she returned to Saba in the 1870s, she taught lace-making, and the art has endured ever since. Every weekday Saban ladies display and sell their creations at the community center in Hell's Gate. Many also sell their wares from their houses; just follow the signs. Collars, tea towels, napkins, and other small items are relatively inexpensive; larger items, such as tablecloths, can be pricey. You should know that the fabric requires some care—it's not drip-dry. Saba Spice is another island buy. Although it *sounds* as delicate as Saba lace and the aroma is as sweet as can be, the base for this liqueur is 151-proof rum.

You'll find souvenirs and gifts in almost every shop. Look for the superlative book *Saban Cottages: A Book of Watercolors,* sold in several stores.

The **Saba Artisan Foundation** (⊠ The Bottom, ☎ 599/416–3260) turns out hand-screened fabrics that you can buy by the yard or that are already made into resort clothing. It also sells T-shirts and spices.

Around the Bend (⊠ Windwardside, ☎ 599/416–2259) carries souvenirs and clothing as well as "gifts, oddments, and pretties." The **Breadfruit Gallery** (⊠ Windwardside, ☎ 599/416–2509) showcases and sells local artists' work. **Jobean Designs** (☎ 599/416–2490) sells intricate, handmade glass-bead jewelry as well as sterling silver and gold pieces by artist-owner Jo Bean. She also offers bead-making workshops. **Katherine's Windwardside Gallery** (⊠ Windwardside, ☎ 599/416–2360) was Saba's first gallery for works by local artist Katherine Maeder, who now works out of Meadowview Cottage on Park Lane. The **Lynn Gallery** (⊠ Windwardside, ☎ 599/416–2435), which is open by appointment or by chance, displays and sells artwork by the multitalented Lynn family, which also has a gallery in St. Martin's Grand Case. **El Momo Folk Art** (⊠ Windwardside, ☎ 599/416–2518) has silk-screened T-shirts and souvenirs. **Sea Saba** (⊠ Windwardside, ☎ 599/416–2246) carries T-shirts, diving equipment, clothing, and books. The **Yellow House** (⊠ Windwardside, ☎ 599/416–2334) sells local books, souvenirs, and lace.

Nightlife

Check the bulletin board in each village for a list of events, which often include parties. **Scout's Place** (⊠ Windwardside, ☎ 599/416–2740) is a popular evening gathering place, with special prices on desserts and coffee from 8 to 10 PM. The convivial bar can get crowded and sometimes there's even dancing.

Exploring Saba

Getting around the island means negotiating the narrow, twisting roadway that clings to the mountainside and rises from sea level to almost 2,000 ft (612 m). Although driving isn't difficult, just be sure to go slowly and cautiously. If in doubt, leave the driving to a cabbie so you can enjoy the scenery. You won't need long to tour the island by car—if you don't stop, you can cover the entire circuitous length of the Road in the space of a morning. If you want to shop, have lunch, and do some sightseeing, plan on a full day.

Numbers in the margin correspond to points of interest on the Saba map.

SIGHTS TO SEE

❻ The Bottom. Sitting in a bowl-shape valley 820 ft (251 m) above the sea, this town is the seat of government and the home of the lieutenant governor. The gubernatorial mansion, next to Wilhelmina Park, has fancy fretwork, a high-pitched roof, and wraparound double galleries. Saba University runs a **medical school** (WEB www.saba.org) in The Bottom, at which about 200 students are enrolled.

On the other side of town is the Wesleyan Holiness Church, a small stone building with white fretwork. It dates from 1919, and although it's no longer used, you can go inside and look around. Stroll by the church, beyond a place called the Gap, to a lookout point where you can see the 400 rough-hewn steps leading down to Ladder Bay. This and Fort Bay were the two landing sites from which Saba's first settlers had to haul themselves and their possessions. Sabans sometimes walk down to Ladder Bay to picnic. Think long and hard before you do: going back requires 400 steps *up* to the Road.

❷ Cove Bay. Near the airport on the island's northeastern side, a 20-ft-long (6-m-long) strip of rocks and pebbles laced with gray sand is really the only place for sunning. There's also a small tidal pool here for swimming.

❶ Flat Point. This is the only place on the island where planes can land. The runway here is one of the world's shortest, with a length of 1,200 ft (366 m). Only STOL (short takeoff and landing) prop planes dare land here, as each end of the runway drops off more than 100 ft (31 m) into the crashing surf below.

❼ Fort Bay. The end of the Road is also the jumping-off place for all of Saba's dive operations and the location of the St. Maarten ferry dock. The island's only gas station is here, as is a 277-ft (84-m) deep-water pier that accommodates the tenders from ships. On the quay are a decompression chamber, one of the few in the Caribbean, and three dive shops. Saba Deep's restaurant, In Two Deep, is a good place to catch your breath while enjoying some refreshments and the view of the water.

❸ Hell's Gate. The Road makes 20 hairpin turns up more than 1,000 vertical ft (305 m) to Hell's Gate. Holy Rosary Church, on Hell's Gate's Hill, is a stone structure that looks medieval but was built in 1962. In the community center behind the church, village ladies sell blouses, handkerchiefs, and tablecloths embellished with the delicate and unique Saba lace. The same ladies make the potent rum-based Saba Spice, each according to her old family recipe. The intrepid can venture to Lower Hell's Gate, where the Old Sulphur Mine Walk leads to bat caves (with a sulfuric stench) that can—with caution—be explored.

❹ Mt. Scenery. Stone and concrete steps—1,064 of them—rise to the top of Mt. Scenery. En route to the mahogany grove at the summit, the steps pass giant elephant ears, ferns, begonias, mangoes, palms, and orchids; there are six identifiable ecosystems in all. Signs name the trees, plants, and shrubs, and the staff at the trail shop in Windwardside can provide a field guide. Have your hotel pack a picnic lunch, wear nonslip shoes, and take along a jacket and a canteen of water. The round-trip excursion will take about three hours and is best begun in the early morning.

Saba Marine Park. Established in 1987 to preserve and manage the island's marine resources, the park circles the entire island, dipping down to 200 ft (61 m), and is zoned for diving, swimming, fishing, boating, and anchorage. One of the unique aspects of Saba's diving is the submerged pinnacles of land at about the 70-ft (21-m) depth mark. Here all·forms of sea creatures rendezvous. The information center offers talks and slide shows for divers and snorkelers and provides literature on marine life. (Divers are requested to contribute $3 a dive to help maintain the park facilities.) Before you visit, call first to see if anyone is around. ⊠ *Harbor Office, Fort Bay,* ☎ *599/416–3295.* ☉ *Weekdays 8–5.*

⑤ **Windwardside.** The island's second-largest village, perched at 1,968 ft (602 m), commands magnificent views of the Caribbean. Here amid the oleander bushes are rambling lanes and narrow alleyways winding through the hills, and clusters of tiny, neat houses and shops. At the village's northern end is the Church of St. Paul's Conversion, a colonial building with a red-and-white steeple. Just down the road is the Saba Tourist Office, where you can pick up books about Saba. You may also want to browse through the town's shops.

Small signs mark the way to the **Saba Museum.** This 150-year-old house, surrounded by lemongrass and clover, replicates a sea captain's home. Period pieces on display include a handsome mahogany four-poster bed, an antique organ, and, in the kitchen, a rock oven. You can also look at old documents, such as a letter a Saban wrote after the hurricane of 1772, in which he sadly says, "We have lost our little all." Don't miss the delightful stroll to the museum down the stone-walled Park Lane, one of the prettiest walks in the Caribbean. ⊠ *Windwardside, no phone.* ▨ *$1 (suggested donation).* ☉ *Weekdays 10–4.*

SABA A TO Z

To research prices, get advice from other travelers, and book travel arrangements, visit www.fodors.com.

AIR TRAVEL

The approach to Saba's tiny airstrip is as thrilling as a roller coaster ride. The strip is only ¼-mi (½-km) long, but the STOL aircraft are built for it, and the pilot needs only half of that length to land properly. Try not to panic; remember that the pilot knows what he's doing and wants to live just as much as you do. (If you're nervous, don't sit on the right. The wing just misses grazing the cliff side on the approach.) Once you've touched down on the airstrip, the pilot taxis an inch or two, turns, and deposits you just outside a little shoe box called the Juancho E. Yrausquin Airport.

➤ AIRLINES AND CONTACTS: **Windward Islands Airways** (☎ 599/416–2255 or 800/634–4907).

AIRPORTS

Saba's Juancho E. Yrausquin Airport is being expanded into a full-fledged airport—the runway has been widened to increase safety and a new terminal has recently been added. Taxi fare from the airport to Hell's Gate is $6; to Windwardside it's $8; and to The Bottom it's $12.50.

➤ AIRPORT INFORMATION: **Juancho E. Yrausquin Airport** (☎ 599/416–2255).

BOAT AND FERRY TRAVEL
FARES AND SCHEDULES

The Edge, a high-speed ferry, leaves St. Maarten's Pelican Marina in Simpson Bay for Fort Bay on Saba on Wednesdays through Sundays at 9 AM and boards for the return trip at about 4 PM. The trip, which can be rough, takes just over an hour each way. Round-trip fare is $60, plus 5% extra if you pay by credit card.

Other options for a trip to or from St. Maarten are the *Voyager I,* a large catamaran that holds 150 people and runs on Tuesdays and Thursdays between Marigot or Philipsburg and Fort Bay, and the *Voyager II,* a large powerboat that can take 100 people and runs on Tuesdays and Thursdays between Marigot and Philipsburg and Fort Bay. The fare on either Voyager boat is $60, plus $2 port fees from Marigot. For any boat travel, it's always best to call ahead to check current schedules.
➤ BOAT AND FERRY INFORMATION: *The Edge* (☎ 599/544–2640). *Voyager I and II* (☎ 599/542–4096).

BUSINESS HOURS
BANKS
The island's two banks are open 8:30–2 (Barclays) or 8:30–3, and until 4 on Fridays (Royal Bank of Trinidad and Tobago).

POST OFFICES
Post offices are open weekdays 8–5.

SHOPS
Shops are open weekdays and Saturday 8–5.

CAR RENTALS
The Road—Saba's one and only—is serpentine, with many a hairpin (read: hair-raising) curve. However, if you dare to drive, you can rent a car (about $45 a day with a full tank of gas and unlimited mileage).
➤ MAJOR AGENCIES: **Hardiana** (✉ The Bottom, ☎ 599/416–2388). **Johnson's Rent A Car** (✉ Juliana's Cottages, Windwardside, ☎ 599/416–2269).

GASOLINE
If you run out of gas, call the island's only **gas station** (☎ 599/416–3272), down at Fort Bay; note that it closes at 3 PM. Gas costs roughly NAf 1.32 per liter ($3 per gallon).

ELECTRICITY
Saba's current is 110 volts, 60 cycles, and visitors from North America should have no trouble using their travel appliances.

EMERGENCIES
The A. M. Edwards Medical Center is a 10-bed hospital with a full-time physician.➤ AMBULANCE AND FIRE: For an **ambulance,** dial ☎ 599/416–3289. To report a **fire,** dial ☎ 599/416–2410.
➤ HOSPITALS: The **A. M. Edwards Medical Center** (✉ The Bottom, ☎ 599/416–3288).
➤ PHARMACIES: The **Pharmacy** (✉ A. M. Edwards Medical Center, The Bottom, ☎ 599/416–3289).
➤ POLICE: **Police** (The Bottom, ☎ 599/416–3237).
➤ SCUBA DIVING EMERGENCIES: **Saba Marine Park Hyperbaric Facility** (✉ Fort Bay, ☎ 599/416–4395).

FESTIVALS AND SEASONAL EVENTS
Saba's Carnival might not be as big as those of other Caribbean islands, but it *is* energetic. This weeklong celebration, which starts in late July and runs through early August, has many special events, local and im-

ported steel-pan bands, food booths, and parades (including the final Grand Carnival Parade). And just so Sabans don't forget what fun is, they hold a Saba Day the first weekend in December—three days of band contests, food tastings, and other events.

HOLIDAYS

Public holidays for 2003 are: New Year's Day, Good Friday (Friday before Easter), Easter Monday (day after Easter), Coronation Day and the Queen's Birthday (April 30), celebrating the birthday and coronation of Holland's Queen Beatrix, Labor Day (May 1), Ascension Day (May 24), Christmas (Dec. 25), and Boxing Day (Dec. 26).

LANGUAGE

Saba's official language is Dutch, but everyone on the island speaks English. Sabans are always willing to help, and they enjoy conversation. If you're open to chatting, you may get some good local advice.

MAIL AND SHIPPING

An airmail letter to North America or Europe costs NAf 2.25; a postcard, NAf 1.10. Book reservations through a travel agent or over the phone; mail can take a week or two to reach the island. The main branch of the post office is in The Bottom in the government administration building; a second office is in Windwardside, near Scout's Place. Both branches offer express mail service. When writing to Saba, don't worry about addresses without post office box numbers or street locations—on an island this size, all mail finds its owner. However, do make sure to include "Netherlands Antilles" and "Caribbean" in the address.

MONEY MATTERS

Prices quoted throughout the chapter are in U.S. dollars unless otherwise noted.

ATMS

There are no ATMs on the island.

CURRENCY

U.S. dollars are accepted everywhere, but Saba's official currency is the Netherlands Antilles florin (NAf; also called the guilder). The exchange rate fluctuates slightly but was around NAf 1.80 to US$1 at press time. The island's two banks provide foreign-exchange services. ➤ BANKS: **Barclays Bank** (✉ Windwardside, ☎ 599/416–2216). **Royal Bank of Trinidad and Tobago** (✉ Windwardside, ☎ 599/416–2631).

PASSPORTS AND VISAS

U.S. and Canadian citizens need proof of citizenship. A valid passport is preferred, but a birth certificate with a raised seal along with a government-issued photo ID will do. British citizens must have a British passport. All visitors must have an ongoing or return ticket.

SAFETY

Take along insect repellent, sunscreen, and sturdy, no-nonsense shoes that get a good grip on the ground. You may encounter the harmless racer snake while hiking. Don't be alarmed; these snakes lie on rocks to sun themselves, but skitter off when people approach.

SIGHTSEEING TOURS

The taxi drivers who meet the planes at the airport or the boats at Fort Bay conduct tours of the island. Tours can also be arranged by dive shops or hotels. A full-day trek costs $40 for one to four passengers and $10 per person for groups larger than four. If you're in from St. Maarten for a day trip, you can do a full morning of sightseeing, stop off for lunch (have your driver make reservations before starting), complete the tour afterward, and return to the airport in time to make the last flight back to St. Maarten. Guides are available for hiking; arrangements may be made through the tourist office or the trail shop in Windwardside.

TAXES AND SERVICE CHARGES

DEPARTURE TAX

You must pay a $5 departure tax when leaving Saba by plane for either St. Maarten or St. Eustatius, or $20 when continuing on an international flight. (Note: when flying home through St. Maarten from here, list yourself as "in transit" and avoid repaying the tax in St. Maarten, which is $20.) There's no departure tax when you leave by boat.

SALES TAX

Several of the larger hotels will tack on a 10%–15% service charge, others will build it into the rates. Call ahead to inquire about service charges. Hotels add a 5% government tax plus a 3% turnover tax to the cost of a room (sometimes it's tacked on to your bill, other times it's built into the room rate). Restaurants on Saba add service charges of 10%–15%.

TAXIS

Taxis meet planes, the ferry, and *Voyager* boats and take you to your destination. They charge a set rate for up to four people per taxi, with an additional cost for each person more than four. The fare from the airport to Hell's Gate is $6, to Windwardside it's $8, and to The Bottom it's $12.50. The fare from the Fort Bay ferry docks to Windwardside is $9.50. A taxi from Windwardside to The Bottom is $6.50.

TELEPHONES

Telephone communications are excellent on the island, and you can dial direct long-distance. There are public phone booths in The Bottom and Windwardside. They take prepaid phone cards, which can be bought at stores throughout the island, or local coins.

COUNTRY AND AREA CODES

To call Saba from the United States, dial 011/599/416, followed by the four digit number.

TIPPING

Even if service charges have been added into your bill, it's customary to tip hotel personnel and restaurant waitstaff; you should tip taxi drivers, as well. About 10%–15% should do it.

TRANSPORTATION AROUND SABA

Carless Sabans get around the old-fashioned ways—walking and hitchhiking (very popular and safe). If you choose to thumb rides, you'll need to know the rules of the Road. To get a lift from The Bottom (which actually is near the top of the island), sit on the wall opposite the Anglican church; to catch one in Fort Bay, sit on the wall opposite the Saba Deep dive center, where the road begins to twist upward.

VISITOR INFORMATION

➤ IN SABA: **Saba Tourist Office** (✉ Box 527, Windwardside, ☎ 599/416–2231 or 599/416–2322, WEB www.turg.com/saba).

18 ST. BARTHÉLEMY

Updated by
Elise Meyer

It's 3:30 PM. Sun-kissed youngsters tumble into the tanned arms of their *mamans* after a twirl on the brightly painted school yard carousel. Traffic along the narrow road stops while the children hop into waiting cars. Nobody cares much about the delay, preferring instead to enjoy the afternoon air perfumed by sea spray and jasmine. The red-tiled roofs along the hillsides glitter in the sun and seem to tumble into the sapphire water. It feels more like a small town in the south of France than an island in the Caribbean.

St. Barthélemy blends the essence of the Caribbean with the essence of France. A sophisticated but unstudied approach to relaxation and respite prevails: you can spend the day on a beach, try on the latest in French fashion, and watch the sun set while nibbling tapas over Gustavia Harbor, then choose from nearly 100 excellent restaurants for an elegant evening meal. You can putter around the island, explore the shops, scuba dive, windsurf on a quiet cove, or just admire the lovely views.

A mere 8 square mi (21 square km), St. Barths has lots of hills and sheltered inlets. The town of Gustavia wraps itself neatly around a lilliputian harbor lined with impressive yachts and rustic fishing boats. Red-roof bungalows dot the hillsides, and beaches run the gamut from calm to "surfable," from deserted to packed. The cuisine is tops in the Caribbean, part of the French *savoir vivre* that prevails throughout the island.

Longtime visitors speak wistfully of the old, quiet St. Barths. Development has quickened the pace of life here, but the island hasn't yet been overbuilt. The largest hotel still has fewer than 100 rooms, and the remaining accommodations are divided among about 40 small hotels. The tiny planes that arrive with regularity still land at the refurbished airport only during daylight hours. And "nightlife" usually means a leisurely dinner and a stargazing walk on the beach.

Christopher Columbus discovered the island—called "Ouanalao" by its native Carib Indians—in 1493; he named it for his brother Bartholomé. The first group of French colonists arrived in 1648, drawn by the ideal location on the West Indian Trade Route, but they were wiped out by the Carib Indians who dominated the area. A small group from Normandy and Brittany arrived in 1694. This time the settlers prospered—with the help of French buccaneers, who took advantage of the island's strategic location and protected harbor. In 1784 the French traded the island to King Gustav III of Sweden in exchange for port rights in Göteborg. The king dubbed the capital Gustavia, laid out and paved streets, built three forts, and turned the community into a prosperous free port. The island thrived as a shipping and commercial center until the 19th century, when earthquakes, fire, and hurricanes brought financial ruin. Many residents fled for newer lands of opportunity, and Oscar II of Sweden decided to return the island to France. After briefly considering selling it to America, Saint-Barthélemy became French once again on August 10, 1877.

Today the island is still a free port and, as a dependency of Guadeloupe, is part of an overseas department of France. Arid, hilly, and rocky, St. Barths was unsuited to sugar production and thus never developed an extensive slave base. Most of the 3,000 current residents are descendants of the tough Norman and Breton settlers of three centuries ago. They are feisty, industrious, and friendly—but insular. However, you will find many new, young French arrivals, predominantly from northwestern France and Provence, who speak English well.

Lodging

There is no denying that hotel rooms carry high prices. You're paying for the privilege of staying on the island, and even at $500 a night the bedrooms tend to be small. Still, if you're flexible—in terms of timing and in your choice of lodgings—you can enjoy a holiday in St. Barths and still afford to send the kids to college.

The most expensive season falls during the holidays (mid-December to early January), when hotels are booked far in advance and may require a 10- or 14-day stay, and can be double the high-season rates. Most quoted hotel rates are per-room, not per-person, and include tax and service charges, and transfers from the airport. More hotels and restaurants here have seasonal closings (from August to September or October) than on other islands, but some places are still open in August. If you're on a budget, look into an off-season stay, when rates can drop by as much as 50% and many properties offer attractive packages. Most top hotels are on four northern beaches: Anse des Flamands, Anse des Cayes, Baie de St-Jean, and Grand Cul de Sac. In the hills away from the beaches are a number of surprisingly reasonable small hotels, guest houses, rental villas, and bungalows that significantly broaden your options. And regardless of the lodgings you choose, you'll want a car to explore the island.

On St. Barths, the term *villa* is used to describe anything from a small cottage to a sprawling manor. Today almost half of St. Barths' accommodations are in villas, and rentals make a lot of sense, especially for longer stays or groups traveling together. Most houses include a small private swimming pool and maid service daily except Sunday. Houses are well equipped with linens, kitchen tools, and such electronic playthings as CD players, satellite TV, and VCRs. In-season rates range from $700 to $25,000 a week. Peak periods are usually booked far in advance. Villa Rental companies have extensive Web sites with virtual tours that simplify the rental process, as most of the companies schedule from off the island. Local offices oversee maintenance and housekeeping. Some provide concierge services to clients.

CATEGORY	COST EP/CP*	COST A.I.**
$$$$	over $350	over $375
$$$	$250–$350	$275–$375
$$	$150–$250	$175–$275
$	under $150	under $175

*EP/CP prices are per night for a standard double room in high season, excluding taxes, service charges, and meal plans
**A.I. (all-inclusive) prices are per person, per night based on double-occupancy during high season, excluding taxes and service charges

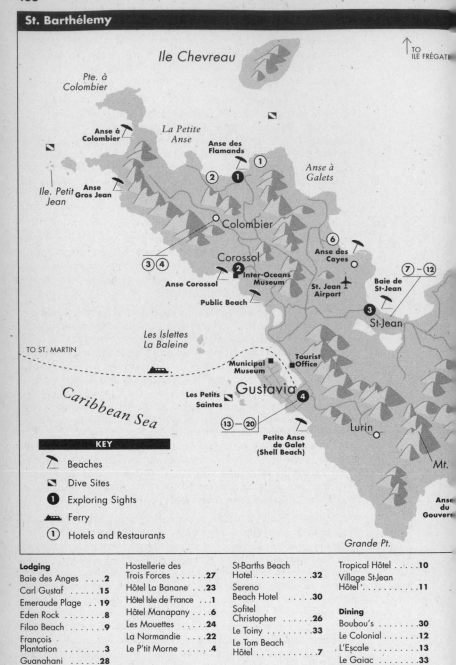

TO
ILE FRÉGATE

Ile Chevreau

Pte. à
Colombier

Anse à
Colombier

La Petite
Anse

Anse des
Flamands

① ①

② ①

Anse à
Galets

Ile. Petit
Jean

Anse
Gros Jean

Colombier

③ ④

Corossol

② ②

Anse des
Cayes

⑥

⑦ — ⑫

Anse Corossol

Inter-Oceans
Museum

St. Jean
Airport

Baie de
St-Jean

③

St-Jean

Public Beach

Les Islettes
La Baleine

TO ST. MARTIN

Tourist
Office

Municipal
Museum

Les Petits
Saintes

Gustavia

④

Caribbean Sea

⑬ — ⑳

Lurin

Petite Anse
de Galet
(Shell Beach)

Mt.

KEY

Anse
du
Gouver

Beaches

Dive Sites

① Exploring Sights

Ferry

① Hotels and Restaurants

Grande Pt.

Lodging
Baie des Anges **2**
Carl Gustaf **15**
Emeraude Plage . . **19**
Eden Rock **8**
Filao Beach **9**
François
Plantation **3**
Guanahani **28**

Hostellerie des
Trois Forces **27**
Hôtel La Banane . .**23**
Hôtel Isle de France . . .**1**
Hôtel Manapany **6**
Les Mouettes **24**
La Normandie **22**
Le P'tit Morne **4**

St-Barths Beach
Hotel **32**
Sereno
Beach Hotel **30**
Sofitel
Christopher **26**
Le Toiny **33**
Le Tom Beach
Hôtel **7**

Tropical Hôtel **10**
Village St-Jean
Hôtel **11**

Dining
Boubou's **30**
Le Colonial **12**
L'Escale **13**
Le Gaiac **33**

ATLANTIC OCEAN

↑ TO
ILE TOC VERS

Les Grenadiers

La Tortue

Pte. Milou

26
25

Anse de
Lorient

23 24

Anse de
Marigot

Anse
Marechal

28

Marigot

Anse de Grand
Cul de Sac

Glorietta
29 32

Lorient

7

22

Anse de Petit
Cul de Sac

Mt. du
Grand Fond

27

Vitet

Toiny

Toiny
Coast

Morne Vitet

33

8

Grand
Fond

Anse á
Toiny

21

Grande
Saline

Pt. à Toiny

6

Anse de
Grand Fond

N
↑

Anse de
Grande
Saline

0 ——————— 1 mile

0 ——————— 1 km

urin

5

Morne
Rouge

ur

Pt. Gouverneur

Hotels

$$$$ ★   🏨 **Carl Gustaf.** One- and two-bedroom suites with private decks and plunge pools spill down a hill overlooking quaint Gustavia harbor. High ceilings and gleaming white rooms are stylishly decorated with nautical marble and baths, tiny kitchens, and such welcome extras as a fax machine, two satellite TVs, stereos. Summer package rates and an excellent honeymoon package are available. Carl Gustaf restaurant, known for its classic French cuisine, is spectacular. ⊠ *Rue des Normands, Gustavia (Box 700, 97133),* ☎ *0590/29–79–00,* FAX *0590/27–82–37,* WEB *www.hotelcarlgustaf.com. 14 suites. Restaurant, piano bar, in-room VCRs, pool, sauna, health club. AE, DC, MC, V. CP.*

$$$$ 🏨 **Eden Rock.** On a craggy bluff that splits Baie de St-Jean is St. Barths' first hotel, originally opened in the 1950s. Cozy, antiques-filled rooms have draped four-poster beds, fine art, sparkling silver fixtures, terracotta floors, and stunning bay views in suites, cabins, or beach cottages. The beach has comfortable chaises, umbrellas, and a sea-water whirlpool. The breakfast buffet is terrific. The Rock, Michael's, and the Sand Bar restaurants are all first-rate. ⊠ *Baie de St-Jean 97133,* ☎ *0590/29–79–89,* FAX *0590/27–88–37,* WEB *www.edenrockhotel.com. 15 rooms. 2 restaurants, 2 bars, minibars, pool, snorkeling, windsurfing, library. AE, MC, V. BP.*

$$$$ ★   🏨 **Guanahani.** The only full-service resort on the island has lovely rooms and suites (some with private pools) in brilliant-colored Creole cottages, all with big bathrooms. Rooms are decorated either in pretty pastel fabrics and stylish rattan furnishings, or luxurious deep tropical colors complemented by plantation-style wood. Units vary in price, privacy, view, and distance from activities; make your preferences known. Service is impeccable. The hotel has two well-regarded restaurants. The hair salon is now run by Clarins. ⊠ *Grand Cul de Sac 97133,* ☎ *0590/27–66–60,* FAX *0590/27–70–70,* WEB *www.leguanahani.com. 47 rooms, 28 suites. 2 restaurants, room-service, cable TV, in-room VCRs, 2 tennis courts, 2 pools, hair salon, boating, windsurfing, piano bar, shop, children's programs (ages 2–6), meeting rooms. AE, MC, V. BP.*

$$$$ ★   🏨 **Hôtel Isle de France.** Everything at this pristine, intimate resort, set on a white sandy beach, says casual refinement. Huge, luxurious rooms furnished with modern four-posters, French fabrics, and fine art have superb marble baths (some with Jacuzzis). La Case de l'Isle restaurant, serving tropic-appropriate nouvelle cuisine, is perched on a pavilion over the beach. Summer packages are available. ⊠ *Baie des Flamands (Box 612, 97098),* ☎ *0590/27–61–81,* FAX *0590/27–86–83,* WEB *www.isle-de-france.com. 12 rooms, 2 suites, 3 junior suites, 13 bungalows. Restaurant, minibars, cable TV, tennis court, 2 pools, gym, bar. AE, MC, V. CP.*

$$$$ ★   🏨 **Hôtel La Banane.** The 2001 redecoration of this intimate garden-set resort will remind you more of NYC or London, but the high-style and hard-edge luxury will please fans of the "W" brand. Ebony walls, honed mahogany furniture, and sisal rugs give private bungalows unusual serenity. Private baths with outdoor showers have every upscale amenity. Lorient beach is within a two-minute walk. Breakfast is served around the shady pool. K'fe Massaï, the on-site African-theme restaurant, is very popular. ⊠ *Quartier Lorient 97133,* ☎ *0590/52–03–00,* FAX *0590/27–68–44. 9 rooms. Restaurant, in-room VCR, 2 pools, bar. AE, MC, V. CP.*

$$$$ 🏨 **Hotel Manapany.** Perched above the white sand of Anse des Cayes, the Manapany cottages tumble down a winding path. At this writing, rooms and suites are in the process of a stylish complete redecoration by new owners, with outdoor porches over the sea, Mexican tile floors, rustic wood furniture, elegant white linen, and brand-new bathrooms, some with private Jacuzzis. Just offshore is a small reef for snorkeling

and a few nice waves in the afternoons for surfing. ⊠ *Anse des Cayes 97098,* ☎ *0590/27–66–55,* FAX *0590/27–75–28,* WEB *www.lemanapany. com. 46 rooms. 2 restaurants, tennis court, gym, pool, beach, bar. AE, MC, V. BP.*

$$$$ ⚃ **Le Toiny.** When perfection is more important than price, choose Le
★ Toiny's romantic villas with mahogany furniture, yards of red toile, and private pools. Rooms have every convenience of home: lush bathrooms, fully equipped kitchenettes, and either a stair-stepper or a stationary bike. Sunday brunch and haute cuisine can be had at the alfresco Le Gaiac, overlooking the Italian-tile pool to the ocean beyond. Summer packages are popular for honeymooning. ⊠ *Anse de Toiny 97133,* ☎ *0590/27–88–88,* FAX *0590/27–89–30,* WEB *www.letoiny.com. 12 villa-suites, 1 3-bedroom suite, 1 cottage. Restaurant, in-room safes, minibars, cable TV, in-room VCRs, pool, exercise equipment, bar, laundry service. AE, DC, MC, V. CP.*

$$$$ ⚃ **Le Tom Beach Hôtel.** Carole Gruson's pretty, compact "boutique" hotel on the beach of St-Jean, continues to up its level of chic. A garden winds around the brightly painted suites, over the pool via a small footbridge, into the hopping open-air restaurant, La Plage. Big, plantation-style rooms: high ceilings, exposed beams, cozy draped beds, nice baths, a TV with both VCR and DVD players, Internet, direct-dial phones, and patios. ⊠ *Plage St-Jean 97133,* ☎ *0590/27–53–13,* FAX *0590/27–53–15,* WEB *www.tombeach.com. 12 rooms. Restaurant, refrigerators, in-room safes, in-room VCRs, minibars, pool, beach, bar AE, MC, V. CP.*

$$$$ ⚃ **Sofitel Christopher.** This Sofitel Coralia hotel, with oversize rooms and a gracious staff, is one of the island's bargains. Two-story colonial-style buildings house spacious, nicely furnished if simple rooms with tiled baths, and either a balcony or terrace. The hotel's pretty swimming pool is the largest on the island, with a wading area. L'Orchidée restaurant serves superb French-creole cuisine. ⊠ *Pointe Milou 97133,* ☎ *0590/27–63–63,* FAX *0590/27–92–92,* WEB *www.accor.com. 41 rooms, 1 suite. 2 restaurants, room service, pool, gym. AE, DC, MC, V. BP.*

$$$ ✕⚃ **Baie des Anges.** Ten clean, fresh, and nicely decorated rooms are right on serene Flamands Beach. Each has a kitchenette and private terrace. Everyone is treated like family at this casual retreat. The food at La Langouste, the hotel's restaurant, is tasty and reasonable. ⊠ *Flamands,* ☎ *0590/27–63–61,* FAX *0590/27–83–44. 10 rooms. Restaurant, pool, beach, car rental. AE, MC, V. EP.*

$$$ ⚃ **Filao Beach.** Excellent service and a location on central Baie de St-Jean keep them coming back to this casual Relais & Châteaux resort. Rooms are in two-room beach bungalows set in a tropical garden. Quarters closer to the beach are the most expensive, but affordable garden rooms are only steps from the sand. Rooms are simple and smallish, with rattan furniture, pastel prints, a compact but tidy bath, and a patio. The restaurant on a deck around the pool serves breakfast, lunch, and killer cocktails. ⊠ *Baie de St-Jean (Box 667, 97099),* ☎ *0590/27–64–84,* FAX *0590/27–62–24,* WEB *www.filaobeach.com. 30 rooms. Restaurant, refrigerators, pool, beach, bar. AE, MC, V. CP.*

$$$ ⚃ **François Plantation.** A colonial-era graciousness pervades this inti-
★ mate, exquisite hillside complex of West Indian–style cottages. Owner and longtime island habitué François Beret is a passionate gardener, discriminating gourmand, and oenophile. A hint of shared interest may result in a tour of the grounds, or of the exceptional wine cellar. The pristine rooms have queen-size mahogany four-poster beds and colorful fabrics. Two larger rooms can accommodate an extra bed. The pool is atop a very steep hill, with magnificent views. La Route Des Epices restaurant, one of the best on the island, serves dinner on a romantic veranda. Low-season packages are available. ⊠ *Colombier 97133,*

☎ 0590/29–80–22, FAX 0590/27–61–26, WEB *www.francois-plantation.com. 12 rooms. Restaurant, refrigerators, pool, gym. AE, MC, V. CP. Closed Aug.–Oct.*

$$$ 🏨 **St-Barths Beach Hotel.** Athletic Europeans and families love this simple, comfortable hotel for its location on a wide, calm beach ideal for windsports (kite-surfing, windsurfing), the complete on-site gym, and its excellent restaurant, Le Rivage. ⊠ *Grand Cul de Sac (Box 580, 97098),* ☎ 0590/27–60–70, FAX 0590/27–75–57, WEB *www.saintbarthbeachhotel.com. 36 rooms, 8 villas. Some kitchens, refrigerators, gym, pool, beach, windsurfing. CP, EP. AE, MC, V.*

$$–$$$ 🏨 **Emeraude Plage.** Right on Baie de St-Jean, these modern and clean bungalows with outdoor kitchenette-patios are convenient, well located, and pleasant. Nice bathrooms add to the comfort. Hotel guests often gather to socialize in the comfortable library-lounge. ⊠ *Baie de St-Jean 97113,* ☎ 0590/27–64–78, FAX 0590/27–83–08, WEB *www.emeraudeplage.com. 24 bungalows, 3 suites, 1 villa. Fans, beach. MC, V. EP.*

$$ 🏨 **Hostellerie des Trois Forces.** High atop the island, this charming "holis-
★ tic New Age inn" is an idiosyncratic delight. Each gingerbread cottage has an astrological color scheme (Libra: blue, Leo: red) and handcrafted furnishings chosen by personable owner/astrologer/international chef Hubert de la Motte, who, when not in the kitchen, may do your chart or lead a yoga session beside the pool. Don't miss a leisurely lunch or dinner at the superb Restaurant des Trois Forces. Breathtaking views, but a four-wheel-drive vehicle is imperative. ⊠ *Morne Vitet 97133,* ☎ 0590/27–61–25, FAX 0590/27–81–38, WEB *www.3forces.net. 7 rooms. Restaurant, fans, minibars, pool, bar. AE, MC, V. EP.*

$$ 🏨 **Sereno Beach Hotel.** New management in 2001 and an upscale renovation by a Miami-based firm have furthered this property's reputation as a destination for younger visitors. Suites overlook the hotel's broad private beach, but garden rooms are half the price. Boubou's restaurant gets a chic crowd throughout the day. The hotel even has a cute boutique. ⊠ *Grand Cul de Sac (Box 19, 97133),* ☎ 0590/27–64–80, FAX 0590/27–75–47, WEB *www.serenobeach.com. 18 rooms, 14 suites. 2 restaurants, in-room safes, refrigerators, pool, health club, beach, snorkeling, boating, bar. AE, MC, V. BP. Closed Sept.–Oct.*

$$ 🏨 **Tropical Hôtel.** Straight up the hill from Baie de St-Jean is a classic example of what the French affectionately call a *hôtel bourgeois:* a simple, stylish place that's also a good value. You'll find well-maintained rooms (those with lower numbers are the best) in a one-story L-shape building. All open onto patios with views of either the ocean or thick tropical foliage and have pristine white walls, linens, and furnishings, beam ceilings, and beds swathed in mosquito netting. Continental breakfast is included in the price. ⊠ *Baie de St-Jean (Box 147, 97133),* ☎ 0590/27–64–87, FAX 0590/27–81–74, WEB *www.st-barths.com/tropical-hotel. 21 rooms. Snack bar, refrigerators, pool, bar, recreation room. AE, MC, V. CP.*

$ 🏨 **La Normandie.** This cozy family-run hotel offers modestly furnished rooms (some with a TV) for well under $100 a night, making it one of the best deals on St. Barths. There's a small pool here, and the beach is within a five-minute walk. ⊠ *Quartier Lorient 97133,* ☎ 0590/27–73–78, FAX 0590/27–98–83. 8 rooms. Pool. MC, V. EP.

$ 🏨 **Les Mouettes.** Six clean, simply furnished, and economical bunga-
★ lows open directly onto the beach. They are also quite close to the road, which can be either convenient for a quick shopping excursion or a bother on account of the noise. Each bungalow has a bathroom with shower, a kitchenette, a patio, two double beds, and a twin bed or fold-out sofa, making this place a good bet for families. ⊠ *Quartier Lorient 97133,* ☎ 0590/27–77–91, FAX 0590/27–68–19. 7 rooms. Kitchenettes, beach, shops, car rental. No credit cards. EP.

$ 🖬 **Le P'tit Morne.** Each of the modestly furnished mountainside studios has a private balcony with panoramic views of the coastline. The small kitchenettes are adequate for creating picnic lunches and other light meals. The snack bar serves breakfast. It's relatively isolated here, however, and the beach is a 10-minute drive away. ⊠ *Colombier (Box 14, 97133),* 🕿 *0590/27–62–64,* FAX *0590/27–84–63.. 14 rooms. Kitchenettes, pool, library. AE, MC, V. CP.*

$$–$$$$ 🖬 **Village St-Jean Hôtel.** For two generations the Charneau family has
★ seen to the high quality of service and the reasonable rates at their small hotel. Handsome, airy stone-and-redwood cottages have high ceilings, sturdy furniture, modern baths, and lovely terraces; one has a Jacuzzi. They also have open-air kitchenettes. The six hotel-style rooms have refrigerators, and most have king-size beds. There is also a three-bedroom villa available. The location is great—you can walk to the beach and town from here—and most accommodations have views. ⊠ *Baie de St-Jean (Box 623, 97098),* 🕿 *0590/27–61–39 or 800/651–8366,* FAX *0590/27–77–96,* WEB *www.villagestjeanhotel.com. 6 rooms, 20 cottages. Restaurant, grocery, some kitchenettes, pool, hot tub, bar, shops, library. AE, MC, V. EP.*

Villas and Condominiums

St. Barth Properties, Inc. (🕿 508/528–7727 or 800/421–3396, FAX 508/528–7789, WEB www.stbarth.com), owned by American Peg Walsh— a regular on St. Barths since 1986—represents more than 100 properties here and can guide you to the perfect place to stay. Weekly peak-season rates range from $1,400 to $40,000 depending on the property's size, location, and amenities. The excellent Web site offers virtual tours of most of the properties and details of availability. An office in Gustavia can take care of any problems you may have and offers some concierge-type services. **ParadiseLodging.com** (⊠ 🕿 888/349–7800, FAX 770/426–5716, WEB www.paradiselodging.com) is an American company that arranges rentals of private villas. You can search and view the panoramic pictures of the offerings on their Web site. **SiBarth Real Estate** oversees more than 200 properties on St. Barths. Bookings are arranged through the company's representative, WIMCO (🕿 800/932–3222, FAX 401/847–6290, WEB www.wimcovillas.com), based in Rhode Island. Properties can be previewed and reserved over the Internet, or you can obtain a catalogue by mail. Rents range from $1,000 to $3,500 per week for one-bedroom villas and $1,800 to $7,000 for two- and three-bedroom villas. Larger villas rent for $7,000 per week and up.

Dining

Dining on St. Barths compares favorably to almost anywhere in the world. Varied and exquisite cuisine, breathtaking natural beauty, a French flair in the decorations, sensational wine, and attentive but unobtrusive service make for a wonderful epicurean experience. St. Barths' style is expressed in dozens of charming places to eat, from beachfront grills to serious five-course meals. Freshly caught local seafood mingles on the plate with top-quality provisions that arrive every afternoon from Paris. Myth has it that St. Barths' restaurants are frightfully expensive—and, certainly, you can spend a small fortune in a number of restaurants by choosing rare vintages and luxury ingredients. However, you can also dine superbly on the island without breaking the bank.

Lunch is usually a less costly meal than dinner, and many casual restaurants are inexpensive. Furthermore, the strength of the U.S. dollar has softened prices. Be sure to sample such local specialties as *accras* (salt cod fritters), usually served with one or more varieties of creole sauce (herbs and crushed, spicy peppers in oil); spiced *christophene* (similar to acorn squash, usually stuffed); *boudin créole* (blood sausage); and lusty *soupe de poissons* (fish soup). Available local fish include *dorade* (mahimahi) and tuna; also look for langouste (spiny lobster). Delicious and interesting variations on *gazpacho,* (cold tomato soup) are common, and a refreshing starter at lunch. Most meat in St. Barths comes from the United States or Argentina.

Reservations are always appreciated and, in high season, essential. If you enter a restaurant without a reservation and find there are empty tables, do not automatically assume the owner will seat you. Restaurant owners on St. Barths take great pride in their service as well as in their food, and they would rather turn you away than slight you on an understaffed evening. You are not being ignored at the end of a leisurely meal; as in France, it is considered rude to present a bill too promptly. Linger at the table and enjoy the complimentary vanilla rum that is sure to appear. Check restaurant bills carefully. A service charge (*service compris*), by law, is always added, but you should leave the server 5%–10% extra. It is generally advisable to charge restaurant meals on a credit card, as the issuer will offer a better exchange rate than the restaurant. As long as exchange rates remain favorable, have your check charged in euros for the best deal. Many restaurants serve locally caught lobster (*langoustine*); priced by weight, it is usually the most expensive item on a menu, and depending on its size and the restaurant, will range in price from $40 to $60. In noting menu prices below, it has been left out of the range.

What to Wear

A bathing suit and *pareu* (sarong) are suitable at lunch. Jackets are never required and rarely worn, but people dress fashionably for dinner. Casual chic is the idea; women wear whatever is hip, tight, and bare. Shorts at the dinner table may label a man *américain,* but many locals have adopted the habit, and nobody cares much. Pack a light sweater or shawl for an after-dinner beach stroll.

CATEGORY	COST*
$$$$	over $30
$$$	$20–$30
$$	$10–$20
$	under $10

per person for a main course at dinner

CARIBBEAN

$$$–$$$$ ✕ **L'Orchidée.** Come here for French-creole haute-cuisine in Sofitel's Hôtel
★   Christopher: sunsets and moonlight vistas, friendly and solicitous service, live music, and serious, beautifully presented food. Try the chef's foie gras, roast duck in demi-glace, or grilled mahimahi with lime. A prix-fixe tasting menu for about $40 changes daily and is an excellent choice. Or just sit at the outdoor bar for a first-rate piña colada. ⊠ *Sofitel Christopher, Pointe Milou,* ☎ *0590/27–63–63. AE, MC, V.*

$$–$$$ ✕ **Gloriette.** This friendly beachside spot serves delicious local creole dishes, such as crunchy accras and a cassoulet of local lobster, grilled fresh fish, meats, and light salads. A daily tasting menu for about $30 features lobster specialties. ⊠ *Grand Cul de Sac,* ☎ *0590/27–75–66. AE, MC, V. Closed Wed.*

$$–$$$ ✕ **Pipiri Palace.** Tucked into a tropical garden, this popular in-town restaurant is known for its barbecued ribs, beef fillet, and rack of lamb. Fish choices include creole fish steamed in a banana leaf. Daily specials like mussels and foie gras are always a good choice here. Pierrot, the friendly owner, is sure to take good care of you. ⊠ *Rue*

Général-de-Gaulle, Gustavia, ☎ *0590 27–53–20. Reservations essential. AE, MC. Closed Sept.*

$$ ✕ **Le Ti St. Barth Caribbean Tavern.** Chef-owner Carole Gruson cap-
★ tures the funky spirit of the island in her wildly popular hilltop hot
spot, as much house party as restaurant. Lounge or dance to great music
with the attractive crowd lingering at the bar; then sit down at one of
the pillow-strewn banquettes at Indian silk-topped tables, or chat on
the torchlit terrace—by the time your appetizers arrive, you'll be best
friends with the next table. Warm, honey-drizzled chèvre salad, house-
smoked fish, grilled duck fillet with mango chutney, ribs, and the best
beef on the island. Extensive wine list. Check to see if one of the fa-
mously raucous full-moon parties will be held during your stay. ⊠ *Pointe
Milou,* ☎ *0590/27–97–71. Reservations essential. MC, V.*

$$ ✕ **Le Rivage.** This popular, affordable restaurant serves wonderful gaz-
★ pacho and huge salads, like warm chèvre (goat cheese) with bacon, cold
mixed seafood, and classic *salade niçoise* (with tuna, olives, green beans,
and hard boiled eggs). Grilled fresh seafood and steaks for heartier appetites—but save room for the warm apple pastry, or warm chocolate
cake with vanilla sauce. Come for lunch and spend the rest of the afternoon sunning or windsurfing on the beautiful beach. ⊠ *St. Barths
Beach Hôtel, Grand Cul de Sac,* ☎ *0590/27–82–42. AE, MC, V.*

CONTEMPORARY

$$$ ✕ **La Mandala.** Boubou, the owner, has popular restaurants all over
the island. All are excellent, fun, attractive, and reasonable, with cute,
friendly staff. Enjoy tasty Thai-influenced food on the sweeping ter-
race over Gustavia harbor. Try the swordfish spring rolls wrapped in
lettuce leaves, pineapple rice, green-curry shrimp, or filet mignon in a
light sate sauce. ⊠ *Rue de la Sous-Préfecture, Gustavia,* ☎ *0590/27–
96–96,* WEB *www.lamandala.com. AE, MC, V.*

$$ ✕ **K'fe Massaï.** Stunning ethnotropical decor and inventive food can
be found at this romantic restaurant. The theme is African, but the food
is basically French. Salmon tartare with grapefruit or creole sausage
tart are good starters. Main courses include thyme-roasted veal and
sesame chicken brochettes. However, these fade into memory the
minute your fork hits the decadent chocolate dessert medley. ⊠ *Lorient,* ☎ *0590/29–76–78. No credit cards.*

ECLECTIC

$$–$$$ ✕ **Boubou's.** At this beachside restaurant, you'll be able to sample more
★ of Boubou's delicious cuisine in a soaring Moroccan tent with Indian-
Berber decor—the ultimate in romantic. Tropical fruit salads, Champagne risotto, ribs, and grilled fish are on tap for lunch, and dinner
has homemade goat cheese ravioli with wild mushrooms and arti-
chokes, grilled shrimp, and fried calamari. Have sorbet if you are too
full for the ricotta cake. Yes, that *is* a bed on the beach. ⊠ *Sereno Beach
Hotel, Grand Cul de Sac,* ☎ *0590/29–83–01. Reservations essential.
AE, MC, V.*

$$ ✕ **La Marine.** In-the-know islanders settle at the popular dockside pic-
nic tables for mussels that arrive from France every Wednesday. The
menu also includes fish, oysters, hamburgers, steaks, and omelets.
Many think that meals here are the best buys on the island. ⊠ *Rue
Jeanne d'Arc, Gustavia,* ☎ *0590/27–68–91. AE, MC, V.*

$$ ✕ **Le Repaire.** This friendly brasserie overlooks Gustavia's harbor and
is a popular spot from 6 AM to 1 AM. Grab a cappuccino, pull a cap-
tain's chair to the street-side rail, and watch the pretty girls. The menu
ranges from cheeseburgers with the island's best fries, to foie gras, grilled
fish, and lobster. The *assiette creole* (creole assortment platter) is a great
introduction to this fine cuisine. Try your hand at the billiards table,

or show up on weekends for live music. ⊠ *Quai de la République, Gustavia,* ☎ *0590/27–72–48. MC, V.*

FRENCH

$$$$ ✕ **La Route des Epices.** Follow the arbor lanterns to a culinary trea-
★ sure of the island, a lovely veranda with sparkling white paint, luxuriant greenery, and buffed mahogany trim. Owner François Beret is
justifiably proud of his wine cellar. You will be lucky, indeed, if he helps
choose wines to enhance the sublime and serious cuisine. Offerings include terrine of foie gras with caramel, served with a perfect sauternes,
smoked salmon and leek "lasagna," and grilled sea bass served with
wild rice risotto and roasted tomato. A vanilla soufflé with chocolate
sauce elicited swooning. ⊠ *Colombier,* ☎ *0590/29–80–22. Reservations essential. AE, DC, MC, V. Closed Sept.–Oct. No lunch.*

$$$–$$$$ ✕ **Le Gaiac.** If you brought a dressy outfit you can wear it to this ele-
gant, restaurant at Le Toiny hotel. Starched blue napery complement
the blue bay view. Lunch includes chilled, spicy mango soup, salads,
and grilled seafood. The dinner menu showcases serious food: roast
rack of lamb in a clay shell with thyme and honey, yellowtail snapper
with curried lentils, and pigeon layered with red cabbage and sweet
potato. Tableside crêpes suzettes are de rigueur. There's a buffet brunch
on Sunday. ⊠ *Le Toiny, Anse de Toiny,* ☎ *0590/29–77–47. AE, DC,
MC, V. Closed Sept.–mid-Oct.*

$$$–$$$$ ✕ **Le Sapotillier.** The brick walls, hand-painted wooden chairs, exquisite
white linen tablecloths, and vivid creole paintings evoke an old-style
private island home. But this is not "Maman's" cooking. This long-
established restaurant serves classic French cuisine like rack of lamb
and roasted Bresse chicken with potato gratin. Sumptuous chocolate
mousse and raspberry soufflé are longtime favorites. ⊠ *Rue de Cen-
tenaire, Gustavia,* ☎ *0590/27–60–28. Reservations essential. MC, V.
Closed May–mid-Oct. No lunch.*

$$$–$$$$ ✕ **Restaurant des Trois Forces.** Make your way to the top of Vitet, the
★ highest hilltop on the island, for a memorable meal at the hands of owner-
chef Hubert de la Motte. Heady *émincés de veau,* homemade bread,
chateaubriand, and exquisite desserts are complemented by rare vin-
tages. ⊠ *Hostellerie des Trois Forces, Morne Vitet,* ☎ *0590/27–62–
25. Reservations essential. AE, MC, V.*

$$–$$$ ✕ **Le Tamarin.** A leisurely lunch here en route to Saline Beach is a St.
★ Barths *must.* Delicious French and creole cuisine is served at this so-
phisticated open-air restaurant. Get to know the parrot, or relax in a
hammock after the house-special carpaccios of salmon, tuna, and beef.
The lemon tart deserves its excellent reputation. ⊠ *Salines,* ☎ *0590/
27–72–12. AE, MC, V. Closed Mon. No dinner weekdays.*

ITALIAN

$–$$ ✕ **L'Escale.** Great food, friendly owners, and up-close harbor views draw
locals and visitors alike to the far side of Gustavia's harbor. The var-
ied menu includes pastas, fresh local fish, veal dishes, steak tartare, and
chicken. Many dishes and 12 different pizzas are cooked in the wood-
burning oven. If it's someone's birthday, don't forget to mention it. ⊠
Rue Jeanne d'Arc, Gustavia, ☎ *0590/27–81–06. Reservations essential. MC, V. No lunch.*

PAN-ASIAN

$–$$ ✕ **Le Colonial.** Delectable Thai, Vietnamese, and Indochinese special-
★ ties served in a red-lacquered pavilion by a charming mother and
daughter team who should have changed the name when they acquired this restaurant from its former owners. Crisp pork or veggie spring
rolls to wrap in lettuce and dip in minty sauce, and Thai duck star as
preludes to the not-to-be-missed desserts like crispy pears with ginger

chocolate sauce, and the world's best banana fritters. Live music some Saturday evenings. ⊠ *Route des Salines, St-Jean,* ☎ *0590-27–53–00. AE, MC.*

$$–$$$ ✕ **La Langouste.** This tiny beachside restaurant in the pool-courtyard of Hotel Baie des Anges lives up to its name by serving fantastic, fresh grilled lobster. Simple, well-prepared fish, pastas, and soups are also available. ⊠ *Hotel Baie des Anges, Flamands Beach,* ☎ *0590/27–63–61. Reservations essential. AE, MC, V. Closed Mon. in summer. Closed Sept.*

Beaches

There are many *anses* (coves) and nearly 20 *plages* (beaches) scattered around the island, each with a distinctive personality and each open to the general public. Even in season you can find a nearly empty beach. Topless sunbathing is common, but nudism is forbidden—although both Saline and Gouverneur are de facto nude beaches. Bear in mind that the rocky beaches around Anse à Toiny are not swimmable.

Anse à Colombier. The beach here is the least accessible, thus the most private, on the island; to reach it you must take either a rocky footpath from Petite Anse or brave the 30-minute climb down (and back up) a steep, cactus-bordered trail from the top of the mountain behind the beach. Boaters favor this beach and cove for its calm anchorage.

Anse Corossol. This is a top boat- and sunset-watching spot.

Anse du Gouverneur. Because it's so secluded, nude sunbathing is popular here; the beach is truly beautiful, with blissful swimming and views of St. Kitts, Saba, and St. Eustatius.

Anse Marechal. Next to the Guanahani Hotel is this tiny beach, which offers some of the island's best snorkeling.

Baie de St-Jean. Like a mini Côte d'Azur—beachside bistros, bungalow hotels, bronzed bodies, windsurfing, and lots of day-trippers—the reef-protected strip is divided by Eden Rock promontory, and there's good snorkeling west of the rock.

Flamands. This is the most beautiful of the hotel beaches—a roomy strip of silken sand.

Grand Cul de Sac. The shallow, reef-protected beach is especially nice for small children, fly fishermen, and windsurfers; it has excellent lunch spots and lots of pelicans.

Grande Saline. Secluded, with its sandy ocean bottom, this is just about everyone's favorite beach and is great for swimmers. Despite the law, young and old alike go nude. It can get windy here, so go on a calm day.

Lorient. This beach is popular with St. Barths families and surfers, who like its rolling waves. Be aware of the level of the tide, which can come in very fast.

Marigot. This tiny, calm beach has good snorkeling along the rocky far end.

Petite Anse de Galet. A five-minute walk from Gustavia, this one is named for the tiny shells on its shore.

Outdoor Activities and Sports

St. Barths is a popular yachting and sailing center thanks to its location mid-way between Antigua and St. Thomas. Gustavia's harbor, 13 to 16 ft deep, has mooring and docking facilities for 40 yachts. There are also good anchorages available at Public, Corossol, and Colombier.

Marine Service (⊠ Gustavia, ☏ 0590/27–70–34) offers full-day outings on a 40-ft catamaran to the uninhabited Ile Fourchue for swimming, snorkeling, cocktails, and lunch; the cost is $100 per person. The company also arranges deep-sea-fishing trips, with a full-day charter of a 30-ft crewed cabin cruiser running $800; an unskippered motor rental runs about $260 a day. Marine Service can also arrange an hour's cruise ($32) on the glass-bottom boat *L'Aquascope*. **Océan Must Marina** (⊠ Gustavia, ☏ 0590/27–62–25) offers all kinds of boat charters. **Ship Chandler du Port Franc** (⊠ Gustavia, ☏ 0590/27–89–27), a ship chandlery, is the place for yachting information and supplies.

FISHING

Most fishing is done in the waters north of Lorient, Flamands, and Corossol. Popular catches are tuna, marlin, wahoo, and barracuda. **Marine Service** (⊠ Gustavia, ☏ 0590/27–70–34) arranges ocean fishing excursions. **Océan Must Marina** (⊠ Gustavia, ☏ 0590/27–62–25) arranges deep-sea-fishing expeditions as well as boat charters. **Caraïbes Yachting** (⊠ Gustavia, ☏ 0590/27–52–48) rents boats and jet skis and can organize all kinds of boat excursions, including a picnic lunch.

HORSEBACK RIDING

Laure Nicolas leads two-hour excursions in the morning and the afternoon for $40 per person from **Ranch des Flamands** (⊠ Anse des Flamands, ☏ 0590/27–80–72; 24-hr notice preferred).

SCUBA DIVING

Several dive shops arrange scuba excursions to local sites. Depending on the weather conditions you may dive at **Pain de Sucre, Coco Island,** or toward nearby **Saba.** There is also an underwater shipwreck to explore, plus sharks, rays, sea tortoises, coral, and the usual varieties of colorful fish. The waters on the island's leeward side are the calmest.

Marine Service operates the only five-star, PADI-certified diving center on the island, called **West Indies Dive** (☏ 0590/27–70–34); scuba trips, packages, resort dives, and certifications start at $50, gear included. **Odysée Caraïbe** (☏ FAX 0590/27–55–94) is recommended for its up-to-the-minute equipment and boat.

TENNIS

If you wish to play tennis at a hotel at which you are not a guest, call ahead to inquire about fees and reservations. There are two lighted tennis courts at the **Guanahani** (⊠ Grand Cul de Sac, ☏ 0590/27–66–60). **Hôtel Isle de France** (⊠ Baie des Flamands, ☏ 0590/27–61–81) has a lighted tennis court. **Hôtel Manapany Cottages** (⊠ Anse de Cayes, ☏ 0590/27–66–55) has a lighted court. **Le Flamboyant Tennis Club** (⊠ Anse de Toiny, ☏ 0590/27–69–82) has two courts.

WINDSURFING

Windsurfing fever has definitely caught on here. You can rent boards for about $20 an hour at water-sports centers along Baie de St-Jean and Grand Cul de Sac beaches. Lessons are offered for about $40 an hour at **Le Centre Nautique** (⊠ Eden Rock Hotel, Baie de St-Jean, ☏ 0590/27–74–77), which also rents boards. **Wind Wave Power** (⊠ St. Barth Beach Hotel, Grand Cul de Sac, ☏ 0590/27–60–70) offers an extensive, six-hour training course. **FWI Watersport** (⊠ Quai du Yacht Club, Gustavia, ☏ 0590/64–47–74) can help you arrange to tour the island on a jet ski or waverunner. On an hour's notice you can have a lesson, then rent by the hour or the half-day.

Shopping

St. Barths is a duty-free port and, with its sophisticated crowd of visitors, shopping is a definite delight, especially for beachwear, accessories, jewelry, and casual wear. Note that stores often close from noon to 2, and many on Wednesday afternoon as well, so plan your shopping day accordingly. A popular afternoon pastime is strolling about the two major shopping areas in Gustavia and St. Jean.

Areas

In **Gustavia,** boutiques line the two major shopping streets, and the **Carré d'Or** plaza is great fun to explore. Shops are also clustered in **La Savane Commercial Center** (across from the airport), **La Villa Créole,** in St-Jean, and **Espace Neptune,** on the road to Lorient. It's worth working your way from one end to the other at both of these shopping complexes—just to see or maybe be seen. Boutiques in all three areas carry the latest in French and Italian sportswear and some haute-couture. Prices, although still on the high side, are often well below those for comparable merchandise in France.

Specialty Items

CLOTHES

Black Swan (⊠ Le Carre d'or, Gustavia, ☎ 0590/27–65–16; ⊠ Villa Creole, St-Jean) has a good selection of bathing suits. **Calypso** (⊠ Le Carre d'or, Gustavia, ☎ 0590/27–69–74) carries resort wear for women by **Chloé. Dovani** (⊠ Rue de la République, Gustavia, ☎ 0590/29–84–70) has elegant leather goods and Baccarat jewelry. Fans of Longchamp handbags and leather goods will find a good selection at about 20% off at **Elysée Caraïbes** (⊠ Le Carre d'or, Gustavia, ☎ 0590/52–00–94). The **Hermès** (⊠ Rue de la République, Gustavia) store in St. Barths is an independently owned franchise, and prices are about 20% below those in the States. **Laurent Effel** (⊠ Rue Général-de-Gaulle, Gustavia) sells beautiful leather belts, colorful linen shirts, bags, and shoes. Don't miss **Lolita Jaca** (⊠ Le Carré d'Or, Gustavia, ☎ 0590/27–59–98) for trendy tailored sportswear by Paul and Joe and other fresh names. **Morgan's** (Villa Créole, St-Jean, ☎ 0590/27–57–22) has a line of popular and wearable casual wear in the trendy vein. **Paradoxe St-Barth** stores (⊠ La Villa Creole, St-Jean, ☎ 0590/27–84–98; ⊠ Rue de la Républic, Gustavia, ☎ 0590/29–21–86) stocks flattering patterned stretch jeans by TARK'1, and pretty chiffon tops. **Pati de ST-BARTH** (⊠ Passage de la Crémaillière, Gustavia, ☎ 0590/29–78–04) is the largest of the three shops that stock the chic, locally made T-shirts that have practically become the "logo" of St. Barths. The newest styles have hand-done graffiti lettering. **Quiksilver Boatriders Club** (⊠ Pelican Plage, St-Jean, ☎ 0590/29–76–66; ⊠ Rue de la République, Gustavia, ☎ 0590/–29–69–40) has the best T-shirts on St. Barths, and is a great source for attractive and popular surfer-inspired beachwear, sunglasses, and waterwear for all ages. **Raffia** (⊠ Boubou's, Sereno Beach Hotel, Grand Cul de Sac; ⊠ St-Jean, ☎ 0590/27–78–39) has great handbags, resort accessories, and current fashions. Across from the airport is **Samaly** (⊠ St-Jean, ☎ 0590/27–54–91), which sells both fashions and accessories. **Stéphane & Bernard** (⊠ Rue de la Républic, Gustavia, ☎ 0590/27–69–13) stocks a large selection of French fashion designers, including Rykiel, Tarlazzi, Kenzo, Feraud, and Mugler. Look to **St. Tropez KIWI** (⊠ St-Jean, ☎ 0590/27–57–08; ⊠ Gustavia, ☎ 0590/27–68–97) for resort wear. **SUD SUD.ETC** (⊠ Galerie du Commerce, St-Jean, ☎ 0590/27–98–75) stocks water-color soft cotton and linen separates for women, as well as unique cast-glass jewelry by English designer Lola Rose. Cute sandals and raffia accessories complete the look. **Terra** (✉ Pelican Plage, ☎ 0590/27–57–50) has pretty, classic styles of resort wear you can even wear back home.

COSMETICS

Superb skin-care products made on-site from local tropical plants by **Ligne de St. Barths** (✉ Rte. de Saline, Lorient, ☎ 0590/27–82–63) are worth buying.

FOODSTUFFS

Match (✉ St-Jean), a supermarket across from the airport, has a wide selection of French cheeses, pâtés, cured meats, produce, and fresh bread. **A.M.C.** (✉ Quai du République, Gustavia) is a bit older than Match but able to supply anything you might need for housekeeping in a villa, or for a picnic. **JoJo Supermarché** (✉ Lorient) is the well-stocked counterpart to Gustavia's two supermarkets and gets daily deliveries of bread and fresh produce. For exotic groceries or picnic fixings, stop by St. Barths' gourmet *traiteur* (take-out) **La Rotisserie** (✉ Rue du Roi Oscar II, Gustavia, ☎ 0590/27–63–13; ✉ Centre Vaval, St-Jean, ☎ 0590/29–75–69) for salads, prepared meats, groceries from Fauchon, and Iranian caviar.

HANDICRAFTS

The ladies of Corossol produce intricate straw work, wide-brim beach hats, and decorative ornaments by hand. Call the tourist office, which can provide information about the studios of other island artists such as Christian Bretoneiche, Robert Danet, Nathalie Daniel, Patricia Guyot, Rose Lemen, and Marion Vinot.

Look for Fabienne Miot's unique gold jewelry at **L'Atelier de Fabienne** (✉ Rue de la République, Gustavia, ☎ 0590/27–63–31). **Chez Pompi** (☎ 0590/27–75–67), on the road to Toiny, is a cottage whose first room is a gallery for the naive paintings of Pompi (also known as Louis Ledee). **Kayali** (✉ Rue de la République, Gustavia, ☎ 0590/27–93–23) shows varied works by other local artists. Local works of art, including paintings, are sold in the bright **Made in St-Barth La Boutique** (✉ Villa Créole, St-Jean, ☎ 0590/27–59–06) shop. Find local stoneware, raku pottery, and other crafts at **St. Barth Pottery** (✉ Gustavia, ☎ 0590/27–69–81), next to the Post Office on the harbor.

JEWELRY

Carat (✉ Quai de la République, Gustavia) has Chaumet and a large selection of Breitling watches. For fine jewelry visit **Cartier** (✉ Quai de la République, Gustavia) harborside. A good selection of watches, including Patek Phillippe and Chanel, can be found at **Diamond Genesis** (✉ Rue Général-de-Gaulle, Gustavia). Next door to Cartier, **Oro del Sol** (✉ Quai de la République, Gustavia) carries beautiful fine accessories by Bulgari, Ebel, and others. **Sindbad** (✉ Carré d'Or, Gustavia, ☎ 0590/27–52–29), at the top, is a tiny shop turned out like a boat with "couture" fashion jewelry by Christian Lacroix, Clio Blue, and others. For under $100, you can bring home a great-looking chunky silver ring with a big faux stone.

LIQUOR AND TOBACCO

La Cave de Saint-Barths (✉ Marigot, ☎ 0590/27–63–21) has an excellent collection of French vintages stored in temperature-controlled cellars. **La Cave du Port Franc** (✉ Rue de la République, Gustavia, ☎ 0590/27–65–27) has a good selection of wine, especially from France. **Le Comptoir du Cigare** (✉ Rue de Général-de-Gaulle, Gustavia, ☎ 0590/27–50–62), run by Jannick and Patrick Gerthofer, is a top purveyor of cigars. The walk-in humidor has an extraordinary selection. Try the Cubans while you are on the island, and take home the Davidoffs. They will ship refills stateside. Be sure to try on the Panama hats.

Nightlife

In clubs change from season to season, so you might ask around for the hot spot of the moment. **Bar de l'Oubli** (⊠ Rue du Roi Oscar II, Gustavia, ☎ 0590/27–70–06) is where young locals gather for drinks. **Carl Gustaf** (⊠ Rue des Normands, Gustavia, ☎ 0590/27–82–83) lures those in search of quiet conversation and sunset watching. **Jungle Café** (⊠ 6 rue Jeanne d'Arc, Gustavia, ☎ 0590/27–67–29), overlooking the harbor, has live music and entertainment during and after dinner. **La Licorne** (⊠ Lorient, ☎ 0590/27–83–94) is hot with a local crowd but open only on Saturday night. **Le Deck Cocktail and Music Bar** (⊠ Gustavia, ☎ 0590/27–86–07) on the Gustavia waterfront is open every night until 2 AM. **Le Petit Club** (⊠ Gustavia, ☎ 0590/27–66–33) is the place to head for late-night dancing. **Le Repaire** (⊠ Rue de la République, Gustavia, ☎ 0590/27–72–48) lures a crowd for cocktail hour. **Le Select** (⊠ Rue du Centenaire, Gustavia, ☎ 0590/27–86–87) is St. Barths' original hangout, commemorated by Jimmy Buffet's "Cheeseburger in Paradise." The boisterous garden is where the barefoot boating set gathers for a brew. **New Feeling** (⊠ Lurin, ☎ 0590/27–88–67) is a disco in the Lurin Hills that has special theme nights on Thursday.

Exploring St. Barthélemy

With a little practice, negotiating St. Barths' narrow, steep roads soon becomes fun. Free maps are everywhere, roads are well-marked, and painted signs will point you where you want to be. Take along a towel, sandals, and a bottle of water on your explorations, and you will surely find a beach upon which to linger.

Numbers in the margin correspond to points of interest on the St. Barthélemy map.

SIGHTS TO SEE

❶ Anse des Flamands. From this wide, white-sand, hotel-lined beach, you can take a brisk hike to the top of the now-extinct volcano believed to have given birth to St. Barths.

❺ Anse du Gouverneur. Legend has it that pirates' treasure is buried at this beautiful beach. The road here from Gustavia offers spectacular vistas. If the weather is clear, you'll be able to see the islands of Saba, St. Eustatius, and St. Kitts from the beach.

❷ Corossol. The island's French provincial origins are most evident in this two-street fishing village with a little rocky beach. Older local women weave Lantana straw into handbags, baskets, hats, and delicate strings of birds. Ingenu Magras's **Inter Oceans Museum** has more than 9,000 seashells and an intriguing collection of sand samples from around the world. You can buy souvenir shells. ⊠ *Corossol,* ☎ *0590/27–62–97.* 🎫 *€3.* 🕙 *Tues.–Sun. 9–12:30 and 2–5.*

❻ Grande Saline. The big salt ponds of Grande Saline are no longer in use, and the place looks a little desolate. Still, you should climb the short hillock behind the ponds for a surprise—the long arc of Anse de Grande Saline.

❹ Gustavia. You can easily explore all of Gustavia during a two-hour stroll. Street signs in both French and Swedish illustrate the island's history. Shops close from noon to 2, so plan lunch accordingly. A good spot to park your car is rue de la République, where catamarans, yachts, and sailboats are moored. The **tourist office** (☎ 0590/27–87–27) on the pier can provide maps and a wealth of information. It's open Monday from 8:30 to 12:30, Tuesday through Friday from 8 to noon and

2 to 5, and Saturday from 9 to noon. On the far side of the harbor known as La Pointe is the charming **Municipal Museum,** where you will find watercolors, portraits, photographs, and historic documents detailing the island's history as well as displays of the island's flowers, plants, and marine life. ☎ 599/29–71–55. ⌑ €2. ☉ *Mon.–Thurs. 8:30–12:30 and 2:30–6, Fri. 8:30–12:30 and 3–6, Sat. 9–11.*

❼ Lorient. Site of the first French settlement, Lorient is one of the island's two parishes; a restored church, a school, and a post office mark the spot. Note the gaily decorated graves in the cemetery. One of St. Barths' treasured secrets is **Le Manoir** (☎ 0590/27–79–27), a 1610 Norman manor that was painstakingly shipped from France and reconstructed in Lorient in 1984 by the charming Jeanne Audy Rowland in tribute to the island's Viking forebears. Look for the entrance by the Ligne St. Barth building.

❸ St-Jean. The ½-mi (¾-km) crescent of sand at St-Jean is the island's most popular beach. Windsurfers skim along the water here, catching the strong trade winds. A popular activity is watching and photographing the hair-raising airplane landings. You'll also find some of the best shopping on the island here, as well as several restaurants.

❽ Toiny coast. Over the hills beyond Grand Cul de Sac is this much-photographed coastline. Stone fences crisscross the steep slopes of Morne Vitet, one of many small mountains on St. Barths, along a rocky shore that resembles the rugged coast of Normandy.

ST. BARTHS A TO Z

To research prices, get advice from other travelers, and book travel arrangements, visit www.fodors.com.

AIR TRAVEL

The principal gateway from North America is St. Maarten's Juliana International Airport. Although it's only 10 minutes by air to St. Barths, the last two may take your breath away. Don't worry when you see those treetops out your window. You're just clearing a hill before dropping down to the runway of Aéroport de St-Jean (St-Jean Airport). Flights leave at least once an hour between 7:30 AM and 5:30 PM on Windward Islands Airways. Air Guadeloupe offers daily service from St. Maarten, Guadeloupe, and Puerto Rico. Air St. Thomas has daily flights to St. Barths from both St. Thomas and Puerto Rico. You must reconfirm your return interisland flight, even during off-peak seasons, or you may very well lose your reservation. Be prepared to fly at a more convenient time for one of the airlines if it doesn't have enough passengers to justify a previously scheduled flight. Do not be upset if your luggage has not made the trip with you. It frequently will arrive on a later flight, and your hotel will send a porter to receive it. It's a good idea to pack a change of clothes and a bathing suit in your carry-on.

➤ CONTACTS: **Air Guadeloupe** (☎ 0590/27–61–90). **Air St. Thomas** (☎ 0590/27–71–76). **Windward Islands Airways** (☎ 0590/27–61–01 or 800/634–4907).

AIRPORTS

Many hotels offer free airport shuttles. When you make your reservations, specify your arrival time. Hotels can be called from a free telephone in the arrivals building. Unmetered taxis cost $5–$20, depending on distance. Drivers set a fare before setting out, and it's usually not negotiable. There are taxi stands at the airport and in Gustavia on the pier. The taxi dispatcher will help. If you have reserved a rental car, your name will be on a blackboard at the appropriate counter.

➤ CONTACTS: **Aéroport de St-Jean** (☎ 0590/27–65–41). **Taxi dispatcher** (☎ 0590/27–66–31).

BIKE AND MOPED TRAVEL

Several companies rent motorbikes, scooters, mopeds, and mountain bikes. Motorbikes go for about $30 per day and require a $100 deposit. Helmets are required.

➤ CONTACTS: **Boutique Harley Davidson** (✉ Gustavia, ☎ 0590/27–70–59). **St. Barths Motobike** (✉ Gustavia, ☎ 0590/27–67–89).

BOAT AND FERRY TRAVEL

Voyager offers ferry service for day trips between St. Barths, St. Maarten (both Phillipsburg and Marigot), and Saba. Round-trips for two are offered for $70. All service is from the Quai République.

➤ CONTACTS: *Voyager* (☎ 0590/87–10–68, WEB www.voyager-st-barths.com).

BUSINESS HOURS

BANKS

Banks are generally open weekdays 8–noon and 2–3:30. There are 24-hour cash machines at most.

POST OFFICES

The main post office on rue Jeanne d'Arc in Gustavia is open Monday–Tuesday and Thursday–Friday 8–3, Wednesday and Saturday 8–noon. The branch in Lorient is open weekdays 7 AM–11 AM and Saturday 8 AM–10 AM. The post office in St-Jean opens Monday–Tuesday 8–2 and Wednesday–Saturday 8–noon.

SHOPS

Stores are generally open weekdays 8:30–noon and 2–5, Saturday 8:30–noon. Some of the shops across from the airport and in St-Jean stay open on Saturday afternoon and until 7 PM on weekdays. Although some shops are closed on Wednesday afternoon, most are open 8:30–noon and 3–6.

CAR RENTALS

In the last two years the dune-buggy-ish minimoke has largely been replaced with small four-wheel-drive vehicles, which provide a welcome increase of power and maneuverability on the steep, narrow roads. Be sure to check the brakes before you head out, and make a careful inventory of the existing dents and scrapes on the rental agreement.

You'll find major rental agencies at the airport, and all accept credit cards. Check with several counters for the best price. You must have a valid driver's license to rent, and in high season there may be a three-day minimum. Be sure to supply the licenses of all who might drive the car. During peak periods, such as Christmas week and February, be sure to arrange for your car rental ahead of time. Charges average about $55 a day; you may be able to bargain if you plan a stay longer than a week. When you make your hotel reservations, ask if the hotel has its own cars available to rent. Though the choice of vehicles may be limited, some hotels provide 24-hour emergency road service—something most rental companies don't offer. Smart of St. Barth rent the tiny, colorful two-seaters called "Smart Cars" that are the rage.

➤ OTHER MAJOR AGENCIES: **Avis** (☎ 0590/27–71–52). **Budget** (☎ 0590/27–67–43). **Europcar** (☎ 0590/27–73–33). **Gumbs** (☎ 0590/27–75–32). **Hertz** (☎ 0590/27–71–14). **Smart of St. Barth** (☎ 0590/29–71–31, WEB www.smartofstbarth.com).

CAR TRAVEL

Roads are sometimes unmarked, so be sure to get a map. Instead of road signs, look for signs pointing to a destination. These will be nailed to posts at all crossroads. Roads are narrow and sometimes very steep, so check the brakes and gears of your rental car before you drive away. Some hillside restaurants and hotels have steep entranceways and difficult steps that require a bit of climbing or negotiating.

GASOLINE

There are two gas stations on the island, one near the airport and one in Lorient. They aren't open after 5 PM or on Sunday, but you can use the one near the airport at any time with some credit cards, including JCB or Carte Blanche—but not Visa, MasterCard, or American Express. A full tank of gas runs $13–$15; considering the short distances, this should last you most of a week.

RULES OF THE ROAD

St. Barths drivers often seem to be in an unending grand prix and thus tend to keep their cars maxed out, especially and inexplicably when in reverse. Parking is an additional challenge.

ELECTRICITY

Voltage is 220 AC, 60 cycles, as in Europe. You can sometimes use American appliances with French plug converters and transformers. Most hotel rooms are conveniently supplied with hair dryers.

EMERGENCIES

The tourist office can provide an up-to-date list of local health professionals.

➤ AMBULANCE AND FIRE: **Ambulance and Fire emergencies** (☎ 18).
➤ HOSPITALS: **Hospital De Bruyn** (✉ Gustavia, ☎ 0590/27–60–35).
➤ PHARMACIES: **Pharmacies** (✉ Quai République, Gustavia, ☎ 0590/27–61–82; ✉ La Savane Commercial Center, St-Jean, ☎ 0590/27–66–61).
➤ POLICE: **Police** (☎ 0590/27–66–66).

FESTIVALS AND SEASONAL EVENTS

In January, St. Barths hosts an international collection of musicians as part of the St. Barths Music Festival. February brings a flood of feasting, dancing, music, and parades during Carnival season. The Caribbean Film Festival takes place in early April. On July 14 Bastille Day is celebrated with a parade, a regatta, parties, and a fireworks display. In early December the annual St. Barths Marble Tournament attracts contestants of all ages.

HOLIDAYS

Public holidays include New Year's Day, Easter weekend, Labor Day (May 1), Pentecost (mid- to late May), Bastille Day (July 14), Pitea Day (commemorates the joining of St. Barths with Pitea in Sweden, Aug. 15), All Saints' Day (Nov. 1), Armistice Day (Nov. 11), and Christmas.

LANGUAGE

French is the official language, so it can't hurt to pack a phrase book and/or a French dictionary. If you speak any French at all, don't be shy. You may also hear Creole, the regional French dialect called patois, and even the Creole of Guadeloupe. Most hotel and restaurant employees speak some English—at least enough to help you find what you need.

MAIL AND SHIPPING

Mail is slow. Correspondence between the United States and the island can take up to three weeks to arrive. Post offices are in Gustavia, St-

Jean, and Lorient. When writing to an establishment on St. Barths, be sure to include "French West Indies" at the end of the address. Faxes are widely used.

➤ CONTACTS: **Main post office** (✉ Rue Jeanne d'Arc Gustavia, ☎ 0590/27–62–00).

MONEY MATTERS

The change from the French franc to the euro in 2002 has not been an especially smooth transition on St. Barths. As of this writing, prices on the island are quoted variously in francs, in euros, and in U.S. dollars. In many cases, euro prices are sometimes "creative" (rounded up to the nearest euro, or even a cover for a price hike). Therefore, please note that quoted prices are approximate. Hopefully the situation will resolve with wider circulation of euro coins and increased familiarity with conversion rates. Don't hesitate to ask to pay in U.S. dollars if you are uncomfortable with the calculations of a transaction.

Prices quoted in this chapter are in U.S. dollars, unless otherwise noted.

ATMS
There are 24-hour cash machines at most banks.

CREDIT CARDS
Credit cards are accepted at most shops, hotels, and restaurants. Paying with a credit card will generally yield a better exchange rate than what the individual restaurant or shop will offer.

CURRENCY
The French franc has been replaced with the euro, but U.S. dollars are accepted in most establishments (though you may receive change in euros). All credit card transactions are charged in Euros.

PASSPORTS AND VISAS
All foreign citizens need a passport and a return or ongoing ticket.

SAFETY
There is relatively little crime on St. Barths. Visitors can travel anywhere on the island with confidence.

SIGHTSEEING TOURS
You can arrange island tours by minibus or car at hotel desks, through the tourist office, or through any of the island's taxi operators in Gustavia or at the airport. Wish Agency can arrange customized tours, as well as take care of airline ticketing, event planning, maid service, and private party arrangements.

TAXES AND SERVICE CHARGES
DEPARTURE TAX
The island charges a $5 departure tax when your next stop is another French island, $10 if you're off to anywhere else.

SALES TAX
Some hotels add an additional 10%–15% service charge to bills; but most include it in their tariffs.

TAXIS
Taxis are expensive and not particularly easy to arrange, especially in the evening. There's a taxi station at the airport and another in Gustavia; from elsewhere you must contact a dispatcher in Gustavia or St. Jean. Technically, there's a flat rate for rides up to five minutes long. Each additional three minutes is an additional amount. In reality, however, cabbies usually name a fixed rate—and will not budge. Fares are 50% higher from 8 PM to 6 AM and on Sunday and holidays.

➤ CONTACTS: **Gustavia taxi dispatcher** (☎ 0590/27–66–31). **St. Jean taxi dispatcher** (☎ 0590/27–75–81).

TELEPHONES

MCI and AT&T services are available. Public telephones do not accept coins; they accept *télécartes*, prepaid calling cards that you can buy at the gas station next to the airport and at post offices in Lorient, St-Jean, and Gustavia. Making an international call using a télécarte is much less expensive than making it through your hotel.

If you would like to retrieve e-mail while you're on the island, the best bet is a visit to the Internet Service at Centre Alizes, which has fax service and 10 computers on line. They are open weekdays, 8:30–12:30 and 2:30–7, as well as Saturday morning. France Télécom can provide you with temporary Internet access that may let you connect your laptop. They can also arrange cellular phone service.

➤ E-MAIL SERVICE CONTACTS: **Centre Alizes** (✉ Rue de la République, Gustavia, ☎ 0590/29–89–89). **France Télécom** (✉ Espace Neptune, St-Jean, ☎ 0590/27–67–00).

COUNTRY AND AREA CODES

The country code for St. Barths is 590. Thus, to phone St. Barths from the United States, dial 011 + 590 + 590 and the local 6-digit number (dial 590 *twice* but omit the 0, which you must dial within the country, before the second 590).

INTERNATIONAL CALLS

To call the United States from St. Barths, dial 001 + the area code + the local 7-digit number.

LOCAL CALLS

For calls on St. Barths, you must dial 0590 + the 6-digit local number; for St. Martin dial just the six-digit number for the French side, for the Dutch side (Sint Maarten) dial 00–599–54 + the five-digit number.

TIPPING

Restaurants include a 15% service charge in their published prices, but it is common French practice to leave 5%–10% *pourboire* (literally: for a drink) and no more on top of this. Keep this in mind that when your credit-card receipt is presented to be signed, the tip space should be blank—just draw a line through it—or you could end up paying a 30% service charge. Most taxi drivers don't expect a tip.

TRANSPORTATION AROUND ST. BARTHS
HITCHHIKING

Hitching rides is a popular, legal, and interesting way to get around. It's widely practiced in the more heavily trafficked areas on the island. But there is more and more traffic, so be careful.

VISITOR INFORMATION

A daily news sheet called *NEWS* that lists local happenings like special dinners or music is available at markets and newsstands. You will also find free, weekly *Journal de Saint-Barth*—although mostly in French—is useful for current events. The small *Ti Gourmet Saint-Barth* is a free pocket-size guidebook that is invaluable for addresses and telephone numbers of restaurants and services; pick one up anywhere.

➤ BEFORE YOU LEAVE: **French West Indies Tourist Board** (✉ 610 5th Ave., New York, NY 10020, WEB www.fgtousa.org). **French Government Tourist Office** (✉ 444 Madison Ave., 16th Floor, New York, NY 10022, ☎ 900/990–0040 [charges a fee]; ✉ 9454 Wilshire Blvd., Suite 303, Beverly Hills, CA 90212, ☎ 213/272–2661; ✉ 645 N. Michigan Ave., Suite 3360, Chicago, IL 60611, ☎ 312/337–6301; in Canada: ✉ 1981 McGill College Ave., Suite 490, Montréal, Québec H3A 2W9, Canada, ☎ 514/288–4264; ✉ 30 St. Patrick St., Suite 700, Toronto, Ontario M5T 3A3, Canada, ☎ 416/593–4723; in the U.K.: ✉ 178 Piccadilly, London W1V OAL, U.K., ☎ 0171/629–9376).

➤ IN ST. BARTHS: **Office du Tourisme** (✉ Quai Général-de-Gaulle, ☎ 0590/27–87–27, FAX 0590/27–74–47).

Updated by
Suzanne
Gordon

Down a country road that seems to lead to nowhere, the rural dwelling of the Berkel family appears. Ismael Berkel wanders through, showing guests his family's heirlooms, photos of his ancestors from a century ago. It's easy to see why he's proud of this property, part of the 82-acre original plantation. The charming clapboard houses, each one room in size, hold the past: the family Bible, old glasses, even the old Singer that Pa gave Ma in 1944. Such was life in Statia's past, but the times here haven't changed all that much.

The tiny Dutch island of St. Eustatius, commonly called Statia (pro-nounced *stay*-sha), in the Netherlands Antilles, is ideal for those with a penchant for quiet times and strolls through history. It was once one of the most powerful merchant centers in the Caribbean; today you'll find only remnants of those times—forts, narrow cobblestone streets, and historic buildings. Statians themselves are reason enough to visit. So is the landing approach: in the distance looms the Quill, an extinct volcano with a primeval rain forest in its crater.

This 12-square-mi (31-square-km) island that Columbus sailed past in 1493 prospered from the day the Dutch Zeelanders colonized it in 1636. In the 1700s a double row of warehouses crammed with goods stretched 1 mi (1½ km) along the bay, and there were sometimes as many as 200 ships tied up at the duty-free port. The island was called the Emporium of the Western World and Golden Rock. There were almost 8,000 Statians in the 1790s (today the population is about 2,700). Holland, England, and France fought over the island, which changed hands 22 times. It has been a Dutch possession, however, since 1816.

During the American War of Independence, when the British block-aded the North American coast, food, arms, and other supplies for the revolutionaries were diverted to the West Indies, notably to neutral Sta-tia (Benjamin Franklin had his mail routed through the island to en-sure its safe arrival in Europe). On November 16, 1776, the brig-of-war *Andrew Doria,* commanded by Captain Isaiah Robinson of the Con-tinental Navy, sailed into Statia's port flying the Stars and Stripes. The ship fired a 13-gun salute to the Royal Netherlands standard, and Gov-ernor Johannes de Graaff ordered the cannons of Ft. Oranje to return the salute. That first official acknowledgment of the new American flag by a foreign power earned Statia the nickname America's Childhood

Friend. In retaliation, British admiral George Rodney attacked and destroyed much of the island in 1781. Statia has yet to recover its prosperity, which, ironically, ended partly because of the American Revolution's success: the island was no longer needed as a trans-shipment port, and its bustling economy gradually came to a stop.

Statia is in the Dutch Windward Triangle, 178 mi (287 km) east of Puerto Rico and 35 mi (56 km) south of St. Maarten. Oranjestad, the capital and only "city," is on the western side, facing the calm Caribbean. On the eastern side are the often-rough waters of the Atlantic. The island is anchored at the north and the south by extinct volcanoes separated by a central, dry plain. The higher elevations are alive with greenery and abloom with flowers—bougainvillea, oleander, and hibiscus.

Statia is a playground for divers and hikers. Colorful coral reefs and myriad ships rest on the ocean floor alongside 18th-century warehouses that were slowly absorbed by the sea. On land, much of the activity involves archaeology and restoration; students come here to study pre-Columbian artifacts, and the island's historical foundation restores local landmarks. Statia is also a way-station for oil, with a 16-million-barrel storage bunker encased in the Boven, an extinct volcano on the island's northern end. On any given day there are several oil tankers at anchor waiting to give or receive the liquid gold.

Most visitors will be content with a day-trip from nearby St. Maarten, exploring some of the historical sights and maybe enjoying a meal. Those who stay longer tend to be collectors of unspoiled islands with a need to relax and a taste for history. Statians are mindful of the potential gold mine of tourism, and, in addition to preserving many historical buildings and forts, they're expanding the island's pier and improving its infrastructure. But it may be the locals themselves who make coming here such a pleasure. Folks in these parts still say hello to strangers, and drivers wave or beep to one another.

Lodging

None of Statia's accommodations could be considered luxurious. Cheerful, tidy, and homey are the best you can expect, and all (at this writing, Statia had only three hotels) have 20 units or less; room decor and furnishing are eclectic but comfortable. If there's a philosophy to owning and running a hostelry on Statia, it's "do what you can with what you have."

Renting an apartment is another lodging alternative. Although Statia has only a handful of them, several are available for $50 or less per night, but don't expect much beyond a bathroom and kitchenette. Check with the tourist office for options.

CATEGORY	COST EP/CP*	COST A.I.**
$$$$	over $350	over $375
$$$	$250–$350	$275–$375
$$	$150–$250	$175–$275
$	under $150	under $175

*EP/CP prices are per night for a standard double room in high season, excluding taxes, service charges, and meal plans

**A.I. (all-inclusive) prices are per person, per night based on double-occupancy during high season, excluding taxes and service charges

$–$$$ ⬚ **The Gin House.** This gracious, historic waterfront building—owned by the same people who run the Holland House hotel on St. Maarten—is a wonderful part of Statia's hotel scene. Most rooms face a courtyard and pool, but four new rooms have opened on the waterfront.

St. Eustatius

KEY

⟋ Beaches

◤ Dive Sites

❶ Exploring Sights

① Hotels and Restaurants

✳ Rain Forest

ATLANTIC OCEAN

Cocoluch Bay

Boven Bay

Fontaan Bay

Boven

Venus Bay

Jenkins Bay

Gilboa Hill

Zeelandia Beach

Zeelandia Bay

Concordia Bay

Great Bay

Compagnie Bay

Lynch Bay

Lynch Bay Beach

Little Mountain

Zeelandia

F.D.R. Airport ✈

Signal Hill

Tumble Down Dick Bay

Fair Play

❸

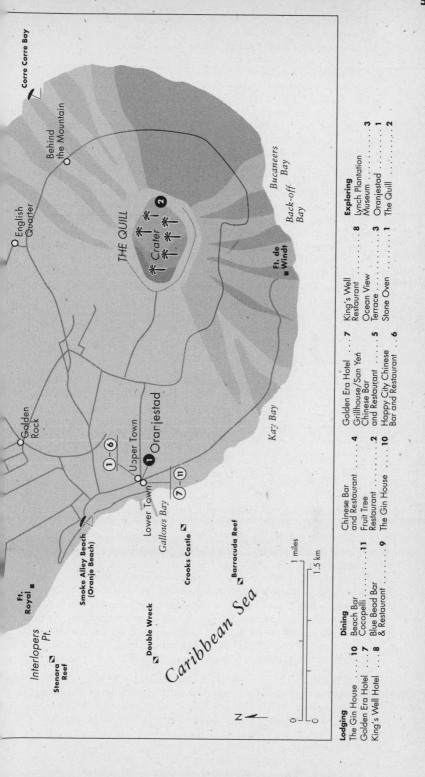

Caribbean Sea

Interlopers Pt.

Stenara Reef

Ft. Royal ■

Smoke Alley Beach (Oranje Beach)

Double Wreck

Crooks Castle

Barracuda Reef

Gallows Bay

Lower Town

Upper Town

Oranjestad

Golden Rock

Kay Bay

Ft. de Windt ■

Back-off Bay

Bucaneers Bay

THE QUILL

Crater

Behind the Mountain

English Quarter

Corre Corre Bay

N

0 — 1 miles
0 — 1.5 km

Lodging
The Gin House 10
Golden Era Hotel . . . 7
King's Well Hotel . . . 8

Dining
Beach Bar
Cocopelli 11
Blue Bead Bar & Restaurant 9
Chinese Bar and Restaurant 4
Fruit Tree Restaurant 2
The Gin House 10
Golden Era Hotel . . . 7
Grillhouse/San Yen Chinese Bar and Restaurant . . . 5
Happy City Chinese Bar and Restaurant . . 6
King's Well Restaurant 7
Ocean View Terrace 3
Stone Oven 1

Exploring
Lynch Plantation Museum 3
Oranjestad 1
The Quill 2

The Gin House restaurant and new beach outlet Beach Bar Cocopelli serve three meals daily. ⊠ *Bay Rd., Lower Town, Oranjestad,* ☎ *599/ 318–2319,* FAX *599/318–2135,* WEB *www.oldginhouse.com. 14 rooms. Restaurant, pool, cable TV, bar. AE, MC, V. EP.*

$ 🏨 **Golden Era Hotel.** Don't be put off by the 1960s-style motel look: this harbor-front hotel has a friendly staff and a central seaside location. Rooms have tile floors, mini-refrigerators, TVs, phones, and little terraces. Just be sure to ask for a room with a view; only half of them have full or partial sea vistas. The Golden Era Hotel restaurant serves great creole food. ⊠ *Bay Rd., Lower Town, Oranjestad (Box 109),* ☎ *599/318–2345 or 800/223–9815,* FAX *599/318–2445. 19 rooms, 1 suite. Restaurant, refrigerators, saltwater pool, bar. AE, D, MC, V. EP, MAP.*

$ 🏨 **King's Well Hotel.** Perched on the cliffs between Upper Town and
★ Lower Town, this small hotel has 14 pleasant rooms with balconies, mini-refrigerators, TVs, and a pool (new in 2001). The four large rooms at the back have queen-size waterbeds and French doors that open to the sea. The make-yourself-at-home atmosphere includes an honor bar in the King's Well Restaurant, which serves guests three meals a day (full breakfast is included in the rates). ⊠ *Bay Rd., Lower Town, Oranjestad,* ☎ FAX *599/318–2538. 14 rooms. Restaurant, refrigerators, pool, bar. D, MC, V. BP.*

Dining

Although you may be surprised with the variety of restaurants, don't expect fine dining. Your best bet is to eat local style; that is, West Indian, and keep your expectations simple. All restaurants are very casual, but do cover up your beachwear.

CATEGORY	COST*
$$$$	over $30
$$$	$20–$30
$$	$10–$20
$	under $10

per person for a main course at dinner

ASIAN

$–$$ ✕ **Grillhouse/San Yen Chinese Bar and Restaurant.** One of several Chinese restaurants on Statia, this one in the heart of town touts its special—a dish combining chicken, scallops, shrimp, beef, and Chinese sausage with vegetables—as the best entrée on the menu. There's a small bar and just a few tables, and a meal here makes you feel as if you're eating at your neighbor's house. ⊠ *Fort Oranjestad, Upper Town, Oranjestad,* ☎ *599/318–2915. No credit cards.*

$–$$ ✕ **Happy City Chinese Bar and Restaurant.** Tucked away in a little in-town mall, this small, simple, clean Chinese restaurant offers a varied Asian menu. Try the *nasi goreng* (Indonesian fried rice), which is the most popular local choice. ⊠ *De Windtweg, Upper Town, Oranjestad,* ☎ *599/318–2540. No credit cards. Closed Wed.*

CARIBBEAN

$$–$$$$ ✕ **Golden Era Hotel.** This somewhat stark establishment (not surprisingly found in the Golden Era Hotel) has excellent creole food, and the large dining room is right on the water. ⊠ *Bay Rd., Lower Town, Oranjestad,* ☎ *599/318–2345. AE, D, MC, V.*

$$ ✕ **Stone Oven.** A Spanish couple runs this cozy eatery, offering such West Indian specialties as "goat water" (goat stew). You can eat inside the little house, which is in a residential neighborhood, or outside on the palm-fringed patio. ⊠ *16A Feaschweg, Upper Town, Oranjestad,* ☎ *599/318–2543. No credit cards.*

$–$$ ✕ **Fruit Tree Restaurant.** The Fruit Tree, named after the papaya, ba-
★ nana, and soursop trees that grow on its grounds, serves heaping plates
of West Indian specialties: bull-foot soup (a stew with vegetables and
beef), goat water, oxtail, and rice. Top it all off with johnnycakes and
bush tea. There are only four tables on the patio, but you won't wait
long, if at all. Next door is a small crafts shop. ⊠ *484 Prinsesweg, Upper
Town, Oranjestad,* ☎ *599/318–2584. No credit cards. Closed Mon.*

ECLECTIC

$$–$$$$ ✕ **King's Well Restaurant.** It's like watching mom and dad make din-
ner to see owners Win and Laura Piechutzki scurry around their open
kitchen preparing the night's meal in this breezy terrace eatery. And
don't expect to eat alone, because a meal here makes you part of the
family at the King's Well Hotel. Overlooking the sea, the restaurant is
run by this fun-loving expatriate couple. The steaks are from Colorado,
the lobster is fresh, and the *rostbraten* (roast beef) and schnitzels are
authentic: Win is German. ⊠ *King's Well Hotel, Bay Rd., Lower
Town, Oranjestad,* ☎ *599/318–2538. D, MC, V.*

$$$ ✕ **The Gin House.** Chef Jan Buyens from Belgium has taken the reigns
of this charming, old-fashioned restaurant inside The Gin House hotel,
turning out his fabulous sauces, homemade breads, fresh lobster, and
rack of lamb. Prix-fixe three- and four-course meals are available in
the main dining room. Reservations are a good idea. ⊠ *Bay Rd.,
Lower Town, Oranjestad,* ☎ *599/318–2319. AE, MC, V. Closed
Mon.–Tue. No lunch.*

$$ ✕ **Blue Bead Bar & Restaurant.** Right on the waterfront, this attrac-
★ tive eatery is the perfect spot for a sunset cocktail. Meals are served
on a cheery, bright blue-and-yellow-trimmed veranda decked with
potted plants; the fare runs the gamut from French-inspired to Italian
pizzas. Don't miss the fried calamari, French-creole stuffed crab, the
local squash (christophene), and salt cod fritters. The daily specials are
recommended, as is a nip of the after-dinner special, homemade vanilla
rum, served by the bottle to each table. Fridays are seafood nights; and
Saturdays for families, when the kids (of any age) can enjoy the Blue
Bead Baby Bimmer Burger. ⊠ *Bay Rd., Lower Town, Oranjestad,* ☎
599/318–2873. AE, D, MC, V. Closed Mon.

$$–$$$ ✕ **Ocean View Terrace.** This patio spot in the courtyard next to the
tourist office serves sandwiches and burgers at lunch, and local cui-
sine—baked snapper with shrimp sauce, spicy chicken, tenderloin
steak—at dinner (you can get breakfast here, too). The courtyard is
surrounded by the beautiful old stone fort and government buildings.
⊠ *Oranjestraat, Upper Town, Oranjestad,* ☎ *599/318–2934. No
credit cards. No lunch Sun.*

$$ ✕ **Chinese Bar and Restaurant.** Owner Kim Cheng serves up tasty Asian
and Caribbean dishes—*bami goreng* (Indonesian noodles with bits of
beef, pork, or shrimp as well as tomatoes, carrots, bean sprouts, cabbage, soy sauce, and spices) and Spanish pork chops, for example—in
hearty portions at his unpretentious establishment. Dining indoors
can be claustrophobic; just ask your waitress if you may tote your
Formica-top table out onto the terrace. She'll probably be happy to
lend a hand and then serve you under the stars. ⊠ *Prinsesweg, Upper
Town, Oranjestad,* ☎ *599/318–2389. No credit cards.*

$–$$ ✕ **Beach Bar Cocopelli.** Part of The Gin House hotel, this outdoor eatery
on the sea is relaxing and fun. Cooking for all meals, all week long,
Chef Jan Buyens serves his homemade breads, pastas, salads, and light
meals on a casual, umbrella-shaded terrace, where you'll find lots of
local conversation. ⊠ *The Gin House Hotel, Bay Rd., Lower Town,
Oranjestad,* ☎ *599/318–2319. AE, MC, V.*

Beaches

Beachcombing on Statia is for the intrepid: the beaches are pristine but unmaintained and occasionally rocky. Sand is mainly volcanic black and gray. The nicest strands are on the Atlantic side, but the surf is generally too rough for swimming. You can (though it's not recommended) hike around the coast at low tide; but driving is the best way to reach remote Atlantic stretches. A big deal on the beaches here is searching for Statia's famed blue-glass beads. Manufactured in the 17th century by the Dutch West Indies Company, these beads were traded for rum, slaves, cotton, and tobacco. Although they're found only on Statia, some researchers believe that it was beads like these that were traded for Manhattan. They're best unearthed after a heavy rain, but as the locals chuckle, "If you find one, it's a miracle, man."

Corre Corre Bay. A 30-minute hike down an easy, marked trail behind the Mountain Road will bring you to this gold-sand cove.

Lynch Bay. Two bends north of Corre Corre Bay, this beach is somewhat protected from the wild swells. On the Atlantic side, especially around Concordia Bay, the surf is rough, and there's sometimes an undertow, making beaches better for sunning than swimming.

Smoke Alley Beach. Also called Oranje Beach, this is the nicest and most accessible beach on the island. The beige-and-black-sand beach is on the Caribbean, off Lower Town, and is relatively deserted until late afternoon, when the locals arrive.

Zeelandia Beach. This 2-mi (3-km) strip of black sand on the Atlantic side has a dangerous undertow, but a small section is considered okay for swimming. It's a lovely, deserted stretch for sunning, walking, and wading.

Outdoor Activities and Sports

Participant Sports

FISHING

By and large, deep-sea fishing is not a major activity off Statia's shores. But it's nice to be out on the water. **Golden Rock Dive Center** (✉ Bay Rd., Lower Town, Oranjestad, ☎ FAX 599/318–2964) offers full- and half-day trips for $500 and $350, respectively, including gear and bait.

HIKING

Trails range from the easy to the "Watch out!" The big thrill here is the Quill, the 1,968-ft (602-m) extinct volcano with its crater full of rain forest. Give yourself two to three hours to make the climb and the return. The tourist office has a list of 12 marked trails and can put you in touch with a guide (whose fee will be about $20). The Quill National Park includes a trail into the crater, which is a long, windy, but safe walk. Maps are available at the Saba Marine Park headquarters on Bay Road. Wear layers: it can be cool on the summit and steamy in the interior.

SCUBA DIVING AND SNORKELING

Statia has more than 30 dive sites protected by the Saba Marine Park, which has an office on Bay Road in Lower Town. Both this park and Quill National Park are under the supervision of STENAPA (St. Eustatius National Parks Foundation). You pay $3 per dive to help offset the costs of preserving the coral and other sea life here.

Barracudas swim around colorful coral walls at **Barracuda Reef,** off the island's southwest coast. At **Double Wreck,** just offshore from Lower Town, you'll find two tall-masted ships that date from the 1700s. The coral has taken on the shape of these two disintegrated vessels, and the site attracts large schools of fish, sting rays, and moray eels. Off the island's western shore, **Stenapa Reef** is an artificial reef created from the wrecks of barges, a harbor boat, and other ship parts. Large grouper and turtles are among the marine life you'll spot here. For snorkelers, **Crooks Castle** has several stands of pillar coral, giant yellow sea fans, and sea whips just southwest of Lower Town.

With 5,000 dives out of Statia each year—and the numbers are growing—the island's three dive shops along Bay Road in Lower Town are busy. They rent all types of gear (including snorkeling gear for about $20 a day), offer certification courses, and organize dive trips. The average cost of a one-tank dive is $35; two-tank dives run around $65. **Dive Statia** (⊠ Bay Rd., Lower Town, Oranjestad, ☎ 599/318–2435), a fully equipped and PADI-certified dive shop (it has received PADI's five-star Gold Palm Designation), is operated by Rudy and Rinda Hees out of a warehouse. In addition to offering standard courses, Dive Statia also offers underwater photography courses and night and multi-level dives. They offer Nitrox diving. **Golden Rock Dive Center** (⊠ Bay Rd., Lower Town, Oranjestad, ☎ FAX 599/318–2964; 800/311–6658 direct to center) is another of Statia's PADI facilities. The staff here specializes in custom dive trips. **Scubaqua** (⊠ Golden Era Hotel, Bay Rd., Lower Town, Oranjestad, ☎ 599/318–2345, FAX 599/318–2160) has dive courses, which are offered in various languages.

WATERSKIING

Dive operators **Dive Statia** and **Scubaqua** will also take you waterskiing for $90 per hour. Scubaqua offers wake boarding (riding on a small, short surfboard, while kneeling or standing and being towed by a boat) for the same price.

Spectator Sports

Cricket and soccer matches are played at the sports complex in Upper Town. Statia hosts teams from other Caribbean islands on weekends; admission is free.

Shopping

Though shopping here is duty-free, it's also very limited. Other than the predictable souvenirs, there's not much to buy. Look for the wonderful book by Saban artist Heleen Cornett *St. Eustatius: Echoes of the Past,* sold in several stores. **Mazinga Gift Shop** (⊠ Fort Oranjestreet, Upper Town, Oranjestad, ☎ 599/318–2245) is a small department store of sorts, selling basic necessities. The **Paper Corner** (⊠ Van Tonningenweg, Upper Town, Oranjestad, ☎ 599/318–2208) sells magazines, a few books, and stationery supplies.

Nightlife

Statia's nightlife is far from brisk. Local bands play around the island on weekends, and the hotels are good places to have a few quiet drinks. **Cool Corner** (⊠ Wilhelminaweg, Upper Town, Oranjestad, ☎ 599/318–2523), a tiny corner bar in the heart of town, across from the St. Eustatius Historical Foundation Museum, is a lively after-work and weekend hangout.

Exploring St. Eustatius

Statia is an arid island consisting of a valley between two mountain peaks. Most sights lie in the valley, making touring the island easy. From the airport you can rent a car or take a taxi and be in historic Oranjestad in minutes; to hike the Quill, Statia's highest peak, you can drive to the trailhead in less than 15 minutes from just about anywhere.

Numbers in the margin correspond to points of interest on the St. Eustatius map.

❸ Lynch Plantation Museum. Also known as the Berkel Family Plantation, this museum consists of two one-room buildings, set up as they were almost 100 years ago. A remarkable collection preserves this family's history—pictures, Bibles, spectacles, original furniture, and farming and fishing implements give a detailed perspective of life on Statia. You'll need either a taxi or a car to visit, and it's well worth the trouble. ✉ *Lynch Bay,* ☎ *599/318–2209 to arrange tour.* 🎫 *Free.*

❶ Oranjestad. Statia's capital and only town sits on the west coast facing the Caribbean. Both Upper Town and Lower Town are easy to explore on foot. History buffs will enjoy poking around the Dutch colonial buildings, which are being restored by the historical foundation. At the tourist office, right in the charming courtyard of the government offices, you can pick up maps, brochures, advice, and a listing of 12 marked trails. You can also arrange for guides and tours.

With its three bastions, **Ft. Oranje** has clutched these cliffs since 1636. In 1976 Statia participated in the U.S. bicentennial celebration by restoring the fort, and now the black cannons point out over the ramparts. In the parade grounds a plaque, presented in 1939 by Franklin D. Roosevelt, reads, HERE THE SOVEREIGNTY OF THE UNITED STATES OF AMERICA WAS FIRST FORMALLY ACKNOWLEDGED TO A NATIONAL VESSEL BY A FOREIGN OFFICIAL.

In the center of Upper Town is the **St. Eustatius Historical Foundation Museum.** It's in the Doncker House, where British admiral Rodney set up his headquarters during the American Revolution. While here, he confiscated everything from gunpowder to port in retaliation for Statia's gallant support of the fledgling country. The house, acquired by the foundation in 1983 and completely restored, is Statia's most important intact 18th-century dwelling. Exhibits trace the island's history from the 6th century to the present. The basement exhibit details Statia's pre-Columbian history with the results of archaeological digs. Statia is the only island thus far where ruins and artifacts of the Saladoid, a newly discovered tribe, have been excavated. ✉ *3 Wilhelminaweg, Upper Town, Oranjestad,* ☎ *599/318–2288.* 🎫 *$2.* 🕐 *Weekdays 9–5, weekends 9–noon.*

The **Dutch Reformed Church,** on Kerkweg (Church Way), was built in 1775. It has been partially restored and has lovely stone arches that face the sea. Ancient tales can be read on the gravestones in the adjacent 18th-century cemetery. On Synagogepad (Synagogue Path), off Kerkweg, is **Honen Dalim** ("She Who Is Charitable to the Poor"), one of the Caribbean's oldest synagogues. Dating from 1738, it's now in ruins but is slated for restoration.

Lower Town sits below Ft. Oranjestraat (Fort Orange Street) and some steep cliffs and is reached from Upper Town on foot via the zigzagging, cobblestone Fort Road or by car via Van Tonningenweg. Warehouses and shops that were piled high with European imports in the 18th century are either abandoned or simply used to store local fishermen's equipment. Along the waterfront is a lovely park with palms, flowering shrubs, and benches—the work of the historical foundation. Peeking out from the shallow waters are the crumbling ruins of 18th-century buildings, from Statia's days as the merchant hub of the Caribbean. The sea has slowly advanced since then, and it now surrounds many of the stone and brick ruins, making for fascinating snorkeling.

❷ The Quill. This extinct 1,968-ft-high (602-m-high) volcano has a primeval rain forest in its crater. If you like to hike, you'll want to head here to see giant elephant ears, ferns, flowers, wild orchids, fruit trees, and birds hiding in the trees. You might also encounter an endangered *iguana delicatissima* (a large—sometimes several feet long—greenish-gray creature with spines down its back). The volcanic cone rises 3 mi (5 km) south of Oranjestad on the main road. Local boys go up to the Quill by torchlight to catch delectable land crabs. The tourist board will help you make hiking arrangements.

ST. EUSTATIUS A TO Z

To research prices, get advice from other travelers, and book travel arrangements, visit www.fodors.com.

AIR TRAVEL

Windward Islands Airways makes the 20-minute flight from St. Maarten to Statia's Franklin Delano Roosevelt Airport several times a day, the 10-minute flight from Saba daily, and the 15-minute flight from St. Kitts twice a week in high season. Be sure to confirm your flight a day or two ahead; schedules change abruptly.

➤ AIRLINES AND CONTACTS: **Windward Islands Airways** (☎ 599/318-2362).

➤ AIRPORT INFORMATION: **Franklin Delano Roosevelt Airport** (☎ 599/318-2362).

BUSINESS HOURS

BANKS

Banks have varying hours: Barclays Bank is open weekdays 8:30–3:30; Windward Islands Bank is open weekdays 8:30–noon and 1–3:30.

POST OFFICES

Post offices are open weekdays 8–noon and 1–4 or 5.

SHOPS

Shops are open 8–6, and grocery stores often stay open until 7.

CAR RENTALS

To explore the island (and there isn't very much of it), car rentals, which cost about $40 to $45 a day, do the job. Brown's rents Mazdas, Suzuki Altos, and sometimes has pick-ups; Walter's rent cars and Jeeps; Rainbow Car Rental has several Hyundais available. Mansion has scooters as well as cars.

➤ MAJOR AGENCIES: **Brown's** (⊠ White Wall Rd. 8, Oranjestad, ☎ 599/318-2266). **Rainbow Car Rental** (⊠ Statia Mall, Oranjestad, ☎ 599/318-2811). **Walter's** (⊠ Chapel Piece, Oranjestad, ☎ 599/318-2719). **Mansion Scooter and Car Rental** (⊠ Golden Rock, ☎ 599/318-2764).

GASOLINE

The island's only gas station—at the south end of Lower Town on the waterfront—is open daily 7:30–7. Gas costs about $1 per liter ($4 per gallon).

ROAD CONDITIONS

Statia's roads, somewhat pocked with potholes, are undergoing resurfacing, but the going is can be slow and bumpy.

ELECTRICITY

Statia, like the other islands of the Netherlands Antilles, uses a 110/120-volt system, the same as in North America.

EMERGENCIES

➤ AMBULANCE AND FIRE: **Fire** (☎ 120). **Ambulance** (☎ 140).
➤ HOSPITALS: **Queen Beatrix Medical Center** (✉ 25 Prinsesweg, Oranjenstad, ☎ 599/318–2211 or 599/318–2371).
➤ PHARMACIES: **Pharmacy** (✉ Queen Beatrix Medical Center, 25 Prinsesweg, Oranjenstad, ☎ 599/318–2211 or 599/318–2371).
➤ POLICE: **Police emergencies** (☎ 599/318–2333 or 111).
➤ SCUBA DIVING EMERGENCIES: **Saba Marine Park Hyperbaric Facility** (✉ Fort Bay, Saba, ☎ 599/416–4395).

FESTIVALS AND SEASONAL EVENTS

Statia celebrates Carnival for a week in July, and the events include parades (culminating in the Grand Carnival Parade), street parties called "jump-ups," local and imported steel-pan bands, sports activities, and food tastings.

HOLIDAYS

Public holidays for the year are: New Year's Day, Good Friday (the Fri. before Easter), Easter Monday (the Mon. after Easter), Coronation Day and the Queen's Birthday (celebrating the birthday and coronation of Holland's Queen Beatrix, Apr. 30), Labor Day (May 1), Ascension Day (Apr. or May, 3 days after Easter), Emancipation Day (July 1), Statia-America Day (commemorating the events of 1776, when Statia became the first foreign government to salute the American flag, Nov. 16), Christmas, and Boxing Day (Dec. 26).

LANGUAGE

Statia's official language is Dutch (it's used in government documents), but everyone speaks English. Dutch is taught as the primary language in the schools, and street signs are in both Dutch and English.

MAIL AND SHIPPING

The post office is in Upper Town, near the police station on Cottagewege. Airmail letters to North America and Europe are NAf2.25; postcards, NAf1.10. When sending letters to the island, be sure to include "Netherlands Antilles" and "Caribbean" in the address.

MONEY MATTERS

Prices quoted throughout this chapter are in U.S. dollars, unless noted otherwise.

ATMS

There are no ATMs on the island.

CURRENCY

U.S. dollars are accepted everywhere, but legal tender is the Netherlands Antilles florin (NAf), also referred to as the guilder, and you shouldn't be surprised to receive change in them. The exchange rate fluctuates slightly but was about NAf1.77 to US$1 at press time. The island's two banks in Upper Town provide foreign-exchange services.
➤ BANKS: **Barclays Bank** (☎ 599/318–2392). **Windward Islands Bank** (☎ 599/318–2846).

PASSPORTS AND VISAS

U.S. and Canadian citizens must have proof of citizenship. A valid passport is best, but a birth certificate with a raised seal along with a government-authorized photo I.D. will do. British citizens need a valid passport. All visitors need a return or ongoing ticket.

SAFETY

Statia is relatively crime-free, but common sense should prevail. Lock your rental car when leaving it, store valuables in the hotel safe, and lock your hotel room door behind you. When driving, particularly at night, be on the lookout for goats and other animals that have wandered onto the road. While hiking you might see the harmless racer snake sunning itself. These snakes are afraid of people and will promptly leave when you arrive.

SIGHTSEEING TOURS

All 10 of Statia's taxis are available for island tours. A two- to three-hour outing costs $40 per vehicle of four (extra persons are $5 each), usually including airport transfer. One of the better taxi tour operators is driver-historian Josser Daniel; ask him to show you his citation from President Clinton for rescuing an American tourist from drowning. The St. Eustatius Historical Foundation Museum sells a sightseeing package that includes a guided walking tour, a booklet detailing the sights, and museum admission. The tour begins in Lower Town at the marina and ends at the museum. You can take it on your own using the booklet (numbered blue signs on most of the sights correspond to signs in the booklet), but a guide may prove more illuminating.

➤ CONTACTS: **Josser Daniel** (☎ 599/318–2358). **The St. Eustatius Historical Foundation Museum** (✉ 3 Wilhelminaweg, Oranjestad, ☎ 599/318–2288).

TAXES AND SERVICE CHARGES
DEPARTURE TAX

The departure tax is $5.65 for flights to other islands of the Netherlands Antilles and $12 to foreign destinations. Note: when flying home through St. Maarten, list yourself as "in transit" and avoid paying the $20 tax levied in St. Maarten, if you are there for less than 24 hours.

SALES TAX

Hotels collect a 7% government tax and 3% turnover tax. Restaurants charge a 3% government tax and a 10% service charge.

TAXIS

Taxis meet all flights from Franklin Delano Roosevelt Airport and charge about $3.50 for the drive into town.

TELEPHONES

Statia has microwave telephone service to all parts of the world. Direct dial is available. There are two pay phones on the island, one near the airport and one in Landsradio. They work with phone cards that you can buy at stores throughout the island.

COUNTRY AND AREA CODES

To call Statia from North America, dial 011 + 599 + 318, followed by the four-digit number.

TIPPING

Although your hotel or restaurant might add a 10%–15% service charge, it's customary to tip maids, waitstaff, and other service personnel, including taxi drivers. About 10% for taxi drivers should do it; hotel maids will appreciate about a dollar or two per day, and members of the waitstaff will be grateful for an extra 5%–10%.

VISITOR INFORMATION

➤ IN ST. EUSTATIUS: **Tourist Office** (✉ Fort Oranjestraat, Oranjestad, ☎ FAX 599/318–2433).

20 ST. KITTS AND NEVIS

Updated by
Jordan Simon

Several couples—men in blazers and slacks, women in flowing cotton dresses—sip cocktails on the patio of a magnificently restored 18th-century plantation great house. A mountain carpeted in lush rain forest towers over the building, and a flawlessly green croquet lawn sweeps down to the sea. Some people sit quietly; others speak into cell phones, checking on stocks or tots back home. It's an incongruous, anachronistic, utterly delightful scene: a Gatsby-esque party transplanted to today's Caribbean.

The sister islands of St. Kitts and Nevis (pronounced *nee*-vis) have developed a sibling rivalry. They're competing for increasingly upscale visitors, and it's a tight race: both islands have uncrowded beaches, lush rain forests, historic ruins; charming if slightly dilapidated capitals in Basseterre (St. Kitts) and Charlestown (Nevis), and restored 18th-century plantation inns. And yet, despite their rivalry, these blissful islands have remained mellow retreats for well-heeled and barefoot travelers alike who appreciate local culture.

Mountainous St. Kitts, the first English settlement in the Leeward Islands, crams some stunning scenery into its 65 square mi (168 square km). Its shape has been compared to a whale, a cricket bat, and a guitar; suffice it to say, it's roughly an oval, with a narrow peninsula trailing off toward Nevis, just 2 mi (3 km) southeast across the strait. Vast, brilliant green fields of sugarcane run to the shore. The fertile, lush island has some fascinating natural and historical attractions: a rain forest replete with waterfalls, thick vines, and secret trails; a central mountain range, dominated by the 3,792-ft (1,378-m) Mt. Liamuiga, whose crater has long been dormant; and Brimstone Hill, known in the 17th century as the Gibraltar of the West Indies.

St. Kitts is known as the mother colony of the West Indies because it was from here that English settlers sailed to Antigua, Barbuda, Tortola, and Montserrat and French settlers dispatched colonizing parties to Martinique, Guadeloupe, St. Martin, and St. Barths. The French, who inexplicably brought a bunch of green vervet monkeys—an African species—with them as pets (the creatures now outnumber the 36,000 residents), arrived on St. Kitts a few years after the British. Still developing tourism, St. Kitts hosts some 75,000 overnight visitors annually—no doubt drawn by the island's rare combination of natural and historic attractions and great beaches.

In 1493, when Columbus spied a cloud-crowned volcanic isle during his second voyage to the New World, he named it Nieves—the Spanish word for "snows"—because it reminded him of the snow-capped peaks of the Pyrenees. Nevis rises from the water in an almost perfect cone, the tip of its 3,232-ft (1,174-m) central mountain smothered in clouds. Even less developed than St. Kitts, Nevis is known for its long beaches with white and black sand, its lush greenery, and its restored sugar plantations that now house charming inns. In 1628 settlers from St. Kitts sailed across the 2-mi (3-km) channel that separates the two islands. At first they grew tobacco, cotton, ginger, and indigo, but with the introduction of sugarcane in 1640, Nevis became the island equivalent of a boomtown. Slaves were brought from Africa to work on magnificent estates, many of them high in the mountains amid lavish tropical gardens.

Restored plantation homes that now operate as inns are true sybaritic lures. Though there's plenty of activity for the energetic—mountain climbing, swimming, tennis, horseback riding, rain forest walks, snorkeling—the going is easy here, with hammocks for snoozing and candlelight dinners in stately dining rooms and on romantic verandas. Each inn has its own ambience, thanks to the delightful, often eccentric owners—either British or American expatriates.

St. Kitts and Nevis, along with Anguilla, achieved self-government as an associated state of Great Britain in 1967. In 1983 St. Kitts and Nevis became an independent nation. Nevis papers sometimes run fiery articles advocating independence, and the sister islands may separate someday (another plebiscite is being considered). However, it's unlikely that a shot will be fired: any war will probably be waged through ad campaigns.

ST. KITTS

Lodging

St. Kitts has an appealing variety of places to stay—beautifully restored plantation inns (where MAP is encouraged, if not mandatory), full-service affordable hotels, simple beachfront cottages, and two all-inclusive resorts. There are also several guest houses and self-serve condos. Increasing development has been touted (or threatened) for years, including a delayed Hyatt resort in South Friar's Bay with a casino, which was slated to begin construction in summer 2002. Meanwhile, in Frigate Bay, the Island Paradise Resort and Casino was scheduled for completion by December 2002, while the entire St. Kitts Royal Beach Resort and Casino complex supposedly will mushroom to 900 units in three phases, including condominiums and a theme park. Another major development, a pre-fabricated small town supporting a tourist development called Whitehall Project, will sprawl in the island's northwest. Should all these projects suddenly materialize, the room base will quadruple, probably taxing the island's current infrastructure. Fortunately, the islandscape shouldn't change until 2004 at the earliest.

CATEGORY	COST EP/CP*	COST A.I.**
$$$$	over $350	over $375
$$$	$250–$350	$275–$375
$$	$150–$250	$175–$275
$	under $150	under $175

*EP/CP prices are per night for a standard double room in high season, excluding taxes, service charges, and meal plans
**A.I. (all-inclusive) prices are per person, per night based on double-occupancy during high season, excluding taxes and service charges

520

St. Kitts

Lodging

Dining

Exploring

Willett's Bay

Dieppe Bay

Sandy Bay

10

Sandy Bay

St. Paul's

9

5 Sadlers

Tabernacle

NORTH WEST RANGE

Newton Ground

Mt. Liamuiga

Ot

Sandy Point Reef

Sandy Point Town

4

Pump Bay

Verchild' Peak

SOUTH EAST RANGE

Half–Way Tree

Middle Island

3

2

7 8

Old Road Town

Challengers

6

Caribbean

Bloody Bay Reef

Coconut Tree Re

Sea

KEY

Beaches

Dive Sites

1 Exploring Sights

Ferry

① Hotels and Restaurants

0   10 miles
0   15 km

Saba
St. Eustatius
St. Kitts
Nevis

N

ATLANTIC OCEAN

Nicola Town
Hermitage Bay
11
ey's
Cayon
Keys

s

Conaree Bay

Monkey Hill

Muddy Pt.

Robert E. Bradshaw Airport

13
Basseterre
12
Frigate Bay
1
15
Basseterre Bay
14
1 - 5
eef
Talata
Frigate Bay
16 - 20
River Taw
Friar's Bay

Sandbank Beach
Mosquito Bluff
St. Anthonys Peak
Great Salt Pond
21
Turtle Bay
White House Bay
Cockleshell Bay
Major s Bay
Banana Bay

Nags Head

TO NEVIS

$$$$ ▦ **Rawlins Plantation Inn.** The views at this idyllic plantation inn, caught
★   between lush Mt. Liamuiga and the cobalt Caribbean, are spectacular. Rooms occupy restored estate buildings (including the original sugar
mill) scattered amid 20 acres of manicured grounds dotted with hammocks and the plantation's original copper syrup vats. Guest quarters
have mahogany four-poster or brass beds, wicker chairs, hardwood
floors, grass mats, and local artworks (including those of Kate Spencer,
the expat Brit whose studio sits on the estate) Rawlins's seclusion, charming owners (Claire and Paul Rawson), and peerless tranquillity invite
total relaxation. ⊠ *St. Paul's (Box 340)*, ☏ *869/465–6221 or 800/346–
5358*, 𝖥𝖠𝖷 *869/465–4954*, 𝖶𝖤𝖡 *www.rawlinsplantation.com. 10 rooms.
Restaurant, fans, tennis court, pool, croquet, laundry service. Closed
mid-Aug.–mid-Oct. AE, MC, V. MAP.*

$$$-$$$$ ▦ **Golden Lemon.** Arthur Leaman, a former decorating editor for *House
★ and Garden,* created this world-renowned retreat. Rooms in the restored
17th-century great house are impeccably decorated with wrought-iron
and four-poster beds swaddled in mosquito netting, armoires, and rock-
ing chairs. Fully equipped one- or two-bedroom town houses (some have
a private pool) are equally stylish. The palm-shaded gray-sand beach
oversees St. Maarten and St. Eustatia. Repeat guests cherish the serene
ambience, almost telepathic service from long-time staffers, and ro-
mantically remote location. All-inclusive packages (just food and bev-
erages) are great value. ⊠ *Dieppe Bay (Box 17)*, ☏ *869/465–7260 or
800/633–7411*, 𝖥𝖠𝖷 *869/465–4019*, 𝖶𝖤𝖡 *www.goldenlemon.com. 9 rooms,
22 villas. Restaurant, fans, tennis court, pool, beach, bar, shop, no kids
under 18. Sept.–mid-Oct. AE, MC, V. BP, MAP, All-inclusive.*

$$$-$$$$ ▦ **Horizons Villa Resort.** These individually owned and decorated
coral, white, and jade duplex villas, most with stunning water views,
have every conceivable amenity, including washer-dryers and CD play-
ers; three- and four-bedroom units have plunge pools. Most have rat-
tan furnishings, vivid local artwork, and pristine white-tile floors.
Frigate Bay Beach is a two-minute walk down the hill and the golf course
(ask about discounted greens fees) within driving range. There are enor-
mous, sparkling if spare oceanview hotel rooms, but the villas, ideal
for families and groups, represent the best value. ⊠ *Fort Tyson, Frigate
Bay (Box 1143)*, ☏ *869/465–0584 or 800/830–9069*, 𝖥𝖠𝖷 *869/465–0785.*
*16 rooms, 48 villas. Restaurant, fans, some kitchens, cable TV, some
in-room VCRs, golf privileges, tennis court, pool, massage. AE, MC,
V. EP.*

$$$-$$$$ ▦ **Ottley's Plantation Inn.** Towering royal palms frame the wild At-
★ lantic at this former sugar plantation. The 18th-century great house
and stone cottages hold spacious guest rooms with hardwood floors,
Laura Ashley–esque fabrics, and wicker and antique furnishings.
Higher-end units feature private plunge pools. You can ramble through
the exquisite 35-acre gardens or the luxuriant adjacent rain forest.
Thoughtful extras include beach and town shuttles, on-call spa services,
and TV/DVDs for rent. The staff is warm yet efficient, while the en-
gaging owners genuinely treat you like family. Ottley's is the model
Caribbean inn: historic yet contemporary, elegant yet unpretentious.
⊠ *Ottley's, southwest of Nicola Town (Box 345)*, ☏ *869/465–7234
or 800/772–3039*, 𝖥𝖠𝖷 *869/465–4760*, 𝖶𝖤𝖡 *www.ottleys.com. 24 rooms.
Restaurant, fans, in-room safes, minibars, no room TVs, tennis court,
pool, croquet, bar, shop, Internet. AE, D, MC, V. BP, MAP.*

$$$ ▦ **St. Kitts Marriott Royal Beach Resort.** St. Kitts's first international-
standard resort opens in November 2002. The main building, a melange
of Mediterranean and neo-classical elements (red barrel-tile roofs,
campaniles, interior gardens, columns, pilasters, circular stairways, and
bas reliefs) flanked by two waterfalls, houses most facilities and half
the "Phase One" units. Fifteen three-story buildings nestle amid lav-

ishly landscaped courtyards with fountains, arcaded walkways, and simulated birds trilling. Enormous beige-tiled rooms have Italian walnut furnishings, cushy carmine armchairs and ottomans, gold lamps, marble accents, peach walls, parrot-green rugs, and floral spreads. As if there weren't enough distractions, an affiliated theme park with miniature golf, an aquarium, and rides should open in 2003. ⊠ *Frigate Bay,* ☎ *800/223–6388,* FAX *800/223–6388,* WEB *www.marriott.com. 237 rooms, 234 villa suites. 5 restaurants, grill, room service, in-room safes, some kitchenettes, refrigerators, cable TV, golf privileges, miniature golf, 5 tennis courts, 3 pools, health club, spa, beach, snorkeling, boating, 6 bars, piano bar, casino, dance club, nightclub, shops, babysitting, children's programs (ages 4–12), laundry service, Internet, business facilities, conference center, meeting rooms. AE, D, MC, V. EP, BP.*

$$–$$$ ⊞ **Ocean Terrace Inn.** This stylish, intimate hotel, nicknamed OTI, of-
★ fers many amenities for business travelers. Room blocks, lovingly tended gardens and a man-made lagoon that feeds the large free-form waterfall pool spill down the hill to the sea. Island touches from masks to murals abound everywhere. Attractively decorated units vary widely in size and style. Several deluxe units, including handsome junior suites, have kitchenettes or whirlpool tubs, while one- and two-bedroom condos down the hill have marvelous ocean views. Both the waterfront Fisherman's Wharf and more elegant hilltop Ocean Restaurant lure lively local crowds. Extras include a shuttle to nearby beaches. ⊠ *Bay Rd., Basseterre (Box 65),* ☎ *869/465–2754 or 800/524–0512,* FAX *869/465–1057,* WEB *www.oceanterraceinn.net. 70 rooms, 8 condominiums. 3 restaurants, in-room safes, some kitchens, some kitchenettes, refrigerators, cable TV, 3 pools, hair salon, 2 outdoor hot tubs, health club, massage, sauna, dock, windsurfing, boating, waterskiing, 4 bars, Internet, meeting rooms. AE, D, MC, V. EP, FAP, MAP.*

$$ ⊞ **Frigate Bay Resort.** The island's golf course adjoins this property, and a complimentary shuttle accesses the nearby Caribbean and Atlantic beaches (or you can walk to the former). The cheerful yellow buildings house standard rooms and condos. Poolside units have nicer views but tend to be noisier. Higher-numbered rooms in the blocks have partial ocean views at the same price. All accommodations have tile floors and sliding glass doors that open onto a terrace or balcony. A thatched, split-level, octagonal restaurant overlooks the pool and swim-up bar; it features raucous buffets with live entertainment in season, but also serves creative Caribbean/Continental fare. ⊠ *Frigate Bay (Box 137, Basseterre),* ☎ *869/465–8935 or 800/266–2185,* FAX *869/465–7050,* WEB *www.frigatebay.com. 40 rooms, 24 studios. Restaurant, fans, refrigerators, some kitchens, cable TV, golf privileges, pool, bar, shop, meeting rooms. AE, D, MC, V. EP, MAP.*

$$ ⊞ **Rex Papillon.** Despite such spiffy touches as an art deco–ish piano bar and a waterfall pool, this all-inclusive can't overcome its predecessor's three distinct styles of architecture, from Antillean-style gingerbreads to ugly "institutional" concrete buildings. Families appreciate the bright one-bedroom cottages. Huge oceanfront rooms gleam with white tile floors and blond-wood and rattan furnishings. Breezes overlooks the golf course and serves buffets. The fancier, vaguely nautical Nautilus offers a United Nations of dishes (from thyme-scented rack of lamb to chili con carne). Though the property borders Frigate Bay's wilder Atlantic beach, it lacks water-sports facilities—a definite minus for an all-inclusive. ⊠ *Frigate Bay (Box 341),* ☎ *869/465–8037 or 800/255–5859,* FAX *869/465–6745. 78 rooms, 22 1-bedroom cottages. 2 restaurants, grocery, fans, cable TV, tennis court, pool, wading pool, gym, beach, 2 bars, shops, children's programs (ages 4–12), meeting rooms. AE, D, MC, V. All-inclusive.*

$–$$ 🏨 **Bird Rock Beach Resort.** This plain but well-maintained resort perched on a bluff consists of pastel two-story buildings snaking through gardens. Rooms have tile floors, rattan and wicker furnishings, and oceanview balconies; suites add kitchenettes and sofa beds. Newer units are more stylish, with throw rugs and mahogany two-poster beds. The tiered sundeck and pool, replete with swim-up bar, boast sterling views of Basseterre, the sea, and the mountains. A complimentary shuttle whisks guests to Frigate Bay and its beach. Dining choices are the alfresco Sunburst or the more informal Tipsy Lobster Cafe. The mix of divers and young Europeans on a budget gives Bird Rock an international flavor. ⊠ *Basseterre Bay (Box 227, Basseterre),* ☎ *869/465–8914 or 800/621–1270,* FAX *869/465–1675,* WEB *www.birdrockbeach.com. 31 rooms, 19 studios. 2 restaurants, fans, some kitchenettes, cable TV, tennis court, 2 pools, volleyball, dive shop, snorkeling, 2 bars, shops. AE, D, MC, V. EP, MAP.*

$–$$ 🏨 **Timothy Beach Resort.** The cordial management is attentive at the sole St. Kitts property directly on the Caribbean. Simple powder-blue stucco buildings hold comfortable, fully equipped, multiple-bedroom units, which can be blocked off to form standard rooms. The original buildings right on the beach are larger and airier and have better views. Units are a hodgepodge of the usual wicker, rattan, and hardwood furnishings, but draperies, fabrics, and wall hangings favor fresh cool blue hues. The beachfront Sunset Café serves tasty Caribbean-Continental fare, and just steps away are an unaffiliated watersports concession and hopping beach bar. ⊠ *Frigate Bay (Box 1198),* ☎ *869/465–8597 or 800/288–7991,* FAX *869/466–7085,* WEB *www.timothybeach.com. 18 rooms, 42 1-bedroom suites. Restaurant, some kitchens, refrigerators, cable TV, pool, beach, bar. AE, MC, V. EP.*

$ 🏨 **Fairview Inn.** This simple inn's main building is an 18th-century French great house, with graceful white verandas and Asian rugs on hardwood floors. Though the smallish, motel-like rooms lack period flair and unimpeded ocean views, they're cozy. Each has a beamed wood ceiling, white-tile floors, wicker furnishings, and light pastel or floral fabrics. Ask for the more atmospheric rooms, like 11: they're built into original foundations and have partial fieldstone walls. The dining room serves authentic island fare. Management lowers rates for longer stays and offers Internet specials. The inn is 7 mi (11 km) north of Basseterre. ⊠ *Off Old Town Rd., Challengers (Box 212, Basseterre),* ☎ *869/465–2472 or 800/223–9815,* FAX *869/465–1056. 30 rooms. Restaurant, room service, fans, refrigerators, pool, bar. AE, D, DC, MC, V. BP, EP, MAP.*

$ 🏨 **Jack Tar Village Royal St. Kitts Resort and Casino.** A raucous atmosphere pervades this all-inclusive, whose bill for billeting and bill-of-fare is low indeed. Shuttles regularly access the beach and golf course, while contests and recreational activities are scheduled daily. Live entertainment, a disco, and a casino keep the place pulsating into the wee hours. Rooms are bright if basic, with pale aquamarine walls, white-tile floors, blond-wood furnishings, and hallucinogenic floral fabrics. However, the parties go on into the wee hours, and the noise carries— the 100 block and rooms numbered higher than 350 are most peaceful. Topaz specializes in theme buffets; dinner-only Caruso's serves competent Italian fare. ⊠ *Frigate Bay (Box 406),* ☎ *869/465–8651 or 800/858–2258,* FAX *869/466–9016,* WEB *www.allegroresorts.com. 267 rooms. 2 restaurants, 2 grills, in-room safes, 2 tennis courts, 2 pools, hair salon, health club, Ping-Pong, shuffleboard, volleyball, dive shop, snorkeling, windsurfing, boating, waterskiing, bicycles, 3 bars, shops, casino, baby-sitting, children's programs (ages 4–12), car rental. AE, D, DC, MC, V. All-inclusive.*

$ ⊞ **Rock Haven Bed and Breakfast.** Judith and Keith Blake have converted their gingerbread house, a two-minute drive from Frigate Bay beaches, into a relaxing, homey B&B. The living and dining rooms have carved mahogany doors, crystal chandeliers, English rugs, and hardwood floors. Two rooms have brass beds draped with mosquito netting. The larger one has a full kitchen and its own patio and entrance. The vast, breezy terrace beckons with white-wicker chaises longues, hammocks, and majestic sea views. Judith prepares sumptuous breakfasts of banana pancakes, Spanish omelets, and pumpkin fritters. Islanders also cherish her homemade ice creams made on-site. ⊠ *Frigate Bay (Box 821),* ☎ FAX *869/465–5503. 2 rooms. Dining room, fans, laundry service. No credit cards. BP.*

Dining

St. Kitts restaurants range from funky beachfront bistros to elegant plantation dining rooms (most with prix-fixe menus); most fare is tinged with the flavors of the Caribbean. Many restaurants offer West Indian specialties such as curried mutton, pepper pot (a stew of vegetables, tubers, and meats), and Arawak chicken (seasoned and served with rice and almonds on breadfruit leaf).

What to Wear

Throughout the island, dress is casual at lunch (but no bathing suits). Dinner, although not necessarily formal, definitely calls for long pants and sundresses.

CATEGORY	COST*
$$$$	over $30
$$$	$20–$30
$$	$10–$20
$	under $10

per person for a main course at dinner

CARIBBEAN

$$ ✕ **Manhattan Gardens.** Even the tangerine, peach, and blueberry exterior of this 17th-century gingerbread creole house looks appetizing. Inside, it's homey, with batik hangings, lace tablecloths, and wood carvings. The rear garden overlooking the sea comes alive for Saturday's Caribbean Food Fest and Sunday's barbecue. The regular menu includes lobster in lemon butter (the one pricey entrée), and wahoo in creole sauce; specials might consist of goat water (goat stew), souse (pickled pigs' trotters), and saltfish. ⊠ *Old Road Town,* ☎ *869/465–9121. No credit cards. No dinner Sun.*

$–$$ ✕ **Chef's Place.** Two things are the draw at this restaurant in a charmingly dilapidated 19th-century house: inexpensive West Indian meals and eavesdropping opportunities (the clientele runs toward local cops, cabbies, and mid-level government workers). Try the St. Kitts version of jerk chicken, the kingfish creole, pig tail and snout soup, or the goat stew. The best tables are outside on the wide, white veranda. ⊠ *Upper Church St., Basseterre,* ☎ *869/465–6176. No credit cards. Closed Sun.*

CONTEMPORARY

$$$$ ✕ **Golden Lemon.** Evenings at the Golden Lemon hotel's restaurant begin with cocktails and hors d'oeuvres on the bougainvillea-draped flagstone patio. A set three-course dinner is served in a tasteful room with crystal chandeliers, white rattan furnishings, Adams and Delft porcelain, and arched doorways. Tempting dishes range from breadfruit puffs in peanut sauce to grilled snapper with eggplant and sweet-pepper relish. Sunday brunch packs the patio with such offerings as banana

pancakes and beef stew made with rum. Owner Arthur Leaman and his partner Martin Kreiner hold clever court (ask them for anecdotes of running a Caribbean hostelry). ⊠ *Golden Lemon, Dieppe Bay,* ☎ *869/465–7260. Reservations essential. AE, MC, V.*

$$$$ ⨯ **Rawlins Plantation.** The refined dining room at the Rawlins Plan-
★   tation Inn has fieldstone walls, lovely family antiques and period furnishings, and high vaulted ceilings. Owner Claire Rawson is one of the
island's most sophisticated chefs. Her prix-fixe four-course dinner emphasizes local ingredients: witness conch ravioli in lobster sauce or shrimp
ceviche with coriander and sour oranges, capped by banana puffs with
lime sauce or chocolate terrine with passion-fruit sauce. The bountiful lunch buffet offers such classic West Indian items as breadfruit salad,
shrimp fritters with mango salsa, and lobster and spinach crepes. ⊠
Rawlins Plantation Inn, St. Paul's, ☎ *869/465–6221. Reservations essential. AE, MC, V.*

$$$$ ⨯ **Royal Palm.** The 65-ft spring-fed pool stretches from the remain-
★   ing walls of the sugar factory beside the elegant, alfresco restaurant at
Ottley's Plantation Inn. Four-course extravaganzas from imaginative
chef Pam Yahn blend indigenous ingredients with Pacific Rim, Mediterranean, southwestern, and Latin touches: for example, Caribbean lobster atop a chili-shrimp corn cake with passion-fruit butter. An à la carte
"Le Bistro" option offers more casual fare like roasted vegetable torte
and creative lobster wraps. The combination of superb food, artful presentation, and warm bonhomie here is unbeatable. ⊠ *Ottley's Plantation Inn, Ottley's, southwest of Nicola Town,* ☎ *869/465–7234.
Reservations essential. AE, D, MC, V.*

$$$ ⨯ **Marshall's.** The pool area of Horizons Villa Resort is transformed
into a romantic eatery thanks to smashing ocean views, potted plants,
and elegantly appointed tables. (The venue may change as the owner
requires more parking.) Jamaican chef Verral Marshall, aided by noted
island chef-consultant, Janice Barber, fuses ultrafresh local ingredients
with global influences. Delectable offerings include conch cutlets with
white-rum lime sauce and black bean salad or Portobello-stuffed
tortellini with lobster and shrimp in creamy tomato basil sauce. Most
dishes are regrettably more orthodox, but the execution is invariably
excellent. ⊠ *Horizons Villa Resort, Frigate Bay,* ☎ *869/466–8245. Reser-
vations essential. AE, MC, V.*

$$–$$$ ⨯ **Stonewall's.** Affable owners Garry and Wendy Steckles practically
built this lush tropical courtyard restaurant by hand. "Our sweat is
varnished into the bar," Garry swears. Banana trees, bougainvillea, and
bamboo grow everywhere. Selections depend on what's fresh and the
cook's mood: it could be a proper roast beef and Yorkshire pudding,
tapenade-crusted wahoo, or chicken breast in sun-dried tomato sauce.
Try the house drink, Stone Against the Wall, concocted from Cavalier
rum, amaretto, coconut rum, triple sec, pineapple and orange juices,
and grenadine. ⊠ *5 Princes St., Basseterre,* ☎ *869/465–5248. AE, MC,
V. No lunch.*

ECLECTIC

$$–$$$ ⨯ **Ballahoo.** This second-floor terrace restaurant draws a crowd for
breakfast, lunch, and dinner. Lilting calypso and reggae on the sound
system, whirring ceiling fans, potted palms, and colorful island prints
are appropriately tropical. Specialties include chili shrimp, conch sim-
mered in garlic butter, madras beef curry, lobster stir fry, and a toasted
rum-and-banana sandwich. Go at lunchtime, when you can watch the
bustle of the Circus and the prices for many dishes are slashed nearly
in half. ⊠ *Fort St., Basseterre,* ☎ *869/465–4197. AE, MC, V. Closed
Sun.*

$$–$$$ ✕ **Mango's.** This cheerful eatery is in the tranquil stone courtyard of the 18th-century Georgian House, and seemingly grows out of the luxuriant garden. The menu runs the gastronomic gamut from conch ceviche and enchiladas to Thai shrimp curry and filet mignon with peppercorn cream. The lunch menu is simpler and cheaper. But the main house, with its glorious parquet floors, brick-and-fieldstone walls, and high-back mahogany is a great place for a romantic dinner despite slapdash service and a pulsating sound system. ✉ *Independence Sq., Basseterre,* ☎ *869/465–4049. AE, MC, V. Closed Sun.*

$$ ✕ **Turtle Beach Bar and Grill.** Treats at this popular daytime watering hole include honey-mustard ribs, coconut-shrimp salad, and grilled lobster. Business cards and pennants from around the world plaster the bar, and the room is decorated with ships' lanterns, harpoons, conch shells, and painted wooden fish. You can snorkel here, spot hawksbill turtles, feed the tame monkeys that boldly belly-up to the bar, schedule a deep-sea fishing trip, laze in a palm-shaded hammock, or rent a kayak, Windsurfer, or mountain bike. On Sunday afternoon, locals come for dancing to live bands and volleyball. It's at the south end of S.E. Peninsula Road. ✉ *S.E. Peninsula Rd., Turtle Beach,* ☎ *869/469–9086. AE, MC, V. No dinner Mon.–Sat.*

ITALIAN

$–$$ ✕ **PJ's Pizza.** "Garbage pizza"—topped with everything but the kitchen sink—is a favorite, or you can create your own pie. Sandwiches and simple but lustily flavored pastas are also served. Finish your meal with delicious, moist rum cake. This casual spot, bordering the golf course and open to cooling breezes, is always boisterous, despite—or perhaps because of—its ironic location atop the Frigate Bay police station. ✉ *Frigate Bay,* ☎ *869/465–8373. AE, MC, V. Closed Mon. and Sept. No lunch.*

SEAFOOD

$$–$$$ ✕ **Fisherman's Wharf.** Part of the Ocean Terrace Inn, this extremely casual waterfront eatery is decorated in swaggering nautical style, with rustic wood beams, rusty anchors, cannons, and buoys. Try the excellent conch chowder, followed by fresh grilled lobster or other shipshape seafood, and finish off your meal with a slice of the memorable banana cheesecake. The tables are long, wooden affairs, and the place is generally hopping, especially on weekend nights. ✉ *Fortlands, Basseterre,* ☎ *869/465–2754. AE, D, MC, V. No lunch.*

$–$$ ✕ **Sprat Net.** This simple cluster of picnic tables, sheltered by a brilliant turquoise corrugated-tin roof and decorated with driftwood and fishnets, sits on a sliver of sand. Nonetheless, it's an island hotspot. There's nothing fancy on the menu: just grilled fish, lobster, and meats—served with mountains of coleslaw and peas and rice. But the fish is amazingly fresh: the fishermen-owners heap their catches on a center table, where you choose your own dinner, as if you were at market, and then watch it grilled to your specification. ✉ *Old Road Town,* ☎ *no phone. No credit cards. Closed Sun. No lunch.*

Beaches

The powdery white-sand beaches, free and open to the public (even those occupied by hotels), are in the Frigate Bay area or on the lower peninsula.

Banana Bay. One of the island's loveliest beaches stretches over a mile (1½ km) at the southeastern tip of the island. Several large hotels, including Banana Bay and Casablanca, were abandoned in the early stages of development—their skeletal structures marring an otherwise idyllic scene.

Cockleshell Bay. Reachable on foot is Banana Bay's twin beach, another eyebrow of glittering sand backed by lush vegetation.

Conaree Bay. On the Atlantic side of the island, this narrow strip of gray-black sand is a good spot for bodysurfing.

Dieppe Bay. Snorkeling and windsurfing are good at this black-sand beach on the north coast, home of the Golden Lemon Hotel.

Friar's Bay. Locals consider the Caribbean (southern) side the island's finest beach, where you will find two hopping beach bars, Monkey and Sunset, which serve excellent inexpensive grilled and barbecued food. You can haggle with fishermen here to take you snorkeling off the eastern point. The waters on the Atlantic (northern) side are rougher, but the beach has a wild, desolate beauty.

Frigate Bay. On the Caribbean side you'll find talcum-powder-fine sand, while on the Atlantic side, the 4-mi-wide (6½-km-wide) stretch is a favorite with horseback riders.

Sandbank Beach. A tiny dirt road, nearly impassable after heavy rains, leads to a long taupe crescent on the Atlantic. The shallow coves are protected here, making it ideal for families, and it's usually deserted.

White House Bay. The beach is rocky, but the snorkeling, taking in several reefs surrounding a sunken tugboat, is superb.

Outdoor Activities and Sports

BOATING

Most operators are on Frigate Bay, known for its gentle currents. Turtle Bay offers stronger winds and stunning views of Nevis. **Mr. X Watersports** (⊠ Frigate Bay, ☎ 869/465–0673) rents small craft, including motorboats (waterskiing and jetskiing are available). Paddleboats are $15 per hour, sailboats (with one free lesson) $20–$25 per hour. Mr. X and his cohorts are usually hanging out at the adjacent open-air Monkey Bar. **Tropical Surf** (also known as Turtle Tours) (⊠ Turtle Bay, ☎ 869/469–9086) rents Sunfish, Hobie Cats, surfboards, kayaks, and boogie boards; the athletically inclined operators offer several soft adventure tours, as well as private snorkeling and fishing charters.

FISHING

The waters surrounding St. Kitts aren't renowned for their big game fish. Still, you can angle for yellowtail snapper, wahoo, mackerel, tuna, dolphinfish, shark, and barracuda. Rates are occasionally negotiable. Figure approximately $350 for a four-hour excursion with refreshments. Most of the large day-sail operators can arrange private charters, usually through the knowledgeable Todd Leypoldt of **Wahoo Water Tours** (⊠ Basseterre, ☎ 869/465–2690), who takes you out on his Robalo, *No Problem*. He's also available for snorkeling charters, beach picnics, and sunset-moonlight cruises.

GOLF

The **Royal St. Kitts Golf Club** (⊠ Frigate Bay, ☎ 869/465–8339) is an 18-hole, par-72 championship course, which underwent a complete redesign to maximize Caribbean and Atlantic views and increase the number of hazards. A branch of the Nick Faldo Gold Academy will open. Full play will resume in November 2002; greens fees with cart rental will likely be around $120, $80 for nine.

HIKING

Trails in the central mountains vary from easy to don't-try-it-by-yourself. Monkey Hill and Verchild's Peak aren't difficult, although the Verchild's climb will take the better part of a day. Don't attempt Mt. Liamuiga without a guide. You'll start at Belmont Estates on horseback, then proceed on foot to the lip of the crater, at 2,600 ft (944 m). You can go down into the crater—1,000 ft (363 m) deep and 1 mi (1½ km) wide, with a small freshwater lake—clinging to vines and roots. Tour rates range from $40 for a rain-forest walk to $65 for a volcano expedition and usually include round-trip transportation from your hotel and picnic lunch.

Addy of **Addy's Nature Tours** (☎ 869/465–8069) offers a picnic lunch and cold drinks during treks through the rain forest; she also discusses the history and folklore relating to native plants. **Greg Pereira** (☎ 869/465–4121), whose family has lived on St. Kitts for well over a century, takes groups on half-day trips into the rain forest and on full-day hikes up the volcano and through the grounds of a private 250-year-old great house, followed by excursions down canyons and past petroglyphs. He and his staff relate fascinating historical, folkloric, and botanical information. **Kriss Tours** (☎ 869/465–4042) takes small groups into the crater, through the rain forest, and to Dos d'Anse Pond, on Verchild's Mountain. **Oliver Spencer's Off the Beaten Track** (☎ 869/465–6314) leads treks to ruins of an abandoned coffee plantation taken over by sprawling banyan trees.

HORSEBACK RIDING

Wild North Frigate Bay and desolate Conaree Beach are great for riding. Guides from **Trinity Stable** (☎ 869/465–3226) offers beach rides ($35) and trips into the rain forest ($45).

SCUBA DIVING AND SNORKELING

St. Kitts has more than a dozen excellent dive sites. **Bloody Bay Reef** is noted for its network of underwater grottoes daubed with purple anemones, sienna bristle worms, and canary-yellow sea fans that seem to wave you in. **Coconut Tree Reef,** one of the largest in the area, includes sea fans, sponges, and anemones. **Nags Head** has strong currents, but experienced divers might spot gliding rays, lobsters, turtles, and reef sharks. Since it sank just over a decade ago in 50 ft (18 m) of water, the *River Taw* makes a splendid site for less-experienced divers. **Sandy Point Reef** has been designated a National Marine Park, including Paradise Reef, with swim-through 90-ft (33-m) sloping canyons, and Anchors Away, where anchors have been encrusted with coral formations. The 1985 wreck of the *Talata* lies in 70 ft (25 m) of water; barracudas, rays, groupers, and grunts dart through its hull.

Auston MacLeod, a PADI-certified dive master-instructor and owner of **Pro-Divers** (☎ 869/466–3483), offers resort and certification courses. His prices are the lowest on the island: $50 less for an open-water certification course. Kenneth Samuel of **Kenneth's Dive Centre** (☎ 869/465–2670) is a PADI-certified dive master who takes small groups of divers with C cards to nearby reefs. Rates average $50 for single-tank dives, $80 for double-tank dives; add $10 for equipment. Night dives, including lights, are $50, and snorkeling trips (four-person minimum) are $35, drinks included. **St. Kitts Scuba** (✉ Frigate Bay, 2 mi [3 km] east of Basseterre, ☎ 869/465–1189) offers competitive prices, friendly dive masters, and a more international clientele.

TENNIS

Unfortunately, options are quite limited unless you're staying at a hotel with a tennis court. **Jack Tar Village Royal St. Kitts Resort and Casino** (✉ Frigate Bay, ☎ 869/465–8651) has two lighted courts, but you must buy a day pass ($50) for the resort in order to play. The fee does include breakfast and lunch, drinks, and other activities (such as nonmotorized watersports).

WINDSURFING

Winds are usually calm on the Caribbean side, meaning beginners won't get into deep water. Turtle Bay, site of the prime outfitter, is particularly well protected. **Tropical Surf,** also known as Turtle Tours (✉ Turtle Bay, ☎ 869/469–9086), rents Windsurfers and offers the best lessons on island.

Shopping

St. Kitts has limited shopping, but there are a few small duty-free shops with good deals on jewelry, perfume, china, and crystal. Several galleries sell excellent paintings and sculptures. The batik fabrics, scarves, caftans, and wall hangings of Caribelle Batik are well known. British expat Kate Spencer is an artist who has lived on the islands for years, reproducing its vibrant colors on everything from silk *pareu* (beach wraps) to note cards to place mats. Other good island buys include crafts, jams, and herbal teas. Don't forget to pick up some CSR, a "new cane spirit drink" that's distilled from fresh sugarcane right on St. Kitts.

Areas and Malls

Most shopping plazas are in downtown Basseterre, on the streets radiating from the Circus. The **Pelican Mall**—a shopping arcade designed to look like a traditional Caribbean street—has 26 stores, a restaurant, tourism offices, and a bandstand. Directly behind it, on the waterfront, is **Port Zante,** the deep-water cruise-ship pier; a much-delayed upscale shopping-dining complex is expected to include at least 25 stores by late 2003. **Shoreline Plaza** is next to the Treasury Building, right on Basseterre's waterfront. **TDC Mall** is just off the Circus in downtown. **All Kind of Tings,** a peppermint-pink edifice on Liverpool Row at College Street Ghaut, functions as a de facto vendor's market where several booths sell local crafts and cheap T-shirts. Its courtyard frequently hosts folkloric dances, fashion shows, poetry readings, and steel pan concerts.

Specialty Items

ART AND ANTIQUES

Spencer Cameron Art Gallery (✉ 10 N. Independence Sq., Basseterre, ☎ 869/465–1617) has historical reproductions of Caribbean island charts and prints, in addition to owner Rosey Cameron's popular Carnevale clown prints and a wide selection of exceptional artwork by Caribbean artists. They will mail anywhere.

CDS AND TAPES

MusicUnltd (✉ TDC Mall, Basseterre, ☎ 869/465–1998) offers a vast selection of island rhythms—lilting *soca* (a mix of soul and calypso) and *zouk* (a bopping beguine from Martinique and Guadeloupe), pulsating salsa and merengue, wicked hip-hop, and mellow reggae and calypso. You can also buy the CDs of some rocking local bands: hard-driving exponents of soca such as Nu-Vybes, Grand Masters, and Small Ave, and the "heavy dancehall" reggae group, House of Judah.

HANDICRAFTS

Caribelle Batik (✉ Romney Manor, Old Road Town, ☎ 869/465–6253) sells batik wraps, T-shirts, dresses, wall hangings, and the like. **Glass Island** (✉ 4–5 Princes St., Basseterre, ☎ 869/466–6771) sells frames, earrings, and blown-art glass vases, bowls, and plates in sinuous shapes and seductive colors. **Island Hopper** (✉ The Circus, Basseterre, ☎ 869/465–2905) is a good place for island crafts, especially wood carvings, pottery, textiles, and colorful resort wear, as well as humorous T-shirts and trinkets. **Kate Designs** (✉ Bank St., Basseterre, ☎ 869/465–5265) showcases the enchanting silk pareus, jewelry, hand-pressed notebooks, prints, greeting cards, and papier-mâché works of Kate Spencer, who also has a studio outside the Rawlins Plantation. **The Potter's House** (✉ West Bay Rd., Basseterre, ☎ 869/465–5947) is the atelier-home of

Carla Astaphan, whose beautifully glazed ceramics and masks celebrate Afro-Caribbean heritage. The **Crafthouse** (⊠ Bay Rd., Southwell Industrial Site, Basseterre, [1//2] mi east of Shoreline Plaza, ☎ 869/465–7754) is one of the best sources for local dolls, woodcarvings, and straw work. **Stonewall's Tropical Boutique** (⊠ 7 Princes St., Basseterre, ☎ 869/466–9124) carries top-of-the-line products from around the Caribbean: hand-painted Jamaican pottery, West Indian photos and artworks, brass jewelry, hand-painted T-shirts, and flowing resort wear by leading Caribbean designer, John Warden.

Nightlife

Most nightlife revolves around the hotels, which host folkloric shows and calypso and steel bands of the usual limbo-rum-and-reggae variety. Check with your hotel or the tourist board for schedules.

BARS

Bambu's (⊠ Bank St., off The Circus, Basseterre, ☎ 869/466–5280) incorporates bamboo everywhere to create an "outdoorsy interior": in the ceiling, railings, bar, lamps, mirrors, benches. The rest is splashed in wild hues such as lemon, lime, tangerine, and raspberry. Local artworks adorn the walls, and the split-level warren of rooms accommodates those who seek intimate conversation, rooting for teams on the big-screen TV, and dancing on a tiny floor weekends. You can order both sophisticated single malt scotches and down-home island food amid the Peace Corps hip ambience. A favorite happy-hour watering hole is the **Circus Grill** (⊠ Bay Rd., Basseterre, ☎ 869/465–0143), a second-floor eatery whose veranda offers views of the harbor and the activity on The Circus.

CASINOS

Jack Tar Village Royal St. Kitts Resort and Casino offers slots and very limited low-stakes action in a rather dingy space. The new **St. Kitts Marriott Royal Beach Resort** will occupy a glitzy 26,000-square-ft (2,400-square-m) space, including *salons privés* for high rollers.

DANCE AND MUSIC CLUBS

Doo-Wop Days (⊠ Memory La., Frigate Bay, ☎ 869/465–1960), owned by Americans Linda and Joe Pozzuolo, is decorated with old 45s, photos, velvet Elvis paintings, guitar-shape pillows, hula hoops, and *Look* magazine covers. There's live music some nights and the inevitable karaoke contests. Try Joe's authentic Philly cheese steaks.

Locals disco down at **Henry's Night Spot** (⊠ Dunn's Cottage, Lower Cayon St., Basseterre, ☎ 869/465–3508).

Exploring St. Kitts

You can explore Basseterre, the capital city, in half an hour or so; allow three to four hours for an island tour. Main Road traces the northwestern perimeter through seas of sugarcane and past breadfruit trees and stone walls. Villages with tiny pastel-color houses of stone and weathered wood are scattered across the island, and the drive back to Basseterre around the island's other side passes through several of them. The most spectacular stretch of scenery is on Dr. Kennedy Simmonds Highway to the tip of the Southeast Peninsula. This ultrasleek modern road twists and turns through the undeveloped grassy hills that rise between the calm Caribbean and the windswept Atlantic, past the shimmering pink Great Salt Pond, a volcanic crater, and seductive beaches.

Numbers in the margin correspond to points of interest on the St. Kitts map.

SIGHTS TO SEE

❶ Basseterre. On the south coast, St. Kitts's walkable capital is graced with tall palms, and although many of the buildings appear run-down, there are interesting shops, excellent art galleries, and some beautifully maintained houses.

The octagonal Circus, built in the style of London's famous Piccadilly Circus, has duty-free shops along the streets and courtyards off from it. There are lovely gardens on the site of a former slave market at **Independence Square** (⊠ off Bank St.). The square is surrounded on three sides by 18th-century Georgian buildings. **St. George's Anglican Church** (⊠ Cayon St.) is a handsome stone building with a crenellated tower originally built by the French in 1670 and called Nôtre-Dame. The British burned it down in 1706 and rebuilt it four years later, naming it after the patron saint of England. Since then it has suffered a fire, an earthquake, and hurricanes, and was once again rebuilt in 1869. **Port Zante** (⊠ Waterfront, behind The Circus) is an ambitious, much-delayed, 27-acre cruise-ship pier-marina reclaimed from the sea. The domed welcome center sports an imposing neoclassical design, with columns and stone arches; when completed (construction will continue through 2003), it will have walkways, fountains, and West Indian–style buildings housing luxury shops, galleries, and restaurants.

❺ Black Rocks. This series of lava deposits was spat into the sea ages ago when the island's volcano erupted. It has since been molded into fanciful shapes by centuries of pounding surf. ⊠ *Atlantic coast, outside town of Sadlers, Sandy Bay.*

❹ Brimstone Hill. The well-restored 38-acre fortress, a UNESCO World Heritage Site, is part of a national park dedicated by Queen Elizabeth in 1985. The steep walk up the hill from the parking lot is well worth it if military history and/or spectacular views interest you. After routing the French in 1690, the English erected a battery here, and by 1736 the fortress held 49 guns. In 1782, 8,000 French troops laid siege to the stronghold, which was defended by 350 militia and 600 regular troops of the Royal Scots and East Yorkshires. When the English finally surrendered, the French allowed them to march from the fort in full formation out of respect for their bravery (the English afforded the French the same honor when they surrendered the fort a mere year later). A hurricane severely damaged the fortress in 1834, and in 1852 it was evacuated and dismantled. The beautiful stones were carted away to build houses.

The citadel has been partially reconstructed and its guns remounted. A seven-minute orientation film recounts the fort's history and restoration. You can see what remains of the officers' quarters, the redoubts, the barracks, the ordinance store, and the cemetery. Its museum collections were depleted by hurricanes, but some pre-Columbian artifacts, objects pertaining to the African heritage of the island's slaves (masks, ceremonial tools, etc.), weaponry, uniforms, photographs, and old newspapers remain. The view from here includes Montserrat and Nevis, to the southeast; Saba and St. Eustatia, to the northwest; and St. Barths and St. Maarten, to the north. Nature trails snake through the tangle of surrounding hardwood forest and savanna (a fine spot to catch the green vervet monkeys skittering about). ⊠ *Main Rd., Brimstone Hill,* ☎ *869/465–2609.* ☞ *$5.* ⊘ *Daily 9:30–5:30.*

❷ Old Road Town. This site marks the first permanent English settlement in the West Indies, founded in 1624 by Thomas Warner. Take the side road toward the interior to find some Carib petroglyphs, testimony of even earlier habitation. The largest depicts a female figure on black volcanic rock, presumably a fertility goddess. Less than a mile east of Old Road Town along Main Road is **Bloody Point,** where French and British soldiers joined forces in 1629 to repel a mass Carib attack; reputedly so many Caribs were massacred, the stream ran red for three days. ⊠ *Main Rd., west of Challengers.*

❸ **Romney Manor.** The ruins of this somewhat restored house and surrounding cottages that duplicate the old chattel-house style are set in 6 acres of gardens, with exotic flowers, an old bell tower, and an enormous gnarled 350-year-old *saman* tree (sometimes called a rain tree). Inside, at **Caribelle Batik,** you can watch artisans hand-printing fabrics by the 2,500-year-old process known as batik. Look for signs indicating a turnoff for Romney Manor near Old Road Town.

NEVIS

Lodging

Most lodgings are in restored manor or plantation houses scattered throughout the island's five parishes (counties). The owners often live at these inns, and it's easy to feel as if you've been personally invited down for a visit. Before dinner you may find yourself in the drawing room having a cocktail and conversing with the family, other guests, and visitors who have come for a meal in the restaurant. Most inns operate on MAP (including complimentary afternoon tea) and offer a free shuttle service to their private stretch on Pinney's Beach. If you require TVs and air-conditioning, you're better off staying at the hotels, and then dining with the engaging inn owners.

For approximate costs, *see* the lodging price chart *in* St. Kitts.

$$$$ **Four Seasons Resort Nevis.** This beachfront beauty offers exemplary
★ business, family, and recreational facilities while exuding romance, from the clubby library bar to 300 acres of exquisitely landscaped grounds. Irreproachable service and services include regular private ferry crossings to St. Kitts and a "beach concierge," dispensing everything from reading materials to CDs. Spacious rooms (550 square ft [51 square m]) are furnished with mahogany armoires and beds, marble bathrooms, botanical prints, genre watercolors, and cushioned rattan sofas and chairs in restrained pastels. Individually designed and owned golf-course villas have cathedral ceilings, open kitchens, and enormous verandas. The resort admirably combines world-class elegance with West Indian hospitality. ⊠ *Pinney's Beach (Box 565, Charlestown),* ☎ *869/469–1111; 800/332–3442 in the U.S.; 800/268–6282 in Canada;* FAX *869/469–1112,* WEB *www.fourseasons.com. 179 rooms, 17 suites, 43 villas. 2 restaurants, grill, room service, fans, in-room safes, minibars, in-room VCRs, 18-hole golf course, 10 tennis courts, 2 pools, aerobics, hair salon, health club, hot tub, spa, beach, dive shop, snorkeling, windsurfing, boating, bicycles, 2 bars, pro shop, library, video game room, shops, baby-sitting, children's programs (ages 2–12), laundry service, laundry facilities, Internet, business services, meeting rooms, car rental. AE, D, MC, V. EP, FAP, MAP.*

$$$–$$$$ **Hermitage Plantation Inn.** A 300-year-old great house—reputedly
★ the Caribbean's oldest wooden house—is the heart of this breeze-swept hillside complex overlooking the distant ocean (beach shuttles are complimentary). The vivacious owners, Maureen and Richard "Loopy" Lupinacci, will introduce you to everyone who's anyone on Nevis. Individually decorated, bougainvillea-draped cottages have hardwood floors, antiques (including four-poster canopy beds swaddled in mosquito netting), and hammock-slung patios or balconies.

Nevis

ATLANTIC OCEAN

Huggins Bay

6

ST. JAMES
WINDWARD

Brick Kiln

Long Haul Bay

Newcastle Beach

9

Newcastle

Newcastle
Airport

8

10

*Tamarind
Bay*

*Mosquito
Bay*

12

11

Oualie Beach

13

*Jones
Bay*

14

The Narrows

*Cades
Bay*

15

Nevis Peak

ST. THOMAS
LOWLAND

Cotton Ground

8

7

ST. PAUL
CHARLESTOWN

1 2 3

16

17

Pinney's
Beach

Jamestown

Saba

St. Eustatius

St. Kitts

Nevis

TO ST. KITTS

KEY

- Beaches
- Dive Sites
- 1 Exploring Sights
- Ferry
- ① Hotels and Restaurants

White Bay

Red Cliff

ST. GEORGE GINGERLAND

Zion ○

⑦

⑥

5

5

4

Saddle Hill

ST. JOHN FIG TREE

4 Fig Tree

3

2

★ Charlestown

Long Pt.

Dogwood Pt.

The Devil's Caves

Caribbean Sea

N

0   5 km
0   5 miles

Lodging

Four Seasons Resort Nevis 16
Golden Rock 7
Hermitage Plantation Inn 4
Hurricane Cove Bungalows 11
Inn at Cades Bay 15
Montpelier Plantation Inn 5
Mt. Nevis Hotel and Beach Club 8
Nisbet Plantation Beach Club 9
Old Manor Estate 6

Oualie Beach Hotel 13
Yamseed Inn 10

Dining

Banaras 12
Four Seasons Dining Room 16
Golden Rock 7
Hermitage Plantation Inn 4
Jamaikey's 1
Le Bistro 3
Miss June's 14
Montpelier Plantation Inn 5

Mt. Nevis Hotel and Beach Club 8
Nisbet Plantation Beach Club 9
Sunshine's 17
Tequila Sheila's 15
Unella's 2

Exploring

Bath Springs 2
Charlestown 1
Eden Brown Estate 6
Ft. Ashby 7
Nelson Museum 3
Nevis Botanical Gardens 5
St. John's Church 4
St. Thomas Anglican Church 8

There's also a two-bedroom replica of a manor house with a private pool. The Hermitage appreciates life's finer things, from the elegant horse-drawn carriage rides to the sparkling dialogue at the bar. ✉ *St. John, Fig Tree Parish,* ☎ *869/469–3477,* FAX *869/469–2481,* WEB *www.hermitagenevis.com. 8 rooms, 8 cottages, 1 house. Restaurant, no air-conditioning, fans, some kitchens, in-room safes, refrigerators, no TV in some rooms, tennis court, pool, horseback riding, bar, shops. AE, MC, V. BP, MAP.*

$$$-$$$$ ⊞ **Nisbet Plantation Beach Club.** From this 18th-century plantation
★   manor house's patio you can see the Atlantic and an old, flower-be-decked sugar mill while enjoying complimentary high tea. Three categories of impeccably maintained accommodations occupy several pale yellow Bermudian-style cottages staggered along a stately coconut palm-lined avenue that sweeps to the beach. All are tastefully appointed with patios, vaulted ceilings, gleaming tile floors, whitewashed wicker and rattan, grass mats, soothing sea-foam and peach fabrics, and abstract tropical prints. In addition to the refined great house restaurant, you'll find a deck bar (terrific sunset watching) and two casual beach eateries. ✉ *Newcastle Beach,* ☎ *869/469–9325 or 800/742–6008,* FAX *869/469–9864,* WEB *www.nisbetplantation.com. 38 rooms. 3 restaurants, fans, in-room safes, refrigerators, no room TVs, tennis court, pool, massage, croquet, beach, snorkeling, 2 bars, library, laundry service. AE, MC, V. MAP.*

$$$ ⊞ **Montpelier Plantation Inn.** You enter this civilized retreat through
★   majestic iron gates, while rusted sugar machinery dots the manicured grounds like abstract sculpture. The fieldstone great house imposingly re-creates the 18th-century original (Horatio Nelson and Fanny Nisbet were married on the grounds). Spare but sparkling hillside cottages hold accommodations with patios, Italian ceramic–tile floors, large bathrooms with exquisite tracery, four-poster or rattan beds, delicate floral spreads, and vivid yellow-and-white-striped curtains. A gorgeous mural decorates one of the walls around the pool; there's a free shuttle to the inn's private Pinney's Beach pavilion. (Do return for the proper complimentary afternoon tea.) Gracious owners James and Celia Gaskell foster an air of incomparable quiet and unpretentious elegance. ✉ *Pond Hill (Box 474, Charlestown),* ☎ *869/469–3462 or 800/ 223–9832,* FAX *869/469–2932,* WEB *www.montpeliernevis.com. 17 rooms. Restaurant, no air-conditioning, fans, no room TVs, tennis court, pool, 2 bars. AE, MC, V. Closed late Aug.–early Oct. BP, MAP.*

$$-$$$ ⊞ **Mt. Nevis Hotel and Beach Club.** The Maguid family blends con-
★   temporary accommodations with typical Nevisian warmth. Deluxe rooms and suites have large balconies, handsome white and natural-wicker furnishings, apricot, mint, and white fabrics, and colorful island prints. Suites have full kitchens and sofa beds, making them fine value for families; standard hotel rooms are comparatively cramped. There are also three fully equipped, individually decorated, oceanview houses. The beach club (free transportation) serves scrumptious pizzas and grilled items. The hotel's verdant site was once a lime plantation; the wild trees' perfume wafts through the air. Invigorating hikes on-site include the 18th-century ruins of the Thomas Cottle Church, unusual in that owners and slaves worshiped together. ✉ *Shaw's Rd., Mt. Nevis (Box 494, Newcastle),* ☎ *869/469–9373 or 800/756–3847,* FAX *869/469–9375,* WEB *www.mountnevishotel.com. 28 units, 3 houses. Restaurant, grill, fans, some kitchens, refrigerators, in-room VCRs, pool, gym, bar, Internet, business services, meeting rooms. AE, D, MC, V. EP, MAP.*

$$-$$$ ⊞ **Old Manor Estate.** Vast tropical gardens surround this former sugar plantation in the shadow of Mt. Nevis. The smokehouse, jail, and other outbuildings have been imaginatively restored as public spaces, the old

cistern is now the pool, and rusting sugar-making equipment forms a virtual sculpture garden/museum. Many enormous guest rooms have exposed wood beams, gorgeous stone, polished hardwood, or tile floors, marble vanities, four-poster beds, antique wardrobes, and colonial reproductions. Others have a monochromatic haute 1970s bachelor pad look. The manor house's respected Cooperage restaurant has splendid sea views and an excellent nouvelle Continental menu. Of all the Nevisian inns, Old Manor probably best re-creates the old-time plantation feel. ⊠ *Charlestown (Box 70),* ☎ *869/469–3445 or 800/892–7093,* FAX *869/469–3388,* WEB *www.oldmanornevis.com. 14 rooms. 2 restaurants, 2 bars, no air-conditioning, fans, refrigerators, no room TVs, pool, shops, library. AE, MC, V. BP, MAP.*

$$–$$$
★
🏨 **Oualie Beach Hotel.** This cozy, congenial beachfront resort consists of white-and-hunter-green gingerbread cottages with views of St. Kitts. Bright, airy rooms are tastefully furnished: deluxe rooms have mahogany four-poster canopy beds, vivid island artworks, and polished granite vanities; studios have full kitchens. Hammocks dangle everywhere, but most people staying here are active types. The on-site dive shop (fine packages available) offers NAUI-certified instruction, and you can rent Sunfish and Windsurfers, charter a sailboat, or take sea-kayaking or turtle-watching tours. Breakfast, lunch, and dinner are served at the informal Oualie Beach Hotel restaurant, best known for its West Indian–themed Saturday nights. ⊠ *Oualie Beach,* ☎ *869/469–9735 or 800/682–5431,* FAX *869/469–9176,* WEB *www.oualie.com. 34 rooms. Restaurant, fans, in-room safes, some kitchens, refrigerators, some in-room VCRs, beach, dive shop, snorkeling, windsurfing, boating, fishing, bar, meeting room. AE, D, MC, V. EP, MAP.*

$$–$$$
🏨 **Golden Rock.** More than 200 years ago, co-owner Pam Barry's great-great-great-grandfather built this estate. It straddles 96 mountainous acres crisscrossed by trails. Rusting cannons placed about the grounds add historic ambience, as do Pam's family heirlooms and the magnificent Eva Wilkin mural in the bar. Oceanview units have mahogany or bamboo four-poster beds and native grass mats. The former sugar mill is a spectacular bi-level suite, the old cistern a spring-fed swimming pool. Free transportation accesses the inn's beach bar on Pinney's. Green vervet monkeys skitter about, and La Rue, a gloriously colored, wolf-whistling Amazona parrot perches wherever he pleases. ⊠ *Gingerland (Box 493),* ☎ *869/469–3346,* FAX *869/469–2113,* WEB *www.golden-rock.com. 16 rooms, 1 suite. Restaurant, grill, no air-conditioning, fans, no room TVs, tennis court, pool, bar, hiking. AE, MC, V. Closed Sept.–early Oct. EP, MAP.*

$$
🏨 **Hurricane Cove Bungalows.** These one-, two-, and three-bedroom bungalows cling precariously to a cliff overlooking lovely Oualie Beach. The glorified treehouse interiors are charmingly rustic, with gleaming terra-cotta floors, hand-carved wood furnishings, batik wall-hangings, and beds swaddled in mosquito netting. All have full kitchens and an enormous enclosed beached-wood patio with breathtaking ocean views (most in-demand, especially for honeymooners, are Sea Biscuit, Baobab, and Williwah). Several have private pools. The postage-stamp-size hotel pool is in the foundation of a 250-year-old fort, under the shade of a baobab tree. The beach is within a five-minute walk. ⊠ *Hurricane Hill, St. James Parish,* WEB *www.hurricanecove.com,* ☎ FAX *869/469–9462. 11 cottages. Fans, pool. AE, MC, V. Closed Sept. EP.*

$$
🏨 **Inn at Cades Bay.** At this complex, each of the tidy peach-colored cottages with sage-green gabled roofs has its own tiny lawn. Sizable rooms have high ceilings, bleached-wood paneling, rattan beds, smart, abstract Spanish fabrics, and terra-cotta patios that overlook the sea. The lovingly tended grounds include 10 varieties of palm trees and a cactus garden. The beach is lined with gazebos with hammocks. Ask

about special "low" high season rates in January and February and Internet deals. ✉ *Cades Bay,* ☎ *869/469–8139,* FAX *869/469–8129,* WEB *www.cadesbayinn.com. 16 rooms. Restaurant, bar, fans, minibars, pool. AE, MC, V. EP, MAP.*

$ 🖥 **Yamseed Inn.** At the end of a very rough access road, this remote pale yellow house's friendly innkeeper, Sybil Siegfried, receives her guests. Hummingbirds on the B&B's beautiful grounds (Sybil is an avid gardener) welcome you to the stylish reception area. Each room is handsomely appointed with a mahogany bed, wood-paneled ceiling, throw rugs, white tile floors, and antiques. Breakfast includes homemade muffins and muesli with grated coconut. The serene white-sand beach stares right at St. Kitts. The only flaw in this almost-paradise is its location in the nearby airport's flight path (fortunately, air traffic is sparse). ✉ *Newcastle Beach,* ☎ *869/469–9361. 4 rooms. Beach. No credit cards. CP. 3-night minimum.*

Dining

Dinner options range from intimate dinners at plantation guest houses (where the menu is often prix fixe) to casual eateries. Seafood is ubiquitous, and many places specialize in West Indian fare.

What to Wear

Dress is casual at lunch, although beach attire is unacceptable. Dress pants and sundresses are appropriate for dinner.

For approximate costs, *see* the dining price chart *in* St. Kitts.

CARIBBEAN

$$$$ ✕ **Golden Rock.** The romantic, dimly lit room's fieldstone walls date from the Golden Rock inn's plantation days. Enchanting Eva Wilkin originals grace the walls, copper sugar-boiling pots are used as planters, and straw mats and unglazed local pottery provide island ambience; distressed French highback chairs, maroon linens, and gold napery contribute colonial accents. The prix-fixe menu might include house favorites like velvety pumpkin soup, raisin curry chicken, and grilled local snapper with *tania* (a type of tuber) fritters. Don't miss the homemade juices, like passion fruit, soursop, and ginger beer. ✉ *Gingerland,* ☎ *869/469–3346. Reservations essential. AE, MC, V. Closed Sun.*

$$$$ ✕ **Miss June's.** While Miss June Mestier, a lady from Trinidad, pre- ★ pares the fare, her son serves drinks—from Miss June's secret rum punch to a proper martini—on the veranda. The dining room's tables are set with mismatched fine china and crystal. The three courses include piquante soup, seafood, and salad. "Now that you've had dinner," Miss June announces, "it's time to have fun!" She then reveals a mahogany buffet laden with 20 dishes. Trinidadian-influenced selections include curries, veggies, seafood, and such meats as ribs in *mauby* (a bark distillation) and pineapple. Wine flows freely. Miss June will join you for coffee and brandy, requesting you to turn the lights out when you leave. ✉ *Jones Bay,* ☎ *869/469–5330. Reservations essential. MC, V.*

$–$$$ ✕ **Unella's.** It's nothing fancy here—just tables on a second-floor porch overlooking Charlestown's waterfront. Stop for exceptional lobster (more expensive than the rest of the menu), curried lamb, island-style spareribs, and steamed conch, all served with local vegetables, rice, and peas. Unella opens shop around 9 AM, when locals and boaters appear waiting for their breakfast, and stays open all day. ✉ *Waterfront, Charlestown,* ☎ *869/469–5574. No credit cards.*

$–$$ ✕ **Jamaikey's.** Tucked away in the downstairs of a quaint gingerbread-trimmed former residence, this humble eatery serves such good, honest Jamaican-inspired fare as stewed saltfish (with sides of "real" rice and peas and ratatouille) and baked chicken, and whatever else is scribbled on the blackboard. The decor is similarly no-frills, save for a striking mural of marine life splashed across one wall. ⊠ *Prince William St., Charlestown,* ☎ 869/469–8748. *No credit cards. Closed Sun.*

$–$$ ✕ **Sunshine's.** Everything about this beach shack is larger than life, in-
★ cluding the Rasta man Llewelyn "Sunshine" Caines himself. Flags from around the world drape the lean-to and complement the inter-national clientele (including many celebrities), who wander over from the adjacent Four Seasons. Picnic tables are splashed with bright sun-rise-to-sunset colors; even the palm trees are painted. Fishermen cruise up with their catch—you might savor lobster rolls or snapper creole. Don't miss the lethal house specialty, Killer Bee rum punch. As Sun-shine boasts, "One and you're stung, two you're stunned, three it's a knockout." ⊠ *Pinney's Beach,* ☎ 869/469–1089. *No credit cards.*

CONTEMPORARY

$$$$ ✕ **Hermitage Plantation Inn.** After cocktails in the inn's antiques-filled parlor (incomparable bartender Shabba's rum punches are legendary, and you could meet all Nevisian society, high and low, at the postage-stamp-size bar), dinner is served on the veranda. The four-course prix-fixe menu might include lemongrass and pumpkin soup, conch cakes with lobster sauce, tuna with guava and rosemary, and a rum soufflé—all lovingly prepared by the local chef, Lovey. Expect an evening of bon mots and bonhomie: the conversation is always lively, thanks to witty, gregarious owners Maureen and Richard Lupinacci. ⊠ *St. John, Fig Tree Parish,* ☎ 869/469–3477. *Reservations essential. AE, MC, V.*

$$$$ ✕ **Montpelier Plantation Inn.** Genial owners James and Celia Gaskell
★ preside over an elegant evening, starting with hors d'oeuvres. Look for the circa-1880 portrait of James's relative, Lady Catherine Gaskell. Can-dlelit dinner is served on the west verandah. The inventive chef, Mark Roberts, utilizes the property's herb gardens and fruit trees and occa-sionally even hauls in the day's catch. The changing menu might present lobster terrine with tarragon chive sauce, seared swordfish in papaya black bean salsa, and a proper herb-crusted rack of lamb in rosemary mustard jus. Simpler lunches (order the lobster salad) are served on the refreshing patio. ⊠ *Pond Hill,* ☎ 869/469–3462. *Reservations essential. AE, MC, V. Closed late Aug.–early Oct.*

$$$$ ✕ **Nisbet Plantation Beach Club.** The great house—an oasis of polished
★ hardwood floors, mahogany and cherry-wood furnishings, straw mats, wicker furnishings, and stone walls—has long been a popular dinner spot. Tables on the veranda look down the palm-tree-lined fairway to the sea. Kevin Hall's five-course menu combines Continental, Pacific Rim, and Caribbean cuisines with local ingredients. Sumptuous choices include blue cheese pumpkin quiche with avocado relish, ginger-crusted mahimahi with lemon parsley rice and beet sauce, and chocolate truf-fle torte. Enjoy cocktails or coffee over silky soft live music in the civ-ilized front bar. ⊠ *Newcastle Beach,* ☎ 869/469–9325. *Reservations essential. AE, MC, V.*

$$$–$$$$ ✕ **Four Seasons Dining Room.** The main restaurant at the Four Sea-
★ sons is imposing yet romantic: beamed cathedral ceiling, imported hardwood paneling, parquet floors, ornate white iron chandeliers, flagstone hearth, china-filled cabinets, hand-carved mahogany chairs, towering floral arrangements, and picture windows overlooking the sea. Chef Joseph Oldham's Southwest/Asian menu changes daily, stress-ing fresh, often organic produce. Stellar offerings might include green tea–smoked salmon with tropical fruit salad and vanilla bean dress-ing and lemongrass-poached lobster with banana spring roll and gin-ger butter sauce. Numerous "spa selections" grace the menu, while the adjacent, less formal Grill Room provides a more classic meat-and-pota-

toes experience. ⊠ *Four Seasons Resort Nevis, Pinney's Beach,* ☎ *869/469–1111. Reservations essential. AE, D, DC, MC, V. No lunch.*

$$–$$$$ ✕ **Mt. Nevis Hotel and Beach Club.** The hotel's airy dining room opens onto the terrace and pool with a splendid view of St. Kitts. The elegant yet light menu deftly blends local ingredients with a cornucopia of cuisines, from Mexican to Thai. Stellar starters are calamari tempura with red peppers and saffron aioli, or Caribbean conch cake with mild basil-chili mayonnaise; excellent entrées include pan-seared salmon with garlic lime butter sauce and superb flambé specials. The service is attentive, the dining room sublime (with lovely Fauvist-hued artworks). ⊠ *Shaws Rd., Mt. Nevis,* ☎ *869/469–9373. AE, D, MC, V.*

ECLECTIC

$$–$$$ ✕ **Bananas.** British expat Gillian Smith, who once worked in various capacities for Disney and Relais et Châteaux, re-opened her funky eatery/bazaar in a complex perched atop a cliff with stunning sunset views. She's added splashes of vivid colors, as well as Turkish copper pots and kilims (many for sale). Scrumptious starters include zucchini cakes with yogurt sauce and crab quesadillas; follow with bourbon-glazed ribs or lobster tails with pineapple and ginger salsa. Jazzy sounds and the scent of wild orchids commingled with Cubanos waft through the lounge. No wonder Gillian fittingly calls it a "Caribbean bistro." ⊠ *Tamarind Bay,* ☎ *869/469–1891. MC, V. Closed Sun. No lunch.*

$$ ✕ **Le Bistro.** Known informally as "Matt's," after owner/chef Matt Lloyd
★ (former chef at Montpelier), this minuscule boîte, set in a 1930s chattel house, is wildly popular, especially during Friday night happy hour. Fare ranges from quiches to curries; coconut chicken's a standout, but opt for the fresh fish specials (Matt usually hauls in the catch himself on his 30-footer, *Deep Venture,* which is available for rent). The impeccable presentation is as colorful as the decor (persimmon floors, plaid tablecloths, and vine-strangled trellises). Local chefs flock here on their nights off—always a promising sign. ⊠ *Chapel St., Charlestown,* ☎ *869/469–5110. MC, V. Closed weekends. No lunch.*

$$ ✕ **Tequila Sheila's.** Right next door to the Inn at Cades Bay, this thatched shack of corrugated tin and wood sits on a beach (there are even palapas) next to a colorful abandoned boat. It has been gussied up with plant-filled baskets, terra-cotta floors, turquoise accents, and billowing windsocks, but the laid-back air remains. The Caribbean-tinged Mediterranean cuisine runs from paella to coconut shrimp to filet mignon in béarnaise sauce. The rollicking Sunday Beach Party Brunch (the crab Benedict is a must) draws locals and tourists alike. ⊠ *Cades Bay,* ☎ *869/469–1633. MC, V. Closed Mon. No lunch Tues.*

Beaches

All the beaches are free to the public, but there are no changing facilities, so wear a swimsuit under your clothes.

Newcastle Beach. This broad swath of soft, ecru sand, shaded by coconut palms, sits at the northernmost tip of the island by Nisbet Plantation, on the channel between St. Kitts and Nevis. It's popular with snorkelers.

Oualie Beach. South of Mosquito Bay and north of Cades and Jones bays, this beige-sand beach is where the folks at Oualie Beach Hotel can mix you a drink and fix you up with water-sports equipment.

Pinney's Beach. The island's showpiece has almost 4 mi (6½ km) of soft, golden sand on the calm Caribbean, lined with a magnificent grove of palm trees. The Four Seasons Resort is here, as are the private cabanas and pavilions of several mountain inns and casual beach bars.

Outdoor Activities and Sports

Participant Sports

BOATING

The seas are usually uncommonly calm, with light breezes. The north-west side of Nevis is particularly delightful, thanks to the sterling views of St. Kitts. You can rent kayaks, Hobie Cats, and Sunfish from **Oualie Beach Club** (✉ Oualie Beach, ☎ 869/469–9518), which also provides excellent instruction. **Nevis Water Sports** (✉ Jones Estate, ☎ 869/469–9060) rents everything from Sunfish ($20 per hour) to power-boats ($100 per hour).

FISHING

Fishing here includes kingfish, wahoo, grouper, tuna, and yellowtail snapper, with marlin occasionally spotted. The best areas are Monkey Shoals and around Redonda. Charters are $350 per half-day. **Nevis Water Sports** (✉ Jones Estate, ☎ 869/469–9060) offers sport fishing aboard its tournament-winning boats, the 31-ft *Sea Brat* and *Sea Troll,* under the supervision of Captain Julian Rigby.

GOLF

Duffers doff their hats to the beautiful, impeccably maintained Robert Trent Jones, Jr.–designed 18-hole, par-72, 6,766-yard championship course at the **Four Seasons Resort Nevis** (✉ Pinney's Beach, ☎ 869/469–1111). The signature hole is the 15th, a 660-yard monster that encompasses a deep ravine; other holes include bridges, steep drops, rolling pitches, and fierce doglegs. The virtual botanical gardens surrounding the fairways almost qualify as a hazard themselves. Greens fees are $100 per person for nine holes, $150 for 18.

HIKING

The center of the island is Nevis Peak, which soars 3,232 ft (967 m) and is flanked by Hurricane Hill on the north and Saddle Hill on the south. If you plan to scale Nevis Peak, a day-long affair, it is highly recommended that you go with a guide. Your hotel can arrange it (and a picnic lunch) for you. The **Upper Round Road Trail** is a 9-mi (14½-km) road constructed in the late 1600s and cleared and restored by the Nevis Historical and Conservation Society. Now a heritage trail, it connects the Golden Rock Hotel, on the east side of the island, with Nisbet Plantation Beach Club, on the northern tip. The trail encompasses numerous vegetation zones, including pristine rain forest, and impressive plantation ruins. The original cobblestones are still evident in many places.

Eco-Tours Nevis (☎ 869/469–2091), headed by David Rollinson, rambles through 18th-century estates and explores what remains of Nevis's last working sugar factory as well as archaeological evidence of pre-Columbian settlements. David also offers treks up Mountravers, a spectacular great-house ruin, and historical walks through Charlestown. The fee is $20 per person, $10 for the Charleston walk. **Michael Herbert** (☎ 869/469–2856) leads four-hour nature hikes up to Herbert Heights, where he offers fresh local juices as you drink in the views of Montserrat; his powerful telescope makes you feel as if you're staring right into that island's simmering volcano. The price is $20; for $25 you can ride one of Herbert's donkeys. Michael also brings people up by appointment to Saddle Hill Battery and Nelson's Lookout, where he has constructed a thatched hut. The festive activities includes crab races, refreshments, rock climbing, and whale-watching in season through a telescope donated by Greenpeace. The **Nevis Historical and Conservation Society** (NHCS; ☎ 869/469–5786) sells an informational guidebook on the Upper Round Road Trail at various shops and the island museums. **Top to Bottom** (☎ 869/469–9080), run by Jim and Nikki Johnston, offers ecorambles (slower tours) and hikes that emphasize Nevis's volcanic and horticultural heritage (including pointing out folkloric herbal medicines). The Johnstons are also keen star- and bird-watchers. Three-hour rambles or hikes are $20 per person (snacks and juice included); it's $30 for a more strenuous climb up Mt. Nevis.

HORSEBACK RIDING

You can arrange for leisurely beach rides or tackle more demanding trail rides through the lush hills ($50 per person) and lessons ($20 per hour) through **Nevis Equestrian Centre** (✉ Clifton Estate, Pinney's Beach, ☎ 869/469–8118). Kids will love the petting zoo, with donkeys, goats, peacocks, and tortoises.

SCUBA DIVING AND SNORKELING

The Devil's Caves are a series of grottoes where divers can navigate tunnels, canyons, and underwater hot springs while viewing lobsters, sea fans, sponges, squirrel fish, and more. The village of Jamestown, which washed into the sea around Fort Ashby, just south of Cades Bay, makes for superior snorkeling and diving. Reef-protected Pinney's Beach offers especially good snorkeling. Single-tank dives are usually $50, two-tank dives $80.

Under the Sea (✉ Tamarind Bay, ☎ 869/469–1291) is the inventive brainchild of Barbara Whitman, a marine biologist from Connecticut. It doubles as a restaurant-bar and snorkeling center, where Barbara gives comprehensive snorkeling lessons and tours, stressing both knowledge and ecological awareness. She has painted a detailed mural of Nevisian marine life on one wall, which she uses for initial familiarization with the various underwater environments, followed by hands-on demonstrations in acrylic "touch-tanks" teeming with over 50 species. The lessons, held twice daily except Mondays, and tours (in sleek trimarans on the small dark-sand beach) are $20 ($35 with snorkel tour included), and profits go to educating local school children. Try **Dive Nevis** (✉ Pinney's Beach, ☎ 869/469–9373) for excellent, affordable dives and packages. **Scuba Safaris** (✉ Oualie Beach, ☎ 869/469–9518) is a PADI five-star facility, NAUI Dream Resort, and NASDS Examining Station, whose experienced dive masters offer everything from a resort course to full certification. They also provide a snorkeling-learning experience that enables you to not only see but listen to sealife, including whales and dolphins.

TENNIS

There are 10 tennis courts (3 lighted), 6 clay and 4 all-weather hardcourts, at the **Four Seasons Resort Nevis** (✉ Pinney's Beach, ☎ 869/469–1111), which also offers instruction by Peter Burwash International pros.

WINDSURFING

Waters are generally calm and winds steady yet gentle, making Nevis an excellent spot for beginners and intermediates. **Windsurfing Nevis** (✉ Oualie Beach Hotel, Oualie Beach, ☎ 869/469–9682) offers top-notch instructors (Winston Crooke is one of the best in the islands) and equipment for $25 per half hour.

Spectator Sports

One of the Caribbean's most unusual events is the occasional "Day at the Races," sponsored by the **Nevis Turf and Jockey Club** (☎ 869/469–3477). The races, which attract a "pan-Caribbean field" (as the club likes to boast), are held on a windswept course called Indian Castle, overlooking the "white horses" of the Atlantic. Last-minute changes and scratches are common; a party atmosphere prevails, with local ladies dispensing heavenly fried chicken and gossip.

Shopping

Nevis is certainly not the place for a shopping spree, but there are some unique and wonderful surprises, notably the island's stamps, batik, and hand-embroidered clothing.

Areas and Malls

Other than a few hotel boutiques and isolated galleries, virtually all shopping is concentrated on or just off Main Street in Charlestown. The lovely old stonework and wood floors of the waterfront Cotton Ginnery Complex make an appropriate setting for stalls of local artisans.

Specialty Items

ART

Nevis has produced one artist of some international repute, the late Dame Eva Wilkin, who for more than 50 years painted island people, flowers, and landscapes in an evocative art naïf style. Her originals sell for $100 and up, and prints are available in some local shops. The **Eva Wilkin Gallery** (⊠ Clay Ghaut, Gingerland, ☎ 869/469–2673) occupies her former atelier. If the paintings, drawings, and prints are out of your price range, consider buying the lovely note cards based on her designs. The front rooms of **Café des Arts** (⊠ Main St., Charlestown, ☎ 869/469–7098) carry Kate Spencer's marvelous hand-painted silk scarves and pareus, prints, notebooks, and place mats; still more island paintings (many from Haiti) and pottery are displayed in the charming interior courtyard, where light lunches and superb croissants and espresso are served. **Robert Humphreys** sells his paintings, flowing bronze sculptures of pirouetting marlins, and clay renderings of local fauna from his studio (⊠ Palm Hill, Brazier Estate, ☎ 869/469–2421). You must call ahead for an appointment.

CLOTHING

Beach Works (⊠ Main St., Charlestown, ☎ 869/469–0620) has become the island's classiest boutique, with an excellent selection of everything from bathing suits to Balinese batik and puppets. You'll find Caribelle batik caftans, scarves, shorts, and blouses, as well as caps, T-shirts, jewelry, steel drums, straw hats, painted fish, and anything conceivable emblazoned with the name Nevis in the **Island Hopper** (⊠ Main St., Charlestown, ☎ 869/469–5430). **Fanny's Closet** (⊠ Hermitage Plantation Inn, St. John) sells John Warden's line of flowing, breathable linen resortwear in eggshell to earth tones, as well as hand-painted baubles and bibelots. **Jerveren's Fashions** (⊠ Cotton Ginnery, Charlestown, ☎ 869/469–0062) carries still more batik resortwear and light cotton sundresses in pastel colors.

FOOD AND WINE

Beekeeping is a buzzing biz, and you'll find beeswax candles (which burn longer than those made of regular wax) and fragrant, tropically flavored honey at many stores. Quentin Henderson, the amiable head of the **Nevis Beekeeping Cooperative** (⊠ Gingerbread, ☎ 869/469–5521), will even arrange trips by appointment to various hives for demonstrations of beekeeping procedures. At **Caribbean Wine** (⊠ Prospect Rd., Fig Tree, ☎ 869/469–3908), Dominique Nelson Ashley, a chemist by trade, produces surprisingly tasty wines by traditional methods from local plants such as soursop, white sorrel, ginger, guava, red plum, passion fruit, cane, mango, and star apple. He then corks and seals them in recycled bottles.

HANDICRAFTS

Caribco Gifts (✉ Main St., Charlestown, ☎ 869/469–1432) sells affordable T-shirts, candles, and pottery emblazoned with Nevis logos. **Knick Knacks** (✉ between Waterfront and Main Sts., next to Unella's Restaurant, Charlestown, ☎ 869/469–5784) showcases top local artisans, including Marvin Chapman (stone and wood carvings) and Jeannie Rigby (exquisite dolls). The **Nevis Handicraft Co-op Society** (✉ Main St., Charlestown, ☎ 869/469–1746), next to the tourist office, offers work by local artisans (clothing, ceramic ware, woven goods) and locally produced honey, hot sauces, and jellies. **AAAC** (✉ Main St., Charlestown, ☎ 869/469–0657) is the acronym for Adams Afro-Caribbean Art & Craft; the name's promise is fulfilled with such striking pieces as drums from Mozambique, hand-carved elephant and lion walking sticks, Nigerian warri boards, Guyanese painted gourds, and various masks and straw mats. **Bocane Ceramics** (✉ Main St., Charlestown, ☎ 869/469–5437) stocks beautifully designed and glazed local pottery, such as platters painted with marine life. Stamp collectors should head for the **Philatelic Bureau** (✉ off Main St., Charlestown, ☎ 869/469–0617), opposite the tourist office. St. Kitts and Nevis are famous for their decorative, and sometimes valuable, stamps. Real beauties include the butterfly, hummingbird, and marine life series.

Nightlife

In season it is usually easy to find a local calypso singer or a steel or string band performing at one of the hotels. Such performances are often in tandem with a special buffet dinner. Scan the posters plastered on doorways announcing informal jump-ups. Though Nevis (blessedly) lacks high-tech discos, many beach bars have live bands or DJs on weekends. Carib Roots plays nightly on the Ocean Terrace at the **Four Seasons Resort Nevis** (✉ Pinney's Beach, ☎ 869/469–1111).

BARS

Beachcomber (✉ Pinney's Beach, ☎ 869/469–1192) offers huge barbecues, happy hours, and occasional live bands in addition to a simple menu of burgers and grilled meats. Two enormous carved pelicans usher you into the quintessential beach bar/cabana, the brightly painted **Booby's** (✉ Newcastle Beach, ☎ no phone), where a hip local crowd parties to righteous sounds, live or taped, Wednesday through Sundays, fueled by scrumptious rotis, curries, and teriyaki stir-fried dishes (ladies drink free Saturday afternoons). The Charlestown lunchtime staple, **Eddy's Bar and Restaurant** (✉ Main St., Memorial Sq., Charlestown, ☎ 869/469–5958), opens Wednesday nights for a raucous West Indian happy hour featuring half-price snacks, including tannia and conch fritters served with terrific hot sauce made by Eddy's mom, Eulalie Williams (you can buy a bottle down the block at the Main Street Supermarket) and dancing, usually to a live string band. **The Water Department Pump House** (✉ Pump St., by the cemetery, Charlestown, ☎ no phone) is the informal name for a lively Friday-night jump-up that's run by two fellows from the local water department. Cars line the streets and the guys dish up fabulous BBQ ribs and chicken—as certain customers lobby to get their water pressure adjusted. It's a classic Caribbean scene.

Exploring Nevis

Nevis's main road makes a 20-mi (32-km) circuit through the five parishes; various offshoots of the road wind into the mountains. You can tour Charlestown, the capital, in a half hour or so, but you'll need three to four hours to explore the entire island. Part of the island's charm is its rusticity: there are no traffic lights, goats still amble through the streets of Charlestown, and local grocers announce whatever's in stock on a blackboard (anything from pig snouts to beer).

Numbers in the margin correspond to points of interest on the Nevis map.

SIGHTS TO SEE

② **Bath Springs.** The springs and the ruins of the Bath Hotel, built by John Huggins in 1778, sustained severe hurricane damage, and reopening has been delayed while the government lobbies the private sector to create a modernized spa (that's the official line, anyway; the full story is a complex web of Caribbean politics). The springs, with temperatures of 104°F–108°F, bubble out of the hillside. Huggins's 50-room hotel, the first hotel in the Caribbean (and allegedly a notorious brothel), was next to the waters. Eighteenth-century accounts reported that a few days of imbibing and soaking in these waters resulted in miraculous cures. Only a miracle could restore the decayed hotel to its former grandeur—it closed down in the late 19th century—but the spring house has been partially restored. Think twice about romping alongside the occasional local (not only are the springs dirty, but they're closed, making access technically illegal). Still, this is a fascinating sight. Follow Main Street south from Charlestown, past Caribbean Cove. ⊠ *Charlestown, on the outskirts.*

① **Charlestown.** About 1,200 of the island's 9,300 inhabitants live in the capital of Nevis. The town faces the Caribbean, about 12½ mi (20 km) south of Basseterre on St. Kitts. If you arrive by ferry, as most people do, you'll walk smack onto Main Street from the pier. It's easy to imagine how tiny Charlestown, founded in 1660, must have looked in its heyday. The weathered buildings still have their fanciful galleries, elaborate gingerbread fretwork, wooden shutters, and hanging plants. The stonework building with the clock tower houses the 1825 courthouse and the second-floor **library** (a cool respite on sultry days), open Monday to Saturday, 9 to 6. A fire in 1873 damaged the building and destroyed valuable records; much of the present building dates from the turn of the 20th century. The little park next to the library is Memorial Square, dedicated to the fallen of World Wars I and II. Down the street from the square, archaeologists have discovered the remains of a Jewish cemetery and synagogue (Nevis reputedly had the Caribbean's second-oldest congregation), but there's little to see. The **Alexander Hamilton Birthplace,** which contains the Museum of Nevis History, is on the waterfront, covered in bougainvillea and hibiscus. This Georgian-style house is a reconstruction of the statesman's original home, built in 1680 and thought to have been destroyed during an earthquake in the mid-19th century. Hamilton was born here in 1755. He left for the American colonies 17 years later to continue his education; he became secretary of the Treasury to George Washington and died in a duel with political rival Aaron Burr. The Nevis House of Assembly occupies the second floor of this building, and the museum downstairs contains Hamilton memorabilia, documents pertaining to the island's history, and displays on island geology, politics, architecture, and cuisine. ⊠ *Low St.,* ☎ *869/469–5786,* WEB *www.nevis-nhcs.com.* ☎ *$3; $2 if admission already paid to affiliated Nelson Museum.* ☉ *Weekdays 9–4, Sat. 9–noon.*

⑥ **Eden Brown Estate.** This government-owned mansion, built around 1740, is known as Nevis's haunted house or, rather, haunted ruins. In 1822 a Miss Julia Huggins was to marry a fellow named Maynard. However, on the day of the wedding, the groom and his best man had a duel and killed each other. The bride-to-be became a recluse, and the mansion was closed down. Local residents claim they can feel the presence of "someone" whenever they go near the eerie old house with its shroud of weeds and wildflowers. You're welcome to drop by; it's always open, and it's free. ⊠ *East Coast Rd., between Lime Kiln and Mannings, Eden Brown Bay,* ☎ *no phone.*

❼ Ft. Ashby. Overgrown with tropical vegetation, this site overlooks the place where the settlement of Jamestown fell into the sea after a tidal wave hit the coast in 1680. Needless to say, this is a favorite scuba-diving site. ⊠ *Main Rd., 1½ mi (2½ km) southwest of Hurricane Hill, Fort Ashby Beach.*

❸ Nelson Museum. This collection merits a visit for its memorabilia of Lord Nelson, including letters, documents, paintings, and even furniture from his flagship. Nelson was based in Antigua but came to Nevis often to court, and eventually to marry, Frances Nisbet, who lived on a 64-acre plantation here. ⊠ *Bath Rd., outside Charlestown,* ☎ *869/ 469–0408.* ⊡ *$3; $2 if admission already paid to affiliated Museum of Nevis History.* ☉ *Weekdays 9–4, Sat. 9–noon.*

❺ Nevis Botanical Gardens. In addition to terraced gardens and arbors, this remarkable 7.8-acre site, in the glowering shadow of Mt. Nevis, has natural lagoons, streams, and waterfalls, as well as superlative bronze mermaids, egrets, and herons, old copper pots used as floral center-pieces, and extravagant fountains. You'll find a proper rose garden, sections devoted to orchids and bromeliads, cacti, and flowering trees and shrubs—even a bamboo garden. The entrance to the Rain Forest Conservatory—which attempts to include every conceivable Caribbean ecosystem and then some—duplicates an imposing Mayan temple. A splendid re-creation of a plantation-style great house contains a tea room with sweeping sea views and a souvenir shop that sells teas, teapots, jams, botanical oils, candles, Caribbean cookbooks, and the like. ⊠ *Montpelier Estate,* ☎ *869/469–3509.* ⊡ *$9.* ☉ *Mon.–Sat. 9–4:30.*

❹ St. John's Church. Among the records of this church built in 1680 is a tattered, prominently displayed marriage certificate that reads: HORA-TIO NELSON, ESQUIRE, TO FRANCES NISBET, WIDOW, ON MARCH 11, 1787. ⊠ *Church Ground, Fig Tree Parish,* ☎ *no phone.*

❽ St. Thomas Anglican Church. The island's oldest church was built in 1643 and has been altered many times over the years. The gravestones in the old churchyard have stories to tell, and the church itself contains memorials to Nevis's early settlers. ⊠ *Main Rd., Jessup's, just south of Cotton Ground,* ☎ *no phone.*

ST. KITTS AND NEVIS A TO Z

To research prices, get advice from other travelers, and book travel arrangements, visit www.fodors.com.

AIR TRAVEL
American flies into San Juan, Puerto Rico, where its commuter arm, American Eagle, flies twice-daily to St. Kitts. Other major domestic airlines fly from their eastern hubs either into Antigua, St. Thomas, or St. Maarten, where connections to St. Kitts (and, less frequently, to Nevis) can be made on American Eagle, LIAT, and Windward Island Airways. British Airways flies daily from London to Antigua; Air Canada, daily in season from Toronto to Antigua. US Airways is expected to fly into each island twice weekly via its St. Maarten route. Nevis Express has daily flights from San Juan to both islands.

➤ AIRLINES AND CONTACTS: **Air Canada** (☎ 800/776–3000). **American/American Eagle** (☎ 869/465–0500). **British Airways** (☎ 800/

247–9297). **LIAT** (☎ 869/465–8613). **Nevis Express** (☎ 869/469–9755). **US Airways** (☎ 800/428–4322). **Windward Island Airways** (☎ 869/465–8010).

AIRPORTS

Taxis meet every flight at the newly expanded and modernized Robert L. Bradshaw Golden Rock Airport on St. Kitts, and at Newcastle Airport on Nevis. The taxis are unmetered, but fixed rates, in EC dollars, are posted at the airport and at the jetty. Note that rates are the same for one to four passengers. On St. Kitts the fare from the airport to the closest hotel in Basseterre is EC$18, to Frigate Bay's resorts EC$29, and to the farthest point EC$72. From the airport on Nevis it costs EC$20 to Nisbet Plantation, EC$37 to the Four Seasons, and EC$55 to Montpelier. Before setting off in a cab, be sure to clarify whether the rate quoted is in EC or U.S. dollars. There's a 50% surcharge for trips made between 10 PM and 6 AM.

➤ AIRPORT INFORMATION: **Robert L. Bradshaw Golden Rock Airport** (✉ Golden Rock, St. Kitts, ☎ no phone). **Newcastle Airport** (✉ Newcastle, Nevis, ☎ no phone).

BOAT AND FERRY TRAVEL

There are three services between St. Kitts and Nevis, all with byzantine schedules that are subject to change. Call the ferry information lines for the most up-to-date schedules. The 150-passenger government-operated ferry M/V *Caribe Queen* makes the 45-minute crossing from Nevis to St. Kitts two to three times daily, except Thursday and Sunday. The former cargo ship, *Sea Hustler,* is larger and makes the trip twice daily. Round-trip fare for both is $8. The faster, air-conditioned, 110-passenger ferry, the M/V *Caribe Breeze,* makes the run twice daily Thursday and Sunday, more frequently other days. The fare is $12 ($15 first class) round-trip.

Sea-taxi service between the two islands is operated by Kenneth Samuel, Nevis Water Sports, Leeward Island Charters, and Auston MacLeod of Pro-Divers for $20 one-way in summer, $25 in winter; discounts can be negotiated for small groups.

Sample taxi fares from the ferry dock in Charlestown are EC$18 to the Four Seasons and EC$27 to Hermitage.

FARES AND SCHEDULES

➤ BOAT FERRY INFORMATION: **Ferry information** (☎ 869/466–4636 and 869/469–9373). **Kenneth Samuel** (☎ 869/465–2670). **Leeward Island Charters** (☎ 869/465–7474). **Nevis Water Sports** (☎ 869/469–9060). **Pro-Divers** (☎ 869/465–3223). *Sea Hustler* (☎ 869/467–9702 or 869/467–9826).

BUSINESS HOURS

BANKS

Hours vary somewhat for banks but are typically Monday–Thursday 8–3 and Friday 8–5. St. Kitts & Nevis National Bank is also open Saturday 8:30 AM–11 AM.

POST OFFICES

Post offices are open Monday–Wednesday and Friday 8–3, Thursday and Saturday 8–noon.

SHOPS

Although shops used to close for lunch noon–1, more and more establishments are remaining open Monday–Saturday 8–4. Some shops close earlier on Thursday.

CAR RENTALS

You'll need a local driver's license, which you can get by presenting yourself, your valid driver's license, and $25 at the police station on Cayon Street in Basseterre (on Nevis the car-rental agency will help you obtain a local license at the police station). The license is valid for one year. Car rentals start at about $35 per day for a compact; expect to pay a few extra bucks for air-conditioning. Most agencies offer substantial discounts when you rent by the week.

Agencies include Avis, which has the best selection of Suzuki and Daihatsu four-wheel-drive vehicles. Delise Walwyn also provides an excellent selection and the option of a replacement car for one day on Nevis if you rent for three days or more on St. Kitts. TDC Rentals has a wide selection of vehicles and outstanding service; it offers a three-day rental that includes a car on both islands.

➤ MAJOR AGENCIES: **Avis** (✉ S. Independence Sq., ☎ 869/465–6507). **Delise Walwyn** (☎ 869/465–8449, WEB www.delisleco.com). **TDC Rentals** (✉ W. Independence Sq., Basseterre, St. Kitts, ☎ 869/465–2991; ✉ Bay Rd., Charlestown, Nevis, ☎ 869/469–5430; WEB www.tdcltd.com).

CAR TRAVEL

One well-kept main road circumnavigates St. Kitts, and signs are usually clearly marked, making it difficult to get lost. If you'd like to dine at the various inns and sightsee for more than one day, a car is advisable. If you plan to stay in the Frigate Bay–Basseterre area on St. Kitts, you can get by using taxis and doing a half-day island tour. Nevis's roads are not in good shape; though driving is on the left, you may be given a right-drive vehicle. And if you deviate from Main Street in Charlestown, you're likely to have trouble finding your way.

GASOLINE

Gasoline is expensive, about $2.60 per gallon.

ROAD CONDITIONS

The main roads on St. Kitts are in admirable condition, especially in the more developed southwestern part, though the northeast can get a bit bumpy, and the access roads to the plantation inns are notoriously rough. The roads on Nevis are pocked with crater-size potholes, and pigs, goats, and cattle command right-of-way.

RULES OF THE ROAD

Driving is on the left.

ELECTRICITY

St. Kitts and Nevis hotels function on 110 volts, 60 cycles, making all North American appliances safe to use.

EMERGENCIES

➤ AMBULANCE AND FIRE: **Ambulance** (☎ 911). **Fire emergencies on St. Kitts** (☎ 869/465–2333). **Fire emergencies on Nevis** (☎ 869/469–5391).

➤ HOSPITALS: **Joseph N. France General Hospital** (✉ Cayon St., Basseterre, St. Kitts, ☎ 869/465–2551). **Alexandra Hospital** (✉ Government Rd., Charlestown, Nevis, ☎ 869/469–5473).

PHARMACIES

There are no 24-hour pharmacies on St. Kitts or Nevis, but several are open seven days a week, usually until at least 5 PM. Call ahead if it's late in the afternoon, though.

➤ CONTACTS: **City Drug** (✉ Fort St., Basseterre, St. Kitts, ☎ 869/465–2156; ✉ Rex Papillon, Frigate Bay, St. Kitts, ☎ 869/465–1803). **Clax-**

ton Medical Centre Pharmacy (✉ Main St., Charlestown, Nevis, ☎ 869/469–5357). **Evelyn's Drugstore** (✉ Main St., Charlestown, Nevis, ☎ 869/469–5278). **Parris Pharmacy** (✉ Central St., Basseterre, St. Kitts, ☎ 869/465–8569).
➤ POLICE: **Police emergencies** (☎ 911).

ETIQUETTE AND BEHAVIOR
People are friendly but shy; always ask before you take photographs. Also, be sure to wear wraps or shorts over beach attire when you're in public places.

FESTIVALS AND SEASONAL EVENTS
ST. KITTS
Carnival is held for 10 days immediately following Christmas Eve and is the usual riot of color and noise, with steel-band and Calypso Monarch competitions and flamboyant parades of the various troupes. The St. Kitts Music Festival, held the last week of June, celebrates everything from R&B to reggae. Among the top international acts to perform have been Chaka Khan, Earl Klugh, Kool and the Gang, and Peabo Bryson. Much of September is devoted to various Independence Celebrations (contact the Government Information Service for information), ranging from beach picnic to military parades and theatrical events.

NEVIS
As on St. Kitts, Carnival is held for 10 days immediately following Christmas Eve. A special Tourism Week is usually held in mid-February and includes horse races, bartender competitions, and jump-ups. Early August's Culturama and mid-September's Heritage Week include pageants, jump-ups, and celebrations of local culture, from food fairs to craft exhibitions.

HOLIDAYS
Public holidays are: New Year's Day, Ash Wednesday (usually during Feb.), Easter Monday (usually Apr. to mid-May), Labour Day (1st Mon. in May), Whit Monday (usually mid-May to late June), Emancipation Day (1st Mon. in Aug.), Independence Day (Sept. 19), Christmas Day, and Boxing Day (Dec. 26).

LANGUAGE
The official language of St. Kitts and Nevis is English, which is spoken with a strong West Indian lilt.

MAIL AND SHIPPING
Airmail letters to the United States and Canada cost EC90¢ per half ounce; postcards require EC80¢; to the United Kingdom letters cost EC$1.20, postcards EC$1; to Australia and New Zealand, letters cost EC$1.60, postcards EC$1.20. Mail takes at least 7 to 10 days to reach the United States. St. Kitts and Nevis issue separate stamps, but each honors the other's.

MONEY MATTERS
Prices quoted throughout this chapter are in U.S. dollars unless otherwise noted.

ATMS
The Royal Bank of St. Kitts has an ATM that accepts CIRRUS and PLUS cards. There are no ATMs on Nevis.
➤ CONTACTS: **Royal Bank of St. Kitts** (✉ Independence Sq., Basseterre, St. Kitts).

CREDIT CARDS

Most large hotels, restaurants, and shops accept major credit cards, but small inns and shops often do not.

CURRENCY

Legal tender is the Eastern Caribbean (EC) dollar. The rate of exchange was EC$2.70 to US$1. U.S. dollars are accepted practically everywhere, but you'll usually get change in EC currency.

CURRENCY EXCHANGE

Exchanging currency is usually not necessary.

PASSPORTS AND VISAS

U.S. and Canadian citizens need a valid passport or must prove citizenship with a birth certificate (with a raised seal) accompanied by a government-issued photo I.D. British citizens must have a passport. A return or ongoing ticket is mandatory.

SAFETY

Crime is not a big problem on either island, but visitors, especially women, should not jog on long, lonely roads. There have been reported incidents of petty theft and break-ins in Basseterre, St. Kitts, but these remain rare.

SIGHTSEEING TOURS

The taxi driver who picks you up will probably offer to act as your guide to the island. Each driver is knowledgeable and does a three-hour tour of Nevis for $50 and a four-hour tour of St. Kitts for $60. He can also make a lunch reservation at one of the plantation restaurants, and you can incorporate this into your tour.

BOAT

In addition to the usual snorkeling, sunset, and party cruises (ranging in price from $35 to $65), nearly all the companies listed below are beginning to offer humpback whale–watching excursions during the winter migrating season, January–April. On St. Kitts, Blue Water Safaris offers half-day snorkeling trips or beach barbecues on deserted cays, as well as sunset and moonlight cruises on its 65-ft catamaran *Irie Lime*. Leeward Island Charters offers day and overnight charters on three catamarans—the 47-ft *Caona*, and two 70-footers *Eagle* and *Spirit of St. Kitts*. Day sails are from 9:30 to 4:30 and include a barbecue, an open bar, and use of snorkeling equipment. Banana Boat Tours provides snorkeling and sunset cruises from Turtle Beach on its 34-ft inflatable, Coast Guard–certified Scarib boat. Private charters, Nevis–St. Kitts shuttles, and deep sea fishing can be arranged. Turtle Tours offers sea kayaking along the Nevis coast, stopping at an otherwise inaccessible beach underneath a towering cliff for snorkeling and at Pinney's for refreshments and a refreshing view of St. Kitts. Tropical Tours offers moonlight cruises on the 52-ft catamaran *Cileca III*, as well as glass-bottom-boat tours. On Nevis, Sea Nevis Charters offers its 44-ft *Sea Dreamer* for snorkeling and island sunset cruises.

➤ ST. KITTS CONTACTS: **Banana Boat Tours** (☎ 869/465–0645 and 869/469–9086). **Blue Water Safaris** (☎ 869/466–4933). **Leeward Island Charters** (☎ 869/465–7474). **Tropical Tours** (☎ 869/465–4167). **Turtle Tours** (☎ 869/469–8503).

➤ NEVIS CONTACTS: **Sea Nevis Charters** (☎ 869/469–9239).

ORIENTATION

Kantours offers general island tours. Tropical Tours can run you around St. Kitts and take you to the rain forest for $45 per person. Norris Martin's Liamuiga Tours offers several tour options and will customize tours as well. On Nevis, Fitzroy "Teach" Williams is recommended: he's the former president of the taxi association—even older cabbies call him "the Dean." TC, a Yorkshire lass who used to drive a doubledecker bus in England and has been married to a Nevisian for over a decade, offers entertaining explorations via TC's Island Tours. Jan's Travel Agency arranges half- and full-day tours of the island. You can also stop by the Nevis Tourist Office for the historical society's self-guided island tour.

➤ St. Kitts Contacts: **Kantours** (☎ 869/465–2098). **Liamuiga Tours** (☎ 869/465–4128). **Tropical Tours** (☎ 869/465–4167).

➤ Nevis Contacts: **Fitzroy "Teach" Williams** (☎ 869/469–1140). **Jan's Travel Agency** (☎ 869/469–5578). **Nevis Tourist Office** (☎ 869/469–1042). **TC's Island Tours** (☎ 869/469–2911).

SPECIAL-INTEREST

Mountain-biking is growing in popularity on both islands. On St. Kitts, Fun Bikes provides three 3-hour excursions daily on all-terrain quad bikes that hold two people. You'll wind through cane fields, rain forest, abandoned plantation ruins, and local villages. Free taxi transfers from Frigate Bay and Basseterre and a complimentary drink are included in the $65 rate. On Nevis, Windsurfing Nevis offers rentals as well as specially tailored tours on its state-of-the-art Gary Fisher, Trek, and Specialised bikes. The tours encompass lush rain forest, majestic ruins, and spectacular views. Rates vary according to itinerary and ability level. Wheel World is run by master windsurfer Winston Crooke, who has also won several bike competitions. Though the shop primarily rents top-notch equipment, Winston and his associates also provide exhilarating tours, generally for experienced riders. Addy's Nature Tours, Greg's Safari, and Kriss Tours specialize in rain-forest and volcano tours on St. Kitts. David Rollinson of Eco-Tours Nevis and the folks at Top to Bottom organize hiking adventures on Nevis.

➤ St. Kitts Contacts: **Addy's Nature Tours** (☎ 869/465–8069). **Fun Bikes** (☎ 869/466–3202 or 869/662–2088). **Greg's Safari** (☎ 869/465–4121). **Kriss Tours** (☎ 869/465–4042).

➤ Nevis Contacts: **Eco-Tours Nevis** (☎ 869/469–2091). **Top to Bottom** (☎ 869/469–5371). **Wheel World** (☎ 869/469–7137). **Windsurfing Nevis** (☎ 869/469–9682).

TAXES

DEPARTURE TAX

The departure tax is $16.50. There's no departure tax when you depart from St. Kitts for Nevis, or vice versa.

SALES TAX

There is no sales tax on either St. Kitts or Nevis. Hotels collect a 7% government tax (8% on Nevis).

TAXIS

Taxi rates are government regulated and are posted at the airport, the dock, and in the free tourist guide. There are fixed rates to and from all the hotels and to and from major points of interest. In St. Kitts you can call the St. Kitts Taxi Association. In Nevis, taxi service is available at the airport, by the dock in Charlestown, and through arrangements made at your hotel. Sample fares from the dock: EC$40 to Nisbet Plantation, EC$18 to the Four Seasons, and EC$27 to Hermitage.

➤ Contacts: **St. Kitts Taxi Association** (☎ 869/465–8487 or 869/465–4253; 869/465–7818 after hrs). **Nevis taxi service** (☎ 869/469–5621 or 869/469–9790; 869/469–5515 after dark).

TELEPHONES

Phone cards, which you can buy in denominations of $5, $10, and $20, are handy for making local phone calls, calling other islands, and accessing U.S. direct lines.

COUNTRY AND AREA CODES

To call St. Kitts and Nevis from the United States, dial the area code 869, then access code 465, 466, 468, or 469 and the local four-digit number.

INTERNATIONAL CALLS

A warning for both islands: many private lines and hotels charge access rates if you use your AT&T, Sprint, or MCI calling card; there's no regularity, so phoning can be frustrating. Pay phones, usually found in major town squares, take EC coins or phone cards.

LOCAL CALLS

To make a local call, dial the seven-digit number.

TIPPING

Hotels add a 10% service charge to your bill. Restaurants occasionally do the same; ask just in case if it isn't printed on the menu; a 15% tip is appropriate when it isn't included. Taxi drivers typically receive a 10% tip, porters and bellhops $1 per bag; if you feel the service was exemplary, leave $3–$4 per night for the housekeeping staff.

TRANSPORTATION AROUND ST. KITTS AND NEVIS

AIRPLANES

LIAT, Carib Aviation, and Nevis Express are reliable charter operations providing service between St. Kitts and Nevis and to other islands. Nevis Express is currently the only carrier with regularly scheduled flights between St. Kitts and Nevis.

➤ CONTACTS: **Carib Aviation** (☎ 869/469–9295 in St. Kitts; 869/465–3055 in Nevis). **LIAT** (☎ 869/465–8613). **Nevis Express** (☎ 869/469–9755).

BUSES

A privately owned minibus circles St. Kitts. Check with the tourist office about schedules and fares.

VISITOR INFORMATION

➤ BEFORE YOU LEAVE: **St. Kitts & Nevis Tourist Board** (In the U.S. ✉ 414 E. 75th St., New York, NY 10021, ☎ 212/535–1234 or 800/582–6208; 866/556–3847 for Nevis alone, WEB www.stkitts-tourism.com; in Canada ✉ 365 Bay St., Suite 806, Toronto, Ontario M5H 2V1, Canada, ☎ 416/368–6707 or 888/395–4887; in the U.K. ✉ 10 Kensington Ct., London W8 5DL, U.K., ☎ 0171/376–0881).

➤ IN ST. KITTS AND NEVIS: **St. Kitts/Nevis Department of Tourism** (✉ Pelican Mall, Bay Rd., Basseterre, St. Kitts [Box 132], ☎ 869/465–2620 or 869/465–4040). **St. Kitts–Nevis Hotel Association** (✉ Liverpool Row, Basseterre, St. Kitts [Box 438], ☎ 869/465–5304). **Nevis Tourism Authority** (✉ Main St., Charlestown, Nevis, ☎ 869/469–7550 or 869/469–1042).

21 ST. LUCIA

Updated by
Jane E. Zarem

Watching the festivities from the porch of the corner bar, the lady seems disappointed with the Friday-night street party. The pounding beat sounds more disco than Caribbean. "Where's the reggae, the calypso?" she wonders aloud. "It's down there, Miss," offers a wiry young man with a broad smile and smooth moves. "You have to be dancing, near the speakers. Come on." Taking her hand, he leads her to the middle of the street, where the melody is loud and clear and the rhythm, definitely Caribbean. To really enjoy the Gros Islet jump-up, you must first jump in.

Historians feel certain that the intrepid Christopher Columbus never set foot on St. Lucia. That was his loss. Today the eye-popping scenery and pristine beaches that Columbus missed are sprinkled with sprawling resorts, small hideaways, and friendly villages—all of which draw more and more visitors to this lush, tropical island.

Settled between Martinique and St. Vincent, and 100 mi (160 km) due west of Barbados, the 27 mi by 14 mi (43½ km by 22½ km) island of St. Lucia (pronounced *loo*-sha) occupies a prime position in the Caribbean, its striking natural beauty easily earning it the moniker of "the Helen of the West Indies." The capital city of Castries and nearby villages in the north are home to 40% of the population and the destination of most vacationers, who stay at posh resorts and play on honey-colored beaches. The south, on the other hand, is dominated by thick jungle and vast banana plantations that cover the hills. A torturously winding road follows the coastline, cutting through mountains, rain forest, and fertile valleys. On the southwest coast, Petit Piton and Gros Piton, the island's unusual twin peaks, rise from the sea to more than 2,600 ft (795 m) and are familiar navigational landmarks for sailors and aviators alike. Divers are attracted to the reefs, found just offshore north of Soufrière, the picturesque French colonial capital of St. Lucia. Most of the natural tourist attractions are, in fact, in this area. "If you haven't been to Soufrière," the local people will tell you, "you haven't been to St. Lucia."

The Arawaks, St. Lucia's first inhabitants, paddled up from South America sometime before AD 200. The aggressive Caribs followed, conquering the Arawaks around AD 800. The Caribs, who named the island Hewanorra (Land Where the Iguana Is Found), still lived on the island when Europeans attempted to establish a settlement. François Le Clerc, a pirate nicknamed Jambe de Bois (Wooden Leg), was actually the first

European settler. In the late 16th century he holed up on Pigeon Island, just off St. Lucia's northernmost point, and attacked passing ships. In 1605, 67 English settlers bound for Guiana were blown off course and landed at the island's southern tip, near Vieux Fort. Within a few weeks, the Caribs had killed all but 19, who escaped in a canoe. More English settlers arrived 30 years later and were met with a similar lack of hospitality. The French arrived in 1651 after the French West India Company purchased the island.

For the next 150 years, battles between the French and the English for possession of the island occurred, with a dizzying 14 changes in power before the British took possession in 1814. The Europeans established sugar plantations, using slaves from West Africa to work the fields. By 1838, when the slaves were emancipated, more than 90% of the population was of African descent—also the approximate proportion of today's 170,000 St. Lucians. Indentured East Indian laborers were brought over in 1882 to help bail out the sugar industry, which suffered when slavery was abolished and all but died in the 1960s, when bananas became the major crop. On February 22, 1979, St. Lucia became an independent state within the British Commonwealth of Nations, with a resident governor-general appointed by the queen. Still, there are many relics of French occupation, notably the island patois (spoken in addition to English), the cuisine, the place names, and surnames.

Lodging

Virtually all St. Lucia's lodgings are along the calm Caribbean coast, concentrated between Castries and Cap Estate in the north, at Marigot Bay a few miles south of Castries, and around Soufrière on the southwest coast. Low-rise resorts and small inns are tucked into lush surroundings on secluded coves, along unspoiled beaches, or in forested hillsides.

A group of small locally owned and operated hotels and guest houses market themselves as The Inns of St. Lucia. Ranging in size from 3 to 71 rooms, with rates starting at just $20 per room at some guest houses, these small inns are a delightful alternative. For more information contact the **St. Lucia Tourist Board** (✉ Pointe Seraphine, Castries, ☎ 758/452–4094, FAX 758/453–1121, WEB www.st.lucia.org). For villa rentals contact **Tropical Villas** (✉ Box 189, Castries, ☎ 758/452–8240, FAX 758/450–8089, WEB www.tropicalvillas.net).

CATEGORY	COST EP/CP*	COST A.I.**
$$$$	over $350	over $375
$$$	$250–$350	$275–$375
$$	$150–$250	$175–$275
$	under $150	under $175

*EP/CP prices are per night for a standard double room in high season, excluding taxes, service charges, and meal plans**A.I. (all-inclusive) prices are per person, per night based on double-occupancy during high season, excluding taxes and service charges*

Castries and the North

$$$$ 🏨 **Papillon St. Lucia.** The all-inclusive Papillon and the Rex St. Lucian, its sister hotel next door, are both on lovely Reduit Beach. Rooms are furnished with one king-size or two twin beds, rattan furniture, tile floors, and tropical-print fabrics in blue and peach. Beachfront rooms have full baths, sitting areas, minibars, and ocean views; rooms with garden or ocean view have a shower only and queen or double beds. The pool is shaped like a butterfly (papillon). Meals are served at The Monarch, the main restaurant, or The Clipper Bar, the informal beach-

side snack bar. Evening entertainment is presented at Tropigala lounge. ✉ *Reduit Beach, Rodney Bay (Box 512, Castries),* ☎ *758/452–0984,* FAX *758/452–9332,* WEB *www.rexcaribbean.com. 140 rooms. Restaurant, bar, snack bar, in-room safes, golf privileges, 2 tennis courts, pool, beach, snorkeling, windsurfing, boating, waterskiing, shuffleboard, shop, baby-sitting, laundry service. AE, DC, MC, V. All-inclusive.*

\$\$\$\$ 🏨 **Royal St. Lucian.** This classy resort, facing Reduit Beach, caters to your every whim. The stunning reception area has a vaulted atrium, marble walls, a fountain, and a sweeping grand staircase. The free-form pool has Japanese-style bridges, a waterfall, and a swim-up bar. Each guest room has an ocean view. Sumptuous suites have sitting areas, luxurious bathrooms, large patios or balconies, soothing pastel color schemes, and background music systems. Massages, hydrotherapy, and other treatments can be arranged at the Royal Spa. Dine at the elegant L'Epicure or two more casual restaurants. Tennis and water-sports facilities are shared with the adjacent Rex St. Lucian. ✉ *Reduit Beach, Rodney Bay (Box 977, Castries),* ☎ *758/452–9999,* FAX *758/452–9639,* WEB *www.rexcaribbean.com. 96 suites. 3 restaurants, 2 bars, room service, in-room safes, minibars, golf privileges, 2 tennis courts, pool, health club, massage, spa, beach, dive shop, snorkeling, waterskiing, windsurfing, boating, fishing, shops, baby-sitting, children's programs (ages 4–12), laundry service, business services, meeting rooms. AE, DC, MC, V. EP, MAP.*

\$\$\$–\$\$\$\$ 🏨 **The Body Holiday at LeSPORT.** Even before arrival, guests can design
★ their own "body holiday"—from robe size to tee time. Indulge in aromatherapy, massages, wraps, yoga, personal trainer services, and more at the splendid Oasis. Otherwise, enjoy the beach, scuba diving, golf, and other sports—with instruction provided, if needed. Rooms have marble floors and king-size four-poster or twin beds. The food is excellent at Cariblue (the main dining room), the casual buffet restaurant, the deli, or top-of-the-line Tao. A separate plantation house, called "Manderley," is available by the week, with or without the resort's all-inclusive amenities. ✉ *Cariblue Beach, Cap Estate (Box 437, Castries),* ☎ *758/450–8551,* FAX *758/450–0368,* WEB *www.thebodyholiday.com. 145 rooms, 9 suites, 1 plantation house. 4 restaurants, 2 bars, refrigerators, golf privileges, tennis court, 3 pools, aerobics, health club, massage, sauna, spa, beach, dive shop, snorkeling, waterskiing, archery, hiking, Ping-Pong, volleyball, piano bar, shops, Internet, airport shuttle, no kids under 16. AE, DC, MC, V. All-inclusive.*

\$\$\$–\$\$\$\$ 🏨 **East Winds Inn.** On a private beach 10 minutes north of Castries, 15 gingerbread-style bungalows, each with two guest rooms, are scattered around 8 acres of gardens. Rooms have king-size beds and patios or terraces; deluxe rooms have TVs, VCRs, and indoor-outdoor showers. Mingle at the clubhouse, in the pool with its swim-up bar, on the sundeck, and on the beach—where kayaks, snorkeling gear, and other water-sports equipment are provided. The international and creole creations of a French chef are served in the thatched-roof restaurant, picnic hampers are available for outings, or dine around in the evening at participating restaurants. ✉ *Labrelotte Bay, Gros Islet (Box 1477, Castries),* ☎ *758/452–8212,* FAX *758/452–9941,* WEB *www.eastwinds.com. 30 rooms. Restaurant, 2 bars, fans, in-room safes, refrigerators, pool, beach, snorkeling, boating, croquet, lawn bowling, shuffleboard, shop, baby-sitting, dry cleaning, laundry service. AE, MC, V. All-inclusive.*

\$\$\$–\$\$\$\$ 🏨 **Rex St. Lucian.** A broad lobby leads to 10 acres of gardens, a pool, and beautiful Reduit Beach. Rooms, each with a patio or balcony, are decorated in rattan and tropical prints. Deluxe rooms have one king-size bed or two twin beds, full baths, minibars, sitting areas, and ocean views. Garden-view rooms are similar but smaller. Poolside rooms have

Lodging

Dining

St. Lucia

KEY

🚢 Cruise Ship Terminal
🔲 Dive Sites
❶ Exploring Sights
⛴ Ferry
① Hotels and Restaurants
🌴 Rain Forest

showers only and no TV. Water sports—including swimming, scuba diving, boating, and fishing—are a major attraction. Book spa treatments at sister resort, the Royal St. Lucian. Enjoy dining at the Oriental restaurant or stroll to any of several area restaurants and nightspots. ⊠ *Reduit Beach, Rodney Bay (Box 512, Castries),* ☎ *758/452–8351, 800/255–5859, or 800/223–9868,* FAX *758/452–8331,* WEB *www.rexcaribbean. com. 120 rooms. 2 restaurants, bar, minibars, no TV in some rooms, golf privileges, 2 tennis courts, pool, beach, dive shop, snorkeling, windsurfing, boating, waterskiing, shops, baby-sitting, children's programs (ages 4–12), laundry service, business services, meeting rooms. AE, DC, MC, V. EP, MAP.*

$$$–$$$$ 🖫 **Sandals Halcyon St. Lucia.** This beachfront resort (for male-female couples only) is 10 minutes north of Castries. Rooms are surrounded by gardens and have king-size mahogany four-poster beds with colorful spreads. The Halcyon is a bit more low-key than its sister resort, Sandals St. Lucia Golf Resort & Spa. You can enjoy water sports, working out in the gym, nightly entertainment, and more. A shuttle runs hourly between the two Sandals resorts, so you can "stay at one, play at two." Three restaurants serve sumptuous buffets, with Italian, Caribbean, and international cuisine at dinner. Seaside weddings are frequent. ⊠ *Choc Bay (Box GM 910, Castries),* ☎ *758/453–0222 or 800/223–6510,* FAX *758/451–8435,* WEB *www.sandals.com. 170 rooms. 3 restaurants, snack bar, 2 bars, golf privileges, 2 tennis courts, 3 pools, gym, hair salon, beach, snorkeling, windsurfing, boating, waterskiing, basketball, billiards, Ping-Pong, shuffleboard, volleyball, piano bar, nightclub, complimentary weddings, airport shuttle, no kids. AE, DC, MC, V. All-inclusive.*

$$$–$$$$ 🖫 **Sandals St. Lucia Golf Resort & Spa.** This expansive resort (for male-female couples only) has one of St. Lucia's two golf courses. Guest rooms are lavishly decorated with rich mahogany furniture, king-size four-poster beds, and colorful fabrics. Many have private plunge pools. The large central pool, with its waterfall and bridges, and the resort's long crescent beach are focal points for socializing and water sports. Massages (single or duet), therapies, scrubs, and wraps are available at the full-service spa (for an additional charge). Six restaurants serve Asian, Continental, French, Mediterranean, Southwestern, or Caribbean cuisine. A free shuttle takes you to sister resort Sandals Halcyon St. Lucia. ⊠ *La Toc Rd., Castries (Box 399),* ☎ *758/452–3081,* FAX *758/453–7089,* WEB *www.sandals.com. 212 rooms, 116 suites. 6 restaurants, 9 bars, room service, in-room safes, 9-hole golf course, 5 tennis courts, 3 pools, gym, hair salon, hot tub, massage, sauna, spa, beach, dive shop, snorkeling, windsurfing, boating, waterskiing, basketball, billiards, boccie, croquet, horseshoes, Ping-Pong, shuffleboard, volleyball, piano bar, shops, nightclub, recreation room, laundry service, complimentary weddings, concierge floor, Internet, business services, meeting rooms, airport shuttle, no kids. AE, DC, MC, V. All-inclusive.*

$$–$$$$ 🖫 **Club St. Lucia by Splash.** This sprawling, all-inclusive family resort has a village concept. Rooms and suites are in color-coordinated buildings along the hillside; each village has its own concierge, or "mayor." Enjoy free use of the adjacent St. Lucia Racquet Club and golf privileges at the Cap Estate course. Children's activities are grouped by age, starting at 6 months. The "Jump Club" for teenagers has a roller-blade track and an e-mail system for keeping in touch with parents. Live entertainment is scheduled nightly. In addition to on-site dining and all-day snacks at pool-side food carts, resort guests receive a discount at the Great House restaurant. ⊠ *Cap Estate (Box 915, Gros Islet),* ☎ *758/450–0551,* FAX *758/450–0281,* WEB *www.splashresorts.com. 297 rooms, 72 suites. 5 restaurants, 5 bars, golf privileges, 9 tennis courts, 5 pools, health club, hair salon, hot tub, spa, beach, snorkeling, wind-*

surfing, boating, waterskiing, nightclub, shops, baby-sitting, children's programs (ages 6 mo.–12 yrs), laundry service, concierge, travel services, car rental. AE, DC, MC, V. All-inclusive.

$$–$$$$ 🏨 **Windjammer Landing Villa Beach Resort.** White stucco villas crowned with tile roofs climb the sun-kissed hillside on one of St. Lucia's prettiest bays. The reception area opens to shops, restaurants, and two pools. Huge, stylishly decorated villas have tile floors and wicker furniture loaded with richly colored pillows. Two- and three-bedroom villas have plunge pools. Eat in the restaurants, make your own meals, or have dinner prepared and served in your villa. Shuttles whoosh you between the villas and activity areas—including two hillside pools connected by a waterfall. Perfect for families or for a romantic getaway, there's lots to do yet plenty of privacy. ✉ *Labrelotte Bay (Box 1504, Castries),* ☎ *758/452–0913,* FAX *758/452–9454,* WEB *www.windjammer-landing. com. 131 villas. 3 restaurants, 3 bars, grocery, room service, fans, in-room safes, kitchens, 2 tennis courts, 2 pools, gym, massage, beach, dive shop, snorkeling, windsurfing, boating, waterskiing, shops, children's programs (ages 4–12), laundry service, concierge, car rental. AE, MC, V. EP, MAP.*

$$–$$$ 🏨 **Rendezvous.** This all-inclusive resort (for male-female couples only) sprawls along Malabar Beach amid 7 acres of gardens opposite the George F. L. Charles Airport runway. The distraction of prop aircraft taking off at the nearby airport is made up for by the luxurious accommodations. Rooms and suites have marble floors, king-size four-poster beds, large marble baths, and balconies or terraces (some with hammocks) facing the sea. Lounge lazily on the beach or actively participate in a host of land and water sports—your choice. Meals are served buffet style at the beachfront terrace restaurant. There's also an air-conditioned dining room, the Trysting Place. ✉ *Malabar Beach, Vigie (Box 190, Castries),* ☎ *758/452–4211,* FAX *758/452–7419,* WEB *www. rendezvous.com.lc. 81 rooms, 11 suites, 8 cottages. 2 restaurants, 2 bars, fans, no room TVs, 2 tennis courts, 2 pools, aerobics, gym, hot tub, massage, sauna, beach, dive shop, boating, waterskiing, bicycles, archery, volleyball, piano bar, shops, complimentary weddings, concierge, airport shuttle, no kids. AE, MC, V. All-inclusive.*

$$–$$$ 🏨 **Wyndham Morgan Bay Resort.** Eight three-story buildings fan out from a central activity area at this all-inclusive resort on 22 landscaped acres along Choc Bay. Rooms, attractively decorated in wicker and tropical pastel florals, have comfortable king-size beds and marble bathrooms. Each room has a veranda or balcony with either a garden or partial sea view. Two open-air restaurants offer informal buffet meals or à la carte French Caribbean cuisine. There's plenty to do—whether you look forward to the early morning aerobics and daily water sports activities or prefer to relax under a palm tree and look forward to the nightly entertainment. ✉ *Choc Bay, Gros Islet (Box 2167, Castries),* ☎ *758/450–2511,* FAX *758/450–1050,* WEB *www.wyndham.com. 238 rooms. 2 restaurants, 2 bars, in-room safes, golf privileges, 4 tennis courts, pool, aerobics, gym, hot tub, sauna, steam room, beach, snorkeling, windsurfing, boating, waterskiing, archery, Ping-Pong, volleyball, billiards, recreation room, shops, children's programs (ages 5–12), dry cleaning, laundry service, concierge, meeting rooms, airport shuttle, car rental. AE, D, MC, V. All-inclusive.*

$–$$ 🏨 **Marigot Beach Club Hotel & Dive Resort.** This quiet spot is 9 mi (14½ km) south of Castries in the yachting center of Marigot Bay. The Firefly Suites climb the steep hillside that forms a backdrop for the resort, and a tram transports you up and down. Studios and one-bedroom suites have kitchenettes, pickled-wood furniture, and patios that overlook the sea. The resort has an excellent water-sports center, and the beach, shaded by coconut palms, is reminiscent of the South Seas. Doolittle's, the open-air waterfront bar and restaurant, offers Caribbean and Continental fare. At Big Bamboo, choose among 50 different burgers. ⊠ *Marigot Bay (Box 101, Castries)*, ☎ *758/451–4974*, FAX *758/451–4973*, WEB *www.marigotdiveresort.com. 9 studios, 23 suites. 2 restaurants, bar, kitchenettes, pool, gym, massage, beach, dive shop, snorkeling, windsurfing, boating, shops. MC, V. EP, MAP.*

$ 🏨 **Auberge Seraphine.** This small, elegant inn, overlooking Vigie Cove, is minutes from George F. L. Charles Airport, Pointe Seraphine, and downtown Castries. Popular among business travelers, it's also a good choice for vacationers who don't require a beachfront location nor the breadth of activities found at a resort. Accommodations are spacious, cheerful, and bright. Most have a view of the cove and nearby marina. A broad tiled sundeck, the center of activity, surrounds a small pool. A shuttle service transports you to and from a nearby beach. The popular restaurant offers fine Caribbean, French, and Continental cuisine and a well-stocked wine cellar. ⊠ *Vigie Cove (Box 390, Castries)*, ☎ *758/453–2073*, FAX *758/451–7001*, WEB *www.sluonestop. com/auberge. 22 rooms. Restaurant, bar, pool, shop, meeting room. AE, MC, V. EP, MAP.*

$ 🏨 **Bay Gardens.** This boutique inn at Rodney Bay—near beautiful Reduit Beach, several popular restaurants, and shops at Rodney Bay Marina—is a favorite of vacationers and regional business travelers alike. Modern and colorful, the lime-green building is studded with flower gardens. Rooms surround a courtyard with a serpentine pool and a Jacuzzi. All are furnished with white wicker furniture and king or twin beds with colorful print spreads in tropical colors. Executive suites are larger, with double or king-size beds, sitting areas, and kitchenettes. Spices restaurant offers a varied menu, along with a weekly barbecue, Caribbean buffet, and Sunday brunch. ⊠ *Rodney Bay (Box 1892, Castries)*, ☎ *758/452–8060*, FAX *758/452–8059*, WEB *www.baygardenshotel. com. 59 rooms, 12 suites. Restaurant, 2 bars, fans, some in-room data ports, in-room safes, some kitchenettes, minibars, refrigerators, 2 pools, hot tub, shops, recreation room, library, business services, meeting rooms. AE, MC, V. EP, MAP.*

Soufrière

$$$$ 🏨 **Anse Chastanet Beach Hotel.** Spectacular hillside rooms blend into
★   the mountainside, with entire walls open to stunning vistas. Each deluxe room has a balcony, tile floor with straw mats, madras cotton fabrics, handmade wooden furniture, and impressive artwork. Other rooms are octagonal gazebos or beachfront cottages, all with similar decor but less drama. This place is magical, as long as you're fit to climb the 100 steps from the beach to the Pitons Restaurant and Bar, followed by another steep climb to most rooms. Diving is a premier draw here. So is lunch at the picturesque Trou au Diable beach restaurant. ⊠ *Anse Chastanet (Box 7000, Soufrière)*, ☎ *758/459–7000*, FAX *758/459–7700*, WEB *www.ansechastanet.com. 49 rooms. 2 restaurants, 2 bars, no air-conditioning, no room phones, fans, in-room safes, refrigerators, no room TVs, tennis court, massage, spa, beach, dive shop, snorkeling, windsurfing, boating, mountain bikes, hiking, shops, airport shuttle, car rental. AE, DC, MC, V. EP, MAP.*

$$$$ 🏨 **Jalousie Hilton Resort & Spa.** Built on the remains of an 18th-century
★   sugar plantation 2 mi (3 km) south of Soufrière, the hillside villas are all but hidden by lush foliage. Sugar Mill Rooms are large, luxurious, and close to the beach. Villas have elegant furnishings, king-size beds, and huge bathrooms; villa suites also have sitting rooms and plunge pools. Shuttle service transports you around the grounds, a blessing given the steep hillside. Meals range from fine dining to beach buffet. The spa offers outdoor massage, aromatherapy, and beauty

treatments; there are also aerobics, weight-training sessions, and exercise classes. The views here are perhaps the most dramatic in all of St. Lucia. ✉ *Anse des Pitons, (Box 251, Soufrière),* ☎ *758/459–7666,* FAX *758/459–7667,* WEB *www.jalousie-hilton.com. 12 rooms, 65 villas, 35 villa suites. 4 restaurants, 4 bars, room service, fans, in-room data ports, in-room safes, minibars, in-room VCRs, 3-hole golf course, putting green, 4 tennis courts, pool, aerobics, health club, hair salon, massage, sauna, spa, beach, dive shop, dock, snorkeling, windsurfing, boating, marina, waterskiing, fishing, basketball, hiking, racquetball, squash, billiards, nightclub, shops, baby-sitting, children's programs (ages 5–17), business services, meeting rooms, airport shuttle, car rental, helipad, no-smoking rooms. AE, D, DC, MC, V. EP, FAP, MAP.*

$$$–$$$$ 🏨 **Ladera Resort.** Nestled high in the mountains, Ladera is one of the
★ most sophisticated small inns in the Caribbean. Each suite or villa is furnished with French colonial antiques and local crafts and has a dazzling view. Villas have private pools fed by waterfalls; eight suites have plunge pools. Dasheene is one of St. Lucia's best restaurants—with a spectacular view of the Pitons. The inn provides shuttle service to Soufrière and nearby beaches and will arrange diving and other activities. Though children 8–15 stay free when sharing a room with an adult, the resort is unsuitable for really young children. ✉ *2 mi (3 km) south of Soufrière (Box 225, Soufrière),* ☎ *758/459–7323, 800/223–9868, or 800/738–4752,* FAX *758/459–5156,* WEB *www.ladera-stlucia.com. 18 suites, 6 villas. Restaurant, 2 bars, no air-conditioning, no room TVs, pool, library, shops, airport shuttle. AE, MC, V. BP, MAP.*

$–$$$ 🏨 **Hummingbird Beach Resort.** This delightful little inn is on the bay of Soufrière. Rooms are in small seaside cabins; most have magnificent views of the Pitons. Rooms are simple—a primitive motif emphasized by African wood sculptures. Four rooms have a mahogany four-poster bed hung with sheer mosquito netting. Most rooms have modern baths; two rooms and a suite share a bath. The two-bedroom country cottage—with a sitting room, kitchenette, and spectacular Piton view—is suitable for a family or two couples vacationing together. The Hummingbird Restaurant is a favorite lunch stop for locals and visitors touring Soufrière. ✉ *Anse Chastanet Rd., Soufrière (Box 280),* ☎ *758/459–7232 or 800/223–9815,* FAX *758/459–7033,* WEB *www.best-caribbean. com/hummingbird. 9 rooms, 1 suite, 1 cottage (some with shared bath). Restaurant, bar, no air-conditioning in some rooms, no room TVs, pool, beach, shops. D, MC, V. EP, MAP.*

$ 🏨 **Still Plantation & Beach Resort.** The simple, inexpensive studios and one- or two-bedroom apartments with sitting rooms and kitchenettes at Still Plantation are a five-minute walk from the waterfront. There are a swimming pool, a boutique, and the Still restaurant, well known for its Caribbean cuisine. The separate Still Beach Resort is also simple and inexpensive, with three small one-bedroom apartments and two studios; all share a veranda with a partial sea view. If you prefer hiking and nature walks, choose the Plantation; if you prefer sand and sea, choose the Beach Resort. A stay at one allows you to use the facilities of the other. ✉ *Lewis St. and Anse Chastanet Rd., Soufrière (Box 246),* ☎ *758/459–7224 or 800/223–9815,* FAX *758/459–7301,* WEB *www.thestillresort.com. 13 apartments, 6 studios. 2 restaurants, 2 bars, no air-conditioning in some rooms, some kitchenettes, no room TVs, pool, beach, shops, laundry service. MC, V. EP.*

Dining

Mangoes, plantains, breadfruit, avocados, limes, pumpkins, cucumbers, papaya, yams, christophenes (a squash-like vegetable), and coconuts are among the fresh local produce that grace St. Lucian menus. The

French influence is strong, and most chefs cook with a creole flair. Resort buffets and restaurant fare run the gamut, from steaks and chops to pasta and pizza, and everything in between. Every menu lists fresh fish along with the ever-popular lobster. Caribbean standards include callaloo, stuffed crab back, pepper-pot stew, curried chicken or goat, and *lambi* (conch). The national dish of salt fish and green fig—a stew of dried, salted codfish, and boiled green banana—is, let's say, an acquired taste. Soups and stews are traditionally prepared in a coal pot, a rustic clay casserole on a matching clay stand that holds the hot coals. Chicken and pork dishes and barbecues are also popular here. As they do throughout the Caribbean, local vendors who set up barbecues along the roadside, at street fairs, and at Friday night "jump ups," do a land-office business selling grilled chicken legs, bakes (biscuits), and beer—all for about $3. Most other meats are imported—beef from Argentina and Iowa, lamb from New Zealand. Piton is the local brew, and Bounty is the local rum.

With so many all-inclusive resorts, guests take most meals at hotel restaurants—which are generally quite good and, in some cases, exceptional. It's fun when vacationing, however, to try some of the local restaurants, as well—for lunch when sightseeing or for a special night out.

What to Wear
Dress on St. Lucia is casual but conservative. Shorts are usually fine during the day, but bathing suits and immodest clothing are frowned on anywhere but at the beach. In the evening the mood is casually elegant, but even the fanciest places generally expect only a collared shirt and long pants for men and a sundress or slacks for women.

CATEGORY	COST*
$$$$	over $30
$$$	$20–$30
$$	$10–$20
$	under $10

*per person for a main course at dinner

Castries and the North
CARIBBEAN
$ ✕ **J. J.'s Paradise.** Not only are the prices right, but the local fare is among the best on the island. Superbly grilled fish with fresh vegetables gets top honors. The welcome is friendly, and the atmosphere is casual. Wednesday is Seafood Night, when owner-chef J. J. prepares an enormous selection of local fish and shellfish. On Friday night the music blares, and the locals come to lime (hang out), eat barbecue, and dance the night away. ✉ *Marigot Bay Rd., Marigot,* ☎ *758/451–4076. No credit cards.*

CREOLE
$$ ✕ **The French Restaurant.** French West Indian cuisine—direct from St. Lucia's neighbor island, Martinique—is the specialty at this Rodney Bay establishment. Choices include wonderful pumpkin or fish soup to start; curried goat, conch, fresh lobster that you select from the tank; and exotic seafood such as octopus and shark. Everything is served with a hot, spicy sauce, but a delicious French pastry or homemade ice cream will quell the fire on your tongue. A creole buffet is the special at lunch. ✉ *Rodney Bay,* ☎ *758/450–0022. D, MC, V. Closed Tues.*

ECLECTIC
$$ ✕ **Green Parrot.** Atop the Morne, acclaimed Chef Harry Edwards prepares a menu of West Indian, creole, and international dishes. There's lively entertainment—a floor show with a belly dancer on Wednesday night and limbo dancing on Saturday—but the best rea-

sons to dine here are the seafood specialties and the romantic view of the twinkling lights in Castries and the harbor. On Monday night, if a lady wears a flower in her hair and is accompanied by a "well-dressed" gentleman, she receives a free dinner. ✉ *Morne Fortune, south of Castries,* ☎ *758/452–3399. Reservations essential. Jacket required. AE, MC, V.*

$–$$ ✕ **The Lime.** A casual bistro with lime-green gingham curtains, straw hats decorating the ceiling, and hanging plants, the Lime's eclectic menu includes char-grilled steaks and fresh-caught fish, along with spicy jerk chicken or pork. The meals are well prepared, the portions are plentiful, and the prices are reasonable, which is perhaps why you often see St. Lucians and visitors alike "liming" at this popular all-day (and most of the night) restaurant. The Late Lime, a club where the crowd gathers as night turns to morning, is next door. ✉ *Rodney Bay,* ☎ *758/452–0761. MC, V.*

FRENCH

$$–$$$ ✕ **Great House.** Elegant, gracious, and romantic all describe the Great
★ House. Reconstructed on the foundation of the original Cap Estate plantation house, the grandeur of those early days has been revived, as well. The waitstaff wear traditional St. Lucian costumes. The chef adds a piquant creole touch to traditional French cuisine. The menu, which changes nightly, might include pumpkin-and-potato soup, local crab back with lime vinaigrette, sautéed Antillean shrimp in a creole sauce, and broiled sirloin with thyme butter and sweet-potato chips. Cocktails at the open-air bar are especially enjoyable at sunset. The Derek Walcott Theatre is next door. ✉ *Cap Estate,* ☎ *758/450–0450 or 758/450–0211. Reservations essential. AE, DC, MC, V. No lunch.*

$$ ✕ **The Coal Pot.** Popular for nearly 40 years, this tiny waterfront
★ restaurant (only 10 tables) is managed by Michelle Elliott, daughter of the original owner, and her French husband, Chef Xavier. For a light lunch opt for Greek or shrimp salad, or broiled fresh fish with creole sauce. Dinner might start with divine pumpkin soup, followed by fresh seafood accompanied by one (or more) of the chef's fabulous sauces—ginger, coconut curry, lemon-garlic butter, or wild mushroom. Hearty eaters may prefer duck, lamb, beef, or chicken laced with peppercorns, red wine and onion, or Roquefort cheese sauce. ✉ *Vigie Marina, Castries,* ☎ *758/452–5566. Reservations essential. AE, D, MC, V. Closed Sun. No lunch Sat.*

ITALIAN

$–$$ ✕ **Capone's.** The French chef at this two-in-one restaurant lends a Gallic twist and Caribbean spice to some of your favorite Italian dishes. Paper-thin carpaccio is drizzled with olive oil and lime, before being treated to shavings of Parmesan cheese. Polenta and local vegetables accompany delicate slices of calves liver that have been gently sautéed with onions. And fresh Caribbean snapper is blessed with ginger and rum en route to your plate. The extensive menu includes pasta dishes, seafood, and Black Angus beef. At the adjacent La Piazza, diners enjoy casual meals of burgers, sandwiches, and pizza from noon to midnight. ✉ *Rodney Bay, across from St. Lucian hotel,* ☎ *758/452–0284. AE, MC, V. Closed Mon.*

$ ✕ **Key Largo.** Gourmet pizzas baked in a wood-fired oven and a long list of pasta dishes are the specialties at this casual eatery near Rodney Bay's many hotels. You're welcome to stop in for an espresso or cappuccino, but the popular Pizza Key Largo—topped with shrimp, artichokes, and what seems like a few pounds of mozzarella—is tough to pass up. Kids love Key Largo, too. ✉ *Rodney Heights,* ☎ *758/452–0282. MC, V.*

PAN-ASIAN

$$$ ✕ **Tao.** For exquisite dining, this small restaurant at The Body Holi-
★   day at LeSPORT resort welcomes nonguests. Perched on a second-floor
balcony at the edge of Cariblue Beach, you're guaranteed a pleasant
breeze and a starry sky while you enjoy fusion cuisine—a marriage of
Asian tastes (borrowed from China, Japan, Indonesia, the Philippines)
with a Caribbean touch. Tender slices of pork loin satay accompanied
by *nasi goreng* rice, scallops steamed in rice paper, hibachi-grilled strip
steak—the choices are mouth-watering. Fine wines accompany the
meal, desserts are extravagant, and service is superb. Seating is lim-
ited, and hotel guests are given priority. ⊠ *Cap Estate,* ☎ *758/450–
8551. Reservations essential. AE, DC, MC, V. No lunch.*

Soufrière

CARIBBEAN

$–$$ ✕ **The Hummingbird.** The chef at this cheerful restaurant-bar in the
Hummingbird Beach Resort specializes in French creole cuisine, start-
ing with fresh seafood or chicken seasoned with local herbs and accompanied by a medley of vegetables just picked from the
Hummingbird's garden. Sandwiches and salads are also available. If
you stop for lunch, be sure to visit the batik studio and art gallery of
proprietor Joan Alexander and her son, adjacent to the dining room.
⊠ *Hummingbird Beach Resort, Anse Chastanet Rd., Soufrière,* ☎ *758/
459–7232. AE, D, MC, V.*

$–$$ ✕ **The Still.** If you're visiting Diamond Waterfall, this is a good lunch
spot. The two dining rooms of the Still Plantation & Beach Resort seat
up to 400 people, so it's a popular stop for tour groups and cruise passengers. The emphasis is on creole cuisine using local vegetables—
christophenes, breadfruits, yams, callaloo—and seafood, but there are
also pork and beef dishes. All fruits and vegetables used in the restaurant are organically grown on the estate. ⊠ *Still Plantation & Beach
Resort, Bay St., Soufrière,* ☎ *758/459–7232. MC, V.*

$ ✕ **Trou au Diable at Anse Chastanet.** The beach restaurant and bar at
the Anse Chastanet Beach Hotel, just 1 mi north of Soufrière, is the
perfect place to take a lunch break after diving, boating, touring, or
sunbathing. The West Indian cuisine is delicious; many specialties are
grilled right before your eyes. Outstanding *rotis* (turnovers filled with
curried meat and/or vegetables) are served with homemade mango chutney you could eat by the jar. Try the pepperpot—pork, beef, or lamb
stewed for hours with local veggies and spices—or have a good old
tuna melt if you're homesick. Stick around for the evening beach barbecue and creole buffet each Tuesday and Friday. ⊠ *Anse Chastanet
Beach Hotel, Anse Chastanet,* ☎ *758/459–7000. AE, DC, MC, V.*

CONTEMPORARY

$$–$$$ ✕ **Dasheene Restaurant and Bar.** The terrace restaurant at Ladera Re-
★   sort has breathtaking close-up views of the Pitons and the sea between
them. (The sunsets are breathtaking!) Casual by day and magical at
night, the creative menu is best described as Nouvelle Caribbean. Appetizers may include smoked kingfish crepes and spicy seafood gazpacho. Typical entrées are shrimps Dasheene, pan-fried with peppers
and herbs, or poulet supreme Ladera, stuffed with seafood and served
on a green banana risotto. Light dishes, salads, and sandwiches are served
at lunchtime. ⊠ *Ladera Resort, 2 mi (3 km) south of Soufrière,* ☎ *758/
459–7323. AE, DC, MC, V.*

Beaches

Beaches are all public, but many of those north of Castries are flanked
by hotels. A few secluded stretches of beach on the west coast south

of Marigot Bay are accessible only by boat and are a popular stop on catamaran or powerboat sightseeing trips. Don't swim along the windward (east) coast, as the Atlantic Ocean is too rough—but the views are spectacular.

Anse Chastanet. In front of the resort of the same name, just north of Soufrière this palm-studded dark-sand beach has a backdrop of green hills, brightly painted fishing skiffs bobbing at anchor, and the island's best reefs for snorkeling and diving. The resort's wooden gazebos are nestled among the palms; its dive shop, restaurant, and bar are on the beach and open to the public.

Anse Cochon. This remote black-sand beach 3 mi (5 km) south of Marigot Bay is accessible only by boat. The waters and adjacent reef are superb for swimming, diving, and snorkeling, but there are no facilities.

Anse des Pitons. South of Soufrière, between the Pitons on Jalousie Bay, is a crescent of white sand that was imported by Jalousie Hilton Resort and spread over the natural black sand. Accessible from the resort or by boat, the beach offers good snorkeling, diving, and a magnificent location.

Anse de Sables. At Vieux Fort, on the southeastern tip of St. Lucia, is a long stretch of white sand with crystal-clear waters protected by reefs.

Choc Beach. In the north, just below Rodney Bay, this beach is easily accessible from the road.

Marigot Beach. Calm waters rippled only by passing yachts lap the finger of sand studded with palm trees at Marigot Bay; dive trips can be arranged nearby, and refreshments are available at adjacent restaurants.

Pigeon Point. At this small beach within Pigeon Island National Historic Park, a restaurant serves snacks and drinks, but this is also a perfect spot for picnicking.

Reduit Beach. This long stretch of golden sand is next to Rodney Bay. The Rex St. Lucian Hotel, which faces the beach, has a water-sports center. Many feel that Reduit (pronounced red-*wee*) is the island's finest beach.

Vigie Beach. This 2-mi (3-km) stretch of white sand runs parallel to the George F. L. Charles Airport runway, in Castries, and continues on to become Malabar Beach, the beachfront for the Rendezvous resort.

Outdoor Activities and Sports

Participant Sports

BOATING AND SAILING

Rodney Bay and Marigot Bay are centers for bareboat and crewed yacht charters. Their marinas offer safe anchorage, shower facilities, restaurants, groceries, and maintenance for yachts sailing the waters of the eastern Caribbean. **Destination St. Lucia (DSL) Ltd.** (✉ Rodney Bay, ☎ 758/453–8531) offers bareboat yacht charters; vessels range in length from 38 ft to 51 ft. The **Moorings Yacht Charters** (✉ Marigot Bay, ☎ 758/451–4357 or 800/535–7289) rents bareboat or crewed yachts ranging from Beneteau 39s to Morgan 60s.

CAMPING

Bay of Freedom Camp Site, St. Lucia's only campsite, is 133 acres of sloping terrain at Anse La Liberté (French for "Bay of Freedom"), on the west coast near the village of Canaries—accessible by boat or by car (a 45-minute drive south from Castries or 15 minutes north from Soufrière). Rough campsites and platforms for tents are available, along with communal toilets and showers, a cooking center, a small secluded beach, and 4 mi of hiking trails. Camping fees are inexpensive, particularly if you bring your own tent, and reservations are required. The camp site is on one of the many sites where former slaves celebrated their emancipation in 1834; it is administered by the St. Lucia National Trust (☎ 758/452–5005).

FISHING

Among the deep-sea creatures you can find in St. Lucia's waters are dolphin (dorado), barracuda, mackerel, wahoo, kingfish, sailfish, and white or blue marlin. Sportfishing is generally done on a catch-and-release basis, but the captain may permit you to take a fish back to your hotel to be prepared for your dinner. Neither spearfishing nor collecting live fish in coastal waters is permitted. Half- or full-day deep-sea fishing excursions can be arranged at either Vigie Cove or Rodney Bay Marina. Rates for a half-day fishing trip are about $100. Beginners are welcome. **Captain Mike's** (✉ Vigie Cove, ☎ 758/452–1216 or 758/452–7044) has a fleet of Bertram fishing boats (up to 38-ft long) that accommodates as many as eight passengers; all equipment and cold drinks are supplied. **Mako Watersports** (✉ Rodney Bay Marina, Rodney Bay, ☎ 758/452–0412) takes fishing enthusiasts out on the well-equipped six-passenger *Annie Baby*.

GOLF

Courses on St. Lucia are scenic and enjoyable, but they're not championship quality. **Sandals St. Lucia Golf Resort & Spa** (✉ La Toc Rd., Castries, ☎ 758/452–3081) has a 9-hole course for Sandals guests only. **St. Lucia Golf and Country Club** (✉ Cap Estate, ☎ 758/452–8523), the island's only public course, is at the island's northern tip and offers panoramic views of both the Atlantic and Caribbean. It's an 18-hole course (6,829 yards, par 72). The clubhouse has a bar and a pro shop where you can rent clubs and shoes and arrange lessons. Greens fees are $65 for nine holes or $85 for 18 holes; carts are included. Reservations are essential.

HIKING

The island is laced with trails, but you shouldn't attempt the challenging peaks on your own. The **St. Lucia Forestry Department** (☎ 758/450–2231) manages trails throughout the rain forest and provides guides who explain the plants and trees you'll encounter and keep you on the right track for a small fee—about $10 per person. The **St. Lucia National Trust** (☎ 758/452–5005) maintains two trails: one is at Anse La Liberté, near Canaries on the Caribbean coast; the other is on the Atlantic coast, from Mandélé Point to the Fregate Islands Nature Reserve. Full-day excursions with lunch cost about $50–$60 per person and can be arranged through hotels or tour operators.

HORSEBACK RIDING

Creole horses, an indigenous breed, are fairly small, fast, sturdy, and even-tempered animals suitable for beginners. Established stables can accommodate all skill levels and offer countryside trail rides, beach rides with picnic lunches, plantation tours, carriage rides, and lengthy treks. Prices run about $35 for one hour, $45 for two hours, and $60 for a three-hour beach ride with picnic. Transportation is usually provided between the stables and nearby hotels. Local people sometimes appear on beaches with their steeds and offer 30-minute rides for $10; ride at your own risk.

Country Saddles (✉ Marquis Estate, Babonneau, ☎ 758/450–5467), 45 minutes east of Castries, guides beginners and advanced riders through banana plantations, forest trails, and along the Atlantic coast. **International Riding Stables** (✉ Beauséjour Estate, Gros Islet, ☎ 758/452–8139 or 758/450–8665) offers either English- or Western-style riding. Their beach picnic ride includes time for a swim—with or without your horse. **Trim's National Riding Stable** (✉ Cas-en-Bas, Gros Islet,

☎ 758/452–8273 or 758/450–9971), the island's oldest establishment, offers four riding sessions per day, plus beach tours, trail rides, and carriage tours to Pigeon Island.

SCUBA DIVING AND SNORKELING

Anse Chastanet, near the Pitons on the southwest coast, is the best beach-entry dive site. The underwater reef drops off from 20 ft to nearly 140 ft (6–42 m) in a stunning coral wall. A 165-ft freighter, *Lesleen M,* was deliberately sunk in 60 ft (18 m) of water near **Anse Cochon** to create an artificial reef; divers can explore the ship in its entirety and view huge gorgonians, black coral trees, gigantic barrel sponges, lace corals, schooling fish, angel fish, sea horses, spotted eels, stingrays, nurse sharks, and sea turtles. **Anse-La-Raye,** midway up the west coast, is one of St. Lucia's finest wall and drift dives and a great place for snorkeling. At the base of the **Petit Piton,** a spectacular wall drops to 200 ft (61 m). You can view an impressive collection of huge barrel sponges and black coral trees; strong currents ensure good visibility. At **The Pinnacles,** four coral-encrusted stone piers rise to within 10 ft (3 m) of the surface.

Buddies (✉ Rodney Bay Marina, Rodney Bay, ☎ 758/452–9086) offers wall, wreck, reef, and deep dives; resort courses and open-water certification with advanced and specialty courses are taught by PADI-certified instructors. **Dive Fair Helen** (✉ Wyndham Morgan Bay Resort, Choc Bay, ☎ 758/450–1640) is a PADI center that offers half-day excursions to wreck, wall, and marine reserve areas, as well as night dives. **Frogs** (✉ Windjammer Landing Villa Beach Resort, Labrelotte Bay, ☎ 758/452–0913; ✉ Jalousie Hilton, Anse des Pitons, ☎ 758/ 452–0913 or 758/459–7666 Ext. 4024), 2 mi (3 km) south of Soufrière, provides resort courses and open-water certification. Two-tank and night dives are also offered, and rental equipment is available. **Rosemond's Trench Divers** (✉ Marigot Bay, ☎ 758/451–4761) offers PADI training, wreck dives, night dives, and special dive packages for yachties. **Scuba St. Lucia** is a PADI five-star training facility, with a dive shop at Anse Chastanet (✉ Soufrière, ☎ 758/459–7755; ✉ Rex St. Lucian Hotel, Rodney Bay, ☎ 758/452–8009). Daily beach and boat dives and resort and certification courses are offered; underwater photography and snorkeling equipment are available. Day trips from the north of the island include round-trip speedboat transportation.

SEA EXCURSIONS

A day sail or sea cruise to Soufrière and the Pitons is a wonderful way to see St. Lucia and, perhaps, the perfect way to get to the island's distinctive natural sites. Prices for a full-day sailing excursion to Soufrière run about $70–$85 per person and include a land tour to the Sulphur Springs and the Botanical Gardens, lunch, a stop at Anse Cochon for swimming and snorkeling, and a visit to pretty Marigot Bay. Two-hour sunset cruises along the northwest coast cost about $40 per person. Most boats leave from either Vigie Cove, Castries or Rodney Bay. The 140-ft tall ship ***Brig Unicorn*** (✉ Vigie Cove, Castries, ☎ 758/452–8644), used in the filming of the TV miniseries *Roots,* is a replica of a 19th-century brig. Day trips along the coast are fun for the whole family. Several nights each week, a sunset cruise, with drinks and a live steel band, sails to Pigeon Point and back. On ***Endless Summer*** (✉ Rodney Bay Marina, Rodney Bay, ☎ 758/450–8651), a 56-ft "party" catamaran, you can take a day trip to Soufrière or a half-day swimming and snorkeling trip. For romantics, there's a weekly sunset cruise, with dinner and entertainment. ***Surf Queen*** (Vigie Cove, Castries, ☎ 758/452– 8232), a trimaran, runs a fast, sleek sail and has a special tour for German-speaking passengers. From Pigeon Island, north of Rodney Bay, you can take a more intimate cruise to the Pitons aboard the 57-ft luxury cruiser MV **Vigie** (☎ 758/452–8232). Customized sea and snorkeling charters can be arranged for small groups (four to six people) through **Captain Mike's** (✉ Vigie Cove, Castries, ☎ 758/452–0216 or 758/452–7044).

TENNIS AND SQUASH

All large resorts have their own tennis courts; most are lighted for night play and often have pros who offer lessons. People staying at small inns without tennis courts or those who wish to play squash can access a few private facilities for a fee. The **Rex St. Lucian Hotel** (✉ Reduit Beach, Rodney Bay, ☎ 758/452–8351) has two tennis courts open to the public at $20 per half hour or $30 per hour; reservations are required. **St. Lucia Racquet Club** (✉ Club St. Lucia, Cap Estate, ☎ 758/450–0106), the site of the St. Lucia Open each December, has seven lighted tennis courts, a pro shop, a restaurant-bar, and a squash court. The club charges $10 per person per hour for use of the facilities; reservations are required. **St. Lucia Yacht Club** (✉ Rodney Bay, ☎ 758/452–8350) has two air-conditioned, wood-floored, glass-backed squash courts; rackets can be rented. The club charges $10 per hour, and you'll need to make reservations. **Windjammer Landing Villa Beach Resort** (✉ Labrelotte Bay, ☎ 758/452–0913) permits nonguests to use its tennis courts for $10 per hour; reservations are required.

WINDSURFING

Major resorts generally offer Windsurfers and instruction. Cas-en-Bas, on the northeast coast, and Vieux Fort, on the southeast, are the most popular windsurfing locations for advanced and intermediate windsurfers. Reduit Beach, near Rodney Bay, and elsewhere along the calmer west coast are the best areas for beginners. Note that from August to October the wind loses strength island-wide. **Island Windsurfing Ltd.** (✉ Anse de Sables Beach, Vieux Fort, ☎ 758/454–7400) has board rentals and instruction; it's open daily from 10 AM until dusk. The **Rex St. Lucian** (✉ Reduit Beach, Rodney Bay, ☎ 758/452–8351) offers board rentals and instruction to nonguests for a fee.

Spectator Sports

CRICKET AND SOCCER

Both of these national pastimes are played at Mindoo Philip Park in Marchand, 2 mi (3 km) east of Castries. Contact the tourist board for details on schedules and tickets.

TENNIS

The **St. Lucia Racquet Club** (✉ Club St. Lucia, Cap Estate, ☎ 758/450–0106) is the site of regional tennis events, the most important being the St. Lucia Open in early December.

Shopping

The island's best-known products are artwork and wood carvings; clothing and household items made from batik and silk-screened fabrics, designed and printed in island workshops; and clay pottery. You can also take home straw hats and baskets and locally grown cocoa, coffee, and spices.

Areas and Malls

Along the harbor in Castries, you can see the rambling structures with bright-orange roofs that house several markets, which are open from 6 AM to 5 PM Monday through Saturday. Saturday morning is the busiest and most colorful time to shop. For more than a century, farmers' wives have gathered at the **Castries Market** to sell produce—which, alas, you can't import to the United States. But you can bring back spices (such as cocoa, turmeric, cloves, bay leaves, ginger, peppercorns, cinnamon sticks, nutmeg, mace, and vanilla essence), as well as bottled hot pepper sauces—all of which cost a fraction of what you'd pay back home. The **Craft Market,** adjacent to the produce market, has aisles and aisles of baskets and other handmade straw items, rustic brooms made from palm fronds, wood carvings and leather work, clay pottery, and souvenirs—all at affordable prices. The **Vendor's Arcade,** across the street from the Castries Craft Market, is a maze of stalls and booths where you can find handicrafts among the T-shirts and costume jewelry.

Gablewoods Mall, on the Gros Islet Highway in Choc Bay, a couple of miles north of downtown Castries, has about 35 shops that sell groceries, wines and spirits, jewelry, clothing, crafts, books and foreign newspapers, music, souvenirs, household goods, and snacks. At the grocery or liquor store at Gablewoods, you might pick up a bottle of Bounty Rum, the local firewater made at a distillery in Roseau, just south of Castries. Along with 54 boutiques, restaurants, and other businesses that sell services and supplies, a large supermarket is the focal point of each **J. Q.'s Shopping Mall;** one is at Rodney Bay, and the other's at Vieux Fort. If you're a die-hard shopper, be sure to visit **Pointe Seraphine,** an attractive Spanish-motif complex on Castries Harbour with more than 20 shops that sell duty-free goods, clothing, and local artwork. **La Place Carenage,** on the opposite side of the harbor, is a smaller duty-free complex with some of the same stores as at Pointe Seraphine. The origin of its French name dates back to its waterfront location, where ships were "careened" to clean, repair, and paint the bottom of their hulls. What was once an old cargo shed is now two floors of inviting boutiques. **William Peter Boulevard,** the capital's main shopping street, is primarily where locals shop for household items.

Most shops in **Soufrière** provide goods for local consumption, although you can also find gift shops, boutiques, and studios at local inns and attractions.

Specialty Items

ART

Artsibit Gallery (⊠ Brazil and Mongiraud Sts., Castries, ☎ 758/452–7865) exhibits and sells moderately priced pieces by St. Lucian painters and sculptors. **Caribbean Art Gallery** (⊠ Rodney Bay Yacht Marina, Rodney Bay, ☎ 758/452–8071) sells original artwork by world-renowned local artist Llewellyn Xavier, along with antique maps and prints and hand-painted silk. **Modern Art Gallery** (⊠ Gros Islet Highway, Bois d'Orange, ☎ 758/452–9079) is a home studio, open by appointment only, where you can buy contemporary and avant-garde Caribbean art. **Snooty Agouti** (⊠ Rodney Bay, ☎ 758/452–0321) sells original Caribbean artwork, wood carvings, prints, and maps; it's adjacent to the bar and restaurant of the same name.

BOOKS AND MAGAZINES

Sunshine Bookshop (⊠ Gablewoods Mall, Castries, ☎ 758/452–3222) has novels and titles of regional interest, including books by Caribbean authors—among them the works of the St. Lucian Nobel laureate, poet Derek Walcott. You can also find current newspapers and magazines. **Valmont Books** (⊠ Corner of Jeremie and Laborie Sts., Castries, ☎ 758/452–3817) has West Indian literature and picture books, as well as stationery items.

CLOTHES AND TEXTILES

Bagshaw Studios (⊠ La Toc Rd., La Toc Bay, Castries, ☎ 758/452–2139 or 758/451–9249) sells clothing and table linens with colorful tropical patterns; the fabric is designed and silk-screened by hand in the adjacent workroom. You can also find Bagshaw boutiques at Pointe Seraphine, La Place Carenage, and Rodney Bay, and a selection of items in gift shops at Hewanorra Airport. **Batik Studio** (⊠ Hummingbird Beach Resort, on the bayfront, north of wharf, Soufrière, ☎ 758/459–7232) has superb batik sarongs, scarves, and wall panels designed and created on site by Joan Alexander and her son, David. At **Caribelle Batik** (⊠ Howelton House, Morne Fortune, Castries, ☎ 758/452–3785), craftsmen demonstrate the art of batik and silk-screen printing. Meanwhile, seamstresses create clothing and wall hangings, which you can purchase in the shop. The studio is in an old Victorian mansion, high atop the Morne overlooking Castries. There's a terrace where you can have a cool drink and there's a garden full of tropical orchids and lilies. Caribelle Batik creations are featured in many gift shops throughout St. Lucia. **Sea Island Cotton Shop** (⊠ Bridge St., Castries, ☎ 758/452–3674; ⊠ Gablewoods Mall, Choc Bay,☎ 758/451–6946; ⊠ J. Q.'s Shopping Mall, Rodney Bay, ☎ 758/458–4220) sells quality T-shirts, Caribelle Batik clothing and other resort wear, and colorful souvenirs.

DUTY-FREE GOODS

Pointe Seraphine and La Place Carenage in Castries, the arcade at the Rex St. Lucian hotel in Rodney Bay, and Hewanorra International Airport are where duty-free goods are sold. You must present your passport and airline ticket to get the duty-free price. If you can forget for a moment that you're in the tropics, try on beautiful wool sweaters at **Benetton** (⊠ Pointe Seraphine, Castries, ☎ 758/452–7685). **Colombian Emeralds** (⊠ Pointe Seraphine, Castries, ☎ 758/453–7721; ⊠ La Place Carenage, Castries, ☎ 758/452–4288; ⊠ Hewanorra Airport, Vieux Fort, ☎ 758/454–7774) has fine-quality gems set in beautiful pieces of jewelry. **Studio Images** (⊠ Pointe Seraphine, Castries, ☎ 758/452–6883; ⊠ La Place Carenage, Castries, ☎ 758/452–0887; ⊠ Hewanorra Airport, Vieux Fort, ☎ 758/454–7884) sells designer fragrances; they also stock watches, cameras, sunglasses, electronics, and gifts. **Little Switzerland** (⊠ Pointe Seraphine, Castries, ☎ 758/452–7587; ⊠ La Place Carenage, Castries, ☎ 758/451–6785) specializes in imported china and crystal, jewelry, and leather goods.

GIFTS AND SOUVENIRS

Caribbean Perfumes (⊠ Morne Fortune, Castries, ☎ 758/453–7249) blends a half dozen lovely scents for women and two aftershaves for men from exotic flowers, fruits, tropical woods, and spices. Fragrances are all made in St. Lucia, reasonably priced, and available at the perfumery and at many hotel gift shops. **Noah's Arkade** (⊠ Jeremie St., Castries, ☎ 758/452–2523; ⊠ Pointe Seraphine, Castries, ☎ 758/452–7488) has hammocks, wood carvings, straw mats, T-shirts, books, and other regional items. Take home a cassette recording or CD by a local band, which you can find at **Sights 'n Sounds** (⊠ 46 Micoud St., Castries, ☎ 758/451–9600; ⊠ Gablewoods Mall, Castries, ☎ 758/451–7300).The **St. Lucia Philatelic Bureau,** at the General Post Office (⊠ Bridge St., Castries, ☎ 758/452–3774), supplies collectors and stamp dealers throughout the world with beautiful St. Lucian commemoratives.

HANDICRAFTS

On the southwest coast, halfway between Soufrière and Vieux Fort, you can find locally made clay and straw items at the **Choiseul Arts & Crafts Centre** (⊠ La Fargue, ☎ 758/454–3226). Many of St. Lucia's artisans come from this area. At Marigot Bay, **Cinnamon Batiks** (⊠ Marigot Bay Beach Club, Marigot Bay, ☎ 758/451–4974) has colorful handmade batik wall hangings and pillow covers depicting island themes, such as fish, parrots, and flowers, which are reasonably priced. **Eudovic Art Studio** (⊠ Morne Fortune, Castries, ☎ 758/452–2747) is a workshop and studio where you can buy trays, masks, and figures sculpted from local mahogany, red cedar, and eucalyptus wood. At **Zaka** (⊠ Rodney Bay, ☎ 758/452–0946), next to Shamrock's Pub, you can find contemporary Caribbean masks and totems carved from local driftwood and painted in brilliant colors. All items are created in a home studio, just down the road, by London-born woodcarver Simon Gajadhar and his wife, St. Lucian artist Sophie Barnard.

Nightlife and the Arts

Nightlife

The large, all-inclusive resort hotels have nightly entertainment—island music, calypso singers, and steel bands, as well as disco, karaoke, and talent shows. Many offer entertainment packages, including dinner, to nonguests. Otherwise, Rodney Bay is the best bet for nightlife. The many restaurants and bars there attract a crowd nearly every night.

BARS

The **Captain's Cellar** (⊠ Pigeon Island, Rodney Bay, ☎ 758/450–0253) is a cozy Old English pub with live jazz on weekends. **Shamrocks Pub** (⊠ Rodney Bay, ☎ 758/452–8725) is an Irish-style pub with pool tables and darts, lots of beer, and music. **The Wharf** (⊠ Choc Bay, ☎ 758/450–4844) has a happy hour every evening, followed by live music or karaoke.

DANCE CLUBS

Most dance clubs with live bands have a cover charge of $6–$8 (EC$15–EC$20), and the music usually starts at 11 PM. **Doolittle's** (⊠ Marigot Bay, ☎ 758/451–4974) has live bands and dance music—calypso, soul, salsa, steel band, reggae, limbo, and jump-up—that changes nightly. At **Indies** (⊠ Rodney Bay, ☎ 758/452–0727) you can dance to the hottest rhythms Wednesday, Friday, and Saturday; dress is casual though smart—no hats or sandals, no shorts or sleeveless shirts for men. There's shuttle bus service to and from most major hotels. The **Late Lime** (⊠ Reduit Beach, Rodney Bay, ☎ 758/452–0761) is a particular favorite of St. Lucians; it's air-conditioned and intimate, with DJ dance music every night but Tuesday.

THEME NIGHTS

For a taste of St. Lucian village life, head south from Castries to the **Anse La Raye "Fish Feast"** on a Friday night. Beginning at 6:30 PM, streets in this tiny fishing village are closed to vehicles, and the residents prepare what they know best: fish cakes for about 40¢ each, fried or stewed fish for $3 a portion, even a whole lobster for $10–$15, depending on size. Walk around, eat, chat with the local people, and listen to live music in the village square until the wee hours of the morning. The **Green Parrot** (⊠ Morne Fortune, ☎ 758/452–3399) is in a class all by itself. On Wednesday and Saturday, Chef Harry Edwards hosts the floor show—singing, dancing, and shimmying under the limbo pole himself. Dress semiformally for these evenings of frolic. The **Gros Islet Jump Up** in Gros Islet is legendary. Every Friday night, starting at about 9 PM, the sleepy fishing village a mile or so north of Rodney Bay becomes a huge street party. A mammoth sound system facing the central intersection beats out pulsating Caribbean rhythms; vendors sell barbecued chicken, conch, and local beverages; and everyone lets their hair down and dances until about 1 AM. It's very crowded and can get rowdy, so it's best to travel in a group—women shouldn't carry a purse. **J. J.'s Friday Night Street Jam** (⊠ Marigot Bay,

☎ 758/451–4076) is the south-side alternative to Gros Islet, with an outdoor barbecue and a band that plays island music.

The Arts

GALLERIES

St. Lucian artist **Llewellyn Xavier** (☎ 758/450–9155) creates modern art, ranging from vigorous oil abstracts that take up half a wall to small objects made from beaten silver and gold. Much of his work has an environmental theme, created from recycled materials. Xavier's work is on permanent exhibit at major museums in New York and Washington, D.C. His studio is in Cap Estate; call to arrange a visit.

THEATER

The small, open-air **Derek Walcott Center Theatre,** next to the Great House restaurant in Cap Estate, seats just 200 people for monthly productions of music, dance, and drama, as well as Sunday brunch programs. The Trinidad Theatre Workshop also presents an annual performance here. For schedule and ticket information contact the Great House (✉ Cap Estate, ☎ 758/450–0551 or 758/450–0450).

Exploring St. Lucia

One main route circles all of St. Lucia, except for a small area in the extreme northeast. The road snakes along the coast, cuts across mountains, makes hairpin turns and sheer drops, and reaches dizzying heights. It would take four or five hours to drive the whole loop. Even at a leisurely pace with frequent sightseeing stops, it would be a tiring drive.

The West Coast Road from Castries to Soufrière has steep hills and sharp turns, but it's well marked and incredibly scenic. South of Castries, the road tunnels through Morne Fortune, skirts the island's largest banana plantation (more than 127 varieties of bananas, called "figs" in this part of the Caribbean, are grown on the island), and passes through tiny fishing villages. Just north of Soufrière is the island's fruit basket, where most of the mangoes, breadfruit, tomatoes, limes, and oranges are grown. In the mountainous region that forms a backdrop for Soufrière, you can see Mt. Parasol and 3,118-ft (954-m) Mt. Gimie (pronounced Jimmy), St. Lucia's highest peak. As you approach Soufrière, you'll also have spectacular views of the Pitons.

The landscape changes dramatically between the Pitons and Vieux Fort, on the island's southeastern tip. Along the South Coast Road, the terrain starts as steep mountainside with dense vegetation, progresses to undulating hills that drop into sleepy fishing villages, and finally becomes rather flat and comparatively arid. Anyone arriving at Hewanorra International Airport and staying at a resort near Soufrière will travel along this route, a journey of just over an hour. From Vieux Fort north to Castries, the East Coast Road twists through Micoud, Dennery, and other villages. It winds up, down, and around mountains, crosses Barre de l'Isle Ridge, and slices through the rain forest. The scenery is breathtaking. The Atlantic pounds against rocky cliffs, and acres and acres of bananas and coconut palms cover the hillsides. If you arrive at Hewanorra and stay at a resort near Castries, you'll travel along the East Coast Road—a 1¼-hour ride.

Numbers in the margin correspond to points of interest on the St. Lucia map.

Castries and the North

Castries, the capital, and the area north of it are the island's most developed areas. The roads are straight, flat, and easy to navigate. The beaches are some of the island's best. This area is the location of most of the resorts and busy Rodney Bay Marina. One of the island's important historical sites, Pigeon Island, is off the northwestern tip.

SIGHTS TO SEE

⑤ Barre de l'Isle Forest Reserve. St. Lucia is divided into eastern and western halves by Barre de L'Isle Ridge. A mile-long (1½-km-long) trail cuts through the reserve, and four lookout points provide panoramic views. Visible in the distance are Mt. Gimie, immense green valleys, the Caribbean and the Atlantic, and coastal communities. The reserve is about a half-hour drive from Castries; it takes about an hour to walk the trail and another hour to climb Mt. La Combe Ridge. Permission from the **Forest and Lands Department** (☎ 758/450–2231 or 758/450–2078) is required to access the trail in Barre de L'Isle; a naturalist or forest officer guide will accompany you.

① Castries. The capital, a busy commercial city of about 65,000 people, wraps around a sheltered bay. Morne Fortune rises sharply to the south of town, creating a dramatic green backdrop. The charm of Castries lies almost entirely in its liveliness, since practically all the colorful colonial buildings were destroyed by four fires that occurred between 1796 and 1948. Freighters (exporting bananas, coconut, cocoa, mace, nutmeg, and citrus fruits) and cruise ships come and go daily, making Castries Harbour one of the Caribbean's busiest ports. **Pointe Seraphine** is a duty-free shopping complex on the north side of the harbor, about a 20-minute walk or two-minute cab ride from the city center; a launch ferries passengers across the harbor when ships are in port. Pointe Seraphine's attractive Spanish-style architecture houses more than 20 upscale duty-free shops, a tourist information kiosk, a taxi stand, and car-rental agencies. **Derek Walcott Square** is a green oasis bordered by Brazil, Laborie, Micoud, and Bourbon streets. Formerly Columbus Square, it was renamed to honor the hometown poet who won the 1992 Nobel prize in literature—one of two Nobel laureates from St. Lucia (the late Sir W. Arthur Lewis won the 1979 Nobel prize in economics). Some of the 19th-century buildings that have survived fire, wind, and rain can be seen on Brazil Street, the southern border of the square. On the Laborie Street side, there's a huge, 400-year-old *samaan* tree with leafy branches that shade a good portion of the square. Directly across Laborie Street from Derek Walcott Square is the Roman Catholic **Cathedral of the Immaculate Conception,** which was built in 1897. Though rather somber on the outside, its interior walls are decorated with colorful murals reworked by St. Lucian artist Dunstan St. Omer in 1985, just prior to the pope's visit. This church has an active parish and is open daily for both public viewing and religious services. At the corner of Jeremie and Peynier streets, spreading beyond its brilliant-orange roof, is the **Castries Market.** Full of excitement and bustle, the market is open every day except Sunday. It is most lively on Saturday morning, when farmers bring their fresh produce and spices to town, as they have for more than a century. Next door to the produce market is the **Craft Market,** where you can buy pottery, wood carvings, and handwoven straw items. Across Peynier Street from the Craft Market, at the **Vendor's Arcade,** there are still more handicrafts and souvenirs. Just 2 mi (3km) south of downtown, visit **Bagshaw Studios** (La Toc Rd., La Toc Bay, ☎ 758/452–7570) to see how Stanley Bagshaw's original tropical designs are turned into colorful silk-screened fabrics, which are fashioned into clothing and household items that are created and sold on site. Admission is free; it's open weekdays 8:30–5, Saturday 8:30–4, and Sunday 10–1. Weekend hours may be extended if a cruise ship is in port.

② Ft. Charlotte. Begun in 1764 by the French as the Citadelle du Morne Fortune, Ft. Charlotte was completed after 20 years of battling and changing hands. Its old barracks and batteries are now government buildings and local educational facilities, but you can drive around and look at the remains, including redoubts, a guardroom, stables, and cells. You can also walk up to the Inniskilling Monument, a tribute to the battle fought in 1796, when the 27th Foot Royal Inniskilling Fusiliers wrested the Morne from the French. At the military cemetery, which was first used in 1782, faint inscriptions on the tombstones tell the tales of French and English soldiers who died here. Six former governors of the island are buried here as well. From this point atop Morne Fortune you can view Martinique to the north and the twin peaks of the Pitons to the south.

④ Marigot Bay. This is one of the prettiest natural harbors in the Caribbean. In 1778 British Admiral Samuel Barrington sailed into this secluded bay-within-a-bay and covered his ships with palm fronds to hide them from the French. Today this picturesque community—where parts of the original movie *Doctor Doolittle* were filmed more than 30 years ago—is a favorite anchorage. You can charter a yacht, swim, snorkel, or mingle with the yachting crowd at one of the bars. There are several small inns and restaurants here. A 24-hour ferry connects the bay's two shores.

⑮ Marquis Estate. If you want a close-up view of a working plantation and are willing to get a little wet and muddy in the process, you can tour the island's largest one. The 600-acre Marquis Estate, situated on the northern Atlantic coast, began as a sugar plantation. Now it produces bananas and copra (dried coconut processed for oil) for export, as well as a number of other tropical fruits and vegetables for local consumption. St. Lucia Representative Services Ltd. conducts the tour and will pick you up at your hotel in an air-conditioned bus. You can see the estate by bus or on horseback; a river ride to the coast and lunch at the plantation house are both included. Self-drive or private taxi tours aren't permitted. Wear casual clothes. ✉ *Marquis Bay,* ☎ *758/452–3762.*

③ Morne Fortune. Morne Fortune forms a striking backdrop for the capital. This "Hill of Good Luck" has seen more than its share of bad luck over the years—including devastating hurricanes and four fires that leveled Castries. The drive to Morne Fortune from Castries will take you past **Government House,** on Government House Road, the official residence of the governor-general of St. Lucia and one of the island's few remaining examples of Victorian architecture.

🐚 **⑰ Pigeon Island.** Jutting out of the northwest coast, Pigeon Island is connected to the mainland by a causeway. Tales are told of the pirate Jambe de Bois (Wooden Leg), who once hid out on this 44-acre hilltop islet— a strategic point during the struggles for control of St. Lucia. Now, it's a national landmark and a venue for concerts, festivals, and family gatherings. There are two small beaches with calm waters for swimming and snorkeling, a restaurant, and picnic areas. Scattered around the grounds are ruins of barracks, batteries, and garrisons that date from 18th-century French and English battles. In the Museum and Interpretative Centre, housed in the restored British officers' mess, a multimedia display explains the island's ecological and historical significance. ✉ *Pigeon Island, St. Lucia National Trust, Rodney Bay,* ☎ *758/452–5005.* 💳 *$4.* ⊙ *Daily 9–5.*

⑯ Rodney Bay. About 15 minutes north of Castries, the 80-acre man-made lagoon—surrounded by hotels and many popular restaurants—is named for British admiral George Rodney, who sailed the English

Navy out of Gros Islet Bay in 1780 to attack and ultimately decimate the French fleet. Rodney Bay Marina is one of the Caribbean's premier yachting centers and the destination of the Atlantic Rally for Cruisers (trans-Atlantic yacht crossing) each December. Yacht charters and sightseeing day trips can be arranged at the marina. The Rodney Bay Ferry makes hourly crossings between the marina and the shopping complex, as well as daily excursions to Pigeon Island.

Soufrière and the South

The southwest coast is the destination of most sightseeing trips. This is where you can see the landmark Pitons and the French colonial town of Soufrière, with its drive-in volcano, botanical gardens, working plantations, and countless other examples of the natural beauty for which St. Lucia is deservedly famous.

SIGHTS TO SEE

⑦ Diamond Botanical Gardens. These splendid gardens are part of Soufrière Estate, a 2,000-acre land grant made in 1713 by Louis XIV to three Devaux brothers from Normandy in recognition of their services to France. The estate is still owned by their descendants; the gardens are maintained by Joan Du Bouley Devaux. Bushes and shrubs bursting with brilliant flowers grow beneath towering trees and line pathways that lead to a natural gorge. Vapor steaming up from La Soufrière volcano and water bubbling up from sulfur springs stream downhill in rivulets to become Diamond Waterfall, deep within the botanical gardens. Through the centuries, the rocks over which the cascade spills have become encrusted with minerals and tinted yellow, green, and purple. Adjacent to the falls, curative mineral baths are fed by underground springs. For $2.50 you can slip into your swimsuit and bathe for 30 minutes in one of the outside pools; a private bath costs $3.75. King Louis XVI of France provided funds in 1784 for the construction of a building with a dozen large stone baths to fortify his troops against the St. Lucian climate. It is claimed that Joséphine Bonaparte bathed here as a young girl while visiting her father's plantation nearby. During the Brigand's War, just after the French Revolution, the bathhouse was destroyed. In 1930 the site was excavated by André Du Boulay, and two of the baths were restored for his use. The outside baths were added later. ✉ *Soufrière Estate, Soufrière, ☎ 758/452–4759 or 758/454–7565.* 🎫 *$2.75.* ☉ *Mon.–Sat. 10–5, Sun. and holidays 10–3.*

⑭ Fregate Island Nature Reserve. A mile-long (1½-km) trail encircles the preserve, which you reach from the East Coast Road near the fishing village of Praslin. In this area, boat builders still fashion traditional fishing canoes, called *gommiers* after the trees from which the hulls are made. The ancient design was used by the original Amerindian people who populated the Caribbean. A natural promontory at Praslin provides a lookout where you can view the two small islets, Fregate Major and Fregate Minor, and—with luck—the frigate birds that nest here in summer. Guided tours of Fregate Island Nature Reserve, which include a ride in a gommier to Fregate Minor for a picnic lunch and swim, are arranged through the **St. Lucia National Trust** (✉ Box 595, Castries, ☎ 758/452–5005). All hikers must be accompanied by a guide. The cost is $18 per person (minimum of two), and trips are by appointment only.

⑬ Maria Islands Nature Reserve. Two tiny islands in the Atlantic, off St. Lucia's southeast coast, comprise the reserve, which has its own interpretive center. The 25-acre Maria Major and the 4-acre Maria Minor, its little sister, are inhabited by two rare species of reptiles (the colorful Maria Island ground lizard and the harmless grass snake) that share their home with frigate birds, terns, doves, and other wildlife.

There's a small beach for swimming and snorkeling, as well as an undisturbed forest, a vertical cliff covered with cacti, and a coral reef for snorkeling or diving. Tours, including the boat trip, cost $35 per person and are arranged by the **St. Lucia National Trust** (⊠ Box 595, Castries, ☎ 758/452–5005). Bring a picnic lunch.☉ *Aug.–mid-May, Wed.–Sun. 9:30–5.*

⑨ **Morne Coubaril Estate.** This 250-acre coconut and cocoa plantation in Soufrière, the first major estate established on St. Lucia, has a rich French history that dates from 1713, when Crown land was granted by King Louis IV to three St. Lucian brothers. Authentic 18th-century plantation life is explained as a guide escorts you along an original mule-carriage pathway and through reconstructed slave quarters. On the fascinating 90-minute tour, you see how cocoa, copra, and manioc were processed in the days before mechanization. The foliage is thick and green, and the tropical flowers are beautiful. The plantation house has been renovated and furnished according to the original plans. You can purchase freshly made cocoa, straw items, and hand-carved wooden items. If you wish to have lunch, a delicious creole buffet is available by reservation for about $10 per person. ⊠ *Soufrière,* ☎ 758/459–7340. ☜ $6. ☉ *Daily 9–5.*

⑧ **The Pitons.** These incredible mountains have become the symbol of St. Lucia. The road south out of Soufrière offers a magnificent view of the twin peaks, which rise precipitously from the cobalt blue Caribbean. The two pyramidal cones, covered with thick tropical vegetation, were formed by lava from a volcanic eruption 30 to 40 million years ago. They are not identical twins since—confusingly—2,619-ft (801-m) Petit Piton is taller than 2,461-ft (753-m) Gros Piton, though Gros Piton is, as the word translates, broader. Gros Piton is currently the only one where climbing is permitted, though the trail up even this shorter Piton is one very tough trek and requires the permission of the **Forest and Lands Department** (☎ 758/450–2231 or 758/450–2078) and a knowledgeable guide—whose services cost about $45.

⑩ **St. Lucia National Rain Forest.** Dense tropical rain forest stretches from one side of the island to the other, sprawling over 19,000 acres of mountains and valleys. It's home to a multitude of exotic flowers and plants, as well as rare birds—including the brightly feathered Jacquot parrot. The Edmund Forest Reserve, on the island's western side, is most easily accessible from just east of Soufrière, on the road to Fond St. Jacques. A trek through the lush landscape, with spectacular views of mountains, valleys, and the sea beyond, can take a full day. It takes an hour or so just to reach the reserve by car from the north end of the island. You'll also need plenty of stamina and sturdy hiking shoes. Permission from the **Forest and Lands Department** (☎ 758/450–2231 or 758/450–2078) is required to access reserve trails, and the department requires a naturalist or forest officer guide ($10 per person) because the vegetation is so dense.

⑥ **Soufrière.** The oldest town in St. Lucia and the former French colonial capital, Soufrière was founded by the French in 1746 and named for the nearby volcano. The wharf is the center of activity in this sleepy town (which currently has a population of about 9,000), particularly when a cruise ship is moored in pretty Soufrière Bay. French colonial influences can be noticed in the architecture of the wooden buildings around the market square, with their second-story verandas and gingerbread trim. The market building is decorated with colorful murals. The **Soufrière Tourist Information Centre** (⊠ Bay St., Soufrière, ☎ 758/459–7200) provides information about area attractions.

🌀 ⑪ **La Soufrière Drive-In Volcano.** As you approach, your nose will pick up the strong scent of the sulfur springs—more than 20 belching pools of muddy water, multicolored sulfur deposits, and other assorted minerals baking and steaming on the surface. Actually, you don't drive in. You drive up within a few hundred feet of the gurgling, steaming mass, then walk behind your guide—whose service is included in the admission price—around a fault in the substratum rock. It's a fascinating, educational half hour that can also be pretty stinky on a hot day. ✉ *Bay St., Soufrière,* ☎ *758/459–5500.* 🎫 *$1.25.* ⊙ *Daily 9–5.*

⑫ **Vieux Fort.** St. Lucia's second-largest city and port is the location of Hewanorra International Airport. From the Moule à Chique Peninsula, the island's southernmost tip, you can see all of St. Lucia to the north and the island of St. Vincent 21 mi (34 km) south. This is where the clear Caribbean waters blend with those of the deeper blue Atlantic.

ST. LUCIA A TO Z

To research prices, get advice from other travelers, and book travel arrangements, visit www.fodors.com.

AIR TRAVEL

Air Canada has direct weekend service to Hewanorra from Toronto and Montréal. Air Jamaica flies direct to Hewanorra via Grenada from New York twice weekly and also offers connecting service to Hewanorra via Montego Bay, Jamaica and to George F. L. Charles Airport via Barbados. American Airlines/American Eagle has daily service to George F. L. Charles via San Juan from New York and other major U.S. cities. British Airways has direct service to Hewanorra from London via Barbados. BWIA has direct service to George F. L. Charles via either Barbados or Trinidad from Miami, New York, Washington, D.C., and London. US Airways has a weekly nonstop flight between Philadelphia and Hewanorra. Virgin Atlantic has a weekly nonstop flight to Hewanorra from London. From other parts of the world, connections must be made through U.S. cities, San Juan, Toronto, or London.

Air Caraïbes flies into George F. L. Charles Airport from Martinique and other islands in the French West Indies. Caribbean Star connects George F. L. Charles with Antigua, Dominica, St. Vincent, and Grenada. HelenAir flies charter service between Barbados and George F. L. Charles. LIAT operates at Hewanorra, as well as at George F. L. Charles, linking St. Lucia with Barbados, Trinidad, Antigua, Martinique, Dominica, Guadeloupe, and other islands.
➤ AIRLINES AND CONTACTS: **Air Canada** (☎ 758/452–3051 or 758/452–2550). **Air Caraïbes** (☎ 758/452–2463 or 758/453–6660). **Air Jamaica** (☎ 758/453–6611). **American Airlines/American Eagle** (☎ 758/452–6777). **British Airways** (☎ 758/452–3951). **BWIA** (☎ 758/452–3778, 758/451–7700, or 758/454–5075). **Caribbean Star** (☎ 758/452–5898). **HelenAir** (☎ 758/453–2777). **LIAT** (☎ 758/452–3051 or 758/452–2348). **US Airways** (☎ 758/454–8186). **Virgin Atlantic** (☎ 758/454–3610).

AIRPORTS

St. Lucia has two airports. Hewanorra International Airport, at Vieux Fort on the southern tip of the island, is a modern airport with a long runway capable of handling wide-body jets. George F. L. Charles Airport, in Castries, is a short airstrip that accommodates small, propeller-driven aircraft used for interisland and charter flights.

The drive from Hewanorra to Castries takes about 1¼ hours; to Soufrière, just over an hour. Although both are long rides, either route follows a picturesque coastline and traverses lush rain forest. George F. L. Charles Airport is only 10 to 20 minutes from resorts in or near Castries; it's about 30 minutes to Marigot and 1¼ hours to Soufrière. Another option is to take a boat between George F. L. Charles Airport (from Vigie Cove Marina) and Soufrière, which shortens the trip to about 40 minutes.

Many resorts include airport transfers in their rates. Taxis are always available at the airports. If you take one, be sure to agree on the fare (and in which currency it's being quoted) before you get in. Between Hewanorra and Soufrière or the resorts near Castries, expect to pay $60–$70 each way; between George F. L. Charles Airport and nearby resorts, $15–$20.

➤ AIRPORT INFORMATION: **George F. L. Charles Airport** (☎ 758/452–1156). **Hewanorra International Airport** (☎ 758/454–6355).

BOAT AND FERRY TRAVEL
Cruise ships from major lines call at Castries and Soufrière. At Port Castries, ships tie up at berths right in town and are convenient to duty-free shops, the market, and transportation for sightseeing excursions. In Soufrière, ships anchor offshore, and passengers are transferred ashore by tenders.

Visitors arriving on private or chartered yachts can find full-service facilities—including duty-free fuel, ship's chandlery, sail and engine repair, telecommunications, groceries, and other services—at the island's two main yachting centers, Port Castries (including Vigie Cove Marina) and Rodney Bay, or at picturesque Marigot Bay. All are official ports of entry to St. Lucia.

FARES AND SCHEDULES
The Rodney Bay Ferry makes the trip between the marina and the shopping complex daily on the hour from 9 to 4 for $4 round-trip. Ferry service to Pigeon Island from Rodney Bay (adjacent to The Lime restaurant) is available twice daily for $50 round-trip, including the entrance fee to Pigeon Island and lunch; snorkel equipment can be rented for $12.

➤ BOAT AND FERRY INFORMATION: **Castries Yacht Centre** (☎ 758/452–6234). **The Moorings Yacht Charters** (☎ 758/451–4357). **Port Castries** (☎ 758/452–3036). **Rodney Bay Ferry** (☎ 758/452–8816). **Rodney Bay Marina Boatyard** (☎ 758/452–0324). **St. Lucia Yacht Services** (☎ 758/452–5057).

BUSINESS HOURS
BANKS
Banks are open Monday–Thursday 8–3, Friday 8–5; a few branches in Rodney Bay are also open Saturday 9–noon.

POST OFFICES
Post offices are open weekdays 8:30–4:30.

SHOPS
Most stores are open weekdays 8:30–12:30 and 1:30–4:30, Saturday 8–12:30; Gablewoods Mall shops are open Monday–Saturday 9–7; Pointe Seraphine shops are open weekdays 9–5, Saturday 9–2. Some hotel gift shops may be open on Sunday.

CAR RENTALS
To rent a car, you must be at least 25 years old and provide a valid driver's license and a credit card. If you don't have an international driver's license, you must buy a temporary St. Lucian driving permit at car-rental firms, the immigration office at either airport, or the Gros Islet police

station. The permit costs $20 (EC$54) and is valid for three months. Car-rental rates are usually quoted in U.S. dollars and range from $45 to $80 per day or $250–$400 per week, depending on the car.

Car-rental agencies generally include free pickup at your hotel and unlimited mileage. Many major U.S. car-rental firms have agencies in St. Lucia. Avis has a main office in Castries and desks at both airports, at the Pointe Seraphine transportation center, and at Rodney Bay Marina. Budget has its main office in Castries and a desk at Hewanorra International Airport. Hertz has desks at both airports.

Local agencies offer competitive service and rates. C. T. L. Rent-a-Car is convenient for people staying at resorts near Rodney Bay or who arrive in St. Lucia by private yacht. Cool Breeze Jeep/Car Rental is convenient for people staying at resorts in the southwest near Soufrière. Courtesy Car Rental has an office north of Rodney Bay and a rental desk at the Bay Gardens Hotel in Rodney Bay. Gibin Rent A Car is convenient for people staying in the north, near Gros Islet. St. Lucia National Car Rental has desks at both airports, at the Pointe Seraphine transportation center, and a desk at The Body Holiday at LeSPORT resort and a few other hotels.

➤ MAJOR AGENCIES: **Avis** (✉ Castries, ☎ 758/452–2700; ✉ Rodney Bay, ☎ 758/452–0782; ✉ Vieux Fort, ☎ 758/454–6325; ✉ Vigie, ☎ 758/452–2046.) **Budget** (✉ Castries, ☎ 758/452–0233; ✉ Vieux Fort, ☎ 758/454–5311). **Cool Breeze Jeep/Car Rental** (✉ Soufrière, ☎ 758/459–7729). **Courtesy Car Rental** (✉ Bois d'Orange, Gros Islet, ☎ 758/452–8140). **C. T. L. Rent-a-Car** (✉ Rodney Bay Marina, ☎ 758/452–0732). **Gibin Rent A Car** (✉ Beausejour, Gros Islet, ☎ 758/ 452–9528). **Hertz** (✉ Castries, ☎ 758/452–0679; ✉ Vieux Fort, ☎ 758/454–9636; ✉ Vigie, ☎ 758/451–7351). **St. Lucia National Car Rental** (✉ Castries, ☎ 758/450–8721; ✉ Vieux Fort, ☎ 758/454–6699; ✉ Vigie, ☎ 758/452–3050; ✉ Pointe Seraphine, ☎ 758/453–0085).

CAR TRAVEL

Driving yourself is a fine idea if you want to do a lot of exploring and try lots of restaurants during your stay. If you're staying at an all-inclusive resort and plan limited excursions off the property, however, taxis would be a better bet. The drive from Castries to Soufrière is magnificent, but the winding roads can be exhausting for the uninitiated; local drivers are accustomed to the trek. You might even prefer to make that trip by boat, which is a popular option.

GASOLINE

Gasoline is expensive: about EC$2 per liter (the equivalent of $2.75 per gallon).

ROAD CONDITIONS

St. Lucia has about 500 mi (800 km) of roads, but only about half (281 mi [450 km]) are paved. All towns and villages are connected by major routes. The highways on both coasts are winding and steep—and often scarred by potholes.

RULES OF THE ROAD

Driving in St. Lucia is on the left, British style. Observe speed limits, particularly the 30-mph limit within Castries. Respect no-parking zones; police issue tickets, and penalties start at about $15 (EC$40). Wear your seat belts.

ELECTRICITY

The electric current on St. Lucia is 220 volts, 50 cycles, with a square three-pin plug. A few large hotels have 110-volt outlets—at least for shavers. To use most North American appliances, however, you'll need a transformer to convert voltage and a plug adapter; dual-voltage computers or appliances will still need a plug adapter. Hotels will sometimes lend you one for use during your stay.

EMBASSIES
➤ UNITED KINGDOM: **British High Commission** (✉ N.I.S. Building, Waterfront Second Floor, Castries, ☎ 758/452–2482).

EMERGENCIES
Victoria Hospital is St. Lucia's main hospital, on the southwest side of Castries harbor heading toward La Toc. Regional medical facilities are located at Dennery Hospital, on the island's east coast, St. Jude's Hospital, near Hewanorra International Airport, and Soufrière Hospital, in the southwest.
➤ AMBULANCE AND FIRE: **Ambulance and fire emergencies** (☎ 911).
➤ HOSPITALS: **Dennery Hospital** (✉ Main Rd., Dennery, ☎ 758/453–3310). **St. Jude's Hospital** (✉ Airport Rd., Vieux Fort, ☎ 758/454–6041). **Soufrière Hospital** (✉ W. Quinlan St., Soufrière, ☎ 758/459–7258). **Victoria Hospital** (✉ Hospital Rd., Castries, ☎ 758/452–2421).
➤ PHARMACIES: **M & C Drugstore** (✉ Bridge St., Castries, ☎ 758/452–2811; ✉ J. Q. Shopping Mall, Rodney Bay, ☎ 758/458–0178; ✉ Gablewoods Mall, Gros Islet Hwy., Choc, ☎ 758/451–7808; ✉ New Dock Rd., Vieux Fort, ☎ 758/454–3760). **Williams Pharmacy** (✉ Bridge St., Castries, ☎ 758/452–2797).
➤ POLICE: Dial ☎ 999. For **marine police** dial ☎ 758/453–0770 or 758/452–2595.
➤ SEA-AIR RESCUE: Dial ☎ 758/452–2894, 758/452–1182, or 758/453–6664.

ETIQUETTE AND BEHAVIOR
Dress conservatively in town and in restaurants. In St. Lucia, as well as throughout the Caribbean, beachwear should be reserved for the beach. If you wish to take photographs of local people or their property, be sure to ask permission first and offer a small gratuity in appreciation. Note that souvenir vendors can be persistent, particularly outside some of the popular attractions in and around Soufrière. Be polite but firm if you're not interested.

FESTIVALS AND SEASONAL EVENTS
For two days in May, the St. Lucia National Trust holds its annual fundraiser, the Festival of Comedy; adult comedy shows are held at the Cultural Centre in Castries, and there's a day of family entertainment, with storytellers and comedians, at Pigeon Island.

In early May the weeklong St. Lucia Jazz Festival, one of the premier events of its kind in the Caribbean, sees international jazz greats entertain at outdoor venues on Pigeon Island and at various hotels, restaurants, and nightspots throughout the island; free concerts are also held at Derek Walcott Square in downtown Castries.

In June, the St. Lucia Golf Open, a two-day tournament held at the St. Lucia Golf and Country Club in Cap Estate, is open to amateurs; it's a handicap event, and prizes are awarded.

St. Lucia's Carnival, the most extravagant two days of the year, is held on the third Monday and Tuesday in July; a costume parade winds through Castries, prizes are awarded for the best band, the calypso king and queen are crowned, and there are endless music and dancing in the streets.

The St. Lucia Billfishing Tournament, held in late September or early October, attracts anglers from all over the Caribbean, with prizes awarded for the biggest fish and the largest catch; the blue marlin is the most sought-after fish, and everyone hopes to find one that beats the 1,000-lb mark.

The last Sunday in October marks Jounen Kweyol Etenasyonnal (International Creole Day), the grand finale of Creole Heritage month; festivities are held in several communities, but musicians always do their stuff at Pigeon Point Park and in the streets in Castries, where vendors set up stalls and sell food and handicrafts.

The annual Atlantic Rally for Cruisers, or ARC, is the world's largest ocean-crossing race. It starts in Las Palmas, Canary Islands, and ends in early December at Rodney Bay; the event is marked by a week of festivities and parties.

HEALTH

Tap water is perfectly safe to drink throughout the island, but you should be sure that fruit is peeled or washed thoroughly before eating it. Insects can be a real bother during the wet season (July–November), particularly in the rain forest; bring along repellent to ward off mosquitoes and sand flies. Manchineel trees have poisonous fruit that looks like a small green apple and leaves that can cause skin blisters on contact. Even raindrops falling off the trees can cause blisters. Manchineels grow near the water; those on hotel property or populated areas are usually marked with a sign or a band of red paint.

HOLIDAYS

Public holidays are: New Year's Day (Jan. 1), Independence Day (Feb. 22), Good Friday (Fri. before Easter), Easter Monday (day after Easter), Labour Day (May 1), Whit Monday (7th Mon. after Easter), Corpus Christi (8th Thurs. after Easter), Emancipation Day (1st Mon. in Aug.), Carnival (3rd Mon. and Tues. in July), Thanksgiving Day (Oct. 25), National Day (Dec. 13), Christmas (Dec. 25), and Boxing Day (Dec. 26).

LANGUAGE

English is the official language of St. Lucia and is spoken everywhere, but you'll often hear local people speaking a French Creole patois (Kweyol) among themselves. If you're interested in learning some patois words and phrases, pick up a copy of *A Visitor's Guide to St. Lucia Patois,* a small paperback book sold in local bookstores for $4.

As in many of the Caribbean islands, to "lime" is to hang out and a "jump-up" is a big party with lots of dance music (often in the street, as in the village of Gros Islet every Friday night). Don't be surprised if people in St. Lucia call you "darling" instead of "ma'am" or "sir"—they're being friendly not forward.

MAIL AND SHIPPING

The General Post Office is on Bridge Street in Castries and is open weekdays 8:30–4:30; all towns and villages have branches. Postage for airmail letters to the U.S., Canada, and the U.K. is EC95¢ per ½ ounce; postcards are EC65¢. Airmail letters to Australia and New Zealand cost EC$1.35; postcards, EC70¢. Airmail can take two or three weeks to be delivered—even longer to Australia and New Zealand.

MONEY MATTERS

Prices quoted in this chapter are in U.S. dollars unless otherwise indicated.

The international Bank of Nova Scotia, or Scotiabank, has its head office in central Castries and branch offices at Rodney Bay and Vieux Fort. Barclays Bank offers international banking services from its two offices in Castries and branches in major towns. National Commercial Bank of St. Lucia is a large regional bank, with two offices in Castries and branches at Hewanorra Airport, Gros Islet, and Soufrière. Royal Bank of Canada has its main office in downtown Castries and a branch at Rodney Bay Marina.

➤ CONTACTS: **Bank of Nova Scotia** (✉ Wm. Peter Blvd., Castries, ☎ 758/452–2100; ✉ Rodney Bay, ☎ 758/452–8805; ✉ Vieux Fort, ☎ 758/454–6314). **Barclays Bank** (✉ Bridge St., Castries, ☎ 758/456–2100; ✉ Rodney Bay Marina, Rodney Bay, ☎ 758/452–9384; ✉ Hewanorra Airport, Vieux Fort, ☎ 758/454–6255; ✉ Soufrière, ☎ 758/459–7255). **National Commercial Bank of St. Lucia** (✉ Bridge St., Castries, ☎ 758/456–6000; ✉ Pointe Seraphine, Castries, ☎ 758/452–4787; ✉ Hewanorra Airport, ☎ 758/454–7780; ✉ Gros Islet, ☎ 758/450–9851; ✉ Soufrière, ☎ 758/459–7450). **Royal Bank of Canada** (✉ William Peter Blvd., Castries, ☎ 758/452–2245; ✉ Rodney Bay Marina, Rodney Bay, ☎ 758/452–9921).

ATMS

Automated teller machines (ATMs) are available 24 hours a day at bank branches, transportation centers, and shopping malls, where you can use major credit cards to obtain cash (in local currency only).

CREDIT CARDS

Major credit cards and traveler's checks are widely accepted.

CURRENCY

The official currency is the Eastern Caribbean dollar (EC$). It's linked to the U.S. dollar at EC$2.67, but stores and hotels often exchange at EC$2.50 or EC$2.60. U.S. currency is readily accepted, but you'll probably get change in EC dollars.

PASSPORTS AND VISAS

U.S., Canadian, and British citizens whose stay does not exceed six months must have a valid passport or prove citizenship with a birth certificate (with a raised seal) and a government-issued photo ID. Visitors from other countries must present a valid passport. Everyone must have a return or ongoing ticket.

SAFETY

Although crime isn't a significant problem, take the same precautions you would at home—lock your door, secure your valuables, and don't carry too much money or flaunt expensive jewelry on the street.

Coastal waters surrounding the island of St. Lucia are protected areas. Spearfishing and collecting live fish are prohibited. Be aware that sea urchins live among the rocks on the coastline; should one's long black spines lodge under your skin, don't try to pull them out. Apply an ammonia-based liquid (such as urine!), and the spine will retreat, allowing you to ease it out. Swimming on the rough Atlantic side of the island is dangerous.

SIGHTSEEING TOURS

Guided half- and full-day land and/or sea tours depart from the Castries area (Pointe Seraphine and Vigie Cove) or Rodney Bay and head north to Pigeon Island or south along the picturesque west coast to the Pitons and the sights in and around Soufrière. Half-day land tours range in price from $35 to $40 per person; full-day land tours, from $120 to $140 for one to four people. Cruises include refreshments and range in price from $40 per person at sunset to $85 for a full day.

BOAT

Board the 140-ft *Brig Unicorn* for a full-day sail to Soufrière or a sunset cruise under full sail, accompanied by champagne, snacks, and live music. Endless Summer Cruises (Cats Inc.) offers full-day tours and champagne sunset cruises aboard its 56-ft catamaran party boat, *Endless Summer.* The 56-ft motor cruiser MV *Vigie* takes passengers for half-day cruises to Pigeon Island or full-day tours to the Pitons and the sights around Soufrière, with lunch, swimming, and snorkeling at Anse Cochon included.

➤ CONTACTS: **Brig Unicorn** (✉ Vigie Cove, Castries, ☎ 758/452–8811). **Endless Summer Cruises** (Cats Inc., ✉ Rodney Bay, ☎ 758/450–8651). **MV *Vigie*** (✉ Rodney Bay Marina, Rodney Bay, ☎ 758/452–9423 or 758/452–8232).

BICYCLE

Although the terrain can get pretty rugged, several tour operators have put together fascinating bicycle and combination bicycle-hiking tours that appeal to novice riders as well as those who enjoy a good workout. It's a marvelous way to enjoy the spectacular scenery throughout the St. Lucia countryside. Prices range from $60 to $100 per person.

Bike St. Lucia takes small groups of bikers on Jungle Biking™ tours along trails that meander through the remnants of an 18th-century plantation near Soufrière. Stops are made to explore the French Colonial ruins, study the beautiful tropical plants and fruit trees, enjoy a picnic lunch, and take dip in a river swimming hole or a swim at the beach. For those staying in the north, transportation to and from the facility is provided by land taxi and boat from Vigie Marina, in Castries.

Island Bike Hikes is suitable for all fitness levels. Jeep or bus transportation is provided across the central mountains to Dennery, on the east coast. After a 3-mi ride through the countryside, bikes are exchanged for shoe leather. The short hike into the rain forest ends with a picnic and a refreshing swim next to a sparkling waterfall—then the return leg to Dennery. All gear is supplied.

➤ CONTACTS: **Bike St. Lucia** (✉ Anse Chastanet, Soufrière, ☎ 758/451–2453). **Island Bike Hikes** (✉ Rodney Bay, Gros Islet, ☎ 758/458–0908).

HELICOPTER

Helicopter sightseeing tours are fascinating ways to get a bird's-eye view of the island. A 10-minute North Island tour ($45 per person) leaves from Pointe Seraphine, in Castries, continues up the west coast to Pigeon Island, then flies along the rugged Atlantic coastline before returning inland over Castries. The 20-minute South Island tour ($120 per person) starts at Pointe Seraphine and follows the western coastline, circling picturesque Marigot Bay, Soufrière, and the majestic Pitons before returning inland over the volcanic hot springs and tropical rain forest. To arrange a helicopter sightseeing trip, contact St. Lucia Helicopters.

➤ CONTACTS: **St. Lucia Helicopters** (✉ Pointe Seraphine, ☎ 758/453–6950, FAX 758/452–1553).

ORIENTATION

Taxi drivers are well informed and can give you a full tour—and often an excellent one, thanks to government-sponsored training programs. From the Castries area, full-day island tours cost $140 for up to four people; sightseeing trips to Soufrière, $120. If you plan your own day, expect to pay the driver $20 per hour plus tip.

St. Lucia Heritage Tourism has put together an "authentic St. Lucia experience," specializing in the local culture and traditions. Groups are small, and some of the off-the-beaten-track sites visited are a 19th-century plantation house surrounded by nature trails, a 20-ft waterfall hidden away on private property, and a living museum where creole practices and traditions are experienced. Plan on paying $65 per person for a full-day tour.

Jungle Tours specializes in rain forest hiking tours for all levels of ability. You're only required to bring hiking shoes or sneakers and have a willingness to get wet and have fun! Prices range from $80 to $90 and include lunch, fees, and transportation via open Land Rover truck.

Sunlink Tours offers dozens of land, sea, and combination sightseeing tours, as well as shopping tours, plantation, and rain forest adventures via Jeep safari, deep-sea fishing excursions, and day trips to other islands. Prices range from $20 for a half-day shopping tour to $120 for a full-day land-and-sea Jeep safari to Soufrière.
➤ CONTACTS: **Jungle Tours** (✉ Cas en Bas, Gros Islet, ☎ 758/450–0434). **St. Lucia Heritage Tours** (✉ Pointe Seraphine, Castries, ☎ 758/451–6058). **Sunlink Tours** (✉ Reduit Beach Ave., Rodney Bay, ☎ 758/452–8232 or 800/786–5465, WEB www.stluciareps.com).

TAXES AND SERVICE CHARGES
DEPARTURE TAX
The departure tax is $20 (EC$54), payable in cash only (either Eastern Caribbean or U.S. dollars).

SALES TAX
A government tax of 8% is added to all hotel and restaurant bills. There is no sales tax on items purchased in shops.

SERVICE CHARGES
Most restaurants add a service charge of 10% to restaurant bills in lieu of tipping.

TAXIS
Taxis are always available at the airports, the harbor, and in front of major hotels. They're unmetered, although nearly all drivers belong to a taxi cooperative and adhere to standard fares. Sample fares for up to four passengers are: Castries to Rodney Bay, $16; Rodney Bay to Cap Estate, $10; Castries to Cap Estate, $20; Castries to Marigot Bay, $24; Castries to Soufrière, $64. Always ask the driver to quote the price *before* you get in, and be sure that you both understand whether it's in EC or U.S. dollars. Drivers are knowledgeable and courteous.

TELEPHONES
COUNTRY AND AREA CODES
The area code for St. Lucia is 758.

INTERNATIONAL CALLS
You can make direct-dial overseas and interisland calls from St. Lucia, and the connections are excellent. To charge an overseas call to a major credit card, dial 811; there is no surcharge. From public phones and many hotels, you can dial AT&T Direct Service 1–800/USA–2881 or MCI Worldcom at 1–800/888–8000 and charge the call to your calling card to avoid expensive rates or hotel surcharges. Phonecards can be purchased at many retail outlets and used from any touch-tone telephone (including pay phones) in St. Lucia.

LOCAL CALLS
You can dial local calls throughout St. Lucia directly from your hotel room by connecting to an outside line and dialing the seven-digit number. Some hotels charge a small fee (usually about EC50¢) for local calls. Pay phones accept EC25¢ and EC$1 coins. Phone cards can be used for local calls, as well as for international calls.

TIPPING

Most restaurants add a 10% service charge to your bill in lieu of tipping; if one has not been added, a 10%–15% tip is appropriate for good service. Tip porters and bellhops $1 per bag, although many of the all-inclusive resorts have a no-tipping policy. Taxi drivers also appreciate a 10%–15% tip.

TRANSPORTATION AROUND ST. LUCIA

Privately owned and operated minivans constitute St. Lucia's bus system, an inexpensive and efficient means of transportation used primarily by local people. Minivan routes cover the entire island and run from early morning until approximately 10 PM. You may find this method of getting around most useful for short distances, between Castries and the Rodney Bay area, for example; longer hauls can be uncomfortable. The fare between Castries and Gablewoods Mall is EC$1; Castries and Rodney Bay, EC$1.50; Castries and Vieux Fort (a trip that takes more than two hours), EC$7. Minivans follow designated routes (signs are displayed on the front window); ask at your hotel for the appropriate route number for your destination. Wait at a marked bus stop or hail a passing minivan from the roadside. In Castries, buses depart from the corner of Micoud and Bridge streets, behind the markets.

Each minivan has a driver and usually a conductor, a young man whose job it is to collect fares, open the door, and generally take charge of the passenger area. If you're sure of where you're going, simply knock twice on the metal window frame to signal that you want to get off at the next stop. Otherwise, just let the conductor or driver know where you're going, and he'll stop at the appropriate place.

Helicopter transfers are much more expensive but a much quicker mode of transport. The cost for the 15-minute flight from Hewanorra to Castries is $100 per person, including luggage; for the 10-minute flight to Soufrière, $85 per person. There are helipads at Pointe Seraphine, Windjammer Landing Villa Beach Resort, Jalousie Hilton Beach Resort & Spa, and Rodney Bay. Contact St. Lucia Helicopters.

➤ CONTACTS: **St. Lucia Helicopters** (✉ Pointe Seraphine, ☎ 758/453–6950, FAX 758/452–1553).

VISITOR INFORMATION

➤ BEFORE YOU LEAVE: **St. Lucia Tourist Board** (In the U.S.: ✉ 800 2nd Ave., Suite 400-J, New York, NY 10017, ☎ 212/867–2950 or 800/456–3984, FAX 212/867–2795, WEB www.stlucia.org; in Canada: ✉ 8 King St. E, Suite 700, Toronto, Ontario M5C 1B5, ☎ 416/362–4242, FAX 416/362–7832; in the U.K.: ✉ 421A Finchley Rd., London NW3 6HJ, ☎ 0171/431–3675, FAX 0171/431–7920).

➤ IN ST. LUCIA: **St. Lucia Tourist Board** (✉ Sureline Bldg., Vide Bouteille, Box 221, Castries, ☎ 758/452–4094 or 758/452–5968, FAX 758/453–1121, WEB www.stlucia.org; ✉ Jeremie St., Castries, ☎ 758/452–2479; ✉ Pointe Seraphine, Castries, ☎ 758/452–7577; ✉ Bay St., Soufrière, ☎ 758/459–7419; ✉ George F. L. Charles Airport, Vigie, Castries, ☎ 758/452–2596; ✉ Hewanorra International Airport, Vieux Fort, ☎ 758/454–6644).

Updated by
Michael de
Zayas

A warm breeze gently caresses the dining room, while lights dance off the water in the canal. A young couple dressed in black, their foreheads almost touching, whispers in French; a Dutch family gathers around a large table for a festive reunion; and four animated Americans just off a charter boat recap the day's adventures. On this island, such multicultural scenes regularly unfold.

There are several advantages to visiting St. Maarten/St. Martin. Airline service is good, so you don't have to spend half your vacation getting here. The 37-square-mi (96-square-km) island is home to two cultures—St. Maarten is Dutch and St. Martin is French—and you can experience both for the price of one. The island is ideal if you like to have an active vacation, and paradisiacal if you like fine dining.

Whatever can be done in or on the water—snorkeling, windsurfing, waterskiing—is available here; golf and tennis are also options. Serious diners will find a different top-class restaurant each night. The duty-free shopping is as good as anywhere in the Caribbean. There's an active nightlife, with discos and casinos. Day trips can be taken by ship or plane to the nearby islands of Anguilla, Saba, St. Eustatius, and St. Barthélemy. There are hotels for every budget—from motel-type units to some of the Caribbean's most exclusive resort accommodations. The standard of living is one of the highest in the Caribbean, so islanders can afford to be honest and treat visitors as welcome guests.

On the negative side, St. Maarten/St. Martin has been thoroughly discovered and exploited; unless you stay in an exclusive resort, you may well end up sharing beachfronts with tour groups (the exception being some of the beaches in Terres Basses, on the French side). Yes, there's gambling, but the table limits are so low that hard-core gamblers have a better time gambling on the beach. As is often the case in the Caribbean, the island infrastructure has not kept pace with development. The governments, however, have upgraded the port area and the airport, and improved the roads—both to better accommodate visitors and to make things more comfortable for islanders.

Lodging

On the Dutch side the main resort areas are along beaches such as Maho Bay, where the swimming is great and the restaurants are abundant; at Simpson Bay, south of the airport where traffic can be heavy; and along Front Street in downtown Philipsburg, where shops and eateries abound. The casinos are still found exclusively on the Dutch side.

The French side's attractive Baie Nettlé and busy, popular Baie Orientale (Orient Bay, with its sports outfitters and beachside bistros) are two resort areas. Others include secluded Anse Marcel (Marcel Cove); Mont Vernon, which has a nice beach a bit removed from the crowds; Marigot, with shops, an open-air market, and fine dining; and Grand Case, which has an excellent beach and dozens of charming restaurants.

In general, the French resorts are more intimate. Most large Dutch resorts have time-share annexes; the units are often available for rental to those who prefer the condo lifestyle.

CATEGORY	COST EP/CP*	COST A.I.**
$$$$	over $350	over $375
$$$	$250–$350	$275–$375
$$	$150–$250	$175–$275
$	under $150	under $175

*EP/CP prices are per night for a standard double room in high season, excluding taxes, service charges, and meal plans
**A.I. (all-inclusive) prices are per person, per night based on double-occupancy during high season, excluding taxes and service charges

Hotels

DUTCH SIDE

$$$–$$$$ 🏨 **Maho Beach Resort & Casino.** This megaresort has the island's largest casino, the Casino Royal; its largest pool; and one of the island's best spots for late night dancing, the Q Disco. Spacious rooms have balconies with sea or garden views—the trick is to get a room far enough from the airport's landing strip (those behind the main lobby are the quietest). Besides the resort's three restaurants, many other eateries and shops are in a modern complex across the street. The beach resort and the nearby strands are among the Dutch side's finest. ✉ *Airport Rd., Maho Bay (Box 834)*, ☎ *599/545–2115 or 800/223–0757*, FAX *599/545–3180*, WEB *www.mahobeach.com. 570 rooms, 25 suites. 3 restaurants, 3 bars, 4 tennis courts, 2 pools, health club, spa, beach, shops, casino, dance club, baby-sitting, business services, car rental. AE, D, DC, MC, V. EP.*

$$–$$$$ 🏨 **Sunterra Royal Palm Beach Club.** A complex of suites and shops on Kimsha Beach, the Royal Palm is an excellent place from which to explore Simpson Bay and beyond. Rooms, which face the sea and can accommodate as many as six people, have two full baths and lots of rattan furniture with floral-pattern fabrics. ✉ *Airport Rd., Simpson Bay (Box 3035)*, ☎ *599/544–3732*, FAX *599/544–3727*, WEB *www.sunterra.com. 142 suites. Restaurant, 2 bars, kitchens, in-room VCRs, pool, beach, shops, baby-sitting, laundry service. AE, D, MC, V. EP.*

$$$ 🏨 **Pelican Resort & Casino.** This large timeshare property has many on-site activities and a wide beach. The white stucco buildings house apartments, suites, and deluxe studios—all with sweeping Caribbean views. ✉ *Off Airport Rd., Simpson Bay (Box 431, Pelican Key)*, ☎ *599/544–2503 or 800/550–7088*, FAX *599/544–2133*, WEB *www.pelicanresort.com. 210 suites, 132 apartments. 2 restaurants, 4 bars, grocery, kitchenettes, 4 tennis courts, 5 pools, spa, beach, dive shop, dock, snorkeling, windsurfing, boating, jet skiing, waterskiing, casino, playground, car rental. AE, D, MC, V. EP.*

$$–$$$ 🏨 **La Vista.** At this intimate property Antillean buildings are connected by brick walkways lined with riotous hibiscus and bougainvillea. All suites have cable TV and balconies. A stay here gets you use of the pool, tennis courts, and spa facilities at the adjacent Pelican Resort & Casino. ✉ *Pelican Key, Simpson Bay (Box 2086)*, ☎ *599/544–*

St. Maarten/St. Martin

KEY

Beaches

Cruise Ship Terminal

Dive Sites

❶ Exploring Sights

Ferry

① Hotels and Restaurants

TO ANGUILLA

B

Pt. Arago

Baie de la Potence

Pt. du Plum

Pte. du Bluff

Baie Rouge

Pte. des Pierres à Chaux

Baie de Marigot

Terres Basses

㊲

Baie Nettlé

㉘ ㉞

㉟

⑨

Marigot

■ Musée de Saint-Martin

㊳ ㊲

㊱

Baie Longue

Simpson Bay Lagoon

Sentry Hill

S T .

Cupecoy Beach

Mullet Bay

㊵

Juliana International Airport

㊷ ㊸

Maho Bay

㊶

Simpson Bay

Koolbaai

Annie

㊴

Caribbean Sea

N

Cole Bay

0 _____ 2 miles

0 _____ 3 km

3005, FAX 599/544–3010, WEB www.lavistaresort.com. 32 suites. Restaurant, kitchenettes, refrigerators. AE, MC, V. EP.

$$–$$$ ⊞ **Mary's Boon Beach Plantation.** This St. Maarten fixture is visible beside the airport when you arrive by plane, but the charm of the plantation-style complex is only evident once you step inside. American owners Karla and Mark have imported Indonesian mahogany furniture and four-poster beds, and patios overlooking the long beach or interior gardens. Nightly dinner service includes an honor bar, and a traditional family-style dinner rotating between island cuisine (lobster creole, shrimp Provencale) and international selections (roast duck, beef tenderloin). ⊠ *17 Simpson Bay Rd., Simpson Bay,* ☎ *599/545–4235,* FAX *599/545–3403,* WEB *www.marysboon.com. 21 rooms. Restaurant, bar, in-room data ports, kitchenettes, minibars, microwaves, pool, beach, Internet. AE, MC, V. EP.*

$$ ⊞ **Divi Little Bay Beach Resort.** Jutting out on a peninsula at the end of Great Bay, this resort offers terrific views of Philipsburg to one side, and is steps from a great private beach to the other. There's a light-blue-and-cream, Dutch colonial motif throughout the modern hotel, and the large rooms have king-size beds, wide balconies with sea views, and small but adequate kitchens. The poolside Sea Breeze Bar hosts weekly barbecues and live music. ⊠ *Little Bay Rd., Philipsburg (Box 961),* ☎ *599/542–2333 or 800/367–3484,* FAX *599/542–4336,* WEB *www.diviresorts.com. 235 rooms. 2 restaurants, 3 bars, grocery, refrigerators, tennis court, 3 pools, beach, snorkeling, boating, laundry service, gym, hair salon, dive shop, shops, car rental. AE, D, DC, MC, V. EP, FAP, MAP.*

$$ ⊞ **Great Bay Beach Hotel & Casino.** A 10-minute walk from the center of Philipsburg, this resort has its own stretch of wonderful beach at the west end of Great Bay. The open-air lobby overlooks the sea, and many of the rooms, in muted pastel color schemes, have views of the ocean. There's a casino on-site, and the fun staff runs organized activities daily. ⊠ *Little Bay Rd., Great Bay (Box 910, Philipsburg),* ☎ *599/ 542–2446 or 800/223–0757,* FAX *599/542–3859,* WEB *www.greatbayhotel. com. 275 rooms, 10 1-bedroom suites. 2 restaurants, 2 bars, tennis court, 2 pools, gym, hair salon, beach, snorkeling, boating, shops, casino, nightclub, car rental. AE, D, DC, MC, V. All-inclusive, EP.*

$$ ⊞ **Holland House Beach Hotel.** The shops of Front Street are at this hotel's doorstep, and the mile-long (1½-km-long) Great Bay Beach is out back. Each room (ask for one with a beach view) has a balcony and most rooms have a kitchenette. The open-air restaurant overlooking the water serves reasonably priced dinners, and the indoor-outdoor patio lounge is a popular spot from which to watch the sunset. There is free 24-hour Internet access in the lobby. ⊠ *43-A Front St., Philipsburg (Box 393),* ☎ *599/542–2572 or 800/223–9815,* FAX *599/ 542–4673,* WEB *www.hollandhousehotel.com. 48 rooms, 6 suites. Restaurant, in-room safes, some kitchenettes, refrigerators, beach, lounge, Internet, meeting room. AE, D, DC, MC, V. BP, FAP, MAP.*

$–$$ ⊞ **Pasanggrahan Royal Inn.** It's entirely appropriate that the bar here is named Sydney Greenstreet. It looks like a set for an old Bogie–Greenstreet film. The green-and-white, Indonesian plantation-style house on Great Bay Beach was formerly the guest house for royal Danish visitors. Wicker peacock chairs, balconies shaded by tropical greenery, and four-post beds with mosquito nets add to the relaxed, tropical allure. ⊠ *15 Front St., Philipsburg (Box 151),* ☎ *599/542–3588 or 599/542– 2743,* FAX *599/542–2885. 27 rooms, 1 suite. Restaurant, bar, in-room safes, refrigerators, beach. AE, MC, V. EP.*

$$ ⊞ **Radisson Vacation Villas St. Maarten at Oyster Bay.** New units with ocean views here provide fully modern apartments good for a week-long stay on the northern edge of the Dutch border. The pool overlooks the sea from a dramatic dropoff level, and you're only steps away from pretty Dawn Beach. ✉ *Emerald Merit Rd. 10, Oyster Pond (Box 239, Philipsburg),* ☎ *599/543–6040 or 877/478–6669,* FAX *599/543–6695,* WEB *www.oysterbaybeachresort.com. 190 condos. Restaurant, bar, some kitchenettes, minibars, some in-room VCRs, pool, beach, bicycles, gym, hot tub, massage, shops, laundry service, car rental. AE, D, MC, V. BP, EP, FAP.*

FRENCH SIDE

$$$$ 🖭 **La Samanna.** Overlooking a perfect white beach and set on 55 acres of lush gardens, this Mediterranean-style retreat is pure luxury. The designer rooms are furnished with mahogany and teak imports, and there are also ultraluxurious penthouses and suites for the chic set. The service is impeccable, the food exquisite. ✉ *Baie Longue (Box 4007), Marigot 97064,* ☎ *590/87–64–00 or 800/854–2252,* FAX *590/87–87–86,* WEB *www.lasamanna.orient-express.com. 81 units. Restaurant, bar, 3 tennis courts, pool, aerobics, health club, massage, beach, windsurfing, waterskiing, shops, library. AE, MC, V. CP, MAP. Closed Sept.–Oct.*

$$$$ 🖭 **Le Méridien.** This bustling yet elegant resort, which consists of two smaller complexes called L'Habitation and Le Domaine, is wildly popular with tour groups and families. There are 1,600 ft (489 m) of white-sand beach and a slew of sports facilities amid beautifully landscaped gardens on enchanting Marcel Cove. All rooms and suites have balconies, and suites on the marina have fully equipped kitchens and patios. A stay here gets you free access to the facilities at Le Privilege Resort & Spa. ✉ *Anse Marcel (Box 581), 97150, bear north at French Cul de Sac, follow signs to Anse Marcel,* ☎ *590/87–67–00 or 800/543–4300,* FAX *590/87–30–38,* WEB *www.lemeridien-hotels.com. 396 rooms, 84 suites. 4 restaurants, 4 bars, 6 tennis courts, miniature golf, 2 pools, some kitchens, refrigerators, aerobics, gym, beach, dive shop, dock, snorkeling, boating, jet skiing, waterskiing, racquetball, squash, shops, dance club, car rental. AE, DC, MC, V. EP.*

$$$$ 🖭 **Le Privilege Resort & Spa.** At this resort, perched above Marcel Cove and Le Méridien, those into the spa life can take advantage of all kinds of treatments. Rooms and suites are spacious and comfortably furnished, with tile floors, marble baths, even CD players. There's a free shuttle down to the beach and the resort's marina, but you'll still need a car—Marcel Cove is isolated from the rest of the island. ✉ *Anse Marcel 97150, bear left at French Cul de Sac, follow signs,* ☎ *590/87–38–38 or 800/874–8541,* FAX *590/87–44–12,* WEB *www.privilege-spa.com. 16 rooms, 18 suites. 2 restaurants, bar, 6 tennis courts, 3 pools, in-room safes, in-room VCRs, hair salon, health club, massage, spa, dive shop, dock, windsurfing, boating, fishing, racquetball, squash, nightclub. AE, MC, V. CP.*

$$$–$$$$ 🖭 **Esmeralda Resort.** The green roofs and stacked configuration make this villa complex look like an American Sun Belt development, but the interiors are tastefully decorated. The 65 rooms and suites in 18 villas can be combined any way you like, from studios to five-bedroom palatial digs. Each villa has a private pool, and all rooms have terraces. Five restaurants on the nearby beach let you charge meals to your room. ✉ *Baie Orientale (Box 5141, 97064),* ☎ *590/87–36–36 or 800/622–7836,* FAX *590/87–35–18,* WEB *www.esmeralda-resort.com. 65 rooms in 18 villas. 6 restaurants, in-room safes, kitchenettes, 2 tennis courts, 17 pools, shops. AE, MC, V. EP.*

$$$–$$$$ 🖭 **Green Cay Village.** Set high above Orient Bay facing the trade
★ winds, this complex is a great choice for small groups or families. Each of the 16 spacious one-, two-, and three-bedroom villas has its own pool, large deck, full kitchen, and dining patio. Daily maid service is included. Although all villas have plenty of privacy, those highest on

the hill enjoy the most seclusion—and the best views. ⊠ *Parc Baie Orientale, Baie Oriental (Box 3006, 97064),* ☎ *590/87–38–63 or 888/ 832–2302,* FAX *590/87–39–27,* WEB *www.greencay.com. 16 villas. Room service, kitchenettes, refrigerators, microwaves, tennis court, baby-sitting, laundry service, cable TV, airport shuttle, in-room VCRs, 16 pools. AE, MC, V. CP, EP.*

$$–$$$$ 🖬 **Blue Bay Club Mont Vernon.** Gingerbread fretwork decorates this rambling hotel, which sits on a bluff over Orient Bay. Rooms in the buildings that face the ocean are slightly larger than the others. All have balconies. This is a big resort that lures package-tour groups and business seminars. ⊠ *On French Cul de Sac, Baie Orientale (Box 1174, 97062),* ☎ *590/87–62–40 or 800/258–3229,* FAX *590/87–37–27,* WEB *www.bluebayresorts.com. 394 rooms. 3 restaurants, 2 bars, 2 tennis courts, 2 pools, gym, beach, snorkeling, windsurfing, shops, baby-sitting, car rental. AE, DC, MC, V. All-inclusive.*

$$$ 🖬 **Grand Case Beach Club.** This superb condo complex combines one
★   of the greatest locations on the island—sharing Grand Case beach and an additional "secret" crescent of sand looking out toward Anguilla and Creole Rock—with a relaxed attitude and excellent, secure facilities. The tastefully furnished studios and one- and two-bedroom apartments have balconies or patios; the 62 oceanfront units are in greatest demand. The aptly named Sunset Café sits over the beach, facing west. ⊠ *21 Rue de Petit Plage, Grand Case, north end of Blvd. de Grand Case (Box 339, 97150),* ☎ *590/87–51–87 or 800/537–8483,* FAX *590/ 87–59–93,* WEB *www.gcbc.com. 77 condos. Restaurant, kitchens, tennis court, beach, dive shop, snorkeling, waterskiing, lounge, shops, laundry facilities, laundry service, Internet, car rental. AE, D, DC, MC, V. CP.*

$$$ 🖬 **Hôtel L'Esplanade Caraïbes.** This complex is on a hillside over-
★   looking Grand Case Bay and is a three-minute walk from the beach. Two curved stone staircases with inlaid tile and brick lead up to the open-air reception area. Tastefully decorated suites are large, and duplexes have cathedral ceilings and mahogany staircases as well as an extra half bath and a loft bedroom. Grand Case's roster of fine restaurants is a three-minute walk away. ⊠ *Grand Case (Box 5007, 97150),* ☎ *590/87–06–55,* FAX *590/87–29–15,* WEB *www.lesplanade.com. 24 units. Kitchens, 2 pools, laundry service, car rental. AE, MC, V. EP. Closed Sept.*

$$–$$$ 🖬 **Alizéa.** The view of Orient Bay from this resort on Mont Vernon hill is stunning. An open-air feeling pervades the hotel, from the Le Mango restaurant—where the food is superb—to the 26 guest apartments with their contemporary light-wood furnishings. Rooms vary in style and design, but all are tasteful and have large balconies. There's a path to the beach, a 10-minute walk away. ⊠ *Mont Vernon 97150, bear right on road to French Cul de Sac,* ☎ *590/87–33–42,* FAX *590/ 87–41–15,* WEB *www.alizeahotel.com. 8 1-bedroom bungalows, 18 studios. Restaurant, bar, kitchenettes, pool. AE, D, MC, V. CP.*

$$–$$$ 🖬 **Hôtel l'Atlantide.** The 10 sun-drenched units here range in size from a studio to a two-bedroom suite. The apartments are airy, with gleaming white-tile floors, crisp pastel-striped or floral upholstery, and balconies that overlook Grand Case Bay and the beach. ⊠ *Blvd. de Grand Case, Grand Case (Box 5140, 97150),* ☎ *590/87–09–80,* FAX *590/87– 30–09. 9 apartments, 1 suite. Kitchenettes, beach. MC, V. EP. Closed Sept.*

$$–$$$ 🖬 **Mercure Simson Beach Coralia.** Budget-conscious Europeans love this place because of such extras as a huge breakfast buffet and nightly local entertainment. Rooms and suites are cheerfully decorated; most have water views, and all have kitchenettes on the balconies. The lagoon is placid, but the beach is thin, and the water rocky. Flanking this resort are two operations with similar quality, price, and configuration: Anse Margot and Le Flamboyant Hotel. ✉ *Sandy Ground Rd., Baie Nettlé (Box 172, 97052),* ☎ *590/87–54–54 or 800/221–4542,* FAX *590/87–92–11,* WEB *www.mercure-simson-beach.com. 132 studios, 46 1-bedroom duplexes. Restaurant, bar, grocery, kitchenettes, tennis court, 2 pools, beach, dive shop, snorkeling, windsurfing, boating, jet skiing, waterskiing, bicycles, shops, laundry facilities, car rental. AE, DC, MC, V. BP.*

$$–$$$ 🏨 **Pavillon Beach Hotel.** Every room and suite here faces the sea and has a balcony. The spacious studios and one-bedroom suites are done in warm pastel colors and have tile floors and elegant rattan furniture. Bathrooms have hair dryers and showers but no tubs. Ground-level rooms have sliding shuttered doors opening right onto the beach. ✉ *Plage de Grand Case, Grand Case, RN 7, (Box 5133, 97070),* ☎ *590/ 87–96–46 or 800/223–9815,* FAX *590/87–71–04,* WEB *www.pavillonbeach. com. 6 rooms, 11 suites. Kitchenettes, beach. AE, MC, V. CP.*

$$ 🏨 **Captain Oliver's.** This property straddles the St. Maarten–St. Martin border: stay in France, and dine in the Netherlands—literally. The suites, all in bungalows, are a good bargain. The main hotel building faces a beautiful horseshoe-shape bay. Sail-and-stay package are popular here. Although there is no beach on site, the hotel's dinghy will transport you to nearby Dawn Beach. ✉ *Oyster Pond 97150, on the east side of Oyster Pond,* ☎ *590/87–40–26,* FAX *590/87–40–84,* WEB *www.captainolivers.com. 50 suites. Restaurant, grill, snack bar, 2 bars, in-room safes, some kitchenettes, minibars, pool, dive shop, marina, shops. AE, DC, MC, V. CP.*

$$ 🏨 **Nettlé Bay Beach Club.** The peach and aqua suites at this large resort, about five minutes from Marigot, are spread across the sands of Nettlé Bay. Four sets of villa suites (one- or two-bedroom) and a set of garden bungalows, each with its own pool, face the waterfront and Dutch St. Maarten across the bay. Rooms and suites are furnished simply but comfortably and have kitchens, and patios or balconies. The on-site restaurants offer South American and French cuisine. ✉ *Sandy Ground Rd., Baie Nettlé (Box 4081, Marigot 97064),* ☎ *590/87–68– 68 or 800/999–3543,* FAX *590/87–21–51. 148 units. 2 restaurants, bar, kitchens, 3 tennis courts, 4 pools, beach, snorkeling, jet skiing, shops, laundry service. AE, MC, V. CP, EP.*

$ 🏨 **La Résidence.** The downtown location and soundproof rooms of this Marigot hotel make it a popular place for business travelers. The intimate restaurant offers a good $28 three-course menu. You'll have to take a cab or drive to the beach, however. ✉ *Rue du Général de Gaulle, Marigot (Box 679, 97150),* ☎ *590/87–70–37 or 800/223–9815,* FAX *590/87–90–44. 22 rooms. Restaurant, minibars, lounge, shops. AE, D, MC, V, CP, MAP.*

$ 🏨 **Le Royale Louisiana.** This hotel's white and pale green galleries overlook a flower-filled courtyard. There's a selection of twin, double, and triple duplexes. Although you may need to take a taxi to the beach (the nearest one is a 20-minute walk away), you'll find plenty of shopping just steps from your door in downtown Marigot's boutique area. ✉ *Rue du Général de Gaulle, Marigot (Box 476, 97055),* ☎ *590/87–86–51,* FAX *590/87–96–49. 58 rooms. Restaurant, snack bar, hair salon. AE, D, MC, V. CP.*

Villas

Both sides of the island have villas of different sizes and for different budgets. In the United States you can get information on villa rentals through **Caribbean Concepts** (✉ 575 Underhill Blvd., Suite 140, Syosset, NY 11791, ☎ 800/423–4433). **French Caribbean International** (✉ 5662 Calle Real, #333, Santa Barbara, CA 93117-2317, ☎ 805/967–

9850 or 800/322–2223, WEB www.frenchcaribbean.com) offers island
condos and villas. **Villas of Distinction** (⊠ Box 55, Armonk, NY 10504,
☎ 914/273–3331 or 800/289–0900, WEB www.villasofdistinction.com)
is one of the oldest villa rental companies serving the island. **WIMCO**
(⊠ Box 1461, Newport, RI 02840, ☎ 401/849–8012 or 800/932–3222,
WEB www.wimco.com) has more villa, apartment, and condo listings
in the Caribbean than just about anyone else. On the island contact
Carimo (⊠ Rue du Général de Gaulle [Box 220], Marigot 97150, ☎
590/87–57–58), which has fabulous villas for rent in the tony Terres
Basses area. **St. Martin Rentals** (⊠ Box 10300, St. Martin, ☎ 599/545–
4330; Box 10300, Bedford, NH 03110, ☎ 800/308–8455) also represents several rental properties.

Dining

It may seem that this island has no monuments, but they're here—all
are dedicated to gastronomy. You'll scarcely find a touch of Dutch; the
major influences are French and Italian. The steep prices reflect both
the island's high culinary reputation and the difficulty of obtaining fresh
ingredients. In high season *make reservations. A month's notice* is
needed for many of the island's top restaurants, especially on the
French side. Many restaurants close during summer months; call ahead
to check hours.

What to Wear

Appropriate dining attire on this island ranges from swimsuits to sport
jackets. For men, a jacket and khakis or jeans take you anywhere; for
women, dressy pants, a skirt, or even fancy shorts are usually acceptable. Jeans are de rigueur in the less formal and trendier eateries. In
the listings below dress is casual (and chic) unless otherwise noted, but
ask when making reservations if you're unsure.

CATEGORY	COST*
$$$$	over $30
$$$	$20–$30
$$	$10–$20
$	under $10

per person for a main course at dinner

Dutch Side

AMERICAN

$$ ✕ **Turtle Pier Bar & Restaurant.** Though the entrance beside a gas sta-
tion may seem unenticing, a passage leads you past monkeys and par-
rots to a relaxing deck area over Simpson Bay Lagoon. The genial owner,
Al Wathey, whose family is one of the island's oldest, offers cheap draft
beer, huge American breakfasts, all-you-can-eat Sunday rib dinners, and
live music several nights a week. ⊠ *114 Airport Rd., Simpson Bay,* ☎
599/545–2562. AE, D, MC, V.

$ ✕ **Ric's Place.** This sports bar is popular with Americans who need a
dose of home and with just about anyone who wants to drool over
one of the biggest burgers in town. Try the nachos *grande* with a cou-
ple of friends while you watch one (or two) of six satellite televisions.
⊠ *Airport Blvd. 12, Simpson Bay,* ☎ *599/545–3630. No credit cards.*

ASIAN

$$ ✕ **Wajang Doll.** Indonesian dishes are served in the garden of this
West Indian–style house. *Nasi goreng* (fried rice) and red snapper in a
sweet soy glaze are standouts, as is *rijsttafel,* a traditional Indonesian
meal of rice accompanied by 15 to 20 dishes. (The name comes from
the *wajang* doll, which is used in Indonesian shadow plays, a tradi-

tional art form.) ✉ *167 Front St., Philipsburg,* ☎ *599/542–2687. AE, MC, V. Closed Sun. No lunch Sat.*

CAFÉ

$ ✕ **Kangaroo Court Caffè.** The Kangaroo might just serve the island's best cup of coffee. Decorated in a whimsical West Indian style with potted plants and colorful tiles and umbrellas, it's in an old salt warehouse off Front Street beside the courthouse. Come for breakfast or a lunch of salads, pastas, and sandwiches. ✉ *6 Hendrickstraat, Philipsburg,* ☎ *599/542–4278. MC, V. No dinner. Closed Sun..*

CONTEMPORARY

$$$–$$$$ ✕ **Le Perroquet.** A cool green-and-white West Indian–style house overlooking a lagoon is where you'll find this peaceful, romantic restaurant. Chef Pierre Castagna prepares exotic specialties, such as grilled breast of ostrich in a bordelaise sauce, as well as savory dishes featuring duck, veal, and beef. ✉ *Airport Rd., Simpson Bay,* ☎ *599/545–4339. AE, MC, V. No lunch. Closed Mon. Closed June and Sept.*

CONTINENTAL

$$–$$$ ✕ **Chesterfield's.** Casual lunches of burgers and salads and more elaborate Continental dinners are served at this informal, nautical-theme marina restaurant. The dinner menu includes French onion soup, roast duckling with fresh pineapple and banana sauce, and several different preparations of shrimp. The Mermaid Bar is popular with yachties. ✉ *Great Bay Marina, Philipsburg,* ☎ *599/542–3484. D, MC, V.*

ECLECTIC

$$$–$$$$ ✕ **Saratoga.** The handsome mahogany-outfitted dining room in the
★ yacht club's stucco and red-tile building has views of the Simpson Bay Marina. The menu changes daily, borrowing from various influences, including Asian and Southwestern. You might start with Malpeque oysters with balsamic-horseradish sauce, then segue into crispy fried roundhead snapper in fermented black bean sauce. The wine list includes 10 to 12 wines by the glass. ✉ *Simpson Bay Yacht Club, Airport Rd., Simpson Bay,* ☎ *599/544–2421. Reservations essential. AE, MC, V. No lunch. Closed Sun. Closed Aug.–Sept.*

$$–$$$$ ✕ **Indiana Beach.** This light-hearted restaurant-bar is fronted by Kimsha Beach at Simpson Bay. The motif is pure adventure and jungle exotic, with cavernous arches and terra-cotta walls painted with designs based on pre-Columbian petroglyphs. The big night here is Thursday, when happy hour runs until the wee hours. You can swim at Kimsha or at the restaurant's own pool. Fare is sandwiches, steaks, and seafood. ✉ *8 Billy Folly Rd., Simpson Bay,* ☎ *599/544–2797. AE, MC, V.* ☻ *Breakfast also served.*

FRENCH

$$–$$$$ ✕ **Antoine.** This elegant spot overlooks Great Bay. Candles glow on tables set with crisp blue-and-white tablecloths and gleaming silver, and the sound of the surf drifts up from the beach. You might start your meal with French onion soup or lobster bisque, then move on to steak au poivre, duck in brandy sauce with cherries, or lobster thermidor. For dessert try the sublime Grand Marnier soufflé. You can also lunch on the thatched roof huts right on the sand. Say hello to accommodating owner Jean-Pierre. ✉ *119 Front St., Philipsburg,* ☎ *599/542–2964. Reservations essential. AE, MC, V.*

$$–$$$$ ✕ **L'Escargot.** A 19th-century house wrapped in verandas houses one of St. Maarten's oldest French restaurants. Starters include frogs' legs in garlic sauce and crepes filled with caviar and sour cream. For a main course try *canard de l'escargot* (duck in pineapple and banana sauce).

There's often cabaret-style entertainment on Wednesday night. ✉ *84 Front St., Philipsburg,* ☎ *599/542–2483. AE, MC, V.*

INDIAN

$$ ✕ **Shiv Sagar.** This large second-floor restaurant emphasizes Kashmiri and Mogul specialties. Marvelous tandooris and curries are offered, but try one of the less familiar preparations, such as *madrasi machi* (red snapper with hot spices). ✉ *20 Front St., Philipsburg,* ☎ *599/542– 2299. AE, D, DC, MC, V. Closed Sun.*

ITALIAN

$$–$$$ ✕ **Spartaco.** Every element of the Northern Italian cuisine served in this 200-year-old stone plantation house is either homemade or imported from Italy. Specialties include black angel-hair pasta with shrimp and garlic, and veal Vesuviana with mozzarella, oregano, and tomato sauce. ✉ *Almond Grove, Cole Bay,* ☎ *599/544–5379. AE, MC, V. No lunch. Closed Mon. Closed June–Oct.*

French Side

CAFÉ

$$ ✕ **Bistrot Nu.** It's hard to top the simple, unadorned fare and reason-
★ able prices you'll find at this adorable restaurant tucked in a Marigot alley. Traditional brasserie-style food—coq au vin, fish soup, snails— is served in a friendly, intimate dining room. The place is enormously popular, and the tables are routinely packed until it closes at midnight. ✉ *Rue de Hollande, Marigot,* ☎ *590/87–97–09. MC, V. Closed Sun. Dinner only.*

CARIBBEAN

$$–$$$$ ✕ **Paradise View.** Perched atop one of the island's most scenic look-
★ outs, this restaurant rewards you with breathtaking views of Orient Beach, the coast, and the sea to St. Baths. The owner regales you with the stories behind her delightful local dishes, which include conch and dumplings, baby-back ribs, traditional beef stew, and the house drink, mango madness colada (free with lunch). ✉ *Hope Hill, Orient Bay,* ☎ *590/29–45–37. AE, MC, V.*

$$–$$$ ✕ **Claude Mini-Club.** This brightly decorated upstairs restaurant on the
★ harbor serves terrific creole and French cuisine. The chairs and madras tablecloths are a mélange of sun-yellow and orange, and the whole place is built (tree house–style) around the trunks of coconut trees. It's the place to be on Wednesday and Saturday nights, when the dinner buf- fet includes roast pig, lobster, roast beef, and all the trimmings. ✉ *Front de Mer, Marigot,* ☎ *590/87–50–69. AE, MC, V. No lunch Sun.*

$$–$$$ ✕ **Yvette's.** The attempts at romance couldn't be more endearing:
★ classical music plays softly, and the tiny eight-table room is bathed in yellow. Creole specialties, such as *accras* (spicy fish fritters), stewed chicken with rice and beans, and conch and dumplings, make this an island favorite. ✉ *Orléans, off the Orléans road,* ☎ *590/87–32–03. No credit cards. Closed Wed.*

$–$$ ✕ **Le Poulet d'Orléans.** Chef Tony and his adorable children—three sons and one daughter—treat you to unsurpassably warm service from the three-table porch of their roadside gingerbread home. The local spe- cialties are excellent, including seafood, conch and dumplings, and the best ribs on the island. Interior rooms of the house are filled with an- tiques, many of which are for sale. ✉ *Orient Bay Hwy., French Quartier,* ☎ *590/87–48–24. No credit cards. Closed Mon. Dinner only, except Sun.*

$ ✕ **Enoch's Place.** Enoch's cooking draws crowds of locals and visitors each day to the blue-and-white-striped awning on a corner of the Marigot Market. Local specialties include garlic and creole shrimp, and fresh lobster. For breakfast, try cod in delicious fried johnnycakes.

✉ *Marigot Market, Front de Mer, Marigot,* ☎ *590/29–29–88. No credit cards. Closed Sun.*

CONTEMPORARY

$$$–$$$$ ✕ **Le Tastevin.** This chic pavilion lookout out on Grand Case bay is filled with tropical plants and cooled by ceiling fans. Owner Daniel Passeri, a native of Burgundy, also founded the homey Auberge Gourmande across the street. The menu here is more ambitious, including foie gras in Armagnac sauce, duck breast in banana-lime sauce, and red snapper fillet with curry and wild-mushroom sauce. ✉ *86 blvd. de Grand Case, Grand Case,* ☎ *590/87–55–45. Reservations essential. AE, MC, V.*

ECLECTIC

$$$–$$$$ ✕ **Le Pressoir.** Many say that presentation is everything. Combine that
★ with excellent food and a setting in a charming West Indies house, where the bill won't break the bank, and you have a great restaurant. French and creole fusion cuisine reigns; go for the fresh local fish prepared with tropical fruit glazes and sauces. The crème brûlée is superb. ✉ *30 blvd. de Grand Case, Grand Case,* ☎ *590/87–76–62. AE, MC, V. No lunch. Closed Sun.*

$$$–$$$$ ✕ **The Rainbow.** In a town of splendid seaside boîtes, this is one of the
★ best. The cobalt-blue-and-white, split-level dining room is strikingly simple. Lapping waves and murmuring guests make for a highly romantic mood. Fleur and David are the stylish, energetic hosts. Specialties include shrimp and scallop fricassee with Caribbean chutney, and dishes are dressed with such fanciful touches as red cabbage crisps. ✉ *176 blvd. de Grand Case, Grand Case,* ☎ *590/87–55–80. AE, MC, V. Closed Sun.*

FRENCH

$$$–$$$$ ✕ **Le Santal.** The approach to this dazzler is through a nondescript work-
★ ing-class suburb of Marigot. The exterior appears ramshackle, but the interior is transformed by soft lighting, china, and crystal. Specialties by chef Marc Daniel, who trained at Paris's Lasserre restaurant, include roasted lobster with shallots and tomatoes, foie gras sautéed in cassis, and lacquered duck. Reserve one of the five cherished waterside tables. ✉ *Sandy Ground Rd., Sandy Ground,* ☎ *590/87–53–48. AE, MC, V. No lunch.*

$$$–$$$$ ✕ **La Vie En Rose.** This island classic on the Marigot waterfront serves classic French with an occasional Caribbean twist, as in the fillet of red snapper in a puff pastry served with fresh herbs and lime sauce. Appetizers include a warm smoked salmon with potatoes and chives, and lobster salad with a touch of ginger. Women are presented a red rose after dinner, a touch in tune with the mood of the candlelit, second-floor dining room. ✉ *On the waterfront, at rue de la République, Marigot,* ☎ *590/87–54–42. Reservations essential. AE, D, MC, V. No lunch Sun.; dinner only mid-June–mid-Oct.*

$$–$$$$ ✕ **Le Mango.** Many claim that this elegant terrace restaurant at the Al-
★ izéa hotel offers the island's best cuisine. The menu has a tantalizing blend of French creole and traditional French specialties, with appetizers like homemade foie gras with red-wine jelly or roasted sea scallops. For the main course, take your pick from the fresh seafood offerings, including mahimahi and tuna, or try the beef tenderloin with stewed shallots in red wine sauce. ✉ *Mont Vernon, bear right on road to French Cul de Sac,* ☎ *590/87–41–20. AE, D, MC, V.*

$$–$$$ ✕ **Mario's Bistro.** This fabulous, romantic eatery earns raves for its fine
★ service and high-quality cuisine. Didier Gonnon and Martyne Tardif are out front, while chef Mario Tardif is in the kitchen creating dishes such as baked salmon in a caramelized onion crust. The open-air country French–style restaurant is on the canal as you enter Marigot from

Sandy Ground, and if you didn't know better, you'd think you were in Venice. ⊠ *Sandy Ground,* ☎ *590/87–06–36. Reservations essential. MC, V. Closed Sun. Closed mid-June–July.*

SEAFOOD

$$–$$$ ✕ **La Plaisance.** Cool strains of jazz waft through this lively open-air brasserie as you sample terrific salads (try the Niçoise or *landaine*— duck, smoked ham, croutons, and fried egg), pizzas (wonderful lobster), pastas (garlic and basil *pistou*), and grilled seafood at unbeatable prices. This is one of several ultracasual eateries at Port La Royale, all offering simple, appetizing food, fixed-price menus, and happy hours. ⊠ *La Marina Port la Royale, Marigot,* ☎ *590/87–85–00. AE, MC, V.*

Beaches

The island's 10 mi (16 km) of beaches are all open to the public. However, you can't enter the beach via a hotel unless you're a paying guest or are renting water-sports equipment there. Topless bathing is virtually de rigueur on the French side, where the beaches are generally better than on the Dutch side. Don't leave valuables unattended on the beach or in your rental car—even in the trunk.

Dutch Side

Cupecoy Beach. Near the Dutch–French border and south of Baie Longue, this small, shifting arc of white sand is fringed by eroded limestone cliffs. You'll find vendors who sell cold sodas and beers, and you can rent chairs and umbrellas. The strip is clothing-optional and attracts the island's gay crowd.

Dawn Beach–Oyster Pond. The approach to this long stretch of white sand is through the grounds of the Dawn Beach Hotel. The long beach is partly protected by reefs (good for snorkeling), but the water isn't always calm. When the waves come rolling in, this is the island's best bodysurfing spot.

Great Bay. This long stretch of white sand runs behind the shops, restaurants, and hotels of Philipsburg's Front Street. There are numerous beachside bistros; some even offer showers and toilets (for a fee) and rent water-sports equipment. The bay is a favorite with cruise-ship passengers, but its east end, near the marinas, can be dirty with detritus from boats.

Maho Bay. Ecru-color sand, palm and sea-grape trees, calm waters, and the roar of jets lowering to nearby Juliana International Airport distinguish this beach.

Mullet Bay. The powdery white sands of this beach are always crowded: people come to bask in its wide spaces and enjoy its great surf. Concession stands offer refreshments.

Simpson Bay. This long half-moon of white sand is near Simpson Bay Village, one of the island's last undiscovered hamlets. In this small fishing village you'll find refreshments, a dive shop, and neat little ultra-Caribbean town homes.

French Side

Baie de Friar. The beach at Friar's Bay is on a small, picturesque cove between Marigot and Grand Case. It attracts a casual crowd of locals and has a small snack bar, Kali's, that's owned by a welcoming gentleman with dreadlocks.

Baie de Grand Case. A gentle surf and plenty of fine restaurants are the draws of the thin beach at Grand Case Bay. You'll find water-sports activities, and, at the north end, small coves. The snorkeling is best at the south end. On the north end you'll find several *lolos,* barbecue huts that serve inexpensive local fare.

Baie Longue. Long Bay's beach is a beautiful 1-mi-long (1½-km-long) curve of white sand on the island's westernmost tip. It's a good place for snorkeling and swimming, but beware of a strong undertow when the waters are rough. You can sunbathe in the buff, and in relative seclusion, though only a few do. There are no facilities.

Baie Orientale. The beach at Orient Bay, the island's best-known clothing-optional beach, is at the top of the agenda for voyeurs from cruise ships. The nude section is to the right on the southern end. Farther down, toward the middle of the beach, is a resort with several restaurants, bars, and chaises (with food and beverage service) for rent. This is a good windsurfing spot, with a couple of on-site rental shops that can help you take advantage of the steady trade winds.

Baie Rouge. Red Bay is right off the main road past Prune Bay. Some consider it the prettiest beach on the island, though the waves here can be rough. You'll find refreshment stands and places to rent beach chairs and umbrellas.

Ilet Pinel. This little speck of land off the northeast coast has about 500 yards of beach that offer a great deal of privacy. Boats can transport you here from French Cul de Sac and the beach at Orient Bay ($5 per person round-trip). A couple of small beachside restaurants offer refreshments.

Outdoor Activities and Sports

BOATING AND SAILING

The island's waters and winds make it ideal for exploring or relaxing by boat. It'll cost you around $500 per day to rent a 20-ft power boat, less for smaller boats. A 35-ft sailboat runs about $700 per day. You can rent motorboats, speedboats, and sailboats at **Aquamania Watersports** (⊠ Pelican Marina, Simpson Bay, ☎ 599/544–2640). **Bobby's Marina** (⊠ Yrausquin Blvd., Philipsburg, ☎ 599/542–4096) has numerous watersports and boat rental options. For the best full-service yacht and watersports rentals on the French side, contact **Marine Time** (☎ 590/87–20–28), behind the tourist office at the port in Marigot. **The Moorings** (⊠ Captain Oliver's Marina, Oyster Pond, ☎ 590/87–32–55 or 888/952–8420) has a fleet of Beneteau yachts as well as bareboat and crewed catamarans. **Sunsail** (⊠ Captain Oliver's Marina, ☎ 590/87–83–41 or 800/327–2276), in Oyster Pond, has a fleet of sailboats for hire. For the thrill of a lifetime, you can join the **St. Maarten America's Cup Challenge** at Bobby's Marina (☎ 599/542–2366 or 800/786–2278). Participants are put on teams and compete using such one-time 36-ft racing machines as Dennis Connor's *Stars and Stripes* and the *Canada II* (yes, the actual boats). The cost to participate in the two-plus hour races, which are held daily, is $65.

FISHING

You can angle for yellowtail snapper, grouper, marlin, tuna, and wahoo on deep-sea excursions. Costs (for four people) range from $400 for a half day to $700 for a full day. Prices usually include bait and tackle, instruction for novices, and an open bar. Contact **Lee Deepsea Fishing** (⊠ Airport Rd., Simpson Bay, ☎ 599/544–4233 or 599/544–4234), which is convenient for hotels in that area. **Rudy's Deep Sea Fishing** (⊠ Airport Rd., Simpson Bay, ☎ 599/545–2177, WEB www.rudysdeepseafishing.com) has been around for years and is one of the more experienced sport angling outfits. **Sailfish Caraïbes** (⊠ Anse Marcel, ☎ 590/87–31–94 or 590/27–40–90) is your best bet on the north side of the island.

GOLF

Mullet Bay Resort (⊠ Airport Rd., north of airport, ☎ 599/545–2801 or 599/545–3069) has an 18-hole course—the island's *only* course.

Greens fees are $52 for 9 holes, and $93 for 18 holes. Club and cart rentals are also available.

HORSEBACK RIDING

All horseback riding outfitters can accommodate novices and experts alike; costs start at $50 for a two-hour ride. You can also arrange rides through most hotels. **Bayside Riding Club** (⊠ Galion Beach Rd., Baie Orientale, ☎ 590/87–36–64) is a long-established outfit. **Caid & Isa** (⊠ French Cul de Sac–Anse Marcel Rd., Anse Marcel, ☎ 590/87–45–70) has been offering guided rides for years. **Crazy Acres Riding Center** (⊠ Wathey Estate, Cole Bay, ☎ 599/544–2793) is your best bet for guided rides in the Philipsburg area.

PARASAILING

On the French side, **Kontiki Watersports** (⊠ Northern beach entrance, Baie Orientale, ☎ 590/87–46–89) offers parasailing rides.

SCUBA DIVING

The water temperature here is rarely below 70°F (21°C), and visibility is usually excellent, averaging about 100 ft (30 m). Beginners and night divers will appreciate the tugboat *Annie,* which lies in 25 ft–30 ft (6 m–9 m) of water in Simpson Bay. Off the north coast, in the protected and mostly current-free Grand Case Bay, is **Creole Rock.** The water here ranges in depth from 10 ft–25 ft (3 m–8 m), visibility is excellent. Other sites off the north coast include **Ilet Pinel,** for its good shallow diving; Green Key, with its vibrant barrier reef; and Tintamarre (Flat Island), for its sheltered coves and geologic faults. One of the most popular sites is **Proselyte Reef,** named for the British frigate HMS *Proselyte.* The ship, initially a Dutch frigate, was captured by the British in 1796 and sank about 1 mi (1½ km) south of Great Bay in 1801. Today the hulk lies 15 ft–45 ft (5 m–14 m) below the surface and is almost completely covered with coral. On average, one-tank dives start at $50, two-tank dives start at $80, and certification courses start at $350.

On the Dutch side, SSI- (Scuba Schools International) and PADI-certified dive centers include **Ocean Explorers Dive Shop** (⊠ 113 E. Walfare Rd., Simpson Bay, ☎ 599/544–5252). **Trade Winds Dive Center** (⊠ Great Bay Marina, Philipsburg, ☎ 599/547–5176) is one of the island's oldest dive operations, and a good choice in the Philipsburg area.

On the French side, **Blue Ocean** (⊠ Sandy Ground Rd., Baie Nettlé, ☎ 590/87–89–73) is PADI- and CMAS-certified. **Octoplus** (⊠ Blvd. de Grand Case, Grand Case, ☎ 590/87–20–62) is a complete PADI-certified dive center. **O2 Limit** (⊠ Blvd. de Grand Case, Grand Case, ☎ 590/64–28–92), in the Grand Case Beach Club, is a complete PADI-certified dive center with the newest equipment and great instructors.

SNORKELING

Some of the best snorkeling on the Dutch side can be found around the rocks below Fort Amsterdam off Little Bay Beach, in the west end of Maho Bay, off Pelican Key, and around the reefs off Dawn Beach and Oyster Pond. On the French side, the area around Orient Bay, Caye Verte (Green Key), Ilet Pinel, and Flat Island is especially lovely and is officially classified, and protected, as a regional underwater nature reserve. The average cost of an afternoon snorkeling trip is $25 per person. **Dive Safaris** (⊠ Bobby's Marina, Yrausquin Blvd., Philipsburg, ☎ 599/544–4056) is a full-service outfit for snorkelers and divers. Arrange rentals and snorkeling trips through **Kontiki Watersports** (⊠ Northern beach entrance, Baie Orientale, ☎ 590/87–46–89). **Ocean Explorers** (⊠ 113 E. Walfare Rd., Simpson Bay, ☎ 599/544–5252) offers diving and snorkeling excursions.

SEA EXCURSIONS

The 50-ft catamaran *Bluebeard II* (☎ 599/545–2898), moored in Simpson Bay, sails around Anguilla's south and northwest coasts to Prickly Pear, where there are excellent coral reefs for snorkeling and powdery white sands for sunning. These excursions cost $45–$65 per person. You can take a daylong picnic sail to nearby islands or secluded coves aboard the 45-ft ketch *Gabrielle* (☎ 599/542–3170). The sleek 76-ft catamaran *Golden Eagle* (☎ 599/543–0068) takes day sailors to outlying islets and reefs for snorkeling and partying. The *Laura Rose* (☎ 599/547–0710) offers half- and full-day sails, ranging from $25 to $65 per person.

A cross between a submarine and a glass-bottom boat, the 34-passenger *Seaworld Explorer* (✉ Blvd. de Grand Case, Grand Case, ☎ 599/542–4078), crawls along the water's surface while you, submerged in a lower chamber, view marine life and coral through large windows. Divers jump off the boat and feed the fish and eels. The cost is $30 for adults, $20 for kids; transport to and from your hotel costs an extra $10 per adult, $7 per child.

In St. Martin, sailing, snorkeling, and picnic excursions to nearby islands can be arranged through **Kontiki Watersports** (✉ northern beach entrance, Baie Orientale, ☎ 590/87–46–89). **Le Méridien's L'Habitation** (✉ Anse Marcel, ☎ 590/87–33–33) is a good choice for those staying in the north.

TENNIS

There are two lighted courts at the **Blue Bay Club Mont Vernon** (✉ East off road to Freneh Cul de Sac, Baie Orientale, ☎ 590/87–62–00). You'll find four lighted courts at the **Maho Beach Resort & Casino** (✉ Airport Rd., Maho Bay, ☎ 599/545–2115). You can use the four lighted courts at the **Pelican Resort & Casino** (✉ Airport Rd., Pelican Key, Simpson Bay, ☎ 599/544–2503). The six lighted courts at **Le Privilège Resort & Spa** (✉ Anse Marcel, ☎ 590/87–38–38) are available to nonguests, as are its four squash and two racquetball courts.

WATERSKIING

Expect to pay $50 per half-hour for waterskiing, and $40–$45 per half hour for jet-skiing. On the Dutch side rent waterskiing and jet-skiing equipment through **Aquamania** (✉ Pelican Marina, Simpson Bay, ☎ 599/544–2640), a water-sports activity center. On the French side, **Kontiki Watersports** (✉ Northern beach entrance, Baie Orientale, ☎ 590/87–46–89) rents windboards, takes water-skiers out, and provides instruction. **Grand Case Beach Club Activities** (✉ 21 rue de Petit Plage, Grand Case, ☎ 590/87–51–87) provides instruction for novice waterskiiers.

WINDSURFING

The **Nathalie Simon Windsurfing Club** (✉ northern beach entrance, Baie Oriental, ☎ 590/29–41–57) offers rentals and lessons. Lessons are $25–$30 per hour.

Shopping

Nearly 200 cruise ships call at St. Maarten each year, and they do so for about 500 reasons. That's roughly the number of duty-free shops on the island. Prices can be 25%–50% below those in the United States and Canada on French perfumes, liquor, cognac and fine liqueurs, cigarettes and cigars, Swedish crystal, Irish linen, Italian leather, cameras, designer fashions, Swiss watches, plus thousands of other things you never knew you wanted. If you're shopping for electronics in Philipsburg, try negotiating for a lower price. Competition is fierce, and some stores will bargain if you pay cash. You'll find more fashion on the French side in Marigot, although stalwarts such as Polo Ralph Lauren, Tommy Hilfiger, and Benetton have Philipsburg outlets. But you'll find Marigot to be a much more pleasant place to shop and stroll.

If you're looking for local crafts, you may be disappointed; they tend to be of the cheesy variety. St. Maarten's best-known local product is its guavaberry liqueur, made from rum and the wild berries that grow only on this island's central mountains.

Prices are quoted in florins, euros, and dollars; shops take credit cards and traveler's checks.

Areas

Front Street, Philipsburg, is one long strip lined with sleek boutiques and colorful shops, but if more than one cruise ship is in port, it's best to avoid this street as you won't be able to move. **Old Street,** near the end of Front Street, has 22 stores, boutiques, and open-air cafés. There's a slew of boutiques in the **Maho** shopping plaza as well as at the **Plaza del Lago,** at the Simpson Bay Yacht Club complex. On the French side, wrought-iron balconies, colorful awnings, and gingerbread trim decorate Marigot's smart shops, tiny boutiques, and bistros in the **Marina Port La Royale** complex and on the main streets, **rue de la Liberté** and **rue de la République.**

Specialty Items

ART GALLERIES

Galerie Lynn (✉ 83 blvd. de Grand Case, Grand Case, ☎ 590/87–77–24) sells stunning paintings and sculptures. **Gingerbread Galerie** (✉ Marina Port La Royale, Marigot, ☎ 590/87–73–21) specializes in Haitian art. **Greenwith Galleries** (✉ 33 Front St., Philipsburg, ☎ 599/542–3842) has Caribbean art. **Minguet** (✉ Rambaud Hill, ☎ 590/87–76–06) carries richly hued paintings, lithographs, posters, and postcards, all depicting island flora and landscapes by the artist Alexandre Minguet. **Roland Richardson Paintings and Prints** (✉ 6 rue de la République, Marigot, ☎ 590/87–84–08) sells oil and watercolor paintings by the well-known local artist Roland Richardson. Richardson, who also works in monoprints, copper etchings, and woodcuts, is famous for his elaborate depictions of the flamboyant, or royal poinciana, tree.

DUTY-FREE GOODS

Carat (✉ 16 rue de la République, Marigot, ☎ 590/87–73–40; ✉ 73 Front St., Philipsburg, ☎ 599/542–2180) sells china and jewelry. **Havane** (✉ Marina Port la Royale, Marigot, ☎ 590/87–70–39) is a good place for designer fashions. **Lipstick** (✉ Plaza Caraibes, rue du Kennedy, Marigot, ☎ 590/87–73–24; ✉ 31 Front St., Philipsburg, ☎ 599/542–6051) has an enormous selection of perfume and cosmetics. **Little Europe** (✉ 80 Front St., Philipsburg, ☎ 599/542–4371; ✉ 1 rue de Général de Gaulle, Marigot, ☎ 590/87–92–64) sells fine jewelry, crystal, and china. **Little Switzerland** (✉ 6 rue de la Liberté, Marigot, ☎ 590/87–09–02; ✉ 52 Front St., Philipsburg, ☎ 599/542–3530) purveys fine crystal and china as well as perfume and jewelry. **Oro Diamante** (✉ 62 Front St., Philipsburg ☎ 599/543–0343) carries loose diamonds, jewelry, watches, perfume, and cosmetics. **Manek's** (✉ Rue de la République, Marigot, ☎ 590/87–54–91) sells, on two floors, luggage, perfume, jewelry, Cuban cigars, duty-free liquors, and tobacco products.

HANDICRAFTS

The **Guavaberry Company Shop** (✉ 8 Front St., Philipsburg, ☎ 599/542–2965, WEB www.guavaberry.com) is the small factory where the famous guavaberry liqueur is made by the Sint Maarten Guavaberry Company; on sale are myriad versions of the liqueur (including one made with jalapeño peppers), as well as spices and batiks. There are free samples. **Shipwreck Shop** (⊠ 42 Front St., Philipsburg, ☎ 599/ 542–2962; ⊠ Marina Port la Royale, Marigot, ☎ 590/87–27–37) stocks Caribelle batiks, hammocks, handmade jewelry, the local guavaberry liqueur, and herbs and spices.

Nightlife

To find out what's doing on the island, pick up *St. Maarten Nights* or *St. Maarten Events,* both distributed free in the tourist office and hotels. The glossy *Discover St. Martin/St. Maarten* magazine, also free, has articles on island history and on the newest shops, discos, and restaurants.

BARS

Axum Café (⊠ 7L Front St., Philipsburg, no phone), a bar and 1960s-style coffee shop, offers cultural activities, dancing, open-mike night, and art exhibits. It's open daily, 11:30 AM until the wee hours. **Le Bar de la Mer** (⊠ Market Sq., Marigot, ☎ 590/87–81–79), on the harbor, is a popular gathering spot in the evening (it's open until 2 AM). **Cheri's Café** (⊠ Airport Rd., Simpson Bay, across from Maho Beach Hotel & Casino, ☎ 599/545–3361) is a local institution, with cheap food and great live bands. **Turtle Pier Bar & Restaurant** (⊠ Airport Rd., Simpson Bay, ☎ 599/545–2230) always hops with a lively crowd.

CASINOS

All the island's casinos—found only on the Dutch side—have craps, blackjack, roulette, and slot machines. You must be 18 years or older to gamble. Dress is casual (most anything goes except bathing suits or skimpy beachwear). Many casinos are in hotels such as Great Bay Beach Hotel, Pelican Resort, and Casino Royal at Maho Beach (which produces the splashy Paris Revue Show). You'll also find independent casinos: **Coliseum** (⊠ Front St., Philipsburg, ☎ 599/543–2101) is small, but you can win or lose as much as you'd like. The **Lightning Casino** (⊠ Airport Rd., Cole Bay, ☎ 599/544–3290) is easily recognized by its gaudy, flashing sign. The **Rouge et Noir Casino** (⊠ Front St., Philipsburg, ☎ 599/542–2952), another Front Street casino, is small but busy.

DANCE CLUBS

Club One (⊠ Marina Port Royale, Marigot Bay, ☎ 590/87–98–41) is a late-night (really, all-night every night but Sunday and Monday) happening spot on the marina. **Greenhouse** (⊠ Front St., Philipsburg, ☎ 599/542–2941) has canned DJ music and a two-for-one happy hour that lasts all night Tuesday. **L'Atmo** (⊠ Marina Port la Royale, Marigot, ☎ 590/87–98–41) is where French nationals and locals flock for salsa and soca on Friday. It's open every night but Monday. **Pink Mango** (⊠ Sandy Ground Rd., Baie Nettlé, ☎ 590/87–91–75) at the Hotel Laguna is a popular gay spot with a young, mixed crowd. **Q Club** (⊠ Airport Rd., Maho Bay, ☎ 599/545–2115) is a popular disco upstairs from the casino at Maho Beach Resort.

Exploring St. Maarten/St. Martin

St. Maarten–St. Martin's roads are very good and are generally well marked, although many of the main routes outside Marigot and Philipsburg don't have official names. With the exception of some annoying congestion, especially in and around Philipsburg and Marigot, the island is easy to traverse (it's best to rent a car, motorcycle, or scooter).

If you're looking for scenic routes on the Dutch side, try the road that leads to Oyster Pond, north of Philipsburg. It winds past soaring hills, turquoise waters, quaint West Indian houses, and wonderful views of St. Barths, and it eventually leads down to Dawn Beach, one of the island's best snorkeling spots. Terres Basses is a western coastal area that runs from Sandy Ground, just south of Marigot, to Cupecoy Beach, on the Dutch side—a short, beautiful stretch of sandstone cliffs and coves. Beaches here also include Baie Rouge and Baie Longue.

Numbers in the margin correspond to points of interest on the St. Maarten/St. Martin map.

Sights to See

⑤ Butterfly Farm. Run by Karin and Willy Slayter, British lovers of lepidoptera, the Butterfly Farm showcases dozens of varieties of colorful insects in various stages of development. At any given time, some 40 species of butterfly, numbering as many as 600, are fluttering around in a garden under a tented net. ✉ *Rte. de Le Galion, Quartier d'Orleans,* ☎ *590/87–31–21,* WEB *www.thebutterflyfarm.com.* ✆ *$10.* ⊙ *Daily 9–4.*

⑦ French Cul de Sac. North of Orient Bay Beach, you'll find the French colonial mansion of St. Martin's mayor nestled in the hills. Little red-roof houses look like open umbrellas tumbling down the green hillside. The scenery here is glorious, and the area is great for hiking. There's a lot of construction, however, as the surroundings are slowly being developed. From the beach here shuttle boats make the five-minute trip to **Ilet Pinel,** an uninhabited island that's fine for picnicking, sunning, and swimming.

⑧ Grand Case. The island's most picturesque town is set in the heart of the French side on a beach at the foot of green hills and pastures. Though it has only a 1-mi-long (1½-km-long) main street, it's known as the "restaurant capital of the Caribbean." More than 27 restaurants serve French, Italian, Indonesian, and Vietnamese fare here. The budget-minded love the half dozen *lolos*—kiosks at the far end of town that sell savory barbecue and seafood. Grand Case Beach Club is at the end of this road and has two beaches where you can take a dip.

② Guana Bay Point. North of Philipsburg, Guana Bay Point offers a splendid view of the island's east coast, tiny deserted islets, and petite St. Barths, which is anything but deserted.

⑨ Marigot. This town is a wonderful place to tarry awhile if you are a shopper, a gourmand, or just a Francophile. Marina Port la Royale is the shopping complex at the port, but rue de la République and rue de la Liberté, which border the bay, are also filled with duty-free shops, boutiques, and bistros. There's less bustle here than in Philipsburg, and the open-air cafés are tempting places in which to stop for a rest. Marigot doesn't die at night, so you might wish to stay here into the evening—particularly on Wednesdays, when the market opens its art, crafts, and souvenir stalls, and on Thursdays, when the shops of Marina Port la Royale remain open until 10 and shoppers enjoy live music. In the harbor's main parking lot you'll find the kiosk for the Anguilla ferry as well as several crafts stalls. Across the parking lot, near the small traffic circle, is the helpful French tourist office. North of town there's a shopping complex on the inland side of the main road. The small, ambitious **Musée de Saint-Martin** (St. Martin Museum), south of town, has artifacts from the island's pre-Columbian days. Included are pottery exhibits, rock carvings, and petroglyphs, as well as displays from the colonial and sugar plantation days. Upstairs is a small art gallery, where you'll find locally produced art, including lithographs and posters. ✉ *Sandy Ground Rd.,* ☎ *590/29–22–84.* 💳 *$5.* ⏱ *Mon.–Sat. 9–1 and 3–6.*

❹ Orléans. North of Oyster Pond and the Étang aux Poissons (Fish Lake) is the island's oldest settlement, also known as the French Quarter. You'll find classic, vibrantly painted West Indian–style homes with elaborate gingerbread fretwork.

❸ Oyster Pond. North of Dawn Beach is the point where two early settlers, a Frenchman and a Dutchman, allegedly began to pace in opposite directions around the island to divide it between their respective countries. Local legend maintains that the obese, sweaty Hollander stopped frequently to refresh himself with gin—the reason the French side is nearly twice the size of the Dutch (the official boundary marker is on the other side of the island).

❶ Philipsburg. The capital of Dutch St. Maarten stretches about a mile (1½ km) along an isthmus between Great Bay and the Salt Pond and has five parallel streets: Front, Back, C. A. Cannegieter, Walter Nisbeth, and Pondfill. Front Street has been recobbled, cars are discouraged from using it, and the pedestrian area has been widened. Shops, restaurants, and casinos vie for the hordes coming off cruise ships. Little lanes called *steegjes* connect Front Street with Back Street, which has fewer shops and is considerably less congested.

Wathey Square (pronounced watty), in the middle of the isthmus on which Philipsburg sits, bustles with souvenir shops and visitors. Directly across from the square are the town hall and the courthouse, in the striking white building with the cupola. The structure was built in 1793 and has served as the commander's home, a fire station, a jail, and a post office. The streets surrounding the square are lined with hotels, duty-free shops, fine restaurants, and cafés—most of them in West Indian cottages gussied up with gingerbread trim. Alleys lead to arcades and flower-filled courtyards where there are yet more boutiques and eateries. The **Captain Hodge Pier,** just off the square, is a good spot to view Great Bay and the beach that stretches alongside. The **Sint Maarten Museum** hosts rotating cultural exhibits and a permanent historical display called Forts of St. Maarten/St. Martin. The artifacts range from Arawak pottery shards to articles salvaged from the wreck of the HMS *Proselyte.* ✉ *7 Front St.,* ☎ *599/542–4917.* 💳 *Free.* ⏱ *Weekdays 10–4, Sat. 10–2.*

❻ Pic du Paradis. From Friar's Bay Beach, a bumpy, tree-canopied road leads inland to this peak. At 1,278 ft (390 m), it's the island's highest point and the Caribbean vistas from it are breathtaking. **Loterie Farm** is a peaceful 150-acre oasis run by American expat B. J. Welch to preserve farm, forest, and mountain land. He's renovated an old farmhouse and welcomes visitors for horseback riding, hiking, mountain biking, eco tours, or such inactivities as meditation. A restaurant is open for lunch and dinner Tuesday through Sunday. ✉ *Route de Pic du Paradis,* ☎ *590/87–86–16,* 🌐 *www.loteriefarm.com.* 💳 *$5 entry fee; 1½-hr tour, $25; 4-hr tour, $35.* ⏱ *Daily sunrise–sunset.*

ST. MARTIN A TO Z

To research prices, get advice from other travelers, and book travel arrangements, visit www.fodors.com.

AIR TRAVEL
Air ALM has daily service from Curaçao, with connections from Aruba, Bonaire, and Caracas, and from Miami via Curaçao. The airline also works with KLM to carry passengers from numerous Euro-

pean cities. Air France offers daily nonstop flights from Paris, with connections from other European cities, as well as connections to and from Martinique and Antigua. Air Caraïbes offers daily flights St. Barths. The airline flies mainly out of L'Espérance, on the French side.

The most convenient carrier from the United States is American Airlines, with daily nonstop flights from New York and Miami, as well as connections via its San Juan hub. BWIA offers service from Trinidad, Jamaica, and Antigua. Continental Airlines has daily nonstop flights from Newark and connections from San Juan. LIAT has daily service from San Juan and several Caribbean islands, including Antigua, the USVI, the BVI, and St. Kitts–Nevis. US Airways has nonstop service from Philadelphia on Saturday and Sunday and from Charlotte on Saturday. Windward Islands Airways (a.k.a. Winair), based on St. Maarten, has daily service to Anguilla, Saba, St. Barths, St. Eustatius, and St. Kitts–Nevis, as well as several weekly flights to Tortola. The company also offers tour and charter services.

➤ AIRLINES AND CONTACTS: **Air ALM** (☎ 599/545–4240). **KLM** (☎ 599/545–4747). **Air France** (☎ 599/545–4212). **Air Caraïbes** (☎ 599/545–2568). **American Airlines** (☎ 599/545–2040). **BWIA** (☎ 599/545–4646). **Continental Airlines** (☎ 599/545–3444). **LIAT** (☎ 599/545–4203). **US Airways** (☎ 599/545–4344). **Windward Islands Airways** (☎ 599/545–2568).

AIRPORTS
Aeroport de L'Espérance, on the French side, is small and handles only island hoppers. Jumbo jets fly into Princess Juliana International Airport, on the Dutch side.
➤ AIRPORT INFORMATION: **Aeroport de L'Espérance** (☎ 590/87–53–03). **Princess Juliana International Airport** (☎ 599/545–4211).

BIKE AND MOPED TRAVEL
A motorbike is a great way get around. Parking is easy, filling the tank with gas is affordable, and you've got that sea breeze in your hair. Scooters rent for $22 a day and motorbikes for $35 a day at Eugene Moto, on the French side. If you're in the mood for a more substantial bike, contact the Harley-Davidson dealer, on the Dutch side, where you can rent a big hog for $90 a day.
➤ CONTACTS: **Eugene Moto** (✉ Sandy Ground Rd., ☎ 590/87–13–97). **Harley-Davidson** (✉ Cole Bay, ☎ 599/544–2779).

BOAT AND FERRY TRAVEL
FARES AND SCHEDULES
The *Voyager I* and *Voyager II* offer daily service from Marigot to St. Barths. Both boats also carry passengers from Bobby's Marina (at the east end of Front Street in Philipsburg) to St. Barths on Wednesday, Thursday, and Friday. The cost for the 75-minute ride is $57 per person round trip, including an open bar, snacks, and port fees. Both boats also make Tuesday (from Marigot) and Thursday (from Philipsburg) runs to Saba, also for $57 per person. Children under 12 are roughly half price, and children under five travel for free. The high-speed 50-passenger ferry *Edge* motors from Simpson Bay's Pelican Marina to Saba on Wednesday, Friday, and Sunday (70 minutes, $60 round-trip) and to St. Barths on Tuesday, Thursday, and Saturday (45 minutes, $50 round-trip). The trips depart at 9 and return by 5 the same day. A ferry makes the 20-minute trip between the Marigot piers and Blowing Point, on Anguilla, departing and returning every half hour from 8 AM until 7 PM daily. The fare is $10 one-way plus $2 departure tax, or $24 round-trip; according to ferry authorities, this fee is due to rise to $15

one-way plus $4 departure tax, or $38 round-trip, in the near but un-determined future.

➤ BOAT AND FERRY INFORMATION: *Voyager I* and *Voyager II* (☎ 599/542–4096 or 590/87–10–68, WEB www.voyager-st-barths.com). *Edge* (☎ 599/544–2640).

BUSINESS HOURS
BANKS
Banks on the Dutch side are open Monday–Thursday 8:30–3:30 and Friday 8:30–4:40. French banks are open weekdays 8:30–12:30 and 2:30–4 and close afternoons preceding holidays.

POST OFFICES
Dutch-side post offices are open Monday–Thursday 7:30–5 and Friday 7:30–4:30. The branch at the Food Center at Cul de Sac keeps Saturday hours 9–1. On the French side post offices are open weekdays 7:30–4:45 and Saturday 7:30–11:30.

SHOPS
Shops on the Dutch side are open Monday–Saturday 8–noon and 2–6; on the French side, Monday–Saturday 9–noon or 12:30 and 2–6. (Many shops on both sides now remain open during lunch; others set their own capricious hours.) Some of the larger shops open on Sunday and holidays when cruise ships are in port.

CAR RENTALS
You can book a car at Juliana International Airport, where all major rental companies have booths. If you don't have a reservation, don't worry: rentals abound on the island. Rates, in general, are low—approximately $40–$50 a day for a subcompact car. All foreign driver's licenses are honored, and major credit cards are accepted. Avis, Budget, Dollar, Hertz, and National (Eurocar) all have cars for rent.

➤ MAJOR AGENCIES: **Avis** (☎ 800/331–1084). **Budget** (☎ 800/472–3325); **Dollar** (☎ 800/800–4000). **Hertz** (☎ 800/654–3131). **National (Eurocar)** (☎ 800/328–4567).

CAR TRAVEL
GASOLINE
Gas costs about $1.10 per liter ($3.85 per gallon).

ROAD CONDITIONS
Most roads are paved and generally well-marked on both sides of the island. In many cases signs will be in either French or Dutch, but they're easy to figure out, and international symbols are used.

ELECTRICITY
Generally, the Dutch side operates on 110 volts AC (60-cycle) and has outlets that accept flat-prong plugs—the same as in North America. The French side operates on 220 volts AC (60-cycle), with round-prong plugs; you'll need an adapter and a converter for North American appliances.

EMERGENCIES
➤ AMBULANCE AND FIRE: **Ambulance or fire emergencies Dutch side** (☎ 911 or 111). **Ambulance or fire emergencies French side** (☎ 15).

➤ HOSPITALS: Dutch side: **St. Maarten Medical Center** (✉ Cay Hill, ☎ 599/543–1111). French side: **Hospital de Marigot** (✉ Rue de l'Hôpital, Marigot, ☎ 590/29–57–57).

➤ PHARMACIES: **Central Drug Store** (✉ Cannegieter St., Philipsburg, ☎ 599/542–5576). **Pharmacie du Port** (✉ Rue de la Liberté, Marigot, ☎ 590/87–50–79).

➤ POLICE: **Police emergencies Dutch side** (☎ 911). **Police emergencies French side** (☎ 17).

ETIQUETTE AND BEHAVIOR

Religion plays an important part in island life, and churches are packed on Sunday. On the streets and in shops, conservative dress is the norm. Take the cue. In addition, a smile and a simple greeting go a long way toward establishing good relations with locals.

FESTIVALS AND SEASONAL EVENTS

The French side's Carnival is a pre-Lenten bash of costume parades, music competitions, and feasts. On the Dutch side, Carnival takes place after Easter, usually in early May. On the French side the Calypso Festival is held in early July. The Caribbean Quest Musical Awards, a festival of regional music from around the islands, is held in early August on the French side. On the Dutch side early March sees the Heineken Regatta, an international sailing regatta around the island.

HEALTH

Mosquitos come out in the early evening, but the gentle sea winds are enough to keep them to a minimum in most places. The biggest problem might be sun exposure. Even on seemingly cloudy days the sun can cause painful burns, so make sure to use sunscreen, and limit your sunbathing to about 15 minutes at a stretch. Drinking water is generally safe, except immediately following a hurricane or storm. If in doubt, buy bottled drinking water, which is plentiful at shops throughout the island.

HOLIDAYS

Both sides of the island celebrate specific holidays related to their government and culture, and some, such as New Year's, the Easter holidays (moveable, Apr. or May), Labor Day (the first Monday in Sept.), Christmas, and Boxing Day (Dec. 26) are celebrated together.

Other French-side holidays are: Ascension Day (May 25), Bastille Day (July 14), Schoelcher Day (July 21), All Saints' Day (Nov. 1), and the Feast of St. Martin (Nov. 11). Other Dutch-side holidays are: Antillean Day (Oct. 21) and St. Maarten Day (Nov. 11; this coincides with Feast of St. Martin on the French side).

LANGUAGE

Dutch is the official language of St. Maarten, and French is the official language of St. Martin, but almost everyone speaks English. If you hear a language you can't quite place, it's Papiamento—a mix of Spanish, Portuguese, Dutch, French, and English—spoken throughout the Netherlands Antilles.

MAIL AND SHIPPING

The main Dutch-side post office is on Walter Nisbeth Road in Philipsburg. Other branches are at the Food Center Mall in Cul de Sac and at Princess Juliana Airport. The main post office on the French side is in Marigot, on rue de la Liberté. Letters from the Dutch side to North America, Europe, and New Zealand cost NAf 2.25; postcards NAf 1.10. A standard letter to Australia is NAf 2.75, a postcard is NAf 1.30. From the French side, letters up to 20 grams and postcards are 3.80F to North America and 5.20F to Europe, New Zealand, and Australia. When writing to Dutch St. Maarten, call it "Sint Maarten" and make sure to add "Netherlands Antilles" to the address. When writing to the French side the proper spelling is "St-Martin," and you add "French West Indies" to the address. Postal codes are only used on the French side.

MONEY MATTERS

Note: prices quoted in this chapter are in U.S. dollars unless otherwise noted.

ATMS

All banks now have automatic teller machines (ATMs) that accept international cards. On the Dutch side try ABN-Amro. Windward Islands Bank has several branches on the island. On the French side, try Banque des Antilles Françaises or Banque Française Commerciale, but they will issue only euros.

➤ CONTACTS: **ABN-Amro** (✉ Emnaplein, Philipsburg, ☎ 599/542–3344; ✉ Union Rd., Cole Bay, ☎ 599/544–3078, WEB www.abnamro.com). **Windward Islands Bank** (✉ Wathey Sq., Front St., Philipsburg, ☎ 599/ 542–2313, WEB www.wib-bank.net). **Banque des Antilles Françaises** (✉ Rue de la République, Marigot, ☎ 590/29–13–30). **Banque Française Commerciale** (✉ rue de la République, Marigot, ☎ 590/87–53–80).

CREDIT CARDS

MasterCard, Visa, and Amex are accepted all over the island; Diners Club and Discover on occasion.

CURRENCY

Legal tender on the Dutch side is the Netherlands Antilles florin (guilder), written NAf; on the French side, the euro (€). The exchange rates fluctuate, but in general they're about NAf 1.80 to US$1 and about €1.13 to US$1. On the Dutch side prices are usually given in both NAf and U.S. dollars, which are accepted all over the island.

PASSPORTS AND VISAS

U.S. and Canadian citizens need proof of citizenship. A passport (valid or not expired more than five years) is always the best document with which to travel, particularly for children. Barring a passport, an original birth certificate with raised seal (or a photocopy with notary seal) *plus* a government-issued photo ID, such as a driver's license, is also acceptable. This is why children are best served by passports, since they are unlikely to have other types of photo ID. British citizens need a valid passport or a national ID card. Citizens of Australia and New Zealand require a valid passport. All visitors must have a confirmed room reservation and an ongoing or return ticket.

SAFETY

Always lock your valuables and travel documents in your room safe or your hotel's front desk safe. When sightseeing in a rental car, keep valuables locked in the trunk or car, and never leave your things unattended at the beach. Despite the romantic imagery of the Caribbean, it's not good policy to take long walks along the beach at night.

SIGHTSEEING TOURS

HELICOPTER

You can arrange island tours and charters through Heli-Inter Caraïbes in Anse Marcel. St. Martin Helicopters also offers transport and tours by helicopter. Tours run upward of $400 for six people.

➤ CONTACTS: **Heli-Inter Caraïbes** (☎ 590/87–35–88). **St. Martin Helicopters** (☎ 599/545–4287).

ORIENTATION

A 2½-hour taxi tour of the island costs $30 for one or two people, $10 for each additional person. Your hotel or the tourist office can arrange it for you. On the Dutch side Calypso Tours has, among other things, three-hour island tours for $20 per person. Elle Si Belle offers tours by van or bus. You can also contact St. Maarten Sightseeing Tours. On the French side R&J Tours will show you the island; a three-hour tour (minimum of five people) is $15 per person.

➤ CONTACTS: **Elle Si Belle** (✉ Airport Blvd., Simpson Bay, ☎ 599/545–2271). **R&J Tours** (✉ North of Marigot, Colombier, ☎ 590/87–56–20). **St. Maarten Sightseeing Tours** (✉ Maho Plaza at Maho Beach Hotel & Casino, Airport Rd., Simpson Bay, ☎ 599/545–2115).

TAXES
DEPARTURE TAX
Departure tax from Juliana Airport is $6 to destinations within the Netherlands Antilles and $20 to all other destinations. Note that if you arrive on the island by plane and depart within 24 hours, you will be considered "in transit" and won't be required to pay the $20 departure tax. It will cost you 15F (about $3, usually included in the ticket price) to depart by plane from L'Espérance Airport, and $4 by ferry to Anguilla from Marigot's pier.

SALES TAX
Hotels on the Dutch side add a 15% service–energy charge to the bill as well as a 5% government tax, for a total of 20%. Hotels on the French side add 10%–15% for service and a *taxe de séjour*; the amount of this visitor tax differs from hotel to hotel, and can be as high as 5%.

TAXIS
The government regulates taxi rates. You can hail cabs on the street, or call the Dutch taxi dispatch on the Dutch side. On the French side of the island, contact the French taxi dispatch for pickups. There's a taxi service at the Marigot port near the tourist information bureau. Fixed fares apply from Juliana International Airport and the Marigot ferry to the various hotels around the island. Fares are 25% higher between 10 PM and midnight, 50% higher between midnight and 6 AM.
➤ CONTACTS: **Dutch taxi dispatch** (☎ 147). **French taxi dispatch** (☎ 590/87–56–54).

TELEPHONES
COUNTRY AND AREA CODES
To call the Dutch side from the United States, dial 011–599/54 plus local number; for the French side, 011–590–590 plus the six-digit local number.

INTERNATIONAL CALLS
At the Landsradio in Philipsburg, there are facilities for overseas calls and an ATT USADirect phone, where you are directly in touch with an ATT operator who will accept collect or credit-card calls. On the French side you can't make collect calls to the United States, and there are no coin phones. If you need to use public phones, go to the special desk at Marigot's post office and buy a Telecarte, which gives you 40 units (it takes 120 units to cover a five-minute call to the United States) for around 31F or 120 units for 93F. There's a public phone at the tourist office in Marigot where you can make credit-card calls: the operator takes your card number (any major card) and assigns you a PIN (Personal Identification Number), which you then use to charge calls to your card.

LOCAL CALLS
To phone from the Dutch side to the French, dial 00–590 plus local number; from the French side to the Dutch, 00–599/54 plus local number. Keep in mind that a call from one side to the other is considered an overseas call, not a local one. To call a French side local number from the French side, dial 0590 plaus the six digit number.

TIPPING

Service charges are added to hotel and restaurant bills all over the island. These are often included in all menu prices on the French side; on the Dutch side most restaurants add 10%–15% to the bill. Still, you should tip as you would at home; taxi drivers, porters, chambermaids, and restaurant waitstaff all expect a tip, even when a service charge is included in the bill. Think about 10%–15% for waitstaff, a couple of dollars for cabbies, a dollar per bag for porters, and $1–$5 per night for chambermaids.

TRANSPORTATION AROUND ST. MARTIN

At a flat rate of $1.50 ($2 after 8 PM), buses are the island's best bargains. They operate frequently between 7 AM and midnight from Philipsburg through Cole Bay to Marigot and on to Grand Case. There are no official stops: you just stand by the side of the road and flag the bus down. Exact change is preferred though not required, and drivers accept both U.S. and local currency.

VISITOR INFORMATION

➤ BEFORE YOU LEAVE: **St. Maarten Tourist Office** (⊠ 675 3rd Ave., Suite 1806, New York, NY 10017, ☎ 800/786–2278 or 212/953–2084, WEB www.st-maarten.com). **St. Maarten Tourist Information** (⊠ 703 Evans Ave., Suite 106, Toronto, Ontario M9C 5E9, Canada, ☎ 416/622–4300). **St. Martin Office of Tourism** (⊠ 675 3rd Ave., Suite 1807, New York, NY 10017, ☎ 877/956–1234 or 212/475–8970, FAX 212/260–8481, WEB www.st-martin.org; ⊠ 9454 Wilshire Blvd., Suite 715, Beverly Hills, CA 90212, ☎ 310/271–6665; ⊠ 676 N. Michigan Ave., Suite 3360, Chicago, IL 60611, ☎ 312/751–7800; ⊠ 1981 McGill College Ave., Suite 490, Montréal, Québec H3A 2W9, Canada, ☎ 514/288–4264; ⊠ 30 St. Patrick St., Suite 700, Toronto, Ontario M5T 3A3, Canada, ☎ 416/593–6427).

➤ IN ST. MARTIN: **Dutch-side Tourist Information Bureau** (⊠ Cyrus Wathey Sq., Philipsburg, ☎ 599/542–2337). **Dutch-side tourist bureau administrative office** (⊠ 33 W. G. Buncamper Rd., Philipsburg, in the Vineyard Park Bldg., ☎ 599/542–2337). **French-side Tourist Information Office** (☎ 590/87–57–21).

23 ST. VINCENT AND THE GRENADINES

Updated by
Jane E. Zarem

Standing on Dorsetshire Hill, above Kingstown, the wily old gentleman points to an island just offshore. On it is a large white cross that glimmers in the sun. "Know what that's about?" he asks. The grin on his weathered face fades to a wry smile as, without pause, he tells the tale. A local land developer, it seems, bought the island and put up the cross. Later, when he died, his body was placed upright inside it so that he could always face his life's work. "You see," says the gent with a shrug, "Vincentians love their country with a passion."

The island of St. Vincent and the string of 32 islands and cays that make up the Grenadines are a single nation—one that's loved passionately by its inhabitants as much for its interesting history as for its natural beauty. SVG, as it's abbreviated, is in the Windward Islands chain in the southern Caribbean. Mountainous St. Vincent, only 18 mi (29 km) by 11 mi (18 km) and just 13° north of the equator, is the largest and the northernmost in the group; the Grenadines extend in a 45-mi (73-km) arc southwest to Grenada. While the island of St. Vincent will appeal to anyone interested in exploring nature, regional history, and ecotourism, the islands of the Grenadines will dazzle you with their secluded white-sand beaches, fine sailing waters, and get-away-from-it-all atmosphere.

St. Vincent's major export is bananas, and these plants, along with coconut palms and breadfruit trees, crowd more of the island than the 110,500 inhabitants (another 10,000 live on the Grenadines). This has obvious charm for nature lovers, who can spend days walking or hiking St. Vincent's well-defined trails, catching a glimpse of the rare St. Vincent parrot in the Vermont Valley, or climbing the active volcano La Soufrière, which last erupted in 1979. Below sea level, snorkeling and scuba landscapes are similarly intriguing.

Historians believe that the Ciboney Indians were the first to journey from South America to St. Vincent, which they called Hairoun (Land of the Blessed). The Ciboney ultimately moved on to Cuba and Haiti, leaving St. Vincent to the agrarian Arawak tribes, who journeyed from coastal South America to islands throughout the Lesser Antilles. Not long before Columbus sailed by in 1492, the Arawaks succumbed to the powerful Carib Indians, who had also paddled their way north from South America, conquering one island after another en route.

St. Vincent's mountains and forests thwarted European settlement. As colonization advanced elsewhere in the Caribbean, many Caribs fled to St. Vincent—making it even more of a Carib stronghold. In 1626 the French managed to settle on the island, but their success was short-lived; England took over a year later. Although "possession" of the island seesawed between France and England for years, the Caribs continued to make complete European colonization impossible. Ironically it was a rift in the Carib community itself that enabled the Europeans to gain a foothold.

In 1675 African slaves who had survived a Dutch shipwreck were welcomed into the Carib community. Over time the Carib nation became, for all intents and purposes, two nations—one composed of the so-called Yellow Caribs, the other of the so-called Black Caribs. Relations between the two groups were often strained. In 1719 tensions rose so high that the Yellow Caribs united with the French (who were the colonizers that year) against the Black Caribs in what is called the First Carib War. The Black Caribs ultimately retreated to the hills, but they continued to resist the Europeans.

The French went on to establish plantations, importing African slaves to work the fertile land. In 1763 the British claimed the island yet again, and a wave of Scottish slave masters and indentured servants from India and Portugal arrived. Although the ethnic groups have mixed over the years to give Vincentians their unique heritage, communities of direct descendents of the Scots live near St. Vincent's Dorsetshire Hill and on Bequia. In 1779 the French surprised the British and reclaimed the island without a struggle; but four years later St. Vincent was back in the British grip. The determined French backed the Black Caribs against the British in 1795's Second Carib War (also known as the Brigands War). British plantations were ravaged and burned on the island's windward coast, and Black Carib chief Chatoyer pushed British troops down the leeward coast to Kingstown. On Dorsetshire Hill, high above the town, Chatoyer subsequently lost a duel with a British officer. The 5,000 remaining Black Caribs were rounded up and shipped off to Honduras and present-day Belize, where their descendents (the Garifuna people) remain to this day. The few remaining Yellow Caribs retreated to the remote northern tip of St. Vincent, near Sandy Bay, where many of their descendents now live. A monument to Chatoyer has been erected on Dorsetshire Hill, where there's a magnificent view over Kingstown and the Caribbean Sea toward Central America.

The Grenadines were historically as free from war and politics as their pristine beaches are today free from crowds. Just south of St. Vincent is Bequia, the largest of the Grenadines. Its Admiralty Bay is one of the most popular anchorages in the Caribbean. With superb views, snorkeling, hiking, and swimming, the island has much to offer the international mix of backpackers and luxury-yacht owners who frequent its shores.

South of Bequia, on the exclusive, private island of Mustique, posh villas are tucked into lush hillsides. Mustique does not encourage wholesale tourism, least of all to those hoping for a glimpse of the rich and famous (Princess Margaret, Mick Jagger, and Tommy Hilfiger, for example) who own villas here. The appeal of Mustique is its seclusion.

Boot-shape Canouan, just over 3 square mi (8 square km) in area, is an unspoiled island where you can relax on the beach, snorkel, or hike. Its 1,000 residents earn their living from farming and fishing. Tiny Mayreau has fewer than 200 residents and one of the area's most beautiful beaches—where the Caribbean Sea is often mirror calm, and just yards away at the narrow northern tip of the island, the rolling Atlantic surf washes the shore.

Union Island is the transportation center of the southern Grenadines, with a busy airport for landlubbers and yacht services for sailors. It took decades to turn the 100-acre, mosquito-infested mangrove swamp called Prune Island into the private resort of Palm Island; now the well-heeled lounge on the island's five palm-fringed white-sand beaches. Petit St. Vincent is another private island, reclaimed from the overgrowth by owner-manager Hazen K. Richardson II. The luxury resort's stone houses are far enough apart that you could spend your vacation without ever seeing another human being.

Although SVG has its share of the poor and unemployed, the super fertile soil allows everyone to grow enough food to eat and trade for necessities. Villages are busy and clean, concrete-block homes are painted in tropical colors, and colorful flowers and bright green foliage grow in profusion. The issue of "possession" of St. Vincent has long since been resolved; fully independent since 1979 (but still a part of the British Commonwealth), it belongs to a diverse, culturally rich people now known only as Vincentians—who truly have good reason to love their homeland with a passion.

ST. VINCENT

Lodging

With few exceptions, tourist accommodations and facilities on St. Vincent are in either Kingstown or the Villa Beach area. Most hotels offer the EP, with the MAP available as an option; at resorts in the Grenadines, the FAP or AI is common. All guest rooms have air-conditioning, TV, and telephone, unless stated otherwise.

CATEGORY	COST EP/CP*	COST A.I.**
$$$$	over $350	over $375
$$$	$250–$350	$275–$375
$$	$150–$250	$175–$275
$	under $150	under $175

*EP/CP prices are per night for a standard double room in high season, excluding taxes, service charges, and meal plans**A.I. (all-inclusive) prices are per person, per night based on double-occupancy during high season, excluding taxes and service charges*

KINGSTOWN

$$ ★ 🖫 **Camelot Inn.** Snuggled in the hills overlooking Kingstown, this stylish inn sits on the site of the island's first French governor's residence, later its first guest house. It's an elegant place with impeccable service; the views are magnificent. Guest rooms are soothing white and deep green, with rattan furniture, antique mirrors and prints, and parquet floors; bathrooms have hand-painted porcelain sinks imported from France. Each spacious room has a patio. Meals are served in the King Arthur dining room or on the terrace. Afternoon tea is served in the garden. Guests may use Young Island Resort's beach and water-sports facilities (transportation included). A city tour and one massage are complimentary. ⊠ *Kingstown Park (Box 787),* ☎ *784/456–2100,* FAX *784/456–2233,* WEB *www.vincy.com/camelot. 19 rooms, 3 suites. 2 restaurants, fans, in-room safes, tennis court, pool, gym, hair salon, massage, sauna, 2 bars, library, shop laundry service, meeting rooms, airport shuttle. AE, DC, MC, V. EP.*

$ 🖫 **Cobblestone Inn.** On the waterfront in "the city," as Vincentians call Kingstown, this small hotel occupies a former sugar and arrowroot warehouse, built in 1814 of local stone. Converted to a hotel in 1970, the historic building has original Georgian architecture, a sunny interior courtyard, and winding cobblestone walkways and arches. Rooms are tiny, but each has stone walls, rattan furniture, and a private bath. Number 5, at the front, is lighter and bigger than most of the other rooms—but noisier, too. A rooftop bar-restaurant serves breakfast and light lunches. The popular Basil's Bar and Restaurant is located at ground level. ⊠ *Upper Bay St. (Box 867),* ☎ *784/456–1937,* FAX *784/456–1938. 21 rooms. Restaurant, bar, shops, laundry service, meeting room. AE, D, MC, V. EP.*

$ 🏨 **The New Montrose Hotel.** Despite no beach, pool, or activities, this is a fine choice for comfortable and reasonable lodgings. Painted a delightful lemon yellow, the rambling hotel is on the northern outskirts of Kingstown. All suites are modern, with fully equipped kitchenettes, table and chairs, and two queen-size beds. The restaurant serves a limited menu of West Indian cuisine, but the food is good, and service is pleasant. This is a quiet, residential part of Kingstown, yet it's just a few minutes from downtown, the beach, the airport, and the botanical gardens. Long-term rates are available. ⊠ *New Montrose (Box 215),* ☎ *784/457–0172,* FAX *784/457–0213,* WEB *www.newmontrosehotel.com. 25 suites. Restaurant, room service, fans, kitchenettes, refrigerators, bar. AE, MC, V. EP, CP.*

VILLA BEACH AREA

$$$–$$$$ 🏨 **Young Island Resort.** St. Vincent's premier resort is on a 35-acre private island 200 yards off Villa Beach and accessible by hotel launch (a five-minute ride). Airy hillside cottages are decorated in ecru, ochre, and green, with bamboo and rattan furniture. Walls of stone and glass have louvred windows surrounding the sitting areas. Each room has a terrace, and bathrooms have open-air showers. All cottages have water views despite being hidden in lush tropical vegetation. Two beachfront cottages have private plunge pools. Enjoy fine dining in the terrace dining room or in a private thatched-roof gazebo. Sailaway packages include five hotel nights and two nights touring the Grenadines on the resort's 44-ft sailboat. ⊠ *Young Island (Box 211),* ☎ *784/458–4826,* FAX *784/457–4567,* WEB *www.youngisland.com. 30 cottages. Restaurant, room service, no air-conditioning, fans, in-room safes, refrigerators, no room TV, tennis court, pool, beach, snorkeling, windsurfing, boating, 2 bars, baby-sitting, laundry service, meeting room, airport shuttle. AE, MC, V. MAP.*

$$ 🏨 **Grand View Beach Hotel.** This 19th-century great house is now Tony and Heather Sardine's grand hotel. Perched just above Indian Bay, it has both extensive facilities and intimate charm—all set on 8 acres that beckon you to explore. Rooms are attractive but not fussy, with plain white walls and hardwood floors, and most offer a sweeping vistas of the Grenadines. Luxury rooms have broad terraces with ocean views; two honeymoon suites have king-size beds and whirlpool tubs. Enjoy West Indian and Continental-style cuisine at Wilkie's restaurant. Sailboats, Windsurfers, and snorkeling equipment are complimentary, but you have to hike down a rather steep hill to the beach. ⊠ *Villa Point,* ☎ *784/458–4811,* FAX *784/457–4174,* WEB *www.grandviewhotel.com. 17 rooms, 2 suites. 2 restaurants, fans, tennis court, pool, health club, massage, sauna, beach, snorkeling, windsurfing, boating, squash, 3 bars, library, baby-sitting, laundry service, meeting room. AE, MC, V. CP, EP, MAP.*

$$ 🏨 **Sunset Shores Beach Hotel.** Down a long, steep driveway off the main road, this lemon-yellow low-rise surrounds a small pool and a gigantic and prolific mango tree (help yourself from January through July). It also faces a lovely curve of Indian Bay beachfront. All rooms are large

St. Vincent

St. Vincent Passage

Caribbean Sea

OCEAN

St. Vincent
The Grenadines

Espagnol Pt.

Commantawana Bay

Porter Pt.

Baleine Bay

Larikai Bay

Dark Head

Chateaubelair Bay

Petit Bordel Bay

Wallilabou Bay

Cumberland Bay

Sandy Bay

Owia Salt Pond

Crater Lake

La Soufrière

Richmond Peak

Grand Bonum

Colonaric

Windward Hwy.

Black Point Tunnel

Fancy

Owia

Overland Village

Georgetown

Colonarie

Richmond

Chateaubelair

Troumaka

Barrouallie

7 Owia

6 Baleine Bay

8 La Soufrière

9

10 Georgetown

11 Black Point Tunnel

5 Wallilabou Bay

6 Cumberland Bay

4 Barrouallie

617

ATLANTIC O

Colonarie Bay
Sans Souci

Grant's Bay
Biabou

Mesopotamia
Argyle

Greiggs

Stubbs Bay

Yambou R.

Vigie Hwy.

Milligan Cay

Mt. St. Andrew

Kingstown

Calliaqua

Villa
Villa Beach
Young Island

Calliaqua Bay

Indian Bay

E. T. Joshua Airport

Kingstown Bay

Leeward Hwy.

Buccament Bay

Layou

Questelle's Bay

Anchor Reef,
New Guinea Reef,
The Forest

TO BEQUIA

N

0   2 miles
0   3 km

KEY

- Cruise Ship Terminal
- Beaches
- Dive Sites
- ❶ Exploring Sights
- Ferry
- ① Hotels and Restaurants

Exploring

Barrouallie 4	Kingstown 1	La Soufrière 8
Black Point Tunnel 11	Layou 3	Wallilabou Bay 5
Falls of Baleine 6	Mesopotamia Valley 12	
Ft. Charlotte 2	Montreal Gardens 13	
Ft. Duvernette 14	Owia 7	
Georgetown 10	Rabacca Dry River 9	

Dining

Basil's Bar and Restaurant 2	Slick's Bar & Restaurant 13
French Restaurant 5	Vee Jay's Rooftop Diner & Pub 4
King Arthur Dining Room 9	Wallilabou Bay Hotel 1
Lime Restaurant & Pub 10	Young Island Resort 12

Lodging

Beachcombers 8	The New Montrose Hotel 2
Camelot Inn 1	Petit Byahout 5
Cobblestone Inn 3	Sunset Shores Beach Hotel 9
Grand View Beach Hotel 7	Young Island Resort 10
Lagoon Marina & Hotel 14	

and comfortable, with patios or balconies. Opt for a room with a water view; otherwise you'll have to amble over to the poolside bar to get a glimpse of the gorgeous sunsets. The restaurant is good, with a small but varied menu featuring fresh local fish and lobster (in season); service is friendly and efficient. ⊠ *Villa Beach (Box 849),* ☎ *784/458–4411,* FAX *784/457–4800,* WEB *www.sunsetshores.com. 32 rooms. Restaurant, room service, pool, beach, snorkeling, boating, Ping-Pong, 2 bars, baby-sitting, laundry service, meeting room. AE, D, MC, V. EP, MAP.*

$ 🏨 **Beachcombers.** This small, family-owned, beachfront hotel is modest but delightful. Half the guest rooms face the sea; the others overlook the Mango Tree Lounge or the garden's frenzy of flowers. Rooms with air-conditioning cost extra, and bathrooms have showers only—insignificant privations when the welcome here is so warm and the rates so low. Best of all, an on-site health spa offers aromatherapy, facials, sauna, steam baths, and aerobics. On weekend evenings, you'll usually find a live band and dancing on the sundeck adjacent to the restaurant and bar. ⊠ *Villa Beach (Box 126),* ☎ *784/458–4283,* FAX *784/458–4385,* WEB *www.beachcombershotel.com. 18 rooms, 2 suites, 1 apartment. Restaurant, no air-conditioning in some rooms, fans, kitchenettes, refrigerator, pool, aerobics, massage, sauna, steam room, Turkish bath, beach, bar, library, baby-sitting, laundry service. AE, MC, V. CP.*

ELSEWHERE ON ST. VINCENT

$$–$$$ 🏨 **Petit Byahaut.** For those with Swiss Family Robinson fantasies, this 50-acre retreat offers accommodations in large deluxe tents, complete with wood floors, private decks, queen-size beds, hammocks, solar-powered lighting, and bathrooms with solar-heated alfresco showers. Meals, including candlelit dinners, are served in the bayfront dining room. This adults-only camp is accessible only by a 20-minute boat ride from Kingstown (complimentary for guests). Once you've settled in, you'll find a selection of other boats with which to play, along with scuba and snorkeling equipment and a private black-sand beach. If you tire of the seclusion, excursions are easily arranged. Weekly rates are available. ⊠ *Petit Byahaut Bay,* ☎ FAX *784/457–7008,* WEB *www.outahere. com/petitbyahaut. 6 tents. Dining room, no air-conditioning, no room phones, no room TVs, hiking, beach, dive shop, snorkeling, boating, bar, shop, meeting room, airport shuttle, no kids. MC, V. Closed July– Oct. FAP. 3-night minimum.*

$ 🏨 **The Lagoon Marina & Hotel.** This hotel overlooking sheltered Blue Lagoon Bay may well be the island's busiest. Thanks to its marina, there are usually seafaring types liming (hanging out) in the terrace bar and plenty of yacht traffic to watch from one of two couches on your big balcony. Sliding patio doors lead onto these perches from the wood-ceilinged, carpeted rooms. Basic wooden furniture, twin beds, dim lighting, tiled bathrooms, and ceiling fans provide an adequate level of comfort, but don't expect luxury. Sloping garden grounds contain a secluded two-level pool, a strip of beach, and a pretty terrace restaurant. ⊠ *Blue Lagoon, Ratho Mill (Box 133),* ☎ *784/458–4308,* FAX *784/457–4308,* WEB *www.lagoonmarina.com. 19 rooms, 2 apartments. Restaurant, room service, grocery, no air-conditioning in some rooms, fans, kitchenettes, pool, beach, dock, snorkeling, windsurfing, boating, marina, bar, baby-sitting, laundry service, meeting room. AE, V. EP.*

Dining

Nearly all the restaurants in St. Vincent specialize in West Indian cuisine, although you'll find chefs with broad culinary experience at the more posh restaurants. Local dishes to try include *callaloo* (similar to spinach) soup, curried goat or chicken, *rotis* (turnovers filled with curried meat or vegetables), seasonal seafood (lobster, kingfish, snapper, and mahimahi), local vegetables (avocados, breadfruit, christophene, and pumpkin) and "provisions" (roots, such as yams or dasheen), and tropical fruit (from mangoes and soursop to pineapples and papaya). Fried or baked chicken is available everywhere, often accompanied by "rice 'n' peas" or *pelau* (seasoned rice). The local beer, Hairoun, is brewed according to a German recipe at Campden Park, just north of Kingstown. Sunset is the local rum.

What to Wear

Restaurants are casual. You may want to dress up a little—long pants and collared shirts for gents, summer dresses or dress pants for the ladies—for an evening out at a pricey restaurant, but none of the places listed below requires gentlemen to wear a jacket or tie. Beachwear should always be reserved for the beach.

CATEGORY	COST*
$$$$	over $30
$$$	$20–$30
$$	$10–$20
$	under $10

per person for a main course at dinner

Kingstown

CARIBBEAN

$–$$ ✕ **Basil's Bar and Restaurant.** This refreshingly air-conditioned restaurant, downstairs at the Cobblestone Inn, is owned by Basil Charles, whose Basil's Beach Bar on Mustique is a hangout for the vacationing rich and famous. It's the Kingstown power-lunch venue, where local business people gather for the daily buffet or a full menu of salads, sandwiches, barbecued chicken, or fresh seafood platters. Dinner entrées of pasta, local seafood, and chicken (try it poached in fresh ginger and coconut milk) are served at candlelit tables. There's a Chinese buffet on Friday, and takeout is available that night only. ✉ *Cobblestone Inn, Upper Bay St.,* ☎ *784/457–2713. AE, MC, V.*

$–$$ ✕ **Vee Jay's Rooftop Diner & Pub.** This eatery, above Roger's Photo Studios (have your pix developed while you eat!) and opposite the Cobblestone Inn, offers downtown Kingstown's best harbor view from beneath a green corrugated-plastic roof. Among the "authentic Vincy cuisine" specials chalked on the blackboard are mutton or fish stew, chicken or vegetable rotis, curried goat, souse, and *buljol* (sautéed codfish, breadfruit, and vegetables). Not-so-Vincy sandwiches, fish and chips, and burgers can be authentically washed down with *mauby,* a bittersweet drink made from tree bark; linseed, peanut, passion fruit, or sorrel punch; local Hairoun beer or cocktails. Lunch is buffet style. ✉ *Upper Bay St.,* ☎ *784/457–2845. Reservations essential. AE, MC, V. Closed Sun.*

CONTEMPORARY

$$–$$$ ✕ **King Arthur Dining Room.** Expect fine cuisine and elegant service when supping at this intimate dining room downstairs in the Camelot Inn. The chef's table d'hôte menu offers you a choice of two to three starters and entrées, which change daily. Dishes—such as fillet of beef, grilled fish with herb sauce, chicken sautéed in white wine—are served with local vegetables. The homemade soups are memorable, and so is the rum-raisin ice cream. There's entertainment in season and a weekly barbecue on the breezy Guinevere Terrace, which overlooks the harbor. ✉ *Camelot Inn, Kingstown Park,* ☎ *784/456–2100. Reservations essential. AE, D, MC, V.*

Villa Beach Area

CONTINENTAL

$$$ ✕ **Young Island Resort.** Even if you're not a resort guest, you can take
★   the ferry (a five-minute ride from Villa Beach) to the island for a pic-
     turesque lunch or a very special romantic evening. Stone paths lead to
     thatched huts with individual candlelit tables; the water laps against the
     shore, and a warm breeze rustles the leaves. Five-course table d'hôte,
     prix-fixe dinners of grilled seafood, roast pork, beef tenderloin, and
     sautéed chicken are accompanied by local vegetables; a board of won-
     derful fresh breads is offered for your selection. Two or three choices
     are offered for each course. Lunch is à la carte—with a choice of soups,
     salads, grilled meats or fish—and served on the beachfront terrace. ⊠
     Young Island, ☎ *784/458–4826. Reservations essential. AE, MC, V.*

ECLECTIC

$$–$$$$ ✕ **Slick's Bar & Restaurant.** On the Villa Beach waterfront's "Restau-
     rant Row," along with The Lime and The French, Slick's offers entrées
     culled from Italian, American, French, and West Indian cuisines.
     Whether you choose shrimp, lobster, steak, lamb chops, or chicken,
     the dish is ultimately determined that day by the chef's preparation and
     accompanying sauces. Dinner is by candlelight, and lunch affords a de-
     lightful view of Young Island, the harbor activity, and the distant
     Grenadines. The restaurant's small playground offers added pleasure
     for young children. ⊠ *Young Island Channel, Villa Harbour,* ☎ *784/
     457–5783. AE, MC, V.*

$–$$$ ✕ **Lime Restaurant & Pub.** Although this sprawling, waterfront restau-
     rant-bar is named for the *pursuit* of liming, its decor also includes a
     great deal of green. An extensive, all-day menu caters to beachgoers
     and boaters, who drop by for a roti and a bottle of Hairoun—or burg-
     ers, curries, sandwiches, gourmet pizzas, pastas, soups, and salads. Din-
     ner choices include fresh seafood, volcano chicken (with a creole sauce
     that's as spicy as lava is hot), curried goat, and pepper steak. Casual
     and congenial during the day, the mood is all candlelight and romance
     at night—enhanced by the twinkling lights of boats at anchor and waves
     quietly breaking against the seawall. ⊠ *Young Island Channel, Villa
     Harbour,* ☎ *784/458–4227. AE, D, DC, MC, V.*

FRENCH

$$–$$$ ✕ **French Restaurant.** "The French" is where yachties go for a quiet
★   waterfront breakfast or lunch—and also when they're in the mood for
     lobster. There's a lobster pool on the terrace, where you can watch the
     staff fish for your supper. As befits a bistro run by a French couple,
     most dishes are the Gallic version of local cuisine. Stuffed crab back,
     for instance, comes in a pastry shell, not a crab shell; steak—au poivre,
     with garlic butter or with béarnaise—is imported; the onion soup and
     lemon tart are French, the way they should be; and the warm, fresh
     bread is a genuine Parisienne-style baguette. ⊠ *Young Island Chan-
     nel, Villa Harbour,* ☎ *784/458–4972. AE, MC, V.*

Elsewhere on St. Vincent

CARIBBEAN

$–$$ ✕ **Wallilabou Bay Hotel.** Halfway up the Caribbean coast of St. Vin-
     cent, this is a favorite anchorage for folks sailing the Grenadines as
     well as daytrippers returning from a visit to the Falls of Baleine. Pretty
     as a picture, it's open all day (from 8 AM), and it's a particularly per-
     fect luncheon or sunset-viewing spot for landlubbers touring the lee-
     ward coast. The bar-and-restaurant serves snacks, sandwiches, tempting
     West Indian dishes, and lobster in season. Ice, telephone, business ser-
     vices, and shower facilities are available to boaters. ⊠ *Leeward Hwy.,
     Wallilabou Bay,* ☎ *784/458–7270. AE, MC, V.*

Beaches

St. Vincent's origin is volcanic, so its beachfront ranges in color from golden-brown to black. Young Island has the only truly white-sand beach; but since the island is private, it's reserved for hotel guests. Otherwise, all beaches are public. On the windward coast dramatic swaths of broad black sand are strewn with huge black boulders, but the water is rough and unpredictable. Swimming is recommended only in the lagoons and bays along the leeward coast.

Buccament Bay. Good for swimming, this tiny black-sand beach is 20 minutes north of Kingstown.

Indian Bay. South of Kingstown it has golden sand but is slightly rocky—a good location for snorkeling.

Questelle's Bay. This beach (pronounced keet-*ells*), north of Kingstown and next to Campden Park, has a black-sand beach.

Villa Beach. Opposite Young Island and 10 minutes south of Kingstown is the island's main beach (although it's hardly big enough to merit such a title). Boats bob at anchor in the channel; dive shops and restaurants line the shore.

Outdoor Activities and Sports

BICYCLING

Bicycles can be rented for about $10 per day, but roads are not particularly conducive to leisurely cycling. Serious bicyclists, however, will enjoy a day of mountain biking in wilderness areas. **Sailor's Wilderness Tours** (⊠ Middle St., Kingstown, ☎ 784/457–1712; 784/457–9207 after hours) takes individuals or groups on half-day bike tours for $25 per person (which includes bike rental).

BOATING, FISHING, AND SAILING

From St. Vincent you can charter a monohull or catamaran (bareboat or complete with captain, crew, and cook) to weave you through the Grenadines for a day or a week of sailing—or a half-day, full-day, or overnight fishing trip. Boats of all sizes and degrees of luxury are available. **Barefoot Yacht Charters** (⊠ Blue Lagoon, Ratho Mill, ☎ 784/456–9526, FAX 785/456–9238) has a fleet of yachts. **Blue Water Charters** (⊠ Aquatic Club, Villa Beach, ☎ 784/456–1232, FAX 784/456–2382) will take you on full-day, half-day, or overnight fishing or sightseeing excursions on its modern 55-ft sportfishing boat. **Crystal Blue Charters** (⊠ Indian Bay, ☎ 784/457–4532, FAX 784/456–2232) offers sportfishing charters on a 34-ft pirogue for amateur and serious fishermen. **Sunsail** (⊠ Blue Lagoon, Ratho Mill, ☎ FAX 784/458–4308) has 44-ft crewed sloops from $200 per day; 7- or 10-day packages are available.

HIKING

St. Vincent offers hikers and trekkers a choice of experiences: easy, picturesque walks near Kingstown; moderate-effort nature trails in the central valleys; and exhilarating climbs through a rain forest to the rim of an active volcano. Bring a hat, long pants, and insect repellent if you plan to hike in the bush.

A hike up **Dorsetshire Hill,** about 3 mi (5 km) from Kingstown, rewards you with a sweeping view of city and harbor. You can also see the monument to Black Carib chief Chatoyer, who lost his life in a duel at this site.

La Soufrière, the queen of climbs, is St. Vincent's active volcano (which last erupted, appropriately enough, on Friday the 13th, April 1979). Approachable from either the windward or leeward coast, this is *not* a casual excursion for inexperienced walkers—the massive mountain covers nearly the entire northern third of the island. Climbs are all-day excursions. You'll need stamina and sturdy shoes to reach the top and peep into the mile-wide (1½-km-wide) crater at just over 4,000 ft (1,219 m). Be sure to check the weather before you leave; hikers have been sorely disappointed to find a cloud-obscured view at the summit. A guide ($25–$30) can be arranged through your hotel, the SVG Board of Tourism, or tour operators. The eastern approach is more popular. In a four-wheel-drive vehicle, you pass through Rabacca Dry River, north of Georgetown, and the Bamboo Forest; then it's a two-hour, 3½-mi (5½-km) hike to the summit. Approaching from the west, near Châteaubelair, the climb is longer—10–12 mi (6–7 km)—and rougher, but even more scenic. If you hike up one side and down the other, arrangements must be made in advance to pick you up at the end.

Trinity Falls, in the north, requires a trip by four-wheel-drive vehicle from Richmond to the interior, then a steep two-hour climb to a crystal-clear river and three waterfalls, one of which forms a whirlpool where you can take a refreshing swim. **Vermont Nature Trails** are two hiking trails that start near the top of the Buccament Valley, 5 mi (8 km) north of Kingstown. A network of 1½-mi (2½-km) loops passes through bamboo, evergreen forest, and rain forest. In the late afternoon, you may be lucky enough to see the rare St. Vincent parrot, *Amazona guildingii.*

SCUBA DIVING AND SNORKELING

Novices and advanced divers alike will be impressed by the marine life in SVG waters—brilliant sponges, huge deepwater coral trees, and shallow reefs teeming with colorful fish. Many sites are still virtually unexplored.

You'll find dive shops on St. Vincent, Bequia, Mustique, Canouan, and Union, as well as at private resorts on Mayreau, Petit St. Vincent, and Palm Island. Most offer three-hour beginner "resort" courses, full certification courses, and excursions to reefs, walls, and wrecks found throughout the Grenadines. A single-tank dive costs about $50; a two-tank, $95; a 10-dive package, $400. All prices include equipment. It can't be emphasized enough, however, that the coral reef is extremely fragile, and you must only look and never touch.

St. Vincent is ringed by one long, almost continuous reef. The best dive spots are in the small bays along the coast between Kingstown and Layou; many are within 20 yards of shore and only 20–30 ft (6–9 m) down. **Anchor Reef** has excellent visibility for viewing a deep-black coral garden, schools of squid, seahorses, and maybe a small octopus. **The Forest,** a shallow dive, is still dramatic, with soft corals in pastel colors and schools of small fish. **New Guinea Reef** slopes to 90 ft (28 m) and can't be matched for its quantity of corals and sponges.

A trip to **Tobago Cays,** in the southern Grenadines, will allow you to experience some of the best snorkeling in the world. A group of four islands surrounds a shallow reef studded with sponges and coral formations, and populated with countless colorful fish. **Young Island** is also a good place for snorkeling. If you're not a resort guest, phone for permission to take the ferry from Villa Beach over to the island and rent snorkeling equipment from the resort's water-sports center.

Dive St. Vincent (⊠ Young Island Dock, Villa Beach, ☎ 784/457–4928) is where NAUI- and PADI-certified instructor Bill Tewes and his staff offer beginner and certification courses and dive trips to the St. Vincent coast and the southern Grenadines. **Dive Fantasea** (⊠ Villa Beach, ☎ 784/457–5560 or 784/457–5577) offers dive and snorkeling trips to the St. Vincent coast and the Tobago Cays. **Wallialabou Dive Ex-**

perience (✉ Wallialabou, ☎ 784/456–0355) offers PADI-certified courses and daily one- or two-tank dives to sites on St. Vincent.

Tennis

Haddon Tennis Club (✉ Murrays Road, Kingstown, ☎ 784/456–1897) has two outdoor courts lighted for night use. **St. Vincent and the Grenadines National Tennis Centre** (✉ Villa, ☎ 784/457–4090) has four lighted outdoor courts.

Shopping

The 12 blocks that hug the waterfront in downtown Kingstown comprise St. Vincent's main shopping district. Among the shops that sell goods to fulfill household needs are a few that sell local crafts, gifts, and souvenirs. Bargaining is neither expected nor appreciated.

CDS, TAPES, AND RECORDS

To bring back sounds of the islands, stop by **Music World** (✉ Egmont St., Kingstown, ☎ 784/547–1884), where you'll find the latest reggae, soca, and calypso music on CD or tape.

DUTY-FREE GOODS

The best place for duty-free shopping is at the **Cruise Ship Terminal** (✉ Upper Bay St., Kingstown, ☎ 784/456–1830). Among its 20 shops are several that specialize in duty-free goods. At **Gonsalves Duty-Free Liquor** (✉ Airport Departure Lounge, Arnos Vale, ☎ 784/456–4781), spirits and liqueurs are available at discounts of up to 40%.

HANDICRAFTS

Artisans Craft Shop (✉ 2nd floor, Bonadie's Plaza, Bay St., Kingstown, ☎ 784/458–2306) sells local crafts, such as straw mats and baskets, woodcraft, pottery, macramé, and hand-painted and tie-dyed clothing. At **FranPaul's Selections** (✉ 2nd floor, Bonadie's Plaza, Bay St., Kingstown, ☎ 784/456–2662), Francelia St. John fashions dresses, pants, and shirts from colorful fabrics she selects in Trinidad. The emphasis is on African, Afro-Caribbean, and casual wear. **Noah's Arkade** (✉ Bay St., Kingstown, ☎ 784/457–1513) sells appealing crafts and gifts from all over the Caribbean, as well as T-shirts and a good selection of books on local customs and history. **Nzimbu Browne** (☎ 784/457–1677) creates original art from dried banana leaves, carefully selecting and snipping bits and arranging them on pieces of wood to depict local scenes. His artwork is sold at Artisans Craft Shop, but he also sets up shop on Bay Street in front of the Cobblestone Inn. **St. Vincent Craftsmen's Centre** (✉ Frenches St., Kingstown, ☎ 784/457–1288), three blocks from the wharf, sells locally made grass floor mats, place mats, and other straw items, as well as batik cloth, handmade West Indian dolls, hand-painted calabashes, and framed artwork. The large grass mats can be rolled and folded for easy transport home. No credit cards are accepted.

Nightlife

Nightlife here consists mostly of once-a-week hotel barbecue buffets with local music and jump-ups, so called because the lively steel-band and calypso music makes listeners jump up and dance. At nightspots in Kingstown and at Villa Beach, you can join Vincentians for late-night dancing to live or recorded reggae, hip-hop, and soca music.

CASINO

Emerald Valley Casino (✉ Peniston Valley, ☎ 784/456–7824) combines the hominess of a small English pub with the gaming of Vegas—

roulette, blackjack, Caribbean stud poker, craps, and slots. It's generally open Wednesday–Monday 9 PM–3 AM, and until 4 AM on Saturday. Call ahead for free transportation.

DANCE AND MUSIC CLUBS

Dance clubs generally charge a cover of $4 (EC$10), slightly more for headliners. At the **Aquatic Club** (⊠ Villa Beach, ☎ 784/458–4205), the rhythmic sounds of soca and reggae reverberate on the waterfront on Saturday night as locals and visitors dance to live music. The **Attic** (⊠ 1 Melville St., Kingstown, ☎ 784/457–2558) is above the KFC; you'll hear international jazz and blues on Thursday night; weekend parties begin at 10 PM. **Touch Entertainment Centre** (⊠ Grenville St., Kingstown, ☎ 784/457–1825) is a dance hall with disco music on Friday and live music on Saturday. It attracts a local crowd of mostly young people.

THEME NIGHTS

Calliaqua Culture Pot (⊠ Main Rd., Calliaqua, ☎ no phone) is a community street party held every Friday evening at 8 PM. Join the crowd for barbecue, beer, dancing to local music, arts and crafts, and cultural performances. On Wednesday and Friday evenings at **Vee Jay's Rooftop Dining Club** (⊠ Bay St., Kingstown, ☎ 784/457–2845), karaoke accompanies dinner, drinks, and the open-air harbor view. **Young Island Resort** (⊠ Young Island, ☎ 784/458–4826) hosts sunset cocktail parties with hors d'oeuvres every Friday evening at adjacent Ft. Duvernette. Hotel guests and nonguests (with reservations) are ferried from Young Island Resort to the tiny island, where the 100 steps up the hill are lighted by flaming torches. The National String Band plays infectious music on guitars and instruments made of bamboo, bottles, and gourds.

Exploring St. Vincent

Kingstown's shopping and business district, historic churches and cathedrals, and other points of interest can easily be seen in a half-day, with another half-day for the Botanical Gardens. The coastal roads of St. Vincent offer spectacular panoramas and scenes of island life. The Leeward Highway follows the scenic Caribbean coastline; the Windward Highway follows the more dramatic Atlantic coast. A drive along the windward coast or a boat trip to the Falls of Baleine each requires a full day. Exploring La Soufrière and the Vermont Trails are also major undertakings, requiring a very early start and a full day's strenuous hiking.

Numbers in the margin correspond to points of interest on the St. Vincent map.

Sights to See

❹ **Barrouallie.** This was once an important whaling village; now, however, the fishermen of Barrouallie (pronounced *bar*-relly) earn their livelihoods trawling for blackfish, which are actually small pilot whales. The one-hour drive north from Kingstown, on the Leeward Highway, takes you along ridges that drop to the sea, through small villages and lush valleys, and beside picturesque bays with black-sand beaches and safe bathing.

⓫ **Black Point Tunnel.** In 1815, under the supervision of British colonel Thomas Browne, Carib and African slaves drilled this 300-ft (90-m) tunnel through solid volcanic rock to facilitate the transportation of sugar from estates in the north to the port in Kingstown. The tunnel, an engineering marvel for the times, links Grand Sable with Byrea Bay, just north of Colonarie (pronounced con-a-*ree*).

6 **Falls of Baleine.** They're impossible to reach by car, so book an escorted, all-day boat trip from Villa Beach or the Lagoon Marina. The boat ride along the coast offers scenic island views. When you arrive, you have to wade through shallow water to get to the beach. Then local guides help you make the easy five-minute trek to the 60-ft (18-m) falls and the rock-enclosed freshwater pool the falls create—plan to take a dip.

2 **Ft. Charlotte.** Started by the French in 1786 and completed by the British in 1806, the fort sits on a dramatic promontory 636 ft (195 m) above sea level, with a stunning view of Kingstown and the Grenadines. Interestingly, cannons face inward—the fear of attack by native peoples was far greater than any threat approaching from the sea; though, truth be told, the fort saw no action. Nowadays the fort serves as a signal station for ships; its ancient cells house paintings, by Lindsay Prescott, depicting early island history.

14 **Ft. Duvernette.** The fort was built around 1800, on a massive rock behind Young Island, to defend the bay. Views from the 195-ft (60-m) summit are terrific, but you'll have to climb about 100 steps carved into the rock to get here. Two complete batteries of rusting armaments remain near the top. Arrange your visit at the Young Island Resort—their little ferry will transport you to the fort and bring you back.

10 **Georgetown.** St. Vincent's second-largest (and former capital) city, halfway up the island's east coast, is surrounded by acres and acres of coconut groves. This is also the site of the now defunct Mount Bentinck sugar factory. A small, quiet town—with a few streets, small shops, a restaurant or two, and modest homes—it is completely untainted by tourism. It's also a convenient place to stop for a cool drink or snack or other essential shopping while traveling along the windward coast.

1 **Kingstown.** The capital city of St. Vincent and the Grenadines is on the island's southwestern coast. The town of 25,000 residents, about a fourth of the nation's population, wraps around Kingstown Bay; a ring of green hills and ridges, studded with homes, forms a backdrop for the city. This is very much a working city, with a busy harbor and few concessions to tourists.

In fact, **Kingstown Harbour,** the only deepwater port on the island, was always more likely to host a freighter than a passenger ship. However, the island's $14-million Cruise Ship Terminal has added a new dimension.

What few gift shops there are can be found on and around **Bay Street,** near the harbor. Upper Bay Street, which stretches along the bay front, bustles with daytime activity—workers going about their business and housewives doing their shopping. Many of Kingstown's downtown buildings are built of stone or brick brought to the island in the holds of 18th-century ships as ballast (and replaced with sugar and spices for the return trip to Europe). The Georgian-style stone arches and second-floor overhangs on former warehouses create shelter from midday sun and the brief, cooling showers common to the tropics.

Grenadines Wharf, at the south end of Bay Street, is busy with schooners loading supplies and ferries loading people bound for the Grenadines. The **Cruise Ship Terminal,** south of the commercial wharf, has a duty-free mall with 20 shops, plus restaurants, a post office, communications facilities, and a taxi/minibus queue.

An almost infinite selection of produce fills the **Kingstown Produce Market,** a two-story building that takes up a whole city block on Upper Bay, Hillsboro, and Bedford streets in the center of town. It's noisy, colorful, and open Monday–Saturday—but the busiest times (and the best times to go) are Friday and Saturday mornings. Upstairs, shops sell clothing, household items, gifts, and other products.

Little Tokyo, so called because funding for the project was a gift from Japan, is a waterfront shopping area with a bustling indoor fish market and dozens of stalls where you can buy inexpensive homemade meals, drinks, ice cream, bread and cookies, clothing, and trinkets, and even get a haircut.

St. George's Cathedral, on Grenville Street, is a pristine, creamy-yellow Anglican church built in 1820. The dignified Georgian architecture includes simple wooden pews, an ornate chandelier, and beautiful stained-glass windows; one was a gift from Queen Victoria, who actually commissioned it for London's St. Paul's Cathedral in honor of her first grandson. When the artist created an angel with a red robe, she was horrified and sent it abroad. The markers in the cathedral's graveyard recount the history of the island. Across the street is **St. Mary's Cathedral of the Assumption** (Roman Catholic), built in stages beginning in 1823. The strangely appealing design, a blend of Moorish, Georgian, and Romanesque styles applied to black brick, was built in stages beginning in 1823. Nearby, freed slaves built the **Kingstown Methodist Church** in 1841. The exterior is brick, simply decorated with quoins (solid blocks that form the corners), and the roof is held together by metal straps, bolts, and wooden pins. **Scots Kirk** (1839–80) was built by and for Scottish settlers but became a Seventh-Day Adventist church in 1952.

Ⓢ A few minutes north of downtown by taxi is St. Vincent's famous **Botanical Garden.** Founded in 1765, it is the oldest botanical garden in the western hemisphere. Captain Bligh—of *Bounty* fame—brought the first breadfruit tree to this island for landowners to propagate. The prolific bounty of the breadfruit tree was used to feed the slaves. You can see a direct descendant of this original tree among the specimen mahogany, rubber, teak, and other tropical trees and shrubs in the 20 acres of gardens. Two dozen rare St. Vincent parrots live in the small aviary. Guides explain all the medicinal and ornamental trees and shrubs; they also appreciate a tip at the end of the tour. ✉ *Off Leeward Hwy., Montrose,* ☎ *784/457–1003.* 🎫 *$3.* ⊙ *Daily 6–6.*

❸ **Layou.** Just beyond this small fishing village, about 45 minutes north of Kingstown, are petroglyphs (rock carvings) left by pre-Columbian people 13 centuries ago. Arrange a visit through the Tourist Board. For $2, Victor Hendrickson, who owns the land, or his wife will escort you to the site.

⓬ **Mesopotamia Valley.** The rugged, ocean-lashed scenery along St. Vincent's windward coast is the perfect counterpoint to the lush, calm west coast. The fertile Mesopotamia Valley (nicknamed "Mespo") offers a panoramic view of dense rain forests, streams, and endless banana and coconut plantations. Breadfruit, sweet corn, peanuts, and arrowroot also grow in the rich soil here. The valley is surrounded by mountain ridges, including 3,181-ft (973 m) Grand Bonhomme Mountain, and overlooks the Caribbean.

⓭ **Montreal Gardens.** Welsh-born landscape designer Timothy Vaughn renovated 7½ acres of neglected commercial flower beds and a falling-apart plantation house into a stunning, yet informal, garden spot. Anthuriums, ginger lilies, birds-of-paradise, and other tropical flowers are planted in raised beds; tree ferns create a canopy of shade along the walkways. The gardens are in the shadow of majestic Grand Bon Homme mountain, deep in the Mesopotamia Valley, about 12 mi from Kingstown. ✉ *Montreal St., Mesopotamia,* ☎ *784/458–1198.* 🎫 *$3.* ⊙ *Mon.–Fri. 9–4. Closed Sept.–Nov.*

❼ Owia. The Carib village of Owia, on the island's far northeast coast about two hours from Kingstown, is the home of many descendents of the Carib people of St. Vincent. It is also the location of the Owia Arrowroot Processing Factory. Used for generations to thicken sauces and flavor cookies, arrowroot is now in demand as a finish for computer paper. Close to the village is the **Owia Salt Pond,** where you can take a dip before the long, scenic ride back to Kingstown.

❾ Rabacca Dry River. This rocky gulch just beyond the village of Georgetown was carved out of the earth by the lava flow from the 1902 eruption of nearby **La Soufrière.** When it rains on La Soufrière, the river is no longer dry—and you can be stranded on one side or the other for an hour or two or, in rare cases, longer.

❽ The volcano **La Soufrière,** which last erupted in 1979, is 4,000 ft (1,219 m) high and so huge in area that it covers virtually the entire northern third of the island. The eastern trail to the rim of the crater, a two-hour ascent, begins at Rabacca Dry River.

❺ Wallilabou Bay. You can sunbathe, swim, picnic, or buy your lunch at Wallilabou (pronounced wally-la-*boo*) Anchorage, on the bay. This is a favorite stop for day-trippers returning from the Falls of Baleine and boaters anchoring for the evening. Nearby there's a river with a small waterfall where you can take a freshwater plunge.

THE GRENADINES

The Grenadine Islands offer excellent spots for sailing, fine diving and snorkeling, magnificent beaches, and unlimited chances to relax with a picnic, watch boats, and wait for the sun to set. Whether you're seeking peace and quiet or active water sports and informal socializing, you'll be happy in the Grenadines—though each island has a different appeal.

Bequia

Bequia (pronounced *beck*-way) is the Carib word for "island of the cloud." Hilly and green, with several gold-sand beaches, Bequia is just 9 mi (14½ km) south of St. Vincent's southwestern shore; with a population of 5,000, it's the largest of the Grenadines.

While boatbuilding, whaling, and fishing have been industries here for generations, sailing and Bequia have become almost synonymous. Bequia's picturesque Admiralty Bay is a favored anchorage for private or chartered yachts. Lodgings range from comfortable resorts to cozy West Indian inns. Bequia's airport and regular, frequent ferry service from St. Vincent make this a favorite destination for day-trippers, as well. The ferry docks in Port Elizabeth, a tiny town with waterfront bars, restaurants, and shops where you can buy handmade souvenirs, including the exquisitely detailed model sailboats for which Bequia is famous.

Lodging

For approximate costs, *see* the lodging price chart *in* St. Vincent.

$$$–$$$$ ☐ **Plantation House.** The peach-pink Plantation House sits on 20 man-
★ icured acres facing Admiralty Bay, with lawn and gardens punctuated by swaying palms, alabaster statuary, hammocks, and lounge chairs. Standard rooms each have a dressing room, twin beds, and a veranda. Deluxe rooms are in the main building, five suites in two beachfront cottages. Buffet breakfast and candlelight dinners are served at the Verandah restaurant in the main house. The informal beachfront Green Flash bar/restaurant serves lunch and is a convivial gathering place in

Caribbean Sea

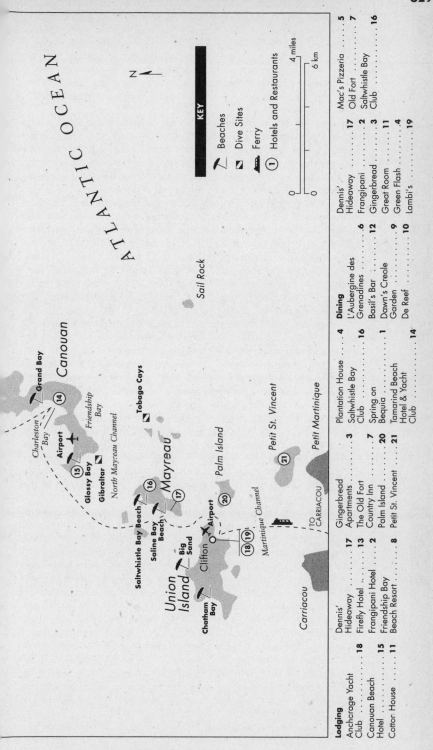

the evening. Taxi-boat service to Princess Margaret Beach (a three-minute ride) is complimentary. ⊠ *Admiralty Bay, Port Elizabeth (Box 16)*, ☎ *784/458–3425,* FAX *784/458–3612,* WEB *www.hotel-plantation.com. 5 rooms, 5 suites, 17 cabanas. 2 restaurants, room service, fans, in-room safes, refrigerator, in-room VCRs, tennis court, pool, beach, snorkeling, windsurfing, boating, waterskiing, bicycling, 2 bars, piano, shops, baby-sitting, laundry service, meeting room, airport shuttle. AE, MC, V. BP, MAP.*

$$ 🏨 **Friendship Bay Beach Resort.** This sprawling hillside complex hugs a mile-long arc of white sand beach. Accommodations are in the main building, with a sweeping view of the sea, and in a group of coral-stone cottages that dot the spacious landscaped grounds. Rooms are small, but each has a terrace with an ocean panorama. The open-air Spicy 'n' Herby beach bar and restaurant serves seafood and creole cuisine. On Saturday night there's a barbecue and jump-up, and the rope-swing seats at the bar will keep you upright even after a potent rum punch. Breakfast and special dinners are served in the Oceanside restaurant. ⊠ *Friendship Bay (Box 9),* ☎ *784/458–3222,* FAX *784/ 458–3840,* WEB *www.friendshipbay.com. 27 rooms, 1 suite. 2 restaurants, room service, no air-conditioning, no room TVs, no phones, fans, tennis court, volleyball, beach, dive shop, dock, snorkeling, wind-surfing, boating, waterskiing, 2 bars, shops, baby-sitting, laundry service, meeting room. AE, MC, V. CP, MAP.*

$–$$ 🏨 **Frangipani Hotel.** The venerable Frangipani, owned by former prime
★ minister James Mitchell, is also known for its friendly waterfront bar and excellent restaurant—both hangouts for the yachting crowd. Five simple, inexpensive rooms in the original shingle-sided sea captain's home have painted-wood walls and floors, grass rugs, and plain furniture; all but one share a bath. Luxurious garden units, built of local stone and hardwoods, rise on a gentle slope filled with fragrant frangipani trees and bushes. These rooms have tile floors, louvered windows and doors, canopy beds, spacious baths with dressing rooms, and verandas with spectacular sunset views of the harbor. ⊠ *Admiralty Bay, Port Elizabeth (Box 1),* ☎ *784/458–3255,* FAX *784/458–3824,* WEB *www.frangipanibequia.com. 15 rooms. Restaurant, room service, no air-conditioning, fans, refrigerator, tennis court, beach, dive shop, snorkeling, boating, bar, shops, baby-sitting, laundry service. MC, V. EP.*

$–$$ 🏨 **Gingerbread Apartments.** Identified by its decorative woodwork,
★ the Gingerbread faces the busy Admiralty Bay waterfront. Suites—suitable for three—are large, modern, and stylishly decorated, with bedroom alcoves, adjoining salons, and full kitchens. Downstairs rooms have twin beds and large bayfront porches; upper rooms have king-size four-poster beds and verandas with harbor views. Decorated and furnished in a sophisticated tropical style, rooms have Italian tile floors, blue-and-white geometric-print bed quilts, sheer mosquito netting gathered over beds, and natural wood and rattan furniture throughout. Bathrooms are large and modern. Gingerbread restaurant serves full meals; for snacks head to the waterfront café. ⊠ *Admiralty Bay, Port Elizabeth (Box 1),* ☎ *784/458–3800,* FAX *784/458–3907,* WEB *www.begos.com/gingerbread. 9 suites. Restaurant, room service, no air-conditioning, café, ice cream parlor, fans, in-room safes, kitchens, beach, dive shop, snorkeling, boating, bar, baby-sitting, travel services. AE, MC, V. EP.*

$–$$ 🏨 **Spring on Bequia.** Nestled on 20 acres of green hills belonging to a 200-year-old plantation, this small hotel is about 1 mi (1½ km) north of Port Elizabeth. Two spacious guest rooms with balconies are in a stone-and-wood building called Fort, highest on the hill, with beautiful views of countless coconut palms and the sea. Four large units are in Gull, halfway up the hill, and have similar full or partial ocean views. Other rooms are convenient to the pool, garden, open-air bar, and restaurant. Strolling down to the beach—a 10-minute walk—you'll pass the ruins of a sugar mill, now overgrown with colorful flowers. ✉ *Spring Bay,* ☎ *784/458–3414,* FAX *784/457–3305; U.S. agent:* ✉ *Spring on Bequia, Box 19251, Minneapolis, MN 55419,* ☎ *612/823–1202. 10 rooms. Restaurant, no air-conditioning, pool, tennis court, beach, snorkeling, hiking, bar. Closed mid-June–Oct. AE, D, MC, V. EP, MAP.*

$$ 🖽 **The Old Fort Country Inn.** Otmar Schaedle turned this historic stone sugar estate into an intimate Provence-style inn. Perched high on a cliff and cooled by trade winds, the location is both remote and stunning. Each guest room has a panoramic Grenadine vista and kitchen facilities. Because the nearest beach, Ravine, is nearly 450 ft (165 m) down a rather steep path and the water is too rough for swimming, the inn is a good choice for romantics and getaway purists who are content with a pool. The Old Fort restaurant is well worth the 10-minute trek from town by car. ✉ *Mt. Pleasant,* ☎ *784/458–3440,* FAX *784/457–3340,* WEB *www.oldfortbequia.com. 6 rooms. Restaurant, room service, kitchenettes, pool, hiking, bar, baby-sitting, laundry service, airport shuttle. MC, V. CP, EP, MAP.*

Dining

Dining on Bequia ranges from casual meals to more elaborate cuisine, and the food and service are consistently good. Barbecues at Bequia's hotels mean spicy West Indian seafood, chicken, or beef, plus a buffet of side salads and vegetable dishes and sweet desserts.

For approximate costs, *see* the dining price chart *in* St. Vincent.

CARIBBEAN

$$ ✕ **Frangipani.** Just before sunset, yachties come ashore to relax and
★ dine at what is arguably the most popular gathering spot in Bequia—the Frangipani Hotel waterfront bar. After a drink and a chat, the mood turns romantic, with candlelight and excellent Caribbean cuisine in the open-air dining room. The à la carte menu emphasizes seafood and local dishes. On Monday nights in high season, a local string band plays catchy tunes on both usual (mandolin, guitar) and unusual instruments (bamboo, bottles, gourds); on Friday nights, folksingers entertain. The Thursday-evening Frangi barbecue buffet (about $30) is accompanied by steel-band music and a jump-up. ✉ *Frangipani Hotel, Belmont Walkway, Admiralty Bay, Port Elizabeth,* ☎ *784/458–3255. Reservations essential. MC, V.*

$$–$$$ ✕ **Old Fort.** Otmar and Sonja Schaedle, owners of The Old Fort Country Inn, restored this mid-1700s estate to its current bougainvillea-shaded, stone-arched, candlelighted beauty and continue to serve food good enough to attract nonguests to its romantic atmosphere with one of the best views—and coolest breezes—on the island. At lunch feast on pumpkin or callaloo soup, crepes, sandwiches, salads, or pasta. At dinner the French creole cuisine focuses on entrées such as spring lamb, tuna steak, langouste Grenadines, or char-grilled whole snapper, accompanied by fresh, homemade bread and curried pigeon peas. ✉ *Old Fort Country Inn, Mt. Pleasant,* ☎ *784/458–3440. Reservations essential. MC, V.*

$–$$$ ✕ **Dawn's Creole Garden.** It's worth the walk uphill to the Creole Garden Hotel for the delicious West Indian food and the view. Lunch options include sandwiches, rotis, fresh mutton, "goat water" (a savory soup, with bits of goat meat and root vegetables), fresh fish, or conch. At dinner, the five-course creole seafood, lobster, or vegetarian specials include the christophene and breadfruit accompaniments for which Dawn's is known. Barbecue is always available on request. The dinner menu changes daily. There's live guitar music most Saturday nights and a barbecue lunch, with live music, right on the beach on Sundays. ⊠ *Creole Garden Hotel, Lower Bay,* ☎ *784/458–3154. Reservations essential. AE, MC, V.*

$–$$ ✕ **De Reef.** This café-restaurant on Lower Bay is the primary feeding station for long, lazy beach days. When the café closes at dusk, the restaurant takes over—if you've made reservations, that is. For breakfast (from 7) or light lunch, the café bakes its own breads, croissants, coconut cake, and cookies—and blends fresh juices to accompany them. For a full lunch or dinner, conch, lobster, whelks, and shrimp are treated the West Indian way, and the mutton curry is famous. Every other Saturday in season, there's a seafood buffet dinner accompanied by live music. Sunday lunch is always popular. ⊠ *Lower Bay,* ☎ *784/458–3484. Reservations essential. No credit cards.*

CONTINENTAL

$–$$$ ✕ **Green Flash.** The informal, waterfront restaurant at the posh Plantation House hotel has an à la carte menu that ranges from pizza and cold buffet at lunch to French, Italian, and local specialties (lobster and fresh grilled fish with regional vegetables) at dinner. On Tuesday evenings check out the creole buffet—a feast of barbecued meats and fish, side salads, vegetable dishes, and excellent pastries—accompanied by live band music. ⊠ *Plantation House, Belmont Beach, Admiralty Bay, Port Elizabeth,* ☎ *784/458–3425. AE, MC, V.*

ECLECTIC

$$–$$$ ✕ **Gingerbread.** The airy dining room verandah at the Gingerbread Apartments overlooks Admiralty Bay and the waterfront activity. The lunch
★   crowd can enjoy barbecued beef kebabs or chicken with fried potatoes or onions, grilled fish, homemade soups, salads, and sandwiches. In the evening, steaks, seafood, and curries are specialties of the house. Save some room for warm, fresh gingerbread—served here with lemon sauce. In season, dinner is often accompanied by live music. ⊠ *Gingerbread Apartments, Belmont Walkway, Admiralty Bay, Port Elizabeth,* ☎ *784/458–3800. Reservations essential. AE, MC, V.*

FRENCH

$$–$$$ ✕ **L'Aubergine des Grenadines.** Owned by the same French couple who've operated The French Restaurant on St. Vincent for years, this quaint restaurant on the waterfront facing Admiralty Bay is convenient for the yachting crowd, daytrippers, and anyone staying awhile. The extensive menu marries French and West Indian cuisines: fresh seafood and local vegetables prepared with a French twist. Lobster is a specialty; select your own from the lobster pool and it will be prepared to taste. Light salads and sandwiches are available at lunch. Delicious baguettes and delicate pastries round out any meal. ⊠ *Belmont Walkway, Admiralty Bay, Port Elizabeth,* ☎ *784/458–3201. Reservations essential. AE, MC, V.*

PIZZA

$–$$ ✕ **Mac's Pizzeria.** Overheard at the dock in Mustique: "We're sailing over to Bequia for pizza." The two-hour sunset sail to Admiralty Bay is worth the trip for Mac's pizza. Choose from 14 mouthwatering toppings (including lobster), or select quiche, pita sandwiches, lasagna, or soups and salads. Mac's home-baked cookies and muffins are great for dessert or a snack. To complement your meal, the outdoor terrace offers fuchsia bougainvillea and water views. ⊠ *Belmont Walkway, Admiralty Bay, Port Elizabeth,* ☎ *784/458–3474. Reservations essential. No credit cards.*

Beaches

Bequia has clean, uncrowded white-sand beaches. Some are a healthy walk from the jetty at Port Elizabeth; others require transportation.

Friendship Bay. This beach can be reached by land taxi. You can rent windsurfing and snorkeling equipment at Friendship Bay Resort and also grab a bite to eat or a cool drink.

Hope Beach. Getting to this beach on the Atlantic side involves a long taxi ride (about $7.50) and a mile-long (1½-km-long) walk downhill on a semi-paved path. Your reward is a magnificent crescent of white sand, total seclusion, and—if you prefer—nude bathing. Be sure to ask your taxi driver to return at a prearranged time. Bring your own lunch and drinks; there are no facilities. Even though the surf is fairly shallow, swimming can be dangerous because of the undertow.

Industry Bay. A nearly secluded beach fringed with towering palms is on the northeast side of the island and requires transportation from Port Elizabeth. This is a good beach for snorkelers, but there could be a strong undertow. Bring a picnic; the nearest facilities are at Spring on Bequia resort, a 10- to 15-minute walk from the beach.

Lower Bay. This wide, palm-fringed beach, reachable by taxi or hiking beyond Princess Margaret Beach, is an excellent location for swimming and snorkeling. There are facilities to rent water-sports equipment here, as well as De Reef restaurant.

Princess Margaret Beach. Quiet and wide with a natural stone arch at one end, the beach is a half-hour hike over rocky bluffs from Belmont Walkway—or you can take a water or land taxi. Though it has no facilities, it's a popular spot for swimming, snorkeling, or snoozing under the palm and seagrape trees.

Outdoor Activities and Sports

BOATING AND SAILING

With regular trade winds, visibility for 30 mi (48 km), and generally calm seas, Bequia is a center for some of the best blue-water sailing you'll find anywhere in the world with all kinds of options: day sails or weekly charters, bareboat or fully crewed, monohulls or catamarans—whatever's your pleasure. Prices for day trips run $60–$75 per person, depending on the destination.

Friendship Rose (☎ FAX 784/458–3373), an 80-ft schooner that spent its first 25 years as a mail boat, was subsequently refitted to take passengers on day trips from Bequia to Mustique and the Tobago Cays. The 60-ft catamaran **Passion** (✉ Belmont, ☎ 784/458–3884), custom-built for day sailing, offers all-inclusive daylong snorkeling and/or sportfishing trips from Bequia to Mustique, the Tobago Cays, and St. Vincent's Falls of Baleine. It's also available for private charter. The Frangipani Hotel (☎ 784/458–3255) owns the **S. Y. Pelangi,** a 44-ft cutter, for day sails or longer charters; four people can be accommodated comfortably, and the cost is $200 per day.

SCUBA DIVING AND SNORKELING

About 35 dive sites around Bequia and nearby islands are accessible within 15 minutes by boat. The leeward side of the 7-mi (11-km) reef that fringes Bequia has been designated a marine park. **The Bullet,** off Bequia's north point, is a good spot for spotting rays, barracuda, and the occasional nurse shark. **Devil's Table** is a shallow dive that's rich in fish and coral and has a sailboat wreck nearby at 90 ft (28 m). **Moonhole** is shallow enough in places for snorkelers to enjoy. **The Wall** is a 90-ft (28 m) drop off West Cay. Expect to pay dive operators $50 for a one-tank and $95 for a two-tank dive. Dive boats welcome snorkelers, but for the best snorkeling in Bequia, take a water taxi to the bay at Moonhole and arrange a pickup time.

Bequia Dive Adventures (✉ Belmont Walkway, Admiralty Bay, ☎ 784/458–3247, FAX 784/665–7088) offers PADI instruction courses and takes small groups on three dives daily; harbor pickup and return is included for customers staying on yachts. **Dive Bequia** (✉ Belmont Walkway, Admiralty Bay, ☎ 784/458–3504, FAX 784/458–3886), at the Gingerbread complex in Port Elizabeth, offers dive and snorkel tours, night dives, and full equipment rental. Resort and certification courses are available. **Dive Paradise** (✉ Friendship Bay, ☎ 784/458–3563, FAX 784/457–3115) has two modern dive boats and offers dive packages and certified instruction for beginners and advanced divers, equipment rental, night and wreck dives, and snorkeling packages (but they don't take credit cards). **Friendship Divers** (✉ Friendship Bay, ☎ FAX 784/458–3422), located near the Bequia Beach Club, offers one- and two-tank dives, instruction, and equipment rental; the dive boat accommodates up to 16 people.

TENNIS
Public tennis courts are located next to the Bequia airport and can be used by anyone at no charge on a first-come, first-served basis.

Shopping
Bequia's shops are mostly on Front Street and Belmont Walkway, its waterfront extension, just steps from the jetty where the ferry arrives in Port Elizabeth. North of the jetty, there's an open-air market and, farther along the road, the model-boat builders' shops. Opposite the jetty, at Bayshore Mall, shops sell ice cream, baked goods, stationery, gifts, and clothing; a liquor store, pharmacy, travel agent, and bank are also on-site. On Belmont Walkway, south of the jetty, shops and studios showcase gifts and handmade items. Shops are open weekdays from 8 to 5, Saturday 8 to noon.

HANDICRAFTS
Long renowned for their boatbuilding skills, Bequians have translated that craftsmanship to model-boat building. In their workshops in Port Elizabeth you can watch as hair-thin lines are attached to delicate sails or individual strips of wood are glued together for decking. Other Bequian artisans work with fabric—designing or hand-painting it first, then creating clothing and gift items for sale.

Crab Hole (✉ Belmont Walkway, Port Elizabeth, ☎ 784/458–3290) sells hand-printed and batik fabric, clothing, and household items. You can see the fabrics being created (and even request your own designs) in the workshop behind the boutique. **Local Color** (✉ Belmont Walkway, Port Elizabeth, ☎ 784/458–3202), above the Porthole restaurant, has an excellent and unusual selection of handmade jewelry, wood carvings, and resort clothing. **Mauvin's Model Boat Shop** (✉ Front St., Port Elizabeth, ☎ no phone) is where you can purchase the handmade model boats for which Bequia is known. You can even special-order a replica of your own yacht. They're incredibly detailed and quite expensive—from a few hundred to several thousand dollars. The simplest ones take about a week to make. **Sargeant's Model Boat Shop** (✉ Front St., Port Elizabeth, ☎ 758/458–3312) is another location where you can buy a handmade model boat or commission one to be built for you. You can visit the studio of French artist **Claude Victorine** (✉ Lower Bay, ☎ 784/458–3150) and admire her delicate hand-painted silk wall hangings and scarves. Large wall hangings cost $100, scarves $50. Her studio is open from noon to 7 PM; closed Fridays.

SOUVENIRS
Bequia Bookshop (✉ Belmont Walkway, Port Elizabeth, ☎ 784/458–3905) has Caribbean literature, plus cruising guides and charts, Caribbean flags, beach novels, souvenir maps, and exquisite scrimshaw and whalebone penknives hand-carved by Bequian scrimshander Sam McDowell. In the Frangipani Hotel, **Noah's Arkade** (✉ Belmont Walk-

way, Port Elizabeth, ☎ 784/458–3424) has gifts, souvenirs, and contemporary arts and crafts from all over the Caribbean.

Exploring Bequia

To see the views, villages, beaches, and boatbuilding sites around Bequia, hire a taxi at the jetty in Port Elizabeth. Several usually line up to meet each ferry from St. Vincent. The driver will show you the sights in a couple of hours, point out a place for lunch, and drop you (if you wish) at a beach for swimming and snorkeling and pick you up later on. Negotiate the fare in advance, but expect to pay about $15 per hour.

Water taxis are available for transportation between the jetty in Port Elizabeth and the beaches. The cost is only a couple of dollars per person each way, but keep in mind that most of these operators are not insured: ride at your own risk.

SIGHTS TO SEE

Admiralty Bay. This huge, sheltered bay, on the leeward side of Bequia, is a favorite anchorage of yachtsmen. Throughout the year, it's filled with boats; in season they're moored, literally, cheek by jowl. It's the perfect spot for watching the sun dip over the horizon each evening— either from your boat or from the terrace bar of one of Port Elizabeth's bay-front hotels.

Hamilton Battery. Just north of Port Elizabeth, high above Admiralty Bay, the 18th-century battery was built to protect the harbor from marauders. Today it's a place to enjoy a magnificent view.

Mt. Pleasant. Bequia's highest point (881 ft [270 m]) is a reasonable goal for a hiking trek. Alternatively, it's a pleasant drive. The reward is a stunning view of the island and surrounding Grenadines.

The Oldhegg Turtle Sanctuary (☎ 784/458–3245), in the far northeast of the island past Park Beach, is where Orton King, a retired fisherman, tends to endangered hawksbill turtles. He'll be glad to show you around and tell you how his project has increased the turtle population in Bequia. A contribution of $5 is requested.

Port Elizabeth. Bequia's capital is on the northeast side of Admiralty Bay. The ferry from St. Vincent docks at the jetty, in the center of the tiny town that's only a few blocks long and a couple of blocks deep. Walk north along Front Street, which faces the water, to the open-air market, where you can buy local fruits and vegetables and some handicrafts; farther along, you'll find the model-boat builders' workshops for which Bequia is renowned. Walk south along Belmont Walkway, which meanders along the bay front past shops, cafés, restaurants, bars, and hotels.

Canouan

Halfway down the Grenadines chain, this tiny boot-shape island—just 3½ mi (5½ km) long and 1¼ mi (2 km) wide—has only about 1,000 residents; however, it does have three resort hotels (though Carenage Bay—with the only golf course and casino on the island—will be closed through most of 2003) and a modern airstrip—with night-landing facilities and regularly scheduled flights from both St. Vincent and Puerto Rico. Canouan (pronounced *can*-no-wan) also claims some of the most pristine white-sand beaches in the Caribbean. Walk, swim, sail, dive, snorkel, or just relax—these are your options.

Lodging

For approximate costs, *see* the lodging price chart *in* St. Vincent.

$–$$$ 🗄 **Tamarind Beach Hotel & Yacht Club.** Thatched roofs are a trademark of this beachfront hotel. Accommodations are in three buildings facing reef-protected Grand Bay Beach. Rooms have natural wood walls and have white wicker furniture; louvered wooden doors open onto a spacious veranda and a beautiful Caribbean vista. Ceiling fans keep you cool. The alfresco Palapa Restaurant serves Caribbean specialties, grilled meat or fish, pizzas, and pasta prepared by a European chef. Barbecues and themed dinners rotate throughout the week. Live Caribbean music is featured fairly regularly at the Pirate Cove bar. A 55-ft catamaran is available for day sails to the Tobago Cays. ⊠ *Charlestown,* ☎ *784/458–8044,* FAX *784/458–8851. 42 rooms. 2 restaurants, ice cream parlor, no air-conditioning, no room TVs, fans, in-room safes, golf privileges, beach, dive shop, snorkeling, windsurfing, boating, marina, fishing, bicycles, 2 bars, shops, baby-sitting, laundry service, meeting room, travel services, airport shuttle, car rental. AE, MC, V. MAP.*

$$ 🖳 **Canouan Beach Hotel.** Perched on a lovely beach at the southwest end of the island, within walking distance of the airport, this all-inclusive hotel attracts repeat French tourists most of the year. Small, very simply furnished, whitewashed cottages with pastel roofs and trim are just steps from the sand. An open-air restaurant specializes in French cuisine, mainly seafood. Included in the rates are soft drinks from the bar, rum punch each evening, and French wine with dinner—as well as all water sports, including a catamaran day sail to the Tobago Cays. Twice a week the hotel hosts live music and dancing. ⊠ *S. Glossy Bay (Box 520),* ☎ *784/458–8888,* FAX *784/458–8875. 30 cottages. Restaurant, some fans, driving range, tennis court, Ping-Pong, volleyball, beach, dive shop, snorkeling, windsurfing, boating, marina, bar, shop, complimentary weddings, airport shuttle. AE, MC, V. All-inclusive.*

Beaches

Glossy Bay. This and other beaches along the southwest (windward) coast of Canouan are absolutely spectacular. To reach them, you cross a narrow ridge that runs the length of the island.

Godahl Beach. This lovely beach is at the south end of the Carenage Bay property.

Grand Bay. In the center of the island on the leeward side is the main beach and the site of Charlestown, the largest settlement, where ferries dock.

Mahault Bay. This lovely but remote expanse of beach (pronounced *ma*-ho) is at the northern tip of the island.

Outdoor Activities and Sports

GOLF

The island's only golf course, at the Carenage Bay Golf Club, will be closed through most of 2003 as the resort is extensively renovated.

SCUBA DIVING AND SNORKELING

The mile-long (1½-km-long) reef and waters surrounding Canouan offer excellent snorkeling as well as spectacular sites for both novice and experienced divers. **Gibraltar,** a giant stone almost 30 ft (9 m) down, is a popular site; plenty of colorful fish and corals are visible. The crystalline waters surrounding the **Tobago Cays** offer marvelous diving and snorkeling.

Blueway International (⊠ Tamarind Beach Hotel, Charlestown, ☎ 784/458–8044, FAX 784/458–8851), a full-service dive facility, offers resort and certification courses and dive and snorkel trips to the Tobago Cays, Mayreau, and Palm Island.

Mayreau

Privately owned Mayreau (pronounced *my*-row) is minuscule—just 1½ square mi (4 square km). Only 200 or so residents live in the hilltop village, and there are no proper roads. Guests at the resort on Saltwhistle Bay enjoy the natural surroundings in one of the prettiest locations in the Grenadines—one of the few spots where the calm Caribbean is separated from the Atlantic surf by only a narrow strip of beach. It's a favorite stop for boaters, as well. Except for water sports and hiking, there's not much to do—but everyone prefers it that way. For a day's excursion, you can hike up Mayreau's only hill (wear sturdy shoes) to a stunning view of the Tobago Cays. Then stop for a drink at Dennis' Hideaway and enjoy a swim at Saline Bay Beach, where you may be joined by a few boatloads of cruise-ship passengers. This pretty little island is a favorite stop for small ships that ply the waters of the Grenadines and anchor just offshore for the day. The only access to Mayreau is by boat (ferry, private, or hired), which you can arrange at Union Island.

Lodging

For approximate costs, *see* the lodging price chart *in* St. Vincent.

$$$$ 🏨 **Saltwhistle Bay Club.** This resort is so cleverly hidden within 22 acres of lush foliage that sailors need binoculars to be sure it's there at all. Gorgeous Saltwhistle Bay is a half-moon of crystal-clear water rimmed by almost a mile of sparkling white, sandy beach. Each roomy cottage is decked out with wooden shutters, ceiling fans, and a circular stone shower. You can dry your hair on the breezy second-story veranda atop each bungalow. Individual dining cabanas with stone tables are protected from sun and the occasional raindrop by thatched roofs. You'll relish turtle steak, duckling, lobster, and à la carte lunches. ⊠ *Saltwhistle Bay,* ☎ 784/458–8444, ℻ 784/458–8944. 10 cottages. Restaurant, no air-conditioning, no room TVs, fans, beach, dive shop, snorkeling, windsurfing, boating, Ping-Pong, volleyball, bar, baby-sitting. MC, V. FAP, MAP. Closed Oct.

$ ✕🏨 **Dennis' Hideaway.** Dennis (who plays guitar two nights a week) is a charmer, the seafood is great, the drinks are strong, and the view is heavenly. The rooms in the guest house are clean but very simple: a bed, a nightstand, a chair, a private bath, and a place to hang some clothes. ⊠ *Saline Bay,* ☎ ℻ 784/458–8594. 7 rooms. Restaurant, bar. No credit cards. EP.

Beaches

Saline Bay Beach. This beautiful 1-mi (1½-km) curve on the southwest coast has no facilities, but you can walk to Dennis' Hideaway. The dock here is where the ferry from St. Vincent ties up.

Saltwhistle Bay Beach. In the north, this beach takes top honors—it's an exquisite half moon of powdery white sand, shaded by perfectly spaced palms, seagrapes, and flowering bushes.

Outdoor Activities and Sports
BOATING, FISHING, AND SAILING

Yacht charters, drift fishing trips, and day sails on a 44-ft sailing yacht can be arranged at **Dennis' Hideaway** (⊠ Saline Bay, ☎ 784/458–8594). Expect to pay $40 per person for drift fishing for 1½ hours and $120–$200 per person (depending on the number of passengers) for a full day of sailing, swimming, and snorkeling—lunch included.

Mustique

This upscale hideaway, 18 mi (29 km) southeast of St. Vincent, is only 3 mi (5 km) by 1½ mi (2 km) at its widest point. The island is hilly and has several green valleys, each with a sparkling white sand beach facing an aquamarine sea. The permanent population is about 300.

Princess Margaret put this small, private island on the map after owner Colin Tennant (Lord Glenconner) presented her with a 10-acre plot of land as a wedding gift in 1960 (Tennant had purchased the entire 1,400-acre island in 1958 for $67,500). The Mustique Company—which Tennant formed in 1968 to develop the copra, sea-island cotton, and sugarcane estate into the glamorous hideaway it has become—now manages the privately owned villas, provides housing for all island employees, and operates a house-rentals department. Arrangements must be made about a year in advance to rent the royal holiday home, Les Jolies Eaux, or one of the other 49 luxury villas that pepper the northern half of the island.

Sooner or later, stargazers see the resident glitterati (e.g., Mick Jagger, Elton John, David Bowie, Tommy Hilfiger) at Basil's Bar, the island's social center. Basil also runs a boutique crammed with clothes and accessories specially commissioned from Bali. A pair of candy-color buildings, the centerpiece of the tiny village, house a gift shop and clothing boutique. There's a delicatessen-grocery to stock yachts and supply residents with fresh Brie and Moët; an antiques shop is stocked with fabulous *objets d'art* for those extraordinary villas.

Lodging

For approximate costs, *see* the lodging price chart *in* St. Vincent.

HOTELS

$$$$ **Cotton House.** The glamorous resort surrounds the island's 18th-
★   century plantation house and stone mill. The Great Room restaurant is in the colonial house, whose wraparound porch functions as lounge, bar, tearoom, and social center. Oceanfront rooms and suites have private walkways leading to the beach. A quartet of elegant ocean-view suites and three poolside cottages have sunken baths, king-size beds with mosquito nets, and terraces affording stunning views. All accommodations have dressing areas, French doors and windows, desks, bathrooms with marble fittings, your choice of bed pillows, and perfect peace. Do as much or as little as you wish. TV/VCRs are available at your request. ⊠ *Endeavour Bay (Box 349),* ☎ *784/456–4777,* FAX *784/456–5887,* WEB *www.cottonhouse.net. 12 rooms, 5 suites, 3 cottages. 2 restaurants, fans, in-room safes, minibars, 2 tennis courts, pool, spa, 2 beaches, dive shop, snorkeling, windsurfing, boating, horseback riding, 2 bars, shops, library, baby-sitting, meeting room, concierge, airport shuttle. AE, D, MC, V. MAP.*

$$$ **Firefly Hotel.** Tiny and charming, this exclusive, reclusive three-story aerie is wedged into thick foliage on a hillside above Britannia Bay. One of the island's original villas is now a romantic hideaway. Each room is unique: one has a private deck with hot tub; another, a plunge pool; yet another; an open-air shower. The inn's two pools are connected by a waterfall, and the beach is just down the (rather steep) garden path. Firefly restaurant serves Caribbean cuisine, gourmet pizza, and pasta dishes. A small motorized buggy is included in the room rate, and private air service from Barbados is reasonably priced. ⊠ *Britannia Bay (Box 349),* ☎ *784/456–3414,* FAX *784/456–3514,* WEB *www.mustiquefirefly.com. 4 rooms. Restaurant, room service, some air-conditioning, fans, minibars, 2 pools, beach, snorkeling, bar, piano, airport shuttle, no children under 12. AE, MC, V. FAP.*

VILLAS

$$$$ **Mustique Villas.** Villa rentals on Mustique are arranged solely through the Mustique Company's house-rentals department, even though the villas are privately owned. Rates are per villa, not per person, and include a full staff (with a cook), laundry service, and a vehicle or two. Houses range from rustic (albeit with en suite bathrooms

for every bedroom, phones, pools, cable TVs, VCRs, CD players, and faxes) to extravagant, expansive, faux-Palladian follies with resident butler. All are designer-elegant and immaculately maintained. Villas accommodate up to 12 people. Weekly rentals run from $3,000 for a two-bedroom villa in the off-season to $30,000 for a palatial seven-bedroom, five-staff, two-jeep, one-whirlpool villa in winter. ⊠ *Mustique Company Ltd., House Rentals Dept., Box 349, St. Vincent,* ☎ *784/458–4621,* FAX *784/456–4565,* WEB *www.mustique-island.com. 50 villas. AE, DC, MC, V. FAP.*

Dining

For approximate costs, *see* the dining price chart *in* St. Vincent.

SEAFOOD

$$$–$$$$ ✕ **Great Room.** Expect a memorable experience when dining at the fine
★ Cotton House resort. The chef pairs fresh island ingredients with excellent wines. Appetizers of conch Napoleon or tuna carpaccio are every bit as tempting as the entrées—which might include grilled barracuda with thyme-braised potatoes or curry-rubbed chicken breast with coconut rice. A vegetarian choice is always available. Homemade ice cream or sorbet may be enough for dessert, if you can blink when the warm chocolate cake is offered. Luncheon pastas, sandwiches, and salads are served by the pool bar or packed in a picnic basket. ⊠ *Endeavour Bay,* ☎ *784/456–4777. Reservations essential. AE, D, MC, V.*

$–$$ ✕ **Basil's Bar.** Basil's is *the* place to be—and only partly because it is
★ the *only* place to be aside from the two hotel restaurants. This rustic eatery has a wooden deck built over the waves, a thatched roof, a congenial bar, and a dance floor that's open to the stars—in every sense. You never know what recognizable face may show up at the next table. The food is simple and good—mostly fish hauled from the water 100 yards away, homemade ice cream, burgers and salads, great French toast, the usual cocktails, and unusual wines. Wednesday is barbecue and party night; on Monday there's live music. ⊠ *Britannia Bay,* ☎ *784/458–4621. Reservations essential. AE, MC, V.*

Beaches

Britannia Bay. This beach is best for day-trippers, since it's next to the jetty, and Basil's Bar is convenient for lunch.

Endeavour Bay. On the northwest coast is the site of the Cotton House, as well as a dive shop and water-sports equipment rental.

Gelliceaux Bay. On the southwest coast is a good beach for snorkelers.

L'Ansecoy Bay. At the island's very northern tip is a broad crescent of white sand with brilliant turquoise water.

Macaroni Beach. Macaroni is Mustique's most famous stretch of fine white sand—offering swimming (no lifeguards) in moderate surf that's several shades of blue, along with a few palm huts and picnic tables in a shady grove of trees.

Outdoor Activities and Sports

Water-sports facilities are available at the Cotton House, and most villas have equipment of various sorts. Four floodlit tennis courts are near the airport for those whose villa lacks its own; there's a cricket field for the Brits (matches on Sunday afternoon); and motorbikes or "mules" (beach buggies) to ride around the bumpy roads rent for $45 per day.

HORSEBACK RIDING

Mustique is one of the few islands where you can find a fine horse. Daily excursions leave from the **Equestrian Centre** (☎ 784/458–4316), which is one block from the airport. Rates are $50 per hour for an island trek, $60 per hour for a surf ride, and $45 per hour for lessons.

All rides are accompanied, and children over five years are allowed to ride.

SCUBA DIVING AND SNORKELING

Mustique is surrounded by coral reefs, and the tiny island has two dive shops. **Basil's Bar** (✉ Britannia Bay, ☎ 784/458–4621) will arrange scuba-diving and snorkeling trips and rent equipment. **Mustique Watersports** (✉ Cotton House, Endeavour Bay, ☎ 784/456–4777) offers PADI instruction and certification and has a 28-ft, fully equipped dive boat. Rates are $65 for a one-tank dive, and multidive packages are available.

Palm Island

A private speck of land only 100 acres in area, exquisite Palm Island used to be an uninhabited, swampy, mosquito-infested spot called Prune Island. One intrepid family put heart and soul—as well as muscle and brawn—into taking the wrinkles out of the prune and rechristened it as Palm Island. They cleaned the five surrounding beaches, built bungalows, planted palm trees, and irrigated the swamp with seawater to kill the mosquitos. The rustic getaway existed for 25 years. More recently, Palm Island has been dolled up to be one of the finest resorts in the Caribbean. Other than the resort, the island has only a handful of private villas. Access is via Union Island, 1 mi (1½ km) to the west and a 10-minute ride on the resort's launch.

Lodging

For approximate costs, *see* the lodging price chart *in* St. Vincent.

$$$–$$$$ 🏨 **Palm Island.** Perfect for a honeymoon, rendezvous, or luxurious es-
★   cape, this palm-studded resort offers pristine white-sand beaches, a calm aquamarine sea for swimming and watersports, nature trails for quiet walks, a pool with waterfall, sophisticated dining, impeccable service, and exquisite accommodations. Choose a beachfront room with stone bathroom, a palm-view "Plantation" suite, or a "Coconut Treehouse"—a remote, private cottage on stilts. All rooms have custom-designed wicker and bamboo furniture, rich fabrics, wooden louvers on three walls to catch every breeze, and original artwork. The dining room offers a varied menu, while restaurant near the dock welcomes both guests and nonguests for seafood, light fare, and drinks. ✉ *Palm Island,* ☎ *784/458–8824,* FAX *784/458–8804,* WEB *www.palmislandresorts.com. 36 rooms, 4 suites, 7 cottages. Dining room, restaurant, no in-room TVs, fans, in-room safes, refrigerator, 5-hole golf course, tennis court, pool, massage, 5 beaches, dock, snorkeling, windsurfing, boating, bicycles, hiking, 2 bars, shop, library, recreation room, airport shuttle. AE, D, DC, MC, V. All-inclusive.*

Petit St. Vincent

The southernmost of St. Vincent's Grenadines, tiny (113-acres), private Petit St. Vincent, affectionately called PSV, is ringed with white-sand beaches and covered with tropical foliage. To get here, you fly into Union Island, where the resort's motor launch meets you for the 30-minute trip.

Lodging

For approximate costs, *see* the lodging price chart *in* St. Vincent.

$$$$ 🏨 **Petit St. Vincent.** Stone-and-glass cottages perch on a bluff or over-
★   look the surf, with stone steps to the beach. Each has a bedroom, a sitting room, and one or two bathrooms with cobblestone shower, fabulous toiletries, robes, beach bags, and an iron. No cottage is more than

a five-minute walk from dinner, yet each is completely private, with a system of signal flags to convey whims to the staff. Hoist your red flag, and nobody *dreams* of approaching; hoist the yellow, and you can promptly receive a meal, drinks, a picnic lunch, or a ride to the jetty. Relax, read, swim, get away from it all in rustic elegance. ⊠ *Petit St. Vincent,* ☎ *784/458–8801,* FAX *784/458–8428,* WEB *www.psvresort.com; U.S. Agent: PSV, Box 12506, Cincinnati, OH 45212,* ☎ *513/242–1333,* FAX *513/242–6951. 22 cottages. Dining room, no air-conditioning, no room phones, no room TVs, tennis court, beach, snorkeling, boating, bar, shop. AE, MC, V. FAP. Closed Sept.–Oct.*

Union Island

The jagged peak of The Pinnacle soars 995 ft (300 m) in the air, distinguishing Union Island from its neighbors. Union is a particularly popular anchorage for French vacationers sailing the Grenadines and a crossroads for others heading to surrounding islands (Palm, Mayreau, and Petit St. Vincent) just minutes away by speedboat. Clifton, the main town, is small and commercial, with a bustling harbor, three simple beachfront inns, a few restaurants, businesses that cater to yachts, and the regional airstrip—perhaps the busiest in the Eastern Caribbean. Taxis and minibuses are available.

Lodging

For approximate costs, *see* the lodging price chart *in* St. Vincent.

$–$$ 🖼 **Anchorage Yacht Club.** Between the airstrip and the waterfront, comfortably furnished seaside rooms and beach bungalows with concealed outdoor showers and terraces offer great bay views. Grounds are attractive, with flower gardens, palm trees, and a large fish pool. You'll find watersports and yacht-charters galore. The full-service marina creates a cosmopolitan buzz throughout the resort. Rates include breakfast at Les Pieds dans l'Eau, the adjoining restaurant, which also serves a barbecue lunch and French and creole cuisine at dinner. There's a pizza and sandwich counter as well. Each night guests and stranded sailors are serenaded by steel-band, reggae, or piano music in the bar. ⊠ *Clifton,* ☎ *784/458–8221,* FAX *784/458–8365,* WEB *www.ayc-hotel-grenadines.com. 10 rooms, 6 bungalows. Restaurant, snack bar, beach, dock, snorkeling, boating, marina, fishing, bar, shop. MC, V. CP, FAP, MAP.*

Dining

For approximate costs, *see* the dining price chart *in* St. Vincent.

CARIBBEAN

$–$$ ✕ **Lambi's.** Overlooking the waterfront in Clifton, enjoy Lambi's specialty—delicious conch creole. Lambi is Creole patois for "conch," and the restaurant's walls are even constructed from conch shells. The menu also offers other local seafood and grilled meats. Yachts and dinghies can tie up at the wharf, and there's steel-band music every night in season. ⊠ *Clifton,* ☎ *784/458–8549. No credit cards.*

Beaches

Big Sand. Union has relatively few good beaches, but the trek here, on the north shore, is worth the effort.

Chatham Bay. The desolate but lovely beach offers good swimming.

Outdoor Activities and Sports

BOATING AND SAILING

Union is a major base for yacht charters and sailing trips. At **Anchorage Yacht Club** (⊠ Clifton, ☎ 784/458–8221), you can arrange crewed yacht or sailboat charters for a day sail or longer treks around the Grenadines. For example, sailing out of Union to the nearby islands of Mayreau, Canouan, and the Tobago Cays for a full day of snorkeling, fishing, and swimming costs about $200 per person for two people or $120 per person for four or more—lunch and drinks included. The marina is also a good place to stock up on fresh-baked bread and croissants, ice, water, food, and other boat supplies.

SCUBA DIVING AND SNORKELING

Grenadines Dive (✉ Sunny Grenadines Hotel, Clifton, ☎ 784/458–8138, FAX 784/458–8851), run by NAUI-certified instructor Glenroy Adams, offers Tobago Cays snorkeling trips and wreck dives at the *Purina*, a sunken World War I English gunboat. A single-tank dive costs $60; multidive packages are discounted. Beginners can take a four-hour resort course, which includes a shallow dive, for $85. Certified divers can rent equipment by the day or week.

ST. VINCENT AND THE GRENADINES A TO Z

To research prices, get advice from other travelers, and book travel arrangements, visit www.fodors.com.

AIR TRAVEL

Travelers from North America and Europe arrive at airports in St. Vincent and the Grenadines via connecting service to major airlines that serve six gateways: Barbados, Grenada, Martinique, St. Lucia, Puerto Rico, or Trinidad. Connections are via Air Caraïbe, BWee Express, Caribbean Star, LIAT, Mustique Airways, and SVG Air.

Air Caraïbe flies between Martinique and St. Vincent, Canouan, and Union islands. American Eagle flies nonstop from San Juan, Puerto Rico, to Canouan. BWIA's BWee Express flies to SVG from Barbados and Trinidad. Caribbean Star flies to St. Vincent from St. Lucia or Grenada. LIAT connects St. Vincent, Bequia, and Union with Grenada and St. Lucia. Mustique Airways operates frequent shared-charter service linking Barbados with St. Vincent and the four airports in the Grenadines. SVG Air has daily scheduled service between Barbados and St. Vincent, Bequia, and Mustique; between Grenada/Carriacou and Bequia, Canouan, and Union; and between St. Vincent and Mustique, Canouan, and Union.

From other parts of the world, connections must be made through major U.S. cities, Toronto, or London and Caribbean hubs, such as San Juan or Barbados.

➤ AIRLINES AND CONTACTS: **American Eagle** (☎ 784/456–5555). **Air Caraïbe** (☎ 784/458–4528 in St. Vincent; 784/458–8888 in Canouan; 784/458–8826 in Union). **BWee Express** (☎ 784/627–6222). **Caribbean Star** (☎ 784/456–5800). **LIAT** (☎ 784/458–4841 in St. Vincent; 784/457–1821 in Bequia; 784/458–8230 in Union). **Mustique Airways** (☎ 784/458–4380; 784/458–3183 in Bequia; 784/458–8325 in Canouan). **SVG Air** (☎ 784/457–5124 in St. Vincent; 784/458–3713 in Bequia; 784/458–8329 in Canouan; 784/458–8882 in Union).

AIRPORTS

St. Vincent's E. T. Joshua Airport is in Arnos Vale, about halfway between Kingstown and Villa Beach. It's a busy airport with night landing equipment, although it only services turboprop aircraft. The St. Vincent Department of Tourism has an information desk in the arrivals hall, where arriving passengers can ask questions or collect maps, brochures, and other information. For departing passengers, there are a snack bar and a few shops that sell souvenirs, handicrafts, and sundry items. The departure lounge has a duty-free liquor shop.

In the Grenadines, Bequia has a small, modern airport with night-landing equipment. Mustique, Canouan, and Union islands each have an airstrip with frequent commercial service.

Taxis and buses are readily available at the airport on St. Vincent. The taxi fare to hotels in either Kingstown or the Villa Beach area is about $8–$10 (EC$20–$25). Taxi service is available from the airports on Bequia, Mustique, Canouan, and Union islands.

➤ AIRPORT INFORMATION: **E. T. Joshua Airport** (✉ Arnos Vale, St. Vincent, ☎ 784/458–4011). On Bequia: **James F. Mitchell Airport** (✉ Bequia, ☎ 784/458–3948). **Canouan Airport** (✉ Canouan, ☎ 784/458–8049). **Mustique Airport** (✉ Mustique, ☎ 784/458–4621). **Union Airport** (✉ Union, ☎ 784/458–8750).

BOAT AND FERRY TRAVEL

St. Vincent's Cruise Ship Terminal is located at Port Kingstown. The berths can accommodate two ships at one time; a broad landing stage accommodates passengers arriving by launch from ships at anchor. The facility has all clearance services; a bank, post office, communications facility, and tourism office; a restaurant and food courts; and 20 retail shops offering local goods (spices and seasonings, shellwork, leather goods, art and wood carvings, clothing, and straw mats) and duty-free items. Tour buses depart from the terminal, and those opting for a day in Bequia can board the ferry at an adjacent wharf.

Cruise ships that call at Port Elizabeth on Bequia, Mayreau, and elsewhere in the Grenadines anchor offshore and tender passengers to beaches or waterfront jetties.

FARES AND SCHEDULES

All scheduled ferries leave St. Vincent from Grenadines Wharf in Kingstown and from Port Elizabeth on Bequia. The one-way trip between St. Vincent and Bequia takes 60 minutes and costs $6 (EC$15) each way or $11 (EC$28) round-trip.

MV *Admiral I* and MV *Admiral II* make several round-trips between Bequia and Kingstown Monday–Saturday beginning at 6:30 AM in Bequia and 8 AM in St. Vincent; the latest departure each day is at 5 PM from Bequia and 7 PM from Kingstown. On Sunday the one round-trip leaves St. Vincent at 9 AM and returns from Bequia at 5 PM.

MV *Barracuda* leaves St. Vincent on Monday and Thursday mornings, stopping in Bequia, Canouan, Mayreau, and Union Island. It makes the return trip Tuesday and Friday. On Saturday it does the round-trip from St. Vincent to each island and returns in a day. Including stopover time, the trip takes 3¼ hours from St. Vincent to Canouan ($5), 4½ hours to Mayreau ($6), and 5¼ hours to Union Island ($8).

MV *Bequia Express* travels between Kingstown and Bequia, making two or three trips daily, including holidays.

➤ BOAT AND FERRY INFORMATION: **MV *Admiral I* and MV *Admiral II*** (☎ FAX 784/458–3348). **MV *Barracuda*** (☎ 784/456–5180). **MV *Bequia Express*** (☎ 784/458–3472).

BUSINESS HOURS

BANKS

Banks are open Monday–Thursday 8–1, 2, or 3, Friday until 5. The bank at the airport is open Monday–Saturday 7–5. Bank branches on Bequia, Canouan, and Union are open Monday–Thursday 8–1 and Friday 8–5.

POST OFFICES

The General Post Office, on Halifax Street in Kingstown, is open daily 8:30–3, Saturday 8:30–11:30.

SHOPS

Shops and businesses in Kingstown are open weekdays 8–4; many close for lunch noon–1. Saturday hours are 8–noon. Shops are closed on Sunday, but supermarkets in Kingstown and Arnos Vale are open Sunday mornings.

BUS TRAVEL

Public buses on St. Vincent are really privately owned, brightly painted minivans with colorful names like *Confidence, Fully Loaded, Irie,* and *Who to Blame.* Bus fares range from 37¢–$2.25 (EC$1–EC$6) on St. Vincent; the 10-minute ride from Kingstown to Villa Beach, for example, costs 58¢ (EC$1.50). Buses operate from early morning until about midnight, and routes are indicated on a sign on the windshield. Just wave from the road or point your finger to the ground as a bus approaches, and the driver will stop. When you want to get out, signal by knocking twice on a window. A conductor rides along to open the door and collect fares; it's helpful to have the correct change in EC coins. In Kingstown, the bus terminal is near Market Square. Buses serve the entire island, although trips to remote villages are infrequent.

CAR RENTALS

Rental cars cost about $55 per day or $300 a week, with some free miles. Unless you already have an international driver's license, you'll need to buy a temporary local permit for $20 (EC$50), valid for six months. To get one, you'll need to present your valid driver's license at the police station on Bay Street or the Licensing Authority on Halifax Street in Kingstown.

Among the car-rental firms on St. Vincent are Avis Rent-A-Car—the one international agency represented on St. Vincent. Avis offers rates that are competitive with local firms. Ben's Auto Rental is located two minutes from the airport and offers all-terrain vehicles as well as cars. David's Auto Clinic, just south of Kingstown and not far from the airport, offers reliable vehicles at reasonable rates. Kims Rentals has been renting cars and jeeps on St. Vincent for nearly 40 years. Star Garage is right in town and rents minivans and buses, in addition to cars and four-wheel-drive vehicles. If you'd prefer "the slow lane," two-seater scooters or mopeds can be rented for $30 per day or $180 per week from Speedway Bike & Scooter Rental.

In Bequia, you can rent a four-wheel drive vehicle from B&G Jeep Rental. For a car during your stay on Bequia, check out Phil's Car Rental.
➤ MAJOR AGENCIES IN ST. VINCENT: **Avis Rent-A-Car** (✉ Airport, Arnos Vale, ☎ 784/456–4389). **Ben's Auto Rental** (✉ Arnos Vale, ☎ 784/456–2907). **David's Auto Clinic** (✉ Sion Hill, ☎ 784/456–4026). **Kims Rentals** (✉ Arnos Vale, ☎ 784/456–1884). **Speedway Bike & Scooter** (✉ Arnos Vale, ☎ 784/456–4894). **Star Garage** (✉ Grenville St., Kingstown, ☎ 784/456–1743).
➤ MAJOR AGENCIES IN BEQUIA: **B&G Jeep Rental** (✉ Port Elizabeth, ☎ 784/458–3760). **Phil's Car Rental** (✉ Port Elizabeth, ☎ 784/458–3304).

CAR TRAVEL

About 300 mi (484 km) of paved road wind around St. Vincent's perimeter, except for a section in the far north with no road at all, precluding a circle tour of the island. A few roads jut into the interior a few miles, and only one east–west road (through the Mesopotamia Valley) bisects the island. It's virtually impossible to get lost.

GASOLINE

Gasoline costs about $2.80 per gallon.

ROAD CONDITIONS

Although major improvements are being made, roads are usually unmarked and not always well maintained. Roads are narrow in the country, often not wide enough for two cars to pass, and people (including schoolchildren), dogs, goats, and chickens often share the roadway. Outside populated areas, they can be bumpy and potholed; be sure your rental car has proper tire-changing equipment and a spare in the trunk.

RULES OF THE ROAD

Be sure to drive on the left, and honk your horn before you enter blind curves out in the countryside—you'll encounter plenty of steep hills and hairpin turns.

ELECTRICITY

Electricity is generally 220/240 volts, 50 cycles; Petit St. Vincent has 110 volts/60 cycles (U.S. standard). Some resorts also have 110-volt current; most have 110-volt shaver outlets. Dual-voltage computers or small appliances will still require a plug adapter. Some hotels will lend transformers and/or plug adapters.

EMBASSIES

➤ UNITED KINGDOM: British High Commission (⊠ Grenville St., Kingstown, St. Vincent [Box 132], ☎ 784/457–1701 or 784/458–4381).

EMERGENCIES

ST. VINCENT

➤ AMBULANCE AND FIRE: Ambulance and fire emergencies (☎ 911).
➤ COAST GUARD: Coast Guard emergencies (☎ 911). Coast Guard non-emergencies (☎ 784/457–4578).
➤ HOSPITALS: Kingstown General Hospital (⊠ Kingstown, ☎ 784/456–1185).
➤ PHARMACIES: Davis Drugmart (⊠ Tyrrell and McCoy Sts., Kingstown, St. Vincent, ☎ 784/456–1174). Deane's (⊠ Middle St., Kingstown, ☎ 784/457–2877). People's Pharmacy (⊠ Bedford St., Kingstown, ☎ 784/456–1170).
➤ POLICE: Police emergencies (☎ 911). Police nonemergencies (☎ 784/457–1211).

THE GRENADINES

➤ AMBULANCE AND FIRE: Ambulance and fire (☎ 911).
➤ HOSPITALS: Bequia Casualty Hospital (⊠ Port Elizabeth, Bequia, ☎ 784/458–3294). Canouan Clinic (⊠ Charlestown, Canouan, ☎ 784/458–8305). Mustique Company Island Clinic (⊠ Adjacent to Mustique Airport, Mustique, ☎ 784/458–4621 Ext. 353). Union Island Health Centre (⊠ Clifton, Union, ☎ 784/458–8339).
➤ PHARMACIES: Imperial Pharmacy (⊠ Front St., Port Elizabeth, Bequia, ☎ 784/458–3373).
➤ POLICE: Police emergencies (☎ 911).

ETIQUETTE AND BEHAVIOR

People are friendly, helpful, and photogenic. But if you wish to photograph them, their families, or their property, ask permission first—and offer a small tip as a gesture of appreciation.

Except in the evenings at the fanciest hotel restaurants, dress is extremely casual—particularly in the Grenadines. Keep in mind, however, that in St. Vincent, as throughout the Caribbean, local people dress modestly and expect visitors to do the same. T-shirts and shorts are fine for shopping or sightseeing, but swimsuits and short-shorts should be reserved for beach and boat.

FESTIVALS AND SEASONAL EVENTS

The National Music Festival is held at Kingstown's Memorial Hall during March and April. The best in Vincentian music and song is presented—folk songs and calypso, solos and duets, choirs and group ensembles. Fisherman's Day (Labour Day, which falls on the first Monday in May) marks the end of a week's activities honoring the fisherman's contribution to the economy. All kinds of fishing competitions take place. Vincy Mas, St. Vincent's Carnival, is the biggest cultural festival of the year, with street parades, costumes, calypso, steel bands, food and drink, and the crowning of Miss Carnival and the Soca Monarch. It begins in late June, builds in intensity through the first two weeks in July, and culminates in a calypso competition on the final Sunday (Dimanche Gras), a huge street party (Jouvert) on the final Monday, and a Parade of Bands on the final Tuesday. The National Dance Festival is held in September each year at Kingstown's Memorial Hall, with presentations of traditional, folk, ballroom, ballet, and tap dancing. Bicycle racing, arts and crafts exhibitions, caroling, and street parties with music and dancing mark Nine Mornings, a pre-Christmas tradition, which occurs during the nine days immediately before Christmas.

On Bequia, the Easter Regatta is held during the four-day Easter weekend. Revelers gather to watch boat races and celebrate Bequia's seafaring traditions with food, music, dancing, and competitive games. The Bequia Carnival, with calypso music and revelry, is a four-day celebration held in late June, just prior to St. Vincent's Carnival. On Canouan, the Canouan Yacht Races are held in August. Besides competitive boat races and sailing events, there are fishing contests, calypso competitions, donkey and crab races, and a beauty pageant. On Union, the Easterval Regatta occurs during the Easter weekend. Festivities include boat races, sports and games, a calypso competition, a beauty pageant, and a cultural show featuring the Big Drum Dance (derived from French and African traditions). Union is one of the few islands (along with Grenada's Carriacou) that perpetuates this festive dance.

HEALTH

Water from the tap is safe to drink, but bottled water is available. Fresh fruits and vegetables from the market are safe to eat, but (as at home) you should wash them first. Cooked food purchased at the market, in small shops, or at village snackettes is wholesome and safe to enjoy.

HOLIDAYS

New Year's Day (Jan. 1), National Heroes Day (Mar. 13), Good Friday (Fri. before Easter), Easter Monday (day after Easter), May Day (1st Mon. in May), Whit Monday (7th Mon. after Easter), Caricom Day/Carnival Monday (2nd Mon. in July), Carnival Tuesday (2nd Tues. in July), Emancipation Day (1st Mon. in Aug.), Independence Day (Oct. 27), Christmas (Dec. 25), and Boxing Day (Dec. 26).

LANGUAGE

English is spoken throughout St. Vincent and the Grenadines. Although there's certainly a Caribbean lilt, you won't hear the Creole patois common on other islands that have a historical French background. One term to listen for is "jump-up," in which case you can expect a party with music and dancing. And if you're going to "lime" at the next "gap," you'll be hanging out (probably at the bar) down the road.

MAIL AND SHIPPING

The General Post Office is on Halifax Street in Kingstown, St. Vincent. Most villages on St. Vincent have branch offices. Bequia's post office is in Port Elizabeth, across from the jetty. Airmail postcards cost EC60¢ to the United States, Canada, the United Kingdom, Australia, and New Zealand; airmail letters cost EC90¢ per ounce to the United States and Canada; EC$1.10 to the United Kingdom, Australia, and New Zealand. When writing to a location in the Grenadines, the address on the envelope should always indicate the specific island name followed by "St. Vincent and the Grenadines, West Indies."

MONEY MATTERS

Prices quoted in this chapter are in U.S. dollars, unless otherwise noted.

ATMS

ATMs are located at banks in Kingstown and at their branches.

BANKS

Branches of several regional and international banks are in Kingstown, with other branches elsewhere on St. Vincent and in the Grenadines. ➤ IN ST. VINCENT: **Bank of Nova Scotia** (Scotiabank) (✉ Halifax St., Kingstown, ☎ 784/457–1601). **Barclays Bank** (✉ Halifax St., Kingstown, ☎ 784/456–1706). **National Commercial Bank of St. Vincent** (✉ Bedford St., Kingstown, ☎ 784/457–1844; ✉ E. T. Joshua Airport, Arnos Vale, Kingstown, ☎ 784/458–4943).
➤ IN THE GRENADINES: **National Commercial Bank of St. Vincent** (✉ Port Elizabeth, Bequia, ☎ 784/458–3700; ✉ Charlestown, Canouan, ☎ 784/458–8595; ✉ Clifton, Union, ☎ 784/458–8347).

CREDIT CARDS

Major credit cards—including Access, American Express, Diners Club, Discover, Eurocard, MasterCard, and Visa—and traveler's checks are accepted by hotels, car-rental agencies, and some shops and restaurants.

CURRENCY

Although U.S. dollars are accepted nearly everywhere, Eastern Caribbean currency (EC$) is the official currency and preferred. The exchange rate is fixed at EC$2.67 to US$1. Price quotes in shops are often given in both currencies. Large U.S. bills may be difficult to change in small shops. U.S. coins are not accepted anywhere.

PASSPORTS AND VISAS

U.S., Canadian, and U.K. citizens need a valid passport or a birth certificate with a raised seal and a government-issued photo I.D. Travelers from other countries must present a valid passport. Everyone must hold return or ongoing tickets.

SAFETY

There's relatively little crime here, but don't tempt fate by leaving your valuables lying around or your room or rental car unlocked. Also, be alert and mindful of your belongings around the wharf areas in Kingstown; it's congested when passengers are disembarking from ferries or cruise ships.

SIGHTSEEING TOURS

Several operators offer sightseeing tours on land or by sea. Per-person prices range from $20 for a two-hour tour to St. Vincent's Botanical Gardens to $140 for a day sail to the Grenadines. A full-day tour around Kingstown and either the leeward or windward coast, including lunch, will cost about $50 per person.

You can arrange informal land tours through taxi drivers, who double as knowledgeable guides. Expect to pay $25 per hour for up to four people.

On St. Vincent, Baleine Tours offers scenic coastal trips to the Falls of Baleine as well as charters to Bequia and Mustique, deep-sea fishing trips, and snorkeling excursions to the Tobago Cays. Calypso Tours has a 42-ft tour boat for trips to the Falls of Baleine, Bequia, Mustique, and the Tobago Cays. Fantasea Tours will take you on a 38-ft power cruiser to the Falls of Baleine, Bequia, and Mustique, or to the Tobago Cays for snorkeling. For bird-watchers, hikers, and ecotourists, HazECO Tours offers wilderness tours and hikes to enjoy the natural beauty and see historic sites throughout St. Vincent. Preference Tours has a 55-ft catamaran for sunset cruises and day trips out of Bequia to the Falls of Baleine and the Grenadines. Sailor's Wilderness Tours run the gamut, from a comfortable sightseeing drive (by day or by moonlight) to mountain biking on remote trails or a strenuous hike up the La Soufrière volcano. Sam Taxi Tours offers half- or full-day tours of St. Vincent, as well as hiking tours to La Soufrière and scenic walks along the Vermont Nature Trails. Sam's also operates on Bequia, where a sightseeing tour includes snorkeling at Friendship Bay. SVG Tours has several hiking itineraries for St. Vincent and sailing day trips to the Grenadines.

➤ CONTACTS: **Baleine Tours** (✉ Villa Beach, St. Vincent, ☎ 784/457–4089). **Calypso Tours** (✉ Blue Lagoon, St. Vincent, ☎ 784/456–1746). **Fantasea Tours** (✉ Villa Beach, St. Vincent, ☎ 784/457–4477). **HazECO Tours** (✉ Kingstown, St. Vincent, ☎ 784/457–8634). **Preference Tours** (✉ Port Elizabeth, Bequia, ☎ 784/458–3197). **Sailor's Wilderness Tours** (✉ Middle St. Kingstown, St. Vincent, ☎ 784/457–1712). **Sam Taxi Tours** (✉ Cane Garden, St. Vincent, ☎ 784/456–4338; 784/458–3686 in Bequia). **SVG Tours** (✉ Kingstown, St. Vincent, ☎ 784/458–4534).

TAXES AND SERVICE CHARGES

DEPARTURE TAX

The departure tax from St. Vincent and the Grenadines is $12 (EC$30), payable in either U.S. or E.C. currency; children under 12 are exempt.

SALES TAX

A government tax of 7% is added to hotel bills.

SERVICE CHARGES

A service charge of 10% is generally added to both hotel and restaurant bills.

TAXIS

Fares are set by the government, but it's smart to settle on the price before entering the taxi—and be sure you know what currency is being quoted. On St. Vincent, the one-way fare between Kingstown and Villa is about $10 (EC$25).

On some islands, most notably Bequia, water taxis can take you between Port Elizabeth and the beaches for a couple of dollars each way. Keep in mind that these taxi operators aren't regulated or insured: travel at your own risk.

TELEPHONES

St. Vincent and the Grenadines has a fully digitized telephone system, with international direct dialing available throughout the entire area. Pay phones are readily available and best operated with the prepaid phone cards that are sold at many stores and can be used on many Caribbean islands.

The area code for St. Vincent and the Grenadines is 784.

E-MAIL
To check your e-mail, Internet access is available for a small fee at **Office Essentials, Ltd.** (✉ Bonadie's Plaza, Middle St., Kingstown, ☎ 784/457–2235).

INTERNATIONAL CALLS
For an international operator, dial ☎ 115; for international operator-assisted credit-card calls, dial ☎ 117.

LOCAL CALLS
Local calls are free from private phones and most hotels. For local directory assistance, dial ☎ 118. Prepaid phone cards, which can be used in special cardphones throughout St. Vincent and other Caribbean islands, are sold at shops, transportation centers, and other convenient outlets. (The phone cards can be used for local or international calls.)

TIPPING
Hotels and restaurants generally add a 10% service charge to the tab. If the charge hasn't been added, a gratuity at that rate is appropriate. Otherwise, tipping is expected only for special service.

VISITOR INFORMATION
➤ BEFORE YOU LEAVE: **St. Vincent and the Grenadines Tourist Office** (✉ 801 2nd Ave., 21st floor, New York, NY 10017, ☎ 212/687–4981 or 800/729–1726, FAX 212/949–5946; ✉ 10 Kensington Ct., London W8 5DL, U.K., ☎ 0207/937–6570, FAX 0207/937–3611; WEB www.svgtourism.com). **St. Vincent Hotels & Tourism Association** (WEB www.svghotels.com).

➤ IN ST. VINCENT AND THE GRENADINES: **St. Vincent and the Grenadines Department of Tourism** (✉ Cruise Ship Terminal, Kingstown, St. Vincent [Box 834], ☎ 784/457–1502, FAX 784/451–2425). **Tourist information desks** (✉ E. T. Joshua Airport, Arnos Vale, St. Vincent, ☎ 784/458–4685; ✉ Union airport, Clifton, Union, ☎ 784/458–8350). **Bequia Tourism Association** (✉ Ferry Jetty Port Elizabeth, Bequia [Box 164], ☎ 784/458–3286, FAX 784/458–3964, WEB www.bequiasweet.com).

24 TRINIDAD AND TOBAGO

Updated by
Vernon O'Reilly-
Ramesar

The boat slides lazily through the brackish waters of the Caroni Bird Sanctuary. On either side of the channel the twisted fairytale roots of the mangrove trees seem locked in some eternal struggle. Curious caimans slice noiselessly through the water, snakes shimmer in the branches of the trees. In the distance the emerald-clad Northern Range rises imperiously toward a cloudless sky. All the world seems at peace. The small boat turns a corner and you're suddenly in a large lake surrounded by the mangrove forest. Then, as if on cue, the sky turns red—confusing the senses—the scarlet ibis have returned home in their thousands to settle in for the evening. Every tree is now cloaked with birds—what was green is now red—squawking in appreciation of their own magnificent show. Thousands of performances behind them and no end in sight.

From the beat of calypso and *soca* (an upbeat, sexy variation of calypso) to the steady tapping of raindrops accompanied by birdsong, Trinidad and Tobago's cultural and natural diversions are refreshing, vivid, and alive. This two-island republic—T&T, as it's commonly called—is the southernmost link in the Antillean island chain, lying some 9 mi (14½ km) off the coast of Venezuela and safely outside the path of all those devastating Caribbean hurricanes. Both Trinidad and Tobago are more geologically akin to continental South America than they are to other Caribbean islands: Tobago's Main Ridge and Trinidad's Northern Range are believed to represent the farthest reaches of the Andes Mountains. But although the two islands are linked geographically and politically, in some ways they could not be more dissimilar.

Trinidad's growth arose out of oil prosperity—it remains one of the largest petroleum producers in the western hemisphere—which makes it a prime destination for business travelers. They enjoy the sophisticated shopping, restaurants, and hotels in the republic's lively capital, Port-of-Spain, partying late into the night to the syncopated steel-band sounds that originated in Trinidad.

Port-of-Spain is still one of the most active commercial cities in the Caribbean. The cultural scene is as vital as ever, especially during the country's riotous Carnival—a period of festivities, concerts, and shows that begins after Christmas and culminates in a two-day street parade that ends on Ash Wednesday. The capital is home to around 300,000 of Trinidad's 1.3 million residents—Africans, Indians, Americans, Europeans, and Asians, each culture with its own language and customs (though the official language is English). About a quarter of the population is Hindu, which is why there's an abundance of East Indian festivals, religious celebrations, and delicious East Indian food. Outside Port-of-Spain you can find good beaches and many other natural attractions, though there are currently few hotels that offer more than bare-bones comfort.

On Tobago, 22 mi (35 km) away, the pace of life is slower, and seclusion easier to find. Though seaside resorts may beckon, you can still lazily explore unspoiled rain forests, coral reefs, and a largely undeveloped coastline—for now, anyway. Tourism is a growing industry, and the number of hotel rooms has been growing dramatically.

Trinidad was called *Iere* (Land of the Hummingbird) by the original Amerindian population. Columbus reached these islands on his third voyage, in 1498. Three prominent peaks around the southern bay of Trinidad prompted him to name the land La Trinidad, after the Holy Trinity. Trinidad was captured by British forces in 1797, ending 300 years of Spanish rule. Tobago's history is more complicated. It was "discovered" by the British in 1508. The Spanish, Dutch, French, and British all fought for it until it was ceded to England under the Treaty of Paris in 1814. In 1962 both islands gained their independence within the British Commonwealth, finally becoming a republic in 1976.

TRINIDAD

Lodging

Trinidad accommodations range from charming guest houses to large business hotels; most acceptable establishments, however, are within the vicinity of Port-of-Spain, far from any beach. Most places include breakfast and dinner for an additional flat rate (MAP). Port-of-Spain has a small downtown core—with a main shopping area along Frederick Street—and is surrounded by inner and outer suburbs. The inner areas include Belmont, Woodbrook, Newtown, St. Clair, St. Ann's, St. James, and Cascade. Regardless of the type of accommodation, be prepared to book far in advance (and to pay a good deal more) for stays during Carnival season.

CATEGORY	COST*
$$$$	over $175
$$$	$100–$175
$$	$60–$100
$	under $60

All prices are for a standard double room, excluding 15% tax and 10% service charge

$$ $$$ ⊞ **Hilton Trinidad and Conference Centre.** Beautifully landscaped
★ grounds and a singular setting are among the draws here. The complex stretches across the top and down the side of a hill overlooking the Gulf of Paria and Queen's Park Savannah. You take an elevator *down* to your room. Each room has a balcony with a fine view of Queen's Park Savannah, the city, the mountains, and the sea or the large, inviting pool. The Hilton is the most upscale hotel in the city. On most nights

Trinidad

ATLANTIC OCEAN

Galera Pt.

Redhead

Salibea Bay

Sans Souci

Toco

Balandra Bay

Guataro Pt.

Grande Rivière

Matelot

Saline Bay

Mattura Bay

Cocos Bay

Manzanilla Beach

(17)

Mt. Oropuche

Madamas Bay

Matura

Sangre Grande

El Cerro del Aripo

Valencia

Eastern Main Rd.

Blanchisseuse Bay

Churchill-Roosevelt Hwy.

Chupara Pt.

Las Cuevas Bay

2 (16)

Arima

Tabaquite

Flanigin Town

3

Piarco International Airport

Chaguanas

Cyril Bay

Tunapuna

(15)

Tyrico Bay

Maracas Bay

El Tucuche

San Juan

Uriah Butler Hwy.

Couva

La Vache Bay

4

1

California

Chaguaramas

Port-of-Spain

1 — (14)

Gulf of Paria

Pointe-a-Pierre

(1)

TO TOBAGO

Caribbean Sea

Dragon's Mouth

TOBAGO

Scarborough

Port-of-Spain

TRINIDAD

VENEZUELA

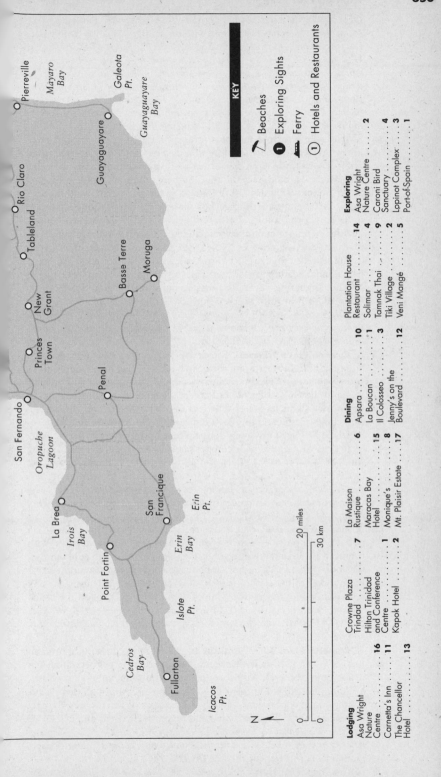

KEY

Beaches

1 Exploring Sights

Ferry

① Hotels and Restaurants

Exploring
Asa Wright
Nature Centre **2**
Caroni Bird
Sanctuary **4**
Lopinot Complex ... **3**
Port-of-Spain **1**

Dining
Apsara **10**
La Boucan **1**
Il Colosseo **3**
Jenny's on the
Boulevard **12**

Plantation House
Restaurant **14**
Solimar **4**
Tamnak Thai **9**
Tiki Village **2**
Veni Mangé **5**

La Maison
Rustique **7**
Maracas Bay
Hotel **15**
Monique's **8**
Mt. Plaisir Estate .. **17**

Lodging
Asa Wright
Nature
Centre **16**
Carnetta's Inn **11**
The Chancellor
Hotel **13**

Crowne Plaza
Trinidad **7**
Hilton Trinidad
and Conference
Centre **1**
Kapok Hotel **2**

20 miles

30 km

N

there is poolside entertainment ranging from calypso to Latin jazz. Two rooms have facilities for people with disabilities. ⊠ *Lady Young Rd., Port-of-Spain (Box 442),* ☎ *868/624–3211; 800/445–8667 in the U.S.,* FAX *868/624–4485,* WEB *www.trinidadhilton.com. 394 rooms, 25 suites. 2 restaurants, 3 bars, room service, in-room safes, minibars, 2 tennis courts, pool, wading pool, health club, massage, sauna, Ping-Pong, shops, baby-sitting, playground, dry cleaning, laundry service, business services, meeting rooms, car rental, travel services, no-smoking rooms. AE, DC, MC, V. All-inclusive, EP, FAP.*

$–$$ ⊞ **Asa Wright Nature Centre.** In this mountain retreat you can swim
★   in cool waterfall pools, explore dim caverns populated by nocturnal oilbirds, or simply sip a cup of tea while enjoying the view from the lodge veranda. Built in 1908, this 200-acre mountain estate is in a rain forest (about two hours east of Port-of-Spain) populated by 400 species of birds. The elegant lounge has mahogany floors, bookcases, antiques, and ornithological artifacts. Three meals a day, afternoon tea, and the evening rum punch are included in the rates as are government taxes and services charges. Note that children under 14 cannot be accommodated. To reach the nature center, drive east from Port-of-Spain past Arima, heading for Wallerfield; turn left at Emmaus Centre after pillars designating Ft. Read; cross Eastern Main Rd. and bear right; drive about ½ hr until you see sign for Centre. ⊠ *Arima Valley (Box 4710),* ☎ *868/667–4655 or 800/426–7781,* FAX *868/667–4540,* WEB *www.asawright.org. 24 rooms, 1 bungalow. Dining room, fans, pond, hiking, shops. MC, V. FAP.*

$–$$ ⊞ **Crowne Plaza Trinidad.** Proximity to the port and Independence Square is both the draw and the drawback here. From any upper-floor room you have a lovely pastel panorama of the old town and of ships idling in the Gulf of Paria, and you're within walking distance of the downtown sights and shops. Bear in mind, however, that with the action comes traffic and noise. Rooms are spacious and tastefully decorated. La Ronde, a revolving rooftop restaurant, offers a striking view of the city at night, which compensates for the generally uninspiring food. ⊠ *Wrightson Rd., Port-of-Spain (Box 1017),* ☎ *868/625–3361 or 800/465–4329,* FAX *868/625–4166. 235 rooms, 10 suites. 2 restaurants, 3 bars, room service, pool, gym, shops, baby-sitting, laundry service, business services, meeting rooms, travel services, no-smoking rooms. AE, MC, V. MAP.*

$–$$ ⊞ **Maracas Bay Hotel.** This hotel sits on the island's most popular beach about ½ hour outside Port-of-Spain. Rooms are simple and clean, with bright, white-painted wood walls, firm double beds, and cool maroon tile floors (but no TVs, radios, or phones). The in-house restaurant serves basic food but the service is very slow, so be patient. During the day you may choose to eat from one of the many food huts on the beach serving local specialties. ⊠ *Maracas Bay,* ☎ *868/669–1914,* FAX *868/ 669–1643. 39 rooms, 1 suite. Dining room, lounge, beach, meeting rooms. AE, MC, V. EP, MAP.*

$ ⊞ **Carnetta's Inn.** When Winston Borrell retired as director of tourism
★   for T&T, he and his wife, Carnetta, opened this inn on their suburban property in Maraval. All rooms have a bath (with shower), a phone, a radio, and cable TV; most have kitchenettes. Although there's air-conditioning, cool breezes usually do the trick. Carnetta uses her garden-grown herbs in her cooking and prepares excellent dinners. ⊠ *99 Saddle Rd., Maraval,* ☎ *868/628–2732,* FAX *868/628–7717,* WEB *carnettas.com. 14 rooms. Restaurant, bar, lounge, cable TV, laundry service, airport shuttle, car rental. AE, DC, MC, V. EP, MAP.*

$ ⊞ **The Chancellor Hotel.** Billing itself as "the first true businessman's hotel in the Caribbean," this beautiful small hotel has Internet access in all rooms and full business services. Rooms are large and well appointed (each with cable TV) and are decorated with original batik hangings. The waterfall cascading into the nearby swimming pool adds a relaxing air to the bar and restaurant area. ⊠ *5 St. Ann's Ave., St. Ann's, Port-of-Spain,* ☎ FAX *868/623–0883,* WEB *www.thechancellorhotel.com. 15 rooms, 7 suites. Restaurant, bar, in-room data ports, pool, business services, meeting rooms. AE, MC, V. EP.*

$ ⭐ ▥ **Kapok Hotel.** Leave it to business travelers to find a well-run hotel that's a good value for the money. Sunlight (front rooms have views of Queen's Park Savannah) complements the pastel color schemes and rattan furniture. If you're into cooking for yourself, take one of the studios, which have kitchenettes. Otherwise, the Tiki Village Asian restaurant has terrific views of the city and is popular with locals. On the second floor, the alfresco coffee and wine bar, *Bois Cano,* is lovely and relaxed. ⊠ *16–18 Cotton Hill, St. Clair, Port-of-Spain,* ☎ *868/622–5765 or 800/344–1212,* FAX *868/622–9677,* WEB *www.kapok.co.tt. 75 rooms, 12 suites, 9 studios. Restaurant, room service, pool, gym, shops, dry cleaning, laundry service, laundry facilities, business services, meeting rooms, no-smoking rooms. MC, V. EP, FAP, MAP.*

$ ▥ **La Maison Rustique.** There's plenty to charm you at this B&B, with its gingerbread detail, its neighborhood, including other wonderful Victorian homes, and its proximity to Queen's Park Savannah. Rooms in the garden cottage are the nicest, but all are clean and presentable. Some have air-conditioning, and a few have private baths. The proprietor, Maureen Chin-Asiong, serves good breakfasts—popovers, croissants, quiche—and also whips up afternoon tea, snacks, and picnic baskets. ⊠ *16 Rust St., St. Clair, Port-of-Spain,* ☎ FAX *868/622–1512. 7 rooms, 3 with bath. No air-conditioning in some rooms. MC, V. CP.*

$ ▥ **Monique's.** Members of the Charbonné family really *like* having guests, as they've been proving for more than two decades. Rooms here are large and spotless, with solid teak floors and furniture as well as cable TV and phones. Ask for a room in "Monique's on the Hill," as each one has a kitchenette and a sizable balcony. All rooms are equipped with data ports. ⊠ *114–116 Saddle Rd., Maraval,* ☎ *868/628–3334 or 868/628–2351,* FAX *868/622–3232,* WEB *moniquestrinidad.com. 20 rooms. Dining room, bar, in-room data ports, laundry service, travel services, airport shuttle. AE, DC, MC, V. EP, MAP.*

$ ⭐ ▥ **Mt. Plaisir Estate.** If getting away from it all appeals to you, then this gem of a hotel is a perfect choice. In remote Grande Riviere with the ocean on one side and the peaks of the rainforest in the backdrop, you may see leatherback turtles nesting by the hundreds in this idyllic spot. Rooms are homey and clean, and the on-site restaurant serves exceptional meals. Owner Piero Guerrini is an internationally renowned photographer and will be happy to advise you on your shots. All in all, this hotel is an excellent value. ⊠ *Grande Riviere,* ☎ *868/670–8381,* FAX *868/670–0057,* WEB *mtplaisir.com. 13 rooms, 2 suites. Dining room, lounge, beach. AE, MC, V. CP, EP, MAP, FAP.*

Dining

The food on T&T is a delight to the senses and has a distinctively creole touch, though everyone has a different idea about what creole seasoning is (just ask around, and you'll see). Bountiful herbs and spices include bay leaf, *chadon beni* (similar to cilantro), nutmeg, saffron, and different varieties of peppers. The cooking also involves a lot of brown sugar, rum, plantain, and local fish and meat. If there's fresh juice on the menu, be sure to try it. You can taste Asian, Indian, African, French, and Spanish influences, among others, often in a single meal. Indian-inspired food is a favorite: *rotis* (sandwiches of soft dough with a filling, similar to a burrito) are served as a fast food; a mélange of curried meat or fish and vegetables frequently makes an appearance as do *vindaloos* (spicy meat, vegetable, and seafood dishes). *Pelau* (chicken stewed in coconut milk with peas and rice), a Spanish-influenced dish, is another local favorite. Crab lovers will find large blue-backs curried, peppered, or in callaloo, a stew made with green dasheen leaves, okra, and coconut milk. Shark-and-bake (lightly seasoned, fried shark meat) is the sandwich of choice.

No Trinidadian or Tobagonian dining experience is complete without a rum punch with fresh fruit and the legendary Angostura bitters, made by the same local company that produces the excellent Old Oak rum (just watch out for the fiendish sugar content). Light, refreshing Carib beer is the local lager; Stag is an even stronger lager, and dark-beer aficionados can try Royal Extra Stout (R. E.).

What to Wear
Restaurants are informal: you won't find any jacket-and-tie requirements. Beachwear, however, is a little too casual for most places. A nice pair of shorts is appropriate for lunch; for dinner you'll probably feel most comfortable in a pair of slacks or a casual sundress.

CATEGORY	COST*
$$$$	over $30
$$$	$20–$30
$$	$10–$20
$	under $10

per person for a main course at dinner

ASIAN
$$–$$$$ ✕ **Tamnak Thai.** In a beautifully renovated former colonial house around Queen's Park Savannah, this upscale restaurant offers the best Thai cuisine on Trinidad. You may choose to sit outside on the patio surrounded by flowing water and lush foliage or pick the elegant inside dining room for a more intimate (and cooler) dining experience. You might well start with the hors d'oeuvres *Tamnak Thai*, a delightful selection of Thai appetizers, and if you can stand the heat move on to *gai pad med manuang, prik tod* (chicken with cashew nuts and fiery chilies). ⊠ *13 Queen's Park East, Port-of-Spain,* ☎ *868/623–7510,* FAX *868/628–4783. AE, MC, V.*

$$–$$$ ✕ **Tiki Village.** Port-of-Spainers in the know flock to this upscale rooftop restaurant on the eighth floor of the Kapok Hotel, where the views of the city day and night are simply spectacular. The dining room is lined with teak, and the menu includes the best of Polynesian and Chinese fare. The dim sum—with tasting-size portions of dishes such as pepper squid and tofu-stuffed fish—is very popular. ⊠ *Kapok Hotel, 16–18 Cotton Hill, St. Clair, Port-of-Spain,* ☎ *868/622–5765. AE, MC, V.*

CARIBBEAN
$$$–$$$$ ✕ **Plantation House Restaurant.** This elegant gem in a late-19th-century building is furnished in colonial style with wrought iron and chintz. The menu concentrates on game and seafood dishes, all beautifully presented and served. Beware of the massive portions. The truly adventurous can order alligator tails (creole style, of course) or stewed agouti (a large local rodent). The conch-souse appetizer (conch strips marinated in a spicy lime-juice mixture) is a must-try. ⊠ *38 Ariapita Ave., Woodbrook, Port-of-Spain,* ☎ *868/628–5551. AE, DC, MC, V. Closed Sun.*

$–$$ ✕ **Veni Mangé.** The best lunches in town are served upstairs in this
★   traditional West Indian house decorated with local art. Credit Allyson Hennessy—a Cordon Bleu–trained chef and local television celebrity—and her friendly, flamboyant sister-partner, Rosemary Hezekiah (Roses).

The creative creole menu changes regularly, and there's always a unique and delicious vegetarian entrée. This place is popular, and reservations are advised; dinner is served only on Wednesday from 7:30 to 10. The bar area is a fun hangout on a Friday evening (5 to midnight) when Allyson and Roses hold court. ✉ *67A Ariapita Ave., Woodbrook, Port-of-Spain,* ☎ *868/624–4597. AE, MC, V. Closed weekends. No dinner except Wed.*

ECLECTIC

$$–$$$$ ✕ **La Boucan.** Trinidadian dancer Geoffrey Holder painted the large mural of a social idyll in Queen's Park Savannah that dominates one wall of this room at the Hilton Trinidad and Conference Centre. A more leisurely Trinidad is also reflected in the old-fashioned charm of silver service, uniformed waiters, soft lighting, and pink tablecloths. The menu is international, including steaks, seafood grills, and other simple preparations, but you can also find such local specialties as callaloo soup, shrimp creole, and West Indian chicken curry. ✉ *Hilton Trinidad and Conference Centre, Lady Young Rd., Port-of-Spain,* ☎ *868/624– 3211. AE, DC, MC, V. Closed Sun.*

$$–$$$$ ✕ **Solimar.** In a series of dimly lit, plant-filled dining areas, chef Joe Brown offers a menu that travels the world in one meal: there's always a choice of a European, Asian, or North American main course. Solimar is popular with expats and is known for being a relaxed and informal spot. Valet parking is available. ✉ *6 Nook Ave., St. Ann's, Port-of-Spain,* ☎ *868/624–6267. AE, MC, V.*

$$–$$$ ✕ **Jenny's on the Boulevard.** Jenny's is in a beautifully restored grand old art nouveau–style home near Port-of-Spain's Queen's Park Savannah. The decidedly eclectic (almost dizzying) interior is filled with antiques, but the excellent American steak-house food and true Cantonese cuisine shine. The Cellar Pub, a blend of British tradition and Hollywood kitsch, is fun, raucous, and upscale—but also tends to be smoke-filled and congested. A no-smoking room and a private dining room are available. ✉ *6 Cipriani Blvd., Port-of-Spain,* ☎ *868/625– 1807. Reservations essential. AE, MC, V. Closed Sun.*

INDIAN

$$–$$$ ✕ **Apsara.** The name means "celestial dancer," and the food is indeed heavenly. The elegant maroon interior is decorated with modern interpretations of Moghul art by local artist Sarah Beckett. Choosing dishes from the comprehensive menu is a bit daunting, so don't be afraid to ask for help. The boneless chicken curry with spinach and fennel is an excellent choice. Owner Marie Kavanagh is a delightful hostess and would be thrilled to give you the history of the restaurant. ✉ *13 Queen's Park East, Port-of-Spain,* ☎ *868/627–7364 or 868/623– 7659. AE, MC, V. Closed Sun.*

ITALIAN

$$–$$$$ ✕ **Il Colosseo.** Calabrian chef Angelo Cofone married a Trinidadian and soon found himself co-owning the island's best Italian restaurant. In the heart of Port-of-Spain—in a remodeled 1940s home—it's popular with locals and visiting businesspeople alike. The innovative Northern Italian menu changes monthly. ✉ *47 Ariapita Ave., Port-of-Spain,* ☎ *868/623–3654. AE, MC, V. Closed Sun.*

Beaches

Although Trinidad is not the beach destination Tobago is, it has its share of fine shoreline along the North Coast Road within an hour's drive of Port-of-Spain. To reach the east coast beaches, you must drive for an hour and take the detour road to Arima. But "goin' behind God's back," as the Trinis say, rewards the persistent traveler with gorgeous vistas and secluded stretches of sand. And, best of all, Trinidad's beaches are all open to the public and free of charge.

Balandra Bay. On the northeast coast, the beach is sheltered by a rocky outcropping and is popular with bodysurfers.

Blanchisseuse Bay. On the North Coast Road you'll find this narrow, palm-fringed beach. Facilities are nonexistent, but it's an ideal spot for a romantic picnic. You can haggle with local fishermen to take you out in their boats to explore the coast.

Grande Riviere. At the end of the road on Trinidad's rugged northeast coast, Grand Riviere is well worth the drive. Swimming is good and there are several guesthouses nearby for refreshments, but the main attraction here is turtles. Every year up to 500 giant leatherback turtles come onto the beach to lay their eggs. If you're here at night, run your hand through the black sand to make it glow—a phenomenon caused by plankton.

Las Cuevas Bay. This narrow, picturesque strip on North Coast Road is named for the series of partially submerged and explorable caves that ring the beach. A food stand offers tasty snacks, and vendors hawk fresh fruit across the road. You can also buy fresh fish and lobster from the fishing depot near the beach. There are basic changing and toilet facilities. It's less crowded here than at nearby Maracas Bay and seemingly serene, although, as at Maracas, the current can be treacherous.

Manzanilla Beach. You'll find picnic facilities and a pretty view of the Atlantic here, though its water is occasionally muddied by the Orinoco River, which flows in from South America. The Cocal road running the length of this beautiful beach is lined with stately palms, whose fronds vault like the arches at Chartres. This is where many well-heeled Trinis have vacation homes.

Maracas Bay. This long stretch of sand has a cove and a fishing village at one end. It's *the* local favorite, so it can get crowded on weekends. Lifeguards will guide you away from strong currents. Parking sites are ample, and there are snack bars and rest rooms. Try a shark-and-bake (which you can choose to top with any of dozens of choices—such as tamarind sauce and coleslaw) at one of the huts (Natalie's is considered the best) on the beach or in the nearby carpark.

Salibea Bay. Past Galera Point, which juts toward Tobago, this gentle beach has shallows and plenty of shade—perfect for swimming. Snack vendors abound in the vicinity.

Tyrico Bay. This small beach is made lively by the surfers who flock here. The strong undertow may be too much for some swimmers. Be sure to pack insect repellent as the sand flies and mosquitoes can be a nuisance in the rainy season.

Outdoor Activities and Sports

BIRD-WATCHING

Trinidad and Tobago are among the top 10 spots in the world in terms of the number of species of birds per square mile—more than 430 altogether, many living within pristine rain forests, lowlands and savannas, and fresh- and saltwater swamps. If you're lucky, you might spot the collared trogon, Trinidad piping guan (known locally as the common pawi), or a rare white-tailed Sabrewing hummingbird. Restaurants often hang feeders outside their porches, as much to keep the birds away from your food as to provide a chance to see them.

You can fill up your books with notes on the native species in Trinidad at the island's major bird sanctuaries. **Asa Wright Nature Centre** (☎ 868/667–4655), a half-hour drive from Blanchisseuse, has more than 170 bird species in residence. **The Caroni Bird Sanctuary** (☎ 868/645–

1305), a half-hour from Port-of-Spain, is a habitat for the scarlet ibis, Trinidad's national bird. The **Point a Pierre Wildfowl Trust** (✉ Petrotrin Complex, Point-a-Pierre, ☎ 868/658–4200 Ext. 2512) is a haven for rare bird species on 26 acres within the unlikely confines of a petro-chemical complex; you must call in advance for a reservation. **Winston Nanan** (☎ 868/645–1305) runs the highly regarded Nanan's Bird Sanctuary Tours to nearby Guyana and Venezuela.

FISHING

The islands off the northwest coast of Trinidad have excellent waters for deep-sea fishing; you may find wahoo, king fish, and marlin, to name a few. The ocean here was a favorite angling spot of Franklin D. Roosevelt. Through **Bayshore Charters** (✉ 29 Sunset Dr., Bayshore, Westmoorings, ☎ 868/637–8711) you can fish for an afternoon or hire a boat for a weekend; the *Melissa Ann* is fully equipped for comfort-able cruising, sleeps six, and has an air-conditioned cabin, refrigera-tor, cooking facilities, and, of course, fishing equipment. Captain Sa Gomes is one of the most experienced charter captains on the islands. Members of the **Trinidad and Tobago Yacht Club** (✉ Western Main Rd., Bayshore, Westmoorings, ☎ 868/637–4260) may be willing to ar-range a fishing trip for you.

GOLF

The best course in Trinidad is the 18-hole **St. Andrew's Golf Club** (✉ Moka, Saddle Rd., Maraval, Port-of-Spain, ☎ 868/629–2314), just out-side Port-of-Spain. Greens fees are approximately $35 for 18 holes. Con-venient tee times are available weekdays.

TENNIS

Several establishments allow nonmembers or nonguests to play tennis on their courts. The **Hilton Trinidad and Conference Centre** (✉ Lady Young Rd., Port-of-Spain, ☎ 868/624–3211) has two asphalt courts. The **Trinidad Country Club** (✉ Long Circular Rd., Maraval, Port-of-Spain, ☎ 868/622–3470) has six asphalt courts. The **Tranquility Square Lawn Tennis Club** (✉ Victoria Ave., Port-of-Spain, ☎ 868/625–4182) has four asphalt courts.

Shopping

Good buys in Trinidad include Angostura bitters, Old Oak or Vat 19 rum, and leather goods, all widely available throughout the country. Thanks in large part to Carnival costumery, there's no shortage of fab-ric shops. The best bargains for Asian and East Indian silks and cot-tons can be found in downtown Port-of-Spain, on Frederick Street, and around Independence Square. Recordings of local calypsonians and steel-pan performances as well as *chutney* (a local East Indian music) are available throughout the islands and make great gifts.

Areas and Malls

Downtown Port-of-Spain, specifically **Frederick, Queen,** and **Henry** streets, is full of fabrics and shoes. **Ellerslie Plaza** is an attractive out-door mall well worth a browse. **Excellent City Centre** is set in an old-style oasis under the lantern roofs of three of downtown's oldest commercial buildings. Look for cleverly designed keepsakes, trendy cot-ton garments, and original artwork. The upstairs food court overlooks bustling Frederick Street. **Long Circular Mall** has upscale boutiques that are great for window-shopping. **The Market** is a small collection of shops that specialize in indigenous fashions, crafts, jewelry, bas-ketwork, and ceramics. You can also have afternoon tea in the elegant little café.

Specialty Items

CLOTHING

A fine designer clothing shop, **Meiling** (✉ Kapok Hotel, Maraval, Port-of-Spain, ☎ 868/627–6975), sells classically detailed Caribbean resort clothing. **Radical** (✉ West Mall, Western Main Rd., Westmoorings, ☎ 868/632–5800; ✉ Long Circular Mall, Long Circular Rd., St. James, Port-of-Spain, ☎ 868/628–5693; ✉ Excellent City Centre, Independence Square, Port-of-Spain, ☎ 868/627–6110), which carries T-shirts and original men's and women's clothing, is something like the Gap of the Caribbean.

DUTY-FREE GOODS

Duty-free goods are only available at the airport upon departure or arrival. **De Lima's** (✉ Piarco International Airport, Piarco, ☎ 868/669–4738) sells traditional duty-free luxury items. **Stecher's** (✉ Piarco International Airport, Piarco, ☎ 868/669–4793) is a familiar name for those seeking to avoid taxes on fine perfumes, china, crystal, handcrafted items, and jewelry.

HANDICRAFTS

The tourism office can provide a list of local artisans who specialize in everything from straw and cane work to miniature steel pans. The **101 Art Gallery** (✉ 101 Tragarete Rd., Port-of-Spain, ☎ 868/628–4081) is Trinidad's foremost gallery, which showcases local artists such as Sarah Beckett (semi-abstracts in oil, some of which are featured on local stamps); Jackie Hinkson (figurative watercolors); Peter Sheppard (stylized realist local landscapes in acrylic); and Sundiata (semi-abstract watercolors). Openings are usually held Tuesday evenings year-round; the gallery is closed Sunday and Monday. For painted plates, ceramics, aromatic candles, wind chimes, and carved wood pieces and instruments, check out **Cockey** (✉ Long Circular Mall, Long Circular Rd., St. James, Port-of-Spain, ☎ 868/628–6546). **Poui Boutique** (✉ Ellerslie Plaza, Long Circular Rd., Maraval, Port-of-Spain, ☎ 868/622–5597) has stylish handmade batik items, Ajoupa ware (an attractive, local terracotta pottery), and many other gift items. The miniature ceramic houses and local scenes are astoundingly realistic, and are all handcrafted by owner Bunty O'Connor.

JEWELRY

The design duo of Barbara Jardine and Rachel Ross creates the Alchemy jewelry line. Their handmade works of art with sterling silver, 18K gold, and precious and semiprecious stones are for sale at **Precious Little** (✉ West Mall, Western Main Rd., Westmoorings, ☎ 868/632–1077).

MUSIC

Just CDs and Accessories (✉ Long Circular Mall, Long Circular Rd., St. James, Port-of-Spain, ☎ 868/622–7516) has a good selection of popular local musicians as well as other music genres. **Rhyner's Record Shop** (✉ 54 Prince St., Port-of-Spain, ☎ 868/625–2476; ✉ Piarco International Airport, Piarco, ☎ 868/669–3064) has a decent (and duty-free) selection of calypso and soca music.

Nightlife and the Arts

Nightlife

There's no lack of nightlife in Port-of-Spain, and spontaneity plays a big role—around carnival time look for the handwritten signs announcing the PANYARD, where the next informal gathering of steel-drum bands is going to be.

Two of the island's top nightspots are on a former American Armed Forces base in Chaguaramas. **The Anchorage** (✉ Point Gourde Rd.,

Chaguaramas, ☎ 868/634–4334) is a good spot for early evening cocktails and snacks. **Pier 1** (✉ Western Main Rd., Chaguaramas, ☎ 868/634–4426) is *the* place for lively late-night action. You can dance through the night on a large wooden deck jutting into the ocean with gentle sea breezes to cool you down. It's about 20 minutes west of Port-of-Spain, so get a party together from your hotel and hire a cab. It opens at 9 PM, Wednesday–Sunday. For the serious partiers, Pier 1 offers a "party boat" that leaves on Friday, Saturday, and Sunday night for a floating party for $10.

At **Club Coconuts** (✉ Cascadia Hotel, St. Ann's, Port of Spain, ☎ 868/623–6887) you can dance 'til the wee hours with a fun crowd. **Mas Camp Pub** (✉ corner of Ariapata Ave. and French St., Woodbrook, Port-of-Spain, ☎ 868/627–4042) is Port-of-Spain's most dependable nightspot. Along with a bar and a large stage where a DJ or live band reigns, the kitchen dishes up hearty, reasonably priced creole lunches, and if one of the live bands strikes your fancy, chances are you can also buy their tape here. **Pelican** (✉ 2–4 Coblentz Ave., St. Ann's, Port-of-Spain, ☎ 868/624–7486), an English-style pub with a mixed gay and straight crowd, gets increasingly frenetic as the week closes. The biggest nights are Wednesday, Friday, and Sunday, when the crowd overflows into the parking lot. There is also seasonal entertainment with calypso at carnival time and *parang* (Spanish-influenced music) at Christmas time. **Smokey and Bunty** (✉ Western Main Rd., St. James, Port-of-Spain) is a unique Port-of-Spain phenomenon. This is the late-night spot to visit when everything else is closed, and although it doesn't amount to much more than standing around on the sidewalk, the people are fun and the drinks are very cheap.

OFF THE
BEATEN PATH

HiRpm (✉ Gulf City Mall, 2nd floor, South Trunk Rd., La Romain, ☎ 868/652–3760) is a great alternative if you want something out of town. Just take the main highway south to the end of the line and then follow South Trunk Road to the mall. This lively, laid-back establishment is a good place to listen to pop music, and you can hear live local pop/rock bands on Wednesday nights performing their covers of the latest hits. The large oval bar (it takes up half the room) is a great place to meet talkative southerners. The owner Selwyn "Bunny" Persad is a race car driver and enthusiast and will be happy to talk to you about his favorite sport.

The Arts

Trinidad always seems to be either anticipating, celebrating, or recovering from a festival. Visitors are welcome at these events, which are a great way to explore the island's rich cultural traditions.

CARNIVAL

Trinidad's version of the pre-Lenten bacchanal is reputedly the oldest in the western hemisphere; there are festivities all over the country, but the most lavish are in Port-of-Spain. Trinidad's Carnival has the warmth and character of a massive family reunion and is billed by locals (not unreasonably) as "The Greatest Show on Earth."

The season begins right after Christmas, and the parties, called fêtes, don't stop till Ash Wednesday. Listen to a radio station for five minutes, and you'll find out where the action is. The Carnival event itself officially lasts only two days, from *J'ouvert* (2 AM) on Monday to midnight the following day, Carnival Tuesday. It's best to arrive in Trinidad a week or two early to enjoy the preliminary events. (Hotels fill up quickly, so be sure to make reservations months in advance, and be prepared to pay premium prices for a minimum five-night stay. Even private homes have been known to rent bedrooms for as much as $225 per night.) If you visit during Carnival, try to get tickets to one of the all-inclusive parties where thousands of people eat and drink to the sound of soca music all night long. One of the best Carnival parties in Trinidad is **Veni Fête,** which attracts about two thousand people.

Carnival is about extravagant costumes. Colorfully attired *mas* (troupes), whose membership sometimes numbers in the thousands, march to the beat set by massive music trucks and steel bands. You can visit the various mas "camps" around Port-of-Spain where these elaborate getups are put together—the addresses are listed in the newspapers—and perhaps join one that strikes your fancy. Fees run anywhere from $35 to $200; you get to keep the costume. You can also buy your costume online at the tourist board's Web site, which has links to all the major camps. Children can parade in a kiddie carnival that takes place on the Saturday morning before the official events.

Carnival is also a showcase for performers of calypso, music that mixes dance rhythms with social commentary—sung by characters with such evocative names as Shadow, the Mighty Sparrow, and Black Stalin—and soca, which fuses calypso with a driving dance beat. As Carnival approaches, many of these singers perform nightly in calypso tents around the city. Many hotels also have special concerts by popular local musicians. You can also visit the city's "panyards," where steel orchestras, such as the Renegades, Desperadoes, Neal and Massy All-Stars, Invaders, and Phase II, rehearse their musical arrangements (most can also be heard during the winter season).

For several nights before Carnival, costume makers display their work, and the steel bands and calypso singers perform in competitions at Queen's Park Savannah. Here the Calypso Monarch is crowned on the Sunday night before Carnival (Dimanche Gras). The city starts to fill with metal-frame carts carrying steel bands, trucks hauling sound systems, and revelers who squeeze into the narrow streets. At midnight on "Carnival Tuesday," Port-of-Spain's exhausted merrymakers go to bed. The next day feet are sore, but spirits have been refreshed. Lent (and theoretical sobriety) takes over for a while.

MUSIC

Trinidadian culture doesn't end with music, but it definitely begins with it. Although both calypso and steel bands are at their best during Carnival, steel bands play at clubs, dances, and fêtes throughout the year. At Christmastime the music of the moment is a Venezuelan-derived folk music called *parang,* sung in Spanish to the strains of a stringed instrument called a *quattro*. The Lopinot Complex in Arouca is a parang center. If you can stomach the steep uphill drive, Paramin, near Port-of-Spain (take Maracas Road and turn off on Paramin Road), is another spectacular location to hear this music.

THEATER

There are always a few plays being performed by local groups. Consult local newspapers for listings.

Exploring Trinidad

The intensely urban atmosphere of Port-of-Spain belies the tropical beauty of the countryside surrounding it. You'll need a car and three to eight hours to see all there is to see. Begin by circling the Queen's Park Savannah to Saddle Road, in the residential district of Maraval. After a few miles the road begins to narrow and curve sharply as it climbs into the Northern Range and its undulating hills of dense foliage. Stop at the lookout on North Coast Road; a camera is a must-have here. You'll pass a series of lovely beaches starting with Maracas. From the town of Blanchisseuse there's a winding route to the Asa Wright Nature Centre that takes you through canyons of towering palms, mossy grottoes, and imposing bamboo. In this rain forest keep an eye out for vultures, parakeets, hummingbirds, toucans, and if you're lucky, maybe red-bellied, yellow-and-blue macaws. Trinidad also has more than 600 native species of butterflies and well over 1,000 varieties of orchids.

Numbers in the margin correspond to points of interest on the Trinidad map.

Sights to See

② **Asa Wright Nature Centre.** Nearly 500 acres here are covered with plants, trees, and multi-hued flowers, and the surrounding acreage is atwitter with more than 400 species of birds, from the gorgeous blue-green motmot to the rare, nocturnal oilbird. If you stay at the center's inn for two nights or more, take one of the center's guided hikes (included in your room price) to the oilbirds' breeding grounds in Dunston Cave. Those who don't want to hike can relax on the inn's veranda and watch birds swoop about the porch feeders—an armchair bird-watcher's delight. This stunning plantation house looks out onto the lush, untouched Arima Valley. Even if you're not staying over, book ahead for lunch (TT$37.50) Monday–Saturday or for the noontime Sunday buffet (TT$62.50). ⊠ *Arima Valley (Box 4710), ½ hr outside Blanchisseuse; take right at fork in road (signposted to Arima) and drive another ½ hr (sign for the center is at milepost 7¼) on Blanchisseuse Rd.; turn right there (for directions from Port-of-Spain, ☞ Lodging),* ☎ *868/667–4655,* WEB *www.asawright.org.* ☞ *$6.* ☉ *Daily 9–5. Guided tours at 10:30 and 1:30; reservations essential.*

④ **Caroni Bird Sanctuary.** This large swamp with maze-like waterways is bordered by mangrove trees, some plumed with huge termite nests. If you're lucky, you may see lazy caimans idling in the water and large snakes hanging from branches on the banks taking in the sun. In the middle of the sanctuary are several islets that are home to Trinidad's national bird, the scarlet ibis. Just before sunset the ibis arrive by the thousands, their richly colored feathers brilliant in the gathering dusk, and as more flocks alight, they turn the mangrove foliage a brilliant scarlet. Bring a sweater and insect repellent.

The only official tour operator for the sanctuary is **Winston Nanan** (☎ 868/645–1305). Tours are $10, children over 5 years old are half price, and ages 5 and under are free. Phone or write him in advance for reservations. ⊠ *½ hr from Port-of-Spain; take Churchill Roosevelt Hwy. east to Uriah Butler south; turn right and in about 2 mins, after passing Caroni River Bridge, follow sign for sanctuary.* ☞ *Free.*

③ **Lopinot Complex.** It's said that the ghost of the French count Charles Joseph de Lopinot prowls his former home on stormy nights. Lopinot came to Trinidad in 1800 and chose this magnificent site to plant cocoa. His restored estate house has been turned into a museum—a guide is available from 10 to 6—and a center for parang, the Venezuelan-derived folk music. ⊠ *Take Eastern Main Rd. from Port-of-Spain to Arouca; look for sign that points north, no phone.* ☞ *Free.* ☉ *Daily 6–6.*

① **Port-of-Spain.** Most tours begin at the port. If you're planning to explore on foot, which will take two to four hours, start early in the day; by midday the port area can be as hot and packed as Calcutta. It's best to end your tour on a bench in the Queen's Park Savannah, sipping a cool coconut water bought from one of the vendors operating out of flatbed trucks. For about 35¢ he'll lop the top off a green coconut with a deft swing of the machete and, when you've finished drinking, lop again, making a bowl and spoon of coconut shell for you to eat the young pulp. As in most cities, take extra care at night; women should not walk alone.

The town's main dock, **King's Wharf,** entertains a steady parade of cruise and cargo ships, a reminder that the city started from this strategic harbor. When hurricanes threaten other islands it's not unusual to see as many as five large cruise ships taking advantage of the safety of the harbor. It's on Wrightson Road, the main street along the water on the southwest side of town.

Across Wrightson Road and a few minutes' walk from the south side of King's Wharf, the busy **Independence Square** has been the focus of the downtown area's major gentrification. Flanked by government buildings and the familiar twin towers of the Financial Complex (they adorn all T&T dollar bills), the square (really a long rectangle) is a lovely park with trees, flagstone walkways, chess tables, and the Brian Lara Promenade (named after Trinidad's world-famous cricketer). On its south side the Cruise Ship Complex, full of duty-free shops, forms an enclave of international anonymity with the Crowne Plaza Trinidad. On the eastern end of the square is the Cathedral of the Immaculate Conception; it was by the sea when it was built in 1832, but subsequent landfill around the port gave it an inland location. The imposing Roman Catholic structure is made of stone from nearby Laventille.

Frederick Street, Port-of-Spain's main shopping drag, starting north from the midpoint of Independence Square, is a market street of scents and sounds—perfumed oils sold by sidewalk vendors and music tapes being played from vending carts—and crowded shops.

At Prince and Frederick streets, **Woodford Square** has served as the site of political meetings, speeches, public protests, and occasional violence. It's dominated by the magnificent Red House, a Renaissance-style building that takes up an entire city block. Trinidad's House of Parliament takes its name from a paint job done in anticipation of Queen Victoria's Diamond Jubilee in 1897. The original Red House was burned to the ground in a 1903 riot, and the present structure was built four years later. The chambers are open to the public.

The view of the south side of the square is framed by the Gothic spires of Trinity, the city's Anglican cathedral, consecrated in 1823; its mahogany-beam roof is modeled after that of Westminster Hall in London. On the north are the impressive public library building, the Hall of Justice, and City Hall.

If the downtown port area is the pulse of Port-of-Spain, the great green expanse of **Queen's Park Savannah,** roughly bounded by Maraval Road, Queen's Park West, Charlotte Street, and Saddle Road, is the city's soul. You can walk straight north on Frederick Street and get there within 20 minutes. Its 2-mi (3-km) circumference is a popular jogger's track. The Grandstand on the southern end is a popular venue for Calypso and cultural shows. The northern end of the Savannah is devoted to plants. A rock garden, known as the The Hollows, and a fishpond add to the rusticity.

A series of astonishing buildings constructed in a several 19th-century styles—and known collectively as the **Magnificent Seven**—flanks the western side of the Savannah. Notable are Killarney, patterned (loosely) after Balmoral Castle in Scotland, with an Italian-marble gallery surrounding the ground floor; Whitehall, constructed in the style of a Venetian palace by a cacao-plantation magnate and currently the office of the prime minister; Roomor, a flamboyantly Baroque colonial house with a preponderance of towers, pinnacles, and wrought-iron trim that suggests an elaborate French pastry; and the Queen's Royal College, in German Renaissance style, with a prominent tower clock that chimes on the hour. Head over to the southeast corner of the Savannah to see the **National Museum and Art Gallery,** especially its Carnival exhibitions, the Amerindian collection and historical re-creations, and the fine 19th-century paintings of Trinidadian artist Cazabon. ⊠ *117 Upper Frederick St.,* ☎ *868/623–5941.* ☞ *Free.* ⊙ *Tues.–Sat. 10–6.* The cultivated expanse of parkland north of the Savannah is the site of the president's and prime minister's official residences and also the **Emperor Valley Zoo and the Botanical Gardens.** A meticulous lattice of walkways and local flora, the parkland was first laid out in 1820 for Governor Ralph Woodford. In the midst of the serene wonderland is the 8-acre zoo, which exhibits mostly birds and animals of the region—from the brilliantly plumed scarlet ibis to slithering anacondas and pythons; you can also see (and hear) the wild parrots that breed in the surrounding foliage. The zoo draws a quarter of a million visitors a year, and more than half of them are children, so admission is priced accordingly—a mere TT$2 for folks under 12. ⊠ *Botanical Gardens,* ☎ *868/622–3530 or 868/622–5343.* ☞ *TT$4 for the zoo, gardens free.* ⊙ *Daily 9:30–5:30.*

TOBAGO

Lodging

On Tobago there are a few modest lodgings in the towns, but the trend is toward seaside resorts, many of them appealingly low-key. If you're staying on the east side of Tobago, accommodations with meal plans are almost essential due to the dearth of restaurants.

For approximate costs, *see* the lodging price chart *in* Trinidad.

$$$$ ⊞ **Plantation Beach Villas.** Nestled on a hillside above a palm-fringed beach, these pink-and-white villas are comfortably furnished in plantation style—four-poster beds, rocking chairs, louvered doors, and lots of West Indian fretwork. The accommodations (and the price) are perfect for large families or other groups: each two-story villa has three bedrooms, three baths, and a teak veranda with a view of the sea. ⊠ *Scarborough (Box 434),* ☎ ℻ *868/639–9377. 6 villas. Bar, kitchenettes, pool, baby-sitting, laundry service. AE, MC, V. EP.*

$$$$ ⊞ **Stonehaven Villas.** This property perches on a hillside adjacent to a bird sanctuary and commands an impressive view of the Caribbean. The complex consists of 14 French-style villas and a club house, which serves as the restaurant and social gathering area. Each villa has three large bedrooms with en suite bathrooms and a private vanishing-edge pool. Have no fear about cleaning, cooking, or ironing because each villa comes complete with all-day maid service. ⊠ *Bon Accord, Grafton Estate, Shirvan Rd., Black Rock (Box 1079),* ☎ *868/639–9887,* ℻ *868/ 639–0102,* 🕸 *www.stonehavenvillas.com. 14 villas. Restaurant, bar, kitchenettes, pool, laundry service, meeting rooms. AE, MC, V. EP.*

$$$ ⊞ **Coco Reef Resort.** Elements of Caribbean, colonial, and Mediterranean architecture blend in an abundance of arches, tiles, and fretwork flourishes; harsh angles have been eliminated to create soothing spaces. Rooms have cool, calming tiles, pretty wall stencils, and handcrafted wicker furniture. If you want to venture off the resort's small beach, Coco Bay, Pigeon Point, and Store Bay are nearby. ⊠ *Coconut Bay, Scarborough (Box 434),* ☎ *868/639–8571 or 800/221–1294,*

Lodging

Arnos Vale Hotel **6**
Blue Waters Inn **4**
Coco Reef Resort . . . **14**
Grafton Beach
Resort **12**
Le Grand Courlan
Resort and Spa **8**
Hilton Tobago **17**

Kariwak Village **15**
Mt. Irvine Bay
Hotel **11**
Plantation
Beach Villas **7**
Stonehaven Villas . . . **9**
Toucan Inn **16**

Dining

Arnos Vale
Waterwheel
Restaurant **5**
Blue Crab **1**
Bonkers **16**
Café Petunia **18**
First Historical
Café/Bar **3**

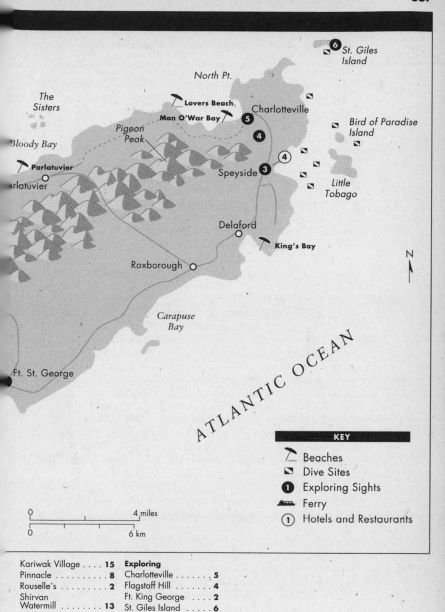

North Pt.

The Sisters

Bloody Bay

Parlatuvier

Pigeon Peak

Lovers Beach

Man O'War Bay

St. Giles Island **6**

Charlotteville

5

4

Speyside **3**

4

Bird of Paradise Island

Little Tobago

Delaford

King's Bay

Roxborough

Carapuse Bay

Ft. St. George

N

ATLANTIC OCEAN

KEY
⚓ Beaches
◩ Dive Sites
❶ Exploring Sights
⛴ Ferry
① Hotels and Restaurants

0 _____ 4 miles
0 _____ 6 km

FAX *868/639–8574 or 305/639–2717,* WEB *www.cocoreef.com. 135 rooms, 35 suites. 2 restaurants, 2 bars, room service, pool, 2 tennis courts, gym, hair salon, spa, beach, dive shop, snorkeling, windsurfing, baby-sitting, business services, meeting rooms, travel services, car rental. AE, D, DC, MC, V. CP, FAP, MAP.*

$$$ 🏨 **Le Grand Courlan Resort and Spa.** This hotel, under the same ownership as—and right next door to—the Grafton Beach Resort, is aiming for a *very* upscale clientele. The spacious rooms have pink-tile floors, oak furniture, and large balconies with fantastic views; the beach is one of the best on the island; and the staff is gracious. The Pinnacle dining room serves lovely dinners in a relaxed setting. The spa offers a variety of services from aromatherapy with essential oil extracts to Swedish massage. Several packages are available including scuba, spa, and golf. ✉ *Shirvan Rd., Black Rock,* ☎ *868/639–9667 or 800/468–3750; 800/424–5500 in Canada,* FAX *868/639–9292. 68 rooms, 10 suites. 3 restaurants, 2 bars, room service, in-room safes, minibars, golf privileges, 2 tennis courts, pool, hair salon, health club, hot tub, massage, sauna, spa, steam room, beach, dive shop, windsurfing, boating, fishing, bicycles, squash, shops, laundry service, business services, meeting rooms, travel services, car rental, no-smoking rooms. AE, MC, V. EP, MAP.*

$$–$$$ 🏨 **Mt. Irvine Bay Hotel.** The advantage of this low-key establishment is golf—guests of the hotel get special rates on the 18-hole, par-72, 127-acre championship course. Since opening in 1972, this resort has had many, many repeat customers (who rave about the staff). The main restaurant, the Sugar Mill, is set inside a 17th-century mill, and there are two more restaurants—a dressy French one, Le Beau Rivage, and the Jacaranda, which serves true Caribbean dishes. You can swim in the large pool, play tennis on the floodlit courts, or take the private trail across the road to the beach and its bar. ✉ *Shirvan Rd., Mt. Irvine Bay (Box 222),* ☎ *868/639–8871,* FAX *868/639–8800,* WEB *www.mtirvine.com. 105 rooms, 6 suites, 46 cottages. 3 restaurants, 6 bars, pool, 18-hole golf course, 2 tennis courts, hair salon, sauna, beach, snorkeling, windsurfing, waterskiing, fishing, shops, meeting rooms, no-smoking rooms. AE, MC, V. CP, EP, MAP.*

$$ 🏨 **Hilton Tobago.** This dazzling property sets a high standard for Tobago. The hotel occupies 20 beachfront acres and boasts, among other things, 200 rooms, an 18-hole championship par-72 golf course, and a massive pool. The huge atrium lobby has floor to ceiling windows that manage to blur the line between hotel and ocean. Rooms are spacious and comfortable, offering amenities that you would expect from any world-class hotel. All rooms have an ocean view; ground floor rooms have a small patio that opens onto the gardens. ✉ *Scarborough (Box 633),* ☎ *868/660–8500,* FAX *868/660–8503,* WEB *www.hilton.com. 178 rooms, 22 suites. 2 restaurants, 3 bars, refrigerators, 18-hole golf course, 2 tennis courts, pool, health club, hair salon, sauna, beach, snorkeling, windsurfing, waterskiing, fishing, shops, meeting rooms, no-smoking rooms. AE, MC, V. All-inclusive, CP, EP, MAP.*

$–$$ 🏨 **Blue Waters Inn.** A 90-minute drive from Scarborough and a trek
★ down a bumpy driveway brings you to this beach hotel, with villas set amid 46 acres of greenery on the northeast Atlantic coast. You're guaranteed the sound of waves all night in each room. The bungalows have one or two bedrooms, a living room, and a kitchen. You can fax in an order for provisions and have the staff stock your room. The restaurant serves the freshest of fish, and the lively bar specializes in exotic drinks. Barbecue dinners are cooked up on the beach patio. ✉ *Bateaux Bay, Speyside,* ☎ *868/660–4077 or 800/742–4276,* FAX *868/660–5195,*

WEB *www.bluewatersinn.com. 28 rooms, 3 suites, 4 bungalows. Restaurant, bar, tennis court, beach, dive shop, snorkeling, boating, baby-sitting, meeting rooms, car rental. AE, MC, V. CP, EP, FAP, MAP.*

$–$$ ⊡ **Grafton Beach Resort.** The palm-fringed hotel sports a huge lobby-
★   bar-restaurant-pool area and the in-room amenities and furnishings (solid-teak furniture and terra-cotta floors) are all first class. A walkway leads directly to a fine beach, where there's another bar. You can learn to dive, play squash, work out in Le Grand Courlan Resort and Spa's gym next door, or go canoeing and sailing, among other things—all included in the rates. Guests here can also use the spa facilities at Le Grand Courlan for a fee. ⊠ *Shirvan Rd., Black Rock,* ☎ *868/639–0191,* FAX *868/639–0030,* WEB *www.grafton-resort.com. 101 rooms, 4 suites. 2 restaurants, 3 bars, pool, beach, dive shop, snorkeling, windsurfing, boating, squash, dance club, shops, business services, meeting rooms. AE, MC, V. All-inclusive.*

$ ⊡ **Arnos Vale Hotel.** Romance isn't hard to find at this Mediterranean-style complex on 400 lush acres (Princess Margaret honeymooned here 40 years ago). Rooms are in white-stucco cottages on a hill; from your quarters you can take a winding path down to a secluded beach, a pool, and a bar. The hilltop restaurant—with antique pieces, iron-lattice tables, and chandelier—has a magnificent patio with sweeping sea views. ⊠ *Arnos Vale and Franklin Rds., Scarborough (Box 208),* ☎ *868/639–2881,* FAX *868/639–4629,* WEB *www.arnosvalehotel.com. 35 rooms, 3 suites. Restaurant, bar, tennis court, pool, beach, snorkeling, shops. AE, DC, MC, V. CP, EP, MAP.*

$ ⊡ **Kariwak Village.** People tend to return to Allan and Cynthia Clo-
★   vis's charming, reasonably priced cabana village, which they describe as the "holistic haven and hotel." This peaceful atmosphere, all-natural cuisine (vegetarians love this place), an outdoor hot tub, and weekly yoga classes in the open-air conference area keep them coming back. A bamboo pavilion houses the highly respected Kariwak Village restaurant. All accommodations are in nicely appointed cabanas featuring high ceilings (designed to maximize your energy potential). The complex is near the airport, Store Bay, and Pigeon Point. ⊠ *Crown Point (Box 27),* ☎ *868/639–8442,* FAX *868/639–8441,* WEB *www.kariwak.co.tt. 24 rooms. Restaurant, bar, pool. AE, MC, V. EP, MAP.*

$ ⊡ **Toucan Inn.** This charming 20-room hotel is in the midst of beautiful gardens. You may choose from garden rooms or the less private cabanas around the pool. Immaculate rooms are well appointed with beautiful local teak furniture. The rates, excellent service, and proximity to the airport make this hotel an unbeatable value. There's great live entertainment Monday, Wednesday and Friday nights. One of the main advantages of staying here is that the hotel's restaurant and bar, Bonkers, is one of Tobago's most popular hangouts. ⊠ *Store Bay Local Rd., Crown Point,* ☎ *868/639–7173,* FAX *868/639–8933,* WEB *www.toucan-inn.com. 20 rooms. Restaurant, bar, pool. AE, MC, V. CP, MAP.*

Dining

Curried crab and dumplings is Tobago's Sunday dinner favorite. Oil-down—a local dish—tastes better than it sounds: it's a gently seasoned mixture of boiled breadfruit and salt beef or pork flavored with coconut milk. Mango ice cream or a sweet and sour tamarind ball makes a tasty finish. You may want to take home some hot-pepper sauce or chutney to a spice-loving friend or relative.

For approximate costs, *see* the dining price chart *in* Trinidad.

CARIBBEAN

$$–$$$$ ✕ **Shirvan Watermill.** For a quiet, romantic dinner, this elegant alfresco restaurant surrounded by lush foliage and a winding fishpond filled with carp is an essential dining experience. The daily changing menu, the bouquets of anthuriums, and the starched navy tableclothes and white napkins add even more charm. A regular specialty is "river lobster" (crayfish) with garlic butter (a mess is expected). ✉ *Shirvan Rd., Mt. Pleasant,* ☎ *868/639–0000. AE, MC, V. No lunch.*

$$–$$$ ✕ **Blue Crab.** Alison Sardinha is Tobago's most ebullient and kindest
★ hostess, and her husband, Ken, one of its best chefs. The menu may include kingfish, curried chicken, or suckling pig. You'll always find callaloo, rotis, and *cou-cou* (a cornmeal dish); sometimes you may find a "cookup"—a pelau-type rice dish with *everything* in it. The place is officially open only on Wednesday and Friday nights, but Miss Alison will open up on other evenings and for weekend lunches if you call in the morning. ✉ *Robinson and Main Sts., Scarborough,* ☎ *868/639– 2737. AE, MC, V. Dinner Wed. and Fri. only. Closed weekends.*

$$–$$$ ✕ **Kariwak Village.** Recorded steel-band music plays gently in the
★ background at this romantic candlelit spot in the Kariwak Village complex. In a bamboo pavilion that resembles an Amerindian round hut, Cynthia Clovis orchestrates a very original four-course menu. Whatever the dish, it will be full of herbs and vegetables picked from Cynthia's organic garden. Saturday buffets, with live jazz or calypso, are a Tobagonian highlight. ✉ *Crown Point,* ☎ *868/639–8442. AE, DC, MC, V.*

$ ✕ **Café Petunia.** This little gem is a true delight—the sort of place that you will brag to your friends that you "discovered." On a little hill and simply decorated in what can only be described as "mauve retro," it's a great place to while away the hours sipping on cappuccino or wine. Owner Petunia Thomas offers light snacks, salads, and fresh juices that she prepares herself. Friday evenings are lively with a band performing jazz, pop, and calypso standards and featuring the song stylings of Petunia herself. ✉ *Old Milford Rd., near the Signal Hill turnoff between Crown Point and Scarborough,* ☎ *868/639–6878. No credit cards.*

$ ✕ **First Historical Café/Bar.** This funky little roadside eatery owned by the Washington family is in a traditional West Indian building. The backporch dining area overlooking the sea has a crushed-rock-and-coral floor, brightly painted yellow, green, and red bamboo walls, time-line posters that present historical tidbits on Tobago, and a thatched roof. The food is simple but good, featuring such island delights as fruit plates, coconut bread, and fish sandwiches. ✉ *Mile Marker 8, Windward Main Rd., in Studley Park area en route to Charlotteville,* ☎ *868/660–2233. No credit cards.*

CONTEMPORARY

$$$$ ✕ **Tamara's.** Here, at the elegant Coco Reef Resort, you dine on contemporary cuisine with an island twist. The peach walls and whitewashed wooden ceiling make the place feel airy and light, and island breezes waft through the palm-tree-lined terrace. The menu changes seasonally, but the fish dishes are sure to please. A full tropical buffet breakfast is served daily; dinner is served nightly. ✉ *Coco Reef Resort, Pigeon Point, Scarborough,* ☎ *868/639–8571. AE, MC, V.*

$$–$$$ ✕ **Arnos Vale Waterwheel Restaurant.** At this popular eatery on landscaped grounds in a rain-forest nature park, gleaming hardwood walkways take you past remnants of an old sugar mill. There's a roof overhead, but otherwise you're completely outdoors (insect repellent is a good idea). Tables and chairs are green wrought-iron, with lights fashioned in the shape of large pineapples overhead. The crayfish and caviar salad with raspberry vinaigrette is a good choice. When you arrive at the park entrance, let the attendants know you're dining here to save the park admission fee. ⊠ *Arnos Vale Estate, Franklyn Rd.,* ☎ *868/660–0815. MC, V.*

ITALIAN

$$$$ ✕ **La Tartaruga.** Milanese owner Gabriele de Gaetano has created a
★ unique dining experience on the island. Sitting on the large patio surrounded by lush foliage with Gabriele rushing from table to table chatting in Italian-laced English is all the entertainment you'll need. The tagliatelli with lobster and capers in wine and cream will give your tastebuds fond memories to last for years to come. The restaurant has an impressive wine cellar stocked with only Italian wines. ⊠ *Buccoo Rd., Buccoo,* ☎ *868/639–0940. Reservations essential. AE, MC, V. Closed Sun.*

ECLECTIC

$$$–$$$$ ✕ **Pinnacle.** The main dining room at Le Grand Courlan Resort and Spa serves pleasant local dishes and international favorites in a large, open, airy space facing the beach. Light dinner music is performed nightly, starting at 8, and service is friendly. ⊠ *Le Grand Courlan Resort and Spa, Shirvan Rd., Black Rock,* ☎ *868/639–9667. AE, MC, V.*

$$–$$$$ ✕ **Rouselle's.** An enchanting terrace high above Scarborough Bay with
★ a big, congenial bar, Rouselle's has a menu that dons different accessories rather than changing completely. Fresh fish and local produce are always prepared in a stylish creole manner. An appetizer, hot garlic bread, and dessert (save room for pineapple pie or homemade ice cream) are included in the entrée price. ⊠ *Old Windward Rd., Bacolet,* ☎ *868/639–4738. AE, MC, V.*

$–$$$ ✕ **Bonkers.** Despite the rather odd name, this restaurant at the Toucan Inn is atmospheric and excellent. Designed by expatriate British co-owner Chris James, the architecture is a blend of Kenyan and Caribbean styles, executed entirely in local teak and open on all sides. The menu is huge; Chris claims it pains him to remove any items, so he just keeps adding more. You can savor your Lobster Rockefeller while enjoying the nightly entertainment. Open for breakfast and lunch seven days a week, this is the busiest eatery on the island. ⊠ *Toucan Inn, Store Bay Local Rd., Crown Point,* ☎ *868/639–7173,* fax *868/639–8933. AE, MC, V.*

Beaches

You won't find manicured country-club sand here. But those who enjoy feeling as though they've landed on a desert island will relish the untouched quality of these shores.

Bacolet Beach. This dark-sand beach was the setting for the films *Swiss Family Robinson* and *Heaven Knows, Mr. Allison.*

Englishman's Bay. This charming beach is usually completely deserted.

Great Courland Bay. Near Fort Bennett, the bay has clear, tranquil waters. Along the sandy beach—one of Tobago's longest—you'll find several glitzy hotels. A marina attracts the yachting crowd.

King's Bay. Surrounded by steep green hills, this is the most visually satisfying of the swimming sites off the road from Scarborough to Speyside—the bay hooks around so severely you'll feel like you're in a lake. The crescent-shape beach is easy to find because it's marked by a sign about halfway between Roxborough and Speyside. Just before you reach the bay, there's a bridge with an unmarked turnoff that leads to a gravel parking lot; beyond that, a landscaped path leads to a waterfall with a rocky pool. You may meet locals who'll offer to guide you to the top of the falls; however, you may find the climb not worth the effort.

Little Rockley Bay. West of Scarborough (take Milford Road off the main highway), the beach is craggy and not much good for swimming or sunbathing, but it's quiet and offers a pleasing view of Tobago's capital across the water.

Lovers Beach. So called because of its pink sand and its seclusion—you have to hire a local to bring you here by boat—it's an isolated and quiet retreat.

Man O' War Bay. In the pretty little fishing village of Charlotteville (just northwest of Speyside), you can lounge on the sand and purchase the day's catch for your dinner.

Mt. Irvine Beach. Across the street from the Mt. Irvine Bay Hotel is this unremarkable beach, but it has great surfing in July and August; the snorkeling is excellent, too. It's also ideal for windsurfing in January and April. There are picnic tables surrounded by painted concrete pagodas and a snack bar.

Parlatuvier. On the north side of the island, the beach is best approached via the road from Roxborough. It's a classic Caribbean crescent, a scene peopled by villagers and fishermen.

Pigeon Point. This stunning locale is often displayed on Tobago travel brochures. Although the beach is public, it abuts part of what was once a large coconut estate, and you must pay a token admission (about TT$10) to enter the grounds and use the facilities. The beach is lined with towering royal palms, and there are food stands, gift shops, a diving concession, and paddleboats for rent. The waters are calm.

Sandy Beach. Along Crown Point, this beach is abutted by several hotels. You won't lack for amenities around here.

Stone Haven Bay. A gorgeous stretch of sand is across the street from the luxurious Grafton Beach Resort.

Store Bay. The beach, where boats depart for Buccoo Reef, is little more than a small sandy cove between two rocky breakwaters, but the food stands here are divine: six huts licensed by the tourist board to local ladies who sell roti, pelau, and the world's messiest dish—crab and dumplings. Miss Jean's is the most popular; but you should try Miss Esmie's crab.

Turtle Beach. Named for the leatherback turtles that lay their eggs here at night between February and June, it's on Great Courland Bay. (If you're very quiet, you can watch; the turtles don't seem to mind.)

Outdoor Activities and Sports

BIRD-WATCHING

Some 200 varieties of birds have been documented on Tobago: look for the yellow oriole, scarlet ibis, and the comical motmot—the male of the species clears sticks and stones from an area and then does a dance complete with snapping sounds to attract a mate. The flora is as vivid as the birds. Purple and yellow *poui* trees and spectacular orange immortelles splash color over the countryside, and something is blooming virtually every season. Naturalist and ornithologist **David Rooks** (☎ 868/639–4276) offers bird-watching walks inland and trips to offshore bird colonies. Call Pat Turpin (☎ 868/660–4327) or Renson Jack (☎ 868/660–5175) at **Pioneer Journeys** for information about their bird-watching tours of Bloody Bay rain forest and Louis D'Or River valley wetlands.

BOATING

Hew's Glass Bottom Boat Tours (✉ Pigeon Point, ☎ 868/639–9058) are perfect excursions for those who neither snorkel nor dive. Boats leave daily at 11:30 AM. **Kalina Kats** (✉ Scarborough, ☎ 868/639–6304) has a 50-ft catamaran on which you can sail around the Tobago coastline with stops for snorkeling and exploring the rain forest. The romantic sunset cruise with cocktails is a great way to end the day.

FISHING

Dillon's Fishing Charter (⌧ Crown Point, ☎ 868/639–8765) is excellent for full- and half-day trips for kingfish, barracuda, wahoo, mahimahi, blue marlin, and others. Trips start at $165 for four hours, including equipment. With **Hard Play Fishing Charters** (⌧ 13, The Evergreen, Auchenskeoch, Buccoo, ☎ 868/639–7108), colorful skipper Gerard "Frothy" De Silva helps you bag your own marlin. Cost is for $275 for two hours on the 38-ft *Hard Play* or $200 on the 31-ft *Hard Play Lite.*

GOLF

The 18-hole course at the **Mt. Irvine Golf Club** (⌧ Mt. Irvine Bay Hotel, Shirvan Rd., Mt. Irvine Bay, ☎ 868/639–8871) has been ranked among the top five in the Caribbean and among the top 100 in the world. Greens fees are $30 for 9 holes; $48 for 18 holes (note that these rates are subject to 15% VAT tax).

HIKING

Eco-consciousness is strong on Tobago, where the rain forests of the Main Ridge were set aside for protection in 1764, creating the first such preserve in the western hemisphere. Natural areas include Little Tobago and St. Giles islands, both major seabird sanctuaries. In addition, the endangered leatherback turtles maintain breeding grounds on some of Tobago's leeward beaches.

They groomed some of the rain forest around the **Arnos Vale Waterwheel** (⌧ Arnos Vale Estate, Franklyn Rd., ☎ 868/660–0815) to insert a series of shiny wooden walkways that take you past the remnants of an old sugar factory. The walkways allow you to see much of the ruins without disturbing nature. There's also a small museum, an excellent restaurant, and several hiking trails around the property, including a 2½-mi (4-km) loop. The remnants of the Buckra Estate house are on a hilltop that has spectacular views of Tobago. There are also two Amerindian sights, remains of a slave village, and a tomb. Guides are available and can make your nature-history walk truly come alive. There's a TT$10 admission charge unless you're dining at the restaurant, so let the attendants know if you plan to have a meal here. Private-tour guide **AJM Tours** (⌧ Crown Point Airport, Crown Point, ☎ 868/639–0610, WEB www.ajmtours.com) offers tours of the Arnos Vale Waterwheel complex as well as guided tours of Tobago and even nearby Venezuela.

SCUBA DIVING

An abundance of fish and coral thrives on the nutrients of South America's Orinoco River, which are brought to Tobago by the Guyana current. Off the west coast is **Arnos Vale Reef,** with a depth of 40 ft (12 m) and several reefs that run parallel to the shore. Here you can spot French and queen angelfish, moray eels, southern stingrays, and even the Atlantic torpedo ray. Much of the diving is drift diving in the mostly gentle current. **Crown Point,** on the island's southwest tip, is a good place for exploring the Shallows—a plateau at about 50–100 ft (15–30½ m) that's favored by turtles, dolphin, angelfish, and nurse sharks. Just north of Crown Point on the southwest coast, **Pigeon Point** is a good spot to submerge. North of Pigeon Point, long sandy beaches line the calm western coast; it has a gradual offshore slope and the popular **Mt. Irvine Wall,** which goes down to about 60 ft (18 m).

A short trip from Charlotteville, off the northeast tip of the island, is **St. Giles Island.** Here are natural rock bridges—London Bridge, Marble Island, and Fishbowl—and underwater cliffs. The **waters off Spey-side** on the east coast draw scuba-diving aficionados for the many manta rays in the area. Exciting sites in this area include Batteaux Reef, Angel Reef, Bookends, Blackjack Hole, and Japanese Gardens—one of the loveliest reefs, with depths of 20–85 ft (6–26 m) and lots of sponges.

There are several places in Tobago to get information, supplies, and instruction. **AquaMarine Dive Ltd.** (✉ Blue Waters Inn, Batteaux Bay, Speyside, ☎ 868/639–4416) is on the northeast coast. **Man Friday Diving** (✉ Windward Rd., Charlotteville, ☎ 868/660–4676) is on the northwest coast. **Tobago Dive Experience** (✉ Manta Lodge, Speyside, ☎ 868/639–7034) is a west coast scuba diving operation. **Tobago Dive Masters** (✉ Windward Rd., Speyside, ☎ 868/639–4697) is on the northeastern end of the island.

SNORKELING

Tobago offers many wonderful spots for snorkeling. Although the reefs around Speyside in the northeast are becoming better known, **Buccoo Reef,** off the island's southwest coast, is still the most popular—perhaps too popular. Over the years the reef has been damaged by the ceaseless boat traffic and by the thoughtless visiting divers who take pieces of coral for souvenirs. Still, it's worth experiencing, particularly if you have children. Daily 2½-hour tours by flat glass-bottom boats let you snorkel at the reef, swim in a lagoon, and gaze at Coral Gardens—where fish and coral are as yet untouched. The trip usually costs about $8, and masks, snorkeling equipment, and reef shoes are provided. Departure is at 11 AM from Pigeon Point. Most dive companies in the Black Rock area also arrange snorkeling tours. There is also good snorkeling near the **Arnos Vale Hotel** and the **Mt. Irvine Bay Hotel.**

TENNIS

The remote enclave of **Blue Waters Inn** (✉ Batteaux Bay, Speyside, ☎ 868/660–4341) on the northeast Atlantic coast has two of the best courts on the island and also allows nonresidents to play. If you're in the Mt. Irvine area, the **Mt. Irvine Bay Hotel** (✉ Shirvan Rd., Mt. Irvine, ☎ 868/639–8871) has great lighted courts and a splendid view (if you can take your eye off the ball). Guests and nonguests can play on one of **Rex Turtle Beach**'s (✉ Courland Bay, Black Rock, ☎ 868/639–2851) two lighted, all-weather courts. Lessons are available for $30 per hour.

Shopping

The souvenir-bound will do better in Trinidad than in Tobago, but determined shoppers should manage to ferret out some things to take home. Scarborough has the largest collection of shops, and Burnett Street, which slopes sharply from the port to St. James Park, is a good place to browse.

FOODSTUFFS

Forro's Homemade Delicacies (✉ The Andrew's Rectory, Bacolet St., opposite the fire station, Scarborough, ☎ 868/639–2485) sells its own fine line of homemade tamarind chutney, lemon or lime marmalade, hot sauce, and guava or golden apple jelly. Eileen Forrester, wife of the Anglican Archdeacon of Trinidad and Tobago, supervises a kitchen full of good cooks who boil and bottle the condiments and pack them in little straw baskets—or even in bamboo. Most jars are small, easy to carry, and inexpensive.

HANDICRAFTS

Cotton House (✉ Bacolet St., Scarborough, ☎ 868/639–2727) is a good bet for jewelry and imaginative batik work. Paula Young runs her shop like an art school. You can visit the upstairs studio; if it's not too busy, you can even make a batik square at no charge. **Souvenir and Gift Shop**

(✉ Port Mall, Wrightson Rd., Scarborough, ☎ 868/639–5632) stocks straw baskets and other crafts.

Nightlife

Tobago is not the liveliest island after dark but there's usually some form of nightlife to be found. Whatever you do the rest of the week, don't miss the huge impromptu party, affectionately dubbed Sunday School, that gears up after midnight on all the street corners of Buccoo and breaks up around dawn. Pick your band, hang out for a while, then move on. In downtown Scarborough on weekend nights you can also find competing sound systems blaring at informal parties that welcome extra guests. In addition, "blockos" (spontaneous block parties) spring up all over the island; look for the hand-painted signs. Tobago also has harvest parties on Sunday throughout the year, when a particular village extends its hospitality and opens its doors to visitors.

Bonkers (✉ Store Bay Local Rd., Crown Point, ☎ 868/639–7173) is lively on most evenings with live entertainment every night except Sunday. **The Deep** (✉ Sandy Point Hotel, Crown Point, ☎ 868/639–8533) is a basement pub/disco that plays an unusual blend of pop, rock and soca on their sound system. **Grafton Beach Resort** (✉ Shirvan Rd., Black Rock, ☎ 868/639–0191) has some kind of organized cabaret-style event every night. Even if you hate that touristy stuff, check out Les Couteaux Cultural Group, which does a high-octane dance version of Tobagonian history. **Kariwak Village** (✉ Crown Point, ☎ 868/639–8442) has hip hotel entertainment and is frequented as much by locals as visitors on Friday and Saturday nights—one of the better local jazz-calypso bands almost always plays.

Exploring Tobago

A driving tour of Tobago, from Scarborough to Charlotteville and back, can be done in about four hours, but you'd never want to undertake this spectacular, and very hilly, ride in that time. The switchbacks can make you wish you had motion-sickness pills (take some along if you're prone). Plan to spend at least one night at the Speyside end of the island, and give yourself a chance to enjoy this largely untouched country and seaside at leisure.

Numbers in the margin correspond to points of interest on the Tobago map.

SIGHTS TO SEE

❺ **Charlotteville.** This delightful fishing village in the northeast is enfolded in a series of steep hills. Fishermen here announce the day's catch by sounding their conch shells. A view of Man O' War Bay with Pigeon Peak (Tobago's highest mountain) behind it at sunset is an exquisite treat.

❹ **Flagstaff Hill.** One of the highest points of the island sits at the northern tip of Tobago. Surrounded by ocean on three sides and with a view of other hills, Charlotteville, and St. Giles Island, this was the site of an American military lookout and radio tower during World War II. It's an ideal spot for a sunset picnic. The turnoff to the hill is located at the major bend on the road from Speyside to Charlotteville. It is largely unpaved so the going may be a bit rough.

❷ **Ft. King George.** On Mt. St. George, a short drive up the hill from Scarborough, Tobago's best-preserved historic monument clings to a cliff high above the ocean. Ft. King George was built in the 1770s and operated until 1854. It's hard to imagine that this lovely, tranquil spot commanding sweeping views of the bay and landscaped with lush tropical foliage was ever the site of any military action, but the prison, officers' mess, and several stabilized cannons attest otherwise. Just to the left of the tall wooden figures dancing a traditional Tobagonian jig is the former barrack guardhouse, now housing the small **Tobago Museum** (☎ 868/639–3970). Exhibits include weapons and other pre-Columbian artifacts found in the area; the fertility figures are especially interesting. Upstairs are maps and photographs of Tobago's past. Be sure to check out the gift display cases for the perversely fascinating jewelry made from embalmed and painted lizards and sea creatures; you might find it hard to resist a pair of bright-yellow shrimp earrings. The museum is open weekdays 9–5; entrance to the museum is TT$5. ⊠ *84 Fort St., Scarborough.* ☜ *Free.*

The **Fine Arts Centre** at the foot of the Ft. King George complex shows the work of local artists.

❻ **St. Giles Island.** The underwater cliffs and canyons here off the northeastern tip of Tobago draw divers to this spot where the Atlantic meets the Caribbean. ⊠ *Take Windward Rd. inland across mountains from Speyside.*

❶ **Scarborough.** Around Rockley Bay on the island's leeward hilly side, this town is both the capital of Tobago and a popular cruise-ship port, but it conveys the feeling that not much has changed since the area was settled two centuries ago. It may not be one of the delightful pastel-color cities of the Caribbean, but Scarborough does have its charms, including several interesting little shops. Whatever you do be sure to check out the busy Scarborough Market, an indoor and outdoor affair featuring everything from fresh vegetables to live chickens and clothing. Note the red-and-yellow Methodist church on the hill, one of Tobago's oldest churches.

❸ **Speyside.** At the far reach of the windward coast of Tobago, this small fishing village has a few lodgings and restaurants. Divers are drawn to the unspoiled reefs in the area and to the strong possibility of spotting giant manta rays. The approach to Speyside from the south affords one of the most spectacular vistas of the island. Glass-bottom boats operate between Speyside and **Little Tobago Island,** one of the most important seabird sanctuaries in the Caribbean.

TRINIDAD AND TOBAGO A TO Z

To research prices, get advice from other travelers, and book travel arrangements, visit www.fodors.com.

AIR TRAVEL

American Airlines offers daily direct flights from both New York and Miami to Trinidad. The national carrier, BWIA West Indies Airways, offers direct flights to Trinidad from Atlanta, Miami, New York, and Washington, D.C., in the U.S.; from Toronto in Canada; and from London in the U.K.; and from many Caribbean islands; it also offers at least six connections to Tobago daily from Trinidad. Air Canada flies nonstop from Toronto to Trinidad; British Airways offers weekly flights to Tobago from London (the number of flights increases in peak season). LIAT offers numerous flights to Trinidad from other Caribbean islands; it also has service from the eastern Caribbean islands to Tobago. Air DCE has direct flights from Curaçao to Trinidad on Tuesday, Thursday, and Sunday; flights from Aruba and Bonaire connect with this Curaçao flight.

➤ Airlines and Contacts: **Air Canada** (☎ 868/664–4065). **Air DCE** (☎ 868/623–6522). **American Airlines** (☎ 868/664–4661). **British Airways** (☎ 800/744–2997). **BWIA West Indies Airways** (☎ 868/ 625–1010 or 868/669–3000). **LIAT** (☎ 868/627–2942 or 868/623– 1838).

AIRPORTS

Trinidad's Piarco International Airport, located about 30 minutes east of Port-of-Spain (take Golden Grove Road north to Arouca and then follow Eastern Main Road west for about 10 mi (16 km) to Port-of-Spain, is a thoroughly modern facility complete with 16 airbridges. Tobago's small Crown Point Airport is the gateway to the island. Taxis are readily available at Piarco Airport; the fare to Port-of-Spain is set at $20 ($30 after 10 PM) and $24 to the Hilton. In Tobago the fare from Crown Point Airport to Scarborough is fixed at $8, to Speyside at $36.

➤ Airport Information: **Piarco International Airport** (☎ 868/669– 4101, WEB www.airporttnt.com). **Crown Point Airport** (☎ 868/639– 0509, WEB www.airporttnt.com).

BOAT AND FERRY TRAVEL

FARES AND SCHEDULES

The Port Authority maintains ferry service every day except Saturday between Trinidad and Tobago, although flying is preferable because the seas can be very rough. The ferry leaves once a day (from St. Vincent Street Jetty in Port-of-Spain and from the cruise-ship complex in Scarborough); the trip takes about five hours. The round-trip fare is TT$50. Cabins, when available, run TT$160 (round-trip, double occupancy).

➤ Boat and Ferry Information: **Port-of-Spain, Trinidad** (☎ 868/625– 3055, WEB www.patnt.com/ferry.htm). **Scarborough, Tobago** (☎ 868/ 639–2181, WEB www.patnt.com/ferry.htm).

BUSINESS HOURS

BANKS

Banks are open Monday–Thursday 8–3, and Friday 8–noon and 3–5. Banks in malls will often stay open until 7 PM.

POST OFFICES

Post offices are open 8–noon and 1–4:30 on weekdays.

SHOPS

Most shops are open weekdays 8–4:30, Saturday 8–noon; malls stay open later during the week and operate all day Saturday.

CAR RENTALS

All agencies require a credit card deposit, and in peak season you must make reservations well in advance of your arrival. Figure on paying $40–$60 per day in both Trinidad and Tobago. In addition to Thrifty, an international company, there are several local agencies operating on either Trinidad or Tobago or both; Auto Rentals is a local company with many locations on Trinidad.

➤ Major Agencies in Trinidad: **Auto Rentals** (✉ Piarco International Airport, Piarco, ☎ 868/669–2277). **Kalloo's Auto Rentals** (✉ Piarco International Airport, Piarco, ☎ 868/669–5673). **Southern Sales Car Rentals** (☎ 868/669–2424; dial ☎ 269 from a courtesy phone in airport baggage area). **Thrifty** (✉ Piarco International Airport, Piarco, ☎ 868/669–0602).

➤ Major Agencies in Tobago: **Rattan's Car Rentals** (✉ Crown Point Airport, Crown Point, ☎ 868/639–8271). **Rollock's Car Rentals** (✉ Crown Point Airport, Crown Point ☎ 868/639–0328). **Singh's Auto**

Rentals (⊠ Grafton Beach Resort, Shirvan Rd., Black Rock, ☎ 868/639–0191 Ext. 53). **Thrifty** (⊠ Rex Turtle Beach Hotel, Courland Bay, Black Rock, ☎ 868/639–8507).

CAR TRAVEL

It's not worth renting a car if you're staying in Port-of-Spain, where the streets are often jammed with drivers who routinely play chicken with one another; taxis are your best bet. If you're planning to tour Trinidad, you'll need some wheels. In Tobago you're better off renting a four-wheel-drive vehicle than relying on expensive taxi service.

GASOLINE

Gas runs about TT$2.60 per liter. There are plenty of gas stations in Trinidad, but in Tobago, don't let your tank get low because there aren't many gas stations on the island.

ROAD CONDITIONS

Trinidad has excellent roads throughout the island. Be careful when driving during the rainy season, as roads often flood. Never drive into downtown Port-of-Spain during afternoon rush hour (generally from 3 to 6:30).

In Tobago, many roads, particularly in the interior or on the coast near Speyside and Charlotteville, are bumpy, pitted, winding, and/or steep (though the main highways are smooth and fast).

RULES OF THE ROAD

Driving is on the left, in the British style, so remember to look to your right when pulling out into traffic.

ELECTRICITY

Electric current is usually 110 volts/60 cycles, but some establishments provide 220-volt outlets.

EMBASSIES

➤ CANADA: **Canadian High Commission** (3-3A Sweet Briar Rd., St. Clair, Port-of-Spain, Trinidad, ☎ 868/622–6232).

➤ UNITED KINGDOM: **British High Commission** (19 St. Clair Ave., St. Clair, Port-of-Spain, Trinidad, ☎ 868/622–2748).

➤ UNITED STATES: **U.S. Embassy** (15 Queen's Park West, Port-of-Spain, Trinidad, ☎ 868/622–6371).

EMERGENCIES

➤ AMBULANCE AND FIRE: **Ambulance and fire emergencies** (☎ 990).

➤ HOSPITALS: **Port-of-Spain General Hospital** (⊠ 169 Charlotte St., Port-of-Spain, Trinidad, ☎ 868/623–2951). **St. Clair Medical Centre** (⊠ 18 Elizabeth St., St. Clair, Port-of-Spain, ☎ 868/628–1451). **Scarborough Hospital** (⊠ Fort St., Scarborough, Tobago, ☎ 868/639–2551).

➤ PHARMACIES: **Bhaggan's** (Charlotte and Oxford Sts., Port-of-Spain, Trinidad, ☎ 868/627–4657). **Kappa Drugs** (Roxy Round-a-bout, St. James, Port-of-Spain, Trinidad, ☎ 868/622–2728). **Scarborough Drugs** (⊠ Carrington St. and Wilson Rd., Scarborough, Tobago, ☎ 868/639–4161).

➤ POLICE: **Police emergencies** (☎ 999).

ETIQUETTE AND BEHAVIOR

Religious and racial tolerance are important to the people of Trinidad and Tobago. You may hear a word used in public that elsewhere might constitute a slur; on these islands, chances are it's being used in jest—but only by locals who know one another well. Many islanders are well educated and well traveled; don't assume they're unfamiliar with international politics and customs. As in many British-influenced Caribbean nations, beach attire isn't appreciated in stores, restaurants, or hotel lobbies.

FESTIVALS AND SEASONAL EVENTS
In addition to the incomparable Trinidad Carnival, there are a number of celebrations throughout the year. During the Tobago Heritage Festival (usually held in late July) villages throughout the island hold events and activities that portray one aspect (music, dance, drama, cooking, costuming) of island arts or culture. Divali, held in October or November and known as the festival of lights, is the climax of long spiritual preparation in the Hindu community. Small lamps beautifully illuminate the night, and there are events involving music, dancing, gift exchanges, and much hospitality.

HEALTH
Insect repellent is a must during the rainy season (June–December) and is worth having around anytime. Trinidad is only 11 degrees north of the equator, and the sun here is intense; bring a strong sun block. If you have a sensitive stomach, you're better off drinking bottled water, though tap water on the islands is generally safe.

HOLIDAYS
Public holidays are: New Year's Day, Good Friday, Easter Monday, Spiritual Baptist Liberation Day (March 30), Indian Arrival Day (May 30), Labor Day (June 19), Emancipation Day (Aug. 1), Independence Day (Aug. 31), Divali (date is announced by government a few months before, but it's usually in October or November), Eid (a Muslim festival whose actual date late in the year varies), Christmas, and Boxing Day (Dec. 26). Carnival Monday and Tuesday are not official holidays, but don't expect anything to be open.

LANGUAGE
The official language of Trinidad and Tobago is English, there's no end of idiomatic expressions used by the loquacious locals (who tend to speak English very fast). If someone invites you for a "lime," by all means go—you're being invited to a party; "limin' " means relaxing and having a good time. To "beat pan" is to play the steel drum; "wine" is a sexy dance style done by rotating the hips. You'll also hear smatterings of French, Spanish, Chinese, and Hindi (Trinidad's population is about 40% Indian).

MAIL AND SHIPPING
Postage to the United States and Canada is TT$3.45 for first-class letters and TT$2.25 for postcards; prices are slightly higher for other destinations. The main post offices are on Wrightson Road (opposite the Crowne Plaza), in Port-of-Spain, and in the NIB Mall on Wilson Street (near the docks), in Scarborough. There are no zip codes on the islands. To write to an establishment here, you simply need its address, town, and "Trinidad and Tobago, West Indies."

MONEY MATTERS
Prices quoted in this chapter are in U.S. dollars unless otherwise noted.

ATMS
Banks (many with ATMs that accept international cards) are plentiful in the towns and cities (branches of the Republic Bank and the Royal Bank are a common sight) but much less so in the countryside. In addition to the banks in Scarborough and Tobago's airport, a couple of grocery stores in the southwest part of Tobago have ATMs.

BANKS

There are four major banks operating on the islands: First Citizens Bank, Republic Bank, Royal Bank, and Scotiabank. Each of these banks has dozens of branches (there are far fewer branches in Tobago and most of those are in Scarborough). Banking hours are 8 AM–2 PM Monday to Thursday, 9–noon and 3–5 on Fridays. Bank branches in shopping malls are usually open until 6 PM on weekdays. First Citizens Bank operates branches at both Piarco and Crown Point airports.

➤ CONTACTS: **First Citizens Bank** (☎ 868/ 623–2576). **Republic Bank** (☎ 809/625–3611). **Royal Bank** (☎ 868/623–1322). **Scotiabank** (☎ 809/625–3566).

CREDIT CARDS

Credit cards and ATM cards are almost universally accepted for payment by businesses, hotels, and restaurants. VISA and MasterCard are ubiquitous, American Express much less so, and Diners Club and Discover rarely accepted. Cash is necessary only in the smallest neighborhood convenience shops and roadside stalls.

CURRENCY

The current exchange rate for the Trinidadian dollar (TT$) is about TT$6.30 to US$1. Most businesses on the island will accept U.S. currency if you're in a pinch.

PASSPORTS AND VISAS

Citizens of the United States, the United Kingdom, and Canada who expect to stay for less than six weeks may enter the country with a valid passport. Citizens of Australia and New Zealand must also obtain a visa before entering the country.

SAFETY

Travelers should exercise reasonable caution in Trinidad, especially in the eastern part of the island and downtown Port-of-Spain, where walking on the streets at night is not recommended unless you're with a group. As a general rule, Tobago is safer than its larger sister island, though this should not lure you into a false sense of security. Petty theft occurs on both islands, so don't leave cash in bags that you check at the airport, and use hotel safes for valuables.

SIGHTSEEING TOURS

IN TRINIDAD

Almost any taxi driver in Port-of-Spain will take you around town and to beaches on the north coast. It costs around $70 for up to four people to go Maracas Bay beach, plus $20 per hour extra if you decide to go farther; but you should haggle for a cheaper rate. For a complete list of tour operators and sea cruises, contact the tourism office. Kalloo's offers tours ranging from a fascinating three-hour tour of Port-of-Spain to an overnight turtle watching tour. Winston Nanan is the only official tour operator at the Caroni Bird Sanctuary; phone or write him in advance for reservations.

➤ CONTACTS: **Kalloo's** (✉ Piarco International Airport, Piarco, ☎ 868/669–5673 or 868/622–9073). **Winston Nanan** (✉ Nanan Bird Sanctuary Tours, 38 Bamboo Grove, No. 1, Uriah Butler Hwy., Valsayn, ☎ 868/645–1305).

IN TOBAGO

Frank's Glass Bottom Boat and Birdwatching Tours offers glass-bottom-boat and snorkeling tours of the shores of Speyside; Frank also conducts guided tours of the rain forest and Little Tobago. As a native of Speyside, he's extremely knowledgeable about the island's flora, fauna, and folklore. Rooks Nature Tours offers rain-forest hikes and bird-watching expeditions, all with ornithologist David Rooks. Tobago Travel is the island's most experienced tour operator, offering a wide variety of services and tours.

➤ CONTACTS: **Frank's Glass Bottom Boat and Birdwatching Tours** (✉ Speyside, ☎ FAX 868/660–5438). **Rooks Nature Tours** (✉ 462 Moses Hill, Lambeau, ☎ 868/639–4276, WEB www.pariasprings.com/rookstours/tours.html). **Tobago Travel** (✉ Scarborough, ☎ 868/639–8778).

TAXES

DEPARTURE TAX

Departure tax, payable at the airport, is TT$100. At press time there were plans in the works to add an additional TT$100 "airport maintenance tax."

SALES TAX

All hotels add a 15% government tax.

VALUE ADDED TAX (V.A.T.)

Almost all goods and services will be charged a 15% V.A.T.

TAXIS

Taxis in Trinidad and Tobago are easily identified by their license plates, which begin with the letter *H*. Passenger vans, called Maxi Taxis, pick up and drop off passengers as they travel and are color-coded according to which of the six areas they cover. Rates are generally less than $1 per trip. (Yellow is for Port-of-Spain, red for eastern Trinidad, green for south Trinidad, and black for Princes Town. Brown operates from San Fernando to the southeast—Erin, Penal, Point Fortin. The only color for Tobago is blue.) They're easy to hail day or night along most of the main roads near Port-of-Spain. For longer trips you'll need to hire a private taxi. Cabs aren't metered, and hotel taxis can be expensive. A new taxi service available in Trinidad, called 628–TAXI, will take you to and from the airport for $11 each way, to the beach for $10, and around town for $4.

➤ TAXI INFORMATION:: **628–TAXI** (☎ 868/628–8294).

TELEPHONES

A digital phone system is in place, bringing with it direct-dial service, a comprehensive cell-phone network, and easy Internet access. Pay phones take phone cards, which you can buy in different denominations at gift shops and newsagents.

COUNTRY AND AREA CODES

The area code for both islands is 868 ("TNT" if you forget). This is also the country code if you're calling to Trinidad and Tobago from another country.

INTERNATIONAL CALLS

Most hotels and guest houses will allow you to dial a direct international call. To dial a number in North America or the Caribbean simply dial "1" and the area code before the number you're calling, but be warned that most hotels add a hefty surcharge for overseas calls. Calls to Europe and elsewhere can be made by checking for the appropriate direct dial codes in the telephone directory. To make an international call from a pay phone you must first purchase a "companion card," which is readily available from most convenience shops—then simply follow the instructions on the card. Cards are available in various denominations.

LOCAL CALLS

To make a local call to any point in the country simply dial the seven-digit local number.

TIPPING

Almost all hotels will add a 10%–15% service charge to your bill. Most restaurants include a 10% service charge, which is considered standard on these islands. If it isn't on the bill, tip according to service: 10%–15% is fine. Cabbies expect a token tip of around 10%. At drinking establishments tipping is optional, and the staff at smaller bars may tell you on your way out that you forgot your change.

VISITOR INFORMATION

➤ BEFORE YOU LEAVE: In the U.S.: **Tourism Hotline** (☎ 888/595–4TNT). **Trinidad and Tobago Tourism Office** (✉ 331 Almeria Ave., Coral Gables, FL 33134, ☎ 800/748–4224; in the U.K.: ✉ Mitre House, 66 Abbey Rd., Bush Park Hill, Enfield, Middlesex EN1 2RQ, ☎ 208/350–1000; in Canada: ✉ Taurus House, 512 Duplex Ave., Toronto, Ontario M4R 2E3, ☎ 416/535–5617 or 416/485–8724, WEB www.visitTNT.com).

➤ IN TRINIDAD: **TIDCO** (✉ 10–14 Phillips St., Port-of-Spain, ☎ 868/623–6023 or 868/623–1932; ✉ Piarco International Airport, Piarco, ☎ 868/669–5196, WEB www.visitTNT.com).

➤ IN TOBAGO: **Tobago Division of Tourism** (✉ N.I.B. Mall, Level 3, Scarborough, ☎ 868/639–2125; ✉ Crown Point Airport, Crown Point, ☎ 868/639–0509, WEB www.visitTNT.com).

25 · TURKS AND CAICOS ISLANDS

Updated by
Kathy Borsuk

"Everything cool, man?" Shadow asks with a laugh as he cuts the speedboat through Crocodile Pass en route to Middle Caicos. A Caribbean renaissance man, Shadow took his nickname from an uncanny ability to sneak up on bonefish. He also bats .500 for the local all-star team, fishes for trophy-size blue marlin in the annual rodeo, plays a mean guitar, and tells a great story. When he reaches the shore, he plans to whip up a batch of seviche using fresh conch, onion, sweet peppers, lime juice, and Tabasco—thus adding "cook" to an impressive, island-style résumé.

Sportfishermen, scuba divers, and beach aficionados have long known about the Turks and Caicos (pronounced *kay*-kos). To them this British Crown colony of more than 40 islands and small cays (only eight of which are inhabited) is a gem that offers dazzling turquoise seas, priceless stretches of sand, and reefs rich in marine life. Whether you're swimming with the fishes or attempting to catch them from the surface, the Turks and Caicos won't disappoint. In an archipelago 575 mi (927 km) southeast of Miami and 90 mi (145 km) north of Haiti, the total landmass of these two groups of islands is 193 square mi (500 square km); the total population is less than 25,000.

The Turks Islands include Grand Turk, which is the capital and seat of government, and Salt Cay. It's claimed that Columbus's first landfall was on Grand Turk. Legend also has it that these islands were named by early settlers who thought the scarlet blossoms on the local cactus resembled the Turkish fez.

Approximately 22 mi (35½ km) west of Grand Turk, across the 7,000-ft-deep (2,141-m-deep) Columbus Passage, is the Caicos group: South, East, West, Middle, and North Caicos and Providenciales (nicknamed Provo). South Caicos, Middle Caicos, North Caicos, and Provo are the only inhabited islands in this group; Pine Cay and Parrot Cay are the only inhabited cays. "Caicos" is derived from *cayos*, the Spanish word for "cay" and is believed to mean, appropriately, "string of islands."

In the mid-1600s, Bermudians began to rake salt from the flats on the Turks Islands, returning to Bermuda to sell their crop. Despite French and Spanish attacks and pirate raids, the Bermudians persisted and established a trade that became the bedrock of the islands' economy. In

1766 Andrew Symmers settled here to hold the islands for England. The American Declaration of Independence left British loyalists from South Carolina and Georgia without a country, causing many to take advantage of British Crown land grants in the Turks and Caicos. Cotton plantations were established and prospered for nearly 25 years until the boll weevil, soil exhaustion, and a terrible hurricane in 1813 devastated the land. Left behind to make their living off the land and sea were the former slaves, who remained to shape the culture.

Today the Turks and Caicos are known as a reputable offshore tax haven whose company formation, banking, trusts, and insurance institutions lure investors from North America and beyond. Provo, in particular, is on its way to becoming a popular Caribbean tourist destination. Mass tourism, however, shouldn't be in the cards; government guidelines promote a quality, not quantity policy, including conservation awareness. And without a port for cruise ships, the islands remain uncrowded and peaceful.

THE TURKS

Grand Turk

Bermudian colonial architecture abounds on this string bean of an island (just 7 mi [11 km] long and 1½ mi [2½ km] wide). Buildings have walled-in courtyards to keep wandering horses from nibbling on the foliage. The island caters to divers, and it's no wonder: the wall, a slice of vertical coral mountain, is less than 300 yards from the beach.

Lodging

Throughout the islands accommodations range from small (sometimes non-air-conditioned) inns to splashy resorts and hotels that are the ultimate in luxury. Most medium and large hotels offer a choice of EP and MAP. Almost all hotels offer dive packages.

CATEGORY	COST EP/CP*	COST A.I.**
$$$$	over $350	over $375
$$$	$250–$350	$275–$375
$$	$150–$250	$175–$275
$	under $150	under $175

*EP/CP prices are per night for a standard double room in high season, excluding taxes, service charges, and meal plans

**A.I. (all-inclusive) prices are per person, per night based on double-occupancy during high season, excluding taxes and service charges

$$ 🏠 **The Arches of Grand Turk.** If you're looking for a home away from home, these immaculate vacation town houses offer space, privacy, and a loving touch. Each of the four two-story suites is fully furnished in clean-cut country style. Kitchen/dining areas are on the lower levels, with two huge bedrooms upstairs. Arched balconies front and back promise breathtaking sunrises and sunsets. Atop the ridge northeast of town, steady breezes keep insects away, and there is an eagle's-eye view of the island. ✉ *Lighthouse Rd., Grand Turk, (Box 226),* ☎ FAX *649/946–2941,* WEB *www.grandturkarches.com. 4 town homes. Kitchens, microwaves, cable TV with movies, bicycles, laundry facilities. D, MC, V. EP.*

$ 🏠 **Arawak Inn and Beach Club.** These newly renovated condo-style accommodations have private bedrooms, full-size baths and kitchens, and living rooms with sofa beds. The complex fronts a fabulous white-sand beach, and there's a seaside freshwater pool and volleyball court. Don't feel like cooking? The restaurant serves delicious Caribbean meals. ✉ *Near White Sands Beach, Grand Turk, (Box 190),* ☎ *649/946–2277,* FAX *649/946–2279. 16 units. Restaurant, bar, kitchens, cable TV with* *movies, pool, beach, snorkeling, horseback riding, volleyball, laundry service. AE, MC, V. CP, MAP.*

$ ⊞ **Island House.** Perched on a breezy hill overlooking North Creek, this Mediterranean-style all-suites inn offers romantic comfort and panoramic views from large porches. One mile (1½ km) from town, gas-powered golf carts are provided free of charge. Relax on the expansive, palm-shaded pool/patio area with barbecue grill. Fishing from the dock and bird-watching are popular at this peaceful retreat, but dive packages are available for active types. ⊠ *Lighthouse Rd., Grand Turk, (Box 36),* ☎ *649/946–1519,* FAX *649/946–2646,* WEB *www. islandhouse-tci.com. 9 suites. Kitchenettes, microwaves, cable TV with movies, pool, dock, fishing, bicycles, laundry facilities, Internet, some pets allowed. AE, MC, V. EP.*

$ ⊞ **Osprey Beach Hotel.** Rooms in this two-story oceanfront building open onto a private veranda overlooking the beach; there are airy cathedral ceilings on the top floors. Deluxe units have brand-new furnishings, king-size beds, and bathrooms; suites include sitting rooms and full kitchens. The pool bar serves drinks and tapas to the sound of breaking waves just steps away. A pleasant touch is the lush foliage lining the walkways. ⊠ *Duke St., Grand Turk, (Box 1),* ☎ *649/946–2888,* FAX *649/946–2817,* WEB *www.ospreybeachhotel.com. 28 rooms. Coffee shop, bar, some kitchens, microwaves, cable TV with movies, golf privileges, pool, beach, snorkeling, meeting rooms. AE, MC, V. EP, FAP, MAP.*

$ ⊞ **Salt Raker Inn.** Across a quaint one-way street from the beach, this inn—once the home of a Bermudian shipwright—was built more than 170 years ago. The renovated rooms are clean and comfortable, all with the original red pine floors. Upstairs suites have balconies overlooking the ocean, and lush tropical gardens at back envelop the Secret Garden restaurant. Hotel service is unpretentious and friendly. Dive packages are available through Blue Water Divers. ⊠ *Duke St., Grand Turk, (Box 1),* ☎ *649/946–2260,* FAX *649/946–2817,* WEB *www. microplan.com. 10 rooms, 3 suites. Restaurant, bar, no phones in some rooms, refrigerators, no TV in some rooms, dive shop, bicycles. AE, MC, V. EP, FAP, MAP.*

$ ⊞ **Turks Head Hotel.** Although thoroughly modernized, the historical Turks Head Hotel has maintained its romantic charm and tranquil ambience. The two-story structure, filled with antique furnishings, was built in 1840 as the home of a prosperous salt miner, and has also served as the American consulate and governor's guest house. Rooms are a comfortable blend of old and new, with a coffeemaker and mini-bar beside the canopied four-poster bed. The hotel bar and Calico Jack's restaurant bustle at night; the beach is only a few strides away, and dive packages are available. ⊠ *Duke St., Grand Turk, (Box 58),* ☎ *649/946–2466,* FAX *649/946–1716,* WEB *www.grand-turk.com. 8 rooms. Restaurant, minibars, cable TV with movies, golf privileges, beach, bicycles, pub. MC, V. EP, CP, FAP, MAP.*

Dining

Like everything else on these islands, dining out is a very laid-back affair, which is not to say it's cheap. Because of the high cost of importing all edibles, the price of a meal is higher than in the United States. Reservations are generally not required, and dress tends to be casual.

CATEGORY	COST*
$$$$	over $30
$$$	$20–$30
$$	$10–$20
$	under $10

*per person for a main course at dinner

Turks and Caicos Islands

Three Mary's Cays

32–34

TO BAHAMAS

30

5

Parrot Cay

Spanish Point

Caicos Passage

Football Fields ☒

Fort George Cay

6

High Cay

Pine Cay

Northwest Point

Little Water Cay

North Caicos

Jun H

31

Providenciales

4

Grace Bay

3

Mid

Southwest Bluff

Juba Point

12–29

C A I C O S

I S L

West Caicos

Vine Point

Oc H

Southwest Reef

☒ **Molasses Reef**

C A I C O S B A N K

N

0 ———————— 14 miles

0 ———————— 21 km

White Cay

A T L A N T I C   O C E A N

ico
nt

Haulover Point

os

Long Bay

Joe Grant Cay

Drum Point

oll Crawl
Point

East Caicos

Big Southern
Bush

Big Cameron Cay

Middle Creek
Cay

Sail Rock Island

D S

Horse Cay

❾ ㊱

❽

South Caicos

Six Hill Cays

High Point

Long Cay

Columbus Passage

Black ◥
Forest

Grand
Turk
Island

① – ⑧

①

Gibb's Cay

**TURKS
ISLANDS**

◥
**The
Library**

Long Cay

Fish Cays

Cotton Cay

Little
mbergris
Cay

Big Ambergris Cay

❾ ⑩ ⑪ ❷

East Cay

Toney Rock

Salt Cay

South Point

AMBERGRIS CAYS

SEAL CAYS

Cay

Bush Cay

Big Sand Cay

Mouchoir Passage

AMERICAN

$$–$$$ ✕ **Water's Edge.** This pleasantly rustic eatery would have to float to be any closer to the ocean. Proprietor Seamus Day is committed to serving conch in any way, shape, or form—conch salad, cracked conch, conch creole, curried conch, and even conch po'boys. Other choices include giant, juicy "Goo Burgers," made-from-scratch pizza, and homemade pies. ✉ *Duke St., Grand Turk,* ☎ *649/946–1680. MC, V. Closed Sun.*

CAFÉS

$ ✕ **Courtyard Café.** Homemade waffles with fresh fruit and whipped cream? Huge omelets and oversized muffins? Submarine sandwiches and pasta salad? It's all at this casual café, where you can enjoy your meal in the cool shade of the garden courtyard. Prices are reasonable and daily specials range from lasagna and quiche to island-style beef patties. ✉ *Duke St., Grand Turk,* ☎ *649/946–1453. AE, MC, V.*

ECLECTIC

$$–$$$ ✕ **Calico Jack's.** The menu changes daily at this lively restaurant—touted by many residents as the best on the island—in the Turks Head Hotel. Look for lobster, steaks, chicken curry, lamb shanks, pizza, and homemade soups on the menu, as well as an excellent selection of wines. On Friday nights there's a courtyard barbecue, with live music by local musicians. The English pub is usually abuzz with local gossip and mirthful chatter. ✉ *Turks Head Hotel, Duke St., Grand Turk,* ☎ *649/946–2466. MC, V.*

SEAFOOD

$$–$$$ ✕ **Secret Garden.** Menu highlights at the Salt Raker Inn's restaurant include local conch and fish dishes and grilled lobster tail. For dessert try the Caribbean bread pudding or Key Lime pie. Morning offerings include a full English breakfast and an island favorite, fish-and-grits. Wednesday- and Sunday-night sing-alongs, featuring local guitarist/divemaster Mitch Rolling, are popular, as are the Wednesday- and Saturday-night barbecues. ✉ *Salt Raker Inn, Duke St., Grand Turk,* ☎ *649/946–2260. AE, MC, V.*

$–$$ ✕ **Regal Begal.** Drop by this local eatery for island specialties such as cracked conch, minced lobster, and fish-and-chips. It's a casual place with unmemorable decor, but the portions are large and the prices easy on your wallet. ✉ *Hospital Rd., Grand Turk,* ☎ *649/946–2274. No credit cards.*

Beaches

There are more than 230 mi (370 km) of beaches in the Turks and Caicos Islands, ranging from secluded coves to miles-long stretches, and most beaches are soft coralline sand. Tiny cays offer complete isolation for nude sunbathing and skinny-dipping. Many are accessible only by boat. **Governor's Beach,** a long white strip on the west coast of Grand Turk, is one of the nicest, with plenty of sparkling, powder-soft sand on which to stroll.

Outdoor Activities and Sports

CYCLING

The island's flat terrain isn't very taxing, and most roads have hard surfaces. Take water with you: there are few places to stop for refreshment. Most hotels in Cockburn Town have bicycles available, but you can also rent them for $10–$15 a day from **Sea Eye Diving** (☎ FAX 649/946–1407).

SCUBA DIVING AND SNORKELING

In these waters you can find undersea cathedrals, coral gardens, and countless tunnels, but note that you must carry and present a valid certificate card before you'll be allowed to dive. As its name suggests, the **Black Forest** offers staggering black-coral formations as well as the occasional black-tip shark. In the **Library** you can study fish galore, including large numbers of yellowtail snapper. At the Columbus Passage separating South Caicos from Grand Turk, each side of a 22-mi-wide (35-km-wide) channel drops more than 7,000 ft (2,141 m). From January through March, thousands of Atlantic humpback whales swim through en route to their winter breeding grounds.

Dive outfitters can all be found in Cockburn Town. Two-tank boat dives generally cost $60–$75. **Blue Water Divers** (⊠ Salt Raker Inn, Duke St., Grand Turk, ☎ FAX 649/946–1226) has been in operation on Grand Turk since 1983. **Oasis Divers** (⊠ Duke St., Grand Turk, ☎ FAX 649/946–1128) specializes in complete gear handling and pampering treatment. It also supplies NITROX. Besides daily dive trips to the wall, **Sea Eye Diving** (⊠ Duke St., Grand Turk, ☎ FAX 649/946–1407) offers encounters with friendly stingrays.

Nightlife

A fun crowd gathers at **Turk's Head Hotel** (⊠ Duke St., Grand Turk, ☎ 649/946–2466) almost every night. On weekends and holidays the younger crowd heads over to the **Nookie Hill Club** (⊠ Nookie Hill, Grand Turk, ☎ no phone) for late-night wining and dancing. There's folk and pop music at the **Salt Raker Inn** (⊠ Duke St., Grand Turk, ☎ 649/946–2260) on Wednesday and Sunday nights.

Exploring Grand Turk

Pristine beaches with vistas of turquoise waters, small local settlements, historic ruins, and native flora and fauna are among the sights on Grand Turk. Fewer than 5,000 people live on this 7½-square-mi (19-square-km) island, and it's hard to get lost as there aren't many roads.

Numbers in the margin correspond to points of interest on the Turks and Caicos Islands map.

❶ **Cockburn Town.** The buildings in the colony's capital and seat of government reflect a 19th-century Bermudian style of architecture. Narrow streets are lined with low stone walls and old street lamps, now powered by electricity. The once-vital salinas have been restored, and covered benches along the sluices offer shady spots for observing wading birds, including flamingos that frequent the shallows. In one of the oldest stone buildings on the islands, the **Turks & Caicos National Museum** (⊠ Duke St., Grand Turk, ☎ 649/946–2160) houses the Molasses Reef wreck of 1513, the earliest shipwreck discovered in the Americas. The natural history exhibits include artifacts left by Taíno, African, North American, Bermudian, French, and Latin American settlers. An impressive addition to the museum is the coral-reef and sealife exhibit, faithfully modeled on a popular dive site just off the island. The museum is open Monday–Tuesday and Thursday–Friday 9–4, Wednesday 9–6, and Saturday 9–1. Admission is $5.

Salt Cay

Fewer than 100 people live on this 2½-square-mi (6-square-km) dot of land, maintaining an unassuming lifestyle against a backdrop of quaint stucco cottages, stone ruins, and weathered wooden windmills standing sentry in the abandoned salinas. There's not much in the way of development, but there are splendid beaches on the north coast. The most spectacular sights are beneath the waves: 10 dive sites are just minutes from shore.

Lodging

For approximate costs, *see* the lodging price chart *in* Grand Turk.

$$$–$$$$ ⊞ **Windmills Plantation.** The attraction here is the lack of distraction.
★   The hotel resembles a romantic's version of a colonial-era plantation.
The great house has four suites, each with a sitting area, a four-poster
bed, ceiling fans, and a veranda or balcony with a sea view. All are fur-
nished in a mix of antique English and wicker furniture. Four other
rooms are housed in adjacent buildings. Managers Jim and Sharon Shafer
bring a sterling reputation as gracious hosts. ⊠ *North Beach Rd., Salt
Cay,* ☎ *649/946–6962 or 800/822–7715,* FAX *649/946–6930,* WEB
*www.windmillsplantation.com. 4 rooms, 4 suites. Restaurant, bar, no
air-conditioning, no room phones, no room TVs, pool, beach, snorkel-
ing, fishing, hiking, horseback riding, library, no kids. AE, MC, V. BP.*

$ ⊞ **Mount Pleasant Guest House.** This simple, somewhat rustic hotel
was a former salt-plantation home, now serving as a guest house cater-
ing to divers. Rooms are bright, clean, and simply furnished. The
premises are filled with memorabilia and artifacts, and the gazebo bar
overlooks a cut-stone cistern pit converted into a palm grove for ham-
mocks. Meals are superb, with dinners including whelk soup, grilled
fresh fish and lobster, buttery cracked conch, and New York strip
steaks. ⊠ *Balfour Town,* ☎ FAX *649/946–6927,* WEB *www.turksand-
caicos.tc/mtpleasant. 8 rooms. Restaurant, bar, no air-conditioning in
some rooms, no room phones, fans, no room TVs, bicycles, horseback
riding, library. MC, V. FAP, MAP.*

$ ⊞ **Salt Cay Sunset House.** Built in 1832, this historic bed-and-break-
fast and oceanfront café is housed in the oldest salt-plantation home
on Salt Cay, lovingly restored by enthusiastic owners Michele Wells
and Paul Dinsmore. All three bedrooms have en suite baths; there's a
shared living room. Period furnishings can be found throughout.
Michelle serves hearty local and Continental fare for breakfast, lunch,
and dinner on the breezy veranda at the Blue Mermaid Café. ⊠ *Bal-
four Town,* ☎ FAX *649/946–6942,* WEB *www.seaone.org. 3 rooms.
Restaurant, no air-conditioning, no room phones, fans, no room TVs,
beach, snorkeling, horseback riding, Internet. MC, V. BP, MAP.*

Beaches

There are superb beaches on the north coast of **Salt Cay. Big Sand Cay,**
7 mi (11 km) south of Salt Cay, is also known for its long, unspoiled
stretches of open sand.

Outdoor Activities and Sports

SCUBA DIVING AND SNORKELING

Scuba divers can explore the **_Endymion,_** a 140-ft wooden-hull British
warship that sank in 1790. It's off the southern point of Salt Cay. **Reef
Runners** (☎ 649/946–6901) conducts daily trips and rents all the nec-
essary equipment. It costs around $80 for a two-tank dive.

Exploring Salt Cay

Salt sheds and salinas are silent reminders of the days when the island
was a leading producer of salt. Island tours are often conducted by mo-
torized golf cart. From January through March whales pass by on the
way to their winter breeding grounds.

❷ **Balfour Town.** What little development there is on Salt Cay is found
here. It's home to several small hotels and a few stores that sell hand-
woven baskets, T-shirts, convenience foods, and beach items.

THE CAICOS

West Caicos

Accessible only by boat, this uninhabited, untamed island has no facilities whatsoever. A glorious white beach stretches for 1 mi (1½ km) along the northwest point, and the offshore diving here is among the most exotic in the islands. The "Wilds of West Caicos" encompass a pristine wall, about ¼ mi (½ km) from shore, which starts at 35–45 ft (11–14 m) and cascades to 7,000 ft (2,141 m). Here, sharks, eagle rays, and turtles are commonly seen on the many dive sites. It's about an hour boat ride from Provo, but well worth the trip. Most dive operators depart from satellite locations on the south side of Provo for the journey.

Providenciales

In the mid-18th century, so the story goes, a French ship was wrecked near here, and the survivors were washed ashore on an island they gratefully christened La Providentielle. Under the Spanish, the name was changed to Providenciales. Today about 20,000 people live on Provo (as everybody calls it); a considerable number are expatriate British, Canadian, and American businesspeople and retirees, or refugees from nearby Haiti. The island's 44 square mi (114 square km) are by far the most developed in the Turks and Caicos.

Along the beach-lined north shore there are no less than a dozen high-end condominium hotels (some currently under construction), three all-inclusive resorts, and the country's first time-share resort. Residential development is also booming, especially in the upscale Leeward and Chalk Sound areas. Although roads are in desperate need of upgrading, power, water, telecommunications and cable TV utilities are modern and well-serviced.

Lodging

For approximate costs, *see* the lodging price chart *in* Grand Turk.

A popular option on Provo is renting a self-contained villa or private home. **Elliot Holdings and Management Company** (⊠ Box 235, Providenciales, ☎ 649/946–5355, ⟨WEB⟩ www.ElliotHoldings.com) offers a wide selection of modest to magnificent villas in the Leeward, Grace Bay, and Turtle Cove areas of Providenciales. **T. C. Safari** (⊠ Box 64, Providenciales, ☎ 649/941–5043, ⟨WEB⟩ www.tcsafari.tc) has exclusive oceanfront properties in the beautiful and tranquil Sapodilla Bay/Chalk Sound neighborhood on Provo's southwest shores. For the best villa selection, plan to make your reservations three to six months in advance.

$$$$ ⛱ **Grace Bay Club.** Staying at this Swiss-owned, Mediterranean-style
★ resort is a little like being the guest of honor of a very gracious host with unbeatable taste. Suites have breathtaking views of stunning Grace Bay and are furnished with rattan and pickled wood, with Mexican-tile floors and elegant Turkish and Indian throw rugs. Activities range from diving to golf to catered picnics on surrounding islands, but relaxing is the major pastime. Elegant French-Caribbean meals are served in the Anacaona restaurant. ⊠ *Grace Bay (Box 128),* ☎ *649/ 946–5757 or 800/946–5757,* ⟨FAX⟩ *649/946–5758 or 800/946–5758,* ⟨WEB⟩ *www.gracebayclub.com. 21 suites. Restaurant, bar, in-room safes, kitchens, cable TV with movies, in-room VCRs, 2 tennis courts, pool, hot tub, massage, beach, snorkeling, windsurfing, boating, parasail-*

ing, bicycles, shop, laundry service, concierge, Internet, no kids under 12. Closed Sept. AE, MC, V. CP, MAP.

$$$$
★ 🏨 **Point Grace.** This boutique hotel raises the bar for luxury resorts on the islands. Majestically designed in British Colonial style, two oceanfront buildings house magnificent two- and three-bedroom suites. All have expansive terraces overlooking Grace Bay and are furnished with Indonesian hardwood and teak. Hand-painted tiles line the bathrooms and Frette linens cover the king-size, four-poster beds. Two four-bedroom penthouse suites have separate massage rooms and rooftop Jacuzzis. Rolls Royce airport transfers can be requested. ✉ *Grace Bay (Box 700),* ☎ *888/682–3705 or 649/946–5096,* 𝖥𝖠𝖷 *649/946–5097,* 𝖶𝖤𝖡 *www.pointgrace.com. 23 suites, 9 cottages, 2 villas. 2 restaurants, 2 bars, in-room fax, in-room safes, some in-room hot tubs, kitchenettes, microwaves, cable TV with movies, in-room VCRs, pool, massage, beach, snorkeling, windsurfing, boating, parasailing, fishing, bicycles, recreation room, baby-sitting, laundry service, concierge, Internet, business services, car rental. Closed Sept. AE, D, MC, V. CP.*

$$$–$$$$
★ 🅒 🏨 **Beaches Turks & Caicos Resort & Spa.** There's plenty to satisfy families at this member of the Sandals chain, including a children's park complete with a video game center, water slides, a swim-up soda bar, a 1950s-style diner, and a teen disco. Nice rooms, lots of activities, extravagant meals, and many kinds of water sports make this beachfront all-inclusive resort an indulgent experience. Rooms are furnished in rich mahogany and warm tropical tones, with king-size beds; honeymoon villas include a Jacuzzi in the bedroom. The spa offers body wraps, massages, and facials. ✉ *Lower Bight Rd., Grace Bay,* ☎ *649/946–8000 or 800/726–3257,* 𝖥𝖠𝖷 *649/946–8001,* 𝖶𝖤𝖡 *www.beaches.com. 359 rooms, 103 suites. 9 restaurants, 8 bars, nightclub, in-room safes, cable TV with movies, 4 tennis courts, 6 pools, gym, hair salon, hot tub, massage, spa, beach, dive shop, snorkeling, windsurfing, boating, parasailing, fishing, bicycles, recreation room, theater, video game room, shops, baby-sitting, children's programs (ages 0–5), concierge, meeting rooms, car rental. AE, MC, V. All-inclusive.*

$$$–$$$$
🏨 **Royal West Indies Resort.** Distinctive British Colonial architecture and extensive gardens highlight this well-run luxury condominium resort. Private balconies front all units to make the most of the sea view, and interiors are an eclectic blend of wood and fabrics from Central and South America. Although the beach is steps away, the 80-ft-long pool surrounded by tropical fruit trees is a peaceful place to relax and sip a drink from the superb on-site Mango Reef restaurant and bar. ✉ *Grace Bay (Box 482),* ☎ *649/946–5004,* 𝖥𝖠𝖷 *649/946–5008,* 𝖶𝖤𝖡 *www.royalwestindies.com. 99 suites. Restaurant, bar, in-room data ports, in-room safes, kitchenettes, microwaves, cable TV with movies, 2 pools, beach, snorkeling, boating, fishing, laundry facilities, baby-sitting, car rental. AE, MC, V. EP.*

$$$–$$$$
★ 🏨 **The Sands at Grace Bay.** "Simply breathtaking" describes the sparkling ocean views from the huge screened patios and floor-to-ceiling windows adorning units at this beach lover's haven. The upscale condominium resort offers units ranging from studios to three bedrooms; larger suites have two TVs, extra sleeper sofas, and washer-dryers. Contemporary furnishings combine Indonesian wood, wrought iron, and wicker with seaside-tone fabrics to emphasize the resort's theme of sophisticated simplicity. Hemingway's, an excellent oceanfront cabana restaurant and bar, is on site. ✉ *Grace Bay (Box 681),* ☎ *649/941–5199,* 𝖥𝖠𝖷 *649/946–5198,* 𝖶𝖤𝖡 *www.thesandsresort.com. 116 suites. Restaurant, bar, in-room data ports, in-room safes, kitchens, microwaves, cable TV with movies, tennis court, 3 pools, gym, spa,*

beach, snorkeling, boating, bicycles, shop, baby-sitting, laundry facilities, concierge, car rental. AE, MC, V. EP.

$$-$$$$ 🏨 **Coral Gardens.** This intimate beachfront resort fronts one of Provo's
★   best snorkeling reefs and is in a tranquil area well west of bustling Grace Bay. The deluxe suites have terraces and floor-to-ceiling walls of sliding glass. Gourmet kitchens open into the dining areas, and bedrooms and baths overlook the luxurious gardens. The beachfront area is accented by two dramatic waterfalls cascading down the face of each building. Fine dining alfresco is offered at Coyaba Restaurant. ✉ *Penn's Rd., The Bight (Box 281),* ☎ *649/941–3713 or 800/532–8536,* FAX *649/ 941–5171,* WEB *www.coralgardens.com. 28 suites. 2 restaurants, 2 bars, room service, in-room data ports, in-room safes, kitchens, microwaves, cable TV with movies, 2 pools, aerobics, massage, beach, snorkeling, boating, fishing, laundry facilities, concierge, Internet, car rental. AE, MC, V. EP.*

$$-$$$$ 🏨 **Ocean Club.** These luxury all-suites condominiums are on a 12-mi
★   (19-km) stretch of pristine beach, a short walk from Provo's only golf course. Units range from efficiency studios to three-bedroom suites with living rooms, dining rooms, kitchens, and screened balconies. Management and service are consistently superb. You can take a free shuttle to use the facilities of sister property, Ocean Club West. The on-site Gecko Grille serves creative island dishes. ✉ *Grace Bay (Box 240),* ☎ *649/946–5880 or 800/457–8787,* FAX *649/946–5845,* WEB *www. oceanclubresorts.com. 86 suites. 2 restaurants, 2 bars, in-room data ports, in-room safes, some kitchens, kitchenettes, microwaves, cable TV with movies, tennis court, 2 pools, gym, spa, beach, dive shop, snorkeling, boating, shops, laundry facilities, concierge, Internet, meeting room, car rental. AE, MC, V. EP.*

$$-$$$$ 🏨 **Ocean Club West.** This sister property to the Ocean Club maintains
★   signature details of the original—breathtaking seascapes, large balconies, and exquisite landscaping—while expanding the oceanfront central courtyard area to include a gazebo-capped island, winding free-form pool, and a seaside café and swim-up bar. Interiors are decorated in subdued sophistication, utilizing whites, light woods, and wicker. Junior one-bedrooms are an especially good value. ✉ *Grace Bay (Box 640),* ☎ *649/946–5880 or 800/457–8787,* FAX *649/946–5845,* WEB *www.oceanclubresorts.com. 90 suites. 1 restaurant, 1 bar, in-room data ports, in-room safes, some kitchens, kitchenettes, microwaves, cable TV with movies, tennis court, 2 pools, gym, spa, beach, dive shop, snorkeling, boating, laundry facilities, concierge, Internet, meeting room, car rental. AE, MC, V. EP.*

$$-$$$ 🏨 **Allegro Resort and Casino Turks & Caicos.** This sprawling beachfront property is an all-inclusive resort that caters primarily to adults (though it still welcomes children). The oversize oceanfront rooms have rattan furniture, a rich Caribbean color scheme, and private balcony or terrace. A pool-patio area and a PADI 5-Star dive facility are on site. Meals range from Caribbean fare to Italian specialties, with unlimited beverages. The American Casino, the island's only gaming facility, is here. ✉ *Grace Bay (Box 205),* ☎ *649/946–5555 or 800/858–2258,* FAX *649/946–5522,* WEB *www.allegroresorts.com. 186 rooms. 3 restaurants, 3 bars, in-room safes, cable TV with movies, 3 tennis courts, pool, aerobics, gym, hot tub, massage, beach, dive shop, snorkeling, windsurfing, boating, fishing, bicycles, volleyball, casino, theater, shops, baby-sitting, children's programs (ages 4–12), laundry service, concierge, Internet, meeting rooms, travel services, car rental. AE, MC, V. All-inclusive.*

$$ 🏨 **Club Med Turkoise.** This village is a major water-sports center, with scuba diving, windsurfing, sailing, and waterskiing on the turquoise waters at the doorstep. Two- and three-story bungalows line a 1-mi

(1½-km) beach, and all the usual sybaritic pleasures are here. This all-inclusive (except drinks) club is geared toward couples, singles age 18 and over, and divers. There are also a flying trapeze, nightly entertainment, dive packages, and excursions offered to sites in the Turks and Caicos. ⊠ *Grace Bay,* ☎ *649/946–5491 or 800/258–2633,* ︎FAX *649/946–5497,* ︎WEB *www.clubmed.com. 288 rooms. 2 restaurants, 3 bars, cable TV with movies, 8 tennis courts, pool, aerobics, gym, hot tub, massage, beach, dive shop, snorkeling, windsurfing, boating, fishing, bicycles, billiards, soccer, volleyball, dance club, theater, shops, laundry services, no kids. AE, MC, V. All-inclusive.*

$–$$ 🏨 **Comfort Suites.** Although Comfort Suites is the island's only "franchise" hotel, the property's exceptional hospitality and superior performance are anything but standard. Suites are housed in two three-story buildings built around an Olympic-size pool and landscaped patio area; frosty drinks are served at the tiki bar. Like the rest of the hotel, rooms are spotless and furnished in bright Caribbean colors. Grace Bay's pearly white beach is just across the street. The hotel flanks the Ports of Call shopping village. ⊠ *Grace Bay (Box 590),* ☎ *649/946–8888 or 888/678–3483,* ︎FAX *649/946–5444,* ︎WEB *www.comfortsuitestci.com. 100 suites. Bar, in-room data ports, in-room safes, refrigerators, cable TV with movies, pool, shops, travel services. AE, MC, V. CP.*

$ 🏨 **Back of Beyond.** As the name suggests, this retreat is set apart from Provo's hustle and bustle on the quiet south shore. A burnished-orange stucco, pueblo-style inn houses the nine rooms, each charmingly decorated by proprietress Coleen Darragh, who with husband Ed designed and built the distinctive building to complement the surrounding cactus-dotted terrain. Rooms and the dining patio overlook the turquoise-green hues of the ocean beyond; a secluded white sand beach is just a stroll away. Coleen's hospitality extends to the on-site restaurant and bar, where she cooks and serves home-style "comfort" fare. ⊠ *Venetian Rd., Discovery Bay,* ☎ *649/941–4555,* ︎WEB *www.backofbeyond.tc. 9 rooms. Restaurant, bar, no air-conditioning, fans, no room TVs, pool. No credit cards. BP.*

$ 🏨 **Turtle Cove Inn.** This pleasant, two-story inn offers affordable, comfortable lodging much in favor with scuba, boating, and fishing enthusiasts. All rooms include a private balcony or patio overlooking either the courtyard's lush tropical gardens and pool or Turtle Cove Marina. Dockside is the Tiki Hut Cabana Bar and Grill, a popular local watering hole; in another corner there's the more upscale Terrace restaurant. You can readily stroll to the snorkeling trail at Smith's Reef, and access the remaining miles of north shore beach from there. ⊠ *Turtle Cove Marina, Turtle Cove (Box 131),* ☎ *649/946–4203 or 800/887–0477,* ︎FAX *649/946–4141,* ︎WEB *www.turtlecoveinn.com. 28 rooms, 2 suites. 2 restaurants, 2 bars, in-room safes, refrigerators, cable TV with movies, pool, marina, fishing, bicycles, shops, car rental, no smoking rooms. AE, MC, V. EP.*

Dining

There are more than 50 restaurants on Provo, ranging from casual to elegant, with cuisine from Continental to Asian (and everything in between). You can spot the islands' own Caribbean influence no matter where you go, exhibited in fresh seafood specials, colorful presentations, and a tangy dose of spice.

For approximate costs, *see* the dining price chart *in* Grand Turk.

CARIBBEAN

$$–$$$ ✕ **Mango Reef.** Third generation restaurateur Doug Camozzi (of Tiki Hut fame) was determined to spotlight Caribbean ingredients when he created the menu for his newest venture, in the Royal West Indies

Resort. The end result is a marvelous medley of flavors, colors, and textures made by marinating meats and seafoods prior to grilling and pairing them with inventive fruit- and vegetable-based chutneys and salsas. Meals are served throughout the day, and the separate bar area is a popular evening spot for residents. ⊠ *Royal West Indies Resort, Grace Bay,* ☎ *649/946–8200. AE, MC, V.*

DELI

$ ✗ **Top o' the Cove New York Style Delicatessen.** You can walk to this tiny café on Leeward Highway, just south of Turtle Cove. Order breakfast, deli sandwiches, salads, and enticingly rich desserts and freshly baked goods. From the deli case you can buy the fixings for a picnic; the shop's shelves are stocked with an eclectic selection of fancy foodstuffs. Open from 6:30 AM on weekdays and Saturday, from 8 to 2 on Sunday. ⊠ *Leeward Hwy., Turtle Cove,* ☎ FAX *649/946–4694. No credit cards.*

ECLECTIC

$$$–$$$$ ✗ **Anacaona.** At the Grace Bay Club, this *palapa*-style restaurant (with
★ tables clustered under large thatched-roof structures) offers a memorable dining experience minus the tie, the air-conditioning, and the attitude. Start with a bottle of fine wine and then enjoy a three- or four-course meal of the chef's light but flavorful cooking, which combines traditional European recipes with Caribbean fare. Oil lamps on the tables, gently circulating ceiling fans, and the murmur of the trade winds add to the Eden-like environment. ⊠ *Grace Bay Club, Grace Bay,* ☎ *649/946–5050. AE, MC, V.*

$$$–$$$$ ✗ **Coyaba Restaurant.** As founding member of the local chapter of the Chaîne des Rôtisseurs, chef Paul Newman lets his talent soar at Coral Gardens' elegantly appointed, terrace-style restaurant. A typical meal (served on Royal Doulton china, no less) might start with truffle mousse, follow with chipotle-glazed maple leaf duck breast, and finish with upside down apple pie, all complemented by wines from the outstanding list. The careful attention to detail makes an evening here live up to its name's translation from the Arawak Indian tongue, "heavenly." ⊠ *Coral Gardens, Penn's Rd., The Bight,* ☎ *649/946–5186. Reservations essential. AE, MC, V. Closed Tues.*

$$–$$$$ ✗ **Gecko Grille.** At this Ocean Club resort restaurant you can eat indoors surrounded by tropical murals or out on the garden patio, where the trees are interwoven with tiny twinkling lights. Creative "Floribbean" fare combines native specialties with exotic fruits and zesty island spices and includes Black Angus steaks grilled to order. There's live music Sunday and Wednesday evenings. ⊠ *Ocean Club, Grace Bay,* ☎ *649/ 946–5885. AE, MC, V. Closed Mon.*

$$$ ✗ **Caicos Café Bar and Grill.** There's a pervasive air of celebration in the tree-shaded outdoor dining terrace of this popular eatery. Choose from fresh grilled seafood, steak, lamb, and chicken served hot off the outdoor barbecue. Owner-chef Pierrik Marziou adds a French accent to his appetizers, salads, and homemade desserts. ⊠ *Across from Allegro Resort, Grace Bay,* ☎ *649/946–5278. AE, MC, V.*

$$$ ✗ **The Terrace.** One of the most popular dining spots on Provo, on the grounds of the Turtle Cove Inn, specializes in creative conch dishes, such as conch ravioli and conch fillets encrusted with ground pecans, as well as fresh local fish served with fruit salsas. The house salad, sprinkled with pine nuts and shaved, aged Parmesan, is excellent, as are the hot bread pockets served with your meal. Top it all off with a classic crème brûlée or scoop of homemade ice cream. ⊠ *Turtle Cove Inn, Turtle Cove Marina, Turtle Cove,* ☎ *649/946–4763. AE, MC, V. Closed Sun.*

ITALIAN

\$\$–\$\$\$ ✕ **Baci Ristoranté.** Aromas redolent of the Mediterranean waft from the open kitchen as you walk into this intimate eatery east of Turtle Cove. Outdoor seating is on a romantic canal-front patio. The menu offers a small, varied selection of Italian delights. Main courses focus on veal, but also include pasta, chicken, and fresh fish dishes. House wines are personally selected by the owners and complement the tasteful wine list. Try the tiramisu for dessert with a flavored coffee drink. ✉ *Harbour Town, Turtle Cove,* ☎ *649/941–3044. AE, MC, V. Closed Mon.*

SEAFOOD

\$\$ ✕ **Banana Boat.** Buoys and other sea relics deck the walls of this lively restaurant/bar on the wharf. Grilled grouper, lobster salad sandwiches, conch fritters, and conch salad are among the options. Tropical drinks include the rum-filled Banana Breeze—a house specialty. ✉ *Turtle Cove Marina, Turtle Cove,* ☎ *649/941–5706. AE, MC, V.*

TEX-MEX

\$–\$\$ ✕ **Hey Jose's Caribbean Cantina.** Frequented by locals, this restaurant, just south of Turtle Cove, claims to serve the island's best margaritas. Customers also return for the tasty Tex-Mex treats: tacos, tostados, nachos, burritos, fajitas, and special-recipe hot chicken wings. Thick, hearty pizzas are another favorite—especially the "Kitchen Sink," with a little bit of everything thrown in! ✉ *Central Square, Leeward Hwy., Turtle Cove,* ☎ *649/946–4812. MC, V. Closed Sun.*

Beaches

A fine white-sand beach stretches 12 mi (19 km) along Provo's **north coast,** where most of the hotels are. There are also good beaches at **Sapodilla Bay** and **Malcolm Roads,** at North West Point, which is accessible only by four-wheel-drive vehicles.

Outdoor Activities and Sports

BICYCLING

Provo has a few steep grades to conquer, but they're short. Unfortunately, traffic on Leeward Highway and rugged road edges make pedaling here a less-than-relaxing experience. Instead, try the less-traveled roads through the native settlements of Blue Hills, the Bight, and Five Cays. Most hotels have bikes available. You can rent mountain bikes at **Provo Fun Cycles** (✉ Ports of Call, Grace Bay, ☎ 649/946–5868) for $15 a day.

BOATING AND SAILING

Provo's calm, reef-protected turquoise seas combine with constant easterly trade winds for excellent sailing conditions. Several multihulled vessels offer charters with snorkeling stops, food and beverage service, and sunset vistas. Prices range from $39 for group trips to $600 or more for private charters. **Atabeyra** (☎ 649/941–5363) is a retired rum runner and the choice of residents for special events. **Sail Provo** (☎ 649/946–4783) runs 57-ft and 48-ft catamarans on scheduled half-day, full-day, and sunset cruises.

FISHING

The island's fertile waters are great for angling—anything from bottom- and reef fishing (most likely to produce plenty of bites and a large catch) to bonefishing and deep-sea fishing (among the finest in the Caribbean). You're required to purchase a $15 visitor's fishing license; operators generally furnish all equipment, drinks, and snacks. Prices range from $100 to $375, depending on the length of trip and size of boat. You can rent a boat with a captain for a half or full day of bottom- or bonefishing through **J&B Tours** (✉ Leeward Marina, Leeward,

☎ 649/946–5047). For deep-sea fishing trips in search of marlin, sailfish, wahoo, tuna, barracuda, and shark, look up *Sakitumi* (✉ Turtle Cove Marina, Turtle Cove, ☎ 649/946–4065). Captain Arthur Dean at **Silver Deep** (✉ Leeward Marina, Leeward, ☎ 649/946–5612) is said to be among the Caribbean's finest bonefishing guides.

GOLF

Provo Golf and Country Club's (☎ 649/946–5991) par-72, 18-hole championship course, designed by Karl Litten, is a combination of lush greens and fairways, rugged limestone outcroppings and freshwater lakes. Fees are $120 for 18 holes with shared cart.

PARASAILING

A 15-minute parasailing flight over Grace Bay is available for $60 (single) or $110 (tandem) at **Turtle Parasail** (☎ 649/231–0643).

SCUBA DIVING AND SNORKELING

For excellent close-to-shore snorkeling, try the **White House Reef,** off Penn's Road in the Bight, and **Smith's Reef,** over Bridge Road east of Turtle Cove. Both offer marked underwater snorkeling trails.

Scuba diving in the crystalline waters surrounding the islands ranks among the best in the Caribbean. The reef and wall drop-offs thrive with bright, unbroken coral formations and lavish numbers of fish and marine life. Mimicking the idyllic climate, waters are warm all year, averaging 76–78°F in the winter and 82–84°F during the summer. With minimal rainfall and soil runoff, visibility is naturally good and frequently superb, ranging from 60 to 150 ft (18 to 46 m) plus. An extensive system of marine national parks and boat moorings, combined with an ecoconscious mindset among dive operators, contributes to an underwater environment little changed in centuries.

Dive operators in Provo regularly visit sites at **Grace Bay** and **Pine Cay** for spur-and-groove coral formations and bustling reef diving. They make the longer journey to the dramatic walls at **North West Point** and **West Caicos,** depending on weather conditions. Instruction from the major diving agencies is available for all levels and certifications.

Art Pickering's Provo Turtle Divers (☎ 649/946–4232 or 800/833–1341), at the Ocean Club, Ocean Club West, and in Turtle Cove Marina, has been on Provo for more than 30 years. The staff is friendly, knowledgeable, and unpretentious. **Big Blue Unlimited** (✉ Leeward Marina, Leeward, ☎ 649/946–5034) specializes in eco-diving adventures, with a certified marine biologist on staff. It also offers Nitrox, Trimix, and rebreathers. **Caicos Adventures** (✉ Caicos Cafe Plaza, Grace Bay, ☎ FAX 649/946–3346) is run by friendly Frenchman Fifi Kuntz, and offers daily West Caicos trips with night dives on the West Caicos wall. **Dive Provo** (✉ Allegro Resort, Ports of Call, Grace Bay, ☎ 649/946–5040 or 800/234–7768) is a resort-based, PADI 5-Star operation that runs daily one- and two-tank dives to popular Grace Bay sites. **Flamingo Divers** (✉ Turtle Cove Landing, Turtle Cove, ☎ 649/946–4193 or 800/204–9282) focuses on small groups and personalized service.

TENNIS

The following hotels have courts open to nonguests. Prices vary, so call before you go. **Club Med Turkoise** (☎ 649/946–5491) has eight courts; four of them are lit for night games. **Erebus Inn** (☎ 649/946–4240) has clay courts, both of them lit. **Grace Bay Club** (☎ 649/946–5754) has two lit courts. The **Ocean Club and Ocean Club West** (☎ 649/946–5880) have one and two lit courts, respectively. You can rent equipment at **Provo Golf and Country Club** (☎ 649/946–5991) and play on their two lit courts.

WATERSKIING AND WINDSURFING

Windsurfers find the calm turquoise water ideal. **Windsurfing Provo** (⊠ Ocean Club, Grace Bay, ☎ 649/946–5649; ⊠ Ocean Club West, Grace Bay, ☎ 649/946–5649) rents windsurfers, kayaks, motorboats, and Hobie Cats and offers windsurfing instruction.

Shopping

Don't expect the variety of goods offered on more developed Caribbean destinations. There are several main shopping areas in Provo: Market Place and Central Square, on the Leeward Highway about ½ mi to 1 mi outside of downtown Providenciales, and the shopping village Ports of Call, in Grace Bay. Delicate woven baskets, polished conch shells, paintings, wood carvings, handmade dolls, and small metalwork are the only crafts native to the area.

The **Bamboo Gallery** (⊠ Market Place, Leeward Hwy., Downtown Providenciales, ☎ FAX 649/946–4748) sells Caribbean art, from vivid Haitian paintings to wood carvings and local metal sculptures. For a large selection of duty-free liquors, visit **Carib West** (⊠ Airport Rd., Downtown Providenciales, ☎ 649/946–4215). **Greensleeves** (⊠ Central Square, Leeward Hwy., Turtle Cove, ☎ FAX 649/946–4147) offers paintings by local artists, island-made rag rugs, baskets, jewelry, and sisal mats and bags. **Marilyn's Craft** (⊠ Ports of Call, Grace Bay, no phone) sells handmade dolls, rag rugs, and wood carvings, plus tropical clothing and knickknacks. **Paradise Gifts** (⊠ Central Square, Leeward Hwy., Turtle Cove, ☎ 649/941–3828) offers a creative selection of decorated T-shirts, handmade jewelry, and paintings by local artists. From outlets at the Provo airport, Allegro Resort, Arch Plaza, Beaches, Club Med, Ocean Club Plaza, and The Sands at Grace Bay, **Royal Jewels** (☎ 649/946–4699) sells gold and jewelry, designer watches, perfumes, fine leather goods and cameras—all duty free.

With more than 20,000 items, including a large fresh produce section, on-site bakery, and extensive meat counter, **IGA Supermarket** (⊠ Leeward Hwy., Grace Bay, ☎ 649/941–5000), Provo's largest, is likely to have what you're looking for. Be prepared: prices are much higher than you would expect at home. If you need to supplement your beach reading stock or are looking for island-specific materials, visit **The Unicorn Bookstore** (⊠ Market Place, Leeward Hwy., Downtown Providenciales, ☎ 649/941–5458) for a wide assortment of books and magazines, including a large children's section.

Termed "the best little watersports shop in Provo," **Seatopia** (⊠ Leeward Hwy., Grace Bay, ☎ 649/941–3355; ⊠ Ports of Call, Grace Bay, no phone) sells reasonably priced scuba and snorkeling equipment, swimwear, beachwear, sandals, hats, and related water gear and swim toys. Besides having a licensed pharmacist on duty, **Super Value Pharmacy** (⊠ South Winds Plaza, Downtown Providenciales, ☎ 649/941–3779), just east of downtown Provo, stocks a super selection of cosmetics, greeting cards, baby care products, souvenirs, household goods, even beer, wine, and liquors.

Nightlife

Residents and tourists flock to **Lattitudes** (⊠ Ports of Call, Grace Bay, ☎ 649/946–5832) on Friday nights to let their hair down. There are a pool table and satellite sports on five TVs in the bar. On Thursday nights you can find a local band and lively crowd at **Sharkbite Bar & Grill** (⊠ Harbour Town, Turtle Cove, ☎ 649/941–5090). Also known as The Nightclub, the new **Stardust & Ashes** (⊠ Leeward Hwy., Grace Bay, ☎ 649/941–5475) sets the stage for a great night out with music and dancing on a torch-lit tropical terrace and luxurious lounge areas for private moments. The sound system and lighting are state of the art and entertainment themes vary nightly.

The only casino on the island is the **American Casino** (✉ Allegro Resort, Grace Bay, ☎ 649/946–5508). It's open to all and includes 80 slot machines and several table games including blackjack, Caribbean stud poker, and roulette. Drinks are free for all players.

Exploring Providenciales

Numbers in the margin correspond to points of interest on the Turks and Caicos Island map.

③ Downtown Providenciales. Near Providenciales International Airport, downtown Provo is really an extended strip mall that houses a grocery store, car-rental and travel agencies, law offices, banks, and other businesses.

④ Caicos Conch Farm. On the northeast tip of Provo, this is a major mariculture operation where mollusks are farmed commercially (more than 3 million conch are here). Guided tours are available; call to confirm times. The small gift shop sells conch-related souvenirs. ✉ *Leeward-Going-Through, Leeward,* ☎ *649/946–5330.* ➭ *$6.* ☉ *Mon.–Sat. 9–4.*

Little Water Cay

This small, uninhabited cay is a protected area under the National Trust of the Turks and Caicos. On these 150 acres are two trails, small lakes, red mangroves, and an abundance of native plants. Boardwalks protect the ground and interpretive signs explain the habitat. The cay is the habitat of about 2,000 rare, endangered rock iguanas. They say the iguanas are shy, but these creatures actually seem rather curious. They waddle right up to you, as if posing for a picture; you can usually get within a foot of them before they move.

Parrot Cay

Once said to be a hideout for pirate Calico Jack Rackham and his lady cohorts Mary Reid and Anne Bonny, the 1,000-acre cay, between Fort George Cay and North Caicos, is now the site of an ultra-exclusive hideaway resort, a holistic health spa, and upscale homesites. Bordered by a wild stretch of pristine beach to the north and mangrove-lined wetlands to the south, tiny Parrot Cay is a natural wonder.

Lodging

For approximate costs, *see* the lodging price chart *in* Grand Turk.

$$$$ ⊡ **Parrot Cay Resort.** Frequented by celebrities and the international
★ ultrachic, this exclusive resort combines natural beauty and elegant simplicity to create a rarified atmosphere of tranquility. Mediterranean-style hillside structures house one- and two-bedroom suites, all with private terraces overlooking the ocean. Seaside villas include some private pools, butler service, and fully equipped kitchens, complete with chef and waitstaff on request. The on-site Shambhala Spa has been ranked among the top 10 in the world. The resort can only be accessed by private boat from Leeward Marina. ✉ *Box 164, Providenciales,* ☎ *649/ 946–7788,* FAX *649/946–7789,* WEB *www.parrot-cay.com. 58 rooms. 2 restaurants, 2 bars, room service, in-room data ports, in-room safes, some kitchens, minibars, cable TV with movies, in-room VCRs, 2 tennis courts, pool, gym, hot tub, Japanese baths, massage, sauna, spa, steam room, beach, snorkeling, windsurfing, boating, waterskiing, fishing, mountain bikes, library, baby-sitting, laundry service. AE, MC, V. BP.*

Pine Cay

One of a chain of small cays linking North Caicos and Provo, 800-acre Pine Cay is where you'll find the Meridian Club—a retreat for people seeking peaceful seclusion. Its 2½-mi (4-km) beach is among the most beautiful in the archipelago. The island has a 3,800-ft (1,162-m) airstrip and electric golf carts for getting around. Offshore is the **Football Fields** dive site, which has been called the Grand Central Station of the fish world.

Lodging

For approximate costs, *see* the lodging price chart *in* Grand Turk.

$$$$ ⊡ **Meridian Club.** Here you can enjoy an unspoiled cay with vast
★ stretches of soft, white sand and a 500-acre nature reserve that lures bird-watchers and botanists. A stay here is truly getting away from it all, as there are no air-conditioners, phones, or TVs. Accommodations are in spacious rooms with king-size beds and patios, as well as cottages that range from rustic to well appointed. Meals and activities are included in the room rate, as is your boat or air-taxi trip from Provo. ✉ *Pine Cay (456 Glenbrook Rd., Stamford, CT 06906),* ☎ *no direct phone to hotel;* 800/331–9154 *or* 203/602–0300 *for reservations only,* ⨎ 649/941–7010 *direct to hotel;* 203/602–2265 *U.S. reservations number,* ⓦⓔⓑ *www.meridianclub.com. 12 rooms, 38 cottages. Restaurant, bar, no air-conditioning, no room phones, fans, no room TVs, tennis court, pool, beach, snorkeling, windsurfing, boating, fishing, bicycles, library, airstrip, no kids under 12. No credit cards. All-inclusive, EP, FAP.*

North Caicos

Thanks to abundant rainfall, this 41-square-mi (106-square-km) island is the lushest of the Turks and Caicos. Bird lovers can see a large flock of flamingos here, and fishermen can find creeks full of bonefish and tarpon. Bring all your own gear; this quiet island has no watersports shops. Although there's no traffic, almost all the roads are paved, so bicycling is an excellent way to sightsee.

Lodging

For approximate costs, *see* the lodging price chart *in* Grand Turk.

$$$ ⊡ **Prospect of Whitby Hotel.** This secluded, all-inclusive retreat is run
★ by an Italian resort chain, Club Vacanze. Miles of beach are yours for sunbathing, windsurfing, or snorkeling. Spacious rooms have elegant Tuscan floor tiles and pastel pink paneling; in true getaway fashion, rooms lack TVs but include minibars. The restaurant, on a veranda overlooking the sea, is excellent, with a selection of local, Italian, and international dishes served buffet style. Scuba diving and daily excursions to nearby natural wonders are included. ✉ *Whitby,* ☎ 649/946–7119; 305/235–4780 *for reservations only,* ⨎ 649/946–7114; 305/235–4781 *for reservations only,* ⓦⓔⓑ *www.prospectofwhitby.com. 23 rooms, 4 suites. Restaurant, bar, piano bar, minibars, in-room safes, no room TVs, tennis court, pool, beach, dive shop, snorkeling, windsurfing, boating, fishing, bicycles. AE, MC, V. All-inclusive.*

$–$$ ⊡ **Ocean Beach Hotel Condominiums.** This unpretentious place provides family-style accommodations on a 10-mi (16-km) stretch of sheltered beach. The spacious units, some with kitchenettes, face the ocean and are cooled by the constant tradewinds. You can learn about local plants from the botanical walk encircling the premises. Diving, snorkeling, and exploring trips are arranged through Beach Cruiser Charters, at the hotel. ✉ *Whitby,* ☎ 649/946–7113 *or* 800/710–5204; 905/690–3817 *in Canada,* FAX *649/946–7386,* WEB *www.turksandcaicos.tc/oceanbeach. 3 rooms, 7 suites. Restaurant, bar, no air-conditioning, fans, some kitchenettes, pool, beach, dive shop, snorkeling, boating, fishing, bicycles, car rental. AE, MC, V. Closed from June to Oct. BP, FAP, MAP.*

$$ 🏨 **Pelican Beach Hotel.** Built and operated by Clifford Gardiner (the Islands' first licensed solo pilot) and his family, this laid-back hotel fronts beautiful expanses of deserted, windswept beach. Large rooms are done in pastels and dark-wood trim; the sound of breaking waves will soothe you in the first-floor beachfront units. Excellent local dishes and homemade bread are served in the airy dining room shaded by a grove of whispering casuarina pines. ⊠ *Whitby,* ☎ *649/946–7112,* FAX *649/ 946–7139. 14 rooms, 2 suites. Restaurant, bar, no room TVs, beach, fishing. MAP.*

Beaches

The beaches of North Caicos are superb for shelling and lolling, and the waters offshore have excellent snorkeling, bonefishing, and scuba diving.

Exploring North Caicos

❺ **Flamingo Pond.** This is a regular nesting place for the beautiful pink birds. They tend to wander out in the middle of the pond, so bring binoculars.

❻ **Kew.** This settlement has a small post office, school, church, and ruins of old plantations—all set among lush tropical trees bearing limes, papayas, and custard apples. Visiting Kew will give you a better understanding of the daily life of many islanders.

Middle Caicos

At 48 square mi (124 square km) and with fewer than 300 residents, this is the largest and least developed of the inhabited Turks and Caicos. A limestone ridge runs to about 125 ft (38 m) above sea level, creating dramatic cliffs on the north shore and a cave system farther inland. Middle Caicos is best suited to those looking to unwind and who enjoy nature.

Lodging

For approximate costs, *see* the lodging price chart *in* Grand Turk.

$$ 🏨 **Blue Horizon Resort.** Breathtaking scenery and sweet seclusion abound in this 50-acre retreat. Cottages (and two villas) come in several different sizes; all have screened-in porches, bleached wood furniture, comfortable beds, and spectacular views of the beachfront cliff, where there's a hillside cave and private ocean swimming cove. Fax a (basic) grocery list ahead of time, and management will stock your refrigerator. Activities by request include spelunking, fishing, and snorkeling with local guides. ⊠ *Mudjin Harbor, Conch Bar,* ☎ *649/946–6141,* FAX *649/946–6139,* WEB *www.bhresort.com. 5 cottages, 2 villas. No air-conditioning in some rooms, no phones in some rooms, fans, some kitchenettes, cable TV with movies in some rooms, no TV in some rooms, beach, snorkeling, fishing, hiking, laundry service. AE, MC, V. EP.*

Exploring Middle Caicos

❼ **Conch Bar Caves.** These limestone caves have eerie underground lakes and milky white stalactites and stalagmites. Archaeologists have discovered Lucayan Indian artifacts in the caves and the surrounding area. It's an easy walk through the main part of the cave, but wear sturdy shoes to avoid slipping. You'll hear, see, and smell some bats, but they don't bother visitors. **J&B Tours** (⊠ Leeward Marina, Leeward, Providenciales, ☎ 649/946–5047, WEB www.jbtours.com) offers boat trips from Provo to the caves.

South Caicos

This 8½-square-mi (21-square-km) island was once an important salt producer; today it's the heart of the fishing industry. Nature prevails, with long, white beaches, jagged bluffs, quiet backwater bays, and salt flats. Diving and snorkeling on the pristine wall and reefs are a treat enjoyed by only a few.

Lodging

For approximate costs, *see* the lodging price chart *in* Grand Turk.

$ 🏨 **South Caicos Ocean Haven.** On Cockburn Harbour, a protected marine sanctuary, this hotel operates as the base from which divers can discover a pristine paradise waters minutes from the dock. Comfortable, air-conditioned rooms have ocean and pool or town views; evenings bring spectacular sunsets overlooking the harbor. The restaurant emphasizes local seafood. Instructors on staff offer PADI courses, with economical dive packages available. ⊠ *West St., Cockburn Harbour,* ☎ 649/946–3444, FAX 649/946–3446, WEB *www.oceanhaven.tc. 22 rooms. Restaurant, bar, saltwater pool, beach, dive shop, snorkeling, windsurfing, boating, fishing. MC, V. EP, FAP.*

Beaches

Due south is **Big Ambergris Cay,** an uninhabited cay about 14 mi (23 km) beyond the Fish Cays, with a magnificent beach at Long Bay. To the north, uninhabited **East Caicos** has a beautiful 17-mi (27-km) beach on its north coast. The island was once a cattle range and the site of a major sisal-growing industry. Both these cays are accessible only by boat.

Exploring South Caicos

Spiny lobster and queen conch are found in the shallow Caicos Bank to the west, and are harvested for export by local processing plants. The bonefishing here is some of the best in the West Indies. **Beyond the Blue** (⊠ Cockburn Harbour, ☎ 649/231–1703, WEB www.beyondtheblue.com) offers bonefishing charters on a specialized airboat, which can operate in less than a foot of water. At the northern end of the island are fine white-sand beaches; the south coast is great for scuba diving along the drop-off; and there's excellent snorkeling off the windward (east) coast, where large stands of elkhorn and staghorn coral shelter several varieties of small tropical fish.

❽ Boiling Hole. Abandoned salinas make up the center of this island—the largest, across from the downtown ball park, receives its water directly from an underground source connected to the ocean through this boiling hole.

❾ Cockburn Harbour. The best natural harbor in the Caicos chain hosts the South Caicos Regatta, held each year in May.

TURKS AND CAICOS A TO Z

To research prices, get advice from other travelers, and book travel arrangements, visit www.fodors.com.

AIR TRAVEL

American Airlines flies three times daily between Miami and Provo, with a fourth flight on Thursdays through Sundays between New York/JFK and Provo. British Airways connects London/Heathrow and Provo on Sundays. Air Canada flies between Toronto and Provo on

Saturdays. Bahamasair flies between Nassau and Provo on Tuesdays, Thursdays, and Sundays. Air Jamaica Express travels to Provo from Montego Bay from Friday through Monday. Turks & Caicos Airways, the national flag carrier, offers regularly scheduled flights between Provo, Grand Turk, and the outer Turks and Caicos Islands. SkyKing connects Provo with Grand Turk and South Caicos several times daily and also offers flights to Cuba, the Dominican Republic, and Haiti. Additionally, in season there are weekly charter flights from a number of North American cities, including Boston, Chicago, Detroit, New York, Philadelphia, Montréal, and Toronto.

➤ AIRLINES AND CONTACTS: **Air Canada** (☎ 888/247–2262 or 800/361–8071). **Air Jamaica Express** (☎ 800/523–5585). **American Airlines** (☎ 649/946–4948 in Turks and Caicos; 800/433–7300). **Bahamasair** (☎ 800/222–4262). **British Airways** (☎ 800/247–9297). **SkyKing** (☎ 649/941–5464). **Turks & Caicos Airways** (☎ 649/946–4255).

AIRPORTS

All international flights currently arrive at Providenciales International Airport. Then you use domestic carriers to fly on to airports in Grand Turk and the out islands of North Caicos, Middle Caicos, South Caicos, and Salt Cay. All have paved runways in good condition and small buildings serving as terminals. Grand Turk International Airport serves the nation's capital, bustling in the early morning and late afternoon with government officials and lawyers returning to Provo. Providenciales International Airport has modern, secure arrival and check-in services. You'll find taxis at the airports, and most resorts provide pickup service. A trip between Provo's airport and most major hotels runs about $15. On Grand Turk a trip from the airport to Cockburn Town is about $8; it's $8–$12 to hotels outside town.

➤ AIRPORT INFORMATION: **Grand Turk International Airport** (☎ 649/946–2233). **Providenciales International Airport** (☎ 649/941–5670).

BIKE AND MOPED TRAVEL

Although scooters are available for rent, in recent years the option has dwindled in popularity with the deteriorating condition of the roads and increase in auto traffic. If you choose to ride a scooter or bicycle, take extra care around steep shoulder drop-offs. Scooter Bob's in Providenciales rents double seater scooters and bicycles (as well as jeeps, SUVs, vans, and cars). Rates are $40 per day for scooters and $20 per day for bicycles.

➤ BIKE AND MOPED RENTALS: **Scooter Bob's** (☎ 649/946–4684).

BOAT AND FERRY TRAVEL

Surprisingly, there is no scheduled boat or ferry service between Provo and the other Turks and Caicos Islands. Instead, islanders tend to catch rides leaving from the marina at Leeward-Going-Through. *Sea Dancer* offers live-aboard diving with weekly trips out of Provo. The *Turks and Caicos Aggressor* live-aboard dive boat plies the islands' pristine sites with weekly charters from Turtle Cove Marina.

➤ BOAT AND FERRY INFORMATION: *Sea Dancer* (☎ 800/932–6237). **The *Turks and Caicos Aggressor*** (☎ 800/348–2628).

BUSINESS HOURS

BANKS

Banks are open Monday–Thursday 9:00–3:00, Friday 9:00–5:00.

POST OFFICES

Post offices are open weekdays from 8 to 4.

SHOPS

Shops are generally open weekdays from 8 or 8:30 to 5.

CAR RENTALS

Car and jeep rental rates average $35–$80 per day, plus a $15-per-rental-agreement government tax. Reserve well ahead of time during the peak winter season. Most agencies offer free mileage and airport pick-up service.

➤ Major Agencies: On Grand Turk: **Tony's Car Rental** (☎ 649/946–1879). On Provo: **Avis** (☎ 649/946–4705). **Budget** (☎ 649/946–4079). **Provo Rent-a-Car** (☎ 649/946–4404). **Rent a Buggy** (☎ 649/946–4158). **Tropical Auto Rentals** (☎ 649/946–5300).

CAR TRAVEL

GASOLINE

Because it must be imported, gasoline runs around $3.00 per gallon.

ROAD CONDITIONS

There are paved, two-lane roads connecting the resort areas, airport, and major settlements on Providenciales. However, they're often pocked with potholes and have steep shoulder drop-offs. A major road rehabilitation project is reportedly in the making. Dusty, rutted side roads are in worse condition. Ironically, the little-traveled roads in Grand Turk and the out islands are, in general, smooth and paved.

RULES OF THE ROAD

Driving here is on the left side of the road; when pulling out into traffic, remember to look to your right.

ELECTRICITY

Electricity is fairly stable throughout the islands, and the current is suitable for all U.S. appliances (120/240 volts, 60 Hz).

EMERGENCIES

➤ Ambulance and Fire: **Ambulance and Fire** (☎ 911).
➤ Hospitals: **Associated Medical Practices** (✉ Leeward Hwy., Glass Shack, Providenciales, ☎ 649/946–4242). **Grand Turk Hospital** (✉ Hospital Rd., Grand Turk, ☎ 649/946–2333).
➤ Pharmacies: **Government Clinic** (✉ Grand Turk Hospital, Grand Turk, ☎ 649/946–2040). **Super Value Pharmacy** (✉ South Winds Plaza, Downtown Providenciales, Providenciales, ☎ 649/941–3779).
➤ Police: Police (☎ 649/946–2499 in Grand Turk; 649/946–7116 in North Caicos; 649/946–4259 in Provo; 649/946–3299 in South Caicos).
➤ Scuba Diving Emergencies: **Associated Medical Practices** (✉ Leeward Hwy., Glass Shack, Providenciales, ☎ 649/946–4242) has a hyperbaric chamber.

HOLIDAYS

Public holidays are: New Year's Day, Commonwealth Day (second Monday in March), Maundy Thursday, Good Friday, Easter Monday, National Heroes Day (last Monday in May), Queen's Birthday (third Monday in June), Emancipation Day (first Monday in August), National Youth Day (last Monday in September), Columbus Day (second Monday in October), International Human Rights Day (last Monday in October), Christmas Day (Dec. 25), and Boxing Day (Dec. 26).

LANGUAGE

The official language of the Turks and Caicos is English. Native islanders (termed "Belongers") are of African descent, though the population—especially on cosmopolitan Provo—also consists of Canadian, British, American, European, Haitian, and Dominican expats.

MAIL AND SHIPPING

The main branch of the post office is in downtown Provo at the corner of Airport Road. It costs 50¢ to send a postcard to the United States, 60¢ to Canada and the United Kingdom, and $1.25 to Australia and New Zealand; letters, per ounce, cost 60¢ to the United States, 80¢ to Canada and the United Kingdom, and $1.40 to Australia and New Zealand. When writing to the Turks and Caicos Islands, be sure to include the specific island and "Turks and Caicos Islands, BWI" (British West Indies). Delivery service is provided by FedEx, with offices in Provo and Grand Turk.

➤ CONTACTS: **FedEx** On Grand Turk (☎ 649/946–2542); on Provo (☎ 649/946–4682).

MONEY MATTERS

Prices quoted in this chapter are in U.S. dollars. Barclays Bank, Scotiabank, and CIBC have offices on Provo, with branches on Grand Turk. Many larger hotels and the casino can take care of your money requests. Bring small denominations to the less-populated islands.

➤ CONTACTS: **Barclays Bank** (☎ 649/946–4245). **CIBC** (☎ 649/946–5303). **Scotiabank** (☎ 649/946–4750).

ATMS

There are few ATMs on the islands.

CREDIT CARDS

Major credit cards and traveler's checks are accepted at many establishments.

CURRENCY

The unit of currency is the U.S. dollar.

PASSPORTS AND VISAS

U.S. and Canadian citizens need some proof of citizenship, such as a birth certificate (original or certified copy), plus a photo ID or a current passport. All other travelers, including those from the United Kingdom, Australia, and New Zealand, require a current passport. Everyone must have an ongoing or return ticket.

SAFETY

Petty crime does occur here, and you're advised to leave your valuables in the hotel safe-deposit box and lock doors in cars and rooms when unattended. Bring along a can of insect repellent: the mosquitoes and no-see-ums can be vicious after rain.

In some hotels on Grand Turk, Salt Cay, and South Caicos, there are signs that read PLEASE HELP US CONSERVE OUR PRECIOUS WATER. These islands have no water supply other than rainwater collected in cisterns, and rainfall is scant. Drink only from the decanter of fresh water your hotel provides.

SIGHTSEEING TOURS

Whether by taxi, boat, or plane, you should try to voyage beyond the resort grounds and beach to better understand the culture and daily life of the islanders. Global Airways specializes in trips to North Caicos. If you want to island-hop on your own schedule, air charters are available through Inter-Island Airways. Nell's Taxi offers taxi tours of the islands; priced between $25 and $30 for the first hour and $25 for each additional hour. J&B Tours offers sea and land tours, including trips to Middle Caicos, the largest of the islands, for a visit to the caves, or to North Caicos to see flamingos and plantation ruins. Aerial photo safaris are provided by Provo Air Charter.

➤ CONTACTS: **Global Airways** (☎ 649/941–3222). **Inter-Island Airways** (☎ 649/941–5481). **J&B Tours** (☎ 649/946–5047, WEB www.jbtours. com). **Nell's Taxi** (☎ 649/231–0051). **Provo Air Charter** (☎ 649/941–0685).

TAXES & SERVICE CHARGES

DEPARTURE TAX

The departure tax is $23, payable only in cash or traveler's checks.

SALES TAX

Hotels add 10%–15% to your bill for service, and restaurants and hotels add a 10% government tax.

TAXIS

Cabs are now metered, and rates are regulated by the government. In Provo call the Provo Taxi and Bus Group for more information.
➤ CONTACTS: **Provo Taxi and Bus Group** (☎ 649/946–5481).

TELEPHONES

To place credit-card calls, dial 810 (English). Cellular phones can be rented through Cable & Wireless. Internet access is available via hotel room phone connections or Internet kiosks on Provo and Grand Turk. Calls from the islands are expensive, and many hotels add steep surcharges for long-distance. Talk fast.
➤ CONTACTS: **Cable & Wireless** (☎ 649/946–2200, WEB www.tcimall.tc).

AREA CODE

The area code for the Turks and Caicos is 649.

INTERNATIONAL CALLS

To make calls from the Turks and Caicos, dial 0, then 1, the area code, and the number.

LOCAL CALLS

To make local calls, dial the seven-digit number.

TIPPING

At restaurants, tip 15% if service isn't included in the bill. Taxi drivers also expect a token tip, about 10% of your fare.

VISITOR INFORMATION

➤ BEFORE YOU LEAVE: **Turks and Caicos Islands Tourist Board** (☎ 649/946–2321 or 800/241–0824, WEB www.turksandcaicostourism.com); in the U.K. **Morris-Kevan International Ltd.** (✉ Mitre House, 66 Abbey Rd., Bush Hill Park, Enfield, Middlesex EN1 2RQ, ☎ 0181/350–1000).
➤ IN TURKS AND CAICOS ISLANDS: **Government Tourist Office** In Grand Turk: (✉ Front St., Cockburn Town, ☎ 649/946–2321). In Provo: (✉ Stubbs Diamond Plaza, The Bight, ☎ 649/946–4970). **Times Publications** (✉ Caribbean Pl., Box 234, ☎ 649/946–4788, WEB www.timespub.tc).

UNITED STATES VIRGIN ISLANDS

Updated by
Carol Bareuther
and Lynda Lohr

Mornings at Lillian's on St. Thomas aren't much different from those in coffee shops back home. A cop stops by to joke with the waitress and collect his first cup of coffee; a high-heeled secretary runs in for the paper and some toast; a store clerk lingers over a cup of tea to discuss politics with the cook. But is the coffee shop back home in a ballast-brick-walled 19th-century building, steps from a park abloom with frangipani—in January? Are bush tea and johnny-cake served alongside oatmeal and omelets?

It's the combination of the familiar and the exotic found in St. Thomas, St. Croix, and St. John—the United States Virgin Islands (USVI)—that defines this "American paradise" and explains much of its appeal. The effort to be all things to all people—while remaining true to the best of itself—has created a sometimes paradoxical blend of island serenity and American practicality in this U.S. territory 1,000 mi (1,600 km) from the southern tip of the U.S. mainland.

The images you'd expect from a tropical island are here: stretches of beach arc into the distance, and white sails skim across water so blue and clear it stuns the senses. Red-roofed houses color the green hillsides as do the orange of the flamboyant tree, the red of the hibiscus, the magenta of the bougainvillea, and the blue stone ruins of old sugar mills. Towns of pastel-tone villas, decorated with filigree wrought-iron terraces, line narrow streets that climb from the harbor. Amid all the images you can find moments of exquisite tranquillity: an egret standing in a pond at dawn, palm trees backlighted by a full moon, sunrises and sunsets that send your spirits soaring with the frigate bird flying overhead.

Chances are that on one of the three islands you'll find your own idea of an ideal Caribbean vacation spot. Check into a beachfront condo on the east end of St. Thomas, eat burgers, and watch football at a beachfront bar and grill. Or stay at an 18th-century plantation great house on St. Croix, dine on Danish delicacies, and go horseback riding at sunrise. Rent a tent or a cottage in the pristine national park on St. John, take a hike, kayak off the coast, read a book, or just listen to the sounds of the forest. Or dive deep into "island time" and learn the art of limin' (hanging out, Caribbean-style) on all three islands.

Idyllic though they may be, these bits of volcanic rock in the middle of the Caribbean Sea haven't entirely escaped such worries of overdevelopment as trash, crime, and traffic. Isolation and limited space

United States Virgin Islands

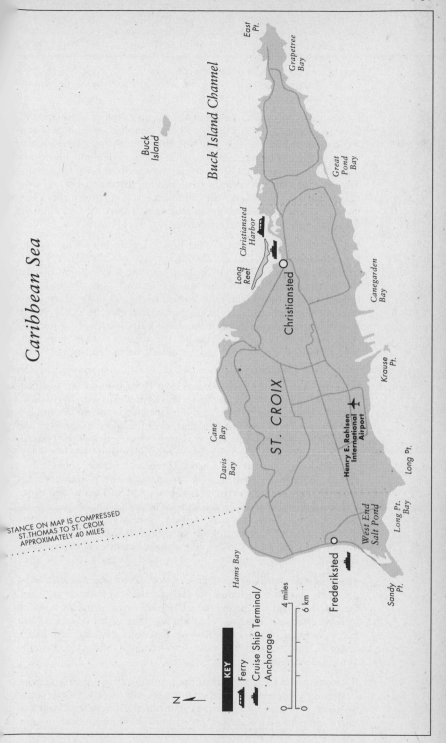

Caribbean Sea

Buck Island Channel

East Pt.

Grapetree Bay

Buck Island

Great Pond Bay

Christiansted Harbor

Long Reef

Christiansted

Canegarden Bay

Krause Pt.

ST. CROIX

Henry E. Rohlsen International Airport

Long Pt.

Cane Bay

Davis Bay

DISTANCE ON MAP IS COMPRESSED
ST. THOMAS TO ST. CROIX
APPROXIMATELY 40 MILES

Hams Bay

West End Salt Pond

Long Pt. Bay

Frederiksted

Sandy Pt.

4 miles

6 km

KEY

Ferry

Cruise Ship Terminal/
Anchorage

N

0

0

have, in fact, accentuated these problems. What, for example, do you do with 76 million cans and bottles imported annually when the nearest recycling plant is across 1,000 mi (1,600 km) of ocean? Despite these dilemmas wildlife has found refuge here. The brown pelican is on the endangered list worldwide but is a common sight in the USVI. The endangered native boa tree is protected, as is the hawksbill turtle, whose females lumber onto the beaches to lay eggs.

Preserving its own culture while progressing as a tourist destination is another problem. The islands have been inhabited by Taíno Indians (on St. John and St. Thomas); Carib Indians (on St. Croix); Danish settlers and Spanish pirates; traders and invaders from all the European powers; Africans brought in as slaves; migrants from other Caribbean islands; and, finally, Americans, first as administrators, then as businesspeople and tourists. All these influences are creating a more homogeneous culture, and with each passing year the USVI lose more of their rich, spicy, Caribbean personality.

Sailing into the Caribbean on his second voyage in 1493, Christopher Columbus came upon St. Croix before the group of islands that would later be known as St. Thomas, St. John, and the British Virgin Islands (BVI). He named St. Croix "Santa Cruz" (called Ay Ay by the Carib Indians already living there), but moved on quickly after he encountered the fierce residents. As he approached St. Thomas and St. John, he was impressed enough with the shapely silhouettes of the numerous islands and cays (including the BVI) to name them after Ursula and her 11,000 virgins, but he found the islands barren and moved on to explore Puerto Rico.

Over the next century, as it became clear that Spain couldn't defend the entire Caribbean, other European powers began to settle the islands. In the 1600s the French were joined by the Dutch and the English on St. Croix, and St. Thomas had a mixture of European residents in the early 1700s. By 1695 St. Croix was under the control of the French, but the colonists had moved on to what is today Haiti. The island lay virtually dormant until 1733, when the Danish government bought it—along with St. Thomas and St. John—from the Danish West India Company. At that time settlers from St. Thomas and St. John moved to St. Croix to cultivate the island's gentler terrain. St. Croix developed a plantation economy, but St. Thomas's soil was ill suited to agriculture. There the harbor became internationally known because of its size and ease of entry; it's still hailed as one of the most beautiful seaports in the world.

Plantations depended on slave labor, of which there was a plentiful supply in the Danish West Indies. As early as 1665, agreements between the Brandenburger Company (which needed a base in the West Indies from which to ship the slaves it had imported from Africa) and the West India Company (which needed the kind of quick cash it could collect in duties, fees, and rents from the slave trade) established St. Thomas as a primary slave market.

It's from the slaves who worked the plantations that most Virgin Islanders are descended. More than likely the salesclerk who sells you a watch and the waitress who serves your rum punch can trace their lineage to ancestors captured in Africa some 300 years ago and brought to the West Indies, where they were sold on the block, priced according to their comeliness and strength. Most were captured along Africa's Gold Coast, from the tribes of Asante, Ibo, Mandika, Amina, and Wolof. They brought with them African rhythms in music and language, herbal medicine, and such crafts as basketry and wood carving. The

West Indian–African culture comes to full bloom at Carnival time, when playing *mas* (with abandon) takes precedence over all else.

Yet you can still see the influence of the early Danish settlers here, too. It's reflected in the language and architecture; in common surnames such as Petersen, Jeppesen, and Lawaetz; and in street names such as Kongen's Gade (King Street) and Kronprindsen's Gade (Prince Street). The town of Charlotte Amalie was named after a Danish queen. The Lutheran Church is the state church of Denmark, and Frederick Lutheran Church on St. Thomas dates from 1666. Other peoples have left their marks on the USVI as well. Jewish settlers came to the territory as early as 1665; they were shipowners, chandlers, and brokers in the slave trade. Today their descendants coexist with nearly 1,500 Arabs—95% of whom are Palestinian. You'll also find many East Indians, who are active members of the business community. Immigrants from Puerto Rico and the Dominican Republic make up close to half of St. Croix's population. Transplants from Caribbean countries to the south continue to arrive, seeking better economic opportunities.

St. Thomas, St. Croix, and St. John were known collectively as the Danish West Indies until the United States bought the territory in 1917 during World War I, prompted by fears that Germany would establish a U-boat base in the western hemisphere. The name was changed to the United States Virgin Islands, and almost immediately thereafter British-held Tortola and Virgin Gorda—previously known simply as the Virgin Islands—hastily inserted "British" on the front of their name.

In the 1960s, Pineapple Beach Resort (today Renaissance Grand Beach Resort) was built on St. Thomas, and the Caneel Bay Resort on St. John, built in 1956, was expanded; and with direct flights from the U.S. mainland, the tourism industry was born. In 1960 the total population of all three islands was 32,000. Today there are about 50,000 people living on 32-square-mi (83-square-km) St. Thomas (about the same size as Manhattan), 51,000 on the 84 square mi (216 square km) of pastoral St. Croix, and about 5,000 on 20-square-mi (52-square-km) St. John, two-thirds of which is a national park. The per capita income in the USVI is the highest in the West Indies. Just over 25% of the total labor force is employed by the government, and about 10% work in tourism.

Agriculture hasn't been a major economic factor since the last sugarcane plantation on St. Croix ceased operating in the 1960s, and today most foods are imported. The islands' cuisine reflects a tradition where root vegetables such as sweet potato, slave rations of cornmeal, and stick-to-your-ribs breads were staples 200 years ago. Their influence is still evident in the sweet potato stuffing (mashed potatoes, spices, and raisins), *fungi* (cornmeal and okra), and johnnycakes (deep-fried dough rounds made of cornmeal and white flour) that are ever-present on menus today. Beverages include not only rum but coconut water, fruit juices, and *maubi*, made from tree bark, and reputedly a virility enhancer.

The backbone of the economy is tourism, but at the heart of the islands is an independent, separate being: a rollicking hodgepodge of West Indian culture with a sense of humor that puts sex and politics in almost every conversation. Lacking a major-league sports team, Virgin Islanders follow the activities and antics of their 15 elected senators with the rabidity of Washingtonians following the Redskins. Loyalty to country and faith in God are the rules in the USVI not the exceptions. Prayer is a way of life, and ROTC is one of the most popular high-school extracurricular activities.

The struggle to preserve the predominantly black Caribbean-influenced culture is heating up in the Virgin Islands. Native Virgin Islanders say they want access to more than just the beach when big money brings in big development. But the three islands are far from united in their goals, especially in light of a $1 billion deficit that threatens the autonomy of the local government and protection of the territory's number-one resource—scenic beauty. The ongoing conflict between progress and preservation here is no mere philosophical exercise, and attempts at resolutions display yet another aspect of the islands' unique blend of character.

ST. THOMAS

Updated by
Carol
Bareuther

If you fly to the 32-square-mi (83-square-km) island of St. Thomas, you land at its western end; if you arrive by cruise ship, you come into one of the world's most beautiful harbors. Either way, one of your first sights is the town of Charlotte Amalie. From the harbor you see an idyllic-looking village that spreads into the lower hills. If you were expecting a quiet hamlet with its inhabitants hanging out under palm trees, you've missed that era by about 300 years. Although other islands in the USVI developed plantation economies, St. Thomas cultivated its harbor, and it became a thriving seaport soon after it was settled by the Danish in the 1600s.

The success of the naturally perfect harbor was enhanced by the fact that the Danes—who ruled St. Thomas with only a couple of short interruptions from 1666 to 1917—avoided involvement in some 100 years' worth of European wars. Denmark was the only European country with colonies in the Caribbean to stay neutral during the war of the Spanish succession in the early 1700s. Thus, products of the Dutch, English, and French islands—sugar, cotton, and indigo—were traded through Charlotte Amalie, along with the regular shipments of slaves. When the Spanish wars ended, trade fell off, but by the end of the 1700s Europe was at war again, Denmark again remained neutral, and St. Thomas continued to prosper. Even into the 1800s, while the economies of St. Croix and St. John foundered with the market for sugarcane, St. Thomas's economy remained strong. This prosperity led to the development of shipyards, a well-organized banking system, and a large merchant class. In 1845 Charlotte Amalie had 101 large importing houses owned by the English, French, Germans, Haitians, Spaniards, Americans, Sephardim, and Danes.

Charlotte Amalie is still one of the most active cruise-ship ports in the world. On almost any day at least one and sometimes as many as eight cruise ships are tied to the dock or anchored outside the harbor. Gently rocking in the shadows of these giant floating hotels are just about every other kind of vessel imaginable: sleek sailing mono- and multi-hulls that will take you on a sunset cruise complete with rum punch and a Jimmy Buffett soundtrack, private megayachts that spirit busy executives away, and barnacle-bottom sloops—with laundry draped to dry over the lifelines—that are home to world-cruising gypsies. Huge container ships pull up in Sub Base, west of the harbor, bringing in everything from cornflakes to tires. Anchored right along the waterfront are picturesque down-island sloops that ply the waters between the Greater Antilles and the Leeward Islands transporting goods like refrigerators, VCRs, and disposable diapers.

The waterfront road through Charlotte Amalie was once part of the harbor. Before it was filled to build the highway, the beach came right up to the back door of the warehouses that now line the thoroughfare.

Two hundred years ago those warehouses contained indigo, tobacco, and cotton. Today the stone buildings house silk, crystal, linens, and leather. Exotic fragrances are still traded—but by island beauty queens in air-conditioned perfume palaces instead of through open market stalls. The pirates of old used St. Thomas as a base from which to raid merchant ships of every nation, though they were particularly fond of the gold- and silver-laden treasure ships heading to Spain. Pirates are still around, but today's versions use St. Thomas as a drop-off for their contraband: illegal immigrants and drugs.

Lodging

Of the USVI, St. Thomas has the most rooms and the greatest number and variety of resorts. You can let yourself be pampered at a luxurious resort—albeit at a price of $300 to more than $500 per night, not including meals. If your means are more modest, you will find fine hotels (often with rooms that have a kitchen and a living area) in lovely settings throughout the island. There are also guest houses and inns with great views (if not a beach at your door) and great service at about half the cost of the beachfront pleasure palaces. Learn more about these properties by calling the St. Thomas–St. John Hotel & Tourism Association by calling 340/774–6835 or via the Internet at www.innparadise.com. Many of these are east and north of Charlotte Amalie, in the Frenchtown area or overlooking hills—ideal if you plan to get out and mingle with the locals. There are also inexpensive lodgings (most right in town) that are perfect if you just want a clean room to return to after a day of exploring or beach-bumming.

Families often stay at an east end condominium complex. Although condos are pricey (winter rates average $240 per night for a two-bedroom unit, which usually sleeps six), they have full kitchens, and you can definitely save money by cooking for yourself—especially if you bring your own nonperishable foodstuffs. (Virtually everything on St. Thomas is imported, and restaurants and shops pass shipping costs on to you.) Though you may spend some time laboring in the kitchen, many condos ease your burden with daily maid service and on-site restaurants; a few also have resort amenities, including pools and tennis courts. The east end is convenient to St. John, and it's a hot for the boating crowd with some good restaurants. The prices below reflect rates in high season, which runs from December 15 to April 15. Rates are 25% to 50% lower the rest of the year.

CATEGORY	COST EP/CP*	COST A.I.**
$$$$	over $350	over $375
$$$	$250–$350	$275–$375
$$	$150–$250	$175–$275
$	under $150	under $175

*EP/CP prices are per night for a standard double room in high season, excluding taxes, service charges, and meal plans **A.I. (all-inclusive) prices are per person, per night based on double-occupancy during high season, excluding taxes and service charges*

Hotels
CHARLOTTE AMALIE

$$ 🏨 **Best Western Emerald Beach Resort.** On a white-sand beach across from the airport, this mini-resort has the feel of its much larger east-end cousins. Each room in the four pink three-story buildings has its own terrace or balcony, palms, and colorful flowers that frame an ocean view. Rooms have modern tropical prints and rattan furniture. A minus: the noise from nearby jets taking off and landing can be heard intermittently over a three-hour period each afternoon. ✉ *8070 Lind-*

St. Thomas

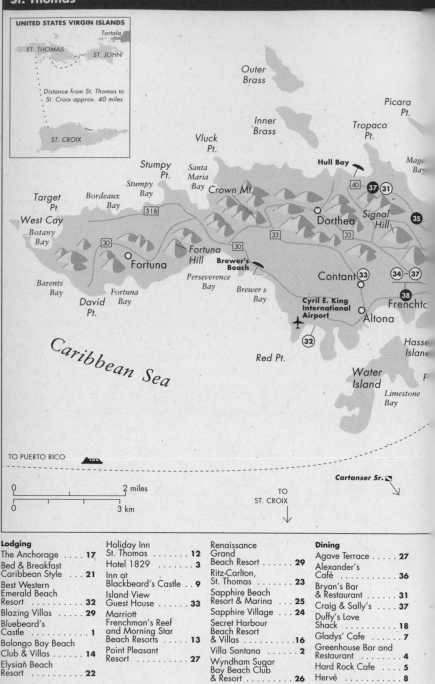

UNITED STATES VIRGIN ISLANDS

Tortola

ST. THOMAS — ST. JOHN

Distance from St. Thomas to
St. Croix approx. 40 miles

ST. CROIX

Outer
Brass

Inner
Brass

Picara
Pt.

Tropaco
Pt.

Vluck
Pt.

Santa
Maria
Bay

Stumpy
Pt.

Hull Bay

Mage
Bay

Stumpy
Bay

Crown Mt.

40 37 31

Target
Pt.

Bordeaux
Bay

Signal
Hill

35

West Cay

318

Dorthea

Botany
Bay

Fortuna
Hill

33

33

**Brewer's
Beach**

30

30

Fortuna

Perseverence
Bay

Contant

33

34 - 37

Barents
Bay

Fortuna
Bay

Brewers
Bay

38

Frenchto

David
Pt.

Red Pt.

**Cyril E. King
International
Airport**

Altona

32

Hasse
Island

Caribbean Sea

Water
Island

Limestone
Bay

TO PUERTO RICO

0 ———— 2 miles

0 ———— 3 km

Cartanser Sr.

TO
ST. CROIX

Lodging

The Anchorage **17**
Bed & Breakfast
Caribbean Style . . . **21**
Best Western
Emerald Beach
Resort **32**
Blazing Villas **29**
Bluebeard's
Castle **1**
Bolongo Bay Beach
Club & Villas **14**
Elysian Beach
Resort **22**

Holiday Inn
St. Thomas **12**
Hotel 1829 . . . . . . **3**
Inn at
Blackbeard's Castle . **9**
Island View
Guest House **33**
Marriott
Frenchman's Reef
and Morning Star
Beach Resorts **13**
Point Pleasant
Resort **27**

Renaissance
Grand
Beach Resort **29**
Ritz-Carlton,
St. Thomas **23**
Sapphire Beach
Resort & Marina . . **25**
Sapphire Village . . **24**
Secret Harbour
Beach Resort
& Villas **16**
Villa Santana **2**
Wyndham Sugar
Bay Beach Club
& Resort **26**

Dining

Agave Terrace **27**
Alexander's
Café **36**
Bryan's Bar
& Restaurant **31**
Craig & Sally's **37**
Duffy's Love
Shack **18**
Gladys' Cafe **7**
Greenhouse Bar and
Restaurant **4**
Hard Rock Cafe . . . **5**
Hervé **8**

KEY

- Beaches
- Cruise Ship Terminal
- Dive Sites
- ① Exploring Sights
- Ferry
- ① Hotels and Restaurants

ATLANTIC OCEAN

Ians ...llick

Lovelund Bay

...'s Bay

Mandal Pt.

The *General* Rogers

Thatch Cay

Grass Cay and Congo Cay →

N

42 Mandal

Tutu Bay

Coki Beach

○ Mafolie

Frydendal

29 ㉝

㉔㉕

29 ㉑ 40

㉙

○ Charlotte Amalie

38 ㉞

㉘ ㉗

Cabes Pt.

㉖

Thomas ...rbor

○ Tutu

38

Sapphire Beach

Redhook Bay

30

Morningstar Beach

㉘ — ㉛

㉓

TO ST. JOHN

⑬

32

㉖ ㉗

Red Hook

㉜ ㉑ ㉒

Cow and Calf Rocks

Nadir

Great Bay

⑭

30

㉛

Secret Harbour

⑮

Jersey Bay

St. James Bay

Coculus Pt

Great St. James Island

Long Pt.

Little St. James Island

❚ **Frenchcap**

TO ST. JOHN

berg Bay, 00802, ☎ *340/777–8800 or 800/233–4936,* FAX *340/776–3426,* WEB *www.emeraldbeach.com. 90 rooms. Restaurant, bar, in-room data ports, refrigerators, no room TVs, tennis courts, pool, gym, beach, boating, volleyball. AE, D, MC, V. CP.*

$$ 🏨 **Bluebeard's Castle.** Though not exactly a castle, this large red-roofed complex offers kingly comforts on a steep hill above town. All rooms are air-conditioned and have terraces. The hotel is a short ride from the shops of Charlotte Amalie and Havensight Mall, and there's free transportation to Magens Bay Beach and to town. ✉ *Bluebeard's Hill (Box 7480, 00801),* ☎ *340/774–1600 or 800/524–6599,* FAX *340/774–5134. 170 rooms. 3 restaurants, bar, minibars, 2 tennis courts, pool, gym, shops, concierge, meeting rooms, car rental. AE, D, DC, MC, V. EP.*

$$ 🏨 **Holiday Inn St. Thomas.** This harbor-front property is comfortable for business travelers as well as vacationers who want to be close to the duty-free shopping. Contemporarily furnished rooms have such amenities as coffeemakers, hair dryers, ironing boards and irons. A daily beach shuttle and an introductory dive lesson are complimentary. ✉ *Waterfront Hwy. (Box 640, 00804),* ☎ *340/774–5200 or 800/524–7389,* FAX *340/774–1231,* WEB *www.holidayinn.st-thomas.com. 140 rooms, 11 suites. 2 restaurants, bar, room service, in-room data ports, in-room safes, refrigerators, room TVs with movies and video games, pool, gym, hair salon, dive shop, shops, laundry services, business services, meeting rooms, car rental. AE, D, DC, MC, V. EP.*

$–$$ 🏨 **Hotel 1829.** This historic Spanish-style inn is popular with visiting ★ officials conducting business at Government House down the street. Rooms, on several levels (no elevator), range from elegant and roomy to quite small but are priced accordingly. Author Graham Greene is said to have stayed here, and it's easy to imagine him musing over a drink in the small, dark bar. The second-floor botanical gardens and open-air champagne bar make a romantic spot for sunset viewing before dinner in the hotel's restaurant. The shops of Charlotte Amalie are within walking distance. ✉ *Government Hill (Box 1567, 00804),* ☎ *340/776–1829 or 800/524–2002,* FAX *340/776–4313,* WEB *www.hotel1829.com. 14 rooms. Restaurant, bar, no room phones, refrigerators, pool. AE, D, MC, V, CP.*

$–$$ 🏨 **Inn at Blackbeard's Castle.** This cozy hilltop inn is laid out around a tower from which, it's said, Blackbeard kept watch for invaders sailing into Charlotte Amalie harbor. It's an informally elegant place, where you can while away a Sunday morning reading the *New York Times.* Mahogany furnishings, including four-poster beds, lend a 17th-century feel to the place, yet each room has many modern conveniences. ✉ *Blackbeard's Hill (Box 6227, 00804),* ☎ *340/776–1234 or 800/334–5771,* FAX *340/776–4521,* WEB *www.blackbeardscastle.com. 16 rooms. Restaurant, bar, no room phones, fans, pool. AE, D, DC, MC, V. CP.*

$–$$ 🏨 **Villa Santana.** Built by General Santa Anna of Mexico, this six-villa ★ landmark (circa 1857) still provides a panoramic view of the harbor and plenty of West Indian charm. Dark-wood furniture, plaster-and-stone walls, shuttered windows, cathedral ceilings, four-poster or cradle beds, and interesting nooks contribute to the sense of romance and history. Villas La Torre and La Mansion are split-level quarters with spiral staircases. ✉ *2D Denmark Hill, 00802,* ☎ *340/776–1311,* FAX *340/776–1311,* WEB *www.st-thomas.com/villasantana. 6 rooms. No air-conditioning in some rooms, no room phones, kitchenettes, pool, croquet. AE. CP.*

$ 🏨 **Island View Guest House.** In tropical foliage 545 ft (166 m) up on ★ the face of Crown Mountain, this simply furnished bed-and-breakfast offers sweeping views of Charlotte Amalie harbor from the pool and shaded terraces. Continental breakfast is served daily; however, six rooms have kitchenettes. The friendly office staff can arrange tours. ✉ *Rte. 332, Estate Contant (Box 1903, 00801),* ☎ *340/774–4270 or 800/524–2023,* ℻ *340/774–6167,* 🌐 *www.st-thomas.com/islandviewguesthouse. 15 rooms. No air-conditioning, fans, kitchenettes in some rooms, pool, no kids under age 14. AE, MC, V. CP.*

EAST END

$$$–$$$$
★   🏨 **Ritz-Carlton, St. Thomas.** This premier luxury resort resembles a villa in Venice and offers stunning ocean views through the lobby's glass doors. Guest rooms, in six buildings that fan out from the main villa, are spacious and tropically furnished. Elegance is everywhere, from the beautiful pool that appears to become one with the sea to the superior dinner restaurant, casual alfresco lunch area, and island-style bush tea served in the opulent living room. A $75 million renovation and expansion project, which was completed in the fall of 2002, added 48 additional rooms, a full-service spa and fitness center, and 80 two- and three-bedroom private club residences. ✉ *Rte. 317 #6900, Estate Great Bay 00802,* ☎ *340/775–3333 or 800/241–3333,* ℻ *340/775–4444,* 🌐 *www.ritzcarlton.com. 196 rooms. 2 restaurants, 3 bars, room service, in-room safes, minibars, 3 tennis courts, pool, health club, hair salon, spa, beach, windsurfing, boating, shops, baby-sitting, children's programs (ages 4–12), laundry services, concierge, Internet, business services, meeting rooms, airport shuttle, no-smoking rooms. AE, D, DC, MC, V. EP.*

$$$–$$$$
🏨 **Sapphire Beach Resort & Marina.** On a clear day the lush, green mountains of the neighboring British Virgin Islands seem close enough to touch from this picturesque, red-roofed resort. Rooms have tropical bold-patterned rugs and comforters and full kitchenettes. This is a fun, family-oriented resort, where highlights are the Sunday beach party that thumps with rock and reggae and MeriStar's Fun Factory™ Kids Klub, which offers activities like arts and crafts, sing-alongs, and sand-castle building. Children under 12 eat free, and teens up to 18 also can sleep in their parents' room at no additional charge. ✉ *Rte. 38, Sapphire Bay (Box 8088, 00801),* ☎ *340/775–6100 or 800/330–8272,* ℻ *340/775–2403,* 🌐 *www.sapphirebeachstthomas.com. 171 suites. 2 restaurants, bar, snack bar, room service, kitchenettes, microwaves, refrigerators, 4 tennis courts, pool, beach, dock, snorkeling, windsurfing, boating, jet skiing, marina, parasailing, volleyball, shop, baby-sitting, children's program (ages 4–12), playground, concierge, meeting room, car rental. AE, MC, V. EP, MAP.*

$$–$$$$
🏨 **Secret Harbour Beach Resort & Villas.** These beige buildings, which contain low-rise studios and suites, are tucked into the hillsides and along an inviting sandy cove. Watch marvelous sunsets from the balconies or the casual restaurant. All units have air-conditioning and maid service. Children under age 13 stay free, making this a family-friendly resort. ✉ *Rte. 317 #6280, Estate Nazareth 00802-1104,* ☎ *340/775–6550 or 800/524–2250,* ℻ *340/775 –1501,* 🌐 *www.secretharbourvi. com. 49 suites, 15 studios. Restaurant, bar, kitchenettes, 4 tennis courts, pool, health club, beach, dive shop, snorkeling, boating, shop. AE, MC, V. CP.*

$$$–$$$$
★   🏨 **Wyndham Sugar Bay Beach Club & Resort.** This warm, terra-cotta hillside resort is one of the island's most attractive. Most rooms overlook water; some have views of the British Virgin Islands. All are spacious and comfortable and have balconies, hair dryers, and coffeemakers. The beach is small, but there's a giant pool with waterfalls. A full-service spa and fitness center opened in the spring of 2002. ✉ *Rte. 38 #6500, Estate Smith Bay 00802,* ☎ *340/777–7100 or 800/927–7100,* ℻ *340/777–7200,* 🌐 *www.wyndham.com. 300 rooms, 9 suites. 2*

restaurants, bar, snack bar, room service, 2 tennis courts, pool, health club, spa, beach, windsurfing, boating, shop, baby-sitting, children's programs (ages 4–12), laundry service, concierge, business services, meeting rooms. AE, D, DC, MC, V. All-inclusive.

$$–$$$$ ⊡ **Renaissance Grand Beach Resort.** The zigzag architectural angles
★ spell luxury, and that's what you'll find everywhere, from the marble atrium lobby to the one-bedroom suites with whirlpool baths. The beach is excellent, and there's a fitness center with Nautilus machines. The resort is favored for convention groups. Families are welcome, and daily activities for children include iguana hunts, T-shirt painting, and sandcastle building. ✉ *Rte. 38, Estate Smith Bay (Box 8267, 00801),* ☎ *340/775–1510 or 800/468–3571,* ℻ *340/775–2185,* ⟦WEB⟧ *www.renaissancehotels.com/sttsr. 290 rooms, 36 suites. 2 restaurants, 2 bars, snack bar, room service, in-room data ports, in-room safes, minibars in some rooms, cable TVs with movies, 6 tennis courts, 2 pools, health club, beach, dock, boating, jet skiing, parasailing, volleyball, shops, baby-sitting, children's programs (ages 4–12), laundry service, concierge, business services, convention center, car rental. AE, D, DC, MC, V. EP, MAP.*

$$$ ⊡ **Point Pleasant Resort.** Stretching up a steep, tree-covered hill and affording a great view of Drake's Channel, this resort offers a choice of accommodations from simple bedrooms to multiroom suites. Although the "beach" is almost nonexistent, three good-size pools surrounded by decks are placed at different levels on the hill. The property also has a labyrinth of well-marked nature trails to explore. Every guest gets four hours free use of a car daily (you do need to pay the $20, per use, fuel and maintenance fee). If you like seafood, don't miss dinner at the Agave Terrace restaurant. ✉ *Rte. 38 #6600, Estate Smith Bay 00802,* ☎ *340/775–7200; 800/524–2300 direct to hotel,* ℻ *340/776–5694,* ⟦WEB⟧ *www.pointpleasantresort.com. 132 suites. 2 restaurants, bar, in-room data ports, in-room safes, kitchenettes, tennis court, 3 pools, gym, beach, shops, laundry facilities, concierge, car rental. AE, D, DC, MC, V. EP.*

$$ ⊡ **Elysian Beach Resort.** The coral-colored villas here are situated along a hill all the way to the edge of Cowpet Bay. All rooms have terraces; some have full kitchens. Activity centers on a kidney-shape pool with a waterfall and thatched-roof pool bar. The Palm Court restaurant has a strong local following for the Sunday buffet brunch. ✉ *Rte. 317, Estate Nazareth (Box 51, 00802),* ☎ *340/775–1000 or 800/753–2554,* ℻ *340/776–0910. 175 rooms. 2 restaurants, bar, minibars, tennis court, pool, health club, outdoor hot tub, beach, boating, volleyball, shops, meeting rooms. AE, MC, V. EP.*

SOUTH SHORE

$$$$ ⊡ **Marriott Frenchman's Reef and Morning Star Beach Resorts.** On a
★ prime harbor promontory east of Charlotte Amalie, you'll find these two sprawling, luxurious, full-service superhotels. Frenchman's Reef suites have ocean and harbor views. The more elegant Morning Star rooms are in buildings nestled surfside along the fine white sand of Morning Star Beach. Dining is alfresco on American or Caribbean fare or oceanfront at the Tavern on the Beach; there's also a lavish buffet served, overlooking the sparkling lights of Charlotte Amalie. Live entertainment and dancing, scheduled activities for all ages, and a shuttle boat to town make having fun easy. ✉ *Rte. 315, Estate Bakkeroe (Box 7100, 00801),* ☎ *340/776–8500 or 800/524–2000,* ℻ *340/715–6191,* ⟦WEB⟧ *www.offshoreresorts.com/stthomas.html. 504 rooms, 27 suites. 6 restaurants, bar, snack bar, room service, in-room data ports, in-room safes, minibars, cable TVs with movies, 4 tennis courts, 2 pools, health club, hair salon, massage, sauna, spa, beach, boating, volleyball, piano*

bar, dance club, shops, baby-sitting, concierge, business services, convention center. AE, D, DC, MC, V. EP.

$$ ⊞ **Bolongo Bay Beach Club & Villas.** This 75-room, beachfront resort also includes the 20-room Bolongo Villas next door and the six-room Bolongo Bayside Inn across the street. All rooms—which include minisuites and one- and two-bedroom units—have kitchens and balconies and are just steps from a strand of white-sand beach. The resort offers a choice of all-inclusive or semi-inclusive plans, which means you can pay less if you opt for fewer activities and no included meals. The all-inclusive rate covers all meals and drinks, the use of tennis courts, and many water-sports activities—including an all-day sail and half-day snorkel trip on a yacht. There's a three-night minimum for the all-inclusive plan. ⊠ *Rte. 30, #50, Estate Bolongo 00802,* ☎ *340/775–1800 or 800/524–4746,* FAX *340/775–3208,* WEB *www.bolongobay.com. 101 units. 2 restaurants, bar, snack bar, kitchenettes, 2 tennis courts, 3 pools, health club, beach, dive shop, dock, windsurfing, boating, volleyball, nightclub, shop, baby-sitting, children's programs (ages 4–12), playground. AE, D, DC, MC, V. All-inclusive.*

Villas and Condominiums

EAST END

$$$$ ⊞ **The Anchorage.** Next to the St. Thomas Yacht Club and facing Cow-
★ pet Bay, these two- and three-bedroom villas are right on the beach. They have washing machines and dryers, and the complex has two lighted tennis courts, a freshwater pool, and an informal restaurant. ⊠ *Rte. 317, Estate Nazareth (Antilles Resorts, Box 8529, 00801),* ☎ *340/775–2600 or 800/874–7897,* FAX *340/775–5901,* WEB *www.antillesresorts.com. 30 rooms. Restaurant, bar, kitchenettes, 2 tennis courts, pool, beach, laundry facilities. AE, D, MC, V. EP.*

$$–$$$ ⊞ **Sapphire Village.** A stay in these high-rise units may take you back to the swinging-singles days of apartment-house living since many of the units are rented out long-term to refugees from northern winters. The best units overlook the marina and St. John; the beach is in sight and just a short walk down the hill. ⊠ *Rte. 38, Sapphire Bay (Antilles Resorts, Box 8529, 00801),* ☎ *340/775–2600 or 800/874–7897,* FAX *340/775–5901,* WEB *www.antillesresorts.com. 35 units. Restaurant, bar, kitchenettes, 2 tennis courts, 2 pools, beach, dock, snorkeling, windsurfing, boating, jet skiing, marina, parasailing, volleyball, laundry facilities. AE, D, MC, V. EP.*

$$ ⊞ **Blazing Villas.** On the Renaissance Grand Beach Resort property,
★ these cool pastel yellow, pink, green, and blue villas have their own garden patios and can be combined with other villas to create a four-bedroom, four-bath unit. Children under 12 free when staying with parents. You can use all the resort's facilities. ⊠ *Rte. 38, Estate Smith Bay (Box 502697, 00805),* ☎ *340/776–0760 or 800/382–2002,* FAX *340/776–3603,* WEB *www.blazingvillas.com. 19 rooms. 2 restaurants, 2 bars, snack bar, room service, microwaves, refrigerators, 6 tennis courts, 2 pools, health club, beach, dock, boating, jet skiing, parasailing, volleyball, shops, baby-sitting, children's programs (ages 4–12), laundry service, concierge, business services, convention center, car rental. AE, MC, V. EP.*

$–$$ ⊞ **Bed & Breakfast Caribbean Style.** Honeymooners will enjoy the ro-
★ mantic feel of these private, elegantly decorated condos. Each unit has a king-size bed, a reading and video library, and a porch with hammock. The kitchen comes stocked with a tempting selection of breakfast foods. There's a small pool on the property, and the beach and water sports are a five-minute walk away. Those seeking to tie the knot will find that making wedding arrangements, including professional photography, is a specialty of the owner. ⊠ *Rte. 317 at Cabrita Point,*

Estate Vessup Bay (6501 Red Hook Plaza, Suite 201, 00802), ☎ 340/715–1117, WEB www.cstyle.co.vi. 4 units. Kitchenettes, pool, beach, snorkeling, windsurfing, boating, no kids, no smoking. AE, MC, V. CP.

Private Homes

You can arrange private-home rentals through various agents that represent luxury residences and usually have both Web sites and brochures that show photos of the properties they represent. Some villas are suitable for travelers with disabilities. **Calypso Realty** (✉ Box 12178, 00801, ☎ 340/774–1620 or 800/747–4858, WEB www.calypsorealty.com) specializes in rental properties in St. Thomas. **McLaughlin-Anderson Villas** (✉ 100 Blackbeard's Hill, Suite 3, 00802, ☎ 340/776–0635 or 800/537–6246, WEB www.mclaughlinanderson.com) handles rental villas throughout the U.S. Virgin Islands, British Virgin Islands, and Grenada.

Dining

The beauty of St. Thomas and its sister islands has attracted a cadre of professionally trained chefs who know their way around fresh fish and local fruits. You can dine on everything from terrific, cheap local dishes such as goat water (a spicy stew) and fungi (a cornmeal polenta-like side dish), to imports such as hot pastrami sandwiches and raspberries in crème fraîche.

In large hotels you'll pay prices similar to those in New York City or Paris. Fancy restaurants may have a token chicken or pasta dish under $20, but otherwise, main courses are pricey. You can, however, find good inexpensive Caribbean restaurants. To snack on some local fare, order a johnnycake or a thick slice of dumb bread (a dense round loaf often cut into triangles and filled with cheddar cheese) from any of the mobile food vans parked all over the island. Familiar fast-food franchises also abound.

If your accommodations have a kitchen and you plan to cook, you'll find good variety in St. Thomas's mainland-style supermarkets. Note, however, that grocery prices are about 20% higher than those on the mainland United States. As for drinking, outside the hotels a beer in a bar will cost between $2 and $3 and a piña colada $4 or more.

What to Wear

Dining on St. Thomas is informal. Few restaurants require a jacket and tie. Still, at dinner in the snazzier places, shorts and T-shirts are inappropriate; men would do well to wear slacks and a shirt with buttons. Dress codes on St. Thomas rarely require women to wear skirts, but you'll never go wrong with something flowing.

CATEGORY	COST*
$$$$	over $30
$$$	$20–$30
$$	$10–$20
$	under $10

per person for a main course at dinner

Charlotte Amalie

AMERICAN

$$–$$$ ✕ **Greenhouse Bar and Restaurant.** Watch the waterfront wake up at this large, bustling open-air restaurant. An eight-page menu offers burgers, omelets, salads, sandwiches, and pizza served all day long, along with more upscale entrées like peel-'n'-eat shrimp, Maine lobster, and certified black Angus prime rib that are reasonably priced. This is generally a family-friendly place, though the Wednesday night live reggae band

that starts thumping at 10 PM draws a lively young-adult crowd. ✉ *Waterfront Hwy. at Storetvaer Gade,* ☎ *340/774–7998. AE, D, MC, V.*

$–$$ ✕ **Hard Rock Cafe.** A hot spot from the day it opened, this waterfront restaurant is pretty much like its namesakes around the world. Rock-and-roll memorabilia abound, and the menu offers hamburgers, sandwiches, salads, and great desserts. Jerk pork tenderloin is a delicious Caribbean addition. Doors are open from 11 AM until 2 AM; there's always a wait for a table during prime meal times. ✉ *International Plaza on Waterfront,* ☎ *340/777–5555. AE, MC, V.*

CARIBBEAN

$–$$ ✕ **Gladys' Cafe.** Even if the local specialties—conch in butter sauce,
★ salt fish and dumplings, hearty red bean soup—didn't make this a recommended café, it would be worth coming for Gladys's smile. While you're here, pick up a $5 or $10 bottle of her hot sauce. ✉ *Waterfront at Royal Dane Mall,* ☎ *340/774–6604. AE. No dinner.*

$–$$ ✕ **Lillian's Caribbean Grill.** This is where the local business community fuels up for their day of selling in Main Street stores. Specialties include dumb bread and cheese, spicy oatmeal and bush tea for breakfast, with everything from hamburgers to conch in butter sauce, fish and fungi, curried chicken and stewed mutton served for lunch. ✉ *Grand Galleria,* ☎ *340/774–7900,* WEB *pws.prserv.net/lillian/. No credit cards. No dinner.*

CONTINENTAL

$$$–$$$$ ✕ **Hotel 1829.** You'll dine by candlelight flickering over stone walls
★ and pink table linens at this restaurant on the terrace of the Hotel 1829. The menu and wine list (325 varieties, 15 available by the glass) are extensive, from Caribbean rock lobster to rack of lamb. Many items—including a warm spinach salad—are prepared table-side, and the restaurant is justly famous for its dessert soufflés: chocolate, Grand Marnier, raspberry, or coconut, to name a few. ✉ *Government Hill near Main St.,* ☎ *340/776–1829. Reservations essential. AE, D, MC, V. No lunch. Closed Sun.*

ECLECTIC

$$–$$$$ ✕ **Hervé.** In the glow of candlelight—at tables impeccably dressed with
★ linen cloths, silver settings, and fine crystal—you can start off with French-trained Hervé Chassin's crispy conch fritters served with a spicy-sweet mango chutney, then choose from such entrées as fresh tuna encrusted with sesame seeds or succulent roast duck with a ginger and tamarind sauce. The passionfruit cheesecake is to die for. ✉ *Government Hill,* ☎ *340/777–9703. AE, MC, V.*

$$–$$$$ ✕ **Tavern on the Waterfront.** White linen tablecloths, silver and crystal table settings, and a rich mahogany interior set the scene for an elegant meal at this second-floor, air-conditioned restaurant that overlooks the harbor. Tiger Woods, Michael Jordan, and Walter Cronkite have all supped here. The menu offers flavors from every corner of the globe. Try the soft-shell crabs with mango salsa or the tuna sushi for lunch. Dinner offerings include a two-pound Caribbean lobster specialty. Sunday is Latin night. ✉ *Waterfront at Royal Dane Mall,* ☎ *340/776–4328. AE, MC, V. Closed Sun.*

ITALIAN

$$$–$$$$ ✕ **Virgilio's.** For the island's best Northern Italian cuisine, don't miss
★ this intimate, elegant hideaway tucked on a quiet side street. Eclectic art covers the two-story-high brick walls, and the sound of Italian opera music sets the stage for a memorable meal. Come here for more than 40 homemade pastas complemented by superb sauces—*cappellini* (very thin spaghetti) with fresh tomatoes and garlic, say, or spaghetti peasant style (in a rich tomato sauce with mushrooms and prosciutto). House

specialties are osso buco and tiramisu for dessert, expertly prepared by chef Ernesto Garrigos. ⊠ *18 Main St.,* ☎ *340/776–4920. Reservations essential. AE, MC, V. Closed Sun.*

East End

ECLECTIC

$$–$$$ ⨯ **Raffles.** In a homey dining room set in a quaint marina, from-
★ scratch creations include a signature coconut shrimp appetizer, and entrées like beef Wellington, mahimahi in a rich lobster sauce, and a two-day Peking duck. There are fresh fish and vegetarian specials daily. For dessert, try the chocolate pâté—Belgian chocolate melted and frozen into a decadent treat. ⊠ *Rte. 32 at Compass Point Marina, Estate Frydenhoj,* ☎ *340/775–6004. Reservations essential. AE, MC, V. No lunch Apr.–Oct. Closed Mon.*

$ ⨯ **Duffy's Love Shack.** If the floating bubbles don't attract you to this zany eatery, the lime-green shutters, loud rock music, and fun-loving wait staff surely will. It's billed as the "ultimate tropical drink shack," and the bartenders shake up such exotic concoctions as the Love Shack Volcano—a 50-ounce flaming extravaganza. Dining selections are just as trendy. Try the grilled mahimahi taco salad or jerk Caesar wrap. Thursday night is usually a theme party complete with giveaways. ⊠ *Rte.32, Red Hook,* ☎ *340/779–2080. No credit cards.*

IRISH

$$–$$$ ⨯ **Molly Molone's.** This casual, alfresco restaurant has a devout following of locals who live and work on boats docked nearby. You'll find such traditional Irish dishes as stew, and bangers and mash (sausage and mashed potatoes), as well as fresh fish, oversize deli sandwiches, and rich soups. Beware: the iguanas like to beg for table scraps—bring your camera. Upstairs, the same owners run A Whale of a Tale, a pricier seafood eatery that also serves freshly made pasta and fine wines. ⊠ *Rte. 32 at American Yacht Harbor, Bldg. D, Red Hook,* ☎ *340/775–1270. MC, V.*

ITALIAN

$$$–$$$$ ⨯ **Romanos.** Inside this huge, old stucco house is a delightful surprise:
★ a spare yet elegant restaurant serving superb Northern Italian cuisine. Owner Tony Romano hasn't advertised since the restaurant opened in 1988, yet it's always packed. Try the pastas, either with a classic sauce or one of Tony's unique creations, such as a cream sauce with mushrooms, prosciutto, pine nuts, and Parmesan. ⊠ *Rte. 388 at Coki Point, Estate Frydendal,* ☎ *340/775–0045. Reservations essential. MC, V. No lunch. Closed Sun.*

SEAFOOD

$$–$$$$ ⨯ **Off The Hook.** The fish is so fresh at this open-air eatery, formerly called Cafe Wahoo, that you may see it coming in from one of the boats tied up at the dock just steps away. For starters, try the crispy conch fritters with sweet-hot banana chili chutney. Entrées include a rib-sticking fish stew with scallops, shrimp, mahimahi, mussels, conch, and salamari swimming in a pineapple coconut curry broth. Steak, poultry, and pasta lovers will find something to please on the menu, too. Children's menu. ⊠ *Rte. 32, Red Hook,* ☎ *340/775–6350. AE, MC, V. No lunch.*

$$–$$$ ⨯ **Agave Terrace.** At this dimly lit, open-air pavilion restaurant in the Point Pleasant Resort, fresh fish is the specialty, served as steaks or fillets, and the catch of the day is listed on the blackboard. There are more than a dozen fish sauces to choose from, including teriyaki-mango and lime ginger. Come early and have a drink at the Lookout Lounge, which has breathtaking views of the British Virgins. The food enjoys as good a reputation as the view. ⊠ *Rte. 38 at the Point Pleasant Resort, Estate Smith Bay,* ☎ *340/775–4142. AE, MC, V. No lunch.*

Frenchtown

AUSTRIAN

$$–$$$ ✕ **Alexander's Café.** This place is a favorite with the people in the restau-
★ rant business on St. Thomas—always a sign of quality. Alexander is
Austrian, and the schnitzels are delicious and reasonably priced; pasta
specials are fresh and tasty. Save room for strudel. Next door is Alexander's Bar & Grill, serving food from the same kitchen but in a more
casual setting and at lower prices. ✉ *24-A Honduras,* ☎ *340/774–4349.*
AE, D, MC, V. Closed Sun.

CARIBBEAN

$$–$$$ ✕ **Victor's New Hide-Out.** Although it's a little hard to find—it's up the
hill between the Nisky shopping center and the airport—this landmark
restaurant is worth the search. Native food—steamed fish, marinated
pork chops, and local lobster—and native music are offered in a casual,
friendly West Indian spot. ✉ *Sub Base,* ☎ *340/776–9379. AE, MC, V.*

ECLECTIC

$$–$$$$ ✕ **The Pointe at Villa Olga.** Set in the old Russian consulate great
house at the tip of the Frenchtown peninsula, this restaurant offers su-
perb views along with fresh fish, teriyaki dishes, lobster, and steaks grilled
to order. A large salad bar, brimming with traditional salad fare, along
with Mediterranean-style roasted vegetables and fresh-baked rustic
breads, offers a meal in itself. ✉ *Villa Olga,* ☎ *340/774–4262. AE,*
D, DC, MC, V. No dinner Sun.

$$–$$$ ✕ **Craig & Sally's.** In the heart of Frenchtown, culinary wizard Sally
★ Darash creates menus with a passionate international flavor using
fresh ingredients and a novel approach that makes for a delightful din-
ing experience at this friendly casual eatery. Husband Craig maintains
a 300-bottle wine list that's received accolades. ✉ *22 Honduras,* ☎
340/777–9949. AE, MC, V. No lunch weekends. Closed Mon.–Tues.

Northside

AMERICAN

$–$$$ ✕ **Sib's Mountain Bar and Restaurant.** Here you'll find live music, foot
ball, burgers, barbecued ribs and chicken, and beer. It's the perfect place
for a casual dinner after a day at the beach. Don't be surprised when
the basil, tomatoes, or hot peppers you see the chef pick from the backyard garden wind up on your plate minutes later. ✉ *Rte. 35, Estate*
Mafolie, ☎ *340/774–8967. AE, MC, V.*

ECLECTIC

$$–$$$$ ✕ **Bryan's Bar & Restaurant.** The dramatic views are of Hull Bay and
Inner Brass Cay. Tuna, wahoo, and dolphinfish—caught daily by the
island's French fishermen—are served grilled, fried, or broiled. Baby-
back ribs, 9-ounce beef burgers, and a kids' menu are the major draws.
Sunday brunch draws a big local crowd for choices ranging from steak
and eggs to salmon quesadillas. Live music and lively billiard games
keep the place jumping on weekends. ✉ *Rte. 37, Estate Hull,* ☎ *340/*
777–1262. AE, MC, V. No lunch.

Beaches

All 44 St. Thomas beaches are open to the public, although you can
reach some of them only by walking through a resort. Hotel guests fre-
quently have access to lounge chairs and floats that are off-limits to
nonguests; for this reason you may feel more comfortable at one of
the beaches not associated with a resort, such as Magens Bay (which
charges an entrance fee to cover beach maintenance) or Coki. Whichever
one you choose, remember to remove your valuables from the car and
keep them out of sight when you go swimming.

Brewer's Beach. This long stretch of powdery white sand is on Route 30 near the airport. Trucks that sell lunch, snacks, and drinks often park along the road bordering the beach.

Coki Beach. Next to Coral World (turn north off Route 38) is this popular snorkeling spot for cruise-ship passengers; it's common to find a group of them among the reefs on the east and west ends of the beach. It's also a good place to dash in for a swim or just to do some people-watching. Don't leave valuables unattended in your car or on the beach.

Hull Bay. This beach on the north shore (Route 37) faces Inner and Outer Brass cays and attracts fishermen and beachcombers. With its rough Atlantic surf and relative isolation, Hull Bay is one of the island's best surfing spots. Take a break from the rigors of sightseeing at the Hull Bay Hideaway, a laid-back beach bar where a local band plays rock on Sunday afternoon.

Magens Bay. On Route 35, Magens Bay is usually lively because of its spectacular crescent of white sand, more than ½ mi (¾ km) long, and its calm waters, which are protected by two peninsulas. It's often listed among the world's most beautiful beaches. (If you arrive between 8 AM and 5 PM, you'll have to pay an entrance fee of $3 per person.) The bottom is flat and sandy, so this is a place for sunning and swimming rather than snorkeling. On weekends and holidays the sounds of groups partying under the sheds fill the air. You'll also find a bar, bathhouses, a nature trail (unmarked and often overgrown), and a snack bar. East of the beach is Udder Delight, a one-room shop of the St. Thomas Dairies that serves a Virgin Islands tradition—a milk shake with a splash of Cruzan rum. Kids can enjoy virgin shakes, which have a touch of soursop, mango, or banana flavoring.

Morning Star Beach. Close to Charlotte Amalie and fronting the Marriott Frenchman's Reef Hotel, this pretty curve of sand is where many young locals bodysurf or play volleyball. Snorkeling is good near the rocks when the current doesn't affect visibility.

Sapphire Beach. You'll find a fine view of St. John and other islands here. The snorkeling is excellent at the reef to the right or east, near Pettyklip Point.

Secret Harbor. The condo resort here doesn't at all detract from the attractiveness of the cove-like beach. Not only is this east end spot pretty, it also has superb snorkeling—head out to the left, near the rocks.

Outdoor Activities and Sports

Participant Sports

BOATING AND SAILING

Calm seas, crystal waters, and nearby islands (perfect for picnicking, snorkeling, and exploring) make St. Thomas a favorite jumping-off spot for day- or weeklong sails or powerboat adventures. With more than 100 vessels from which to choose, St. Thomas is the charter-boat center of the U.S. Virgin Islands. You can go through a broker to book a sailing vessel with a crew or contact a charter company directly. Crewed charters start at $1,200 per person per week, while bareboat charters are less expensive and can start at $600 to $800 per person on a weekly basis, not including provisioning.

Fan Fare Charters (⌗ 6501 Red Hook Plaza, Suite 201, Red Hook, ☎ 340/715–1326, WEB www.fanfarecharters.com), at the Vessup Bay Marina, is the only yacht rental business in the Virgin Islands to offer sailboats by the day as well as week. Day charter rates range from $220 to $450 for 30-ft to 50-ft yachts. **Island Yachts** (⌗ 6100 Red Hook Quarter, 18B, Red Hook, ☎ 340/775–6666 or 800/524–2019, WEB www.islandyachts.com), offers sail or power boats on either a bareboat or crewed basis. **Paradise Connections** (✉ #41, Water Island, ☎ 340/774–1111 or 877/567–9350, WEB www.paradiseconnections.com) is run by long time sailors, Bob and Sheila Wise, who are expert at matching clients with yachts for a week-long crewed charter holidays. Bareboat sail and power boats, including a selection of stable trawlers, are available at **VIP Yacht Charters** (✉ Rte. 32, #6118, Estate Frydenhoj, ☎ 340/776–1510 or 800/524–2015, WEB www.vipyachts.com), near Red Hook.

Awesome Powerboat Rentals (✉ 6100 Red Hook Qtr., Red Hook, ☎ 340/775–0860, WEB www.powerboatrentalsvi.com), at "P" dock next to Cafe Wahoo, offers 22-ft to 26-ft twin engine catamarans for day charters. Rates range from $185 to $375 for half- or full-day. **Nauti Nymph** (✉ 6501 Red Hook Plaza, Suite 201, Red Hook, ☎ FAX 340/775–5066 .or ☎ 800/734–7345, WEB www.bookitvi.com/nauti.htm) has a large selection of powerboats for rent. Rates vary from $255 to $390 a day, including snorkel gear, water skis, and outriggers.

CYCLING

Water Island Bike Tours (✉ Water Island, ☎ 340/714–2186 or 340/775–5770) is a cycling adventure to the USVI's "newest" Virgin. You'll take a 10-minute ferry ride from Crown Bay Marina to Water Island before jumping on a Cannondale M-200 18-speed mountain bike for a three-hour tour over rolling hills on mostly paved roads. Explore the remains of the Sugar Bird Hotel, the inspiration for Herman Wouk's book, *Don't Stop the Carnival*, the site of a 17th-century plantation and beautiful Honeymoon beach for a cooling swim. Helmets, water, a guide, and ferry fare are included in the $60 cost.

FISHING

Fishing here is synonymous with blue marlin angling—especially from June through October. Four 1,000-pound-plus blues, including three world records, have been caught on the famous North Drop, about 20 mi (32 km) north of St. Thomas. If you're not into marlin fishing, try hooking up sailfish in the winter, dolphinfish come spring, and wahoo in the fall. To really find the trip that will best suit you, walk down the docks at either American Yacht Harbor or Sapphire Beach Marina in the late afternoons and chat with the captains and crews.

At the **American Yacht Harbor** (✉ 6100 Red Hook Plaza, Red Hook, ☎ 340/775–6454), you'll find the charter boats *Blue Fin II, Marlin Prince*, and *Prowler*. The **Charter Boat Center** (✉ 6300 Red Hook Plaza, Red Hook, ☎ 340/775–7990 or 800/866–5714) is a major source for sport fishing charters. Capt. Red Bailey's *Abigail III* bases out of the **Sapphire Beach Marina** (✉ Sapphire Bay, ☎ 340/775–6100), along with several other charter operations.

GOLF

The **Mahogany Run Golf Course** (✉ Rte. 42, Estate Lovenlund, ☎ 340/777–5000, WEB www.mahoganyrungolf.com) underwent extensive renovation in 2001, which included re-grassing the green and doubling the size of the 15th hole so that the green spans 6,000 square ft. The attraction for golfers is a spectacular view of the British Virgin Islands and the challenging 3-hole Devil's Triangle on this Tom and George Fazio–designed par-70, 18-hole course. There's a fully stocked pro shop, snack bar, and open-air club house. The course is open daily and there are frequently informal weekend tournaments.

PARASAILING

The Caribbean waters are so clear here that the outlines of coral reefs are visible from high in the sky. Parasailers sit in a harness attached to a parachute that lifts them off a boat deck until they're sailing up in the air. Parasailing trips average a 10-minute ride in the sky that costs $55 per person. Friends who want to ride along and watch pay $10 for the boat trip. **Caribbean Parasail and Watersports** (✉ 6501 Red Hook Plaza, Red Hook, ☎ 340/775–9360) makes parasailing pick-ups from every beachfront resort. They also rent jet skis, kayaks, and floating battery-powered chairs.

SCUBA DIVING AND SNORKELING

Popular dive sites include such wrecks as the *Cartanser Sr.,* a beauti-fully encrusted World War II cargo ship sitting 35-ft deep (11 m deep), and the *General Rogers,* a 65-ft-deep (21-m-deep) Coast Guard cut-ter with a gigantic resident barracuda. Reef dives offer hidden caves and archways at **Cow and Calf Rocks,** coral-covered pinnacles at **French-cap,** and tunnels where you can explore undersea from the Caribbean to the Atlantic at **Thatch Cay, Grass Cay,** and **Congo Cay.** Many resorts and charter yachts offer dive packages. A one-tank dive starts at $50; two-tank dives are $70 or more. There are plenty of snorkeling pos-sibilities, too. Nick Aquilar's *At-A-Glance Snorkeller's Guide to St. Thomas,* available at local souvenir shops, describes 15 idyllic spots in detail.

Admiralty Dive Center (✉ Waterfront Hwy., Charlotte Amalie, ☎ 340/777–9802, WEB www.admiraltydive.com), at the Holiday Inn St. Thomas, provides boat dives, rental equipment and a retail store. Six-tank to 12-tank packages are available if you want to dive over sev-eral days. **Aqua Action** (✉ 6501 Red Hook Plaza, Red Hook, ☎ 340/775–6285, WEB www.aadivers.com) is a full-service, PADI five-star shop that offers all levels of instruction at Secret Harbour Beach Re-sort. **Blue Island Divers** (✉ Rte. 304 at Crown Bay Marina, Estate Con-tant, ☎ 340/774–2001, WEB www.blueislanddivers.com) is a full-service dive shop that offers both day and night dives to wrecks and reefs. **Chris Sawyer Diving Center** (☎ 340/775–7320 or 877/929–3483, WEB www.sawyerdive.vi) is a PADI five-star outfit that specializes in dives to the 310-ft-long *Rhone,* in the British Virgin Islands. Hotel/dive packages are offered through the Renaissance Grand Beach Resort, Wyn-dham Sugar Bay Beach Club & Resort, and Colony Point Pleasant Re-sort. **Snuba of St. Thomas** (✉ Rte. 388 at Coki Point, Estate Frydendal, ☎ 340/693–8063, WEB www.visnuba.com) offers a cross between snorkeling and scuba diving: a 20-ft (6-m) air hose connects you to the surface.

SEA EXCURSIONS

Landlubbers and seafarers alike will enjoy the wind in their hair and salt spray in the air while exploring the waters surrounding St. Thomas. Several businesses can effortlessly book you on a half-day inshore light-tackle fishing trip for $300 to $400 for two anglers; a snorkel-and-sail to a deserted cay for the day that costs on the average $75 to $90 per person; or an excursion over to the British Virgin Islands starting at $100 per person plus $12 custom's fees. For a soup-to-nuts choice of sea tours, contact the **Adventure Center** (✉ Rte. 315 at Mar-riott French's Reef Hotel, Estate Bakkeroe, ☎ 340/774–2990). The **Char-ter Boat Center** (✉ 6300 Red Hook Plaza, Red Hook, ☎ 340/775–7990 or 800/866–5714) specializes in day trips to the British Virgin Islands and day or weeklong sailing charters. **Limnos Charters** (✉ 6100 Red Hook Plaza, Red Hook, ☎ 340/775–3203, WEB www.limnoscharters.com) offers one of the most popular British Virgin Is-lands day-trips, complete with lunch, open bar, and snorkel gear. Jimmy Loveland at **Treasure Isle Cruises** (✉ Rte. 32, #6616, Estate Nadir, ☎ 340/775–9500, WEB www.treasureislecruises.com) can set you up with everything from a half-day sail to a 10-day multi-island sailing adventure.

SEA KAYAKING

Fish dart, birds sing, and iguanas lounge on the limbs of dense mangroves deep within a marine sanctuary on St. Thomas's southeast shore. Many resorts on St. Thomas's eastern end have kayaks. **Virgin Islands Ecotours** (⊠ Rte. 32, Estate Nadir, ☎ 340/779–2155, 〔WEB〕 www. usvi-on-line.com/partners/vieco/vieco.html) offers 2½-hour guided trips on two-person sit-atop ocean kayaks; there are stops for swimming and snorkeling. The cost is $50 per person.

STARGAZING

Without the light pollution so prevalent in more densely populated areas, the heavens appear supernaturally bright. On a **Star Charters Astronomy Adventure** (☎ 340/774–9211), you can peer into the Caribbean's largest telescope—an 18-inch Newtonian reflector—and learn the science and lore of the stars from a well-informed celestial guide.

SUBMARINING

Dive 90 ft (28 m) under the sea to one of St. Thomas's most beautiful reefs without getting wet. The ***Atlantis* Adventures** (⊠ Havensight Shopping Mall, Bldg. VI, Charlotte Amalie, ☎ 340/776–5650, 〔WEB〕 www. goatlantis.com/stthomas) submarine is a 46-passenger, air-conditioned conduit to a watery world teeming with brightly colored fish, vibrant sea fans, and an occasional shark. A guide narrates the two-hour journey, while a diver makes a mid-tour appearance for a fish-feeding show. The cost is $72. No children shorter than 36 inches tall are allowed.

TENNIS

The Caribbean sun is hot, so be sure to hit the courts before 10 AM or after 5 PM (many courts are lighted). You can indulge in a set or two even if you're staying in a guest house without courts, since most hotels rent time to nonguests. **Marriott Frenchman's Reef Resort** (⊠ Rte. 315, Estate Bakkeroe, ☎ 340/776–8500 Ext. 6818) has two courts, with nonguests charged $10 per hour per court. There are six courts at **Renaissance Grand Beach Resort** (⊠ Rte. 38, Estate Smith Bay, ☎ 340/775–1510) that are lighted until 8 PM and rent for $8 per hour. Three courts are available at the **Ritz-Carlton, St. Thomas** (⊠ Rte. 317, #6900, Estate Great Bay, ☎ 340/775–3333), where nonguests can reserve lessons for $60 per hour and $35 per ½ hour. **Sapphire Beach Resort** (⊠ Sapphire Bay, ☎ 340/775–6100 Ext. 8135) has four courts that fill up fast in the cool early morning hours. The cost for nonguests is $10 per hour. Tennis pro Cecil Phillips gives lessons to nonguests at **Wyndham Sugar Bay** (⊠ Rte. 38, #6500, Estate Smith Bay, ☎ 340/777–7100) by appointment. Rates start at $40 for a half-hour lesson.

Lindberg Bay Park (⊠ Rte. 302, Estate Lindberg Bay) has two courts that are open to the public; it's opposite the Cyril E. King Airport. There are two public tennis courts at **Sub Base** (⊠ Rte. 306, next to the Water and Power Authority, Estate Contant), open on a first-come, first-served basis for no cost. Lights are on until 10 PM.

WINDSURFING

Expect some spills, anticipate the thrills, and try your luck clipping through the seas. Most beachfront resorts rent Windsurfers and offer one-hour lessons for about $60. One of the island's best-known independent windsurfing companies is **West Indies Windsurfing** (⊠ Vessup Beach, No. 9, Estate Nazareth, ☎ 340/775–6530).

Spectator Sports

HORSE RACING

The **Clinton Phipps Racetrack** (⊠ Rte. 30, Estate Nadir, ☎ 340/775–4555) schedules races—especially on local holidays—with sanctioned betting. Be prepared for large crowds.

Shopping

St. Thomas lives up to its billing as a duty-free shopping destination. Even if shopping isn't your idea of how to spend a vacation, you still may want to slip in on a quiet day (check the cruise-ship listings—Monday and Saturday are usually the least crowded) to browse. Among the best buys are liquor, linens, china, crystal (most stores will ship), and jewelry. The amount of jewelry available makes this one of the few items for which comparison shopping is worth the effort. Local crafts include shell jewelry, carved calabash bowls, straw brooms, woven baskets, fragrances, and dolls. Creations by local doll maker Gwendolyn Harley— like her costumed West Indian market woman—have been goodwill ambassadors bought by visitors from as far away as Asia. Spice mixes, hot sauces, and tropical jams and jellies are other native products.

There's no sales tax in the USVI, and you can take advantage of the $1,200 duty-free allowance per family member (remember to save your receipts). Although you'll find the occasional salesclerk who will make a deal, bartering isn't the norm.

Areas and Malls

The prime shopping area in **Charlotte Amalie** is between Post Office and Market squares; it consists of three parallel streets that run east–west (Waterfront Highway, Main Street, and Back Street) and the alleyways that connect them. Particularly attractive are the historic **A. H. Riise Alley, Royal Dane Mall, Palm Passage,** and pastel-painted **International Plaza**—quaint alleys between Main Street and the Waterfront.

Vendors Plaza, on the waterfront side of Emancipation Gardens in Charlotte Amalie, is a central location for vendors selling handmade earrings, necklaces, and bracelets; straw baskets and handbags; T-shirts; fabrics; African artifacts; and local fruits. Look for the many brightly colored umbrellas.

West of Charlotte Amalie, the pink-stucco **Nisky Center,** on Harwood Highway about ½ mi (¾ km) east of the airport, is more of a hometown shopping center than a tourist area, but you'll find a bank, pharmacy, record shop, and Radio Shack.

Havensight Mall, next to the cruise-ship dock, may not be as charming as downtown Charlotte Amalie, but it does have more than 60 shops. You'll find an excellent bookstore, a bank, a pharmacy, a gourmet grocery, and smaller branches of many downtown stores. The shops at **Port of Sale,** which adjoins the Havensight Mall (its buildings are pink instead of the brown of the Havensight shops), sell discount items.

East of Charlotte Amalie on Route 38, **Tillett Gardens** is an oasis of artistic endeavor across from the Tutu Park Shopping Mall. The late Jim Tillett and then-wife Rhoda converted this old Danish farm into an artists' retreat in 1959. Today you can watch artisans produce silk-screen fabrics, pottery, candles, watercolors, jewelry, and other handicrafts. Something special is often happening in the gardens as well: the Classics in the Gardens program is a classical music series presented under the stars, Arts Alive is a visual-arts and crafts festival held four times yearly, and the Pistarckle Theater holds its performances here.

Tutu Park Shopping Mall, across from Tillett Gardens, is the island's one and only enclosed mall. The 47 stores and food court are anchored by a Kmart and the Plaza Extra grocery store. Archaeologists have discovered evidence that Arawak Indians once lived near the mall grounds.

Red Hook has **American Yacht Harbor,** a waterfront shopping area with a dive shop, a tackle store, clothing and jewelry boutique, and a few restaurants. Don't forget **St. John.** A ferry ride (an hour from Charlotte Amalie or 20 minutes from Red Hook) will take you to the charming shops of **Mongoose Junction** and **Wharfside Village,** which specialize in unique, often island-made items.

Specialty Items

ART

A. H. Riise Caribbean Print Gallery. Historic and contemporary prints, posters, and photo notecards depicting West Indian life are sold here. ⊠ *37 Main St., Charlotte Amalie, at Riise's Alley,* ☎ *340/776–2303.*

Blue Turtle Gallery. Best known for her vivid tropical landscapes, local artist Lucinda Schutt not only exhibits her artwork but uses the gallery to teach and showcase water color paintings by students. ⊠ *Government Hill, two buildings west of Hotel 1829, Charlotte Amalie,* ☎ *340/774–9440,* WEB *www.blueturtlegallery.net.*

Camille Pissarro Art Gallery. This second-floor gallery, in the birthplace of St. Thomas's famous artist, offers a fine collection of original paintings and prints by local and regional artists. ⊠ *14 Main St., Charlotte Amalie,* ☎ *340/774–4621.*

Mango Tango. Works by popular local artists—originals, prints, and notecards—are displayed (there's a one-person show at least one weekend a month) and sold here. You'll also find the island's largest humidor and a brand-name cigar gallery. ⊠ *Al Cohen's Plaza, atop Raphune Hill, ½ mi (¾ km) east of Charlotte Amalie,* ☎ *340/777–3995.*

BOOKS AND MAGAZINES

Dockside Bookshop. This place is packed with books for children, travelers, cooks, and historians, as well as a good selection of paperback mysteries, best-sellers, art books, calendars, and prints. It also carries a selection of books written in and about the Caribbean and the Virgin Islands. ⊠ *Rte. 30 at Havensight Mall, Charlotte Amalie,* ☎ *340/774–4937.*

Island Newsstand. This place has the largest selection of magazines and newspapers on St. Thomas. Expect to pay about 20% above stateside prices. ⊠ *Grand Galleria, Tolbod Gade at Norre Gade, Charlotte Amalie,* ☎ *340/774–0043.*

CAMERAS AND ELECTRONICS

Boolchand's. Brand-name cameras, audio and video equipment, and binoculars are sold here. ⊠ *31 Main St., Charlotte Amalie,* ☎ *340/776–0794;* ⊠ *Rte. 30 at Havensight Mall, Charlotte Amalie,* ☎ *340/776–0302.*

Royal Caribbean. Shop here for cameras, camcorders, stereos, watches, and clocks. ⊠ *33 Main St., Charlotte Amalie,* ☎ *340/776–4110;* ⊠ *Rte. 30 at Havensight Mall, Charlotte Amalie,* ☎ *340/776–8890,* WEB *www.royalcaribbean.vi.*

CHINA AND CRYSTAL

The Crystal Shoppe. All is glitter at this family-run store that sells Swarovski and Waterford crystal, figurines by Hummel, Daum, and Royal Copenhagen, and china by Belleek, Kosta Boda, and several Limoges factories. ⊠ *14 Main St., Charlotte Amalie,* ☎ *340/777–9835.*

The English Shop. This store offers figurines, cutlery, and china and crystal from major European and Japanese manufacturers, including Spode, Royal Doulton, Portmeirion, Noritaki, and Wedgwood. You can choose what you like from the catalogs here, and shopkeepers will order and factory-ship it for you. (Be sure to keep your receipts in case something goes awry.) ⊠ *Rte. 30 at Havensight Mall, Charlotte Amalie,* ☎ *340/776–1555.*

Little Switzerland. All of this establishment's shops carry crystal from Baccarat, Waterford, Orrefors, and Riedel; china from Villeroy &

Boch, Rosenthal, and Wedgwood, among others. There's also an assortment of cut-crystal animals, china, and porcelain figurines—including Lladro figurines, and many other affordable collectibles. They also do a booming mail-order business; ask for a catalog. ✉ *Tolbod Gade, across from Emancipation Garden, Charlotte Amalie,* ☎ *340/776–2010;* ✉ *3B Main St., Charlotte Amalie,* ☎ *340/776–2010;* ✉ *5 Main St., Charlotte Amalie, inside A. H. Riise Gift Mart,* ☎ *340/776–2303;* ✉ *Rte. 30 at Havensight Mall, Charlotte Amalie, located dockside,* ☎ *340/776–2198,* WEB *www.littleswitzerland.com.*

CLOTHING

Cosmopolitan. At this sophisticated clothing emporium, look for such top lines as Paul and Shark, Bally, Timberland, Sperry Topsider, Givenchy, and Nautica. ✉ *Drake's Passage at the Waterfront, Charlotte Amalie,* ☎ *340/776–2040.* WEB *www.cosmopolitan.vi.*

Local Color. Men, women, and children will find something to choose from among brand name wear like Jams World, Urban Safari, and St. John artist Sloop Jones's colorful, hand-painted island designs on cool dresses, T-shirts, and sweaters. There are also tropically oriented accessories like big-brimmed straw hats, bold-color bags, and casual jewelry. ✉ *Royal Dane Mall, Charlotte Amalie, at the Waterfront,* ☎ *340/774–2280.*

Lover's Lane. With the motto "Couples that play together, stay together," this romantic second-floor shop sells sensuous lingerie, sexy menswear, and provocative swimwear. ✉ *Waterfront Hwy. at Raadets Gade, Charlotte Amalie,* ☎ *340/777–9616,* WEB *www.loverslane.com.*

Pusser's Tropical & Nautical Co. Store. Here, tropical sports and travel clothing for men, women, and children all have a nautical theme. Look for bottles of Pusser's rum at the sales counter. Find discounted items at the Havensight location. ✉ *Waterfront Hwy. at Riise's Alley, Charlotte Amalie,* ☎ *340/777–9281;* ✉ *Rte. 30 across from Havensight Mall, Charlotte Amalie,* ☎ *340/774–9680.*

Tommy Hilfiger Boutique. Stop by this shop for classic American jeans and sportswear as well as trendy bags, belts, ties, socks, caps, and wallets. ✉ *Waterfront Hwy. at Trompeter Gade, Charlotte Amalie,* ☎ *340/777–1189.*

FOODSTUFFS

Caribbean Chocolate. Everything at this confectionery tastes as good as it smells. A wide assortment of Godiva chocolates shares space with Caribbean rum balls, tropical-flavor saltwater taffy, colorful jelly beans, homemade fudge, and Caribbean coffees. ✉ *Trompeter Gade, Charlotte Amalie,* ☎ *340/774–6675.*

Cost-U-Less. This store sells everything from soup to nuts, but in giant sizes and case lots. The meat and seafood department, however, has smaller, family-size portions. ✉ *Rte. 38, 1 mi (1½ km) east of Charlotte Amalie and ¼ mi (½ km) west of Rte. 39 intersection, Estate Donoe,* ☎ *340/777–3588.*

Fruit Bowl. For fresh fruits and vegetables, this is the place to go. ✉ *Rte. 38 and 313 intersection at the Wheatley Center, Charlotte Amalie,* ☎ *340/774–8565.*

Gourmet Gallery. Visiting millionaires buy their caviar here. There's also an excellent and reasonably priced wine selection, as well as specialty ingredients for everything from tacos to curries to chow mein. A full-service deli offers imported meats, cheeses, and in-store prepared foods that are perfect for a gourmet picnic. ✉ *Rte. 304 at Crown Bay Marina, Estate Contant,* ☎ *340/776–8555;* ✉ *Rte. 30 at Havensight Mall, Charlotte Amalie,* ☎ *340/774–4948.*

Grandma Sandy's Island Cookie Company. The heavenly aroma wafting through the alleyways will pull you into this bake shop for creative yet decidedly homespun-tasting cookies. Owner Sandra Davis's famous tropical medley oatmeal cookies are bigger than the palm of your hand and studded with raisins, walnuts and dried mango bits. Gourmet coffees and teas are also available. ⊠ *Royal Dane Mall, Charlotte Amalie,* ☎ *340/776–7546.*

Marina Market. You won't find a better fresh-meat and seafood department anywhere on the island. ⊠ *Rte. 32 across from the Red Hook ferry, Red Hook,* ☎ *340/779–2411.*

Plaza Extra. This large U.S.-style supermarket has everything you need from produce to meat, including fresh seafood, a fresh foods deli, and a bakery. There's a bulk-size section and liquor department, too. ⊠ *Rte. 38 at Tutu Park Shopping Mall, Estate Tutu,* ☎ *340/775–5646.*

Pueblo Supermarkets. You'll find stateside brands of most products at these large supermarkets—but at higher prices because of shipping costs to the islands. ⊠ *Rte. 38 at Four Winds Plaza, across from Tillett Gardens, Estate Tutu,* ☎ *340/775–4655;* ⊠ *Sub Base, 1 mi (1½ km) north of Havensight Mall, Estate Contant,* ☎ *340/774–4200;* ⊠ *1 mi (1½ km) north of Havensight Mall, Estate Thomas,* ☎ *340/774–2695.*

U.S. Virgin Islands Rum Cake Centre. Pirate-outfitted sales staff will tell you the 17th-century secrets behind these scrumptious rum cakes, available in several flavors. Samples are available, as are gift tins. ⊠ *Rte. 30 at Havensight Shopping Mall, Charlotte Amalie,* ☎ *340/714–2936.*

HANDICRAFTS

Arabella's. St. Croix artist Jan Mitchell displays her vibrantly colored fused-glass platters and ornaments in this cheery store. You'll also find pottery, batik, baskets, and watercolors from Virgin Islands and Caribbean artists, not to mention hot sauces, jams, and jellies, too. ⊠ *Trompeter Gade, Charlotte Amalie,* ☎ *340/774–8041.*

Caribbean Marketplace. This is a great place to buy handicrafts from the Caribbean and elsewhere. Also look for Sunny Caribee spices, soaps, coffee, and teas from Tortola, and coffee from Trinidad. ⊠ *Rte. 30 at Havensight Shopping Mall, Charlotte Amalie,* ☎ *340/776–5400.*

Down Island Traders. These traders deal in hand-painted calabash bowls; finely printed Caribbean note cards; jams, jellies, spices, hot sauces, and herbs; teas made of lemongrass, passion fruit, and mango; coffee from Jamaica; and handicrafts from throughout the Caribbean. ⊠ *Waterfront Hwy. at Post Office Alley, Charlotte Amalie,* ☎ *340/ 776–4641.*

Native Arts and Crafts Cooperative. More than 40 local artists—including schoolchildren, senior citizens, and people with disabilities—create the handcrafted items for sale here: African-style jewelry, quilts, calabash bowls, dolls, carved-wood figures, woven baskets, straw brooms, note cards, and cookbooks. ⊠ *Tolbod Gade, across from Emancipation Garden and next to visitor center, Charlotte Amalie,* ☎ *340/ 777–1153.*

Tropical Memories. The emphasis here is on Virgin Islands artists. There are prints, pottery, gorgeous glass trays, carved mahogany bowls, and scented soaps. ⊠ *Royal Dane Mall, Charlotte Amalie,* ☎ *340/776– 7536.*

JEWELRY

Amsterdam Sauer. Many fine one-of-a-kind designs are displayed and this jeweler's three locations. The Imperial Topaz Collection at the Main Street store is a stunner. ⊠ *14 Main St., Charlotte Amalie,* ☎ *340/774– 2222;* ⊠ *Rte. 30 at Havensight Shopping Mall, Charlotte Amalie,* ☎ *340/776–3828;* ⊠ *Ritz-Carlton Resort, Rte. 317, #6900, Estate Great Bay,* ☎ *340/779–2308.*

Blue Carib Gems. At family-owned and -run Blue Carib Gems, watch Alan O'Hara, Sr., polish Caribbean amber and larimar, agate, and other gems and mount them into gold and silver settings. ✉ *2–3 Back St., Charlotte Amalie,* ☎ *340/774–8525.*

Cardow Jewelry. A "chain bar"—with gold chains in several lengths, widths, sizes and styles—awaits you here, along with diamonds, emeralds, and other precious gems. You're guaranteed 40%–60% savings off U.S. retail prices, or your money will be refunded within 30 days of purchase. ✉ *33 Main St., Charlotte Amalie,* ☎ *340/776–1140;* ✉ *Rte. 30 at Havensight Shopping Mall, Charlotte Amalie,* ☎ *340/774–0530 or 340/774–5905;* ✉ *Rte. 315 at Marriott Frenchman's Reef Resort, Estate Bakkeroe,* ☎ *340/774–0434.*

Colombian Emeralds. Well known in the Caribbean, this store offers set and unset emeralds as well as gems of every description. The watch boutique carries upscale Ebel, Tissot, and Jaeger LeCoultre brands. ✉ *30 Main St., Charlotte Amalie,* ☎ *340/777–5400;* ✉ *Waterfront at A. H. Riise Mall, Charlotte Amalie,* ☎ *340/774–1033;* ✉ *Rte. 30 at Havensight Mall, Charlotte Amalie,* ☎ *340/774–2442.*

Diamonds International. Choose a diamond, emerald, or tanzanite gem and a mounting, and you'll have your dream ring set in an hour. Famous for having the largest inventory of diamonds on the island, this shop welcomes trade-ins, has a U.S. service center, and offers free diamond earrings with every purchase. ✉ *31 Main St., Charlotte Amalie,* ☎ *340/774–3707;* ✉ *3 Drakes Passage, Charlotte Amalie,* ☎ *340/775–2010;* ✉ *7AB Drakes Passage, Charlotte Amalie,* ☎ *340/774–1516;* ✉ *Rte. 30 at Havensight Mall, Charlotte Amalie,* ☎ *340/776–0040;* ✉ *Wyndham Sugar Bay Beach Club & Resort, Rte. 38, #6500, Estate Smith Bay,* ☎ *340/777–7100.*

H. Stern Jewelers. The World Collection of jewels set in modern, fashionable designs and an exclusive sapphire watch have earned this Brazilian jeweler a stellar name. ✉ *12 Main St., Charlotte Amalie,* ☎ *340/776–1939;* ✉ *32AB Main St., Charlotte Amalie,* ☎ *340/776–1146;* ✉ *Rte. 30 at Havensight Mall, Charlotte Amalie,* ☎ *340/776–1223;* ✉ *Marriott Frenchman's Reef Resort, Estate Bakkeroe,* ☎ *340/776–3550.*

Rolex Watches at A. H. Riise. As the Virgin Islands official Rolex retailer, find one of the largest selections of these fine timepieces in the Caribbean. An After Sales Service Center assures your Rolex keeps on ticking for its lifetime. ✉ *37 Main St., at Riise's Alley, Charlotte Amalie,* ☎ *340/776–2303;* ✉ *Rte. 30 at Havensight Mall, Charlotte Amalie,* ☎ *340/776–4002.*

LEATHER GOODS

Purses and Things. This "house of handbags" has a wide selection of sizes and great prices (you can buy a five-in-one leather clutch for only $20). Bargains are equally good on eel-skin goods. ✉ *International Plaza, Charlotte Amalie,* ☎ *340/777–9717.*

Zora's. Fine leather sandals made to order are the specialty here. There's also a selection of made-only-in-the-Virgin-Islands backpacks, purses, and briefcases in durable, brightly colored canvas. ✉ *Norre Gade across from Roosevelt Park, Charlotte Amalie,* ☎ *340/774–2559.*

LINENS

Fabric in Motion. Fine Italian linens share space with Liberty's of London silky cottons, colorful batiks, cotton prints, ribbons, and accessories at this small shop. ✉ *Storetvaer Gade, Charlotte Amalie,* ☎ *340/774–2006.*

Mr. Tablecloth. The friendly staff here will help you choose from the floor-to-ceiling selection linens, from Tuscany lace tablecloths to Irish linen pillowcases. The prices will please. ✉ *6–7 Main St., Charlotte Amalie,* ☎ *340/774–4343.*

A. H. Riise Liquors. This Riise venture offers a large selection of tobacco (including imported cigars), as well as cordials, wines, and rare vintage Armagnacs, cognacs, ports, and Madeiras. It also stocks fruits in brandy and barware from England. ⊠ *37 Main St., at Riise's Alley, Charlotte Amalie,* ☎ *340/776–2303;* ⊠ *Rte. 30 at Havensight Mall, Charlotte Amalie,* ☎ *340/776–7713.*

Al Cohen's Discount Liquor. The wine selection at this warehouse-style store is very large. ⊠ *Rte. 30 across from Havensight Mall, Charlotte Amalie,* ☎ *340/774–3690.*

Rio Cigars. Find a wide selection of premium cigars and accessories, including A. Fuente, Romeo Y Juleta, Havana, and more. ⊠ *Royal Dane Mall, Charlotte Amalie,* ☎ *340/774–5877.*

MUSIC

Modern Music. Shop for the latest stateside and Caribbean CD and cassette releases, plus oldies, classical, and New Age music. ⊠ *Rte. 30 across from Havensight Shopping Mall, Charlotte Amalie,* ☎ *340/774–3100;* ⊠ *Rte. 30 at Nisky Center, Charlotte Amalie,* ☎ *340/777–8787.*

Parrot Fish Records and Tapes. A stock of standard stateside tapes and CDs, plus a good selection of Caribbean artists, including local groups, can be found here. Write them for a catalog of calypso, *soca* (up-tempo calypso), steel band, and reggae music. ⊠ *Back St., Charlotte Amalie (Box 9206, St. Thomas, USVI 00801),* ☎ *340/776–4514.*

PERFUME

Tropicana Perfume Shoppes. Tropicana has the largest selection of fragrances for men and women in all of the Virgin Islands, including those locally made by Gail Garrison from the essential oils of tropical fruits and flowers like mango and jasmine. ⊠ *2 Main St., Charlotte Amalie,* ☎ *340/774–0010.*

SUNGLASSES

Fashion Eyewear. Take your pick from among name-brand eyewear. A real plus here is prescription sunglasses, copied from your present eyewear, ready in a half hour for $99. ⊠ *International Plaza, Charlotte Amalie,* ☎ *340/776–9075.*

TOYS

Quick Pics. Birds sing, dogs bark, and fish swim in this animated toyland that is part of a larger electronics and souvenir store. Adults have as much fun trying out the wares as do kids. ⊠ *Rte. 30 at Havensight Mall, Charlotte Amalie,* ☎ *340/774–3500.*

Nightlife and the Arts

On any given night, especially in season, you'll find steel-pan orchestras, rock-and-roll, piano music, jazz, broken-bottle dancing (dancing atop broken glass), disco, and karaoke. Pick up a copy of the free, bright yellow *St. Thomas–St. John This Week* magazine when you arrive (you'll see it at the airport, in stores, and in hotel lobbies); the back pages list who's playing where. The Thursday edition of the *Daily News* carries complete listings for the upcoming weekend.

Nightlife

BARS

Agave Terrace. Island-style steel-pan bands are a treat that should not be missed. Pan music resonates after dinner here on Tuesdays and Thursdays. ⊠ *Rte. 38 at the Point Pleasant Resort, Estate Smith Bay,* ☎ *340/775–4142.*

Bolongo Beach House. There's a Carnival night complete with steel pan music on Wednesdays. ⊠ *Rte. 30, #50, Estate Bolongo,* ☎ *340/775–1800.*

Duffy's Love Shack. A live band and dancing under the stars is a big draw for locals and visitors alike. ⊠ *Red Hook Plaza parking lot, Red Hook,* ☎ *340/779–2080.*

Epernay Bistro. This intimate night spot has small tables for easy chatting, wine and champagne by the glass, and a spacious dance floor. Mix and mingle with island celebrities. The action runs from 4 PM until the wee hours from Mondays through Saturdays. ⊠ *24-A Honduras, Frenchtown,* ☎ *340/774–5348.*

The Greenhouse. Once this favorite eatery puts away the salt and pepper shakers at 10 PM, it becomes a rock-and-roll club with a DJ or live reggae bands raising the weary to their feet six nights a week. ⊠ *Waterfront Hwy. at Storetvaer Gade, Charlotte Amalie,* ☎ *340/774–7998.*

Iggies Beach Bar. Sing along karaoke-style to the sounds of the surf or the latest hits at this beachside lounge. There's live bands on the weekends where you can dance inside or kick up your heels under the stars. ⊠ *Rte. 30, #50, Estate Bolongo,* ☎ *340/775–1800.*

Old Mill Entertainment Complex. In—you guessed it—an old mill, this is a rock-'til-you-drop late-night spot Thursday through Sunday. There's also a tamer piano bar and jazz club in the complex, as well as billiards and foosball tables. ⊠ *193 Contant, Charlotte Amalie,* ☎ *340/774–7782.*

Raffles. There's steel pan and calypso on Thursdays, jazz and blues Fridays, live guitar Saturdays and open-mike night Sundays. ⊠ *Rte. 32 at Compass Point Marina, Estate Frydenhoj,* ☎ *340/775–6004.*

Ritz-Carlton. On Monday nights, catch pan music at this resort's bar. ⊠ *Rte. 317, #6900, Estate Great Bay,* ☎ *340/775–3333.*

The Arts

THEATER

Pistarkle Theater. The air-conditioned theater with more than 100 seats, nestled in Tillett Gardens, is the site of a dozen or more productions annually, plus a children's drama summer camp. ⊠ *Rte. 38 across from Tutu Park Shopping Mall, Estate Tutu,* ☎ *340/775–7877.*

Reichhold Center for the Arts. This amphitheater has its more-expensive seats covered by a roof. Schedules vary, so check the paper to see what's on when you're in town. Throughout the year there's an entertaining mix of local plays, dance exhibitions, and music of all types. ⊠ *Rte. 30 across from Brewers Beach, Estate Lindberg Bay,* ☎ *340/693–1559.*

Exploring St. Thomas

St. Thomas is only 13 mi (21 km) long and less than 4 mi (6½ km) wide, but it's extremely hilly, and even an 8- or 10-mi (13- or 16-km) trip could take several hours. Don't let that discourage you, though; the mountain ridge that runs east to west through the middle and separates the island's Caribbean and Atlantic sides has spectacular vistas.

Charlotte Amalie

Look beyond the pricey shops, T-shirt vendors, and bustling crowds for a glimpse of the island's history. The city served as the capital of Denmark's outpost in the Caribbean until 1917, an aspect of the island often lost in the glitz of the shopping district.

Emancipation Gardens, right next to the fort, is a good place to start a walking tour. Tackle the hilly part of town first: head north up Government Hill to the historic buildings that house government offices and have incredible views. Several regal churches line the route that runs west back to the town proper and the old-time market. Virtually all the alleyways that intersect Main Street lead to eateries that serve

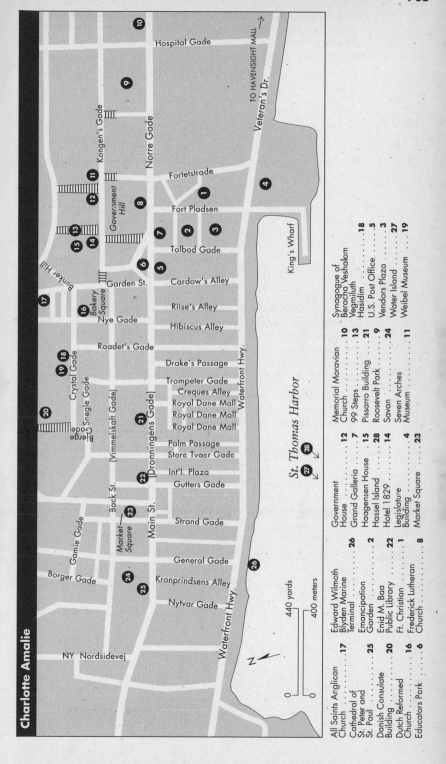

Charlotte Amalie

Hospital Gade
TO HAVENSIGHT MALL →
Veteran's Dr.
Kongen's Gade
Norre Gade
Fortetstrade
Government Hill
Fort Pladsen
Tolbod Gade
Garden St.
Cardow's Alley
Riise's Alley
Hibiscus Alley
Bakery Square
Nye Gade
Raadet's Gade
Bunker Hill
Drake's Passage
Crystal Gade
Trompeter Gade
Creques Alley
Royal Dane Mall
Royal Dane Mall
Royal Dane Mall
Bjerge Gade
Snegle Gade
(Vimmelskaft Gade)
(Dronningens Gade)
Palm Passage
Store Tvaer Gade
Int'l. Plaza
Gutters Gade
Back St.
Main St.
Strand Gade
Market Square
Gamle Gade
General Gade
Borger Gade
Kronprindsens Alley
Nytvar Gade
NY Nordsidevej
Waterfront Hwy.

King's Wharf

St. Thomas Harbor

440 yards
400 meters

All Saints Anglican Church 17
Cathedral of St. Peter and St. Paul 25
Danish Consulate Building 20
Dutch Reformed Church 16
Educators Park 6

Edward Wilmoth Blyden Marine Terminal 26
Emancipation Garden 2
Enid M. Baa Public Library 22
Ft. Christian 1
Frederick Lutheran Church 6

Government House 12
Grand Galleria . . . 7
Haagensen House . . . 15
Hassel Island 28
Hotel 1829 14
Legislature Building 4
Market Square 23

Memorial Moravian Church 10
99 Steps 13
Pissarro Building . . 21
Roosevelt Park 9
Savan 24
Seven Arches Museum 11

Synagogue of Beracha Veshalom Vegmiluth Hasidim 18
U.S. Post Office . . . 5
Vendors Plaza 3
Water Island 27
Weibel Museum . . . 19

frosty drinks, sandwiches and burgers, and West Indian fare. You'll find public rest rooms in this area, too. Allow an hour for a quick view of the sights, two hours if you plan to tour Government House.

A note about the street names: in deference to the island's heritage, the streets downtown are labeled by their Danish names. Locals will use both the Danish name and the English name (such as Dronningens Gade and Norre Gade for Main Street), but most people refer to things by their location ("a block toward the Waterfront off Main Street" or "next to the Little Switzerland Shop"). It's best to ask for directions by shop names or landmarks.

Numbers in the margin correspond to points of interest on the Charlotte Amalie map.

SIGHTS TO SEE

⑰ All Saints Anglican Church. Built in 1848 from stone quarried on the island, the church has thick, arched window frames lined with the yellow brick that came to the islands as ballast aboard ships. Merchants left the brick on the waterfront when they filled their boats with molasses, sugar, mahogany, and rum for the return voyage. The church was built in celebration of the end of slavery in the USVI. ⊠ *Domini Gade,* ☎ *340/774–0217.* ⊙ *Mon.–Sat. 9–3.*

㉕ Cathedral of St. Peter and St. Paul. This building was consecrated as a parish church in 1848 and serves as the seat of the territory's Roman Catholic diocese. The ceiling and walls are covered with murals painted in 1899 by two Belgian artists, Father Leo Servais and Brother Ildephonsus. The San Juan–marble altar and side walls were added in the 1960s. ⊠ *Lower Main St.,* ☎ *340/774–0201.* ⊙ *Mon.–Sat. 8–5.*

⑳ Danish Consulate Building. Built in 1830, this structure once housed the Danish Consulate. Today, it serves is the office of the territory's governor. ⊠ *Take stairs north at corner of Bjerge Gade and Crystal Gade to Denmark Hill.*

⑯ Dutch Reformed Church. This church has an austere loveliness that's amazing considering all it has been through—founded in 1744, it has been rebuilt twice in the last 200 years following fires and hurricanes. The unembellished cream-colored hall gives you a sense of peace—albeit monochromatically. The only other color is the forest green of the shutters and the carpet. Call ahead if you need to visit at a particular time; the doors are sometimes locked. ⊠ *Nye Gade and Crystal Gade,* ☎ *340/776–8255.* ⊙ *Weekdays 9–5.*

⑥ Educators Park. A peaceful place amid the town's hustle and bustle, the park has memorials to three famous Virgin Islanders: educator Edith Williams, J. Antonio Jarvis (a founder of the *Daily News*), and educator and author Rothschild Francis. The latter gave many speeches from here. ⊠ *Main St. across from U.S. Post Office.*

㉖ Edward Wilmoth Blyden Marine Terminal. Locally called "Tortola Wharf," it's where you can catch the *Native Son* and other ferries to the BVI. The restaurant upstairs is a good place to watch the Charlotte Amalie harbor traffic and sip an iced tea. Next door is the ramp for the *Seaborne* seaplane, which offers commuter service and flightseeing tours to St. Croix, the BVI, and Puerto Rico. ⊠ *Waterfront Hwy.*

② Emancipation Garden. Built to honor the freeing of slaves in 1848, the garden was the site of a 150th anniversary celebration of emancipation. A bronze bust of a freed slave blowing a symbolic conch shell commemorates this anniversary. The gazebo here is used for official ceremonies. Two other monuments show the island's Danish-American tie—a bust of Denmark's King Christian and a scaled-down model of the U.S. Liberty Bell. ⊠ *Between Tolbod Gade and Ft. Christian.*

㉒ Enid M. Baa Public Library. Like so many structures on the north side of Main Street, this large pink building is a typical 18th-century town house. Merchants built their houses (stores downstairs, living quarters above) across from the brick warehouses on the south side of the street. The library was once the home of merchant and landowner Baron von Bretton. It's the island's first recorded fireproof building, meaning it was built of ballast brick instead of wood. Its interior of high ceilings and cool stone floors is the perfect refuge from the afternoon sun. You can browse through historic papers or just sit in the breeze by an open window reading the paper. ⊠ *Main St.,* ☎ *340/774–0630.* ⊙ *Weekdays 9–5, Sat. 9–3.*

① Ft. Christian. St. Thomas's oldest standing structure, this monument anchors the shopping district. It was built in 1672–1680 and now has U.S. National Landmark status. The clock tower was added in the 19th century. This remarkable building has, over time, been used as a jail, governor's residence, town hall, courthouse, and church. Ft. Christian now houses **The Virgin Islands Museum,** where you can see exhibits on USVI history, natural history, and turn-of-the-20th-century furnishings. Local artists display their works monthly in the gallery. A gift shop sells local crafts, books, and other souvenir items. This is also the site of the Chamber of Commerce's Hospitality Lounge, where you'll find public rest rooms, brochures, and a place you can stash your luggage for some last-minute shopping on the way to the airport. ⊠ *Waterfront Hwy. just east of shopping district,* ☎ *340/776–4566.* 🎫 *Free.* ⊙ *Weekdays 8:30–4:30.*

⑧ Frederick Lutheran Church. This historic church has a massive mahogany altar, and its pews—each with its own door—were once rented to families of the congregation. Lutheranism is the state religion of Denmark, and when the territory was without a minister, the governor—who had his own elevated pew—filled in. ⊠ *Norre Gade,* ☎ *340/776–1315.* ⊙ *Mon.–Sat. 9–4.*

⑫ Government House. Built as an elegant residence in 1867, today Government House serves as the governor's office, with the first floor open to the public. The staircases are of native mahogany, as are the plaques hand-lettered in gold with the names of the governors appointed and, since 1970, elected. Brochures detailing the history of the building are available, but you may have to ask for them.

The three murals at the back of the lobby were painted by Pepino Mangravatti in the 1930s as part of the U.S. government's Works Projects Administration. They depict Columbus's landing on St. Croix during his second voyage in 1493; the transfer of the islands from Denmark to the United States in 1917; and a sugar plantation on St. John.

A deputy administrator can take you on a tour of the second floor. You can call ahead for an appointment, or you can take a chance that an official will be in. It's worth the extra effort, if for no other reason than the terrace view. Imagine colonial affairs of state being conducted in the grandeur of the high-ceiling, chandeliered ballroom. In the reception room are four small paintings by Camille Pissarro, but unfortunately they're hard to appreciate because they're enclosed in frosted-glass cases. More interesting—and visible—is the large painting by an unknown artist that was found in Denmark and purchased by former governor Ralph M. Paiewonsky, who then gave it to Government House: it depicts a romanticized version of St. Croix. ⊠ *Government Hill,* ☎ *340/774–0001.* 🎫 *Free.* ⊙ *Weekdays 8–5.*

7 Grand Galleria. This imposing building stands at the head of Main Street. Once the island's premier hotel, it has been converted into offices and shops. ⊠ *Tolbod Gade at Norre Gade,* ☎ *340/774–7282.* ☉ *Weekdays 8–5, Sat. 9–noon.*

15 Haagensen House. Behind Hotel 1829, this lovingly restored home was built in the early 1800s by Danish entrepreneur Hans Haagensen and is surrounded by an equally impressive cookhouse, outbuildings, and terraced gardens. A lower-level banquet hall now showcases an antique-print and photo gallery. ⊠ *Government Hill,* ☎ *340/774–5541,* W̄Ē̄B̄ *haagensenhouse.com.* ⊡ *$8.* ☉ *Daily 9–4.*

28 Hassel Island. East of Water Island in Charlotte Amalie harbor, Hassel Island is part of the Virgin Islands National Park, as it has the ruins of a British military garrison (built during a brief British occupation of the USVI during the 1800s) and the remains of a marine railway (where ships were hoisted into drydock for repairs). There's a small ferry that runs from the Crown Bay Marina to the island; departure times are posted at Tickles Dockside Pub, and the fare is $3.50 or $7 round-trip.

14 Hotel 1829. As its name implies, it was built in 1829, albeit as a residence of a prominent merchant named Lavalette rather than as a hotel. The building's bright coral-color exterior walls are accented with fancy black wrought iron, and the interior is paneled in a dark wood, which makes it feel delightfully cool. From the dining terrace there's an exquisite view of the harbor framed by tangerine-color bougainvillea. Be sure to visit Haagensen House, just behind the hotel, for a peek at another wonderfully restored 19th-century home. ⊠ *Government Hill,* ☎ *340/776–1829.*

4 Legislature Building. Its pastoral-looking lime-green exterior conceals the vociferous political wrangling of the Virgin Islands Senate going on inside. Constructed originally by the Danish as a police barracks, the building was later used to billet U.S. Marines, and much later it housed a public school. You're welcome to sit in on sessions in the upstairs chambers. ⊠ *Waterfront Hwy. across from Ft. Christian,* ☎ *340/774–0880.* ☉ *Daily 8–5.*

23 Market Square. Formally called Rothschild Francis Square, this is a good place to find produce. A cadre of old-timers sells mangoes and papayas, strange-looking root vegetables, and herbs; sidewalk vendors offer African fabrics and artifacts and tie-dyed cotton clothes at good prices. ⊠ *North side of Main St. at Strand Gade.*

10 Memorial Moravian Church. Built in 1884, it was named to commemorate the 150th anniversary of the Moravian Church in the VI. ⊠ *17 Norre Gade,* ☎ *340/776–0066.* ☉ *Weekdays 8–5.*

☙ **13 99 Steps.** This staircase "street," built by the Danes in the 1700s, leads to the residential area above Charlotte Amalie and Blackbeard's Castle. The castle's tower, built in 1679, was once used by the notorious pirate Edward Teach. Today this lookout serves at the backdrop for a trendy restaurant. If you count the stairs as you go up, you'll discover, as have thousands before you, that there are more than 99. ⊠ *Look for steps heading north from Government Hill.*

21 Pissarro Building. Housing several shops and an art gallery, this was the birthplace and childhood home of Camille Pissarro, who later moved to France and became an acclaimed impressionist painter. In the art gallery you'll find three original pages from Pissarro's sketchbook and two pastels by Pissarro's grandson, Claude. ⊠ *Main St., between Raadets Gade and Trompeter Gade.*

9 **Roosevelt Park.** You'll see members of the local legal community head to the nearby court buildings while you rest on a bench in this park—a good spot to people-watch. The small monument on the park's south side is dedicated to USVI war veterans. Kids enjoy the playground made of wood and tires. ⊠ *Norre Gade.*

24 **Savan.** A neighborhood of small streets and houses, it was first laid out in the 1700s as the residential area for a growing community of middle-class black artisans, clerks, and shopkeepers. You'll find a row of Rastafarian shops along the first block and restaurants that sell *pate*—a delicious turnover-type pastry stuffed with meat or vegetables. It's best not to walk here at night and to exercise caution even in daylight. ⊠ *Turn north off lower Main St. onto General Gade.*

11 **Seven Arches Museum.** This restored 18th-century home is a striking example of classic Danish–West Indian architecture. There seem to be arches everywhere—seven to be exact—all supporting a "welcoming arms" staircase that leads to the second floor and the flower-framed front doorway. The Danish kitchen is a highlight: it's housed in a separate building just off the main house, as were all cooking facilities in the early days (in case of fire). Inside the house you'll find mahogany furnishings and gas lamps. ⊠ *Government Hill, 3 bldgs. east of Government House,* ☎ *340/774–9295.* ⊡ *$5, suggested donation.* ☉ *10–4. By appointment only Aug.–Sept.*

18 **Synagogue of Beracha Veshalom Vegmiluth Hasidim.** The synagogue's Hebrew name translates to the Congregation of Blessing, Peace, and Loving Deeds. The small building's white pillars contrast with rough stone walls, as does the rich mahogany of the pews and altar. The sand on the floor symbolizes the exodus from Egypt. Since the synagogue first opened its doors in 1833, it has held a weekly Sabbath service, making it the oldest synagogue building in continuous use under the American flag and the second-oldest (after the one on Curaçao) in the western hemisphere. Guided ½ hour tours are offered weekdays beginning at 10:30 AM. Next door, the Weibel Museum showcases Jewish history on St. Thomas. ⊠ *15 Crystal Gade,* ☎ *340/774–4312.* ☉ *Weekdays 9–4.*

5 **U.S. Post Office.** While you buy your postcard stamps, contemplate the murals of waterfront scenes by *Saturday Evening Post* artist Stephen Dohanos. His art was commissioned as part of the Works Project Administration (WPA) in the 1930s. ⊠ *Tolbod Gade and Main St.*

3 **Vendors Plaza.** Here merchants sell everything from T-shirts to African attire to leather goods. Look for local art among the ever-changing selections at this busy market. ⊠ *West of Ft. Christian at the waterfront.* ☉ *Weekdays 8–6, weekends 9–1.*

27 **Water Island.** This island, once owned by the U.S. Department of the Interior and about ¼ mi (½ km) out in Charlotte Amalie Harbor, was once a peninsula of St. Thomas. A channel was cut through so that U.S. submarines could get to their base in a bay just to the west, known as Sub Base. Today, this is the fourth-largest U.S. Virgin Island. A ferry goes between Crown Bay Marina and the island several times daily, at a cost of $3.50 or $7 round-trip.

19 **Weibel Museum.** In this museum next to the synagogue, 300 years of Jewish history on St. Thomas are showcased. The small gift shop sells a commemorative silver coin celebrating the anniversary of the Hebrew congregation's establishment on the island in 1796. There's also tropically inspired items like a shell seder plate and palm tree painted menorahs. ⊠ *15 Crystal Gade,* ☎ *340/774–4312.* ⊡ *Free.* ☉ *Weekdays 9–4.*

Around the Island

To explore outside Charlotte Amalie, you'll need to rent a car or hire a taxi. Your rental car should come with a good map; if not, pick up the "St. Thomas–St. John Road Map" at a tourist information center. Roads are marked with route numbers, but they're confusing and seem to switch numbers suddenly. If you stop to ask for directions, it's best to have your map in hand because locals probably know the road you're looking for by another name. Allow yourself a day to explore, especially if you want to stop for picture taking or to enjoy a light bite or refreshing swim. Most gas stations are on the island's more populated eastern end, so fill up before heading to the north side. And remember to drive on the left.

Although the eastern end has many major resorts and spectacular beaches, don't be surprised if a cow or a herd of goats crosses your path as you drive through the relatively flat, dry terrain. The north side of the island is more lush and hush—fewer houses and less traffic. Here you'll find roller-coaster routes (made all the more scary because the roads have no shoulders) and incredible vistas. Leave time in the afternoon for a swim at the beach. Pick up some sandwiches from delis in the Red Hook area for a picnic lunch, or enjoy a slice of pizza at Magens Bay. A day in the country will reveal the tropical pleasures that have enticed more than one visitor to become a resident.

Numbers in the margin correspond to points of interest on the St. Thomas map.

SIGHTS TO SEE

31 **Compass Point Marina.** It's fun to park your car and walk around this marina. The boaters—many of whom have sailed here from points around the globe—are easy to engage in conversation. Turn south off Route 32 at well-marked entrance road just east of Independent Boat Yard. ⊠ *Estate Frydenhoj.*

33 **Coral World Marine Park.** Coral World has an offshore underwater observatory that houses the Predator Tank, one of the world's largest coral-reef tanks, and an aquarium with more than 20 portholes providing close-ups of Caribbean sea life. *Sea Trekkin'* lets you tour the reef outside the park at a depth of 15 ft (4½ m) under the sea thanks to specialized high-tech headgear and a continuous air supply that's based on the surface. A guide leads the ½-hour tour and the narration is piped through a specialized microphone inside each trekker's helmet; the cost is $50 per person. The park also has several outdoor pools where you can touch starfish, pet a baby shark, feed stingrays, and view endangered sea turtles. In addition you'll find a mangrove lagoon and a nature trail full of lush tropical flora. Daily feedings and talks take place at most every exhibit. ⊠ *Coki Point, turn north off Rte. 38 at sign, Estate Frydendal,* ☎ *340/775–1555,* WEB *www.coralworldvi.com.* ⊠ $18. ⊙ *Daily 9–5:30.*

36 **Drake's Seat.** Sir Francis Drake was supposed to have kept watch over his fleet and looked for enemy ships from this vantage point. The panorama is especially breathtaking (and romantic) at dusk, and if you arrive late in the day you'll miss the hordes of day-trippers on taxi tours who stop here to take a picture and buy a T-shirt from one of the many vendors. ⊠ *Rte. 40, Estate Zufriedenheit.*

37 **Estate St. Peter Greathouse & Botanical Gardens.** This unusual spot is perched on a mountainside 1,000 ft (306 m) above sea level, with views of more than 20 other islands and islets. You can wander through a gallery displaying local art, sip a complimentary rum or Virgin Punch while looking out at the view, or follow a nature trail that leads through nearly 200 varieties of trees and plants, including an orchid jungle. ⊠ *Rte. 40, Estate St. Peter,* ☎ *340/774–4999,* WEB *www.greathouse-mountaintop.com.* 🎟 *$10.* ⊗ *Mon.–Sat. 9–4:30.*

38 **Frenchtown.** Popular for its several bars and restaurants, Frenchtown is also the settling place of the descendants of immigrants from St. Barthélemy (St. Barths). You can watch them pull up their brightly painted boats and display their equally colorful catch of the day along the waterfront. If you chat with them, you'll hear speech patterns slightly different from those of other St. Thomians. Get a feel for the residential district of Frenchtown by walking west to some of the town's winding streets, where tiny wooden houses have been passed down from generation to generation. ⊠ *Turn south off Waterfront Hwy. at the U.S. Post Office.*

35 **Mountain Top.** Stop here for a banana daiquiri and spectacular views from the observation deck more than 1,500 ft (459 m) above sea level. There are also shops that sell everything from Caribbean art to nautical antiques, ship models, and T-shirts. Kids will like talking to the parrots—and hearing them answer back. ⊠ *Head north off Rte. 33; look for signs.* WEB *www.greathouse-mountaintop.com.*

30 **Paradise Point Tramway.** Fly skyward in a gondola to Paradise Point, an overlook with breathtaking views of Charlotte Amalie and the harbor. There are several shops, a bar, and a restaurant. A ¼-mi (½-km) hiking trail leads to spectacular sights of St. Croix to the south. Wear sturdy shoes; the trail is steep and rocky. ⊠ *Rte. 30 across from Havensight Mall, Charlotte Amalie,* ☎ *340/774–9809,* WEB *www.paradisepointtramway.com.* 🎟 *$15.* ⊗ *Daily 7:30–4:30.*

32 **Red Hook.** In this nautical center you'll find fishing and sailing charter boats, dive shops, and powerboat rental agencies at the American Yacht Harbor marina. There are also several bars and restaurants, including Molly Molone's, Duffy's Love Shack, and Cafe Wahoo. One grocery store and two delis offer picnic fixings—from sliced meats and cheeses to rotisserie-cooked chickens, prepared salads, and fresh baked breads.

34 **Tillett Gardens.** Clustered in a booming shopping area, you'll find a colony where local artisans craft stained glass, pottery, gold jewelry, and ceramics. Tillett's paintings and silk-screened fabrics are also on display and for sale. The gardens encircle a shaded courtyard with fountains. ⊠ *Rte. 38 across from Tutu Park Shopping Mall, Estate Tutu,* ☎ *340/775–1929,* WEB *www.tillettgardens.com.* 🎟 *Free.*

ST. CROIX

Updated by
Lynda Lohr

St. Croix, the largest of the three USVI at 84 square mi (218 square km), lies 40 mi (65 km) south of St. Thomas. But unlike the bustling island-city of St. Thomas, its harbor teeming with cruise ships and its shopping district crowded with bargain hunters, St. Croix has a slower pace and a more diverse economy, mixing tourism with light and heavy industry on rolling land that was once covered with waving carpets of sugarcane.

St. Croix's population has grown dramatically over the last 30 years, and its diversity reflects the island's varied history. The cultivation of sugarcane was more important here than on St. Thomas or St. John and continued as an economic force into the 1960s. After the end of slavery in 1848, the need for workers brought waves of immigrants from other Caribbean islands, particularly nearby Puerto Rico. St. Croix was divided into plantation estates, and the ruins of great houses and the more than 100 sugar mills that dot the land are evidence of an era when St. Croix was one of the greatest producers of sugar in the West Indies.

Tourism began and boomed in the 1960s, bringing both visitors and migrants from the mainland United States (whom locals refer to as Continentals). In the late 1960s and early 1970s industrial development brought St. Croix yet another wave of immigrants. This time they came mostly from Trinidad and St. Lucia to seek work at the Hess oil refinery or at the south shore aluminum-processing plants.

St. Croix is a study in contrasting beauty. The island isn't as hilly as St. Thomas or St. John. A lush rain forest envelops the northwest, the eastern end is dry, and palm-lined beaches with startlingly clear aquamarine water ring the island. The capital, Christiansted, is a restored Danish port on a coral-bound northeastern bay. The tin-roof 18th-century buildings in both Christiansted and Frederiksted, on the island's western end, are either pale yellow, pink, or ocher—resplendent with bright blazes of bougainvillea and hibiscus. The prosperous Danes built well (and more than once, as both towns were devastated by fire in the 19th century), using imported bricks or blocks cut from coral, fashioning covered sidewalks (galleries) and stately colonnades, and leaving an enduring cosmopolitan air as their legacy.

Lodging

From plush resorts to simple beachfront digs, St. Croix's accommodations are bound to suit every type of traveler. If you sleep in either the Christiansted or Frederiksted area, you'll be close to shopping, restaurants, and nightlife. Any of the island's other hotels will put you just steps from the beach. St. Croix has several small but special properties that offer personalized service. If you like all the comforts of home, you may prefer to stay in a condominium or villa. Room rates on St. Croix are competitive with those on other islands, and if you travel off-season, you'll find substantially reduced prices. Many properties offer honeymoon and dive packages that are also big money savers. Whether you stay in a hotel, a condominium, or a villa, you'll find up-to-date amenities. Most properties have room televisions, but at some bed and breakfasts, you'll find one only in the common room.

Although a stay right in historic Christiansted may mean putting up with a little urban noise, you probably won't have trouble sleeping. Christiansted rolls up the sidewalks fairly early and air-conditioners drown out any noise. The Frederiksted area is perfect for folks who want peace. A small, charming town—hardly more than a village—with a lovely waterfront, it has beaches within walking distance of its shops and restaurants. Solitude is guaranteed at hotels and inns outside the main towns.

For approximate costs, *see* the lodging price chart *in* St. Thomas.

Hotels
CHRISTIANSTED

$–$$ **Hotel Caravelle.** The fetching, three-story Caravelle offers moderately priced in-town lodgings. Rooms are tasteful with white walls and floral-print bedspreads and curtains. Baths are clean and fresh, though the unique tile in the showers is a holdover from when the hotel was built in 1968. Most rooms have some sort of ocean view; the best overlook the harbor. Owners Sid and Amy Kalmans are friendly and helpful. The Rum Runners, a casual terrace eatery, serves local and Continental cuisine. ⊠ *44A Queen Cross St., 00820,* ☎ *340/773–0687 or 800/524–0410,* FAX *340/778–7004,* WEB *www.hotelcaravelle.com. 43 rooms, 1 suite.*

Restaurant, bar, refrigerators, cable TV, pool, massage, Internet, meeting room, no-smoking rooms. AE, D, DC, MC, V. EP.

$–$$ ⊞ **King's Alley Hotel.** In the center of Christiansted's hustle and bustle, this small hotel (part of the King's Alley shopping and restaurant complex) mixes convenience with charm. The 12 premium rooms in the section across the courtyard have mahogany four-poster beds, Mexican tile floors, and Indonesian print fabrics. French doors open onto balconies with a view of the waterfront and the shopping arcade. The 23 standard rooms in the older section are a tad less interesting but still attractive. ⊠ *57 King St. (Box 4120, 00822),* ☎ *340/773–0103 or 800/843–3574,* FAX *340/773–4431,* WEB *www.kingsalley.com. 35 rooms. Some in-room data ports, cable TV with movies, pool, meeting room. AE, D, DC, MC, V. EP.*

$ ⊞ **Breakfast Club.** This rambling guest house is within walking distance of downtown, but a taxi is a good idea if you're heading back late at night. Rooms of various sizes are clean with colorful print spreads. Twin hammocks beckon, offering sea and town views. Guests like to gather at the bar, and owner Toby Chapin includes hearty breakfasts (featuring banana pancakes) in the room rates. ⊠ *18 Queen Cross St., 00820,* ☎ *340/773–7383,* FAX *340/773–8642,* WEB *www.nav.to/thebreakfastclub. 7 rooms. No air-conditioning in some rooms, no room phones, fans, kitchens, no room TVs, Internet, no children under 6. MC, V. BP.*

$ ⊞ **Pink Fancy Hotel.** Listed on the National Register of Historic Places, this venerable small hotel dates to 1780. Thanks to a total refurbishment that began in 1999, it now has up-to-date amenities as well as gracious service. The rooms are furnished with antiques, mahogany pieces, and oriental carpets, and lush gardens meander around the fenced-in compound. Both create a comfortable base for folks who like to get out and about. Guests gather poolside for breakfast and conversation. This hotel shines brightly in a neighborhood that's a bit on the run-down side, so take a taxi back after nighttime excursions. ⊠ *27 Prince St., 00820,* ☎ *340/773–8460 or 800/524–2045,* FAX *340/773–6448,* WEB *www.pinkfancy.com. 13. Fans, in-room data ports, kitchenettes, cable TV with movies, no-smoking rooms. AE, MC, V. CP.*

OUTSIDE CHRISTIANSTED

$–$$ ⊞ **Innparadise.** A stay here is like a visit with your favorite relatives— if you are lucky enough to have kinfolk with a surburban-style home in St. Croix, that is. Transplanted southerners Paula and Tommie Broadnax dish up exuberant hospitality complete with hugs goodbye. The rooms are squeaky clean, with tile floors or carpeting, colorful spreads, and fanciful names that reflect the island's plantation past. Some rooms share a bathroom. The common room sports expansive views of the sea and surburban sprawl, comfy couches, a bar, and large dining room table, where a generous breakfast is offered each morning. A rental car is a necessity. ⊠ *1 Estate Golden Rock, Golden Rock (Box 428, Christiansted 00821),* ☎ *340/713–9803 or 866/800–9803,* FAX *340/713–8722,* WEB *www.innparadisestcroix.com. 4 rooms and 1 suite with a kitchenette. Fans, no room phones, refrigerators, Internet, no smoking. AE, MC, V. BP.*

$ ⊞ **Carringtons Inn.** This spacious B&B exudes style. Once the winter
★ home of a well-off family, the inn has many nice touches. Each room is different, with a decorating theme that reflects its floral name. Wicker furniture, oriental carpets and balconies in some rooms, colorful spreads, and sea or pool views are inviting touches. Hosts Claudia and Roger Carrington conjure up delicious breakfasts—rum-soaked French toast is a house specialty. In a hillside suburban neighborhood, a stay here requires a rental car. ⊠ *4001 Estate Hermon Hill, Christiansted 00820,*

KEY

- ⌇ Beaches
- ⛴ Cruise Ship Terminal
- ◩ Dive Sites
- ❶ Exploring Sights
- ① Hotels and Restaurants
- 🌴 Rain Forest

Lodging

Breakfast Club **3**
The Buccaneer . . . **17**
Carringtons Inn **16**
Chenay Bay
Beach Resort **20**
Divi Carina Bay
Resort **22**
Hibiscus Beach
Hotel **27**

Hilty House **15**
Hotel Caravelle **2**
Innparadise **26**
King's Alley
Hotel **10**
Pink Fancy Hotel **1**
Sandcastle on the
Beach **33**
Schooner Bay **13**
Sugar Beach **25**

Sunterra
Carambola
Beach Resort **30**
Tamarind
Reef Hotel **18**
Villa Madeleine . . . **21**
Waves at Cane
Bay **28**

Dining

Blue Moon **32**
Breezez **24**
Café Christine **12**
The Galleon **19**
Harvey's **4**
Indies **5**
Kendricks **9**
Morning Glory
Coffee and Tea **14**

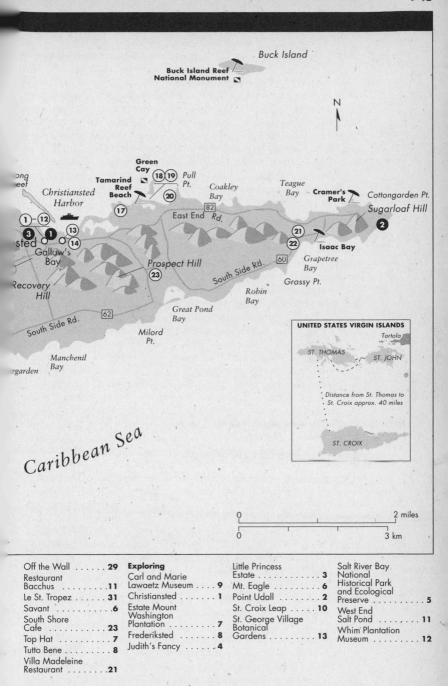

Buck Island

Buck Island Reef National Monument

N

Green Cay
⑱ ⑲ Pull Pt.
Tamarind Reef Beach
⑳
⑰

Coakley Bay

Teague Bay

Cramer's Park
Cottongarden Pt.
Sugarloaf Hill

ong eef

Christiansted Harbor

① ⑫
❸ ①
⑬
⑭

East End Rd.

82

② ❷

Gallow's Bay

Prospect Hill
㉓

Recovery Hill

㉑
㉒
Isaac Bay
Grapetree Bay
Grassy Pt.

South Side Rd.
60

Robin Bay

62

South Side Rd.

Great Pond Bay

Milord Pt.

Manchenil Bay

egarden

Caribbean Sea

UNITED STATES VIRGIN ISLANDS

Tortola
ST. THOMAS
ST. JOHN

Distance from St. Thomas to St. Croix approx. 40 miles

ST. CROIX

0   2 miles
0   3 km

☎ *340/713–0508 or 877/658–0508,* 𝙵𝙰𝚇 *340/719–0841,* 𝚆𝙴𝙱 *www. carringstoninn.com. 5 rooms. Fans, some kitchenettes, refrigerators, no room TVs, pool, Internet, no smoking. AE, MC, V. BP.*

$ 🏠 **Hilty House.** For an alternative to beach and in-town lodgings, try this tranquil hilltop B&B. Built on the ruins of an 18th-century rum factory, it has the feel of a Florentine villa. You can escape to a patio and while away an afternoon in sun or shade, or mingle with others in the immense great room, where a prix-fixe dinner is served on Friday (reservations essential). Unless you want to spend your entire vacation reading or sunning at the large tiled pool, however, you'll need a rental car to venture forth from here. ☒ *Queste Verde Rd., Hermon Hill (Box 26077, Gallows Bay 00824),* ☎ 𝙵𝙰𝚇 *340/773–2594,* 𝚆𝙴𝙱 *www.hiltyhouse.com. 3 rooms, 2 cottages. No air-conditioning in some rooms, no phones in some rooms, some microwaves, cable TV in some rooms, pool, no children under 12, no smoking. No credit cards. CP.*

EAST END

$$$–$$$$ 🏠 **The Buccaneer.** On the grounds of an old, 300-acre sugar plantation, this complex has it all: sandy beaches, swimming pools, golf, and many activities. A palm tree–lined main drive leads to the large, pink main building atop a hill; shops, restaurants, and guest quarters are scattered about rolling manicured lawns. Rooms have a Mediterranean feel, with tile floors, four-poster beds, massive wardrobes of pale wood, pastel fabrics, spacious marble baths, and local works of art. All rooms have such modern conveniences as hair dryers and irons. ☒ *Rte. 82, Shoys (Box 25200, 00824),* ☎ *340/773–2100 or 800/255–3881,* 𝙵𝙰𝚇 *340/778–8215,* 𝚆𝙴𝙱 *www.thebuccaneer.com. 138 rooms. 4 restaurants, bar, in-room safes, refrigerators, cable TV, 18-hole golf course, 8 tennis courts, 2 pools, gym, spa, 3 beaches, snorkeling, hiking, video game room, shops, children's programs (ages 4–12), Internet, meeting rooms, no-smoking rooms. AE, D, DC, MC, V. BP.*

$$–$$$$ 🏠 **Chenay Bay Beach Resort.** The beachfront location and complimentary tennis and water-sports equipment (including kayaks) make this resort a real find—especially for families with active kids. Rooms are basic, with ceramic-tile floors, bright peach or yellow walls, rattan furnishings, and front porches. Gravel paths connect the terraced wood or stucco cottages with the shore, where you'll find a large L-shape pool, a protected beach, a picnic area, and a casual restaurant. The hotel offers a shuttle to grocery stores and shopping areas. ☒ *Rte. 82, Green Cay (Box 24600, Christiansted 00824),* ☎ *340/773–2918 or 800/548–4457,* 𝙵𝙰𝚇 *340/773–6665,* 𝚆𝙴𝙱 *www.chenaybay.com. 50 rooms. Restaurant, bar, picnic area, kitchenettes, cable TV, 2 tennis courts, pool, outdoor hot tub, beach, snorkeling, volleyball, baby-sitting, children's programs (ages 4–12). AE, MC, V. EP.*

$$–$$$$ 🏠 **Divi Carina Bay Resort.** Opt for a bottom-floor room at this oceanfront resort, and you're just steps from the water's edge. The rooms are fresh, with rattan and wicker furniture, white tile floors, sapphire and teal spreads, and sea-tone accessories that compliment the white walls. You're a long way from anywhere here, so if you're not content to just read a good book on your balcony or patio, hit the casino across the street, or lounge at the pool or beach, you'll need a car to get around. ☒ *25 Rte. 60, Estate Turner Hole 00820,* ☎ *340/773–9700 or 800/ 823–9352,* 𝙵𝙰𝚇 *340/773–6802,* 𝚆𝙴𝙱 *www.divicarina.com. 124 rooms, 2 suites, 20 villas. 2 restaurants, 3 bars, fans, in-room data ports, in-room safes, microwaves, refrigerators, 2 tennis courts, pool, outdoor hot tub, gym, beach, dock, snorkeling, billiards, casino, video game room. AE, D, DC, MC, V. EP.*

$$ 🏠 **Tamarind Reef Hotel.** At this casual, motel-like seaside spot, you can sunbathe at the large pool and sandy beach or snorkel in the reef, which

comes right to the shore (serious swimming here is difficult). The spacious, modern rooms have rattan furniture, tropical-print drapes and spreads, and either a terrace or a deck with views of the water and St. Croix's sister islands to the north. Many rooms have basic kitchenettes—handy for preparing light meals. There's a snack bar just off the beach and a restaurant at the adjacent Green Cay Marina. ⊠ *5001 Tamarind Reef, off Rte. 82, Annas Hope 00820,* ☎ *340/773–4455 or 800/619–0014,* FAX *340/773–3989,* WEB *www.usvi.net/hotel/tamarind. 46 rooms. Snack bar, in-room data ports, some kitchenettes, refrigerators, pool, snorkeling, meeting rooms, no-smoking rooms. AE, DC, MC, V. EP.*

OUTSIDE FREDERIKSTED

$–$$ ⊞ **Sandcastle on the Beach.** Right on a gorgeous strand of white beach, this resort caters mainly to gay men and lesbians. Most are couples, but singles also enjoy the house-party atmosphere. There are several categories of rooms; some put you steps from the water, and most have sea views. Room refurbishments are on-going; finished rooms have a modern look with Mexican tile floors; although the others are still a bit old-fashioned, all are comfortable. ⊠ *127 Smithfield, Rte. 71, Frederiksted 00840,* ☎ *340/772–1205 or 800/524–2018,* FAX *340/772–1757,* WEB *www.gaytraveling.com/onthebeach. 6 rooms, 11 suites, 4 villas. Fans, kitchenettes, cable TV, in-room VCRs, 2 pools, beach, snorkeling, no kids. AE, D, MC, V. CP.*

NORTH SHORE

$$$–$$$$ ⊞ **Sunterra Carambola Beach Resort.** The 25 quaint, two-story, red-roofed villas are connected by lovely, lush walkways. Rooms are identical except for the view—ocean or garden. Rooms have terra-cotta floors, ceramic lamps, mahogany ceilings and furnishings, and rocking chairs and sofas. Each room has a patio and a huge bath (shower only). The beach is beautiful and the remote location peaceful, but maintenance at this luxury resort has slipped due to bankruptcy proceedings. Things are on the upswing, but it has a way to go to again reach perfection. ⊠ *Rte. 80, Davis Bay (Box 3031, Kingshill 00851),* ☎ *340/778–3800 or 888/503–8760,* FAX *340/778–1682. 150 rooms, 1 cottage. 2 restaurants, deli, fan, kitchenettes, cable TV, in-room VCRs, golf course, 4 tennis courts, pool, gym, massage, spa, beach, dive shop, snorkeling, meeting rooms. AE, D, DC, MC, V. CP.*

$$ ⊞ **Hibiscus Beach Hotel.** Rooms here are in five pink two-story buildings—each named for a tropical flower. Most rooms have ocean views, but those in the Hibiscus Building are closest to the water. All have roomy balconies, and all are tastefully decorated with white-tile floors, white walls, pink-striped curtains, floral spreads, and fresh-cut hibiscus blossoms. Bathrooms are clean but nondescript—both the shower stalls and the vanity mirrors are on the small side. ⊠ *4131 Estate La Grande Princesse, off Rte. 752, La Grand Princesse 00820-4441,* ☎ *340/773–4042 or 800/442–0121,* FAX *340/773–7668,* WEB *www.1hibiscus. com. 37 rooms. Restaurant, in-room data ports, in-room safes, cable TV, minibars, pool, beach, snorkeling. AE, D, MC, V. EP.*

$–$$ ⊞ **Waves at Cane Bay.** Lapping waves lull you to sleep at this isolated inn. Although the beach here is rocky, Cane Bay Beach is next door, and the world-famous Cane Bay Reef is just 100 yards offshore (divers take note: this is a PADI resort). You can also sunbathe on a small patch of sand beside the very unusual pool: it's carved from the coral along the shore, and waves crash dramatically over its side, creating a foamy whirlpool on blustery days. Two peach and mint-green buildings house enormous, balconied guest rooms that are done in cream and soft pastel prints. ⊠ *Rte. 80, Kingshill (Box 1749, Cane Bay 00851),* ☎ *340/778–1805 or 800/545–0603,* FAX *340/778–4945,* WEB *www.canebaystcroix. com. 12 rooms, 1 suite. Restaurant, fans, in-room data ports, in-room* *safes, kitchenettes, cable TV, pool, dive shop, snorkeling, Internet. AE, MC, V. EP.*

Cottages and Condominiums

$$–$$$ ⊡ **Sugar Beach.** A stay here puts you on the beach at the north side of the island and five minutes from Christiansted. The apartments, which range from studios to four-bedroom units, are immaculate and breezy. Each has a full kitchen and a large patio or balcony with an ocean view; larger units have washers and dryers. Though the exteriors of these condos are ordinary beige stucco, the interiors are lovely (white with tropical furnishings). The pool is amid the ruins of a 250-year-old sugar mill. ⊠ *Rte. 752, Estate Golden Rock 00820,* ☎ *340/773–5345 or 800/524–2049,* FAX *340/773–1359,* WEB *www.sugarbeachstcroix.com. 46 apartments. Fans, kitchens, cable TV, pool, 2 tennis courts, beach, meeting rooms. AE, D, MC, V. EP.*

$$$ ⊡ **Villa Madeleine.** A West Indian plantation great house is the centerpiece
★   of this exquisite resort complex. Richly upholstered furniture, Asian rugs, teal walls, and whimsically painted driftwood set the mood in the billiards room, the library, and the sitting room. Each villa has a full kitchen and a pool, but only bedrooms are air-conditioned. Villas are all done up in tropical: rattan furniture with plush cushions, rocking chairs, and, in some, bamboo four-poster beds. Special touches include pink-marble showers and hand-painted floral wall borders. Enjoy fine dining on the terrace at the Villa Madeleine Restaurant. ⊠ *Off Rte. 82, Teague Bay (52 King St., Christiansted 00820),* ☎ *340/773–4850 or 800/237–1959,* FAX *340/773–8989,* WEB *www.teaguebayproperties.com. 43 villas. Restaurant, bar, fans, kitchens, cable TV, tennis court, 43 pools, meeting room. AE, MC, V. EP.*

$$ ⊡ **Schooner Bay.** This red-roof condo village climbs a hill above Gallows Bay shopping center. Each modern two- or three-bedroom apartment has a balcony, a washer and dryer, and lovely sea views. Rattan furnishings are set on beige-tile floors; floral-print fabrics add splashes of color. Three-bedroom units have spiral staircases. Sun worshipers might be disappointed that the nearest beach is east, at the Buccaneer, but those with a yen to explore Christiansted will find the location ideal—within walking distance of downtown yet away from its bustle. ⊠ *5002 Gallows Bay, Gallows Bay 00820,* ☎ *340/778–7670 or 888/868–7798,* FAX *340/773–4740,* WEB *www.stayinstcroix.com/schooner_bay.html. 40 apartments. Fans, kitchens, cable TV, in-room VCRs, tennis court, 2 pools. AE, MC, V. EP.*

Private Homes and Villas

Renting a house gives you the convenience of home as well as top-notch amenities. Many houses have pools, hot tubs, and deluxe furnishings. Most companies meet you at the airport, arrange for a rental car, and provide helpful information. **Caribbean Property Management** (☎ 340/778–8782 or 800/496–7379, WEB www.enjoystcroix.com) has villas across the island. **The Collection** (☎ 856/751–2413) specializes in villas at Carambola. **Island Villas** (☎ 340/773–8821 or 800/626–4512, WEB www.stcroixislandvillas.com) rents villas across St. Croix. **Rent A Villa** (☎ 800/533–6863, WEB www.rentavillavacations.com) specializes in villas on the island's east end. **Vacation St. Croix** (☎ 340/778–0361 or 877/788–0361, WEB www.vacationstx.com) has villas island-wide.

Dining

Seven flags have flown over St. Croix, and each has left its legacy in the island's cuisine. You can feast on Italian, French, Danish, and American dishes; there are even Chinese and Mexican restaurants in

Christiansted. Fresh local seafood is plentiful and always good; wahoo, mahimahi, and conch are popular. Island chefs often add Caribbean twists to familiar dishes. For a true island experience, stop at a local restaurant for goat stew, curry chicken, or fried pork chops. Regardless of where you eat, your meal will be an informal affair. But be forewarned, prices are a lot higher than you'd pay on the mainland.

For approximate costs, *see* the dining price chart *in* St. Thomas.

Christiansted

CARIBBEAN

$$–$$$ ✕ **Indies.** You'll have a wonderful dining experience in this historic court-
★   yard full of tables covered with handmade floral-print cloths. The menu of island-inspired dishes changes each day to take advantage of St. Croix's freshest bounties. Indulge in the crab cakes or the spicy Caribbean spring rolls to start, then the spice-rubbed chicken (every bite reveals a new, subtle flavor) or spiny lobster fresh from the sea. Enjoy live jazz Saturday evenings. ⊠ *55–56 Company St.,* ☎ *340/692-9440. AE, D, MC, V. No lunch weekends.*

$–$$ ✕ **Harvey's.** The plain, even dowdy dining room has just 14 tables, and plastic floral tablecloths constitute the sole attempt at decor. But who cares? The food is delicious. Daily specials, such as mouthwatering goat stew and tender whelks in butter, served with heaping helpings of rice, fungi, and vegetables, are listed on the blackboard. Genial owner Sarah Harvey takes great pride in her kitchen, bustling out from behind the stove to chat and urge you to eat up. ⊠ *11B Company St.,* ☎ *340/773-3433. No credit cards. Closed Sun. No dinner.*

CONTEMPORARY

$$–$$$$ ✕ **Restaurant Bacchus.** On the chic side, this restaurant is as famous
★   for its wine list as it is for its food. Named after the god of wine, its cellars hold an impressive variety. The menu is imaginative with new twists on old favorites. Try the escargots served over an artichoke half with a brandy sauce or an eggplant napoleon with Portabella mushrooms, spinach and fresh mozzarella. Dessert might be rum-drenched sourdough bread pudding. ⊠ *Queen Cross St., off King St.,* ☎ *340/692-9922. AE, D, MC, V. Closed Sun.–Mon. No lunch.*

$$–$$$ ✕ **Kendricks.** The chef at this open-air restaurant—a longtime favorite
★   with locals—conjures up creative, tasty cuisine. Try the Alaskan king crab cakes with lemon black pepper aioli to start, or the warm chipotle pepper with garlic and onion soup. Move on to the house specialty: pecan-crusted roast pork loin with ginger mayonnaise. ⊠ *21–32 Company St.,* ☎ *340/773-9199. AE, MC, V. Closed Sun. No lunch.*

$$–$$$ ✕ **Savant.** Savant is one of those small-but-special spots that locals love.
★   The cuisine is a fusion of Mexican, Thai, and Caribbean, a combination that works well. Everything from a veggie dish dripping with Thai red coconut curry sauce, to enchiladas stuffed with chicken, beef, or seafood, to maple teriyaki pork tenderloin comes out of the tiny kitchen. With only 10 candlelit tables tucked cheek and jowl, diners call early for reservations. ⊠ *4C Hospital St.,* ☎ *340/713-8666. AE, MC, V. No lunch.*

CONTINENTAL

$$–$$$ ✕ **Top Hat.** Owned by a delightful Danish couple, this restaurant has
★   been serving international cuisine (with Danish specialties, of course) since 1970. Dishes include roast duck stuffed with apples and prunes, *frikadeller* (savory meatballs in a tangy cocktail sauce), conch beignets, and smoked eel. The signature dessert is a rum-ice-cream-filled chocolate windmill whose blades turn. ⊠ *52 Company St.,* ☎ *340/773-2346. AE, D, DC, MC, V. No lunch.*

ECLECTIC

$ ✕ **Morning Glory Coffee and Tea.** Stop by this cozy spot in a popular shopping center for light fare. Lunch runs to wrap sandwiches filled with veggies, cheeses, and lunchmeats, turkey clubs, and panini (filled, pressed, and grilled to create a new twist on a grilled-cheese-like favorite). For breakfast, the chef conjures up waffles, beignets, croissants, and eggs cooked any way. Smoothies are a house specialty. ⊠ *Gallows Bay Marketplace,* ☎ *340/773–6620. No credit cards. Closed Sun. No dinner.*

FRENCH

$–$$ ✕ **Café Christine.** A favorite with the professionals who work in downtown Christiansted, Café Christine's presentation is as lovely as the food. The small menu changes daily, but look for dishes like a green salad with salmon and shrimp drizzled with a lovely vinaigrette dressing or a vegetarian plate with quiche, salad, and lentils. Desserts are perfection. If the pear pie topped with chocolate is on the menu, don't hesitate. This tiny restaurant has both air-conditioned indoor tables and an outside porch that overlooks historic buildings. ⊠ *Apothecary Hall Courtyard, 4 Company St.,* ☎ *340/713–1500. No credit cards. Closed weekends. No dinner.*

ITALIAN

$$–$$$ ✕ **Tutto Bene.** Its yellow walls, brightly striped cushions, and painted trompe l'oeil tables make Tutto Bene look more like a sophisticated Mexican cantina than an Italian cucina. One bite of the food, however, will clear up any confusion. Written on hanging mirrors is the daily menu, which includes such fare as veal Parmesan and veal chops with fresh mozzarella and sun-dried tomato pesto. Desserts, including a decadent tiramisu, are on the menu as well. ⊠ *2 Company St.,* ☎ *340/773–5229. AE, MC, V.*

Outside Christiansted

ECLECTIC

$–$$ ✕ **Breezez.** This aptly named restaurant sits poolside at Club St. Croix condominiums. Visitors and locals are drawn by its reasonable prices and good food. This is *the* place to be for Sunday brunch, where the menu includes lobster rolls, burgers, and blackened prime rib with Cajun seasonings and horseradish sauce. For dessert, try the flourless chocolate torte—a wedge of rich chocolate served with a river of chocolate sauce. ⊠ *Club St. Croix, 3220 Golden Rock, off Rte. 752, Golden Rock,* ☎ *340/773–7077. AE, D, MC, V.*

East End

CONTEMPORARY

$$–$$$ ✕ **Villa Madeleine Restaurant.** The elegant restaurant at the Villa Madeleine resort serves such diverse cuisine as red curry roasted rack of lamb with fire-roasted root vegetables that's a tad on the spicy side as well as other equally inventive fare. The wine list is extensive. Take Route 82 out of Christiansted, turn right at Reef Condominiums. ⊠ *19A Teague Bay, Teague Bay,* ☎ *340/778–7377. AE, D, MC, V. No lunch.*

ECLECTIC

$$$ ✕ **The Galleon.** This dockside restaurant is popular with both locals and visitors. Start with the Caesar salad or gravlax (fresh salmon with dill and pepper). Pasta lovers should sample the pasta primavera, a delightful dish made with fresh pasta, whatever vegetables the chef brings home, and olive oil and garlic or a cream sauce. The osso buco and rack of lamb are legendary. Take Route 82 out of Christiansted, turn left at the sign for Green Cay Marina. ⊠ *Annas Hope,* ☎ *340/773–9949. AE, MC, V. No lunch.*

$$–$$$ ✕ **South Shore Cafe.** This casual bistro sits near the Great Salt Pond on the island's south shore. Popular with locals for its good food, the restaurant's menu includes dishes drawn from several different cuisines. Meat lovers and vegetarians can find common ground with a menu that runs from handmade pasta to prime rib. The selection isn't extensive, but the chef puts together a blackboard full of specials every day. ⊠ *Rte. 62 at Rte. 624, Sally's Fancy,* ☎ *340/773–9311. V. Closed Mon.–Tues. No lunch.*

Frederiksted

ECLECTIC

$$–$$$ ✕ **Blue Moon.** This terrific little bistro, popular for its live jazz on Friday night, has a changing menu that draws on Asian, Cajun, and local flavors. Try the spicy gumbo with andouille sausage or crab cakes with a spicy aioli as an appetizer; the roasted vegetables and shrimp scampi loaded with garlic and served over pasta as an entrée; and the Almond Joy sundae for dessert. ⊠ *17 Strand St.,* ☎ *340/772–2222. AE, MC, V. Closed Mon.*

$$–$$$ ✕ **Le St. Tropez.** A ceramic-tile bar and soft lighting set the mood at this pleasant Mediterranean bistro, tucked into a courtyard off Frederiksted's main thoroughfare. Seated either inside or on the adjoining patio, you can enjoy such items as grilled meats in delicate French sauces. The menu changes daily, often taking advantage of local seafood. The fresh basil, tomato, and mozzarella salad is heavenly. ⊠ *227 King St.,* ☎ *340/772–3000. AE, MC, V. Closed Sun. No lunch Sat.*

Cane Bay

ECLECTIC

$–$$ ✕ **Off the Wall.** Divers fresh from a plunge at the north shore's popular wall gather at this breezy spot right on the beach. If you want to sit a spell before you order, a hammock beckons. Burgers, fish sandwiches, quesadillas, and Philly steak sandwiches join pizza and hotdogs on the menu. The potato salad that comes with your sandwich is as good as you'd get at home. You might find blues and jazz Tuesday through Sunday nights. ⊠ *Rte. 80,* ☎ *340/778–4771. AE, MC, V.*

Beaches

Buck Island. A visit to this island, part of the U.S. National Park system, is a must. The beach is beautiful, but its finest treasures are those you can see when you plop off the boat and adjust your mask, snorkel, and flippers. To get here, you'll have to charter a boat or go on an organized trip.

Cane Bay. The waters aren't always gentle at this breezy north shore beach, but there are seldom many people around, and the scuba diving and snorkeling are wondrous. You'll see elkhorn and brain corals, and less than 200 yards out is the drop-off called Cane Bay Wall.

Cramer's Park. This USVI territorial beach on the northeast coast (Route 82) is very popular with locals. It's a good spot for beach picnics and camping. Because of its isolation, though, it's not a good place to linger if you're traveling solo.

Isaac's Bay. This east-end beach is almost impossible to reach without a four-wheel-drive vehicle, but it's worth the effort. You'll find secluded sands for sunbathing, calm waters for swimming, and a barrier reef for snorkeling. You can also get here via footpaths from Jack's Bay.

Tamarind Reef Beach. Small but attractive Tamarind Reef Beach is east of Christiansted. Both Green Cay and Buck Island seem smack in front of you—an arresting view. The snorkeling is good.

West End Beaches. There are several unnamed beaches along the coast road north of Frederiksted. Just pull over at whatever piece of powdery sand catches your fancy. The beach at the Rainbow Beach Club, a five-minute drive outside Frederiksted on Route 63, has a bar, a casual restaurant, water sports, and volleyball.

Outdoor Activities and Sports

CYCLING

A bike tour to some of the island's top sights adds a new dimension to your vacation and helps you stay in shape. **St. Croix Bike and Tours** (⊠ Strand Square Courtyard, Frederiksted, ☎ 340/773–2343) offers two tours; both cost $35. One heads through historic Frederiksted before cycling on a fairly flat road to Hamm's Bluff. The second takes bikers to a remote beach with a snorkel stop included. Bikes rent for $7.50 for the first hour; $2.50 for each additional hour.

BOAT TOURS

Day sail to Buck Island aboard a charter boat. Most leave from the Christiansted waterfront or from Green Cay Marina. They stop for a snorkel at the island's eastern end before dropping anchor off a gorgeous sandy beach for a swim, a hike, and lunch. A full-day sail runs about $65 with lunch included on most trips. A half-day sail costs about $50. **Big Beard's Adventure Tours** (☎ 340/773–4482) takes you on a catamaran, the *Renegade* or the *Flyer,* from the Christiansted Waterfront to Buck Island for snorkeling before dropping anchor at a private beach for a barbecue lunch. **Mile Mark Watersports** (☎ 340/773–2628) departs from the Christiansted waterfront for half- and full-day trips on various boats. **Teroro Charters** (☎ 340/773–3161) trimaran *Teroro II* leaves Green Cay Marina for full- or half-day sails. Bring your own lunch.

FISHING

In the past quarter century, some 20 world records—many for blue marlin—have been set in these waters. Sailfish, skipjack, bonito, tuna (allison, blackfin, and yellowfin), and wahoo are abundant. A charter runs about $100 an hour per person, with most boats going out for four-, six- or eight-hour trips. **Captain Peter's Sportfishing** (⊠ St. Croix Marina, Gallows Bay, ☎ 340/773–1123) will take you fishing his 27-ft *The Louis G.* **Mile Mark Charters** (⊠ 59 King's Wharf, Christiansted, ☎ 340/773–2628) will take you out on a 38-ft powerboat, the *Fantasy.*

GOLF

St. Croix's courses welcome you with spectacular vistas and well-kept greens. Check with your hotel or the tourist board to determine when major celebrity tournaments will be held. There's often an opportunity to play with the pros. The **Buccaneer** (⊠ Rte. 82, Shoys, ☎ 340/773–2100) has an 18-hole course that is conveniently close to Christiansted. The **Reef Golf Course** (Teague Bay, ☎ 340/773–8844), in the northeastern part of the island, has 9 holes. The spectacular 18-hole course at **Sunterra Carambola Beach Resort** (⊠ Rte. 80, Davis Bay, ☎ 340/778–5638), in the northwest valley, was designed by Robert Trent Jones, Sr.

HIKING

Although you can set off by yourself on a hike through a rain forest or along a shore, a guide will point out what's important and tell you why. The nonprofit **St. Croix Environmental Association** (⊠ Arawak Bldg., Suite 3, Gallows Bay 00820, ☎ 340/773–1989) offers treks through several ecological treasures, including Estate Mt. Washington, Mt. Victory, the rain forest, and Salt River. The cost is $20 per person for a 2½-hour hike.

HORSEBACK RIDING

Well-kept roads and expert guides make horseback riding on St. Croix pleasurable. At Sprat Hall, just north of Frederiksted, Jill Hurd runs **Paul and Jill's Equestrian Stables** (✉ Rte. 58, Frederiksted, ☎ 340/772–2880 or 340/772–2627) and will take you clip-clopping through the rain forest, pastures, and hilltops (explaining the flora, fauna, and ruins on the way). A 1½-hour ride costs $50.

KAYAKING

Caribbean Adventure Tours takes you on trips through Salt River National Park and Ecological Preserve, one of the island's most pristine areas. A daytime ecotour runs $45, and a moonlight trip is $40. (✉ Columbus Cove Marina, Rte. 80, Salt River, ☎ 340/773–4599).

SCUBA DIVING AND SNORKELING

At **Buck Island,** a short boat ride from Christiansted or Green Cay Marina, the reef is so nice that it's been named a national monument. You can dive right off the beach at **Cane Bay,** which has a spectacular drop-off. **Frederiksted Pier** is home to a colony of seahorses, creatures seldom seen in the waters off the Virgin Islands. At **Green Cay,** just outside Green Cay Marina in the east end, you'll see colorful fish swimming around the reefs and rocks. Two exceptional **north shore sites** are North Star and Salt River, which you can reach only by boat. You can float downward through a canyon filled with colorful fish and coral.

The island's dive shops take you out for one- or two-tank dives. Plan to pay about $50 for a one-tank dive and $70 for a two-tank dive, including equipment and an underwater tour. **Anchor Dive Center** (✉ Salt River Marina, Rte. 801, Salt River, ☎ 340/778–1522 or 800/532–3483) takes divers to 35 sites, including the wall at Salt River Canyon and Buck Island Reef National Monument. It also offers PADI certification. **Cane Bay Dive Shop** (✉ Rte. 80, Cane Bay, ☎ 340/773–9913 or 800/338–3843) takes you on boat and beach dives along the north shore. The famed wall is just 150 yards from their shop. **Dive Experience** (✉ 40 Strand St., Christiansted, ☎ 340/773–3307 or 800/235–9047) is a five-star PADI training facility that offers everything from introductory dives to certification. It also runs trips to the north shore walls and reefs. **Scuba West** (330 Strand St., Frederiksted, ☎ 340/772–3701 or 800/352–0107) operates out of Frederiksted. Although it runs trips to reefs and wrecks, its specialty is the seahorses that live around the Frederiksted Pier. **St. Croix Ultimate Bluewater Adventures** (14 Caravelle Arcade, Christiansted, ☎ 340/773–5994 or 877/567–1367) is a PADI international outfit that will take you to your choice of over 20 sites.

TENNIS

The public courts in Frederiksted and out east at Cramer Park are in questionable shape. It's better to pay a fee and play at one of the hotel courts. Costs vary by resort, but count on paying at least $10 an hour. **The Buccaneer** (✉ Rte. 82, Shoys, ☎ 340/773–2100) has eight courts (two lighted), plus a pro and a full tennis shop. **Chenay Bay Beach Resort** (✉ Rte. 82, Green Cay, ☎ 340/773–2918) has two courts (no lights). **Club St. Croix** (✉ Rte. 752, Estate Golden Rock, ☎ 340/773–4800) has three lighted courts. **Sunterra Carambola Beach Resort** (✉ Rte. 80, Davis Bay, ☎ 340/778–3800) has four lighted courts.

WINDSURFING

St. Croix's trade winds make windsurfing a breeze. Most hotels rent Windsurfers and other water-sports equipment to nonguests. **St. Croix Watersports** (✉ Hotel on the Cay, Christiansted, ☎ 340/773–7060) offers Windsurfer rentals, sales, and rides; parasailing; and water-sports equipment, such as Sea Doos and kayaks. Renting a windsurfer runs about $25 an hour.

Shopping

Areas and Malls

Although the shopping on St. Croix isn't as varied or extensive as that on St. Thomas, the island does have several small stores with unique merchandise. In Christiansted the best shopping areas are the **Pan Am Pavilion** and **Caravelle Arcade** off Strand Street, **Kings Alley Walk,** and along **King** and **Company streets.** These streets give way to arcades filled with boutiques. **Gallows Bay** has a blossoming shopping area in a quiet neighborhood. Stores are often closed on Sunday.

The best shopping in Frederiksted is along **Strand Street** and in the side streets and alleyways that connect it with **King Street.** Most stores close Sunday except when a cruise ship is in port.

Specialty Items

BOOKS

The Bookie. This shop carries paperback novels, stationery, newspapers, and cards. Stop in for the latest gossip and to find out about upcoming events. ⊠ *1111 Strand St., Christiansted,* ☎ *340/773–2592.*
Undercover Books. For Caribbean books or the latest good read, try this bookstore across from the post office in the Gallows Bay shopping area. ⊠ *5030 Anchor Way, Gallows Bay,* ☎ *340/719–1567.*

CLOTHING

Coconut Vine. Pop into this store at the start of your vacation, and you'll leave with enough comfy cotton or rayon batik men's and women's clothes to make you look like a local. Although the tropical designs and colors originated in Indonesia, they're perfect for the Caribbean. ⊠ *King's Alley, Christiansted,* ☎ *340/773–1991.*
From the Gecko. Come here for the hippest clothes on St. Croix, from superb batik sarongs to hand-painted silk scarves. ⊠ *1233 Queen Cross St., Christiansted,* ☎ *340/778–9433.*
The White House/Black Market. This contemporary store sells clothes in all-white, black, and natural colors. Look for exquisite lingerie, elegant evening wear, and unusual casual outfits. ⊠ *8B Kings Alley Walk, Christiansted,* ☎ *340/773–9222.*

FOODSTUFFS

If you've rented a condominium or a villa, you'll appreciate that St. Croix offers excellent shopping at its stateside-style supermarkets. Fresh vegetables, fruits, and meats arrive frequently. Try the open-air stands strung out along Route 70 for island produce.

Cost-U-Less is a warehouse-type store across from Sunshine Mall. It does not charge a membership fee. It's just outside Frederiksted, across from Kmart. ⊠ *Rte. 70, Hogensborg,* ☎ *340/692–2220.*
Plaza Extra sells Middle Eastern foods in addition to the usual grocery store items. ⊠ *United Shopping Plaza, Rte. 70, Sion Farm,* ☎ *340/778–6240;* ⊠ *Rte. 70, Mount Pleasant,* ☎ *340/719–1870.*
Pueblo is a stateside-style market with locations all over the island. ⊠ *Orange Grove Shopping Center, Rte. 75, Christiansted,* ☎ *340/773–0118;* ⊠ *Sunny Isle Shopping Center, Rte. 70, Sunny Isle,* ☎ *340/778–5005;* ⊠ *Villa La Reine Shopping Center, Rte. 75, La Reine,* ☎ *340/778–1272.*
Schooner Bay Market is on the smallish side, but has good quality deli items. ⊠ *Rte. 82, just outside of town, Mount Welcome,* ☎ *340/773–3232.*

GIFTS

Gone Tropical. Whether you're looking for inexpensive souvenirs of your trip or a special, singular gift, you'll probably find it here. On her travels about the world, owner Margo Meacham keeps her eye out for items with which to stock her shop—from tablecloths and napkins in bright Caribbean colors to carefully crafted metal birds. ⊠ *5 Company St., Christiansted,* ☎ *340/773–4696.*

Island Webe. The coffees, jams, and spices—produced locally or elsewhere in the Caribbean—here will tempt your taste buds. Small *mocko jumbie* dolls depict an African tradition transported to the islands during slave days (they represent the souls of the ancestors of African slaves). The fabric dolls wearing Caribbean costumes will delight kids of all ages. Turn the double dolls upside down to see a white face on one side and a black one on the other. ⊠ *210 Strand St., Frederiksted,* ☎ *340/772–2555.*

Mitchell-Larsen Studio. Carefully crafted glass plates, sun-catchers, and more grace the shelves of this interesting store. All made on-site by two St. Croix glassmakers, the items are often whimsically adorned with tropical fish, flora, and fauna. ⊠ *58 Company St., Christiansted,* ☎ *340/719–1000.*

Royal Poinciana. You'll find island seasonings and hot sauces, West Indian crafts, bath gels, and herbal teas at this attractive shop. Shop here for tablecloths and paper goods in tropical brights. ⊠ *1111 Strand St., Christiansted,* ☎ *340/773–9892.*

Soul of Africa. The African masks, wine glasses with African motifs, and aromatherapy candles will catch your eye. Elegant silk jackets, classy sandals, and batik bedspreads in unique patterns also fill the shelves. ⊠ *Kings Alley, Christiansted,* ☎ *340/773–3099.*

Tradewinds Shop. Whatever the wind blew in seems to land here. Glass sailboats glide across the shelves while metal fish sculptures swim nearby. Candles with tropical motifs, note cards, and costume jewelry jostle for space with Naot sandals. ⊠ *53 King St., Christiansted,* ☎ *340/719–3920.*

HOUSEWARES

St. Croix Landmarks Museum Store. If a mahogany armoire or cane-backed rocker catches your fancy, the staff will arrange to have it shipped to your mainland home at no charge from its mainland warehouse. Furniture aside, this store has one of the largest selections of local art along with Caribbean-inspired bric-a-brac in all prices ranges. ⊠ *5A King St., Christiansted,* ☎ *340/713–8102.*

Textiles with a Story. Oriental rugs mingle with island-inspired batiks at this store that speaks of an Arabian souk. Comfy pillows in varied motifs and colors invite you to rest. ⊠ *52 King St., Christiansted,* ☎ *340/692–9867.*

JEWELRY

Crucian Gold. This store carries the unique gold creations of St. Croix native Brian Bishop. His trademark piece is the Turk's Head ring (a knot of interwoven gold strands), but the chess sets with Caribbean motifs as the playing pieces are just lovely. ⊠ *59 King's Wharf, Christiansted,* ☎ *340/773–5241.*

The Gold Shop. Specializing—of course—in gold jewelry, this store also carries diamonds, emeralds, rubies, sapphires, and gold. Jewelers will create one-of-a-kind pieces to your design. ⊠ *1102 Strand St., Christiansted,* ☎ *340/773–0365 or 800/416–9078.*

Karavan West Indies. The owner here designs her own jewelry and also sells an assortment of tchotchkes, including handmade Christmas ornaments. ⊠ *5030 Anchor Way, Gallows Bay,* ☎ *340/773–9999.*

Sonya's. Sonya Hough invented the hook bracelet, popular among locals as well as visitors. With hurricanes hitting the island so frequently, she has added an interesting decoration to these bracelets: the swirling symbol used in weather forecasts to indicate these storms. ⊠ *1 Company St., Christiansted,* ☎ *340/778–8605.*

LIQUOR AND TOBACCO

Baci Duty Free Liquor and Tobacco. A walk-in humidor with a good selection of Arturo Fuente, Partagas, and Macanudo cigars is the centerpiece of this store. It also carries sleek Danish-made watches and Lladro figurines. ⊠ *55 Company St., Christiansted,* ☎ *340/773–5040.*
Cruzan Rum Distillery. A tour of the company's factory culminates in a tasting of its products, all sold here at bargain prices. ⊠ *West Airport Rd., Estate Diamond,* ☎ *340/692–2280.*
Kmart. The two branches of this discount department store—a large one in the Sunshine Mall and a smaller one mid-island at Sunny Isle Shopping Center—carry a huge line of discounted, duty-free liquor. ⊠ *Sunshine Mall, Rte. 70, Frederiksted,* ☎ *340/692–5848;* ⊠ *Sunny Isle Shopping Center, Rte. 70, Sunny Isle,* ☎ *340/719–9190.*

PERFUMES

Violette Boutique. Perfumes, cosmetics, and skin-care products are the draws here. ⊠ *Caravelle Arcade, 38 Strand St., Christiansted,* ☎ *340/773–2148.*

Nightlife and the Arts

The island's nightlife is ever-changing, and its arts scene is eclectic—ranging from Christmastime performances of the *Nutcracker* to whatever local group got organized enough to put on a show. Folk-art traditions, such as quadrille dancers, are making a comeback. To find out what's happening, pick up the local newspapers—*V.I. Daily News* and *St. Croix Avis*—which are available at newsstands. Christiansted has a lively and eminently casual club scene near the waterfront. Frederiksted has a couple of restaurants and clubs offering weekend entertainment.

Nightlife

Hotel on the Cay (⊠ Protestant Cay, Christiansted, ☎ 340/773–2035) has a West Indian buffet on Tuesday night in the winter season, when you can watch a broken-bottle dancer (a dancer who braves a carpet of broken bottles) and mocko jumbie characters. Easy jazz flows from the courtyard bar at **Indies** (⊠ 55–56 Company St., Christiansted, ☎ 340/692–9440) Thursday, Friday, and Saturday evenings. The **2 Plus 2 Disco** (⊠ 17 La Grande Princesse, Christiansted, ☎ 340/773–3710) spins a great mix of calypso, soul, disco, and reggae; there's live music on weekends in the winter.

Blue Moon (⊠ 17 Strand St., Frederiksted, ☎ 340/772–2222), a waterfront restaurant, is the place to be for live jazz on Friday 9 PM–1 AM.

Outside Frederiksted, **Off the Wall** (⊠ Rte. 80, Cane Bay, ☎ 340/778–4471) has blues or jazz Tuesday–Sunday from 6 PM to 9 PM.

The Arts

The **Whim Plantation Museum** (⊠ Rte. 70, Estate Whim, ☎ 340/772–0598), which is just outside of Frederiksted, hosts classical music concerts during the winter season.

Exploring St. Croix

Though there are things to see and do in St. Croix's two towns, Christiansted and Frederiksted (both named for Danish kings), there are lots of interesting spots in between them and to the east of Christiansted. Just be sure you have a map in hand (pick one up at rental-car agencies, or stop by the tourist office for an excellent one that's free). Many secondary roads remain unmarked; if you get confused, ask for help.

Numbers in the margin correspond to points of interest on the St. Croix map.

Christiansted and the East

Christiansted is a historic Danish-style town that always served as St. Croix's commercial center. Your best bet is to see the historic sights in the morning, when it's still cool. This two-hour endeavor won't tax your walking shoes and will leave you with energy to poke around the town's eclectic shops. Break for lunch at an open-air restaurant before spending as much time as you like shopping.

An easy drive (roads are flat and well marked) to St. Croix's eastern end takes you through some choice real estate. Ruins of old sugar estates dot the landscape. You can make the entire loop on the road that circles the island in about an hour, a good way to end the day. If you want to spend a full day exploring, you'll find some nice beaches and easy walks, with places to stop for lunch.

SIGHTS TO SEE

❶ **Christiansted.** In the 1700s and 1800s this town was a trading center for sugar, rum, and molasses. Today you'll find law offices, tourist shops, and restaurants, but many of the buildings, which start at the harbor and go up into the gentle hillsides, still date from the 18th century. You can't get lost. All streets lead gently downhill to the water. Still, if you want some friendly advice, stop by the **Visitor Center** (⊠ 53A Company St., ☎ 340/773–0495) weekdays between 8 and 5 for maps and brochures. Large, yellow **Ft. Christiansvaern** dominates the waterfront. Because it's so easy to spot, it makes a good place from which to begin a walking tour. In 1749 the Danish built the fort to protect the harbor, but the structure was repeatedly damaged by hurricane-force winds and was partially rebuilt in 1771. It's now a national historic site, the best preserved of the five remaining Danish-built forts in the Virgin Islands, and houses the park's Visitor Center. ⊠ *Hospital St.,* ☎ *340/773–1460,* WEB *www.nps.gov/chrii.* ⊠ *$2, includes admission to Steeple Bldg.* ⊗ *Daily 8–4:45.* When you're tired of sightseeing, stop at **D. Hamilton Jackson Park**—on the street side of Ft. Christiansvaern—for a rest. It's named for a famed labor leader, judge, and journalist who started the first newspaper not under the thumb of the Danish crown. ⊠ *Between Ft. Christiansvaern and the Danish Customs House.* Built in 1830 on foundations that date from 1734, the **Danish Customs House**—near Ft. Christiansvaern—originally served as both a customs house and a post office (second floor). In 1926 it became the Christiansted Library, and it has been a National Park office since 1972. ⊠ *King St.,* ☎ *340/773–1460,* WEB *www.nps.gov/chrii.* ⊗ *Weekdays 8–5.* Constructed in 1856, the **Scale House** was once the spot where goods passing through the port were weighed and inspected. Park staff now sells a good selection of books about St. Croix history and its flora and fauna. ⊠ *King St.,* ☎ *340/773–1460,* WEB *www.nps.gov/chrii.* ⊗ *Daily 8–5.* Built by the Danes in 1753, the **Steeple Building** was the first Danish Lutheran church on St. Croix. It's now a national park museum and contains exhibits that document the island's Indian habitation. It's worth the short walk from Ft. Christiansvaern to see the building's collection of archaeological artifacts, displays on plantation life, and exhibits on the architectural development of Christiansted, the early history of the church, and Alexander Hamilton, the first secretary of the U.S. Treasury, who grew up in St.

Croix. ⊠ *Church St.,* ☎ *340/773–1460.* ☞ *$2, includes admission to Ft. Christiansvaern.* ☉ *Daily 9–4:30.* The **Post Office Building,** built in 1749, was once the Danish West India & Guinea Company warehouse. ⊠ *Church St.* One of the town's most elegant structures, **Government House,** was built as a home for a Danish merchant in 1747. Today it houses USVI government offices. If the building is open, slip into the peaceful inner courtyard to admire the still pools and gardens. A sweeping staircase leads you to a second-story ballroom, still the site of official government functions. ⊠ *King St.,* ☎ *340/773–1404.* ☉ *Weekdays 8–5.* Around the corner and down a block from Government House, the tanks at the **St. Croix Aquarium** contain a selection of local sea creatures. Children are invited to explore the discovery room, with its microscopes, interactive displays, and educational videos. Children will enjoy the petting tank, where they can feel starfish relax to their touch. ⊠ *13 Caravelle Arcade,* ☎ *340/773–8995.* WEB *www.geocities.com/stcroixaquarium.* ☞ *$5.* ☉ *Tues.–Sat. 11–4.* Built in 1735 as a slave market, today **the market,** housed in a wood and galvanized aluminum structure, is where farmers and others sell their goods every Wednesday and Saturday from 8 to 5. ⊠ *Company St.* The **Buck Island Reef National Monument,** off the northeast coast, has pristine beaches that are just right for sunbathing, but there's enough shade for those who don't want to fry. The snorkeling trail set in the reef allows close-up study of coral formations and tropical fish. It's suffered some in the spate of hurricanes that have hit the island since 1989, but scientists consider it to be on the mend. There's an easy hiking trail to the island's highest point, where you'll be rewarded for your efforts by spectacular views of the reef and St. John. Charter-boat trips leave daily from the Christiansted waterfront or from Green Cay Marina, about 2 mi (3 km) east of Christiansted. Check with your hotel for recommendations. ⊠ *Buck Island, off the north shore of St. Croix,* ☎ *340/773–1460 (park headquarters),* WEB *www.nps.gov/buis.*

➋ Point Udall. This rocky promontory, the easternmost point in the United States, is about a half-hour's drive from Christiansted. A paved road takes you to an overlook with glorious views. More adventurous folks can hike down to the pristine beach below. On the way back, look for The Castle, an enormous mansion that can only be described as a cross between a Moorish mosque and the Taj Mahal. It was built by an extravagant recluse known only as the Contessa. ⊠ *Rte. 82, Et Stykke.*

Between Christiansted and Frederiksted

A drive through the countryside between these two towns will take you past ruins of old plantations, many bearing whimsical names (Morningstar, Solitude, Upper Love) bestowed by early owners. The traffic moves quickly—by island standards—on the main roads, but you can pause and poke around if you head down some side lanes. It's easy to find your way west, but driving from north to south requires good navigation. Don't leave your hotel without a map. Allow an entire day for this trip so you'll have enough time for a swim at a north shore beach. Although you'll find lots of casual eateries on the main roads, pick up a picnic lunch if you plan to head off the beaten path.

SIGHTS TO SEE

➍ Judith's Fancy. In this upscale neighborhood you'll find the ruins of an old great house and tower of the same name, both remnants of a circa-1750 Danish sugar plantation. The "Judith" comes from the first name of a woman buried on the property. From the guard house at the neighborhood entrance, follow Hamilton Drive past some of St. Croix's loveliest homes. At the end of Hamilton Drive the road overlooks Salt River Bay, where Christopher Columbus anchored in 1493. On the way back, make a detour left off Hamilton Drive onto Caribe Road for a close look at the ruins. ⊠ *Turn north onto Rte. 751, off Rte. 75.*

❸ Little Princess Estate. If the old plantation ruins decaying here and there around St. Croix intrigue you, a visit to this Nature Conservancy project will give you even more of a glimpse into the past. The staff has carved walking paths out of the bush that surrounds what's left of a 19th-century plantation. It's easy to stroll among well-labeled fruit trees and see the ruins of the windmill, the sugar and rum factory, and the laborers' village. This is the perfect place to reflect on St. Croix's agrarian past fueled with labor from African slaves. The property also has a community garden. ⊠ *Just off Rte. 75; turn north at the Five Corners traffic light,* ☎ *340/773–5575.* 🎫 *Free.* ☉ *Tues. and Thurs. 3–5.*

❻ Mt. Eagle. This is St. Croix's highest peak (1,165 ft [356 m]). Leaving Cane Bay and passing North Star Beach, follow the coastal road that dips briefly into a forest, then turn left on Route 69. Just after you make the turn, the pavement is marked with the words THE BEAST and a set of giant paw prints. The hill you're about to climb is the location of the famous Beast of the St. Croix Half Ironman Triathlon, an annual event during which participants must bike this intimidating slope. ⊠ *Rte. 69.*

❺ Salt River Bay National Historical Park and Ecological Preserve. This joint national and local park commemorates the area where Christopher Columbus's men skirmished with the Carib Indians in 1493 on his second visit to the new world. The peninsula on the bay's east side is named for the event: Cabo de las Flechas (Cape of the Arrows). Although the park is not developed, it has several sights with cultural significance. A ball court, used by the Caribs in worship ceremonies, was discovered at the spot where the taxis park. Take a short hike up the dirt road to the ruins of an old earthen fort for great views of Salt River Bay and the surrounding countryside. The area also encompasses a biodiverse coastal estuary with the largest remaining mangrove forest in the USVI, a submarine canyon, and several endangered species, including the hawksbill turtle and the roseate tern. ⊠ *Rte. 75 to Rte. 80, Salt River,* ☎ *340/773–1460,* 🌐 *www.nps.gov/sari.*

Frederiksted and Environs

St. Croix's second-largest town, Frederiksted, was founded in 1751. A stroll around its historic sights will take you no more than an hour. Allow a little more time if you want to browse in the few small shops. The area just outside town has old plantations, some of which have been preserved as homes or historic structures that are open to the public.

SIGHTS TO SEE

❾ Carl and Marie Lawaetz Museum. For a trip back in time, tour this circa-1750 farm. Owned by the prominent Lawaetz family since 1899, just after Carl arrived from Denmark, the lovely two-story house is in a valley at La Grange. A Lawaetz family member shows you the four-poster mahogany bed Carl and Marie shared, the china Marie painted, the family portraits, and the fruit trees that fed the family for several generations. Initially a sugar plantation, it was subsequently used to raise cattle and produce. ⊠ *Rte. 76, Mahogany Rd., Estate Little La Grange,* ☎ *340/772–1539,* 🌐 *www.stcroixlandmarks.com/lawaetz.* 🎫 *$6.* ☉ *Wed.–Sat. 10–4.*

❼ Estate Mount Washington Plantation. Several years ago, while surveying the property, the owners discovered the ruins of a sugar plantation beneath the rain-forest brush. The grounds have since been cleared and opened to the public. You can take a self-guided walking tour of the mill, the rum factory, and other ruins, and there's an antiques shop in what were once the stables (watch for antiques shop sign). ⊠ *Rte. 63,*

Mount Washington, ☎ *340/772–1026.* ☼ *Ruins open daily dawn–dusk antiques shop open by appointment only.*

8 Frederiksted. The town is noted less for its Danish than for its Victorian architecture, which dates from after the slave uprising and the great fire of 1878. One long cruise-ship pier juts into the sparkling sea. It's the perfect place to start a tour of this quaint city. The **Visitor Center** (⌂ Waterfront, ☎ 340/772–0357), right on the pier, was built in the late 1700s; the two-story gallery was added in the 1800s. The building once served as the customs house; today you can stop in weekdays from 8 to 5 and pick up brochures or view the exhibits on St. Croix. On July 3, 1848, 8,000 slaves marched on the red-brick **Ft. Frederik** to demand their freedom. Danish governor Peter von Scholten, fearing they would burn the town to the ground, stood up in his carriage parked in front of the fort and granted them their freedom. The fort, completed in 1760, houses a number of interesting historical exhibits as well as an art gallery and a display of police memorabilia. It's within earshot of the Visitor Center. ⌂ *Waterfront,* ☎ *340/772–2021.* ⌸ *Free.* ☼ *Weekdays 8:30–4:30.* **St. Patrick's** Roman Catholic church, complete with three turrets, was built in 1843 of coral. Wander inside, and you'll find woodwork handcrafted by Frederiksted artisans. The churchyard is filled with 18th-century gravestones. ⌂ *Prince St.* **St. Paul's Anglican Church** (circa 1812) is a mix of Georgian and Gothic Revival architecture. The bell tower of exposed sandstone was added later. The simple interior has gleaming woodwork and a tray ceiling (it looks like an upside-down tray) popular in Caribbean architecture. ⌂ *Prince St.* Built in 1839, **Apothecary Hall** is a good example of 19th-century architecture; its facade has both Gothic and Greek Revival elements. ⌂ *King Cross St.* Stop at the **market** for fresh fruits and vegetables (be sure to wash or peel this produce before eating it) sold each morning, just as they have been for more than 200 years. ⌂ *Queen St.*

10 St. Croix Leap. This workshop sits in the heart of the rain forest, about a 15-minute drive from Frederiksted. It sells mirrors, tables, bread boards, and mahogany jewelry boxes crafted by local artisans. ⌂ *Rte. 76, Brooks Hill,* ☎ *340/772–0421.* ☼ *Weekdays 8–5:30, Sat. 10–5.*

13 St. George Village Botanical Gardens. At this 17-acre estate you'll find lush, fragrant flora amid the ruins of a 19th-century sugarcane plantation village. There are miniature versions of each ecosystem on St. Croix, from a semiarid cactus grove to a verdant rain forest. ⌂ *Rte. 70, turn north at the sign, St. Georges,* ☎ *340/692–2874,* WEB *www.sgvbg.com.* ⌸ *$6.* ☼ *9–5.*

11 West End Salt Pond. A bird-watcher's delight, this salt pond attracts a large numbers of winged creatures, including flamingos. ⌂ *Veteran's Shore Dr., Hesselberg.*

☞ **12 Whim Plantation Museum.** The lovingly restored estate, with a windmill, cook house, and other buildings, will give you a sense of what life was like on St. Croix's sugar plantations in the 1800s. The oval-shape great house has high ceilings and antique furniture and utensils. Notice its fresh, airy atmosphere—the waterless stone moat around the great house was used not for defense but for gathering cooling air. If you have kids, the grounds are the perfect place for them to stretch their legs, perhaps while you browse in the museum gift shop. It's just outside of Frederiksted. ⌂ *Rte. 70, Estate Whim,* ☎ *340/772–0598,* WEB *www.stcroixlandmarks.com.* ⌸ *$6.* ☼ *Mon.–Sat. 10–4.*

ST. JOHN

Updated by
Lynda Lohr

Beautiful and largely undisturbed St. John is 3 mi (5 km) east of St. Thomas across the Pillsbury Sound (a 20-minute ferry ride from Red Hook). In 1956 Laurance Rockefeller, who founded the Caneel Bay Res ort, bought up much of St. John's 20 square mi (53 square km) to donate to the United States for a national park. The park now encompasses about two-thirds of the island. Because of this, the island comes close to realizing that travel-brochure dream of "an unspoiled tropical paradise." It's covered with vegetation, including a bay-tree forest that once supplied St. Thomas with the raw material for its fragrant bay rum. Along St. John's north shore, clean, gleaming white-sand beaches fringe bay after bay, each full of iridescent water perfect for swimming, fishing, snorkeling, diving, and underwater photography.

In 1675 Jorgen Iverson claimed the unsettled island for Denmark. The British residents of nearby Tortola, however, considered St. John theirs, and when a small party of Danes from St. Thomas moved onto the uninhabited island, the British "invited" them to leave (which they did). Despite this, in 1717 a group of Danish planters founded the first permanent settlement at Coral Bay. The question of who owned St. John wasn't settled until 1762, when Britain decided that maintaining good relations with Denmark was more important than keeping St. John.

By 1728 St. John had 87 plantations and a population of 123 whites and 677 blacks. By 1733 there were more than 1,000 slaves working more than 100 plantations. In that year the island was hit by a drought, hurricanes, and a plague of insects that destroyed the summer crops. Everyone felt the threat of famine, particularly the slaves, whose living and working conditions were already harsh. Sensing the growing desperation, the landowners enacted even more severe measures in a misguided attempt to keep control. On November 23 the slaves revolted. With great military prowess, they captured the fort at Coral Bay, took control of the island, and held on to it for six months. During this time nearly a quarter of the island's population—black and white—was killed. The rebellion was eventually put down by 100 Danish militia and 220 Creole troops brought in from Martinique. Slavery continued until 1848, when slaves in St. Croix marched on Frederiksted to demand their freedom from the Danish government. After emancipation, St. John fell into decline, with its inhabitants eking out a living on small farms. Life continued in much the same way until the national park was established in 1956 and tourism became an industry.

Today St. John may well be the most racially integrated of the three USVI. Its 5,000 residents, black and white, have a strong sense of community that seems rooted in a desire to protect the island's natural beauty. While the middle portion of the island remains undeveloped thanks to its status as a national park, the western end has boomed from the village of Cruz Bay into a small, sprawling town. On busy days it can suffer from traffic and parking woes. Coral Bay, at the eastern end of the island, is blossoming as the hillsides above it fill with homes and restaurants and shops appear at its shoreline. But, despite the growth, there are still many pockets of tranquillity. Here you can truly escape the pressures of modern life for a day, a week—perhaps, forever.

Lodging

St. John doesn't have many beachfront hotels, but that's a small price to pay for all the pristine sand. However, the island's two world-class resorts—Caneel Bay Resort and the Westin Resort, St. John—*are* on the beach. Sandy, white beaches string out along the north coast, which

KEY

- Beaches
- Dive Sites
- Exploring Sights
- Ferry
- Hotels and Restaurants

Lodging
Caneel Bay Resort **18**
Cinnamon Bay Campground **19**
Coconut Coast Villas **17**
Concordia Studios & Eco–tents **26**
Estate Zootenvaal **24**
Gallows Point Resort **2**
Garden by the Sea Bed & Breakfast . . . **16**
Harmony Studios . . . **21**
Maho Bay Camps **20**
Serendip **14**
St. John Inn **12**
Westin Resort, St. John **15**

Dining
Asolare **3**
Café Roma **1**
Chateau Bordeaux **22**
Fish Trap **4**
Lime Inn **5**
Miss Lucy's Restaurant **25**
Morgan's Mango . . . **6**
Panini Beach Trattoria **7**
Paradiso **8**
Skinny Legs Bar and Restaurant **23**
Stone Terrace Restaurant **10**
Sun Dog Cafe **11**
Tamarind Court Restaurant **9**
Uncle Joe's Barbecue **13**
Zozo's Ristorante **2**

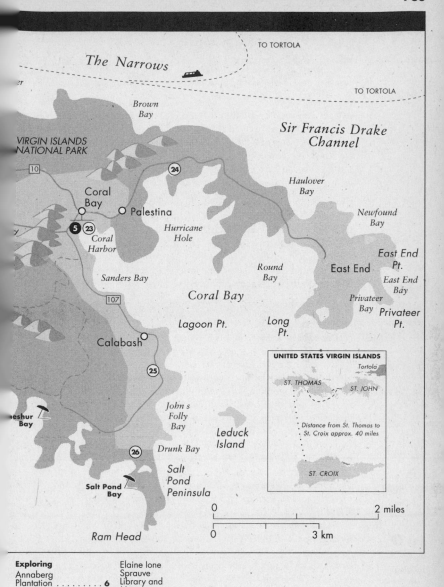

The Narrows

TO TORTOLA

TO TORTOLA

Brown
Bay

*Sir Francis Drake
Channel*

VIRGIN ISLANDS
NATIONAL PARK

10

Haulover
Bay

Coral
Bay

Palestina

Newfound
Bay

24

5 23

*Hurricane
Hole*

Coral
Harbor

East End
Pt.

Sanders Bay

Round
Bay

East End

East End
Bay

107

Coral Bay

Privateer
Bay

Privateer
Pt.

Calabash

Lagoon Pt.

Long
Pt.

25

John s
Folly
Bay

Leduck
Island

UNITED STATES VIRGIN ISLANDS

Tortola

26

Drunk Bay

ST. THOMAS

ST. JOHN

eshur
Bay

Salt
Pond
Peninsula

*Distance from St. Thomas to
St. Croix approx. 40 miles*

**Salt Pond
Bay**

ST. CROIX

Ram Head

0   2 miles

0   3 km

is popular with sunbathers and snorkelers and is where you'll find the Caneel Bay Resort and Cinnamon and Maho Bay campgrounds. Most villas are in the residential south shore area, a 15-minute drive from the north shore beaches. If you head east you'll come to the laid-back community of Coral Bay, where you'll find a few villas and cottages. A stay outside of Coral Bay will be peaceful and quiet.

If you're looking for West Indian–village charm, there are a few inns in Cruz Bay. Just know that when bands play at any of the town's bars (some of which stay open till the wee hours), the noise can be a problem. Your choice of accommodations also includes condominiums and cottages near town; two campgrounds, both at the edges of beautiful beaches (bring bug repellent); ecoresorts; and luxurious villas, often with a pool or a hot tub (sometimes both), and a stunning view.

If your lodging comes with a fully equipped kitchen, you'll be happy to know that St. John's handful of grocery stores sells everything from the basics to sun-dried tomatoes and green chilies—though the prices will take your breath away. If you're on a budget, consider bringing some staples (pasta, canned goods, paper products) from home. Hotel rates throughout the island, though considered expensive by some, do include endless privacy and access to most water sports.

For approximate costs, *see* the lodging price chart *in* St. Thomas.

Hotels and Inns

$$$$ ★ ☒ **Caneel Bay Resort.** Set on 170 lush peninsular acres—originally part of the Danish West India Company's Durloo plantation—Caneel Bay Resort mixes a good bit of peace and quiet into its luxurious air. You won't find crowds or glitz; your room won't have a TV, or even a phone (though management will loan you a cellular). Instead, you'll discover spacious, restful rooms that are open to the breezes and are tastefully decorated with tropical furnishings; seven beaches, each more gorgeous than the last; and an attentive staff that will fill your every need. ✉ *Rte. 20, Caneel Bay (Box 720, Cruz Bay 00830),* ☎ *340/776–6111 or 888/767–3966,* ℻ *340/693–8280,* WEB *www.caneelbay.com. 166 rooms. 4 restaurants, no room phones, fans, minibars, no room TVs, 11 tennis courts, beach, dive shop, dock, snorkeling, windsurfing, boating, billiards, children's programs (ages infant–12), meeting rooms. AE, DC, MC, V. EP, FAP, MAP.*

$$$$ ☒ **Westin Resort, St. John.** Spread over 47 beachfront acres adjacent to Great Cruz Bay, the Westin Resort has lushly planted gardens, a white sandy beach that beckons sunbathers, comfortable rooms with tropical touches, and enough amenities to make stepping off the grounds unnecessary. You can keep very busy here with tennis and watersports or you can idle away a good portion of the day at the pool or beach. If you want to get out and about, though, taxi jaunts into Cruz Bay are a breeze. ✉ *Rte. 104, Great Cruz Bay (Box 8310, Cruz Bay 00831),* ☎ *340/693–8000 or 800/808–5020,* ℻ *340/693–8888,* WEB *www.westinresortstjohn. com. 282 rooms and 67 villas. 3 restaurants, fans, in-room data ports, in-room safes, minibars, refrigerators, cable TV, 6 tennis courts, pool, gym, outdoor hot tub, massage, beach, dive shop, snorkeling, windsurfing, boating, fishing, shops, children's programs (ages 3–12), meeting rooms, no-smoking rooms. AE, D, DC, MC, V. EP.*

$$ ☒ **Garden by the Sea Bed and Breakfast.** An easy walk from Cruz Bay, this cozy spot has rooms that reflect the sea and sky. White spreads and curtains provide pristine counterpoints. Enjoy views of a salt pond and the sea as you enjoy your piña colada French toast on the front porch. It's perfect for folks who enjoy peace and quiet—there are no phones or TVs in the rooms, but each room does have a small tabletop fountain. (If the gurgle of water over rocks annoys you, the fountain has an off switch.) ✉ *Enighed (Box 1469, Cruz Bay 00831),* ☎ ⒻⒶⓍ *340/779–4731,* ⓌⒺⒷ *www.gardenbythesea.com. 3 rooms. No air-conditioning, no room phones, fans, no room TVs, no-smoking rooms. No credit cards. BP.*

$–$$ 🖭 **St. John Inn.** Within walking distance of Cruz Bay's shops and restaurants, this inn offers not only a convenient location but also affordable accommodations with a touch of charm. You might find a four-poster bed or an antique-style armoire in rooms painted in lush hues. ✉ *Off Rte. 104, Cruz Bay (Box 37, 00831),* ☎ *340/693–8688 or 800/666–7688,* ⒻⒶⓍ *340/693–9900,* ⓌⒺⒷ *www.stjohninn.com. 13 units. Fans, some kitchenettes, refrigerators, cable TV, pool. AE, D, MC, V. EP.*

Campgrounds

$–$$ ⚠ **Cinnamon Bay Campground.** Camping here puts you in Virgin Islands National Park, surrounded by trees and at the edge of lovely Cinnamon Bay Beach. Amenities are basic and include propane stoves and bed linens. Only the unlockable screened cottages have electric lights; tenters depend on propane lanterns. Bring your own tent and gear for the bare sites (a steal at $27 a night). The showers (on the cool side) and flush toilets, as well as a restaurant and a small store, are a short walk away. Hiking, water sports, and ranger-led evening programs are at your doorstep. ✉ *Rte. 20, Cinnamon Bay (Box 720, Cruz Bay 00830-0720),* ☎ *340/776–6330 or 800/539–9998,* ⒻⒶⓍ *340/776–6458,* ⓌⒺⒷ *www.cinnamonbay.com. 44 tents, 40 cottages, 26 bare sites. Restaurant, no air-condtioning, no room phones, no room TVs, hiking, beach, snorkeling, windsurfing. AE, MC, V. EP.*

$ ⚠ **Maho Bay Camps.** Tucked into the greenery along the island's north shore, this seaside ecocamp is a lush hillside community of rustic structures. The tents (wooden platforms protected from the elements by canvas and screening) are linked by wooden stairs, ramps, and walkways—all of them elevated—so that you can trek around camp, down to the beach and to the coolish public showers without disturbing the terrain. The tents have some amenities like real beds and electricity, but ice-filled coolers keep your food from spoiling. ✉ *Maho Bay (Box 310, Cruz Bay 00830),* ☎ *340/776–6240 or 800/392–9004,* ⒻⒶⓍ *340/ 776–6504,* ⓌⒺⒷ *www.mahobay.com. 114 tent cottages. Restaurant, no air-conditioning, no in-room phones, no room TVs, beach, snorkeling, windsurfing, Internet. AE, D, MC, V. EP.*

Condominiums and Cottages

Many of the island's condos are just minutes from the hustle and bustle of Cruz Bay, but you'll find more condos and cottages around the island.

$$$–$$$$ 🖭 **Gallows Point Resort.** These soft-gray buildings are clustered on a peninsula a 10-minute walk south of the Cruz Bay ferry dock. The upper-level apartments have loft bedrooms and good views. The harborside villas get better trade winds, but they're also a tad noisier. Rooms have tropical rattan furniture and pastel tropical accents. The entranceway is bridged by Ellington's restaurant, which serves contemporary cuisine. ✉ *Gallows Point, Cruz Bay (Box 58, 00831),* ☎ *340/776–6434 or 800/323–7229,* ⒻⒶⓍ *340/776–6520,* ⓌⒺⒷ *www.gallowspointresort.com. 52 rooms. Restaurant, fans, kitchens, cable TV, pool, beach, snorkeling. AE, MC, V. EP.*

$$–$$$ 🖭 **Estate Zootenvaal.** Set at the far reaches of the island, outside Coral Bay, this small complex provides modest cottages right at the water or across the street from the beach. It's a quiet spot perfect for people who like to sit in the chaise and read. ✉ *Rte. 10, Hurricane Hole, Zootenvaal 00830,* ☎ *340/776–6321,* ⓌⒺⒷ *www.usviguide.com/zootenvaal. 3*

units. No air-conditioning, fans, kitchens, no room TVs, beach. No credit cards. EP.

$$ 🏨 **Harmony Studios.** The condominium-style units sit hillside at Maho Bay. They have the usual decks, sliding glass doors and great sea views, but the carpets are attractively made of recycled milk cartons, the pristine white walls of old newspapers, and the energy comes from the wind and the sun. Each unit has a laptop computer programmed to monitor energy consumption. Tile floors, undyed cotton linens, and South American handicrafts are in keeping with the ideals. ⊠ *Maho Bay (Box 310, Cruz Bay 00830),* ☎ *340/776–6240 or 800/392–9004,* FAX *340/776–6504,* WEB *www.mahobay.com. 12 units. Restaurant, no air-conditioning, no room phones, fans, kitchens, no room TVs, beach, snorkeling, windsurfing, Internet, no-smoking rooms. AE, D, MC, V. EP.*

$–$$ 🏨 **Coconut Coast Villas.** Within walking distance of Cruz Bay's shops and restaurants, this small condominium complex—with studio, two- and three-bedroom units—sits so close to the water you'll fall asleep to the sound of waves. ⊠ *Turner Bay (Box 618, Cruz Bay 00831),* ☎ *340/693–9100 or 800/858–7989,* FAX *340/779–4157,* WEB *www.coconutcoast.com. 9 units. Kitchens, fans, cable TV, pool, beach. MC, V. EP.*

$–$$ 🏨 **Serendip.** This complex offers modest units on lush grounds with lovely views. You definitely need a rental car if you stay here, though; it's about 1 mi (1½ km) up a killer hill out of Cruz Bay. If air-conditioning is important to you, be sure to mention it when booking, as some units have only ceiling fans. ⊠ *Enighed (Box 273, Cruz Bay 00831),* ☎ *340/776–6646 or 888/800–6445,* WEB *www.st-john.com/serendip. 10 units. Air-conditioning in some rooms, fans, cable TV, kitchens. MC, V. EP.*

$ 🏨 **Concordia Studios and Eco-tents.** An ecofriendly resort in the Maho Bay Camps family, these studios and ecotents sit hillside on 51 acres near remote Salt Pond Bay. The spacious units are casually comfortable with tile floors and lovely sea views. They're made of recycled materials, and energy for all the appliances (even the ice makers) is wind- and solar-generated. Next door are five eco-tents, upscale camping structures made of environmentally friendly materials, equipped with solar power and composting toilets. ⊠ *20–27 Estate Concordia, Concordia 00830,* ☎ *340/693–5855 or 800/392–9004,* FAX *340/693–5960,* WEB *www.mahobay.com. 20 studios, 5 tents. No air-conditioning, no room phones, kitchens, no room TVs, pool, no-smoking rooms. AE, D, MC, V. EP.*

Villas

Tucked here and there between Cruz Bay and Coral Bay are about 350 villas (prices range from $ to $$$$). With pools and/or hot tubs, full kitchens, and living areas, they provide a home away from home. They're perfect for couples and extended groups of families or friends. You'll need a car since most are up in the hills (very few are at the beach). Villa managers usually pick you up at the dock, arrange for your rental car, and answer questions you have upon arrival as well as during your stay.

To rent a luxury villa, contact one of the following rental agents:

Caribbean Villas and Resorts (⊠ Box 458, Cruz Bay 00831, ☎ 340/776–6152 or 800/338–0987, FAX 340/779–4044, WEB www.caribbeanvilla.com) handles condo rentals for Cruz Views, Lavender Hill, and Gallow's Point Resort, as well as for private villas. **Catered To, Inc.** (⊠ Box 704, Cruz Bay 00830, ☎ 340/776–6641, FAX 340/693–8191, WEB www.cateredto.com) has luxury homes in Creat Cruz Bay and Chocolate Hole areas. **Destination St. John** (⊠ Box 8306, Cruz Bay 00831, ☎ FAX 340/779–4647 or ☎ 800/562–1901, WEB www.destinationstjohn.com) manages villas within a 10-minute drive of Cruz Bay. **Park Isle Villas** (⊠ Box 1263, Cruz Bay 00831, ☎ FAX 340/693–8261 or ☎ 800/

416–1205, WEB www.batteryhill.com) handles Battery Hill and Villa Caribe condos. **Private Homes for Private Vacations** (✉ Mamey Peak 00830, ☎ FAX 340/776–6876, WEB www.privatehomesvi.com) has homes across the island. **Star Villa** (✉ Box 599, Cruz Bay 00830, ☎ 340/776–6704 or 888/897–9759, FAX 340/776–6183, WEB www.starvillas.com) has cozy villas just outside Cruz Bay. **Vacation Homes** (✉ Box 272, Cruz Bay 00831, ☎ 340/776–6094, FAX 340/693–8455) has luxury homes from outside Cruz Bay to mid-island. **Vacation Vistas** (✉ Box 476, Cruz Bay 00831, ☎ 340/776–6462, WEB www.vacationvistas.com) manages villas in the Chocolate Hole and Great Cruz Bay area. **Windspree** (✉ 7924 Emmaus, Cruz Bay 00830, ☎ 340/693–5423, FAX 340/693–5623, WEB www.windspree.com) handles villas mainly in the Coral Bay area.

Dining

The cuisine on St. John seems to get better every year, with culinary school–trained chefs vying to see who can come up with the most imaginative dishes. There are restaurants to suit every taste and budget—from the elegant establishments at Caneel Bay Resort (where men may be required to wear a jacket at dinner) to the casual in-town eateries of Cruz Bay. For quick lunches try the West Indian food stands in Cruz Bay Park and across from the post office. The cooks prepare fried chicken legs, pates (meat- and fish-filled pastries), and callaloo.

For approximate costs, *see* the dining price chart *in* St. Thomas.

Bordeaux
CONTEMPORARY

$$$–$$$$ ✕ **Chateau Bordeaux.** This rustic restaurant with a to-die-for view of Coral Bay is made elegant with lace tablecloths, candlelight, and stylish dinner presentations. You might start with a dill crepe stuffed with Caribbean lobster and melted Brie and drizzled with a lemon butter sauce; then segue into New Zealand rack of lamb with a honey-Dijon-pecan crust in a port wine cream sauce or salmon crusted with pistachio and macadamia nuts and finished with a green curry-coconut cream sauce. Save room for dessert—the fresh berry cups with Chambord and caramel are wonderful. ✉ *Rte. 10, Bordeaux,* ☎ *340/776–6611. AE, MC, V. No lunch.*

Coral Bay and Environs
AMERICAN

$ ✕ **Skinny Legs Bar and Restaurant.** Sailors who live aboard boats an-
★ chored just off shore and an eclectic coterie of residents gather for lunch and dinner at this funky spot. If owners Doug Sica and Moe Chabuz are around, take a gander at their gams; you'll see where the restaurant got its name. It's a great place for burgers, fish sandwiches, and watching whatever sports event is on cable TV. ✉ *Rte. 10, Coral Bay,* ☎ *340/779–4982. AE, D, MC, V.*

CARIBBEAN

$ ✕ **Miss Lucy's Restaurant.** Sitting seaside at remote Friis Bay, Miss Lucy's
★ dishes up Caribbean food with a contemporary flair. Dishes like tender conch fritters, a spicy West Indian stew called callaloo, and fried fish make up most of the menu, but you'll also find a generous pot of seafood, as well as sausage and chicken paella on the menu. Sunday brunches are legendary, and if you're around on the full moon, stop by for the monthly full moon party. The handful of small tables near the water are the nicest, but if they're taken or the mosquitoes are bad, the indoor tables do nicely. ✉ *Rte. 107, Friis Bay,* ☎ *340/693–5244. AE, D, MC, V. Closed Mon. No dinner Sun.*

Cruz Bay

BARBECUE

$–$$ ✕ **Uncle Joe's Barbecue.** Juicy ribs and tasty chicken legs dripping with the house barbecue sauce make for one of St. John's best dining deals. An ear of corn on the cob, rice, and a generous scoop of macaroni salad or coleslaw round out the plate. This very casual spot crowds the edge of a busy sidewalk in the heart of Cruz Ba y. Even though there are a few open-air tables for dining in, the ambience is more than a tad on the pedestrian side, so take-out is a better bet. ⊠ *North Shore Rd., across from post office,* ☎ *340/693–8806. No credit cards.*

CONTEMPORARY

$$$–$$$$ ✕ **Stone Terrace Restaurant.** A delightful harbor view, soft lantern light, and white linen tablecloths provide the backdrop for chef Aaron Willis's imaginative cuisine. To standards like a roasted half duck, he adds a spiced orange glaze and a pablano pepper stuffed with mashed sweet potatoes. The salad course takes on a new twist with a tomato napoleon made with roasted peppers, boursin cheese, and roasted garlic sauce layered between crisp tortillas. The desserts change daily, but are always as intriguing as the other courses. ⊠ *Bay St.,* ☎ *340/693–9370. AE, D, MC, V. Closed Mon. No lunch.*

$$–$$$ ✕ **Lime Inn.** Mainland transplants who call St. John home as well as visitors flock to this alfresco spot for the congenial hospitality and good food, including all-you-can-eat shrimp on Wednesday nights. There are shrimp and steak dishes and such specials as pistachio chicken breasts with plantains and Thai curry cream sauce. Fresh lobster is the specialty every night. ⊠ *Lemon Tree Mall, King St.,* ☎ *340/776–6425. AE, MC, V. Closed Sun. No lunch Sat.*

$$–$$$ ✕ **Morgan's Mango.** A long flight of stairs leads you to this alfresco eatery, but good food makes it worth the climb. Although fish is the specialty—try the voodoo snapper topped with a many-fruit salsa—the chef also creates a vegetarian platter with black beans, fried plantains, salad, and even an ear of corn. ⊠ *North Shore Rd., across from V.I. National Park's Visitors Center,* ☎ *340/693–8141. AE, MC, V. No lunch.*

ECLECTIC

$$–$$$$ ✕ **Fish Trap.** The rooms and terraces here all open to the breezes and buzz with a mix of locals and visitors. Chef Aaron Willis conjures up such tasty appetizers as conch fritters and Fish Trap chowder (a creamy soup of snapper, white wine, paprika, and secret spices). The menu also includes an interesting pasta of the day, steak and chicken dishes, and hamburgers. ⊠ *Bay and Strand Sts., next to Our Lady of Mount Carmel Church,* ☎ *340/693–9994. AE, D, MC, V. Closed Mon. No lunch.*

$$$ ✕ **Paradiso.** This popular spot is on the upper level of the island's largest shopping complex. The menu is a mix of everything, including pork tenderloin with a tomato, bacon, and onion marmalade; and garlic rosemary–basted mahimahi. You can dine indoors, in air-conditioned comfort, or outdoors on a small terrace overlooking the street. ⊠ *Mongoose Junction shopping center, North Shore Rd.,* ☎ *340/693–8899. AE, MC, V.*

$–$$$ ✕ **Tamarind Court Restaurant.** This casual courtyard restaurant at the Inn at Tamarind Court sees a different chef in the kitchen every night. The menus are always small, but the modest prices make this a popular spot with locals. All the food is good, but Monday's Greek night is the standout, with dishes like spanakopita and gyros on the menu. On Tuesdays, the menu is Asian; sushi chefs take to the kitchen on Wednesdays. Try the southern cooking on Thursdays and prime rib on Fridays and Sundays. Chefs also conjure up waffle and pancake breakfasts. ⊠ *Inn at Tamarind Court, Route 104,* ☎ *340/776–6378. AE, D, MC, V. No lunch; no dinner Sat.*

$ ✕ **Sun Dog Cafe.** You'll find an unusual assortment of dishes at this charming restaurant tucked into a courtyard in the upper reaches of the Mongoose Junction shopping center. Kudos to the white artichoke pizza with roasted garlic, artichoke hearts, mozzarella cheese, and capers. The Jamaican jerk chicken sub or the black bean quesadilla are also good choices. ⊠ *Mongoose Junction shopping center, North Shore Rd.,* ☎ *340/693–8340. AE, MC, V.* ☉ *Lunch only.*

ITALIAN

$$$ ✕ **Zozo's Ristorante.** Creative takes on old standards coupled with lovely presentation are what draw the crowds to this restaurant. The baked jumbo shrimp comes with an artichoke and crabmeat tapenade served over a porcini mushroom risotto, and the rack of lamb sports a pistachio crust in a tasty rosemary and port sauce. The pastas are equally imaginative. The lobster ravioli is stuffed with wild mushrooms and tasted pine nuts swimming in a tomato cream sauce. Opt for inside seating. While the terrace looks tempting, street noise can be a distraction. ⊠ *Across from school ballfield on unnamed street that heads inland from ferry dock,* ☎ *340/693–9200. AE, MC, V. No lunch.*

$$–$$$ ✕ **Café Roma.** This casual second-floor restaurant in the heart of Cruz Bay is *the* place for traditional Italian cuisine: lasagna, spaghetti and meatballs, chicken Parmesan. There are also excellent pizzas. Marscapone mango crepes are a dessert specialty. ⊠ *Vesta Gade,* ☎ *340/776–6524. MC, V. No lunch.*

$$–$$$ ✕ **Panini Beach Trattoria.** Taking its name from the pressed and grilled Italian sandwich, available only at lunch, this cozy seaside bistro serves delightful Northern Italian fare. Lunch includes basics like pizza and soup and salads, but at dinner the menu runs to fresh pasta and chicken dishes cooked with herbs and spices. Save room for dessert. The chocolate panini is from dessert heaven. You can dine inside in air-conditioned comfort, although the alfresco beachfront tables are the nicest bets. ⊠ *Wharfside Village shopping center, Strand St.,* ☎ *340/693–9119. AE, MC, V. No lunch weekends.*

PAN-ASIAN

$$$–$$$$ ✕ **Asolare.** Contemporary Asian cuisine dominates the menu at this
★ elegant open-air eatery in an old St. John house. Come early and relax over drinks while you enjoy the sunset over the harbor. Start with an appetizer such as pork spring rolls served with sticky rice and a baby greens salad. Entrées include such delights as seared yellowfin tuna served with sweet jasmine rice, sautéed summer squash, snow peas, and a sesame vinaigrette. If you still have room for dessert, try the chocolate pyramid, a luscious cake with homemade ice cream melting in the middle. ⊠ *Rte. 20 on Caneel Hill,* ☎ *340/779–4747. AE, MC, V. No lunch.*

Beaches

St. John is blessed with many beaches, and all of them fall into the good, great, and don't-tell-anyone-else-about-this-place categories. Those along the north shore are all within the national park. Some are more developed than others—and many are crowded on weekends, holidays, and in high season—but by and large they're still pristine. Beaches along the south and eastern shores are quiet and isolated.

Caneel Bay. Caneel Bay is actually a catch-all name for seven white-sand north-shore beaches, six of which can be reached only by water if you aren't a guest at the Caneel Bay Resort. (Access to beaches is a civil right in the USVI, but access to land that leads to the beaches is not.) The seventh, **Caneel Beach,** is open to the public and is easy to reach from the main entrance of the resort; just ask for directions at the gatehouse. Nonguests can also dine at three of the hotel's four restaurants and browse in its gift shop.

Cinnamon Bay. This long, sandy beach faces beautiful cays and abuts the national park campground. The facilities are open to the public and include cool showers, toilets, a commissary, and a restaurant. You can rent water-sports equipment here—a good thing because there's excellent snorkeling off the point to the right; look for the big angelfish and large schools of purple triggerfish. Afternoons on Cinnamon Bay can be windy, so arrive early to beat the gusts. The Cinnamon Bay hiking trail begins across the road from the beach parking lot; ruins mark the trailhead. There are actually two paths here: a level nature trail (signs along it identify the flora) that loops through the woods and passes an old Danish cemetery, and a steep trail that starts where the road bends past the ruins and heads straight up to Route 10.

Hawksnest Beach. Sea-grape trees line this narrow beach, and there are rest rooms, cooking grills, and a covered shed for picnicking. It's the closest beach to town, so it's often crowded.

Lameshur Bay. This nifty beach is toward the end of a very long dirt road on the southeast coast. It offers solitude, good snorkeling, and a chance to spy on some pelicans. The ruins of the old plantation are a five-minute walk down the road past the beach.

Maho Bay. This popular beach is below the Maho Bay Camps—a wonderful hillside enclave of tent cabins. The campground offers informal talks and slide and film presentations on nature, environmentally friendly living, and whatever else crosses the manager's mind.

Salt Pond Bay. If you're adventurous, this somewhat rocky beach on the scenic southeastern coast—next to Coral Bay and rugged Drunk Bay—is worth exploring. It's a short hike down a hill from the parking lot, and the only facilities are an outhouse and a few picnic tables scattered about. There are interesting tidal pools, and the snorkeling is good. Take special care to leave nothing valuable in your car; reports of thefts are common.

Trunk Bay. St. John's most-photographed beach is also the preferred spot for beginning snorkelers because of its underwater trail. (Cruise-ship passengers interested in snorkeling for a day come here, so if you're looking for seclusion, come early or late in the day.) Crowded or not, this stunning beach is sure to please. There are changing rooms, a snack bar, picnic tables, a gift shop, phones, lockers, and snorkeling equipment rentals.

Outdoor Activities and Sports

BOATING AND SAILING

For a speedy trip to offshore cays and remote beaches, a powerboat is a necessity. It can cost you around $300 per day with gas and oil charges, depending on how far you are going. More leisurely day sails to islands not far offshore or longer sails to points east are also possibilities. If you're boatless, book with one of the island's agents. Most day sails include lunch, beverages, and at least one stop to snorkel. A full-day sail with lunch runs around $90 per person.

Adventures in Paradise (⊠ Cruz Bay, across from the post office, ☎ 340/779–4527) books fishing, sailing, and scuba trips on most of the island's charter boats. **Connections** (⊠ Cruz Bay, a block up from the ferry dock and catercorner from Chase Manhattan Bank, ☎ 340/776–6922) pairs you up with the sailboat that suits you. Have simple tastes? The smiling staff can help. If luxury is more your style, they can book that, too. **Ocean Runner** (⊠ Cruz Bay, on the waterfront, ☎ 340/693–8809) rents one- and two-engine boats for fast trips around the island's seas. **Proper Yachts** (✉ Caneel Bay, ☎ 340/776–6256) books day sails and longer charters on its fleet of luxury yachts that depart from Caneel Bay Resort.

FISHING

Well-kept charter boats head out to the north and south drops or troll along the inshore reefs. The captains usually provide bait, drinks, and lunch, but you'll need your hat and sunscreen. Fishing charters run around $100 per hour per person. The **Charter Boat Center** (☎ 340/775–7990), in Red Hook on St. Thomas, also arranges fishing trips for folks in St. John. **Gone Ketchin'** (☎ 340/693–8657), in St. John, arranges trips with old salt Wally Leopold. **St. John World Class Anglers** (☎ 340/779–4281) offers light-tackle shore and offshore half- and full-day trips.

HIKING

Although it's fun to go hiking with a Virgin Islands National Park guide, don't be afraid to strike out on your own. To find a hike that suits your ability, stop by the park's visitor center in Cruz Bay and pick up the free trail guide; it details points of interest, dangers, trail lengths, and estimated hiking times. Although the park staff recommends pants to protect against thorns and insects, most people hike in shorts because pants are too hot. Wear sturdy shoes or hiking boots even if you're hiking to the beach. Don't forget to bring water and insect repellent.

The **Virgin Islands National Park** (☎ 340/776–6201, WEB www.nps.gov/viis) maintains more than 20 trails on the north and south shores and offers guided hikes along popular routes. A full-day trip to Reef Bay is a must; it's an easy hike through lush and dry forest, past the ruins of an old plantation, and to a sugar factory adjacent to the beach. Take the public Vitran bus or a taxi to the trailhead, where you'll meet a ranger who will serve as your guide. The park provides a boat ride back to Cruz Bay for $15 to save you the walk back up the mountain. The schedule changes from season to season; call for times and reservations, which are essential.

HORSEBACK RIDING

Clip-clop along the island's byways for a slower-pace tour of St. John. **Carolina Corral** (☎ 340/693–5778) offers horseback trips down quiet roads as well as riding lessons. Rates start at $45 for a one-hour ride.

SCUBA DIVING AND SNORKELING

Although just about every beach has nice snorkeling—Trunk Bay, Cinnamon Bay, and Waterlemon Cay at Leinster Bay get the most praise—you'll need a boat to head out to the more remote snorkeling locations and the best scuba spots. Sign on with any of the island's water-sports operators to get to spots farther from St. John. Their boats will take you to hot spots between St. John and St. Thomas, including the tunnels at **Thatch Cay,** the ledges at **Congo Cay,** and the wreck of the *General Rogers.* Dive off St. John at **Stephens Cay,** a short boat ride out of Cruz Bay, where fish swim around the reefs as you float downward. At **Devers Bay,** on St. John's south shore, fish dart about in colorful schools. Count on paying $65 for a one-tank dive and $80 for a two-tank dive. Rates include equipment and a tour.

Cruz Bay Watersports (☎ 340/776–6234) has three locations: in Cruz Bay, at the Westin Resort, and in the Palm Plaza Shopping Center. Owners Marcus and Patty Johnston offer regular reef, wreck, and night dives and USVI and BVI snorkel tours. **Low Key Watersports** (☎ 340/693–8999 or 800/835–7718), at Wharfside Village, offers PADI certification and resort courses, one- and two-tank dives, and specialty courses.

SEA KAYAKING

Poke around crystal bays and explore undersea life from a sea kayak **Arawak Expeditions** (☎ 340/693–8312 or 800/238–8687) professional guides use traditional kayaks to ply coastal waters. Prices start at $40 for a half-day trip.

TENNIS

With hot weather the norm, tennis players take to the courts in the morning or late afternoon. The **Westin Resort, St. John** (✉ Rte. 104, Great Cruz Bay, ☎ 340/693–8000), has six lighted courts. Nonguests are welcome to play here for a fee of $15 an hour. The **public courts,** near the fire station in Cruz Bay, are lit until 10 PM and are available on a first-come, first-served basis.

WINDSURFING

Steady breezes and expert instruction make learning to windsurf a snap. Try **Cinnamon Bay Campground** (✉ Rte. 20, Cinnamon Bay, ☎ 340/776–6330), where rentals are available for $20–$30 per hour. Lessons are available right at the waterfront; just look for the Windsurfers stacked up on the beach. The cost for a one-hour lesson is about $60.

Shopping

Areas and Malls

You'll find luxury items and handicrafts on St. John. Most shops carry a little of this and a bit of that, so it pays to poke around. The Cruz Bay shopping district runs from **Wharfside Village,** just around the corner from the ferry dock, through the streets of town to North Shore Road and **Mongoose Junction,** an inviting shopping center with stonework walls (its name is a holdover from a time when those furry island creatures gathered at a garbage bin that was here). Steps connect the two sections of the center, which has unique upscale shops. Out on Route 104, stop in at **The Marketplace** to explore its handful of gift and crafts shops. At the island's other end, you'll find a few stores—selling clothes, jewelry, and artwork—here and there from the village of **Coral Bay** to the small complex at **Shipwreck Landing.**

Specialty Items

ART

Bajo el Sol. A cooperative gallery, Bajo el Sol sells Aimee Trayser's expressionistic Caribbean scenes, Les Anderson's island scenes in oil, Kat Sowa's watercolors, and works by a handful of other artists. ✉ *Mongoose Junction, North Shore Rd., Cruz Bay,* ☎ *340/693–7070.*
Coconut Coast Studios. This waterside shop, a five-minute walk from Cruz Bay, showcases the work of Elaine Estern. She specializes in undersea scenes. ✉ *Frank Bay, Cruz Bay,* ☎ *340/776–6944.*

BOOKS

MAPes MONDe. Here you'll find a good selection of books on the Caribbean, including the exquisite-looking publications that are the hallmark of Virgin Islands publisher MAPes MONDe. You'll also find many reproductions of old maps as well as contemporary prints and greeting cards. ✉ *Mongoose Junction, North Shore Rd., Cruz Bay,* ☎ *340/779–4545.*
National Park Headquarters. The headquarters sells several good histories of St. John, including *St. John Back Time,* by Ruth Hull Low and Rafael Lito Valls, and for linguists, Valls's *What a Pistarckle!*—an explanation of the colloquialisms that make up the local version of English (*pistarckle* is a Dutch Creole word that means "noise" or "din," which pretty much sums up the language here). ✉ *The Creek, near Cruz Bay bulkhead and baseball field, Cruz Bay,* ☎ *340/776–6201.*

CLOTHING

Big Planet Adventure Outfitters. You knew when you arrived that some place on St. John would cater to the outdoor enthusiasts that hike up and down the island's trails. Well, this outdoor-clothing store is where you'll find the popular Noats sandals, along with colorful and durable cotton clothing and accessories by Patagonia, the North Face, Columbia, and others. The store also sells children's clothes. ⊠ *Mongoose Junction, North Shore Rd., Cruz Bay,* ☎ *340/776–6638.*

Bougainvillea Boutique. If you want to look like you stepped out of the pages of the resort-wear spread in an upscale travel magazine, try this store. Owner Susan Stair carries *very* chic men's and women's resort wear, straw hats, leather handbags, and fine gift items. ⊠ *Mongoose Junction, North Shore Rd., Cruz Bay,* ☎ *340/693–7190.*

The Clothing Studio. Several talented artists hand-paint original designs on clothing for all members of the family. You'll find T-shirts, beach cover-ups, pants, shorts, and even bathing suits with beautiful hand-painted creations. ⊠ *Mongoose Junction, North Shore Rd., Cruz Bay,* ☎ *340/776–6585.*

Jolly Dog. Stock up on the stuff you forgot to pack at this store. Sarongs in cotton and rayon, beach towels with tropical motifs, and hats and T-shirts sporting the Jolly Dog logs fill the shelves. ⊠ *Rte. 107, Shipwreck Landing, Sanders Bay,* ☎ *340/693–5333.*

St. John Editions. Shop here for nifty cotton shifts that go from beach to dinner with a change of shoes and accessories. Owner Ann Soper also carries attractive straw hats and inexpensive jewelry. ⊠ *North Shore Rd., Cruz Bay,* ☎ *340/693–8444.*

FOODSTUFFS

If you're renting a villa, condo, or cottage and doing your own cooking, there are several good places to shop for food; just be aware that prices are much higher than those at home.

Marina Market. Although this market usually has the best prices, its selection is small. ⊠ *Rte. 104, Cruz Bay,* ☎ *340/779–4401.*

Starfish Market. The island's largest store usually has the best selection of meat, fish, and produce. ⊠ *Marketplace Shopping Center, Rte. 104, Cruz Bay,* ☎ *340/779–4949.*

Tropicale. You can get great take-out meals here in addition to its rather smallish selection of groceries. ⊠ *Palm Plaza, Rte. 104, Cruz Bay,* ☎ *340/693–7474.*

GIFTS

Bamboula. Owner Jo Sterling travels the Caribbean and the world to find unusual housewares, rugs, bedspreads, accessories, shoes, and men's and women's clothes for this multicultural boutique. ⊠ *Mongoose Junction, North Shore Rd., Cruz Bay,* ☎ *340/693–8699.*

The Canvas Factory. If you're a true shopper who needs an extra bag to carry all your treasures home, this store offers every kind of tote and carrier imaginable—from simple bags to suitcases with numerous zippered compartments—all made of canvas, naturally. It also sells great canvas hats. ⊠ *Mongoose Junction, North Shore Rd., Cruz Bay,* ☎ *340/776–6196.*

Donald Schnell Studio. In addition to pottery, this place sells unique hand-blown glass, wind chimes, kaleidoscopes, fanciful water fountains, and more. Your purchases can be shipped worldwide. ⊠ *Mongoose Junction, North Shore Rd., Cruz Bay,* ☎ *340/776–6420.*

Fabric Mill. Shop here for handmade dolls, place mats, napkins, and batik wraps. Or take home a bolt of tropical brights from the upholstery-fabric selection. ⊠ *Mongoose Junction, North Shore Rd., Cruz Bay,* ☎ *340/776–6194.*

Pink Papaya. This store is the home of longtime Virgin Islands resident M. L. Etre's well-known artwork plus a huge collection of one-of-a-kind gift items, including bright tablecloths, unusual trays, dinnerware, and unique tropical jewelry. ⊠ *Lemon Tree Mall, King St., Cruz Bay,* ☎ *340/693–8535.*

Wicker, Wood and Shells. Shop the second floor of this store for lovely sculptures and other objets d'art, all with a tropical theme. On the first floor, you'll find the island's best selection of greeting cards, notepaper, and other interesting items to tuck in your suitcase for friends back home. ⊠ *Mongoose Junction, North Shore Rd., Cruz Bay,* ☎ *340/776–6909.*

JEWELRY

Blue Carib Gems. Here you'll find custom-made jewelry, loose gemstones, and old coins as well as hand-crafted jewelry from local and other artists. ⊠ *Wharfside Village, Strand St., Cruz Bay,* ☎ *340/693–8299.*

Caravan Gallery. Owner Radha Speer creates much of the unusual jewelry you'll find here. And the more you look, the more you see—folk art, tribal art, and masks for sale cover the walls and tables, making this a great place to browse. ⊠ *Mongoose Junction, North Shore Rd., Cruz Bay,* ☎ *340/779–4566.*

Colombian Emeralds. This branch of a St. Thomas store has high-quality emeralds and also sells rubies, diamonds, and other jewels set in attractive gold and silver settings. ⊠ *Mongoose Junction, North Shore Rd., Cruz Bay,* ☎ *340/776–6007.*

Free Bird Creations. Head here for the unique handcrafted jewelry—earrings, bracelets, pendants, chains—as well as the good selection of waterproof watches great for your excursions to the beach. ⊠ *Wharfside Village, King St., Cruz Bay,* ☎ *340/693–8625,*

R&I Patton Goldsmiths. Rudy and Irene Patton design most of the unique silver and gold jewelry in this shop. The rest comes from various jeweler friends of theirs. Sea fans (those large, lacy plants that sway with the ocean's currents) in filigreed silver, lapis set in long drops of gold, starfish and hibiscus pendants in silver or gold, and gold sand dollar–shape charms and earrings are tempting choices. ⊠ *Mongoose Junction, North Shore Rd., Cruz Bay,* ☎ *340/776–6548.*

Nightlife

St. John isn't the place to go for glitter and all-night partying. Still, after-hours Cruz Bay can be a lively little town in which to dine, drink, dance, chat, or flirt. Notices posted on the bulletin board outside the Connections telephone center—up the street from the ferry dock in Cruz Bay—or listings in the island's two small newspapers (the *St. John Times* and *Tradewinds*) will keep you apprised of special events, comedy nights, movies, and the like.

After a sunset drink at **Ellington's** (⊠ Gallows Point Resort, ☎ 340/693–8490), up the hill from Cruz Bay, you can stroll here and there in town (much is clustered around the small waterfront park). Many of the young people from the U.S. mainland who live and work on St. John will be out sipping and socializing, too.

Duffy's Love Shack (⊠ Veste Gade, Cruz Bay, ☎ 340/776–6065) is the wild and crazy place to go. Loud music and drinks like the shark tank (rum and 3 tropical liquers) make this Cruz Bay's hottest late-night spot. There's calypso and reggae on Wednesday and Friday at **Fred's** (⊠ King St., Cruz Bay, ☎ 340/776–6363). The **Inn at Tamarind Court** (⊠ Rte. 104, Cruz Bay, ☎ 340/776–6378) serves up country rock on Friday. On the far side of the island, check out the action at **Skinny Legs Bar and Restaurant** (⊠ Rte. 10, Coral Bay, ☎ 340/779–4982). Young folks like to gather at **Woody's** (✉ Ferry Rd., Cruz Bay, ☎ 340/779–4625). Its sidewalk tables provide a close-up view of Cruz Bay's action.

Exploring St. John

St. John is an easy place to explore. One road runs along the north shore, another across the center of the mountains. There are a few roads that branch off here and there, but it's hard to get lost. Pick up a map at the visitor center before you start out, and you'll have no problems. Few residents remember the route numbers, so have your map in hand if you stop to ask for directions. Bring along a swimsuit for stops at some of the most beautiful beaches in the world. You can spend all day or just a couple of hours exploring, but be advised that the roads are narrow and wind up and down steep hills, so don't expect to get anywhere in a hurry. There are lunch spots at Cinnamon Bay and in Coral Bay, or you cando what the locals do—picnic. The grocery stores in Cruz Bay sell Styrofoam coolers just for this purpose.

If you plan to do a lot of touring, renting a car will be cheaper and will give you much more freedom than relying on taxis, which are reluctant to go anywhere until they have a full load of passengers. Although you may be tempted by an open-air Suzuki or Jeep, a conventional car can get you just about everywhere on the paved roads, and you'll be able to lock up your valuables. You may be able to share a van or open-air vehicle (called a safari bus) with other passengers on a tour of scenic mountain trails, secret coves, and eerie bush-covered ruins.

Numbers in the margin correspond to points of interest on the St. John map.

Sights to See

⑥ Annaberg Plantation. In the 18th-century sugar plantations dotted the steep hills of the USVI. Slaves and free Danes and Dutchmen toiled to harvest the cane that was used to create sugar, molasses, and rum for export. Built in the 1780s, the partially restored plantation at Leinster Bay was once an important sugar mill. Though there are no official visiting hours, the National Park Service has regular tours, and some well-informed taxi drivers will show you around. Occasionally you'll find a living-history demonstration—someone making johnnycake or weaving baskets. For information on tours and cultural events, contact the St. John National Park Service Visitors Center. ✉ *Leinster Bay Rd., Annaberg,* ☎ *340/776–6201,* WEB *www.nps/gov/viis.* 🖼 *$4.*

④ Bordeaux Mountain. St. John's highest peak rises to 1,277 ft (391 m). Route 10 passes near enough to the top to offer breathtaking views. Drive nearly to the end of the dirt road for spectacular views at Picture Point and for the trailhead of the hike downhill to Lameshur. Get a trail map from the park service before you start. ✉ *Rte. 10.*

⑦ Catherineberg Ruins. At this fine example of an 18th-century sugar and rum factory, there's a storage vault beneath the windmill. Across the road, look for the round mill, which was later used to hold water. In the 1733 slave revolt, Catherineberg served as headquarters for the Amina warriors, a tribe of Africans captured into slavery. ✉ *Rte. 10, Catherineberg.*

⑤ Coral Bay. This laid-back community at the island's dry, eastern end is named for its shape rather than for its underwater life—the word *coral* comes from *krawl,* Dutch for "corral." It's a small, quiet, neighborhoody settlement—a place to get away from it all. You'll need a Jeep if you plan to stay at this end of the island, as some of the rental houses are up unpaved roads that wind around the mountain. If you come just for lunch, a regular car will be fine.

1 **Cruz Bay.** St. John's main town may be compact (it consists of only several blocks), but it's definitely a hub: the ferries from St. Thoma and the BVI pull in here, and it's where you can get a taxi or rent a car to travel around the island. There are plenty of shops in which to browse, a number of watering holes where you can stop for a breather many restaurants, and a grassy square with benches where you can sit back and take everything in. Look for the current edition of the handy, amusing "St. John Map" featuring Max the Mongoose. To pick up a handy guide to St. John's hiking trails, see various large maps of the island, and find out about current park service programs, including guided walks and cultural demonstrations, stop by the **V. I. National Park Visitors Center.** ⊠ *In an area known as the Creek, near Cruz Bay bulkhead and baseball field, Cruz Bay 00831,* ☎ *340/776–6201.* ⊞ *www.nps.gov/viis.* ⊠ *Free.* ☉ *Daily 8–4:30.*

2 **Elaine Ione Sprauve Library and Museum.** On the hill just above Cruz Bay is the **Enighed Estate Great House,** built in 1757. *Enighed* is the Danish word for "concord" (unity or peace). The great house and its outbuildings (a sugar-production factory and horse-driven mill) were destroyed by fire and hurricanes, and the house sat in ruins until 1982. Today it houses a library and museum that contains a dusty collection of Indian pottery and colonial artifacts. ⊠ *Rte. 104, make a right past Texaco station, Cruz Bay,* ☎ *340/776–6359.* ⊠ *Free.* ☉ *Weekdays 9–5.*

8 **Peace Hill.** It's worth stopping at this spot just past the Hawksnest Bay overlook for great views of St. John, St. Thomas, and the BVI. On the flat promontory you'll find an old sugar mill. ⊠ *Off Rte. 20, Denis Bay.*

3 **Reef Bay Trail.** Although this is one of the most interesting hikes on St. John, unless you're a rugged individualist who wants a physical challenge (and that describes a lot of people who stay on St. John), you'll probably get the most out of the trip if you join a hike led by a park service ranger, who can identify the trees and plants on the hike down, fill you in on the history of the Reef Bay Plantation, and tell you about the petroglyphs on the rocks at the bottom of the trail. If you're without a car, take a taxi or the public Vitran bus from the Cruz Bay ferry dock to the trailhead on Route 10, where you'll meet a ranger for the hike downhill. A boat will take you to Cruz Bay, saving you the uphill return climb. ⊠ *Rte. 10, Reef Bay,* ☎ *340/776–6201 Ext. 238 reservations,* ⊞ *www.nps.gov/viis.* ☉ *Tours at 10 AM; days change seasonally.* ⊠ *Free; return boat trip to Cruz Bay $15.* The **Reef Bay Plantation,** according to architectural historian Frederik C. Gjessing, is the most architecturally ambitious structure of its kind on St. John. Though gutted, the great house is largely intact, and its classical beauty is still visible. It sits on a side trail to the north, off the trail to Lameshur Bay, and the sugar works are near the beach. Reef Bay was the last working plantation on St. John when it stopped production in 1920. ⊠ *Rte. 10 between Cruz Bay and Coral Bay; parking area is on the left, trail is to the right.*

U.S. VIRGIN ISLANDS A TO Z

To research prices, get advice from other travelers, and book travel arrangements, visit www.fodors.com.

AIR TRAVEL

One advantage to visiting the USVI is the abundance of nonstop and connecting flights to St. Thomas and St. Croix that can have you at the beach in three to four hours from easternmost United States departures. Small island-hopper planes and a seaplane connect St. Thomas and St. Croix, and a ferry takes you from St. Thomas to St. John.

American is the territory's major carrier with flights from Miami and New York. Continental flies from Newark. Delta flies from Atlanta. United flies from Chicago and Washington, D.C. US Airways flies from Philadelphia. American Eagle has frequent flights throughout the day from San Juan. Cape Air flies from San Juan to both St. Thomas and St. Croix. It has code-sharing arrangements with all major airlines so your luggage can transfer seamlessly. Seaborne Airlines flies between St. Thomas and St. Croix.

➤ AIRLINES AND CONTACTS: **American Airlines** (☎ 340/774–6464 or 340/778–1140). **American Eagle** (☎ 340/776–2560 or 340/778–2000). **Cape Air** (☎ 800/352–0714 or 340/774–2204, WEB flycapeair.com). **Continental Airlines** (☎ 800/231–0856). **Delta Airlines** (☎ 340/777–4177). **Seaborne Airlines** (☎ 340/773–6442, WEB www.seaborneairlines.com). **United Air Lines** (☎ 340/774–9190). **US Airways** (☎ 340/774–7885).

AIRPORTS

St. Thomas's Cyril E. King Airport sits at the western end of the island. There is no airport on St. John. St. Croix's Henry Rohlsen Airport sits outside Frederiksted, a 10-minute drive away. It takes about a half-hour to reach Christiansted from the airport.

Most hotels on St. Thomas do not have airport shuttles, but taxi vans at the airport are plentiful. From the airport, fees (set by the VI Taxi Commission) for two or more people sharing a cab are: $12 to the Ritz-Carlton, $9 to Renaissance Grand Beach Resort, $7.50 to Marriott Frenchman's Reef, and $5 to Bluebeard's Castle. Expect to be charged 50¢ per bag and to pay a higher fee if you're riding alone. During rush hour the trip to east end resorts can take up to 40 minutes, but a half-hour is typical. Driving time from the airport to Charlotte Amalie is 15 minutes.

Getting from the airport to St. Croix hotels by taxi costs about $10–$20. You'll spend a half-hour getting to the hotels in the Christiansted area, but those in the Frederiksted area are only about 10 minutes away. It takes about 45 minutes to get to the hotels on the East End.

Visitors to St. John fly into St. Thomas and take a taxi to either Charlotte Amalie or Red Hook, where they catch a ferry to Cruz Bay, St. John. The ferry from Charlotte Amalie makes the 45-minute trip several times a day and costs $7 a person. From Red Hook the ferry leaves on the hour; the 20-minute trip costs $3 a person.

➤ AIRPORT INFORMATION: **St. Croix's Henry Rohlsen Airport** (☎ 340/778–0589, WEB www.viport.com/aviation.html). **St. Thomas's Cyril E. King Airport** (☎ 340/774–5100, WEB www.viport.com/aviation.html).

BOAT AND FERRY TRAVEL

Virtually every type of ship and major cruise line calls at St. Thomas; only a few call at St. Croix. Many ships that call at St. Thomas also call in St. John or offer an excursion to that island.

Ferries are a great way to travel around the islands; there's service between St. Thomas and St. John and their neighbors, the BVI. There's something special about spending a day on St. John and then joining your fellow passengers—a mix of tourists, local families, and construction workers on their way home—for a peaceful, sundown ride back to St. Thomas. Sometimes one of the St. John ferry services offers a special weekend trip to Fajardo, Puerto Rico. Such junkets depart from the waterfront in St. Thomas on a Friday evening and return to the same locale on Sunday afternoon.

Ferries to Cruz Bay, St. John, leave St. Thomas from either the Charlotte Amalie waterfront west of the U.S. Coast Guard dock or from
Red Hook. From Charlotte Amalie ferries depart at 9, 11, 1, 3, 4, and
5:30. To Charlotte Amalie from Cruz Bay, they leave at 7:15, 9:15, 11:15
1:15, 2:15, and 3:45. The one-way fare for the 45-minute ride is $7
for adults, $3 for children. From Red Hook, ferries to Cruz Bay leave
at 6:30 AM and 7:30 AM. Starting at 8 AM, they leave hourly until midnight. Returning from Cruz Bay, they leave hourly starting at 6 AM until
11 PM. The 15- to 20-minute ferry ride is $3 one-way for adults, $1
for children under 12.

Car ferries, called barges, run about every half-hour between Red
Hook, St. Thomas, and Cruz Bay, St. John. The ride takes a half-hour
(one way) and costs $27 (round-trip). Plan to arrive 15 minutes be-
fore departure.

Reefer is the name of both of the brightly colored 26-passenger skiffs
that run between the Charlotte Amalie waterfront and Marriott Frenchman's Reef hotel daily every hour from 9 to 4, returning from the Reef
from 9:30 until 4:30. It's a good way to beat the traffic (and is about
the same price as a taxi) to Morning Star Beach, which adjoins the Reef.
And you get a great view of the harbor as you bob along in the shadow
of the giant cruise ships anchored in the harbor. The captain of the *Reefer*
may also be persuaded to drop you at Yacht Haven, but check first.
The fare is $4 one-way, and the trip takes about 15 minutes.

There's daily service between either Charlotte Amalie or Red Hook,
on St. Thomas, and West End or Road Town, Tortola, BVI, by either
Smiths Ferry or Native Son, Inc., and to Virgin Gorda, BVI, by Smiths
Ferry. The times and days the ferries run change, so it's best to call for
schedules once you're in the islands. The fare is $22 one-way or $40
round-trip, and the trip from Charlotte Amalie takes 45 minutes to an
hour to West End, up to 1½ hours to Road Town; from Red Hook the
trip is only half an hour. The twice-weekly 2¼-hour trip from Charlotte Amalie to Virgin Gorda costs $28 one-way and $40 round-trip.
There's also daily service between Cruz Bay, St. John, and West End,
Tortola, aboard the *Sundance*. The half-hour one-way trip is $21.
You'll need to present proof of citizenship upon entering the BVI; a
passport is best, but a birth certificate with a raised seal in addition to
a government-issued photo ID will suffice.

➤ BOAT AND FERRY INFORMATION: **Native Son, Inc.** (☎ 340/774–8685).
Reefer (☎ 340/776–8500 Ext. 6814). **Smiths Ferry** (☎ 340/775–7292).
Sundance (☎ 340/776–6597).

BUS TRAVEL

On St. Thomas, the island's 20 deluxe mainland-size buses make public transportation a very comfortable—though slow—way to get from
east and west to Charlotte Amalie and back (service to the north is limited). Buses run about every 30 minutes from stops that are clearly
marked with VITRAN signs. Fares are $1 between outlying areas and
town and 75¢ in town.

Privately owned taxi vans crisscross St. Croix regularly, providing reliable service between Frederiksted and Christiansted along Route 70.
This inexpensive ($1.50 one-way) mode of transportation is favored
by locals, and though the many stops on the 20-mi (32-km) drive between the two main towns make the ride slow, it's never dull. The public Vitran buses aren't the quickest way to get around the island, but
they're comfortable and affordable. The fare is $1 between Chris-
tiansted and Frederiksted or to places in between.

Modern Vitran buses on St. John run from the Cruz Bay ferry dock through Coral Bay to the far eastern end of the island at Salt Pond, making numerous stops in between. The fare is $1 to any point.

BUSINESS HOURS

BANKS

Bank hours are generally Monday–Thursday 9–3 and Friday 9–5; a handful have Saturday hours (9–noon). Walk-up windows open at 8:30 on weekdays.

POST OFFICES

Hours may vary slightly from branch to branch and island to island, but they are generally 7:30 or 8 to 4 or 5:30 weekdays and 7:30 or 8 to noon or 2:30 Saturday.

SHOPS

On St. Thomas, stores on Main Street in Charlotte Amalie are open weekdays and Saturday 9–5. The hours of the shops in the Havensight Mall (next to the cruise-ships dock) are the same, though occasionally some stay open until 9 on Friday, depending on how many cruise ships are at the dock. You may also find some shops open on Sunday if a lot of cruise ships are in port. Hotel shops are usually open evenings, as well.

St. Croix shop hours are usually Monday–Saturday 9–5, but you'll find some shops in Christiansted open in the evening.

On St. John, store hours run from 9 or 10 to 5 or 6. Wharfside Village and Mongoose Junction shops in Cruz Bay are often open into the evening.

CAR RENTALS

Any U.S. driver's license is good for 90 days on the USVI, as are valid driver's licenses from other countries; the minimum age for drivers is 18, although many agencies won't rent to anyone under the age of 25. At the height of the winter season, it may be tough to find a car and, occasionally, all rental companies run out of cars at once; reserve well in advance to ensure you get the vehicle of your choice.

ST. THOMAS

➤ MAJOR AGENCIES: **ABC Rentals** (☎ 340/776–1222 or 800/524–2080). **Anchorage E-Z Car** (☎ 340/775–6255). **Avis** (☎ 340/774–1468 or 800/331–1084). **Budget** (☎ 340/776–5774 or 800/626–4516). **Cowpet Rent-a-Car** (☎ 340/775–7376). **Dependable Car Rental** (☎ 340/774–2253 or 800/522–3076). **Discount** (☎ 340/776–4858). **Hertz** (☎ 340/774–1879 or 800/654–3131).

ST. CROIX

Atlas is located outside Christiansted but provides pickups at hotels. Avis is located at the airport. Budget has locations at the airport and in the King Christian Hotel in Christiansted. Midwest is located outside Frederiksted, but picks up at hotels. Olympic and Thrifty are located outside Christiansted, but will pick up at hotels.
➤ CONTACTS: **Atlas** (☎ 340/773–2886 or 800/426–6009). **Avis** (☎ 340/778–9355 or 800/897–8448). **Budget** (☎ 340/778–9636 or 888/227–3359, WEB www.budgetstcroix.com). **Midwest** (☎ 340/772–0438 or 877/772–0438, WEB www.midwestautorental.com). **Olympic** (☎ 340/773–2208 or 888/878–4227). **Thrifty** (☎ 340/773–7200).

ST. JOHN

Best is just outside Cruz Bay near the public library off Route 10. Cool Breeze is in Cruz Bay across from the Creek. Delbert Hill Taxi Rental Service is in Cruz Bay around the corner from the ferry dock across from Wharfside Village. Denzil Clyne is across from the Creek. O'Connor Jeep is in Cruz Bay at the Texaco Station. St. John Car Rental is at the Creek in Cruz Bay. Spencer's Jeep is across from the Creek in Cruz Bay. V.I. Sun and Sand is in Cruz Bay across from the Creek.

➤ CONTACTS: **Best** (☎ 340/693–8177). **Cool Breeze** (☎ 340/776–6588, WEB www.coolbreezecarrental.com). **Delbert Hill Taxi and Jeep Rental Service** (☎ 340/776–6637). **Denzil Clyne** (☎ 340/776–6715). **O'Connor Jeep** (☎ 340/776–6343). **St. John Car Rental** (☎ 340/776–6103, WEB www.stjohncarrental.com). **Spencer's Jeep** (☎ 340/693–8784 or 888/776–6628). **Sun and Sand Car Rental** (☎ 340/776–6374).

CAR TRAVEL

Even at a sedate speed of 20 mph, driving can be an adventure—for example, you may find yourself in a Jeep slogging behind a slow tourist-packed safari bus at a steep hairpin turn. Give a little beep at blind turns. Note that the general speed limit on these islands is only 25–35 mph, which will seem fast enough for you on most roads. If you don't think you'll need to lock up your valuables, a Jeep or open-air Suzuki with four-wheel drive will make it easier to navigate potholed dirt side roads and to get up slick hills when it rains. All main roads are paved.

GASOLINE

Gas is pricey on St. John and St. Thomas: about $2 per gallon. But on St. Croix, where the big Hess refinery is, the prices are much closer to what you might expect to pay stateside, about $1.25 per gallon.

ROAD CONDITIONS

In St. Thomas, traffic can get pretty bad, especially in Charlotte Amalie at rush hour (7–9 and 4:30–6). Cars often line up bumper to bumper along the waterfront. If you need to get from an east end resort to the airport during these times, find the alternate route (starting from the east end, Route 38 to 42 to 40 to 33) that goes up the mountain and then drops you back onto Veterans Highway. If you plan to explore by car, be sure to pick up the latest edition of "Road Map St. Thomas–St. John" that includes the route numbers *and* the names of the roads that are used by locals. It's available anywhere you find maps and guidebooks.

St. Croix, unlike St. Thomas and St. John, where narrow roads wind through hillsides, is relatively flat, and it even has a four-lane highway. The speed limit on the Melvin H. Evans Highway is 55 mph and ranges 35–40 mph elsewhere. Roads are often unmarked, so be patient—sometimes getting lost is half the fun.

In St. John, use caution. The terrain is very hilly, the roads are winding, and the blind curves numerous. You may suddenly come upon a huge safari bus careening around a corner or a couple of hikers strolling along the side of the road. Major roads are well paved, but once you get off a specific route, dirt roads filled with potholes are common. For such driving a four-wheel-drive vehicle is your best bet.

RULES OF THE ROAD

Driving is on the left side of the road (although your steering wheel will be on the left side of the car). The law requires *everyone* in a car to wear seat belts: many of the roads are narrow, and the islands are dotted with hills, so there's ample reason to put safety first.

ELECTRICITY

The USVI use the same current as the U.S. mainland—110 volts. Since power fluctuations occasionally occur, bring a heavy-duty surge protector (available at hardware stores) if you plan to use your computer.

EMERGENCIES

➤ AMBULANCE AND FIRE: **Air Ambulance Network** (☎ 800/327–1966). **Ambulance and fire emergencies** (☎ 911). **Medical Air Services** (☎ 340/777–8580 or 800/643–9023).

➤ COAST GUARD: **Marine Safety Detachment** (☎ 340/776–3497 in St. Thomas and St. John; 340/772–5557 in St. Croix). **Rescue Coordination Center** (☎ 787/289–2040 in San Juan, Puerto Rico).

➤ HOSPITALS ON ST. THOMAS: **Roy L. Schneider Hospital & Community Health Center** (⊠ Sugar Estate, 1 mi [1½ km] east of Charlotte Amalie, ☎ 340/776–8311).

➤ HOSPITALS ON ST. CROIX: **Gov. Juan F. Luis Hospital and Health Center** (⊠ 6 Diamond Ruby, north of Sunny Isle Shopping Center on Rte. 79, Christiansted, ☎ 340/778–6311). **Ingeborg Nesbitt Clinic** (⊠ 516 Strand St., Frederiksted, ☎ 340/772–0260).

➤ HOSPITALS ON ST. JOHN: **Myrah Keating Smith Community Health Center** (⊠ Rte. 10, about 7 mins east of Cruz Bay, Susannaberg, ☎ 340/693–8900).

➤ PHARMACIES ON ST. THOMAS: **Havensight Pharmacy** (⊠ Havensight Mall, Charlotte Amalie, ☎ 340/776–1235). **Kmart Pharmacy** (⊠ Tutu Park Mall, Tutu, ☎ 340/777–3854). **Sunrise Pharmacy** (⊠ Red Hook, ☎ 340/775–6600; ⊠ Vitraco Park, near Havensight Mall, ☎ 340/776–7292).

➤ PHARMACIES ON ST. CROIX: **D&D Apothecary Hall** (⊠ 501 Queen St., Frederiksted, ☎ 340/772–1890). **Kmart Pharmacy** (⊠ Sunshine Mall, Cane Estate, ☎ 340/692–2622). **People's Drug Store, Inc.** (⊠ Sunny Isle Shopping Center, Rte. 70, Christiansted, ☎ 340/778–5537).

➤ PHARMACIES ON ST. JOHN: **Chelsea Drug Store** (⊠ The Marketplace Shopping Center, Rte. 104, Cruz Bay, ☎ 340/776–4888).

➤ POLICE: **Police emergencies** (☎ 911).

➤ SCUBA-DIVING EMERGENCIES: **Roy L. Schneider Hospital & Community Health Center** (Sugar Estate, 1 mi [1½ km] east of Charlotte Amalie, ☎ 340/776–2686).

ETIQUETTE AND BEHAVIOR

A smile and a "good day" greeting will start any encounter off on the right foot. Dress is casual throughout the islands, but cover up when you're sightseeing or shopping in town; bare chests and bathing suit tops are frowned upon.

FESTIVALS AND SEASONAL EVENTS

ST. THOMAS

January–April sees Classics in the Garden, a chamber-music series at Tillett Gardens where young musicians from all over the world perform. Tillett Gardens hosts annual Arts Alive festivals in November, March, and August. During Easter weekend, St. Thomas Yacht Club hosts the Rolex Cup Regatta, which is part of the three-race Caribbean Ocean Racing Triangle (CORT) that pulls in yachties and their pals from all over. Carnival is a weeklong major-league blowout of parades, parties, and island-wide events. The dates change from year to year, following the Easter calendar. Marlin mania begins in May and so do the sportfishing tournaments. There are also several locally sponsored fishing events throughout summer and fall.

The St. Thomas Gamefishing Club hosts its July Open Tournament over the Fourth of July weekend. There are categories for serious marlin anglers, just-for-fun fishermen, and even kids who want to try their luck from docks and rocks. The mid-July celebration of Bastille Day—which commemorates the French Revolution—is marked by a mini-carnival in Frenchtown. During full moon in August, anglers compete for big-money prizes in the USVI Open/Atlantic Blue Marlin Tournament. September's Texas Society Chili Cook-Off is a party on Sapphire Beach—you'll find country music performances, dancing, games, and, of course, chili tasting. In November the St. Thomas Agricultural Fair showcases fresh produce, home-grown herbs, and local dishes, such as callaloo, salt fish and dumplings, and fresh fish simmered with green banana, pumpkin, and potatolike *tannia*.

➤ CONTACTS: **Arts Alive Festival** (☎ 340/775–1405). **Carnival** (☎ 340/776–3112). **Classics in the Garden** (☎ 340/775–1405). **July Open Tournament** (☎ 340/775–9144). **Rolex Cup Regatta** (☎ 340/775–6320). **St. Thomas Agricultural Fair** (☎ 340/693–1080). **Texas Society Chili Cook-Off** (☎ 340/776–3595). **USVI Open/Atlantic Blue Marlin Tournament** (☎ 340/775–9500).

ST. CROIX

The island celebrates Carnival with its Crucian Christmas Festival, which starts in late December. After weeks of beauty pageants, food fairs, and concerts, the festival wraps up with a parade in early January. In February and March the St. Croix Landmarks Society House Tours visit some of the island's most exclusive and historic homes and give you a chance to peek inside places you can usually view only from the road.

The St. Croix Half Ironman Triathlon attracts international-class athletes as well as amateurs every May for a 1-mi (2-km) swim, a 7-mi (12-km) run, and a 34-mi (55-km) bike ride; it includes a climb up The Beast, on Route 69. Serious swimmers should join island residents in late October for the Coral Reef Swim. Participants swim about 5 mi (8 km) from Buck Island to Christiansted. The event also includes an awards dinner. The International Regatta sets sail in February at the St. Croix Yacht Club. Sailors converge on Teague Bay for three days of sailing and parties.

➤ CONTACTS: **Coral Reef Swim** (☎ 340/773–2100 Ext.739). **International Regatta** (☎ 340/773–9531, WEB www.stcroixyc.org). **St. Croix Half Ironman Triathlon** (☎ 340/773–4470, WEB www.stcroixtriathlon.com). **St. Croix Landmarks Society House Tours** (☎ 340/772–0598, WEB stcroixlandmarks.org).

ST. JOHN

The island dishes up its own version of Carnival with the July 4th Celebration. Weeks of festivities—including beauty pageants and a food fair—culminate in a parade through the streets of Cruz Bay on July 4. On the two days after Thanksgiving an eclectic group of sailors takes to the waters of Coral Bay for the annual Coral Bay Thanksgiving Regatta. Some boats are "live-aboards," whose owners only pull up anchor for this one event; other boats belong to Sunday sailors; and a very few are owned by hotshot racers. If you'd like to crew, stop by Skinny Legs Bar and Restaurant.

➤ CONTACTS: **Coral Bay Thanksgiving Regatta** (☎ 340/779–4994).

HOLIDAYS

Public holidays, in addition to the U.S. federal holidays are: Three Kings Day (Jan. 6); Transfer Day (commemorates Denmark's 1917 sale of the territory to the United States, Mar. 31); Holy Thursday and Good Friday (always precedes Easter); Emancipation Day (when slavery was abolished in the Danish West Indies in 1848, July 3); Columbus Day and USVI–Puerto Rico Friendship Day (always on Columbus Day weekend); and Liberty Day (honoring David Hamilton Jackson, who secured freedom of the press and assembly from King Christian X of Denmark, Nov. 1).

Although the government closes down for 26 days a year, most of these holidays have no effect on shopping hours. Unless there's a cruise ship arrival, expect most stores to close for Christmas and a few other holidays in the slower summer months.

LANGUAGE

English is the official language, though island residents often speak it with a lilting Creole accent, so you might not recognize certain words at first. If you have trouble understanding someone, ask them to speak slowly.

MAIL AND SHIPPING

The main U.S. Post Office on St. Thomas is near the hospital, with branches in Charlotte Amalie, Frenchtown, Havensight, and Tutu Mall; there are post offices at Christiansted, Frederiksted, Gallows Bay, and Sunny Isle, on St. Croix, and at Cruz Bay, on St. John. The postal service offers Express Mail next-day service to major cities if you mail before noon; outlying areas may take two days. Letters to the United States are 33¢ and postcards are 20¢. Sending mail home to Canada you'll pay 46¢ for a letter and 40¢ for a postcard. To the United Kingdom and Australia, letters are 60¢, postcards 50¢.

On St. Thomas, Federal Express offers overnight service if you get your package to the office before 5 PM. Parcel Plus, across from Havensight Mall, also has express mail service. The Federal Express office on St. Croix is in Peter's Rest Commercial Center; try to drop off your packages before 5:30 PM. On St. John, Sprint Courier Service connects to all major couriers.

➤ CONTACTS: **Federal Express** (✉ Cyril E. King Airport, St. Thomas, ☎ 340/777–4140, WEB www.fedex.com; ✉ Peter's Rest Commercial Center, Rte. 708, Peter's Rest, St. Croix, ☎ 340/778–8180). **Parcel Plus** (✉ across from Havensight Mall on Rte. 30, Charlotte Amalie, St. Thomas, ☎ 340/776–9134). **Sprint Courier Service** (✉ off Rte. 104 across from the basketball court, Cruz Bay, St. John, ☎ 340/693–8130).

MONEY MATTERS

Prices quoted in this chapter are in U.S. dollars.

BANKS AND ATMS

Each of the islands has several banks. On St. Thomas, First Bank is near Market Square. There are waterfront locations for both Banco Popular and V.I. Community Bank.

St. Croix has branches of Banco Popular in Orange Grove and Sunny Isle Shopping Centers. V.I. Community Bank is in Orange Grove Shopping Center and in downtown Christiansted. Scotia Bank has branches in Sunny Isle Frederiksted, Christiansted, and Sunshine Mall.

St. John's two banks are located near the ferry docks. Chase is one block up from the ferry dock, and Scotia Bank is in a trailer just east of Chase.

➤ CONTACTS: **Banco Popular** (☎ 340/693–2777, WEB www.bancopopular. com). **Chase Manhattan Bank** (☎ 340/775–7777). **First Bank** (☎ 340/776–9494, WEB www.firstbankpr.com). **Scotia Bank** (St. Croix, ☎ 340/778–5350, WEB www.scotiabank.com; St. John, ☎ 340/776–6552).

CREDIT CARDS

All major credit cards and traveler's checks are generally accepted. Some places will take Discover, though it is not as widely accepted as Visa, MasterCard, and American Express.

CURRENCY

The American dollar is used throughout the territory, as well as in the neighboring BVI. If you need to exchange foreign currency, you'll need to go to the main branch of major banks.

PASSPORTS AND VISAS

If you're a U.S. or Canadian citizen, you can prove citizenship with a current or expired (but not by more than five years) passport or with an original birth certificate (with a raised seal) along with a government-issued photo I.D. A valid passport, however, is best. Citizens of other countries need a passport.

SAFETY

Vacationers tend to assume that normal precautions aren't necessary in paradise. They are. Though there isn't quite as much crime here as in large U.S. mainland cities, it does exist. To be safe, stick to well-lighted streets at night and use the same kind of street sense (don't wander the back alleys of Charlotte Amalie or Christiansted after five rum punches, for example) that you would in any unfamiliar territory. If you plan to carry things around, rent a car—not a jeep—and lock possessions in the trunk. Keep your rental car locked wherever you park. Don't leave cameras, purses, and other valuables lying on the beach while you snorkel for an hour (or even for a minute), whether you're on the deserted beaches of St. John or the more crowded Magens and Coki beaches on St. Thomas. St. Croix has several remote beaches outside Frederiksted and on the east end; it's best to visit them with a group rather than on your own.

SIGHTSEEING TOURS

AIR TOURS

Air Center Helicopters, on the Charlotte Amalie waterfront (next to Tortola Wharf) on St. Thomas, has 30-minute island tours priced at $375 (for up to four passengers) per trip. You can also arrange longer flights that loop over to the neighboring BVI, as well as photography tours. Seaborne Airlines offers narrated flightseeing tours of the USVI and the BVI from its Havensight base on St. Thomas and from the Christiansted waterfront in St. Croix. The 30-minute "Round-the-Island" tour is $79–$99 per person.

➤ CONTACTS: **Air Center Helicopters** (✉ Waterfront, Charlotte Amalie, St. Thomas, ☎ 340/775–7335). **Seaborne Adventures** (✉ 5305 Long Bay Rd., Charlotte Amalie, St. Thomas, ☎ 340/773–5991; ✉ Christiansted Waterfront [west of downtown], Christiansted, St. Croix, ☎ 340/773–6442 or 888/359–8786; WEB www.seaborneairlines.com).

BOAT TOURS

Caribbean Pelican Rides offers a unique land and sea tour of Charlotte Amalie aboard an amphibious British Alvis Stalward vessel. Tours depart from the Coast Guard dock opposite Vendor's Plaza. The 55-minute excursions costs $55 for adults, $15 for children ages 12 and under.

St. Thomas's *Kon Tiki* party boat is a kick. Put your sophistication aside, climb on this big palm-thatch raft, and dip into bottomless barrels of rum punch along with a couple of hundred of your soon-to-be closest friends. Dance to the steel-drum band, sun on the roof (watch out: you'll fry), and join the limbo dancing on the way home from an afternoon of swimming and beachcombing at Honeymoon Beach on Water Island. This popular 3½-hour afternoon excursion costs $29 for adults, $15 for children under 13 (although few come to this party).

➤ CONTACTS: **Caribbean Pelican Rides** (✉ Coast Guard Dock, opposite Vendor's Plaza, Charlotte Amalie, St. Thomas, ☎ 340/774–7808). *Kon Tiki* (✉ Gregorie Channel East Dock, Frenchtown, St. Thomas, ☎ 340/775–5055).

BUS AND TAXI TOURS

V. I. Taxi Association St. Thomas City-Island Tour gives a two-hour $45 tour for two people in an open-air safari bus or enclosed van; aimed at cruise-ship passengers, this tour includes stops at Drake's Seat and Mountain Top. For just a bit more money (about $45–$50 for two) you can hire a taxi and ask the driver to take the opposite route so you'll avoid the crowds. But do see Mountain Top: the view is wonderful.

Tropic Tours offers half-day shopping and sightseeing tours of St. Thomas by bus six days a week ($25 per person). The company also has a full-day ferry tour to St. John that includes snorkeling and lunch. The cost is $70 per person.

St. Croix Safari Tours offers van tours of St. Croix. They depart from Christiansted, last about three hours, cost from $25 per person plus admission fees to attractions. St. Croix Transit offers van tours of St. Croix. They depart from Christiansted, last about three hours, cost from $25 per person plus admission fees to attractions.

In St. John, taxi drivers provide tours of the island, making stops at various sites including Trunk Bay and Annaberg Plantation. Prices run around $15 a person. The taxi drivers congregate near the ferry in Cruz Bay. The dispatcher will find you a driver for your tour.
➤ CONTACTS: **St. Croix Safari Tours** (☎ 340/773–6700). **St. Croix Transit** (☎ 340/772–3333). **Tropic Tours** (☎ 340/774–1855 or 800/524–4334). **V. I. Taxi Association St. Thomas City-Island Tour** (☎ 340/774–4550).

WALKING TOURS

The *St. Thomas–St. John Vacation Handbook,* available free at hotels and tourist centers, has an excellent self-guided walking tour of Charlotte Amalie on St. Thomas. The St. Thomas Historical Trust has published a self-guided tour of the historic district; it's available in book and souvenir shops for $1.95. A two-hour guided historic walking tour is available by reservation. It begins (at 9 AM) at the Emancipation Garden, covers all the in-town sights, and can be narrated in Spanish, Danish, German, and Japanese as well as in English. The cost is $35 per person; wear a hat and comfortable walking shoes.

Possible nature tours on St. Thomas include bird-watching, whale-watching, and waiting hidden on a beach while the magnificent hawksbill turtles come ashore to lay their eggs. Contact EAST (Environmental Association of St. Thomas–St. John).

St. Croix Heritage Tours leads walks through the historic towns of Christiansted and Frederiksted, detailing the history of the people and the buildings. Custom tours that cover the island are also available.

Along with providing trail maps and brochures about Virgin Islands National Park, the park service also gives several guided tours on- and off-shore. Some are only offered during particular times of the year, and some require reservations. For more information, contact the National Park Service on St. John.
➤ CONTACTS: **EAST** (Environmental Association of St. Thomas–St. John; ⊠ Box 12379, St. Thomas 00801, ☎ 340/776–1976). **St. Croix Heritage Tours** (⊠ Box 7937, Sunny Isle 00823, ☎ 340/778–6997, WEB www.stcroixtours.com). **St. Thomas Historical Trust** (☎ 340/776–2726). **V.I. National Park Visitors Center** (⊠ at area known as the Creek; across from Cruz Bay bulkhead and adjacent to ball field, Cruz Bay, ☎ 340/776–6201, WEB www.nps.gov/viis).

TAXES AND SERVICE CHARGES
TAXES

There's no sales tax, but there is an 8% hotel-room tax in the USVI. The St. John Accommodations Council members ask that hotel and villa guests voluntarily pay a $1-a-day surcharge to help fund school and community projects and other good works.

TAXIS

USVI taxis don't have meters, but you needn't worry about fare gouging if you check a list of standard rates to popular destinations (required by law to be carried by each driver and often posted in hotel and airport lobbies and printed in free tourist periodicals, such as *St. Thomas This Week* and *St. Croix This Week*) and settle on the fare before you start out. Fares are per person, not per destination, but drivers taking multiple fares (which often happens, especially from the airport) will charge you a lower rate than if you're in the cab alone.

ST. THOMAS

On St. Thomas taxi vans line up along Havensight and Crown Bay docks when a cruise ship pulls in. If you booked a shore tour, the operator will lead you to a designated vehicle. Otherwise, there are plenty of air-conditioned vans and open-air safari buses to take you to Charlotte Amalie or the beach. The cab fare from Havensight to Charlotte Amalie is $2.50 per person; you can, however, make the 1½-mi (2½-km) walk into town in about 30 minutes along the beautiful waterfront. From Crown Bay to town the taxi fare is $2.50 per person whether you travel solo or you share; it's a 1-mi (1½-km) walk, but the route passes along a busy highway. Transportation from Havensight to Magens Bay for swimming is $6.50 per person ($4 if you share).

Additionally, taxis of all shapes and sizes are available at various ferry, shopping, resort, and airport areas, and they also respond to phone calls. There are taxi stands in Charlotte Amalie across from Emancipation Garden (in front of Little Switzerland, behind the post office) and along the waterfront. But you probably won't have to look for a stand, as taxis are plentiful and routinely cruise the streets. Walking down Main Street, you'll be asked "Back to ship?" often enough to make you never want to carry another shopping bag.
➤ CONTACTS: **East End Taxi** (☎ 340/775–6974). **Islander Taxi** (☎ 340/774–4077). **VI Taxi Association** (☎ 340/774–4550).

ST. CROIX

Taxis, generally station wagons or minivans, are a phone call away from most hotels and are available in downtown Christiansted, at the Henry E. Rohlsen Airport, and at the Frederiksted pier during cruise-ship arrivals.

In Frederiksted, all the shops are just a short walk away, and you can swim off the beach in Frederiksted. Most ship passengers visit Christiansted on a tour; a taxi will cost $20 for one or two people.
➤ CONTACTS: **Antilles Taxi Service** (☎ 340/773–5020). **Cruzan Taxi and Tours** (☎ 340/773–6388). **St. Croix Taxi Association** (☎ 340/778–1088).

ST. JOHN

Taxis meet ferries arriving in Cruz Bay. Most drivers use vans or open-air safari buses. You'll find them congregated at the dock and at hotel parking lots. You can also hail them anywhere on the road. You're likely to travel with other tourists en route to their destinations. It's very difficult to get taxis to respond to a phone call. If you need one to pick you up at your rental villa, ask the villa manager for suggestions on who to call or arrange a ride in advance.

Some cruise ships stop at St. John to let passengers disembark for a day. The main town of Cruz Bay is near the area where the ships drop off passengers. If you want to swim, the famous Trunk Bay is a $9 taxi ride (for two) from town.

TELEPHONES

On St. Thomas, AT&T has a state-of-the-art telecommunications center (it's across from the Havensight Mall) with 15 desk booths, fax and copy services, video phone, and TDD equipment (for people with hearing impairments). Islander Services and East End Secretarial Services offer long-distance dialing, copying, and fax services. Parcel Plus in St. Thomas has three computers available for accessing e-mail; the cost is $5 per half hour. Express mail service, international calling, and phone cards are also available here. On St. John, the place to go for phone or message needs is Connections.

➤ CONTACTS: **AT&T** (✉ Across from Havensight Mall, Charlotte Amalie, St. Thomas, ☎ 340/777–9201). **Connections** (✉ Cruz Bay, St. John, ☎ 340/776–6922, WEB www.connectionsstjohn.com; ✉ Coral Bay, St. John, ☎ 340/779–4994). **East End Secretarial Services** (✉ Upstairs at Red Hook Plaza, Red Hook, St. Thomas, ☎ 340/775–5262). **Islander Services** (✉ 5302 Store Tvaer Gade, behind the Greenhouse Restaurant, Charlotte Amalie, St. Thomas, ☎ 340/774–8128). **Parcel Plus** (✉ Across from Havensight Mall, Charlotte Amalie, St. Thomas, ☎ 340/776–9134).

COUNTRY AND AREA CODES

The area code for all of the USVI is 340. If you are calling from within the U.S., you need only dial 1 plus the area code and number. If you are calling from outside the United States, dial the U.S. country code 01.

INTERNATIONAL CALLS

You can dial direct to and from the mainland United States, and to and from Australia, Canada, New Zealand, and the United Kingdom from most phones.

LOCAL CALLS

Local calls from a public phone cost up to 35¢ for each five minutes. If you have a cell phone, you can dial 6611 for information about how to use it locally.

TIPPING

Many hotels add a 10% to 15% service charge to cover the room maid and other staff. However, some hotels may use part of that money to fund their operations, passing on only a portion of it to the staff. Check with your maid or bellhop to determine the hotel's policy. If you discover you need to tip, give bellhops and porters 50¢ to $1 per bag and maids $1 or $2 per day. Special errands or requests of hotel staff always require an additional tip. At restaurants bartenders and waiters expect a 10%–15% tip, but always check your tab to see whether service is included. Taxi drivers get a 15% tip.

VISITOR INFORMATION

➤ BEFORE YOU LEAVE: **USVI Government Tourist Office** (✉ 245 Peachtree St., Center Ave. Marquis One Tower MB-05, Atlanta, GA 30303, ☎ 404/688–0906; ✉ 500 N. Michigan Ave., Suite 2030, Chicago, IL 60611, ☎ 312/670–8784; ✉ 3460 Wilshire Blvd., Suite 412, Los Angeles, CA 90010, ☎ 213/739–0138; ✉ 2655 Le Jeune Rd., Suite 907, Coral Gables, FL 33134, ☎ 305/442–7200; ✉ 1270 Ave. of the Americas, Room 2108, New York, NY 10020, ☎ 212/332–2222; ✉ Hall of Streets, #298, 444 N. Capital St. NW, Washington, DC 20006, ☎ 202/624–3590; ✉ 268 Ponce deLeon Ave, Suite 1101, Hato Rey, Puerto Rico 00918, ☎ 787/763–3815; ✉ 3300 Bloor St. W, Suite 3120, Toronto, Ontario, Canada M8XC 2X3, ☎ 416/233–1414; ✉ Molasses House, Clove Hitch Quay, Plantation Wharf, York Place, London SW11 3TW, U.K., ☎ 020/7978–5262; WEB www.usvi.org/tourism).

➤ IN THE U.S. VIRGIN ISLANDS: **USVI Division of Tourism** (✉ 78-123 Estate Contant, Charlotte Amalie, St. Thomas 00804, ☎ 340/774–8784 or 800/372–8784; ✉ 53A Company St., Christiansted, St. Croix 00822, ☎ 340/773–0495; ✉ Strand St., Frederiksted, St. Croix 00840, ☎ 340/772–0357; ✉ Henry Samuel St. [next to the Post Office], Cruz Bay, St. John, ☎ 340/776–6450). **V.I. National Park** (✉ at the Creek, Cruz Bay, St. John 00831, ☎ 340/776–6201, WEB www.nps.gov/viis).

INDEX

NOTES

NOTES

NOTES

NOTES

NOTES

NOTES

NOTES

NOTES

Fodor's Key to the Guides

America's guidebook leader publishes guides for every kind of traveler. Check out our many series and find your perfect match.

Fodor's Gold Guides
America's favorite travel-guide series offers the most detailed insider reviews of hotels, restaurants, and attractions in all price ranges, plus great background information, smart tips, and useful maps.

Fodor's Road Guide USA
Big guides for a big country—the most comprehensive guides to America's roads, packed with places to stay, eat, and play across the U.S.A. Just right for road warriors, family vacationers, and cross-country trekkers.

COMPASS AMERICAN GUIDES
Stunning guides from top local writers and photographers, with gorgeous photos, literary excerpts, and colorful anecdotes. A must-have for culture mavens, history buffs, and new residents.

Fodor's CITYPACKS
Concise city coverage with a foldout map. The right choice for urban travelers who want everything under one cover.

Fodor's EXPLORING GUIDES
Hundreds of color photos bring your destination to life. Lively stories lend insight into the culture, history, and people.

Fodor's POCKET GUIDES
For travelers who need only the essentials. The best of Fodor's in pocket-size packages for just $9.95.

Fodor's To Go
Credit-card–size, magnetized color microguides that fit in the palm of your hand—perfect for "stealth" travelers or as gifts.

Fodor's FLASHMAPS
Every resident's map guide. 60 easy-to-follow maps of public transit, parks, museums, zip codes, and more.

Fodor's CITYGUIDES
Sourcebooks for living in the city: Thousands of in-the-know listings for restaurants, shops, sports, nightlife, and other city resources.

Fodor's AROUND THE CITY WITH KIDS
68 great ideas for family days, recommended by resident parents. Perfect for exploring in your own backyard or on the road.

Fodor's ESCAPES
Fill your trip with once-in-a-lifetime experiences, from ballooning in Chianti to overnighting in the Moroccan desert. These full-color dream books point the way.

Fodor's FYI
Get tips from the pros on planning the perfect trip. Learn how to pack, fly hassle-free, plan a honeymoon or cruise, stay healthy on the road, and travel with your baby.

Fodor's Languages for Travelers
Practice the local language before hitting the road. Available in phrase books, cassette sets, and CD sets.

Karen Brown's Guides
Engaging guides to the most charming inns and B&Bs in the U.S.A. and Europe, with easy-to-follow inn-to-inn itineraries.

Baedeker's Guides
Comprehensive guides, trusted since 1829, packed with A–Z reviews and star ratings.
